The Palgrave Companion to Oxford Economics

Robert A. Cord
Editor

The Palgrave Companion to Oxford Economics

palgrave
macmillan

Editor
Robert A. Cord
Researcher in Economics
London, UK

ISBN 978-3-030-58470-2   ISBN 978-3-030-58471-9   (eBook)
https://doi.org/10.1007/978-3-030-58471-9

This Palgrave Macmillan imprint is published by the registered company Springer Nature Switzerland AG.
The registered company address is: Gewerbestrasse 11, 6330 Cham, Switzerland

For Sissi and Herbert

Introduction

This is a volume about the economics and economists associated with the University of Oxford. It is the third in a series to be published by Palgrave examining the many and varied contributions made by important centres of economics. With only a very few exceptions, the focus of most history of economic thought studies, at least in terms of books,[1] has been on schools of thought. Such an approach provides valuable insights into how competing schools interact and how some come to predominate, for whatever reason and length of time, while others fall out of fashion or indeed never attain any particular notoriety. However, a key deficiency of such a *modus operandi* is that it often fails to illuminate the many processes and tensions that can and do occur at the level of the individual university, the personnel of which may be fighting internal battles for supremacy whilst trying to establish external hegemony.

Each volume in the series consists of two parts. The first contains a set of chapters which consider the contributions made by a centre where these contributions are considered to be especially important, this subject to a mixture of personal preferences and soundings from those who know better. The second, longer part is made up of chapters discussing the contributions of individual economists attached to a particular centre. 'Attached' is the crucial word. Some economists are easy to identify with a single institution as they may, for example, have spent their whole academic careers at it. Those who have moved from institution to institution are the more difficult case. One way forward in these instances is to place an economist in the institution

---

[1] Articles are of course another matter.

where they carried out their most important work, although this, in its turn, carries with it the danger of disagreement over what 'their most important work' was or is perceived to be and how this has changed over time. Another factor perhaps worthy of consideration is an economist's education. Where such an education has been received at the knee of a master, to what extent has this influenced the subsequent work of the noted pupil and how should this be considered when that pupil has flown the nest and settled at another institution? Issues of leadership style, discipleship, loyalty and access to publication outlets and to financing also enter the frame. Finally, there are issues of practicality, including space constraints and unavailability of contributors, among others. Given this matrix of possibilities, disagreement about who should be in which volume is inevitable. However, I hope that the outrage will not be too great given the overarching goal of the series.

The next volume in the series will examine the University of Chicago.

Robert A. Cord

Contents

List of Figures

List of Tables

Part I

Themes in Oxford Economics

1

Oxford's Contributions to Econometrics

David F. Hendry and Bent Nielsen

1 Introduction[1]

The name econometrics was a neologism created by Ragnar Frisch to characterise a discipline concerned with advancing economic theory in its relation to statistics and mathematics. As a founding member of the Econometric Society and its journal *Econometrica* in the early 1930s, Frisch wanted to promote research that unified 'the theoretical-quantitative and the empirical-quantitative approach to economic problems' (Frisch 1933: 1). Since then, however, the term econometrics has come to signify just the statistical aspects of quantitative economics research as with *A Textbook of Econometrics* (Klein 1953) or just *Econometrics* (as in Valavanis 1959). There remained a branch emphasising the more general aspect, in that textbooks were titled *Statistical Methods of Econometrics* (see Malinvaud 1966), which was also the name of the main econometrics course for the Master of Philosophy (MPhil) degree in Economics at the University of Oxford when the first author arrived there in 1982.

---

[1] We are grateful to Steve Bond, John Creedy, Christopher L. Gilbert, Grayham E. Mizon, James Poterba and Jan Toporowski for helpful information about Oxford econometrics and recollections from their time at the University and to John Gittins for permission to quote from his history of Oxford statistics (Gittins 2013).

D. F. Hendry (✉) • B. Nielsen
Department of Economics and Nuffield College, Oxford University, Oxford, UK
e-mail: david.hendry@nuffield.ox.ac.uk; bent.nielsen@economics.ox.ac.uk

© The Author(s), under exclusive license to Springer Nature Switzerland AG 2021
R. A. Cord (ed.), *The Palgrave Companion to Oxford Economics*,
https://doi.org/10.1007/978-3-030-58471-9_1

Given the relatively recent definition of econometrics, and its subsequent narrowing, much of the early history of the discipline must be conceptualised as economics in relation to statistics, as we do here, including the creation and curation of observations on economic phenomena. Moreover, "statistics" still refers both to the discipline which studies methods of statistical analysis (as in a department of statistics) and to summary measures of observations (as in the statistics of crime). Schumpeter (1933: 5) claimed that in contrast to the physical sciences that had to create their measures, 'Some of the most fundamental economic facts, on the contrary, already present themselves to our observation as quantities made numerical by life itself'. However, that still requires that such facts be recorded and combined over events, time and people to be useful for analysis. We include researchers who undertake such invaluable tasks as econometricians, which leads to a surprisingly rich history of the subject at Oxford before the 1930s.

General histories of econometrics are provided by Morgan (1990) and Qin (1993, 2013), with an overview and selected reprints of key papers in *The Foundations of Econometric Analysis* by Hendry and Morgan (1995). Thomas (2018) records the important role the London School of Economics (LSE) played in the development of econometrics in the twentieth century and also in beginning the study of the history of econometrics. Oxford econometricians continued that development of the history of their discipline. In addition to the two books by Qin and that by Hendry and Morgan, see Qin and Gilbert (2001) and Gilbert and Qin (2006, 2007), both of whom had been doctoral students or faculty at Oxford.

The structure of this chapter is as follows. Section 2 describes the early history of contributions to quantitative economics as embryonic econometrics from the seventeenth to the nineteenth centuries. Section 3 discusses econometrics at Oxford over 1900-1980, including major advances in creating aggregate economic measurements. Section 4 updates the history from 1980 to 2000, before Section 5 records Oxford econometrics in the twenty-first century to about 2010, after which point it is no longer "history", although such time divisions are arbitrary and many individuals span several of these sections. Section 6 describes contributions to data provision in the twenty-first century before Section 7 considers the most recent addition of climate econometrics, developing and applying econometric tools for analysing climate data, which is driven by human economic behaviour and so faces much the same slew of econometric problems as macroeconomic time series.

2   Early Days: Seventeenth–Nineteenth Century Contributions

2.1   Sir William Petty

One of the earliest records of advances in economics related to statistics, later to become econometrics, can be attributed to the Oxford graduate Sir William Petty (1623-1687). Petty came from a relatively humble background and was largely self-taught initially, sufficient to study medicine at Oxford, and indeed become anatomy tutor at Brasenose College as well as being a physician. As antecedents, he had acted as personal secretary to Thomas Hobbes through whom he was able to meet many of the prominent European philosophers of the time. At Oxford, he became a friend of Robert Boyle and was a member of the Oxford Philosophical Club, a precursor to the Royal Society of London of which he was a Founding Fellow. He seems to have been influenced by the empirical scientific approach of Francis Bacon, so Petty was a man with wide interests (see McCormick 2009).

However, it was only after moving permanently to Ireland that he became interested in economics. These earlier influences had led to Petty deciding that mathematics and the senses must be the basis of all rational sciences based on Bacon's *Novum Organum*. A desire to achieve that goal focused his interests on empirical phenomena that were measurable and so could be quantified, rather than merely described, leading to the creation of a new discipline that he called *Political Arithmetick*, published posthumously in a book of that title in 1690 (see Petty 1690). Consequently, Petty has a strong claim to be viewed as one of the first quantitative economists. He discerned what he viewed as a seven-year business cycle, suggesting a possible basis for systematic economic forecasts, although historically, cycles 'vary greatly in duration and intensity' (Zarnowitz 2004: 1). Petty was later to prove a considerable influence on Colin Clark, as we discuss in Section 3.

2.2   Florence Nightingale

In his history of Oxford statistics written to celebrate the 25th anniversary of the Department of Statistics in 2013, Professor John Gittins notes:

> Florence Nightingale, the pioneer of modern nursing, following her experiences during the Crimean war, was also an enthusiast for statistical methods. In the 1870s, she discussed the possibility with her friend Benjamin Jowett, Master of Balliol College, of endowing a Professorship of Statistics in Oxford to which

they both agreed to contribute, and later further discussed the idea with Francis Galton, another pioneer of applied statistics. Writing to Galton in 1891, she suggested that the professorship should address the need for statistics relating to education, penology, workhouses and India. In his response, Galton stressed the importance of the new professor doing research as well as teaching, and also questioned the suitability of Oxford as the home for this venture. Neither comment blended well with Miss Nightingale's vision and, partly for these reasons, sadly the proposal foundered (Gittins 2013: 4).

Nevertheless, the Department of Statistics at Oxford now has a Florence Nightingale Bicentennial Fellowship and Tutor in Statistics and Probability as well as a Florence Nightingale Lecture: 2020 being her bicentenary may see other forms of recognition. Her role in statistics is not as well known as that in nursing, but Nightingale was a pioneer in using graphical presentations of statistical data, such as the pie chart, to convey persuasive messages. She is credited with developing the polar-area diagram (which she called a "coxcomb") to illustrate seasonal mortality in the Crimean War hospital she managed (see Nightingale 1858: 310–311). Nightingale was elected the first female member of the Royal Statistical Society in 1859 and became an Honorary Member of the American Statistical Association in 1874.

2.3   Francis Ysidro Edgeworth

However, the University of Oxford did appoint someone we would now call an econometrician to a chair in 1891, namely Francis Ysidro Edgeworth (see Bowley 1934). This was not to a chair in statistics, but as the Drummond Professor of Political Economy at All Souls. Edgeworth was an Irish philosopher and political economist who had previously been Tooke Professor of Economic Science and Statistics in London and made many significant contributions to statistical methods. Earlier in life, he had been a student in philosophy at Balliol College, Oxford, from 1867 to 1869, so was doubly connected with the University.

In statistics, Edgeworth's name is remembered through Edgeworth series, which approximate a probability density function in terms of its cumulants. He published many papers on statistics and his principle of maximum probability is an early version of likelihood (Edgeworth 1887). He also contributed to index number analysis. Stigler (1978: 295) viewed Edgeworth's plan as to 'adapt the statistical methods of the theory of errors to the quantification of uncertainty in the social, particularly economic, sciences' and provides an excellent discussion of its implementation. The Royal Statistical Society awarded Edgeworth the Guy Medal in 1907 and he served as its President during 1912-1914. Edgeworth was also influential in the development of neoclassical economics, perhaps best known for the Edgeworth-Bowley box diagram. In 1891, he was appointed as the founding editor of the *Economic Journal*, where he continued as editor or joint editor until his death 35 years later (for more details on Edgeworth, see Chapter 11 in this volume by Creedy).

3 Econometrics at Oxford, 1900–1980

3.1 Colin Clark

Colin Clark is the next important econometrician at Oxford. Clark compiled the first modern set of national income accounts (NIAs) for the UK and pursued data collection on a worldwide scale. He was born in London and studied chemistry at Brasenose College (1924-1928), Petty's old college, where he became a Fellow for a time, and later was Director of the Agricultural Economics Research Institute at Oxford. His hero was indeed Petty, and like Petty, he started academically as a scientist so was self-taught in economics, with a similar creative imagination, also displaying brilliance and originality from an early age. Clark was first appointed Lecturer in Statistics at the University of Cambridge in 1931, before moving to Australia, where he spent a year at the Universities of Melbourne and Sydney, then as Director of the Queensland Bureau of Industry and as the Queensland Government Statistician between 1938 and 1953 before he returned to England, but settled permanently in Australia from 1978.

His Herculean data collection efforts in the 1930s remain unparalleled to the modern day. He was inspired by Bowley (1895, 1913), and built on key contributions by Marshall (1890), who had considered an aggregate idea of national income, leading to the modern measure of gross domestic product (GDP). Alfred Flux (1924, 1929) was another precursor who, with Bowley, pioneered the Census of Production to create a measure from the supply side as well as estimating the national income, as was Stamp (1916) (see Tily 2009). Tily as well as Millmow (2019) and Chapter 16 of the current volume provide excellent discussions of Clark's major contributions to the development of national income accounts, and as Tily remarks: 'The breadth and depth of Colin Clark's work in the 1930s–funded from his own resources, it should be added—marked him out as the most resourceful and innovative National Accountant of them all' (Tily 2009: 356). (See Darnell (2018) for more detail on Bowley.)

Clark is credited with inventing the concept of "gross national product" before Kuznets (1946) invented GDP, and later was influential in setting up the national accounts for Australia. He produced many journal papers and books, including *The National Income, 1924–1931*, published in 1932 (Clark 1932), and *National Income and Outlay*, in 1937 (Clark 1937). Clark also developed a system of equations explaining the US trade cycle during the period 1921–1941 (Clark 1949), an embryonic macroeconomic model and contributed to development studies (see Maddison 2004).

3.2   Oxford Institute of Statistics

The next significant step in the development of Oxford statistics was again by its economists, who were increasingly keen to build economic theory on a foundation of sound data analysis. This led to the creation in 1935 of an Institute of Statistics financed by the Rockefeller Foundation with a Director holding a new Readership in Statistics (see Chapter 6 in this volume by Toporowski). As Oxford's first research institute in statistics, the new organisation was concerned with economics as well as statistics in relation to economic data, features made more obvious in 1962 when it was renamed the Institute of Economics and Statistics (IES). Chester (1986) provides a history of IES to 1985.

The first Director of the Institute of Statistics in 1935 was the econometrician Jacob Marschak, who was born in Kiev in 1898 as the son of a Jewish jeweller. Marschak had lived an eventful life in Russia and Germany until coming to Oxford fleeing Hitler. He moved to the USA in 1938 where he had a distinguished career at the Cowles Commission.

During the war years, the Acting Director of the Institute was Sir Arthur Bowley, the distinguished economic statistician who had recently retired from a chair at LSE. Although not primarily a statistician, Michał Kalecki was also housed at the Institute from 1939 to 1945 where he contributed to analysing data on many aspects of the Second World War, publishing in the *Bulletin*. Hubert Henderson, Acting Director of the Institute at the time, recorded his appreciation for Kalecki when he left: '[T]he repute that the Institute has won as a war-time centre of lively, yet scientific and realistic economic study, owes much to your stimulating influence' (Henderson quoted in Toporowski 2018: 141). David Worswick (see Chapter 19 in this volume by Seneca) was at the Institute from 1940 to 1960, but did not regard econometrics favourably, arguing that it made 'pretend-tools' (Worswick 1972: 79) while trying to achieve Frisch's aims.

The Readership was then filled by David Champernowne, who also became Director of the Institute from 1945 to 1948 and Professor of Statistics from 1948 to 1959, after which he returned to Cambridge where he had read mathematics and then economics, graduating in 1934. Champernowne went on to do research on income distribution, for which he was the first to provide a statistical model. In 1937, this work earned him a Prize Fellowship at King's College, Cambridge. He continued to work on income distribution for the rest of his academic career (see Boianovsky 2017 for more details).

The Oxford Institute of Statistics then became home to a steady stream of distinguished economic statisticians and econometricians. In roughly chronological order, Frank Burchardt was the Director after Champernowne in 1948, and he helped attract Lawrence Klein, later a Nobel Prize winner. Klein worked at the Institute from 1954 to 1958 during the McCarthy era, and helped develop the first UK macroeconometric model with James Ball, Arthur Hazlewood and Peter Vandome (Klein et al. 1961a). Klein spoke of his association with the Institute in its early days in his Nobel Prize autobiography.[2]

Some of the papers related to Klein's macroeconomic modelling were published in the *Bulletin of the Oxford Institute of Economics and Statistics*, established in 1939, changing its name in 1973 to the *Oxford Bulletin of Economics and Statistics*. Ball et al. (1959) published "Econometric Forecasts for 1959" (for the UK) in the February issue of 1959, while the February 1961 issue contained "Re-estimation of the Econometric Model of the UK and Forecasts for 1961" by Klein et al. (1961b). That issue also published "A Post-Mortem on Econometric Forecasts for 1959" by Hazlewood and Vandome.

Next, IES was home to Gerhard Stuvel (see, for example, Stuvel 1965), Christopher Winsten (whose serial correlation correction method in a 1954 Cowles Discussion Paper with Sig Prais became widely cited (Prais and Winsten 1954)), N. Schwartz and John Hammersley (at Oxford from 1961 and whose excellent 1964 book on Monte Carlo methods with David Hanscomb (Hammersley and Handscomb 1964) helped Hendry and Pravin Trivedi develop their 1972 paper: Hendry and Trivedi 1972). They were followed by a non-econometrician, Teddy Jackson, as Director, then Hendry (who was Director from 1982 to 1984) and Stephen Nickell, who was its final Director from 1984 to 1997.

3.3   James Meade

James Meade (later another Nobel Prize Laureate) was born in Swanage, Dorset, in 1907 and attended Oriel College, Oxford, in 1926 to read Greats,

---

[2] See https://www.nobelprize.org/prizes/economic-sciences/1980/ldcin/biographical/.

but switched to Philosophy, Politics and Economics (PPE), securing an outstanding First. During 1930-1931, he was a postgraduate at Christ's and Trinity Colleges, Cambridge, where he had discussions with Dennis Robertson and John Maynard Keynes among other distinguished economists. Meade was a Lecturer at Hertford College, Oxford, from 1931 to 1937 before going to the League of Nations. In the Second World War, he was a member of the Economic Section of the War Cabinet Secretariat. It was in that role that together with Richard Stone (see Barker 2017) they developed estimates of UK national income accounts (NIAs) under Keynes, who perhaps had understood the crucial role of data from his (1920) calculations of the impossibility of Germany paying the reparations imposed in the Treaty of Versailles, as well as Keynes's desire to know what resources the UK had available to fight the Second World War (see Howson 2017 for more details).

The Oxford Savings Surveys were another major data resource, first analysed by Fisher (1956), reinforcing Oxford economics role in data curation. That paper led to the complete May 1957 issue of the *Bulletin* being devoted to empirical studies of the consumption function with a galaxy of contributors, including Albert Ando and Franco Modigliani, Milton Friedman, Trygve Haavelmo, Lawrence Klein, Denis Sargan and James Tobin, making five Nobel Laureates (Hendry and Phillips (2018) provide more detail about Sargan).

3.4   Martin Feldstein

Martin Feldstein was a Fellow of Nuffield from 1964 to 1967, the year in which he received his DPhil (doctorate) supervised by Terence Gorman (and later became an Honorary Fellow). Feldstein's research pioneered the empirical analysis of production functions for hospitals using differences in location and time within the National Health Service (NHS) to estimate the costs and benefits of various medical procedures. His findings were published in both medical and economics journals, as well as a book (Feldstein 1967), helping shift analyses of healthcare productivity from studies of specific cases to population data sets (see https://voxeu.org/article/ideas-and-influence-martin-feldstein-1939-2019).

3.5   Grayham Ernest Mizon

Grayham Mizon was the RTZ Research Fellow at St Catherine's College, Oxford, from 1970 to 1973 during which time he published important research on estimation and inferential procedures in non-linear models, before returning to LSE (see Mizon 1974, 1977). He remained a long-term collaborator of Hendry and was a key participant in most of the Economic and Social Research Council (ESRC)-funded econometrics research programmes at Nuffield College from 1988 to 2002 and an Associate at the Institute for New Economic Thinking at the Oxford Martin School from 2012 to 2018.

3.6   Alan Brown

Alan Brown moved to Oxford in 1970 and was associated with IES and as editor of the *Bulletin* until his death in 1984 (see, for example, Aitchison and Brown 1957, and Brown and Deaton 1972). Stone (1985: 194) refers to Brown as 'a mainstay of advanced studies in econometrics and development economics' and Creedy (2008: 8) admired him as a thesis supervisor (Brown had examined Hendry's PhD thesis).

3.7   Other Faculty

Other faculty who also taught econometrics at Oxford before (and after) 1980 included Michael Dempster who did so during the 1970s, as did Michael Surrey (see Surrey 1971), Robert Bacon (see, for example, Bacon 1991), followed by David Begg (see Corker and Begg 1985), and Christopher Gilbert (see Gilbert 1976, 1986). Jerry Hausman was a doctoral student then, graduating in 1973 (see Hausman 1974—later also an Honorary Fellow of Nuffield). As a lead into the next section, Jim Poterba was a doctoral student supervised by Hendry, graduating in 1983 when he was already a Junior Research Fellow at Nuffield (see, for instance, Poterba and Summers 1983).

4   Oxford Econometrics, 1980–2000

When Teddy Jackson retired as IES Director in 1982 after focusing on development economics, the University proposed closing the Institute as part of the savings it needed, but offered the first author (newly arrived from LSE) the chance to run it (unpaid) to see if it could pay its way. By renegotiating the royalties accruing to its *Bulletin* sufficiently to fund a full-time Director, in 1984 Steve Nickell (see Ours 2018 for more detail) was attracted to that role, which he held until IES was merged into the new Department of Economics. IES and the *Bulletin* quickly returned to their statistical roots by being at the forefront of the cointegration wave, and by 1986 the *Bulletin* was becoming one of the most cited "statistics" journals, though read by few non-economics statisticians! While he was Director, Hendry started a tradition of fortnightly econometrics lunches where all interested faculty and graduate students could meet and discuss their teaching and research, which still continues. Throughout, there has also been a fortnightly econometrics seminar as a venue for non-Oxford speakers.

It often surprises readers that despite having existed for hundreds of years, Oxford did not have a department of economics until almost the end of the twentieth century (for a brief history, see https://www.economics.ox.ac.uk/about/about-homepage). Before 1997, economics teaching was college based, with colleges having their own fellows who taught PPE. There was a taught BPhil degree for graduates from 1945, which became an MPhil in 1979, with much more technical economics and econometrics content. Over this period, economics had a "sub-faculty" status with IES and Nuffield College being focal points. By way of comparison, the Department of Statistics was only created in 1988.

4.1   Nuffield College

Somewhat earlier, Nuffield College had been founded in 1937 as a graduate college of the University specialising in the social sciences, particularly economics, politics (especially psephology) and sociology. Nuffield had close ties with IES, many of whose members were fellows of the College. Before the creation of an Economics Department, Nuffield acted in lieu of a department as it had the largest number of economics faculty, with many of the main graduate lecture courses taught in the College. Statisticians and econometricians have also often served as its Warden, including Sir David Cox, 1988-1994, Sir Tony Atkinson, 1994-2005 (see Jenkins 2017 for more details), Sir Stephen Nickell, 2006-2012, and Sir Andrew Dilnot since then. Other statisticians who were fellows have included Klim McPherson, Clive Payne, Lucy Carpenter, David Firth, Garett Fitzmaurice and Tom Snijders; and its econometricians included Terence Gorman (see Chapter 21 in this volume by Neary and Honohan), John Muellbauer (see Chapter 26 by Duca), Hendry (see Chapter 24 by Ericsson) and Bent Nielsen (see, for example, Harbo et al. 1998 and Johansen and Nielsen 2009) in addition to those mentioned elsewhere. Nielsen has collaborated with many other Oxford faculty (see, for instance, Hendry and Nielsen 2007 and Vanessa Berenguer-Rico and Nielsen 2020) and contributed to a wide range of econometric theory developments as well as to teaching.

Neil Ericsson joined Nuffield from LSE in 1982 as a Research Officer on an ESRC award with Hendry, starting another long collaboration from Hendry and Ericsson (1983), eventually published in 1991 as Hendry and Ericsson (1991). Adrian Neale followed in 1986, helping develop a menu-driven program for Monte Carlo simulation experiments (see Hendry and Neale 1987). Olympia Bover was a Research Officer, 1985-1987, then Research Fellow, 1987–1989, at Nuffield and Manuel Arellano was also a Research Fellow at Nuffield, 1986-1989, and Research Lecturer at IES, 1985-1989. Together with Steve Bond, Fellow at Nuffield since 1990 and previously a student there from 1984, he published the much-cited Arellano and Bond (1991) paper. This provided an estimation method for dynamic panels where the time-series dimension was relatively short. Gavin Cameron came in 1992 and mainly published with Muellbauer (see Cameron and Muellbauer 1998). Hans-Martin Krolzig joined as a Research Officer at IES and an Associate at Nuffield for a decade from 1995 and published extensively on Markov-switching and business-cycle modelling (see Krolzig 1997) as well as on econometric modelling with Hendry (see, for example, Hendry and Krolzig 1999). Stan Hurn, 1996–1998, and Katy Graddy also researched econometrics.

Two other long collaborations for Hendry that began in IES were with Mike Clements and Jurgen Doornik. That with Clements started with his doctorate, leading to a paper by Clements and Hendry (1993) (where the discussion was longer than the paper!), and numerous publications since, including Clements and Hendry (1998), as well as his participating in many of the ESRC research programmes at Nuffield (see ibid.). That with Doornik began in 1989, initially as a Research Officer on ESRC research programmes and then a Research Fellow at Nuffield College from 1996 on, developing Ox, an object-oriented matrix language (see https://doornik.com/ox/, leading to Doornik and Hendry 1992, applied in Hendry and Doornik 1994; also see the much-used test in Doornik and Hansen 2008).

Neil Shephard was a Fellow of Nuffield over 1991-2013 and Professor of Economics, 1999-2013, actively researching financial econometrics (see, for example, Ole Barndorff-Nielsen and Shephard 2001, 2002, 2004a, b, 2006, for which he received the Royal Statistical Society's Guy Medal in Silver). He contributed importantly to econometric modelling of realised volatility, and developed stochastic volatility models, as well as methods for handling jumps in financial time series in research linked to similar advances for modelling breaks in macroeconomic data. Shephard also formulated methods for non-Gaussian and non-linear models, and with Michael Pitt, developed filtering by simulation using auxiliary particle filters (see Pitt and Shephard 1999). While at Nuffield, he was awarded a number of ESRC grants where Tina

Rydberg (see, for instance, Rydberg and Shephard 2003) and Frank Gerhard (see Gerhard and Hautsch 2002) were Research Officers. He co-founded the *Econometrics Journal* with David Hendry and his later research is discussed in Section 5.

Richard Spady was an Official Fellow of Nuffield over 1992-1999, and a regular visitor since then, researching non- and semi-parametric methods. Oliver Linton, a Research Fellow there from 1991 to 1993, also researched non-parametric methods. Bronwyn Hall, Professor of Economics and Professorial Fellow, Nuffield College, 1996-2001, brought a strong interest in econometric computing, and her Time Series Processor (TSP) software was linked into OxMetrics.

4.2   Doctoral Students

A major driving force behind advances in econometrics across a vast range of topics during the period from 1980 was a succession of brilliant DPhil students adding to those mentioned above, including Anindya Banerjee (later a Fellow of Wadham College), Gregor Smith, John Galbraith, Juan Dolado (see, for example, Banerjee et al. 1986, 1993), Kate Desbarats, Carlo Favero (see Favero and Hendry 1992), Andreas Fischer (see Fischer 1989), Kivilcim Metin (see Metin 1995), Karim Abadir (see, for instance, Abadir 1992), Rebecca Emerson (see Emerson and Hendry 1996), Steven Cook (see Cook and Hendry 1993), Claudio Lupi (see Brunello et al. 2001), Pekka Pere (see Pere 2000) and Edmund Cannon (see Cannon and Tonks 2004).

In addition, some of the DPhil econometricians went into the commercial and public sectors, including Fritz Struth (state-space modelling), Massimo Fuggetta (financial econometrics: founder of Bayes Investments), Ian Harnett (consumption expenditure: founder of Absolute Strategy Research) and Lamin Leigh (money demand: who joined the IMF).

4.3   Research Funding

Over the period 1984-2000, numerous ESRC-funded research grants were attracted to Nuffield by research teams, including various econometricians from Arellano, Banerjee, Clements, Doornik, Hendry, Mizon, Muellbauer, Nielsen, Shephard and John Walker, totalling almost £2 million in nominal terms. In rough chronological order from 1984, grants investigated included *Expectational Variables and Feedback Mechanisms, Structural Change, Model Evaluation, Economic Policy, Cointegration, Modelling Non-stationarity,*

Financial Econometrics and *Forecasting*, the last of which was then supported by a five-year Leverhulme Personal Research Professorship for Hendry.

Links to economic historians continued to be important to the econometricians, especially with major data creators like Charles Feinstein (see Feinstein 1972) and Stephen Broadberry (see Section 6 in Offer 2017 and Chapter 4 in this volume by Offer), including joint teaching of a quantitative approach to the UK's inter-war experience.

Nuffield also acted as a venue for many visiting econometricians, including several visits by (amongst others) Clive Granger, Rob Engle, Adrian Pagan, who was also a Nuffield Fellow for a period (see their interviews by Phillips 1997, Diebold 2003 and Skeels 2016 respectively in *Econometric Theory*), Paul Ruud, Tom Rothenberg, Anders Rahbek and Gunnar Bårdsen.

5   Oxford Econometrics in the Twenty-First Century

With the creation of the Department of Economics in Manor Road, the institutional framework for Oxford econometrics changed. At the same time, the number of graduate students grew dramatically across the University and in economics, where a new MSc in Financial Economics was created jointly with the Saïd Business School in 2003. The Nuffield post-doc programme expanded as a joint venture with the Department. A compulsory econometrics component was introduced in the undergraduate PPE programme.

The econometricians who arrived in Oxford at the faculty level over this period included Valérie Lechene, 1999–2006, Adrian Pagan, 2000–2003, Kevin Shephard, 2004, Martin Browning, 2006–2019, Debopam Bhattacharya, 2009–2015, Jennifer Castle, 2009, Sophocles Mavroeidis, 2011, Michael Keane, 2012–2017, James Wolter, 2013–2018, Vanessa Berenguer-Rico, 2015, James Duffy, 2016, Anders Kock, 2017, Frank DiTraglia, 2019, Max Kasy, 2020 and Frank Windmeijer, 2020. There has been a constant flow of post-docs in econometrics, including Ola Elerian, 2001–2002, Jeremy Large, 2005–2008, Jennifer Castle, 2006–2009, Brendan Beare, 2007–2008, Mika Meitz, 2006–2008, Shin Kanaya, 2008–2012, Vitaliy Oryshchenko, 2011–2014, Vanessa Berenguer-Rico, 2012–2014, Daniel Gutknecht, 2012–2015, James Wolter, 2012–2013, Liang Chen, 2013–2016, Yingying Lee, 2013–2016, Marianne Bruins, 2014–2018, James Duffy, 2014–2016, Ryoko Ito, 2015–2017, Felix Pretis, 2015–2018, Stefan Hubner, 2016, Sander Barendse, 2018, Xiyu Jiao, 2019, and Susana Martins, 2019. Research Officers included Marianne Sensier, Anthony Murphy and

Luca Nunziato. Following the 2008 financial crisis, Hendry received funding from the Institute for New Economic Thinking to set up a Program for Economic Modelling and to develop tools for forecasting after crises, which partly funded a number of the post-docs.

DPhil students in econometrics included Sule Akkoyunlu, Mavroeidis, Domenico Lombardi, Michael Massmann, Guillaume Chevillon, Castle, Carlos Santos, James Reade, Nicholas Fawcett, Julia Giese, Sonja Keller Canto, Pretis, Andrew Martinez, Oleg Kitov, Michael Pitt, Carlos Caceras, Taka Kurita, Diaa Noureldin, Qianzi Zeng, Heiko Hesse, Jiao, Matthias Qian, Aurora Manrique, Cavit Pakel and Clive Bowsher.

Neil Shephard's research in financial econometrics continued to flourish. The returns on financial assets were modelled using volatility models driven by a Lévy process (see Barndorff-Nielsen and Shephard 2002). These are processes allowing a continuous component and both large and many small jumps. The jumps can be estimated by power and bipower variation (see Barndorff-Nielsen and Shephard 2004a) and multivariate features can be estimated by realised covariation (see ibid. 2004b). Shephard was involved in the creation of the MSc in Financial Econometrics and also in teaching the core financial economics paper. He attracted funding from the Man hedge fund to found the Oxford-Man Institute to study quantitative finance, and was its first Director in 2007–2011. Neil is currently Chair of the Department of Statistics at Harvard University.

In 2010, Sophocles Mavroeidis returned to a faculty position from Brown University, working on identification in macroeconomic models. Previously, he had worked on the problem of weak instruments in forward-looking models (Mavroeidis 2004, Kleibergen and Mavroeidis 2009). He next considered the empirical evidence on inflation expectations in the New Keynesian Phillips curve (Mavroeidis et al. 2014), identification using stability restrictions (Magnusson and Mavroeidis 2014) and how learning in representative-agent forward-looking models can generate long memory endogenously (Chevillon and Mavroeidis 2018). This research was supported by a European Research Council (ERC) consolidator grant in 2015. Mavroeidis brought the 30th EC2 conference back to Oxford in 2019 after a long absence since the 4th EC2 conference hosted by Hendry in 1993.

5.1   Software Developments

Research in econometric computing took a new direction with the development of automated software for model selection and detection of outliers and step shifts. Inspired by Hoover and Perez (1999), Hendry and Krolzig (1999, 2005) developed the PcGets software, later replaced by Autometrics by

Doornik (2008) and accompanied by Gets in R by Pretis et al. (2018a). An asymptotic theory for outlier detection was initiated by Hendry et al. (2008) and Johansen and Nielsen (2009). The model selection project continues and involves a number of other researchers, students, post-docs and faculty, including Berenguer-Rico, Castle, Jiao and Qian.

Several new teaching courses were introduced, including Quantitative Economics in 2009 and Environmental Economics and Climate Change for PPE, and, as mentioned above, an MSc in Financial Economics with a financial econometrics core course. Research funding matched the change in emphasis to *Economic Forecasting, Modelling, Forecasting and Policy in the Evolving Macro-economy, Economic Modelling in a Rapidly Changing World, Rebalancing Theory and Evidence in Macroeconomics, Automatic Tests of Model Specification, Extending the Boundaries of Econometric Modelling, Our World in Data, New Approaches to the Identification of Macroeconomic Models* and *Climate Econometrics*.

5.2   Easter Schools

Over the period 2001–2008, Hendry, Nielsen and Shephard organised a series of annual Easter Schools in econometrics funded by the Royal Economic Society and ESRC. The Schools had prominent speakers and attracted many students from across the world:

* *Financial Econometrics*: Enrique Sentana and Neil Shephard
* *Micro-econometrics*: Martin Browning and Hidehiko Ichimura
* *Linear and Non-linear Non-stationary Time Series*: Søren Johansen and Anders Rahbek
* *Financial Econometrics*: Torben Andersen, Tim Bollerslev and Nour Medahi
* *Causality*: David Cox, Nancy Cartwright, David Hendry, Jim Heckman and Steffen Lauritzen
* *Panel Data*: Manuel Arellano and Steve Bond
* *Model Selection*: Kevin Hoover, David Hendry, Benedikt Pötscher and Halbert White

6   Contributions to Data Provision in the Twenty-First Century

Oxford econometrics has continued its interest in data construction and organisation. The vast, easily accessed and immensely useful provision in Our World in Data (see https://ourworldindata.org/) by Max Roser and his team

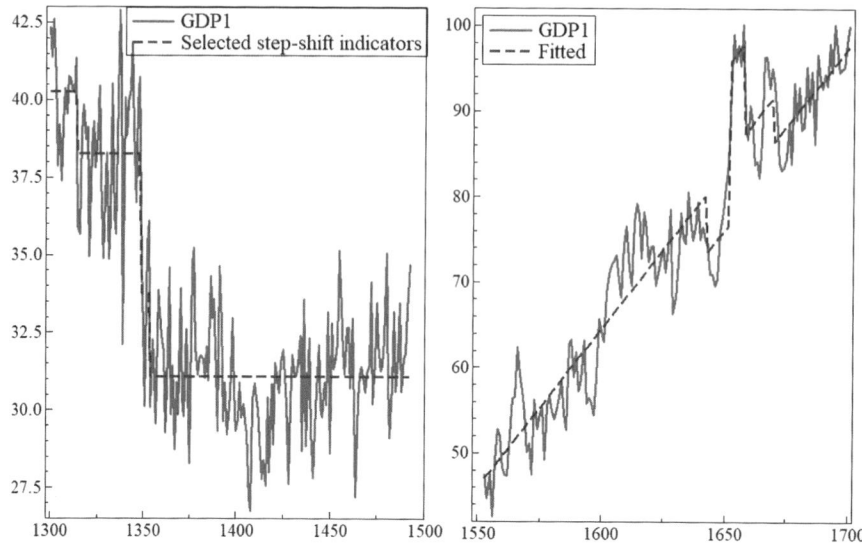

Figure 1.1   UK GDP reconstructions, 1300–1700

is a major contribution to understanding the evolution of the world. Their database has curated many thousands of time series and maps from Age through Antibiotics and Biodiversity to Working Hours, covering economics, politics, climate, health, gender, sustainability, poverty and inequality, all beautifully presented graphically.

Recently, Apostolides et al. (2008) have performed the enormous task of estimating English GDP from 1300-1700, providing an incredibly long run of historical time series data, shown for what the authors call "GDP1" in Figure 1.1, pre- and post- their missing data period.[3] The downward location shift following the Black Death starting in 1348 is very marked in the left-hand panel, as is the relative stagnation through to about 1500, both highlighted by using step-indicator saturation (SIS: see Castle et al. 2015). On the right-hand panel (note the different scales), the strong and relatively constant absolute growth from around 1550 onwards is equally obvious, and now SIS picks up the drop in GDP during the English Civil War (1642-1651), and the boom following its ending, as well as another boom over 1664-1672. While it may be thought to be anachronistic to create GDP data for a period where the concept was unknown, the authors' detailed and extensive archival research is an important contribution to understanding the past, and builds on a long Oxford tradition in data curation.

---

[3] For an update and continuous time series, see Broadberry et al. (2015).

7   Climate Econometrics

The Climate Econometrics (CE)[4] project at Nuffield (co-directed by Hendry and Pretis) brings together a multi-disciplinary group of researchers from economics, econometrics, computing, climate science, political science and geography. The aim is to develop and apply econometric tools to empirical modelling in order to better understand both how humanity has affected the global climate and how humanity has been affected in turn. Econometrics has proved a useful toolkit for statistically modelling high-dimensional dynamic economic systems subject to wide-sense non-stationarity (from stochastic trends and location shifts), outliers, potential non-linearities and simultaneous interactions, based on relevant but incomplete economic theory, so requiring model selection. Figure 1.2 illustrates the extreme wide-sense non-stationarity and huge outliers for UK domestic carbon dioxide (CO_2) emissions in tons per person per year from 1860 to 2017, also showing dramatic recent reductions following the Climate Change Act of 2008, with emissions now below levels recorded in the 1860s when the UK was the "workshop of the world".

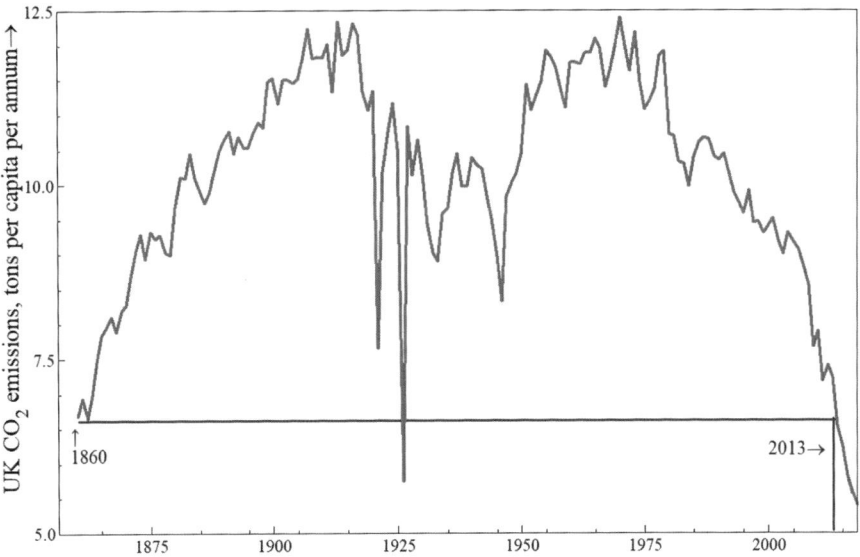

Figure 1.2   UK domestic CO_2 emissions in tons per person per year, 1860–2018

[4] Funded by the Robertson Foundation and Nuffield College: see http://www.climateeconometrics.org for more information.

Since climate change is driven by economic activity creating greenhouse gas emissions (primarily CO_2), similar econometrics modelling tools are proving valuable. Castle and Hendry (2019) and Castle et al. (2019) provide non-technical explanations of the modelling tools and forecasting methods respectively. Empirical examples include linking econometric models and climate systems (see Pretis 2020); damage caused by hurricanes (see Martinez https://sites.google.com/view/andrewbmartinez/current-research/damage-prediction-tool); modelling data on UK and global CO_2 emissions (see Figure 1.2 for the former and Hendry and Pretis 2013 for the latter); the impact of volcanic eruptions on temperatures (see Pretis et al. 2016) and of temperature rises on output worldwide (see Pretis et al. 2018b); and even the role of CO_2 during past ice ages (Castle and Hendry 2020).

Post-doctoral researchers on the climate team include Doornik (econometrics and computing: see Doornik 2008), Luke Jackson (oceanography: see Jackson and Jevrejeva 2016), Ryan Rafaty (climate policy: see Farmer et al. 2019), Sam Rowan (climate policy: see Rowan 2019), with Susana Martins (financial econometrics) and Jiao (econometrics) just joining, as well as DPhil students Moritz Schwarz and Jonas Krule, and research assistant Lisa Thalheimer. Angela Wenham is the communications officer and DPhil graduate Martinez recently left (econometrics and forecasting: see Castle et al. 2017).

Such a project also reflects a number of general developments in econometrics which have led from single topics to multi-disciplinary studies, from single authors to multiple, and spreading from being primarily economics focused to seeing applications in many other observational-data disciplines. An interesting future for Oxford econometrics lies ahead.

References

Abadir, K.M. (1992). 'A Distribution Generating Equation for Unit-Root Statistics'. *Oxford Bulletin of Economics and Statistics*, 54(3): 305–323.

Aitchison, J. and J.A.C Brown (1957). *The Lognormal Distribution with Special Reference to Its Uses in Economics*. Cambridge: Cambridge University Press.

Apostolides, A., S. Broadberry, B. Campbell, M. Overton and B. van Leeuwen (2008). 'English Gross Domestic Product, 1300–1700: Some Preliminary Estimates'. Discussion Paper, University of Warwick. Available at: https://warwick.ac.uk/fac/soc/economics/staff/sbroadberry/wp/pre1700v2.pdf.

Arellano, M. and S.R. Bond (1991). 'Some Tests of Specification for Panel Data: Monte Carlo Evidence and an Application to Employment Equations'. *Review of Economic Studies*, 58(2): 277–297.

Bacon, R.W. (1991). 'Rockets and Feathers: The Asymmetric Speed of Adjustment of UK Retail Gasoline Prices to Cost Changes'. *Energy Economics*, 13(3): 211–218.

Ball, R.J., A. Hazlewood and L.R. Klein (1959). 'Econometric Forecasts for 1959'. *Bulletin of the Oxford Institute of Economics and Statistics*, 21(1): 3–16.

Banerjee, A., J.J. Dolado, J.W. Galbraith and D.F. Hendry (1993). *Co-integration, Error Correction, and the Econometric Analysis of Non-Stationary Data*. Oxford: Oxford University Press.

Banerjee, A., J.J. Dolado, D.F. Hendry and G.W. Smith (1986). 'Exploring Equilibrium Relationships in Econometrics Through Static Models: Some Monte Carlo Evidence'. *Oxford Bulletin of Economics and Statistics*, 48(3): 253–277.

Barker, T. (2017). 'Richard Stone (1913–1991)'. Chapter 37 in R.A. Cord (ed.) *The Palgrave Companion to Cambridge Economics*. Volume 2. London: Palgrave Macmillan: 835–855.

Barndorff-Nielsen, O.E. and N. Shephard (2001). 'Non-Gaussian Ornstein–Uhlenbeck-Based Models and Some of Their Uses in Financial Economics (with Discussion)'. *Journal of the Royal Statistical Society, Series B*, 63(2): 167–241.

Barndorff-Nielsen, O.E. and N. Shephard (2002). 'Econometric Analysis of Realised Volatility and Its Use in Estimating Stochastic Volatility Models (with Discussion)'. *Journal of the Royal Statistical Society, Series B*, 64(2): 253–280.

Barndorff-Nielsen, O.E. and N. Shephard (2004a). 'Power and Bipower Variation with Stochastic Volatility and Jumps (with Discussion)'. *Journal of Financial Econometrics*, 2(1): 1–48.

Barndorff-Nielsen, O.E. and N. Shephard (2004b). 'Econometric Analysis of Realized Covariation: High Frequency Based Covariance, Regression and Correlation in Financial Economics'. *Econometrica*, 72(3): 885–925.

Barndorff-Nielsen, O.E. and N. Shephard (2006). 'Econometrics of Testing for Jumps in Financial Economics Using Bipower Variation'. *Journal of Financial Econometrics*, 4(1): 1–30.

Berenguer-Rico, V. and B. Nielsen (2020). 'Cumulated Sum of Squares Statistics for Nonlinear and Nonstationary Regressions'. *Econometric Theory*, 36(1): 1–47.

Boianovsky, M. (2017). 'David Gawen Champernowne (1912–2000)'. Chapter 34 in R.A. Cord (ed.) *The Palgrave Companion to Cambridge Economics*. Volume 2. London: Palgrave Macmillan: 767–794.

Bowley, A.L. (1895). 'Changes in Average Wages (Nominal and Real) in the United Kingdom Between 1860 and 1891'. *Journal of the Royal Statistical Society*, 58(2): 223–285.

Bowley, A.L. (1913). 'The Census of Production and the National Dividend'. *Economic Journal*, 23(89): 53–61.

Bowley, A.L. (1934). 'Francis Ysidro Edgeworth'. *Econometrica*, 2(2): 113–124.

Broadberry, S., B.M.S. Campbell, A. Klein, M. Overton and B. van Leeuwen (2015). *British Economic Growth, 1270–1870*. Cambridge: Cambridge University Press.

Brown, J.A.C. and A.S. Deaton (1972). 'Surveys in Applied Economics: Models of Consumer Behaviour'. *Economic Journal*, 82(328): 1,145–1,236.

Brunello, G., C. Lupi and P. Ordine (2001). 'Widening Differences in Italian Regional Unemployment'. *Labour Economics*, 8(1): 103–129.

Cameron, G. and J. Muellbauer (1998). 'The Housing Market and Regional Commuting and Migration Choices'. *Scottish Journal of Political Economy*, 45(4): 420–446.

Cannon, E.S. and I. Tonks (2004). 'UK Annuity Rates, Money's Worth and Pension Replacement Ratios, 1957–2002'. *The Geneva Papers on Risk and Insurance: Issues and Practice*, 29(3): 371–393.

Castle, J.L., M.P. Clements and D.F. Hendry (2019). *Forecasting: An Essential Introduction*. New Haven and London: Yale University Press.

Castle, J.L., J.A. Doornik, D.F. Hendry and F. Pretis (2015). 'Detecting Location Shifts During Model Selection by Step-Indicator Saturation'. *Econometrics*, 3(2): 240–264.

Castle, J.L. and D.F. Hendry (2019). *Modelling our Changing World*. Palgrave Macmillan. Open access. Available at: https://link.springer.com/content/pdf/10.1007%2F978-3-030-21432-6.pdf.

Castle, J.L. and D.F. Hendry (2020). 'Climate Econometrics: An Overview'. *Foundations and Trends in Econometrics*, 10(3–4): 145–322.

Castle, J.L., D.F. Hendry and A.B. Martinez (2017). 'Evaluating Forecasts, Narratives and Policy Using a Test of Invariance'. *Econometrics*, 5(3), article 39. Open access. Available at: https://www.mdpi.com/2225-1146/5/3/39.

Chester, N. (1986). *Economics, Politics and Social Studies in Oxford, 1900–85*, especially Chapter 10 'The Institute of Economics and Statistics'. Basingstoke: Macmillan: 144–160.

Chevillon, G. and S. Mavroeidis (2018). 'Perpetual Learning and Apparent Long Memory'. *Journal of Economic Dynamics and Control*, 90(May): 343–365.

Clark, C.G. (1932). *The National Income, 1924–1931*. London: Macmillan.

Clark, C.G. (1937). *National Income and Outlay*. London: Macmillan.

Clark, C.G. (1949). 'A System of Equations Explaining the United States Trade Cycle, 1921 to 1941'. *Econometrica*, 17(2): 93–124.

Clements, M.P. and D.F. Hendry (1993). 'On the Limitations of Comparing Mean Squared Forecast Errors (with Discussion)'. *Journal of Forecasting*, 12(8): 617–637.

Clements, M.P. and D.F. Hendry (1998). *Forecasting Economic Time Series*. Cambridge: Cambridge University Press

Cook, S. and D.F. Hendry (1993). 'The Theory of Reduction in Econometrics'. In B. Hamminga and N.B. De Marchi (eds) *Idealization VI: Idealization in Economics*. Poznań Studies in the Philosophy of the Sciences and the Humanities, 38. Amsterdam: Rodopi: 71–100.

Corker, R.J. and D.K.H. Begg (1985). 'Rational Dummy Variables in an Intertemporal Optimisation Framework'. *Oxford Bulletin of Economics and Statistics*, 47(1): 71–78.

Creedy, J. (2008). 'J.A.C. Brown (1922–1984): An Appreciation'. Research Paper 1027, Economics Department, University of Melbourne.

Darnell, A. (2018). 'Arthur Lyon Bowley (1869–1957)'. Chapter 8 in R.A. Cord (ed.) *The Palgrave Companion to LSE Economics*. London: Palgrave Macmillan: 215–238.

Diebold, F.X. (2003). 'The ET Interview: Professor Robert F. Engle'. *Econometric Theory*, 19(6): 1,159–1,193.

Doornik, J.A. (2008). 'Encompassing and Automatic Model Selection'. *Oxford Bulletin of Economics and Statistics*, 70(S1): 915–925.

Doornik, J.A. and D.F. Hendry (1992). *PCGIVE 7: An Interactive Econometric Modelling System*. Oxford: Institute of Economics and Statistics, University of Oxford.

Doornik, J.A. and H. Hansen (2008). 'An Omnibus Test for Univariate and Multivariate Normality'. *Oxford Bulletin of Economics and Statistics*, 70(S1): 927–939.

Edgeworth, F.Y. (1887). *Metretike, Or the Method of Measuring Probability and Utility*. London: Temple.

Emerson, R.A. and D.F. Hendry (1996). 'An Evaluation of Forecasting Using Leading Indicators'. *Journal of Forecasting*, 15(4): 271–291.

Farmer, J.D., C. Hepburn, M.C. Ives, T. Hale, T. Wetzer, P. Mealy, R. Rafaty, S. Srivastav and R. Way (2019). 'Sensitive Intervention Points in the Post-Carbon Transition'. *Science*, 364(6,436): 132–134.

Favero, C. and D.F. Hendry (1992). 'Testing the Lucas Critique: A Review'. *Econometric Reviews*, 11(3): 265–306.

Feinstein, C.H. (1972). *National Income, Expenditure and Output of the United Kingdom, 1855–1965*. Cambridge: Cambridge University Press.

Feldstein, M.S. (1967). *Economic Analysis for Health Service Efficiency: Econometric Studies of the British National Health Service*. Amsterdam: North-Holland.

Fischer, A.M. (1989). 'Policy Regime Changes and Monetary Expectations: Testing for Super Exogeneity'. *Journal of Monetary Economics*, 24(3): 423–436.

Fisher, M.R. (1956). 'Exploration in Savings Behaviour'. *Bulletin of the Oxford University Institute of Economics and Statistics*, 18(3): 201–277.

Flux, A.W. (1924). 'The Census of Production'. *Journal of the Royal Statistical Society*, 87(3): 351–390.

Flux, A.W. (1929). 'The National Income'. *Journal of the Royal Statistical Society*, 92(1): 1–25.

Frisch, R. (1933). 'Editorial'. *Econometrica*, 1(1): 1–4.

Gerhard, F. and N. Hautsch (2002). 'Volatility Estimation on the Basis of Price Intensities'. *Journal of Empirical Finance*, 9(1): 57–89.

Gilbert, C.L. (1976). 'The Original Phillips Curve Estimates'. *Economica*, New Series, 43(169): 51–57

Gilbert, C.L. (1986). 'Professor Hendry's Econometric Methodology'. *Oxford Bulletin of Economics and Statistics*, 48(3): 283–307.

Gilbert, C.L. and D. Qin (2006). 'The First Fifty Years of Modern Econometrics'. Chapter 4 in T.C. Mills and K.D. Patterson (eds) *Palgrave Handbook of*

Econometrics—Volume 1: Econometric Theory. Basingstoke: Palgrave Macmillan: 117–155.

Gilbert, C.L. and D. Qin (2007). 'Representation in Econometrics: A Historical Perspective'. Chapter 10 in M.A. Boumans (ed.) *Measurement in Economics: A Handbook.* Amsterdam: Elsevier: 251–269.

Gittins, J. (2013). 'Oxford University Department of Statistics A Brief History'. Available at: http://www.stats.ox.ac.uk/wp-content/uploads/2017/07/History_of_Statistics_Department_3_5_13.pdf.

Harbo, I., S. Johansen, B. Nielsen and A. Rahbek (1998). 'Asymptotic Inference on Cointegrating Rank in Partial Systems'. *Journal of Business and Economic Statistics,* 16(4): 388–399.

Hammersley, J.M. and D.C. Handscomb (1964). *Monte Carlo Methods.* London: Chapman and Hall.

Hausman, J.A. (1974). 'Full Information Instrumental Variables Estimation of Simultaneous Equations Systems'. *Annals of Economic and Social Measurement,* 3(4): 641–652.

Hazlewood, A. and P. Vandome (1961). 'A Post-Mortem on Econometric Forecasts for 1959'. *Bulletin of the Oxford Institute of Economics and Statistics,* 23(1): 67–81.

Hendry, D.F. and J.A. Doornik (1994). 'Modelling Linear Dynamic Econometric Systems'. *Scottish Journal of Political Economy,* 41(1): 1–33.

Hendry, D.F. and N.R. Ericsson (1983). 'Assertion Without Empirical Basis: An Econometric Appraisal of "*Monetary Trends in…the United Kingdom*" by Milton Friedman and Anna Schwartz'. In *Monetary Trends in the United Kingdom.* Bank of England Panel of Academic Consultants, Panel Paper No. 22. London: Bank of England: 45–101.

Hendry, D.F. and N.R. Ericsson (1991). 'An Econometric Analysis of UK Money Demand in *Monetary Trends in the United States and the United Kingdom* by Milton Friedman and Anna J. Schwartz'. *American Economic Review,* 81(1): 8–38.

Hendry, D.F., S. Johansen and C. Santos (2008). 'Automatic Selection of Indicators in a Fully Saturated Regression'. *Computational Statistics,* 23(2): 317–335. Erratum: 337–339.

Hendry, D.F. and H.-M. Krolzig (1999). 'Improving on "Data Mining Reconsidered" by K.D. Hoover and S.J. Perez'. *Econometrics Journal,* 2(2): 202–219.

Hendry, D.F. and H.-M. Krolzig (2005). 'The Properties of Automatic *GETS* Modelling'. *Economic Journal,* 115(502): C32–C61.

Hendry, D.F. and M.S. Morgan (eds) (1995). *The Foundations of Econometric Analysis.* Cambridge: Cambridge University Press.

Hendry, D.F. and A.J. Neale (1987). 'Monte Carlo Experimentation Using PC-NAIVE'. In T. Fomby and G.F. Rhodes (eds) *Advances in Econometrics.* Volume 6. Greenwich, CT: JAI Press: 91–125.

Hendry, D.F. and B. Nielsen (2007). *Econometric Modeling: A Likelihood Approach.* Princeton: Princeton University Press.

Hendry, D.F. and P.C.B. Phillips (2018). 'John Denis Sargan (1924–1996)'. Chapter 27 in R.A. Cord (ed.) *The Palgrave Companion to LSE Economics*. London: Palgrave Macmillan: 667–695.

Hendry, D.F. and F. Pretis (2013). 'Anthropogenic Influences on Atmospheric CO_2'. Chapter 12 in R. Fouquet (ed.) *Handbook on Energy and Climate Change*. Cheltenham: Edward Elgar: 287–326.

Hendry, D.F. and P.K. Trivedi (1972). 'Maximum Likelihood Estimation of Difference Equations with Moving-Average Errors: A Simulation Study'. *Review of Economic Studies*, 39(2): 117–145.

Hoover, K.D. and S.J. Perez (1999). 'Data Mining Reconsidered: Encompassing and the General-to-Specific Approach to Specification Search'. *Econometrics Journal*, 2(2): 167–191.

Howson, S. (2017). 'James Meade (1907–1995)'. Chapter 32 in R.A. Cord (ed.) *The Palgrave Companion to Cambridge Economics*. Volume 2. London: Palgrave Macmillan: 723–746.

Jackson, L.P. and S. Jevrejeva (2016). 'A Probabilistic Approach to 21st Century Regional Sea-Level Projections Using RCP and High-End Scenarios'. *Global and Planetary Change*, 146(November): 179–189

Jenkins, S.P. (2017). 'Anthony B. Atkinson (1944–)'. Chapter 52 in R.A. Cord (ed.) *The Palgrave Companion to Cambridge Economics*. Volume 2. London: Palgrave Macmillan: 1,151–1,174. (Title altered following Atkinson's death in 2017.)

Johansen, S. and B. Nielsen (2009). 'An Analysis of the Indicator Saturation Estimator as a Robust Regression Estimator'. Chapter 1 in J.L. Castle and N. Shephard (eds) *The Methodology and Practice of Econometrics: A Festschrift in Honour of David F. Hendry*. Oxford: Oxford University Press: 1–36.

Kleibergen, F. and S. Mavroeidis (2009). 'Weak Instrument Robust Tests in GMM and the New Keynesian Phillips Curve (with discussion)'. *Journal of Business & Economic Statistics*, 27(3): 293–311.

Klein, L.R. (1953). *A Textbook of Econometrics*. Evanston, IL: Row, Peterson, and Co.

Klein, L.R., R.J. Ball, A. Hazlewood and P. Vandome (1961a). *An Econometric Model of the United Kingdom*. Institute of Statistics, Monograph No. 6. Oxford: Basil Blackwell.

Klein, L.R., A. Hazlewood and P. Vandome (1961b). 'Re-estimation of the Econometric Model of the UK and Forecasts for 1961'. *Bulletin of the Oxford Institute of Economics and Statistics*, 23(1): 49–66.

Krolzig, H.-M. (1997). *Markov-Switching Vector Autoregressions: Modelling, Statistical Inference, and Application to Business Cycle Analysis*. Lecture Notes in Economics and Mathematical Systems, 454. Berlin: Springer-Verlag.

Kuznets, S. (1946). *National Income: A Summary of Findings*. New York: National Bureau of Economic Research.

Maddison, A. (2004). 'Quantifying and Interpreting World Development: Macromeasurement Before and After Colin Clark'. *Australian Economic History Review*, 44(1): 1–34.

Magnusson, L.M. and S. Mavroeidis (2014). 'Identification Using Stability Restrictions'. *Econometrica*, 82(5): 1,799–1,851.

Malinvaud, E. (1966). *Statistical Methods of Econometrics*. Chicago: Rand McNally & Company.

Marshall, A. (1890). *Principles of Economics*. London: Macmillan.

Mavroeidis, S. (2004). 'Weak Identification of Forward-Looking Models in Monetary Economics'. *Oxford Bulletin of Economics and Statistics*, 66(S1): 609–635.

Mavroeidis, S., M. Plagborg-Møller and J.H. Stock (2014). 'Empirical Evidence on Inflation Expectations in the New Keynesian Phillips Curve'. *Journal of Economic Literature*, 52(1): 124–188.

McCormick, T. (2009). *William Petty: And the Ambitions of Political Arithmetic*. Oxford: Oxford University Press.

Metin, K. (1995). 'An Integrated Analysis of Turkish Inflation'. *Oxford Bulletin of Economics and Statistics*, 57(4): 513–531.

Millmow, A.J. (2019). 'The Economist Who Changed His Mind: The Life and Times of Colin Clark'. Unpublished typescript, Federation Business School, Australia.

Mizon, G.E. (1974). 'The Estimation of Non-Linear Econometric Equations: An Application to the Specification and Estimation of an Aggregate Putty-Clay Relation for the United Kingdom'. *Review of Economic Studies*, 41(3): 353–369.

Mizon, G.E. (1977). 'Inferential Procedures in Nonlinear Models: An Application in a UK Industrial Cross Section Study of Factor Substitution and Returns to Scale'. *Econometrica*, 45(5): 1,221–1,242.

Morgan, M.S. (1990). *The History of Econometric Ideas*. Cambridge: Cambridge University Press.

Nightingale, F. (1858). *Notes on Matters Affecting the Health, Efficiency, and Hospital Administration of the British Army, Founded Chiefly on the Experience of the Late War*. London: Harrison and Sons.

Offer, A. (2017). 'Charles Hilliard Feinstein (1932–2004)'. Chapter 46 in R.A. Cord (ed.) *The Palgrave Companion to Cambridge Economics*. Volume 2. London: Palgrave Macmillan: 1,027–1,044.

Ours, J.C. (2018). 'Stephen J. Nickell (1944–)'. Chapter 27 in R.A. Cord (ed.) *The Palgrave Companion to LSE Economics*. London: Palgrave Macmillan: 667–695.

Pere, P. (2000). 'Adjusted Estimates and Wald Statistics for the AR(1) Model with Constant'. *Journal of Econometrics*, 98(2): 335–363.

Petty, W. (1690). *Political Arithmetick*. London: Clavel.

Phillips, P.C.B. (1997). 'The ET Interview: Professor Clive Granger'. *Econometric Theory*, 13(2): 253–303.

Pitt, M.K and N. Shephard (1999). 'Filtering via Simulation: Auxiliary Particle Filters'. *Journal of the American Statistical Association*, 94(446): 590–599.

Poterba, J.M. and L.H. Summers (1983). 'Dividend Taxes, Corporate Investment, and "Q"'. *Journal of Public Economics*, 22(2): 135–167.

Prais, S.J. and C.B. Winsten (1954). 'Trend Estimators and Serial Correlation'. Cowles Commission Discussion Paper 383. Chicago: Cowles Foundation.

Pretis, F. (2020). 'Econometric Modelling of Climate Systems: The Equivalence of Energy Balance Models and Cointegrated Vector Autoregressions'. *Journal of Econometrics*, 214(1): 256–273.

Pretis, F., L. Schneider, J.E. Smerdon and D.F. Hendry (2016). 'Detecting Volcanic Eruptions in Temperature Reconstructions by Designed Break-Indicator Saturation'. *Journal of Economic Surveys*, 30(3): 403–429.

Pretis, F., J.J. Reade and G. Sucarrat (2018a). 'Automated General-to-Specific (GETS) Regression Modeling and Indicator Saturation for Outliers and Structural Breaks'. *Journal of Statistical Software*, 86(3). Open access. Available at: https://www.jstatsoft.org/article/view/v086i03.

Pretis, F., M. Schwarz, K. Tang, K. Haustein and M.R. Allen (2018b). 'Uncertain Impacts on Economic Growth when Stabilizing Global Temperatures at 1.5°C or 2°C Warming'. *Philosophical Transactions of the Royal Society A*, 376: 20160460.

Qin, D. (1993). *The Formation of Econometrics: A Historical Perspective*. Oxford: Clarendon Press.

Qin, D. (2013). *A History of Econometrics: The Reformation from the 1970s*. Oxford: Clarendon Press.

Qin, D. and C.L. Gilbert (2001). 'The Error Term in the History of Time Series Econometrics'. *Econometric Theory*, 17(2): 424–450.

Rowan, S.S. (2019). 'Pitfalls in Comparing Paris Pledges'. *Climatic Change*, 155(4): 455–467.

Rydberg, T.H. and N. Shephard (2003). 'Dynamics of Trade-by-Trade Price Movements: Decomposition and Models'. *Journal of Financial Econometrics*, 1(1): 2–25.

Schumpeter, J.A. (1933). 'The Common Sense of Econometrics'. *Econometrica*, 1(1): 5–12.

Skeels, C.L. (2016). 'The ET Interview: Adrian Pagan'. *Econometric Theory*, 32(5): 1,055–1,094.

Stamp, J. (1916). *British Incomes and Property: The Application of Official Statistics to Economic Problems*. London: P.S. King & Son.

Stigler, S.M. (1978). 'Francis Ysidro Edgeworth, Statistician'. *Journal of the Royal Statistical Society, Series A*, 141(3): 287–322.

Stone, J.R.N. (1985). 'James Alan Calvert Brown: An Appreciation'. *Oxford Bulletin of Economics and Statistics*, 47(3): 191–197.

Stuvel, G. (1965). *Systems of Social Accounts*. Oxford: Clarendon Press.

Surrey, M.J.C. (1971). *The Analysis and Forecasting of the British Economy*. London: Cambridge University Press.

Thomas, J.J. (2018). 'LSE and Econometrics'. Chapter 1 in R.A. Cord (ed.) *The Palgrave Companion to LSE Economics*. London: Palgrave Macmillan: 3–33.

Tily, G. (2009). 'John Maynard Keynes and the Development of National Accounts in Britain, 1895–1941'. *Review of Income and Wealth*, 55(2): 331–359.

Toporowski, J. (2018). *Michał Kalecki: An Intellectual Biography, Volume II, By Intellect Alone 1939–1970*. Basingstoke: Palgrave.

Valavanis, S. (1959). *Econometrics*. New York: McGraw-Hill.

Worswick, G.D.N. (1972). 'Is Progress in Economic Science Possible?'. *Economic Journal*, 82(325): 73–86.

Zarnowitz, V. (2004). 'An Important Subject in Need of Much New Research'. *Journal of Business Cycle Measurement and Analysis*, 1(1): 1–7.

2

Development Economics at Oxford, 1950–2020

Frances Stewart and Valpy FitzGerald

1   Introduction

Development economics as a distinct branch of economics emerged after the Second World War as newly independent countries and other poor countries sought assistance—finance, technology and policy advice—in realising their economic goals. Broadly, development economics is directed at understanding how developing economies work and providing policy advice. New institutions were established in response to the post-colonial context—in particular, specialised UN agencies, the Bretton Woods institutions and developed countries' aid ministries. Naturally—and particularly in the UK—this new and specialised field of economics built on the foundations of colonial economics in general and empirical knowledge of Africa and South Asia in particular. However, the new field also had important foundations in the European approach to the study of the process of industrialisation, socio-economic

We have greatly benefited from generous contributions and comments from many colleagues, including Judith Heyer, Rosemary Thorp and Barbara Harriss-White, who commented on the chapter as a whole, and Chris Adam, Cheryl Doss, Xiaolan Fu, Douglas Gollin, John Knight, Diego Sánchez-Ancochea, Francis Teal and Adrian Wood, who helped us understand their own work. Needless to say, we alone are responsible for the text, and we apologise to anyone who feels we have misrepresented them.

F. Stewart (✉) • V. FitzGerald
Oxford Department of International Development, Queen Elizabeth House, Oxford, UK
e-mail: Frances.stewart@qeh.ox.ac.uk; edmund.fitzgerald@qeh.ox.ac.uk

© The Author(s), under exclusive license to Springer Nature Switzerland AG 2021
R. A. Cord (ed.), *The Palgrave Companion to Oxford Economics*,
https://doi.org/10.1007/978-3-030-58471-9_2

transformation and how to "catch up" with the most advanced nations. Both traditions were (and still are) represented in Oxford development economics, as we shall see.

During the war years, Oxford's Institute of Economics and Statistics (which had been established in 1935 in order to construct economic theory on the basis of a sound foundation of data analysis) gave a home to leading European refugee economists, among them founders of development economics in their own political economy tradition such as Michał Kalecki and Kurt Mandelbaum, as well as other key theorists of industrialisation such as Ernst Schumacher and Josef Steindl. The experience of British wartime controls and post-war reconstruction also provided the justification for State intervention, economic planning and basic needs provision which were to profoundly affect heterodox development economists at Oxford.

The post-war influence of Keynesianism in Oxford, through Roy Harrod and John Hicks, was also directly relevant to development economics—due to Harrod's emphasis on growth and capital accumulation on the one hand, and Hicks on incomes and employment on the other. The notion that output and productivity growth, full employment and rising living standards for the population as a whole could and should be the goal of macroeconomic policy was important to the new generation of development economists at Oxford.

Nonetheless, the Oxford chair explicitly devoted to the study of the economies of developing countries was only created in 1963, when Herbert Frankel became Professor of the Economics of Underdeveloped Countries, a post he was to hold until his retirement in 1971. His title had initially been Professor of Colonial Economic Affairs on its creation in 1944, and subsequently Commonwealth Professor of Economic Affairs. Meanwhile, the Institute of Colonial Studies became the Institute of Commonwealth Studies and eventually the Oxford Department of International Development (ODID).

Development economics at Oxford has made major contributions to the analysis of development economics worldwide. Oxford development economics was never monolithic. For much of the time, two schools can be distinguished: one reflecting mainstream economics and using neoclassical assumptions applied to developing countries, the other more critical, adopting institutional and political economy approaches, often drawing in and working with various disciplines. The two schools had distinct intellectual roots, broadly corresponding to the colonial/neoclassical and Keynesian/European traditions sketched above. They were occasionally in direct conflict, often worked on parallel lines, but usually cooperated, particularly in teaching the subject to generations of undergraduates and postgraduates. This chapter traces the story from 1950 to the present day.

Section 2 of the chapter surveys the changing context and the institutional evolution of development economics in Oxford. Section 3 reviews the contributions of development economists which we interpret to include scholars studying the economies of what are commonly known as developing countries—hence, we include those working on topics of direct relevance to developing countries, some of whom also worked on other issues and might not describe themselves as development economists. Section 4 concludes with some reflections on the nature of this field of economics, the Oxford contribution in both theory and practice, and possible directions for the future.

2   Context and Institutions

2.1   The Changing Context

During the seven decades covered in this chapter, both the prevailing economic environment facing developing countries and dominant thought among economists changed significantly. As far as the social and economic environment is concerned, the period starts with deep and rather uniform underdevelopment in the colonies and newly independent countries of the Third World, as well as countries in Latin America which, though formally independent for many decades, were subject to "informal colonisation". Very low incomes and poor social indicators, a heavy dependence on agricultural production and primary commodity exports, weak and deteriorating terms of trade, and small "modern" sectors presented the main challenges facing developing countries, while the developed countries still showed the scars of the Second World War and their economies remained subject to the controls and restrictions introduced during the war. For about three decades after the Second World War, most developing countries remained inward-looking with many constraints on production, trade and capital, in contrast to developed countries where government intervention in both internal and external markets was progressively reduced. However, from around 1980, marketisation accelerated in developed countries in response to political changes, while a debt crisis greatly increased the influence of the international financial institutions (IFIs) over policy-making in many developing countries, and consequently government intervention in the economy were radically reduced and international integration of product and capital (but not, of course, labour) markets followed in a process which came to be described as "globalisation".

The pace and nature of economic development varied considerably among countries over the succeeding decades, so that by 2000, the Third World was far less homogeneous, with differences among countries providing abundant material for the analysis of causes and consequences of structural and policy change. Social indicators showed considerable improvement almost everywhere; the gap between developed and developing countries narrowed, and some countries effectively caught up with developed countries in industrialisation and incomes (Nayyar 2013). However, over one-and-a-half billion remained in extreme poverty, many in so-called middle-income as well as low-income countries and poverty incidence was particularly high and persistent in Sub-Saharan Africa (Ravallion 2016).

Mainstream economics also changed over these decades. For three decades after the Second World War, Keynesianism was dominant. However, it was largely displaced in the late 1970s, partly due to the theoretical work of Friedrich Hayek and Milton Friedman, but also as a result of political changes. The neoclassical paradigm became dominant in economics departments from then on, albeit challenged by unorthodox economists such as Joe Stiglitz. This radical change in mainstream economics undoubtedly affected the teaching of and research into development economics. Despite this, it should be emphasised that many development economists adopted a neoclassical approach throughout this period, while others stuck to a broadly Keynesian approach. This is illustrated by the differences in approach of economists working on development in Oxford.

Another change that affected development economics at least in the UK was the British government's policies towards development cooperation generally and development research in particular. With decolonisation, the government was concerned to promote relations with the newly independent countries through commercial, cultural and academic relations, and a government department devoted to development was initiated. Its status—whether independent or part of the Foreign and Commonwealth Office—changed according to which government was in power. Resources devoted to aid rose, culminating in a statutory commitment to the achievement of the United Nations target of 0.7% of annual gross national income in 2015. Consequently, there was financial support for area and development studies centres, for research and for training, as well as numerous consultancy opportunities to assist in the disbursement of aid. Research funding increased substantially, gradually switching from support for relatively small projects to large grants administered competitively. Development economics in the UK generally flourished in this environment.

2.2   Institutional Evolution in Oxford

The institutional centres in Oxford where development economists congregate have been of considerable importance in generating collaborative research and the fertilisation of ideas, as well as in encouraging interdisciplinarity. The main institutions of relevance were the Institute of Economics and Statistics, later evolving into the Economics Department, Queen Elizabeth House (QEH), eventually becoming the ODID, Nuffield College, and a number of regional studies centres.

QEH was constituted by Royal Charter in 1954 as a residential centre affiliated to the University which people concerned with the study of Commonwealth affairs could visit in order to make contacts and exchange ideas. In 1961, the Institute for Commonwealth Studies moved into QEH, bringing with it Oxford academic positions from a number of disciplines, mainly non-economists. In 1968, the economist Paul Streeten became Director, and it was then that QEH became a focus for development economics. The Agricultural Economics Research Institute was subsumed into QEH in 1986 when the latter became a fully fledged department of the University. Subsequently, QEH introduced graduate degrees, including the multidisciplinary MPhil in Development Studies, a doctorate in Development Studies and, over time, several other Master's programmes, as well as becoming responsible for the MSc in Economics for Development. The Department was renamed the Oxford Department for International Development in 2008.

Nuffield College is a multidisciplinary graduate college—covering economics, politics and sociology—founded in 1937. Prominent economists associated with the College at various times who have contributed to development economics include Ian little, James Mirrlees, Nicholas Stern and Amartya Sen.

In the 1960s, the University established regional studies for Latin America, the Middle East, Japan, Russia and Eastern Europe and appointed young research-driven economists. They made a valuable contribution to development research through their knowledge of the economies of particular regions, combined with a concern for historical, institutional, socio-political and policy issues.

The two centres most relevant to development were the Latin American Centre (LAC), created in 1964, and the Centre for the Study of African Economies (CSAE), established in 1991. In LAC, economists have adopted a historical and institutional approach, often conducting multidisciplinary collaborative work, usually involving an extensive international collaborative network with colleagues from both the Americas. Oxford economists associated with the Centre have included Rosemary Thorp, Valpy FitzGerald and Diego Sanchez-Ancochea. CSAE was set up with an ambitious research agenda covering both macro- and microeconomic questions, all with a central focus on understanding how poverty in Africa could be reduced, using advanced theory and statistical techniques, particularly household surveys to investigate poverty, and firm-level data to investigate sources of low productivity within manufacturing firms. The Centre was initially directed by Paul Collier[1] with Francis Teal as Deputy. Besides them, senior researchers included Chris Adam, Abigail Barr, David Bevan, Marcel Fafchamps and John Knight, as well as many younger researchers, including a number of African scholars. It became a focal point for collaborative work among numerous African countries and produced both detailed country-level research and comparative work across these countries. The major innovation, for an African-focused research agenda, was that household and firm surveys were designed to generate panel data.

Although there was no centre for Asian studies as such, South Asia was a focus of extensive study throughout the period.

3   The Contributions of Oxford Development Economists

3.1   The Early Years

In the 1950s and 1960s, Herbert Frankel, Hla Myint, Colin Clark, Thomas Balogh, Peter Ady, Ursula Hicks and Peggy (Margaret) Haswell were the most active of the development economists at Oxford. Echoing later developments, they (and those who worked with them) fell broadly into different categories: Frankel and Myint were strong (and at the time unfashionable) advocates of the merits of the market and highly critical of State intervention. However, as Toye states of Frankel, 'he found few Oxford colleagues who shared his veneration of the market mechanism' (Toye 2009: 175). Balogh was much more critical of market economics, believing that State intervention was essential to generate development; Clark adopted a statistical approach, aiming to detect broad trends in national income and sectoral shares; and Ady, Hicks and Haswell provided careful analysis in their respective fields (national income

---

[1] This chapter covers some of Paul Collier's work, but is not comprehensive, as he is also the subject of a separate chapter in this volume.

accounting in the case of Ady; taxation in that of Hicks; and Haswell worked on peasant agriculture).

Frankel was a South African and a dislike of the paternalism of the apartheid semi-colonial State there inspired his ideas. While at the London School of Economics (LSE), he had also been influenced by laissez-faire anti-State economists, such as Hayek, Frank Paish and Lionel Robbins. A precursor of the conditionality later practiced by the IFIs, Frankel argued that aid should be dependent on 'the integration of their countries into the free world economy' (Frankel 1952: 324). However, unlike many in this school of economics, he was suspicious of mathematics and believed that 'economic behaviour was inherently embedded in the peculiarities of individual societies' (Toye 2009: 176). Myint became Lecturer in Colonial Economics at Oxford in 1950 later renamed Lecturer in Underdeveloped Countries and left in 1965. Like Frankel, he was greatly influenced by Hayek (his doctoral supervisor) and by his experience in Burma where he worked intermittently as an economic adviser. He shared Frankel's suspicion of planning and other government intervention and broadly supported a laissez-faire approach (Myint 1964). His major original contribution was the application of Adam Smith's notion of trade as a "vent for surplus": departing from the assumption of full employment, he argued that free trade would enable developing countries to find a market for their surplus agricultural output which would otherwise be unused (Myint 1958).

Balogh, who became a Fellow of Balliol in 1940, was a heterodox political economist, an adviser to numerous governments and central banks, including those of India, Malta, Jamaica, Greece, Mauritius, Algeria and the Sudan, as well as being Adviser on Economic Affairs in the Cabinet Office of the UK during Harold Wilson's premiership. His contributions to development economics were mostly critical rather than creative, showing the weaknesses in a variety of models and policies. He was welcomed by progressive governments for his ability to understand the politics of decision-making and to identify equitable solutions (Balogh 1963, 1966).

Clark was Director of the Agricultural Economics Research Institute at Oxford from 1953 to 1969. In contrast to Frankel and Balogh, he was not primarily interested in theory, but in the accumulation of facts, drawing conclusions from broad trends. His approach can be seen as a precursor of Irving Kravis, Simon Kuznets and Hollis Chenery. The first edition of Clark's most well-known contribution, *Conditions of Economic Progress* (Clark 1940), predated his Oxford appointment, although the third and final edition appeared in 1957. He was pioneering in comparing income per capita and agricultural productivity across countries, and in exploring trends in sectoral shares in national income. Substantive conclusions included the observation that the share of agriculture declined as incomes rose, and the share of industry and services increased; he also pointed to increasing agricultural productivity as necessary for industrial development (Clark and Haswell 1964). More controversially, he questioned the role of investment in economic growth, noting that it was a necessary but not sufficient condition (Clark 1961); and he argued that population growth and density could have a positive impact on growth (Clark 1967). This contrasted with Balogh's view that rapid population growth was one of the reasons for the slow growth in per capita income (Balogh 1966).

Hicks specialised in the public finances of developed countries, particularly the UK, writing a widely used textbook on the issue (Hicks 1947). She applied this expertise to developing countries, visiting, advising and writing, often with her husband, the eminent economist John Hicks. Hers was among the first analytic discussions of local government and local revenue raising in developing countries (Hicks 1961).[2] She also contributed to the analysis of federal systems of government, exploring factors that led to such systems and those that accounted for their breakdown (Hicks 1978).

Ady was appointed the first Lecturer in Development Economics at Oxford in 1947 and a stand-in Director of QEH in 1976. She made significant contributions to national income accounting in developing countries, first helping to create integrated social accounts in Burma (Ady 1951) and subsequently reviewing accounts in a number of African countries, making the French and British approaches consistent, and pointing to data deficiencies and requirements (Ady and Courcier 1960).

Haswell became Lecturer in Tropical Economics in 1959. She conducted village studies both in West Africa and India, revisiting a village in the Gambia over four decades, from 1947 to 1987, as well as writing a textbook on tropical agriculture (Haswell 1967, 1973, 1991). Her village studies led to two important conclusions: first, the need to take a holistic approach to the analysis of rural change; and second, the importance of analysing changes as they occur over time, rather than taking a snapshot (Haswell and Hunt 1991). Her work carefully traced how production patterns were affected by changing demography, investments in modern infrastructure, including roads and schools, and worsening environmental factors. Hers was the first of a number

---

[2] A review stated 'had this book been published a few years ago it would have adorned the shelves of every District Commissioner's office in the British administered territories in Africa and Asia, and what is more it would have been in constant use' (Gunn 1962: 74).

of important long-term village studies by Oxford economists, as we shall see later, and the only one of an African village.

Thus, while Oxford economists made important contributions to development analysis over these early years, they were largely individual contributions and not collaborative efforts as occurred subsequently.

3.2 Flourishing of Development Economics from the Late 1960s

With the establishment of a government department in Britain specifically devoted to development in 1964, which supported development research in a variety of ways, development economics (and development studies more generally) became more organised and respected as a subdiscipline throughout the UK.[3] From 1968, with the appointment of Paul Streeten as Director, QEH flourished as a centre for development research and, soon after, in 1971, Ian Little became Professor of the Economics of Underdeveloped Countries.

Streeten had been critical of orthodox micro-theory from his first writings in the 1940s. He was heavily influenced by Gunnar Myrdal, some of whose works he translated, and by his former tutor, the iconoclastic Balogh, who had a room in QEH. Streeten had also worked with Dudley Seers (in the Ministry of Overseas Development) who, like Myrdal, took a highly critical view of the use of Western economic concepts and models for analysing developing countries.

At QEH, Streeten, Balogh and Ady held a weekly development economics seminar which became the centre for critical analysis. Streeten attracted a group of younger scholars as students and research associates, including, Keith Griffin, Sanjaya Lall, Deepak Nayyar, Akbar Noman and Frances Stewart. Although the work of this group covered a large range of issues, they shared some common presumptions: that orthodox assumptions must be carefully and critically analysed with an emphasis on identifying hidden biases and values; and that analysis must be empirically grounded in developments in particular developing countries.

At the same time, at the other geographical end of Oxford—in Nuffield—Ian Little attracted another talented group of development economists who took a more orthodox view. The group included Jim Mirrlees, Maurice Scott, Christopher Bliss, Max Corden (on Visiting Fellowships), and, among the young scholars, Vijay Joshi and Deepak Lal. The view shared among this

---

[3] The Institute of Development Studies at Sussex was founded in 1966 with support from the Ministry as Oxford did not make a sufficiently attractive offer when approached by Whitehall.

group was that developing countries had made a grave mistake (as had their non-orthodox advisers) in neglecting the role of prices and the market in the allocation of resources. While the QEH team frequently collaborated with the United Nations, including United Nations Conference on Trade and Development (UNCTAD), United Nations Industrial Development Organization (UNIDO), United Nations Research Institute for Social Development (UNRISD) and the UN Centre for Transnational Companies (and occasionally the World Bank), the Nuffield group's institutional links were largely with the OECD—Organisation for Economic Co-operation and Development—and the World Bank. The two groups worked on parallel lines and rarely clashed openly: the one notable exception was the debate between Stewart and Streeten on the one hand, and Little and Mirrlees on the other, on the appraisal of public investment projects in developing countries.

The underlying approach at QEH was a questioning of the automatic transfer of Western-designed concepts and theory to the different conditions of developing countries, developing an alternative analysis with an emphasis on institutional factors; and an attempt to include political as well as economic elements. As Streeten wrote: 'The main conclusion is to beware of the simple transfer of fairly sophisticated concepts from one setting to another, without close scrutiny of the institutional differences' (Streeten 1972: 127). He himself had questioned Western concepts of employment presaging the later focus on the informal sector in his appendix to Myrdal's 1968 *Asian Drama*. The QEH group adopted a similar critical approach to understanding the role of foreign investment, aid and technology. Particular contributions in the 1970s included analysis of foreign direct technology (Lall and Streeten), technological learning and capabilities (Lall), the role of appropriate technology (Stewart), and the impact of aid (Griffin and Enos). Griffin and Heyer analysed agricultural strategies in an Asian and African context respectively, while Griffin, Stewart and Streeten explored alternative development strategies.

Foreign Investment, Technology, and Aid: Lall and Streeten's analysis of multinational investment was the outcome of an empirical study of the costs and benefits of foreign direct investment (FDI) in six developing countries. They questioned two views then prevalent: on the one hand, that FDI had only positive benefits (Reuber et al. 1973); on the other, the views of nationalists and *dependencia* theorists that foreign investment was mainly destructive. The Lall/Streeten conclusion was that FDI could make a positive contribution, but that careful analysis of costs and benefits as well as regulation was needed, especially in relation to the hidden costs of technology transfer. This study initiated Lall's lifelong work on technology transfer, FDI and learning, on which he made major and lasting contributions.

These contributions took three forms. First, he provided careful empirical analysis of the transfer pricing practiced, in particular, among pharmaceutical firms, involving large losses of tax revenue for developing countries (Lall 1979). Second, he was among the first to notice the growing significance of Third World multinationals, investing in the North as well as other developing countries. Moreover, Lall showed that these investments were not only concentrated in small-scale labour-intensive activities, but some involved quite sophisticated capital-intensive processes, and he predicted rightly—in contrast to other observers—that this was likely to be of growing importance (Lall 1983). This led him to assume a major and long-lasting research interest in why, when and how developing country firms created technological capacity of their own and were not simply passive recipients of Western technology. Lall's analysis of the phenomenon of "technological capability"—its causes and consequences, all based on in-depth empirical analysis of particular firms in a range of countries—was path-breaking (Lall 1982, 1987, 1992). It had strong policy implications, including supporting a certain type of selective industrial policy and questioning the free trade approach that was supported by the World Bank, especially from the 1980s, and widely advocated by mainstream economists. Later, after his untimely death, Lall's work was carried on at Oxford by Xiaolan Fu, as we shall see below.

Stewart, too, questioned the generally accepted approach to technology, but from a different angle, criticising the neoclassical assumption of the existence of a range of efficient technical choices of varying labour and capital intensity (Stewart 1977). Rather, she showed, again based on empirical cases, that capital-intensive technologies generally dominated, being much more efficient than most labour-intensive ones. This arose because the technologies were developed in high-income countries to suit their own conditions. She showed that this lack of choice explained the limited modern-sector employment opportunities, and argued, along with Schumacher (1973), that there was a need for efficient appropriate technology reflecting conditions in developing countries; moreover, Stewart developed the concept of "appropriate products"—consumer goods specifically designed to meet the needs of poor people—arguing that the absence of such products further impoverished such consumers.

The role of aid was also subject to critical scrutiny by Griffin and Enos (Griffin 1970; Griffin and Enos 1970)—Griffin had been a student of Streeten and Balogh and was closely associated with QEH, becoming its Director from 1978 to 1979. Enos and Griffin concluded—on the basis of theoretical arguments and empirical evidence—that aid might not promote economic growth and might indeed retard it, partly because of a negative impact on domestic savings. They were among the first to make this point, and a large theoretical and empirical literature ensued, much of it confirming their arguments, though problems of the direction of causality were not fully resolved.

Griffin also produced an important book on the Green Revolution of the 1950s and 1960s, in parallel with a growing literature by Indian economists. New hybrid seeds introduced and promoted by the Consultative Group on International Agricultural Research in the 1970s were expected to transform agriculture and reduce poverty as a result of a large increase in agricultural productivity (Brown 1970). However, in one of the first challenges to the unqualified positive view of the impact of the new seeds, Griffin (1974) suggested that they were '"landlord-biased" … suitable only for those who had access to good irrigation facilities and plenty of working capital' (Griffin in Boyce 2011: 271). Griffin argued that the nature and impact of technology change depended on the institutional context, and that in the South Asian case this meant that the technology was unequalising, leaving out most poor people. In contrast, a study of the village of Palanpur (described below) showed an equalising impact (Bliss and Stern 1982). Twenty years later, a review of over 300 studies of the impact of the Green Revolution showed that 80% of the studies confirmed Griffin's view (Freebairn 1995).

Rural development in Sub-Saharan Africa was analysed by Heyer et al. (1981). On the basis of extensive country studies from the region, they argued that "rural development" was *imposed* by outside agencies, notably the World Bank, and like the Green Revolution analysed by Griffin, this was rarely in the interests of African peasant farmers, which largely accounted for the near-universal failure of the programmes.

Joseph Stiglitz was a Visiting Fellow at St Catherine's College (1973–1974) and held the Drummond Professorship of Political Economy from 1976 to 1979. During his Fellowship, Stiglitz's work reflected his penetrating insights into market imperfections arising from their very structure, drawing on research in Kenya. Thinking about development problems led him to rethink the way that real markets work in a world characterised by asymmetric information and unequal asset distribution. This was shown in two papers from his time at St Catherine's: one on the determinants of wages and unemployment (Stiglitz 1974a), and the second on the functioning of sharecropping (Stiglitz 1974b). While holding the Drummond Chair, he produced an important paper on surplus labour and the distribution of income in developing countries which explored the implications of the efficiency wage hypothesis for shadow prices in the urban sector, showing that under certain circumstances the opportunity cost could be negative (Stiglitz 1976). He also analysed commodity price stabilisation schemes with David Newbery: they showed that long- and short-run implications could differ and that any conclusions depended on behavioural assumptions (Newbery and Stiglitz 1979).

Strategies of Development: In the course of the 1970s, problems with the import-substituting, growth-oriented strategy of development then adopted became apparent—in particular, although countries' economic growth was generally quite good, poverty and inequality were high and too few jobs were created for the growing workforce. The strategy was criticised by both Nuffield and QEH groups albeit from different perspectives.

The main emphasis of the Nuffield group was on inefficiencies in the market interventions of the strategy. The first major contribution was the work of Ian Little and Jim Mirrlees, who produced a new method of social cost-benefit analysis for project evaluation (Little and Mirrlees 1969, 1974). Existing methods of evaluating public investment focused on estimating the monetary value of unpriced externalities, measuring a project's net benefit in terms of its contribution to domestic consumption, and taking domestic prices (market prices) as a guide to costs and benefits. Little and Mirrlees argued that with high levels of protection, then prevalent in most developing countries, a project might show high values at domestic prices, yet be uneconomic since the country could consume more by importing the product and exporting some other commodity. They therefore advocated valuing project costs and benefits on the basis of opportunity costs, using border or world prices for tradable commodities and social marginal costs for non-traded commodities taking into account both the low marginal productivity of labour and the additional consumption that wage employment generated. This procedure would show that many of the industries that had developed in the presence of high import tariffs and quotas had a negative present value—in effect, they were arguing that world prices would broadly give the correct signals. In contrast to most methods of social cost-benefit analysis, Little and Mirrlees downplayed the role of externalities and, initially, gave limited attention to income distribution.

Their method was criticised by some Oxford economists—for example, for assuming full capacity domestically so that extra output would not be a net addition but would displace other potential production, and for understating linkage and dynamic effects of projects (Joshi 1972; Stewart and Streeten 1972; Stewart 1978). Nonetheless, as Healey stated: 'The Little-Mirrlees methodology is a major contribution to the theory and practice of cost-benefit analysis' (Healey 1972: 150).

For a while, the approach was quite widely adopted—for example, it became the standard approach in Kreditanstalt für Wiederaufbau, the German state-owned development bank. Oxford economists, including Maurice Scott, Nick Stern and Deepak Lal, then a Research Officer at Oxford, adopted the method for particular evaluations (Stern 1972; Lal 1972; Little and Scott 1976; Scott et al. 1976), but UNIDO and the World Bank each developed their own methodologies (Dasgupta et al. 1972; Squire and Van Der Tak 1975).

In the long run, the publication of *Industry and Trade in Some Developing Countries* by Little, Scitovsky and Scott in 1970 had a more profound effect than the work on social cost-benefit analysis (Little et al. 1970). This book was based on six country studies. It argued 'that trade controls, and inward-looking policies more generally, impose large economic costs and reduce employment and growth. It advocated radical trade liberalisation, but not laissez-faire: it was explicitly in favour of using taxes and subsidies to offset domestic market failures' (Bliss and Joshi 2014: 321). The book made an important contribution to the growing number of critiques of the planning and market interventions in developing countries then prevalent—others included Balassa (1965, 1971), Krueger (1966, 1974) and Ranis (1972). Written in an accessible style, it was very widely read, and had a significant influence on the radical change in perspectives on development that occurred in the late 1970s, with a switch away from planning towards market reforms. This changing perspective in turn led to the dismantling of import protection that occurred in the 1980s and 1990s, as the debt crisis—as noted earlier—empowered the International Monetary Fund (IMF) and World Bank to insist on such reforms. In 1982, Little wrote a textbook on economic development, *Economic Development: Theory, Policy and International Relations* (Little 1982), which carefully laid out the reasoning behind this neoclassical view of economic development, while criticising structuralist views.

In QEH, Stewart, Streeten, Griffin and James also criticised prevalent development strategies, but from a very different angle. Stewart and Streeten argued that to deal with the evident problems of unemployment, inequality and poverty, a three-pronged approach was required 'combining signals and incentives, institutional reforms directed at the redistribution of assets (including education) and technical and institutional innovation' (Stewart and Streeten 1976: 403), while Griffin and James (1981) urged that radical asset redistribution was essential for a substantial reduction in poverty and explored ways of achieving this. The focus remained on incomes, but widely shared and employment-creating, in contrast to existing patterns of development.

The questioning of accepted approaches in this period also extended to the role of the international system more broadly, beyond aid and foreign investment to the entire relationship between countries and regions of different wealth, with the imbalances in power relations that followed. The awareness of power relations coming from many scholars interacted with a particular sensitivity to the role of institutions and history, which originated in Area Studies. The LAC's work on the economic history of the region, in a succession of case studies centred on Oxford conferences, was a prime example (Thorp 1984; Thorp and Whitehead 1987; Cárdenas et al. 2000a, b) to all of which FitzGerald and Thorp contributed.

Over the 1960s and 1970s, there was increasing recognition that monetary income per capita—even if well distributed—was an inadequate measure of progress (Seers 1969), and Oxford economists contributed to the identification of alternative development objectives. Streeten and Mahbub ul Haq led a team at the World Bank (including Javed Burki, Norman Hicks and Frances Stewart) aiming to replace an income-oriented approach by the basic needs approach, which (temporarily) had a major impact on World Bank policy (Streeten et al. 1981; Stewart 1985).

Amartya Sen was a Professor at Oxford from 1977 to 1988 (Drummond Professor from 1980). He cannot be categorised in terms of the two schools of thought noted above, but can be connected with both. He made two fundamental contributions in this area. First, he focused on famine prevention, and showed how massive famine could occur even when food output was increasing (Sen 1981). He argued that people's "entitlements" were critical in determining whether they starved or not. Entitlements are essentially people's legal claims on food through incomes from work and other sources which can fall below survival level even when food supplies are adequate if, for example, inflation reduces real purchasing power as happened in the massive Bengal famine of 1943 due to wartime colonial policy. Sen's approach transformed the analysis of famine and was further developed by Martin Ravallion, when at Oxford in the 1980s, adding speculation to Sen's framework (Ravallion 1987).

Secondly, Sen's highly influential work on capabilities was initiated while he was at Oxford (Sen 1980). In his Tanner Lecture, entitled *Equality of What?*, Sen played down the role of income. He argued that inequality should be measured not in terms of utility or incomes but rather people's capabilities—or what they can do or be. The capabilities approach was developed further after Sen left Oxford and has become an established framework of analysis. With elements drawn from basic needs analysis, it formed the theoretical underpinning of the human development approach, embodied in the publication of the *Human Development Reports* of the United Nations

Development Programme (UNDP), the first of which appeared in UNDP (1990). John Knight also worked on human development (with Keith Griffin), coming to similar conclusions to those in the UNDP report (Griffin and Knight 1990).

Sen, Anand and Stewart contributed to the first *Report* and many later ones, analysing numerous aspects of human development. Sudhir Anand—in collaboration with Sen—contributed to the methodology underlying measures of human development, notably to the way income was treated in the Human Development Index (HDI), the inequality-adjusted HDI and measures of gender inequality (Anand and Sen 1994, 1995, 2000; Anand 2018). He also explored the relative contribution of private incomes and public services to human development outcomes (Anand and Ravallion 1993). Stewart and others explored the two-way relationship between human development and economic growth and the important role of social institutions and social capabilities (Stewart et al. 2018).

Oxford contributions to the human development approach were continued by a later generation. Sabina Alkire made a significant contribution to the theory and application of the capability approach (Alkire 2002) and to the measurement of multidimensional poverty to be discussed below. Diego Sánchez-Ancochea focused on the political economy of inequality, moving beyond the narrow, anti-poverty approach long promoted by international institutions like the World Bank and paying particular attention to universal social policy. His work proposes more pragmatic and holistic ways to build universal social policy, considering alternative public interventions, the contradictory role of the private sector and the need to build cross-class alliances more explicitly (Franzoni and Sánchez-Ancochea 2016). Sánchez-Ancochea also analysed the lessons from Latin America's history of vertical and horizontal inequality for the rest of the world. Negative processes currently observed in developed countries, like weakening democracies and dual labour markets, have been present in Latin America for more than a century (Sánchez-Ancochea 2020).

Since the first *Human Development Report*, global concern with human aspects of development has increased dramatically, as shown by the Millennium Development Goals agreed on a global basis in 2000, followed by the Sustainable Development Goals in 2015. Although income growth remains a dominant objective, there has been a substantial enlargement of development objectives. Oxford development economists played an important role in this change.

3.3 The 1980s and 1990s: Debt Crises and Adjustment Policies

In the 1980s, many of the policies advocated by Little, Scott and Scitovsky were adopted by developing countries, under pressure from the IMF and World Bank, whose influence greatly expanded as countries sought their help to deal with the debt crisis, and the role of the State in the economy was rolled back. Moreover, stabilisation policies were introduced, cutting government expenditure to reduce budget deficits.

Already in the 1970s, Thorp had criticised the orthodox monetarist policies in IMF programmes implemented in Latin America. Studies of various Latin American economies showed how the crude monetarism behind the stabilisation policies being urged by the IMF was leading to costly recession and often a worsening of the structural bottlenecks and policy weaknesses which were at the root of the inflation they were meant to cure (Thorp and Whitehead 1979). This contributed to the growing international literature on monetarism versus structuralism. As the 1980s unfolded, the harsh social consequences of the programmes were revealed. Stewart was a co-author of UNICEF's critique of adjustment policies which focused on the rising poverty and worsening social indicators associated with them (Cornia et al. 1987).

Adopting a more orthodox approach, Little contributed to the design of a major World Bank-financed study of macroeconomic policies in seventeen developing countries, organised by Anne Krueger. With Vijay Joshi, he wrote one of the volumes in the study, looking at economic reforms in India, and a subsequent follow-up volume (Joshi and Little 1994, 1996). These publications, in turn, undoubtedly contributed to India's ongoing economic reforms. Other Oxford contributors were David Bevan and Paul Collier who undertook the Kenya and Nigeria studies. Little was also co-author of the overview book, *Boom, Crisis, and Adjustment* (Little et al. 1993). As the title indicates, the study went beyond an assessment of stabilisation and adjustment policies to consider how best to manage booms and busts. Amongst its conclusions were the need to assert firm overall budgetary control and budgetary accountability; to resist euphoria when export prices rise exceptionally, new resources are discovered or new borrowing opportunities open; to avoid using import controls, except in extremis, and then to remove them as soon as macroeconomic circumstances permit; to avoid jerky movements in the real exchange rate; and to maintain flexibility in policy, and, in particular, to correct policy mistakes quickly.

The analysis of booms and busts in natural resources was carried forward, also from a neoclassical perspective, by Bevan, Collier and Jan Gunning of CSAE in a series of publications on macro policies to deal with commodity price fluctuations in African economies. They made use of the natural experiment in which Kenya (predominantly market based) and Tanzania (centrally planned), both big coffee producers and exporters, were assailed by the same unanticipated (temporary) terms of trade shock arising from the loss of the Brazilian coffee crop to frost in 1976, and investigated differences in macro policy response and outcomes (Bevan et al. 1990). They developed a general equilibrium model, including some structural features and aspects of political economy (ibid.; Bevan et al. 1993). Subsequently, they conducted a sixteen-country study, paying attention to the micro-foundations of macro-development, notably the savings behaviour of peasants (Collier and Gunning 1999). Their main conclusions were that the "normal" policy advice to countries should be reversed: with positive booms it was better to allow the peasant sector to secure the benefits of the boom since in most countries they found that the peasant sector saved much of the bonanza, whereas allowing the public sector to tax the extra revenue (as commonly recommended) led to high government spending which was difficult to reverse subsequently, leading to fiscal crises. With negative shocks, they argued that government dissaving to compensate losers might be justified but could come up against credibility issues, potentially leading to fiscal and exchange rate crises (Bevan et al. 1990).

Scholars within the Keynesian/structuralist tradition reached similar conclusions about the importance of governance, but with a greater focus on why policy was so consistently inappropriate. The influence of the Area Studies focus on history and interdisciplinary dimensions was apparent. Rosemary Thorp and Geoff Bertram produced an economic history of Peru going back to the 1890s, showing how the country's wealth of natural resources consistently biased policy choices away from diversification and a more sustainable development path (Thorp and Bertram 1978). Later, Thorp and others undertook an economic history of Latin America (at the request of Enrique Iglesias then President of the Inter-American Development Bank), which emphasised the consequences of dependence driven by resource endowment and unequal power in the international economy in a historical context (Thorp 1998). In this major project, Valpy FitzGerald and Pablo Astorga made an important contribution in providing long-run statistical foundations; and from this quantitative initiative grew the Oxford Latin American History Database (OxLAD) and a series of influential econometric papers, including Astorga et al. (2005) and Astorga et al. (2011). Another study on the nature and consequences of natural resource dependence again found that policy decisions were undermined by a reliance on unstable commodities, with adverse consequence for equity (Thorp et al. 2012).

Meanwhile, Maurice Scott, working largely on his own, undertook a major analysis of the causes of economic growth, critiquing the Solow approach (Solow 1956). In the classic Solow model, technical progress was assumed to be independent of investment and to occur year by year in an unexplained way. When applied empirically—with particular neoclassical assumptions—the model showed that technical progress accounted for around three-quarters of the increase in output in developed countries. Balogh and Streeten had termed this large contribution of unexplained technical progress as a "coefficient of ignorance" (Balogh and Streeten 1963). Scott set out to explain technical progress as the product of investment, not only in research and development, but importantly also in capital equipment, essential to embody new technologies. He showed the positive empirical association between investment and increases in productivity (Scott 1989). His approach—which applied to both developed and developing countries—had strong policy implications, suggesting that the rate of investment was the most important determinant of economic growth, as economies could not wait passively and expect technical progress to occur without new investment. Later empirical explorations of the causes of economic growth across the world have shown that the only significant robust correlate with growth is the rate of investment, confirming Scott's views, and challenging Clark's (Barro 1996). Scott's analysis of technology and growth was similar to that of Romer (1990) and Alesina and Perotti (1994), but with a much firmer empirical basis. However, it was less influential, perhaps because he wrote a book rather than articles in well-known journals and did not employ much mathematics.

Two decades later, John Knight and Sai Ding explored the factors underlying China's remarkable growth (Knight and Ding 2012). They also showed the significance of the extremely high investment ratio. But going further than Scott or Barro, they sought to explain this, not only in terms of demand and supply factors, but mostly as a result of the underlying prevailing political economy—the "developmental state" that enabled China to adapt institutions and provide incentives which were responsible for the economy's dynamism.

3.4   The 1990s and Beyond

The 1990s and 2000s saw continued work by Oxford development economists on macro issues; there was also a renewed focus on sectoral issues and on technology; and micro research—both quantitative and qualitative—blossomed.

Macro-Analysis: Chris Adam, working both at CSAE and ODID, and David Bevan at CSAE, continued the analysis of the macroeconomy of developing countries, incorporating both a neoclassical framework and sensitivity to institutions and political economy. They were partly inspired by the Bevan, Collier and Gunning approach—in particular, adopting conventional techniques of modern macroeconomics to understand the dynamic behaviour of small, open, shock-prone economies, starting from a recognition of the critical importance of understanding the structure and political economy of fiscal and monetary institutions in the relevant countries. This research led to a range of policy applications, and Adam has worked with the Department for International Development (DFID) in Britain and the IMF, among others, advising on macro policies and institutions in low-income countries. Significant and influential policy conclusions covered policy requirements for fiscal adjustment and sustainability in low-income countries, and macro policy responses to sudden aid inflows, such as those associated with the Heavily Indebted Poor Countries (HIPC) initiative.

On fiscal reforms—on the basis of work in Zambia in the 1990s—Adam and Bevan concluded that, in low-income countries, reforms which directly addressed revenue mobilisation underpinned sustained fiscal adjustment, as against a focus on expenditure control which was central to reforms in Latin America and Europe (Adam and Bevan 2004, 2005). They also stressed the critical role of the political economy for protecting recurrent spending on operations and maintenance (Adam and Bevan 2014). Adam and others working with DFID and the IMF explored efficient fiscal and monetary responses to large aid inflows in circumstances where countries had poor histories of macroeconomic stability and were progressively liberalising the capital account of the balance of payments, stressing the need to anticipate private sector responses (asset demand in particular) to debt relief and aid inflows when setting their fiscal and monetary policies. Dogmatic or simple rule-based approaches (as were being recommended by the IMF at the time) raised the risk of excess volatility in interest rates and exchange rates (Buffie et al. 2008, 2010).

In parallel, Vijay Joshi worked on India's macroeconomy for many decades, as well as advising central economic institutions. With Robert Cassen and others, he analysed India's economic reforms of the early 1990s (Cassen and Joshi 1995). More recently, Joshi's 2017 book, *India's Long Road: The Search for Prosperity*, provides a long-term analysis of the Indian economy, arguing that the foundations of rapid, durable and inclusive economic growth in India are weak. He suggests that for India to realise its huge potential, the relations among the State, the market and the private sector need to be comprehensively realigned. Deeper liberalisation is required but far from sufficient. In addition, the State needs to perform its core tasks much more effectively.

Matthew McCartney (who joined the Oxford South Asia Programme in 2011) has also been concerned with India's macroeconomy, taking a political economy approach, more critical of the contribution of liberalisation, exploring the role of class interests and the economic impact of geography, regional diversity and discrimination (McCartney 2019). Adopting a similar approach, he has also analysed the social dynamics underlying the Pakistani economy (McCartney and Zaidi 2019).

Sectoral Studies: Recent analysis of agriculture and industry has encompassed both micro and comparative cross-country analysis.

Analysing agricultural productivity, Douglas Gollin (who joined ODID in 2012) and others showed that low agricultural productivity was a key element explaining income differences across countries (Dercon and Gollin 2014), which he found was partly due to barriers resulting from remoteness and poor spatial connectivity (Gollin and Rogerson 2014). In work with David Lagakos and Michael Waugh, Gollin showed that the gap in agricultural productivity in African economies relative to other countries is a real one and that only a fraction can be explained by omissions and measurement errors (Gollin et al. 2014).

Industry and Productivity in Africa: The 1990s saw a transformation in the fortunes of many African countries. Nonetheless, there was a pervasive failure to create a successful industrial sector. Why this was so formed the central focus of Francis Teal's survey work at CSAE which covered Ghana, Ethiopia and Tanzania. He found, unsurprisingly, that firm labour productivity was, on average, very low. Size emerged as a central issue from the research. Large firms were different in almost all respects from their smaller cousins. They were far more likely to export, they paid higher wages, their capital-labour ratios were much higher, they were far more likely to have paid employees rather than depend on apprentices, and their skill levels were much higher. How these outcomes were related to firm size and how firms became large thus emerged as key research questions.

Panel data helped explain why and how firms grow. It appeared very clearly that the answer was not increasing returns to scale, while skills, as conventionally measured by the education and experience of the workforce, played only a small part in differences in productivity. What mattered overwhelmingly for increased labour productivity was the higher capital-labour ratio of larger firms. Panel data showed the importance of fixed effects—time-invariant unobservables—as determinants of both firm productivity and worker earnings. Moreover, country differences were persistent. Research showed that a worker's earnings also depended on these unobservables in a major way—the country where the worker was employed and the size and characteristics of the firm mattered enormously. This suggested the need to focus less on generating skills through more education and more on exploring how firms and workers are matched in a way that gives rise to the enormous dispersion of earnings observed (Söderbom and Teal 2004; Baptist and Teal 2014). The research showed that rather than a divide between a formal and an informal sector, a much better "picture" of the labour market was of a spectrum from small-scale, low-skill, low-productivity employment to high-skill, high-productivity employment, a transition facilitated by changing firm size. The central failure of policy-making in Africa remains its inability to move its people along this spectrum.

Gollin has also been concerned with the relative failure of industrialisation in Africa, despite rapid urbanisation. Using cross-country data, he found that a heavy dependence on natural resources was one explanation (Gollin et al. 2016), while a high rate of urbanisation was due to the significantly higher living standards in urban than in rural areas (Gollin et al. 2018).

Xiaolan Fu brought QEH research back to the issue of *technology*. She extended the work of both Lall and Stewart, mainly using evidence from China. Exploring China's industrial policy, she challenged the Washington consensus of the unqualified positive role of FDI and the market and explored the transmission mechanisms through which trade and FDI affect economic development (Fu 2004, 2015). Examining the relationship between foreign technology transfer and indigenous innovation in technology upgrading, Fu et al. (2011) found, in line with the findings of Lall (1992), that 'despite the potential offered by globalization and a liberal trade regime, the benefits of international technology diffusion can only be delivered with parallel indigenous innovation efforts … In this sense, indigenous and foreign innovation efforts are complementary' (Fu et al. 2011: 1,204).

Fu also extended the theory of appropriate technology to the sector level taking into account sector specificity in technology intensity and dynamics, and demonstrating the critical importance of indigenous innovation in technological upgrading in developing (especially middle-income) countries (Fu and Gong 2011). Technologies created in the South are shown to be more appropriate for developing countries which have similar economic and technological resources and industrial structure (Fu et al. 2011). She has also explored the determinants of innovation in low-income countries, extending her investigations to the informal sector, a seriously under-researched area, for example in Fu et al. (2018). Her work on innovation suggests that countries should adopt an "open national innovation system", with multiple drivers, market and State, national and international (Fu 2015).

International Dimensions: Developing countries have always been greatly affected by the behaviour of the global economy. Until the 1970s, this influence was mainly through aid flows, FDI and the terms of trade. The debts of developing countries became a major issue in the 1980s as a result of excessive lending and borrowing in the 1970s, leading to stringent adjustment policies and, eventually, some debt write-off. Accelerated growth of trade and capital flows after 1980—"globalisation"—gave developing countries more influence on the world economy, but also created new concerns. How could private capital flows be managed to avoid the major financial crises observed in Asia in the 1990s and recurrently in Mexico? How would changes in the global division of labour affect income inequalities? These were topics explored at QEH by Valpy FitzGerald and Adrian Wood.

FitzGerald came to Oxford in 1992, bringing to ODID and LAC an academic interest in the macroeconomics and finance of middle-income "open economy" developing countries, and professional experience as an economic adviser to Latin American governments. His work at Oxford started with the working out of the original insights of Kalecki into investment finance, fiscal balance and income distribution (FitzGerald 1993). This represented a new approach to development economics, with significant implications for the critique of stabilisation policy and structural adjustment on the one hand, and the role of IFIs such as the IMF and the World Bank on the other (FitzGerald 2003). He then developed an original approach to the analysis of international capital flows to developing countries, focusing on the determinants of investor demand for emerging-market assets as the driver of financial instability and debt crises, in contrast to the conventional approach (FitzGerald 2007).

FitzGerald's interest in income distribution led him to focus on the role of the progressive taxation of corporations and private wealth as central to the construction of a stable and equitable macroeconomic strategy in support of sustainable development, which in turn had significant implications for international tax cooperation (FitzGerald 2012; FitzGerald and Dayle Siu 2018). He showed that higher taxation of profits would not depress investment or growth, but that achieving it would require much greater collaboration in the regulation of offshore financial centres—his work, including advice to UNCTAD, the OECD and the G24, contributed to the ongoing process of the reform of global tax rules (FitzGerald 2002, 2012). From these theoretical and policy analyses, a fundamental rethinking of the conventional approach to public finance in developing countries followed, taking into account the consequences of their integration in global capital markets (FitzGerald 2019).

Wood became a Professor of International Development at QEH in 2005, working mainly on the causes and effects of the global division of labour. In Wood (1994), he had analysed North-South trade in a Heckscher-Ohlin model in which comparative advantage depended on endowments of four factors of production—skilled labour, literate unskilled labour, illiterate labour, and natural resources—but not on capital because of its international mobility. At QEH, he extended this analysis to show how cheaper communication and travel, by assisting highly skilled workers in the North to cooperate with workers in the South, had widened the wage gap in the North between highly skilled and other workers while narrowing the North-South gap in the wages of other workers (Anderson et al. 2006). He proposed improvements to Heckscher-Ohlin theory (Wood 2011) and estimated the size of the shift in the comparative advantage of the rest of the South away from manufacturing and towards primary production as a result of China's entry into world markets (Wood and Mayer 2011). In another work, Wood showed how the impact of aid on world poverty could be increased by allocating it in a way that took account of differences among developing countries not only in terms of current poverty levels but also in probable rates of poverty decline in the absence of aid (Wood 2008).

Micro Studies: Two approaches can again be distinguished: on the one hand, use of large samples and econometric analysis; on the other, more qualitative and multidisciplinary approaches. In the more quantitative vein, CSAE and the Department of Economics made a large contribution in this area. Prominent economists here were Paul Collier, Marcel Fafchamps, Francis Teal, John Knight, Stefan Dercon and Abigail Barr. Research methods included analysis of cross-section and panel data; randomised experiments; and experimental games. Here, we only give some highlights of the very extensive output.

Household Econometrics, Risk and Uncertainty: Fafchamps (in Oxford from 1999 to 2013) covered a large range of issues, including agricultural markets and market institutions, risk sharing, and analysis of self-help groups, social networks and political violence, as well as child labour, rural poverty and crime. He used a variety of methods, including surveys, randomised experiments and game playing (with Barr), often investigating underexplored areas. For example, with others he showed that social networks were effective in transmitting information (Fafchamps and Vicente 2013); that firms in Africa learn by exporting (Bigsten et al. 2004); that there were negative effects of workday taboos on agricultural output (Stifel et al. 2011); that, controlling for population composition and other risk factors, crime in Madagascar 'increases with distance from urban centres and, with few exceptions, decreases with population density' (Fafchamps and Moser 2003: 625; see also Fafchamps and Ferrara 2012); that informal associations have an insurance and redistributive function, using evidence from urban Kenya; and other research showed that child labour decreases with urban proximity, using data from Nepal (Fafchamps and Wahba 2006).

Knight (with Richard Sabot) undertook major surveys of education in Kenya and Tanzania, contrasting secondary school education policies. The research showed that returns to education were not simply due to "signalling", then a fashionable view, but to the cognitive skills acquired (Knight and Sabot 1990). Analysis of education in Ethiopia found high production externalities to rural education while internal returns were relatively low, helping to explain the low level of education (Weir and Knight 2007). Further work in Africa included analysis of the very high open unemployment rate in South Africa, which he and Kingdon explained by barriers to entry to the small informal sector (Kingdon and Knight 2004).

In the 1990s, partly stimulated by Chinese students at Oxford, Knight joined the China Household Income Project (CHIP), then co-directed by Keith Griffin. His research on China covered poverty, inequality, the labour market, migration, education and happiness, based largely on microdata. Knight and Lina Song were among the first to provide comprehensive coverage of the widening rural-urban divide in incomes and services, a paradox in an economy emerging from a peasant revolution. Once the early rural reforms had narrowed the income gap, the divide grew for a quarter of a century, assisted by institutional constraints and government policies. The high ratio of urban to rural income per capita began to decline about 2010, essentially because of emerging rural labour scarcity (Knight and Song 1999, 2005).

A key focus of Dercon's extensive research has been the relationship between risks and poverty, conducting surveys in a number of East African countries. He shows that poor rural households adopt a variety of methods to cope with risks, but these are often insufficient to prevent adverse events, leading to extreme poverty among vulnerable households. Women often bear the brunt of the resulting hardship. Macro policies to reduce fluctuations and a variety of State-supported safety nets can be helpful, though care is needed as the latter may undermine self-insurance mechanisms and worsen the position of those not covered (Dercon and Krishnan 2000; Dercon 2002, 2004). Dercon has extended his work on risk to the analysis of the role of social protection mechanisms in humanitarian crises (Clarke and Dercon 2016). Analysis over time has shown that the deleterious effects of shocks are long-lasting

(Dercon et al. 2005; Dercon and Porter 2014; Weerdt et al. 2017). Dercon has also made contributions in many other areas, including African agricultural development strategies, the impact of industrial jobs on health and incomes, and informational flows and social externalities, among others. He also made a direct contribution to British aid and development policy as Chief Economist at DFID from 2011 to 2017.

Research by Barr (in Oxford, mainly at CSAE, from 1996 to 2011) focused on issues such as how to set up mutually beneficial agreements, what determines individual values and the role of "other-regarding preferences" in decisions. She researched these topics by designing incentivised games to generate data: conducting experiments among students, villagers, nurses and doctors in a large number of countries in Africa, Latin America and Europe. For example, she investigated the role of cultural background, or social norms, in determining the propensity to be corrupt; the influence of networks on enterprise productivity; and the determinants of trust in communities, differentiating between local communities and new settlements (Barr 2002, 2003).

A Case-Study Approach—Village and Town Studies in India: A more qualitative approach, developed over several decades, blossomed in this period as findings accumulated. These came from a number of path-breaking long-term village studies in India, revisiting the same village(s) over decades and thereby capturing the process of dynamic change. Again, differences in approach can be seen, with some primarily concerned with economic relationships and outcomes—the Palanpur studies and those of Dercon—and others—Heyer and Harriss-White—adopting a more multidisciplinary approach and viewing village and town economies as embedded in social relations and the surrounding area.

Bliss and Stern first surveyed Palanpur, a small village in Uttar Pradesh in 1974–1975 (Bliss and Stern 1982). This was the baseline survey which provided a benchmark source of comparison with subsequent surveys, conducted at roughly decadal intervals, but with new participants from outside Oxford, many still involving Stern, who had moved to LSE. To date, seven successive surveys have shown rising incomes at a steady 2% per annum, changing contractual arrangements with a decline in sharecropping and an increase in rentals, but no clear difference in productivity between the two types of contract, while cropping intensity and mechanisation in agriculture increased. There was a shift of households into a plurality of activities with agriculture providing a declining share of income and sources outside the village a rising share. Inequality decreased up to the mid-1980s but subsequently increased and there was some shift in average incomes among castes, with some castes seizing new opportunities to a greater extent than others. Intergenerational mobility declined (Himanshu et al. 2018).

Dercon and others examined changes in living conditions in six villages in Andhra Pradesh and Maharashtra, initially surveyed during 1975–1984. They found that both monetary and non-monetary indicators of well-being improved considerably. Migrants experienced faster welfare improvements than non-migrants, but more analysis is needed to confirm whether this was due to their initial characteristics or to migration. Surprisingly, lower caste groups experienced faster poverty declines, although this effect was largely confined to Mahbubnagar in Andhra Pradesh (Badiani et al. 2007).

Judith Heyer studied villages near to Tiruppur, a small town in Western Tamil Nadu in South India, over a thirty-year period, visiting them every decade from 1980. Initially, her concern was with the impact of government-targeted interventions aimed at increasing the assets of poor households, but later examining the drivers of asset distribution over time. She found that the 1970s and 1980s programmes worked reasonably well for small farmers but not for agricultural labourers because they did not have enough of the other resources needed to make assets productive. Food for work and other employment programmes that were also a feature of the 1970s and early 1980s largely excluded Dalits, or included them on less advantageous terms. Poorer households did better under food subsidy programmes which started in the early 1980s (Heyer 2013). From 2008, poorer households also benefited substantially from the national employment guarantee programme (MGNREGA—Mahatma Gandhi National Rural Employment Guarantee Act). The fact that Dalits and other poorer households benefited more in the later years was partly a result of changing hierarchies of power at the village level which were less strongly loaded against Dalits as time went on.

In later work, the role of caste and gender became central. The village study was important in demonstrating that caste discrimination did not weaken significantly with industrialisation, as had been widely expected. Moreover, this occurred in a State that was known for its political and social movements in the 1920s and 1930s which were celebrated for breaking down caste power.

The surprising strength of gender discrimination also emerged from Heyer's fieldwork. It had generally been assumed that gender discrimination was much less serious in South India than in the rest of India. Heyer showed both that patriarchal structures put very strong limits on what women could do, and also that female infanticide and foeticide were both significant correlates with capitalist development in the area studied (Heyer 1992, 2016).

Heyer's village-level work showed the importance of rural-urban interactions and the need to understand the regional context of village developments.

The villages studied were part of a regional economy in which industrialisation was proceeding apace, and the villages became increasingly integrated into these economic processes of change (Heyer 2013).

Barbara Harriss-White came to Oxford in 1987, already known for her work on agricultural markets. Unlike the earlier research of Griffin and Heyer, she focused on the unequal relationship of producers and traders and showed that traders were responsible for much of the inequality in India's agricultural sector (Harriss-White 1996; Harriss-White and Janakarajan 2004).

From the early 1970s, Harriss-White also undertook long-term studies of ten villages and a small town, Arni, in northern Tamil Nadu. These village studies showed the growth in productivity due to the Green Revolution and subsequent agricultural diversification and then stagnation as a water crisis hit village economies, as well as many aspects of the economics of agrarian poverty, and the drivers and impact of rapid institutional change on rural development (ibid.).

Her research into the long-term development of a small-town economy and its rural hinterland in India from 1973 to 2012 is a rare case study of small-town change. She tracked the changing nature of local business and the workforce, their urban-rural relations, their regulation through civil society organisations and social practices, and their relations to the State and to India's accelerating and dynamic growth (ibid.; Harriss-White 2015). This research showed that plans do not reflect realities on the ground; and, like Heyer, it also showed the persistence of institutions, such as caste and gender, which had been expected to wither, and the ways that rural development is dynamised by the urban economy.

Arising from these studies, Harriss-White produced an influential body of work on the importance of the informal economy and the way that social structures regulated accumulation in both the informal and the formal economies (Harriss-White 2003).

3.5 New Issues in the Twenty-First Century

The twenty-first century has seen a focus on several areas which had hitherto been relatively neglected. These came to the fore in response both to developments on the ground and to changing global concerns. They include the study of conflict, gender issues, multidimensional poverty and some work on the environment.

Conflict: Analysis of human development and poverty across countries showed that the worst performers were almost invariably in conflict. Moreover, the end of the Cold War saw an escalation in the number of civil wars. As a result, analysis of the economic causes and consequences of war was initiated by Collier and Hoeffler at CSAE and FitzGerald and Stewart at QEH.

Collier and Hoeffler's work on the causes and consequences of conflict has been widely recognised. Famously, they differentiated between "greed" and "grievance" as a cause of conflict and, in one of the early econometric exercises to identify causes, argued that grievances—in the form of inequality, political rights and ethnic or religious polarisation—were insignificant, whereas per capita income and growth, primary commodities as a share of exports and the size of the diaspora population were significantly associated with the outbreak of conflict. They interpreted the latter variables as proxies for opportunity or greed, although they agreed that low incomes might also be a form of grievance (Collier and Hoeffler 2004). Later work focused on "feasibility" as the main explanation of conflict, arguing with empirical evidence that grievance was unimportant, and conflict occurred where it was feasible financially and from a military perspective (Collier et al. 2009). However, Collier also led an influential World Bank study on conflict which argued that poverty (i.e. low average per capita incomes) was both cause and consequence of conflict (Collier et al. 2003). Collier and Hoeffler also investigated the optimal timing and level of aid for poverty reduction in post-conflict economies, among other issues (Collier and Hoeffler 2002).

Two major studies on conflict were undertaken at QEH: First, a multi-country study directed by FitzGerald and Stewart on the economics of war-affected economies, showing the macro and meso mechanisms which lead to the negative economic and social impact of conflict, which extend far beyond the immediate deaths. The study suggested a number of policies which might mitigate these effects, even during war (Stewart 1993; Stewart and FitzGerald 2000). Second, Stewart led a research centre at ODID—the Centre for Research on Inequality, Human Security and Ethnicity—investigating the causes of conflict, including eight country studies. The main conclusion of these studies was that multidimensional "horizontal" inequalities (inequalities across a variety of identity groups) were significantly associated with the outbreak of conflict, even though vertical inequality (inequality among individuals) had been shown *not* to be significantly associated with conflict by Collier and Hoeffler, among others. The Centre analysed the policy implications of this finding for conflict-prevention and post-conflict policies, with a particular focus on policies towards affirmative action and the special issues for policy in resource-abundant economies (Stewart 2008; Thorp et al. 2012). The significant role of horizontal inequalities in raising the risk of conflict, initiated by Stewart at Oxford (Stewart 2000), has been supported by much subsequent empirical research (Cederman et al. 2011; Hillesund et al. 2018). Work on horizontal inequalities continued beyond analysis of conflict to considering the causes of persistent horizontal inequality, the relationship with democracy, and issues of justice, as well as policy analysis (Stewart and Langer 2008; Thorp and Paredes 2010; Brown et al. 2012; Stewart 2014).

Gender Aspects of Rural Transformation: Gender aspects of development were very much present in Heyer and Harriss-White's investigations into village and small-town India, as noted above, but the importance of gender was brought to the fore in Oxford by Cheryl Doss who joined ODID in 2016. The central focus of her work is on gender aspects of rural transformation. Through a series of collaborative projects, using both qualitative and quantitative data, Doss is involved in shifting our understanding of rural households and how they engage with processes of structural transformation. Her research has three strands: First, women's access to and ownership of land and other assets. Using data from the Gender Asset Gap Project, which she and others initiated in 2009, she has analysed how the gender wealth gap is related to marital and inheritance laws and norms, comparisons of men's and women's responses regarding the market value of their dwelling, and analyses of how men and women acquire assets, considering both inheritance and market purchases. Following this work, data on individual ownership is being incorporated in many large sample surveys (Doss et al. 2019).

A second theme concerns understanding gender and rural transformation, with a particular focus on the impact of men's migration on women left behind. Using mixed methods, she has explored the impact on female empowerment in Nepal, showing how patterns differ depending on whether the women live in nuclear households or are the mother-in-law or daughter-in-law in a joint household.

Third, Doss is moving beyond the traditional approach to household surveys, in which survey data is collected from one member of the household, typically the household head, to interview multiple people in the household. This approach generated new challenges, since husbands and wives often report different answers. In particular, in many contexts when wives report that they co-own land and housing with their husbands, their husbands report themselves as the sole owners. Similarly, different answers occur with respect to who is involved in household decision-making. She is exploring explanations for these differences, arguing that it is not due simply to measurement error or different understandings of the question, but asymmetric information and the fact that neither spouse has full information about the other. She also draws on analyses of collective action in natural resource management for understanding household decision-making, and uses new methods to try to work out why a particular person makes a decision (Doss and Meinzen-Dick 2015; Ambler et al. 2021).

Analysis and Measurement of Poverty: The widening of development objectives associated with Sen's capability analysis and the human development approach led to a recognition that the definition and measurement of poverty should be correspondingly enlarged. At QEH, Susana Franco, Harriss-White, Caterina Ruggeri Laderchi, Ruhi Saith and Stewart showed that alternative definitions of poverty—monetary, capability and participatory as well as measures of social exclusion—gave very different answers to the question of who was poor on the basis of research in India and Peru (Ruggeri Laderchi et al. 2003; Stewart et al. 2007).

Alkire investigated the variety of conceptions of well-being among poor women in India with the aim of giving practical meaning to the objective of widening capabilities (Alkire 2002). Adopting a capability approach, the work of Alkire and the Oxford Poverty and Human Development Initiative (OPHI) (a centre at ODID initiated by Alkire) has been largely devoted to the development of a multidimensional measure of capability poverty and its application across the world. In path-breaking work, Alkire and Foster produced a new method for measuring multidimensional poverty—the multidimensional poverty index (MPI) (Alkire and Foster 2008, 2011; Alkire 2015). The method allows decomposition across ethnicities and regions and measures of inequalities among the poor (OPHI and UNDP 2019). The MPI is now applied globally as well as nationally, where it has guided policy in several countries, including Mexico and Nepal. The global MPI, which is produced jointly by OPHI and the UNDP, covered 101 countries in 2019.

Environment: Rather little research has been done on this topic by Oxford economists. Joshi has worked on "fairness" in climate change mitigation generally and in relation to India (Joshi and Patel 2009), while Harriss-White led a major study of the carbon footprint of different rice production and distribution systems in India (Harriss-White et al. 2019). This was followed by a study of the waste economy in a small town in South India (Harriss-White 2020). Harriss-White also wrote on Karl Marx's and Justus von Liebig's ideas on ecological restitution in theoretical work arising from this (Harriss-White 2019).

4   Conclusions

This chapter has shown the enormous amount of work done by development economists at Oxford, spanning the whole period in which development economics has been practised, the very rich array of concepts, theories and evidence produced, and the attention to every level of economic development, from the global, to macro, to village studies, to micro analysis of firms and the household. The methodology adopted has evolved towards the use of more sophisticated methods, and towards recognition of the need for a multidisciplinary approach. Economists at Oxford have contributed to almost every major issue confronted by developing countries and development economists over the years. These include the role of technology in development; redefining development objectives; innovating methods for cost-benefit analysis; challenging inward and interventionist policies; exploring the impact of macro adjustment policies on poverty; analysing the causes of conflict; introducing new ways of measuring poverty; and exploring gender roles within the household, among many other issues touched on above. However, perhaps the weakest aspect of development economics at Oxford has been a neglect of environmental issues.

In this survey, we have shown that there is no single school of development economics at Oxford. Rather, we have observed several approaches, with two often dominant—one emphasising Keynesian, structuralist and interventionist approaches, and the other adopting a neoclassical framework and arguing for market orientation.

Development economists at Oxford have contributed to policy-making nationally and internationally. Many have advised the UK's development ministry, some in prominent positions, such as Paul Streeten in the 1960s and Stefan Dercon, Adrian Wood and Valpy FitzGerald fifty years later, while Paul Collier has been a regular adviser to UK governments at the highest level. Also, Oxford economists have advised numerous governments in developing countries in every region of the world. Internationally, Oxford economists have worked with the World Bank, the IMF and many UN agencies. They have helped determine the policies of UNDP, UNCTAD, UNIDO, UNICEF, the International Labour Organization (ILO), UNRISD, the Inter-American Development Bank, the Asian Development Bank and the African Economic Research Consortium, as well as chairing and guiding the UN's Committee on Development Policy. In so doing, they have helped transform the terms of the global debate, contributing to changes in policy, such as the basic needs approach taken up by the World Bank in the late 1970s, the move away from interventionist policies towards the market adopted by the World Bank in the 1980s, a focus on the rising poverty associated with adjustment policies also in the 1980s, the human development approach of the UNDP in the 1990s and after, and multidimensional poverty measurement adopted by the UNDP and many governments in the 2000s.

With these undoubted achievements in mind, it is time now to consider the role of development economics over the coming decades.

When economists started to analyse the economies of developing countries in the early post-colonial era, most thought it was obvious that development economics was "different" from economics applied to so-called advanced countries because of differences in resources, knowledge, flexibility and adaptability, social constraints and human behaviour. Hence, the call for different concepts, models and theories—exemplified by Streeten at Oxford—and the need to take into account structural factors and inequality as they affected economic relations, especially at the international level, a particular focus of economists working on Latin America.

Yet, this view was increasingly challenged by economists adopting a neoclassical framework, such as Ian Little, Deepak Lal and others, which gained strength with the displacement of Keynesianism by neoclassical economics in economics departments of the developed world generally. Indeed, Albert Hirschman and Lal, from very different perspectives, both wrote of the "death" of development economics in the 1980s (Hirschman 1982; Lal 1983). At Oxford, this was exemplified by the change in name of the MSc devoted to developing economies from an MSc in "Development Economics" to an MSc in "Economics for Development". The transformation of many developing economies that occurred over three-quarters of a century covered in this chapter perhaps also endorses the view that a "different" type of economics is no longer appropriate or needed.

A more universal approach, encompassing rich as well as poor countries, is emerging. The changes in objectives—first, from growth to capabilities and human development, and then to *sustainable* (environmentally responsible) development (to which Oxford development economists have contributed)—apply to *all* countries. Many of the concepts, initially developed in the context of developing economies, such as the "informal sector", "horizontal inequalities", "structural constraints", have turned out to be equally applicable to developed country economies. A number of the problems confronting economists examining developing economies are universal—such as inequality, poverty, inadequate employment opportunities, and environmental destruction. The political obstacles to what seems to be rational policy do not respect North-South boundaries. The importance of context for understanding change applies the world over. Methodologies—the use of mixed methods, including anthropological and historical studies, game playing, randomised approaches, and the use of panel data—are universally applicable. The need for multidisciplinarity, drawing on history, anthropology, political science and sociology, is as compelling in advanced as in developing country contexts.

A further reason for universalising development economics is the neo-colonial aroma that hangs over the idea of development economics in which people in one part of the world (the richer part) analyse what is happening in the poorer part, and tell the governments there how their economies work and what they should do. This approach was a natural one as colonialism ended, which left many countries with very limited skills and education, and power still firmly in the North. But today, the dominantly one-way flow involved is becoming increasingly unacceptable, especially as economists in developing countries are numerous and sophisticated.

All this suggests that we now need to move beyond development economics to a more universal approach, and, from this point of view, development economics as such is becoming outdated. This is not to endorse the view that neoclassical economics has all the answers, as Deepak Lal implied—indeed the reverse. Rather, we need to draw on the findings of development economists about understanding context and structural constraints for economics in general.

Oxford development economics is indeed already moving in this direction. Joint work with scientists in developing countries is becoming more common; analysis of developed countries along with developing is beginning to occur; and most economists would agree that context matters. However, institutions have not caught up, in Oxford or elsewhere. Over the next seventy years, it is likely that we will develop problem-oriented institutions—such as those already in existence in the energy, environmental, area studies and social policy fields in Oxford—and that we transform the institutions devoted to development studies to institutions which study economic structures, constraints and change the world over.

References

Adam, C.S. and D.L. Bevan (2004). 'Fiscal Policy Design in Low-Income Countries'. Chapter 3 in T. Addison and A. Roe (eds) *Fiscal Policy for Development: Poverty, Reconstruction and Growth*. Houndmills, Basingstoke, Hampshire: Palgrave Macmillan: 46–71.

Adam, C.S. and D.L. Bevan (2005). 'Fiscal Deficits and Growth in Developing Countries'. *Journal of Public Economics*, 89(4): 571–597.

Adam, C.S. and D.L. Bevan (2014). 'Public Investment, Public Finance, and Growth: The Impact of Distortionary Taxation, Recurrent Costs, and Incomplete Appropriability'. IMF Working Paper WP14/73. Washington, D.C.: IMF. Available at: https://www.imf.org/en/Publications/WP/Issues/2016/12/31/Public-Investment-Public-Finance-and-Growth-The-Impact-of-Distortionary-Taxation-Recurrent-41518.

Ady, P. (1951). *Economic Statistics in Burma: Report and Recommendations of a United Nations Expert.* New York: United Nations Technical Assistance Administration.

Ady, P. and M. Courcier (1960). *Systems of National Accounts in Africa.* Paris: Organisation for European Economic Co-operation.

Alesina, A. and R. Perotti (1994). 'The Political Economy of Growth: A Critical Survey of the Recent Literature'. *World Bank Economic Review*, 8(3): 351–371.

Alkire, S. (2002). *Valuing Freedoms: Sen's Capability Approach and Poverty Reduction.* Oxford: Oxford University Press.

Alkire, S. (2015). *Multidimensional Poverty Measurement and Analysis.* Oxford: Oxford University Press.

Alkire, S. and J. Foster (2008). 'Counting and Multidimensional Poverty Measurement'. Working Paper No. 07, Oxford Poverty & Human Development Institute. Available at: https://www.ophi.org.uk/wp-content/uploads/ophi-wp7_vs2.pdf.

Alkire, S. and J. Foster (2011). 'Counting and Multidimensional Poverty Measurement'. *Journal of Public Economics*, 95(7–8): 476–487.

Ambler, K., C. Doss, C. Kieran and S. Passarelli (2021). 'He Says, She Says: Spousal Disagreement in Survey Measures of Bargaining Power'. *Economic Development and Cultural Change*, 9(2): 765–788.

Anand, S. (2018). 'Recasting Human Development Measures'. Working Paper 23, International Inequalities Institute. London: LSE.

Anand, S. and M. Ravallion (1993). 'Human Development in Poor Countries: On the Role of Private Incomes and Public Services'. *Journal of Economic Perspectives*, 7(1): 133–150.

Anand, S. and A.K. Sen (1994). 'Human Development Index: Methodology and Measurement'. Occasional Paper No. 12, United Nations Development Programme. Available at: http://hdr.undp.org/sites/default/files/oc12.pdf.

Anand, S. and A.K. Sen (1995). 'Gender Inequality in Human Development: Theories and Measurement'. Occasional Paper No. 19, United Nations Development Programme. Available at: http://hdr.undp.org/sites/default/files/sudhir_anand_amartya_sen.pdf.

Anand, S. and A.K. Sen (2000). 'The Income Component of the Human Development Index'. *Journal of Human Development*, 1(1): 83–106.

Anderson, E., P.J.G. Tang and A. Wood (2006). 'Globalization, Co-operation Costs, and Wage Inequalities'. *Oxford Economic Papers*, New Series, 58(4): 569–595.

Astorga, P., A.R. Bergés and E.V.K. FitzGerald (2005). 'The Standard of Living in Latin America During the Twentieth Century'. *Economic History Review*, New Series, 58(4): 765–796.

Astorga, P., A.R. Bergés and E.V.K. FitzGerald (2011). 'Productivity Growth in Latin America Over the Long Run'. *Review of Income and Wealth*, 57(2): 203–223.

Badiani, R., S. Dercon, P. Krishnan and K.P.C. Rao (2007). 'Changes in Living Standards in Villages in India, 1975–2004: Revisiting the ICRISAT Village Level Studies'. CPRC Working Paper 85. Queen Elizabeth House, Oxford, Chronic Poverty Research Centre. Available at: http://www.chronicpoverty.org/uploads/publication_files/WP85_Badiani_et_al.pdf.

Balassa, B. (1965). 'Tariff Protection in Industrial Countries: An Evaluation'. *Journal of Political Economy*, 73(6): 573–594.

Balassa, B. (1971). *The Structure of Protection in Developing Countries*. Baltimore: Johns Hopkins Press.

Balogh, T. (1963). *Unequal Partners*. Two volumes. Oxford: Basil Blackwell.

Balogh, T. (1966). *The Economics of Poverty*. London: Weidenfeld & Nicolson.

Balogh, T. and P. Streeten (1963). 'The Coefficient of Ignorance'. *Bulletin of the Oxford University Institute of Economics and Statistics*, 25(2): 99–107.

Baptist, S. and F. Teal (2014). 'Technology and Productivity in African Manufacturing Firms'. *World Development*, 64(December): 713–725.

Barr, A.M. (2002). 'The Functional Diversity and Spillover Effects of Social Capital'. *Journal of African Economies*, 11(1): 90–113.

Barr, A.M. (2003). 'Trust and Expected Trustworthiness: Experimental Evidence from Zimbabwean Villages'. *Economic Journal*, 113(489): 614–630.

Barro, R.J. (1996). 'Determinants of Economic Growth: A Cross-Country Empirical Study'. NBER Working Paper No. 5698. Cambridge, MA: National Bureau of Economic Research.

Bevan, D.L., P. Collier and J.W. Gunning (1990). 'Temporary Trade Shocks and Dynamic Adjustment'. Economics Series Working Papers 9993. Department of Economics, University of Oxford.

Bevan, D.L., P. Collier and J.W. Gunning (1993). 'Trade Shocks in Developing Countries: Consequences and Policy Responses'. *European Economic Review*, 37(2–3): 557–565.

Bigsten, A., P. Collier, S. Dercon, M. Fafchamps, B. Gauthier, J.W. Gunning, A. Oduro, R. Oostendorp, C. Pattillo, M. Söderbom, F. Teal and A. Zeufack (2004). 'Do African Manufacturing Firms Learn from Exporting?'. *Journal of Development Studies*, 40(3): 115–141.

Bliss, C. and V. Joshi (2014). 'Ian Malcolm David Little, 1918–2012'. *Biographical Memoirs of Fellows of the British Academy*. XIII. London: Oxford University Press: 315–349.

Bliss, C.J. and N.H. Stern (1982). *Palanpur: The Economy of an Indian Village*. Oxford: Clarendon Press.

Boyce, J.K. (2011). 'Keith Griffin'. *Development and Change*, 42(1): 262–283.

Brown, L.R. (1970). *Seeds of Change. The Green Revolution and Development in the 1970s*. London: Pall Mall.

Brown, G., A. Langer and F. Stewart (eds) (2012). *Affirmative Action in Plural Societies: International Experiences*. London: Palgrave.

Buffie, E.F., C.S. Adam, S.A. O'Connell and C. Pattillo (2008). 'Riding the Wave: Monetary Responses to Aid Surges in Low-Income Countries'. *European Economic Review*, 52(8): 1,378–1,395.

Buffie, E.F., S.A. O'Connell and C. Adam (2010). 'Fiscal Inertia, Donor Credibility, and the Monetary Management of Aid Surges'. *Journal of Development Economics*, 93(2): 287–298.

Cárdenas, E., J.A. Ocampo and R. Thorp (eds) (2000a). *Industrialization and the State in Latin America: The Black Legend and the Post-War Years*. London: Macmillan.

Cárdenas, E., J.A. Ocampo and R. Thorp (2000b). 'The Export Age: The Latin American Economies in the Late Nineteenth and Early Twentieth Centuries'. Chapter 1 in E. Cárdenas et al. (eds) *An Economic History of Twentieth-Century Latin America: Volume 1—The Export Age*. London: Macmillan: 1–31.

Cassen, R. and V. Joshi (eds) (1995). *India: The Future of Economic Reform*. Delhi: Oxford University Press.

Cederman, L.-E., N.B. Weidmann and K.S. Gleditsch (2011). 'Horizontal Inequalities and Ethnonationalist Civil War: A Global Comparison'. *American Political Science Review*, 105(3): 478–495.

Clark, C. (1940). *The Conditions of Economic Progress*. London: Macmillan.

Clark, C. (1961). *Growthmanship: A Study of the Mythology of Investment*. London: Institute of Economic Affairs.

Clark, C. (1967). *Population Growth and Land Use*. London: Macmillan.

Clark, C. and M. Haswell (1964). *The Economics of Subsistence Agriculture*. London: Macmillan.

Clarke, D.J. and S. Dercon (2016). *Dull Disasters?: How Planning Ahead Will Make A Difference*. Oxford: Oxford University Press.

Collier, P., V.L. Elliott, H. Hegre, A. Hoeffler, M. Reynal-Querol and N. Sambanis (2003). *Breaking the Conflict Trap: Civil War and Development Policy*. Washington, D.C.: World Bank.

Collier, P. and J. Gunning (1999). *Trade Shocks in Developing Countries*. Two volumes. Oxford: Oxford University Press.

Collier, P. and A. Hoeffler (2002). 'Aid, Policy, and Growth in Post-Conflict Societies'. World Bank Policy Research Working Paper No. 2902, World Bank. Available at: http://documents.worldbank.org/curated/en/648621468739472948/pdf/multi0page.pdf.

Collier, P. and A. Hoeffler (2004). 'Greed and Grievance in Civil War'. *Oxford Economic Papers*, New Series, 56(4): 563–595.

Collier, P., A. Hoeffler and D. Rohner (2009). 'Beyond Greed and Grievance: Feasibility and Civil War'. *Oxford Economic Papers*, New Series, 61(1): 1–27.

Cornia, G.A., R. Jolly and F. Stewart (1987). *Adjustment With A Human Face*. Oxford: Clarendon Press.

Dasgupta, P., S. Marglin and A.K. Sen (1972). *Guidelines for Project Evaluation in Developing Countries*. Vienna: United Nations Industrial Development Organisation.

Dercon, S. (2002). 'Income Risk, Coping Strategies, and Safety Nets'. *World Bank Research Observer*, 17(2): 141–166.

Dercon, S. (2004). *Insurance Against Poverty*. Oxford: Oxford University Press.

Dercon, S. and D. Gollin (2014). 'Agriculture in African Development: Theories and Strategies'. *Annual Review of Resource Economics*, 6: 471–492.

Dercon, S. and P. Krishnan (2000). 'In Sickness and in Health: Risk Sharing within Households in Rural Ethiopia'. *Journal of Political Economy*, 108(4): 688–727.

Dercon, S. and C. Porter (2014). 'Live Aid Revisited: Long-Term Impacts of the 1984 Ethiopian Famine on Children'. *Journal of the European Economic Association*, 12(4): 927–948.

Dercon, S., J. Hoddinott and T. Woldehanna (2005). 'Shocks and Consumption in 15 Ethiopian Villages, 1999–2004'. *Journal of African Economies*, 14(4): 559–585.

Doss, C.R. and R. Meinzen-Dick (2015). 'Collective Action Within the Household: Insights from Natural Resource Management'. *World Development*, 74(October): 171–183.

Doss, C.R., H. Swaminathan, C.D. Deere, J.Y. Suchitra, A.D. Oduro and B. Anglade (2019). 'Women, Assets, and Formal Savings: A Comparative Analysis of Ecuador, Ghana and India'. *Development Policy Review*, 8(2): 180–205.

Fafchamps, M. and E.L. Ferrara (2012). 'Self-Help Groups and Mutual Assistance: Evidence from Urban Kenya'. *Economic Development and Cultural Change*, 60(4): 707–733.

Fafchamps, M. and C. Moser (2003). 'Crime, Isolation and Law Enforcement'. *Journal of African Economies*, 12(4): 625–671.

Fafchamps, M. and P.C. Vicente (2013). 'Political Violence and Social Networks: Experimental Evidence from a Nigerian Election'. *Journal of Development Economics*, 101(March): 27–48.

Fafchamps, M. and J. Wahba (2006). 'Child Labor, Urban Proximity, and Household Composition'. *Journal of Development Economics*, 79(2): 374–397.

FitzGerald, E.V.K. (1993). *The Macroeconomics of Development Finance: A Kaleckian Analysis of the Semi-Industrialised Economy*. New York: Palgrave Macmillan.

FitzGerald, E.V.K. (2002). 'International Tax Co-operation and Capital Mobility'. *CEPAL Review No. 77*: 65–78.

FitzGerald, E.V.K. (2003). *Global Markets and the Developing Economy*. New York: Palgrave.

FitzGerald, E.V.K. (2007). 'International Risk Tolerance, Capital Market Failure and Capital Flows to Emerging Markets'. Chapter 16 in G. Mavrotas and A. Shorrocks (eds) *Advancing Development: Core Themes in Global Economics*. New York: Palgrave: 299–318.

FitzGerald, E.V.K. (2012). 'Global Capital Markets, Direct Taxation and the Redistribution of Income'. *International Review of Applied Economics*, 26(2): 241–252.

FitzGerald, E.V.K. (2019). 'Development Economics and Public Economics: Emerging Analytical Interface and Practical Policy Implications'. Chapter 5 in M. Nissanke and J.A. Ocampo (eds) *The Palgrave Handbook of Development Economics*. Cham: Palgrave: 143–176.

FitzGerald, E.V.K. and E. Dayle Siu (2018). 'The Effects of International Tax Competition on National Income Distribution'. Chapter 9 in J.A. Ocampo (ed.) *International Policy Rules and Inequality: Implications for Global Economic Governance*. New York: Colombia University Press: 243–272.

Frankel, S.H. (1952). 'United Nations Primer For Development'. *Quarterly Journal of Economics*, 66(3): 301–326.

Franzoni, J.M. and D. Sánchez-Ancochea (2016). *The Quest for Universal Social Policy in the South: Actors, Ideas, and Architectures*. Cambridge: Cambridge University Press.

Freebairn, D.K. (1995). 'Did the Green Revolution Concentrate Incomes? A Quantitative Study of Research Reports'. *World Development*, 23(2): 265–279.

Fu, X. (2004). *Exports, Foreign Direct Investment and Economic Development in China*. London: Palgrave Macmillan.

Fu, X. (2015). *China's Path to Innovation*. Cambridge: Cambridge University Press.

Fu, X. and Y. Gong (2011). 'Indigenous and Foreign Innovation Efforts and Drivers of Technological Upgrading: Evidence from China'. *World Development*, 39(7): 1,213–1,225.

Fu, X., P. Mohnen and G. Zanello (2018). 'Innovation and Productivity in Formal and Informal Firms in Ghana'. *Technological Forecasting & Social Change*, 131(June): 315–325.

Fu, X., C. Pietrobelli and L. Soete (2011). 'The Role of Foreign Technology and Indigenous Innovation in the Emerging Economies: Technological Change and Catching-Up'. *World Development*, 39(7): 1,204–1,212.

Gollin, D., R. Jedwab and D. Vollrath (2016). 'Urbanization With and Without Industrialization'. *Journal of Economic Growth*, 21(1): 35–70.

Gollin, D., D. Lagakos and M.E. Waugh (2014). 'The Agricultural Productivity Gap'. *Quarterly Journal of Economics*, 129(2): 939–993.

Gollin, D., M. Martina Kirchberger and D. Lagakos (2018). 'Measuring Living Standards Across Space in the Developing World'. Oxford: Oxford Department of International Development.

Gollin, D. and R. Rogerson (2014). 'Productivity, Transport Costs and Subsistence Agriculture'. *Journal of Development Economics*, 107(March): 38–48.

Griffin, K.B. (1970). 'Foreign Capital, Domestic Savings and Economic Development'. *Bulletin of the Oxford University Institute of Economics and Statistics*, 32(2): 99–112.

Griffin, K.B. (1974). *The Political Economy of Agrarian Change: An Essay on the Green Revolution*. Cambridge, MA: Harvard University Press.

Griffin, K.B. and J.L. Enos (1970). 'Foreign Assistance: Objectives and Consequences'. *Economic Development and Cultural Change*, 18(3): 313–327.

Griffin, K.B. and J.B. Knight (eds) (1990). *Human Development and the International Development Strategy for the 1990s*. Basingstoke: Palgrave Macmillan.

Griffin, K.B. and J. James (1981). *The Transition to Egalitarian Development: Economic Policies for Structural Change in the Third World*. London: Macmillan.

Gunn, I. (1962). 'Review of *Development From Below*, by U.K. Hicks'. *African Affairs*, 61(242): 74–75.

Harriss-White, B. (1996). *A Political Economy of Agricultural Markets in South India*. New Delhi: Sage.

Harriss-White, B. (2003). *India Working: Essays on Society and Economy*. Cambridge: Cambridge University Press.

Harriss-White, B. (ed.) (2015). *Middle India and Urban-Rural Development: Four Decades of Change*. New Delhi: Springer.

Harriss-White, B. (2019). 'Making the World a Better Place: Restitution and Restoration'. In L. Panitch and G. Albo (eds) *Socialist Register 2020: Beyond Market Dystopia—New Ways of Living*. London: The Merlin Press: 30–53.

Harriss-White, B., A. Gadthorne-Hardy and G. Rodrigo (2019). 'Towards Lower-Carbon Indian Agricultural Development: An Experiment in Multi-Criteria Mapping'. *Review of Development and Change*, 24(1): 5–30.

Harriss-White, B. (2020). 'Waste, Social Order, and Physical Disorder in Small-Town India'. *Journal of Development Studies*, 56(2): 239–258.

Harriss-White, B. and S. Janakarajan (2004). *Rural India Facing the 21st Century*. London: Anthem Press.

Haswell, M. (1967). *Economics of Development in Village India*. London: Routledge & Kegan Paul.

Haswell, M. (1973). *Tropical Farming Economics*. London: Longman.

Haswell, M. (1991). 'Population and Change in a Gambian Rural Community 1947–1987'. Chapter 8 in M. Haswell and D. Hunt (eds) *Rural Households in Emerging Societies: Technology and Change in Sub-Saharan Africa*. Oxford: Berg: 141–171.

Haswell, M. and D. Hunt (1991). 'Introductory Chapter'. Chapter 1 in M. Haswell and D. Hunt (eds) *Rural Households in Emerging Societies: Technology and Change in Sub-Saharan Africa*. Oxford: Berg: 1–7.

Healey, J.M. (1972). 'An Aid Economist's Evaluation of the Little-Mirrlees Manual'. *Bulletin of the Oxford University Institute of Economics and Statistics*, 34(1): 135–152.

Heyer, J. (1992). 'The Role of Dowries and Daughters' Marriages in the Accumulation and Distribution of Capital in a South Indian Community'. *Journal of International Development*, 4(4): 419–436.

Heyer, J. (2013). 'Integration into a Global Production Network: Impacts on Labour in Tiruppur's Rural Hinterlands'. *Oxford Development Studies*, 41(3): 307–321.

Heyer, J. (2016). 'Loosening the Ties of Patriarchy with Agrarian Transition in Coimbatore Villages: 1981/2–2008/9'. Chapter 7 in B.B. Mohanty (ed.) *Critical Perspectives on Agrarian Transition: India in the Global Debate*. London: Routledge: 199–221.

Heyer, J., P. Roberts and G. Williams (eds) (1981). *Rural Development in Tropical Africa*. Basingstoke: Macmillan.

Hicks, U.K. (1947). *Public Finance*. London: Nisbet.

Hicks, U.K. (1961). *Development From Below: Local Government and Finance in Developing Countries of the Commonwealth*. London: Oxford University Press.

Hicks, U.K. (1978). *Federalism: Failure and Success—A Comparative Study*. London: Macmillan.

Hillesund, S., K. Bahgat, G. Barrett, K. Dupuy, S. Gates, H.M. Nygård, S.A. Rustad, H. Strand, H. Urdal and G. Østby (2018). 'Horizontal Inequality and Armed Conflict: A Comprehensive Literature Review'. *Canadian Journal of Development Studies*, 39(4): 463–480.

Himanshu, P.L., P. Lanjouw and N.H. Stern (2018). *How Lives Change: Palanpur, India, and Development Economics*. Oxford: Oxford University Press.

Hirschman, A.O. (1982). 'The Rise and Decline of Development Economics'. Chapter 22 in M. Gersovitz, C.F. Diaz-Alejandro, G. Ranis and M.R. Rosenzweig (eds) *The Theory and Experience of Economic Development: Essays in Honour of Sir W. Arthur Lewis*. London: George Allen & Unwin: 372–390.

Joshi, H. (1972). 'World Prices as Shadow Prices: A Critique'. *Bulletin of the Oxford University Institute of Economics and Statistics*, 34(1): 53–73.

Joshi, V. (2017). *India's Long Road: The Search for Prosperity*. Oxford: Oxford University Press.

Joshi, V. and I.M.D. Little (1994). *India: Macroeconomics and Political Economy, 1964–1991*. Washington, D.C. and Delhi: Oxford University Press.

Joshi, V. and I.M.D. Little (1996). *India's Economic Reforms, 1991–2001*. Oxford and Delhi: Clarendon Press.

Joshi, V. and U.R. Patel (2009). 'India and Climate-Change Mitigation'. Chapter 9 in D. Helm and C. Hepburn (eds) *The Economics and Politics of Climate Change*. Oxford: Oxford University Press: 167–196.

Kingdon, G.G. and J.B. Knight (2004). 'Unemployment in South Africa: The Nature of the Beast'. *World Development*, 32(3): 391–408.

Knight, J.B. and S. Ding (2012). *China's Remarkable Economic Growth*. Oxford: Oxford University Press.

Knight, J.B. and R.H. Sabot (1990). *Education, Productivity, and Inequality: The East African Natural Experiment*. New York: Oxford University Press.

Knight, J.B. and L. Song (1999). *The Rural-Urban Divide: Economic Disparities and Interactions in China*. Oxford: Oxford University Press.

Knight, J.B. and L. Song (2005). *Towards a Labour Market in China*. Oxford: Oxford University Press.

Krueger, A.O. (1966). 'Some Economic Costs of Exchange Control: The Turkish Case'. *Journal of Political Economy*, 74(5): 466–480.

Krueger, A.O. (1974). 'The Political Economy of the Rent-Seeking Society'. *American Economic Review*, 64(3): 291–303.

Lal, D. (1972). *Wells and Welfare: An Exploratory Cost-Benefit Study of the Economics of Small-Ccale Irrigation in Maharashtra*. Paris: Organisation for Economic Co-operation and Development.

Lal, D. (1983). *The Poverty of "Development Economics"*. London: Institute of Economic Affairs.

Lall, S. (1979). 'Transfer Pricing and Developing Countries: Some Problems of Investigation'. *World Development*, 7(1): 59–71.

Lall, S. (1982). *Developing Countries as Exporters of Technology: A First Look at the Indian Experience*. London: Macmillan.

Lall, S. (1983). *The New Multinationals: The Spread of Third World Enterprises*. Chichester: Wiley.

Lall, S. (1987). *Learning to Industrialize: The Acquisition of Technological Capability by India*. Basingstoke: Macmillan.

Lall, S. (1992). 'Technological Capabilities and Industrialization'. *World Development*, 20(2): 165–186.

Little, I.M.D. (1982). *Economic Development: Theory, Policy, and International Relations*. New York: Basic Books.

Little, I.M.D., R.N. Cooper, W.M. Corden and S. Rajapatirana (1993). *Boom, Crisis, and Adjustment: The Macroeconomic Experience of Developing Countries*. New York: Oxford University Press.

Little, I.M.D. and J.A. Mirrlees (1969). *Manual of Industrial Project Analysis in Developing Countries, II, Social Cost-Benefit Analysis*. Paris: OECD.

Little, I.M.D. and J.A. Mirrlees (1974). *Project Appraisal and Planning for Developing Countries*. London: Heinemann.

Little, I.M.D., T. Scitovsky and M. FG. Scott (1970). *Industry and Trade in Some Developing Countries: A Comparative Study*. London: Oxford University Press.

Little, I.M.D. and M. FG. Scott (1976). *Using Shadow Prices*. London: Heinemann Educational.

McCartney, M. (2019). *The Indian Economy, 1947–2017*. London: Agenda.

McCartney, M. and A. Zaidi (eds) (2019). *New Perspectives on Pakistan's Political Economy: State, Class and Social Change*. New Delhi: Cambridge University Press.

Myint, H. (1958). 'The "Classical Theory" of International Trade and the Underdeveloping Countries'. *Economic Journal*, 68(270): 317–337.

Myint, H. (1964). *The Economics of the Developing Countries*. London: Hutchinson.

Myrdal, G. (1968). *Asian Drama: An Inquiry into the Poverty of Nations*. London: Allen Lane.

Nayyar, D. (2013). *Catch Up: Developing Countries in the World Economy*. Oxford: Oxford University Press.

Newbery, D.M.G. and J.E. Stiglitz (1979). 'The Theory of Commodity Price Stabilisation Rules: Welfare Impacts and Supply Responses'. *Economic Journal*, 89(356): 799–817.

OPHI and UNDP (2019). *Global Multidimensional Poverty Index 2019: Illuminating Inequalities*. Oxford and New York: Oxford Poverty & Human Development Initiative and United Nations Development Programme.

Ranis, G. (1972). 'Relative Prices in Planning for Economic Development'. Chapter 5 in D.J. Daly (ed.) *International Comparisons of Prices and Output*. New York: National Bureau of Economic Research: 287–331.

Ravallion, M. (1987). *Markets and Famines*. Oxford: Clarendon Press.

Ravallion, M. (2016). *The Economics of Poverty: History, Measurement and Policy*. Oxford: Oxford University Press.

Reuber, G.L., H. Crookell, M. Emerson and G. Gallais-Hamonno (1973). *Private Foreign Investment in Development*. Oxford: Clarendon Press.

Romer, P. (1990). 'Endogenous Technological Change'. *Journal of Political Economy*, 98(5): S71–S102.

Ruggeri Laderchi, C., R. Saith and F. Stewart (2003). 'Does It Matter That We Do Not Agree on the Definition of Poverty? A Comparison of Four Approaches'. *Oxford Development Studies*, 31(3): 243–274.

Sánchez-Ancochea, D. (2020). *The Costs of Inequality in Latin America: Lessons and Warnings for the Rest of the World*. London: I.B.Tauris.

Schumacher, E.F. (1973). *Small Is Beautiful: A Study of Economics As If People Mattered*. New York: Harper & Row.

Scott, M. FG. (1989). *A New View of Economic Growth*. Oxford: Clarendon Press.

Scott, M. FG., J. MacArthur and D.M.G. Newbery (1976). *Project Appraisal in Practice: The Little/Mirrlees Method Applied in Kenya*. London: Heinemann.

Seers, D. (1969). 'The Meaning of Development'. *International Development Review*, 11(4): 3–4.

Sen, A.K. (1980). 'Equality of What?'. In S.M. McMurrin (ed.) *The Tanner Lectures on Human Values, Volume 1*. Cambridge: Cambridge University Press: 195–220.

Sen, A.K. (1981). *Poverty and Famines: An Essay on Entitlement and Deprivation*. Oxford: Clarendon Press.

Söderbom, M. and F. Teal (2004). 'Size and Efficiency in African Manufacturing Firms: Evidence from Firm-Level Panel Data'. *Journal of Development Economics*, 73(1): 369–394.

Solow, R.M. (1956). 'A Contribution to the Theory of Economic Growth'. *Quarterly Journal of Economics*, 70(1): 65–94.

Squire, L. and H.G. Van Der Tak (1975). *Economic Analysis of Projects*. Maryland: Johns Hopkins University Press.

Stern, N.H. (1972). 'Experience With the Use of the Little/Mirrlees Method For An Appraisal of Small-Holder Tea in Kenya'. *Bulletin of the Oxford University Institute of Economics and Statistics*, 34(1): 93–123.

Stewart, F. (1977). *Technology and Underdevelopment*. London: Macmillan.

Stewart, F. (1978). 'Social Cost-Benefit Analysis in Practice: Some Reflections in the Light of Case Studies Using Little-Mirrlees Techniques'. *World Development*, 6(2): 153–165.

Stewart, F. (1985). *Planning to Meet Basic Needs*. London: Macmillan.

Stewart, F. (1993). 'War and Underdevelopment: Can Economic Analysis Help Reduce the Costs?'. *Journal of International Development*, 5(4): 357–380.

Stewart, F. (2000). 'Crisis Prevention: Tackling Horizontal Inequalities'. *Oxford Development Studies*, 28(3): 245–262.

Stewart, F. (ed.) (2008). *Horizontal Inequalities and Conflict: Understanding Group Violence in Multiethnic Societies*. London: Palgrave.

Stewart, F. (2014). 'Justice, Horizontal Inequality, and Policy in Multi-Ethnic Societies'. Chapter 7 in G.A. Cornia and F. Stewart (eds) *Towards Human*

Development: New Approaches to Macroeconomics and Inequality. Oxford: Oxford University Press: 122–147.

Stewart, F. and E.V.K. FitzGerald (2000). *War and Underdevelopment: Volume 1— The Economic and Social Consequences of Conflict*. Oxford: Oxford University Press.

Stewart, F. and A. Langer (2008). 'Horizontal Inequalities: Explaining Persistence and Change'. Chapter 4 in F. Stewart (ed.) *Horizontal Inequalities and Conflict: Understanding Group Violence in Multiethnic Societies*. London: Palgrave: 54–82.

Stewart, F., G. Ranis and E. Samman (2018). *Advancing Human Development: Theory and Practice*. Oxford: Oxford University Press.

Stewart, F., R. Saith and B. Harriss-White (eds) (2007). *Defining Poverty in the Developing World*. Basingstoke: Palgrave Macmillan.

Stewart, F. and P. Streeten (1972). 'Little-Mirrlees Methods and Project Appraisal'. *Bulletin of the Oxford University Institute of Economics and Statistics*, 34(1): 75–91.

Stewart, F. and P. Streeten (1976). 'New Strategies for Development: Poverty, Income Distribution, and Growth'. *Oxford Economic Papers*, New Series, 28(3): 381–405.

Stifel, D., M. Fafchamps and B. Minten (2011). 'Taboos, Agriculture and Poverty'. *Journal of Development Studies*, 47(10): 1,455–1,481.

Stiglitz, J.E. (1974a). 'Alternative Theories of Wage Determination and Unemployment in LDC's: The Labor Turnover Model'. *Quarterly Journal of Economics*, 88(2): 194–227.

Stiglitz, J.E. (1974b). 'Incentives and Risk Sharing in Sharecropping'. *Review of Economic Studies*, 41(2): 219–255.

Stiglitz, J.E. (1976). 'The Efficiency Wage Hypothesis, Surplus Labour, and the Distribution of Income in LDC's'. *Oxford Economic Papers*, New Series, 28(2): 185–207.

Streeten, P. (1972). *The Frontiers of Development Studies*. London: Macmillan.

Streeten, P., S.J. Burki, M. ul Haq, N. Hicks and F. Stewart (1981). *First Things First: Meeting Basic Human Needs in Developing Countries*. New York: Oxford University Press.

Thorp, R. (ed.) (1984). *Latin America in the 1930s: The Role of the Periphery in World Crisis*. London: Macmillan.

Thorp, R. (1998). *Progress, Poverty and Exclusion: An Economic History of Latin America in the 20th Century*. Washington, D.C.: Inter-American Development Bank.

Thorp, R., S. Battistelli, Y. Guichaoua, J.C. Orihuela and M. Paredes (2012). *The Developmental Challenges of Mining and Oil: Lessons from Africa and Latin America*. London: Palgrave Macmillan.

Thorp, R. and G. Bertram (1978). *Peru, 1890–1977: Growth and Policy in an Open Economy*. London and New York: Macmillan and Columbia University Press.

Thorp, R. and M. Paredes (2010). *Ethnicity and the Persistence of Inequality: The Case of Peru*. Basingstoke, Hampshire: Palgrave Macmillan.

Thorp, R. and L. Whitehead (eds) (1979). *Inflation and Stabilisation in Latin America*. London: Macmillan.

Thorp, R. and L. Whitehead (eds) (1987). *Latin American Debt and the Adjustment Crisis*. London: Macmillan.

Toye, J. (2009). 'Herbert Frankel: From Colonial Economics to Development Economics'. *Oxford Development Studies*, 37(2): 171–182.

UNDP (1990). *Human Development Report 1990*. Oxford: Oxford University Press.

Weerdt, J. De, K. Beegle and S. Dercon (2017). 'Orphanhood and Self-Esteem: An 18–Year Longitudinal Study From an HIV-Affected Area in Tanzania'. *Journal of Acquired Immune Deficiency Syndrome*, 76(3): 225–230.

Weir, S. and J.B. Knight (2007). 'Production Externalities of Education: Evidence from Rural Ethiopia'. *Journal of African Economies*, 16(1): 134–165.

Wood, A. (1994). *North-South Trade, Employment, and Inequality: Changing Fortunes in a Skill-Driven World*. Oxford: Oxford University Press.

Wood, A. (2008). 'Looking Ahead Optimally in Allocating Aid'. *World Development*, 36(7): 1,135–1,151.

Wood, A. (2011). 'Better-Behaved Heckscher-Ohlin Models Through More Consistent Treatment of Trade Costs'. QEH Working Paper No. 185. Oxford: Queen Elizabeth House. Available at: https://www.qeh.ox.ac.uk/sites/www.odid.ox.ac.uk/files/qehwps185.pdf.

Wood, A. and J. Mayer (2011). 'Has China De-Industrialised Other Developing Countries?'. *Review of World Economics*, 147(2): 325–350.

3

Oxford's Contributions to Industrial Economics from the 1920s to the 1980s

Lise Arena

1   Introduction

Industrial economics is usually defined as the study of the structure of markets, the economic performance of industries, the behaviour of both and the manner in which they interact. The discipline did not emerge as a separate subject area until the inter-war period in the United States and in England.[1] Embryonic forms of industrial economics can be found in earlier economic theories, with the earliest example in the United Kingdom probably being *The Economics of Industry* by Alfred and Mary Paley Marshall (1879). Four decades later, a number of US economists, including Frank Knight (1921) and John Maurice Clark (1922), had succeeded in introducing some central concepts, such as specific forms of imperfect competition and the role of uncertainty and risk in the context of innovation.

While industrial economics focuses on the aggregate analysis of sectors and industries, the theory of the firm is primarily concerned with the internal organisation of firms and firm behaviour. Until the end of the nineteenth century, questions relating to firm organisation were subsumed within the

---

[1] As Hay and Morris remarked in their internationally known textbook on the subject, 'people have been interested in the economic behaviour and performance of industries since the beginning of the industrial revolution, but the delineation of a specific area of economics under the title of industrial economics is a phenomenon of the last forty years' (Hay and Morris 1979: 3).

L. Arena (✉)
CNRS-Université Côte d'Azur Research Institute GREDEG, Nice, France
e-mail: lise.arena@univ-cotedazur.fr

theory of prices and value and were, at best, concerned with sector- or industry-level analysis (see Marshall and Marshall 1879): firms were "empty boxes" governed by cost curves (Clapham 1922). The concept of the internal organisation of a firm remained neglected, especially after Pigou and Robertson's highly abstract neoclassical analysis effectively eliminated the Marshallian concern with the actual workings of the firm (Pigou and Robertson 1924). In a well-known survey of the theory of the firm, Kenneth Boulding (1942: 791) attributed early developments in the field to 'extensive transformations' in the basic theory of value in the 1930s.[2] At the same time, empirical studies, which were increasingly concerned with the separation of ownership from management (see Berle and Means 1932), highlighted the separate existence of firms from markets, and the importance of their internal forms of organisation for overall economic performance.

Since the inter-war period, industrial economics and the theory of the firm have constituted a significant part of applied microeconomics. This chapter seeks to provide a better understanding of Oxford's contributions to the emergence and the institutionalisation of industrial economics as an academic discipline. It falls into four main parts: "Premises", triggered by David Macgregor's contribution and the Oxford Economists' Research Group (OERG) (1921–1965); "Roots", illustrated by the research on the Courtauld Inquiry and Philip Andrews' contribution (1943–1947); "Institutionalisation", evidenced by the creation of the *Journal of Industrial Economics* (1952–1968); and "Transformation", exemplified by the shift of the discipline towards industrial organisation (1979–1991). Despite the prominent position of its researchers in their respective fields, Oxford's leading role in the emergence of industrial economics is not attributable to any specific school of thought it produced, as could be argued was the case at Cambridge. Rather, the Oxford case stands out because of its contribution to the emergence and development of institutions that are still internationally central to the discipline.

2   Premises: From Macgregor's (Isolated) Contribution to the OERG in the Analysis of Industrial Firms (1921–1965)

Until the post-war period, there was no established form of industrial economics at Oxford, despite a significant number of scholars interested in the study of industrial structures and firms. The premises of the academic

---

[2] Boulding was specifically referring to Chamberlin (1933) and Robinson (1933), noting that 'these volumes mark the explicit recognition of the theory of the firm as an integral division of economic analysis upon which rests the whole fabric of equilibrium theory' (Boulding 1942: 791).

discipline were fostered by a relatively obscure economist, David Hutchison Macgregor, who was involved in the creation of an informal group of Oxford economists known as the Oxford Economists' Research Group (OERG).

2.1   Macgregor and Embryonic Industrial Economics

This section considers the life and work of Macgregor who published a substantial amount on the theory of the firm and contributed to the development of Oxford industrial economics. Macgregor studied economics at Cambridge where he obtained a BA in 1901. There, he became 'one of Marshall's favourite students and became quite attached to his method, i.e. to the use of theory tempered by empirical investigation' (Lee 1989: 23). In particular, it was argued that if Macgregor 'used Marshallian methods that was because, testing them as far as he could against the facts of ordinary life they seemed to him the best available' (Andrews 1953: 348). During his stay at Cambridge, Macgregor prepared his *Industrial Combination*, which was published in 1906 and resulted in him being elected a Fellow of Trinity College, Cambridge, in 1904. According to Lee's biography of Macgregor, at this time he was 'employed as a university lecturer in general economics and was paid, unofficially, by Marshall for the work' (Lee 2008: 3). In 1908, Macgregor left Cambridge to become Professor of Political Economy at the University of Leeds.

Macgregor's *Report of Travels* (1913) expressed his interest in studying forms of industrial organisation in different countries, such as China, Japan, India, Russia and the United States. In particular, Macgregor 'had in view specially the relation of foreign nations to the great industrial changes which occurred in England nearly a century and a half ago—changes to which we owe the nature and the problems of our present industrial life' (ibid.: 8). In 1919, Macgregor moved to Manchester where he became Stanley Professor of Political Economy He stayed there for only two years, as in 1921, Edgeworth vacated the chair at Oxford, and according to Young and Lee (1993: 12), although Macgregor 'did not formally apply for the Drummond', the 'electors offered it to him'. Immediately after his appointment, Macgregor engaged in extensive research concerned with a wide range of economics topics, such as: unemployment (Macgregor 1923); consumption (Macgregor 1924); agriculture (Macgregor 1925); and family allowances (Macgregor 1926). He also pursued his research interests in industrial economics and prepared the final revision of his 1906 book. In addition, towards the end of the 1920s, Macgregor published his research on cartels and other industrial combinations (Macgregor 1927a, 1929, 1930) and became interested in proposals for the rationalisation of industry (Macgregor 1927b). From 1925 until 1937, he was joint editor of the *Economic Journal*, with John Maynard Keynes.[3]

Macgregor's concern with an empirical approach to economics was reflected by the statistical investigations conducted in his various articles. Although his intellectual orientation and personality made him, to some extent, an isolated figure, he still contributed to the development of the theory of the firm and industrial economics at Oxford, both at the teaching and research level. Macgregor's analysis did not follow the usual methods of pure maximisation and equilibrium concepts. Rather, he was more interested in the growth of firms and the way that they were able to reproduce themselves. His main idea was that new competition came about from skilled businessmen who had learnt the trade, who promoted existing relations with customers and suppliers and who used their savings (and personal connections) to start their own businesses.

By the mid-1930s, Macgregor had published *Enterprise Purpose & Profit* (1934)—concerned with the behaviour of firms over the trade cycle under risk and uncertainty—where he 'used the formations of new joint stock companies to represent the course of enterprise' to discover that 'variations of this index precede variations of both prices and employment' (Todd 1935: 544). To him, variations in financial and stock market conditions reflected variations in company formations. Hence, the concept of strategic behaviour is implicitly used at the heart of Macgregor's contribution: once a firm has entered into competition and is established in the market, it then follows long-term policies, such as stable prices, balanced with more short-term ones, such as decisions to expand.

Despite his research, Macgregor's message did not take hold at Oxford at the time, his contribution eclipsed by the then evolving mainstream of microeconomics. This situation made him, as recently argued by Warren Samuels, 'an "applied" economist in a new world dominated by "pure" economics' (Samuels 2008: 150).[4] Yet, he could not be completely ignored by mainstream economists due to his steady flow of books and journal articles principally published in the *Economic Journal* and more occasionally in *Economica* until

---

[3] Further information about this can be found in Macgregor's correspondence with Roy Harrod. See in particular Letter 119R, Macgregor to Harrod, 18 September 1926 (Besomi 2003: 74); Letter 150, Harrod to Macgregor, 7 July 1928 (ibid.: 95); Letter 337, Keynes to Harrod, 30 December 1933 (ibid.: 259); Letter 456R, Macgregor to Harrod, 12 July 1935 (ibid.: 397).

[4] This view is also reinforced by Maurice Allen who argued that '[Macgregor] was in the old-fashioned Marshall tradition and had…little interest in rigorous analysis that came into vogue in the later years of his life. In my view, he was none the worse for that. I should say that in his books…and in his teaching he gave students a sounder understanding of the problems of the economy of his time than contemporary dons give them at present … It seems to me that…the value of his contribution was underestimated because the newer trends (fashions?) in economics passed him by' (Allen in Lee 2008: 1).

the mid-1930s. Furthermore, *Industrial Combination* still constituted an early significant account of industrial economics, which was reprinted on several occasions and was used as an economics textbook by subsequent generations of students inside and outside Oxford.[5]

2.2   The Role of the OERG in the Analysis of Industrial Firms

Despite his isolated position, Macgregor became an 'active and enthusiastic member' of the OERG shortly after its creation (Andrews 1953: 346). The Group was created in 1936 and was initially led by Sir Hubert Henderson who was the sole Professor of Economics at Oxford. The earliest members were all economists and teaching fellows at Oxford at the time. They are listed in Appendix 1 at the end of this chapter. Andrews, who came to Oxford in 1937 as a member of the research staff, became Secretary of the OERG.

A couple of years after the establishment of the first Sub-Faculty in Economics at Oxford in 1932, All Souls College offered a Readership in Economic Statistics to promote systematic empirical work in social studies. Oxford economists—who were already developing the work of the Oxford Institute of Statistics (OIS)—took the opportunity to approach the Rockefeller Foundation. In 1937, the financial assistance given by the Foundation to Roy Harrod enabled the Group to grow, in two years, from a relatively small number of participants to more than nineteen members.

The meetings of the OERG were quite informal and their studies basically consisted of sets of inquiries or research projects which usually took about eighteen months and which were based upon questionnaires. These questionnaires were sent in advance and then formed the basis for after-dinner interviews with businessmen who were invited to come to Oxford to dine and spend an evening answering members' questions. Intensive questioning and discussions often took place until the small hours of the morning. A record was kept of what was said at each meeting and sent back to the guest, allowing him to alter his comments. This procedure was considered to be a completely new methodology at the time and broke with traditional deductive methods.

---

[5] For example, in 1937, the "Current Notes" section in the *Journal of the Royal Statistical Society* states that: 'Middle-aged students of industrial combinations will remember the publication in 1906 of an important work on that subject by D.H. Macgregor ... It has been for some time out of print, and we are indebted to the London School of Economics and Political Science for securing its re-issue as the first of a series of reprints of scarce works on political economy ... Even after thirty years it will repay perusal, for it differs from the usual books confined to description or denunciation and is a dispassionate study of the economic aspects of the movement' (Current Notes 1937: 144–145).

While the topics studied within the Group were diverse and not only focused on firms and industries, its most notable research concerned the influence of interest rates on investment, and the pricing policies of firms. It was found that investment decisions taken by businessmen were influenced very little by changes in the rates of interest. Regarding pricing policies, many of the businessmen participants claimed to set prices according to the "full-cost" principle, that is, calculating the average cost of production and then adding a margin. In October 1938, the Group published its results in the first issue of *Oxford Economic Papers*. Indeed, a key purpose of the journal was to make public the empirical research being carried out by the OERG and the OIS.

In 1939, the OERG published papers on pricing, in particular the famous Hall-Hitch exposition of the full-cost principle. It was the first time that theorists had examined actual business practice. They used questionnaires for a sample of thirty-eight firms, with the results showing that a significant proportion of these companies did indeed set their prices according to full-cost. Typically, a company would make an ex-ante estimate of its output for the coming year, then determine average cost (direct costs, e.g. labour, materials, energy, per unit of product) and then add to it percentage margins for profit— the "mark-up". The firms in question insisted that this pricing mechanism was a "rule of thumb" and could result in maximum profits by accident only. Hence, the results of the survey appeared to conflict with the received doctrine of the time. In other words, this exercise tested the conventional assumption of maximisation in terms of equalisation of marginal cost and marginal revenue. In fact, Hall and Hitch justified the full-cost principle by arguing that 'producers cannot know their demand or marginal revenue curves' (Hall and Hitch 1939: 22). Thus, the evidence obtained from the businessmen showed that they did not and could not use marginal revenue and cost (i.e. any forms of marginalism) to set prices. Rather, it indicated 'that they [were] thinking in altogether different terms' (ibid.: 18).

After the publication of the articles in *Oxford Economic Papers*,[6] the Group was full of intellectual vitality and raring to take their research forward, but when the war started in September 1939, members were dispersed, disrupting the OERG, which became inactive for the duration of hostilities.[7]

The conventional wisdom on the post-war OERG is that it had a limited effect on Oxford economics in terms of influence and direction of research.

---

[6] These publications were reprinted in *Oxford Studies in the Price Mechanism* in 1951 edited by Wilson and Andrews.

[7] One of the difficulties for scholars in collecting archival evidence from this period is the lack of documentation. The rumour, which was still circulating many decades later, was that concerns about a Nazi invasion and confidentiality issues led Harrod and Andrews to burn the files which contained the entire proceedings of the Group in the boilers of Christ Church College, Oxford.

According to some of its former members, the OERG tried to resurrect itself after the war, but the drive and interest that existed before 1939 had gone. Nevertheless, the Group did reform, and some new members played an active part in its reconstruction. Roy Harrod took the chair and was accompanied by some new and some old members, listed in Appendix 2. As can be seen in this Appendix, Frank Burchardt, Hubert Henderson and Edward Hugh-Jones still attended meetings, along with Philip Andrews, who became the new Secretary of the Group and was assisted by Elizabeth Brunner, one of the very few female members.

During the post-war period, the members of the OERG were more concerned with researching the internal organisation of the firm. Work on pricing had been completed before the war and the post-war Group began to look at issues such as productivity and factors affecting capital expenditure (Andrews and Brunner 1950: 197). Between 1950 and the end of the OERG, four main themes were studied: pricing policy of exporters when the exchange rate altered; relationships between firms; business investment; and the sources of growth. Papers looking at the last of these were published in the March 1964 number of *Oxford Economic Papers* (Leyland 1964; Richardson 1964; Richardson and Leyland 1964).

At the beginning of the 1960s, the links that had been developed with businessmen were still growing, especially with the help of Harrod, Richardson, Leyland and Andrews, and the reputation of Oxford itself. Meanwhile, in November 1962, Roger Opie became Secretary of the Group in place of Norman Leyland. At the same time, however, the Group's members started showing some loss of interest in its work and the decision to try to increase membership and invite new economists was taken. This did not work, however, and by the summer of 1964 the Group started to seriously question its relevance. A meeting in 1965 examined forecasts and business decisions, this turning out to be the last gathering of the OERG.

3 Roots: From the Courtauld Inquiry to the Publication of *Manufacturing Business* (1943–1949)

The outbreak of war transformed economics research at Oxford and provided some new war-related research topics for the OERG and the OIS. This new range of issues soon became institutionally based and gave rise to new developments within the University, such as the Nuffield College Post-War

Reconstruction Survey (1941–1944) which led to the Courtauld Inquiry (1943–1947). Later on, the publication of *Manufacturing Business* by Philip Andrews in 1949 ushered in a new period of institutionalisation.

3.1   Courtauld Inquiry (1943–1947)

In 1937, the philanthropist, Lord Nuffield, expressed his desire to fund the creation of a new postgraduate residential college at Oxford which would be devoted to the study of both engineering and accountancy. While the form of the offer proposed by Nuffield did not match the University's desire, it was still seen as a major opportunity to provide some coherence within social studies at Oxford. Nuffield's offer was discussed between Alexander Dunlop Lindsay (Vice-Chancellor of Oxford) and the economist William Beveridge (then Master of University College), the latter clearly disapproving the idea of Nuffield's project on the grounds that it was not sensible to focus exclusively on the type of research being suggested. Eventually, Lindsay convinced Nuffield to fund a college just concerned with social studies, to the exclusion of engineering.

In May 1940, the Warden of Nuffield, Harold Butler, proposed to the College Committee a project which would look at the problems of post-war economic and social reconstruction. At this stage, G.D.H. Cole and Lindsay (also members of the Committee) suggested that Butler's proposal was too focused on a post-war context, and should rather deal with the changes then taking place in the economy, such as the effects of the redistribution of population. During the following months, Cole and Lindsay went in search for financial support for their project from the government. By April 1941, funding had been secured, and under Cole's enthusiastic direction, work began on examining the economic and social prospects of Britain's main industrial regions (see Young and Lee 1993: 142). Over the next two years, Cole invested the majority of his time and energy in this effort. However, the purpose of this Social Reconstruction Survey was soon being criticised by senior members of the University and by some of Cole's colleagues at Nuffield who questioned its practicality.

The "failure" of the Survey did not help with the promotion of social studies at Oxford. Shortly before Cole's resignation in 1944, he received a letter in March 1943 from Samuel Courtauld, Visiting Fellow at Nuffield and wealthy textile industrialist, expressing his doubts about the dictum "bigger is better". Courtauld offered to partially finance an investigation which would aim to collect evidence among firms and their accountants on the issue of the growth of firms. In 1943, it was decided that a six-month pilot investigation should be undertaken. This became known as the "Courtauld Inquiry" and was placed under a special committee called the "Courtauld Committee" within the College Committee at Nuffield.[8] The theoretical investigation—concerned with the optimum size of a firm—was conducted by Josef Steindl, J.R.L. Schneider and Arthur Bowley and worked out of the OIS.

In May 1944, the first report of the Courtauld Committee was sent to Courtauld who particularly liked the statistical investigation conducted by Andrews, 'because it dealt with Courtauld's data obtained from the [Courtauld] accountants' (ibid.: 149). As a result, Henry Clay, who had taken over from Butler as Warden of Nuffield in 1945, agreed with Courtauld that Andrews should continue his statistical investigation. The latter went one step further, proposing to Clay and Courtauld that he expand his study to the clothing and shoe industries. Over the next two years, Andrews, along with the help of the OIS, carried out this additional investigation with the assistance of his collaborator, Elizabeth Brunner. Although Courtauld died in 1947, funding for the project went on until 1949 and led Andrews to publish his results in *Manufacturing Business*.

3.2   Phillips Andrews' Contribution and the Publication of *Manufacturing Business*

Manufacturing Business was published in 1949 in a very specific context. It constituted, on the one hand, a reaction to the well-known Cambridge Cost Controversies of the 1920s and 1930s and was, on the other hand, to a large extent a continuation of the famous Hall and Hitch empirical investigation which appeared in 1939. The Cost Controversies questioned the theoretical meaning of Marshall's work and especially Pigou's specific interpretation of it. Hall and Hitch, however, as shown earlier, followed a more empirical critique and sought to demonstrate that the assumption of short-run profit maximisation which formed the basis of Pigou's interpretation clearly contradicted the pricing practices of businessmen.

In addition to this theoretical background, it is relevant to recall that *Manufacturing Business* emerged from the initial Courtauld Inquiry and was

---

[8] Archival documents about the Courtauld Inquiry can be found in the Andrews and Brunner Archive held at the London School of Economics (LSE). See, in particular, Box 56, which contains an interesting note on the relative efficiency of small and big businesses; Box 58, which contains some documents about big and small business; Box 60, which contains a report to the Courtauld Committee written by Andrews in 1945; and Box 63.

also an attempt to provide some "practical" tools and empirical evidence for the few existing theories on the internal organisation of the firm. Andrews made clear his theoretical inspiration:

> This mention of a wider experience gives me an opportunity to pay a tribute to a major element in my education as an industrial economist—my association with the pre-war Oxford Economists' Research Group … It was the work of this Research Group that developed so strongly the conviction that the behaviour of business men was consistent, and that, accordingly, even though, on many points, it might not seem directly explicable by generally accepted economic theory, there was hope that one would arrive at a consistent theory by studying individual businesses (Andrews 1949: xv).

In the volume, Andrews used an approach based on observed industrial realities at the expense of elementary mathematical formalism. Andrews' first objective was to illustrate the combination of both deductive and inductive approaches, and to emphasise their complementarities. Thus, accordingly, *Manufacturing Business* was largely concerned with the complex facts of business life, expressed by a detailed investigation of specific firms and industries.

At the same time, however, Andrews tried to develop analytical foundations to go with Hall and Hitch's empirical results. In fact, he was strongly in favour of an integrative approach, combining the full-cost principle (reshaped as "normal cost") with a revival of the Marshallian framework. Andrews' main idea was that in his analysis of the short run, Marshall could clearly be interpreted with the help of marginal tools. His analysis of the long period was, however, considered to be incompatible with these tools and their individualistic foundations.[9] Andrews' interpretation of Marshall's theory in particular stressed the existence of long-run supply curves, including economies of scale. The expansion of a firm's operations over the long run could not be supported by a marginal approach, which only admitted increasing average costs across such a time period.

Andrews' expression of normal costs in the long run was, to a large extent, influenced by Marshall's long-period theoretical framework, and especially by his concept of the representative firm. By contrast with the marginal

---

[9] To a large extent, therefore, Andrews' innovations were analytically rooted. In this context, some years after the publication of *Manufacturing Business*, he wrote: 'As I interpret Marshall, the root cause of his treatment of long run supply at the level of the individual firm is that he thinks of falling, rising or constant cost as being equally conceivable conditions in what he wishes to analyse as competitive industries and—as so many passages show—he thinks of manufacturing industry as typically showing falling average costs as expanded outputs are maintained in the long run' (Andrews' Lecture Notes IV, 2 December 1968, Andrews and Brunner Archive, LSE: 2).

interpretation of the representative firm, which considered this concept as an equilibrium firm, Andrews considered it as a firm which represented the reality of industry. He made it clear in the following note:

> This [concept of the representative firm] was his [Marshall's] new semi-historical concept which he brought into his analysis. In Book IV, Ch. XIII, p. 317 when he refers to the long period, he talks about <u>normal</u> expenses of production and says that for these we must refer to the representative firm, not to any particular competitive firm (Andrews' Lecture Notes IV, 2 December 1968, Andrews and Brunner Archive, LSE: 3; underlining in original).

Hence, Andrews refused to see Marshall's contribution to economics as a "static marginalist equilibrium theory"[10] extended to the long run. Marshall's representative firm was rather an industrial concept and 'in effect he [Marshall] is saying that we must refer the industrial supply curve to industrial conditions and not disaggregate it to purport to get long run marginal cost curves for individual businesses' (ibid.: 4). Thus, the content and methodology of *Manufacturing Business* was a direct attack on the marginalist theory of the firm.

From *Manufacturing Business* emerged a series of further work on industries which led, in turn, to the establishment of industrial economics as an academic discipline at Oxford.

4   Institutionalisation: From the Creation of the *Journal of Industrial Economics* to Further Developments Towards Information- and Knowledge-Based Approaches to the Firm (1952–1968)

Philip Andrews' contribution to the development of industrial economics at Oxford went one step further after the publication of *Manufacturing Business* with his creation of the *Journal of Industrial Economics* in 1952. In parallel, further developments in the discipline in terms of information- and knowledge-based approaches to the analysis of the behaviour of industrial firms helped to propel Oxford's importance in the field.

---

[10] Or "SMET", as Andrews referred to the marginalist approach in his Lecture Notes.

4.1   Creation of the *Journal of Industrial Economics*

As a response to the wave of interest in empirical studies of industries described earlier, the first issue of the *Journal of Industrial Economics* in 1952 represented the confirmation of industrial economics as a stand-alone discipline. The aim of the *Journal* was to drive the new discipline forward, not only based upon industrial facts, but also supported by general theoretical assertions:

> Then in 1952 he [Andrews] founded the *Journal of Industrial Economics.* Did not mean just the old economics of industries. The new term for a new subject was not established then as it is now…searching about whether we could use the term and not be misunderstood. It is very definitely not just an "applied" subject. The heart of it is the study of the individual business unit and the decision-making process—investment, pricing, etc.—and also of course the relationships between businesses, which brings in the study of industrial structure, restrictive practices and environment generally (talk given by E. Brunner to Frank Friday Group (c.1961), Andrews and Brunner Archive, LSE, Box 529: 1–2).

The first issues of the *Journal* were largely concerned with industrial matters, often supported by case studies. For instance, the first article of the first issue, which was written by Edward Mason, mainly focused on the specific case of the raw products industry in the United States (Mason 1952). In the same issue, Fred Stones wrote about "Price Policy in a Nationally Administered Industry" (Stones 1952) while Robert Shone considered "Steel Price Policy" (Shone 1952). The making of business decisions—particularly those studied by Frank Friday in the first issue with his paper on "The Problem of Business Forecasting" (Friday 1952)—was also a central issue for the *Journal*.

4.2   The Information- and Knowledge-Based Approaches to the Firm: Contributions by Richardson and Malmgren

Less than a decade after the emergence of the *Journal of Industrial Economics*, a new trend in the economics of industry and competition emerged with the contributions made by two Oxford economists: George Richardson and Harald Malmgren, both students of John Hicks. The development of the Richardson-Malmgren view of the behaviour of industrial firms was not a coincidence or an unintended consequence of their respective work, but on the contrary was largely influenced by the intellectual context of Oxford in the late 1950s and early 1960s. Indeed, Richardson and Malmgren were not aware of each other's work until quite late on.

The Richardson-Malmgren approach stressed the role of information and knowledge in explaining industrial behaviours. Several remarks can be made about the similarities between both authors.

George Richardson contributed to a new strand of thinking in the field of industrial economics, stressing the role of information in the evolution of firms. Richardson opened *Information and Investment* (1960) with a critique of the concept of perfect competition and of the Walrasian general economic equilibrium (GEE) theory. This stressed the fundamental importance of information and knowledge and led to Richardson's more general critique of the suppression of the co-ordination problem in neoclassical microeconomics. In fact, according to Richardson, informational factors within the firm are essential, mainly because 'no direct connection can exist between objective conditions and purposive activity; the immediate relationship is between *beliefs* about relevant conditions and *planned* activities which it may or may not prove impossible to implement' (Richardson 1959: 224; italics in original). Thus, Richardson's critique of GEE theory was made on the basis of the existence of informational factors. Company performance largely depends on what Richardson called the "market conditions" in the GEE. This includes both "primary" conditions (concerned with technical production possibilities and the current state of consumer preferences) and "secondary conditions" meaning the 'relevant projected activities' of other economic agents (ibid.: 229). As Richardson puts it, '[firms'] mutual interdependence clearly presents, for entrepreneurs, a barrier to obtaining the necessary secondary information, and, if we are to hope to show how a system can work, we cannot escape the obligation to explain how the barrier is overcome' (ibid.: 230). This concept of mutual interdependence providing more information to the firm represents the rationale behind the emergence of co-ordination.

Harald Malmgren worked on very similar issues but seems not to have been aware of Richardson's work until he was very far advanced in writing his thesis.[11] He spent much time discussing period analysis with his supervisor, John Hicks, after the publication of *Value and Capital* (1939). In line with Richardson's argument, Malmgren's work on the concept of time periods led to insights regarding the importance of new flows of information in the process of decision-making and located informational factors at the heart of his theory of industries. In fact, Malmgren argued that firms entered into

---

[11] Malmgren (private correspondence, 2008).

co-operation to stabilise the expectations of managers and could therefore reduce transaction costs (as also argued by Richardson). Malmgren's contribution was original and constituted a first attempt in paving the way to a new kind of industrial organisation, mainly based on organisational and firm theory. His contributions favoured a multi-disciplinary approach, incorporating ideas not only from economics, but also from organisational theory, game theory and information theory.

The desire for realism expressed by the co-ordination approach to industrial economics does not, however, imply that Richardson's and Malmgren's contributions were purely empirical. On the contrary, their publications remain theoretically grounded, especially regarding their insights on the importance of co-ordination and individual interactions in a decision-making process. A modern theorist of the firm, reading their texts for the first time, may be tempted to link their examination of decision-making to early game theory in that they consider the importance of strategic interactions. However, this interpretation would be misleading as Richardson and Malmgren made it clear that, even though they were aware of game theory, they did not explicitly employ it in their research.

Richardson's work could not be framed in terms of game theory mainly because, in his framework of investment co-ordination, before "placing their bets", entrepreneurs are first trying to improve the information they have about other agents, since the actions of others necessarily influence the outcomes of their own choices (see Earl 1998: 18). In other words, Richardson was much more interested in the way that agents search for and collect information than by their strategic choices per se. Similarly, in his DPhil thesis, Malmgren made clear his rejection of game theory. Indeed, he argued that the solution to strategic interactions could only depend on the initial nature of the information available to each competitor and, therefore, on the degree of communication between these competitors. In this respect, Malmgren rejected the "theory of games" approach, 'which ordinarily requires perfect information', and which realistically 'turns out to be a non-zero-sum game' with an indeterminate solution (Malmgren 1961: 253).

The novelty of Richardson's and Malmgren's approaches to Oxford industrial economics was mainly due to their success in providing an alternative framework to GEE theory, which remained predominant at Oxford after having been revived by the publication of Hicks's *Value and Capital*, twenty years before. The Richardson-Malmgren co-ordination view of the firm, as it stood, also offered an alternative to contemporary developments in game theory, which were mainly concerned with strategic choices and much less with the nature of information and knowledge at an individual level.

5   Transformation: From Industrial Economics to Industrial Organisation (1979–1991)

Two Oxford economists influenced the general orientation of the subject of industrial economics at Oxford during the last part of the twentieth century. Donald Hay's and Derek Morris's roles in Oxford economics are often associated with their landmark textbook, *Industrial Economics: Theory and Evidence*, which is considered as important historical evidence regarding the evolution of industrial economics. The increasing weight of new microeconomics at Oxford is seen as highly influential in the theoretical generalisations made by the discipline, which moved further away from the hitherto empirical approach to the firm.

5.1   A Comparison of the Successive Editions of *Industrial Economics: Theory and Evidence*—A Shift from Industrial Economics to Industrial Organisation

The first edition of Hay and Morris's textbook on industrial organisation in 1979 constituted a landmark in the development of the subjects of industrial economics and industrial organisation in the United Kingdom. It served as a basis for teaching even decades after its publication and, as such, exemplified the orientation taken by the discipline at Oxford and more generally in England. In the preface of the book, Hay and Morris made the objective of their volume explicit:

> In recent years Industrial Economics has emerged as a major area of economic analysis both in terms of theoretical and empirical research and in terms of the number of courses at undergraduate and graduate level. This book, stemming originally from lecture and seminar series at both levels, is designed for those pursuing such courses (Hay and Morris 1979: v).

This first edition was a standard textbook in which industrial economics was described as a field in which debates and controversies were ongoing. It tried to provide students with synthetic overviews of different approaches. In their introduction, Hay and Morris outlined the difficulty in finding a single definition of industrial economics and raised two particular matters related to it: the disagreements on both theoretical and empirical issues and the confusion over the scope, concepts and methodology of the subject.[12] They made it clear that industrial economics had emerged as a distinct approach from the traditional theory of the firm. In particular, they claimed that:

> First, there is an important sense in which the traditional theory of the firm represents a long detour in the history of the study of firms' economic behaviour. Second, the development of industrial economics can partly be seen as a consequence of several inadequacies and faults of analysis in the theory of the firm. Third, while the latter provides a main foundation for the study of industrial economics, several important influences from outside have given a totally different character to industrial economics (ibid.).

Nevertheless, while Hay and Morris's approach to firms and industries rejected the standard version of the theory of the firm, their contribution to the subject still constituted a break from the Oxford tradition of industrial economics, as shaped by Andrews and the *Journal of Industrial Economics* of the 1950s. This judgement is reinforced by comparing the first edition, which appeared in 1979, with the second edition, published in 1991, under a slightly different title, *Industrial Economics and Organisation: Theory and Evidence*. The 1979 edition referred only twice to Andrews' normal cost theory. The first reference appeared in a chapter dedicated to "pricing behaviour" in which *Manufacturing Business* was mentioned only for its empirical evidence on pricing. The book was depicted as a series of empirical investigations, which supported the validity of the cost-pricing principle and tried to incorporate this into a theory of competition. It is clear, however, that in the authors' minds, Andrews' book only constituted new evidence to support the 1939 Hall and Hitch article on pricing. As regards Marshall, Hay and Morris adopted a very cautious approach while arguing that Post-Marshallians had lost a part of Marshall's message in dedicating too much work to purely empirical studies. Finally, they indicated their support for an approach to industrial organisation that would, once again, combine empirical and theoretical aspects, as Marshall had done.

The second edition of Hay and Morris's textbook confirmed these comments. Andrews was again mentioned infrequently, with *Manufacturing Business* only being considered among various empirical contributions, its theoretical aspects being completely neglected. Marshall received more or less the same treatment as he did in the first edition. The main difference between

---

[12] 'First, as in several areas of economics, there is often disagreement on both the theoretical and empirical issues involved … Second, and more serious, there is both confusion and conflict over the three main elements of this (or any) discipline—its scope or purpose, its concepts and its methodology' (ibid.: 3).

the editions was in the ebbing of controversy within the field of industrial organisation between 1979 and 1991, mainly because of the increasing domination of game theory in the theory of imperfect competition and strategic interaction. Interestingly, the change in title between the two editions did not merit comment or explanation from the authors. However, the second edition indicated a shift away from empirical studies towards formalisation, which had initially emerged in the United States. Overall, the publication of Hay and Morris's textbook depicted the waning influence of Marshall and to the empirical approach to the firm.

5.2 Developments in Applied Microeconomics and Their Influence on Industrial Organisation (1950s–1980s)

The development of industrial organisation by Hay and Morris was conducted in harmony with advances in general microeconomics. At Oxford, microeconomics was taught at undergraduate level in Philosophy, Politics and Economics (PPE) and at graduate level in the BPhil in Engineering Science and Economics and in the BPhil in Economics. The first microeconomics lecture addressed to PPE students was introduced as late as 1968 and was taught by Peter Oppenheimer. Before then, studies of firms' behaviour were encapsulated in the "Theory of the Firm", "Structures of Industry", "Industrial Organisation", "Theory of Prices", "Welfare Economics" and the "Theory of Demand".[13] From 1968, microeconomic theory was taught by Oppenheimer and George Richardson to PPE students; by Christopher Allsopp, Nicholas Dimsdale and Laurie Baragwanath to BPhil students in Engineering Science and Economics; and by Richardson, James Mirrlees, Max Corden and occasionally by John Hicks to BPhil students in Economics.[14] The first lectures in the theory of games were introduced in the Hilary term of 1954. This increasing amount of teaching of microeconomics, applied microeconomics and game theory confirms the new orientation taken by industrial organisation, suggested by the successive editions of Hay and Morris's textbook, and

---

[13] Lectures about the theory of the firm and industries were mainly taught by Andrews and Brunner (1952–1968). John Jewkes was mostly in charge of the lectures entitled "Structures of Industry" (1952–1969) and "Industrial Organization" with Edward Hugh-Jones (1953–1955). "Industrial Organization" was also taught by Norman Leyland (essentially during the year 1954). The "Theory of Prices" was successively taught by Paul Streeten (1952), John Hicks (1952–1953/1958), George Richardson (1953–1954) and Mr Wright (1955–1960). "Welfare Economics" was taught by Hicks (1954–1958/1961–1963); he also taught the "Theory of Demand" (1961–1963).

[14] In particular, Hicks taught "Microeconomics IV: 'Value and Capital' Revisited" during the Hilary term of 1970.

reflected a general tendency in the mid-1970s and early 1980s towards developing more deductive and normative approaches in the discipline.

When Andrews and Brunner left Oxford in 1968, David Stout was left in charge of the BPhil seminar on industrial economics before he, in turn, left Oxford in the early 1970s. Derek Morris then became its organiser and pushed the seminar in a different direction. For instance, in 1974 the seven weeks of the first term were structured as follows:

1. The principles and significance of company accounts
2. The profit-maximising hypothesis
3. Price formation
4. Game theory and oligopoly
5. Mergers and concentration
6. The organisational structure of the modern corporation
7. Multinational corporations

A closer look at the reading lists for each topic shows that Week 2 includes references to Berle and Means (1932), Marris (1964) and Williamson (1964), as contributions to the extension of the profit-maximising hypothesis without referring at all to Hall and Hitch or to any work made by the OERG at Oxford. It has been argued elsewhere that Marris and Williamson developed approaches to the firm supported by concepts of optimum and equilibrium, far from Andrews' interpretation of industrial economics (see Arena 2004).

As a comparison with the first-term topics examined by the seminar, the programme for the Michaelmas term of 1957 was concerned with industrial economics as defined by Andrews:

1. Profits in accountancy and in economic theory
2. Empirical cost functions and their theoretical implications
3. Competition and the conditions of entry
4. Competition and the structure of markets
5. The growth of the firm and the concentration of industry
6. Oligopolies

This Oxford orientation could be contextualised within a broader picture. The introduction of the theory of contestable markets by Baumol et al. (1982) was indeed considered a generalisation of the theory of perfectly competitive markets in which the determination of industry structure was made endogenous. According to Baumol, 'in the limiting case of perfect contestability, oligopolistic structure and behaviour are freed entirely from their previous dependence on the conjectural variations of *incumbents* and, instead, these are generally determined uniquely...by the pressures of *potential* competition' (Baumol 1982: 2; italics in original).

The concept of "potential competition" that is central to the theory of contestable markets had already been referred to by Marshall and Walras before it was systematised by Baumol and his colleagues as the key to their theory of industrial structures. The new research programme in industrial organisation also highlighted the need to understand economics not only as the production of theoretical knowledge but also as policy. The formulation of a competition policy as needing to maintain the threat of potential competitors in order to ensure the efficiency of new entries/exits contrasted with the structure-conduct-performance paradigm which was clearly more concerned with the stabilisation of structures through insiders' behaviour. This new line of reasoning enlarged the validity conditions of theories of perfectly competitive markets questioned by some industrial economists, especially with the introduction of multi-product firms based on differentiation.

In addition, new models of strategic interaction were also seen as an alternative to standard microeconomics and as a contribution to industrial organisation, as shown in Hay and Morris (1991). Price strategies were now studied in the context of duopolies and oligopolies with the help of emerging modelling techniques. These issues in strategic interaction—developed with an intensive use of game theory—corresponded to a new and substantial methodological element in industrial organisation.

The theoretical and empirical orientation taken by the *Journal of Industrial Economics* after Brunner had left the editorial board was also indicative of the increasing interest in applied microeconomics and game theory. In particular, when Hay took over the editorship, he made a specific effort to align the *Journal's* aims and objectives with research in game theory. He was convinced that such a reorientation was the only strategy that would help to keep the *Journal* successful within the academic community.[15] As a result, the issues published from the beginning of the 1980s became increasingly formalised and less and less empirical in Andrews' initial sense of industrial economics.

6   Conclusion

Until the beginning of the twentieth century, economists were mostly focused on the theory of value and of income distribution whereas studies of firms and industries were conducted within the framework of price theory. However,

---

[15] Oral conversation between Brunner and Hay mentioned in an interview with Hay on 18 July 2006, Social Sciences Faculty, University of Oxford.

the evolution of management techniques led scholars to shift their attention towards the internal organisation of the firm and industrial dynamics. From a theoretical perspective, the separation of the theory of the firm from the theory of value resulted from the Cost Controversy in Cambridge accompanied by a new interpretation of the work of Alfred Marshall.

This chapter has shown that Oxford's contribution to industrial economics is not attributable to any specific school of thought that it produced, as could be argued was the case for Cambridge. The lack of emblematic figures at Oxford and/or the relative isolation of successive individuals elected to the Drummond Chair (in particular Edgeworth and Macgregor) did not produce a unified body of knowledge until, perhaps, the innovations made by the OERG which, despite its heterogeneous interests, still paved the way for a more homogenous methodology and theoretical orientation. Hence, although industrial economics today does not resemble the discipline as Philip Andrews knew it, his legacy was to institutionally establish it at Oxford.

Oxford took a unique approach to industrial economics due to the OERG and the empirical analysis of the firm, this a reaction to the theory of imperfect competition popularised at Cambridge in the 1930s. The methodology, in particular the use of questionnaires, was at the time specific to Oxford. The development of industrial economics at Oxford was also strongly influenced by George Richardson and Harald Malmgren who focused on information and knowledge between firms and contributed to a deeper understanding of the organisation of firms. In this way, they shed light on the emergence of more recent knowledge-based economies. The modern evolutionary theory of the firm is based on the concepts of capabilities and competences as proposed by Richardson and Malmgren which views the firm as a complex and organised set of competences and resources that is continuously faced with uncertainty. Later on, two key players in the development of industrial economics at Oxford were Donald Hay and Derek Morris, whose *Industrial Economics: Theory and Evidence* served as a foundation for the teaching of the subject and which represented an important manifestation of the direction taken by the discipline at the University.

Finally, industrial economics was shaped by the institutions of Oxford itself. The BPhil seminar on industrial economics and the *Journal of Industrial Economics*, both introduced by Andrews in the 1950s, exemplify the applied orientation of the discipline based on an empirical methodology. Saying this, Andrews' influence did later wane with the rise of industrial organisation based on game theory exported from the United States.

Appendix 1: Pre-War Members of OERG

Name and affiliation	Years in the group	Main research interests	Reasons for departure
Maurice Allen (Balliol College)	1936–1948	Monetary economics and economic theory	Adviser and Executive Director, Bank of England, 1950–1970
Marian Bowley (OIS)	1936–1937	Industrial economics, especially building material industries	To focus on research into the building material industries
Russell Bretherton (Wadham)	1936–1939	Macroeconomics, especially public finance	
Arthur Brown (Hertford)	1936–1939	Industrial economics, applied economics and statistics	
Frank Burchardt (All Souls)	1936–1958	Applied economics and statistics; Director of the OIS, 1940–1958	
Robert Hall (Trinity)	1936–1947	Macroeconomics, especially consumption and pricing theory	
Roy Harrod (Christ Church)	1936–1965	Macroeconomics, especially business cycle theory	Never left the Group
Hubert Henderson (All Souls)	1936–1950	Applied economics and statistics	
Charles Hitch (Queen's)	1936–1939	Macroeconomics, especially pricing theory	
Edward Hugh-Jones (Keble)	1936–1955	Industrial economics and history	
Jacob Marschak (OIS)	1936–1939	Applied economics and statistics; Director of the OIS, 1935–1939	
James Meade (Hertford)	1936–1937	International economics	Member (1938–1940) and Director (1940–1947) of the Economic Section of the League of Nations
Roger Opie (Magdalen/ New)	1936–1964	International economics	
Henry Phelps Brown (New)	1936–1947	Labour economics and history	Professor of Economics of Labour at LSE, 1947–1968

(*continued*)

(continued)

Name and affiliation	Years in the group	Main research interests	Reasons for departure
Edward Radice	1936–?	Monetary economics; macroeconomics, especially savings issues	
Richard Sayers (Pembroke)	1936–1947	British monetary economics	Cassel Professor of Economics at LSE, 1947–1968
George Shackle (OIS)	1936–1939	Macroeconomics, especially the theory of uncertainty and business cycle theory	

Appendix 2: Post-War Members of OERG

Name and affiliation	Years in the group	Main research interests
Philip Andrews (Nuffield)	1937–1960	Industrial economics, especially the theory of the firm
Laurie Baragwanath (St Catherine's)	1961–1965	Microeconomics
Elizabeth Brunner (Nuffield)	1948–1960	Industrial economics, especially the theory of the firm
Frank Burchardt (All Souls)	1936–1959	Applied economics and statistics; Director of the OIS, 1940–1958
David Champernowne (OIS)	1948–1959	Macroeconomics, especially unemployment issues
Norman Chester (Nuffield)	1948–1949	Politics and unemployment issues
Henry Clay (Nuffield)	1948–1950	Macroeconomics, especially unemployment issues
Theo Cooper (St Hugh's)	1964–1965	Public finance
John Fforde (Nuffield)	1950–1959	Monetary economics
Terence Gorman (Nuffield)	1963–1964	Mathematical macroeconomics
Margaret Hall (Somerville)	1948–1962	Industrial economics
Eric Hargreaves (Oriel)	1948–1959	Industrial economics
Roy Harrod (Christ Church)	1935–1965	Macroeconomics, especially business cycle theory
Arthur Hazlewood (Pembroke)	1963	Development economics
Hubert Henderson (All Souls)	1935–1959	Statistics and applied economics
John Hicks (All Souls)	1950–1965	Trade cycle theory

(continued)

(continued)

Name and affiliation	Years in the group	Main research interests
Edward Hugh-Jones (Keble)	1935–1955	Industrial economics and history
John Jewkes (Merton)	1950–1959	Industrial economics
Charles Kennedy (Queen's)	1950–1959	Macroeconomics
Kenneth Knowles (OIS)	1960–1962	Labour economics
Norman Leyland (Brasenose)	1950–1965	Industrial economics
Ian Little (Nuffield)	1960–1964	Macroeconomics
Donald MacDougall (Nuffield)	1950–1959	Macroeconomics, especially trade cycle theory
Grigor McClelland (Balliol)	1963–1965	Management studies
Denys Mundy (Nuffield)	1960–1964	Macroeconomics
M.E. Paul	1963–?	Macroeconomics
George Richardson (St John's)	?–1965	Microeconomics, especially the information theory of the firm
Derek Robinson (OIS)		Macroeconomics
Dick Sargent (Worcester)	1950–1959	Applied macroeconomics
Maurice Scott (Nuffield)	1960–1965	Macroeconomics, especially economic growth
David Stout (University)	1960–1965	Industrial economics, especially the theory of the firm
Paul Streeten (Balliol)	1961–?	International macroeconomics
Peter Vandome (OIS)	1964	Econometrics
Charles Ward-Perkins (Pembroke)	1950–1959	Economic history
Tom Wilson (University)	1950–1959	Industrial economics, especially pricing policy
David Worswick (Magdalen)	1964	Statistics
John Wright (Trinity)	1960–1965	Industrial economics

References

Andrews, P.W.S. (1949). *Manufacturing Business*. London: Macmillan.

Andrews, P.W.S. (1953). 'Obituary: D.H. Macgregor, 1877–1953'. *The Oxford Magazine*, 71(22), 4 June: 346–348.

Andrews, P.W.S. and E. Brunner (1950). 'Productivity and the Business Man'. *Oxford Economic Papers*, New Series, 2(2): 197–225.

Arena, L. (2004). *Post-Marshallian Approaches to Firms and Competition: The Cases of J. Robinson, E. Brunner and E. Penrose*. MSc thesis, University of Oxford.

Baumol, W.J. (1982). 'Contestable Markets: An Uprising in the Theory of Industry Structure'. *American Economic Review*, 72(1): 1–15.

Baumol, W.J., J.C. Panzar and R.D. Willig (1982). *Contestable Markets and the Theory of Industrial Structure*. New York: Harcourt Brace Jovanovich.

Berle, A.A. and G.C. Means (1932). *The Modern Corporation and Private Property*. New York: Macmillan.

Besomi, D. (ed.) (2003). *The Collected Interwar Papers and Correspondence of Roy Harrod*. Three volumes. Cheltenham: Edward Elgar.

Boulding, K.E. (1942). 'The Theory of the Firm in the Last Ten Years'. *American Economic Review*, 32(4): 791–802.

Chamberlin, E. (1933). *The Theory of Monopolistic Competition*. Cambridge, MA: Harvard University Press.

Clapham, J.H. (1922). 'Of Empty Economic Boxes'. *Economic Journal*, 32(127): 305–314.

Clark, J.M. (1922). *Studies in the Economics of Overhead Costs*. Chicago: University of Chicago Press.

Current Notes (1937). *Journal of the Royal Statistical Society*, 100(1): 144–148.

Earl, P.E. (1998). 'George Richardson's Career and the Literature of Economics'. Chapter 2 in N.J. Foss and B.J. Loasby (eds) *Economic Organization, Capabilities and Co-ordination: Essays in Honour of G.B. Richardson*. London: Routledge: 14–43.

Friday, F.A. (1952). 'The Problem of Business Forecasting'. *Journal of Industrial Economics*, 1(1): 55–71.

Hall, R.L. and C.J. Hitch (1939). 'Price Theory and Business Behaviour'. *Oxford Economic Papers*, 2(May): 12–45.

Hay, D.A. and D.J. Morris (1979). *Industrial Economics: Theory and Evidence*. Oxford: Oxford University Press.

Hay, D.A. and D.J. Morris (1991). *Industrial Economics and Organization: Theory and Evidence*. Oxford: Oxford University Press.

Hicks, J.R. (1939). *Value and Capital*. Oxford: Clarendon Press.

Knight, F.H. (1921). *Risk, Uncertainty, and Profit*. New York: Houghton Mifflin Company.

Lee, F.S. (1989). 'D.H. Macgregor and the Firm: A Neglected Chapter in the History of the Post Keynesian Theory of the Firm'. *British Review of Economic Issues*, 11(24): 21–47.

Lee, F.S. (2008). 'D.H. Macgregor and the Marshallian Tradition at Oxford, 1920–1945'. Paper presented at an international workshop on "Marshall and Marshallians on Industrial Economics", March, Hitotsubashi University, Tokyo.

Leyland, N.H. (1964). 'Growth and Competition'. *Oxford Economic Papers*, New Series, 16(1): 3–8.

Macgregor, D.H. (1906). *Industrial Combination*. London: George Bell & Sons.

Macgregor, D.H. (1913). *Report of Travels of D.H. Macgregor as A.K. Travelling Fellow: September 1911–September 1912*. London: University of London Press.

Macgregor, D.H. (1923). 'Public Authorities and Unemployment'. *Economica*, 7(January): 10–18.

Macgregor, D.H. (1924). 'Consumer's Surplus: A Reply'. *Economica*, 11(June): 131–134.

Macgregor, D.H. (1925). 'The Agricultural Argument'. *Economic Journal*, 25(3): 389–397.

Macgregor, D.H. (1926). 'Family Allowance'. *Economic Journal*, 36(1): 1–10.

Macgregor, D.H. (1927a). 'Recent Papers on Cartels'. *Economic Journal*, 37(2): 247–254.

Macgregor, D.H. (1927b). 'Rationalisation of Industry'. *Economic Journal*, 37(4): 521–550.

Macgregor, D.H. (1929). 'Joint Stock Companies and the Risk Factor'. *Economic Journal*, 39(4): 491–505.

Macgregor, D.H. (1930). 'The Coal Bill and the Cartel'. *Economic Journal*, 40(1): 35–44.

Macgregor, D.H. (1934). *Enterprise, Purpose & Profit*. Oxford: Clarendon Press.

Malmgren, H.B. (1961). *Information, Expectations and the Nature of the Firm*. DPhil thesis, University of Oxford.

Marris, R. (1964). *The Economic Theory of 'Managerial' Capitalism*. London: Macmillan.

Marshall, A. and M.P. Marshall (1879). *The Economics of Industry*. London: Macmillan.

Mason, E.S. (1952). 'An American View of Raw Materials Problems: The Report of the President's Materials Policy Commission'. *Journal of Industrial Economics*, 1(1): 1–20.

Pigou, A.C. and D.H. Robertson (1924). 'Those Empty Boxes'. *Economic Journal*, 34(133): 16–31.

Richardson, G.B. (1959). 'Equilibrium, Expectations and Information'. *Economic Journal*, 69(274): 223–237.

Richardson, G.B. (1960). *Information and Investment: A Study in the Working of the Competitive Economy*. London: Oxford University Press.

Richardson, G.B. (1964). 'The Limit to a Firm's Rate of Growth'. *Oxford Economic Papers*, New Series, 16(1): 9–23.

Richardson, G.B. and N.H. Leyland (1964). 'The Growth of Firms'. *Oxford Economic Papers*, New Series, 16(1): 1–2.

Robinson, J.V. (1933). *The Economics of Imperfect Competition*. London: Macmillan.

Samuels, W.J. (ed.) (2008). 'Notes from D.H. Macgregor's Seminar on Trade Cycle Theory and Lectures on Economic Analysis, Oxford University, 1932–1933'. In W.J. Samuels (ed.) *Documents from F. Taylor Ostrander at Oxford, John R. Commons' Reasonable Value and Clarence E. Ayres' Last Course. Research in the History of Economic Thought and Methodology, Volume 26-B*. Bingley, UK: JAI Press: 149–196.

Shone, R. (1952). 'Steel Price Policy'. *Journal of Industrial Economics*, 1(1): 43–54.

Stones, F. (1952). 'Price Policy in a Nationally Administered Industry'. *Journal of Industrial Economics*, 1(1): 32–42.

Todd, G.F. (1935). 'Professor Macgregor on Enterprise and the Trade Cycle'. *Journal of the Royal Statistical Society*, 98(3): 544–552.

Williamson, O.E. (1964). *The Economics of Discretionary Behaviour: Managerial Objectives in a Theory of the Firm*. Englewood Cliffs, NJ: Prentice Hall.

Wilson, T. and P.W.S. Andrews (1951). *Oxford Studies in the Price Mechanism*. Oxford: Clarendon Press.

Young, W. and F.S. Lee (1993). *Oxford Economics and Oxford Economists*. London: Macmillan.

4

Economic History at Oxford, 1860–2020

Avner Offer

1   Introduction[1]

Economics and economic history in Britain came into being together, inter-twined in Adam Smith's *The Wealth of Nations* (1776). Towards the end of the nineteenth century they began to diverge. Jevons, Marshall and Edgeworth reached for a "Great Theory", worked up from first principles, 'complete and self-sufficient, able, on its own terms, to answer all questions which those terms allowed' (Shackle 1967: 4). In contrast, economic history is a part of "the other canon" of inductive, evidence-based economic investigation (Reinert and Daastøl 2004). Its central subject is "the wealth of nations"—modern economic growth, how it came about, how it kept going, and how it affected people at every level. For earlier times and other places, the discipline imposes the questions and concepts of political economy. Unlike economics, however, economic history is discovered, not created. If it sometimes takes an ideological inflection, evidence usually wins out.

---

[1] This chapter is derived from biographical sources, the archive of All Souls College, Oxford, University Lecture Lists and examination decrees, postholder publications, Google Scholar citations (tabulated with Harzing's *Publish or Perish*), comments by colleagues, critical readings by friends and my own experience. Thanks to Cormac O'Grada for a line from Thomas Gray's "Elegy Written in a Country Churchyard", to Jane Humphries for an apt quotation from Toynbee and to Urvi Khaitan for skilful research.

A. Offer (✉)
All Souls College, Oxford, UK
e-mail: avner.offer@all-souls.ox.ac.uk

© The Author(s), under exclusive license to Springer Nature Switzerland AG 2021
R. A. Cord (ed.), *The Palgrave Companion to Oxford Economics*,
https://doi.org/10.1007/978-3-030-58471-9_4

It comes as a surprise to find that its most persistent theme is how the economy affects the household. This is not motivated by middle-class guilt (as per Coleman 1987: 65), but by an intuition that what the economy produces holds out the incentives for the next round of production: 'Consumption is the sole end and purpose of all production' (Smith 1776, 2: 159). Productivity and welfare interact with each other, and this interaction gives the discipline its hidden coherence.

It is easy to construct a kings and queens history of the discipline around professors and readers, but their writ did not run far—when they led (which was not always) it was by example and suasion. Instead, the story here is of problems and preoccupations, each with a lineage of investigators. The first theme is how economic output affected the experience of ordinary life. A second one is craft, commerce and industry, production, exchange and finance, in their specific detail and local cause and effect. Agricultural organisation is a subset of the previous two in a low-density environment which antedates modern economic growth. How to measure and validate is a methodological challenge and has a lineage of its own. Coming out of Victorian laissez-faire, the discipline implicitly assumes the primacy of getting and spending, self-interest and market exchange. This epistemological legacy, the history of economic thought, forms another lineage. Government and the State appear to the discipline mostly as agents of taxation and war; social policy has been outsourced (especially in Oxford) to other kinds of historians. The final lineage is what drives economic growth and what holds it back.

The University of Oxford is a federation of wealthy institutions which hire accomplished scholars and send young ones into the world. Postholders do not appoint their successors, hence there is no dynastic "Oxford School". There is, however, a mode of production. In the enlightenment model of progress, valid knowledge is revealed by inspired individuals. Academic courses and examinations order it into a syllabus. Continuity comes from teaching, which is particularly inflexible in Oxford. Examination rubrics persist for decades, courses are examined externally (i.e. not by their teacher), and content changes only slowly. Until recent years, most designated economic history posts were University ones with reduced teaching loads. College fellows in history or economics had to cover a larger syllabus, but could focus their research. Together, these two groups provided a rich but narrow array of undergraduate courses, focused mostly on the British experience.

From the 1930s onwards, economic history had at least two or three earmarked University posts. Tenures were short: postholders arrived with reputations already made (in Oxford or elsewhere) and stayed for a decade or two, sometimes to retirement and beyond. Scholars typically published one or two landmark works over their tenure, making one or more for the discipline in every decade except the 1890s. These beacons signalled the validity of the discipline, were widely discussed, and are cited hundreds and even thousands of times. More humble publications make up for lower resonance with larger numbers. Knowledge is a web, not a race: everything connects and even an uncited publication, born to 'waste its sweetness on the desert air', may be cherished by its author and vital to their development. Only research carried out or published in Oxford is covered here. This undervalues dowries brought over from previous posts and also the vast output of postgraduate research, most of which was published (if it was) after authors had moved elsewhere.

2   Beginnings

Despite our intentions, in the long early decades which stretch from 1860 to 1930 it is more convenient to follow individual scholars: the themes took a while to get going. The discipline of economic history at Oxford began at one of its pinnacles. James Edwin Thorold Rogers (Drummond Professor of Political Economy, 1862–1867, 1888–1890, Tooke Professor at King's College, London, Lecturer in History at Worcester College, Oxford—all part time) was an eminent Victorian who did much to create the discipline in its modern form. Educated in the classics, ordained then de-ordained, he published editions of Aristotle's *Ethics* (1865) and of *The Wealth of Nations*, two collections of economic history lectures, and many contributions in classics, religion, political economy and party polemic, a total of 84 items in Oxford libraries, some reprinted several times. Rogers was a Liberal Radical close to Richard Cobden, an editor of John Bright, a friend of John Stuart Mill and an MP from 1880 to 1885. He was inspired by the early Victorian statistical movement to extend Thomas Tooke and William Newmarch's *A History of Prices* backwards from 1793 to the Middle Ages. His great achievement is *A History of Agriculture and Prices in England* (1866–1902, seven volumes), with a midway commentary on *Six Centuries of Work and Wages* (1884, two volumes). Rogers transcribed an unmatched amount of archival evidence and established a grand narrative. Some interpretations have been superseded but the work endures, and the volumes remain in print. Robert Allen (a more recent Oxford authority) wrote to me that 'Other scholars have added to it … No one has replaced it'. In Rogers' own words, 'genuine facts are far more valuable than the inferences of any individual who uses them' (Rogers 1866–1902, 4: vi).

Arnold Toynbee was a precocious young Lecturer at Balliol in the late 1870s and a favourite of the Master, Benjamin Jowett. Toynbee's *Lectures on the Industrial Revolution in England* (1884) was a short and influential text assembled posthumously from student notes. In a burst of eloquence, it defines the main issues of economic history in Britain since the Industrial Revolution: it asks why it started there in the first place, and what effects it had on welfare; and it set the benefits of prosperity against rural displacement and factory disciplines. Together with much larger studies by Rogers, Adolf Held in Germany and William Cunningham in Cambridge, it laid some of the foundations for the nascent discipline.

Toynbee inspired a group of students at Oxford to take up economic and social research. Like their teacher, they wanted to confront classical political economy with historical evidence. One of their models was the *Verein für Sozialpolitik*, a German academic association whose historical and institution-alist approach provoked a "battle of the methods" with more analytical Austrian economists. Like their mentors in Germany, these Oxford aspirants combined archival narratives with current developments and government policy in a neomercantilist vein. It was difficult to obtain an Oxford position in those years and some of them embarked on University extension lectures in the industrial North before going on to posts in other universities (Goldman 1995; Kadish 1982, Kadish and Tribe 1993; Koot 1987; Tribe 2002).

The most accomplished of this group was William James Ashley who pub-lished an important *Introduction to English Economic History and Theory* (1888). His work extended from the Middle Ages to current politics and policy, recognised by a succession of chairs in Toronto, Harvard and Birmingham. Another member, Edwin Cannan, led economics at the London School of Economics (LSE), edited a landmark edition of *The Wealth of Nations* and wrote a profound critique of classical economics. E.C.K. Gonner in Liverpool edited Ricardo and wrote a history of *Common Land and Inclosure* (1912) while in 1910 the younger George Unwin obtained in Manchester the first chair in economic history not only in Britain but also the first in the British Empire (Corley 2002: 16). In the tariff reform controversies of the Edwardian period, most of this cohort weighed in on the side of protection, giving the argument some weight.

L.L. Price, the one who returned to Oxford, established the first qualifica-tion in economics and political science, a one-year diploma (1904), and became the first University Lecturer in Economic History (1907; Reader 1909–1921). Oxford had already offered a Political Economy module in both Modern History and *Literae Humaniores* (Classics) since the 1870s, with lec-tures in political economy, the history of economic thought and economic history (the latter from 1898). This anticipated the separate Philosophy, Politics and Economics (PPE) undergraduate degree which Price helped to start in 1921. The discipline deepened its affinity with adult working-class learners in the Edwardian period. Ruskin College opened in Oxford in 1899 to take in such students, and the Workers' Educational Association (WEA) for extra-mural teaching was also founded there in 1903, supported in part by the colleges. The University economics diploma was taken by some Ruskin students and extension lecture graduates. In 1908, All Souls College contributed £1,200 (enough to support four or five extension tutors) and appointed R.H. Tawney, a Classics graduate of Balliol, to lecture two terms a year to working men in the North West, and one term in Oxford. Workers 'wanted to know something of the forces which had made them what they were' (Goldman 1995: 130) and economic history was their favourite subject. Thus began an illustrious career, and also an enduring association of All Souls with the discipline. Sir William Anson, Warden of the College and Liberal Unionist MP, was once seen at a WEA party near to midnight keeping time to "Auld Lang Syne" 'with hands clasping those of burly trade unionists on either side of him' (ibid.: 145).

Also at All Souls was its chaplain, A.H. Johnson, 'a country gentleman in holy orders…a hunting, shooting and fishing don' (ibid.: 33), a tutor at many colleges and author of many books. In 1909, he gave the prestigious James Ford Lectures in British history on *The Disappearance of the Small Landowner* (1909) from the Middle Ages to his own time, deftly defining a central issue in agrarian history. It is remarkably judicious, is written from primary sources and remains in print today. He also wrote a detailed history of the Worshipful Company of Drapers, originally a medieval London trade guild but by then a club for wealthy businessmen.

Tawney followed some of his 1880s forerunners into LSE, but, unlike them, he was on the left. His landmark book *Religion and the Rise of Capitalism* (1926) inspired a classic debate which largely took place in Oxford. In 1941, Tawney identified some sources of the English Civil War in the "rise of the gentry" as a capitalist class in the countryside. In 1948, he received able support from Lawrence Stone, a Lecturer at University College. Tawney was challenged by Stone's former tutor, Hugh Trevor-Roper, soon to be elected Regius Professor of Modern History, with statistical evidence provided by J.P. Cooper of Trinity. Contemporaries thought that Trevor-Roper had won, but that is not the view of posterity. Stone became a History Fellow at Wadham (1950–1963), and capped the debate with a magnum opus, *The Crisis of the Aristocracy, 1558–1641* (1965). It is the most highly cited Oxford work named here and was published shortly after Stone left for a distinguished career at Princeton.

Retracing our steps, Ephraim Lipson (Reader in Economic History after Price, 1922–1931) graduated from Cambridge and came to Oxford initially as a private tutor. His *The Economic History of England* (1915–1931, three volumes) extended from the Middle Ages to the onset of the Industrial Revolution in thematic style, by industry and sector. This comprehensive and detailed text, highly cited and last reprinted in 1964, became a standard work and is still worth dipping into. It was an early statement of the view that the Industrial Revolution of the eighteenth century was not a sharp break in economic development. The style is that of German historical economics and the narrative builds on the foundations laid by Rogers and Cunningham. Lipson, together with Tawney, founded and edited the *Economic History Review*. Julia de Lacy Mann (Tutor in Economics at St Hilda's, Oxford, from 1923 and then Principal 1928–1955) served as assistant editor. English wealth from medieval times to the nineteenth century was founded on textiles. Lipson wrote a history of the woollen and worsted industries which de Lacy Mann complemented with *The Cotton Trade and Industrial Lancashire, 1600–1780* (1931, with A.P. Wadsworth). Her doctoral student, G.D. Ramsay (Fellow in History, St Edmund Hall, Oxford, 1937–1974), rounded off the subject with several studies of the early modern woollen export trade.

Labour wage rigidity is central to interpretations of inter-war unemployment. Christina Violet Butler, an early social investigator and Director of Barnett House, Oxford (now the Department of Social Policy and Intervention), taught classes in labour and urban history in the 1920s and 1930s. G.D.H. Cole brought industrial relations into the centre of Oxford economics teaching. He graduated from Balliol like Tawney, also in Classics. At the age of 24, he published *The World of Labour* (1913) which held out a vision of guild socialism, that is, worker control of industry for the public good by means of occupational guilds. During the war and afterwards, he built up a large reputation on the political left. In 1925, Cole obtained a Readership in Economics (like Lipson's, at New College). A prolific and much-translated author, he also wrote (with his wife, Margaret Cole) twenty-nine detective novels. It is customary to think of Cole as a political theorist, and indeed in 1944 he was appointed to the Chair of Political Theory at All Souls. Of his fifteen most cited works, ten are historical, the top one being a social history of *The Common People, 1746–1938* (1938, with Raymond Postgate). His economics was institutional and inductive, in defiance of current economic theory. From time to time, he also lectured on economic history, and on the adult education circuit. He published a great deal on the history of socialist thought, the labour movement, and consumer co-operatives and his elegant biographies of William Cobbett and Robert Owen are of lasting value. Cole's publication record is broad rather than deep but still adds up to a great deal. His doctoral student Hugh Clegg (student, then Fellow of Nuffield College, 1947–1967) co-founded the Oxford School of Industrial Relations and published the first of three volumes of *A History of British Trade Unions Since 1889* in 1964 (with Alan Fox and A.F. Thompson).

At the end of the 1920s, All Souls put up housing on some of its North London farmland and conferred part of the windfall on a new Chichele Chair of Economic History (named after the College founder). Lipson, who had a strong claim, was passed over and left Oxford in a huff. The person appointed was George Clark (in post from 1931 to 1943). Like Tawney and his own friend and contemporary Cole, Clark was a Balliol Classics graduate and had lectured to the WEA. He was a safe pair of hands: a lucid writer of broad surveys, successively editor of the *English Historical Review*, the *Oxford History of England*, the *New Cambridge Modern History* and the *Home University Library*. He moved on to become Regius Professor of History at Cambridge, Provost of Oriel College and President of the British Academy. Clark was a distinguished historian, no more and no less. He wrote a great deal over a long career, but his research contribution to economic history at Oxford was modest: a great facilitator but less of a pacemaker. Between the wars, Oxford had no economic historians of the stature of John Clapham and Michael Postan at Cambridge. In consequence, it had to import much of its talent from Cambridge after 1945.

3   Welfare

Thorold Rogers was outraged by the pre-industrial degradation of labourers, which he attributed not to market conditions but to policies 'which were designed or adopted with the express purpose of compelling the labourer to work at the lowest rates of wages possible' (Rogers 1884: 7). How much is labour oppression caused by asymmetries of power and how much by the workings of the market? The theme is an abiding one at Oxford. Arnold Toynbee wrote that: '[I]n the early days of competition the capitalists used all their power to oppress the labourers, and drove down wages to starvation point. This kind of competition has to be checked' (Toynbee 1884: 66). The issue migrated out of Oxford and eventually came back half a century later in the next great controversy, the standard of living debate on the welfare of manual workers during the Industrial Revolution.

The main polemical thrust of Rogers' work was that 'It is vain to rejoice over the aggregate of our prosperity, and to forget that the great part of the nation has no share in its benefits' (Rogers 1866–1902, 1: viii). In two articles published in 1949 and 1957, Eric Hobsbawm reopened the long-standing distinction (coined as such by T.S. Ashton) between "optimists", who celebrated the benefits of economic development and "pessimists", who lamented its cost. In response to Hobsbawm, the case for optimism was taken up by Max Hartwell (Reader in Recent Social and Economic History, 1956–1977). He revisited the initial controversy that took place in the early nineteenth century, with its discordant voices of suffering and celebration. How was it possible to reconcile such different narratives from similar evidence? Hartwell calculated that the commodity standard of living was rising. The protagonists, who remained civil throughout, faced each other from opposite corners. Hobsbawm was an unrepentant member of the Communist Party, Hartwell a follower of Friedrich Hayek, a member of his neoliberal Mont Pèlerin Society and later its President. His official history of the Society is his most cited work.

The standard of living debate became a proxy for the stand-off between two visions of society, social democracy and market liberalism, against the backdrop of the Cold War. Neither Hobsbawm nor Hartwell were expert quantifiers, but the discipline came to think that the optimists had the numbers on their side. In response, the pessimists reached for a broader conception of well-being. E.P. Thompson, the most charismatic of them, set it out in his great article "Time, Work-Discipline and Industrial Capitalism" (1967). Budgets and commodities were only instrumental to ends, namely mental stimulation and existential meaning. Smith and Marx had already described how factory discipline diminished and debased the mental lives of its workers. Thompson was in tune with some critical voices in economics, notably John Kenneth Galbraith's *The Affluent Society* (1958), William Nordhaus and James Tobin's "Is Growth Obsolete?" (1972) and Richard Easterlin's "Does Economic Growth Improve the Human Lot?" (1974). He anticipated subsequent developments by decades. In "The Moral Economy of the English Crowd in the Eighteenth Century" (1971), Thompson interpreted a transition from paternalism to impersonal markets in terms of a dishonoured contract between the elites and the people (there is a similar argument in Rogers). The issues have never gone away. Thompson was hugely influential: The 1967 and 1971 articles were cited twenty and nineteen more times respectively than Hartwell's best, and endure as staples of the syllabus. These are academic votes—the popular vote for Thompson would have been larger still. Hartwell is remembered fondly in Oxford as an impartial teacher and supervisor, for his Australian wit and convivial presence.

Thompson's disciple and New Left comrade Raphael Samuel, charismatic in his own way and also a graduate of Balliol, taught at Ruskin from 1962. Like Thompson, he left the Communist Party in 1956, and applied a similar holistic approach, economic, social and cultural, to the experience of working-class lives in the Victorian period. He co-founded the left-leaning *History Workshop Journal* which promoted "history from below".

In the late 1960s and early 1970s, the Cold War erupted violently in South East Asia. Young people engaged with the counterculture, the New Left, and the student rebellions, which affected Oxford as well. At the same time, Western societies began their slow swerve towards market liberalism. Economic history seemed to be relevant: its popularity peaked in the early 1970s (see Coleman 1987: 96–98).

In the 1960s, the best left-wing scholars (Thompson, Hobsbawm, Sidney Pollard) were kept out of the top professorships. Oxford did its bit when Hobsbawm applied in 1967. Trevor-Roper, the Regius Professor of Modern History, dominated the selection committee. After its meeting, the Oxford historian Keith Thomas heard Trevor-Roper boast 'that he had that day succeeded in keeping Eric out of the Chichele Chair of Economic History' (Thomas quoted in Evans 2019: 429). Peter Mathias, the successful candidate (Chichele Professor, 1969–1987) was suitably accomplished: the author of excellent histories of brewing and of a grocery chain (the latter commissioned), he arrived in Oxford with a judiciously meliorist and very successful textbook on *The First Industrial Nation* (1969a). He was last in the line of Oxford institutional economic historians, a descendant of the free-trade lineage of John Clapham and Charles Wilson in Cambridge, a dignified presence, a reliable doctoral supervisor, co-editor of two volumes of *The Cambridge Economic History of Europe* (1978, 1989), President of the International Economic History Association, and Master of Downing College, Cambridge, after early retirement in 1987.

At a time of intellectual ferment and existential dread, some of the discipline's senior professors in Cambridge, London and beyond found nothing more important to do than to write corporate histories, implicit celebrations of things as they are, all the more so for being commissioned and paid for. They followed the lead of Wilson in Cambridge, author of a three-volume *History of Unilever* (1954, 1968), into what one of them described as 'a form of outdoor relief for indigent economic historians' (Coleman 1987: 139). Ironically perhaps, one of the main teaching and research themes in those years was Britain's industrial decline. During eighteen years in the Chichele Chair, Mathias published a handful of articles, only one of which (jointly with Patrick O'Brien) had much of an impact. Hobsbawm outpaced him in lifetime citations by sixty to one. D.C. Coleman, the Chair at Cambridge and a business historian himself, wrote a valedictory book on the decline of the discipline (ibid.). He conceded that commissioned volumes were not much read and did not quicken anybody's pulse; he acknowledged that they lacked the penetration or panache of Alfred Chandler's concurrent work on North American corporations. Coleman remained hopeful for business history, but for the discipline it was a dead end. Barry Supple, another accomplished business historian, followed Hartwell as Reader (1978–1981) but published little in this short time. The business turn might have been a refuge from the left but another challenge was looming.

In the 1960s, economic historians in the United States reclaimed the discipline for economics by applying statistical inference and economic theory to the time-series data of the past, which they worked to expand and enrich. Economic theory provided models of cause and effect in terms of maximising behaviour, and econometric analysis estimated and ranked the causal effect of different variables. Robert Fogel deployed this method (known colloquially as "cliometrics") to argue that modern economic growth was not driven by a single technological breakthrough, and more specifically not by the railways, by calculating a counterfactual in which railways did not exist (1964). In another landmark book (with Stanley Engerman), he argued controversially that American slavery was formidable because it was economically efficient (1974). Cliometrics was a powerful innovation with a polemical undertone, assuming (like the rest of economics) the normative primacy of markets. The method provided rich data, crisp explanations, and a new sense of scientistic rigour. It was even recognised by a Nobel Prize in Economics (for Fogel and Douglass North) in 1993.

Cliometrics challenged teachers more than students. It replaced narrative with the toolkits of economics. Thatcher's market liberalism constructed its legitimacy with the same tools. Many British economic historians were reluctant to go along, partly from attachment to legacy methods, and partly because it was hard to retool. From the 1980s onwards, the discipline, with one foot in each of these two discordant approaches, has existed in a mild state of dissonance. As history departments turned away from politics and society towards culture and language, economic history in the United States and Britain moved out of them. In the former, the discipline found a home in economics but in Britain it was out on a limb. Its student appeal diminished and it lost much of its academic purchase, although not in Oxford, Cambridge or LSE.

Oxford opened up early to cliometrics. Three significant doctorates were written at Nuffield College in the 1960s. Several American cliometricians came over and a graduate seminar with two of them ran weekly in 1968. In Chicago, Donald McCloskey played on British anxieties by asking "Did Victorian Britain Fail?" (1970) and answered counter-intuitively that it did not because failure was impossible in a competitive neoclassical economy. However, that might not have passed muster for the subsequent Edwardian period. Nicholas Crafts (Economics Fellow at University College, 1977–1986) led British cliometrics by example, and moved on to eminence at Warwick and LSE. In Oxford, he supervised some remarkable doctorates and ran a stimulating cliometrics seminar in the 1980s. His initial book and still most highly cited publication, *British Economic Growth During the Industrial Revolution* (1985), did not overtly deploy the cliometric trademark technique of regression analysis. It refined some of the older price and wage data, investigated sectoral composition, and added microeconomics and growth theory, but its main finding came from a native British tradition of national accounting, revising prior work by Phyllis Deane, W.A. Cole and Charles Feinstein to argue persuasively that growth had been lower than the term "revolution" might imply. It followed therefore that the rise of income per head was also slow, and slow to take off.

National accounting received three Nobel Prizes in Economics (Simon Kuznets, Wassily Leontief and Richard Stone), but by the 1980s had been forsaken by economists who handed it over to central statistical offices. As an academic discipline it lives on in economic history. Charles Feinstein (Reader, then Chichele Professor 1987–1999) compiled a definitive *National Income, Expenditure and Output of the United Kingdom, 1855–1965* (1972) while still in Cambridge. Stephen Broadberry (Professor of Economic History at Nuffield, 2015) has continued in this line, extending the investigation all the way back to 1270 in *British Economic Growth, 1270–1870* (2015, with several co-authors).

From the 1970s onwards, there was always at least one cliometrician at Oxford in the Department of Economics, and sometimes more than one. Nicholas Dimsdale (Economics Fellow at The Queen's College, 1961–2004) wrote important studies of British monetary policy and of unemployment and real wages during the inter-war years, several studies of finance and an initial volume of *UK Business and Financial Cycles Since 1660* (2019, with Ryland Thomas). In the 1990s, the University Lecturer in Economic History at St Antony's College was James Foreman-Peck, whose *Public and Private Ownership of British Industry, 1820–1990* (1994, with Robert Millward) showed that urban utilities owned privately were not more efficient than municipal ones. He was followed in post by Charles Knickerbocker ("Knick") Harley (Lecturer, 2005–2011), a prolific cliometrician from Canada who detected concurrently with Crafts that growth was slow in the Industrial Revolution. He was a strong critical presence in seminars, an excellent teacher, supervisor and colleague.

By the time Harley retired, cliometrics was taking a new direction, introduced in Oxford by his successor, James Fenske (Associate Professor, St Antony's 2011–2016). His focus was on African economic history, investigating inter alia the pre-colonial determinants of African development and retardation. An empirical turn was taking place in economics, which set economic theory aside. The method was to construct a laboratory or field experiment in two comparable settings and to determine local causation by applying an intervention to one but not to the other. Fenske applied this counterfactual method sequentially to determine whether antecedent conditions could explain later outcomes. His successor, Eric Chaney (St Antony's, since 2018) specialises in the Islamic world before the modern period. Two other cliometricians in the most recent decade were Rui Esteves (Fellow in Economics at Brasenose, with a specialisation in international finance in the nineteenth century) and Brian A'Hearn at Pembroke, who writes mostly on Italy. A'Hearn is also known for applying (with co-authors, and not for the first time) a numeracy test to populations all the way back to the Middle Ages by identifying whether people could specify their year of birth (suggesting competence) or whether they rounded it up or down ("heaping").

The impulses that drove the standard of living debate appeared to be spent by the 1990s. A premature sense of closure was provided by Feinstein. In response to a particular outburst of standard of living optimism, his Tawney Lecture of 1997 was a compelling re-estimation of the commodity standard of living. Maximising economic growth is taken in economics to be the measure of policy success. Did growth improve the lives of those who enabled it? Reaching for the essence, Feinstein wrote (in words that echoed those of Rogers) that the majority of workers 'had to endure almost a century of hard toil with little or no advance from a low base before they really began to share in any of the benefits of the economic transformation they had helped to create' (Feinstein 1998: 652).

The issue lives on, I have argued, because distribution affects not only equity, but also efficiency. Jane Humphries (Reader and Professor of Economic History, 1998–2013), a Cambridge graduate in economics, initially made her mark as an early feminist economist in North America before returning to Cambridge. Ever since Rogers, welfare was approached through a masculine lens. The long time series used to study it were almost entirely of male wages.

Humphries transformed a male breadwinner story into a family one: '[T]he standard of living', she wrote, 'is determined by the household's access to all resources—including the contributions of other family members and welfare subsidies' (Horrell and Humphries 1992: 850). At Oxford, she studied the experience of women, children and households during the Industrial Revolution and the nineteenth century, using both numbers and archives to endorse a pessimistic view. In recent years, she has revisited family standards of living all the way from the Middle Ages to the 1850s. In addition to household work, consumption and incomes, Humphries opened up the mental experience of adolescence by means of working people's autobiographies in *Childhood and Child Labour in the British Industrial Revolution* (2010). Rogers had already written that conventional accounts exaggerated welfare by assuming full-time working (see Rogers 1884, 2: 481). Humphries incorporated the wage and household work of women and children to suggest that family standards of living had been exaggerated. This has been amplified recently from other sources by Judy Stephenson, a Junior Research Fellow at Wadham. Further doubt on the optimist case had been cast by the decline of adult heights (an objective indicator of well-being) during the 1830s and 1840s. Deborah Oxley (Lecturer and then Professor of Social History, since 2008) has been collecting body measurements of nineteenth-century convicts. She highlights the large gap between men and women—some of whom actually gained weight in prison—as an indication of how hard their lot had been outside. Humphries and Oxley have both studied welfare (diets, children, poor relief) as well as human capital formation (health, apprenticeship, schooling).

Since the 1990s, an expanding body of work has shown that well-being can diverge from income and expenditure in both material and cognitive terms. Avner Offer (Reader, 1992–2000; Chichele Professor, 2000–2011) scrutinised the welfare impact of capitalism in more recent times. His most-cited work, *The Challenge of Affluence* (2006) shows how myopic bias in consumers (under the influence of marketing) has diminished welfare in both American and British consumer societies since the 1950s, and the extent to which quality of life is partly a matter of active choice. Cognitive biases undermine the economics of self-interest, giving rise to choices that consumers might come to regret, for example, the overeating that gives rise to obesity. Following Smith, Rogers and Thompson, he reaffirmed the role of non-market reciprocal exchange as a driver of individual choice.

4   Medieval, Agrarian and Demographic

After Rogers and Ashley, medieval economic history at Oxford resumed with the formidable figure of the Russian Paul Vinogradoff (Corpus Professor of Jurisprudence, 1903–1925), who added to the reputation of his *Villainage in England* (1892) with *The Growth of the Manor* (1905) and *English Society in the Eleventh Century* (1908). His student, A.E. Levett (History Fellow and Vice-Principal, St Hilda's, 1910–1923), the first woman economic historian in an Oxford post, wrote on monasteries and manors, most notably on the Black Death on the Winchester diocesan estates, but ranged into the early modern period and even published a text on *Europe since Napoleon* (1913). Ephraim Lipson covered the Middle Ages at the same time, in the first volume of his *Economic History of England*. R.V. Lennard, a medieval agricultural historian, began to teach in Oxford before the First World War, lectured in the School of Agriculture and succeeded Lipson as Reader (1932–1951). Like many Oxford scholars of the time, he published little in post but a good *Rural England, 1086–1135* (1959) after retirement.

Exceeding Lennard in portentous silence was Trevor Aston (History Fellow at Corpus, 1952–1985), a specialist in the manorial economy with a significant reputation but only one important article. He also edited the important social history journal *Past and Present* for twenty-five years. In contrast with Aston, Lennard's prolific successor, W.G. Hoskins (Reader, 1951–1965), wrote *The Making of the English Landscape* (1955), a foundational work in environmental history, as well as many highly cited articles and books on late medieval and early modern agrarian and urban history, without however engaging much with the questions of dispossession and agrarian development during the transition to modern growth. Barbara Harvey (History Fellow at Somerville, 1956–1993) followed Levett with studies of *Westminster Abbey and its Estates in the Middle Ages* (1977) and of the monastic experience (1993). Rosamond Faith (independent scholar) writes on the English peasantry and the growth of lordship and, more recently, on the moral economy in the countryside in Anglo-Saxon and Anglo-Norman England. Nicholas Mayhew of the Ashmolean Museum, an expert on numismatics, has written extensively on money and the money supply from the Middle Ages to the end of the early modern period while Pamela Nightingale also writes on medieval money and credit. Chris Wickham (Chichele Professor of Medieval History, 2005–2016) ventured into the deeper past: his landmark work on *Framing the Early Middle Ages* (2005) came out at the point of his arrival and was followed by other studies of early medieval Italy and Europe. Alan Bowman and Andrew Wilson, both of them classical archaeologists, study the economy of the Roman Mediterranean.

Hoskins was followed by Joan Thirsk (Reader, 1965–1983), an early modernist. She preferred small differences to large movements, and traced them in probate records of household inventories, parish registers of birth and marriage, regional differences in soils and handicraft industries, the everyday experience of a distant and unfamiliar past, before the onset of factory industry. Probate records in particular provide a rich insight into status differentials, occupations, standards of living and material culture. Her most important achievement was as general editor from 1974 of *The Agrarian History of England and Wales* which she brought to completion (1967–2000, eight volumes). As editor of the three volumes spanning 1500 to 1750, she assembled a detailed account of the period by its foremost scholars, including herself. Her *Economic Policy and Projects: The Development of a Consumer Society in Early Modern England* (1978) is an engaging account of material cultures and household experiences. In retirement, she retrieved early modern diets and occasionally served the staple barley bread to dinner guests.

Agricultural enclosure and innovation were another saga of immiseration and enrichment. Working the land was still the largest economic sector at the end of the eighteenth century, and its transformation in Britain initially affected more people than the industrial one. Rogers' *Six Centuries* was a story of lost contentment. The largest disaster in British history, the Black Death of 1348–1349, was followed by relatively good times on the land as a shortage of hands drove up farming incomes and wages. By the nineteenth century, however, agricultural labourers had become the poorest of all manual workers.

Agricultural development in England took the form of enclosing common land and the privately owned strips scattered on the open fields. Marx called this "primitive accumulation", the initial big push of capitalist enterprise. It had two aspects: a conversion of long-term leasehold quasi-property into annual tenancy, and privatisation of common land that provided families with subsistence in kind. In the nineteenth century these transitions still had a bearing on the Radical struggle for political, economic and social democracy against the landed elite. Christopher Orwin became Director of the Oxford Agricultural Economics Research Institute at the very end of this period (1913–1945), and mostly directed surveys of current farming conditions. With his wife Christabel, he wrote *The Open Fields* (1938) about the sole remaining English unenclosed field system in Laxton, Northamptonshire. What they found was not a prelapsarian community, but a pragmatic arrangement by enterprising farmers. E.M. Ojala of the same Institute wrote an important and underappreciated work, *Agriculture and Economic Progress*

(1952), a rich analytical account of development which provided estimates of farm output over the previous century in the United States, Britain and Sweden.

Hrothgar John Habakkuk (Chichele Professor, 1950–1967) made his mark initially in Cambridge as an historian of English landownership in the seventeenth and eighteenth centuries, also publishing several articles on the subject while in the chair. His magnum opus, *Marriage, Debt, and the Estates System* (1994), investigates legal arrangements and property rights. His other main contribution, noted later, was in another field altogether.

Richard Smith (Lecturer, then Reader in Population History, 1983–1994) approached medieval and early modern agrarian history from a demographic aspect. As Director of the Wellcome Unit for the History of Medicine he considered the interface between demography and health care as well as informal support within the family. He was a large positive presence as teacher and research leader. Smith was followed by John Landers (Lecturer in Historical Demography, 1991–2005) whose most important publication was *Death and the Metropolis* (1993) which examined the demography of London from 1670 to 1830. Tony Wrigley (Senior Research Fellow, All Souls College, 1988–1994), Britain's foremost historian of population, spent most of his academic life in Cambridge. He is prolific and very highly cited.

Finally, Robert Allen (Reader and Professor of Economic History, 2001–2013) had already contributed to the early history of enclosure before his arrival, with the argument that agricultural improvement was the work of farmers more than landlords and had largely preceded the eighteenth century. He subsequently investigated another big push, this time into State capitalism: the industrialisation of Russia and the collectivisation of its agriculture between the wars (*From Farm to Factory* (2003)).

5   Economic Thought and Political Economy

Thorold Rogers opens *The Economic Interpretation of History* (1888) with a limpid exposition of Smith's early doctrine of reciprocity as motivation. Toynbee's *Industrial Revolution* engaged polemically with Ricardo and Mill. Ashley, Cannan and Gonner published outstanding editions of Mill, Smith and Ricardo respectively. L.L. Price wrote a popular *Short History of Political Economy in England* (1891) and included the history of thought as one of three equal components in the first Oxford diploma, together with economics and economic history. Lectures in vintage economic thought have been offered continuously at Oxford since before the First World War, and during the 1960s were given by John Hicks, who won the Nobel Prize in Economics soon afterwards in 1972. G.D.H. Cole wrote a much-cited five-volume *History of Socialist Thought* (1953–1960). Walter Eltis (Economics Fellow, Exeter College, 1958–1988) published a neoclassical interpretation of *The Classical Theory of Economic Growth* (1984) and other studies in that vein. Hartwell's *History of the Mont Pèlerin Society* (1995) has already been mentioned. More recently, James Forder (Economics Fellow, Balliol College) has shed light on the Friedman-Keynesian debates of the 1960s in *Macroeconomics and the Phillips Curve Myth* (2014) which shows that an inflation-unemployment policy trade-off was not part of the original reception of the Phillips model, and that the expectations argument on the Friedman side was a commonplace in economics two decades earlier. Avner Offer wrote on Smith, Ricardo and Hayek, and published a book-length political and policy interpretation of the Nobel Prize in Economics.

The political economy of taxation, tariffs and war is a constant preoccupation, ever since the Edwardian tariff reform controversy. Free trade came to be associated with Cambridge. Price, like most of the late-Victorian cohort, was a protectionist. G.D.H. Cole published a book in 1923 on labour regulation in coal mining during the First World War. W.K. Hancock was Chichele Professor from 1944 to 1949 and during his short tenure he published the *British War Economy* (1949) with Margaret Gowing, the first volume in a series of "civil histories" on the United Kingdom that had been authorised in 1942 by the war cabinet. However, most of his prolific writing took place elsewhere. Peter Dickson's *The Financial Revolution in England* (1967) is the foundational modern study of the origins of public debt in Britain (History Fellow, Reader and Professor at St Catherine's, 1960–1996). The political economy of the British fiscal state in the eighteenth century was the subject of Patrick O'Brien's Oxford DPhil (Lecturer, then Reader, St Antony's College, 1970–1992) and also of several of his most cited contributions. Offer wrote a book on war and empire (1989) before returning to Oxford, and several articles afterwards. Tim Mason (co-founder of *History Workshop Journal*, History Fellow at St Peter's, 1971–1984) published mostly in German. He argued that Hitler was forced into the Second World War by the pressure of working-class material expectations which he had stoked up previously. Patricia Clavin (History Fellow at Jesus from 2003) wrote *Securing the World Economy: The Re-invention of the League of Nations, 1920–1946* (2013). Kevin O'Rourke (Chichele Professor, 2011–2019) is renowned as an authority on growth and international trade. At Oxford, he wrote most notably on the economic determinants of political extremism between the wars, on currency unions, and *A Short History of Brexit* (2019). Mary Cox, a Junior Research Fellow at Brasenose, combined demographics and war in *Hunger in War & Peace:*

Women and Children in Germany, 1914–1924 (2019). Finally, Nicholas Dimsdale wrote on taxation and its economic effect between the wars, and Gregg Huff (Senior Research Fellow, Pembroke, 2014–2018) has brought together years of work for his definitive *World War II and Southeast Asia: Economy and Society under Japanese Occupation* (2020). Catherine Schenk, Jane Humphries' successor (Professor of Economic and Social History, St Hilda's, since 2017), specialises in financial history.

6   Drivers of Economic Development

Economic development in Britain and overseas, its causes not its consequences, is the final lineage. Paul Slack (Fellow in History at Exeter College from 1973, then Professor of Early Modern History and Principal of Linacre College until 2010), who is a prolific social historian, published *The Invention of Improvement* (2014), a fine study of the ideology of development from the sixteenth to the eighteenth centuries in Britain, encompassing the emergence of political economy and early estimates of national income. A descriptive narrative had held sway from Toynbee to Mathias, but a break was made by the latter's predecessor, John Habakkuk, whose genius was to connect welfare causally with productivity. In the post-war years, an abiding question in current policy was why labour productivity was so much higher in the United States than in Britain, despite their similarities in other respects. In *American and British Technology in the Nineteenth Century* (1962), Habakkuk argued that the United States suffered a shortage of industrial labour because workers could move west and set up as independent farmers with little need for hired hands. To economise on labour, American capitalists reached out for new technologies. Peter Temin, an American cliometrician, wrote that this account was inconsistent with economic theory and with some known stylised facts about the two economies (Temin 1966). Habakkuk later reflected that an invitation in 1967 to become Principal of Jesus College, Oxford, came in the nick of time to prevent a serious collapse in his self-confidence under the impact of this criticism, on the face of it demonstrating the superiority of American over British technology (Thompson 2004: 103–104). But Temin had argued mostly from theory, and theory is a premise, not a finding. Any mismatch with reality might arise from defective theory rather than historical induction. Habakkuk's book is cited seven times more than Temin's influential critique.

How much did British economic growth benefit from empire and slavery? Sugar from West Indian slave plantations enriched merchants and planters, sweetened life a little for the labourers and stimulated the economy. Nevertheless, nowhere was wealth more detached from welfare. Figuring out this enterprise was part of the life work of Richard Pares, a Fellow of All Souls (1924–1945, 1954–1958, among several academic and government positions) and 'perhaps the most admired and looked up to Oxford teacher of his generation' (Berlin 2001: 122), author most notably of *War and Trade in the West Indies, 1739–1763* (1936), and *Merchants and Planters* (1960). He continued to write and to teach in defiance of a disabling disease which cut his career short. Did the profits of slavery also provide seed capital for British industrial growth? Eric Williams (later Prime Minister of Trinidad) made the case that it did in an Oxford DPhil published as the landmark *Capitalism and Slavery* (1944). British merchants also made fortunes in the slave trade, and the textile industry depended on raw cotton grown by slaves on millions of offshore "ghost acres" in the American South. Charles Feinstein, then a Marxist, wanted to study this question for his doctoral dissertation in 1952 but had no answer when asked by Joan Robinson, 'How can you explain the prosperity of the Scandinavian economies if it is all due to Empire?' (Robinson quoted in Thomas 2008: 289). Patrick O'Brien took a similar approach, applying the counterfactual method and finding that '*if* the British economy had been excluded from trade with the periphery, gross annual investment expenditures would have fallen by not more than 7 per cent' (O'Brien 1982: 17; italics in original). It could be argued in response that this conception of development was too narrow in its focus on investment before the railways, when capital was not so critical (and also leaving out the heavy compensation received by planters for the abolition of slavery). O'Brien also compared British performance with that of other countries, notably in *Economic Growth in Britain and France, 1780–1914: Two Paths to the Twentieth Century* (with Caglar Keyder, 1978). He reprised Habakkuk's point that ownership of land by those who worked it affected the choice of technique and induced slower urban growth in France. Its economy nevertheless arrived at similar levels of prosperity, albeit at a lesser pace but with not as much social harm.

In 1969, Peter Mathias asked "Who Unbound Prometheus?" about the relation between science, technology and economic growth (Mathias 1969b). Nicholas Crafts, just before arriving in Oxford, speculated whether the occurrence of the Industrial Revolution in Britain rather than France, which had a similar endowment of talent and innovation, might not have been a matter of chance. In a class of his own in this area, Paul David (Senior Research Fellow, All Souls College, 1993–2002, Oxford Internet Institute, 2002–2008) continues to study the economics of technology. He came to prominence in the 1980s with his concept of "path dependence", a claim that an industry might be locked into inferior technologies at an early stage because users committed prematurely to its inflexible routines. His example was famously the QWERTY typewriter keyboard. At Oxford, he continued to publish a stream of highly cited articles on the economics of science in historical settings and is cited almost five times more than any other Oxford economic historian.

In the post-war decades, several East Asian economies converged with those of the West, none more impressively than China. This motivated historians to speculate about a possible previous divergence. Kenneth Pomeranz's *The Great Divergence* (2000) argued that the West only began to draw ahead of Asia in the eighteenth century. This stimulated a remarkable enterprise in Oxford, a synthesis of welfare and growth developed by Robert Allen. His innovation was to use microeconomic price and wage observations to infer macroeconomic trends. The initial step followed the example of Rogers and used some of his data. Allen set out to establish long-run trends of prices and wages in terms of a standard subsistence basket of commodities. With a global network of collaborators, Allen constructed standard of living time series from the Middle Ages to modern times in a large number of countries. This defined the Great Divergence more precisely in terms of manual labour consumption patterns. It also provided more granular resolution to the "little divergence" between Northern and Southern Europe which persists to this day. Allen found that wages doubled in England and the Netherlands between 1500 and 1800, whereas in peripheral Europe they stagnated or declined. This led to an interpretation of the Industrial Revolution somewhat similar to the Habakkuk thesis on the relation between productivity and welfare: high wages in Britain incentivised its entrepreneurs to seek labour-saving innovations. As in North America, there was also a natural resource, cheap and accessible coal in the United Kingdom versus extensive land in the United States, except that nature worked for capital in Britain, not for labour. The combination of technical innovation and natural resources delivered a productivity breakthrough whose magnitude gave Britain a head start in development that lasted for almost a century.

Oxford scholars of non-British economic history had prepared some of the ground for this work. Mark Elvin published *The Pattern of the Chinese Past: A Social and Economic Interpretation* (1973). D.C.M. Platt wrote in the 1960s and 1970s on the British involvement in Latin American development, Valpy FitzGerald and Rosemary Thorp on the region in more recent decades, and David Washbrook on colonial India. Pamela Nightingale, the medieval historian, wrote two books on India in the eighteenth century (1970, 1985), and one on Sinkiang, in Chinese Central Asia in the nineteenth century (with Clarmont Skrine, 1973). Roger Owen laid the foundations for his eminence as an economic historian of the Middle East, Michael Kaser edited a three-volume economic history of Eastern Europe since 1919 (with E.A Radice, 1986–1987), David Fieldhouse wrote several influential works on the political economy of imperialism, William Beinart wrote on environmental history, landownership and population in black South Africa while Feinstein's *An Economic History of South Africa* (2005) was another profound investigation of how oppression can defeat markets.

Free labour markets will pay enough to motivate immediate effort, but not always to support its long-term requirements for education, health care, housing and support for disability and old age. In late Victorian Britain, almost a third of the population went short of food, shelter, clothing and fuel. It requires collective action, and ultimately government intervention, to compensate for market failures. Hence, it is odd that social policy is so incidental to economic history at Oxford, perhaps reflecting a bias against non-market arrangements. Instead, the subject is mostly taught and studied at Oxford by other kinds of historians, lawyers or social scientists. Already, Toynbee advocated municipal housing in 1884. In 1888, the Liberal statesman William Harcourt affirmed the same principle when he famously stated that 'We are all socialists now'. That social policy is not primarily a matter of compassion but of national efficiency explicitly motivated Edwardian social insurance (Searle 1971). Alfred Venn Dicey (Vinerian Professor of Law, 1882–1909), a star of Anson's All Souls College, described what he called the growth of collectivism (the curtailment of "freedom of contract" in favour of labour, of which he disapproved) in his magisterial *Lectures on the Relation Between Law and Public Opinion in England During the Nineteenth Century* (1905). Legal norms, he said, were not exogenous but always in England an expression of public opinion.

Social history is part of the official rubric of the economic history group where it is usually taken with some analytical or quantitative twist. Another strand within the Faculty of History at Oxford largely falls outside social science. It is a substantial department whose achievements are beyond my scope here, but several contributions have been salient for economic history. Asa Briggs, a giant of the discipline, was in Oxford for a decade from 1945 and from 1951 as the first Reader in Recent Social and Economic History set up for PPE. Apart from *Victorian People* (1954) and an excellent volume on the history of Birmingham (1952) (the first of several commissioned works), most of his immense contribution was made after he left and before he came back as Provost of Worcester College. Between them Paul Slack, Joanna Innes and Jose Harris depicted the unfolding of social policy from the early modern period and beyond the First World War. Finally, Charles Webster wrote a political history of the National Health Service (2002).

7   Teaching

Oxford never had a separate first degree in economic history. An 1870s paper in *Literae Humaniores* was the first examined course in political economy. The subject was taught sporadically, for example, by Toynbee at Balliol and by Rogers in the Hall of Worcester College. 'These lectures', wrote Rogers' son, 'were attended by an extremely small audience'. Had they been given in some industrial centre, he wrote, 'hundreds of workmen would, I believe, have paid to listen to them' (A.G.L. Rogers 1891: vii). Ashley, Cannan, Gonner et al. found their audiences at extension lectures in industrial towns, followed later by Unwin, Price, Tawney, Cole, G.N. Clark and many others.

At the end of the nineteenth century, the Modern History School at Oxford was offering a module of half a dozen lectures in political economy. A single course in economic history (from 1898) extended to four or five a term after 1907. When PPE began in 1921, it included an optional paper in "British Social and Economic History Since 1770". A hundred years later, this paper is still being taught, with the initial date moved up a century. Undergraduate teaching in the discipline is a rich seam: For the period 1920 to 1980, there were always around half a dozen course offerings in the Lecture List (mostly both in History and PPE) during the first two terms of the academic year (fewer in the third), covering British history from medieval to modern, with a single paper on European economic history being taught from 1941. Written recollections by inter-war PPE students claim that they did almost all of their work in tutorials and rarely went to any lectures—but they still felt able to pass judgement on the lecturers (Lee 1993). In Modern History, it was still possible to take papers in political economy up to the 1930s. In 1940, this fell to a single paper, "The Economic Policy of Peel", which remains on the books today albeit in a different form. Undergraduate lectures on economic history continued to be offered at about the same intensity up to the 1980s, when they began to wither. A separate joint Honours School in History and Economics began in 1970. It admits a strong contingent of around twenty students a year.

Training for research was an apprenticeship, primarily the DPhil: an incoming candidate would be assigned a supervisor and then left largely on their own. Such was my own experience in the 1970s. A weekly seminar was introduced by Habakkuk in the 1950s complete with full minutes of each paper and its discussion (see Thompson 2004: 104), and was still running in the 1960s. Hartwell convened one for doctoral students at Nuffield in the late 1950s. Today's weekly staff-graduate seminar first appears in the Lecture List in 1970, and many other seminar series came and went, often several of them every week. Postgraduate and doctoral research is the beating heart of the discipline. Every year, a young and eager cohort arrived and measured itself anxiously against the challenge. It could be a lonely experience and connections were not always easy to make. Half an hour of sherry after the seminar was the main opportunity. As a graduate student, I used to see a distinctive young face across the seminar table but only learned his name when he turned up as my host at a seminar in Melbourne several years later.

In the 1970s, the core of the discipline in Oxford stabilised. There were four permanent posts: The Chichele Chair at All Souls (in the Faculty of Modern History), Max Hartwell's Readership in Recent Social and Economic History at Nuffield (Faculty of Social Studies), Joan Thirsk's Readership at St Hilda's (History) and Patrick O'Brien's Lectureship at St Antony's (Social Studies). Another was added in the 1980s, namely Richard Smith's Lectureship in Population History, also at All Souls. Area Studies (mostly at St Antony's) appointed economic historians of other continents and regions, who did not mix much with the disciplinary core (their achievements have already been mentioned). A few tutors in the Faculties of Economics and History also engaged with the subject. Chris McKenna and Rowena Olegario plough their field in the Business School studying the development of management consultancy, credit agencies, brand management, and Jewish traders in the United States while Joshua Getzler in the Faculty of Law wrote an important *History of Water Rights at Common Law* (2004).

In the 1980s, economic history went out of fashion in British universities and most independent departments closed. In this dismal setting, economic history at Oxford recovered in response to an external nudge. The Economic and Social Research Council laid down that students should undergo a year of training before going on to doctoral work. In 1991–1992, Feinstein (with Offer) devised a taught Master's degree which for the first time imposed a structure on the discipline in Oxford. Graduate instruction fell outside the rigid conventions of Oxford teaching and it was possible to design a course from the ground up. Two core courses in methodology and quantitative methods were combined with an array of options arranged around the teachers' own research interests, and a thesis. The course attracted a cosmopolitan entry of twenty to thirty students a year, about half of them from North America and Europe, one-fifth from Britain and the rest from elsewhere. Everyone acquired some statistical competence and every lecture on theory was linked to a class which applied it to an historical episode. Course progression promoted bonding, this in part serving to change the local culture. A community of up to fifty graduate students interacted frequently at lectures, classes, seminars and informally with postdocs and postholders. A norm of methodological pluralism accepted any line of inquiry as legitimate if aspirations were high. Undergraduate teaching continued, but the focus of the subject had shifted to graduate work.

The practical purpose of this effort is to equip students and their older selves with the capacity to make informed judgements by means of argument and evidence. More than five hundred graduates have gone forth to responsible positions around the world in universities, public service, business, law, advocacy, even in medicine and art.

The experience is also a good in itself. The past is lost. It comes alive when somebody holds it in their mind, perhaps while reading a book, or while composing thoughts in conversation and writing. Meeting together week after week in a lecture room or seminar, people bond together. In the shared quest for understanding, and when the magic works, history can light up in their heads.

8   Conclusion

In 160 years, what has the discipline of economic history achieved at Oxford? In several respects, it has gone full circle. It emerged in the twilight years of classical economics. The rising neoclassical approach took several decades to get established, and eventually expelled economic history. But a 140 years after Toynbee, the ladder of esteem in the discipline leans again towards economics. A new empirical turn in economics is as inductive as history and takes the past as a quarry for its natural experiments. Economic history has declined from its peak as an undergraduate subject, and now thrives as a research discipline.

Economic and social development over historical time is too important a subject to ever fall by the wayside and finds a home in a variety of academic settings, and altogether outside them. Is it merely a subject or is it also a method? At its best, it is a vantage point on the human condition. In Oxford, for 160 years, a succession of scholars and their students have striven to stand taller and see further. In the discipline of economic history, this collective effort has had few equals.

References

Allen, R.C. (2003). *From Farm to Factory: A Reinterpretation of the Soviet Industrial Revolution*. Princeton, NJ: Princeton University Press.

Aristotle (1865). *Ethica Nicomachea*. Edited by J.E.T. Rogers. London: Apud Rivington.

Ashley, W.J. (1888). *Introduction to English Economic History and Theory*. London: Rivingtons.

Berlin, I. (2001). *Personal Impressions*. Expanded edition, edited by Henry Hardy. Princeton, NJ: Princeton University Press.

Briggs, A. (1952). *History of Birmingham: Volume 2, Borough and City, 1865–1938*. Oxford: Oxford University Press.

Briggs, A. (1954). *Victorian People: Some Reassessments of People, Institutions, Ideas and Events, 1851–1867*. London: Odhams Press.

Broadberry, S., B.M.S. Campbell, A. Klein, M. Overton and B. van Leeuwen (2015). *British Economic Growth, 1270–1870*. Cambridge: Cambridge University Press.

Clavin, P. (2013). *Securing the World Economy: The Re-invention of the League of Nations, 1920–1946*. Oxford: Oxford University Press.

Clegg, H.A., A. Fox and A.F. Thompson (1964). *A History of British Trade Unions Since 1889*. Oxford: Clarendon Press.

Cole, G.D.H. (1913). *The World of Labour: A Discussion of the Present and Future of Trade Unionism*. London: G. Bell.

Cole, G.D.H. (1923). *Labour in the Coal-Mining Industry, 1914–1921*. Oxford: Clarendon Press.

Cole, G.D.H. (1953–1960). *A History of Socialist Thought*. Five volumes. London: Macmillan.

Cole, G.D.H. and R. Postgate (1938). *The Common People, 1746–1938*. London: Methuen.

Coleman, D.C. (1987). *History and the Economic Past: An Account of the Rise and Decline of Economic History in Britain*. Oxford: Clarendon Press.

Corley, T.A.B. (2002). 'George Unwin: A Manchester Economic Historian Extraordinary'. Henley Business School, University of Reading. Available at: https://www.reading.ac.uk/web/files/management/435.pdf.

Cox, M.E. (2019). *Hunger in War & Peace: Women and Children in Germany, 1914–1924*. Oxford: Oxford University Press.

Crafts, N.F.R. (1985). *British Economic Growth During the Industrial Revolution*. Oxford: Clarendon Press.

Dicey, A.V. (1905). *Lectures on the Relation Between Law and Public Opinion in England During the Nineteenth Century*. London: Macmillan.

Dickson, P.G.M. (1967). *The Financial Revolution in England: A Study in the Development of Public Credit, 1688–1756*. London: Macmillan.

Dimsdale, N. and R. Thomas (2019). *UK Business and Financial Cycles Since 1660: Volume 1—A Narrative Overview*. Cham: Palgrave Macmillan.

Easterlin, R.A. (1974). 'Does Economic Growth Improve the Human Lot?: Some Empirical Evidence'. In P.A. David and M.W. Reder (eds) *Nations and Households in Economic Growth: Essays in Honor of Moses Abramovitz*. New York: Academic Press: 89–125.

Eltis, W.A. (1984). *The Classical Theory of Economic Growth*. London: Macmillan.

Elvin, M. (1973). *The Pattern of the Chinese Past: A Social and Economic Interpretation.* Stanford: Stanford University Press.

Evans, R.J. (2019). *Eric Hobsbawm: A Life in History.* London: Little, Brown.

Feinstein, C.H. (1972). *National Income, Expenditure and Output of the United Kingdom, 1855–1965.* Cambridge: Cambridge University Press.

Feinstein, C.H. (1998). 'Pessimism Perpetuated: Real Wages and the Standard of Living in Britain During and After the Industrial Revolution'. *Journal of Economic History*, 58(3): 625–658.

Feinstein, C.H. (2005). *An Economic History of South Africa: Conquest, Discrimination and Development.* Cambridge: Cambridge University Press.

Fogel, R.W. (1964). *Railroads and American Economic Growth: Essays in Econometric History.* Baltimore: Johns Hopkins Press.

Fogel, R.W. and S.L. Engerman (1974). *Time on the Cross: Volume 1, The Economics of American Negro Slavery, Volume 2, Evidence and Methods.* Boston: Little Brown and Company.

Forder, J. (2014). *Macroeconomics and the Phillips Curve Myth.* Oxford: Oxford University Press.

Foreman-Peck, J. and R. Millward (1994). *Public and Private Ownership of British Industry, 1820–1990.* Oxford: Clarendon Press.

Galbraith, J.K. (1958). *The Affluent Society.* Boston: Houghton Mifflin.

Getzler, J. (2004). *A History of Water Rights at Common Law.* Oxford: Oxford University Press.

Goldman, L. (1995). *Dons and Workers: Oxford and Adult Education Since 1850.* Oxford: Clarendon Press.

Gonner, E.C.K. (1912). *Common Land and Inclosure.* London: Macmillan.

Habakkuk, H.J. (1962). *American and British Technology in the Nineteenth Century: The Search for Labour-Saving Inventions.* Cambridge: Cambridge University Press.

Habakkuk, H.J. (1994). *Marriage, Debt, and the Estates System: English Landownership, 1650–1950.* Oxford: Clarendon Press.

Hancock, W.K. and M.M. Gowing (1949). *British War Economy.* London: HMSO.

Hartwell, R.M. (1995). *History of the Mont Pèlerin Society.* Indianapolis: Liberty Fund.

Harvey, B. (1977). *Westminster Abbey and its Estates in the Middle Ages.* Oxford: Clarendon Press.

Harvey, B. (1993). *Living and Dying in England, 1100–1540: The Monastic Experience.* Oxford: Clarendon Press.

Hobsbawm, E.J. (1949). 'Trends in the British Labou Movement Since 1850'. *Past & Present*, 13(4): 289–312.

Hobsbawm, E.J. (1957). 'The British Standard of Living, 1790–1850'. *Economic History Review*, New Series, 10(1): 46–68.

Horrell, S. and J. Humphries (1992). 'Old Questions, New Data, and Alternative Perspectives: Families' Living Standards in the Industrial Revolution'. *Journal of Economic History*, 52(4): 849–880.

Hoskins, W.G. (1955). *The Making of the English Landscape*. London: Hodder & Stoughton.

Huff, G. (2020). *World War II and Southeast Asia: Economy and Society under Japanese Occupation*. Cambridge: Cambridge University Press.

Humphries, J. (2010). *Childhood and Child Labour in the British Industrial Revolution*. Cambridge: Cambridge University Press.

Johnson, A.H. (1909). *The Disappearance of the Small Landowner: Ford Lectures 1909*. Oxford: Clarendon Press.

Kadish, A. (1982). *The Oxford Economists in the Late Nineteenth Century*. Oxford: Clarendon Press.

Kadish, A. and K. Tribe (1993). *The Market for Political Economy: The Advent of Economics in British University Culture, 1850–1905*. London: Routledge.

Kaser, M.C. and E.A Radice (eds) (1986–1987). *The Economic History of Eastern Europe, 1919–1975: Volume 1, Economic Structure and Performance Between the Two Wars, Volume 2, Interwar Policy, the War and Reconstruction, Volume 3, Institutional Change Within a Planned Economy*. Oxford: Clarendon Press.

Koot, G.M. (1987). *English Historical Economics, 1870–1926: The Rise of Economic History and Neomercantilism*. Cambridge: Cambridge University Press.

Landers, J. (1993). *Death and the Metropolis: Studies in the Demographic History of London, 1670–1830*. Cambridge: Cambridge University Press.

Lee, F.S. (ed.) (1993). *Oxford Economics and Oxford Economists, 1922–1971: Recollections of Students and Economists*. Oxford: Bodleian Library.

Lennard, R.V. (1959). *Rural England, 1086–1135: A Study of Social and Agrarian Conditions*. Oxford: Clarendon Press.

Levett, A.E. (1913). *Europe since Napoleon*. London: Blackie & Son.

Lipson, E. (1915–1931). *The Economic History of England*. Three volumes. London: Adam and Charles Black.

Mathias, P. (1969a). *The First Industrial Nation: An Economic History of Britain, 1700–1914*. London: Methuen.

Mathias, P. (1969b). 'Who Unbound Prometheus?: Science and Technical Change, 1600–1800'. *Bulletin of Economic Research*, 21(1): 3–16.

Mathias, P. and S. Pollard (eds) (1989). *The Cambridge Economic History of Europe: Volume 8, The Industrial Economies—The Development of Economic and Social Policies*. Cambridge: Cambridge University Press.

Mathias, P. and M.M. Postan (eds) (1978). *The Cambridge Economic History of Europe: Volume 7, The Industrial Economies—Capital, Labour and Enterprise, Part 1, Britain, France, Germany and Scandinavia; Part 2, The United States, Japan and Russia*. Cambridge: Cambridge University Press.

McCloskey, D.N. (1970). 'Did Victorian Britain Fail?'. *Economic History Review*, New Series, 23(3): 446–459.

Nightingale, P. (1970). *Trade and Empire in Western India, 1784–1806*. London: Cambridge University Press.

Nightingale, P. (1985). *Fortune and Integrity: A Study of Moral Attitudes in the Indian Diary of George Paterson, 1769–1774*. Delhi: Oxford University Press.

Nordhaus, W.D. and J. Tobin (1972). 'Is Growth Obsolete?'. In *Economic Growth*. Fiftieth Anniversary Colloquium V. New York: National Bureau of Economic Research: 1–80.

O'Brien, P. (1982). 'European Economic Development: The Contribution of the Periphery'. *Economic History Review*, New Series, 35(1): 1–18.

O'Brien, P. and C. Keyder (1978). *Economic Growth in Britain and France, 1780–1914: Two Paths to the Twentieth Century*. London: George Allen & Unwin.

Offer, A. (1989). *The First World War: An Agrarian Interpretation*. Oxford: Clarendon Press.

Offer, A. (2006). *The Challenge of Affluence: Self-Control and Well-Being in the United States and Britain Since 1950*. Oxford: Oxford University Press.

Ojala, E.M. (1952). *Agriculture and Economic Progress*. London: Oxford University Press.

O'Rourke, K. (2019). *A Short History of Brexit*. London: Pelican.

Orwin, C.S. and C.S. Orwin (1938). *The Open Fields*. Oxford: Clarendon Press.

Pares, R. (1936). *War and Trade in the West Indies, 1739–1763*. Oxford: Clarendon Press.

Pares, R. (1960). *Merchants and Planters*. Cambridge: Cambridge University Press.

Pomeranz, K. (2000). *The Great Divergence: China, Europe, and the Making of the Modern World Economy*. Princeton, NJ: Princeton University Press.

Price, L.L. (1891). *A Short History of Political Economy in England: From Adam Smith to Arnold Toynbee*. London: Methuen.

Reinert, E.S. and A.M. Daastøl (2004). 'The Other Canon: The History of Renaissance Economics'. Chapter 1 in E.S. Reinert (ed.) *Globalization, Economic Development and Inequality: An Alternative Perspective*. Cheltenham: Edward Elgar: 21–70.

Rogers, J.E.T. (1866–1902). *A History of Agriculture and Prices in England: From the Year After the Oxford Parliament (1259) to the Commencement of the Continental War (1793)*. Seven volumes. Oxford: Clarendon Press.

Rogers, J.E.T. (1884). *Six Centuries of Work and Wages: The History of English Labour*. Two volumes. London: W.S. Sonnenschein.

Rogers, J.E.T. (1888). *The Economic Interpretation of History (Lectures Delivered in Worcester College Hall, Oxford, 1887–1888)*. London: T. Fisher Unwin.

Rogers, A.G.L. (1891). 'Preface'. In J.E.T. Rogers (1891). *The Industrial and Commercial History of England (Lectures Delivered to the University of Oxford)*. Edited by A.G.L. Rogers. London: T. Fisher Unwin: v–vii.

Searle, G.R. (1971). *The Quest for National Efficiency: A Study in British Politics and Political Thought, 1899–1914*. Oxford: Basil Blackwell.

Shackle, G.L.S. (1967). *The Years of High Theory: Invention and Tradition in Economic Thought, 1926–1939*. Cambridge: Cambridge University Press.

Skrine, C.P. and P. Nightingale (1973). *Macartney at Kashgar: New Light on British, Chinese and Russian Activities in Sinkiang, 1890–1918*. London: Methuen.

Slack, P. (2014). *The Invention of Improvement: Information and Material Progress in Seventeenth-Century England*. Oxford: Oxford University Press.

Smith, A. (1776). *The Wealth of Nations*. Two volumes. London: W. Strahan and T. Cadell.

Stone, L. (1965). *The Crisis of the Aristocracy, 1558–1641*. Oxford: Clarendon Press.

Tawney, R.H. (1926). *Religion and the Rise of Capitalism*. London: John Murray.

Temin, P. (1966). 'Labor Scarcity and the Problem of American Industrial Efficiency in the 1850s'. *Journal of Economic History*, 26(3): 277–298.

Thirsk, J. (ed.) (1967). *The Agrarian History of England and Wales: Volume IV, 1500–1640*. Cambridge: Cambridge University Press.

Thirsk, J. (1978). *Economic Policy and Projects: The Development of a Consumer Society in Early Modern England*. Oxford: Clarendon Press.

Thomas, M. (2008). 'Charles H. Feinstein, interviewed by Mark Thomas'. In J.S. Lyons, L.P. Cain and S.H. Williamson (eds) (2008). *Reflections on the Cliometrics Revolution: Conversations with Economic Historians*. London and New York: Routledge: 286–300.

Thompson, E.P. (1967). 'Time, Work-Discipline and Industrial Capitalism'. *Past & Present*, 38(1): 56–97.

Thompson, E.P. (1971). 'The Moral Economy of the English Crowd in the Eighteenth Century'. *Past & Present*, 50(February): 76–136.

Thompson, F.M.L. (2004). 'Hrothgar John Habakkuk, 1915–2002'. *Proceedings of the British Academy*, 124: 90–114.

Toynbee, A. (1884). *Lectures on the Industrial Revolution in England: Popular Addresses, Notes and Other Fragments*. London: Rivingtons.

Tribe, K. (2002). 'Historical Schools of Economics: German and English'. Keele Economics Research Papers, KERP 2002/02, Department of Economics, Keele University. Available at: https://ssrn.com/abstract=316689.

Vinogradoff, P. (1892). *Villainage in England: Essays in English Mediaeval History*. Oxford: Clarendon Press.

Vinogradoff, P. (1905). *The Growth of the Manor*. London: W.S. Sonnenschein.

Vinogradoff, P. (1908). *English Society in the Eleventh Century: Essays in English Mediaeval History*. Oxford: Clarendon Press.

Wadsworth, A.P. and J. de Lacy Mann (1931). *The Cotton Trade and Industrial Lancashire, 1600–1780*. Manchester: University Press.

Webster, C. (2002). *The National Health Service: A Political History*. Oxford: Oxford University Press.

Wickham, C. (2005). *Framing the Early Middle Ages: Europe and the Mediterranean, 400–800*. Oxford: Oxford University Press.

Williams, E.E. (1944). *Capitalism and Slavery*. Chapel Hill: University of North Carolina Press.

Wilson, C. (1954). *The History of Unilever: A Study in Economic Growth and Social Change*. Two volumes. London: Cassell.

Wilson, C. (1968). *Unilever, 1945–1965: Challenge and Response*. London: Cassell.

5

PPE and Oxford Economics

Warren Young and Frederic S. Lee

1   Introduction

Over the century since its inception, the Oxford Philosophy, Politics and Economics (PPE hereafter) degree has been the focus of admiration and controversy alike. Originally conceived as "Modern Greats", a portmanteau undergraduate degree parallel to Oxford's *Literae Humaniores*, or "Greats", PPE has evolved over time, as has its influence. Many universities in Britain and worldwide have copied it (see Brennan et al. 2010). On the other hand, its societal impact—as a breeding ground for the British political elite—has come to be increasingly criticised especially in recent years (see Kelly 2010; Cohen 2014; Beckett 2017). Moreover, as a result of its intrinsic nature, that is to say, without a direct focus on economics, the role of the degree in the development of Oxford economics, as against those who taught economics within its framework, has been problematic. One observer has noted:

Fred Lee (1949–2014) was my co-author on *Oxford Economics and Oxford Economists* (1993). This essay would have been co-authored with him, and is based on many of his writings, so it is a posthumous joint publication.

W. Young (✉)
Bar-Ilan University, Ramat Gan, Israel

F. S. Lee (1949–2014)

© The Author(s), under exclusive license to Springer Nature Switzerland AG 2021
R. A. Cord (ed.), *The Palgrave Companion to Oxford Economics*,
https://doi.org/10.1007/978-3-030-58471-9_5

While Cambridge was Marshall and then Pigou, economics at Oxford had long been dominated by the English Historical School…which called into question the universal propositions of mathematical model building. PPE in the 1920s relied at least as much on Mill's *Political Economy* as on Marshall's *Principles*. The enterprise had the stigma of being a soft option (Reisman 2018: 4–5).

Even as late as 1968, a left-wing critic of PPE and its impact upon Harold Wilson, one of its most prestigious graduates, wrote in his biography of Wilson:

The Oxford School of Politics, Philosophy and Economics is based on two unalterable principles: first, everything written about politics and philosophy by Karl Marx…is out of date and dangerously biased, while everything written by John Stuart Mill…is modern, vigorous and untainted by bias; secondly, everything written about economics by Karl Marx…is out of date and dangerously biased, while everything written by Alfred Marshall is modern, vigorous and untainted by bias (Foot 1968: 32).

After the establishment of PPE, some Oxford economists even lobbied for a separate degree in economics and the formation of a School of Economics such that, early on, there was little support for the degree in Oxford, especially amongst the economists themselves (see Young and Lee 1993: 26). Indeed, an Economics Department was established in Oxford only in 1999, and there is still no Oxford BA in the subject. This lack of led to critiques of PPE by some of its most prominent graduates who became economists, including Hicks and Meade. In his Nobel Prize Lecture, Hicks said, 'My move (in 1923) to "philosophy, politics and economics", the "new school" just being started at Oxford, was however not a success. I finished with a Second-Class degree, and no adequate qualification in any of the subjects I studied' (Hicks 1992: 133). Meade, another laureate in economics, described PPE as being a 'Jack-of-three-trades' degree (Meade quoted in Reisman 2018: 5).

In any case, the overall pedagogical aims and objectives of the Oxford PPE have remained consistent since its inception. It was first established 'to promote the study of the structure, and philosophical, political and economic principles, of modern society' (Chester 1986: 35). In 1960, according to the *Handbook to the University of Oxford*, it was 'designed to be a well-balanced course of study of the social problems of the modern world' (*Handbook to the University of Oxford* 1960: 158). The following description, on the occasion of its centenary, appeared on the PPE website in March 2020:

PPE was born of the conviction that study of the great modern works of economic, social, political and philosophical thought would have a transformative effect on students' intellectual lives, and thereby on society at large. This conviction remains as firm today as it was then. As the world has evolved, so has PPE. The course brings together some of the most important approaches to understanding the world around us, developing skills useful for a wide range of careers and activities (PPE website n.d.).

However, immediately under this appeared, a photograph of the famous door 10 Downing Street, illustrating the dissonance that has affected PPE over the past century. On the one hand, it became perhaps the world's most famous undergraduate academic degree, attracting from the beginning American Rhodes Scholars. According to one account of the relationship between the Rhodes Scholar programme and Oxford, PPE was in fact set up partly to meet the needs of Rhodes Scholars. It was purposely constructed for those who sought careers in public service but had little or no knowledge of Greek required for acceptance into the Greats programme (see Schaeper and Schaeper 2010: chapter 7). Moreover, one of the early arguments put forth in 1919 in support of establishing the degree was 'the expectation of foreign students, especially from America, of finding in Oxford a complete apparatus of systematic training in social studies' (Briggs 1991: 320). On the other hand, it served as a training ground for what turned out to be the British political elite and future leaders in many other countries.

The University awards degrees—undergraduate and graduate—based on examination and/or dissertation. University faculties, schools and departments are the framework for lectures. Instruction also includes seminars, lab work (in the physical and biological sciences) and other types of learning. Colleges provide small group undergraduate teaching known as tutorials, which are 'central to teaching at Oxford' (University of Oxford website n.d.). This has been the case for the past century of PPE. However, a caveat is necessary here. While tutoring takes place in colleges, in some cases, students have been tutored by dons in colleges other than their own at the initiative of the college economics tutors themselves. Moreover, different tutors often have their own subject preferences. Responsibility for lectures was sub-Faculty, and, after 1999, Department of Economics based. The bipartite PPE structure after the first year of study was introduced in 1971, focusing on the combination of either economics and politics, economics and philosophy, or politics and philosophy. The structure of the economics component of the PPE degree is described by the Department of Economics website thus:

The economics element of the degree begins with Introductory Economics in the first year. This is a compulsory course and introduces students to micro and macroeconomic theory. In the second and third years, students continuing with Economics on a bipartite basis are required to take at least three courses in Economics and at least one of these must be Microeconomics, Macroeconomics or Quantitative Economics. Students studying Economics on a tripartite basis are required to take at least two courses in Economics and at least one of these must be Microeconomics, Macroeconomics, Quantitative Economics or Development of the World Economy Since 1800. Students may choose from a range of optional courses in areas such as Behavioural and Experimental Economics, Money and Banking, Labour Economics and Inequality and Economics of Developing Countries. Students thinking of pursuing a demanding higher degree in pure Economics (for example the MPhil in Economics at Oxford) normally take Econometrics and either Game Theory and/or Microeconomic Analysis (Department of Economics website n.d.).

The history of PPE has been dealt with in detail by Chester (1986), Young and Lee (1993) and Currie (1994). Here, we will limit our study to a purposive survey of PPE economic studies and the development of what we have called "Oxford Economics". Before proceeding, however, an account of the development of political economy before the advent of PPE is warranted in order to better understand the background to, and problematic nature and historical context of, economics within the degree.

2   Pre-PPE Political Economy at Oxford

Political economy and the teaching of its principles at Oxford had a long and problematic history. In May 1825, Oxford accepted an offer by Henry Drummond to endow a Chair in Political Economy at All Souls. While opposed by some, the supporters of the idea of a chair, led by Richard Whately, urged acceptance. Political economy, they maintained, was rapidly becoming an indispensable field for statesmen. Indeed, as Whately is reported to have said, 'before long political economists of some sort or other must govern the world' (Whately quoted in Briggs 1991: 320). As Oxford was perceived as a place to educate the future leaders of Britain, a failure to teach economics would mean that they would fall under the influence of Ricardians and Utilitarians, an outcome which would be anathema to Oxford's High Church *weltanschauung*. Moreover, since 1816, Cambridge already had a lecturer in political economy.

Whately was instrumental in securing the appointment of his former pupil and friend, Nassau William Senior, as the first Drummond Professor of Political Economy in June 1825. Senior presented the theoretical and policy positions of what can be called the "Oxford-Dublin School", as a proto-marginalist challenge to classical economics. After Senior's five year-term ended in 1830, Whately took over the Drummond Professorship himself, but stayed for only a year before accepting a position as the new Archbishop of Dublin in late 1831. Whately's departure led to the appointment of William Forster Lloyd to the Drummond. Although himself a proto-marginalist, Lloyd was not quite of the school of Whately-Senior (see Moore and White 2010). He was succeeded by Herman Merivale and then Travers Twiss. Senior returned to Oxford for a second five-year tenure as holder of the Drummond from 1847 to 1852. Succeeding holders of the Chair were George Kettilby Rickards, Charles Neate and James Edwin Thorold Rogers (see Kadish 1982: 181–183; see also Young and Lee 1993: 1–4).

The integration of economics in the Oxford curriculum was tentative. From the outset, it was originally merely an optional subject within Classics. There was rarely more than one question on economics on the Classics exam, and it was under-weighted in any case. The Drummond Professorship was organised under the School of History. As a result of reforms in 1854, a new honours course in Law and Modern History was introduced, for which political economy was a subject. History was strengthened by the establishment of the Chichele Professorship of Modern History in 1862, and the separation of the law component into its own course in 1873. Modern History (containing economics) quickly became the second most popular honours course, behind Classics. Familiarity with political economy was also a subject for the general non-honours examination. In 1873, the recommended textbooks were Smith's *Wealth of Nations* and Mill's *Principles* (see ibid.: 267).

The terms of the Drummond were also revised. After Rogers' first tenure, the two-year interval condition was revoked in December 1867, to allow Bonamy Price to serve consecutive terms. In 1877, the University of Oxford statutes were revised, and the University added to Drummond's original endowment, taking the stipend up to £300, supplemented by an additional £200 Fellowship at All Souls (see ibid.: 172–173).

The English Historical School, notably in the form of Rogers and Price in economics, and T.H. Green and Arnold Toynbee in modern history, generated interest in economics that grew throughout the 1880s. Alfred Marshall became a Tutor and Lecturer in Political Economy at Balliol College, from 1883 to 1884, replacing Toynbee, who died in 1883 (see ibid.: 145, 198). Marshall was a popular tutor and lecturer. He influenced many Oxford students, notably L.L. Price. Indeed, as the *Oxford Magazine* wrote of Marshall on 21 January 1885 after his appointment at Cambridge (cited in Whitaker 1975: 27): 'Coming to tutorial work little more than a year ago, he has been energetic in the teaching of his subject, and has had his reward in large and appreciative audiences. He has done much to stimulate the study of Economics in Oxford and will be much missed'. Marshall recommended John Neville Keynes as his replacement.

Some of the new group of economics-oriented students included William Ashley, J.A. Hobson, George Goschen, Price and Edwin Cannan. Many stayed on at Oxford, whether as fellows or as lecturers, and went on to form organisations like the Social Science Club and the Oxford Economic Society (see Kadish 1982: 53–59, 203–204).

The arrival of Francis Ysidro Edgeworth as Drummond Professor in 1891 changed matters. An economic theorist, Edgeworth deflated the historicist energy that had bubbled up during the 1880s. He primarily relied on the theoretical economics of Mill and Marshall for the lion's share of his lectures. Partly as a result, economic history was gradually reduced to a single course out of seven (see ibid.: 200; see also Young and Lee 1993: 2).

L.L. Price, while a Fellow at Oriel College and afterwards, took the position that Oxford should offer a degree in economics. In 1902, he complained to the Oxford Hebdomadal Council (Governing Board of the University) that the study of economics had fallen to a point of near extinction among students. Price pointed to Cambridge's growing strength in the subject and the imminent introduction of the Economics Tripos there, suggesting that Oxford needed to catch up and consider a degree in economics. This led to the establishment of a special postgraduate "Diploma in Economics", overseen by a special seven-member Committee for Economics, to encourage more systematic study of economics at Oxford. Diploma lectures and examinations began in 1905 and consisted of five papers, three required papers on economic theory, the history of economic thought and economic history, and two elective papers on any mix of these (including applied topics) (see Chester 1986: 6–10).

However, while the Diploma was introduced in 1905, it took until 1920 for the establishment of PPE, which institutionalised economics teaching at Oxford, albeit not in the framework of a specific economics degree. Meanwhile, not all of the economists at Oxford were impressed by the new degree, with Price viewing it as a continuation of Oxford's tradition of treating economics as 'pretty…but unimportant' (Department of Economics website n.d.).

3 PPE Economics at Oxford in the Inter-War Years

As noted above, the teaching of economics in Oxford prior to the establishment of the Final Honours School of PPE in 1920 was more historical and applied in orientation, such as to label it the "Oxford approach" to political economy. Marshallian supply and demand theory was broadly accepted, but where many Oxford dons and lecturers differed from Marshall was in its usefulness. On the one hand, they argued that the theory was specific to a particular historical period of capitalism; thus, when those conditions changed, the theory's theoretical conclusions would not necessarily or likely be appropriate. On the other hand, they argued that if political economy was to be useful, it must be applied to pressing economic and social problems. Thus, Oxford dons were most interested in applying theory to practical questions of socialism, State interference in the marketplace, fair wages, tariffs, unions and cooperatives, land reform and the poor law system. In this context, students were asked to learn only the rudiments of supply and demand before moving on rapidly to historical and applied topics. Hence, it was a Millian version of supply and demand as modified and interpreted by J. Shield Nicholson's *Principles of Political Economy*, Henry Rogers Seager's *Introduction to Economics* and Charles Gide's *Principles of Political Economy* that dominated Oxford economics at this time; Marshall's *Principles*, although accepted as authoritative, was only presented to advanced students, if at all (see Young and Lee 1993: 12–18).

The establishment of PPE combined with students' interest in economic questions led to an increasing need to provide lectures and tutorials in economics. In turn, this led to a nearly two-decade-long spree of hiring young, Marshallian-educated and Marshallian-inclined economists, such as Roy Harrod, Lionel Robbins, Robert Hall, Eric Hargreaves, Henry Phelps Brown, James Meade, Lindsay Fraser, Redvers Opie, Maurice Allen, Richard Sayers and Thomas Balogh. Consequently, Marshallian supply and demand theory became more dominant as the core material to be taught, with all applied and historical topics secondary, especially if they were not based on the theory. By 1939, the emphasis on historical process disappeared. In particular, lectures on economic history declined by nearly 50% between 1920–1921 and 1938–1939 (from 11 to 6), whereas lectures on the history of economic thought initially fluctuated between one and seven, stood at six in 1932–1933, but then declined to just one when its status was demoted to an elective paper. In contrast, lectures in economic theory fluctuated at around 14 on average and applied topics rose dramatically from an average of nine in 1920–1923 to 21 in 1936–1939 (see ibid.: 19–22).

The increasing emphasis on and interest in economic theory are reflected in the transformation of the economics portion of the PPE examination during this period. That is, while many exam questions during the inter-war period were concerned with "real-world" questions, what became more and more evident were that these questions were dressed up in a theoretical guise, so the students were actually dealing with theory rather than the real world per se. As many of the real world qua theoretical questions dealt with money, credit, unemployment and the Great Depression, they largely drew upon the work of economists other than Marshall. However, there was also a steady stream of micro-oriented questions. In the 1920s, these examined issues such as interest and the productivity of capital, whether the interest rate could actually be explained as the result of a preference for present over future income, and the distinction between long and short periods in an analysis of costs of production. But in the 1930s, the questions were more directed towards utilising marginalist theory. Perhaps the smoking gun transition question came in the 1933 examination when students were faced with a question asking them to delineate the "equilibrium price" and whether it could be distinguished from the older expression of "normal price". When, in 1939, an examination question was set asking about the "representative enterprise", there was a protest about expecting students to know new terminology (see ibid.: 73–80).

Marshallian economics was clearly taught at Oxford in the inter-war period: students had tutorials where they ploughed through the *Principles*, others remember lectures derived from the *Principles* and working through it in preparation for exams, and some even read the *Principles* during the long (or summer) holiday (see Lee 1993). In addition, in the 1928–1929 academic year, D.H. Macgregor gave lectures based on the *Principles*. As the prescribed books required students to undertake a historical survey of the classical economists, many tutors, such as Robert Hall, who accepted Marshall's continuity thesis (or the non-marginal revolution thesis), directed such surveys so that they would inexorably lead up to Marshall (see Lee 1993: 108). Finally, students were directed to read volumes from the Cambridge Economic Handbook series, including Hubert Henderson's *Supply and Demand* and Dennis Robertson's *Money* and *The Control of Industry*, as well as books and articles penned by John Maynard Keynes, A.C. Pigou, Cannan, Gustav Cassel and other non-Oxford economists which, at least in the 1920s, were thought to be compatible with Marshall. The basic point was that many components of Marshall's *Principles*, such as utility, marginal utility, supply and demand curves, scarcity, price elasticity of demand, quasi-rents, diminishing returns, increasing returns, economies of scale, real costs, marginal productivity and support for capitalism, were all part of the instruction at Oxford and hence part of Oxford economics.

With the influx of new fellows throughout the inter-war period, Oxford became populated by young economists who were not tied to the old ways of theorising and who were eager to arrive at 'practical maxims for economic policy' (Sayers quoted in Young and Lee 1993: 186) using marginalist tools. Much of this work was beyond Marshall's *Principles* and hence did not concern the theoretical core of his supply and demand analysis of prices. However, Oxford economists did reject Marshall's analysis of prices, his concept of the market supply curve and his representative firm. As early as 1924, Harrod had started formulating his ideas about the problems associated with supply curves, especially with regard to diminishing and increasing returns, a research agenda that eventually led to his publications on imperfect competition (see, in particular, Harrod 1931). However, Harrod was not of the view that he was dismissing Marshall's supply and demand analysis and his portrayal of the business enterprise, but was rather improving on them:

> The main doctrines of imperfect competition were worked out largely independently by myself and Joan Robinson … The main motive prompting me was to get nearer to reality. Orthodox theory had its monopoly theory and its theory of competition: the latter assumed an infinite number of producers working for a perfect market. This seemed so highly unrealistic that it seemed worth exploring what would happen if one made some intermediate assumption. No doubt any theory of this sort is only an abstract skeleton, a structure that will have to be revised in many particulars, only a very imperfect model of reality. But I do think it is an immense improvement on the old doctrine (Harrod 1936).

Of course, Harrod's 'improvements' *did* constitute a rejection of Marshall's analysis. It is clear that all the economists at Oxford, bar Macgregor, accepted the reformulation of supply and demand in marginalist terms and hence the models of perfect and imperfect competition and the equilibrium firm. For example, in his lectures on "Questions in Advanced Economic Theory" delivered in Trinity term 1935, Hall dealt with the determinacy of prices. Arthur Brown's notes of the lectures indicate that Hall drew liberally from Edward Chamberlin's *The Theory of Monopolistic Competition* and Robinson's *The Economics of Imperfect Competition*. Consequently, marginal cost and revenue, optimality, equilibrium, the individual firm, diagrams and mathematics were central to Hall's lectures; and what was entirely absent was any notion of a representative firm or any other Marshall-like industrial analysis. Later, Hall gave lectures on "Imperfect Competition" (Michaelmas term 1936) and "Competition, Imperfect Competition, and Monopoly" (Michaelmas term 1938), while Allen gave lectures on "Monopoly and Imperfect Competition" (Trinity term 1937). As noted above, Hall's lectures were viewed by Oxford students as being up-to-date and not old-fashioned. Oxford postgraduate students, such as Henry Smith, also fell under the influence of Chamberlin and Robinson and the use of geometry as a tool of analysis (see Smith 1992: 76).

The replacement of Marshall's mode of analysis of prices, price determination and the business enterprise with marginalism is best seen in the work of the Oxford Economists' Research Group. The events leading to the formation of the Group, its purpose and its research into pricing have been told at length elsewhere (see Young and Lee 1993: 128–136). What is important to emphasise is the theoretical role that Chamberlin, Robinson, Harrod and marginalism played in framing the Oxford economists' understanding and analysis of businessmen's responses to questions dealing with price determination. That is, the responses of businessmen with regard to prices and price determination could lend themselves to a theoretical interpretation that was distinct from marginalism, as with Philip Andrews' theory of normal-cost pricing. However, with the exception of Macgregor and Henderson, all members of the Group were confirmed marginalists and accepted the imperfect competition/monopolistic competition approaches to price determination. On the other hand, the feedback that they received from businessmen clearly indicated that the latter thought of prices in terms of some relationship to average total costs and totally ignored the marginalist approach to pricing. In fact, severe questioning by the Group failed to uncover any evidence that businessmen paid any attention to marginal revenue or costs and that they had only the vaguest ideas about anything remotely resembling price elasticities of demand. However, this did not prevent the framing of the responses and evidence in marginalist terms.

In November 1937, Hall read a paper to the group on "Notes on the Behaviour of Entrepreneurs During Trade Depression", which was an interpretative-theoretical analysis of the responses of businessmen. In particular, Hall argued:

> In my opinion, the most usual type of competition among the firms which we have been considering is a modified form of oligopolistic competition, the governing factor being the idea of what one of the entrepreneurs called a reasonable remuneration. Using very rough figures, I should say that in the absence of a cartel, competitors will not follow you if you raise your price above total average

cost plus a quantity of the order of 10%, so that over a reasonable period the individual demand curve is highly elastic for prices higher than this, or in Harrod's terminology becomes greater than this in the short period. But they are compelled to follow you if you lower your prices below this, because if they do not do so you will gradually get their trade, the individual demand curve again becoming highly elastic in a reasonable period. Thus each individual firm has a demand curve which is highly elastic (the more competitors the more elastic) above full cost plus normal profit, but with an elasticity similar to the market elasticity below this. (See Chamberlin, *Monopolistic Competition*, Chapter V, for analysis of this effect.) If this is so, then profit should be maximized by getting the price as high as you can persuade your competitors to put it unless there is an unusual degree of elasticity about the market. But receipts may well be maximized at a much lower price (Hall 1937: 4–5).

In a subsequent version of the paper, "The Business View of the Relation Between Price and Cost", which was presented at the 1938 meetings of the British Association for the Advancement of Science, Hall makes it even clearer that the marginalist approach framed the analysis of businessmen's responses:

[O]ur investigations throw some doubt upon the account of business behaviour usually given in textbooks on economics … The facts on which this paper is based may be stated briefly[:] many businessmen appear to base their prices on average or full cost irrespective of the state of the market, and many others think that this should be the normal procedure. According to economic theory, this would be the most profitable course only (a) in perfect competition when this price corresponded to the optimum output (b) in imperfect competition when marginal cost equalled marginal revenue at the point where price equalled average cost. Thus, it appears that the statement of economists about business behaviour is too simple (Hall 1938: 2–3).

This view was retained in the famous published version, "Price Theory and Business Behaviour" (Hall and Hitch 1939). So, from the beginning, Hall and Hitch's kinked demand curve was a marginalist response and explanation of why businessmen do not use marginal analysis when determining prices, which was the way it was seen at Oxford. What was missing from the discussion was any reference to Marshall and his representative firm. By 1939, then, Marshall's industrial analysis had no place in the theoretical thinking of Oxford economists (see Lee 1991: 489–497; Young and Lee 1993: 195–197).

4   PPE Economics During Wartime and Post-War

During the Second World War, the study and teaching of economics at Oxford, as with so many other subjects, were reduced significantly both by the drafting of prospective students into military service and by the movement of economics tutors into the military or government service. Among those economics tutors who went into the military or "war-work" were Allen, Fraser, Harrod, Hall, Hargreaves, Meade, Opie, Phelps-Brown, Robbins and Sayers (see Young and Lee 1993: 151). Balogh, for his part, remained in Oxford, teaching and working at the University's Institute of Economics and Statistics (see Streeten 2001: 28; see also the chapter in this volume on Balogh by Andrew Graham).

In the 1950s, most economics tutors concentrated on teaching only one of the three PPE components; prior to this, many had also taught politics. However, they had to teach all aspects of economics—theoretical, institutional and historical. Prior to the 1950s, PPE students were obliged to study all three component subjects for all three years of study. By the early 1950s, pressure increased to cut this to two areas of study after the first year, to enable the introduction of advanced topics in the third year of the degree. In conjunction, a graduate BPhil degree in Economics was introduced a few years earlier, in 1945, to provide a bridge leading to DPhil research. Now, while most non-philosophers at Oxford favoured the bipartite economics and politics PPE degree structure after the first year, the philosophers were powerful enough to ensure that Modern Greats, including philosophy, was tripartite, to parallel Greats, this being the case at least until 1971. Establishment of a single subject BPhil was thus an important development for economics. This was later transformed into the MPhil in Economics (see Chester 1986: 161–184).

The nature of tutorials, lectures and examinations in economics also changed in the post-war period. Tutorials were directly linked to lecture materials, and examinations consisted of three types of questions—essays, short answers and mathematical—rather than essay questions only. Recommended texts, once based on Marshall and other neoclassical materials for microeconomics and John Maynard Keynes and related materials for macroeconomics, changed to Hal Varian for microeconomics and Charles Jones for macroeconomics respectively.

5 Economics Tutors, Their Students and PPE's Influence in Post-War Britain

Twenty-eight British Prime Ministers have been Oxford graduates; three studied PPE: Harold Wilson, Edward Heath and David Cameron. In addition, economics tutors influenced a generation of Chancellors of the Exchequer and other senior British politicians from the 1930s onwards. Those who received the PPE degree between 1923 and 1939 reads like a Who's Who of modern British politicians, public servants and academics, along with prominent personalities of other nationalities (see Young and Lee 1993: 81–82). Moreover, in the post-war period, as many Rhodes Scholars opted for PPE (there were no Scholars appointed during 1940–1946), the result was an increasing number of leading US academics and others who were PPE-trained (see Schaeper and Schaeper 2010: chapter 9).

Regarding PPE economics tutors, the pre-war group had a significant post-war impact as follows. Robbins tutored Evan Durbin and Hugh Gaitskell; Harrod tutored Nigel Lawson; Hall tutored Anthony Crosland; Fraser, Opie and Allen tutored Wilson and Heath; and Balogh tutored Roy Jenkins. However, there are some qualifications to this influence. For example, in his first term at Oxford, Gaitskell went to Robbins for tutoring in elementary economics. Although Robbins was a critic of Labour, he 'enjoyed tutoring' the future leader of the Party (Howson 2011: 128, 131).

Jenkins wrote in his autobiography that Balogh 'was by far the best teacher I had', even if Balogh was shocked by the First Class degree that Jenkins obtained (see Jenkins 1991: 42–43). Jenkins went on to recall that while he was recruited 'as an economist' after the war to work for the British Industrial and Commercial Financial Corporation, he was 'a product of the Oxford PPE school with no…specialist training' in economics (ibid.: 60). That Jenkins decided to pursue PPE is not surprising since, as his biographer noted, the degree had been the 'course of choice for aspiring politicians' as early as the 1930s (Campbell 2014: 25). Opie tutored both Wilson and Heath. According to one Wilson biographer, Opie rated Wilson higher than Heath (see Ziegler 1993: 21), and indeed Wilson had a promising start to his career as an Oxford don. In the view of another of Wilson's biographers, if he had not been seconded into war work, later deciding to go into politics rather than academia, he might well have had a distinguished, albeit unorthodox, academic career, along the lines of Kaldor or Balogh, who later advised him as Prime Minister (see Smith 1964: 72). On the other hand, some tutors had a direct influence on the formation of their student's ideas. Reisman wrote in his study of

Crosland, who was tutored by Hall: 'It may have made a difference that Crosland was writing his Oxford essays on supply and demand for a Trinity tutor who, coincidentally, was himself a Labour Party man' at the time (Reisman 1997: 69). Crosland, in turn, tutored Anthony Wedgwood Benn in economics while at Oxford (see ibid.: 8).

Perhaps the most outstanding evidence in support of the influence of PPE in post-war Britain and up to the present is to be found in the February 2017 *Guardian* listing of just some of those who have studied the degree. The list includes former UK Prime Ministers; Deputy Prime Ministers, Chancellors, Foreign, Education, Health, Justice, Energy, and Work and Pensions Secretaries; UK Party Leaders; four non-UK Prime Ministers (two Australian, one Pakistan, one Myanmar); one US President; numerous economics and political journalists, columnists, editors and a media mogul. Whether or not this is a measure of the success of PPE economics per se is a moot point. It is, however, an indication of the success of PPE as founded, that is, as a degree designed, in the early 1920s, for the future leaders of Britain and the world.

References

Beckett, A. (2017). 'PPE: The Oxford Degree That Runs Britain'. *The Guardian*. 23 February. Available at: https://www.theguardian.com/education/2017/feb/23/ppe-oxford-university-degree-that-rules-britain.

Brennan, G., A. Hamlin and H. Kliemt (2010). 'PPE: An Appraisal'. *Politics, Philosophy & Economics*, 9(4): 363–365.

Briggs, A. (1991). 'Cerberus and the Sphinx: Modern Greats in Oxford'. Chapter 18 in A. Briggs, *Serious Pursuits: Communications & Education—Volume III, The Collected Essays of Asa Briggs*. Urbana and Chicago: University of Illinois Press: 320–326.

Campbell, J. (2014). *Roy Jenkins: A Well-Rounded Life*. London: Jonathan Cape.

Chester, N. (1986). *Economics, Politics and Social Studies in Oxford, 1900–85*. Basingstoke: Macmillan.

Cohen, N. (2014). 'How An Oxford Degree—PPE—Created a Robotic Governing Class'. *The Spectator*, 27 September. Available at: https://www.spectator.co.uk/article/how-an-oxford-degree-ppe-created-a-robotic-governing-class.

Currie, R. (1994). 'The Arts and Social Studies, 1914–1939'. Chapter 5 in B. Harrison (ed.) *The History of the University of Oxford: Volume VIII, The Twentieth Century*. Oxford: Clarendon Press: 109–138.

Department of Economics website, University of Oxford. Available at: https://www.economics.ox.ac.uk/undergraduate/b-a-hons-in-philosophy-politics-economics.

Foot, P. (1968). *The Politics of Harold Wilson*. Harmondsworth: Penguin.

Hall, R.L. (1937). 'Notes on the Behaviour of Entrepreneurs During Trade Depression'. P.W.S. Andrews Papers. London: London School of Economics.

Hall, R.L. (1938). 'The Business View of the Relation Between Price and Cost'. P.W.S. Andrews Papers. London: London School of Economics.

Hall, R.L. and C.J. Hitch (1939). 'Price Theory and Business Behaviour'. *Oxford Economic Papers*, 2(May): 12–45.

Handbook to the University of Oxford (1960). Oxford: Clarendon Press.

Harrod, R.F. (1931). 'The Law of Decreasing Costs'. *Economic Journal*, 41(164): 566–576.

Harrod, R.F. (1936). 'Letter to Hubert Henderson. 23 February 1936'. Hubert Henderson Papers. Nuffield College, University of Oxford.

Hicks, J.R. (1992). 'Biography of Sir John R. Hicks'. In A. Lindbeck (ed.) *Nobel Lectures in Economic Sciences 1969–1980*. Singapore: World Scientific: 132–134.

Howson, S. (2011). *Lionel Robbins*. Cambridge: Cambridge University Press.

Jenkins, R. (1991). *A Life at the Center: Memoirs of a Radical Reformer*. New York: Random House.

Kadish, A. (1982). *The Oxford Economists in the Late Nineteenth Century*. New York: Oxford University Press.

Kelly, J. (2010). 'Why Does PPE Rule Britain?'. *BBC News Magazine*. 1 September. Available at: https://www.bbc.co.uk/news/magazine-11136511.

Lee, F.S. (1981). 'The Oxford Challenge to Marshallian Supply and Demand: The History of the Oxford Economists' Research Group'. *Oxford Economic Papers*, New Series, 33(3): 339–351.

Lee, F.S. (1991). 'The History of the Oxford Challenge to Marginalism, 1934–1952'. *Banca Nazionale Del Lavoro Quarterly Review*, 44(179): 489–511.

Lee, F.S. (1993). 'Oxford Economics and Oxford Economists 1922–71: Recollections of Students and Economists'. Bodleian Archives and Manuscripts, University of Oxford: File MS. Eng. c 4819.

Moore, G.C.G. and M.V. White (2010). 'Placing William Forster Lloyd in Context'. In N.F.B. Allington and N.W. Thompson (eds) *Research in the History of Economic Thought and Methodology*. Volume 28(Part 2). Greenwich, CT: JAI Press: 109–141.

PPE website, University of Oxford. Available at: http://www.ox.ac.uk/admissions/undergraduate/courses-listing/philosophy-politics-and-economics.

Reisman, D. (1997). *Anthony Crosland: The Mixed Economy*. Basingstoke: Palgrave Macmillan.

Reisman, D. (2018). *James Edward Meade*. Basingstoke: Palgrave Macmillan.

Schaeper, T.J. and K. Schaeper (2010). *Rhodes Scholars, Oxford, and the Creation of an American Elite*. New York and Oxford: Berghahn Books.

Smith, H. (1992). *The Impersonal Autobiography of an Economist: How You Appear to Me*. Stroud, Gloucestershire: Sutton.

Smith, L. (1964). *Harold Wilson*. London: Fontana.

Streeten, P. (2001). 'Thomas Balogh'. In P. Arestis and M.C. Sawyer (eds). *A Biographical Dictionary of Dissenting Economists*. Second edition. Cheltenham: Edward Elgar: 28–35.

University of Oxford website. Available at: http://www.ox.ac.uk/admissions/undergraduate/student-life/exceptional-education/personalised-learning.

Whitaker, J.K. (ed.) (1975). *The Early Economic Writings of Alfred Marshall, 1867–1890*. Volume I. London: Palgrave Macmillan.

Young, W. and F.S. Lee (1993). *Oxford Economics and Oxford Economists*. London: Macmillan.

Ziegler, P. (1993). *Harold Wilson*. London: Weidenfeld & Nicolson.

6

The Oxford Institute of Statistics, 1935–1962

Jan Toporowski

1   An Uncertain Start[1]

The Institute of Statistics at the University of Oxford was established in 1935 with the appointment of the econometrician Jacob Marschak to a Lectureship in Statistics at All Souls College. In 1933, the Rockefeller Foundation had given the University a grant of $350,000 to create such an institute. The money was to be spent over the next seven years in establishing statistics teaching and research at Oxford. From the beginning, it was believed that 'it is undesirable to divorce the study of statistics and statistical method from the cognate study of Economic Theory and Organisation', and the appointment of Marschak as its first Director confirmed this orientation in the work of the Institute (Arena 2011: 110–111).

Marschak was an unusual choice for this position. He had been born in Kiev in 1898 and had participated as a Left Menshevik in the October Revolution, rising to the position of a Minister in the Caucasian Republic of Terek. Marschak left Russia in 1919, and went to Berlin, where he studied under Ladislaus von Bortkiewicz, and then under Emil Lederer in Heidelberg. He went on to work with Adolph Lowe at the Kiel Institute for the World Economy

[1] I wish to thank David Hendry and the Librarians of the Bodleian Library for assisting me with finding the papers of the Oxford Institute of Statistics. I am grateful to Robert Cord for directing me to other material on the history of the Institute. Any remaining errors are mine.

J. Toporowski (✉)
Department of Economics, SOAS University of London, London, UK
e-mail: jt29@soas.ac.uk

© The Author(s), under exclusive license to Springer Nature Switzerland AG 2021
R. A. Cord (ed.), *The Palgrave Companion to Oxford Economics*,
https://doi.org/10.1007/978-3-030-58471-9_6

(*Institut für Weltwirtschaft*). German economic theory was highly regarded at that time in Britain, and the Kiel Institute was an outstanding example of a new direction of research that had emerged in the economic and financial turbulence that followed the First World War, gathering economic data and interpreting it with a view to assisting business and government in decision-making and other strategies. Similar institutions had been established in France, Poland and even Russia. The one in Vienna, the *Institut für Konjunkturforschung* that had been established by Ludwig von Mises, was already world famous. A notable feature was that such institutes were not based in universities, but were supposed to be closer to business and government.

Apart from their service in providing information to business and government, the new research institutes reflected another trend in economic theory towards mathematical formalisation and the systematic creation of data on changes in the economy, in particular the business cycle. At the League of Nations, a British economist Alexander Loveday headed an Economic Intelligence Service that published important data on the changing economic fortunes of member countries.

Britain lagged behind Europe in this kind of research. John Maynard Keynes wrote on commodities and stocks for the London and Cambridge Economic Service that brought together contributions from the London School of Economics and Cambridge University (see Cord 2017). But national income estimates were not collected until the Second World War. In part, this was the outcome of a system of higher education that was organised around teaching undergraduates, in particular with the tutorial system in the ancient universities of Oxford and Cambridge where college fellowships were the prize for postgraduate research, rather than the doctorates that had recently been introduced to bring British academic standards up to the level of German universities. When Michał Kalecki's Rockefeller Fellowship expired in 1937, his friends in Cambridge found only a handful of university departments where research in economics was being conducted (see Toporowski 2013: 111).[2]

The Oxford Institute of Statistics was supposed to remedy this, at least for the University of Oxford. However, it seems to have had difficulty in getting itself started. The possible explanations for this range from the personal to the institutional. Among the latter was the alternative focus of research in economics at Oxford provided by Hubert Henderson at All Souls College.

---

[2] Keynes eventually obtained a scholarship for Kalecki at Cambridge to tide him over through 1938, after which Kalecki was transferred to the payroll of the National Institute of Economic and Social Research, which had been set up with a grant from the British Treasury in 1938.

Henderson had assisted with the establishment of the Institute of Statistics. But he also had his own research agenda. He brought together a group of the younger, most research-ambitious economists at Oxford to enquire into prices and interest by means of interviews with businessmen. Henderson's collaborators included Maurice Allen, Eric L. Hargreaves, Frank A Burchardt, Marian Bowley, P.W.S. Andrews, Arthur J. Brown, George Shackle, Roy Harrod, James Meade and others (see Besomi 1998). The relative size of their undertakings was reflected in the staff employed by the two research centres. Marschak wrote to Richard Kahn at Cambridge that at the Institute 'only 1½ of its researchers are paid…the rest are voluntary workers…[whereas] two men work under the "Economists' Research Group"' (Marschak quoted in Toporowski 2013: 112).

A possible personal factor in the slow start was Marschak's own insecurity, or at least his desire to be elsewhere. Having reached Berlin to escape the Russian Civil War, and then England to escape the Nazi takeover in Germany, Marschak was unwilling to test the limits of Germany's expansion, while in America even larger funds (from Rockefeller and the Cowles Commission) were available to beef up economics research with statistics. In December 1938, he left Oxford to go to the United States on a Rockefeller Travelling Scholarship. This left the Institute without a Director. Eventually, on 28 August 1939, two days before Germany's attack on Poland, Marschak resigned his position. However, he then changed his mind and four weeks later, on 26 September, asked for a further year's leave of absence. The Standing Committee of the Institute decided that no further leave would be granted, whereupon Marschak resigned for a second time (see Papers of the Oxford Institute of Statistics (hereafter OIS), University Archives, Bodleian Library: UR/SI/1, File 1).

2   The Wartime Institute

The outbreak of the war gave the Institute the boost that Marschak had failed to deliver. In the first instance, Henderson returned to London, where the government was building up a bureaucracy adequate to the economic and social demands of conflict, taking a number of his fellow researchers from the Oxford Economists' Research Group with him into official service. Second, wartime regulations placed restrictions on the movements and activities of "aliens" from hostile powers and occupied parts of Europe, residing in parts of eastern England, leading to a movement of foreign and refugee economists away from Cambridge. One arrival at the Oxford Institute in February 1940 was the Polish economist Michał Kalecki, followed in due course by other exiled economists keen to engage their professional skills in the war effort. On 31 July 1940, Oxford finally appointed a replacement for Marschak in the shape of Arthur Bowley, the retired Professor of Statistics from the London School of Economics. Bowley's appointment was only part-time, on the basis that he attended for work only four days a week, from Tuesdays to Fridays. He was responsible to a Standing Committee of the Institute that met monthly and usually included Sandie Lindsay, the Master of Balliol College, Bowley, G.D.H. Cole, David Macgregor (the Professor of Political Economy at Oxford) and Charles Hitch. Hitch had survived the call-up of economists to serve in the government because he was an American citizen and therefore exempt from service, that is until the United States entered the war in December 1941 (see OIS: UR/SI/1, File 1).

Kalecki and Bowley were joined at the Institute by a research assistant, the statistician John Leonard Nicholson. Other researchers employed were Thomas Balogh and David Worswick, while in February 1941 the Austrian economist, Josef Steindl, was transferred from Balliol College. They were joined from time to time by occasional researchers such as Kurt Rothschild, Frank Burchardt and Josef Goldmann. The staff of the Institute worked initially at the New Bodleian Library (now the Weston Library) at the bottom of Broad Street, Oxford. In September 1943, it was decided that the Institute should move to Balliol. The Institute by now had a small library, the first specialist economics library at the University, and Kalecki's wife, Adela, was appointed as a part-time librarian. Kalecki's pre-eminence was reflected in the fact that he was paid more than Bowley: In 1943, Kalecki's salary totalled £483, 6 shillings and 8 pence, while Bowley remained on a salary of £400 (see Minutes of the Meeting of the Standing Committee of the Oxford Institute of Statistics, 12 May 1944, OIS: UR/SI/1, File 2). To some extent, his generous salary reflected Kalecki's seniority as the dominant figure, 'the inspiration of the Institute' (Steindl 1984: 245; see also Worswick 1977).

Arguably, it was during the war years that the Institute enjoyed a peak in its activity and its professional standing. With little competition, since British experts were now mostly working for the government and subject to official secrecy requirements, the Institute became an important source of authoritative comment on economic policy and the financing of the war. The scarcity of independent and informed commentary on official economic policy increased still further the value of the articles that appeared in the Institute's monthly *Bulletin* which provided virtually the only regular critical comment on such policy. The consistency of the Institute's work was enhanced by its researchers' deference to the new economics of Kalecki.

Successive issues of the *Bulletin*, and then the collection (edited by Nicholson) of its most important articles, published in 1947 under the title *Studies in War Economics*, confirm the outstanding quality of the Institute's work and Kalecki's leading position among its researchers: His name appears more than that of any other author (see Oxford University Institute of Statistics 1947). The *Studies in War Economics* grouped the most important articles under the following headings: "Economic Mobilization and General Controls", including controls on money and foreign exchange; "War Finance", consisting mostly of Kalecki's comments on successive government budgets during the war, and the question of government debt; "Consumer's Rationing and Price Controls", of which four out of twelve articles were by Kalecki; "Wages and National Income", made up of four articles, of which three were written by Nicholson and one by Kalecki; "Consumption and Prices", of which three out of eight articles were by Goldmann; "Industrial Organisation", seven articles of which three were by Balogh and three by Worswick; and finally "War Contracts and Efficiency", with an article by Steindl, two by Kalecki and two by Worswick.

A notable absence from Nicholson's selection are a handful of papers discussing the plans put forward by Keynes and Harry Dexter White for clearing international payments after the war, and famously discussed at the Bretton Woods Conference in July 1944. On publication of the two plans, the Oxford Institute of Statistics put out a special Supplement of its *Bulletin* on "New Plans for International Trade", dated 7 August 1943. The introduction, "Lessons of the Past" by an anonymous "Editor" summarises precisely the way in which the Institute addressed its technical work to a wider public. The rationale for the Supplement was given as follows:

> The subject matter of international trade and finance is of a highly technical nature and discussions of these problems tend, therefore, to be confined to "experts", city circles and businessmen. It is, of course, appropriate that the efforts to come to a satisfactory plan should be left to the experts of the Allied Nations whenever technical details are concerned. It is important, however, that a wider circle than the mere experts should understand the general issues involved and help to shape the line along which agreement should be sought by the experts. For, although questions of social security and full employment would appear to affect the life of the average citizen more immediately and fundamentally, there can be no doubt that his welfare and standard of living will be greatly influenced by the sort of international order or disorder in the economic relations between States which will emerge after the war ("Lessons of the Past" 1943: 3).

The Supplement represented contributions from members of the Joint Committee of Nuffield College and the Oxford Institute of Statistics. The longest contribution was an article by Ernst ("Fritz") Schumacher summarising the key mechanisms of the plans proposed by Keynes and White (see Schumacher 1943a). As the author of an earlier paper on multilateral clearing (Schumacher 1943b), he was well qualified to summarise Keynes's and White's proposals.[3] Schumacher considered that both plans were inadequate to provide the liquidity necessary to maintain multilateralism and this brought with it the danger that individual governments would revert to rationing foreign exchange or bilateralism, that is, settlements between central banks on a net basis, which would impart deflationary pressure throughout the world. In another paper, written with Kalecki, Schumacher put forward a plan to remedy the defects in both the Keynes and White plans to make them more supportive of development efforts in the less industrialised countries, and more supportive of industrial countries, like the UK, that found themselves with chronic deficits (Kalecki and Schumacher 1943). The third contributor was Balogh, who pointed out how deflationary forces may emerge where governments are less concerned with full employment and more concerned with balanced trade (see Balogh 1943). The Bretton Woods Agreement provoked a further article by Schumacher and Balogh, criticising the absence of adequate reserve provisions and therefore the inevitable continuation of wartime controls after the conflict had ended (see Schumacher and Balogh 1944). Balogh's criticisms were a particular source of annoyance to Keynes, who was responsible for British policy at the Conference (see Skidelsky 2000: 445).

3   Aliens Exposed

A reader looking just at the publications of the Institute might be forgiven for thinking that it provided a congenial intellectual milieu for its researchers to do applied work using statistics to verify trends in economic activity. As usual, this reflects the less visible nature of the vexations that emerged with the war. Among those working at the Institute was the industrial economist P.W.S. Andrews. According to a note by Kalecki, Andrews was working on a

---

[3] Schumacher had been a German Rhodes Scholar at Oxford, but ended up as an agricultural labourer working on the farm of Robert Brand, the Managing Director of Lazard Brothers, who was, with Keynes, one of the British delegations to the Bretton Woods Conference. In 1941, Brand passed on to Keynes a memorandum written by his farm labourer entitled "Some Aspects of Post-War Economic Planning" (see Keynes 1980: 21). Schumacher later became better known, of course, for his volume *Small Is Beautiful*, where he supported the greater use of intermediate (or appropriate) technology.

study examining changes in the stocks of consumption goods (Kalecki 1941). However, it seems that Andrews was a conscientious objector (personal communication from John King; see also King 1988: 190). This may explain why, after a brief note on rationing in the fourth issue of the Institute's *Bulletin* in 1940 (Andrews 1940), no further articles appear in Andrews' name, and there are no articles by him in *Studies in War Economics*. In the late 1940s, Andrews resumed his publishing.

Relations with government and the rest of the University were not helped by the concentration in the Institute of so many foreign researchers with distinctly left-wing political views. They had an ally on the Standing Committee in the form of G.D.H. Cole, Reader in Economics at University College and recently appointed the Sub-Warden of the newly founded Nuffield College. In 1941, Cole put forward the idea of a Social Reconstruction Survey. The Survey was to enquire into social conditions and shifts of population in various regions and industries in Britain as a result of the war. It was established with funding from the Treasury at the newly founded Nuffield College that was then still looking for premises. Andrews was appointed Chief Statistician to the Survey.

Cole's reputation as a radical socialist did not endear him to the man who was paying for the College, the industrialist Lord Nuffield, a man of strongly conservative views. Anxieties about the political direction of the Survey were supposed to be allayed by having it managed by a Joint Committee consisting of representatives of Nuffield College, the Royal Institute of International Affairs (Chatham House) and the Oxford Institute of Statistics. However, opposition to Cole's influence continued in the Hebdomadal Council that governs the University of Oxford. In the summer of 1943, that opposition hardened and it was proposed that the Survey should be transferred to the Oxford Institute of Statistics, whose then Director, Bowley, was appointed to a small committee to investigate the academic value of the Survey ("Introduction" to Papers of the Nuffield College Social Reconstruction Survey).

It was in this context of political and institutional rivalry over the Survey that, on 9 April 1943, J.D. Denniston, a Classics Fellow at Hertford College, wrote to Sir Douglas Veale, the Registrar of the University of Oxford, concerning the confidentiality of the material being received by the Survey, in view of the proximity of the Survey to the Institute of Statistics where so many "aliens", the peculiar term then used by the British for foreigners in the United Kingdom, were working.

Denniston's letter must have been of some importance because Veale referred the matter immediately to Bowley. A handwritten note by Bowley to

Veale, dated 13 April 1943, (OIS: UR6/CQ/SI/, File 1, Part 2) lists two British citizens as working for the Institute, Worswick and Nicholson, fourteen aliens with names and ages and two naturalised aliens, that is, foreigners with British citizenship, Balogh, formerly Hungarian, and M.J. Elsas, a German refugee. Bowley noted that 'in fact no Govt. Department is directly concerned with the Institute, but its Bulletin is circulated and there are occasional enquiries'. On the following day, Veale wrote to Denniston to reassure him that the aliens at the Institute were strictly controlled in their access to confidential government material. In fact, such material was handled by an employee of Chatham House which, together with Nuffield and the Institute, participated in the Joint Committee managing the Survey. Veale attached a "List of Aliens" employed by the Institute. This contained the two naturalised aliens, Balogh and Elsas, seven Germans (including Burchardt and Schumacher), two Austrians (including Steindl), three Czechs (including Goldmann), two Poles (Kalecki and Herbert Frankel, who was called up for military service in November), along with a Mrs Miller who was German-born but British by marriage. The Germans and the Austrians were of course "enemy aliens" two of whom, Rothschild and Steindl, had recently been released from internment (Veale to Denniston, 14 April 1943, OIS: UR6/CQ/SI/, File 1, Part 2). Shortly afterwards, however, the work of the Survey was wound down, its remaining research transferred to the Institute.

4   The Transition to Peace

Bowley retired at the end of 1944 and was replaced by Hubert Henderson as Acting Director of the Institute until a new person was appointed. The Institute needed to secure funding for its research and required a Director who could attract such funding, as well as taking up the position of what was now a Readership in Statistics at All Souls, with the obligation to lecture on statistics. Kalecki harboured hopes of succeeding Bowley (see Osiatyński 1997: 483). However, despite the pre-eminence of his research and policy analysis, and his ingenuity in handling data, Kalecki was a diffident teacher and his personal interests lay in pure mathematics rather than in statistical theory (see Toporowski 2018: 137–138).

The upgrade of the All Souls position to a Readership had been reported to the Standing Committee at its meeting on 12 May 1944. But there were plans now for an even more ambitious appointment. On 1 June, Douglas Veale revealed a proposal in the University to turn the Readership into a full Professorship. He reported that the Vice-Chancellor of the University, Sir

Richard Livingstone, wanted R.A. Fisher, the Galton Professor of Eugenics at University College London and a specialist in biological statistics, to be considered for the position, together with Udny Yule, who lectured in statistics at Cambridge. Henry Clay, economic adviser to the Bank of England, and shortly to be appointed Warden of Nuffield College, recommended Harry Campion, the head of the Central Statistical Office. Other names put forward were Alexander Aitken, Reader in Statistics at Edinburgh University and inventor of the generalised least squares method of statistical estimation, and Egon Pearson, Reader in Statistics at University College London (see OIS: UR6/CQ/SI/, File 1, Part 2).

Pearson did not apply, but was drafted onto a Board of Electors (selection committee) that included Keynes, who excused himself from its meetings because he was out of the country at Bretton Woods, Sir Harold Butler, the Warden of Nuffield College, Sir William Beveridge, the Master of University College, D.H. Macgregor, the Drummond Professor of Political Economy at All Souls College, William Adams, the Warden of All Souls and Livingstone. On 2 September 1944, they agreed to advertise in *The Times*, *The Times Educational Supplement* and *The Economist* for a 'Reader who will also act as Director of the Institute of Statistics' to start from 1 January 1945, with a combined salary of £1,000. Applicants included David Champernowne, then working at the Ministry of Aircraft Production, and Donald MacDougall (see ibid.).

On 20 October 1944, Veale wrote to Bowley to inform him that the Rockefeller Foundation had offered a grant to cover the expenses of the Institute for two years but would then cease further funding. This made more urgent the need to appoint a Director able to secure funding after 1947. Four days later, the Master of Balliol, Sandie Lindsay, wrote to Beveridge to inform him that Roy Allen had dropped out of the competition, and that the shortlist comprised Maurice Bartlett, formerly at Cambridge, now working for the Ministry of Supply, Champernowne, and Edmund Rhodes, Reader in Statistics at the London School of Economics. Maurice Kendall, a distinguished statistical theorist then working for the British Chamber of Shipping, and Harry Campion were still being sounded out in informal discussions. On 24 October, Lindsay wrote to Beveridge that:

> There seems to be a definite view that Champernowne has not the qualities suitable for the head of an institution, that Rhodes is not inspiring, and that Bartlett is probably the best of the three, but not interested in the economic side. I hope you think you have taken the right course (Lindsay to Beveridge, OIS: UR6/CQ/SI/, File 1, Part 2).

In the event, Kendall pulled out. A.C. Pigou from Cambridge and James Meade at the War Cabinet sent in references for Champernowne stating that he was an excellent statistician, but with reservations about his administrative ability. Bowley went further. He declared Champernowne a brilliant mathematician and indicated that Keynes thought highly of his aptitude for economics. Following this, on 18 November, Champernowne was appointed to the position of Reader in Statistics and Director of the Oxford Institute of Statistics.

David Champernowne fitted Oxford perfectly. His father had been Bursar of Keble College. Already before the war, Champernowne had made original contributions to mathematics and statistical theory. He had excellent connections in the government, which were nurtured in wartime. In 1948, Champernowne was appointed Professor of Statistical Economics at Oxford. His main interests were more in statistical theory and the application of statistics to economic theory, rather than in the analysis of economic data and policy. These interests now set the direction for the work of the Institute, a process that was accelerated by the departure of Kalecki and most of the other émigrés, technological progress with more powerful data processing, and political conditions that favoured the technical over the political.

Not all the work of the Institute was concerned with statistical theory. In 1945, it provided a new focus for research with the start of a series of monographs put out by the Oxford publisher Basil Blackwell. The first of these was a study of the financing conditions of firms by Joseph Steindl called *Small and Big Business: Economic Problems of the Size of Firms* (Steindl 1945). Steindl had been recruited in 1943 to undertake an investigation of firm size financed by the textile industrialist Samuel Courtauld, a Visiting Fellow at Nuffield. With the publication of Steindl's monograph, Champernowne introduced the series with a short statement offering

an outlet for research results too long for journals but too short to form a complete book. They are intended to present work of outstanding interest, sometimes even when it is still incompletely developed, in the hope that its early publication will suggest and stimulate research on related subjects and will provoke critical discussion. The monographs will be published at irregular intervals and will deal with problems in applied economics and statistics (Champernowne 1945: ii).

It was another two years before the next monograph appeared in the form of *The Industrialisation of Backward Areas*, by Kurt Mandelbaum (Mandelbaum 1947) and a further five years before the third monograph emerged, K.G.J.C. Knowles's *Strikes: A Study in Industrial Conflict* (Knowles 1952).

Knowles's study covered industrial disputes up to 1947, suggesting delays in the publication process. Steindl's classic, *Maturity and Stagnation in American Capitalism*, also appeared in 1952 (Steindl 1952). Steindl's introduction thanks Miss B.M. Gisborne for reading and correcting proofs. It is dated "Summer 1949". In 1949, Steindl had left Oxford and returned to Vienna. Monographs continued to emerge occasionally. Klein's important *An Econometric Model of the United Kingdom* appeared in 1961 (Klein et al. 1961). Klein had arrived in Oxford in 1954 as a refugee from McCarthyism, staying for four years before returning to the United States to join the Department of Economics at the University of Pennsylvania.

Champernowne served as Director of the Institute from 1945 to 1948, with Frank Burchardt taking over the role in January 1949. Thereafter, the Institute's research depended very much on the enthusiasm and projects brought to it by particular individuals, such as Klein (see Chester 1986: 160). The Institute was then housed in a variety of locations in Oxford, before moving into a new building in 1964, having been renamed the Institute of Economics and Statistics in 1962. With that, the Institute finally succeeded in establishing statistics at Oxford as the legitimate vehicle for economic research, putting behind it the struggle for a new economics for a better society that was the common goal of its wartime researchers.

References

Andrews, P.W.S. (1940). 'Food Rationing and the Present Emergency'. *Bulletin of the Oxford Institute of Statistics*, 2(1): 2–6.

Arena, L. (2011). *From Economics of the Firm to Business Studies at Oxford: An Intellectual History (1890s-1990s)*. DPhil thesis, University of Oxford. Available at: https://tel.archives-ouvertes.fr/tel-00721620/document.

Balogh, T. (1943). 'The Foreign Balance and Full Employment'. *Bulletin of the Oxford Institute of Statistics*, 5(Supplement No. 5): 33–39.

Besomi, D. (1998). 'Roy Harrod and the Oxford Economists' Research Group's Inquiry on Prices and Interest, 1936–39'. *Oxford Economic Papers*, 50(4): 534–562.

Champernowne, D.G. (1945). 'Monograph Series of the Oxford University Institute of Statistics'. In *Small and Big Business: Economic Problems of the Size of Firms*, by J. Steindl. Institute of Statistics, Monograph No. 1. Oxford: Basil Blackwell.

Chester, N. (1986) *Economics, Politics and Social Studies in Oxford, 1900–85*. Basingstoke: Macmillan.

Cord, R.A. (2017). 'The London and Cambridge Economic Service: History and Contributions'. *Cambridge Journal of Economics*, 41(1): 307–326.

Kalecki, M. (1941). 'Changes in Stocks of Commodities'. *Bulletin of the Oxford Institute of Statistics*, 3(15): 335–338.

Kalecki, M. and E.F. Schumacher (1943). 'International Clearing and Long-Term Lending'. *Bulletin of the Oxford Institute of Statistics*, 5(Supplement No. 5): 29–33.

Keynes, J.M. (1980). *Activities 1940–1944, Shaping the Post-War World: The Clearing Union*. Volume XXV of *The Collected Writings of John Maynard Keynes*. London: Macmillan.

King J.E. (1988). 'P.W.S. Andrews (1914–1971)'. Chapter 9 in *Economic Exiles*, by J.E. King. Basingstoke: Macmillan: 187–211.

Klein, L.R., R.J. Ball, A. Hazlewood and P. Vandome (1961). *An Econometric Model of the United Kingdom*. Institute of Statistics, Monograph No. 6. Oxford: Basil Blackwell.

Knowles, K.G.J.C. (1952). *Strikes: A Study in Industrial Conflict, with Special Reference to British Experience Between 1911 and 1947*. Institute of Statistics, Monograph No. 3. Oxford: Basil Blackwell.

'Lessons of the Past' (1943). *Bulletin of the Oxford Institute of Statistics*, 5(Supplement No. 5): 3–8.

Mandelbaum, K. (1947). *The Industrialisation of Backward Areas*. Institute of Statistics, Monograph No. 2. Oxford: Basil Blackwell.

Osiatyński, J. (1997). 'Editorial Notes'. In J. Osiatyński (ed.) *Collected Works of Michał Kalecki: Volume VII. Studies in Applied Economics 1940–1967 Miscellanea*. Oxford: Clarendon Press: 479–585.

Oxford University Institute of Statistics (1947). *Studies in War Economics*. Oxford: Basil Blackwell.

Papers of the Nuffield College Social Reconstruction Survey. Available at: https://www.nuffield.ox.ac.uk/media/2223/ncsrs.pdf.

Schumacher, E.F. (1943a). 'The New Currency Plans'. *Bulletin of the Oxford Institute of Statistics*, 5(Supplement No. 5): 8–29.

Schumacher, E.F. (1943b). 'Multilateral Clearing'. *Economica*, New Series, 10(38): 150–165.

Schumacher, E.F. and T. Balogh (1944). 'An International Monetary Fund'. *Bulletin of the Oxford Institute of Statistics*, 6(6): 81–93.

Skidelsky, R. (2000). *John Maynard Keynes, Volume Three: Fighting for Freedom, 1937–1946*. New York: Viking.

Steindl, J. (1945). *Small and Big Business: Economic Problems of the Size of Firms*. Institute of Statistics, Monograph No. 1. Oxford: Basil Blackwell.

Steindl, J. (1952). *Maturity and Stagnation in American Capitalism*. Institute of Statistics, Monograph No. 4. Oxford: Basil Blackwell.

Steindl, J. (1984). 'Reflections on the Present State of Economics'. *Banca Nazionale del Lavoro Quarterly Review*, 37(148): 3–14. Reprinted as Chapter 18 in J. Steindl (1990) *Economic Papers 1941–88*. Basingstoke: Macmillan: 241–252.

Toporowski, J. (2013). *Michał Kalecki: An Intellectual Biography, Volume I, Rendezvous in Cambridge 1899–1939*. Basingstoke: Palgrave.

Toporowski, J. (2018). *Michał Kalecki: An Intellectual Biography, Volume II, By Intellect Alone 1939–1970*. Basingstoke: Palgrave.

Worswick, G.D.N. (1977). 'Kalecki at Oxford, 1940–44'. *Oxford Bulletin of Economics and Statistics (Special Issue): Michał Kalecki Memorial Lectures*, 39(1): 19–29.

Part II

Some Oxford Economists

7

Nassau Senior (1790–1864)

John Vint

1   Introduction

Nassau William Senior was born in Compton Beauchamp in Berkshire on 26 September 1790, the firstborn child of the Reverend John Raven Senior (1764–1824), the son of a merchant trading overseas, and his wife, Mary, daughter of Henry Duke, solicitor-general of Barbados. Senior's father was the vicar of Durnford and the first name Nassau was given to the child in remembrance of his grandfather Nassau Thomas Senior. The greater part of his childhood was spent in the village of Uffington in the Vale of the White Horse in Berkshire. He was educated at home by his father who had graduated at Merton College, Oxford, in 1785 and from whom, according to Leslie Stephen in the *Dictionary of National Biography*, he 'imbibed a permanent love of classical literature' (Stephen 1897: 246). Senior's grandfather was a wealthy man who owned Baldrick's and Pool's plantations in Barbados as well as significant cash, bonds and other securities. He died in 1786 and his widow Frances Senior passed away a month before her grandson was born. Nassau Senior's parents inherited the entire fortune.

Senior entered Eton College at the age of twelve in May 1803. His tutor was John Bird Sumner, a future Archbishop of Canterbury, who at the time

J. Vint (✉)
Manchester, UK
e-mail: j.vint@mmu.ac.uk

© The Author(s), under exclusive license to Springer Nature Switzerland AG 2021
R. A. Cord (ed.), *The Palgrave Companion to Oxford Economics*,
https://doi.org/10.1007/978-3-030-58471-9_7

was only twenty-three. Later in life, he served with Senior on the Poor Law Commission. Senior did not distinguish himself initially at Eton but was triumphant at the age of sixteen when he defeated more than thirty candidates to be elected to a demyship at Magdalen College, Oxford. A demyship was an undergraduate fellowship which provided free education and living facilities but which also carried with it a number of duties and restrictions relating to the wearing of academic dress, attendance at chapel and limits on theatre attendance. The curriculum at Magdalen in those days was based almost exclusively on the classical languages, theology and a little ancient and modern geography. In his final examination in Spring 1811, Senior passed in Classics but failed in Theology and he then had six months in which to repair the damage by retaking the examination. He was introduced to Richard Whately, a Fellow at Oriel College, who agreed to become his tutor. Whately records his pupil as working assiduously from morning to night for the whole period before the examination. The result was that Senior was awarded First Class Honours in Classics which, after the demyship, was the second victory in his young career. The third, perhaps, was that Senior and Whately became firm friends for more than half a century.

In the following sections, I discuss Senior's career in conveyancing; his two periods as Drummond Professor at Oxford; his contributions to economic theory; some of his key papers in the run up to the period of Poor Law reform; his work on the Poor Law in England from 1832; his contributions to the Irish Poor Law and famine debates; his controversial papers on combinations, hand-loom weavers and factory legislation; his arguments in favour of education reform; a review of his opinion on the role of government; and a conclusion.

2   An Affluent Conveyancer

While he was still an undergraduate, Senior decided to follow in his grandfather's footsteps and take up the law as a profession; as part of this, he was admitted as a member of Lincoln's Inn in 1810. After graduation in 1812, Senior moved into lodgings in Bedford Square, London, although he was required to reside for part of the time in Oxford in order to meet MA requirements. Planning to practice in the Court of Chancery, Senior began to study the law of conveyancing and property. Conveyancers were principally concerned with the drawing up of deeds and mortgages, and in the conveyancing of estates. This was a very profitable branch of the law which usually involved searching for estates to purchase and the organisation and management of any related transactions. Senior's father arranged a pupillage with an eminent conveyancer, Edward Sugden of Lincoln's Inn (later Lord Chancellor), and at the end of 1813, Senior became embroiled with the laws and practices of his planned profession. In the same year, he also won an Oxford scholarship in Law founded by Charles Viner in the middle of the eighteenth century. As a Vinerian Scholar, Senior was entitled to receive an income of £30 per annum for ten years and was obliged to attend the lectures on common law given by the Vinerian Professor William Blackstone, son of Sir William Blackstone, author of the famous book *Commentaries on the Laws of England* (see Levy 1943: 78).

As Senior's period of pupillage was drawing to a close in the middle of 1816, Sugden announced that he was planning to give up a substantial part of his conveyancing business to concentrate on chancery practice. Senior realised that an opportunity presented itself to take over some of Sugden's business. He had not yet been called to the Bar but was able to become a certified conveyancer allowing him to practice. Much of Sugden's work was then divided between another pupil and Senior, who thereafter worked separately. Senior's business prospered and after two years provided him with £400 per year and links with three dozen attorneys. In June 1819, he was called to the Bar and in April 1821 felt prosperous enough to marry Mary Charlotte Mair. For the sake of his bride who disliked the sooty air in London the couple took a house in the then more countrified area and air of Kensington Square. From its windows, they could see William Cobbett working in his nursery gardens and James Mill was also a near neighbour.

Their son Nassau John was born in 1822 and their daughter Mary Charlotte Mair, nicknamed Minnie, was born in 1825. A few years later, Senior built a larger house at 13 Hyde Park Gate where they entertained a variety of friends and colleagues from home and abroad from 1827 until 1863. Mary was moved by the later destruction of the house to 'write down some recollections of the society once gathered within its walls' (Simpson 1898: vii). Malthus was 'a great deal in the house' and she recalled John Stuart Mill striding up and down the dining room 'talking energetically in his calm, measured tones' (ibid.: 8–10).

In 1833, a young man arrived at Senior's chambers unexpectedly and introduced himself as Alexis de Tocqueville, declaring that he would like to make his acquaintance. Despite the fact that they had never met before and that Tocqueville was at that time unknown, Senior took to the young man and they began a long friendship, with mutual visits and an extensive correspondence on economics, politics, international relations and a wide range of other topics which lasted for twenty-five years.

In 1836, Senior reached the height of his profession by being made a Master in Chancery by the Prime Minister Lord Melbourne. The post carried an annual salary of £2,500 (over £300,000 in today's terms). There were a dozen or so masters and one of their tasks, taken in turn, was to assist the Lord Chancellor who presided over the House of Lords.

3   Professor of Political Economy at the University of Oxford

Leon Levy maintains that the impression of one of Nassau's earliest friends in the legal profession was that he began the study of political economy at Oxford (Levy 1943: 76). According to an obituary notice in *The Cornhill Magazine*, Senior had said to his daughter that he was about twenty-five when he determined that he would 'reform the condition of the poor in England' (Thackeray 1864: 253–256). During his pupillage, Senior made a number of friendships with distinguished people in London and had also been introduced to Whately's associates and friends at Oriel College. In 1815, Whately succeeded in publishing his first article on Jane Austen's novels in the October issue of the *Quarterly Review*. Perhaps driven to emulate his close friend, Senior also published *his* first article on the early novels of Sir Walter Scott in the same journal in January 1817. He continued to write and publish essays on fiction in various literary journals until the late 1850s (Senior 1864).

Soon after being called to the Bar, Senior resolved to remain as a conveyancer rather than seek his fortune as an attorney; this would also free him to pursue work in other fields such as politics or literature (see Levy 1970: 96). Having already made a connection with the *Quarterly Review*, he now joined its staff as a reviewer and contributed five articles between July 1821 and July 1822. One of these was his first article on political economy—a review of the Corn Laws and agricultural distress which appeared in the *Quarterly Review* in 1821. Levy (ibid.: 110) maintains that there is no doubt that it was this article which persuaded James Mill to recommend Senior as a member of the newly established Political Economy Club, to which he was elected unanimously in February 1823. The following year he was one of the early members of the Athenaeum Club, a private members' club in London.

In 1825, Senior was elected to the Drummond Chair of Political Economy at the University of Oxford. This was the first professorship in political economy in the country and the first time that the subject had been given recognition as part of the curriculum of an English university. Senior was a strong candidate for the professorship. His publications in the *Quarterly Review* and membership of the Political Economy Club plus his support from important Oxford figures—including Whately at Oriel and Martin Routh, the long-serving President of Magdalen College—were significant. Moreover, statutory requirements relating to Oxford degrees and residence disqualified most recognised economists of the time, such as Malthus, Torrens, James Mill, McCulloch and Tooke. Given the speed of events, it was not until 1827 that Senior had prepared enough material to begin lecturing. Nevertheless, he found time to write an article on "Some Ambiguous Terms Used in Political Economy" (Senior 1826), which was added to the appendix to Whately's *Elements of Logic*, published in *Encyclopedia Metropolitana* in 1826. The article contained 'the germs of Senior's theory of interest and capital formation' (Levy 1943: 112–113).

Senior was required to give at least nine lectures in every course and he offered four courses between 1826 and 1830.[1] The other requirement under the founder's terms was the publication of one lecture per year, but Senior managed to publish twelve in all during the period of his professorship. They were: *An Introductory Lecture on Political Economy* (Senior 1827); *Three Lectures on the Transmission of the Precious Metals from Country to Country* (Senior 1828a); *Two Lectures on Population* (Senior 1829); *Three Lectures on the Rate of Wages* (Senior 1830a); and *Three Lectures on the Cost of Obtaining Money* (Senior 1830b). Senior also delivered *Three Lectures on the Value of Money* at Oxford University in 1829 which were published later (Senior 1840). Levy argued that these lectures increased Senior's reputation not only among economists but also among wealthy clients which, in turn, enhanced his increasingly profitable conveyancing business especially in connection with large estates (see ibid.: 123). Senior's *An Outline of the Science of Political Economy*, which was based on lectures he delivered from 1827 to 1830, was published in 1836.

From 1830 until the mid-1840s, Senior was actively at work on social and economic policy issues, including advising governments, chairing commissions and preparing reports. In 1840, he was appointed Examiner in Political Economy at the recently established University of London, and in 1847 was appointed as Examiner in Law at the same institution. The Political Economy post he held until 1857 and that in Law until 1860. In 1846, Senior became dissatisfied with his literary output which consisted of reports, pamphlets or other physically small contributions. 'I want to put my name to a book', he wrote to the editor of the *Edinburgh Review*, Macvey Napier, on the 18 August, writing to him again on 27 January 1847 that:

> I feel that in writing on so many subjects I have in some measure wasted my opportunities and that if I were now to die I should leave behind me only

---

[1] See Bowley (1937: 341–343) for full details of Senior's lectures offered from 1826 to 1830.

scattered fragments and no great book. I have resolved therefore to write my "great book" which must be on Political Economy, as quickly as possible (Senior quoted in Levy 1970: 154).

Sadly, the 'great book' was not to be—for a number of reasons. First of all, Senior wrote ten articles for the *Edinburgh Review* between 1848 and 1852, including a long review of both Mill's *Essays on Some Unsettled Questions of Political Economy* and his *Principles of Political Economy* (Senior 1848a). Senior also wrote articles on foreign affairs for *The Economist*, which was established in 1843 (see Levy 1943: 279). He was responsible for the paper's news and views on foreign affairs under the first editor James Wilson (editor: 1843–1857) and for a time under the second editor Walter Bagehot (1859–1877).[2]

Second, the impact of Mill's *Principles* may have dampened Senior's spirit for his own venture. He summed up Mill's book at the end of his review: 'It is not an attempt to advance human knowledge in one direction, to be superseded hereafter by more comprehensive treatises. It is a magazine of truths and of precepts from which philosophers and statesmen will, for centuries to come, draw theory and practice' (Senior 1848a: 339).

By his own account, Senior could hardly follow that.

Third, he was once again elected to the Drummond Professorship for the period 1847–1852. This meant that he was committed to thirty-six university lectures.[3] In this second period at Oxford, he had an opportunity to review his position on the scope and method of economics.

Finally, towards the end of his tenure, events conspired to distract him. He became increasingly concerned and involved in the happenings in France. The overthrow of King Louis Philippe's government by republicans on 24 February 1848 led to an article in the *Edinburgh Review* in April entitled "The French Republicans" (Senior 1848b). For two weeks in May 1848, Senior visited colleagues in France, including Tocqueville and Horace Émile Say, son of Jean-Baptiste, and while he was there he began to take notes of things he both heard and saw. This was the beginning of a regular journal which continued through later travels until the end of his life. It is noteworthy that Senior made an extensive visit to France and Italy between October 1850 and the end of May 1851, and it was probably due to his anticipation of this period of absence that he resigned from the Political Economy Club in December 1849 (see Levy 1943: 311).

Meanwhile, events in France were developing further. Tocqueville wrote to Senior on 28 November 1851 saying that the present condition could only end

---

[2] For more details, see *The Economist 1843–1943: A Centenary Volume* (1943), especially the chapter written by Graham Hutton, "The Economist and Foreign Affairs" (Hutton 1943).

[3] See Bowley (1937: 343–344) for full details of Senior's lectures from 1847 to 1852.

by 'some great catastrophe'. Louis-Napoléon Bonaparte carried out a self-coup on 2 December, and news was flashed via the recently installed electric telegraph that a number of persons had been arrested, including Tocqueville. Senior rushed to Paris on 20 December and spent three weeks there visiting the now released Tocqueville and his family before returning home to wind up his final course of lectures. Not surprisingly, therefore, given these distractions, the final lecture course to be delivered between 1851 and 1852 fell somewhat by the wayside with only elements of material prepared (see ibid.: 314). Notwithstanding all these delays and pressures, Levy argued that there was evidence that Senior never gave up on his plan to publish his masterpiece and that he was still working on it just before his death (see Levy 1970: 159).

4 Senior on Theory

Senior's discussion of the fundamental premises in economics was the most significant difference between his treatment of method compared with his predecessors. They were first outlined in an *Introductory Lecture* delivered in Oxford in 1826 and published in 1827. The analysis comprised a definition of wealth and four fundamental propositions or postulates which can be summarised briefly as follows: 'Wealth consists of all those things, and of those things only which are transferable: which are limited in quantity; and which, directly or indirectly, produce pleasure or prevent pain'. The importance of this definition became evident immediately he stated the four fundamental propositions: (1) 'That every person is desirous to obtain, with as little sacrifice as possible, as much as possible of the articles of wealth'. (2) 'That the power of labour, and of the other instruments of production which produce wealth, may be indefinitely increased by using their products as the means of further production'. (3) 'That agricultural skill remaining the same, additional labour employed on the land within a given district produces a less proportionate return'. (4) 'That the population of a given district is limited only by moral or physical evil, or by deficiency in the means of obtaining those articles of wealth, or, in other words those necessaries, decencies, and luxuries, which the habits of each class of the inhabitants of that district lead them to require' (Senior 1827: 35–36). The first two propositions are based primarily on principles of human nature, and the last two on general empirical observation.

Senior's approach changed in his *Outline of the Science of Political Economy* which appeared in 1836. He then argued that economics should be restricted to the field of pure theory—the science which treats of the nature, the production and the distribution of wealth. The economist is not even allowed to offer advice but merely to state general economic principles to which the legislator may agree or ignore. In his *Four Introductory Lectures on Political Economy* of 1852, Senior once more returned to the question of scope and method. He now defined the science of political economy as 'the science which states the laws regulating the production and distribution of wealth, so far as they depend on the action of the human mind' (Senior 1852: 26). In addition to the science of economics, Senior also put forward a definition of the *art* of economics, 'which points out the institutions and habits most conducive to that production, accumulation, and distribution of wealth, which is most favourable to the happiness of mankind' (ibid.). However, he refused to accept that it was justifiable to discuss the art of economics and its implications as an economist. On the other hand, they could be discussed from the standpoint of a moralist or a statesman and he gave an example from the Poor Law:

> I shall think myself justified, for instance, in showing how the natural distribution of wealth may be affected by the institution of poor laws. And I shall not confine myself to their effects upon wealth. I shall consider how far a well-framed poor-law may promote the moral as well as the material welfare of the labouring classes, and an ill administered poor-law may produce moral, intellectual, and physical degradation. But these discussions must be considered as episodes. They form no part of the science which I profess. I shall enter into them, not as a political economist, but as a statesman or a moralist; and I shall expect from those who do me the honour of listening to them, not the full conviction which follows scientific reasoning, but the qualified assent which is given to the precepts of an art (ibid.: 55–56).

It is refreshing to be able to read the link between Senior's own personal assessment of his approach to economic theory and his real-world efforts on policy. It is also interesting to note that in his review of Mill's *Essays on Unsettled Questions* and the *Principles of Political Economy*, Senior points out that Mill seems to have been on a similar journey with regard to methodology: 'The four years which passed between the publication of the *Essays* and of the *Principles* seem to have somewhat modified Mr Mill's views. In the *Essays* political economy is a hypothetical science: in the *Principles* it is a positive art' (Senior 1848a: 304).

In 1860, the British Association for the Advancement of Science held its thirtieth annual meeting in Oxford. Senior delivered the Opening Address before Section F (Economic Science and Statistics) over which he presided (Senior 1860). He spoke on the scope of political economy and its relation to statistics and the art of government (see Levy 1943: 334).

Senior made a significant contribution to value theory. In the *Outline of the Science of Political Economy* (1836), he defined wealth has having three constituents: utility, limitation in supply and transferableness of which limitation in supply is most important. He argued that the desires of people aim not so much at quantity as at diversity and correctly outlined the principle of diminishing marginal utility, although he did this, somewhat confusingly, under the heading "Limitations in Supply":

> It is obvious, however, that our desires do not aim so much at quantity as at diversity. Not only are there limits to the pleasure which commodities of any given class can afford, but the pleasure diminishes in a rapidly increasing ratio long before those limits are reached. Two articles of the same kind will seldom afford twice the pleasure of one, and still less will ten give five times the pleasure of two. In proportion, therefore, as any article is abundant, the number of those who are provided with it, and do not wish, or wish but little, to increase their provision, is likely to be great; and, so far as they are concerned, the additional supply loses all, or nearly all, its utility. And in proportion to its scarcity the number of those who are in want of it, and the degree in which they want it, are likely to be increased; and its utility, or, in other words, the pleasure which the possession of a given quantity of it will afford, increases proportionally (Senior 1836: 11–12).

However, as O'Brien has argued, Senior did not take this further by, for example, using it to derive a demand curve or the notion of effectual demand in the Smithian sense (see O'Brien 2004: 118).

Senior is well known for his concept of abstinence. In his discussion of "Instruments of Production", he includes labour and natural agents (land, mines, forests, rivers, animals) as the primary productive powers. He also included abstinence as a third instrument of production: '[A] term by which we express the conduct of a person who either abstains from the unproductive use of what he can command, or designedly prefers the production of remote to that of immediate results' (Senior 1836: 58). He then went on to outline the links with the four fundamental propositions:

> It was to the effects of this Third Instrument of Production that we adverted, when we laid down, as the third of our elementary propositions, that *the Powers of Labour and of the other Instruments which produce Wealth may be indefinitely increased by using their Products as the means of further Production.* All our subsequent remarks on abstinence are a development and illustration of this proposition; we say development and illustration, because it can scarcely be said to require formal proof (Senior 1836: 58–59; italics in original).

Senior then argued that capital is the result of all three productive instruments combined: 'By the word Abstinence, we wish to express that agent, distinct from labour and the agency of nature, the concurrence of which is necessary to the existence of Capital, and which stands in the same relation to Profit as Labour does to Wages' (ibid.: 59).

Later in the *Outline*, he provided further clarification:

> Perhaps the best plan might appear to be, to apply the term wages to the remuneration of mere labour, the term interest to the remuneration of mere abstinence, and the term profit to the combination of wages and interest, to the remuneration of abstinence and labour combined. This would make it necessary to subdivide capitalists into two classes, the inactive and the active: the first receiving mere interest, the second obtaining profit (ibid.: 133).

Marian Bowley argued that Senior's introduction of the idea of abstinence had more influence on later theory than any of his other contributions. John Stuart Mill took up the idea presenting it in his *Principles* and thereby incorporating it more or less permanently in English capital theory (see Bowley 1937: 163).[4]

In 1830, Senior published *Three Lectures on the Rate of Wages* which comprised the lectures delivered at Oxford in the Easter term of that year together with a "Preface on the Causes and Remedies of the Present Disturbances". At the beginning of the "Preface", Senior briefly outlined the simple "wages fund doctrine" proposition 'that the *rate of wages depends on the extent of the fund for the maintenance of labourers, compared with the number of labourers to be maintained*' (Senior 1830: iii–iv; italics in original) The rest of the "Preface" examined the role of the Poor Law in the agricultural riots of 1830 which were protests against agricultural machinery and rural poverty mainly in southern and eastern England.

In the first chapter of *Three Lectures on the Rate of Wages*, Senior outlined his definitions of high and low wages and the factors that influence the level of wages. In chapters two and three, he went on to argue that the wages fund proposition is 'inconsistent with opinions which are entitled to consideration, some from the number and others from the authority of those who maintain them' (ibid.: 18–62). Examples of 'opinions' included matters such as the

---

[4] See Mill (1848 [1965]: 34, 37). However, Mill had argued differently in his notes on Senior's *Outline of the Science of Political Economy*: 'I question if abstinence can be called an agent or an instrument of production. Could not you call it a *condition*? And might not the word *saving* be used, not to supersede but occasionally to alternate with the term abstinence? Labour, natural agents, & *saving*. Besides, in order to employ productively what serves to feed me, I do not *abstain* from the enjoyment of it, I merely labour *while* I consume it' (Mill in Hayek 1945: 135; italics in original).

effects of the non-residence of landlords; the introduction of machinery; the impact of imports; the consequences of unproductive consumption; and the proposition later known as the 'demand for commodities is not demand for labour' (see Mill 1848 [1965]: 78–88). All of these opinions or examples involved two time periods and as such were *not* inconsistent with the wages fund doctrine. In fact, they were applications of the wages fund doctrine as it was often used in its two-period format. Mill presented a similar list in the *Principles* eighteen years later (see Vint 1994: 124–175).

Senior argued strongly against the Malthusian orthodoxy on population. In 1829, he published *Two Lectures on Population (To Which Is Added a Correspondence Between the Author and the Rev. T.R. Malthus)* (Senior 1829). The lectures were numbers seven and eight of the second lecture course delivered in Easter term at Oxford 1828. The first strand of Senior's argument in the lectures was that the desire of man to improve his position himself was at least as important as sexual desire. He was quite clear that this went against the prevailing orthodoxy. In a letter to Malthus of 15 March 1829, reproduced in the *Lectures*, Senior argued that Malthus's argument was opposed by the tendency of man to try to better himself.

The second strand in Senior's argument in the *Lectures* is that productivity in agriculture may increase with population and offset the tendency towards diminishing returns. Picking up the theme of his 15 March letter in another to Malthus dated 26 March 1829, Senior argued that when he said 'subsistence *has generally* increased in a greater ratio than population' (ibid.: 73; italics in original) he meant that looking back through the history of the world, and comparing the state of each country every two or three hundred years, one can see that there have been periods where subsistence has grown faster than population for a number of reasons, including mechanical inventions and improved modes of cultivation and transport. These periods may be followed by periods where population growth exceeds the growth of subsistence, but the 'retrogression would not be to the point at which food and population relatively stood before' (ibid.: 75). Thus, there may be a "ratchet effect" at work, leading to rising living standards over time.[5] None of these arguments were accepted by Malthus.

Why then did Senior adopt this "heretical" position? There was some empirical evidence. Thus, Barton argued in *An Inquiry into the Causes of the Progressive Depreciation of Agricultural Labour in Modern Times* that it was not

---

[5] Malthus's *An Essay on the Principle of Population* was discussed just after his death at the Political Economy Club in February 1835. At the meeting, Tooke, McCulloch and Torrens spoke along similar lines to Senior (see the entry for 1835 under "Diaries J.L. Mallet" in the *Political Economy Club Centenary Volume, 1821–1920* (1921): 265–266).

a rising birth rate but a falling death rate which was responsible for the increase in population (see Barton 1820: 40–43). More recently, Routh has noted that Malthusianism was a doctrine which was likely to 'enrage rather than subdue the rick-burning, machine-wrecking mobs that were beginning to terrify and terrorise farmers and manufacturers and against whom the agencies of law and order offered a very uncertain defence' (Routh 1989: 151).

The important point about Senior's views on population is that they went on to underpin his approach to the Poor Law and his role in and contribution to its reform.

5   Corn Laws, Poor Laws, the Wages Fund and Emigration

Senior's publications in the 1820s reveal the steady development of the intellectual ingredients of his later approach to economic and social policy. His first publication was a review of the first Report of the Select Committee on Agricultural Distress dated 14 June 1821. The article was published in the *Quarterly Review* (Senior 1821). The curtailment of imports during the Napoleonic Wars had led to a huge extension of tillage on increasingly less productive land with low yielding crops. There was widespread concern amongst landowners who had invested in these lands that with the cessation of hostilities they may have to compete with more bountiful harvests from overseas. As a result of very good Irish harvests in 1819 and 1820, prices dropped significantly and some farmers began to complain that their activities were no longer remunerative. Senior rejected Ricardo's premise that agriculture was taxed more highly than manufacturing and he was against permanent protection for the former. However, he was in favour of the introduction of a twelve-year period during which taxes would be gradually reduced thereby providing opportunities for capital to be withdrawn from the least productive land (see ibid.: 496–497). Senior also rejected Ricardo's claim that increases in the price of corn would equal the whole amount of the tax. He argued that the *immediate* effect of the tax would be to raise the corn price but claimed that its *ultimate* effect would be to diminish the consumption and production of raw produce leaving the price unaffected (Senior 1836: 122–123). Senior also disagreed with Ricardo's view that a rise in the corn price would mean that wages would inevitably rise. He argued that the wages of labour are determined by supply and demand and that the demand for labour would be reduced under the circumstances and it would be unlikely that wages would rise (see Levy 1970: 223).

In 1828, Senior, Whately and others established a new quarterly journal entitled *The London Review*, under the editorship of the Reverend Blanco White. Senior wrote an early article for the journal entitled "On the Corn Laws and the Poor Laws" (Senior 1828b; see also Levy 1970: 229–234).[6] In this article, Senior argued that with diminishing returns and an increasing population, labourers may have to resort to food of an inferior quality and ultimately to potatoes which support six times as many people per acre as corn. However, he argued that, for the present, the Poor Laws would keep that disaster at bay. While the Corn Laws continued, any alteration in the Poor Laws would be an injustice: 'To prohibit the poor man from purchasing his food at the cheapest market, and at the same time to take from him the subsistence to which he is by law entitled would excite, and would deserve to excite, an insurrection' (Senior in Levy 1970: 232).

He went on to argue that while the Poor Laws were useful in preventing the worst consequences of the Corn Laws, they did this at the high cost of weakening, and often destroying, 'the industry, the providence, the self-respect and the social affections of the labourer' (ibid.: 233). In addition, there are burdens on the farmers who have to support first, the aged and the infirm, second, the unemployed, and third, the making up of wages of those who are employed but are on wages insufficient for subsistence. Referring to the last group and using strong language, Senior argues that the 'evil began' (ibid.) when relief was given to the able-bodied. He also made the point that in addition to the Poor Laws acting as a brake on the consequences of the Corn Laws, they had often been suspended and that the importation of cattle and sheep which provided wool, hides, butter, cheese and so on had also assisted in delaying the impact of the laws. Notwithstanding this, Senior was pessimistic about the long run if the Corn Laws were not repealed. The possibility of a large population supported by the cheapest food available was 'perhaps the worst calamity to which a civilized community can be exposed' (ibid.: 232).

In the summer of 1830, there were widespread revolts in the southern counties of England, with the burning of corn ricks and mills and the destruction of machinery. Senior published *Three Lectures on the Rate of Wages* with a preface which examined the riots. He put the cause of these disturbances down to the Poor Laws which had changed the relationship between the labourer and his employer from an open bargain in which the labourer knows what his services are worth to one where the labourer is paid not according to his value but his wants. He then ceases to be a freeman and acquires the

---

[6] The substance of the article was contained in Senior's sixth lecture of the second lecture course delivered at Oxford in 1828.

'indolence, the improvidence, the rapacity, and the malignity but not the subordination of the slave' (Senior 1830: x–xi). Senior went on to analyse the riots in terms of the wages fund doctrine. The Poor Laws had encouraged idleness and inefficiency which reduced the wages fund; if the workers destroyed the corn ricks, they destroyed the fund for future wages. If they destroyed machinery, they destroyed the means by which their work is made more productive and which would therefore increase the wages fund. He argued that this was a short-run problem which could not be solved by recourse to the argument for population restraint for this would take too long. As such, emigration must be encouraged. This would be used in order to remove those whose labour had ceased to be profitable towards a country that will afford room for their exertions. Senior cites the case of the hand-loom weavers—a topic to which he returned at length later (ibid.: xv–xvi).

In January 1831, Senior co-authored a pamphlet with the title *Remarks on Emigration, With a Draft of a Bill* (Senior et al. 1831). The subject was assisted emigration and the draft was of a Bill which Lord Howick was to introduce in Parliament in the same year. Senior wrote the pamphlet with Robert Wilmot-Horton and James Stephen, although it was published anonymously. It proposed a change in the law to allow parishes to support emigration as a means of reducing suffering and the Treasury would make loans to parishes which could be paid back later. Unusually, should the emigrant return there would be no requirement to pay back the passage but there would be a requirement to renounce all further claims on the parish for support. The cost of maintaining a family as paupers was estimated to be about £25 per annum, while the cost of transporting the family to, say, Canada would be about £70 or two to three years of parish support. Howick's Bill was defeated but Senior was not put off. In the Poor Law Amendment Bill, which he helped to draft, he inserted a clause on emigration which, as he wrote to Horton in 1836, 'contained the essence' of the Bill which they had developed five years before (Senior quoted in Winch 1965: 67).

These early papers set up what was to come in the next quarter of a century.

6   The New Poor Law in England

With regard to the Poor Law in England there were perceived to be two key problems, namely the continual increase in the burden of the poor rates due to the growth and scope of relief to the able-bodied, and abuses in the system. Bowley has also pointed out that the problem was primarily one of the agricultural areas, and the concern was over reducing the rates rather than depauperising the labourer (see Bowley 1937: 282). Senior's main contribution was in altering 'class-reform dictated by political necessity, to one of a large-scale social reform based on a philosophy of a free society' (ibid.: 283), and that the key to this was to free the labourer from pauperism. Howick conferred with the leaders of the Whig administration and it was agreed that something ought to be done about the Poor Law abuses in England. On 19 January 1832, Senior's friend (and Secretary to the Board of Control) Thomas Hyde Villiers wrote to Howick suggesting the establishment of a Royal Commission to investigate pauperism and make recommendations for reform. He recommended Senior as a 'practical Political Economist, who has written well on the subject' (Villiers quoted in Bowley 1937: 286).[7] Lord Chancellor Brougham suggested that the Commission be divided into a Central Board, made up of Commissioners, and itinerant Assistant Commissioners who would collect facts and opinions. The Board would digest the information collected and produce proposals based on the evidence. It would also prepare "Instructions" for the Assistant Commissioners; Senior was given this task (see Senior 1832, 1832 [1970]). However, so much time was taken in preparing the questions and Instructions as well as in appointing the Assistant Commissioners that few of them had actually begun to work before August 1832.

Brougham demanded that the results of the Commission's work should be sent to him piecemeal. Senior was given the early results (some 600 replies) and took the opportunity of digesting these for Brougham and presenting his own proposals for reform based on these initial findings. The results were presented in a letter to Brougham dated 14 September 1832—barely a month after the majority of assistants had begun their work. In this letter, Senior focused on five problems: the Allowance System which destroyed productivity; the diminution of the wages and rates funds; the settlement laws; corruption; and the question of bastardy (see Levy 1970: 247–262).

Senior's fundamental objection to the Poor Laws can be seen from this letter in which he argued against the practice which had developed of giving allowances to the able-bodied working poor. The consequences of these allowances for the workforce were to reduce their wages, morale and productivity. The reason why the demands on the funds were increasing was that the people who should have known better, such as farmers, the clergy and the magistrates, subscribed to the 'monstrous' (Senior in ibid.: 249) doctrines that wages were a matter of right and not contract and that the amount for their payment and the payment of poor relief was inexhaustible. Extravagant rates of wages and allowances had been granted as a result. Senior's fundamental

---

[7] See next section.

objection to the Poor Laws was not that they were likely to *increase the rate of growth of population*, but that they were likely to *reduce the rate of growth of the wages fund* from which labour could be supported. He argued for the repeal of the Relief of the Poor Act (Gilbert's Act) of 1782 which forbade the placing of the able-bodied in workhouses. Allowances would be abolished and in future anyone seeking relief would have to enter the workhouse. He also recommended changes to the law relating to bastardy. Having made detailed comparisons, Levy argued that 'many portions of the Commissioners' Report of 1834 were taken verbatim' from Senior's 1832 letter (Levy 1970: 83).

The main point of the reforms eventually outlined in the 1834 Report was to reduce claims for relief from the able-bodied and this was to be achieved by making the system a harsh one. Central to this was the principle of "less eligibility" and the workhouse test. Less eligibility meant that the situation of an able-bodied pauper 'on the whole shall not be made really or apparently so eligible as the situation of the independent labourer of the lowest class' (Senior 1834: 228). This could be enforced by making the able-bodied and their families go into a workhouse as a "test" of their destitution. Conditions there would involve strict discipline, hard work, monotonous food and the separation of families. The final Report of 1834 reflected much of Senior's approach but whilst the reforms were harsh, they were better than the outright abolition proposed by Ricardo and Malthus.

Senior wrote a letter to Brougham in January 1833 (Senior 1833) concerning the administration of the Poor Law Commission (see Levy 1970: 255–262). He argued strongly against the government taking full responsibility for relief, stating that to do so would make the government the general insurer against 'misfortunes, idleness, improvidence and vice' (ibid.: 60). Instead, his scheme combined central inspection with local financial responsibility. In March 1835, Tocqueville wrote from Paris requesting some assistance with work he was preparing on pauperism. Senior duly obliged by sending him a number of pamphlets from the work on the Poor Law Reform Bill. Tocqueville published his *Memoir on Pauperism* in 1835, a work which was influenced by his visit to England and discussions with Senior (de Tocqueville 1835 [1997]).

In 1841, Senior published an article entitled "English Poor Laws" in the *Edinburgh Review* (Senior 1841a) in which he traced the history of the English Poor Laws from the fourteenth century until the reforms of 1834. Also in 1841, Senior authored an anonymous pamphlet called *Remarks on the Opposition to the Poor Law Amendment Law Amendment Bill* (Senior 1841b). He endeavoured to vindicate the 1834 Bill and, accepting that it would never be popular with everyone, made a plea for its continuation and renewal. Much of Senior's focus was on the danger of a possible revival of the Allowance System.

In December 1846, Senior wrote a letter to the then Prime Minister Lord John Russell (Senior 1846a) regarding the reorganisation of the English Poor Law Commission (see Levy 1970: 274–279). This concerned the question of local management versus centralisation. It was local management, Senior argued, which brought on the problems of the pre-1834 position. On the other hand, there were dangers inherent in centralisation, especially if it were in the form of a government department subject to the politics of the House of Commons. The Poor Law Amendment Act had steered a middle course with its organisational machinery comprising Commissioners and Assistant Commissioners. Senior made a plea for a possible increase in the numbers of Assistant Commissioners who had become overloaded with work.

For his efforts with regard to the Poor Law, Senior was offered a knighthood which he turned down. He was also offered and declined the Governorship of Upper Canada.

7   Senior, the Irish Poor Law and the Famine

A few months after he was called to the Bar, Senior made a tour through Scotland and Ireland. In the latter, he travelled from Belfast to Wexford and was shocked by the economic and social conditions he saw. The problem of poor relief in Ireland in the early years of the nineteenth century was considerable and assistance was almost entirely based on private charity. An Act passed in 1772 proposed the setting up of corporations with the responsibility of poor relief with funds raised from lands and estates. Funding was difficult and the scheme was only partially successful especially outside the cities (see Cousins 2013). The issue came to the fore after the end of the Napoleonic Wars with the partial famine in Ireland in 1817. There was some discussion about poor relief at this time but the real public debate did not begin until after 1828 (see Black 1960: 89–90).

In 1830, the Whigs took office and in 1831 Lord Howick suggested to Senior that he examine the question of the advisability of enacting legislation for compulsory relief of the poor (Poor Laws) in Ireland. As a result, Senior wrote *A Letter to Howick* in July 1831 dealing with the matter and in it the role of government is seen in a different light (Senior 1831). Senior began by asserting that evidence from earlier reports indicated that a large proportion of the inhabitants of Ireland were in a state of habitual privation and subject occasionally to severe distress. Senior was opposed to the introduction of the Poor Law in Ireland on the grounds of the existing conditions, not on principle. The Law had been introduced in England to assist the poor affected by the accidents and contingencies of life, not to raise the general standard of living, which is what was required in Ireland. While Senior was sympathetic to the poverty of the able-bodied due to illness or crop failure, he was against the use of allowances which, under the English Poor Law, had created the greatest difficulties. Senior maintained that the effects of the Old Poor Law in England had been bad enough, but to introduce them to Ireland would be worse. The fundamental problem was the deep poverty of the labouring population; the introduction of the English system would have no impact on this while bringing with it a host of other difficulties.

Senior further argued that the wages fund was the result of workers' industry and is 'in a great measure proportioned to it' (ibid.: 52). If effort is reduced so will be the wages fund while the number to be maintained by it grows. Senior went on to outline a series of proposals the aim of which was enlarging the wages fund and lowering the number of claimants. The specific measures were the building of roads, railways, harbours, docks and canals; the draining of bogs; and the reclamation of waste. The principal aim was not to provide employment directly but to increase the productive capacity of the country so that the workforce would be more productive, although employment would also be created in the process. In addition, Senior advocated emigration to reduce the size of the population in order to take pressure off the wages fund while it was being regenerated. He realised that these measures would not solve Ireland's problems quickly, but the aim was to break the vicious circle of poverty. Fundamentally, Senior was, unlike Malthus, an optimist who believed that continuous progress was possible.

In 1833, after the passage of the Great Reform Act in 1832 and the debate on the Poor Law in England from the same year onwards, pressure grew for some official consideration of the introduction of a Poor Law in Ireland. A commission was established in 1833 with Archbishop Whately in the chair. The final report did not appear until 1836 and in it Whately and his colleagues rejected the idea of following the New Poor Law in England, preferring to rely on emigration to relieve the labour market and public works to promote employment. Russell, at that time Home Secretary, was not entirely convinced by the Report and consulted Senior who was broadly sympathetic given that the new document resembled his earlier report in 1831. However, there was significant support for the workhouse system to be introduced and pressure from England to do something to reduce the possibility of increasing numbers of Irish migrants into England. George Nicholls, formerly a member of the Poor Law Commission in England, put forward a set of proposals in January

1836, recommending the adoption of the New Poor Law system in Ireland. After an investigatory tour of Ireland, Nicholls submitted another report to Russell urging the building of workhouses but removing any possibility of outdoor relief. Russell introduced a Bill based on that report in February 1837 and, after some delay, the Irish Poor Law Act based on the Bill was passed in July 1838. Commenting later in 1846, Senior was very positive about the 1838 legislation, arguing that it was a system of legal charity carefully restricted.

In the winter of 1845–1846, there was a failure of the potato crop in Ireland which was seen as a temporary problem. As Black argued, there was nothing in the 1838 Act that considered even the possibility of a partial famine let alone the calamity which was to come. However, previous experience with famines had established an ad hoc policy relief via public works plus private charity; action along these lines was now deemed to be urgent (see Black 1960: 112–113). There was no suggestion that relief should be given via the Poor Law. In this context, Senior wrote a somewhat extraordinary note to the Comptroller General of the Exchequer Lord Monteagle on 14th November 1845 once again arguing for public expenditure:

A portion of the Irish population must be considered to be an army to be fed and employed—and fortunately the means of employing them are ready. We need not *dig holes and fill them in again* or look out for public works. The railways are ready. Could not Government contract for finishing certain lines, and be entitled to participate in the profits (ibid.: 113, fn. 4; italics added) (Senior to Monteagle, 14 November 1845, Monteagle Papers, National Library of Ireland; italics added).

The government did not carry out Senior's proposal, although had they done so immediately there could have been benefits (see Black 1960: 189–202). Peel did however did introduce a system of public works and in November 1845 authorised the purchase of £100,000 of Indian corn by the Treasury to be sold at low prices at depots in Ireland so that those on low wages from public works could be provided for.

The Whigs came into power at the end of June 1846 and maintained Peel's policy until the corn ran out at the end of the year. In the winter of 1846–1847, the crop failed very seriously. Russell's policy was that public works were to be maintained and food was to be supplied by private dealers. The result was rising prices and an inability of the poor to purchase an adequate diet leading to starvation and disease which produced widespread mortality. The idea of the Irish Poor Law being extended to become the main channel of relief was gaining some traction. George Julius Poulett Scrope MP wrote a number of letters to Russell in May 1846 (see Scrope 1846: 3–91). In the series of seven letters, he argued that the Poor Law should be extended to all destitute persons and that relief need not necessarily be provided in the workhouse. There should also be a programme of public works focusing on the reclamation and reallocation of wastelands. Senior argued strongly against this in an article in the *Edinburgh Review* in October 1846 claiming that it would necessitate the levying of rates which would put an end to all private schemes of employment (see Senior 1846b: 267–314). As Black pointed out, the 1846 article was at odds with Senior's attitude in his earlier letter to Lord Howick and his correspondence with Monteagle (see Black 1960: 123).

The situation which Senior had foreseen subsequently came about when from the autumn of 1847 the whole burden of relief was placed on the ratepayer under the Poor Law Extension Act. Use was made of the "quarter-acre clause" which prevented any person holding more than a quarter of an acre of land from claiming relief until he gave up the land; this was a powerful force for the process of clearance. The workhouses were full to capacity by the summer of 1847 and resort to outdoor relief increased. The potato harvest was poor again in 1848 and by 1849 there were 215,000 people in the workhouses and 769,000 on outdoor relief (see ibid.: 120–133). Senior wrote another article in the *Edinburgh Review* in October 1849, reviewing the events of 1847 and 1848. He was very pessimistic about the situation and feared that 'if we allow the cancer of pauperism to complete the destruction of Ireland, and then throw fresh venom into the already predisposed body of England, the ruin of all that makes England worth living in is only a question of time' (Senior 1849: 268).

In 1861, Senior wrote a preface to *Journals, Conversations and Essays Relating to Ireland*, which was in fact published posthumously in 1868. He took the opportunity to review his role in the events that had taken place in Ireland, stating that:

> A Poor Law has been introduced—I believe the best which any country has ever adopted … In 1831, when I first wrote on Irish affairs, no Poor Law was known, except the unreformed Scotch Poor Law and the unreformed English one … I firmly believe, that if a Poor Law, on the English or on the Scotch system, had been introduced into Ireland in 1832—and one of those models would certainly have been adopted—the ruin which I predicted would have followed (Senior 1868: x–xiv).

8   Combinations, Hand-Loom Weavers and the Factory Acts

As soon as Lord Melbourne became Home Secretary in November 1830, he asked Senior to look at the question of the law of combinations. In his memorandum, Senior argued that in this case the duty of government was to maintain law and order. He concluded that the law should be left as it was but that there should be increases in punishment for the use of violence or intimidation, prohibition of picketing and other strong measures. The report was never published but the Webbs had sight of it and reported as follows:

> They[8] accordingly conclude with a series of astounding proposals for the amendment of the law. The Act of 1825 could not conveniently be openly repealed; but its mischievous results were to be counteracted by drastic legislation. They recommend that a law should be passed clearly reciting the common law prohibitions of conspiracy and restraint of trade. The law should go on to forbid, under severe penalties, "all attempts or solicitations, combinations, subscriptions, and solicitations to combinations" to threaten masters, to persuade blacklegs, or even simply to ask workmen to join the Union. Picketing, however peaceful, was to be comprehensively forbidden and ruthlessly punished. Employers or their assistants were to be authorised themselves to arrest men without summons or warrant, and hale them before any justice of the peace. The encouragement of combinations by masters was to be punished by heavy pecuniary penalties, to be recovered by any common informer (Webb and Webb 1898: 125).

The report was regarded as politically impossible to implement and was therefore not acted upon.

In 1837, Senior also became involved in two important new subjects, concerned with the hand-loom weavers and the Factory Acts, which were later to be associated with his name to an extent almost equal to that of the Poor Law Report.

The plight of the weavers had its origins in the eighteenth century. The development of machine spinning in the 1770s had led to a huge supply of cheap yarn and, as a result, the employment of weavers expanded rapidly to nearly a quarter of a million during the Napoleonic Wars. The power loom for weaving was first invented in the 1780s but was slow to develop. Reasonably high weavers' wages meant that more power looms which were less advanced

---

[8] The report was in fact written by Senior and a legal expert.

could be used commercially than would have been the case had wages remained at their earlier, lower levels. These less advanced machines could not be used on some types of yarn and this served initially to maintain the weavers in work. However, as power looms advanced and were able to weave many kinds of fabrics, hand-loom weaving declined, resulting in lower wages and poorer working conditions. Early in September 1837, a Royal Commission of Inquiry was established to examine the condition of the weavers who had become unemployed. Senior was appointed to head the Commission which sought evidence from witnesses in principal weaving districts. The work took four years and it is probable that Senior himself was responsible for writing the report which was published in 1841 (see Bowley 1937: 258).

The first important point made in the *Report of the Commissioners* was that although the original wording of the Commission's task was to look into the 'condition of the unemployed hand-loom workers', initial enquiries revealed that in fact there were not many unemployed workers but that those who were employed suffered from 'great privation and distress, arising…from insufficient wages and excessive toil' (Senior 1841c: 1). The *Report* has been noted for the quality of its classical economic analysis applied to a concrete case (see Stigler 1949: 25–36). The causes of the weavers' plight were divided into those affecting demand and supply respectively followed by a discussion of possible remedies. On the demand side, a tax on power looms and duties on imports were considered but rejected on the grounds of doing more harm than good. On the supply side, hand-loom weaving allowed for independent working at home and the possibility of other family members' participation, making it very desirable compared with the regimentation of factory work. Workers were therefore very reluctant to move into factories even at low wages and supply tended to run ahead of demand particularly during downturns. The effects of the Corn Laws were also considered as leading to sudden and unforeseen changes in the state of trade and to increases in the price of food in times of poor harvests. The Commission conceded that the Corn Laws were harmful but argued that their removal would not improve the main cause of distress which was perceived to be the competition from power looms. It was sympathetic to measures which might alleviate the conditions of the workers such as improvements to dwellings and the provision of education. Emigration was also considered but was rejected.

One last consideration with regard to the hand-loom weavers was Senior's insistence on inserting into the *Report of the Commissioners* elements of his earlier report on trades unions. In a note at the beginning of a reproduction of *Historical and Philosophical Essays* published posthumously in 1865, Senior maintained that 'the lapse of thirty years has not diminished its interest …

The law remains as defective as it was in 1831' (Senior 1865, 2: 116). In fact, Senior's arguments for enabling "free labour" in 1841 were even more repressive than a decade earlier (see Curthoys 2004: 24).

Senior involved himself in the controversy concerning factory legislation and in particular what was to become the Factories Act 1847 (also known as the Ten Hours Act). Under the Factories Act (Althorp's) Act of 1833, those aged between nine and thirteen were restricted to eight hours of work per day. Children in this age group were required to assist adults. It was envisaged that there would be a "relay system" for children with two shifts covering the permitted working day and that, as a result, adults would be able to work a long day. Members of the Ten Hours Movement objected to this on the grounds that it was simply a way of getting adults to work fifteen hours. Lord Ashley, who represented the Ten Hours Movement in parliament, expressed his intention of bringing in a Bill which would reduce adult hours to ten a day.

On 17 March 1837, Senior began a tour of the northern manufacturing districts. Ensconced in the York Hotel in Manchester, he wrote three letters to Charles Poulett Thomson, the President of the Board of Trade. In the first, written on 28 March, he explained that he and his party had been in the centre of the cotton district inquiring into the effects of the Factory Regulations Act on cotton manufacture and any future effects from further legislative *interference*. He went on to write that 'as Lord Ashley's motion is at hand…I think you may not be unwilling to hear the results to which we have as yet come' (Senior 1837: 11). He then put forward his well-known, not to say infamous, argument that if the hours of working in a mill were reduced by one hour per day (prices remaining the same), *net* profit would be destroyed— if they were reduced by an hour and a half, even *gross* profit would be destroyed. Senior also argued that increasing proportions of fixed capital in buildings and machinery in relation to circulating capital will require longer hours of work but that 'the exceeding easiness of cotton-factory labours renders long hours of work *practicable*' (ibid.: 14; italics in original). He ended the letter by stating that 'a ten hours' bill would be utterly ruinous' (ibid.: 16).

Senior argued in the second letter, written on 2 April, that the relay system had failed, that parents were losing money because of the reduction in children's hours and that the duty of educating children should pass from mill owners to the government. In a third letter of 4 April, he registered his 'alarm' (ibid.: 26) at the government's proposals to enforce the factory acts by more stringent inspection and ended by stating that the only matters for enactment are 'ventilation and drainage' and providing 'means and motives to education' (ibid.: 29).

Back in London, Senior attended a meeting of the Political Economy Club on 4 May and reported on his tour. Leonard Horner, the highly respected Inspector of Factories for Lancashire and Yorkshire, was also present. Senior began by taking the audience through his analysis of the capital structures of cotton mills and laid out his argument concerning the "last hour". He then went on to state that the attempt to use relays of young people had failed. Asked to speak, Horner pointed out that a large number of manufacturers had been using the relay system quite satisfactorily and argued against some other of Senior's statements. Senior was not convinced and asked Horner to put his arguments in writing and forwarded to him his correspondence with the President of the Board of Trade. Horner's letter of reply of 23 May gave further substance to his remarks on relays and his disagreement concerning the effect on parental income. Understandably, his strongest arguments came in defending the role of the inspectorate. However, he did agree with Senior on the importance of interfering as little as possible in 'the productive powers of…fixed capital' (ibid.: 30), and although Horner made no explicit reference to the last hour, he did stress 'the fatal consequences' (ibid.: 31) of a reduction in the hours worked to ten a day. Senior was critical of Althorp's Act which Horner broadly defended, but both were at one with regard to Ashley's Bill. Horner's letter together with Senior's Manchester correspondence and a preface were published on 8 June 1837 as *Letters on the Factory Act*.

Senior received both support and criticism concerning the last hour right through the 1840s in the run up to the eventual passing of the Factories Act in 1847 (see Levy 1970: 110–114). Later criticism by Marx in Volume 1 of *Das Kapital* (Marx 1909: 248–254) triggered further discussion of the proposition which continued into the twentieth century.[9]

9   Senior on Education

Senior frequently turned his attention to the condition of elementary education in Britain with a special focus on poor and pauper children. In 1837, in *Letters on the Factory Act*, he argued that 'the Factory Act, by driving many children into other employment, makes the expediency of adopting a general system for the education of all children even more urgent than it was before' (Senior 1837: 23). Following this, in the *Report on the Hand-Loom Weavers* in 1841, he argued that

---

[9] See, in particular, Schumpeter (1954: 485–486) and papers in Blaug (1991) by Johnson, DeLong, Anderson et al. and Pullen.

in the matter of education the Government of this country owes a duty to its people which it has not performed … If we might hazard another suggestion, it would be, that a further step should be made towards the introduction of a general system of education, by the issuing of a Royal Commission to inquire into the state of education of the poorer classes in Great Britain, and to suggest measures for its improvement and for the establishment of a system of national education … A comparison of our methods and of our extent of instruction with those of nations on whose civilization we presume to look down, would be a useful stimulus to the exertions of some, and a useful sedative to the national vanity of others (Senior 1841c: 121–124).

The Royal Commission for which Senior had argued was eventually set up in 1858 with him as a member and in 1859 he submitted a memorandum to his colleagues entitled *On the Education of Pauper Children in Unions*[10] in which he argued:

The pauper children who receive no education, or one which trains them to pauperism, vice, and crime, are precisely the children for whom the Government is responsible. Their parents are dead, or have deserted them, or are unable to feed them, much less to educate them. To them the State is *loco parentis* (Senior in Levy 1970: 179).

In his contribution to the Commission's report and in testimony to a parliamentary select committee in 1862, Senior was critical of the existing Poor Law authorities for their lack of action (see ibid.: 180–182). There was also division in the Commission concerning the role of government. The minority argued against intervention, preferring a reliance on private duty and benevolence. Senior agreed with the majority who were against this "laissez-faire" position (see ibid.: 182–185). In 1861, Senior published a volume entitled *Suggestions on Popular Education* (Senior 1861). Much of it was dedicated to the educational provision of poor and pauper children.[11]

---

[10] The reference is to "workhouse unions".

[11] Senior's daughter-in-law, Jeanie Senior, became the first female civil servant in Britain when she was appointed as an Assistant Inspector of Workhouses in 1873.

10   The Role of Government

In his 1830 memorandum on the trade unions, Senior proposed a narrow role for government, limiting it to the protection of property and the maintenance of law and order. In a change of mind just a year later in his letter to Howick on the Irish Poor, he argued for expenditure on transport and the drainage of bogs as a means of increasing the country's productive capacity. He also proposed the provision of health care for the disabled and the mentally ill (see Bowley 1937: 242–248). There was a clear difference in Senior's attitude to government intervention between the case of Ireland in 1831 and that in England from 1832. In Ireland, there was chronic poverty among the labouring poor, and Senior argued that a Poor Law would not be feasible. In England, he was concerned that the existing Poor Law, with arrangements for outdoor relief, could eventually pauperise the whole agricultural labour force via a downward pressure on wages. Less eligibility was a reform that could be brought into England but not Ireland.

In 1836, Senior's definition of economics changed. He now argued that economics should be restricted to pure theory and the economist was not allowed to offer advice but just explain any economic principles, if required. In the following year, he used economic theory in his arguments against the reduction of hours in factories to ten and in the question of the hand-loom weavers. However, in both cases, Senior also argued for legislation to provide housing and improve living conditions. It seems that Senior found his strictures against advice difficult to conform to. Moreover, it was from 1837 that he advocated a role for government in education.

When Senior became Drummond Professor for the second time, his views had changed again. In two lectures both entitled "The Power of Government to Alter the Degree in Which Wealth Is Desirable",[12] he maintained that 'the only foundation of a right to govern and of a correlative duty to obey, is expediency—the general benefit of the community. It is the duty of a Government to do whatever is conducive to the welfare of the governed' (Senior quoted in Bowley 1937: 265). The sacred principle of non-interference is now thrown over. It is on the same footing as interference, that is, whether it was expedient or not (Bowley 1937: 266). Bowley argued that Senior's view in 1847 was essentially the same as that taken by John Stuart Mill in 1848 and that, this being the case, why it had not been more widely recognised in the former case while it had been in the latter. The answer she put forward was that most of Senior's writings demonstrating the development of his views were contained

---

[12] Lectures, 1847–1852, Course 1, Lectures 6–7.

in reports on social and economic matters written for various members of governments, or they were contained in unpublished lectures or articles. Had Senior had the time and opportunity to write his 'great book' perhaps the history of his own thought may have been different.

11   Conclusion

Senior's second period as Drummond Professor ended in 1852. The post of Master in Chancery was abolished in the same year, although Senior was not released from his duties until 1853. He was entitled to receive during his life, by way of pension, the full amount of his salary as Master in Chancery (see Levy 1943: 319, fn. 340). He was then, at the age of sixty-three, free from all academic duties, business commitments and financial worries until the end of his life. In 1853, he was re-elected by ballot as a member of the Political Economy Club and continued to participate at meetings (see ibid.: 315). The ten years or so left to him were split into two broadly equal parts. The period up until 1859 was a time for long-distance overseas travel and journal writing. The period thereafter was spent on his usual annual trips to France; a longer visit around Scotland and Ireland; and in reflecting upon and in editing work he had already produced.

The first long visit (from the end of February until early June 1855) was to France and Algeria and was quickly followed by an even longer visit (from early November 1855 to late April 1856) to France, Egypt and Malta. The visit to Egypt was as a result of an invitation to join an international commission of engineers investigating the possible construction of the Suez Canal (see Levy 1970: 174–177). At the time, Britain was politically and economically closer to India than any other European power. Senior's view was that if the project was practical then any opposition would be ineffectual and that Britain would be behaving selfishly to attempt to shut off Europe from easier communications with India as well as China. The last long visit (from the beginning of September 1857 until early May 1858) was to Turkey (Asia Minor), Greece and France. On all of these major tours, Senior took the opportunity to speak with many prominent people on a very wide range of topics, including literature, art, history, politics, religion and economics. He acted almost as a roving ambassador with excellent connections, and whenever relevant he pressed the importance of free trade and competition.

Alexis de Tocqueville died in April 1859 and his death prompted Senior to write a preface to the correspondence and conversations between them which had lasted for over a quarter of a century (see Simpson 1872). Also in 1859,

Senior published a journal of his travels in Turkey and Greece which alone out of all his journals and conversations was published in his lifetime (Senior 1859). All of the others were edited and published after his death by Senior's daughter, Mary Simpson (Simpson 1871, 1878, 1882, 1898). Dimand (2004) provides interesting insights into Senior's Eastern travels, outlining his views and attitudes towards local cultures. He also makes a very important point concerning Senior's singular position among his contemporaries which is reinforced by his travel journals:

> Senior's account of these countries as seen by a leading classical economist is unique, and therefore not typical of classical political economy: had Senior been more like his fellow classical economists, he would not have been there, and would not have produced that remarkable (and vast) body of documents, his journals, and conversations (ibid.: 74–75).

In 1861, Senior prepared a preface to his *Journals, Conversations and Essays Relating to Ireland* and in 1863 he wrote supplements to several old articles which were included in his *Historical and Philosophical Essays*.

Senior's address on education, delivered in October 1863 at the National Association for the Promotion of Social Science at which he again made a plea for State intervention in popular education, was his last contribution to public debate (Senior 1863). In January 1864, he fell ill and steadily deteriorated until his death aged seventy-three on 4 June. He had worked almost right up to his death, totalling fifty-one years since the start of his pupillage with Edward Sugden.

It seems appropriate, given his contributions to the magazine, to let *The Economist*, edited by Walter Bagehot, have the last word on their faithful contributor:

> A man has just parted from among us who, though scarcely to be described as a prominent political or social character, rendered in his day and generation more important and various services to his country than many whose names are far more widely known and will, by the public at large, be much longer remembered. Our interest in him and England's concern with him were as a sound political economist and a very sagacious and persistent social reformer … For years he was an active and voluminous writer on nearly all questions which could interest a cultivated mind—on literature, politics, law reform, and social progress … Without being precisely a genial man he was eminently a kindly-natured man; those who lived with him and knew him intimately loved him much; he had no disturbing or unfriendly passions of any sort towards any one; and no prejudices to pervert an intellect singularly cool and clear. Few men have ever made more out of life. Not many are in the habit of turning it to better purposes (*The Economist*, 18 June 1864: 770–771).

References

Main Works by Nassau Senior

Senior, N.W. (1821). 'Review of the *Report of the Select Committee Considering the Depressed State of Agriculture in the United Kingdom*'. *Quarterly Review*, 25(Jul.): 466–504.

Senior, N.W. (1826). 'Some Ambiguous Terms Used in Political Economy'. Added to the Appendix to Richard Whately's *Elements of Logic* in *Encyclopedia Metropolitana*. London: J. Mawman: 309–322.

Senior, N.W. (1827). *An Introductory Lecture on Political Economy*. London: J. Mawman.

Senior, N.W. (1828a). *Three Lectures on the Transmission of the Precious Metals From Country to Country and the Mercantile Theory of Wealth*. London: John Murray.

Senior, N.W. (1828b). 'On the Corn Laws and the Poor Laws'. *The London Review*.

Senior, N.W. (1829). *Two Lectures on Population*. London: Saunders and Otley.

Senior, N.W. (1830a). *Three Lectures on the Rate of Wages*. London: John Murray.

Senior, N.W. (1830b). *Three Lectures on the Cost of Obtaining Money, and on Some Effects of Private and Government Paper Money*. London: John Murray.

Senior, N.W. (1831). *A Letter to Lord Howick*. London: John Murray.

Senior, N.W. (1832). *Instructions from the Central Board of Poor Law Commissioners to Assistant Commissioners*. London: HMSO.

Senior, N.W. (1832) [1970]. 'Senior's Letter of 14 September 1832 to Lord Chancellor Brougham on Poor Law Reform'. Reprinted as Appendix X in S.L. Levy *Nassau W. Senior, 1790–1864*. Newton Abbot: David & Charles: 247–254.

Senior, N.W. (1833) [1970]. 'Senior's Letter of 7 January 1833 to Lord Chancellor Brougham on Poor Law Reform'. Reprinted as Appendix XI in S.L. Levy *Nassau W. Senior, 1790–1864*. Newton Abbot: David & Charles: 255–262.

Senior, N.W. (1834). *Poor Law Commissioners' Report of 1834*. London: HMSO.

Senior, N.W. (1836). *An Outline of the Science of Political Economy*. London: W. Clowes and Sons.

Senior, N.W. (1837). *Letters on the Factory Act*. London: B. Fellowes.

Senior, N.W. (1840). *The Value of Money*. London: B. Fellowes.

Senior, N.W. (1841a). 'English Poor Laws'. *Edinburgh Review*, October. Reprinted as Chapter 6 in N.W. Senior (1865) *Historical and Philosophical Essays*. Volume Two. London: Longman, Green, Longman, Roberts, & Green: 45–115.

Senior, N.W. (1841b). *Remarks on the Opposition to the Poor Law Amendment Bill*. London: John Murray.

Senior, N.W. (1841c). *Report of the Commissioners for Inquiring into the Condition of the Unemployed Hand-Loom Weavers in the United Kingdom*. London: HMSO.

Senior, N.W. (1846a). 'Letter to Lord John Russell on Reorganisation of the English Poor Law Commission'. December. Reprinted in S.L. Levy (1970). *Nassau W. Senior, 1790–1864: Critical Essayist, Classical Economist and Adviser of Governments*. Newton Abbot: David and Charles: 274–279.

Senior, N.W. (1846b). 'Proposals for Extending the Irish Poor Law'. *Edinburgh Review*, 84(October): 267–314.

Senior, N.W. (1848a). 'Review of J.S. Mill, "Essays on Some Unsettled Questions of Political Economy; and Principles of Political Economy, with Some of Their Applications to Social Philosophy"'. *Edinburgh Review*, 88(October): 293–339.

Senior, N.W. (1848b). 'The French Republicans'. *Edinburgh Review*, 87(April): 565–600.

Senior, N.W. (1849). 'Relief of Irish Distress in 1847 and 1848'. *Edinburgh Review*, 89(January): 221–268. Reprinted in N.W. Senior (1868) *Journals, Conversations and Essays Relating to Ireland*. Volume 1. London: Longman, Greene and Co.: 208–282.

Senior, N.W. (1852). *Four Introductory Lectures on Political Economy*. London: Longman, Brown, Green, and Longmans.

Senior, N.W. (1859). *A Journal Kept in Turkey and Greece in the Autumn of 1857 and the Beginning of 1858*. London: London, Brown, Green, Longmans, and Roberts.

Senior, N.W. (1860). 'Opening Address of Nassau W. Senior, Esq., as President of Section F (*Economic Science and Statistics*), at the Meeting of the British Association, at Oxford, 28 June, 1860'. *Journal of the Statistical Society of London*, 23(3): 357–361.

Senior, N.W. (1861). *Suggestions on Popular Education*. London: John Murray.

Senior, N.W. (1863). 'Address by Mr Nassau Senior: President of the Department of Education'. In *The National Association for the Promotion of Social Science: Report of Proceedings at the Seventh Annual Congress*. Edinburgh: William P. Nimmo: 44–66.

Senior, N.W., J. Stephen and R. Wilmot-Horton (1831). *Remarks on Emigration, With a Draft of a Bill*. London: R. Clay.

Works by Nassau Senior Published Posthumously

Senior, N.W. (1864). *Essays on Fiction*. London: Longman, Green, Longman, Roberts, & Green.

Senior, N.W. (1865). *Historical and Philosophical Essays*. Two volumes. London: Longman, Green, Longman, Roberts, & Green.

Senior, N.W. (1868). *Journals, Conversations and Essays Relating to Ireland*. Two volumes. London: Longman, Green, and Co

Simpson, M.C.M. (ed.) (1871). *Journals Kept in France and Italy From 1848 to 1852 with a Sketch of the Revolution of 1848 by the Late Nassau William Senior*. Two volumes. London: Henry S. King and Co.

Simpson, M.C.M. (ed.) (1872). *Correspondence & Conversations of Count Alexis de Tocqueville with Nassau William Senior From 1834 to 1859*. Two volumes. London: Henry S. King and Co.

Simpson, M.C.M. (ed.) (1878). *Conversations with M. Thiers, M. Guizot, and Other Distinguished Persons During the Second Empire by the Late Nassau William Senior*. Two volumes. London: Hurst and Blackett.

Simpson, M.C.M. (ed.) (1880). *Conversations with Distinguished Persons during the Second Empire From 1860 to 1863 by the Late Nassau William Senior*. Two volumes. London: Hurst and Blackett.

Simpson, M.C.M. (ed.) (1882). *Conversations and Journals in Egypt and Malta by the Late Nassau William Senior*. London: Sampson Low, Marston, Searle & Rivington.

Simpson, M.C.M. (1898). *Many Memories of Many People*. London: Edward Arnold.

Other Works Referred To

Barton, J. (1820). *An Inquiry into the Causes of the Progressive Depreciation of Agricultural Labour in Modern Times: With Suggestions for its Remedy*. London: Arch and Co.

Black, R.D.C. (1960). *Economic Thought and the Irish Question, 1817–1870*. Cambridge: Cambridge University Press.

Blaug, M. (ed.) (1991). *Ramsay McCulloch (1789–1864), Nassau Senior (1790–1864) and Robert Torrens (1780–1864)*. Aldershot: Edward Elgar.

Bowley, M. (1937). *Nassau Senior and Classical Economics*. London: Allen & Unwin.

Cousins, M.E.L. (2013). 'The Irish Parliament and Relief of the Poor: The 1772 Legislation Establishing Houses of Industry'. *Eighteenth-Century Ireland*, 28: 95–115.

Curthoys, M. (2004). *Governments, Labour, and the Law in Mid-Victorian Britain: The Trade Union Legislation of the 1870s*. Oxford: Clarendon Press.

Dimand, R.W. (2004). 'Classical Political Economy and Orientalism: Nassau Senior's Easter Tours'. Chapter 3 in S. Charusheela and E. Zein-Elabdin (eds) *Postcolonialism Meets Economics*. Abingdon: Routledge: 73–90.

Hayek, F.A. (1945). '"Notes on N.W. Senior's *Political Economy*", by John Stuart Mill'. *Economica*, New Series, 12(47): 134–139.

Hutton, G. (1943). 'The Economist and Foreign Affairs'. Chapter 6 in *The Economist, 1843–1943: A Centenary Volume*. London: Oxford University Press: 73–100.

Levy, S.L. (1943). *Nassau W. Senior: The Prophet of Modern Capitalism*. Boston: Bruce Humphries, Inc.

Levy, S.L. (1970). *Nassau W. Senior, 1790–1864: Critical Essayist, Classical Economist and Adviser of Governments*. Newton Abbot: David and Charles.

Marx, K. (1909). *Capital: A Critique of Political Economy—Volume 1: The Process of Capitalist Production*. Chicago: Charles H. Kerr & Company.

Mill, J.S. (1848) [1965]. *Principles of Political Economy*. Volume II of *The Collected Works of John Stuart Mill*. Edited by J.M. Rogers. Toronto: University of Toronto Press.

O'Brien, D.P. (2004). *The Classical Economists Revisited*. Princeton, NJ: Princeton University Press.

Political Economy Club Centenary Volume, 1821–1920 (1921). London: Macmillan.

Routh, G. (1989). *The Origin of Economic Ideas*. Second edition. Basingstoke: Macmillan.

Schumpeter, J.A. (1954). *History of Economic Analysis*. London: Allen & Unwin.

Scrope, G.P. (1846). *Letters to the Right Hon. Lord John Russell on the Expediency of Enlarging the Irish Poor-Law to the Full Extent of the Poor-Law of England*. London: James Ridgway.

Stephen, L. (1897). 'Senior, Nassau William (1790–1864)'. *Dictionary of National Biography, 1885–1900: Volume 51*. London: Smith, Elder & Co.: 245–248.

Stigler, G.J. (1949). 'The Classical Economists: An Alternative View'. Lecture 3 in *Five Lectures on Economic Problems*. London: Longmans, Green and Co.: 25–36.

The Economist, 1843–1943: A Centenary Volume (1943). London: Oxford University Press.

The Economist (1864). 'Obituary: Nassau Senior'. 18 June. London: Economist Newspaper Ltd: 770–771.

Thackeray, A.I. (1864). 'The End of a Long Day's Work'. *The Cornhill Magazine*, 10(August): 253–256.

Tocqueville, A. de (1835) [1997]. *Memoir on Pauperism*. Chicago: Ivan R. Dee.

Vint, J. (1994). *Capital and Wages: A Lakatosian History of the Wages Fund Doctrine*. Aldershot: Edward Elgar.

Webb, S. and B. Webb (1898). *The History of Trade Unionism*. London: Chiswick Press.

Winch, D. (1965). *Classical Political Economy and Colonies*. London: G. Bell & Sons.

8

William Forster Lloyd (1794–1852)

Vincent Barnett

1   Introduction

William Forster Lloyd (1794–1852) was born in Bradenham, Buckingham-shire, and attended Westminster School and then Christ Church College, Oxford, graduating with a BA in Mathematics and Classics in 1815 and an MA in 1818. He eventually became Drummond Professor of Political Economy at the University of Oxford, occupying this post between 1832 and 1837, having succeeded Nassau Senior and Richard Whately, and 'delivered a celebrated series of lectures, challenging many of the accepted doctrines of the day' (Smith 1997: 59). Some of Lloyd's lectures were not published at the time of their formal presentation and are now lost, those lost being estimated at 24 in number (see Moore and White 2009: 34; Romano 1977). He was (or became) a member of what has subsequently been called the Oxford-Dublin School of proto-marginalist political economists, the other members being Senior and Whately as well as Samuel Longfield, W. Neilson Hancock and W.E. Hearn (see Senior 1836; Whately 1831).

Lloyd was, unusually for an economist, ordained as a minister in the Church of England in 1822, his books being designated on their title pages as authored 'by The Rev. W.F. Lloyd, Student of Christ Church, Professor of Political Economy'. His brother was the Bishop of Oxford. After leaving his

V. Barnett (✉)
London, UK

post at Oxford in 1837, Lloyd produced no new publications. His most significant work in economics was undoubtedly *Two Lectures on the Checks to Population* of 1833, but he also composed *A Lecture on the Notion of Value as Distinguishable Not only from Utility, but Also from Value in Exchange* of 1834, *Four Lectures on Poor-Laws* of 1835, *Two Lectures on Poor-Laws* of 1836 and then *Two Lectures on the Justice of Poor-Laws and One Lecture on Rent* of 1837. These works were all initially presented as lectures delivered at Oxford between 1832 and 1836, as it was a condition of Lloyd's Professorship that he was to publish at least one lecture per year.

However, Lloyd's first published work had been *Prices of Corn in Oxford in the Beginning of the Fourteenth Century* of 1830, which is in some ways anomalous, as it was much more narrowly and empirically focused than his other works in political economy. He cited two main reasons for publishing this volume. The first was to be able to better estimate 'the condition of the labouring poor in former periods of our history' by means of the facilitation of more accurate price and wage data comparisons (Lloyd 1830: iv). The second was to better understand whether and to what extent the equalisation of prices across different parts of the country occurred, and whether this price equalisation process depended on the facility of communication between regions.

Lloyd concluded that, in general, the price data showed that the prices of wheat and malt usually rose and fell together, but that the price of wheat usually varied more than the price of malt (see ibid.: 11). The book also contained much factual information on the legal controls that were placed on bread and other food products at the time, for example, in regulating the size of loaves, but it gave no indication whatsoever of the type of work in economics that Lloyd would go on to publish. Consequently, this chapter will examine both Lloyd's most well-known contributions to political economy, such as his work on the problems of common land ownership and on marginal utility, and also some of his less recognised ideas in fields such as behavioural economics.

2   The Tragedy of the Commons

Lloyd's most well-known idea has come to be known as the tragedy of the commons, although this was not a phrase used by him at any time. The basic issue and idea as originally presented was developed in response to two related questions. Lloyd asked, why was the cattle reared on commonly owned land often so stunted, and why was the plant life on the common itself often so worn, compared to cattle kept on privately owned land, the latter usually being in much better condition? He answered as follows:

The difference depends on the difference of the way in which an increase of stock in the two cases affects the circumstances of the author of the increase. If a person puts more cattle into his own field, the amount of the subsistence which they consume is all deducted from that which was at the command, of his original stock … But if he puts more cattle on a common, the food which they consume forms a deduction which is shared between all the cattle, as well that of others as his own … In an inclosed pasture, there is a point of saturation… beyond which no prudent man will add to his stock. In a common, also, there is in like manner a point of saturation. But the position of the point in the two cases is different (Lloyd 1833 [2017]: 28).

In modern formulation, individual behaviour that is detrimental to society as a whole, but which benefits an individual or a smaller sub-set of society, will sometimes be undertaken whenever the detrimental effects (or costs) are not directly coupled with the associated benefits.

The solution proposed by a well-known twentieth-century author on the issue, Garrett Hardin, who first coined the phrase "the tragedy of the commons", was better sustainable management of commonly held resources, together with the enforcement of the actual cost-benefit association of using them (see Hardin 1968). Hardin later clarified that by the phrase "the tragedy of the commons", he had really meant the tragedy of the unregulated commons, and went on to link this topic to unrestricted population growth (see Hardin 1995).

It should be noted that the tragedy of the commons is not limited to human affairs, but extends into the animal world as well. Predators that over-deplete their prey animal stock can face the issues of either heightened scarcity of the prey or, in extreme cases, prey extinction, either directly by over-hunting or indirectly by disturbing the natural habitat of the prey. In addition, it has been pointed out that pre-industrialised human communities also sometimes suffered from similar commons-depletion issues, especially when power was very unequally distributed between the various parties involved in using the commonly held resources. As such, the tragedy of the commons has a very long history (see Ruttan and Borgerhoff Mulder 1999).

Finally, it is worth pointing out that Lloyd transferred his analysis of the commons in metaphoric terms to the operation of the labour market, judging about this market that 'the field for the employment of labour is in fact a common, the pasture of which is free to all … In the common for man, the child begins…by the possession of a pair of hands competent to labour' (Lloyd 1833 [2017]: 29). For Lloyd, this meant in turn that the labour market conceived as a commons pasture was always and invariably stocked at saturation point, putting pressure on both the price of labour and the capacity to supply the growing population with necessary food.

3   Marginal Utility and Value

As has been outlined elsewhere, Lloyd's work on value 'has moved some leading historians of economic thought to hail Lloyd as one of the first writers to articulate the marginal utility theory of value' (Gordon 2008: 170; see also Harrod, 1927). In his *A Lecture on the Notion of Value* of 1834, Lloyd clearly articulated the concept of diminishing marginal utility. He considered an example of this as follows:

> Let us suppose the case of a hungry man having one ounce, and only one ounce of food at his command. To him, this ounce is obviously of very great importance. Suppose him now to have two ounces. These are still of great importance; but the importance of the second is not equal to that of the single ounce. In other words, he would not suffer so much from parting with one of his two ounces … The importance of the third ounce is still less than that of the second (Lloyd 1834 [1968]: 11).

This was a clear statement of the law of diminishing marginal utility; that the marginal utility of a commodity declines as its supply increases. To further outline his case, Lloyd used the metaphor of a spring or a watch spring, which when fully compressed, had the greatest capacity for expansion. Demand, when entirely unsatiated, had the greatest capacity for being satisfied, but as this demand gradually unwinds (or is fulfilled), the ability to satisfy it gradually diminishes (a coiled spring gradually loses its tension). Lloyd's use of a spring metaphor in this way can be interpreted in modern terminology as suggesting the idea of demand elasticity (see Whittaker 1940: 443).

Although it was not explicitly noted by Lloyd, his articulation of a diminishing marginal utility conception of value put him in direct opposition to David Ricardo's labour theory of value. Lloyd also commented on Malthus's question on the nature of value, 'whether in a country with nothing but deer, a deer could be said to be without value, because there would be no other object with which to compare it' (Lloyd 1834 [1968]: 30). Lloyd answered that an object certainly could have absolute value independently of all comparisons with other objects or animals, although he disputed the idea that objects had intrinsic value, separate from their practical or aesthetic functions.

However, the lack of influence of Lloyd's proto-marginalism across the nineteenth century as a whole can be indicated by the fact that Stanley Jevons's *The Theory of Political Economy* (1871), despite containing an extensive discussion of the history of mathematical economics, does not mention Lloyd's work on marginal utility at all, although Alfred Marshall did mention Lloyd very briefly in a footnote in the seventh edition of his *Principles of Economics* (see Marshall 1890 [1916]: 101). Joseph Schumpeter subsequently noted about the delayed arc of diffusion of Lloyd's work that it was 'strange that an Oxford professor of economics should have needed rediscovering. Nevertheless, that was the case [with W.F. Lloyd]. The merit of having rescued Lloyd's name from oblivion belongs to the late Professor [E.R.A.] Seligman' in 1903 (Schumpeter 1954: 1055; see also Seligman 1903a, b). Seligman considered Lloyd as one part of a wider group of neglected economists from the nineteenth century that had come back into focus (and relevance) at the beginning of the twentieth century.

4   Poor Laws

Although Lloyd is today most associated with the idea of the tragedy of the commons, by far his most extensively analysed topic in his various lectures was issues relating to the efficacy of the UK poor laws (see Lloyd 1836 [1968]). Lloyd was in general in favour of providing relief for the poor and destitute partly on social justice grounds, this being a sympathy articulated against the Malthusian ideas of the period. He also justified them in part as a positive aid to business and by the use of a mechanical analogy: 'Poor-laws are to the living instruments of a manufacturing society as oil to its machines' (Lloyd 1835 [1968]: 102), this insurance-grade oil allowing the continued shifting of labour across different branches of industry, without the evils that would attend this process in the absence of any poor relief.

He also provided some more concrete arguments for maintaining the poor laws, given that in most situations, 'population is always pressing against the means of subsistence' (ibid.: 57). For example, he argued against the idea that, because there might be insufficient resources available to feed absolutely everyone who did not have an income, then no one should be provided with poor relief, this idea being,

> as absurd as to say, that, because all the thousand persons could not be maintained, therefore not one could be, in fact, maintained, out of the given supply of food … A thousand cannot be maintained. Therefore a thousand have not a right to be maintained. But nine hundred can be maintained. Therefore, for all we know to the contrary, nine hundred may have a right to be maintained (ibid.: 39).

Lloyd was sympathetic to the plight of the poor in relation to population growth and the operation of the so-called preventive check, as he believed this check was often overwhelmed by circumstances, and he supported the provision of poor relief in most situations. He also distinguished between poor relief given for the suppression of what he called 'begging and vagrancy', that is, for those without any real means of supporting themselves through labour, and poor relief given to those who temporarily found themselves in distress for contingent reasons, such as temporarily becoming unemployed (ibid.: 80–82).

More generally, he was concerned to study the structure of the society in which the different industrial classes lived in relation to both the operation of the labour market, and the influence of this structure on individual well-being. For example, he wrote in this respect:

> [T]he simple fact of a country being over populous, by which I mean its population pressing too closely against the means of subsistence, is no, of itself, sufficient evidence that the fault lies in the people themselves, or a proof of the absence of a prudential disposition. The fault may rest…with the constitution of society, of which they form a part (Lloyd 1833 [2017]: 22).

In consequence, Lloyd asserted the progressive principle that the institutions of property ownership in a given society should be designed, at least in part, with regard to their 'tendency to promote the general happiness, and, as often as it is discovered that they can be made for effectual to that end, ought to be modified and amended' (Lloyd 1835 [1968]: 51). Elsewhere, he discussed the comparison between slavery and free labour, pointing out some of the similarities between them, and suggested how slavery has differed in different societies and contexts, such as in the English as against the French colonies and then in Ancient Rome (see Lloyd 1837 [1968]: 20–24).

However, it would be wrong to conclude from all this that Lloyd should be seen as an anticipator of the Marxian treatment of capitalism (see Romano 1971: 285), as Marxism has a much more extensive and comprehensive denunciation of capitalism as an economic system than anything that may have been suggested by Lloyd. Instead, Lloyd's political economy is more accurately described as akin to that of a paternalistic Tory (see Romano 1977). For example, he consistently argued in favour of extensive poor laws, but argued that support for the poor enlarged 'the field for the profitable employment of capital' (Lloyd 1835 [1968]: 127).

5   Behavioural Economics

In addition to his more recognised work on poor laws, Lloyd can be seen to have anticipated some important ideas that have been much more recently articulated in the field of behavioural economics. For example, he wrote on the question of the relation between relative and absolute conceptions of value:

> Such then is the notion of absolute as distinguished from comparative or exchangeable value … In this sense of value, it may be remarked, that to a poor man, the same things are more valuable than to a rich man … "No one would be absurd enough to maintain, that a guinea has the same value, and therefore would become an equal forfeiture to two persons, the one having a thousand and the other only ten of these" (Lloyd 1834 [1968]: 28–29; source of quote unnamed).

In their work on prospect theory, the behavioural economists Daniel Kahneman and Amos Tversky similarly maintained that the real carriers of value to individuals were relative changes in wealth and welfare, rather than final or absolute states (see Kahneman and Tversky 1982). The same absolute degree of wealth could connote extreme poverty for one person and great wealth for another, depending on the particular context of their lives. For example, the billionaire whose total wealth was suddenly reduced to only $10,000 would feel like they had been greatly impoverished, whereas if a rich benefactor gave a homeless individual with no possessions at all $10,000 as a gift, then that individual would feel almost like a millionaire (see Barnett 2019).

In addition, Lloyd was well aware of some cognitive distortions that affected human perception and human understanding in certain instances. For example, he wrote that:

> The human eye is incapable of taking a clear view of many objects at once. When it is fixed on one object, all other objects are necessarily overlooked. In like manner, the mind can only attend at one time to a definite number of considerations: and it follows, that, where the thoughts and feelings are deeply engaged on a present benefit, little power of attention remains to be bestowed upon the future (Lloyd 1833 [2017]: 46).

In the nineteenth century, such illusions of perception and attention were beginning to be documented and studied by some psychologists, although few economists realised their true significance for understanding economic behaviour (see Sully 1887: 86). However, Lloyd did understand their significance, albeit at a more general level, pointing out, for example, that a 'great source of error in all human enquiries' was the tendency to generalise prematurely from insufficient facts (Lloyd 1837 [1968]: 18), this being a particular version of what behavioural economists now call anchoring biases. He also understood that the motives for human behaviour were more complex than simply rational self-interest. Many decades before Thorstein Veblen, Lloyd stressed the importance of the 'spirit of emulation, and the desire of rising in the world' as a powerful motive of human economic behaviour (Lloyd 1833 [2017]: 58), just as Veblen expressed the belief that the 'motive that lies at the root of ownership is emulation' (Veblen 1899 [1925]: 25).

In more general terms and similar to contemporary formulations of the subject of evolutionary psychology (see Barnett 2015, 2018), it is clear that Lloyd believed that the human mind contained some important fixed, inbuilt capacities (or instincts), what he termed 'dispositions'. He explained on this topic that:

> It is convenient, here, to distinguish between the motives and the disposition to prudence. By the motives, I mean circumstances external to the minds of the individuals … By the disposition, I mean something internal to the mind itself, namely, the strength of the reasoning faculty, combined with the degree of self-command possessed by the individual … The disposition, which depends on the reasoning faculty, will vary according as that faculty is improved by education and experience (Lloyd 1833 [2017]: 40).

In addition, this prudential disposition was seen by Lloyd as part of what he explicitly called 'human nature' (ibid.: 52), elsewhere considering a hypothetical 'change in the constitution of human nature' (Lloyd 1835 [1968]: 117). Human nature was, therefore, for Lloyd, the sum total of all of these inbuilt dispositions and also the various 'natural passions', such as those expressed in marriage (Lloyd 1833 [2017]: 32), as evolutionary psychologists currently maintain.

6   Animal Intelligence

One area of political economy which Lloyd has not usually been connected to is the relevance of comparative animal studies and comparative animal psychology to economic behaviour. However, he did on occasion venture into this field, as the following passage attests:

Adam Smith remarks, that man is the only animal which makes exchanges. "Nobody", he says, "ever saw one dog make a fair and deliberate exchange of one bone for another, with another dog" ... But we may observe, that dogs have a sense of value ... Though nobody has ever seen two dogs making an exchange, yet a dog has been often seen to hide a bone. The dog does this from a sense of its value...because he knows that a bone is a good thing which is not always to be had when wanted ... In Constantinople, where the dogs act the part of scavengers, and, it is said, have their regular beats, like beggars in London, no individual dog ever presuming to trespass beyond his own territory (Lloyd 1834 [1968]: 26).

At the end of the nineteenth century, the evolutionary psychologist George Romanes noted various examples of dogs that had been trained to take coins to a shop and purchase particular items in exchange, such as buns or biscuits. Romanes commented on this in turn that some 'dogs have an instinctive idea of giving peace-offerings, and that the step from this to the idea of barter may not be large' (Romanes 1878 [1898]: 452). The anthropocentric approach to studying animal behaviour has recently experienced a resurgence in the psychology literature and also has some crossovers with the fields of behavioural economics and neuroeconomics (see Shettleworth 2012: 529–530; Barnett 2019). Lloyd explicitly characterised human beings at one point as the 'reasoning animal' (Lloyd 1833 [2017]: 12), with ordinary American citizens described as often settling in the woods, indicating the anthropocentric parallel he was here seeking to apply.

7   Conclusion

Overall, Lloyd's methodology has been described as realist and as conceptually distinct from both Ricardo and Malthus (see Moore and White 2009: 40), and his work on value as placing him in the utility school (see Roll 1938 [1989]: 339). Given the greater recognition awarded to him today, it is worth noting that Lloyd had no separate entry in the original nineteenth-century edition of the *Palgrave Dictionary of Political Economy*. Neither was he listed at all in its index, although Lloyd was mentioned in an "appendix" to a later corrected version of this edition (see Moore and White 2009: 40). However, he certainly did receive his own entry in the most recent edition of the *Palgrave Dictionary* and he was also listed in the index (see Gordon 2008: 170–171). Lloyd's ideas on the tragedy of the commons are now even discussed in technology publications such as *Wired* (see Highfield 2018).

In addition, the latest version of the Palgrave *Dictionary* also contained an entry entitled "Tragedy of the Commons", which related that 'Hardin's [1968] article is one of the most cited publications of recent times', although bizarrely, W.F. Lloyd is not mentioned in it at all (Ostrom 2008: 360). The fact that Lloyd's rediscovery was nearly a full century after he first published his various lectures suggests that he was not particularly influential across the remainder of the nineteenth century as a whole.

That was undoubtedly true, but the fact that his ideas about the dangers of the overuse of commonly held property have more recently become a key part of wider environmental concerns more than makes up for this neglect, and this in turn signifies Lloyd's real and lasting importance. This importance is further demonstrated by the fact that Elinor Ostrom was awarded the Nobel Prize in Economics in 2009 chiefly for her book entitled *Governing the Commons: The Evolution of Institutions for Collective Action*, which illustrated how some particular communities willingly cooperate in order to protect resources that are held in common (Ostrom 1991). Ostrom argued that real-world situations were often far more complex than either Lloyd or Hardin allowed, and that even when governments attempt to regulate or control commonly held assets, resource over-depletion can still sometimes occur. One part of the solution proposed by Ostrom was to facilitate greater communication amongst users so as to assist them in reaching collective solutions by themselves while another part was the establishment of clear and effectively enforced boundary rules regarding rights and responsibilities (Ostrom 2008: 361–362).

Given that wider environmental concerns about the state of planet Earth are now some of the most difficult and pressing problems facing human beings in the early twenty-first century, the significance of Lloyd's initial nineteenth-century articulation of the problem of "the tragedy of the commons" in his *Two Lectures on the Checks to Population* of 1833 cannot now be overestimated.

References

Main Works by William Forster Lloyd

Lloyd, W.F. (1830). *Prices of Corn in Oxford in the Beginning of the Fourteenth Century: Also from the Year 1583 to the Present Time*. Oxford: University Press.
Lloyd, W.F. (1833) [2017]. *Two Lectures on the Checks to Population*. London: Rise of Douai.

Lloyd, W.F. (1834) [1968]. *A Lecture on the Notion of Value as Distinguishable Not only from Utility, but Also from Value in Exchange.* New York: Kelley.

Lloyd, W.F. (1835) [1968]. *Four Lectures on Poor-Laws.* New York: Kelley.

Lloyd, W.F. (1836) [1968]. *Two Lectures on Poor-Laws.* New York: Kelley.

Lloyd, W.F. (1837) [1968]. *Two Lectures on the Justice of Poor-Laws and One Lecture on Rent.* New York: Kelley.

Other Works Referred To

Barnett, V. (2015). 'Evolutionary Psychology and Economics'. In F. Wherry and J. Schor (eds) *The SAGE Encyclopedia of Economics and Society.* Volume 2. Thousand Oaks, CA: Sage: 651–656.

Barnett, V. (2018). 'Economists and Evolutionary Psychology'. In T.K. Shackelford and V.A. Weekes-Shackelford (eds) *Encyclopedia of Evolutionary Psychological Science.* Switzerland: Springer. Available at: https://doi.org/10.1007/978-3-319-16999-6_3836-1.

Barnett, V. (2019). 'Behavioral Economics'. In T.K. Shackelford and V.A. Weekes-Shackelford (eds) *Encyclopedia of Evolutionary Psychological Science.* Switzerland: Springer. Available at: https://doi.org/10.1007/978-3-319-16999-6_2806-1.

Gordon, B. (2008). 'William Forster Lloyd'. In S.N. Durlauf and L.E. Blume (eds) *The New Palgrave Dictionary of Economics.* Volume 5. London: Palgrave Macmillan: 170–171.

Hardin, G. (1968). 'The Tragedy of the Commons'. *Science*, 162(3,859): 1,243–1,248.

Hardin, G. (1995). *Living Within Limits: Ecology, Economics, and Population Taboos.* New York: Oxford University Press.

Harrod, R.F. (1927). 'An Early Exposition of "Final Utility": W.F. Lloyd's Lecture on "The Notion of Value" (1833) Reprinted'. *Economic History*, 2(May): 168–183.

Highfield, R. (2018). 'Climate Change Will Get a Whole Lot Worse Before It Gets Better, According to Game Theory'. *Wired*. Available at: https://www.wired.co.uk/article/climate-change-prediction-game-theory-tragedy-of-commons.

Jevons, W.S. (1871). *The Theory of Political Economy.* London: Macmillan.

Kahneman, R. and A. Tversky (1982). *Judgment under Uncertainty: Heuristics and Biases.* New York: Cambridge University Press.

Marshall, A. (1890) [1916]. *Principles of Economics.* Seventh edition. London: Macmillan.

Moore, G.C.G. and M.V. White (2009). 'Placing William Forster Lloyd in Context'. Conference of the History of Economic Thought Society of Australia, University of Notre Dame, 14–17 July.

Ostrom, E. (1991). *Governing the Commons: The Evolution of Institutions for Collective Action.* Cambridge: Cambridge University Press.

Ostrom, E. (2008). 'Tragedy of the Commons'. In S.N. Durlauf and L.E. Blume (eds) *The New Palgrave Dictionary of Economics*. Volume 8. London: Macmillan: 360–362.

Roll, E. (1938) [1989]. *A History of Economic Thought*. London: Faber and Faber.

Romanes, G. (1878) [1898]. *Animal Intelligence*. London: Kegan Paul.

Romano, R.M. (1971). 'W.F. Lloyd: A Comment'. *Oxford Economic Papers*, 23(2): 285–290.

Romano, R.M. (1977). 'William Forster Lloyd: A Non-Ricardian?'. *History of Political Economy*, 9(3): 412–441.

Ruttan, L.M. and M. Borgerhoff Mulder (1999). 'Are East African Pastoralists Truly Conservationists?'. *Current Anthropology*, 40(5): 621–652.

Schumpeter, J. (1954). *History of Economic Analysis*. London: Allen & Unwin.

Seligman, E.R.A. (1903a). 'On Some Neglected British Economists—I'. *Economic Journal*, 13(51): 333–363.

Seligman, E.R.A. (1903b). 'On Some Neglected British Economists—II'. *Economic Journal*, 13(52): 511–535.

Senior, N.W. (1836). *An Outline of the Science of Political Economy*. London: Clowes.

Shettleworth, S.J. (2012). 'Darwin, Tinbergen, and the Evolution of Comparative Cognition'. In J. Vonk and T.K. Shackelford (eds) *The Oxford Handbook of Comparative Evolutionary Psychology*. Oxford: Oxford University Press: 529–546.

Smith, I. (1997). 'Lloyd, William Forster'. In *Economics: Bernard Quaritch Ltd, Catalogue 1246*. London: Quaritch: 59.

Sully, J. (1887). *Illusions: A Psychological Study*. London: Kegan Paul.

Veblen, T. (1899) [1925]. *The Theory of the Leisure Class*. London: Allen & Unwin.

Whately, R. (1831). *Introductory Lectures in Political Economy*. London: Fellowes.

Whittaker, E. (1940). *A History of Economic Ideas*. New York: Longmans.

9

Bonamy Price (1807–1888)

Robert J. Bigg

1   Introduction

History has not been kind to Bonamy Price; a detached alien, a genial nonentity, holding back the development of mid-to-late-nineteenth-century economics in Oxford. He left no great oeuvre, in the manner of Mill or Marshall, but rather, like Nassau Senior, collections of lectures and a notable volume of articles covering churchmanship, constitutional questions, education and political economy, albeit that many were recycled. A man slightly out of his time, a classicist and mathematician, more inclined to the former, and a sceptic of applying a scientific method to something where he thought enlightened common sense should prevail. A prospective reformer of tradition in Oxford tuition who, nonetheless, left no great mark on its teaching.[1] Yet he was often quoted as an authority in the Parliament of his day, and his death was widely reported across the English-speaking world.

He was closest to the English Historical School of Economics, but not quite congruent. Certainly, he rejected the Ricardian and the scientific/mathematical approach of the Marginalists, but he was neither historical nor statistical in his approach. Adam Smith was his constant touchstone. So, whilst to some extent he continued in the vein of his predecessor in the Drummond

---

[1] To be fair, most Oxford reforms since the seventeenth century had come largely from external pressures rather than internal movements.

R. J. Bigg (✉)
Retired Scholar and Author, Newbery, UK

© The Author(s), under exclusive license to Springer Nature Switzerland AG 2021
R. A. Cord (ed.), *The Palgrave Companion to Oxford Economics*,
https://doi.org/10.1007/978-3-030-58471-9_9

Chair, Thorold Rogers, his advantage to the electors was his innate conservatism compared to Rogers' growing radicalism. Rogers would, however, be re-elected to the Chair on Price's death in 1888.

As the entry on Price in Palgrave's original *Dictionary* noted: 'An economist, interesting for the independence of his views, and for the spirit with which he expounds them. The animating principle of his writings is, that for an economist, practical instincts are more needed than speculative ability' (Mozley 1899: 188). A far harsher verdict was given by Coats: 'Oxford economics lacked an effective intellectual leader, for the professor of political economy from 1868 to 1888 was Bonamy Price, a genial nonentity who denied that economics was a science and asserted that it was merely a practical, common-sense subject employing rule-of-thumb methods and enunciating familiar truisms' (Coats 1967: 714).

In examining the development of the later nineteenth century Oxford group of younger economists (Ashley, Cannan, L.L. Price, et al.), Kadish notes that Bonamy Price 'seems to have left no noticeable impression … He is not mentioned in any of their biographical works as a source of inspiration' (Kadish 1982: 172). Perhaps, asks Kadish, the younger economists had little contact with Price, as most Oxford teaching was done through the college lecturers, or perhaps in a wide variety of areas their points of disagreement were either trivial or of limited interest and relevance. Price himself often balanced both sides of an argument, rarely taking an outspoken position, whilst his belief in the underlying unity of interest between the economic classes would not have been in conflict with the views of this younger generation. Perhaps then he was not worth attacking nor referencing as support. Kadish also notes that Price's main interests of currency and banking did not attract a great deal of interest in Oxford.

2   Life

Bonamy Price was born in St Peter Port, Guernsey, on 22 May 1807. From the age of 14, he was privately tutored by the Reverend Charles Bradley, the curate of High Wycombe.[2] In 1825, he went up to Worcester College, Oxford, where he gained a Double First in Classics and Mathematics in 1829. One examiner later noted: 'His examination was brilliant' (the Venerable J. Garbett, Testimonial of 19 December 1851 in Anon 1851: 18). During this time, he was an occasional pupil of Thomas Arnold at Laleham and formed friendships

---

[2] Bradley combined parish work with being a personal tutor.

with the Newman brothers and other members of the Tractarians, although he later attacked their Anglo-Catholic position in the *Edinburgh Review* (see Price 1851).

Price was appointed Mathematical Master at Rugby School in 1830 under the headship of Arnold and was promoted to a Classical Master in 1832; he subsequently took charge of the fifth form. In 1834,[3] he married Lydia Rose. They were to have five daughters. In 1838, Price succeeded James Prince Lee[4] as master to "the twenty", the select cadre of fifth formers from whom the vacancies in the sixth form were decided by competition. He would remain at Rugby until 1850. As a teacher, he was reputed to be stimulating and encouraging, but impartial and open to different viewpoints. Certainly, his former pupils flocked to provide testimonials when he applied for the Greek Chair at Edinburgh University in 1851.[5]

However, this application was unsuccessful, and Price moved to London devoting himself to business and literary work. During this second period of his career, he developed an interest in currency and banking, though somewhat at variance with the prevailing views in the City, as noted by Kadish (1989). He was also a member of two government commissions—on the Scottish Fisheries and the Queen's Colleges in Ireland.

Price was a warm Liberal, but became a strong constitutionalist insisting on the importance of the Lords as a second chamber.[6] A vivid thinker, a lively talker, he was generally acknowledged as a great school teacher, but neither really a scholar nor an academic, despite his own self-estimation in that respect. As Kadish comments, 'he was hardly of the calibre to either change, or come to terms with, the institutional constraints imposed on the professoriate. And he certainly lacked the scholarly stature of Rogers' (Kadish 1989: 40). Whilst Kadish suggests that Price made efforts to adapt his courses to both Oxford's curriculum and subjects of current popular debate, such as

---

[3] The *Dictionary of National Biography* gives 1864 as the year of marriage but this is clearly a typographical error from the original edition, especially as the National Portrait Gallery has a photograph dated 1861 of the whole family as adults.

[4] Lee had been appointed headmaster of King Edward's School, Birmingham, and later would become the Bishop of Manchester.

[5] '*The Times*, in writing of his power as a teacher, has used the phrase that his influence was rather "electric" than "magnetic" ... For Bonamy Price certainly awakened others to the full sense of their power without in any degree subduing them by imparting his own bias. Indeed, the vivacity with which he entered into a view differing from his own was one of the most refreshing of his characteristics' (Anon 1888: 10). See also the testimonials in Anon (1851).

[6] He was still being quoted in the early twentieth century on the role of the House of Lords: 'I cite the authority of Mr. Bonamy Price, a constitutional writer, who during the Irish land law debates was commended to the attention of the House and the country because of the peculiarly detached character of his opinions' (Mr Mitchell-Thomson, MP for Lanarkshire, N.W., Hansard HC Debate, 25 June 1907, vol. 176, c. 1208).

bimetallism, he nonetheless concludes that 'his influence as a teacher had been minimal. His manner was considered more suitable for schoolboys than for university students … Other factors were the eccentricity of his views and his inability to offer any clear insights into the treatment of current problems' (ibid.: 44).

Price favoured the expansion of women's education, signing some prominent petitions, and in the 1870s at the invitation of the secretary, Catherine Winkworth, he lectured in support of the Committee on Higher Education for Women. He was made an Honorary LLD by Edinburgh University in 1881, and in 1883 was elected an Honorary Fellow of Worcester College, Oxford. He died on 8 January 1888 after many months of declining health, at his London home, 29 Michael's Grove, Brompton.

3   Early Government Commissions

Price, together with James Heywood and Arthur Stanley, was behind a petition to Lord Russell, the Prime Minister, in 1848 calling for a Royal Commission into the Universities of Oxford and Cambridge. The Commission, despite some resistance from within the universities, was formed in 1850 and reported in 1852. Price gave evidence to the inquiry in which he supported reform that would cut the costs of university education; reduce the distinctions between noblemen, gentleman-commoners and ordinary undergraduates; increase the number of places by allowing the expansion of new halls and colleges; improve examinations and integrate professorial teaching into the curriculum; and dispense with the requirements of Holy Orders and celibacy for the fellowship. His ideas evolved in the following years, moving closer to the German model where students were first taught by college lecturers and then by professorial instruction. This would also create a career structure where university teachers would provide a pool of talent to become the next generation of the professoriate, and would thus be encouraged to build up their own expertise and research skills (see Kadish 1989: 36–39).

In June 1856, Price was appointed as one of the three Treasury Commissioners to examine the application of grants to the Scottish Board of Fisheries and the future of the herring brand. Price took pride in claiming credit for swaying the Commissioners to retain the branding on Scottish herring barrels which he argued gave an equal chance to the small curers, against the advantages of the larger ones, and helped promote the perceived quality of the product in export markets. The Protected Designation of Origin of its day! The brand was also seen as aiding efficiency and improving storage conditions by minimising the need for the repeated reopening of barrels for inspection. The existence of the brand was likely to increase the number of German merchants willing to buy Scottish white herring as it reduced their risks as to the quality of the supply. On the recommendation of the majority of the Commissioners,[7] a fee was adopted in 1859.[8] Price and St John suggested that the fee would also be an empirical test of the benefits attributed to the brand, since the Crown Brand would come at a cost against rivals which were free. The Select Committee on the Herring Brand in 1881 concluded that this test had indeed been passed.[9]

In February the following year, reflecting his wider interests in education and earlier evidence to the Oxford University Commission (1850–1852), Price was appointed to the Royal Commission into the Queen's Colleges in Belfast, Cork and Galway. This reported in 1858, though ill health prevented Price from contributing to the final report.

4   Election to the Drummond Chair

The later nineteenth century terms of Oxford's Drummond Chair of Political Economy provided for a five-year maximum tenure with re-election possible after the first two. Initially, the electorate was the University Convocation consisting of all doctors and masters, whether resident or not; this was later replaced by a Board of Electors. Price had first sought election in 1862 but had lost out narrowly to Thorold Rogers,[10] who held the post from 1863 to 1868. When Rogers let it be known in 1867 that he would seek re-election, Price also stood and a vote was scheduled for 6 February 1868. The campaign rapidly became highly politicised (as has been described by de Marchi 1976 and Rashid 1978). A conservative anti-Rogers faction actively solicited votes for Price whilst also distributing press and other accounts of Rogers' more radical political views.

Both men were free traders and supporters of religious toleration and of university reform. They were both also sceptical of a scientific rather than a historical or common-sense approach to political economy. So, as Rashid (1978) points out, the differences were largely ones of degree rather than of

---

[7] Admiral Sullivan dissented.

[8] The original suggestion for a brand fee had come from Sir John Lefevre in 1848.

[9] See Report from the Select Committee on Herring Brand (Scotland), 21 June 1881, House of Commons, London and Price and St. John (1857).

[10] By 161 votes to 150 (see *The Times*, 6 June 1862: 12).

kind. Undoubtedly though, Rogers was becoming more politically radical, and Price, whilst a Liberal, more innately conservative.

In the early stages of the election, support was fairly evenly divided. However, as Rashid demonstrates, Rogers' public supporters were largely resident college fellows and, apart from six college chaplains, there was a notable absence of clerical support for their fellow clergyman. Price, on the other hand, had some 56 clerics in support and none apparently from the college fellowships. This could be key as the non-resident electorate of the Convocation was dominated by country clergy.

Whilst the election could be seen as divided along resident and non-resident lines, this would overlook the considerable resident Oxford faction against Rogers; it was these people who had, after all, latched onto Price's campaign. A growing role for political economy in the curriculum would be at the expense of classical studies. Rogers had argued against preferment in the Oxford system and his view on landlords would be uncomfortable for the colleges with large endowments. Whether or not it was Rogers' offence to the Oxford High Church Tories through his toleration of dissenters or his growing political radicalism (as was also adduced by *The Spectator* in Price's obituary of 1888[11]), Price was the ultimate victor with 620 votes to Rogers' 193.[12] He was just the safer option, although Price did not escape some criticism, and even misrepresentation, over his position on banking and monetary issues.[13]

The fact that political and religious factions had played a part in his election is clear from Price's Inaugural Lecture. He was at great pains to distinguish between the recommendations of the science of political economy and the moral judgements required of the politicians to make the final decisions. The lecture was an impassioned plea not only for the general everyday importance of political economy but also for the impartiality of the economist and to let others decide the wider issues on moral grounds. The truths of political economy are the result of the 'investigation of general laws, and its status is professional and subordinate; for these very reasons it admits of dispassionate and scientific study. Its reports should be placed on the same level with the reports of legal and sanitary commissions' (Price 1868: 18).

---

[11] Price it was said was 'as much afraid of revolutionary ideas and new departures taken abruptly in an unhistorical spirit, as he was of reactionary or despotic ideas … Thus, from being an ardent reformer when reform was urgently needed, he became towards the end of his life not a little alarmed at the facility with which the educated classes gave way to abstract principles of the vaguest kind, and it was no doubt to this dread of a somewhat raw Radicalism that he owed his election to the Professorship' (Anon 1888: 11).

[12] See *The Times*, 7 February 1868: 12.

[13] Charles Neate (a former holder of the Drummond Chair), letter to *The Times* 25 January 1868: 12.

Political economy is not supreme over man's destinies on earth. It rules over material objects; but man's existence is something infinitely greater than material. To accumulate riches was not the sole nor the chief end of the creation of man; and this truth should never be absent from the mind of every political economist who values the true honour of his science. On the other hand, to upbraid the investigation of the laws which govern the production of wealth as irreligious is a simple absurdity, unless it be irreligious to be anything else than poor. It is a mere truism to say that the material part of civilisation has high importance for man; but if it is a right thing to be industrious…it cannot but be right also to search out the methods by which this inevitable function may be most successfully performed (ibid.: 19).

Price argued, for example, against the exploitation of child labour, and in favour of education, on moral rather than economic grounds:

The moral and social circumstances which accompany any particular form of the mechanical production can never, and ought never to, be kept out of sight. There are means of generating wealth so destructive of human life, or of all that renders it worth possessing, as to deserve immediate reprobation at the hands of the inquirer (ibid.: 20).

Nonetheless, he felt that:

The economist must strive not to render social aspects the governing principles of his investigation; and the politician and the socialist must labour to prevent their special ideas and aims from guiding researches into the working of industrial arrangements. Each is bound to keep his own end primarily in view: the economist to inquire into the production of wealth, checking afterwards his results by so much of an appeal to social considerations as is inevitable (ibid.: 21).

It was to be this independence of thought that was to become Price's hallmark.

Finally, he complained that the subject, unlike any other, seemed to suffer from an inability to learn from its previous development; it seemed fated to have the same debates over and over again. In this sense, it was different from the progress in the natural sciences: 'Some of the positions reached by Political Economy attain the quality of demonstration: and yet they are denied or ignored as readily as if they were the hypothesis of an empiric. They are not argued against and refuted … They are simply passed over' (ibid.: 22).

It is notable that during Price's lifetime there was no known contender for the Drummond Chair even when the appointment system was changed to a

Board of Electors after 1881 (see Kadish 1982: 175). He was to be re-elected three times in 1873, 1878 and 1883. Nonetheless, there remained those who felt that Price could not continue being returned to the position, particularly as he grew older. Among these was the influential Benjamin Jowett, Master of Balliol.

In 1883, Jowett was urging Alfred Marshall (then at Bristol) to come to Oxford where the death of Arnold Toynbee had freed up a Lectureship at Balliol. He also held out the prospect of succeeding the ageing Price as Drummond Professor. The Marshalls did indeed go to Oxford in the autumn of 1883. His classes drew in many men from other colleges and outside of the Indian Civil Service Probationers who were the primary audience. However, Henry Fawcett died in November 1884, and Marshall was appointed to the Cambridge Chair in December.

Jowett wrote on Christmas Day 1884 thanking Marshall but also scouting out possible candidates for his replacement, yet again holding out the potential to succeed Price:

> We shall greatly miss you at Oxford: the Undergraduates say to me "Who will teach Political Economy to us now?" I have no doubt that there is an excellent field for teaching it…partly because it is "in the air" now, & also because it enters so largely into various University examinations (Jowett to Marshall, 25 December 1884, quoted in Whitaker 1975: 27).

Jowett continued: 'But the lecturer if he succeeds would have a good chance of obtaining Price's chair which must be vacant in 2 or 3 years time, as Price is not likely to be reelected' (ibid.: 28).

In the Michaelmas term of 1884, Price had lectured on a "Summary of Political Economy" twice a week, whereas Marshall had given double that amount covering "Production, Rent &c" and "Economic Theory". Thus in the following Hilary term of 1885, Price lectured alone on "Money, Banking, Socialism, Wages".

5   *The Principles of Currency* (1869)

The year after his election Price published six of his lectures as *The Principles of Currency* (1869a). It comprised his Inaugural Lecture with five others. To this were added appendices on rates of discount, a letter from Michel Chevalier on the treaty of commerce with France and a related paper by Charles Gairdner.

On metallic money, Price argued that money was not sought for its own sake but simply for its role as a medium of exchange. Money was as much on sale as another good; however, its utility lay solely in its transactional use. So 'money hoarded or not used is for the time annihilated as money … [I]t ceases to be a portion of the nation's capital' (Price 1869a: 45). The underlying real value of goods was determined by the relative labour or production costs. In turn, the quantity and circulation of money had no real effect. The quantity used is the quantity needed; any excess would have to be stored or exported to countries with a further use for it. Price's world was characterised by the veil of money: it was goods that bought other goods; money was the convenient intermediary that could make no real difference.

The cheques and bills which make up the majority of the business of the banks were not money. Thus, bankers deal in and transfer debts. The whole business does not affect the quantity of money. Whilst admitting that these debts, in terms of cheques, bills and loans could also be described as purchasing power, Price does not see them as real capital or wealth:

A bank possesses no capital beyond the coin in its till and its house with the furniture contained in it. Capital is not what a bank deals in or lends: it cannot lend what it does not possess. What it has to give is the right and power to buy capital … It bestows this power by transferring the right to demand gold (ibid.: 76).

Price saw wealth as only what was realised when sold; there was no such thing as intangible wealth. Whilst there could be crises of confidence and defaults on debt, 'Mercantile crises never have their origin in a deficiency of currency, of coin, and notes of legal tender' (ibid.: 79). What Price was objecting to was the conflation in the press and popular terminology of what were, to him at least, two separate things, money and loans of money. At the same time, he clearly realised the importance of these wider means of payment: 'The rising flood of cheques, as it is a sign of the activity, so also is it the usual mark of the profitableness of business; their ebb too surely announces the drooping resources of commerce. Great is the note, I admit; but far greater yet is the cheque' (ibid.: 95).

Price's view was that whoever held such bills, cheques and loans of money rather than money itself

has for the time lost wealth; he recovers it only when the bill is paid. For the moment he has a piece of paper, and no other wealth than the intrinsic worth of that piece of paper, that is, nothing at all. That piece of paper is purchasing power; it can buy, it can procure wealth; but wealth and the power to get wealth are two most different things (ibid.: 102).

Banknotes, he went on to argue, were nothing more than a cheque drawn by a banker on himself. So what made this money, where cheques were not? The difference was in their general circulation, in their use in multiple transactions, unlike a cheque which was used but once before ceasing to exist. In turn, that difference was determined by the perceived creditworthiness of the issuer. There was limited knowledge of the standing for a personal cheque, but the banker is widely known and trusted in his area. What was also important was the guarantee of convertibility of banknotes.

In looking at the quantity of banknotes in circulation, Price came to the same conclusion as he had for coin:

> So many banknotes as the public wants and can use will circulate and no more. Neither the bankers, nor Parliament, nor the law, nor the need of borrowers, nor any other power, but the wants and convenience of the public, the number and amount of the specific payments in which banknotes are used, can determine how many convertible banknotes will remain in circulation (ibid.: 110).

Therefore, 'An expanded or inflated circulation of banknotes is an absurdity, nothing better than pure nonsense' (ibid.). Currency is not the regulator, but simply a humble instrument of trade. So in these terms the contemporary debate over free banking was largely irrelevant, except in terms of confidence in the note issue, which would make convertible notes always superior to an inconvertible currency.

Price fully realised, however, that loans are rarely made in actual currency: 'Most advances are given by a line placed in a ledger to the credit of the borrower, who then draws out by degrees this power of buying and paying' (ibid.: 116). Furthermore:

> The City is but one great accountant's office. Its merchants, its bankers…are only clerks employed in the distribution of wealth … The wealth and capital of England are not in the merchants' offices or bankers' ledgers; not in bills and balances; they are spread over the whole land: they are England itself, and all that it contains (ibid.: 121–122).

Turning to his discussion on Mill, Price rejected the quantity theory that Mill outlined. Yes, it was true there was a total supply of money, and that there was a total amount of goods for sale and a volume of transactions made in money. But Price totally opposed the conjecture that this latter element constituted the demand for money. The purchases could be made in a wide variety of ways, for example, bills or forward promises, many of which involved no actual quantity of money. The

> true demand for money, as for every other commodity which men desire to purchase, consists in those requirements for money in which money is actually used … The actual quantity of the goods sold, the size and importance of the trade, have no direct and necessary connection with the use of money (ibid.: 165).

On the other hand, he welcomed Mill's conclusions on the effect of an expansion of credit on prices. For Price, it was not the circulation of banknotes nor cheques and bills that matter but credit and the wider concept of "buying". 'What raises prices universally is buying … [T]he greater the buying…the stronger will be the tendency of the articles in demand to rise in price' (ibid.: 168).

Price was opposed to bimetallism as it set a false fixed conversion rate between silver and gold, whereupon Gresham's Law would operate (see Price 1881a, 1882, and the material reproduced in Gibbs and Grenfell 1886). He approved, in principle, of Clarmont Daniell's plan, published in 1879,[14] to extend the legal tender status of silver coin, as subsidiary to gold, but at a properly regulated metals market-based conversion rate. This would make an expansion of metallic coinage possible to meet the demands of a growing world population without an undue rise in the price of gold (see Price 1882: 575).

In a letter to Henry Grenfell, a leading member of the Bimetallic League and a Governor of the Bank of England, Price wrote:

> An artificial ratio of value between two metals in the coinage is perfectly possible, and may easily be, and is, involved in the present bimetallist proposal; but the power of purchasing commodities lies quite in another region, namely, in the worth of the coined metals as commodities. I have no fear: the actual proposition of bimetallism is irrational (Price to Grenfell, 5 October 1882, in Grenfell and Price 1886: 300).

In addition:

---

[14] Daniell, a monometallist, joined the Bengal Civil Service in 1855. In his later years, he published a number of works on Indian currency and economic issues (see, for example, Daniell 1879).

I did say, and do say, that the value of money is determined by the cost of production of the metal, like the value of a loaf of bread is determined by what it costs to produce. And I say further, that at particular times, the state of supply and demand will alter the value of the metal in exchanging, precisely as the character of the seasons may largely affect the price of wheat in a particular year (Price to Grenfell, 12 November 1882, in ibid.: 323).

6   Is Economics a Science?

From the initial doubts expressed about the progress of political economy in his Inaugural Lecture, Price became increasingly sceptical of a scientific approach to economics through the 1870s. Most notable was his Presidential Address to the Department of Economy and Trade of the National Association for the Promotion of Social Science in Cheltenham in October 1878. He warned of a current crisis in economic thought and teaching. Despite the previous gains of free trade, Price warned that 'The mercantile theory still survives with great vitality in the language of the city and of commercial exchanges' (Price 1878a: 638). Traders failed to understand the nature of money, favourable exchanges were still seen as the best indicator of a prosperous trade, and protectionist calls grew in the face of depression. Where in all this, he asked, were the political economists? One factor was a failure to explain the problems in terms that the people of the market and workshop could understand: political economy was inherently polemical. The other was 'the grave mistake made by economists in attempting to give a scientific form to [their] teaching' (ibid.: 641), and 'The language in which this scientific teaching was couched was as remote from common life as that of the mathematician' (ibid.: 642).

Price's 1878 collection of lectures used the term "Practical Political Economy", which was 'intended to indicate a mode of treatment which not only does not claim to be scientific, but which supposes the strictly scientific method to be a mistake' (Price 1878b: 1). Political economy, therefore, was something of everyday life, open to common sense, simply a means of explaining complexities and exposing error. Attempting to do this in mathematical terms such as proposed by Ricardo, Mill and others was to move away from the essence of what Adam Smith had started. Price pointed out that it was a self-evident truth that if more goods are made than wanted, their price must fall or not be sold at all: 'There is little else in the economical discussions of supply and demand but expansions and applications of these very obvious and instinctively observed facts. To call them scientific principles is nothing but inflated language' (ibid.: 15) and:

The truths proclaimed by Political Economy are ultimately truisms—processes which have always been known to all the world; and when Political Economy has explained them, the hearer is rightly apt to exclaim, that everyone knew that before. It is an excellent test of real economical teaching that it should land the pupil in the perception that it is made up of familiar truisms. A right understanding of them is worth all that scientific treatises have ever constructed (ibid.: 16).

Not scientific laws, then, but simply rules in an art that seeks to explain what is wealth, in terms that anyone would understand, which did not therefore need the precision of a science. Political economy, for Price, is an 'Inquiry into some general processes in the production and distribution of wealth' (ibid.: 19). As such, Ricardo's false path should be abandoned to return to the Smithian method of *The Wealth of Nations*. Price uses very much the same set of arguments in his 1879 article for a US audience, stating: 'Whatever else Political Economy may be, most assuredly it is not the science of value' (Price 1879a: 573).

7   Chapters on Practical Political Economy (1878)

A much larger collection of lecture material was published in 1878 as *Chapters on Practical Political Economy* (Price 1878b), running to a second edition in 1882. This covered political economy as a science, value, exchange, capital, profit, wages, trade unions, free trade and rent as well as the earlier subjects of currency and banking.

With respect to value, Price notes that 'it lies in utility and in feeling (or want), the market value in terms of money is then the consequence of these influences: the relative interplay of wants and satisfactions between the two parties of a transaction' (ibid.: 47). Value is not an actual attribute or property of the good itself. Whilst values are commonly expressed in money terms, that is simply the result of a comparison to a common yardstick. How should value be measured independently? For this, once again, Price turns to Smith and examines the idea of a labour value, the amount of time someone would work to obtain any given item. But Price suggests that seeking any universal measure of value 'is a dream; it has no existence' (ibid.: 58). He suggests that the existence of rent (the excess of market price over costs of production including profit)[15] is sufficient to refute the labour-based doctrine. In the end, it is feeling that determines values but cannot ever measure them.[16]

---

[15] See also the chapter on rent in Price (1878b).
[16] Ibid.: 61.

Nonetheless, in his letters and articles, Price continually returns to the concept that values are determined by the costs of production including profit: '[T]he value of a loaf of bread is determined by what it costs to produce' (Price in Grenfell and Price 1886: 323). Supply and demand factors may create temporary divergences, but in the longer run average values will reflect this fundamental principle, or else producers would simply cease making that particular good.[17]

Price does not reject the idea of competitive markets in determining prices, but argues that they are not sufficient to explain all the observable behaviour and variance in retail prices between different sellers at the same point in time: 'The grand idea of constructing a science of Political Economy on a law of human nature, that men will steadily pursue what most promotes their interest through the agency of competition, rests on a foundation of sand' (Price 1878b: 74). 'Economic teaching can give tendencies only' (ibid.: 75). Indeed, Price goes as far as rejecting the principles of competitive behaviour:

> Men, in buying and selling, are not uniformly governed by the desire of making as large a gain, or saving as much money as possible, however much this principle is fondly laid down by Economists, as the foundation of their science. There are indestructible elements in human nature which come into play here as disturbing forces. Men will not uniformly buy in the cheapest though they generally strive most vigorously to sell in the dearest market (ibid.: 73–74).

Price suggests additional factors which help determine supply and demand, such as loyalty to a trader and the dislike of cheapness. The two countervailing forces are the desire and ability to buy or sell at a given price. Moreover, the desire to sell can take a crucial role, with the farmer deciding to take his stock home to sell another day. The basis of Price's whole model is that ultimately it is goods that are exchanged for other goods: '[P]urchasing power resides in the supply of goods' (ibid.: 90); even rents are just the share of the goods produced on the landowner's farms. Thus 'aggregate demand of any country is the quantity of goods it has to offer in exchange for others' (ibid.). If, however, a country produces more than it consumes, then there is saving and an increase in wealth. With this one exception, any increased spending in one area, whether current or capital, must reduce spending in another. From this, Price derives the idea that, for example, additional railway capital investment, not matched by saving, would have to be financed out of other capital or wealth, thus reducing overall demand. This is the essence of his over-consumption

---

[17] As, for example, outlined in some of Price's 1882 correspondence on bimetallism (see Grenfell and Price 1886: 324).

theory, that even spending on railway construction could consume wealth if it was in excess of the level of savings that the country was willing to make.

In his *Contemporary Review* article of 1876, Price briefly spells out his argument in the form of a simple one-good, agricultural corn economy, with no stocks (see Price 1876a: 787). In such a case, deciding to over-consume this year's corn would lead to too little being set aside as saving for planting and wages in the following year, which would then lead to a reduction in subsequent output and future growth. If we were then to allow for stocks, the over-consumption, assuming an unchanged level of investment, reduces the existing stock of corn, which can thus be seen as consuming out of wealth. An increased level of investment to meet the higher consumption demand would then further erode the existing corn stock/wealth.

There can be no multiplier effect in a simple corn economy as output is fixed by the previous year's investment in planting the seed corn and the weather; that would come solely from increased saving generating increased investment:

> A young nobleman is said to have ordered twenty waistcoats, for which he had no use, under the belief that he was doing good to trade. It did not occur to him that if he had saved what they cost and lent it to a producer, there would have been the same immediate good to trade and as much profit; but there would also have been ever afterwards, an additional income of wealth for employing labourers and buying at shops (Price 1878b: 128–129).

Capital is wealth used for producing further wealth. It is thus used up and destroyed, over varying periods of time, but in doing so it produces new wealth. This distinguishes it from consumption which produces nothing new, just gratification. Land is clearly capital therefore. Labour is also logically capital, though the labourer is not a capitalist (see ibid.: 107) and Price decides in the end that, for all practical purposes, labour is neither capital nor not-capital! The use of goods could be either, so corn that was milled was consumed whilst corn that was replanted was capital. Thus, Price distinguished between two sorts of consumption, productive and non-productive. He also distinguished between types of saving; hoarding was not true saving which was the application of wealth to increase production. On this basis, the building of great houses or ornamental gardens was just hoarding, not productive.

Similarly with capital goods, wealth is consumed, or at least tied up and made unavailable, in the initial construction of fixed assets. Its value then comes from the part that is used up in each period that contributes to the production of new goods for exchange, which can be measured in terms of depreciation, interest costs, maintenance and repairs. Capital formation thus becomes a two-edged sword. To be productive, savings must be so invested,[18] but the over-production of capital goods has the effect of consuming wealth with no return and thus can create a depression. Over-construction takes goods out of the economy and, as a result, there are fewer things to exchange, less trade and less profit:

> This excess of creation of fixed capital—of capital, be it remembered, which is destroyed, and is not, for a long time, practically restored by wealth available for use commonly follows a season of exceptional prosperity. Men are then hopeful, profits are good and abound, extension of business fascinates, trade is active, and demand for goods ever on the rise. At such times, as happened a few years ago, in the iron and coal trades, new works are commenced in profusion. All this while the consumption of the national wealth proceeds rapidly in maintaining many labourers and in the development of luxurious consumption in the fine weather of large profits; and it is followed by the consequences just described. Amongst these offenders none are so mischievous as railways; promoters, desirers of premium, stock-brokers, and many others, eagerly excite one another. The railway works are begun, and often the revulsion overtakes them before they are completed: the nation is stricken with poverty by their construction (Price 1878b: 119).

Profit is the reward for the creation of and for the employment of capital. By giving up some luxury now the capitalist is rewarded by a future higher income. Price stresses that this reflects real things produced, not just money: 'A portion of the cotton spun and sold is the true profit' (ibid.: 130), but Price rejects the idea from Mill that profit is in any part an indemnity or reward for risk, which could be seen as an insurance cost, and the capitalist's own time and labour, which he would count as wages as if a manager had been hired in the capitalist's place. He reached the conclusion that true profit consists 'in the clear surplus gain which the employment of capital creates … [T]here is a remainder, something over and above compensation for every charge…and because there is such a balance…labourers are able to make assaults on profits to the benefit of wages' (ibid.: 133). There is useful insight here by Price, only slightly obscured by a rather pedantic interpretation of the term profit, just as he was very narrow in his definition of what was and was not money above.

---

[18] In 1876, Price asked: 'But what are savings? The surplus of wealth made over wealth consumed. If it is turned into capital and applied to increased production, the nation becomes richer; if it is expended on any luxury or any folly, the nation is where it was. But if the outlay, however wise and ultimately profitable, once passes the limit of saving, harm instantly begins. There arises a loss of wealth which is taken from capital; the means of producing are diminished; fewer goods are made' (Price 1876a: 788).

He does not deny a reward for risk taking, for example, but just does not count it to be a part of profit, in the same way that he does not deny an important role for an expansion of credit, but does not define it as a change in the quantity of money.

Price defended the role of traders: even though they create no new goods, they provide a service at a risk which deserves a margin in return: 'By anticipating demand, and so acting on prices, he [the trader] brings a force of great power into play. He checks consumption; he gives practical warning of the deficiency and its consequences; he diminishes waste and extravagance, and thereby enables the stock in store to hold out longer' (ibid.: 141–143).

Interest rates appear to play no part in the savings and investment discussion. They relate to the supply of the service of lending, together with a risk premium. Once again, Price turns to the relative feelings of the borrower and lender to explain the wide variety of rates and their fluctuations:

> The character of the demander, the opinion framed of the certainty of the exchange being completed by the payment of the interest, and the repayment of the debt, are most governing factors in fixing the rate of interest. It is mind which estimates and judges and gives its form to the feeling called value; it is this feeling which rules that one loan must pay 5%, another granted at the same time 50 (ibid.: 150).

On wages, Price also emphasised the market, and the forces of supply and demand, but he saw the outcome of this in real terms: 'The substantial reward for his [the worker's] efforts is the goods he buys with his wages; it was to procure these goods that he sold his labour. It is a vital matter to grasp firmly that the worth of wages is not money, but what the wages can buy' (ibid.: 182). These wages are, however, paid out of capital, not from current production, that is to say from the goods previously set aside, exactly as they would be in the corn economy:

> The cost of production is first provided out of the consumption of pre-existing capital. But there is, on the other hand, a real and essential connection between what industry at work produces and wages. The employer must recover from new wealth made what he had destroyed in keeping up the labour or he will give up the business … In this sense wages clearly depend on the future results of industry (ibid.: 199).

Thus, Price managed to move beyond the wages fund doctrine. Indeed, he explicitly rejected the idea of fighting over the division of the common fund ... [W]hat one set wins the other loses ... [O]ne fatal fallacy pervades this doctrine. Mr Mill, and before him Ricardo, did not know that profit was a remainder—what is left after all the charges have been paid. He did not see that wages is one of these charges ... [T]he capitalist bargains for labour as he bargains for everything else (ibid.: 136–137).

Nonetheless, Price had some very Malthusian concerns about the growth of population and thus the supply of labour. Such an excess of supply of labour could not be simply made to disappear as was the case in the oversupply of goods. An excess supply of labour would have to be fed and clothed from total output, thereby lowering the average standard of living (see ibid.: 222). Decisions about marriage and childbearing were taken in the light of past economic conditions, so a few years of prosperous trade would increase the marriage rate, especially among the poorer classes. Price believed that as living standards rose, the birth rate would eventually fall, whilst emigration could also improve the balance of supply and demand more immediately, as was the case in Ireland following the potato famine (see ibid.: 226).

Price was, unsurprisingly, no supporter of restraints from either trade unions or employers, which he saw as introducing an unwanted element of antagonism into the labour market. He saw the natural working of the market as a mutual cooperation of interests for, 'The consumers are the source from which flow all the reward, the profits and the wages; the cheaper the goods, the more of them will be bought' (ibid.: 233). Given that labourers make up the largest part of consumers, it follows that efficient labour and higher production also benefit them the most. So, restrictive practices and artificially inflated wages, costs and prices are bad policies, whereas a fair employer rewarding increased productivity out of his higher production can only benefit everyone. The source of this is the increase in production and thereby wealth: 'And it must not be forgotten that, as an almost universal rule, industrial fortunes are not made out of a high rate of profit, but out of moderate profits earned by large operations' (ibid.: 236). What he set his hope on was enlightened mutual interest. However, Price acknowledged an important social and moral role for trade unions to improve working conditions, for example, safety, excessive hours, exploitation of female and child labour, and greater education. He noted that political economy taught quite correctly that such restraints would diminish wealth, but that would be to ignore the moral dimension, since equally he held that political economy 'does not teach that wealth must be acquired at all costs ... It nowhere denies that there are things better than wealth, and that wealth ought to be sacrificed to obtain more worthy ends, or to avert evils for which wealth can give no atonement' (ibid.: 245).

On balance, therefore, unionisation could be a potential benefit to the economy, if it avoided antagonism; then it could ease discussions about particular working conditions, such as the fair rate of wages. But, in going too far beyond this role, unions could be detrimental if they called for equal treatment and pay regardless of ability, and other similarly restrictive practices. Money illusion prevented the unions from understanding that lower prices could encourage higher production, and that the increased quantity of goods made the stock of wealth greater for the whole population.

Turning to trade, Price reaffirmed his absolute commitment to free trade: 'Free trade is the one subject in Political Economy which is susceptible of complete demonstration' (ibid.: 299). Nonetheless, despite the clear argument for free trade having been won from Adam Smith onwards, Price laments that due to 'renewed vigour and progress of protection in the practical world', it is necessary to argue in its favour again from first principles since, 'Protection seems to be indestructible—a weed that no intellectual or social culture can root up—a principle that is a part of human nature itself' (ibid.: 300).

Price first disassociates the term "free trade" from the idea of a lack of governmental regulation of trade, and even from the idea of abolishing customs duties in general (which he associates instead with an argument over indirect taxation). Instead, he concentrates on the idea that free trade is the opposite of protection, and that:

> Protection affirms the policy of differences of duties on the same goods. It inquires into the geographical and national origin of these goods ... Free Trade is the direct contradictory of this principle. It asks no question as to where the foods were made; the same goods must be treated all alike—is its doctrine (ibid.: 302).

Price again argued from his premise of money neutrality that all trade is ultimately the exchange of goods produced. There is simply substitution of production between industries and countries: 'Under Free Trade, foreign countries give in every case as much employment to English workmen and capitalists as if nothing had been brought abroad. English goods of the same value must be purchased by the foreigner, or the trade comes to an end' (ibid.: 307). His second argument was that of the division of labour and comparative advantage: 'Put countries in the place of individual men ... Each country, by taking a single commodity for its work to perform, makes it better and more cheaply, by the very fact that it concentrates its energy and directs its skill on one single operation' (ibid.: 308). Price makes no separate distinction between domestic trade conducted by different towns and international trade. Protection, on the other hand, reduces the consumer surplus and distorts markets through the intervention of the State (his term 'nursery government' has quite a modern ring): 'Protection takes from others what belongs to them, and takes it by force, by the force of law' (ibid.: 319). We have then, ultimately, Say's Law:

> Trade is merely an exchange of goods, and it is practically unlimited if there are more goods to be exchanged on both sides. What is true of the labourer is equally true of the capitalist … The limit to the employment of capital consists in the physical difficulty of obtaining returns for its use. Capital may be applied to a field in such quantity that at last the field yields no return for it that can compensate for the effort of saving capital; but the world has many ages yet to run ere capital encounters the insuperable limit to its further accumulation (ibid.: 322).

8   Teaching in Oxford

From 1870, Oxford started to publish a regular *Oxford University Gazette* of official proceedings, examination results, professorial lectures and other notices. By the early 1880s, this included a wider lecture list for each term. It thus became much easier to trace the timeline of the courses being given, beyond the content reproduced in Price's published collections.

In the three years prior to his re-election to the Drummond Chair in 1873, Price lectured twice weekly every term, excepting the Hilary term of 1873 when the election was held in February. Following his unopposed re-election, the same pattern continues, excepting that the Michaelmas term lectures on Adam Smith were cancelled at the last minute[19] and he gave no lectures again in the Easter term of 1876.

The year 1878 was again an election year for the Drummond and so there were no lectures in Hilary term. However, from 1879, Price gives no lectures at all in the Easter term, thus teaching only in the first two terms of each academic year. In 1882–1883, he only lectured in the first term, giving no lectures in either of the Hilary or Easter terms. The lecture lists show that more teaching was gradually being done by college lecturers.

---

[19] See *Oxford University Gazette*, 16 October 1874: 263.

In the Easter term of 1883, W.A.B. Coolidge was giving a course on "Political Economy, with illustrations from English History" at Magdalen. Then, from the Michaelmas term of the new academic year, Alfred Marshall gave two sets of lectures at Balliol on a variety of topics including "Production and Value", "Foreign Trade", "Wages and Profits" and "Adam Smith". After Marshall had returned to Cambridge, additional lectures where again given by Coolidge, as well as John Neville Keynes and W.J. Ashley in 1885. By 1886, W.A. Spooner, C.R.L. Fletcher and P.F. Willert also contributed, to be joined by L.R. Phelps in 1887 who would take over Price's lectures during and after his final illness. Thorold Rogers also makes a return to lecture on the "Economical Interpretation of History in England" from the Easter term of 1887.

Prince Leopold, Duke of Albany, frequently attended Price's lectures during the early 1870s, and Price's main collection of lectures in 1878 was dedicated to him. Nonetheless, in retrospect, it seems hard to justify *The Spectator's* obituary claim that, 'At Oxford, Bonamy Price's loss will be, and, indeed, has already been, severely felt' (Anon 1888: 11).

9   Later Royal Commissions

Following the bad weather of 1879 and the urging of Henry Chaplin MP, the government established the Royal Commission on the Depressed State of the Agricultural Interest (1879–1882). Besides the President, the Duke of Richmond, the Commission comprised the Duke of Buccleugh, Earl Spencer, Lord Vernon, seven MPs, the political economists Sir William Stephenson and Professor Bonamy Price, farming interests, two Irish representatives and two from Scotland.

A preliminary report of 1881 concentrated on Ireland where there was 'the most conspicuous difference between the relations of landlord and tenant' (Royal Commission on Agriculture 1881: 5). The report found that the effect of the agricultural depression had been made worse by a lack of manufacturing industries and alternative sources of employment. In particular, the impact had been the greatest for smaller farmers. The reasons for the depression lay in the poor weather leading to the failure of the potato crop; foreign competition; an undue inflation of credit due partly to the increased security afforded by the 1870 Land Act; and excessive competition for land, leading to rent increases, higher payments for tenant-right, overcrowding and the minute subdivision of farms. One obvious solution was some managed process of migration and emigration, but also a programme of public works and, the most contentious issue, an examination of the land tenure system, where it was felt that some legislation would be useful to protect tenants from arbitrary rent increases. The Commissioners had heard much evidence on the so-called Three Fs: fixity of tenure, free sale and fair rents, but found mainly that their implementation would be an injustice to landlords.

For his part, Price wrote a dissenting memorandum to the report on the suggestion of additional legislation for rents. He argued that the 1870 Land Act already gave protection against arbitrary rent increases as these could only be enforced by eviction which could then be challenged in court as capricious. The suggestion of legislative interference with rental valuations was

> a direct violation of the fundamental principle of all soundly constituted industry, freedom of contract; and soundly constituted industry is the root of national prosperity. The State might as well dictate what the price of corn, or coals, or cloth shall be. Such an idea would be held to be irrational; why is it less irrational in the business of farming? (ibid.: 10).

He then addressed each of the Three Fs.

Fixity of tenure, Price observed, would effectively deprive landowners of their property without compensation, turning them, in effect, into a mortgagee, as nominal absentee landlords. Furthermore, owners would be discouraged from making any improvements to their estates, further reducing the injection of capital and 'intelligent agriculture' that Ireland needed. It would also perpetuate the number of small-holdings and subdivided farms that engendered poor farming practices.

Price found free sale to be a curious concept as the only thing that a tenant had to sell was improvements to the land and 'goodwill'. This goodwill, as something over and above the value of any improvements, Price described as a 'myth' (ibid.: 11). He pointed out there is no security that the purchasing tenant would know how to farm, whilst the cost of purchasing a tenancy reduced the capital available to invest by any incoming farmer. Finally, as with the first F, free sale 'perpetuates the land miseries of Ireland as they actually exist—the starvation holdings, the bad farming, the wretched dwellings, the living on the verge of starvation' (ibid.).

Finally, on fair rents, Price argued that no government machinery could ever justly value rents. Nor should rents be based on affordability:

> What a particular tenant can pay is no rule for determining the fair rent—the rent which, if he understood his business, he ought to and would be able to pay … [T]his determination of fair rent other than by free contract—strikes at

the root of all improvement in the agriculture of Ireland. It takes as its standard the ignorance, the indolence, the apathy, the want of capital, of the unhappy tenant, who is protected in his want of industry by the adjustment of the rent to his state and habits (ibid.).

The Three Fs were thus fundamentally flawed and ultimately counter-productive. Whilst there had been some great abuses in raising rents by some landlords, the solution lay in education and cooperation, not in 'a legal inter-ference with business, which is unnatural and mischievous' (ibid.).

By February 1881, Price's comments had been republished as a separate pamphlet by the Irish Land Committee (a patrician landowners' organisation) with an explanatory preface, including other opposition to the Three Fs (see Price 1881b).

By contrast, Prime Minister William Gladstone in his speech to Parliament supporting the first reading of the Land Law (Ireland) Bill in 1881, ridiculed, somewhat unfairly, Price's opposition and famously remarked:

> Mr. Bonamy Price, is the only man—and to his credit be it spoken—who has had the resolution to apply, in all their unmitigated authority, the principles of abstract political economy to the people and circumstances of Ireland exactly as if he had been proposing to legislate for the inhabitants of Saturn or Jupiter.[20]

The Commission's final report, the following year, found that whilst all areas of the country had been affected by economic downturn, there were considerable regional variations. The Commissioners also found that depres-sion was not limited to the UK, but had been international. As to the causes, the report concluded that the immediate problem was bad weather (too little sun and too much rain); yields and quality of output were thus lower. After the weather, there was the impact of new competition from abroad that meant prices no longer rose when a bad harvest reduced domestic production. Among the complaints discussed were rates, rents, tenant rights and the effects of security on investment. The Commission called for the establishment of a single government department and minister with responsibility for agricul-ture. Subsequently, Henry Chaplin became the first President of the Board of Agriculture in 1889.

Price served on another of the inquiries engendered by the Long Depression of 1873–1896. The Royal Commission on the Depression in Trade and Industry was set up by the minority Conservative government of Lord

---

[20] Hansard HC Debate, 7 April 1881, vol. 260, c. 895.

Salisbury in August 1885 and completed its work in December 1886. The Commission was seen as a move to ameliorate the pressure on the Conservatives of the "fair traders" against the prevailing "free trade" orthodoxy.

There were many pages of dissenting views to the final report. Price's was short and to the point[21]:

> I beg to express my dissent from paragraph 82. It contains a specific repudiation of the great doctrine of free trade. Shorter hours of labour do not, and cannot, compensate to a nation for increased cost of production or diminished output. They tax the community with dearer goods in order to confer special advantages on the working man. They protect him, and that is a direct repudiation of free trade. The country is sentenced to dearer and fewer goods (Royal Commission Appointed to Inquire into the Depression of Trade and Industry 1886: xlii).

This is the same argument on free trade that Price had made earlier which had been referenced in Parliament in 1877 during a debate on the cotton trade:

> [B]ut what said Professor Bonamy Price in a pamphlet which he wrote a short time ago? Talking of Protectionists, he said—What is it they seek to accomplish? Nothing less than to raise a charity tax on the whole people for the benefit of those employed in a few particular trades. Protection, under the plausible disguises of not throwing poor people out of work…sends round a begging cap to all buyers of goods to make charitable contributions to particular individuals.[22]

On the causes of depression itself, Price had declared himself an *over-consumptionist* both in his *Principles* and in an 1879 article (Price 1879a). Over-consumption caused a shortfall in savings and net consumption rather than the creation of wealth. If capital spending continued in excess of savings, it destroyed net wealth; like digging holes and filling them in again, it produced nothing physically extra in the world. Put another way, Price proposed a theory of over-investment, and his railway boom example has exactly that flavour (save for the effect on interest rates). The excessive investment boom leads to the subsequent depression. But it is not so much the stopping of the investment projects and the subsequent fall off in other orders that he sees as the cause of depression, but rather the destruction of net wealth; the boom fails to produce real things in some lasting sense.

---

[21] Price was objecting to the argument in the report that the Commission did not want to see a loss of leisure enjoyed by workers as a result of demands for longer working hours to combat foreign competition.

[22] Hansard HC Debate, 10 July 1877, vol. 235, c. 1105.

10   Conclusion

Irving Fisher noted that Bonamy Price made the same mistake as Tooke and Jevons in confusing real and nominal rates of interest and overlooked the fact that interest, unlike prices, is not an instantaneous but rather a time-based phenomenon (see Fisher 1896: 69–70). Likewise Price did not grasp the concepts of a bank credit multiplier or the better liquidity of a paper loan note; he just saw bits of paper that changed nothing. His sometimes needless, pedantic nature could often miss the wider point.

On the determination of prices, he reached the same conclusion as the marginalists but by a different route. If prices do not reflect average costs of production plus profit then producers will reduce their output. However, Price's approach lacked the power to show how the levels of profit and output could then be determined. There was little, if anything, gained from his introduction of the other factors that play a part in economic decisions as he then left them too vague and ill-defined.

From a modern perspective, Price came intriguingly close to various insights on human capital and behavioural economics only to then veer steadfastly away from them. Much, if not all, of this derives from his reading of Smith.[23] There are germs of promise in an over-consumption theory that could lead to an overshooting of production beyond realised demand as a factor leading to a cyclical downturn, but that is abandoned for an eccentric view of excess capital formation consuming wealth. Price's approach to money and purchasing power enabled him to reject the quantity theory, but he failed then to build on his own insights. Price's use of common sense did not help develop economics. His was a framework for explanation, review and teaching, but not necessarily one for investigation, exploration and the advancement of knowledge. It is hard to escape the conclusion of the *Dictionary of National Biography*, that, whilst naturally a teacher, Price added nothing to the progress of economics itself (see Hewins and Curthoys 2004).

Although the original writer went on to dismiss the argument, one testimonial from 1851 raised the point 'that even the highest success as a schoolmaster is no guarantee for like success as a Professor' (Shairp in Anon 1851: 8). Perhaps then, Price's greatest lasting achievements lay in those early years where 'he shewed himself at Rugby one of the most successful teachers in England' (Tait in ibid.: 1).

---

[23] See, for example, the discussion of Smith's thought in Norman (2018).

References

Main Works by Bonamy Price

Gibbs, H.H. and B. Price (1877). *Correspondence between Henry Hucks Gibbs, Esq. and Professor Bonamy Price, on the Reserve of the Bank of England*. London: Bank of England.

Grenfell, H. and B. Price (1886). 'Bimetallism Again: Correspondence between Mr Grenfell and Professor Bonamy Price, September 1882'. In H.C. Gibbs and H.R. Grenfell *The Bimetallic Controversy*. London: Effingham Wilson, Royal Exchange: 293–333.

Price, B. (1850). *Suggestions for the Extension of Professorial Teaching in the University of Oxford*. London: Whittaker and Company; Rugby: Crossley and Billington.

Price, B. (1851). 'The Anglo-Catholic Theory'. *The Edinburgh Review*, 94(October): 527–557.

Price, B. (1852). *The Anglo-Catholic Theory*. London: Longman, Brown, Green, and Longmans.

Price, B. (1860). 'What is the House of Lords?'. *The National Review*, 11(July): 110–130.

Price, B. (1861). *Venetia*. Reprinted from the *Army and Navy Gazette* 1860/1861 with additions. London: James Ridgway.

Price, B. (1863). 'The Principles of Currency'. *Fraser's Magazine for Town and Country*, 67(May): 581–599.

Price, B. (1863). 'The Great City Apostasy on Gold'. *Macmillan's Magazine*, 8(June): 124–137.

Price, B. (1863). *Venetia and the Quadrilateral: A Lecture*. London: Royal United Service Institution, printed by Harrisons & Sons.

Price, B. (1868). *Inaugural Lecture* [as Professor of Political Economy in the University of Oxford]. London: Macmillan.

Price, B. (1869a). *The Principles of Currency: Six Lectures Delivered at Oxford with a Letter from M. Michel Chevalier on the History of the Treaty of Commerce with France*. Oxford and London: J. Parker & Co.

Price, B. (1869). 'Credit and Crises'. *Fraser's Magazine for Town and Country*, 80(August): 207–222.

Price, B. (1869). 'The Land Question of Ireland'. *Blackwood's Edinburgh Magazine*, 106(November): 563–579.

Price, B. (1870). 'University Tests'. *Blackwood's Edinburgh Magazine*, 107(February): 139–160.

Price, B. (1870). 'Free Trade and Reciprocity'. *The Contemporary Review*, 13(March): 321–345.

Price, B. (1870). 'Trade-Unions (No. I)'. *Blackwood's Edinburgh Magazine*, 107(May): 554–569.

Price, B. (1870). 'What Is Money? And Has It Any Effect On the Rate of Discount?'. *The Contemporary Review*, 14(May): 236–259.

Price, B. (1871). 'Commercial Crises'. *The North British Review*, 53(January): 450–478.

Price, B. (1871). 'The House of Lords'. *Blackwood's Edinburgh Magazine*, 110(December): 771–785.

Price, B. (1872). 'The Nine-Hours Movement'. *Blackwood's Edinburgh Magazine*, 111(January): 68–83.

Price, B. (1872). 'The Manchester Nonconformists and Political Philosophy'. *Blackwood's Edinburgh Magazine*, 111(March): 334–347.

Price, B. (1874). *Our Currency: The Reign of Panics*. New York: New York News Company.

Price, B. (1875). *The Principles of Currency, and the Error of "Inflation": An Abstract of the Oxford Lectures, Applicable to Financial Questions in the United States*. New York: H.L. Hinton & Co.

Price, B. (1876a). 'One Per Cent'. *The Contemporary Review*, 29(December): 778–799.

Price, B. (1876). *Currency and Banking*. New York: D. Appleton and Co.; London: H.S. King.

Price, B. (1878a). 'Address of the President of the Department of Economy and Trade of the National Association for the Promotion of Social Science, at the Twenty-Second Annual Congress held at Cheltenham, in October, 1878'. *Journal of the Statistical Society of London*, 41(4): 637–653.

Price, B. (1878b). *Chapters on Practical Political Economy being the Substance of Lectures Delivered in the University of Oxford*. London: C.K. Paul & Co. Second edition, 1882.

Price, B. (1879a). 'Is Political Economy a Science?'. *The North American Review*, 129(277): 570–587.

Price, B. (1879). 'Is Political Economy a Science?'. *The Quarterly Review*, 147(January): 182–202.

Price, B. (1879). 'Commercial Depression and Reciprocity'. *The Contemporary Review*, 35(May): 269–288.

Price, B. (1879). 'The Stagnation of Trade and Its Cause'. *The North American Review*, 128(271): 587–604.

Price, B. (1881a). 'Buying and Selling: Its Nature and its Tools'. *Journal of the Society for Arts*, 29(1,485): 526–533.

Price, B. (1881b). *Mr Bonamy Price on the Three Fs*. Dublin: The Irish Land Committee.

Price, B. (1882). 'Address of the President of the Department IV, "Economy and "Trade", of the National Association for the Promotion of Social Science, at the Twenty-Sixth Annual Congress, held at Nottingham, in September 1882'. *Journal of the Statistical Society of London*, 45(4): 558–576.

Price, B. and F. St. John (1857). 'Fishery Board (Scotland): Copy of Reports Addressed to the Lords Commissioners of Her Majesty's Treasury in 1856, or the Present Year, on the Subject of the Fishery Board of Scotland'. *House of Commons Parliamentary Papers*.

Other Works Referred To

Anon (1851). *Additional Testimonials in Favour of…Bonamy Price*. Edinburgh: Bodleian Library.

Anon (1888). 'Professor Bonamy Price'. *The Spectator*, 14 January: 2, 10–11.

Coats, A.W. (1967). 'Sociological Aspects of British Economic Thought (ca. 1880–1930)'. *Journal of Political Economy*, 75(5): 706–729.

Daniell, C.J. (1879). *Gold in the East*. London: Strahan.

Fisher, I. (1896). *Appreciation and Interest*. New York: American Economic Association and Macun.

Gibbs, H.H. and H.R. Grenfell (1886). *The Bimetallic Controversy*. London: Effingham Wilson, Royal Exchange.

Hewins, W.A.S. and M.C. Curthoys (2004). 'Price, Bonamy (1807–1888), economist'. *Oxford Dictionary of National Biography*. Available at: https://www.oxforddnb.com/view/10.1093/ref:odnb/9780198614128.001.0001/odnb-9780198614128-e-22742.

Kadish, A. (1982). *The Oxford Economists in the Late Nineteenth Century*. Oxford: Clarendon Press.

Kadish, A. (1989). *Historians, Economists and Economic History*. London: Routledge.

de Marchi, N.B. (1976). 'On the Early Dangers of Being Too Political an Economist: Thorold Rogers and the 1868 Election to the Drummond Professorship'. *Oxford Economic Papers*, New Series, 28(3): 364–380.

Mozley, J.R. (1899). 'Price, Bonamy (1807–1888)'. In R.H.I. Palgrave (ed) *Dictionary of Political Economy*. London: Macmillan: 188–189.

Norman, J. (2018). *Adam Smith: What He Thought, and Why it Matters*. London: Allen Lane.

Rashid, S. (1978). 'The Price-Rogers Election: Politics or Religion'. *Oxford Economic Papers*, New Series, 30(2): 310–312.

Royal Commission Appointed to Inquire into the Depression of Trade and Industry (1886). *Final Report*. London: Her Majesty's Stationery Office.

Royal Commission on Agriculture (1881). *Preliminary Report from Her Majesty's Commissioners on Agriculture*. London: George Edward Eyre and William Spottiswoode for Her Majesty's Stationery Office.

Whitaker, J.K. (1975). *The Early Economic Writings of Alfred Marshall, 1890*. Volume 1. London: Macmillan.

10

Thorold Rogers (1823–1890)

Robert A. Cord

1   Introduction

James Edwin Thorold Rogers, known as Thorold Rogers, was a member of the
English Historical School of Economics, historian and politician who was
closely associated with Oxford, first as an undergraduate and then as the
holder on two separate occasions of the prestigious Drummond Professorship
of Political Economy. His most important work was the multi-volume *A
History of Agriculture and Prices in England* (hereafter *A History*), which
appeared between 1866 and 1902. Rogers' reputation rests on the painstaking
research carried out over many decades contained in these volumes. Despite
the achievement represented by *A History*, Rogers did not attain the recognition he may have perhaps deserved in his lifetime or subsequently. Various
reasons can be identified which help to explain why this was the case, among
them Rogers' fiery character, his tendency of belittling the work of other economists, and his failure to make any significant contributions to economic
theory. Section 2 of this chapter outlines Rogers' life and career. Section 3
provides an account of *A History* and, as part of this, Rogers' theory of rent.
Section 4 looks at some other aspects of Rogers' work as an economist and his
often-hostile views on the workings of Oxford University. Section 5 concludes.

R. A. Cord (✉)
Researcher in Economics, London, UK
e-mail: robert_cord@cantab.net

© The Author(s), under exclusive license to Springer Nature Switzerland AG 2021
R. A. Cord (ed.), *The Palgrave Companion to Oxford Economics*,
https://doi.org/10.1007/978-3-030-58471-9_10

2   Life and Career

Thorold Rogers was born on 23 March 1823 in the village of West Meon in Hampshire, England. He was the eleventh son of the surgeon, George Vining Rogers, and his wife, Mary Blyth Rogers.[1] Rogers proudly claimed a Northumbrian heritage, although his schooling took place in Southampton on the south coast of England, followed by King's College, London, and matriculation at the age of nineteen at Magdalen Hall (now Hertford College) at the University of Oxford in March 1843. Rogers secured a First Class BA in *Literae Humaniores* (Classics) in 1846 and an MA in 1849. Indeed, before he became an economist, Rogers' academic standing was founded on his reputation as a classicist, even if his academic record was not strong enough to secure a college fellowship.[2]

Rogers' brother John had married Emma Cobden. She was the sister of the Liberal statesman and campaigner for free trade, Richard Cobden, who became one of Rogers' great heroes, possibly his only one. Although Cobden was nearly twenty years older than Rogers, the two quickly struck up a close friendship, regularly visiting each other's homes. As a result, Rogers adopted many of Cobden's economic and political views, perhaps most notably the latter's espousal of a free market and free trade, especially in land as a means of breaking the power of the aristocracy but to also increase capital investment in the agricultural sector and to address growing demographic pressures on Britain's cities and towns. Cobden encouraged Rogers' research, with Rogers becoming a devoted member of the Manchester School and a regular attendee at the Cobden Club, founded the year after Cobden's death.[3] Rogers also delivered the sermon at Cobden's funeral at West Lavington Church, West Sussex, in 1865. It was through Cobden that Rogers got to know Liberal politician, John Bright, working with him on Cobden's *Speeches on Questions of Public Policy* (Bright and Rogers 1870).[4]

---

[1] One of Rogers' elder brothers was the well-known physician and campaigning medical officer, Joseph Rogers. Thorold edited Joseph's *Reminiscences of a Workhouse Medical Officer*, which appeared in 1889.

[2] Being in a hall rather than a college at Oxford counted against Rogers as very few fellowships were ever awarded to members of the former (see Kadish 1989: 19).

[3] Rogers contributed to the publications of the Club, one example being his *Free Trade and Fair Trade: What Do the Words Mean?*, which appeared in 1885 as leaflet number 28. Apart from claiming the superiority of free trade over fair trade, Rogers at one point also makes what might perhaps be interpreted as a pre-Keynesian comment in the leaflet: 'If everything is dearer, there must be stint [less spending]. If everyone is stinted, he has less to spend. If he has less to spend, he can buy less. *If he buys less, he causes less employment to be given*' (Rogers 1885a: 2; italics added).

[4] A few years later, Rogers also edited *Public Addresses by John Bright* (Rogers 1879a).

Another great influence on Rogers was Frédéric Bastiat, a member of the French Liberal School, who supported free trade but who had become less popular by the time of Rogers' death. Bastiat's friendship with Cobden seems to have been the conduit by which Rogers was influenced by the Frenchman, this most clearly seen with respect to the Ricardian theory of rent and the Malthusian theory of population.

Rogers' youth was marked by a number of important events which would go on to shape his political views. These included the Bristol Riots of 1831, the Reform Bill of 1832, the Factory Acts, the series of 90 theological publications written by the English Oxford Movement (the Tractarians) between 1833 and 1841 under the title "Tracts for the Times" (Rogers became a follower of the Tractarians as an undergraduate,[5] although he later distanced himself from them), and Cobden's great triumph, the repeal of the Corn Laws in 1846. Taking holy orders, Rogers was the curate of St Paul's, Oxford, from 1848 to 1851 and then assistant curate at Headington Quarry from 1856, his annual remuneration for the latter role being four shillings and, in the same year, he became an ordained priest. In December 1850, Rogers married Anna Peskett, the only daughter of surgeon William Peskett; this marriage ended on Anna's death in January 1853. Rogers' second marriage was to Anne Reynolds in December 1854. Reynolds was the daughter of the British government's Treasury Solicitor, Henry Reynolds. Together they had five sons and a daughter.[6]

With Rogers putting down roots in Oxford, he decided to become a private tutor in classics[7] and philosophy whilst also being an examiner at the University in the final classical school in 1857 and 1858 and classical moderations in 1861 and 1862 and holding various unpaid administrative offices, before being elected in June 1859 as the Tooke Professor of Economic Science and

---

[5] A number of Rogers' historian contemporaries at Oxford were also attracted to Tractarianism, amongst the most notable being William Stubbs and Edward Augustus Freeman.

[6] Their daughter was Annie Rogers, who went on to become a well-known pioneer of women's education. One of their sons was the mathematician Leonard James Rogers, notable for, amongst other things, discovering and proving the Rogers-Ramanujan identities.

[7] As noted above, for the first part of his academic career, Rogers' main focus was on the classics, one of his earliest publications being an edited edition of Aristotle's *Ethics* (Rogers 1865a). However, he would have been disappointed by a decision by the Clarendon Press to not meet the costs of publishing his Aristotelian dictionary. As a private tutor who had been successful in *Literae Humaniores*, Rogers probably made a reasonably good living. To get a sense of this, Kadish (1989: 19) cites the example of the naval historian Montagu Burrows, who would eventually become the first holder of the Chichele Professorship in Modern History at Oxford. Before taking up this post, Burrows was able to earn up to £600 a year through the private teaching of undergraduates, the equivalent of around £60,000 today. For a time starting from 1872, Rogers also delivered history classes to candidates for the Indian Civil Service examinations at the celebrated crammer school of Walter Wren in Bayswater, London. Edgeworth would later teach at the same establishment.

Statistics at King's College in the University of London. Rogers was the first holder of the Tooke, seeing off a number of other candidates and despite not having published anything of note in the sphere of economics at the time of his appointment. Carrying an annual emolument of just £50, he was obliged to give a minimum of twenty lectures each year, with at least ten of these delivered in the evening so that the working public could attend. Rogers' lectures, the first of which was delivered on 23 January 1860, ranged over a variety of topics, including "The Revenue of the Norman and Earliest Plantagenet Kings" and "Theories of Direct Taxation" (see S.J. 1859). Rogers held the Tooke until his death in 1890.

In 1862, Rogers succeeded Charles Neate to the Drummond Professorship at Oxford. He dedicated himself to the duties required of the office and was keen to serve another five years when the Chair came up for election again in early 1868.[8] Given the extensive research that he had already carried out as part of his investigations into the history of prices in Britain, Rogers' re-election might have been regarded as something of a formality. However, this proved to be far from the case. The circumstances around the election have been extensively discussed by De Marchi (1976) who argues that the main reason for Rogers' defeat was his political views. There is certainly some support for this view. For example, the leader of the group opposing Rogers', the Reverend Henry Wall, who was the first holder of the Wykeham Professorship in Logic, stated that he objected to Rogers' apparent use of his university position to advance his political opinions (see Kadish 1989: 32). In addition, there was Rogers' support for changes in the Oxford curriculum (see De Marchi 1976: 373), including a greater role for political economy, and his criticism of the Oxford system of educating its students (see Section 4.2). Responding to De Marchi, Rashid (1978) posits that Rogers' failure to be re-elected to the Drummond was as much down to his attendance at a particular Baptist missionary meeting, this being regarded by some of those voting in the election as disloyalty to the Church of England. In reality, all of these factors, plus some others, probably played a part in Rogers not being re-elected.

The person who beat Rogers in 1868 was Bonamy Price, a schoolmaster at Rugby School, who lacked distinction as an economist. Notwithstanding this, Price would go on to be Drummond Professor for twenty years, being three times re-elected.[9] Losing the Drummond and searching for a new career,

---

[8] Originally, an individual could occupy the Drummond for a single period of five years and would only become eligible for re-election after an interval of two years. However, this was changed by statute in 1867 to allow for consecutive terms of five years to be served.

[9] Price had stood as a candidate for the Drummond in 1862, but lost out to Rogers.

Rogers turned to politics. In fact, his involvement in the political realm had started a few years previously, founded on his enlightened views on certain issues. One example was his support for the Reform League, which campaigned for one man, one vote in Britain. The League had been established in February 1865, receiving financial backing from a number of luminaries, including John Stuart Mill, Henry Fawcett, Titus Salt and Rogers himself (who also founded the League's Oxford branch in 1866), its activities helping to bring about the vote for all male heads of household in 1867.[10] Meanwhile, Rogers favoured the Clerical Disabilities Relief Act 1870, becoming the first person to benefit from the legislation, withdrawing from his clerical vows on 10 August 1870, the day after the Act had become law.

Standing as a Liberal, Rogers unsuccessfully fought the seat for Scarborough in the February 1874 general election, before being elected for the borough of Southwark in London in 1880. In 1885, a redistribution of seats took place, after which he became the MP for Bermondsey in south-east London, albeit with a majority of just 83 votes over the Conservative candidate, Alfred Lafone. Rogers did not hold the seat for very long, losing to Lafone at the election of July 1886 when he was voted out seemingly for his support for the policy of Irish Home Rule adopted by the Gladstone government.

By all accounts, Rogers was a devoted constituency member of parliament. However, he seems to have found the experience of representing a London constituency disagreeable, arguing that the capital should be run by a centralised body rather than a group of MPs. He was in regular attendance at the House of Commons, although rarely spoke, perhaps aware that his style of debating may cause offence to others. Indeed, it is reported that in his maiden speech which was part of a debate on Charles Bradlaugh's refusal to swear an oath of allegiance to the Crown, Rogers referred to Bradlaugh as 'vermin'.

One of Rogers' most notable parliamentary victories took place in March 1886 when he pushed through a motion which separated the payment of local rates between owners and occupiers. Rogers' other political positions and activities included being a vocal critic of the House of Lords, favouring the extension of employer liability, strengthening protections for friendly societies, backing the North in the American Civil War, supporting the co-operative movement (he served as the presiding officer on the first day of the

---

[10] Many years later, Rogers was a champion of the Representation of the People Act 1884 (the Third Reform Act), which gave to people residing in the countryside the same voting rights that existed for people living in towns. Rogers' backing for the legislation along with that of some other Liberal MPs attracted the ire of Queen Victoria, who wrote a number of letters on the issue to Prime Minister William Gladstone, the main theme of which was her view that the House of Lords had every right to reject the Bill. In fact, Rogers wanted Gladstone to go further by granting the vote to all women, this proposal being rebuffed on the grounds that its inclusion would threaten the whole legislation.

seventh annual meeting of the Co-operative Congress in 1875), and criticising the brutal suppression by Governor Edward John Eyre of the Morant Bay rebellion in Jamaica in October 1865. Overall, however, Rogers' parliamentary career did not live up to the expectations of those who knew him.

Maintaining his connections with Oxford whilst he pursued a political career, Rogers had been appointed as a Lecturer in Political Economy at Worcester College in 1883. This bridge to the University seems to have paid off as Rogers was re-elected to the Drummond in March 1888 following Price's death. However, even this was a close-run thing. The Board of Electors was made up of the Chancellor of Oxford, Lord Salisbury, the Chancellor of the Exchequer, George Goschen, the Regius Professor of Modern History, Edward Augustus Freeman, the Whyte Professor of Moral Philosophy, William Wallace, and a member of All Souls, John Andrew Doyle. Goschen was late to the Board's meeting which had already voted but was tied between Rogers and L.R. Phelps of Oriel College who had taken on Price's teaching duties when he fell ill in 1887. Rogers' victory was secured when immediately upon arriving at the meeting Goschen declared that he was the only man in England who could be the next Drummond Professor (see Kadish 1989: 67).[11]

This later period as Drummond Professor was not a particularly positive one as far as Rogers' relationship with his colleagues and students was concerned. For instance, he refused to teach even the basics of economic theory, this leading to resentment amongst college lecturers who had to fill in the gaps. One perhaps inevitable consequence was that undergraduates were advised by their colleges to not attend Rogers' lectures, this sometimes leading to as few as half a dozen students being in attendance (see ibid.: 68).

Rogers died at Oxford on 14 October 1890, aged 67. Having left little wealth at his death, his wife was granted a civil list pension in 1893.

3   A History of Agriculture and Prices in England

Rogers was part of the English Historical School of Economics, an important goal of which was to overturn the classical approach, founded on deduction, and replace it with inductive methods, based on empirical observation. Although the English School was not as well-known as its German

---

[11] If the recollections of John Neville Keynes are anything to go by, the fact that Phelps, much like Price before him, was even in the running for the Drummond is something of a surprise. In 1885, Keynes dined with Phelps when he was lecturing at Oxford, noting in his *Diary* that Phelps 'does not profess to know a great deal of Political Economy' (John Neville Keynes quoted in Tullberg 2017: 417, fn. 38).

counterpart, it did attract a number of highly regarded figures, including Walter Bagehot, Arnold Toynbee and William Whewell, who regarded themselves as the intellectual heirs to the likes of Francis Bacon and David Hume. The first attempt by Rogers to clearly separate himself from the theories of previous economists, Ricardo in particular, was in the *Manual of Political Economy for Schools and Colleges*, which appeared in 1868, two years after the first volume of *A History*.[12] But it is really to *A History* that we should look in order to get a clearer understanding of Rogers' research agenda and how this shaped his economics.

Prior to Rogers, various studies had examined the development of prices in Britain, notably Fleetwood (1707), Eden (1797), Shuckburgh-Evelyn (1798), Young (1812), Mundell (1829), Porter (1836) and Tooke and Newmarch (1838–1857).[13] However, none of these contained both the depth and breadth of data and analysis that was to appear in *A History*. Granted, Tooke and Newmarch's monumental six-volume study, which attempted to show that changes in prices *precede* changes in the money supply, is regarded as a milestone in the field and, in a nod to this, the period covered by Rogers' research ended in 1793, the first year examined by Tooke and Newmarch. This aside, Tooke and Newmarch only looked at the four or so *decades* up to 1837, a much shorter span of analysis than the nearly five and a half *centuries* surveyed by Rogers.

A number of other factors help to explain why Rogers embarked on *A History*. Despite the various studies that preceded it, investigators had focused much of their attention on the lives of important people rather than the state of the masses in determining the course taken by the economy. It was Rogers' firm belief that only by compiling and interpreting price data could the social ills of the general population be better understood, the same ills that he would have observed when he was assistant curate in the relatively poor district of Headington.

Equally important was a direct challenge laid down by Newmarch (1860) at the International Statistical Congress held in London in 1860 which Rogers attended. He describes what happened at the meeting and subsequently:

---

[12] Despite his hostility to Ricardo, Rogers did occasionally lapse into Ricardianisms. For instance, in the later *The Economic Interpretation of History* he stated that: 'If the ownership of land remains in private hands, and it would be an evil time should it cease to be in private hands, the *inexorable law* which limits profits to an average on the calling would develop rent' (Rogers 1888a: 165–166; italics added). Earlier in the same volume, he insisted that *all* economists agreed that profit is made up of interest, insurance and wages of superintendence and that the purpose of capital was to equalise prices and profit (see ibid.: 17, 19).

[13] Even though these predecessors laboured in the same field as Rogers, they did not escape his wrath. To take one example, Rogers tells us that Young was a 'careful and diligent collector of facts … But he was [also]…an exceedingly bad reasoner, and his economical inferences are perfectly worthless' (Rogers 1866–1902, 1: 690).

I was led in the first instance to enter upon this branch of history in consequence of some suggestions made at the meeting of the [Congress], as to the importance of researches into ancient values, and the relations which might be determined between the prices of labour and food. On returning to Oxford, as I was obliged to remain during the long vacation at home, I searched in the Bodleian Library, and found a little evidence for the fourteenth century, and much for the sixteenth. At first it was my intention to confine my researches to the change of values which took place in the sixteenth century, and thinking that information might be obtained from the account books of the Colleges, I investigated in the first instance those of All Souls. Subsequently I obtained permission to examine the muniment room at Merton, and here I found a vast store of the most valuable documents. I resolved therefore to begin as early as I could, and to make use of the archives in the Public Record Office. I have thus become an antiquary by accident (Rogers 1866–1902, 2: xi).

As well as the sources listed by Rogers, he would also go on to inspect records at, amongst others, Cambridge University, York Minster, the Tower of London, the British Museum, the schools of Eton and Winchester and the private records of individual families, with the most detailed information derived from the rolls of farm bailiffs and the accounts of college bursars. As an indicator of the level of detail that Rogers went into, volume I of *A History* contains corn prices for over five hundred districts in Britain, while no less than eighty thousand documents had to be consulted in order to arrive at the statistics provided in volume IV. Newmarch for one was pleased with the initial results of Rogers' research, commenting in an 1866 review of the first two volumes of *A History* that they were amongst the 'most extraordinary, successful, and remarkable publications which [have] ever appeared in connection with the application of statistics to illustrations of the economical history and progress of a country' and that Rogers had constructed 'probably the first really economical history of our own or of any European country' (Newmarch 1866: 544, 547).

What did Rogers discover? He himself regarded his views and findings on rent as the most important of his contributions to economics. The subject was of interest to Rogers as he was of the opinion that Ricardo's theory of rent was the 'ark of the deductive economists' (Rogers 1880: 673) and so set his sights on disproving it through the data contained in *A History*.[14] Rogers acknowledged that Ricardo's theory was correct insofar as where competitive

---

[14] As alluded to above, a strong statement of Rogers' views on rent can also be found in *A Manual of Political Economy*. Saying this, Schumpeter (1954: 822, fn. 21) referred to the volume as 'not very brilliant', even if it did reach its third edition very quickly as a result of its use in schools and was, according to Ashley (1889: 384) at least, 'a little…idealized' by Henry Sidgwick.

conditions exist, rent can be defined as the excess realised over the costs of production plus the ordinary rate of profit on capital investment. However, this truism was, in Rogers' opinion, hardly a great theoretical innovation in the history of economics as it had already been known to the Egyptians.

The claim that was far more contentious for Rogers was Ricardo's proposition that increases in population drove the cultivation of lands possessed of differing levels of fertility and that, given the same amounts of labour and capital, rents would be influenced by the amount of excess production taking place on the best soil compared to the "margin". It was this aspect of Ricardo's theory which motivated Rogers' research, and which resulted in him showing that, contrary to Ricardo, during the eighteenth century when there was the most significant increase in rents in the history of English agriculture (and when the prices of agricultural products were either stable or fell), the cause was to be found in advances in land management for growing crops rather than population increases (see Gibbins 1890: 606).[15] Coupled with other empirical findings by Rogers, his broad position was that any failings in agriculture were often attributable to factors such as a lack of investment in production-enhancing techniques or the poor protection of tenants' rights (see Koot 1987: 71). As Kadish notes (1989: 62), many of the objections which Rogers levelled against Ricardo's theory had already been made by Wakefield and Torrens, but it was Rogers who provided the empirical evidence to back them up.

Rogers was a passionate defender of laissez-faire, the obvious counterpart to this being his dislike of government involvement in the economy. Rogers used *A History* to identify periods when he thought that the laws of supply and demand operated most purely, without distortion from the State. He argued that the best example of this was to be found in the Middle Ages, in particular the mid-thirteenth century to the mid-fifteenth century, as 'governments had not developed to any marked extent that protective system, that perpetual interference with the freedom of trade which has characterised their later activity' (Rogers 1866–1902, 1: ix–x). Measured in terms of real wages, labourers were better off during this period because, amongst other things, the feudal system operated to the mutual benefit of landowners and those who worked the land and because land ownership was widely distributed (see De Marchi 1976: 368).

The ending of this age of prosperity was precipitated, as Rogers saw it, by the onset of legislation being used by the aristocracy to advance its own

---

[15] As Rogers acknowledged, raising the productivity of land may not be the only factor behind higher rents. Lower wages for labourers (Rogers 1884, 2: 482) and higher prices as a result of food scarcity (ibid.: 486) can also play a part. These points were made by Rogers in *Six Centuries of Work and Wages*, a popular account of the first four volumes of *A History*.

interests,[16] a period which he identified as beginning from the reign of Elizabeth I, lasting through to the early nineteenth century:

> I contend that from 1563 to 1824, a conspiracy, concocted by the law and carried out by parties interested in its success, was entered into, to cheat the English workman of his wages, to tie him to the soil, to deprive him of hope, and to degrade him into irremediable poverty (Rogers 1884, 2: 398).

Rogers focuses specifically on 1563 as it was the year in which the Statute of Artificers became law, restricting workers' freedom of movement and imposing maximum wages. However, Hewins (1898: 341) for one was sceptical about the emphasis that Rogers placed on the Statute, arguing that it was actually meant to *raise* real wages and that Rogers had not fully accounted for the fact that from as early as the fourteenth century, justices of the peace had wide powers in the regulation of wages.[17]

A History was subject to various other criticisms. Rogers himself acknowledged that there were some fundamental issues which the reader had to be aware of. For instance, it was not always easy to work out the precise time of year when purchases of a particular commodity had been made (Rogers uses the example of corn), and there were some lingering problems around the use of weights and measures, such as ambiguity about the size of a bushel. In addition, there were questions over Rogers' treatment of the impact that the Black Death had on the population of Britain, with economic historian Frederic Seebohm arguing that Rogers had significantly underestimated it (see Seebohm 1865, 1866, and a response by Rogers 1866a). Others questioned Rogers' dating of the ending of the system of villeinry[18] and his possible miscalculation of the value of the pound in the fourteenth and fifteenth centuries. Finally, it was pointed out that Rogers was perhaps not as forthcoming as he might have been with regard to acknowledging previous research. Thus, discussing volumes V and VI of *A History*, Nicholson (1889: 169) notes that Rogers makes no reference to the well-regarded work of Georg Schanz on the conduct of commerce in medieval England, this in spite of the fact that Schanz had actually acknowledged Rogers in the preface to the said work (see Schanz 1881: viii).

---

[16] Rogers also objected to the right of primogeniture, seeing it as a perpetuation of the privileged economic position enjoyed by the landed classes (see Rogers 1864a, b).

[17] In another criticism, Brentano asserted that 'as long as the regulations of the Statute…were maintained, the position of the workmen was secure' (Brentano 1870: 103–104). Brentano also argued, however, that it was the *non-observance* of the regulations contained in the Statute that led directly to the creation of the trade union movement (see ibid.).

[18] A villein was a type of serf in the Middle Ages who paid dues to a landlord in return for the use of land. In terms of rights, a villein was between a freeman and a slave.

Notwithstanding these criticisms, Rogers' work became the inspiration for similar research both in the UK and abroad. Perhaps the most prominent example of the latter was Georges d'Avenel's seven volumes examining the development of property prices, wages and general prices in France from 1200 to 1800 (see d'Avenel 1894–1926). In Britain, a notable study was William Beveridge's *Prices and Wages in England from the Twelfth to the Nineteenth Century* (1939), which uncovered a number of sources that had been missed by Rogers (see Hamilton 1942: 54). Beveridge's volume was part of a series published under the auspices of the International Scientific Committee on Price History (of which Beveridge was the Chairman) (see Cole and Crandall 1964). *A History* did not contain any index numbers or moving averages but rather average annual prices by locality. Although Rogers did occasionally provide estimates of changes in the general price level between two periods, a lack of index numbers was an admission that any attempt to come up with accurate weightings for long series of data could be subject to wide margins of error. Beveridge took the same view, although as one reviewer noted, it would not have taken much effort to calculate index numbers for key commodities covering time intervals of say, twenty-five or fifty years (see Hamilton 1942: 55). One advantage that the Beveridge study did have over *A History* was that it used statistics compiled in the same local area. Although this limited the number of series that could be accurately reported, it was a superior approach to that used in *A History* where data sources sometimes had little or no connection with each other. Finally, in another study, Phelps Brown and Hopkins (1961) used statistics on builders' wages dating back to 1264 in order to compare their results with those of Rogers. They found broad agreement between the two data sets, in particular that by the 1880s, wages had recovered to the level previously seen in the fifteenth century (see also Phelps Brown and Hopkins 1956).[19]

4   Other Work

4.1   Other Work as an Economist

The First Nine Years of the Bank of England was published by Rogers in 1887. It was essentially a reprint of the weekly price of Bank of England stock for the period running from 17 August 1694 to 17 September 1703, a series that had

---

[19] For a study contemporaneous with *A History* but which only examined the development of British prices between the 1850s and 1880s, see Mulhall (1885).

been discovered by Rogers seemingly by accident in the Bodleian Library, and also contains his extensive explanations for the movements in such prices. The data itself was derived from a statistical paper compiled by London apothecary, John Houghton, and was supplemented by Bank stock price data found in Narcissus Luttrell's *Diary*, a work kept at All Souls which had already been used by Lord Macaulay. The Bank of England had no record of its own stock for the nine years in question.

Amongst the various contributions made by the volume was a new explanation for the Great Recoinage of 1696 under King William III. Widespread currency fraud, in particular the clipping of silver coins, meant that the value of the pound was in decline in the closing years of the seventeenth century, one result being that English bills were being traded at a significant discount, especially in Amsterdam. This was happening at the same time as William was conducting military operations in the Low Countries, making necessary significant and ongoing remittances. Recoinage was therefore used by the King, argued Rogers, to increase the value of English bills, an objective which had been achieved by the end of 1696 when bills were trading at par.[20]

Rogers' final major volume was *The Economic Interpretation of History*, which appeared in 1888; a second edition was published in 1891. The book was based on lectures that Rogers had delivered at Worcester College, Oxford, and was an attempt to blend economics with the daily workings of government. However, it was not very well received by some of his colleagues, with Ashley asserting that the volume was a jumble of 'hasty assertions and partisan bitterness' (Ashley 1889: 405). On full display was Rogers' usual forceful language and his distaste for some elements of current economic thinking: 'By this study, I began to discover that much which popular economists believe to be natural is highly artificial; that what they call laws are often too hasty, inconsiderate, and inaccurate deductions; and that much which they consider to be demonstrably irrefutable is demonstrably false' (Rogers 1888a: vi–vii). Furthermore, 'two things have discredited political economy—the one is its traditional disregard for facts; the other, its strangling itself with definitions … [I]t is appalling to think of what the consequences would have been if some so-called economical verities had been translated into law' (ibid.: viii).

Rogers used *The Economic Interpretation of History* to revisit the question of the role of the State in the economy. In Chapter 23, entitled "The Policy of Government in Undertaking Service and Supply", he lays outs his case for non-interference, stating that 'There is always a disposition on the part of

---

[20] However, the wider recoinage programme failed due to difficulties in maintaining a financial system based on bimetallism, in this case gold and silver.

governments to allege that the Administration can carry out the business of private life and private action better than individuals can' (ibid.: 501). Rogers then proceeds to give numerous instances where State involvement would lead to sub-optimal outcomes, notably the railways, where the result would be shorter hours and higher pay. Despite this particular example, Rogers was in fact a supporter of an economy-wide shortening of the working day to eight hours, even if such a change should, in his view, be achieved by the actions of workers rather than through legislation (see ibid.: 353).

Combining his positions on non-interference by the State and free trade, *The Economic Interpretation of History* also contains a discussion of the protection of infant industries, with Rogers using this to launch a scathing attack on John Stuart Mill's views on the topic. Instead of granting protection to infant industries, Rogers argues that they should be allowed, if they are fit enough, to come to the fore spontaneously, with the pressures of competition the deciding factor in whether they survive or fail. Rogers also points out that if protection is in fact granted, it can be difficult to subsequently remove, not least because there will inevitably be a question over who decides if and when such protection is ended. The industry enjoying protection is unlikely to argue for its own possible termination. Mill's position was that the shielding of an infant industry from foreign competition was the only situation in which protective duties could justifiably be applied (see Mill 1848, 2: 487–488), Rogers' robust response being that there has perhaps been 'no passage in any work which exhibits so much ignorance of human nature, and so much ignorance of facts' (Rogers 1888a: 386).[21]

4.2   Views on Oxford

As this is a volume about Oxford economics, it is interesting to briefly examine some of the opinions that Rogers held about the workings of the University, not least because he seems to have gone out of his way to express them. In 1861, he published *Education in Oxford: Its Method, Its Aids, and Its Rewards* (Rogers 1861a). In just under 270 pages, he dissects various aspects of life at

---

[21] In *The Economic Interpretation of History*, Rogers also dismissed the wages fund doctrine, the classic statement of which was presented by Mill in his *Principles of Political Economy*. He accused Mill of being in 'total ignorance' (Rogers 1888a: 308) of the history of labour and wages. This aside, there is some debate about whether Mill later recanted his support for the doctrine (see, for example, West and Hafer 1978).

the University, including the relationship between it and its students, the college system, scholarships, fellowships and endowments.

Some insight into the relative merits of different British universities can be gleaned from Rogers' remarks early on in the volume about the time he spent studying at King's College, London, between leaving school and going to Oxford:

> [King's] gives much the same instruction as that at the best Oxford and Cambridge colleges. I can only say, for my own part, that the advantages I derived from a year and a half's study at King's College were larger and more suggestive than any which I ever procured from academical instruction (Rogers 1861a: 19).

As far as Oxford was concerned, Rogers focused in particular on the deficiencies, as he saw them, in the distribution of endowments between different colleges and the college-based teaching system which he regarded as being an unwelcome monopoly (see ibid.: 60–61), with lectures described as 'perfunctory, repressive, irritating' (ibid.: 61). Instead, Rogers argued that only professors should be allowed to deliver lectures (as was the case in Germany) and that only those holding at least an MA degree be permitted to instruct undergraduates.

It seems remarkable that Rogers was first elected to the Drummond only a year after the appearance of *Education in Oxford*. Either way, being a professor at the University did not seem to dim his hostility. One of the likely reasons for this was the influence of Cobden, who often expressed an antipathy towards Oxford (and Cambridge) especially when it came to what he thought was the unsuitability of graduates of these universities for the intellectual demands of political life:

> What Cobden did comment on…is the utter ignorance, on subjects of great political importance, which prevails among young men who have graduated at the older universities, and who…are presented to seats in the House of Commons, or purchase admission into it, or succeed to analogous positions in the House of Lords … Cobden used to argue that the particular knowledge which the older universities impart to such people is of absolutely no use to them in the responsible place which they occupy (Rogers in Bright and Rogers 1870: ix).

Even in 1881, many years after he had served his first term as Drummond Professor but still seven years away from the beginning of his second term, Rogers felt the need to again go on the offensive with an attack on Oxford's tutoring system:

The monopoly of instruction given by college tutors was greatly assisted by their possessing a monopoly of examination, and the right of conferring distinctions in the class list. In other words, they audited, and audit, their own accounts … It is very seldom that anyone except a college tutor is allowed to be an examiner. As a consequence, the gravest scandals have not infrequently arisen. It is a common saying in Oxford that the clever men are to be found in the third class, the dull and industrious in the second, the examiners' friends being put into the first. The statement is undoubtedly an exaggeration, but there is nothing to prevent it being a reality, and if it were a reality, there is not enough public conscience in Oxford to reprobate it (Rogers 1881: 73–74).

5   Conclusion

Thorold Rogers did not make any meaningful theoretical contributions to economics and in particular failed to discover any inductive laws of economic history. Rather, his forte was the hunting down of historical data, using this to help explain poverty especially amongst agricultural labourers. Some of Rogers' contemporaries excelled as much as he did in their respective fields. However, it remains the case that few, if any, reached the heights of *A History of Agriculture and Prices* in terms of the length of time it took to compile, the period that it covers and its level of detail. Riding the wave of the Victorian fad for statistics, it took six years to complete the first two volumes and it was to be another sixteen years before volumes III and IV were published, this long gap being the result of Rogers' political commitments but also because there was less data available for the sixteenth and seventeenth centuries. Volumes V and VI appeared in 1887, a year after Rogers ceased being an MP, while the two parts of volume VII were published in 1902, two years after his death. Even so, Rogers admitted that the research involved was 'costly beyond my expectations' (Rogers 1866–1902, 4: vi).

Even though *A History* would not be familiar to the vast majority of today's students, it was certainly still being used in the decades after it was finally completed. For instance, Nicholson quoted from it in various places in his three-volume *Principles of Political Economy* (see Nicholson 1893–1901) while Clark stated in 1932 that the volumes were 'still in constant use as a book of reference' (Clark 1932: 99). Anyone examining *A History* and Rogers' other work in economics will get a keen insight into the main pillars of his thinking, including his theory that rent is not determined by prices but by profits, the allegedly destructive role played by government in the economy, a dislike of all forms of privilege, support for the role that trade unions play in equalising the respective levels of bargaining power possessed by labour and capital, and perhaps, above all, an increasing hostility, as the volumes progressed, towards orthodoxy in economics. However, it would also be apparent to the reader that Rogers had a tendency to interpret the development of British economic history as being merely made up of a series of key events, such as the Black Death and the Peasants' Revolt. This was at the expense of other possible explanatory processes, notably social evolution. It was also the case that Rogers would sometimes claim originality, even if this was not necessarily borne out by the facts.

Rogers' gruff manner made it difficult for others to support him. His only disciple was Henry de Beltgens Gibbins, who became a schoolmaster after attending Oxford and wrote popular books on aspects of the history of England in the nineteenth century, even if these same volumes were often frowned upon by the community of academic historians at Oxford. Rogers did establish the Oxford University Political Economy Club. However, his unappealing personality meant that he was not able to found a school at the University.

Perhaps it is best to end with a quote from Beveridge:

> Prices and wages are the social phenomena most susceptible of objective statistical record over long periods of time. They reflect and measure the influence of changes in population, in supply of precious metals, in industrial structure and agricultural methods, in trade and transport, in consumption and in the technical arts … A comprehensive co-ordinated history of prices and wages is a framework which should underlie all studies of economic development (Beveridge 1939: xxi).

Despite his shortcomings, Rogers appreciated all of this, dedicating most of his academic life to pursuing such a 'co-ordinated history'. As such, he should be recognised as a noteworthy Oxford economist and perhaps as one of the founders of modern British economic history.

References

Main Works by Thorold Rogers

Bright, J. and J.E.T. Rogers (eds) (1870). *Speeches on Questions of Public Policy by Richard Cobden, MP*. Two volumes. London: Macmillan.

Rogers, J.E.T. (1861a). *Education in Oxford: Its Method, Its Aids, and Its Rewards*. London: Smith & Elder.

Rogers, J.E.T. (1861). 'Facts and Observations on Wages and Prices in England During the Sixteenth and Seventeenth Centuries, and More Particularly During the Thirty-Nine Years 1582–1620'. *Journal of the Royal Statistical Society*, 24(4): 535–585.

Rogers, J.E.T. (1864). 'On a Continuous Price of Wheat for 105 Years, From 1380 to 1484'. *Journal of the Statistical Society of London*, 27(1): 70–81.

Rogers, J.E.T. (1864a). *Primogeniture and Entail: Letters of J.E.T. Rogers and Henry Tupper and Others on the History and Working of the Laws of Primogeniture and Entail in Their Moral, Social and Political Aspects*. Manchester: Alexander Ireland.

Rogers, J.E.T. (1864b). 'The Laws of Settlement and Primogeniture'. *Transactions of the National Association for the Promotion of Social Science*, York Meeting. London: Longman Green: 117–129.

Rogers, J.E.T. (ed.) (1865a). *Aristotelis Ethica Nicomachea*, by Aristotle. London: Rivington.

Rogers, J.E.T. (1865). 'On the Statistical and Fiscal Definitions of the Word "Income"'. *Journal of the Statistical Society of London*, 28(2): 242–260.

Rogers, J.E.T. (1866a). 'England Before and After the Black Death'. *Fortnightly Review*, 3(December): 191–196.

Rogers, J.E.T. (1866). 'On the Social and Local Distribution of Wealth During the First Half of the Fourteenth Century'. *Macmillan's Magazine*, 13(January): 249–259.

Rogers, J.E.T. (1866). 'Opening Address of the President of Section F (Economic Science and Statistics) of the British Association for the Advancement of Science, at the Thirty-Sixth Meeting, at Nottingham, August 1866'. *Journal of the Statistical Society of London*, 29(4): 493–503.

Rogers, J.E.T. (1866–1902). *A History of Agriculture and Prices in England, From the Year After the Oxford Parliament (1259) to the Commencement of the Continental War (1793), Compiled Entirely from Original and Contemporaneous Records*. Seven volumes: Volume I (1866): 1259–1400; Volume II (1866): 1259–1400; Volume III (1882): 1401–1582; Volume IV (1882): 1401–1582; Volume V (1887): 1583–1702; Volume VI (1887): 1583–1702; Volume VII, Part 1 (1902): 1703–1793; Volume VII, Part 2 (1902): 1703–1793. Oxford: Clarendon Press.

Rogers, J.E.T. (1867). 'On the Funds Available for Developing the Machinery of Education in England'. *Journal of the Statistical Society of London*, 30(4): 557–561.

Rogers, J.E.T. (1867). 'Bribery'. Essay IX in F.H. Hill et al. *Questions for a Reformed Parliament*. London: Macmillan: 259–276.

Rogers, J.E.T. (1868). *The Free Trade Policy of the Liberal Party*. Manchester: Guardian.

Rogers, J.E.T. (1868). *A Manual of Political Economy for Schools and Colleges*. Second edition, 1869; third edition, 1875. Oxford: Clarendon Press.

Rogers, J.E.T. (ed.) (1869). *An Inquiry Into the Nature and Causes of the Wealth of Nations*, by A. Smith. Oxford: Clarendon.

Rogers, J.E.T. (1869). *Historical Gleanings: A Series of Sketches—Montagu, Walpole, Adam Smith, Cobbett*. London: Macmillan.

Rogers, J.E.T. (1870). *Historical Gleanings: A Series of Sketches—Wiklif, Laud, Wilkes, Horne Tooke*. London: Macmillan.

Rogers, J.E.T. (1870). 'On the Incidence of Local Taxation'. *Journal of the Statistical Society of London*, 33(2): 243–263.

Rogers, J.E.T. (1871). *Social Economy*. London: Cassell, Petter & Galpin.

Rogers, J.E.T. (1872). 'The Colonial Question'. In *Cobden Club Essays: Second Series, 1871–1872*. London: Cassell, Petter, and Galpin: 399–455.

Rogers, J.E.T. (1873). *Cobden and Modern Political Opinion: Essays on Certain Political Topics*. London: Macmillan.

Rogers, J.E.T. (ed.) (1875). *Complete Collection of the Protests of the Lords, With Historical Introductions*. Three volumes. Oxford: Clarendon.

Rogers, J.E.T. (ed.) (1879a). *Public Addresses by John Bright*. London: Macmillan.

Rogers, J.E.T. (1879). 'English Agriculture'. *The Contemporary Review*, 35(May): 303–323.

Rogers, J.E.T. (1879). 'Review of *Essays in Political and Moral Philosophy*, by T.E. Cliffe Leslie'. *The Academy*, 7 June: 489–491.

Rogers, J.E.T. (1879). 'Causes of Commercial Depression'. *The Princeton Review*, 1(January–June): 211–238.

Rogers, J.E.T. (1879). 'Labour and Wages in England'. *The Princeton Review*, 55(July): 1–26.

Rogers, J.E.T. (1880). 'The History of Rent in England'. *The Contemporary Review*, 37(April): 673–690.

Rogers, J.E.T. (1881). 'Parliament and the Higher Education'. *Fraser's Magazine*, 24(July): 68–83.

Rogers, J.E.T. (1883). *Ensilage in America: Its Prospects in English Agriculture*. London: W. Swan Sonnenschein.

Rogers, J.E.T. (1884). *Six Centuries of Work and Wages: The History of English Labour*. Two volumes. London: W. Swan Sonnenschein.

Rogers, J.E.T. (1885a). *Free Trade and Fair Trade: What Do the Words Mean?* Leaflet Number 28. London: Cobden Club.

Rogers, J.E.T. (1885). *Eight Chapters on the History of Work and Wages*. London: W. Swan Sonnenschein.

Rogers, J.E.T. (1885). *The Agricultural Question*. London: Land Nationalisation Society.

Rogers, J.E.T. (1885). *The British Citizen: His Rights and Privileges—A Short History*. London: Society for Promoting Christian Knowledge.

Rogers, J.E.T. (1886). *Local Taxation, Especially in English Cities and Towns*. London: Cassell & Company.

Rogers, J.E.T. (1887). *The First Nine Years of the Bank of England: An Enquiry into a Weekly Record of the Price of Bank Stock from August 17, 1694 to September 17, 1703*. Oxford: Clarendon Press.

Rogers, J.E.T. (1888a). *The Economic Interpretation of History*. London: T. Fisher Unwin.

Rogers, J.E.T. (1888). *Holland*. London: T. Fisher Unwin.

Rogers, J.E.T. (1888). *The Relations of Economic Science to Social and Political Action*. London: W. Swan Sonnenschein.

Rogers, J.E.T. (1890). 'The Four Oxford History Lecturers'. *The Contemporary Review*, 57(March): 454–456.

Rogers, J.E.T. (ed.) (1891). *Oxford City Documents: Financial and Judicial, 1268–1665*.

Rogers, J.E.T. (1892). *The Industrial and Commercial History of England*. Edited by A.G.L. Rogers. London: G.P. Putnam's Sons.

Other Works Referred To

Ashley, W.J. (1889). 'James E. Thorold Rogers'. *Political Science Quarterly*, 4(3): 381–407.

d'Avenel, G. (1894–1926). *Histoire Économique de la Propriété, des Salaires, des Denrées et de Tous les Prix en Général, Depuis l'an 1200 Jusqu'en l'an 1800*. Paris: Imprimerie Nationale.

Beveridge, W.H. (1939). *Prices and Wages in England from the Twelfth to the Nineteenth Century* (with the collaboration of L. Liepmann, F.J. Nicholas, M.E. Rayner, M. Wretts-Smith and others). London: Longmans.

Brentano, L. (1870). *On the History and Development of Gilds, And the Origin of Trade-Unions*. London: Trübner & Co.

Clark, G.N. (1932). 'The Study of Economic History'. *History*, New Series, 17(66): 97–110.

Cole, A.H. and R. Crandall (1964). 'The International Scientific Committee on Price History'. *Journal of Economic History*, 24(3): 381–388.

De Marchi, N.B. (1976). 'On the Early Dangers of Being Too Political an Economist: Thorold Rogers and the 1868 Election to the Drummond Professorship'. *Oxford Economic Papers*, New Series, 28(3): 364–380.

Eden, F. (1797). *The State of the Poor: Or An History of the Labouring Classes in England From the Conquest to the Present Period*. Three volumes. London: J. Davis.

Fleetwood, W. (1707). *Chronicon Preciosum: Or An Account of English Money, the Price of Corn and Other Commodities For the Last 600 Years*. London: C. Harper.

Gibbins, H.B. de (1890). 'Professor Thorold Rogers'. *The Westminster Review*, 134(6): 603–610.

Hamilton, E.J. (1942). 'Review of *Prices and Wages in England from the Twelfth to the Nineteenth Century*, by Sir William Beveridge with the collaboration of L. Liepmann, F.J. Nicholas, M.E. Rayner, M. Wretts-Smith and Others'. *Economic Journal*, 52(205): 54–58.

Hewins, W.A.S. (1898). 'The Regulation of Wages by the Justices of the Peace'. *Economic Journal*, 8(31): 340–346.

Kadish, A. (1989). *Historians, Economists, and Economic History*. London: Routledge.

Koot, G.M. (1987). *English Historical Economics, 1870–1926: The Rise of Economic History and Neomercantilism*. Cambridge: Cambridge University Press.

Mill, J.S. (1848). *Principles of Political Economy*. Volume II. London: John W. Parker.

Mulhall, M.G. (1885). *History of Prices Since the Year 1850*. London: Longmans, Green and Co.

Mundell, A. (1829). *Tables Showing the Amount, According to Official and Declared Value, of Every Article of Home Produce and Manufacture Exported in Every Year, From 1814 to 1828*. London: Longman.

Newmarch, W. (1860). 'On Methods of Investigation as Regards Statistics of Prices, and Of Wages in the Principal Trades'. *Journal of the Statistical Society of London*, 23(4): 479–497.

Newmarch, W. (1866). 'A Notice of Professor J.E.T. Rogers' *History of Agriculture and Prices in England, 1259–1400*'. *Journal of the Statistical Society of London*, 29(4): 542–548.

Nicholson, J.S. (1889). 'Review of *A History of Agriculture and Prices in England, Volumes V and VI, 1583–1702*'. *English Historical Review*, 4(13): 167–170.

Nicholson, J.S. (1893–1901). *Principles of Political Economy*. Three volumes. London: Adam and Charles Black.

Phelps Brown, E.H. and S.V. Hopkins (1956). 'Seven Centuries of the Prices of Consumables, Compared with Builders' Wage-Rates'. *Economica*, New Series, 23(92): 296–314.

Phelps Brown, E.H. and S.V. Hopkins (1961). 'Seven Centuries of Wages and Prices: Some Earlier Estimates'. *Economica*, New Series, 28(109): 30–36.

Porter, G.R. (1836). *The Progress of the Nation, In Its Various Social and Economical Relations, From the Beginning of the Nineteenth Century to the Present Time*. London: Charles Knight & Co.

Rashid, S. (1978). 'The Price–Rogers Election: Politics or Religion?'. *Oxford Economic Papers*, New Series, 30(2): 310–312.

S.J. (1859). 'First Course of Lectures by the Tooke Professor of Economic Science and Statistics, in King's College, London'. *Journal of the Statistical Society of London*, 22(4): 506.

Schanz, G. (1881). *Englische Handelspolitik Gegen Ende Des Mittelalters*. Leipzig: Verlag von Duncker & Humblot.

Schumpeter, J.A. (1954). *History of Economic Analysis*. London: Allen & Unwin.

Seebohm, F. (1865). 'The Black Death, and Its Place in English History'. *The Fortnightly Review*, 2: 149–160.

Seebohm, F. (1866). 'The Population of England Before the Black Death'. *The Fortnightly Review*, 4: 87–89.

Shuckburgh-Evelyn, G. (1798). 'An Account of Some Endeavours to Ascertain a Standard of Weight and Measure'. *Philosophical Transactions of the Royal Society of London*, 88: 133–182.

Tooke, T. and W. Newmarch (1838–1857). *A History of Prices and of the State of Circulation, 1793–1856*. Six volumes (Tooke was joined by Newmarch for volumes V and VI). London: Longman.

Tullberg, R.M. (2017). 'John Neville Keynes (1852–1949)'. Chapter 18 in R.A. Cord (ed.) *The Palgrave Companion to Cambridge Economics*. London: Palgrave Macmillan: 401–421.

West, E.G. and R.W. Hafer (1978). 'J.S. Mill, Unions, and the Wages Fund Recantation: A Reinterpretation'. *Quarterly Journal of Economics*, 92(4): 603–619.

Young, A. (1812). *An Enquiry into the Progressive Value of Money in England*. London: B. McMillan.

11

Francis Ysidro Edgeworth (1845–1926)

John Creedy

1   Introduction

Francis Ysidro Edgeworth was born in Edgeworthstown in County Longford, Ireland. His large family background is fascinating, and has been richly described by Barbé (2010). His grandfather was the energetic and colourful Richard Lovell Edgeworth, whose life was documented in a two-volume memoir by his eldest daughter, the famous novelist Maria Edgeworth (1820); see also Butler and Butler (1927). Richard Lovell carried out many scientific and mechanical experiments, and was a member of the Lunar Society of Birmingham, whose members included James Watt, Matthew Boulton, Josiah Wedgwood, Joseph Priestley, Erasmus Darwin and Samuel Galton. In addition, Maria's scientific acquaintances included Humphry Davy, Alexander von Humboldt, William Herschel, Charles Babbage, Joseph Hooker and Michael Faraday. The marriage of Francis Ysidro Edgeworth's cousin Harriet Jessie Edgeworth (daughter of Richard Lovell's seventh and youngest son Michael Pakenham) to Arthur Gray Butler provided links with another eminent family. Furthermore, Butler's sister, Louisa, married Francis Galton, a cousin of Charles Darwin.

J. Creedy (✉)
SACL, Victoria University of Wellington, Wellington, New Zealand
e-mail: john.creedy@vuw.ac.nz

© The Author(s), under exclusive license to Springer Nature Switzerland AG 2021
R. A. Cord (ed.), *The Palgrave Companion to Oxford Economics*,
https://doi.org/10.1007/978-3-030-58471-9_11

Richard Lovell's sixth son, and seventeenth surviving child, was Francis Beaufort Edgeworth, who in 1831 met his wife, Rosa Florentina Eroles, from Catalonia and then aged sixteen, while on the way to Germany to study philosophy: they married three weeks later. Francis Ysidro was their fifth son. With his family background and considerable linguistic skills, Edgeworth had wide international sympathies.

Edgeworth was educated by tutors until 1862, when he entered Trinity College Dublin to study languages. His first association with Oxford came in 1867, when he entered Exeter College. After one term he transferred to Magdalen Hall, and then to Balliol in 1868, where in Michaelmas 1869 he obtained a First in *Literae Humaniores*. During the viva Edgeworth apparently replied, 'Shall I answer briefly or at length?', whereupon he spoke for half an hour to convert what was to be a Second into a First.

His career after graduation was varied. He was called to the Bar in 1877, the year in which his first book, *New and Old Methods of Ethics*, was published. Edgeworth applied unsuccessfully for a Professorship of Greek at Bedford College, London, in 1875, but later lectured there on English language and literature for a brief period from late 1877 to mid-1878. He had earlier lectured on logic, mental and moral sciences and metaphysics to prospective Indian civil servants, at a private institution run by a Mr Walter Wren. In 1880, he applied for a chair of philosophy, also unsuccessfully, but began lecturing on logic to evening classes at King's College London. Soon after the publication of his second book, *Mathematical Psychics*, in 1881, he applied for a professorship of logic, mental and moral philosophy and political economy at Liverpool. Edgeworth had to wait until 1890 to obtain a professorial appointment. This was at King's College London, where he succeeded Thorold Rogers in the Tooke Chair of Economic Science and Statistics. In the next year, he again succeeded Rogers, this time to become Drummond Professor, a position he held until his retirement in 1922, and Fellow of All Souls College, Oxford.

In addition to his work in economics, Edgeworth began a series of statistical papers in 1883, and was secretary to the British Association *Report on Index Numbers* (1887–1889). He was President of Section F of the British Association in 1889, a position he held again in 1922. Edgeworth's work on mathematical statistics took an increasingly important role. Indeed, of about 170 papers which he published, approximately three-quarters were concerned with statistical theory: many are collected in McCann (1996). He became a Guy Medalist (Gold) of the Royal Statistical Society in 1907 and was President of the Society from 1912 to 1914. His third and final book was *Metretike: or, The Method of Measuring Probability and Utility* (Edgeworth 1887); on his statistics contributions, see Bowley (1928) and Stigler (1978). Near the end of his life, some of the vast stream of his economics papers were collected in three volumes of *Papers Relating to Political Economy* (Edgeworth 1925).

2 Edgeworth at Oxford

Edgeworth finally settled in Oxford at the age of 46 in one of the most illustrious British chairs in economics. In the same year, he also became the first editor of the *Economic Journal* and was editor or co-editor from its first issue until his death. He was buried in Holywell Cemetery, St Cross Church (next to Holywell Manor), which contains the graves of many notable Oxford people. Edgeworth has a professorship named after him at Nuffield College, Oxford. This distinction in economics is shared only with Nobel Prize winners, Sir John Hicks and James Meade (the other named professorship in Oxford is the Drummond at All Souls, but Drummond was not himself an economist).

At Oxford, Edgeworth was firmly established as the leading economist, after Marshall, in Britain. However, unlike Marshall at Cambridge, Edgeworth devoted little energy to improving the undergraduate teaching of economics. His influence at Oxford was described briefly by Bowley (1934: 123), and at greater length by Price (1946: 37) who complained that 'economics at Oxford looked like slumbering quietly or in effect at least must languish comparatively as it rested, so to say, inert in Edgeworth's keeping. There was no active stir of a resonant hive of busy students gathering honey under his helping regime'. Harrod said of his tutorials with Edgeworth, 'we used to sit side by side at a little table, and he'd go through my various diagrams' (Harrod quoted in Phelps Brown 1981: 662). It is indeed impossible to imagine, on the basis of his literary style, how Edgeworth could lecture clearly to undergraduates. He wrote always for fellow researchers, and even here his style was influenced by his attitude to the subject. As Price (1946: 35) argued, 'Edgeworth…convinced that Economics as he conceived it was so intrinsically hard a study that it could not possibly be made popularly plain…increased repellent difficulty'.

While Edgeworth was in no sense part of an Oxford group, Price (1946), Keynes (1933 [1972]) and Bowley (1934: 122) all stressed his generous hospitality, resulting in him having 'the widest personal acquaintance in the world with economists of all nations' (Keynes ibid.: 264). His complex character was described in the following terms by Keynes (ibid.: 265): 'He was kind, affectionate, modest, self-deprecatory, humorous, with a sharp and candid eye for human nature; he was also reserved, angular, complicated, proud, and touchy, elaborately polite, courteous to the point of artificiality, absolutely unbending and unyielding in himself to the pressure of the outside world'.

He was said to have inherited 'the Edgeworthstown convention of rather formal good manners and conversation' (Butler 1972: 136). The poet Robert Graves (1960: 247) reported that Edgeworth avoided conversational English, persistently using words and phrases that one expects to meet only in books. One evening, T.E. Lawrence returned to All Souls College from a visit to London, and Edgeworth met him at the gate, asking, 'Was it very caliginous in the Metropolis?'; Lawrence replied gravely, 'Somewhat caliginous, but not altogether inspissated'.

3   Edgeworth's Approach to Economics

The obvious dominant characterised of Edgeworth's approach to economics is that it is mathematical, characterised by an original use of techniques, although he does not appear to have received a formal training in mathematics. However, he came to economics from moral philosophy. The central question of distributive justice, rather than simply the application of mathematics, dominated his attitude towards economics. His main argument was that mathematics provided powerful assistance to "unaided" reason, and could check the conclusions reached by other methods. For example, he suggested that 'he that will not verify his conclusions as far as possible by mathematics, as it were bringing the ingots of common sense to be assayed and coined at the mint of the sovereign science, will hardly realise the full value of what he holds' (Edgeworth 1881: 3).

The contrast between Edgeworth and Marshall was sharp. Although both men turned to economics from mathematics and moral philosophy, Marshall generally used biological analogies, and was concerned with developing maxims. In contrast, Edgeworth generally used mechanical analogies, and was more concerned with arriving at theorems. Pigou commented that, 'during some thirty years until their recent deaths in honoured age, the two outstanding names in English economics were Marshall…and Edgeworth … Edgeworth, the tool-maker, gloried in his tools … Marshall, on the other hand, had what almost amounted to an obsession for hiding his tools away' (Pigou quoted in Pigou and Robertson 1931: 3). Edgeworth's interest in the natural sciences often led him to make comparisons with scientific laws, and especially to show that the physical sciences also relied on abstraction and approximation.

Edgeworth argued carefully that the assumptions used in economics are often untestable, and he therefore took precautions against the accusation of "plucking assumptions from the air". He was conscious of the fact that the difficulty is in making the crucial abstractions which make the particular problem under consideration tractable, but which are not question-begging. His attitude to many a priori assumptions was influenced by his approach to statistical inference. He referred to, 'the first principle of probabilities, according to which cases about which we are equally undecided…count as equal' (Edgeworth 1881: 99). Thus, the appropriate assumption was that all feasible values, say of elasticities, were equally likely, until evidence is obtained or reference may be made to 'the consensus of high authorities' (Edgeworth 1925, ii: 391). This also illustrates Edgeworth's attitude to authority and his many allusions to the views of other leading economists. Price (1946: 38) referred to his frequent 'reference to authority for…support of tentative opinion waveringly advanced'.

Edgeworth was also prone to stressing negative results. For example, in discussing taxation, where the criterion of minimum sacrifice does not alone provide a simple tax formula, he stated:

> Yet the premises, however inadequate to the deduction of a definite formula, may suffice for a certain negative conclusion. The ground which will not serve as the foundation of the elaborate edifice designed may yet be solid enough to support a battering-ram capable of being directed against simpler edifices in the neighbourhood (Edgeworth 1925, ii: 261).

4   Early Work in Moral Philosophy

Edgeworth's first book, *New and Old Methods of Ethics*, published in 1877, was strongly influenced by the great Cambridge philosopher Henry Sidgwick. It examined in detail the implications of utilitarianism for optimal distribution. Edgeworth's original contribution was to apply advanced mathematics to this problem. His approach was dominated by utilitarianism, but the influence of contemporary psychological research and the impact of evolutionary ideas can also be seen here. Both aspects led to an explicit consideration of differences between individuals and changes over time.

On considering the major fierce debates in the second half of the nineteenth century between egoism, evolutionism, idealism and intuitionism, Edgeworth's brand of utilitarianism became extremely eclectic. It embraced the majority of other principles, except for those of the Hegelian idealists, while regarding utilitarianism as the "sovereign principle". Writing of this book, Keynes (1933 [1972]: 257) commented that:

> Edgeworth's peculiarities of style, his brilliance of phrasing, his obscurity of connection, his inconclusiveness of aim, his restlessness of direction, his courtesy, his caution, his shrewdness, his wit, his subtlety, his learning, his reserve—all are there full-grown. Quotations from the Greek tread on the heels of the differential calculus.

Edgeworth generally distinguished between "impure" and "pure" utilitarianism. In the latter case, individuals are assumed to be concerned with the welfare of society as a whole. The former case in fact corresponds more closely with a short-term version of egoism. Economic exchange can usefully be analysed in terms of "jostling egoists", but he believed that ultimately individuals would evolve to become pure utilitarians. A reason for believing that individuals would make such a transition was later to be developed by Edgeworth in the form of his contractarian justification of utilitarianism as the appropriate principle of distributive justice.

Edgeworth's early utilitarianism was influenced by his wide knowledge of work in experimental psychology. In his books of 1877 and 1881, there are many references to the work of Joseph Delboeuf, Gustav Fechner, Hermann von Helmholtz, Ernst Weber and Wilhelm Wundt. These references occur in the context of the nature of utility functions and, although Edgeworth at this time was not aware of the earlier work of Stanley Jevons, the same range of work was also cited by Jevons. In 1877, Edgeworth explicitly suggested, in connection with Fechner, that an additive form would not be appropriate.

A further aspect of Edgeworth's utilitarianism is his attitude towards authority. An important issue for early utilitarians involved the nature of inductive evidence about the consequences of acts. Most people cannot know the full consequences of their acts, so that rules of moral conduct must be followed (in contrast with intuitionism where individuals are assumed to have immediate consciousness of moral rules). In arriving at such rules, the opinions of highly regarded individuals are taken to be credible even though it may not be possible to show conclusively that they are "correct". Edgeworth argued, for example, that 'we ought to defer even to the undemonstrated dicta and opinions of the wise, who have a power of mental vision acquired by experience' (Edgeworth 1925, ii: 149).

Edgeworth defined the problem of determining the optimal utilitarian distribution as follows: '[G]iven a certain quantity of stimulus to be distributed among a given set of sentients...to find the law of distribution productive of the greatest quantity of pleasure' (Edgeworth 1877: 43). In treating this problem mathematically, he used Lagrange multipliers, without any explanation, and concluded that 'unto him that hath greater capacity for pleasure shall be added more of the means of pleasure' (ibid.). In using Lagrange multipliers, Edgeworth was also careful to discuss possible complications, referring to the possibility of multiple solutions and explicitly discussing corner solutions and inequality constraints.

Further complexities were then examined, where Edgeworth emphasised that utilitarianism implies equality of the 'means of pleasure' only under a special set of assumptions, and in the general case the prescribed solution will be some form of inequality. In a more general treatment of the problem, Edgeworth used the calculus of variations, but again provided the reader with virtually no help in following his mathematical argument. His analysis of the utilitarian optimal distribution was continued in his paper on "The Hedonical Calculus" (Edgeworth 1879), which was later reprinted as the third part of *Mathematical Psychics* (Edgeworth 1881).

5   Early Work in Economics

The turning point in Edgeworth's work was his introduction to Jevons in 1879 by a mutual friend James Sully, who in 1878 moved to Hampstead, London, where Edgeworth had lodgings in Mount Vernon and where Jevons also lived; see Sully (1918: 180, 223). Directly stimulated by Jevons's treatment of exchange, Edgeworth became interested in the problem of the indeterminacy of the rate of exchange, arising from the existence of only a small number of traders. This led rapidly to Edgeworth's second and most important book *Mathematical Psychics: An Essay on the Application of Mathematics to the Moral Sciences* (Edgeworth 1881), which was obviously written in a state of considerable enthusiasm for his new subject. Marshall's review began, 'This book shows clear signs of genius, and is a promise of great things to come' (Marshall quoted in Whitaker 1975: 265). Jevons began by stating that 'Whatever else readers of this book may think about it, they would probably all agree that it is a very remarkable one' (Jevons 1881: 581). However, this slim volume of 150 pages was long known only to a small group of experts, and it was not until the middle of the twentieth century that many of its central ideas began to be more fully appreciated.

Part 1 of *Mathematical Psychics* (Edgeworth 1881: 1–15) was devoted mainly to a justification of the use of mathematics in economics where precise data are not available. There is probably no other "apology" in the whole of economic literature which compares with Edgeworth's plea for the application of mathematics. For example, when considering individual utility maximisation:

> Atoms of pleasure are not easy to distinguish and discern; more continuous than sand, more discrete than liquid; as it were nuclei of the just-perceivable, embedded in circumambient semi-consciousness. We cannot count the golden sands of life; we cannot number the "innumerable smile" of seas of love; but we seem to be capable of observing that there is here a greater, there a less, multitude of pleasure-units; mass of happiness; and that is enough (ibid.: 8–9).

Great stress was placed on comparison with Lagrange's "Principle of Least Action" in examining the overall effects produced by the interactions among many particles. The connection with Edgeworth's analysis of competition, involving interaction among a large number of competitors to produce a determinate rate of exchange, is central. The fact that in the natural sciences so much could be derived from a single principle was important for Jevons, but Edgeworth took this to its ultimate limit in arguing that the comparable single principle in social sciences, that of maximum utility, would produce results of comparable value. Referring to Laplace, he suggested (ibid.: 12) that "*Mécanique Sociale*" may one day take her place along with "*Mécanique Celeste*", throned each upon the double-sided height of one maximum principle, the supreme pinnacle of moral as of physical science'.

Jevons's work in the *Theory of Political Economy* involved the application of mathematics to the analysis of exchange in competitive markets. The crucial development following Edgeworth's contact with Jevons was not simply the realisation that mathematics can be used to examine equilibrium in exchange. Rather, in his analysis, Jevons explicitly assumed, through his "law of indifference", that all individuals take equilibrium prices as given and outside their control. In using this law as 'one of the central pivots of the theory', Jevons (1957: 87) stated that 'there can only be one ratio of exchange of one uniform commodity at any moment'. His theory was explicitly limited to static equilibrium conditions and Jevons excluded the role of the number of competitors from his analysis via the awkward notion of the "trading body". This followed correspondence with Fleeming Jenkin, who could not see why two isolated individuals should accept the price-taking equilibrium; see Black (1977: 166–178). However, Jevons wished to consider the behaviour of two typical individuals in a large market.

In a section on "Failure of the Laws of Exchange", Jevons discussed cases in which some indeterminacy would result; for details of complex cases considered by Jevons, see Creedy (1992). His most notable example was house sales, where it was suggested that indeterminacy would result from the discrete nature of the good being exchanged. A reviewer suggested instead that indeterminacy 'is really owing in our opinion to the assumed absence of competition' (Anonymous reviewer quoted in Black 1981: 157). It was this gap in Jevons's analysis which Edgeworth set out to fill. He examined how competition between buyers and sellers, through a barter process, leads to a "final settlement" which is equivalent to one in which all individuals act independently as price takers. As he later stated (Edgeworth 1925, ii: 453), 'the existence of a uniform rate of exchange between any two commodities is perhaps not so much axiomatic as deducible from the process of competition in a perfect market'. Edgeworth's highly original analysis is discussed in the following section.

6   Exchange, Contract and Indeterminacy

In modern economic analysis, the analytical tools invented by Edgeworth in 1881, such as the indifference map and the contract curve, are now used in a vast range of contexts. They were introduced by Edgeworth to examine the nature of barter among individuals. He wanted to see if a determinate rate of exchange would result in barter situations where it is assumed only that individuals wish to maximise their own utility, considered solely as a function of their own consumption. Given individuals' utility functions and their initial endowments of goods, would it be possible to work out a "determinate" rate of exchange at which trade would take place? Edgeworth's statement is as follows:

> The PROBLEM to which attention is specially directed in this introductory summary is: How far contract is indeterminate—an inquiry of more than theoretical importance, if it show not only that indeterminateness tends to [be present] widely, but also in what direction an escape from its evils is to be sought (Edgeworth 1881: 20; upper case in original).

Edgeworth began his analysis by taking the case of two individuals, A and B, exchanging quantities, x and y, of two goods. The framework is that described by Jevons, where the first individual holds all of the initial stocks of the first good, and the second individual holds all the stocks of the second good. Edgeworth wrote the utility functions of each individual in terms of the amounts exchanged, rather than consumed. He then immediately defined the general (rather than additive) utility function, the contract curve and indifference curves.

Following Edgeworth's introduction of the general utility function, he raised the question of the equilibrium which may be reached with, 'one or both refusing to move further'. In barter the conditions of exchange must be reached by voluntary agreement, or contract, between the two parties, and of course it is fundamental that egoists would not agree to a contract which would make them worse off than before the exchange. The question thus concerns the nature of the settlement reached by two contracting parties. He immediately answered that contract supplies only part of the answer so that 'supplementary conditions…supplied by competition or ethical motives' are required, and then wrote the equation of his famous contract curve (ibid.: 20–21).

The problem of obtaining the equilibrium values of x and y which, 'cannot be varied without the consent of the parties to it' was stated as follows: 'It is required to find a point (x, y) such that, in whatever direction we take an infinitely small step, [utilities] do not increase together, but that, while one increases, the other decreases' (ibid.: 21). The locus of such points, 'it is here proposed to call the contract-curve'. Edgeworth's alternative derivations of the contract curve involved the movement, from an arbitrary position, along one person's indifference curve. He stated, 'motion is possible so long as, one party not losing, the other gains' (ibid.: 23). Here, Edgeworth used the Lagrange multiplier method of maximising one person's utility subject to the condition that the other person's utility remains constant. After presenting the results for the two-person two-good case, Edgeworth (ibid.: 26) examined the contract curve in the case where three individuals exchange three goods. This involved an early use of determinants in economics.

The concept of the contract curve helps to specify a range of "efficient exchanges". The essential feature of the analysis from Edgeworth's point of view is that there is a range, rather than a unique point, so that 'the settlements are represented by an *indefinite number* of points' along the contract curve (ibid.: 29; italics in original). At any particular settlement, the rate of exchange is expressed in terms of the amount of one good which is given up in order to obtain a specified amount of the other good. Hence, the existence of a range of efficient contracts means that the rate of exchange (or effective price ratio) is "indeterminate". The rate achieved in practice depends on bargaining strength. This result led Edgeworth (ibid.: 30) to make his often-quoted remark that 'an accessory evil of indeterminate contract is the tendency, greater than in a full market, towards dissimulation and objectionable arts of higgling'.

Edgeworth argued that his analysis of indeterminacy in contract between two traders can be applied to a wide variety of contexts, including trade unions and employers' associations. Having shown the possibilities of indeterminacy, Edgeworth went on to show how 'the escape from its evils' requires either competition or arbitration. He quickly moved on to the introduction of further traders.

In Edgeworth's problem of two traders exchanging two goods, the definition of a range of efficient exchanges along the contract curve is analytically separate from the question of whether or not two isolated traders would actually reach a settlement on the contract curve, through barter. However, these two aspects were not clearly separated by Edgeworth because at the beginning of his analysis he introduced his stylised description of the process of barter: this is the "recontracting" process. Edgeworth did not wish to assume that individuals initially have perfect knowledge. Instead, he supposed that 'there is free communication throughout a normal competitive field' (ibid.: 18). Knowledge of the other traders' dispositions and resources is obtained by the formation of tentative contracts, which are not assumed to involve actual transfers and can be broken when further information is obtained. Edgeworth introduced this in typical style, alluding to Alfred Tennyson's poem "Maud; A Monodrama": "'Is it peace or war?', asks the lover of Maud, of economic competition, and answers hastily: it is both, pax or pact between contractors during contract, war, when some of the contractors without the consent of others recontract' (ibid.: 17).

The recontracting process thus enables the dissemination of information among traders. It allows individuals who initially agree to a contract, which is not on the contract curve, to discover that an opportunity exists for making an improved contract according to which at least one person gains without another suffering. The importance of the recontracting process lies in the fact that it allows for Edgeworth's analysis of the role of the number of individuals in a market. With numerous individuals, the process makes it possible to analyse the use of collusion among some of the traders. Individuals can form coalitions in order to improve bargaining strength. Recontracting enables the coalitions to be broken up by outsiders who may attract members of a group away with more favourable terms of exchange.

Edgeworth's analysis was extremely terse. He introduced a second person A and a second person B, assumed to be exact replicas of the initial pair, with identical tastes and endowments. This simplification allows the same diagram to be used as in the case when only two traders are considered in isolation. Two basic points can be stated immediately. First, in the final settlement all individuals will be at a common point in the Edgeworth box. Second, the settlement must be on the contract curve. The first property arises because if two individuals have identical tastes, their total utility is maximised by sharing resources equally.

The question at issue is whether the range of indeterminacy along the contract curve is reduced by the addition of these traders. Suppose with just one pair, the type-B trader has all the bargaining power and pushes the A trader to the limit of the contract curve where B obtains all the gains from trade. With the two pairs of traders no longer in isolation, the ability of a type-A trader to turn to someone else (or form a coalition), rather than deal with a single trader, means that the Bs now compete against each other. The stylised process of recontracting with the two Bs competing against each other will produce a final settlement with all traders at a common point on the contract curve, where the limit has moved inwards along the old contract curve. The analysis can be repeated by starting with an alternative situation whereby the As are initially assumed to be able to appropriate all the gains from trade. This extreme point would no longer qualify as a point on the new contract curve. Hence, the introduction of the additional pair of traders means that the contract curve shrinks.

With many pairs of such traders, Edgeworth showed that a final settlement is on the contract curve, and looks just like a price-taking equilibrium. If there are multiple equilibria, the recontracting process causes the number of final settlements to shrink to the number of price-taking equilibria. For a discussion of utility functions involving multiple equilibria, and a comparison of bargaining, competitive and utilitarian solutions, see Creedy (1994a).

This argument relating to the shrinking contract curve, first established by Edgeworth, is often referred to as the Edgeworth limit theorem; for a more detailed exposition, see Creedy (1986). The fact that the price-taking solution is necessarily on the contract curve gives rise to what is now referred to as the "First Fundamental Theorem" of welfare economics, that a price-taking equilibrium is Pareto efficient. Furthermore, the use of price-taking, compared with recontracting, provides a considerable reduction in the amount of information required by traders. Given an equilibrium set, individuals only need to know the prices of goods, whereas in the recontracting process they have to learn a considerable amount of information about other individuals' preferences and endowments. However, Edgeworth placed most stress on the equivalence of the competitive price-taking solution with a barter process involving large numbers.

Given that coalitions among traders are allowed in the recontracting process, a price-taking equilibrium cannot be blocked by a coalition of traders, and the competitive equilibrium is robust. The argument that a process of bargaining among a large number of individuals produces a result which replicates a price-taking equilibrium, allowing for the free flow of information using recontracting and enabling coalitions of traders to form and break up, is an important result that is far from intuitively obvious. The recontracting process can be said to represent a competitive process, and the contract curve shrinks essentially because of the competition between suppliers of the same good, although it is carried out in a barter framework in which explicit prices are not used (although rates of exchange are equivalent to price ratios).

The price-taking equilibrium, in contrast, does not actually involve a competitive process. Individuals simply believe that they must take market prices as given and outside their control. They respond to those prices without any reference to other individuals. However, the result is that the price-taking equilibrium looks just like a situation in which all activity is perfectly co-ordinated.

Edgeworth (1881: 28) also derived, from his indifference curves, the reciprocal demand curve, or offer curve, of each individual, although such curves (introduced by Marshall as diagrammatic representations of Mill's model of international trade) were then called 'demand-and-supply curves'. Edgeworth's contribution was to define offer curves in terms of indifference curves, 'the locus of the point where lines from the origin touch curves of indifference' (ibid.: 113). He mentioned them only briefly in the text (ibid.: 39), but the lack of emphasis is understandable, since in imperfect competition they are not relevant. When there is a lack of competition, giving rise to indeterminacy, there is nothing to ensure that individuals will trade on their offer curves and, as Edgeworth argued, 'the conceptions of demand and supply at a price are no longer appropriate' (ibid.: 31). It is this general preference, in favour of the analysis of barter in non-competitive situations, to which Marshall later objected.

7   The Utilitarian Calculus

Having shown how indeterminacy can be removed by increasing the number of traders, Edgeworth turned to consider the role of arbitration in resolving the conflict between traders, in a 'world weary of strife' (ibid.: 51). The need for arbitration was stated by Jevons as follows:

> The dispositions and force of character of the parties…will influence the decision. These are motives more or less extraneous to a theory of economics, and yet they appear necessary considerations in this problem. It may be that indeterminate bargains of this kind are best arranged by an arbitrator or third party (Jevons 1957: 124–125).

Edgeworth's statement of the same point was as usual rather less prosaic: 'The whole creation groans and yearns, desiderating a principle of arbitration, and end of strifes' (Edgeworth 1881: 51).

The principle of arbitration examined by Edgeworth was, not surprisingly, the utilitarian principle, which he had earlier used to examine optimal distribution. However, the new context of indeterminacy led him to a deeper justification of utilitarianism as a principle of distributive justice. Having arrived at this new link between "impure" and "pure" utilitarianism, Edgeworth had only to reorientate his earlier analysis of optimal distribution discussed above. His argument involved two steps. First, he showed that the principle of utility maximisation places individuals on the contract curve, because the first-order conditions are equivalent to the tangency of indifference curves. He exclaimed, 'It is a circumstance of momentous interest that one of the in general indefinitely numerous settlements between contractors is the utilitarian arrangement…the contract tending to the greatest possible total utility of the contractors' (ibid.: 53).

Edgeworth recognised that this result was not sufficient to justify the use of utilitarianism as a principle of arbitration. It is only a necessary condition of a principle of arbitration that it should place the parties somewhere on the contract curve. His justification of utilitarianism was as follows:

> Now these positions lie in a reverse order of desirability for each party; and it may seem to each that as he cannot have his own way, in the absence of any definite principle of selection, he has about as good a chance of one of the arrangements as another…both parties may agree to commute their chance of any of the arrangements for…the utilitarian arrangement (ibid.: 55).

The important point about this statement is that Edgeworth viewed distributive justice in terms of choice under uncertainty. He argued that the contractors, faced with uncertainty about their prospects, would choose to accept an arrangement along utilitarian lines. A crucial component of this argument, also clearly stated by Edgeworth in this quotation, is the use of equal a priori probabilities. The importance to him of this new justification of utilitarianism cannot be exaggerated. Indeed, the whole of *Mathematical Psychics* is imbued with a feeling of excitement generated by his discovery of a justification based on a social contract. This provided the crucial link between "impure" and "pure" utilitarianism in a more satisfactory way than his earlier appeal to evolutionary forces.

Edgeworth believed that he had provided an answer to an age-old question, stating, 'by what mechanism the force of self-love can be applied so as to support the structure of utilitarian politics, neither Helvetius, nor Bentham, nor any deductive egoist has made clear' (ibid.: 128). Nevertheless, this argument was neglected until restatements along similar lines were made by Harsanyi (1953, 1955) and Vickrey (1960). The maximisation of expected utility, with each individual taking the a priori view that any outcome is equally likely, was shown to lead to the use of a social welfare function which maximises the sum of individual utilities. This approach is now described as "contractarian neo-utilitarianism".

In discussing the utilitarian solution as a principle of arbitration in indeterminate contract, Edgeworth did not indicate in 1881 that the utilitarian solution of maximum total utility could specify a position making one of the parties worse off than in the no-trade situation. This was later made explicit when, after proposing arbitration along utilitarian lines, he added, 'subject to the condition that neither should lose by the contract' (Edgeworth 1925, ii: 102). This possibility depends largely on the initial endowments of the individuals.

8   Later Work in Economics

After the publication of *Mathematical Psychics*, Edgeworth concentrated increasingly on mathematical statistics, in particular, on the problem of statistical inference but, following his appointment to the Drummond Chair at Oxford, he again made important contributions to economics, although this work mainly involved reactions to, and discussions arising from, the work of other authors. This section discusses a number of these issues.

8.1   Demand and Exchange

In the *Principles of Economics* (1890: Appendix F) Marshall included a brief discussion of Edgeworth's analysis of barter, and produced a figure showing the contract curve. During the following year, in the course of a review written in Italian, Edgeworth criticised Marshall for not having dealt sufficiently with the problem of indeterminacy. The basic problem was that Marshall, using a model in which a series of trades are allowed to take place at disequilibrium prices, believed he had shown that prices eventually settle at the price-taking equilibrium. However, the argument was not transparent. The adjustment process involves moving from the initial endowment point in a series of trades, where trading at "false" prices is allowed at each step. The process must conclude with both individuals at a point on the contract curve. A feature of the process is the assumption that each stage or iteration of the sequence involves Pareto improvements: individuals trade only if it makes them better off. Furthermore, it involves trading at the "short end" of the market, that is, the minimum of supply and demand. This arises from the impossibility of forcing any individual either to buy or sell more than desired at any price. Starting from a disequilibrium price, trade takes place at the short end of the market, and endowments change. At the next trading stage, the price of the good with an excess supply must be lowered. At each trade, there is a Pareto improvement. The combination of Pareto-efficient moves at each stage, combined with an adjustment process such that an excess supply leads to a price reduction, and vice versa, produces a stable process that converges to an equilibrium somewhere on the contract curve. Interestingly, this type of sequence of disequilibrium trades was later used by Launhardt in examining total utility and price-taking (see Creedy 1994b).

Marshall believed that his assumption of an additive utility function, combined with the assumption that the marginal utility of one good is constant for both individuals, guaranteed a determinate price, if the good having constant marginal utility is money. This case was mentioned by Edgeworth (1925, ii: 317, fn. 1). The contract curve is a straight line parallel to the axis for the good with constant marginal utility, along which the rate of exchange is constant. So the equilibrium price does not depend on the sequence of trades. However, Edgeworth's point was that the total amount spent on the good remains indeterminate.

There was a later disagreement between Marshall and Edgeworth over the so-called Giffen good. In a book review, Edgeworth argued that 'Even the milder statement that the elasticity of demand for wheat *may* be positive, though I know it is countenanced by high authority, appears to me so contrary to a priori probability as to require very strong evidence' (Edgeworth 1909: 105; italics in original). The authority was of course Marshall (1890: 132), who replied directly to Edgeworth that I don't want to 'argue ... But... the matter has not been taken quite at random' (Marshall quoted in Pigou 1925: 438). Marshall gave a numerical example involving a journey travelled by two methods, where the distance travelled by the cheaper and slower method must increase when its price increases; for details, see Creedy (1990).

It was mentioned above that Edgeworth introduced the generalised utility function. An implication is that it allows for complementarity, although he did not explicitly consider this in 1881. It was used by Edgeworth in his paper on the pure theory of monopoly. The concept amounts to what is now called gross complementarity, defined in terms of cross-price elasticities. The first major criticism came from Johnson (1913), who pointed out that the criterion is not invariant with respect to monotonic transformations of the utility function. His treatment was extended by Hicks and Allen (1934), so that the modern definition involves net complements in terms of compensated price changes. There is no symmetry between gross substitutes and complements as only the matrix of (compensated) substitution elasticities is assumed to be symmetric.

8.2   Monopoly and Oligopoly

In a paper first published in Italian in 1897, and not translated until the collected *Papers* (Edgeworth 1925), Edgeworth examined several problems relating to monopoly. He began with Cournot's (1838) example of the "source minerale" in which there are "two monopolists" (i.e. duopolists), each owning a spring of mineral water. It would be natural for Edgeworth to expect an indeterminate price in this "small numbers" context. Cournot arrived at a determinate solution for price and output, but Edgeworth showed that 'when two or more monopolists are dealing with competitive groups, economic equilibrium is indeterminate' (Edgeworth 1925, i: 116). He argued that '[A]t every stage…it is competent to each monopolist to deliberate whether it will pay him better to lower his price against his rival as already described, or rather to raise it to a higher…level for that remainder of customers of which he cannot be deprived by his rival' (ibid.: 120).

Edgeworth went on to define (what are now called) reaction curves and isoprofit lines, for variations in prices. However, it was not until Bowley's (1924) discussion that these matters began to be presented in a more transparent manner.

Edgeworth then considered the case of complementary demand within the context of bilateral monopoly, where the two goods are demanded in fixed proportions for use in the production of a further article. A feature is that he wrote the equations of the reaction curves and explicitly dealt with what came to be called conjectural variations, reflecting the extent to which one duopolist is expected to change price in response to changes made by the second duopolist. In discussing this problem, Edgeworth also introduced the concept of a "saddle point", which he called the "Hog's Back", indicating its importance for stability.

Walras (1874: 225) had introduced the concept of the entrepreneur who neither gains nor loses. This result applied only to the competitive equilibrium, where there are no incentives for entrepreneurs to enter any industry.

This does not of course mean that there are no profits, in the accounting sense, since the returns to homogeneous units of inputs of organisation and management services are subsumed in the costs of the firm. Edgeworth's criticisms of this concept of the no-profit entrepreneur, reproduced in his *Papers* (Edgeworth 1925, i), recognised that with Walras's assumptions there is nothing illogical about the argument. The theory simply means that nothing remains, 'after the entrepreneur has paid a normal salary to himself' (ibid.: 26). Furthermore, 'If [the general expenses] are taken into account, the argument becomes a fortiori. For why should not a substantial remuneration for the entrepreneur be included in the general expenses of the business' (Edgeworth 1925, ii: 469–470). Edgeworth's difference with Walras was to some extent "only verbal", but he was also unhappy with the idea that entrepreneurship is homogeneous and divisible.

8.3   Surveys of Taxation and International Values

In the 1890s, Edgeworth produced two surveys of considerable importance. These surveys, of the pure theory of taxation and of the pure theory of international values, were both published in the *Economic Journal* and subsequently reproduced (with alterations) in his *Papers* (Edgeworth 1925, ii). Each survey consisted of three separate parts. They represent his most serious attempts to produce any kind of synthesis of a branch of economic literature. Edgeworth began his taxation survey with the statement that 'The science of taxation comprises two subjects to which the character of pure theory may be ascribed; the laws of incidence, and the principle of equal sacrifice' (ibid.: 64). He then considered a variety of special cases and contexts of tax incidence. The framework for incidence analysis is the simple partial equilibrium approach, still used in many basic textbooks, in which the incidence depends on the relative values of supply and demand elasticities.

The approach to incidence analysis actually stemmed from Jenkin (1871/1872), who suggested that in general the price of the taxed good will either remain constant (in the extreme case of inelastic supply) or will increase. However, this result ignores interrelationships among commodities. Edgeworth showed that when such interrelationships are considered, there are circumstances in which the price of the taxed good will fall. When discussing this "paradox", Edgeworth reproduced his argument, which had in fact been explored in more detail in his paper on monopoly, published in Italian in the same year, 1897. Edgeworth first stated his "tax paradox" in the following terms:

[W]hen the supply of two or more correlated commodities—such as the carriage of passengers by rail first class or third class—is in the hands of a single monopolist, a tax on one of the articles—e.g. a percentage of first class fares—may prove advantageous to the consumers as a whole ... The fares for all the classes might be reduced (Edgeworth 1925, i: 139).

Edgeworth regarded this result as an example of a situation where 'the abstract reasoning serves as a corrective to what has been called the "metaphysical incubus" of dogmatic laisser faire' (ibid.; see also Edgeworth 1925, ii: 93–94). Essentially the two commodities must be substitutes in consumption and production, and the result arises partly because the monopolist has an incentive to increase the supply of the untaxed commodity. Edgeworth (ibid.: 63) also recognised that the result could occur in competitive markets. As with many of Edgeworth's original results, this tax paradox was not a subject of continuous development. Its main practical importance perhaps arises from the fact that it attracted the attention of Hotelling (1932); for further details, see Creedy (1988).

Edgeworth discussed the various sacrifice theories of the distribution of the tax burden, giving qualified support for progressive taxation. His attitude to taxation was similar to that of the major classical economists in that he rejected a benefit approach, on the argument that taxation is not an economic bargain governed by competition. Thus in his view the problem was to determine 'the distribution of those taxes which are applied to common purposes, the benefits whereof cannot be allocated to particular classes of citizens' (Edgeworth 1925, ii: 103). A principle of justice is thus required. His approach marks a crucial stage in the transition towards a welfare economics view of public finance, rather than using a special set of tax maxims such as those laid down by Adam Smith.

Not surprisingly, Edgeworth (1925, ii: 102–103) argued along neo-contractarian lines that the utilitarian arrangement would be accepted by individuals who are uncertain of their own prospects and take an equal a priori view of the probabilities. He suggested that

each party may reflect that, in the long run of various cases…of all the principles of distribution which would afford him now a greater, now a smaller proportion of the sum-total utility obtainable…the principle that the collective utility should be on each occasion a maximum is most likely to afford the greatest utility in the long run to him individually.

Having established the use of utilitarianism as a principle of distribution justice, Edgeworth (ibid.: 103) succinctly argued that maximisation of total net utility reduces to the condition that the total disutility should be a minimum, and hence the marginal disutility of each taxpayer should be the same.

The implication is that if all individuals have the same cardinal utility function, after-tax incomes would be equalised. Edgeworth also recognised that if there is considerable dispersion of pre-tax incomes relative to the total amount of tax to be raised, where there is, 'not enough tax to go round' (ibid.), the equi-marginal condition cannot be fully satisfied unless there is a "negative income tax" which raises the incomes of the poorest individuals to a common level. Thus, 'the acme of socialism is for a moment sighted' (ibid.: 104). However, Edgeworth immediately considered the practical limitations to such high progressive taxation. The following quotation illustrates one of his favourite metaphors, his respect for Henry Sidgwick, his attitude to authority, his views on utilitarianism and the applicability of pure theory, and of course his unmistakable style:

> In this misty and precipitous region let us take Professor Sidgwick as our chief guide. He best has contemplated the crowning height of the utilitarian first principle, from which the steps of a sublime deduction lead to the high table-land of equality; but he also discerns the enormous interposing chasms which deter practical wisdom from moving directly towards that ideal (ibid.).

Among the various limitations, Edgeworth noted differences in individual utility functions, population effects, the disincentives to work, growth of culture and knowledge, savings, and of course the problem of evasion.

Edgeworth's survey of the pure theory of international values contributed to a change of emphasis in the approach to trade theory, despite the fact that it contained few original analytical contributions. Indeed, he said that 'Mill's exposition of the general theory is still unsurpassed' (Edgeworth 1925, ii: 20), and acknowledged further that '[W]hat is written…after a perusal of [Marshall's] privately circulated chapters…can make no claim to originality' (ibid.: 47). Edgeworth saw trade theory as an application of the general theory of exchange:

> The fundamental principle of international trade is that general theory…the Theory of Exchange…which…constitutes "the kernel" of most of the chief problems in economics. It is a corollary of the general theory that all the parties to a bargain look to gain by it … This is the generalised statement of the theory of comparative cost (ibid.: 6).

Thus the gains from trade are analogous to the gains from exchange in simple barter. Hence, trade theory is one more application of the general method of *Mathematical Psychics*. In directly applying the theory of exchange to that of trade, Edgeworth was content to use community indifference curves without clearly specifying how aggregation might be carried out. He said only that, 'By combining properly the utility curves for all the individuals, we obtain what may be called a collective utility curve' (ibid.: 293–294).

One of Edgeworth's criticisms of Mill (1848) was that the latter took as his measure of the gain from trade the change in the ratio of exchange of exports against imports. Thus Mill in this case 'confounds "final" with integral utility' (ibid.: 22). The same point had in fact been made by Jevons (1957: 154–156). However, Edgeworth, while preferring total utility, admitted that Mill was not otherwise led to serious error in using his own measure.

Edgeworth's survey was wide-ranging, though for later developments the most interesting parts are concerned with his elucidation of Mill's 'recognition of the case in which an impediment may be beneficial—or an improvement prejudicial—to one of the countries' (Edgeworth 1925, ii: 19). These cases would now be discussed under the headings of "optimal tariff" and "immiserising growth". In the case of an optimal tariff, a country acts as monopolist and imposes a price which enables that country to attain its highest indifference curve, subject to the other country's offer curve. However, this position is not on the contract curve. The detailed specification of the optimum tariff in terms of elasticities had to wait until Bickerdike (1906), Pigou (1908) and the later revivals of interest in the 1940s. Edgeworth's judgement of Bickerdike was that he had 'accomplished a wonderful feat. He has said something new about protection' (Edgeworth 1925, ii: 344).

Edgeworth did not support the use of such tariffs in practice. He acknowledged the possibility of retaliation. Also, for one nation to benefit itself at the expense of others 'is contrary to the highest morality … But in an abstract study upon the motion of projectiles in vacuo, I do not think it necessary to enlarge upon the horrors of war' (ibid.: 17, fn. 5). The 'highest morality' was, of course, the principle of utilitarianism.

9   Conclusion

After a varied beginning to his career, Edgeworth begin working and writing in economics when in his mid-thirties. In common with the majority of neo-classical economists, he pursued an academic career as a professor of economics. Indeed, in a period which saw the rapid and widespread professionalisation of the subject, Edgeworth's academic position in Oxford was regarded as second only to that of Alfred Marshall. In spite of his wide range of reading and sympathies, Edgeworth's work was virtually all addressed to his fellow professional economists. He was uncompromising in his view that economics is a difficult subject offering only remote and nearly always negative policy advice. It may be said that his work was addressed to a small number of "fellow travellers" in the rarefied atmosphere of the "higher regions" of pure theory. However, Edgeworth imposed no geographical limitations and, with his considerable linguistic skills and international sympathies, was in contact with the majority of leading economists around the world.

The distinguishing feature of the neoclassical "revolution" was its emphasis on exchange as the central economic problem. The success of this shift of focus from production and distribution to exchange was closely associated with the fact that it had as its foundation a model based on utility maximisation. This allowed for a deeper treatment of the gains from exchange and the wider considerations of economic welfare. Schumpeter summarised the point by stating that utility analysis must be understood in terms of exchange as the central 'pivot' and 'the whole of the organism of pure economics thus finds itself unified in the light of a single principle' (Schumpeter 1954: 913). This is indeed the context in which Edgeworth's work in economics must be seen. Schumpeter's remark is merely a more prosaic expression of Edgeworth's view quoted above that "'*Méchanique Sociale*" may one day take her place along with "*Méchanique Celeste*", throned each upon the double-sided height of one maximum principle'. The central theme of Edgeworth's work is also clear in his revealing statement, taken from his Presidential Address to Section F of the Royal Society, that, 'It may be said that in pure economics there is only one fundamental theorem, but that is a very difficult one: the theory of bargain in a wide sense' (Edgeworth 1925, ii: 288).

With this perspective, the thread running through all Edgeworth's work in economics can be seen. His earlier mathematical analysis, of the implications of utilitarianism for optimal distribution, laid the foundation for his future research. The transition from *New and Old Methods of Ethics* to *Mathematical Psychics* was not a shift in major preoccupations but rather a change of emphasis. For Edgeworth, distribution was seen as an important concomitant of exchange, so that the analysis of contract became central. Edgeworth's emphasis on the indeterminacy—the inability of utility maximisation alone to determine the rate of exchange, only a range of efficient exchanges—which results from the existence of a small number of traders, led to his path-breaking analysis of the role of numbers in competition, along with the efficiency properties of competitive equilibria.

The analysis of the utilitarian objective as an arbitration rule led Edgeworth directly to his social contract argument in explaining the acceptance of utilitarianism as a principle of social justice. It was the realisation of this justification of utilitarianism, using his newly developed analytical tools, which generated the excitement that is evident in his first work in economics. While *Mathematical Psychics* developed the techniques of indifference curves and the contract curve within the eponymous box diagram—tools which are now ubiquitous in economic analysis—Edgeworth himself was driven mainly by his ability to link the analysis of private contracts in markets to that of a social contract in which utilitarianism is the "sovereign principle". The integration of his analysis of barter, and the effects of the introduction of additional traders into the market, with the demonstration that the utilitarian arrangement prescribes a point on the contract curve of efficient exchanges and is acceptable to risk-averse traders, was to Edgeworth nothing short of momentous.

The results are of course highly abstract. In discussing their ultimate value, he suggested that:

> Considerations so abstract it would of course be ridiculous to fling upon the flood-tide of practical politics … It is at a height of abstraction in the rarefied atmosphere of speculation that the secret springs of action take their rise, and a direction is imparted to the pure foundation of youthful enthusiasm whose influence will ultimately affect the broad current of events (Edgeworth 1881: 128–129).

The intellectual pleasure derived from being able to draw together so many different subjects of analysis, and strands of Edgeworth's enormous range of learning, is clearly evident. However, it is precisely this wide field of vision, combined with the technical level and idiosyncratic style of writing, which made *Mathematical Psychics* so difficult for his contemporaries, and which continue to make the book seem so strange to the modern reader. When discussing, in *Mathematical Psychics*, the results of barter among a large number of competitors in a market, Edgeworth borrowed (without attribution) a line from Alexander Pope's *Essay on Man*, and described the market as, 'A mighty maze! but not without a plan'. This could just as appropriately be applied to Edgeworth's many contributions to economics.

References

Main Works by Francis Ysidro Edgeworth

Edgeworth, F.Y. (1877). *New and Old Methods of Ethics: or, 'Physical Ethics' and 'Methods of Ethics'*. Oxford: Parker.

Edgeworth, F.Y. (1879). 'The Hedonical Calculus'. *Mind*, 4(15): 394-408.

Edgeworth, F.Y. (1881). *Mathematical Psychics: An Essay on the Application of Mathematics to the Moral Sciences*. London: Kegan Paul.

Edgeworth, F.Y. (1887). *Metretike: or, The Method of Measuring Probability and Utility*. London: Temple.

Edgeworth, F.Y. (1909). 'Review of *Free Trade in Being*, by Russell Rea'. *Economic Journal*, 19(73): 102-106.

Edgeworth, F.Y. (1925). *Papers Relating to Political Economy*. Three volumes. London: Macmillan, for the Royal Economic Society.

Other Works Referred To

Barbé, L. (2010). *Francis Ysidro Edgeworth: A Portrait with Family and Friends*. Cheltenham: Edward Elgar Publishing.

Bickerdike, C.F. (1906). 'The Theory of Incipient Taxes'. *Economic Journal*, 16(64): 529-535.

Black, R.D.C. (ed.) (1977). *Papers and Correspondence of William Stanley Jevons, Vol. III, Correspondence 1863–1872*. London: Macmillan, for the Royal Economic Society.

Black, R.D.C. (ed.) (1981). *Papers and Correspondence of William Stanley Jevons, Vol. VII, Papers on Political Economy*. London: Macmillan, for the Royal Economic Society.

Bowley, A.L. (1924). *The Mathematical Groundwork of Economics*. Oxford: Clarendon Press.

Bowley, A.L. (1928). *Edgeworth's Contributions to Mathematical Statistics*. London: Royal Statistical Society.

Bowley, A.L. (1934). 'Francis Ysidro Edgeworth'. *Econometrica*, 2(2): 113–124.

Butler, M.S. (1972). *Maria Edgeworth: A Literary Biography*. Oxford: Oxford University Press.

Butler, J.H. and H.E. Butler (1927). *The Black Book of Edgeworthstown and Other Edgeworth Memories 1585–1817*. London: Faber & Gwyer.

Cournot, A.A. (1838). *Researches into the Mathematical Principles of the Theory of Wealth*. Translated in 1927 by N.T. Bacon and edited by I. Fisher. London: Stechert-Hafner.

Creedy, J. (1986). *Edgeworth and the Development of Neoclassical Economics*. Oxford: Basil Blackwell.

Creedy, J. (1988). 'Wicksell on Edgeworth's Tax Paradox'. *Scandinavian Journal of Economics*, 90(1): 101–112.

Creedy, J. (1990). 'Marshall and Edgeworth'. *Scottish Journal of Political Economy*, 37(1): 18–39.

Creedy, J. (1992). 'Jevons's Complex Cases in the Theory of Exchange'. *Journal of the History of Economic Thought*, 14(1): 55–69.

Creedy, J. (1994a). 'Exchange Equilibria: Bargaining, Utilitarian and Competitive Solutions'. *Australian Economic Papers*, 33(62): 34–52.

Creedy, J. (1994b). 'Launhardt's Model of Exchange'. *Journal of the History of Economic Thought*, 16(1): 40–60.

Edgeworth, M. (1820). *Memories of Richard Lovell Edgeworth Esq., Begun by Himself and Concluded by his Daughter, Maria Edgeworth*. Two volumes. London: Hunter.

Graves, R. (1960). *Goodbye to All That*. Second edition. London: Penguin.

Harsanyi, J.C. (1953). 'Cardinal Utility in Welfare Economics and in the Theory of Risk-Taking'. *Journal of Political Economy*, 61(5): 434–435.

Harsanyi, J.C. (1955). 'Cardinal Welfare, Individualistic Ethics, and Interpersonal Comparisons of Utility'. *Journal of Political Economy*, 63(4): 309–321.

Hicks, J.R. and R.G.D. Allen (1934). 'A Reconsideration of the Theory of Value, Parts I and II'. *Economica*, New Series, 1(1 and 2): 52–76 and 196–219.

Hotelling, H. (1932). 'Edgeworth's Taxation Paradox and the Nature of Demand and Supply Functions'. *Journal of Political Economy*, 40(5): 577–616.

Jenkin, F. (1871/1872). 'On the Principles which Regulate the Incidence of Taxes'. *Proceedings of the Royal Society of Edinburgh*, 7: 618–631. Reprinted as Chapter 14 in R.A. Musgrave and C.S. Shoup (eds) (1959) *Readings in the Economics of Taxation*. London: Allen & Unwin: 227–239.

Jevons, W.S. (1881). 'Review of *Mathematical Psychics*, by F.Y. Edgeworth'. *Mind*, 6(24): 581–583.

Jevons, W.S. (1957). *The Theory of Political Economy*. Fifth edition. Edited by H.S. Jevons. New York: Augustus Kelly.

Johnson, W.E. (1913). 'The Pure Theory of Utility Curves'. *Economic Journal*, 23(92): 483–513.

Keynes, J.M. (1933) [1972]. *Essays in Biography*. Volume X of *The Collected Writings of John Maynard Keynes*. London: Macmillan.

Marshall, A. (1890). *Principles of Economics*. Two volumes. Variorum edition (1961), edited by C.W. Guillebaud. London: Macmillan.

McCann, C.R. (ed.) (1996). *F.Y. Edgeworth: Writings in Probability, Statistics and Economics*. Three volumes. Cheltenham: Edward Elgar Publishing.

Mill, J.S. (1848). *Principles of Political Economy*. Reprinted in 1920, with editorial material by W.J. Ashley. London: Longmans, Green.

Phelps Brown, H. (1981). 'Henry Roy Forbes Harrod 1900–1978'. *Proceedings of the British Academy*, 65: 652–696.

Pigou, A.C. (1908). *Protective and Preferential Import Duties*. London: Macmillan.

Pigou, A.C. (ed.) (1925). *Memorials of Alfred Marshall*. London: Macmillan.

Pigou, A.C. and D.H. Robertson (1931). *Economic Essays and Addresses*. London: King.

Price, L.L. (1946). *Memoirs and Notes on British Economists 1881–1946*. MSS, Brotherton Library, University of Leeds.

Schumpeter, J.A. (1954). *History of Economic Analysis*. London: Allen & Unwin.

Stigler, S.M. (1978). 'Francis Ysidro Edgeworth, Statistician'. *Journal of the Royal Statistical Society, Series A (General)*, 141(3): 287–322.

Sully, J. (1918). *My Life and Friends*. London: Fisher Unwin.

Vickrey, W.S. (1960). 'Utility, Strategy, and Social Decision Rules'. *Quarterly Journal of Economics*, 74(4): 507–535.

Walras, L. (1874). *Elements of Pure Economics*. English translation by W. Jaffe (1954). London: Allen & Unwin.

Whitaker, J.K. (ed.) (1975). *The Early Economic Writings of Alfred Marshall*. Volume 2. London: Macmillan.

12

David Hutchison Macgregor (1877–1953)

Lowell Jacobsen

1   Introduction

David Hutchison Macgregor is a member of the pantheon of British economists during the early decades of the twentieth century. The leading lights of
this time were, of course, Alfred Marshall, the Cambridge Professor of Political
Economy, and Francis Ysidro Edgeworth, Oxford's Drummond Professor of
Political Economy. Both held the two most venerable economics chairs in
Great Britain. A.C. Pigou would succeed Marshall in 1908 and Macgregor
would succeed Edgeworth in 1922. Like Marshall at Cambridge, Macgregor's
tenure at Oxford would last for 23 years. Further, Macgregor would succeed
Edgeworth as joint editor (along with John Maynard Keynes) of the *Economic
Journal* upon Edgeworth's death in 1926, a position he held until 1934.[1]

The author is most appreciative of the kindness and courtesies shown by Simon Frost and Clare Trowell
at the Marshall Library, Cambridge University, in providing access to the collected papers of Alfred
Marshall and Austin Robinson as well as Grant Buttars and Laura Cooijmans-Keizer at the Centre for
Research Collections, Main Library, University of Edinburgh, for their research assistance.

[1] Hicks (1953: 120) in his Inaugural Lecture as Drummond Professor stated: 'We go to Marshall for the
answers, but for the questions—the questions which still have to be asked after Marshall—we go to
Edgeworth'. Roy Harrod remarked in his 1967 retirement speech that Edgeworth was likely 'the greatest
Oxford economist of all time' (Harrod quoted in Young and Lee 1993: viii).

L. Jacobsen (✉)
Baker University, Baldwin City, Kansas, USA
e-mail: Ljacobsen@bakeru.edu

Though Keynes and Pigou were Marshall's most famous students, Macgregor was one of Marshall's favourites (see Lee 2011; Groenewegen 2012). Schumpeter (1954: 833) observed that Keynes and Pigou were 'formed by [Marshall's] teaching and started from his teaching, however far they may have travelled beyond it'. Much the same could be said about Macgregor whose priority of thought was industrial economics 'where Marshall's originality among his contemporaries shines unrivalled' (Raffaelli et al. 2006: xv). The centrepiece of *Principles* is arguably industrial economics. Marshall (1920: 1) at the outset famously stated: 'Political Economy or Economics is a study of mankind in the ordinary business of life', adding that, 'For man's character has been moulded by his every-day work' (ibid.). Macgregor notably advanced Marshall's industrial economics with a masterly analysis of modern industry featuring 'vast enterprises' or what today are commonly referred to as conglomerates. Indeed, his 1906 *Industrial Combination* is a classic in the field. Gerald Shove (1942: 320), another dedicated Marshallian, observed that such enormous entities 'find little or no place' in *Principles* while their treatment in *Industry and Trade* is 'almost entirely historical and descriptive'. (Of course, *Industry and Trade* was not published until 1919.)

Macgregor was born and bred a Scot. He was born on 10 May 1877 in Monifieth, Forfarshire. Macgregor was very much an "Edinburgh man" having studied at George Watson's College, an independent school in the city, for two years prior to entering Edinburgh University where he distinguished himself with a First Class Honours MA in Philosophy in 1898. During his four years at Edinburgh he studied Latin, Greek, Mathematics, Natural Philosophy, Moral Philosophy, Logic and Mental Philosophy. Edinburgh awarded Macgregor an Honorary LLD (Doctor of Laws) in 1945.

In 1898, Macgregor went on to Cambridge University for three years to study economics under Marshall where he again distinguished himself with First Class Honours in the Moral Sciences Tripos. (The Economics Tripos was not established until 1903.) He was elected President of the Cambridge Union, the famous debating society, in 1902.

After completing his degree, Macgregor stayed in Cambridge, and with Marshall's financial support, lectured in economics and assisted Marshall in the marking of student papers. Macgregor proved to be a daunting lecturer and acquired the reputation as a taskmaster amongst the students. In a letter to his colleague Herbert Foxwell, dated 8 February 1906, Marshall wrote: 'I know that Macgregor is inclined to seek out difficulties overmuch; though he is trying to smooth his mind out. But men who found him too hard would get what they want from Green [G.E. Green's *Elementary Political Economy*]'. In a subsequent letter to Foxwell, dated 12 February 1906, Marshall added: 'I agree with you that the young men ought to do some drudgery; and I had that in mind when I suggested that Macgregor should give a full first years course, pitched rather higher than Green's' (Marshall to Foxwell, quoted in Whitaker 1996, 3: 124 and 126 respectively).

In 1904, Macgregor particularly impressed Marshall with his entry for the prestigious Cobden Club Essay Prize. The "Subjects for Cobden Club Essays 1904" contained a list of six subjects on economics. The list began with "The causes and effects of Commercial and Industrial Trusts, and the extent to which it is possible and desirable to introduce legislative restrictions on their operations" (Alfred Marshall Papers, Marshall Library, Cambridge: Section 2/8, 1904). This was the subject Macgregor chose to address, his essay finishing second in the competition with Marshall as one of the three judges. Marshall thought Macgregor's essay deserved the award and exclaimed in a private letter that 'its 420! typed pages contain an extraordinary amount of original thought' (Marshall to Tanner, 7 December 1904, in Whitaker 1996, 3: 98). The essay was likely the basis for Macgregor's successful fellowship dissertation for Trinity College, Cambridge, in the same year of 1904. Macgregor's signature *Industrial Combination* was a modified version of his dissertation, appearing in 1906. In the book's preface, Macgregor expressed his heartfelt appreciation 'to Professor Marshall, to whom I owe my guidance in economic study' (Macgregor 1906: vi).

In 1908, the year in which Marshall retired, Macgregor succeeded John Clapham (who returned to Cambridge) as Professor of Political Economy at Leeds University. This appointment was likely on the strength of the critically acclaimed *Industrial Combination* and, Marshall's enthusiastic support. For someone so young as Macgregor to receive a professorship was extraordinary and suggested much promise for the years to come.

The Great War, however, would intervene. Despite being nearly 40-years-old, Macgregor fought for King and Country and no less than on the front line in and out of the trenches for which he won the Military Cross for "exemplary gallantry". The experience, including a severe head wound (and, in later years, the grievous loss of his wife and a daughter), would have adverse consequences for his health during the remainder of his life. Most noticeably, he lost the ability to give his customary eloquent lectures. Austin Robinson, another devout Marshallian industrial economist, reflected that Macgregor 'in his last years at Oxford…had somewhat lost the capacity to inspire others. But all this seems strange because there was real life and penetration in [Macgregor's] books themselves'. Later, Robinson wrote in another letter: 'Macgregor was one of the ablest of Marshall's pupils. By the time I knew him he was a dull dog, but he had been a very different sort of person when young'

(Robinson to Lee, 6 September 1980 and Robinson to Hubback, 9 July 1982 respectively, Austin Robinson Papers, Marshall Library, Cambridge University: Section 2/6).

In 1919, Macgregor became the Stanley Jevons Professor of Political Economy at Manchester. Just two years later, he was invited by the electors to take up the Drummond Professorship of Political Economy at Oxford, this without even having made a formal application. Those who did apply included Edwin Cannan, who was at the time the leading professor at LSE. Macgregor would hold the Drummond Chair until his retirement in 1945. He was succeeded by fellow Scot and Cambridge man, Sir Hubert Henderson, followed by John Hicks, who would later become a Nobel Laureate.

Sadly, in 1953, Macgregor tragically died in a street accident in Oxford. May he be long remembered as far from being a "dour Scot" as 'his friends will never forget the light which seemed to come from within his handsome Scots features and the kindly humour which he never lost. Those who talked with Macgregor generally came away feeling they had been with a great man' (Andrews 1953: 346).[2]

2   In and Out of Marshall's Shadow

Peter Groenewegen (2012), the late eminent Marshallian scholar, wondered if possibly Joseph Shield Nicholson, Edinburgh Professor of Political Economy, advised Macgregor upon finishing his MA degree at Edinburgh to go to Cambridge to study with Marshall. After all, Nicholson was also an outstanding student of Marshall as he had won the Cobden Prize as well as received First Class Honours in the Moral Sciences Tripos. Though quite plausible, this possibility is nevertheless speculative, as Groenewegen admitted. Interestingly enough, Macgregor during his second year at Cambridge did cite in his own handwritten "Student Assessment" (including his signature) Nicholson's *Political Economy* and *Money and Monetary Problems* as books he had read (Alfred Marshall Papers, Marshall Library, Cambridge: Section 2/5, 1899). However, first, Macgregor (1942: 313), on the centenary of Marshall's birth and writing in the capacity of one of his former students, referred only to Professor John Stuart Blackie, Professor of Classics at Edinburgh, and not Nicholson. Secondly, Macgregor reflected that '*Principles* is the first book on economics I ever read' (ibid.). Moreover, he

---

[2] In addition to Andrews' poignant obituary of Macgregor, other biographical sources consulted for this section include Lee (1989, 2011), Groenewegen (1995, 2012), Whitaker (1996) and Cristiano (2011).

added that it was the *only* economics book that needed to be studied at Cambridge. Apparently, not even Adam Smith's *Wealth of Nations* was required reading!

Macgregor (ibid.: 314) vividly expressed the following: 'We were soaked and stewed in the theory of Value'. Nevertheless, he recalled there was no easy route, including reading *Economics of Industry*, to properly comprehending *Principles* as 'you had to master it yourself' (ibid.: 313). In his remarkable memoir of Marshall, Keynes echoed Macgregor's sentiments in that despite its 'pervading charm' (Keynes 1924 [1972]: 212), *Principles* required 'much study and independent thought' (ibid.) by the reader; there were no shortcuts to discovering the knowledge and insights 'in the concealed crevices' (ibid.) of Marshall's masterpiece. Yet, as Keynes added and Macgregor certainly appreciated, *Principles* is brimming with 'suggestions, starting points for many investigations' (ibid.: 370), as well as being stocked with analytical tools to apply to economic reality.

Macgregor (1942: 313) reminisced that Marshall's lectures were of little aid to understanding *Principles* as they were intended to stoke interest, not enlighten. Marshall could be quite mischievous and after speaking for a time in what sounded reasonable and measured, with 'perfect gravity', he would suddenly stop and exclaim: 'All I have been saying up to now is perfect nonsense[!]'.

Like nearly everyone around Marshall, Macgregor was in awe of his towering intellect. In thinking back to Marshall's last lecture that Macgregor and other 'colts in the stable' (including Keynes) attended, Macgregor (ibid.: 314) with the utmost gratitude, respect and admiration remarked: 'Then, as always, his sense of dignity was great; also his impression of authority; he could not help knowing that there was as nearly as possible nobody else in the economic leadership'. Even Keynes (1924 [1972]: 198) in his memorial acknowledged that near the end of the nineteenth century there was no one close to Marshall's stature, reigning as the authoritative figure in economics until the end of his life. Keynes (ibid.: 222), of course, memorably exalted that 'Marshall was the first great economist *pur sang* that there ever was' as he dedicated his life to the elevation of economics to a science.

Macgregor (1942) proceeded to dispassionately offer an incisive, balanced, constructive critique of *Principles*. He did so with an adroit, contextual analysis featuring numerous intellectual influences, including both obvious (e.g. Smith, Ricardo, Mill and Jevons) as well as obscure (e.g. Whewell, Moffatt and Jenkin) figures in the history of economic thought. Macgregor's thoroughness went so far as to gently chastise Marshall for his neglect in not citing some notable influences, including the eminent psychologist Alexander Bain (whom Jevons had cited). For example, he illustrated (including with some mathematical detail) the evolution of the price elasticity of demand, commencing with Whewell (whom Marshall did not cite) in the early nineteenth century. Jevons, despite being aware of the concept, chose to ignore, not appreciating its importance. Cournot embraced it while others, including Mill, recognised it but did not give it a name. Further, Marshall did not include it in *Economics of Industry*; however, he would feature it in *Principles*, deploying both algebraic and graphical expression. Macgregor went on to note that in *Industry and Trade*, demand elasticity was described by Marshall as 'a gradual and sometimes uncertain process' (ibid.: 316).

Macgregor (ibid.) gave equally detailed attention to some of the other key concepts in *Principles*, including consumer surplus, substitution, decreasing costs and the representative firm. He also supported Marshall's resistance to the idea of pure or perfect competition in preference for 'free' competition as, no matter how competitive an industry might be as reflected in the movement towards normal price, firms would maintain at least some degree of monopoly power typically in recognition of custom or goodwill. As such, equilibrium occurs where price equals average cost, which does not necessarily mean marginal revenue equals marginal cost. Macgregor agreed with Marshall that the typical business, despite likely possessing an element of monopoly, is conditioned by competition in setting its price as it prefers to maintain, rather than myopically take advantage of, customer goodwill. In keeping with Marshall, Macgregor warned that analytical rigour had its limitations; in the case of the profit maximisation rule, for example, 'it is possible to work this principle too hard' (ibid.: 320). Some relaxation of determinateness may be justified to ensure relevance.[3]

Macgregor constructively defended Marshall's representative firm for not being simply a necessary abstraction to reconcile increasing returns with long-period equilibrium. Such a firm could be identified in any industry as one that provided price leadership given its normal costs. Yes, some firms would have lower costs whilst others have higher costs. This firm was not the *marginal* firm that entered a market given the signal of price exceeding average cost. But, of course, Marshall's introduction of the representative firm could well be (and has been) interpreted as an abstraction as Marshall (1920: 316) somewhat misleadingly explained that real firms are either at any given moment in ascendancy or decline, 'constant rise and fall'. At the same time,

---

[3] Hicks (1939: 84), in stark contrast, warned that in order to uphold perfect competition and its determinate equilibrium, unrealistic assumptions were necessary as 'it must be remembered that the threatened wreckage is that of the greater part of economic theory'.

Marshall (ibid.: 318) goes on to explain that the representative firm of an industry is identified after 'a broad survey' of the companies in an industry—including those that are joint-stock, 'which often stagnate, but do not readily die' (ibid.: 316)—recognising the extent to which such organisations have realised both internal and external economies. A representative firm could hardly be the nascent company at the margin as it has probably enjoyed 'a fairly long life, and fair success' (ibid.: 317). Later in *Principles*, Marshall (ibid.: 367) argued that the representative firm is that which is found in the fiction of a stationary state of long-period equilibrium where everything is constant, including firm size, internal and external economies, and production. However, Marshall likely 'worked this principle too hard' as well given the admission that the long-period representative firm is an 'extreme' (ibid.: 349), indeed an abstraction, where the law of constant returns matches value with production cost.

Macgregor acknowledged the broad criticism of Marshall's treatment of industry structure as out of date and naive especially given the instabilities associated with the rise of trusts and cartels. As Macgregor (1942: 322) explained:

> Consider the items. The small firm is, by a good margin, inefficient, but it is supported by the external economies which are associated with large-scale production. Its place is, to offer a ladder for the rise of new men in search of capital, and is, on the whole, expensively retained with that offset. The private firm has the inherent disadvantage of exhaustion of the business ability which creates it, its rise and fall, like the trees of the forest, being described as a normal result. In spite of the vivid picture of the alert business man, the result appears socially wasteful, since the qualities of such private enterprise are not maintained from one generation to another. If, to avoid this decadence a Joint-Stock Company is formed, that "stagnates but does not decay". Co-operation is mainly suited to retail trade, and public enterprise to local services, and transport.

Interestingly, Marshall was fully aware that *Principles* did not effectively address the evolving nature of industry in which the amalgamation of large businesses (viz. joint-stock companies) into 'vast enterprises' transformed the structure of industries. Beginning with the fifth edition of *Principles* published in 1907, Marshall (1920: xiv) candidly acknowledged in the preface that industrial conglomerates such as trusts 'cannot be fitly discussed in a volume on Foundations: they belong to a volume dealing with some part of the Superstucture'. Such vast and complex enterprises as trusts with intricate interdependencies required a separate, comprehensive analysis that Marshall was working on but which would not appear in print until 1919. This, of course, would be *Industry and Trade*, what Marshall referred to as a "continuation" of *Principles* as noted in the 1920 eighth edition. In "The Theory of Monopolies", Chapter XIV, Book V, Marshall (1920: 477) stated: 'In a later volume a study will be made of the Protean shapes of modern trade combinations and monopolies, some of the most important of which, as for example "Trusts", are of very recent growth'. The substance of this statement was intact from the first edition to the eighth. Only the first four words replaced 'At a later stage', beginning in the fourth (1898) edition (see Guillebaud 1961: 534).

Marshall (1920: 417, fn. 1) regarded industrial combination such as a trust to be a rather incoherent 'semi-monopolistic business aggregate [that] is often "over-capitalized"' and complex, thereby highly confounding in relation to *Principles* where firms are quite normal and hence subject to analysis (particularly, dynamic partial equilibrium) where uniformities are logically deduced. To be sure, *Principles* is about *principles*. Though Marshall (ibid.: xiv) famously wrote that, 'the Mecca of the economist lies in economic biology' (where complexity and change rules), *Principles* is necessarily '*a volume on Foundations [which] must therefore give a relatively large place to mechanical analogies; and frequent use is made of the term "equilibrium"*'which requires that '*predominant attention [is] paid…to [the] normal conditions of life*', including that of industry (italics added).

Marshall (ibid.: 304), although he did not significantly address the novel challenges of 'giant businesses', including joint-stock companies and trusts in *Principles*, acknowledged that such attention was nevertheless 'urgent', particularly in understanding how such sizeable enterprises with far-reaching scope are managed. Further, he expressed amazement at how quickly innovations of process and technique as well as management acumen could be introduced. This was particularly so in the United States where industrial combinations featuring trusts first emerged.

Shove (1942), in his equally authoritative critical assessment of *Principles* in observance of Marshall's centenary birth, more than echoed Macgregor in arguing that the book is obsolete notably with regard to modern industry structure. Though Shove applauded *Principles* for it 'stands with Smith's *Wealth of Nations* and Ricardo's *Principles* as one of the three great watersheds in the development of economic ideas' (ibid.: 313), it failed to effectively address the middle ground between free competition, featuring atomic competition and pure monopoly. The trees in the forest analogy seemed less than satisfactory as large enterprises grew even larger in both scale and scope and became even more dominant and undeterred by old age. Shove (ibid.: 320) enumerated many aspects of modern industry informed by industrial combination that Marshall's theoretical framework was ill-equipped to address, including: the conflict of interests within the firm; the interpenetration of interests between firms through interlocking directorates, shareholdings, subsidiary concerns and the like; the domination of an industry by a few large units; and the inter-mixture of public and private control as seen in the various types of semi-public corporation and of regulating boards and other devices.

Too many complexities, too much instability, too many market imperfections and, perhaps, too much indeterminateness. Maybe there was a limit to Marshall's 'restless quest after realism' combined with a diminished ability to apply the mechanical or even biological approaches to economic development. Moreover, by 1919 when *Industry and Trade* was finally published, Marshall's influence had considerably waned with the "years of high theory" approaching. *Industry and Trade* proved too little, too late or perhaps, more aptly, too much, too late as this 'continuation' volume of *Principles* was 875 pages of small print. Marshall's health issues associated with old age and the distractions of the Great War delayed *Industry and Trade* by some six years. Keynes (1924 [1972]: 228) argued that the volume's three books would have been better published separately. Nevertheless, despite its descriptive and historical emphasis, the volume, particularly Book III, served to highlight the evolution of industrial combination. The matter of trusts caused Marshall the 'greatest trouble' (Whitaker 1990: 220) in terms of his biological life-cycle analysis as maintained in *Principles*.

Macgregor's work on trusts and cartels dating back to his studies under Marshall, fellowship dissertation and the highly regarded *Industrial Combination* first published in 1906 was never explicitly referenced in the fifth (1907) through eighth (1920) editions of *Principles*. Nor is there any evidence of correspondence between Marshall and Macgregor after 1908 when Macgregor left Cambridge for Leeds (see Whitaker 1996). Marshall, nevertheless, should not be thought to have slighted Macgregor. In the preface of the fifth through eighth editions, Marshall (1920: xiv) admitted that trusts 'cannot be fitly discussed in a volume on Foundations'. Starting with the preface to the sixth (1910) edition, Marshall (ibid.: xiii) newly emphasised that *Principles* was concerned with 'normal' behaviour where 'economic evolution is gradual' and where progress is 'never sudden' and the businessman is a creature of 'habit, partly conscious, partly unconscious'. The 'manifestations' of large businesses featuring trusts, however, were conveniently thought rather 'spasmodic, infrequent, and difficult of observation', hence not 'representative' and thereby not amenable to complete economic analysis at least by that offered in *Principles*. Such a 'special examination' of trusts and other amalgamations was contained in *Industry and Trade*, which appeared a year before the eighth edition of *Principles*.

Marshall's *Industry and Trade* was, to be sure, influenced by Macgregor's *Industrial Combination* (see Giocoli 2012). Indeed, Macgregor was explicitly cited in *Industry and Trade* and positively so. In Book III, "Monopolistic Tendencies…", Chapter XI, "Aggregation…", Marshall (1919: 577) began by saluting 'several excellent accounts' of 'giant businesses' with *Industrial Combination* being listed first. (Interestingly, in the index, 'Macgregor, Prof 577n' rather than 'Macgregor, D.H. 577n', is recorded, suggesting a certain level of respect.) Marshall's personal annotated copy of *Industrial Combination* (which is held at Cambridge's Marshall Library) shows that he conducted a careful read of the volume. The notes are very specific and supportive. To the extent that they are critical, the criticism is primarily levelled, not against Macgregor, but his sources. For example, in Macgregor's application of Cournot's mathematics, Marshall wrote in the margin: 'C. made a mistake'. Elsewhere, Marshall wrote: 'I hold Walker to be substantially wrong on this point'. Finally, although, as noted, there is no evidence of any written correspondence between them, Macgregor did attend Marshall's last lecture as Cambridge Professor of Political Economy as well as his funeral.

Macgregor's writings reflected Marshall's enduring inspiration and guidance. *Industrial Combination* was likely motivated in part by Marshall's Presidential Address to the Economic and Statistics Section of the British Association in Leeds in 1890 entitled 'Some Aspects of Competition'. In this, Marshall focused on the 'action of competition and…the attitude of economists towards it' (Marshall 1890 [1925]: 256). In doing so, he made clear his appreciation that combinations, including trusts, were encouraged by the law of increasing returns and artificially so by tariff protection, particularly in America. The nature and scope of competition fundamentally altered in favour of combination, hence the tendency towards monopoly. Yet, industrial reorganisation in the form of trusts could falter and break up if they charged too high a price as both existing and potential rivals, including other trusts, would act as countervailing forces offering products at lower prices or better quality or both.

Trusts, initially at least, are a confederation of typically joint-stock companies fused together by limited contract rather than absorbed by ownership consolidation. Marshall (ibid.: 271) explained: 'Trusts have very many forms and methods, but their chief motive in every case is to take away from the several firms in the combination all inducements to compete by indirect means with one another'. Should there be a tendency towards permanent consolidation whereby competition is unduly constrained, government might well intervene, though not to the extent of managing companies. More than likely, the tendency towards consolidation was actuated by the centralisation of executive power over time. For Marshall, this was how both American and British economists viewed the growing concern over combination.

Marshall advised much patience and forethought before government chose to intervene. First, he had much faith in both actual and potential competition to discipline growing monopoly power. Second, he understood that there is a fine line between intervention and management, which is easily crossed, particularly by a government agency prone to act. Further, the State control of industries turns private firms into 'semi-public concerns' that are ipso facto unnatural and risk forfeiting increasing returns and wider economic progress. To quote Marshall (ibid.: 275; italics added): 'We believe that a private company which stands to gain something by vigorous and efficient management, by promptness in inventing, as well as in adopting and perfecting improvements in processes *and organisation*, will do much more for progress than a public department'. He added that governments should be particularly circumspect before intervening in industry as the law of increasing returns is dynamic and not easily realised in terms of delivering future benefits to consumers, not just in terms of lower prices but product improvements. Marshall, however, emphasised that nascent, small entrepreneurial firms were a requisite 'superior inventive force' that would preserve or, if need be, restore free competition and, intrinsically, the freedom of individualism in the long period.[4]

Marshall (ibid.: 283) had reservations about socialism, particularly in Germany at the time, arguing that socialists 'think too much of competition as the exploiting of labour by capital, of the poor by the wealthy, and too little of it as the constant experiment by the ablest men for their several tasks, each trying to discover a new way in which to attain some important end'. He also questioned whether or not a socialist perspective, although admirably expressed with a 'generous heart', would allow for 'serious contributions to economic science' (ibid.: 284). Specifically, in addressing the determinants of real wages and the causes of their possible suppression, Marshall made the plea for much greater attention to and analysis of industrial combination by economists whereby government officials and indeed the public would be enlightened of its impact on workers, competition and the economy.

---

[4] Marshall (1919: 581) did argue that 'small business must be out of place in the new age: for that belongs to large business'. Yet, he remained optimistic that 'an enterprising man, who sees his way to fitting the work of a small business into the large frame of national industry, may render as high service to the country now as ever' (ibid.: 582).

Marshall concluded in his 1890 Presidential Address: 'Thus the growth of combinations and partial monopolies has in many ways increased, and in no way diminished, the practical importance of the careful study of the influences which the normal forces of competition exert on normal value' (Marshall 1890: 288). Such growth was at a much more rapid pace than previous evolutionary changes in industry organisation, in turn fostering greater complexity. As a result, Marshall emphatically called forth considerable economic investigation and analysis of combinations as the need was no less than 'urgent' (ibid.: 291).

Industrial Combination was a pioneering work by which 'it is doubtful if the general problem of industrial combination has ever been better surveyed' (Andrews 1953: 348). Moreover, it was highly influential in the field of industrial economics 'for nearly a quarter of a century after its publication' (Lee 1989: 23). Ronald Coase (1936: 133), who would later become a Nobel Laureate, in reviewing the volume's reprint three decades after its first publication, praised *Industrial Combination* as 'the standard work on its subject'. Coase noted that Macgregor provided a detailed account of the complexity and analytical rationale for combinations, recognising the otherwise underappreciated role of external economies which of course the pure theory of standard economics had neglected. However, Coase expressed some regret, not that Macgregor would resurrect Marshall's representative firm in the form of a 'representative organisation' as an analytical device or 'method', but rather that he did so when, following Marshall's death in 1924, the representative firm would come under attack and be abandoned in value theory and indeed the industrial economics literature. Coase would add, albeit with the utmost admiration, that Macgregor's book was not always an easy read as 'Professor Macgregor is too aware of the nature of questions he poses to give simple answers. Moreover, there is a wealth of meaning in every sentence and one is liable to miss qualifications or only to see their import after many readings' (ibid.: 135). High praise indeed.[5]

Henry Macrosty (1907) also offered a persuasive, indeed authoritative, endorsement of *Industrial Combination* in his review. Macrosty's 1907 *Trust Movement in British Industries* was rated second to Macgregor's volume in significance by Marshall (1919: 577) with respect to industrial 'aggregations

---

[5] In Coase's Nobel Lecture, "The Institutional Structure of Production", he lamented the dominance of price theory and its refined abstraction focusing on price and output whereby firms' organisational structures are unnecessary. Coase (1991 [1994]: 5) stated: 'The firm in mainstream economic theory has often been described as a "black box". And so it is. This is very extraordinary given that most resources in a modern economic system are employed within firms, with how these resources are used dependent on administrative decisions and not directly on the operation of a market'.

and federations'. Macrosty highly approved of Macgregor's 'representative method' of employing a framework rather than a model that allows analysis featuring assiduous detail and consequential insights to the organisation of combinations. Macgregor, for example, recognised that enormous enterprises, with or without being a combination ipso facto embody monopoly power, but may or may not be monopolies. Such distinctions matter in terms of method and results as well as policy. Macrosty (1907: 105–107) applauded Macgregor for having 'written a very good book', one that is 'very interesting' as well as 'a thoroughly useful piece of work'. He noted that the book is 'full of suggestive criticism' and 'praised' it for its examination of the causes of combinations.

Garrett Droppers' (1907) review of *Industrial Combination* was, however, less than glowing in comparison to those by Coase and Macrosty. He acknowledged Macgregor's skilful analysis of the evolution of modern industrial organisations and how this filled a gap in the work of Marshall. This aside, Droppers felt that the volume was left wanting in terms of additional, more compelling explanation for the inception and growth of trusts. This he found the 'least satisfactory portion' (ibid.: 121) of the book. Though Droppers considered *Industrial Combination* to be a fair and balanced treatment which 'is wholly admirable' (ibid.: 122), he concluded that it suffered from the 'serious handicap' of being too theoretical, 'as if [Macgregor] did not see the wood for the trees' (ibid.: 122). This criticism is perhaps rather harsh and misplaced as Macgregor's approach was steeped in Marshall's organon, featuring a combination of inductive and deductive analysis (rather than theory), blending contemporary and historical concrete facts with a priori reasoning.[6] Consider the following passage from Macgregor (1906: 30):

> But, so far as productive efficiency alone is concerned, this is not the case for all trades, and special circumstances must decide the possibilities of economies on this basis. Thus combinations of dealers are difficult to maintain, because they take slight risk of fixed capital, and a competitor can start easily, if he can obtain only a good-will which rests largely on personal causes. The Cordage combinations had a chequered history because it was "very easy" for a rival to start. A capital of 200,000 dollars is adequate for a representative salt factory. The distilling trade is specially liable to periods of overproduction, because the cost of establishing a distillery of reasonable size is slight, a distillery consuming 1500

---

[6] Marshall preferred analysis over theory with pure theory, in his view, having no place in economics. In a letter to Foxwell (25 January 1897 in Whitaker 1996, 2: 178), Marshall wrote that in economics, 'I do not think there is any "theory" to speak of: & analysis is unprofitable when separated from the study of facts'. Marshall was willing to accept all investigative methods, including induction, deduction, and the use of history, provided they were used constructively.

bushels per day being on a good competitive basis. The Doscher refineries, with a capacity of 3000 barrels per day, claim to run as cheaply as the Trust with its capacity of 45,000; and this is admitted by the Trust. The Wire Nail Pool of 1895–1896 was broken, because "with 10,000 dollars and six weeks' time any one can become a manufacturer of wire nails". Similar evidence was given for Tin-plate and other industries.

Macgregor's *Industrial Combination* was first published in 1906, a time when the aggregation or amalgamation of gigantic businesses was still the exception and the subject of few economic studies. Even though exceptional, combinations made a pronounced adverse impression on the psyche of government officials, in particular, as trusts and cartels were possibly perilous by-products of tariffs and other artificial interferences. Such 'vast enterprises' led by industrial magnates (e.g. Carnegie and Rockefeller) were perceived to have heralded the decline of capitalism, if not the so-called March into Socialism. Government intervention could after all be the logical and desired response to such powerful capitalist elites. Veblen (1904) frequently referred to industrial powers as 'parasitical'. Marshall (1920: 495) even warned that 'monopolistic cartels', in particular, were 'treacherous'. Economic welfare could be at risk.

Macgregor (1906: v), at the outset of his magnum opus, regarded industrial combinations as the 'most pressing question of industrial organisation'. He believed that trusts and other combinations do not necessarily lead to socialism, a view that contrasted with Macrosty's 1904 *Trusts and the State*. Combination is defined by Macgregor as a type of commercial enterprise in which there is unified control across select firms—that is, 'many parts but one common control' (ibid.: 2). Combination is an organisational result of a historical process. Expansion in both domestic and foreign markets with an eye on global rivals in the late nineteenth century was typically the motivation or objective. Though such combinations would have enormous scale under natural evolving conditions, they should not be feared as 'treacherous parasites'.

Macgregor employed Marshall's representative firm to remind the reader that internal scale economies alone should not be the sole criterion of efficiency; indeed, external conditions also needed to be considered in determining the limits to growth. In the case of combinations, the efficient firm was dependent on the readjustment of the combined firms' relations. 'Combination may be the "representative method" of organisation in the twentieth century' (ibid.: 4). Combinations rather than independent firms alone were the new natural form of competition that had evolved. Hence, combinations should not be thought of as monopolies. The extent to which combinations enjoy growth as they outcompete rivals is paradoxically a measure of vibrant competition. Macgregor (ibid.: 6) noted that the situation is akin to one where 'moral laws are of no effect in Paradise'! He thereby concluded that a new economic analysis was needed for a modern age in which laissez-faire should no longer be thought of as free competition featuring independent, atomic firms acting in accordance with the invisible hand. Competition needed to be understood in various ways as the method of organisation of industry had evolved to where productive efficiency was but one of many factors to consider. This was entirely natural, not artificial, in a new century.

Macgregor (ibid.: 16; italics in original) prescribed an analytical framework, rather than model, by which to examine 'what possibilities combination has of becoming the "representative *method*" of industrial enterprise'. Frameworks are preferable when many variables are importantly involved in a dynamic process wherein the precision of equilibrium has no place. Profit maximisation is no longer the sole objective, if an objective at all. Frameworks permit the economist to methodically and meticulously assess the firm in the context of its other-than-simplistic, evolving competitive environment. Firms, particularly 'vast enterprises', behave intentionally whilst they navigate a course of action in coping with various competitive forces. Being strategic reflects intent and an ability to proactively secure and sustain what Macgregor (ibid.: 4) coined 'competitive advantages' over continuous, not discrete, points in time.[7]

Macgregor's (ibid.: 13) comprehensive framework for analysing industrial combinations is composed of four 'factors of competing strength', including productive efficiency, element of risk, bargaining strength with buyers and suppliers, and resources, which considers a firm's strategy and tactics with regard to its rivals. Efficiency alone was viewed as entirely insufficient in trying to understand modern industry. The economic variables of price and quantity are severely, if not absurdly, limited in appreciating competition. Each of these factors is addressed with considerable care and detail, ever mindful and respectful of the prevailing economic doctrine and its limitations. With Marshallian flair, Macgregor's framework is presented with an admixture of detailed facts and analysis which provides an informative, if not compelling, cognisance of industrial combination.

First, the growth of a combination's productive efficiency is a function of both internal and external economies. External economies are derived from

---

[7] Competitive advantage is the central concept in strategic management, a discipline that emerged in the 1960s and, to be sure, one with Marshallian roots (see Jacobsen 2013, 2015).

various entities acting in cooperation. Such entities account for the organisation of economic activity and include communication, transportation facilities, financial services and information networks. They collectively serve as an industry infrastructure and one with excess capacity wherein combination may naturally emerge. Further, there is what Macgregor coined 'collective supply' (ibid.: 21) in which independent firms within the same trade operate in close proximity and benefit from shared interests and intimate informal relationships which generate economies of localisation. This is the preliminary stage before combination. Management is pivotal for realising productive efficiency particularly given the competition from other producer combinations which is more acute than that from independent producers. Combination is a stern test of management but also one that develops their capabilities given the broader, more elaborate, scope of combination.

Secondly, risk as it pertains to fluctuations and uncertainty must not be overlooked. Of course, capital is at risk. Yet, combinations are also 'specially provocative' of competition (ibid.: 63). Lateral integration may be a defensive measure to ameliorate risk whilst vertical, especially forward, integration may increase risk as the 'risks of one industry are heaped upon the special risks of combination in another; the whole structure is liable to be unwieldy and inorganic' (ibid.: 65). Risks fall into two categories, namely static and dynamic. The former applies to interrelationships with other producers and customers. The latter is concerned with the uncertainties introduced by product and process innovation. Combination is a reaction to, as well as a creator of, risk. Hence, appropriate market knowledge, vision, and especially the ability to act decisively are required.

Thirdly, the bargaining strength of buyers and suppliers may matter whenever at least some element of monopoly exists. It may matter a great deal when combination exists. Macgregor took exception to the prevailing wisdom that the buyer at each stage from the production of raw materials to the purchase of final goods has the upper hand in terms of bargaining power. He (ibid.: 68) observed: 'This theory is paradoxical; it would give the conclusion that the persons whose bargaining strength is normally greatest are those who do not bargain at all—the final consumers of goods, or the general mass of the people'. Such misunderstanding of 'real conditions', for example, does not allow for the recognition of consumers' associations and cooperatives that exist to empower the buying public who would otherwise be at a disadvantage in negotiating purchasing terms, including price. Macgregor further recognised Edgeworth's analysis wherein combinations are responsible for indeterminateness as they have the advantage as *both* buyer and supplier. He countered that this is not consistent with the evidence. Rather, 'great organisations' are engaged in robust competition with each other as they leverage decreasing costs in a quest for increased market share. Hence, they will concede bargaining power to both their suppliers and buyers by offering concessions. 'Relative fewness' (ibid.: 69) is too simplistic in determining bargaining strength. Both context and time matter. Somewhat surprisingly, perhaps, Macgregor's analysis of bargaining included the use of several graphs depicting comparative static analysis with respect to the consideration of increasing and decreasing costs.

Fourthly, the factor of resource pertains to what Macgregor labelled 'costs of competition' as opposed to 'costs of production'. Costs of production pertain to *normal* or operational activities that do not alter the behaviour or strategic position of rivals. Costs of competition, for example, advertisements directed at a rival, however, are strategic as the objective is to tilt the competitive landscape in an enterprise's favour. Methods of bargaining may advance to resource status if there is a change in *normal* bargaining power. Such a change is reflected in an alteration of the strategic position of rivals. Integration, both vertical and horizontal, as a strategy that is either defensive or offensive in purpose and which affects the strategic reconfiguration of rivals also falls into the category of resource.

Macgregor (ibid.) then turns to the causes of combination concerning both trusts and cartels. This was a subject that had hitherto received insufficient attention by economists and government policy makers. Rather, their focus had been on preventative and ameliorative measures in addressing markets under abnormal conditions, for example, over-capitalisation and tariffs.

Macgregor (ibid.) proceeds to offer a comparative analysis of various structures of combination using two methods, historical evolution in the same country and the preferred lateral comparison across countries, namely England, America and Germany. The distinctions between trusts and cartels are clearly delineated and deftly considered in his comparative analysis. Then, Macgregor carefully addressed the matter of 'labour combination' as a response to combination. As a competitive response, not only do cartels beget cartels and trusts beget trusts, industrial combinations beget trade unions. Bargaining power is the primary motive for organised labour.

A thorough consideration of the effects of industrial combination on a nation, including public policy, are attended to in the final portion of Macgregor's volume. Combination has had a transformative impact not only on industries and countries but also on the way in which they should be analysed. Combination often fosters innovation with respect to both product and process. Macgregor's (ibid.: 195) evidence supports the notion that traditional monopoly analysis should not be so quickly applied as it is 'rarely applicable'. Further, combinations generally evolve not because of productive efficiency but rather as defensive or offensive competitive manoeuvres. Competition is anything but impersonal, atomistic and determinate; rather, it is strategic, even woolly, and indeed natural. Macgregor concluded that government should be particularly circumspect in addressing combination. He (ibid.: 232) warned that in America, trusts, not just cartels, may be subject to the Sherman Act of 1890 which forbade 'monopoly, or the attempt to do so'. Macgregor feared England would blindly follow America's legislative example, leading him to recommend that, 'The best advice for the period of transition is to avoid passion, and prejudgment, and the terrorism of mere size; to perceive that the extortion of a few strong producers can be remedied otherwise than by drastic interference with economic tendencies' (ibid.: 241).[8]

Macgregor provided a new introduction for the 1938 reprint of *Industrial Combination*.[9] By this time, the "Trust Problem" had become benevolently referred to as "Rationalization". Trusts were to be encouraged rather than deterred as they had proven to be the fittest method of competition; moreover, they were a common feature of the industrial landscape by 1938. In this new introduction, Macgregor observed 'there is a similarity with the history of the Joint Stock, which at first attracted much attention as it superseded the private firm, and then fell into line as an approved and normal development' (Macgregor 1938: page unnumbered).

Imperfect competition, notably oligopoly, had indeed superseded perfect competition. Such is the result of the natural evolution of industry, as Macgregor long argued and anticipated. Market forces mattered. Macgregor (1934: 6) stipulated that '"Evolutionism" does not mean merely letting things take their course'. Rather, it is 'purposes and ideas' dictated by the *conditions* of technological advancements and the organisation of industry as set forth by entrepreneurs and "captains of industry".

---

[8] Interestingly, Marshall later echoed Macgregor's concern of government possibly acting rashly in following the American example regarding monopolies. In a 1918 letter to John Hilton, Secretary to the Commission on Trusts, Marshall wrote: 'I trust that nothing will be done of a far-reaching character without a careful study of the toilsome steps by which American expedients have been developed' (Marshall quoted in Pigou 1925: 492).

[9] Macgregor (1906) was reprinted in 1935 and this did not include the new introduction that was included in the 1938 reprint.

3   The Drummond Professor of Political Economy, 1922–1945

Macgregor accepted the Drummond Chair a few days after it was offered to him in late July 1921 by the electors of the Professorship. Macgregor took up the position upon Edgeworth's retirement at the beginning of the 1922 academic year, one he would hold for twenty-three years until his retirement. He was considered both a logical and obvious choice as he was invited by the electors without even having made an application. Although his credentials were impeccable, including professorships at Manchester and Leeds as well as being a first-class Marshall protégé as evident in his celebrated *Industrial Combination*, one cannot help but think that Edgeworth himself had at least some say, directly or indirectly, in who would succeed him.

Edgeworth was a huge admirer of Marshall referring to him as the 'prime orb' (Edgeworth 1894: 443). They shared 'a lifelong personal and intellectual friendship' (Keynes 1926 [1972]: 255), one that was initiated *and* 'cemented' by Marshall's 1881 affirmative review of Edgeworth's seminal *Mathematical Psychics* (Groenewegen 1995: 402). In his "Reminiscences", Edgeworth in particular noted Marshall's extraordinary ability to temper the application of his 'supreme skill' in abstract reasoning including mathematical application in order 'above all things to be useful' (Edgeworth 1925: 67). Under Edgeworth's leadership, Oxford economists were well versed and intentionally so in adopting Marshall's organon (see Harrod 1953; Stigler 1990; Lee 2011). Edgeworth was, of course, second only to Marshall in stature in British economics and arguably Oxford's only prominent economist at the time.[10]

An Oxford professor had modest lecturing responsibilities in that typically thirty-two lectures were presented in any given academic year (see Worswick 1953). This gave professors, including Macgregor, ample time to pursue research and other activities both within and without Oxford that served to promote the stature of both the professor and the University. Macgregor, of course, lectured on industrial economics but also numerous other courses, such as economic principles, analytical economics, public finance, international trade, and the theory of interest and profit. His many articles primarily appearing in the *Economic Journal* reflected the diversity of his courses. Amongst these articles were "Some Ethical Aspects of Industrialism" (Macgregor 1909a), "The Poverty Figures"

---

[10] In 1920–1921, the only other economists at Oxford included Henry Clay, T.H. Penson, J.A. Todd and F.W. Ogilvie. Clay and Ogilvie would prove to be the most accomplished of the four. However, both were very much junior lecturers following their appointments in 1919. Clay left Oxford for Manchester to fill the Jevons Chair vacated by Macgregor in 1922. Ogilvie would later accept a chair at Edinburgh in 1926 (see Young and Lee 1993).

(Macgregor 1916), "Rationalisation of Industry" (Macgregor 1927a), and "Sanctions for Discount Policy" (Macgregor 1924a). Such a broad interest across economics was in keeping with the newly established degree of Philosophy, Politics and Economics (PPE). Of course, Macgregor's principal research interest in industrial combination, a subject which featured a mixture of economics and government policy interlaced with ethical considerations, was well suited to PPE. As Macgregor (1932: ix) expressed:

> We are continually discussing one policy or another by reference to some effect which it may have on costs and prices. Advances in wages; local rates; the level of income tax; the policy of free trade; all of these are closely considered as problems which finally issue in the effects they have on the fighting front of industry, the buying power of the consumers.

Moreover, cartels, trusts and other amalgamations were international in scope whereby the consideration of intergovernmental relations and policies were of pronounced merit. Additionally, the variety of the courses in which Macgregor lectured also reflected the fact that there were, as noted, only a few economists in Oxford at the time. Macgregor clearly embraced PPE as he was actively involved in the creation of its Final Honours School. PPE quickly proved to be enormously successful: In 1923, there were 85 students, with this growing to 141 by 1927 and 275 by 1933. Such tremendous growth in such a short period of time necessitated the number teaching economics increasing from five to fifteen (see Andrews 1953; Young and Lee 1993).

Consequently, the intellectual fabric altered in favour of a more mathematically informed theoretical approach and ahistorical character. The ascendancy of Pigouvian-refined value theory particularly with respect to its mathematical exposition along with the emergence of imperfect competition theory relegated Marshall's *Principles* to the status of a first-year textbook (see Young and Lee 1993). Harrod reflected in his 1967 retirement speech that Oxford economics had become rather detached from Marshall. Elsewhere, Harrod (1953: 59) observed that Oxford had also become liberated from 'the great edifices of Marshall and Pigou' by an 'eclectic' disposition which gave economics a fresh start.[11]

Hicks (1953: 120), interestingly enough, in his Inaugural Lecture as Drummond Chair spoke very highly of PPE as being perfectly suitable for undergraduates' 'general education in the "principles and structure of modern

---

[11] Harrod in conversation with Jacob Marschak in 1939 regarding the latter leaving Oxford for the United States did not even mention Macgregor even though they both referred to possibly every other economist in Oxford (see Young and Lee 1993). Indeed, Macgregor's influence in Oxford had nearly vanished by the time of his retirement in 1945.

society"'. He remarked that Oxford's PPE, being interdisciplinary, was superior to the Economics Tripos that Marshall had 'imposed upon Cambridge'. For Hicks, the political and the historical were often inseparable from economic issues. He went on to note that the study of economics can suffer from a prejudice in favour of the abstract and nonhistorical. Hicks (ibid.) memorably stated: 'I am quite sure that it is impossible to be a good economist unless one is more than an economist!' So, he cautioned against overspecialisation that only fostered parochial interests. Hicks, *however*, proceeded to admit he was very much a theorist 'content to walk in the footsteps' (ibid.: 121) of his Drummond predecessors, both Senior and Edgeworth. The Chair allowed for such freedom, he believed. Hicks then concluded in his introductory remarks: 'But theory, if it is to be of any use, must be about something' (ibid.), though not identifying what exactly. Had they had the chance, Marshall and Macgregor may simply have pointed out that the 'something' should be about 'the ordinary business of life' (in *Principles*' opening line).[12]

Macgregor was involved with Harrod and Henderson in establishing the Institute of Statistics at Nuffield College, where he was appointed Professorial Fellow, and the Oxford Economists' Research Group (OERG), of which he was a member. His involvement in these significant initiatives in the 1930s was a natural one for him given the focus of advancing empirical work especially with respect to industry. However, there is little evidence to be found of the particulars of Macgregor's participation and indeed contributions. For example, he did not publish in *Oxford Economic Papers*, the vehicle by which the OERG's research was primarily disseminated, including the famous Hall and Hitch article concerning the kinked demand curve published in 1939. Further, it was rare for Macgregor or his work to be referenced in the work of OERG members or, for that matter, they or their work being cited in his work (e.g. Wilson and Andrews 1951). The notable exception was P.W.S. Andrews, a particularly active OERG member and a thoroughly Marshallian industrial economist, who dedicated his landmark *Manufacturing Business* to Macgregor. Andrews (1949: xviii) graciously wrote in the introduction: 'The dedication to Professor Macgregor is entirely without his permission. I think that all economists will sympathize with my desire to offer my tribute to his work in the field with which I am concerned' (see also Lee 2011; Jacobsen 2017, 2019).

---

[12] Hicks's Inaugural Lecture was given on 8 May 1953 at All Souls College, the same day that Macgregor was killed in a street accident in Oxford. Some coincidence. Apparently, the tragedy occurred after the lecture or Hicks was unaware at the time of his lecture as in the one reference to Macgregor in his lecture he stated: 'Professor Macgregor, who succeeded Edgeworth in 1921, is still with us[3]' (Hicks 1953: 120). The footnote read: '[3](He died on 8 May 1953.)'.

4   Concluding Remarks

David Hutchison Macgregor's first book was *Lord Macaulay* published in 1901, five years before *Industrial Combination*. His prize-winning biography offers a splendid appreciation of the richness of the English language, presented in a most lucid, vivid and indeed elegant style. Macgregor, in the opening page, averred: 'The influences of his [Macaulay's] work have not passed away. They are not yet perfected and may not be fully judged' (Macgregor 1901: 1). Such a view could well be expressed about Macgregor himself today, more than a century later. Macgregor (ibid.: 138) poignantly concluded his volume on Macaulay: 'The study of Macaulay has been a labour of love. To enter into his mind is to be refreshed and inspired'. Such sentiment could also well apply to Macgregor. For those interested in industrial economics and from a Marshallian perspective, Macgregor continues to offer the promise of refreshment and inspiration.

References

Main Works by David Hutchison Macgregor

Macgregor, D.H. (1901). *Lord Macaulay*. London: C.J. Clay and Sons.

Macgregor, D.H. (1906). *Industrial Combination*. London: George Bell & Sons.

Macgregor, D.H. (1907). 'Labour Exchange and Unemployment'. *Economic Journal*, 17(4): 585–589.

Macgregor, D.H. (1908). 'Earnings and Surplus'. *Economic Journal*, 18(4): 532–540.

Macgregor, D.H. (1909a). 'Some Ethical Aspects of Industrialism'. *International Journal of Ethics*, 19(3): 284–296.

Macgregor, D.H. (1909). 'Shipping Conferences'. *Economic Journal*, 19(4): 503–516.

Macgregor, D.H. (1910). 'The Poverty Figures'. *Economic Journal*, 20(4): 69–72.

Macgregor, D.H. (1911). *The Evolution of Industry*. London: Williams and Norgate.

Macgregor, D.H. (1914). 'The Development and Control of German Syndicates'. *Economic Journal*, 24(1): 24–32.

Macgregor, D.H. (1914). 'Review of *The Relations of Capital and Labour*, by W. Layton'. *Economic Journal*, 24(95): 449–450.

Macgregor, D.H. (1924a). 'Sanctions for Discount Policy'. *Economic Journal*, 34(4): 638–643.

Macgregor, D.H. (1924). 'Consumer's Surplus: A Reply'. *Economica*, 11(June): 131–134.

Macgregor, D.H. (1925). 'The Agricultural Argument'. *Economic Journal*, 25(3): 389–397.

Macgregor, D.H. (1926). 'Family Allowance'. *Economic Journal*, 36(1): 1–10.

Macgregor, D.H. (1927a). 'Rationalisation of Industry'. *Economic Journal*, 37(4): 521–550.

Macgregor, D.H. (1927). 'Recent Papers on Cartels'. *Economic Journal*, 37(2): 247–254.

Macgregor, D.H. (1927). 'International Cartels'. League of Nations, Economic and Financial Section. Geneva: League of Nations.

Macgregor, D.H. (1929). 'Joint Stock Companies and the Risk Factor'. *Economic Journal*, 39(4): 491–505.

Macgregor, D.H. (1930). 'The Coal Bill and the Cartel'. *Economic Journal*, 40(1): 35–44.

Macgregor, D.H. (1932). 'Introduction'. In *Cartels, Concerns and Trusts*, by R. Liefmann. London: Methuen and Co.: vii–xxix.

Macgregor, D.H. (1933). 'Taxation of Cooperative Dividend'. *Economic Journal*, 43(1): 40–55.

Macgregor, D.H. (1934). *Enterprise, Purpose & Profit*. Oxford: Clarendon Press.

Macgregor, D.H. (1935). 'Review of *Economics in Practice*, by A.C. Pigou'. *Economic Journal*, 45(179): 518–520.

Macgregor, D.H. (1938). *Industrial Combination* (with a new introduction). London: University of London.

Macgregor, D.H. (1939). *Public Aspects of Finance*. Oxford: Clarendon Press.

Macgregor, D.H. (1942). 'Marshall and His Book'. *Economica*, New Series, 9(36): 313–324.

Macgregor, D.H. (1949). *Economic Thought and Policy*. London: Oxford University Press.

Other Works Referred To

Andrews, P.W.S. (1949). *Manufacturing Business*. London: Macmillan.

Andrews, P.W.S. (1953). 'Obituary: D.H. Macgregor, 1877–1953'. *The Oxford Magazine*, 71(22): 346–348.

Coase, R.H. (1936). 'Review of *Industrial Combination*, by D.H. Macgregor'. *Weltwirtschaftliches Archiv*, 44: 133–135.

Coase, R.H. (1991) [1994]. 'The Institutional Structure of Production'. Chapter 1 in R.H. Coase, *Essays on Economics and Economists*. Chicago: University of Chicago Press: 3–14.

Cristiano, C. (2011). 'Two Marshallians: Layton and the Early Macgregor'. Chapter 8 in T. Raffaelli, T. Nishizawa and S. Cook (eds) *Marshall, Marshallians and Industrial Economics*. London: Routledge: 163–180.

Droppers, G. (1907). 'Review of *Industrial Combination*, by D.H. Macgregor'. *Journal of Political Economy*, 15(2): 120–122.

Edgeworth, F.Y. (1894). 'Theory of International Values'. *Economic Journal*, 4(15): 424–443.

Edgeworth, F.Y. (1925). 'Reminiscences'. Chapter 2 in A.C. Pigou (ed.) *Memorials of Alfred Marshall*. London: Macmillan: 66–77.

Giocoli, N. (2012). 'British Economists on Competition Policy (1890–1920)'. *Munich Personal RePEc Archive*, MPRA Paper No. 39245. Available at: https://mpra.ub.uni-muenchen.de/39245.

Groenewegen, P. (1995). *A Soaring Eagle: Alfred Marshall 1842–1924*. Cheltenham, UK: Edward Elgar.

Groenewegen, P. (2012). *The Minor Marshallians and Alfred Marshall*. London: Routledge.

Guillebaud, C.W. (1961). *Marshall's Principles of Economics: Volume II: Notes*. Ninth (variorum) edition. London: Macmillan.

Harrod, R.F. (1953). 'The Pre-War Faculty'. *Oxford Economic Papers*, 5(Supplement): 59–64.

Hicks, J.R. (1939). *Value and Capital*. Oxford: Clarendon Press.

Hicks, J.R. (1953). 'An Inaugural Lecture'. *Oxford Economic Papers*, New Series, 5(2): 117–135.

Jacobsen, L. (2013). 'On Robinson, Penrose, and the Resource-Based View'. *European Journal of the History of Economic Thought*, 20(1): 125–147.

Jacobsen, L. (2015). 'On Robinson, Robertson, and the Industrial Organization View'. *History of Political Economy*, 47(1): 41–89.

Jacobsen, L. (2017). 'P.W.S. Andrews' *Manufacturing Business* Revisited'. *Review of Political Economy*, 29(2): 190–208.

Jacobsen, L. (2019). 'Robinson, Andrews, *and* Marshall: A Case of Arguing at Cross Purposes?'. *History of Economics Review*, 72(1): 35–58.

Keynes, J.M. (1924) [1972]. 'Alfred Marshall'. Chapter 14 in *Essays in Biography*. Volume X of *The Collected Writings of John Maynard Keynes*. London: Macmillan: 161–231.

Keynes, J.M. (1926) [1972]. 'Francis Ysidro Edgeworth, 1845–1926'. Chapter 16 in *Essays in Biography*. Volume X of *The Collected Writings of John Maynard Keynes*. London: Macmillan: 251–266.

Lee, F.S. (1989). 'D.H. Macgregor and the Firm: A Neglected Chapter in the History of the Post Keynesian Theory of the Firm'. *British Review of Economic Issues*, 11(24): 21–47.

Lee, F.S. (2011). 'David H. Macgregor and Industrial Economics at Oxford, 1920–1945'. Chapter 12 in T. Raffaelli, T. Nishizawa and S. Cook (eds) *Marshall, Marshallians and Industrial Economics*. London: Routledge: 231–249.

Macrosty, H.W. (1907). 'Review of *Industrial Combination*, by D.H. Macgregor'. *Economic Journal*, 17(65): 105–107.

Marshall, A. (1890) [1925]. 'Some Aspects of Competition'. Chapter 11 in A.C. Pigou (ed.) *Memorials of Alfred Marshall*. London: Macmillan: 256–291.

Marshall, A. (1919). *Industry and Trade*. London: Macmillan.

Marshall, A. (1920). *Principles of Economics*. Eighth edition. London: Macmillan.

Pigou, A.C. (ed.) (1925). *Memorials of Alfred Marshall*. London: Macmillan.

Raffaelli, T., G. Becattini and M. Dardi (2006). 'Introduction'. *The Elgar Companion to Alfred Marshall*. Cheltenham: Edward Elgar: xiii–xxiv.

Schumpeter, J.A. (1954). *History of Economic Analysis*. New York: Oxford University Press.

Shove, G.F. (1942). 'The Place of Marshall's *Principles* in the Development of Economic Theory'. *Economic Journal*, 52(208): 294–329.

Stigler, G.J. (1990). 'The Place of Marshall's *Principles* in the Development of Economics'. Chapter 1 in J.K. Whitaker (ed.) *Centenary Essays on Alfred Marshall*. Cambridge: Cambridge University Press: 1–13.

Veblen, T. (1904). *The Theory of Business Enterprise*. New York: Charles Scribner's Sons.

Whitaker, J.K. (1990). 'What Happened to the Second Volume of the *Principles*? The Thorny Path to Marshall's Last Books'. Chapter 8 in J.K. Whitaker (ed.) *Centenary Essays on Alfred Marshall*. Cambridge: Cambridge University Press: 193–222.

Whitaker, J.K. (1996). *The Correspondence of Alfred Marshall, Economist*. Three volumes. Cambridge: Cambridge University Press.

Wilson, T. and P.W.S. Andrews (eds) (1951). *Oxford Studies in the Price Mechanism*. Oxford: Clarendon Press.

Worswick, G.D.N. (1953). 'Drummond Professor of Political Economy, 1945–51'. *Oxford Economic Papers*, New Series, 5(Supplement): 65–79.

Young, W. and F.S. Lee (1993). *Oxford Economics and Oxford Economists*. London: Macmillan.

13

Roy F. Harrod (1900–1978)

Walter Eltis

1   An Extended Introduction

Roy Harrod was born in February 1900 and died in March 1978. His father, Henry Dawes Harrod, was a businessman and author of two historical monographs. His mother, Frances (née Forbes-Robertson) was a novelist, and sister of the notable Shakespearean actor-manager, Sir Johnson Forbes-Robertson. Henry Harrod's business failed in 1907, but Roy won a scholarship to St Paul's School in 1911 and a King's Scholarship to Westminster in 1913. He became Head of his House, and in 1918 won a scholarship in History to New College, Oxford, his father's college. He enlisted in September 1918 and was commissioned in the Royal Field Artillery, but the war ended before his training was completed.

Harrod went up to Oxford in early 1919 and first read *Literae Humaniores* (Classical Literature, Ancient History and Philosophy). He might well have devoted his career to academic philosophy, and he valued his publications in that subject more highly than his seminal contributions to economics. Harrod once remarked that significant economic problems have only attracted the attention of profound thinkers for about 200 years, and interest in them

This chapter is reprinted from Eltis (2008) with the permission of Palgrave Macmillan.

W. Eltis (1933–2019)

R. A. Cord (ed.), *The Palgrave Companion to Oxford Economics*,
https://doi.org/10.1007/978-3-030-58471-9_13

might well disappear in another 200. In contrast, deep thought has been devoted to the great philosophical problems (e.g. the validity of inductive methods of thought) for more than 2000 years and new contributions will be read for so long as civilised life remains. But his philosophy tutor at New College, H.W.B. Joseph, deterred him from devoting his life to that subject, by reacting extremely negatively to his essays. Harrod has left an account of a seminar on Einstein's theory of relativity in Oxford in 1922 where Joseph drew attention to a few terminological problems and believed this had undermined the theory. Einstein's theory of relativity survived, but Harrod was persuaded not to pursue a career in academic philosophy. In later years he published in the distinguished philosophical journal, *Mind*, and his *Foundations of Inductive Logic* (Harrod 1956a) has received serious critical attention from philosophers as distinguished as A.J. Ayer (1970), although his main scholarly work was not to be in philosophy.

He followed his First Class Honours in *Literae Humaniores* in 1922 with a First Class in Modern History just one year later, and in 1923, Christ Church, Oxford, elected him to a Tutorial Fellowship (confusingly described as a Studentship in that College) to teach the novel subject, economics, which was to be part of Oxford's new Honour School of Philosophy, Politics and Economics (PPE).

Harrod was allowed two terms away from Oxford so that he could learn enough economics to teach it, and it was suggested that he might spend this time in Europe, but he first went to Cambridge where he attended a wide range of lectures and wrote weekly essays on money and international trade for John Maynard Keynes. He was equally fortunate when he returned to Oxford, for while he was critically discussing the economics essays of Christ Church's undergraduates, he was himself writing weekly microeconomic essays for the Drummond Professor of Political Economy, Francis Ysidro Edgeworth.

In addition to his new academic work, Harrod took a notable part in the administration of his College (where he was Senior Censor in 1929–1931, the most responsible office a student of Christ Church can be called upon to discharge), and also the University where he was elected to Oxford's governing body (the Hebdomadal Council) in 1929 before he was 30. In the University and in Christ Church, he fought powerful campaigns on behalf of Professor Frederick Lindemann (subsequently Lord Cherwell) who held Oxford's Chair of Experimental Philosophy (Physics) and became principal scientific adviser to Winston Churchill's wartime government and a member of his post-war cabinet.

By 1930, Harrod's economics had developed to the point where he was able to publish an important and original contribution, "Notes on Supply" (Harrod 1930a), in which he was the first twentieth-century economist to derive the marginal revenue curve. This should have appeared in 1928 to produce a claim for international priority, but Keynes, the editor of the *Economic Journal*, sent the article to Frank Ramsey, who first believed there were difficulties with the argument. Ramsay subsequently appreciated that his objections rested on a misunderstanding, but Harrod's innovation was less startling in 1930 than it would have been in 1928. He followed this initial contribution to the imperfect competition literature with an important article, "Doctrines of Imperfect Competition" (Harrod 1934a), in which he summarised the essential elements of the new theories of Edward Chamberlin and Joan Robinson.

During the 1930s, Harrod frequently stayed with Keynes and he was increasingly drawn into the group of brilliant young economists which included Richard Kahn and Joan Robinson who were helping Keynes develop the new theories which culminated in *The General Theory of Employment, Interest and Money*. Harrod had written a number of important and influential articles in the press advocating new reflationary policies in the early 1930s and these, together with his extension of Kahn's employment multiplier to international trade in his *International Economics* (Harrod 1933a), prompted Schumpeter to write in 1946 in his obituary article on Keynes that 'Mr Harrod may have been moving independently toward a goal not far from that of Keynes, though he unselfishly joined the latter's standard after it had been raised' (Schumpeter 1946: 509, fn. 24).

Shortly after *The General Theory* appeared, Harrod published *The Trade Cycle* (Harrod 1936a) in which he developed some of the dynamic implications of the new theory of effective demand. The conditions where output would grow were a central theme in Adam Smith's *The Nature and Causes of the Wealth of Nations*, and it had been much analysed in the great nineteenth-century contributions of Malthus, Ricardo, Mill and Marx, but the long-term dynamic implications of immediate changes to particular economic variables received virtually no attention in the neoclassical work that followed the marginal revolution. In *The General Theory*, Keynes mostly went no further than to work through completely the immediate effects *on a formerly stationary economy* of a variety of disturbances such as an excess of the saving which would occur at full employment over the investment that businessmen considered it prudent to undertake. Harrod went a vital step further and showed what could be expected to occur if saving was *permanently high* in relation to *the long-term opportunity to invest*. In 1939, he followed *The Trade Cycle* with "An Essay in Dynamic Theory" (Harrod 1939a), and after the war he developed his growth theory further in the book, *Towards a Dynamic Economics* (Harrod 1948a). Important articles followed including a "Second Essay in Dynamic Theory" (Harrod 1960a) and "Are Monetary and Fiscal Policies Enough?" (Harrod 1964a). It is almost certainly because of Harrod's rediscovery of growth theory in the 1930s and his notable contributions to it that Assar Lindbeck, the Chairman of the Nobel Prize Committee, chose to state that he was among those who would have been awarded a Nobel Prize in Economics if he had lived a little longer (see Lindbeck 1985: 52). The nature of Harrod's original contributions and the gradual evolution of his theory from 1939 to 1964 are set out in the second part of this chapter. The detailed technical characteristics of Harrod's growth model are the subject of Eltis (1987).

In the Second World War, Harrod's friendship with Lindemann and his increasing distinction as an economist led to an invitation to join the Statistical Department of the Admiralty (S Branch) which Churchill set up when he again became First Lord in 1939. This moved to Downing Street when Churchill became Prime Minister in 1940, but Harrod did not have a particular talent for detailed statistical work and he developed an increasing interest in the international financial institutions, the International Monetary Fund and the World Bank, which would need to be set up as soon as the war was won, and from 1942 onwards he pursued this work in Christ Church. In the immediate post-war years, he took a strong interest in national politics, and stood for Parliament unsuccessfully as a Liberal in the general election of 1945 and for a time he was a member of that party's Shadow Cabinet. He had served on Labour Party committees before the war, and in the 1950s with Churchill's support he unsuccessfully sought adoption as a Conservative parliamentary candidate: his economic advice was warmly welcomed by Harold Macmillan, Conservative Prime Minister from 1957 to 1963. Harrod received the honour of a knighthood in 1959 in recognition of his public standing and his notable academic achievements in the pre-war and post-war decades. Meanwhile, he had succeeded Keynes as editor of the *Economic Journal* in 1945, and in partnership with Austin Robinson (who looked after the book reviews), he sustained its reputation and quality until his retirement from the editorship in 1966.

Harrod's post-war academic work included important contributions in three areas. In addition to the continuing development and refinement of his pre-war research on dynamic theory, he published extensively on the theory of the firm and on international monetary theory which had been his particular concern during the war.

The Oxford Economists' Research Group had begun to meet prominent British industrialists before the war. A group of Oxford economists which generally included Harrod invited individual industrialists to dine in Oxford, and after dinner they were questioned extensively on the considerations which actually influenced their decisions. This led to the publication of a number of much cited articles and the book, *Oxford Studies in the Price Mechanism* (Wilson and Andrews 1951), although Harrod did not contribute to the volume. Propositions which emanated from these dinners included the notion that businessmen took little account of the rate of interest in their investment decisions, and that they did not seek to profit maximise, but priced instead by adding a margin they considered satisfactory to their average or "full" costs of production. In his important articles, "Price and Cost in Entrepreneurs' Policy" (Harrod 1939b) and "Theory of Imperfect Competition Revised" (Harrod 1952a), Harrod set out a theoretical account of how firms price in which industrialists follow something like these procedures. Their object is especially to achieve a high market share, and by setting prices low enough to deter new entry, they actually succeed in maximising their long-run profits and avoid the excess capacity that Chamberlin and Robinson had considered an inevitable consequence of monopolistic or imperfect competition. This attempt to reconcile the "rules of thumb" that the businessmen revealed with the propositions of traditional theory was more highly regarded outside Oxford than some of the books and articles in the new tradition.

Harrod's work on the world's international monetary problems occupied a good deal of his time and attention in the post-war decades. Keynes himself had considered the breakdown in international monetary relations a crucial element in the collapse of effective demand in so many countries in the 1930s, and he devoted much of the last years of his life to the creation of new institutions which would avoid a repetition of these disasters. Harrod believed he was continuing this vital work when he devoted much thought and energy to these questions. He arrived at the conclusion that there was bound to be some inflation in a world which was successfully pursuing Keynesian policies, and that the liquidity base of the world's financial system was bound to become inadequate if the price of gold failed to rise with other prices. Harrod believed that underlying world liquidity which rested on gold in the last resort must be allowed to rise in line with the international demand for money. He therefore came to focus on the price of gold, and in his book, *Reforming the World's Money* (Harrod 1965), he proposed that a substantial increase in the price of gold would be needed if subsequent international monetary crises were to be avoided. Harry Johnson (1970) has summarised Harrod's contribution to this debate.

Harrod took a great interest in actual developments in the UK economy, and published seven books and collections of articles in the first two post-war decades which were directly concerned with the policies that Britain should follow. There was, in addition, an immense range of articles in academic journals, bank reviews and the press on these questions, not to mention monthly stockbrokers' letters for Phillips & Drew. Harrod argued strongly and powerfully that nothing was to be gained by running the economy below full employment, which meant an unemployment rate of less than 2% in the 1950s and the 1960s. In the late 1950s, he was deeply concerned that the removal of import controls would render it increasingly difficult for Britain to pursue such Keynesian policies, and he was a vigorous opponent of European Common Market entry. He attached more significance than some distinguished Keynesians to holding down inflation but he published statistics in *Towards a New Economic Policy* (Harrod 1967a) to show that in Britain this had tended to be faster when the economy was in recession than when output was allowed to expand. Harrod argued therefore that deflationary policies could play no useful role in policies to control the rate of cost inflation, which he considered the essential element in inflation in Britain. Policy swung sharply away from this Keynesian tradition in the last years of Harrod's life, and he wrote a final letter to *The Times* on 21 July 1976 in which he praised the economics of Tony Benn and Peter Shore for their opposition to the Labour government's public expenditure cuts, for, 'To cut public spending when there is an undesirably high rate of unemployment is crazy' (Harrod 1976: 15).

Harrod's advocacy of import controls and his adverse reaction to deflationary policies at all times might suggest that he was an economist of the left, but his willingness to support each of the British political parties at various times underlines how his approach to economic and social problems cannot be typecast. The lines of policy he supported always followed directly from his understanding of the significance of the major interrelationships, and it was his belief that Keynesian theory (which he had so notably helped to refine and develop) provided the appropriate tools for the analysis of Britain's economic problems that led him towards the expansionist policies he so consistently advocated. But further theoretical and empirical relationships which he believed were equally well founded led him to advocate a series of social policies to which very right-wing labels can be attached.

Just before the 1959 general election, Harrod's article "Why I Shall Vote Conservative", which appeared in the 20 September edition of *The Observer*, put forward the startlingly unfashionable argument that only the Conservatives would allow more money to go to the better off who had most to contribute to the future of Britain (see Harrow 1959a). Harrod's strong belief in the importance of the *quality* of the country's population stock (which, he held, mattered no less than the physical capital stock) lay behind this article. He thought the quality of the population would be bound to deteriorate if the middle classes continued to have fewer children than the poor. Harrod was a strong believer in the inheritance of every kind of ability, and a provocative conversational conclusion he drew was that in an ideal world one-third of Christ Church's much sought-after undergraduate places should be sold to the rich. Their children often had insufficient academic ability to perform well in examinations, but they had inherited abilities of other kinds which would take them to the highest positions, so they should go to Oxford first. Harrod's reasoning on the inheritance of ability and its implications is set out in detail in the *Memorandum* he submitted to the Royal Commission on Population in 1944 (see Harrod 1950). There he suggested that a difficulty in finding servants was one reason why the middle classes had fewer children. Among his suggestions to remedy this state of affairs was that Diplomas in Domestic Service should be established, and that it should become common practice for servants to have latch-keys and the same rights as their mistresses to enjoy social lives with no questions asked. His *Memorandum* reads strangely nowadays when it is widely regarded as unacceptable that any practical conclusions may be drawn from the proposition that human abilities are inherited. Harrod never hesitated to carry his arguments to their limits, and he always went where his reasoning took him, irrespective of the predictable reactions of others.

The unselfconsciousness of both his academic and his public writing comes out especially in his two biographical volumes, the official life of Keynes (commissioned by the executors) which he published in 1951 (Harrod 1951a) and *The Prof* (Harrod 1959b), his personal sketch of Lord Cherwell. As well as providing magnificent accounts of their subjects from the standpoint of one who had known them intimately (and who profoundly understood the economic problems that Keynes had wrestled with), these books contain extensive autobiographical passages which will enable later generations to know more of Harrod than any biographer can begin to convey.

Harrod ceased to lecture at Oxford in 1967 upon reaching the statutory retirement age of 67, but as a Visiting Professor he continued to teach in several distinguished North American universities. He died at his Norfolk home in 1978, eleven years after his Oxford work came to an end.

2   Harrod's Revival of Growth Theory and His Contribution to Keynesian Macroeconomics

Harrod was intimately involved in the origins and development of Keynesian economics. As the galley proofs of *The General Theory* emerged from the printers from June 1935 onwards, copies were sent to Harrod, Kahn and Joan Robinson, and with their assistance, Keynes rewrote extensively for final publication. Harrod helped to clarify the relationship between Keynes's new theory of the rate of interest and the then ruling neoclassical theory where this depended upon the intersection of the ex ante saving and investment schedules. In the course of their correspondence, Harrod showed Keynes how well he understood the essence of *The General Theory* by setting out its novelty and its principal elements in a few lines on 30 August 1935:

> Your view, as I understand it is *broadly* this:
> Volume of investment determined by:
> Marginal efficiency of capital schedule
> and
> Rate of interest.
> Rate of investment determined by:
> Liquidity preference schedule
> and
> Quantity of money.
> Volume of employment determined by:
> Volume of investment
> and
> Multiplier.
> Value of multiplier determined by:
> Propensity to save (Harrod to Keynes, 30 August 1935, in Keynes 1973: 553; italics in original).

Keynes responded: 'I absolve you completely of misunderstanding my theory. It could not be stated better than on the first page of your letter' (Keynes to Harrod, 10 September 1935, in ibid.).

Almost immediately after the appearance of *The General Theory*, Harrod published *The Trade Cycle* (Harrod 1936a) which contained for the first time in the Keynesian literature the concept of an economy growing at a steady rate. Keynes wrote of it to Robinson on 25 March 1937: 'I think he has got hold of some good and important ideas. But, if I am right, there is one fatal mistake' (Keynes 1987: 149), and to Harrod himself on 31 March: 'I think that your theory in the form in which you finally enunciate it is not correct, being fatally affected by a logical slip in the argument' (ibid.: 151). Harrod replied devastatingly on 6 April: 'There is no slip … The fact is that you in your criticism are still thinking of *once over* changes and that is what I regard as a static problem. My technique relates to steady growth' (ibid.: 163; italics in original). Harrod's 'slip' was in fact the first step towards the reinstatement of growth theory into mainstream economic analysis.

Harrod convinced Keynes, who on 12 April congratulated him for 'having invented so interesting a theory' (ibid.: 170), but with the reservation that, 'I should doubt whether any reader who has not talked or corresponded with you could be aware that the whole of the last half of the book was intended to be in relation to a moving base of steady progress' (ibid.). Keynes added that it was vital that Harrod carry his ideas further and restate them more comprehensibly.

Harrod made important progress in the next 15 months, and on 3 August 1938 he sent Keynes a preliminary draft of the article, "An Essay in Dynamic Theory", and wrote in his accompanying letter that:

> My re-statement of the "dynamic" theory…is, I think, a great improvement on my book … I have been throwing out hints in a number of places of the possibility of formulating a simple law of growth and I want to substantiate the claim. It is largely based on the ideas of the general theory of employment; but I think it gets us a step forward (ibid.: 301).

A lengthy correspondence then developed between Harrod and Keynes in which the two most original elements in Harrod's contribution which later excited much interest and controversy in the economics profession were extensively discussed. Harrod's principal innovation was the invention of a *moving equilibrium growth path* for the economy, and he described this as the "warranted" line of growth. He had perceived before he wrote *The Trade Cycle* that there was a fundamental contradiction between the assumptions prevalent in the microeconomic theory of the firm and industry, to which he had made notable contributions, and the new Keynesian macroeconomics. In the theory of the firm, long-term investment was zero, for firms had no motivation to undertake further investment once they were in long-period equilibrium. But the new Keynesian macroeconomics required that there be net investment by firms or the government whenever there was any net saving in the macroeconomy. A theory compatible with both macro- and microeconomic equilibrium therefore required that firms invest all the time, so that they can continually absorb total net saving. Harrod's formulation of the warranted rate of growth, his novel discovery, was an attempt to set out this necessary equilibrium growth path that industrial and commercial investment decisions must all the time follow in order to achieve a complete economic equilibrium.

Harrod's moving equilibrium or warranted growth path required that saving (of s% of the national income) be continually absorbed into investment, so he asked the question: At what rate of growth will firms all the time choose to invest the s% of the national income, which equilibrium growth requires? To answer this question, he made use of the acceleration principle or "the relation", as he called it, that firms need say, C_r units of additional capital to produce an extra unit of output. It follows from these premises that the warranted rate of growth of output will be s/C_r% per annum. Since each rise in output by 1 unit entails that C_r extra units be invested, a rise in output by s/C_r% of the national income will call for an equilibrium investment of C_r times this, which is precisely s% of the national income, the ratio of ex ante saving in the national income. In Harrod's examples, he suggested a typical s of 10% of the national income and a C_r of 4, to produce a warranted rate of growth of 2.5%.

This idea that if there is continual saving, then equilibrium entails a continual geometric growth in production, came as a considerable surprise to Keynes and the other members of the Cambridge "Circus". As Harrod had already explained in April 1937: 'The static system provides an analysis of what happens where there is no increase [in output] which entails (as in Joan Robinson's long-period analysis) that saving = 0. Now I was on the lookout for a steady rate of advance, in which the rates of increase would be mutually consistent' (ibid.: 164).

But Harrod's second discovery had equally radical implications. Suppose the actual growth of output is marginally above the equilibrium or warranted rate of growth. In Harrod's numerical example with s at 10% and C_r at 4, it can be supposed that output actually grows 0.1 of a percentage point faster than the warranted rate, that is by 2.6% instead of 2.5%. Then with 2.6% output growth, the acceleration principle or relation will entail that 4 times 2.6% be added to the capital stock, so that ex ante investment is 10.4% of the national income. With ex ante saving limited to 10.0%, the 0.1 of a percentage point excess of actual growth over warranted growth then produces an excess in ex ante investment over ex ante saving of 0.4% of the national income. Any excess in ex ante investment over ex ante saving will be associated with extra expansion of the national income according to the economics of *The General Theory*. Thus, if the actual rate of growth exceeds the warranted rate of s/C_r%, the tendency will be for actual growth to rise and rise, for as soon as actual growth rises from 2.6% to say, 3.0%, required investment will rise further to 4 times 3.0% which equals 12% and so exceed the 10.0%

savings ratio by a still greater margin. Conversely, when actual growth comes out at a rate just short of the warranted 2.5%, ex ante investment will be below the 10.0% savings ratio, which will cause the rate of growth to decline. This second discovery, which became known as Harrod's "knife-edge", meant therefore that any rate of growth in excess of the equilibrium or warranted path he had discovered would set off a continual acceleration of growth, while any shortfall would set off a deceleration. He wrote to Keynes of this discovery on 7 September 1938:

> If in static theory producers produce too little, they will be well satisfied with the price they get and feel happy; but this is not taken to be the *right* amount of output; they will be stimulated to produce more. The equilibrium output is taken to be that which *just* satisfies them and induces them to go on as before. Similarly, the warranted rate [of growth] is that which just satisfies them and leaves them going on as before. The difference between the warranted rate and the old equilibrium (i.e. the difference between dynamic and static theory) is, in my view, that if they produce above the warranted rate, they will be more than satisfied and be stimulated, and conversely, while in the case of equilibrium in static conditions the opposite happens. The "field" round the [static] equilibrium contains centripetal, that round the warranted centrifugal forces (ibid.: 336–337; italics in original).

It took Keynes time to absorb Harrod's startling discovery. On 19 September, he proposed a counter-example in which C_r was merely one-tenth, while s was also one-tenth. With this counter-example, a deviation of output by a small amount from the warranted path, say by δx, which would raise planned investment above the level at which it would otherwise be by $C_r\delta x$ would merely raise this by $0.10\delta x$, which would equal the rise in planned saving of $s\delta x$, which would also come to $0.10\delta x$, so there would be no tendency towards an explosive growth in effective demand. This would grow explosively if C_r was one-ninth (in which case planned investment would rise by $0.11\delta x$ and saving by only $0.10\delta x$) but the further growth of output would be damped if C_r was merely one-eleventh, so, Keynes insisted, 'neutral, stable or unstable equilibrium' (ibid.: 341).

Harrod protested on 22 September that 'it is absurd to suppose extra capital required [C_r] only 1/10 of annual output, when the capital required in association with the pre-existent level of incomes in England today is 4 or 5 times annual output' (ibid.: 344). The probability that C_r would exceed s so that ex ante investment would rise by more than ex ante saving in order to produce instability was therefore overwhelming. But several qualifications emerged. In comparing the increase in ex ante investment to the increase in ex ante saving following a small deviation of output from the warranted rate:

1. The relevant marginal capital coefficient (C_r) which determines how much planned investment will rise is the net new requirement of *induced* investment. In so far as investment decisions are autonomous of short-term fluctuations in output, the relevant C_r will be lower than the economy's overall capital-output ratio.
2. The relevant coefficient which determines the increase in planned saving is the *marginal* and not the average propensity to save. Planned saving will rise more where output deviates upward from the warranted rate, the greater is the marginal propensity to save in relation to the average propensity.

The circumstances that could produce a stable upward deviation of growth from the warranted rate and the avoidance of Harrod's knife-edge are therefore a very high marginal propensity to save in combination with a situation where most investment is autonomous so that the induced investment coefficient, C_r, is considerably less than 1. In "An Essay in Dynamic Theory", Harrod covered this possibility with the caveat that, 'when long-range capital outlay is taken into account…the attainment of a neutral or stable equilibrium of advance may not be altogether improbable in certain phases of the cycle' (Harrod 1939a: 26). The possibility he had in mind here is that in the early stages of a cyclical recovery there may be so much excess industrial capacity that C_r will be quite low for a time, and therefore quite possibly lower than the marginal propensity to save. But, in general, any deviation of growth from the warranted line of advance would raise ex ante investment by a greater margin than ex ante saving with the result that the rate of growth would deviate further.

In addition to establishing the existence of the warranted line of advance and its instability, Harrod had to define the equilibrium investment behaviour by businesses which would actually lead to expansion at the requisite rate. In his 1939 article, he omitted to offer any behavioural rule but simply asserted that the warranted rate was 'that rate of growth which, if it occurs, will leave all parties satisfied that they have produced neither more nor less than the right amount' (ibid.: 16). That is no more than a description of equilibrium growth, and much the same can be said of his definition of the warranted rate in *Towards a Dynamic Economics* (Harrod 1948a) as 'that overall rate of advance which, if executed, will leave entrepreneurs in a state of mind in which they are prepared to carry on a similar advance' (ibid.: 82). It was only in the article "Notes on Trade Cycle Theory" (Harrod 1951b) that Harrod arrived at a behavioural assumption that matched his algebraic formulation of the warranted rate:

> Let the representative entrepreneur on each occasion of giving an order repeat the amount contained in his order for the last equivalent period, adding thereto an order for an amount by which he judges his existing stock to be deficient, if he judges it to be deficient, or subtracting therefrom the amount by which he judges his stock to be redundant, if he does so judge it (ibid.: 274).

With this assumption, an economy which once achieves growth at the warranted rate will sustain it, while any upward or downward deviations will lead to still greater deviations wherever C_r exceeds the marginal propensity to save. However, it emerged by 1964, when Harrod published "Are Monetary and Fiscal Policies Enough?", that even that assumption fails to define growth at the warranted rate, for it must also be assumed that the representative entrepreneur will expand at a rate of precisely s/C_r when he judges his capital to be neither deficient nor redundant. This requires an expectation by the representative entrepreneur that his market will grow at a rate of precisely s/C_r. Hence the full requirement for growth along Harrod's warranted equilibrium path is that entrepreneurs expect growth at this rate and expand and continue to expand at that rate so long as their capital stock continues to grow in line with their market so that it is neither deficient nor redundant. They will of course increase their rate of expansion if their capital should prove deficient, and curtail it if part of their stock becomes redundant.

The warranted rate of growth and its instability were Harrod's great innovations. From 1939 onwards, he contrasted this equilibrium rate with the natural rate of growth, 'the rate of advance which the increase of population and technological improvements allow' (Harrod 1948a: 87), which was entirely independent of the warranted rate. Harrod defined the rate of technical progress more precisely as the increase in labour productivity 'which, at a constant rate of interest, does not disturb the value of the capital coefficient' (ibid.: 23). This then entered the language of economics as Harrod-neutral technical progress, which, together with growth in the labour force, determines the natural rate of growth, that is, the rate at which output can actually be increased in the long run. This raised few theoretical problems, and there was nothing novel in the proposition that long-term growth must depend on the rate of increase of the labour force and technical progress. Keynes himself had said as much several years earlier in "Economic Possibilities for Our Grandchildren" (Keynes 1930 [1972]). But the contrast between this natural rate and Harrod's innovatory warranted rate offered entirely new insights.

If the warranted rate exceeds the feasible natural rate, the achievement of equilibrium growth must be impractical because the economy cannot continue to grow faster than the natural rate. It must deviate downwards from the warranted rate towards the natural rate far more than it deviates upwards with the result that 'we must expect the economy to be prevailingly depressed' (Harrod 1948a: 88). If the natural rate is greater, output will tend to deviate upwards towards the natural rate with the result that the economy should enjoy 'a recurrent tendency to develop boom conditions' (ibid.).

Keynes's own reaction to the dichotomy between the warranted and natural rates was characteristically that the warranted rate always exceeded the natural:

> In actual conditions…I suspect the difficulty is, *not* that a rate in excess of the warranted is unstable, but that the warranted rate itself is so high that with private risk-taking no one dares to attain it … I doubt if, in fact, the warranted rate—let alone an unstable excess beyond the warranted—has ever been reached in USA and UK since the war, except perhaps in 1920 in UK and 1928 in USA. With a stationary population, peace and unequal incomes, the warranted rate sets a pace which a private risk-taking economy cannot normally reach and can never maintain (Keynes to Harrod, 26 September 1938 in Keynes 1987: 349–350; italics in original).

This is characteristic Keynes, but Harrod had persuaded him to express his familiar analysis in the language of his new theory of growth. In the immediate post-war decades when full employment and creeping inflation prevailed, it was widely argued that the natural rate had come to exceed the warranted. The richness of Harrod's model is demonstrated by its ability to illuminate both kinds of situation.

Evsey Domar's growth model, which has a good deal in common with Harrod's, was published seven years after "An Essay in Dynamic Theory", and a considerable literature emerged in the next 15 years on the stability conditions and other important features of what came to be known as the Harrod–Domar growth model (see Domar 1946, 1947). This is elegantly summarised by Frank Hahn and Robin Matthews in their celebrated 1964 survey article.

The development of neoclassical growth theory in the 1950s led to an increasing realisation that the warranted and natural growth rates could be equated by an appropriate rate of interest. If the warranted rate was excessive so that oversaving led to slump conditions, a lower interest rate which raised C_r sufficiently would bring it down to the natural rate. Conversely, the inflationary pressures that resulted from an insufficient warranted rate would be eliminated if higher interest rates reduced C_r sufficiently. If the real rate of interest and C_r responded in this helpful way, s/C_r, the warranted rate could always be brought into equality with the natural rate.

Harrod's response included his "Second Essay in Dynamic Theory" (Harrod 1960a), a title which underlines its significance. He proposed that there was an optimum real rate of interest r_n which would maximise utility, with a value of G_p/e, G_p being the economy's long-term rate of growth of labour productivity and e the elasticity of the total utility derived from real per capita incomes with respect to increases in these. If a 1.0% increase in real per capita incomes raises per capita utility by 0.5%, e will be 0.5, and r_n the optimum rate of interest which maximises utility will be $Gp/0.5$, namely twice the rate of growth of labour productivity. If the marginal utility of income does not fall at all as real per capita incomes rise, per capita utility will grow by 1.0% when incomes rise by 1.0% so that e is unity, and r_n equals G_p. The more steeply the marginal utility of incomes fall, the more e will fall below unity, and the more the optimum real rate of interest, G_p/e, will exceed the rate of growth of labour productivity.

If a society actually seeks to establish the optimum rate of interest determined in this kind of way, the value of C_r will depend upon this optimum rate of interest, so it will not also be possible to use the rate of interest to equate the natural and warranted rates of growth in the manner that the neoclassical growth models of, for instance, Robert Solow (1956) and Trevor Swan (1956) propose. There will therefore still be difficulties because the warranted rate of growth with real interest rates at their optimum level will not in general be equal to the natural rate. Therefore, as Harrod suggested in the final articles he published in 1960 and 1964, governments will have to run persistent budget deficits or surpluses if they are to avoid the difficulties inherent in discrepancies between the natural and the warranted rates of growth.

3   Conclusion

So Harrod remained a convinced Keynesian who continued to believe that a long-term imbalance between saving, the main determinant of the warranted rate, and investment opportunity would call for persistent government intervention. When that approach to economic policy again becomes fashionable, economists may learn a good deal from Harrod's later articles which have not yet received the same attention from the economics profession as his seminal work in the 1930s and the 1940s.

References

Main Works by Roy F. Harrod[1]

Harrod, R.F. (1930a). 'Notes on Supply'. *Economic Journal*, 40(158): 232–241.

Harrod, R.F. (1930). 'Progressive Taxation and Equal Sacrifice'. *Economic Journal*, 40(160): 704–707.

Harrod, R.F. (1931). 'The Law of Decreasing Costs'. *Economic Journal*, 41(164): 566–576. Addendum: 42(167): 490–492.

Harrod, R.F. (1933a). *International Economics*. Cambridge: Cambridge University Press. First revised edition, 1939; second revised edition, 1957; Third revised edition, mainly rewritten, 1974.

Harrod, R.F. (1933). 'A Further Note on Decreasing Costs'. *Economic Journal*, 43(170): 337–341.

Harrod, R.F. (1934a). 'Doctrines of Imperfect Competition'. *Quarterly Journal of Economics*, 48(3): 442–470.

Harrod, R.F. (1934). 'Professor Pigou's Theory of Unemployment'. *Economic Journal*, 44(173): 19–32.

Harrod, R.F. (1934). 'The Equilibrium of Duopoly'. *Economic Journal*, 44(174): 335–337.

Harrod, R.F. (1934). 'The Expansion of Credit in an Advancing Community'. *Economica*, New Series, 1(3): 287–299. Rejoinders: 1(4): 476–478 and 2(5): 82–84.

Harrod, R.F. (1936a). *The Trade Cycle: An Essay*. Oxford: Oxford University Press.

Harrod, R.F. (1936). 'Utilitarianism Revised'. *Mind*, 45(178): 137–156.

Harrod, R.F. (1936). 'Imperfect Competition and the Trade Cycle'. *Review of Economics and Statistics*, 18(2): 84–88.

Harrod, R.F. (1937). 'Mr. Keynes and Traditional Theory'. *Econometrica*, 5(1): 74–86.

Harrod, R.F. (1938). 'Scope and Method of Economics'. *Economic Journal*, 48(191): 383–412.

Harrod, R.F. (1939a). 'An Essay in Dynamic Theory'. *Economic Journal*, 49(193): 14–33. Errata: *Economic Journal*, 49(194): 377.

Harrod, R.F. (1939b). 'Price and Cost in Entrepreneurs' Policy'. *Oxford Economic Papers*, 2(May): 1–11.

Harrod, R.F. (1939). 'Modern Population Trends'. *Manchester School of Economic and Social Studies*, 10(1): 1–20.

Harrod, R.F. (1939). 'Review of *Value and Capital*, by J.R. Hicks'. *Economic Journal*, 49(194): 294–300.

---

[1] The "Bibliography of the Works of Sir Roy Harrod" (Scott 1970) includes all the articles that Harrod published in books, journals and magazines from 1928 to 1969, and some of his most influential newspaper articles. The present list of selected works is confined to his books and academic articles.

Harrod, R.F. (1940). 'The Population Problem: A Rejoinder'. *Manchester School of Economic and Social Studies*, 11(1): 47–58.

Harrod, R.F. (1942). 'Memory'. *Mind*, 51(201): 47–68.

Harrod, R.F. (1943). 'Full Employment and Security of Livelihood'. *Economic Journal*, 53(212): 321–342.

Harrod, R.F. (1945). *Memorandum to the Royal Commission on Equal Pay for Men and Women*. Appendix IX in the Fourth Volume of Memoranda of Evidence. London: HMSO.

Harrod, R.F. (1946). *A Page of British Folly*. London: Macmillan.

Harrod, R.F. (1946). 'Review of *Price Flexibility and Employment*, by Oscar Lange'. *Economic Journal*, 56(221): 102–107.

Harrod, R.F. (1946). 'Professor Hayek on Individualism'. *Economic Journal*, 56(223): 435–442.

Harrod, R.F. (1947). 'A Comment on R. Triffin's "National Central Banking and The International Ecs7.

Harrod, R.F. (1947). *Are These Hardships Necessary?* London: Rupert Hart-Davis.

Harrod, R.F. (1948a). *Towards a Dynamic Economics: Some Recent Developments of Economic Theory and their Application to Policy*. London: Macmillan.

Harrod, R.F. (1948). 'The Economic Consequences of Atomic Energy'. Chapter III in M.L. Oliphant et al. *The Atomic Age*. London: Allen & Unwin: 52–80.

Harrod, R.F. (1948). 'The Fall in Consumption'. *Bulletin of the Oxford University Institute of Statistics*, 10(5): 162–167. Rejoinders: 10(7–8): 235–244 and 10(9): 290–293.

Harrod, R.F. (1950). *Memoranda* (submitted in August and December 1944). Papers of the Royal Commission on Population. Volume 5. London: HMSO.

Harrod, R.F. (1951a). *The Life of John Maynard Keynes*. London: Macmillan.

Harrod, R.F. (1951b). 'Notes on Trade Cycle Theory'. *Economic Journal*, 61(242): 261–275.

Harrod, R.F. (1951). *And So It Goes On: Further Thoughts on Present Mismanagement*. London: Rupert Hart-Davis.

Harrod, R.F. (1952a). 'Theory of Imperfect Competition Revised'. Chapter 8 in *Economic Essays*, by R.F. Harrod. London: Macmillan: 139–187.

Harrod, R.F. (1952). 'Supplement on Dynamic Theory'. Chapter 14 in *Economic Essays*, by R.F. Harrod. London: Macmillan: 278–290.

Harrod, R.F. (1952). 'Currency Appreciation as an Anti-Inflationary Device: Comment'. *Quarterly Journal of Economics*, 66(1): 102–116.

Harrod, R.F. (1952). *Economic Essays*. London: Macmillan.

Harrod, R.F. (1952). *The Pound Sterling*. Princeton Essays in International Finance No. 13. Princeton: Princeton University Press.

Harrod, R.F. (1953). *The Dollar*. London: Macmillan. Second edition with new introduction (1963). New York: The Norton Library.

Harrod, R.F. (1953). 'Imbalance of International Payments'. *International Monetary Fund Staff Papers*, 3(1): 1–46.

Harrod, R.F. (1953). 'Foreign Exchange Rates and Monopolistic Competition: A Comment'. *Economic Journal*, 63(250): 294–298.

Harrod, R.F. (1953). 'The Pre-War Faculty'. *Oxford Economic Papers*, 5(Supplement): 59–64.

Harrod, R.F. (1953). 'Full Capacity vs. Full Employment Growth: Comment'. *Quarterly Journal of Economics*, 67(4): 553–559.

Harrod, R.F. (1955). 'Les Relations entre l'Investissement et la Population'. *Revue Économique*, 6(3): 356–367.

Harrod, R.F. (1956a). *Foundations of Inductive Logic*. London: Macmillan.

Harrod, R.F. (1956). 'The British Boom, 1954–55'. *Economic Journal*, 66(261): 1–16.

Harrod, R.F. (1956). 'Walras: A Re-Appraisal'. *Economic Journal*, 66(262): 307–316.

Harrod, R.F. (1957). 'The Common Market in Perspective'. *Bulletin of the Oxford Institute of Statistics*, 19(1): 51–55.

Harrod, R.F. (1957). 'Review of *International Economic Policy, Volume II: Trade and Welfare*, by J.E. Meade'. *Economic Journal*, 67(266): 290–295.

Harrod, R.F. (1957). 'Clive Bell on Keynes'. *Economic Journal*, 67(268): 692–699.

Harrod, R.F. (1958). *The Pound Sterling, 1951–58*. Princeton Essays in International Finance No. 30. Princeton: Princeton University Press.

Harrod, R.F. (1958). 'The Role of Gold Today'. *South African Journal of Economics*, 26(1): 3–13. Rejoinder: 27(2): 16–22.

Harrod, R.F. (1958). *Policy Against Inflation*. London: Macmillan.

Harrod, R.F. (1958). 'Questions for a Stabilization Policy in Primary Producing Countries'. *Kyklos*, 11(2): 207–211.

Harrod, R.F. (1958). 'Factor-Price Relations under Free Trade'. *Economic Journal*, 68(270): 245–255.

Harrod, R.F. (1959a). 'Why I Shall Vote Conservative'. *The Observer*, 20 September: 16.

Harrod, R.F. (1959b). *The Prof: A Personal Memoir of Lord Cherwell*. London: Macmillan.

Harrod, R.F. (1959). 'Domar and Dynamic Economics'. *Economic Journal*, 69(275): 451–464.

Harrod, R.F. (1959). 'Inflation and Investment in Underdeveloped Countries'. In J. Bergvall (ed.) *Ekonomi Politik Samhälle: En Bok Tillägnad Bertil Ohlin*. Stockholm: Bokförlaget Folk och Samhälle: 96–107.

Harrod, R.F. (1960a). 'Second Essay in Dynamic Theory'. *Economic Journal*, 70(278): 277–293. Comment: 70(280): 851. Rejoinder: 72(288): 1,009–1,010.

Harrod, R.F. (1960). 'New Arguments for Induction: Reply to Professor Popper'. *British Journal for the Philosophy of Science*, 10(40): 309–312.

Harrod, R.F. (1960). 'Keynes's Attitude to Compulsory Military Service: A Comment'. *Economic Journal*, 70(277): 166–167.

Harrod, R.F. (1960). 'Evidence Submitted to the Radcliffe Committee on the Working of the Monetary System', May 1958. *Principal Memoranda of Evidence*. Volume 3. London: HMSO.

Harrod, R.F. (1960–1961). 'The General Structure of Inductive Argument'. *Proceedings of the Aristotelian Society*, New Series, 61: 41–56.

Harrod, R.F. (1961). 'The Dollar Problem and the Gold Question'. In S.E. Harris (ed.) *The Dollar in Crisis*. New York: Harcourt, Brace & World: 46–62.

Harrod, R.F. (1961). *Topical Comment: Essays in Dynamic Economics Applied*. London: Macmillan.

Harrod, R.F. (1961). 'Real Balances: A Further Comment'. *Economic Journal*, 71(281): 165–166.

Harrod, R.F. (1961). 'A Plan for Increasing Liquidity: A Critique'. *Economica*, New Series, 28(110): 195–202.

Harrod, R.F. (1961). 'The "Neutrality" of Improvements'. *Economic Journal*, 71(282): 300–304.

Harrod, R.F. (1961). 'Review of *Production of Commodities by Means of Commodities*, by P. Sraffa'. *Economic Journal*, 71(284): 783–787.

Harrod, R.F. (1962). 'Economic Development and Asian Regional Cooperation'. *Pakistan Development Review*, 2(1): 1–22.

Harrod, R.F. (1962). 'Dynamic Theory and Planning'. *Kyklos*, 15(3): 68–79.

Harrod, R.F. (1963). *The British Economy*. New York: McGraw-Hill.

Harrod, R.F. (1963). 'Themes in Dynamic Theory'. *Economic Journal*, 73(291): 401–421. Corrigendum: 73(292): 792.

Harrod, R.F. (1963). 'Desirable International Movements of Capital in Relation to Growth of Borrowers and Lenders and Growth of Markets'. Chapter 5 in R.F. Harrod (ed.) *International Trade Theory in a Developing World*. London: Macmillan: 113–141.

Harrod, R.F. (1963). 'Liquidity'. Chapter 10 in H.G. Grubel (ed.) *World Monetary Reform: Plans and Issues*. Stanford: Stanford University Press: 203–226.

Harrod, R.F. (1964a). 'Are Monetary and Fiscal Policies Enough?'. *Economic Journal*, 74(296): 903–915.

Harrod, R.F. (1964). *Plan to Increase International Monetary Liquidity*. Brussels: European League for Economic Co-operation.

Harrod, R.F. (1964). 'Comparative Analysis of Policy Instruments: Comment'. In W. Baer and I. Kerstenetzky (eds) *Inflation and Growth in Latin America*. Homewood, IL: Richard Irvin: 418–422.

Harrod, R.F. (1964). 'Retrospect on Keynes'. In R. Lekachman (ed.) *Keynes's General Theory*. New York: Macmillan: 139–152.

Harrod, R.F. (1965). *Reforming the World's Money*. London: Macmillan.

Harrod, R.F. (1966). 'International Liquidity'. *Scottish Journal of Political Economy*, 13(2): 189–204.

Harrod, R.F. (1966). 'Optimum Investment for Growth'. In *Problems of Economic Dynamics and Planning: Essays in Honour of Michał Kalecki*. Oxford: Pergamon Press: 169–179.

Harrod, R.F. (1967a). *Towards a New Economic Policy*. Manchester: Manchester University Press.

Harrod, R.F. (1967). 'Increasing Returns'. Chapter 3 in R.E. Kuenne (ed.) *Monopolistic Competition Theory: Studies in Impact: Essays in Honour of Edward H. Chamberlin*. New York: Wiley: 63–76.

Harrod, R.F. (1967). 'Methods of Securing Equilibrium'. *Kyklos*, 20(1): 24–33.

Harrod, R.F. (1967). 'World Reserves and International Liquidity'. *South African Journal of Economics*, 35(2): 91–103.

Harrod, R.F. (1967). 'Assessing the Trade Returns'. *Economic Journal*, 77(307): 499–511.

Harrod, R.F. (1968). 'What Is A Model?'. Chapter 6 in J.N. Wolfe (ed.) *Value, Capital and Growth: Papers in Honour of Sir John Hicks*. Edinburgh: Edinburgh University Press: 173–191.

Harrod, R.F. (1969). *Money*. London: Macmillan.

Harrod, R.F. (1970). *Sociology, Morals and Mystery*. Chichele Lectures, All Souls College, Oxford. London: Macmillan.

Harrod, R.F. (1970). 'Reassessment of Keynes's Views on Money'. *Journal of Political Economy*, 78(4, Part 1): 617–625.

Harrod, R.F. (1970). 'Replacements, Net Investment, Amortisation Funds'. *Economic Journal*, 80(317): 24–31.

Harrod, R.F. (1972). 'Imperfect Competition, Aggregate Demand and Inflation'. *Economic Journal*, 82(325): 392–401.

Harrod, R.F. (1973). *Economic Dynamics*. London: Macmillan.

Harrod, R.F. (1976). 'Letter to the Editor'. *The Times*, 21 July: 15.

Other Works Referred To

Ayer, A.J. (1970). 'Has Harrod Answered Hume?'. Chapter 2 in W.A. Eltis, M. FG. Scott and J.N. Wolfe (eds) *Induction, Growth and Trade: Essays in Honour of Sir Roy Harrod*. Oxford: Oxford University Press: 20–37.

Domar, E.D. (1946). 'Capital Expansion, Rate of Growth, and Employment'. *Econometrica*, 14(2): 137–147.

Domar, E.D. (1947). 'Expansion and Employment'. *American Economic Review*, 37(1): 34–55.

Eltis, W. (1987). 'Harrod-Domar Growth Model'. In J. Eatwell, M. Milgate and P. Newman (eds) *The New Palgrave: A Dictionary of Economics*. Volume 2. London: Macmillan: 602–604.

Eltis, W. (2008). 'Harrod, Roy Forbes (1900–1978)'. In S.N. Durlauf and L.E. Blume (eds) *The New Palgrave Dictionary of Economics*. Second edition. Volume 3. Basingstoke and New York: Palgrave Macmillan: 836–845.

Hahn, F.H. and R.C.O. Matthews (1964). 'The Theory of Economic Growth: A Survey'. *Economic Journal*, 74(296): 779–902.

Johnson, H.G. (1970). 'Roy Harrod on the Price of Gold'. Chapter 18 in W.A. Eltis, M. FG. Scott and J.N. Wolfe (eds) *Induction, Growth and Trade: Essays in Honour of Sir Roy Harrod*. Oxford: Oxford University Press: 266–293.

Keynes, J.M. (1930) [1972]. 'Economic Possibilities for Our Grandchildren'. In *Essays in Persuasion*. Volume IX of *The Collected Writings of John Maynard Keynes*. London: Macmillan: 321–332.

Keynes, J.M. (1973). *The General Theory and After. Part I: Preparation*. Volume XIII of *The Collected Writings of John Maynard Keynes*. London: Macmillan.

Keynes, J.M. (1987). *The General Theory and After. Part II: Defence and Development*. Volume XIV of *The Collected Writings of John Maynard Keynes*. London: Macmillan.

Lindbeck, A. (1985). 'The Prize in Economic Science in Memory of Alfred Nobel'. *Journal of Economic Literature*, 23(1): 37–56.

Schumpeter, J.A. (1946). 'John Maynard Keynes 1883–1946'. *American Economic Review*, 36(4): 495–518.

Scott, M. FG. (1970). 'Bibliography of the Works of Sir Roy Harrod'. Chapter 25 in W.A. Eltis, M. FG. Scott and J.N. Wolfe (eds) *Induction, Growth and Trade: Essays in Honour of Sir Roy Harrod*. Oxford: Oxford University Press: 361–376.

Solow, R.M. (1956). 'A Contribution to the Theory of Economic Growth'. *Quarterly Journal of Economics*, 70(1): 65–94.

Swan, T.W. (1956). 'Economic Growth and Capital Accumulation'. *Economic Record*, 32(2): 334–361.

Wilson, T. and P.W.S. Andrews (1951). *Oxford Studies in the Price Mechanism*. Oxford: Oxford University Press.

Additional References of Interest

Besomi, D. (1999). *The Making of Harrod's Dynamics*. London: Macmillan.

Phelps Brown, H. (1980). 'Sir Roy Harrod: A Biographical Memoir'. *Economic Journal*, 90(357): 1–33.

Rampa, G., L. Stella and A. Thirlwall (eds) (1998). *Economic Dynamics, Trade and Growth: Essays on Harrodian Themes*. London: Macmillan.

Young, W. (1989). *Harrod and his Trade Cycle Group: The Origins and Development of the Growth Research Programme*. London: Macmillan.

14

Robert Lowe Hall (1901–1988)

Warren Young

1   Introduction

Robert Lowe Hall (1901–1988) was an economist "for all seasons"; academic, teacher, adviser, administrator and economic spokesperson as Lord Roberthall. His activities spanned many fields including: Oxford don and tutor; member of the Oxford Economists' Research Group (OERG) and co-author of a seminal study on pricing; head of the Economic Section in the UK Cabinet Office and Chief Economic Adviser to Chancellors of the Exchequer; and service in the House of Lords. We divide this chapter into the following sections. Section 2 covers biographical details. The third deals with Hall's early activities at Oxford: tutor, lecturer and author. Section 4 covers his work as an "Oxford Economist", member of the OERG and the influential paper he co-authored with Charles Hitch. The next section deals with Hall's government service and tenure in the Lords. Section 6 examines Hall's retrospective views on engineering, economics and policy-making. The final section concludes.

W. Young (✉)
Bar-Ilan University, Ramat Gan, Israel

© The Author(s), under exclusive license to Springer Nature Switzerland AG 2021
R. A. Cord (ed.), *The Palgrave Companion to Oxford Economics*,
https://doi.org/10.1007/978-3-030-58471-9_14

2   Biographical Details

Born in Australia in 1901, Robert Hall took a degree in Civil Engineering at the University of Queensland and was then awarded a Rhodes Scholarship to study at Oxford, where he was awarded a First in Philosophy, Politics and Economics (PPE) ("Modern Greats") at Magdalen College in 1926. His PPE tutor at Magdalen was T.D. ("Harry") Weldon, who specialised in philosophy and politics, and was not an economist. According to Hall's biographer, 'the fact that there was no specialist economics tutor meant that Hall's tuition in economics was inadequate' (Jones 1994: 28). Despite this, Hall was appointed Economics Lecturer and Fellow of Trinity College, Oxford (1926–1947). Indeed, as his biographer noted (ibid.: 33):

> Aware that his training in economics had been inadequate, he took the view that he had been appointed because he had got a First, rather than for his knowledge of economics…[but] the engineering course in Queensland had given him a good mathematical foundation, and he found the elements of theory…were easy enough for him. But he found teaching the subject much more difficult. He had to teach himself in order to teach his students.

During the Second World War, Hall worked first in London (1939–1942), then in Washington, D.C. (1942–1945) for the Ministry of Supply (MoS), and later as a part-time Economic Adviser at the Board of Trade (1945–1947). As a representative of the MoS and working on post-war commodity problems, Hall took part in an important session on "The Future of International Investment", and a roundtable discussion of papers by Victor Schoepperle, Frank Fetter and Charles Kindleberger, at the 55th annual meeting of the American Economic Association in January 1943 (see Hall 1943: 355–357). Over the period 1945–1949, he was the first British representative on the Economic and Employment Commission established by the Economic and Social Council of the UN (see Jones 1994: 67–68).

Hall returned to Oxford after the war to resume his teaching and lecturing duties. He succeeded James Meade as Director of the Economic Section in 1947, serving in this position until 1953, and over the period 1953–1961 served as Chief Economic Adviser to the Treasury and various Chancellors of the Exchequer.

Hall was knighted in 1954, and became a Life Peer in 1969, taking the title Lord Roberthall. He actively served in the House of Lords, from 1970 to 1981 on the crossbenches, then, from 1981 to 1986, as economic spokesman for the Social Democratic Party. Hall was President of the Royal Economic

Society from 1958 to 1960, giving as his Presidential Address what was to become his well-known *Economic Journal* article "Reflections on the Practical Application of Economics" (Hall 1959). He also gave the Sidney Ball Lecture "The Place of the Economist in Government" at Oxford in 1954 (Hall 1955), and the Rede Lecture on "Planning" at Cambridge in 1962 (Hall 1962).

Hall also served as a member of the Plowden Committee on Public Expenditure (1961–1962) and the Franks Commission on the reform of the University of Oxford. After leaving public service, he became a Director at Tube Investments, and an Advisory Director at Unilever. In 1963, Hall became Chairman of the National Institute of Economic and Social Research and between 1964 and 1967 he was Principal of Hertford College, Oxford. He died in September 1988 (see Arndt et al. 1988; Jones 1994).

3   Oxford Don: Tutor, Lecturer and Author

Hall was considered 'an excellent tutor and a kind, polite and charming man by his students', albeit he was not considered by them a good lecturer (Young and Lee 1993: 39, 52). Among those who took PPE under his tutelage were Anthony Crosland, and this in 1945 after Crosland resumed his studies at Oxford, transferring from *Literae Humaniores* ("Greats") to PPE at the advanced age of 27. According to one observer, Crosland, who would go on to be a member of both the Wilson and Callaghan cabinets, 'wrote his Oxford essays on supply and demand for a Trinity tutor [Hall] who…coincidently was a Labour party man' (Reisman 1997: 69). A decade or so earlier, Hall is reported to have said that 'Laissez faire is a lost cause which finds no home in Oxford' (Crosland quoted in Harrison 1994: 387). Moreover, by this time, Hall was tutoring Crosland using Marshall's *Principles*, Pigou's *Economics of Welfare* and Keynes's *General Theory*. In 1947, when Hall left Oxford to take over from Meade as Director of the Economic Section, Crosland replaced Hall as PPE tutor at Trinity College, Oxford, tutoring, among others, Anthony Wedgwood Benn, before moving into politics himself.

Over the period from his appointment in 1926 onwards, Hall lectured on the entrepreneur system, wages, the theory of production, prices and the theory of distribution (see Young and Lee 1993: 42). From 1930 to 1939, he gave lectures on the economic functions of the State, equilibrium analysis, the economics of welfare, international trade, the price system in a collectivist economy, the forces determining price and output within an industry, questions in advanced economic theory, imperfect competition, and competition, imperfect competition and monopoly (see ibid.: 44). After the war, in 1946.

Hall also lectured on "Economic Planning in Great Britain", and on price and output policy (see ibid.: 154).

Hall published two books derived from his lectures. The first was based on a lecture he gave in Michaelmas term 1933, entitled *Earning and Spending* (1934). Heavily influenced by Pigou's writings, it did not receive much attention. Hall's second book, *The Economic System in a Socialist State* (1937), was based on lectures given during Hilary term 1934. The book attracted interest, being reviewed favourably by Maurice Dobb in the *Economic Journal* (Dobb 1937), by Jan Tinbergen (in German) in *Weltwirtscaftliches Archiv* (Tinbergen 1938), and by Frank Knight in the *Journal of Political Economy* (Knight 1938). Knight's review was perhaps the most important and influential as it was part of a joint review of Pigou's *Socialism Versus Capitalism* (Pigou 1937) and Hall's book, which Knight called 'scientifically more important' (Knight 1938: 241). Knight went on:

> It is an important book for anyone interested in theoretical—or, as I should prefer to say, "analytical"—economics, whether or not he is particularly concerned with collectivism as such … In this book we not only find unusually sound and penetrating economic theory in the technical sense; in addition, the work is sprinkled with penetrating common-sense observations about the probable workings of economic arrangements as affected by "human nature" (ibid.: 243–244).

Over the period 1930–1939, Hall himself reviewed books for various publications, including *Economica*, the *Economic Journal* and *International Affairs*.

4   Oxford Economist: OERG and Hall and Hitch

The history and output of the Oxford Economists' Research Group (OERG) has been dealt with in detail (see Young and Lee 1993: 128–136), and thus will not be surveyed here. Rather, we focus on one of its most influential and controversial products, which was the paper written by Hall and Hitch entitled "Price Theory and Business Behaviour", published in *Oxford Economic Papers* in May 1939. The paper was based upon a detailed questionnaire and in-depth interviews with what today would be called a "purposive sample" of 38 "entrepreneurs". This sample was made up of '33 manufacturers…3 retailers and 2 builders' (Hall and Hitch 1939: 13). Preliminary results of the survey and the "full-cost pricing" principle developed by members of the OERG were earlier presented in papers by Roy Harrod and Hall in 1937 and 1938 respectively at the Economics Section of the British Association (see ibid.: 12).

The results of the Oxford survey appeared to conflict with the received doctrines of the time, marginalism and imperfect competition alike. As noted above, Hall and Hitch used the questionnaire method and gathered an "unrepresentative" sample of 38 firms. They had found that a high proportion of firms set prices using a full cost method. In other words, the firm would estimate average costs ex ante, as determined by its notion of "normal" output, and then add to it a percentage margin (the "mark-up").

Hall and Hitch did not consider how margins could vary according to demand. They asserted that the pricing mechanism they proposed was a rule of thumb, which could only result, by accident, in maximum profit. Their approach thus went against both the received marginalist theory of the firm, and the "new" theory of imperfect competition. Hall and Hitch justified their full-cost pricing model based on the view that producers did not know their demand or marginal revenue curves (see Hall and Hitch 1939: 18–19). In other words, they not only disregarded existing theory, but they set out an alternative model of industrial pricing.

In the process of explaining their model, they used a kinked demand curve, introduced independently by Sweezy (1939). This curve illustrated a quirk exhibited by oligopolistic markets, that is, an increase in one firm's price would *not* be followed by its competitors, but by a fall in demand for the output of the price-cutting firm. On the other hand, a price decrease *would* be followed by competitors, resulting in a limited rise in demand. Thus, the demand curve facing the firm in an oligopolistic market exhibits a kink at the prevailing market price. This could then be used to account for price rigidity in oligopolistic markets. Indeed, it was proposed as a possible solution to the conundrum—falling output rather than falling prices—that characterised some sections of the economy in the 1930s (see Hall and Hitch 1939: 22–28; Efroymson 1943: 102–103).

What is also important to recall here is that the paper was reprinted in 1951 in the volume *Oxford Studies in the Price Mechanism*, edited by Tom Wilson and Philip Andrews (see Hall and Hitch 1951), and in the view of at least one observer, catalysed, along with other critiques of the theory of the firm, Milton Friedman's famous 1953 essay on "positive" economics. According to this view (Moss 1984: 314–315; italics in original), Friedman's essay was clearly intended as a 'reply to Hall and Hitch (1951)…and others who attacked the theory of the firm for having *demonstrably* unrealistic assumptions'.

The 1939 version of Hall and Hitch with its full-cost pricing principle and critique of both 'current doctrine of the equilibrium of the firm' *and* monopolistic competition approaches (Hall and Hitch 1939: 14–17) was the focus of some support, but mostly severe criticism from mainstream economists in the

American Economic Review and the *Journal of Political Economy* in the post-war period. While their views were supported by Lester (1946) and Gordon (1948), the theory, methodology and conclusions of Hall and Hitch were attacked by Machlup (1946) and Stigler (1947).

Edward Chamberlin replied to the critique of Hall and Hitch in his note "'Full Cost' and Monopolistic Competition" in the *Economic Journal* (1952). In this, he sets out what he saw as 'the relation of the full-cost principle to the theories of imperfect and monopolistic competition' by reference to 'Hall and Hitch in whose well-known article the principle of setting prices in accord with full cost is…presented in sharp contrast to "current doctrine" including specifically my own work [*Monopolistic Competition*]' (Chamberlin 1952: 318). He went on to say (ibid.: 319):

> It seems to have been overlooked by all concerned that the principle in question, far from being at odds with the theory of monopolistic competition, has been from the first an integral part of it. Unless I have badly misunderstood the principle, it is clearly (if briefly) described and contrasted with the principle of maximum profits…and is the basis, together with several closely related factors such as custom, traditional mark-ups, etc. (also oligopolistic influences), of my analysis of the important phenomenon of excess capacity. In so far as the full cost principle is an acceptable part of price theory there is no difficulty whatever about assimilating it into a system of monopolistic competition—it is, in fact, a further development of the theory.

However, as will be seen below, Hall rejected Chamberlin's position (see Hall 1970: 4–5).

In 1946, after his return to Oxford, Hall reviewed a book by George Katona on price controls and business in the US for the *Economic Journal*. As it was based on a survey and interviews—similar to the methodology used by the OERG and Hall and Hitch—Hall reviewed it very positively (see Hall 1946).

5   Government Service and the House of Lords

Hall's tenure as Director of the Economic Section of the Cabinet Office (1947–1953) and Chief Economic Adviser at the Treasury (1953–1961) has been dealt with in detail by Cairncross in his edited volumes of Hall's diaries (Cairncross 1989, 1991), Cairncross and Watts in their history of the Economic Section published in 1989, and Jones in his biography of Hall, *An Economist Among Mandarins* (1994), and thus will not be surveyed in detail here.

Hall took up the post as part-time Director of the Economic Section in June 1947, becoming full-time in September 1947. Meade had left the position in April of that year due to illness. At the Section, Hall worked with a number of people who were to go on to make their mark on economics. Among these were his Deputy Director, Marcus Fleming, Trevor Swan, Christopher Dow, George Shackle and Bryan Hopkin, among others. During the economic crisis in Britain and nationalisation of industries over the period July 1947–December 1948, as Meade and his staff had done previously, Hall and his staff produced discussion papers, including the "Balance of Payments Crisis", "Import Replacement", "Devaluation" "Fiscal Policy and Economic Planning", "Interest Rate Policy" and "The Pricing Policy of Nationalised Industries" (see *Treasury Papers*). Indeed, as Chick commented (1997: 132):

> Concerned to improve the influence of the Section, Hall sought to make its ideas more accessible to non-economists. Some simple improvements could be made, such as dissuading the Section from continuing to write "briefs that are too long" … Hall sought to improve both the presentation of the Section's arguments and to reduce their perception as being a gathering of merely academic theorists. Emphasising "the points on which there is substantial agreement" rather than the irreconcilable differences, Hall also attempted to get the economists and industrialists to meet one another.

Hall's integration into his new position was enabled by the establishment of a good working relationship with Edwin (later Lord) Plowden, who headed the Central Economic Planning Staff from 1947 to 1953. As Jones put it (1994: 95), their 'friendship and method of working closely…was of a kind that was extremely rare in Whitehall'. Also, according to Jones, as Plowden himself later recalled, their respective advice was given 'in tandem': Hall providing the idea or analysis, and after discussion between them, it would be presented by Plowden to the Chancellor of the Exchequer or relevant Treasury committee for their consideration (ibid.).

Reflecting their close working relationship, Plowden and Hall made a joint contribution entitled "The Supremacy of Politics" (1968) to a symposium in 1968 initiated by the editors of *The Political Quarterly* on priorities in the allocation of national resources, focusing in particular on the determination of public expenditure. With the journal's editors arguing for the need for a table of priorities and stressing 'the limited role of rationality', Plowden and Hall wrote:

Although the electorate cannot be expected to understand the technicalities of the management of the economy, it does take into account, in the considerations which lead to the outcome of elections, a view about how the national resources have been managed. But we think that many of the pleas for more research, a more technically trained higher Civil Service, and a reorganisation of the processes of government, are really pleas for a different political system which will hand over the management of public affairs to experts in particular skills or professions. In politics there is no market as there is in economic life, where values which are objectively commensurable are established (at any rate as a first and useful approximation) by the market process, or by calculations about what might be expected to happen if markets which took account of social values could be made to operate. The purpose of a great deal of public intervention is to bring about situations other than those which would result from market forces: there is no scale other than political judgment which can make the factors which are taken into account commensurable. The only expert in the world of politics is a politician. Parliament and the Cabinet are the agents to whom the electorate has handed over the task of weighing these factors against one another and they cannot delegate the task of "assembling a table of priorities" to any other bodies (Plowden and Hall 1968: 368).

Regarding Hall's influence on policy-making from the early 1950s onwards, the following may be said. Britain faced balance of payments and inflation problems during Hall's entire tenure at both the Economic Section and the Treasury. By 1952, the joint problems of sterling convertibility and the balance of payments came to a head. A plan to combine the restoration of sterling convertibility and a flexible exchange rate—called ROBOT[1]—was suggested and rejected because of its employment implications. Hall, for his part, opposed the plan as it included sterling convertibility. In 1957, Chancellor of the Exchequer, Harold Macmillan, reconsidered the idea of floating, in the hope that it could reduce exchange rate volatility. Hall supported the float idea, but it was not implemented at the time, or in 1963, after Hall had left the Treasury, when Macmillan, who had become Prime Minister, again considered floating if the balance of payments situation necessitated it (see Jones 1994: 116–121).

Incomes policy was also considered in the early 1950s to counter inflation. Hall strongly advocated it as a tool for wage restraint and argued *at the time* that it was the only policy that could reconcile price stability and full employment However, the policy was not utilised as the government did not want to

---

[1] Derived from the names of its three civil servant creators, Leslie ROwan, George Bolton and OTto Clarke.

antagonise the unions and bring about industrial strife (see Cairncross and Watts 1989: 337). By 1956, wage inflation had significantly increased, and a public sector price freeze was introduced rather than dealing with inflation via an increase in unemployment. The government also asked companies in the private sector to stabilise prices. In 1957, Macmillan's new Chancellor of the Exchequer, Peter Thorneycroft, brought before the Cabinet proposals made by Hall regarding a wages policy, but this resulted only in the setting up of a Council on Prices, Productivity and Incomes, which would ostensibly issue reports that could provide a benchmark for wage settlements. Although not considered effective by Hall, as it actually put the blame for inflation on government-led demand inflation in most of its reports, the Council lasted until the end of 1961 (see Jones 1994: 148–149).

However, there is another side to the story of Hall's tenure as head of the Economic Section. While the defeat of the Bank of England and the Treasury over the ROBOT plan for sterling convertibility in 1952 is usually attributed to Hall and Plowden, it was actually the Paymaster General, Lord Cherwell, who did most to block the plan in Cabinet and, while Cherwell consulted Hall, he relied mainly on his own economic adviser, Donald MacDougall. Moreover, Macmillan, both as Chancellor of the Exchequer and as Prime Minister, was in direct contact with Roy Harrod, who was his ex officio informal adviser, something which upset Hall. In addition, in 1957, Thorneycroft consulted Lionel Robbins, leading Hall to seriously consider leaving public service (see Peden 2003: 119).

After his elevation to the House of Lords in 1969, Hall began a second career, first, as a crossbencher between 1970 and 1981 and then as economic spokesperson for the new Social Democratic Party (SDP) over the period 1981–1986. He was an active member of the Lords, giving speeches, engaging in debates, and serving on committees and chairing them. Over the period 1970–1981, he spoke on Britain and the EEC, sterling and the decision to float the pound (1972), and inflation, economic policy and OPEC I (1973). In 1975, he was a member of the Lords committee that issued a report on the EEC. In 1976, he gave major speeches on economic policy on wage agreements. In 1976–1977, he chaired the Lords Select Committee on Commodity Prices, which issued its report in July 1977. He also spoke on housing policies in 1977 and in 1978 on European monetary union and EMS, and on productivity and dividends. The next year, he participated in various debates on wages and unemployment, industrial recovery and competitiveness, the EEC budget, and the impact of OPEC II. In 1980, he spoke on the retail price index and commodity price stabilisation, the EEC budget, on problems of gas and electricity supply, and on social security (see Jones 1994: 177–179).

As noted, from 1981 until 1986, Hall was SDP economic spokesperson in the Lords. In 1981, he spoke on social security and workforce expansion, and on the EEC's Common Agricultural Policy, following this in 1982 by speaking on the Lords Select Committee's Report on Unemployment, as well as on social security, economic and social policies in developing countries, housing policy, wage councils and the current account. Between 1983 and 1986, he offered his opinions on a host of subjects, including the world economy and currency stability, unemployment in the UK compared to the OECD, trade with Germany, employment policy and monetary policy (see ibid.: 179–180).

6   Engineering, Economics and Policy-Making: Retrospect and Prospect

In August 1967, Hall gave a paper at a conference on "Economic Policy" at the University of Queensland where, as noted, he had taken a degree in Civil Engineering before being awarded a Rhodes Scholarship to study PPE at Oxford. This paper, entitled "Problems of Aggregation and Dis-Aggregation in Macro-Economic Policy", was later published in the first issue of *Economic Analysis and Policy* (Hall 1970). It retrospectively summed up Hall's *weltanschauung*, reflecting the nexus between his two areas of academic training, and his economic writings and outlook. Due to its importance, we cite from it here at length. He opened by outlining the planning problem and how to deal with it from an engineering and then an economic perspective. Hall wrote (Hall 1970: 1–2):

> This paper does not deal with the mathematical problems or conditions involved. What it attempts to do is to look at the nature of the problems with which an economist engaged in planning is likely to be involved … We may first glance at the question as it confronts the engineer … An example recalled from my own days as a student of Civil Engineering is the "run-off" problem—what is the greatest volume of water which will flow past a given point from a given catchment area … The problem is first to get the data, and then to decide the point at which additional accuracy is not worth the trouble and how much to add to allow for the remaining uncertainty … The economist has to deal with economic behaviour and in macroeconomics the main aggregates are expressed in terms of money and of people; the most interesting ones are usually National Income per head and the rate of growth of this income. Such calculations imply, if they are to be meaningful, that there is a system of allocating real resources which is accepted as valid for the purposes for which these aggregates are being discussed.

Hall then returned to arguments he had made three decades before in his 1937 book *The Economic System in a Socialist State* (Hall 1970: 2–3):

All this led to planning, either in a socialist sense in which the judgment of planners is substituted for market prices or in the form in which it is mainly practised in countries which still have an enterprise system, on lines systematised by Pigou, affecting income distribution or the use of resources in production. The planner is then faced with a sort of engineer's problem, that he has to work in aggregates and that he has to take the units as they come … A description of a market economy which assumed that men were activated by economic motives, and that the proviso that other things should be equal was one that could generally be made, was pragmatically useful, and could indeed construct a model for a planned economy as well as for a market one as long as the objective was the efficient use of resources.

Hall then turned to issues of competition and pricing, this time referring to his 1939 paper with Hitch, and answering Chamberlin (1952) cited above. He wrote (Hall 1970: 4–5):

Although from a planning point of view it is not very important, the problem can be illustrated by considering the question of imperfect competition … The difficulties arise, both in analysis and in making useful models, because the consumers are not homogeneous … In the analysis of perfect competition, it was basic that all potential buyers would prefer a cheaper to a dearer unit of the same commodity and that all commodity units were perfect substitutes for one another. Thus the original imperfect competition models were very unsatisfactory. They showed the change in sales which corresponded to price variations, but not the gain or loss of sales which resulted from blocks of buyers transferring from one producer to another, nor of course the effect on other producers, who were not even shown on the demand curve for the firm. Chamberlin tried to overcome this by shifting the whole curve towards or away from the origin as the share of the market changed between firms, but it is a rather clumsy device … In practice all these situations end in the establishment of a common price— some variant of the full-cost price originally studied by myself and C.J. Hitch— and competition takes the form of selling expenditure.

Hall summed up his arguments as follows (ibid.: 12):

To repeat in brief the thesis of this paper which I have tried to illustrate by a few examples, we cannot expect fine performance from blunt instruments. Planning, which takes as its task the improvement of performance, soon runs into difficulties because of the lack of knowledge about the dis-aggregations needed to do better. It is no good expecting more from an economy than the means at our disposal allow: if we raise our targets, we must improve our instruments.

In a series of articles between 1981 and 1983, Hall set out his views on incomes policy, monetarism, full employment and international economic co-operation. In the April 1981 issue of the Institute of Economic Affairs' magazine, *Economic Affairs*, he published an article on the problem posed by trade unions in the policy nexus relating employment, wages and inflation under the balance of payments constraint in the UK. In the article, he explained his change of opinion regarding the efficacy of incomes policy to combat inflation (see Hall 1981a).

In November 1981, he published an essay in the *London Review of Books* which the magazine titled "Lord Roberthall, Economic Adviser to Macmillan's Government, Looks at the Failure of Monetarism" (Hall 1981b). In it, he essentially repeated the position given in his testimony as Chief Economic Adviser to the Treasury before the Radcliffe Committee almost 25 years before, in 1957, at the high point of the Macmillan government's application of monetary policy to combat inflation. He testified that 'by and large the government has not used monetary policy as an instrument primarily to be used to secure stable prices', asserting that there was 'an institutional factor' causing inflation that had 'been behind' its ongoing requests for restraint of wages (Hall 1960: 98–99).

In 1982, in a retrospective essay entitled "The End of Full Employment", Hall surveyed economic and political developments during the period of his tenure in the Cabinet Office and Treasury from 1947 to 1961 and the subsequent period of increasing economic instability up to the second oil price shock.

Finally, in a popular article in *History Today* entitled "International Economic Co-operation After 1945", Hall published his recollections as the British representative on the UN's Economic and Employment Commission from 1945 to 1949 and his views on post-war developments in international organisations (see Hall 1983).

7   Conclusion

While not the most famous of Oxford's PPE graduates, or its academic personages, Robert Hall, later Lord Roberthall, was perhaps one of its most multifaceted. Starting out in Australia as a civil engineering graduate, he was awarded a Rhodes Scholarship to study at Oxford, taking a First in PPE, became an Oxford don and was an active member of the OERG. In this capacity, Hall published, with Charles Hitch, a paper on full-cost pricing and the kinked demand curve in 1939, which subsequently became the focus of much Transatlantic debate amongst economists in the post-war period.

After his wartime service for the British government in Washington, D.C., Hall returned to Oxford and later was Director of the Economic Section in the Cabinet Office from 1947 to 1953 and then Chief Economic Adviser to the Treasury during 1953–1961. During his tenure in Whitehall, Hall's influence on policy-making was significant, ranging from the rejection of ROBOT, the setting of relevant pricing policies for the post-war nationalisation programme, to the issue of implementation of incomes policy.

Upon leaving government service, Hall returned to Oxford to resume academic activities, becoming Principal of Hertford College, Chairman of the NIESR and President of the RES. Awarded a peerage in 1969, he started what was essentially a new career in politics. After a decade as an independent member of the Lords, Hall became an economic spokesperson for the SDP, active almost until his death in 1988. In light of the above, it may be concluded that he was indeed an economist "for all seasons".

References

Main Works by Robert Hall

Hall, R.L. (1934). *Earning and Spending*. London: Centenary Press.

Hall, R.L. (1937). *The Economic System in a Socialist State*. London: Macmillan.

Hall, R.L. (1943). 'Discussion'. *American Economic Review*, Papers and Proceedings (Supplement), 33(1, Part 2): 355–357.

Hall, R.L. (1946). 'Review of *Price Control and Business*, by George Katona'. *Economic Journal*, 56(222): 297–300.

Hall, R.L. (1955). 'The Place of the Economist in Government'. *Oxford Economic Papers*, New Series, 7(2): 119–135.

Hall, R.L. (1959). 'Reflections on the Practical Application of Economics'. *Economic Journal*, 69(276): 639–652.

Hall, R.L. (1960). 'Testimony of 17 October 1957'. In Minutes of Evidence, *Committee on the Working of the Monetary System* (Radcliffe Committee). London: HMSO: 98–99.

Hall, R.L. (1962). *Planning: The Rede Lecture*. Cambridge: Cambridge University Press.

Hall, R.L. (1970). 'Problems of Aggregation and Dis-Aggregation in Macro-Economic Policy'. *Economic Analysis and Policy*, 1(1): 1–13.

Hall, R.L. (1981a). 'Are the Unions Usurping Parliament?: Why I Have Changed My Mind on Incomes Policy'. *Economic Affairs*, 1(3): 149–155.

Hall, R.L. (1981b). 'Lord Roberthall, Economic Adviser to Macmillan's Government, Looks at the Failure of Monetarism'. *London Review of Books*, 19 November. Available at: https://www.lrb.co.uk/the-paper/v03/n21/lord-roberthall/lord-roberthall-economic-adviser-to-macmillan-s-government-looks-at-the-failure-of-monetarism.

Hall, R.L. (1982). 'The End of Full Employment'. Chapter 7 in C.P. Kindleberger and G. di Tella (eds) *Economics in the Long View: Essays in Honour of W.W. Rostow – Volume 3: Applications and Cases, Part II*. London: Macmillan: 155–174.

Hall, R.L. (1983). 'International Economic Cooperation After 1945'. *History Today*, 12 December. Available at: https://www.historytoday.com/archive/international-economic-co-operation-after-1945.

Hall, R.L. and C.J. Hitch (1939). 'Price Theory and Business Behaviour'. *Oxford Economic Papers*, 2(May): 12–45.

Hall, R.L. and C. Hitch (1951). 'Price Theory and Business Behaviour'. Chapter 3 in T. Wilson and P.W.S. Andrews (eds) *Oxford Studies in the Price Mechanism*. Oxford: Clarendon Press: 107–140.

Plowden, Lord and R.L. Hall (1968). 'The Supremacy of Politics'. *The Political Quarterly*, 39(4): 366–371.

Other Works Referred To

Arndt, H.M., D.M. Bensusan Butt and T.W. Swan (1988). 'An Appreciation of Robert Hall, 1901–1988'. *Economic Record*, 64(4): 360–361.

Cairncross, A. (ed.) (1989). *The Robert Hall Diaries, 1947–53*. Volume 1. London: Unwin Hyman.

Cairncross, A. (ed.) (1991). *The Robert Hall Diaries, 1954–61*. Volume 2. London: Unwin Hyman.

Cairncross, A. and N. Watts (1989). *The Economic Section, 1939–1961: A Study in Economic Advising*. London: Routledge.

Chamberlin, E.H. (1952). '"Full Cost" and Monopolistic Competition'. *Economic Journal*, 62(246): 318–325.

Chick, M. (1997). *Industrial Policy in Britain, 1945–1951: Economic Planning, Nationalisation and the Labour Governments*. Cambridge: Cambridge University Press.

Dobb, M. (1937). 'Review of *The Economic System in a Socialist State*, by Robert Hall'. *Economic Journal*, 47(186): 345–347.

Efroymson, C.W. (1943). 'A Note on Kinked Demand Curves'. *American Economic Review*, 33(1, Part 1): 98–109.

Gordon, R.A. (1948). 'Short-Period Price Determination in Theory and Practice'. *American Economic Review*, 38(3): 265–288.

Harrison, B. (1994). 'Politics'. Chapter 14 in B. Harrison (ed) *The History of the University of Oxford: Volume VIII, The Twentieth Century*. Oxford: Clarendon Press: 377–412.

Jones, K. (1994). *An Economist Among Mandarins: A Biography of Robert Hall, 1901–1988*. Cambridge: Cambridge University Press.

Knight, F.H. (1938). 'Two Economists on Socialism'. *Journal of Political Economy*, 46(2): 241–250.

Lester, R.A. (1946). 'Shortcomings of Marginal Analysis for Wage-Employment Problems'. *American Economic Review*, 36(1): 63–82.

Machlup, F. (1946). 'Marginal Analysis and Empirical Research'. *American Economic Review*, 36(4): 519–554.

Moss, S. (1984). 'The History of the Theory of the Firm from Marshall to Robinson and Chamberlin: The Source of Positivism in Economics'. *Economica*, New Series, 51(203): 307–318.

Peden, G.C. (2003). 'New Revisionists and the Keynesian Era in British Economic Policy: A Comment'. *Economic History Review*, 56(1): 118–124.

Pigou, A.C. (1937). *Socialism Versus Capitalism*. London: Macmillan.

Reisman, D. (1997). *Anthony Crosland: The Mixed Economy*. Basingstoke: Palgrave Macmillan.

Stigler, G.J. (1947). 'The Kinky Oligopoly Demand Curve and Rigid Prices'. *Journal of Political Economy*, 55(5): 432–449.

Sweezy, P.M. (1939). 'Demand Under Conditions of Oligopoly'. *Journal of Political Economy*, 47(4): 569–573.

Tinbergen, J. (1938). 'Review of *The Economic System in a Socialist State*, by R.L. Hall'. *Weltwirtschaftliches Archiv*, 48: 38–40.

Treasury Papers. Series One: Part 1, Reels 8–9, T230/26–28, EC(S)(47)–(49); July 1947–December 1948.

Young, W. and F.S. Lee (1993). *Oxford Economics and Oxford Economists*. London: Macmillan.

15

Thomas Balogh (1905–1985)

Andrew Graham

1   Introduction[1]

'Do you know any Baloghian economics?' It would have been a challenging enough question at any time, but the context piled on the pressure. The questioner was Theo Cooper, then Tutorial Fellow in Economics at St Hugh's, Oxford, known for being both 'crushingly intelligent' and so manifestly honest that she was incapable of hiding her disdain for stupidity. Worse still, I had never met Theo before, nor Thomas Balogh, and I could not have written a sentence about him or his economics. Despite never having met Balogh, it was my first day working for him. The date was Monday, 3 October 1966 and the place…10 Downing Street.

Fortunately, I had the wit only to say 'not much' and, after a few moments of terrifying scrutiny, she pushed a clutch of brown folders across to me saying, 'You had better read these'. They were labelled "Economic Adviser's Office only. Top Secret".

Baloghian economics, it transpired, involved…well, just about anything. After only an hour of skim reading I had come across memos about microprocessor technology, Rhodesian sanctions, the psychology of the

[1] I am grateful to Frances Stewart and Vijay Josh for comments, to Robert Cord for eagle-eyed editing and to Yasmin Rafiei for assistance with the bibliography. As usual, all errors remain my responsibility.

A. Graham (✉)
Oxford Internet Institute, Oxford, UK
e-mail: andrew.graham@balliol.ox.ac.uk

© The Author(s), under exclusive license to Springer Nature Switzerland AG 2021
R. A. Cord (ed.), *The Palgrave Companion to Oxford Economics*,
https://doi.org/10.1007/978-3-030-58471-9_15

347

French, the stupidity of the civil servants at the Board of Trade, foreign exchange controls, awards to university students, international liquidity, public purchasing, the funding and organisation of research councils, changes to the Selective Employment Tax, company law, balance of payments forecasts and car prices.

In his academic writings, Balogh's sinners (and his very occasional saints) are condemned to the depths of his incomparable footnotes, but in his Whitehall minutes, sprayed around like a machine gun, the human agents were in the thick of the action. It was X who was responsible for this piece of damage, Y with this foolish idea, Z who, if promoted, might just possibly put it right.

I rapidly learned that Balogh was formidably clever, totally unconventional and accepted no boundaries to academic disciplines. I recall him growling at me in his inimitable Hungarian accent, 'Why is the female always more deadly than the male?' The object of his attention was not Mrs Thatcher—despite the appropriateness of his remark—but a traffic warden, stabbing a ticket onto a Rolls-Royce in Parliament Street. 'Dressed like a "vasp", you see'. The warden was clearly meant to hear. She could also hardly avoid his unflinching inspection: a penetrating gaze out of small slanted brown eyes over the top of his glasses. The occasion was typical. He was a detailed observer (especially of people and every aspect of their behaviour); he cared little for what other people thought (or, rather, he liked to give this impression); and he said what he thought or what he thought would provoke.

Typical it may have been. Representative it cannot be. Thomas Balogh, or "Tommy" as he was known to most of his friends, was too colourful and too talented to be captured in a single example. Paul Streeten compared conversation with him to wandering through a well-stocked department store: 'One never quite knows what wares will turn up next, but each department presents an array of beautiful and useful items. The moves were sometimes vertical, sometimes horizontal, sometimes diagonal, but always unpredictable' (Streeten 2000: 35).

On another occasion, I was with him at a meeting in the Ministry of Power (as it then was) discussing with the civil servants how much gas the oil companies might actually be finding under the North Sea and he suddenly hissed to me in a stage whisper, 'You know they are all in ze pay of the oil companies' and then left the meeting, leaving me to face the glares of the 'they'.

2 Balogh's Life

Curiously, apart from those who met him—*all* of whom have stories about him—few people today know much about Thomas, later Lord, Balogh. Born in Budapest on 2 November 1905 (only a street away from Nicky Kaldor),[2] he attended a gymnasium, a 'classical grammar school', as he called it, that had been founded by his great-uncle.[3] (Nicky attended the same school two years later.) While his family appears to have been reasonably well off—his father was a civil servant and the family had a governess—Balogh was conscious from an early age of the damage of inflation. The 'adolescent trauma', he said, 'was not unemployment and crisis, but impoverishment and loss of class status as a result of monetary chaos'. With the Austro-Hungarian Empire in final decline, the presence of poverty or the threat of poverty was ubiquitous. He spoke of even the privileged carrying, rather than wearing their shoes, so that they would not become worn out too quickly.

As a result, when Balogh left school, he was conscious of the need to earn his living and so 'instead of studying physics I worked at a bank and read economics'. He attended Budapest University. His thesis on the German inflation of 1921–1923 earned him a fellowship to study in Berlin in 1927–1928 which he combined with work for the Reichsbank. He found in Berlin a 'freedom of manners and thought and sex not to be paralleled for thirty years'. For him 'the sense of liberation from the constrictive conventionality of Budapest was inebriating'.

Subsequently, he won a Rockefeller Fellowship to Harvard (1928–1930). While in the USA he managed to do research for the Federal Reserve, but part of his Fellowship was spent in London and part in Paris (working for the Banque de France). During a visit to London, he sent Keynes a letter of introduction provided for him by Schumpeter. Amongst Balogh's jottings, he records that in June 1930, 'Keynes invited me to lunch. Kingsley Martin was the other guest. Keynes had spent the morning at the Macmillan Committee. After lunch he asked me to stay on'. Three months later, Keynes published in the *Economic Journal* the first article that Balogh had written in English, namely "The Import of Gold into France" (Balogh 1930a).

---

[2] Professor Nicholas Kaldor, later Lord Kaldor (born 12 May 1908, died 30 September 1986) was an equally well-known Hungarian economist who emigrated to the UK at a similar time to Balogh.

[3] Quotes by Balogh in this chapter come from three sources: the excellent biography by June Morris (2007), Balogh's (uncatalogued) papers in the Balliol Archives, Oxford, and my memories of conversations with him. It is a pleasure to acknowledge how greatly the writing of this chapter has been aided by the presence of the work by June Morris.

1931 found Balogh working for the League of Nations. He had hoped to take up a combined academic and banking career in Germany, but the financial crisis and Hitler's dramatic success in the September 1930 federal election had closed that option. He found himself forced to move to England, temporarily unemployed until Keynes assisted him to obtain a job. This was in the City under O.T. "Foxy" Falk, Keynes's successor as Treasury Representative at Versailles, and one of the few people whom Balogh continued to admire throughout his life.

Thus, by the age of 26, Balogh had worked for the central banks of the USA, France and Germany. However, neither then, nor later, did he work for the Bank of England. By the early 1940s, by which time he had taken a post at the Institute of Economics and Statistics at Oxford, he had become such a critic of the Bank that it is rumoured that they tried, unsuccessfully, to prevent him being appointed to a Lectureship at Balliol in 1940. Indeed, he was not elected to a fellowship until 1945 when the then Master, A.D. (Sandy) Lindsay, backed him strongly. He remained connected with Balliol for the rest of his life, first as a Tutorial Fellow from 1945 to 1968, then as a Senior Research Fellow from 1968 to 1973 and, finally, as an Emeritus Fellow until his death. Throughout this period, he also held a University appointment, being elected, in 1960, to a Readership in Economics.

Balogh, alongside his full-time teaching and research at Oxford, either advised or worked in every Labour administration from 1945 to 1979. Indeed, during the Attlee government, he advised almost all of the economics ministers. Not that this was always to his liking. Many years later, he spoke of working for 'buffoons like Shinwell, whose brain I was for ten years'. However, during this time, a much more fruitful relationship was developing with Harold Wilson. Balogh had met Wilson as early as 1937 when Wilson, then only 21, became a Lecturer in Economics at New College, Oxford, and he acted as an unofficial adviser when Wilson was President of the Board of Trade (1947–1951). When the Labour Party went into opposition in the 1950s, and especially when Wilson became Shadow Chancellor and then Leader of the Opposition, they continued to work closely. As a result of his work on development economics, Balogh travelled extensively, but, when not abroad, he would see Wilson about once a week, sometimes more. He not only provided Wilson with a stream of briefs, but also peppered all parts of the Labour Party with his views via phone calls, letters and articles. He was particularly close friends with Aneurin Bevan, Dick Crossman, Barbara Castle and Peter Shore and his ties were strengthened through his membership (from 1943 to 1964) of the Labour Party's Economic and Financial Committee.

Balogh married twice. The first, in 1945, was to Penelope Gatty (née Tower), a psychotherapist and the widow of Oliver Gatty, a Fellow of Balliol. This marriage was dissolved in 1970 and the same year he married Catherine Storr (née Cole), a psychologist and a well-known author of children's books.

However, the bare facts of Balogh's life convey little of the man. The titles of his main books, and still more so those of his articles, listed in the bibliography, indicate something of his range of interests, but even these do not display the power of his intelligence nor the trenchancy of his personality. As June Morris has well described, his deep engagement with economic policy captures only a fraction of Balogh's interests. He was deeply interested in history, art and science, especially applied science.[4] Balogh also had multiple affairs, including an especially intense one with Iris Murdoch. He was fascinated by people's psychology and sexuality and saw few boundaries between this and their political and economic views, asserting to Roger Opie,[5] that as I, Andrew Graham, had an attractive wife, I was bound to be in favour of expansionist policies!

Allied to his intellect was an uncanny ability to absorb ideas, information and gossip about everything. Wilfred Beckerman recalls Balogh arriving in Athens when Beckerman was economic adviser to the Greek government and within an hour Balogh knew more than Beckerman did about everything going on in Greece. Even Keynes, coming to London from Cambridge, is reputed to have used Balogh to find out what was what. Balogh was also constantly on the attack, especially against the Establishment and against what he regarded as stupidity and injustice. For him, everything and everybody was black or white and he was loved and hated in equal measure.

A particular object of attack, in addition to his many criticisms of all traditional "schools" of economics, was the British Civil Service. His 1959 essay "The Apotheosis of the Dilettante"—was a blistering assault on what he regarded as the amateurishness of most civil servants and hence, according to Balogh, the incompetence of their advice.

Yet, Thomas Balogh's economic and political interests were never confined to the UK. In 1955, he and Dudley Seers wrote a report for Dom Mintoff, the Prime Minister of Malta. From that time onwards, as he states:

I rarely spent university vacations and sabbatical leaves at home. The Governments of Jamaica, British Guiana, Mauritius, India, Greece and various

---

[4] He was, for example, a close friend of Margaret Gowing, the first occupant of a chair in the history of science at Oxford.

[5] Fellow and Tutor in Economics, New College, Oxford, 1961–1992.

United Nations agencies, especially the Food and Agriculture Organization, the Special Fund, and the Latin American Economic Commission, as well as the Organization for European Economic Co-operation and the Organization for American States gave me opportunities to work on problems of stunted development.

His advice was constantly sought at the highest levels. He was friends with, as well as adviser to, Michael Manley (Prime Minister of Jamaica), Jawaharlal Nehru (Prime Minister of India) and, as noted, Dom Mintoff. On one occasion when a ferry to Malta had broken down, Mintoff sent a destroyer to collect Balogh from Sicily! He was also a friend of H.C. ("Nugget") Coombs, the first Governor of the Commonwealth Bank of Australia (CBA), later the Reserve Bank, and for the whole period 1942 to 1964, he was a consultant to the CBA, writing a regular newsletter.

In 1964, Balogh was appointed Economic Adviser to the British Cabinet. In practice, he ran what was effectively the first "policy unit" in Downing Street. It was officially called the Economic Adviser's Office and was located at first in the Cabinet Office, but, following the March 1966 general election, it moved into 10 Downing Street. There was a tiny staff, at most two or three other economists at any one time. Despite the small staff,[6] the Office involved itself in the full range of economic policy. During these years, Balogh was seen not only as the éminence grise behind the Prime Minister, but also as the particular scourge of companies developing North Sea gas and, later, oil.

Indeed, at the time, he and Nicky Kaldor became the butt of the right wing "tabloids". With Bulganin and Khrushchev in power in the Soviet Union, the two Hungarians (Balogh at No. 10 and Kaldor at the Treasury) were labelled "B and K, the terrible twins" or, sometimes, "Buda" and "Pest"—which I leave to your imagination. They were the closest of friends, sharing a flat in Gordon Square when Balogh first came to London in the early 1930s, as well as the greatest of competitors both intellectually and socially. They were also both passionately pro-British. Harold Lever tells how Tommy in one his many outbursts against the Board of Trade exclaimed, 'Why should they always be on the side of the bloody foreigners?' (Lever 1985).

In 1968, Balogh was created a life peer and when Wilson returned to power in March 1974 he was appointed Minister of State at the Department of

---

[6] Michael Stewart, later Reader in Economics at University College London; Theo Cooper, Tutorial Fellow in Economics, St Hugh's College, Oxford; Stuart Holland, later Professor at the European University in Florence; Richard Pryke (for just a few weeks), later Senior Lecturer in Economics, University of Liverpool; Margaret Joan Anstee, later Dame Margaret Joan Anstee and Under-Secretary-General, United Nations, and myself.

Energy. In 1976, he became Deputy Chairman of the British National Oil Corporation, the two successive positions thus giving him the opportunity to influence both the policy and the practice of introducing North Sea oil.

Over the whole of his very active life, Balogh travelled endlessly, carried on an enormous correspondence and remained deeply interested in how his former students were faring.[7] He produced more than fifteen books, made numerous contributions to others and wrote something in excess of a thousand articles on every aspect of political economy.

3   Baloghian Economics

With such a colourful and energetic background, why is Balogh so relatively unknown today? Why also would no more than a handful of contemporary economists have heard of 'Baloghian economics', still less be able to describe it? What lasting impact, either for good or ill, did this talented and controversial economist make? Also, for what ought he to be remembered? For today's mainstream economists, the answer is simple enough. Balogh is forgotten because, in their eyes, even at his very best, he was no more than an intemperate critic. Monetarists, Marxists, Keynesians, Austrians and neoclassicists were condemned with equal vigour—or almost equal. Marxists and Austrians received less attention simply because they had much less influence on UK policy.

Even Keynes did not escape. In 1945, notwithstanding their earlier friendship, there was a furious row. Balogh took issue with Keynes over the Bretton Woods Agreement, daring to disagree with him in talks, articles, pamphlets and letters to *The Times*. He even took on Keynes indirectly in the House of Lords by briefing three out of the four who spoke against what Keynes was recommending. In addition to this argument, Balogh criticised Keynes more generally over the neglect of the international dimension of his theory.

His disagreements with the neo-Keynesians went even deeper, the venom made more bitter by his acute sense of a missed opportunity. Keynesian economics, he believed, had offered a brief period of hope. In Balogh's view, Keynes had laid out a theory in which the three central "propensities" around

---

[7] His students loved or, occasionally, hated him, as his tutorials never provided explanations but always challenges, provocations or acerbic comments. Al Steppan, who went on to become, inter alia, the Gladstone Professor of Government at Oxford, said that Balogh loved to shock American students and his first essay was "Why do Americans have such big tits on their cars?", and Steven Lukes, later Tutorial Fellow in Politics at Balliol, tells how Balogh initially simply ignored his essay advocating devaluation, but when he pressed, Balogh snorted, 'Darling, it is like masturbation, it becomes a habit'.

which the structure of *The General Theory* rotates—to save, to invest and to hold liquidity—were all social psychological characteristics, not laws.[8] Moreover, Keynes's framework not only allowed the monetary and real sectors of the economy to interact, as Balogh believed all historical evidence suggested, but also did so without laying down rigid pathways of causation.

However, to Balogh's great regret, Keynes's mobile and suggestive form of theorising was rapidly replaced by formal models. Amongst economists, Hicks, who froze Keynes's potentially open-ended system into a set of simultaneous equations in his IS-LM curves, was the subject of particular attack. So also were Phillips and Paish and their followers, with their claim of a stable relationship between the level of unemployment and the rate of inflation. In both cases, Balogh's central critique was that economic relationships were presented as if the economy were a machine (instead of the evolving organism which he saw it to be).

Balogh was equally scathing of politicians, especially those on the Gaitskellite wing of the Labour Party who swallowed the textbook version of Keynesianism more or less whole. Tony Crosland's influential book, *The Future of Socialism* (Crosland 1956), was a particular source of irritation. Balogh never believed, as Crosland did, that all the main economic problems could be largely solved provided only that there continued to be a relatively small amount of intelligent fiscal and monetary manipulation. In particular, in Balogh's view, in the absence of an incomes policy, either full employment had to be abandoned as a goal, or inflation would not only persist, but also gradually increase—as, indeed, it did. Investment, Balogh also thought, would never be a sufficient share of gross domestic product (GDP) if it were to be left largely to the market.

However, for Balogh, if the neo-Keynesians were bad, monetarists were much worse. For them, the economic levers did not even have to be pulled. Once the dials had been set, they expected the economy to run on autopilot, at worst deviating only "temporarily" from the "natural" rate of unemployment. In this, Balogh accused them of a double error. First, they were wrong even to suppose that the dial could be set. Thus, sometime around 1970, I recall him saying, 'You can't control vot you also measure—ze buggers vill change'. Being translated, this is Goodhart's Law, but many years earlier. Second, Balogh was infuriated because they, like the neoclassicists, simply assumed that the economy was either at equilibrium or, if disturbed, returned quickly to it—an

---

[8] Multiple theses have been written on what Keynes intended. Suffice to say that Keynes described his propensities as both 'psychological' and as 'laws', but was careful to stress that these were not 'laws of necessity'.

assumption that he regarded as not only totally without theoretical support, but also at odds with all the historical evidence of substantial trade cycles.

Is it right to say that Balogh was 'infuriated'? Definitely. To Balogh, what mattered about economics was that it held such power for good or evil over people's lives. This was no academic game. What made him mad about the monetarists was that he felt, and felt passionately, that they were misleading everyone. The solutions they advocated would not be painless, far from it, nor would the difficulties be merely temporary, as their theory implied. Indeed, they would not, in his view, be solutions at all.

For Balogh, neoclassical economics presented exactly the same Panglossian optimism. Again, it was influential and therefore potentially dangerous and based on assumptions, which to him, were so obviously wrong that he found it hard to understand how anyone could take such theories seriously. How, he asked, could the everyday observation that, in the great majority of industries, firms were in the driving seat as price-setters, not price-takers, be squared with a theory which assumed precisely the opposite? Why, equally, were all the models static, when the history of capitalism displayed dramatic change? Why was technology normally ignored? Or, if technical progress was recognised, why was it so frequently assumed to be "disembodied", descending neutrally like manna from heaven? On and on the questions went.

The replies, both old and new, are well known. Then, it would have been said in defence that all theories are abstractions, one has to start from somewhere and what matters is not whether a theory is right (an impossible test), but whether it is illuminating. Today, it might be conceded that many of Balogh's points were well taken, but the reply would be that others had made the same criticisms with greater clarity and that, in any case, such criticisms were of the early textbook models, when the subject was young and naive. Indeed, the responders might well add that Balogh's observations were precisely why the subject had had to become more technical. Only when the power of the mathematics was ramped up, they would say, would it be possible to include the extra complexity which he stressed.

The crunch point, both then and now, is the question: What is the alternative? After all, even Paul Streeten, one of Balogh's closest of allies, has conceded that 'it takes a model to kick out a model' (P. Streeten quoted in H. Streeten 1986: 8). Here we come to the nub of the issue. Was Balogh, despite his phenomenal energy and his obvious talents, not really an economist to be taken seriously; an intemperate and acute critic of others, but with nothing significant to add in the longer run? Or are his methods, his observations and his contributions of enduring interest and significance?

These questions cannot be answered without discussing the fundamental nature of economics. If the subject is a science with discoverable laws that can be modelled mathematically then Balogh has no place because he has no alternative theoretical framework to offer. The best that can be hoped is that his criticisms will lead to small amendments to mainstream theory. Far more likely, however, is that his critical observations, not being easily related to the existing framework, will be disregarded. There is, as Wittgenstein said, a 'contemptuous attitude towards the particular case' (Wittgenstein 1958: 18).

Conversely, if, as Balogh argued, economics, despite its apparent ability to quantify so many things, is not a science based on the belief that there are underlying laws about human behaviour to be discovered, then the picture shifts markedly. Theory no longer holds pride of place at the centre of the citadel, the hard core that has to be protected in its constant skirmishes with the facts. Instead, careful observation is what drives the subject and induction, the process of generalising from such observation, replaces deduction as the primary skill. Economists would then need an education which encompassed history and social psychology, and, above all, to value the ability of the detective higher than that of the mathematician. Of course, theoretical perspectives are still required, but these are no longer formal mathematical models but "organising insights". Theory is a way of looking at the evidence in order to make sense of it, useful for the purpose in hand, but no more than that.

Seen from the second viewpoint, I suggest that Balogh's observations, especially when combined, rather than seen individually, are of more importance than might at first appear. They offer both a useful set of organising insights and a coherent critique of mainstream theory.

Amongst the inductive generalisations that Balogh emphasised were the prevalence of economies of scale, oligopolistic industry, firms as price-setters, poor information, the uneven incidence and take up of technology and the fallibility of human expectations. Taken individually, each of these is a criticism of one part of existing theory, but, taken together, they offer a different perspective. If economies of scale are widespread, if information is poor and if the incidence of technology is not random, then many industries are likely to be oligopolistic. If oligopoly is prevalent, then firms will be price-setters, not price-takers, and mark-up pricing may well be the norm. If prices are determined mainly by costs, and costs are L-shaped in the short run, then demand will almost certainly have its main influence not on prices, but on output, profits and investment.

Moreover, at the centre of Balogh's view of the world lies the elusive concept of power. The starting points for all his work on international development were the massive inequalities that exist both between and within countries. On the dedication page of the first volume of *Unequal Partners*, Balogh cites an 1885 quote by the Indian politician Lala Murlidhar which compares the 'fairness' of free trade between 'impoverished India and the bloated capitalist England' to a meeting between 'a rabbit and a boa constrictor' (Balogh 1963a: dedication page). To Balogh, the problems in measuring power were irrelevant when, in his view, the results of its existence were manifest everywhere.

What is more, if you start within a framework consisting of inequalities of income and wealth and take on board the massive differences in access to power that result, and then add other Baloghian features such as economies of scale, it becomes a relatively trivial matter to construct a convincing story of cumulative causation. Once this is the case, then history matters and multiple equilibria are the norm, not the exception. Also, when history matters, expectations are central, not the generalised perfect foresight of rational expectations, but the fallible particular foresight of the case-by-case approach. Bygones are then no longer bygones, but the stuff from which the future path of history is made.

Of course, many others have covered this ground and perhaps with greater patience, persuasion and illumination, than Balogh. But not many said all of this so early, nor so consistently, nor, above all, over such a wide range and so forcibly. Moreover, it is not just that Balogh *said* these things, but also, that he *used* his insights and used them effectively. This is the litmus test by which a political economist ought to be judged and by which, he, in particular, would want to be judged. As Keynes said describing Marshall's views, 'the bare bones of economic theory are not worth much in themselves … The whole point lies in applying them to the interpretation of current economic life' (Keynes 1924: 342).

4   Balogh's Contributions

The relevant question to ask about Balogh is, therefore, not what theoretical innovations did he make, but what were his key contributions to applied political economy? In the long period up to 1964, before he worked full time in government, four stand out. First, in the 1930s, there is his work on German rearmament. As is well known, the dominant view in the Treasury at that time was steadfastly pre-Keynesian and strongly laissez-faire. They therefore rejected out of hand the possibility that national output could rise massively—and without inflation—by bringing millions of people out of unemployment via State investment, physical controls and rearmament. As Morris (2007: 24–27) recounts, Balogh was one of the very few who understood early on what was happening and wrote and spoke about it whenever and wherever he could (see, for example, Balogh 1938, 1939). He also made calculations of how large the German war effort might be, but the senior civil servants in the Treasury dismissed them. In fact, according to Balogh, the documents released at the end of the war showed that even *his* figures fell 'appreciably short of the truth' (Balogh 1963b: 4).

Second, and of much longer-term significance, there was his understanding of inflation within the context of a world in which, post-Keynes, the macro-economy could be stabilised. He saw earlier than anyone else the need for an incomes policy based on social consensus for the Keynesian policy revolution to be complete. In 1938, Joan Robinson had noted that the guarantee of full employment would fundamentally alter the bargaining position of employ-ees, but it was Balogh who not only noticed what she said, but also saw its implications for policy. As early as 1941, Balogh wrote of the need, if full employment was to be maintained in the post-war period, for 'a co-ordinated price and wage policy, with tribunals to enforce equity and prevent hardship' (Balogh 1941: 13). Later, in 1970, he was the originator (at least in this con-text) of the term "social contract" and a tireless advocate of it within the Labour Party (see especially Balogh 1963c).

Here, as in so much else of Balogh's work, we see his understanding of the importance and complexity of power. Full employment gave fresh power to both employers and employees and so, he argued, in return for guaranteeing full employment, the State had the right to expect that unions and major firms would keep to their sides of the bargain—the power of the three groups being held together in a social contract. That such an incomes policy, mostly voluntary but 'buttressed' (a favourite word of his) by State institutions, should prove so difficult to establish does not in any way diminish the force of the insight.

Third was Balogh's work on international payments. Out of his many con-tributions in this field undoubtedly the most dramatic and the most impor-tant was his campaign in 1945 against Keynes's view of Bretton Woods. Kaldor's comment was that was this was 'one of the rare occasions I know of when Keynes was clearly in the wrong' (Kaldor 1985). Here, we see one of Balogh's best moments as well as one of the clearest examples of his approach.

In a nutshell, his criticism of Bretton Woods was that it entirely ignored the context. It attempted to impose a generalised move to free trade and an early abolition of capital controls and so a return to exchange rate convertibility combined with a system of international reserves proportional to world trade. Fine, in theory, but Balogh's point was that this took no account of the par-ticular situation at the end of the Second World War when the world econ-omy was in fundamental disequilibrium in international payments. The war had strengthened and increased the capital stock of the USA, but seriously damaged that of Europe. It had also placed the UK, in particular, in a position of extreme illiquidity (since sterling was still a reserve currency, massive bank deposits were held in sterling, capable, at a moment's notice, of being switched to other currencies). Balogh predicted that, given this starting point, the application of Bretton Woods would cause either a currency crisis and/or deflation and unemployment in Western Europe.

Today, many people still write as if the Bretton Woods system ran relatively smoothly from 1944 until its demise in 1971, the implicit assumption being that Balogh was proved wrong. Yet the reverse is the case. First, there was the convertibility crisis in the UK in mid-1947; second, there was the Marshall Plan of 1948 for Europe; and third, that this plan had already been preceded by nearly $16 billion of US piecemeal aid in the years 1945–1947. None of these were remotely envisaged by the architects of Bretton Woods. All are vindications of Balogh's predictions.

Balogh's fourth contribution lies in his work on development and international trade. Here he emphasised the importance of agriculture at a time when many countries were paying too much attention to industry. Alongside this, he was a constant advocate of rural education—as well as a critic of those countries which wanted to develop expensive hospitals and universities before they had provided for basic skills or primary health care. Moreover, there is a connection between his ideas on the role of education, training and technology in the process of development and his approach to international trade. Taking it for granted that technical progress would not be random, he saw, far earlier than most, how, if technology could be harnessed and mobilised, this would have positive and cumulatively beneficial effects on a country's share of trade, on investment and on growth.

Together with Paul Streeten, he also produced devastating critiques of the highly influential mathematical growth models, such as the one introduced by Solow (1956). Their joint article, "The Coefficient of Ignorance" (Balogh and Streeten 1963), demonstrates all too clearly how much the extent to which these theoretical articles were fundamentally a cover for how little economists actually knew about the processes of development.

When, in October 1964, Balogh moved into government[9] there was, of course, no sudden disjuncture in his thinking. Both his strengths and his weaknesses were on full display: a brilliant critic, but a dreadful contributor to committee proceedings or Civil Service papers; unmatchable antennae and an

---

[9] De jure he was Economic Adviser to the Cabinet, but, de facto, he was Economic Adviser to the Prime Minister.

extraordinary ability to see to the heart of things, but too impatient and with interests too diverse to bring about lasting change. Just as in his academic work, there was too much activity. He spread his energies far too wide and too thin. In the course of this, he not only exhausted himself, he also reduced his impact. Too many people received too many intemperate notes—and notes that were far from self-explanatory (even when the recipient was sympathetic to the Baloghian point of view).

The truth is that, in his interaction with the Whitehall machine, Balogh was, in many areas, running against the whole grain of thought—'pissing into the wind', as he would have described it. This was especially so where he was demanding ever tighter exchange controls, and the imposition of import rationing. On exchange controls, he made much less progress than he wished and on import controls no impact at all. The government chose an import surcharge instead.

Yet despite all this, the case for regarding Balogh's work during his period within government as being of significance remains impressive. First, there were many policies that can either be directly attributed to him or where he played a significant role. The centrality of incomes policy, the formation of the Department of Economic Affairs, the creation of the Industrial Reorganisation Corporation (the IRC), the emphasis on indicative planning plus the need for changes in the industrial structure, and the frequent attempts to tighten exchange controls, all bear his mark.

Second, there was his anticipation of, and his role in, the gold crisis of March 1968. The UK had devalued in November 1967. What has passed almost unremarked was how close Britain came to a second devaluation just months later. Two factors led in this direction. One was the well-known J-curve effect of devaluation which meant that, in the months immediately following November 1967, the UK current account deficit increased, increasing the loss of reserves. The other, much more significant, was that, with the Vietnam War in full swing, the Americans were also losing reserves as dollar holders switched into gold. Balogh warned Wilson of the dangers as early as January 1968, but the British Treasury seemed unwilling to listen. The situation came to a head in March of that year when the USA threatened to withdraw unilaterally from the London Gold Pool. Balogh saw immediately that, if the threat were to be carried out, the result would be to throw the whole strain onto the UK's tiny gold reserves and so cause a second sterling devaluation. He urged that the only way out was for the UK to counter-threaten the USA. As a result, the UK let the USA know that, if the USA were to withdraw from the Gold Pool, the sterling balances would be blocked—a truly massive disruption of international payments.

As we now know, the eventual outcome was one in which gold was allowed to float on the private markets but remained fixed for official settlements. According to Morris (2007: 150), the Chancellor of the Exchequer at the time, Roy Jenkins, was irked by Balogh's interventions, as were some of the Treasury mandarins. Yet the fact remains that it was Balogh who first warned the Prime Minister of the threat, that it was Balogh who pressed for the contingency planning of severe exchange controls, and that, if no such plans had been prepared, the UK would have had no leverage whatsoever.[10]

A third Balogh contribution, in my judgement substantially his largest, is the role that he played in maximising the benefits to the UK of the discovery in the North Sea, first of gas and then of oil. Balogh's first concern was with the question: 'How much of the North Sea belongs to the UK and how much to Scandinavia?' In 1958, the UN Convention on the Law of the Sea had proposed that the dividing line should be halfway between the relevant shorelines (see UN 1958). However, Balogh discovered that, in the particular case of the North Sea, the shallow shelf that extends from each coast is much wider on the UK side so that the deep trench is much further to the east. On geological grounds, it could therefore have been argued that this trench would have been just as much the "natural" place to draw the line as halfway between the shores. Of course, if this view had been listened to and carried any weight, a much larger proportion of the subsequent discoveries in the North Sea, including the major finds of Ekofisk, Frigg and Statfjord, would have belonged to the UK. However, to his dismay, Balogh discovered that, just before the Labour Government came to power in 1964, the UK had ratified the Convention. For him, this confirmed his worst expectations. As he saw it, it was typical of the amateurish approach of British civil servants that they failed to show any interest in the relevant geological facts, preferring instead a simple layman's view of where to draw the line. That, in reality, he could do nothing about it did not stop Balogh from complaining vociferously.

Blocked on this front, Balogh turned his attention to maximising the benefits to the UK from those discoveries of gas which did lie on the British side of the line. This led him into a second battle. Most of the civil servants dealing with the problem had been imbued with the supposed beauty of the unfettered benefits of the price mechanism and so felt that the market should be left to itself. Balogh, in contrast, saw that, with prevailing gas and oil prices being well above extraction costs, there were potentially huge monopoly

---

[10] This account is based on (a) conversations between the author and Balogh in 1968, (b) Balogh's papers in the Balliol Archives and (c) Hamilton (2008).

profits to be made. His solution was to use the power of British Gas, then publicly owned, as the single purchaser to impose a monopsony price.

This sounds obvious. However, two struggles were required. First, even when the likelihood of large profits had been established, the "conventional wisdom" of the Civil Service still held that using monopsony power in this way was neither needed nor justified. Second, and more difficult, was the question: At what level should the price be set? Balogh's view was that multinational companies would inevitably understate the size of hydrocarbon discoveries and overstate the true cost of extraction.[11] Alongside this was his fear that civil servants would be over-persuaded of the views of the companies, either because, as he saw it, they were amateurs, or, more dangerously, as his stage whisper to me implied, they would be thinking too much about possible lucrative employments once they retired from the Civil Service.

That Balogh's interventions had a major effect is hardly in doubt. In 1966, an agreement was reached for a delivered price of 5 old pence per therm. By 1967, following much tougher negotiations, the price was close to being settled at 3.2 old pence, but Balogh briefed Wilson against this and in 1968 a settlement of only 2.87 old pence was achieved, with resulting savings to the UK of billions of pounds (see Morris 2007: 162).

The third area in which Balogh intervened was with the exploitation of oil in the 1970s. Here, again, he made major contributions, particularly in the face of fresh problems. To start with, there was no monopsony buyer of oil so this route to capturing the monopoly profits for the UK did not exist. Second, the other obvious alternative, taxation, faced a difficulty. In 1973, the Public Accounts Committee (PAC), a select committee of the British House of Commons, uncovered the fact that major oil companies were operating a highly successful tax avoidance scheme. Their accounting arrangements were such that they showed sufficient "apparent" losses on their non-UK operations to more than offset any UK profits. The result was that they hardly ever paid any UK tax (see Public Accounts Committee 1973). How did this come to light? Only because the then Chair of the PAC (Harold Lever, followed by Edmund Dell), plus the special adviser to the PAC, Professor Robert Neild, had received intensive briefing by Balogh and, to a much smaller extent, by me.

In 1974, Balogh, by now a Lord, was made a Minister of State at the Department of Energy and so given the opportunity to tackle the problem directly. His solution was to argue for a special, ring-fenced, petroleum

---

[11] There is no doubt that the difficulties of drilling in the North Sea were exceptional. Nevertheless, someone of sceptical frame of mind might still wonder whether the multiple news reports which appeared at the time, endlessly depicting how horrendous it was, were all driven by the pure snow of factual reporting.

revenue tax (PRT) and the creation of the British National Oil Corporation (BNOC). This latter development was an essential accompaniment to PRT as, without it, the State would have had no direct information on costs. When Wilson resigned in March 1976, Balogh moved to become Deputy Chair of BNOC with the effect that he was able to continue to oversee the direct implementation of the policies he favoured.

Overall, there is no doubt at all that these three interventions—the use of the monopsony power available to British Gas, the introduction of PRT and the creation of BNOC—secured multiple billions of pounds for the UK and they must go down as the area in which Balogh's unique blend of applied theory, intuition, passion, energy, courage, patriotism and practical policy-making ability were best fused.

Nonetheless, Balogh had his weaknesses. There were inconsistencies in his views, he was far too intemperate, much too intolerant of people less clever than him, and he made mistakes. With such trenchant views, this was inevitable. Balogh himself thought that he had been especially wrong in his fear that the USA would revert to unemployment after the Second World War. He also underestimated the speed at which Western Europe would recover. More generally, he prophesied doom far more frequently than proved to be the case. But are prophesies that are confounded by the facts a mistake or a success? A prophesy can be a warning of what to avoid as much as a prediction of the future.

Balogh was also, I believe, always aware of contradictions within himself. What mobilised him above all else was the belief that the world could be made a better place (especially if he had anything to do with it). It was not necessary for people to be ignorant or stupid, nor was it required that the world should be run by knaves and fools, yet his melancholic nature combined with his awareness of the grip of history made him constantly doubt whether a better world could be brought about.

He was also accused by his enemies as well as by some of his friends of being wrong about markets. If this is taken to mean that he did not understand markets, then it is mistaken. When I worked for him in government, I was constantly surprised by the variety of his insights into markets. This was, of course, no more than the Baloghian case-by-case method. For example, he stressed the prevalence and the danger of oligopoly, yet he also noticed the long tail of tiny firms in the machine tool industry and supported measures to rationalise them.

Moreover, once a Baloghian perspective is adopted, it becomes obvious that the joint existence of the IRC and a Monopolies Commission were complementary rather than competitive instruments of economic policy. There were two differing objectives: securing the benefits of economies of scale for lower costs, and securing the passing on of these lower costs to consumers. One needed the IRC, the other the Monopolies Commission.

He was equally aware that in the banking sector the situation was, yet again, different. Here, there was a strong oligopoly with no tail of small potential competitors. As a result, Balogh advocated more competition, but from the public sector in the shape of the Girobank. While in relation to the organisation of research and even more so in the structure of universities, he was passionately in favour of all possible forms of decentralisation of power and was opposed to monopoly of any kind, regarding it as a fundamental threat to new ideas.

If, on the other hand, criticism of Balogh's view of markets is taken to mean that he was too optimistic about how much could be planned and controlled in a non-wartime economy then the criticism is much more warranted. He never really allowed for the complexity that would be involved. No doubt he felt that since he could see what needed to be done, so also could others. Yet, as Paul Streeten has correctly noted, here too there was a contradiction. Balogh denounced administrators in general (and, as we have seen, the British Civil Service in particular) with the same passion that he advocated administrative controls. By the same token, he was too optimistic about the progress that he thought the Soviet Union would continue to make.

One of his best-known works, "The Apotheosis of the Dilettante" (Balogh 1959), is particularly open to this criticism. Indeed, some of those most firmly within mainstream economics might even regard the very title as ironic. Balogh, they could say, was himself a dilettante, always skirmishing on the edges of economics, never offering a new perspective. If this is a claim that Balogh did not know his economics, it is fundamentally wrong. His strength was that he could always see straight through the mathematical flummery to the falsity of the assumptions on which it was based. I vividly recall him accosting me in the early 1970s saying, well before Lucas's work on rational expectations had become at all well known, 'Wot is all zis stuff about rational expectations? It is just perfect information by another name'.

However, while Balogh undoubtedly knew his economics, it remains the case that "The Apotheosis" produced a highly ironic outcome. Partly as a result of his criticism of the amateur nature of the Civil Service, there was an increase in their professional intake and, most particularly, the founding in 1964 of the Government Economic Service, most members of which come from the mainstream in economics with its ever greater reliance on mathematical models. In short, the exact opposite of what Balogh would have wished.

5   Conclusion

Finally, it is worth re-emphasising that, for Thomas Balogh, economics was not, and could never be, a science. No matter how much the power of the econometric microscope might be turned up, it could never discover the laws of human behaviour, because for him there were no such laws. Interesting regularities there might be, constraints there certainly were, but each of these was a product of the habits, history and institutions of the country concerned. Such factors had to be taken into account both because they varied from case to case and because they might change. Economic science was therefore no more than pseudoscience. Political economy was the only proper subject.

If today's heterodox economists wish to take away one thing from Baloghian economics, it is this: What matters above all else is context. Mainstream economists study economis*ing*—which can take as much mathematics as you care to throw at it. Political economists study econom*ies*—and here the maths has to take second place to the complexity of reality.

It is worth recalling at this point Keynes's remark in his obituary of Marshall:

> [T]he amalgam of logic and intuition and the wide knowledge of facts, most of which are not precise, which is required for economic interpretation in its highest form, is, quite truly, overwhelmingly difficult for those whose gift mainly consists in the power to imagine and pursue to their furthest points the implications and prior conditions of comparatively simple facts which are known with a high degree of precision (Keynes 1924: 333, fn. 2).

At a commemoration for Balogh held in the Palace of Westminster in 1985, with three former Prime Ministers in attendance (Wilson, Callaghan and Heath), Lord (Harold) Lever paid tribute to his role above all as 'a devoted public servant' (Lever 1985). Balogh, the scourge of the establishment, would have regarded this as highly ironic, Yet, if we add to this the power of his insights and the flamboyancy (his enemies would say the impossibility) of his character, the verdict is not unfair.

Certainly, Balogh's energies on behalf of his adopted country truly deserve that recognition. But, he was more than a devoted public servant, far more. His multiple contributions make him a political economist extraordinaire. To be blessed with Balogh's intuition is given to very few. To have that intuition, combined with what Streeten (1985a: 19) has called his 'Zivilcourage' (the capacity to speak one's mind when all around are of an opposite opinion), is a gift which should not pass unnoticed in the history of political economy.

References

Main Works by Thomas Balogh

Balogh, T. (1930a). 'The Import of Gold Into France: An Analysis of the Technical Position'. *Economic Journal*, 40(159): 442–460.

Balogh, T. (1930). 'Absorption of Credit by the Stock Exchange'. *American Economic Review*, 20(4): 658–663.

Balogh, T. (1938). 'The National Economy of Germany'. *Economic Journal*, 48(191): 461–497.

Balogh, T. (1939). 'The Economic Background in Germany'. *International Affairs (Royal Institute of International Affairs)*, 18(2): 227–248.

Balogh, T. (1940). 'Foreign Exchange and Export Trade Policy'. *Economic Journal*, 50(197): 1–26.

Balogh, T. (1940). 'The Drift Towards a Rational Foreign Exchange Policy'. *Economica*, New Series, 7(27): 248–279.

Balogh, T. (1941). 'The First Necessity in the New Britain: Work for All'. *Picture Post*, 4 January: 10–13.

Balogh, T. (1944). 'The International Aspects of Full Employment'. Chapter V in F.A. Burchardt et al. *The Economics of Full Employment*. Oxford: Basil Blackwell and the Oxford University Institute of Statistics: Oxford. 126–180.

Balogh, T. (1945). 'Some Theoretical Problems of Post-War Foreign Investment Policy'. *Oxford Economic Papers*, 7(March): 93–110.

Balogh, T. (1945). 'The Planning and Control of Investment'. *Bulletin of the Oxford University Institute of Economics and Statistics*, 7(14): 244–251.

Balogh, T. (1946). 'The United States and the World Economy'. *Bulletin of the Oxford University Institute of Economics and Statistics*, 8(10): 309–322.

Balogh, T. (1946–1947). 'A New View of the Economics of International Readjustment'. *Review of Economic Studies*, 14(2): 82–94.

Balogh, T. (1947). 'Note on the Deliberate Industrialisation for Higher Incomes'. *Economic Journal*, 57(226): 238–241.

Balogh, T. (1947). 'The Problem of the British Balance of Payments'. *Bulletin of the Oxford University Institute of Economics and Statistics*, 9(7): 211–227.

Balogh, T. (1947). *Studies in Financial Organization*. Cambridge: Cambridge University Press.

Balogh, T. (1948). 'Britain's Foreign Trade Problem: A Comment'. *Economic Journal*, 58(229): 74–85.

Balogh, T. (1948). 'Exchange Depreciation and Economic Readjustment'. *Review of Economics and Statistics*, 30(4): 276–285.

Balogh, T. (1949). *The Dollar Crisis: Causes and Cure; a Report to the Fabian Society*. Oxford: Blackwell.

Balogh, T. (1950). 'Problems of Western Unification'. *Bulletin of the Oxford University Institute of Economics and Statistics*, 12(10): 299–314.

Balogh, T. (1954). 'The Dollar Crisis Revisited'. *Oxford Economic Papers*, New Series, 6(3): 243–284.

Balogh, T. (1955). 'Factor Intensities of American Foreign Trade and Technical Progress'. *Review of Economics and Statistics*, 37(4): 425–427.

Balogh, T. (1957). 'Productive Investment and the Balance of Payments: The British Case'. *Review of Economic and Statistics*, 39(1): 84–88.

Balogh, T. (1958). 'Productivity and Inflation'. *Oxford Economic Papers*, New Series, 10(2): 220–245.

Balogh, T. (1959). 'The Apotheosis of the Dilettante'. In H. Thomas (ed.) *The Establishment*. London: New English Library: 81–126.

Balogh, T. (1960). 'International Reserves and Liquidity'. *Economic Journal*, 70(278): 357–377.

Balogh, T. (1961). 'Agricultural and Economic Development: Linked Public Works'. *Oxford Economic Papers*, New Series, 13(1): 27–42.

Balogh, T. (1962). 'Equity and Efficiency: The Problem of Optimal Investment in a Framework of Underdevelopment'. *Oxford Economic Papers*, New Series, 14(1): 25–35.

Balogh, T. (1962). 'Misconceived Educational Programmes in Africa'. *Higher Education Quarterly*, 16(3): 243–249.

Balogh, T. (1962). 'The Mechanism of Neo-Imperialism: The Economic Impact of Monetary and Commercial Institutions in Africa'. *Bulletin of the Oxford University Institute of Economics and Statistics*, 24(3): 331–362.

Balogh, T. (1963a). *Unequal Partners. Volume One*. Oxford: Blackwell.

Balogh, T. (1963b). *Unequal Partners. Volume Two*. Oxford: Blackwell.

Balogh, T. (1963c). *Planning for Progress: A Strategy for Labour*. London: Fabian Society.

Balogh, T. (1964). *The Economic Impact of Monetary and Commercial Institutions of a European Origin in Africa*. Cairo: National Bank of Egypt.

Balogh, T. (1964). 'A Note on the Wealth Tax'. *Economic Journal*, 74(293): 221–224.

Balogh, T. (1964). 'Education and Economic Growth'. *Kyklos*, 17(2): 261–274.

Balogh, T. (1966). '*Planning for Progress*'. *Economica*, New Series, 33(132): 499.

Balogh, T. (1967). 'Multilateral v. Bilateral Aid'. *Oxford Economic Papers*, New Series, 19(3): 328–344.

Balogh, T. (1970). 'Old Fallacies and New Remedies: The SDRs in Perspective'. *Bulletin of the Oxford University Institute of Economics and Statistics*, 32(2): 81–98.

Balogh, T. (1970). *Labour and Inflation*. London: Fabian Society.

Balogh, T. (1973). *Facts and Fancy in International Economic Relations*. Oxford: Pergamon.

Balogh, T. (1974). *The Economics of Poverty*. Second edition. London: Weidenfeld & Nicolson.

Balogh, T. (1977). 'Monetarism and the Threat of a World Financial Crisis'. *Challenge*, 20(2): 40–47.

Balogh, T. (1978). 'Failures in the Strategy Against Poverty'. *World Development*, 6(1): 11–22.

Balogh, T. (1978). 'Monetarism and the Oil Price Crisis'. *Journal of Post Keynesian Economics*, 1(2): 27–46.

Balogh, T. (1982). *The Irrelevance of Conventional Economics*. London: Weidenfeld & Nicolson.

Balogh, T. and A. Graham (1979). 'The Transfer Problem Revisited: Analogies Between the Reparations Payments of the 1920s and the Problems of the OPEC Surpluses'. *Oxford Bulletin of Economics and Statistics*, 41(3): 183–191.

Balogh, T. and P. Streeten (1950). 'The Inappropriateness of Simple "Elasticity" Concepts in the Analysis of International Trade'. *PSL Quarterly Review*, 3(15): 239–248.

Balogh, T. and P. Streeten (1960). 'Domestic Versus Foreign Investment'. *Bulletin of the Oxford University Institute of Economics and Statistics*, 22(3): 213–224.

Balogh, T. and P. Streeten (1963). 'The Coefficient of Ignorance'. *Bulletin of the Oxford University Institute of Economics and Statistics*, 25(2): 99–107.

Balogh, T. and P. Streeten (1968). 'The Planning of Education in Poor Countries'. Chapter 18 in M. Blaug (ed.) *Economics of Education 1: Selected Readings*. Harmondsworth: Penguin: 383–395.

Streeten, P. and T. Balogh (1957). 'The Monetary and Credit System: A Reconsideration of Monetary Policy'. *Bulletin of the Oxford University Institute of Economics and Statistics*, 19(4): 331–339.

Other Works Referred To

Crosland, C.A.R. (1956). *The Future of Socialism*. London: Jonathan Cape.

Hamilton, A. (2008). 'Beyond the Sterling Devaluation: The Gold Crisis of March 1968'. *Contemporary European History*, 17(1): 73–95.

Keynes, J.M. (1924). 'Alfred Marshall, 1842–1924'. *Economic Journal*, 34(135): 311–372. Reprinted as Chapter 14 in *Essays in Biography* (1972). Volume X of *The Collected Writings of John Maynard Keynes*. London: Macmillan: 161–231.

Lever, H. (1985). 'Memorial for Lord Balogh'. House of Lords.

Morris, J. (2007). *The Life and Times of Thomas Balogh: A Macaw Among Mandarins*. Eastbourne: Sussex Academic Press.

Public Accounts Committee (1973). *North Sea Oil and Gas: First Report from the Committee of Public Accounts Session 1972/1973*. London: HMSO.

Solow, R.M. (1956). 'A Contribution to the Theory of Economic Growth'. *Quarterly Journal of Economics*, 70(1): 65–94.

Streeten, P. (1985a). 'Speech at Memorial for Thomas Balogh at Balliol'. *Balliol College Annual Record, 1985*. Oxford: Oxford University Press: 17–19.

Streeten, P. (2000). 'Thomas BALOGH'. In P. Arestis and M. Sawyer (ed.) *A Biographical Dictionary of Dissenting Economists*. Second edition. Cheltenham: Edward Elgar: 28–35.

Stretton, H. (1986). 'Paul Streeten: An Appreciation'. Chapter 1 in S. Lall and F. Stewart (eds) *Theory and Reality in Development: Essays in Honour of Paul Streeten*. London: Palgrave: 1–27.

UN (1958). *Report of the First United Nations Conference on the Law of the Sea*. Cmnd. 584. London: HMSO.

Wittgenstein, L. (1958). *The Blue and Brown Books*. New York: Harper & Row.

Books and Articles about Thomas Balogh

Csikós-Nagy, B. (1985). 'Lord Thomas Balogh, 1905–1985'. *Acta Oeconomica*, 35(1/2): 213–215.

Davis, J. (2007). *Prime Ministers and Whitehall 1960–74*. London: Hambledon Continuum: 1, 7–8.

Evans, M. and D. Morgan (2002). *The Battle for Britain: Citizenship and Ideology in the Second World War*. London: Routledge: 77, 110.

George, C. and S. Bewlay (1964). *Advice and Dissent: Two Men of Influence – A New Look at Professor Kaldor and Professor Balogh*. London: Aims of Industry.

Graham, A. (1992). 'Thomas Balogh (1905–85)'. *Contemporary Record*, 6(1): 194–207.

Kaldor, N. (1985). 'Memorial for Lord Balogh'. House of Lords.

Kandiah, M.D. and A. Seldon (eds) (2013). *Ideas and Think Tanks in Contemporary Britain*. Volume 1. London: Routledge: 153–154.

Morris, J. (1998). 'Thomas Balogh and the Fight for North Sea Revenue'. *Contemporary British History*, 12(2): 105–129.

Simon, Á. (2012). 'Intellectual Migration and Economic Thought: Central European Émigré Economists and the History of Modern Economics'. *History of European Ideas*, 38(3): 467–482.

Streeten, P. (ed.) (1970). *Unfashionable Economics: Essays in Honour of Lord Balogh*. London: Weidenfeld & Nicolson.

Streeten, P. (1985). 'In Memory of Thomas Balogh'. *World Development*, 13(4): 465–466.

16

Colin Clark (1905–1989)

Alex Millmow

1   Introduction

It may surprise some that the Anglo-Australian economist, Colin Clark, could be regarded as an Oxford economist. He is barely mentioned, for instance, in Warren Young and Fred Lee's anthology *Oxford Economics and Oxford Economists* (1993). However, his university education, including an exposure to statistics and economics, was forged at Oxford as well as an introduction to socialism and Labour politics. In mid-career, Clark was appointed as Director of Oxford's Agricultural Economics Research Institute (AERI), a post he held from 1953 to 1969. That position allowed him to become a Fellow of his old college, Brasenose. Appropriately, on the 100th anniversary of his birth, Brasenose hosted a colloquium in 1905 celebrating Clark's life and contributions. In his presentation, David Hendry hailed Clark as an 'Oxford-trained economist whose Herculean data collection remain unparalleled to the modern day'.[1]

It will come as less of a surprise to many that Clark was a world figure in the economics discipline over two distinct periods, first in the 1930s for his

---

[1] Colloquium held to celebrate the 100th anniversary of Clark's birth, Brasenose College, Oxford, 2 November 2005 (mimeo).

A. Millmow (✉)
Federation Business School, Mt Helen, VIC, Australia
e-mail: a.millmow@federation.edu.au

371

work on national income accounting. The Australian economist, Duncan Ironmonger, rightly hailed Clark as 'the father of the national accounts' because he was the first to measure national product, growth and distribution.[2] That milestone was quickly followed by another major undertaking looking at international comparisons of national income and finding that most of the world was desperately poor and that "the age of plenty" would be a long time in coming. These pioneering efforts led one newspaper to deem Clark 'a kind of one-man central statistical office for the world' (*The Daily Telegraph* 1989: 21).

During his time at the Institute, Clark walked again into the international spotlight for his work on development economics, particularly his controversial thesis that rapid population growth was a positive factor for economic prosperity. Being in the limelight was part of Clark's nature as an economist, either in writing for the popular press or, indeed, making headlines himself. His work had already made, for instance, the front page of *The New York Times* in 1949 disproving claims that the Soviet Union was outpacing the West in terms of economic performance. In fact, American productivity was eight-and-a-half times greater than the Soviet rate (Clark 1949a). He again figured prominently in the American press when he warned that the US economy was in danger of falling headlong into recession in 1954. Clark (1949b) had an econometric model of the American business cycle to fortify his projections. His facility with statistics and their interpretation led to him becoming one of the founding fathers of econometrics, yet he is barely mentioned in anthologies on the history of economic thought.

While Clark spent 16 years as the Director of the AERI, he was strangely detached from the Department of Economics at Oxford. Indeed, he found it to be 'intellectually stultifying'.[3] At the time, Oxford economics was dominated by a left-wing Keynesian clique that encompassed demand management, redistribution of income and wealth, nationalisation, and microeconomic intervention (see Young and Lee 1993: 204). Few Oxford economists had interest in the 'data-grubbing' efforts of Clark.[4] However, Clark rubbed shoulders with the likes of Roy Harrod, I.M.D. Little and J.R. Hicks; he sparred intellectually with Thomas Balogh over British economic policy and with Peter Wiles over Soviet economics. Incidentally, it was Hicks who was instrumental in alerting the relevant Oxford authorities to Clark's availability to

---

[2] "Colin Grant Clark 1905–1989", Colin Clark Papers, Brasenose College, Oxford University (CCP, BC, UO hereafter).

[3] This is what Clark told his son, David Clark, who, in turn, relayed it to the author.

[4] As Hendry described Clark's approach to his work at the Colloquium on Clark at Brasenose.

head up the AERI. When that appointment was announced it was likened by the Cambridge agricultural economist, Ruth Cohen, to 'dropping a land mine on a quiet back street' (Cohen quoted in Healey and McFarlane 1979: 20). It was not just because Clark was not renowned as an agricultural economist, but because he had a reputation as a rational antagonist, someone who loved to be outspoken. That said, even he agreed that it was an odd appointment since his research speciality was, in fact, long-run economic change (see Peters 2001: 9–10). However, Clark was underselling himself. At Cambridge, he had written a few pieces on British agricultural policy but, more importantly, in 1935 he had presented a paper at the British Association for the Advancement of Science where he argued that the world's food supply had caught up and overtaken the world's population to the extent that relative food prices were now falling. The paper had opened with the line 'Was Malthus wrong?' and went on to demonstrate Clark's early suspicion about the validity of Malthusianism but also portended a future research interest about the true extent of world hunger.

2   Beginnings

Born in London in 1905, Colin was the first of four children of James and Marion Clark. His father had been a Scottish-born merchant adventurer who had spent 20 years abroad, mostly in Australia, and was involved in the meat export trade. James Clark made and lost three fortunes in his lifetime; here was an early exposure for Colin of the capriciousness of the business cycle. He would later say that you could not understand economics unless you understood the nature of business. Inordinately bright, Colin won a scholarship to Winchester and went up to Oxford to study chemistry. He gained Second Class Honours which suggested that his mind was focused elsewhere. Clark had, in fact, began auditing economics lectures and reading economic tracts. According to Lionel Robbins, a young economics tutor at New College, Clark had quickly become 'disillusioned' with chemistry. He recalled how Clark would turn up to the Adam Smith Society 'with large sheaves of statistical material, worked up in his spare time, to illuminate and bring down to earth the theoretical discussions of his fellow members' (Robbins 1971: 119).

Clark's interest in economics had been sparked by his strong political beliefs and early embrace of Fabian socialism and the Labour Party. It was G.D.H. Cole who introduced him to the world of guild socialism. Clark featured in debates at the Oxford Union during 1927 and 1928 and was described by one colleague, John Parker (1982: 16), as 'one of the most original and striking

Labour Club personalities'. He used his facility at handling statistical data to buttress his arguments. Auspiciously, his first publication, "A Graphical Analysis of the Unemployment Position, 1920–1928" (Clark 1929), merited the Royal Statistical Society's Frances Wood Memorial Prize in 1928. He later described it as a rather 'laborious compilation' of monthly movements in unemployment statistics (Clark to Arndt, 4 September 1978, Heinz Arndt Papers, National Library of Australia). For the moment, a political career beckoned; Clark ran as a Labour Party candidate in three general elections. All met with failure with Clark realising that he did not have 'the right personality' for politics. He realised that he was at heart 'a scientist. Whereas politicians have to deal with action. It is a fundamental distinction' (Clark in Higgins 1989: 297). Clark would become instead a backroom boy, working on Labour policy and those bodies associated with the party.

After Robbins, another academic mentor was Allyn Young of Harvard who had a visiting post at the London School of Economics (LSE). For a few months, Clark worked as his research assistant. He combined this with helping William Beveridge, Director of LSE undertake a "Survey of London Life and Labour", focusing on the urban poor. Under Young, Clark was tasked with finding empirical proof of this hypothesis using American manufacturing statistics. However, his research came up empty-handed (Clark to Blitch, 7 December 1972, Colin Clark Papers, Fryer Library, University of Queensland (CCP, FL, UQ hereafter)). In his Inaugural Lecture at LSE, Young had spoken of how, 'Economic theory, divorced from its functional relations to economic problems, or with those relations obscured, is no better than an interesting intellectual game … But it cannot advance knowledge, for it leads up a blind alley' (Young 1928: 4–5) and of how economics would have to 'make room for new conceptions and new sorts of abstractions if it is to make effective use of the new facts which the statisticians are uncovering' (ibid.: 10).

Clark left LSE in 1929 to take up an appointment as a research assistant with the distinguished sociologist and demographer, Alexander Carr-Saunders, the Charles Booth Professor of Social Science at the University of Liverpool. This meant doing similar work to that which he had undertaken in London, in this case looking at living conditions of people in the slums of Liverpool. The fieldwork opened Clark's eyes to urban squalor and set his mind upon improving urban life. It also exposed him to Carr-Saunders' work on sociology and demographics. This social survey work on Merseyside would culminate much later in a research paper which found that urban population density fell by a negative exponential the greater the distance from the city centre (see Clark 1951a). The work on the urban poor also gave Clark an interest in national income, particularly the distribution between wages and other incomes.

3   The Economic Advisory Council and Keynes

Two of Clark's mentors, G.D.H. Cole and Hugh Dalton, recommended him to work as a secretary to the Economic Advisory Council, which was created in 1930 and reported to the Cabinet on economic matters. It served as an illuminating and unforgettable entrée into the world of economic policy-making. Clark, just 24, described the Council as 'a weird and wonderful organisation indeed' (Clark quoted in Castles 2014: 276), but was dismissive of its overall worth. However, the position allowed Clark to specialise in economic statistics. His first foray was to find that industrial product per man had increased during the 1920s, a discovery which none of the economists on the Council believed other than Keynes. He then turned his attention to estimating national income with a first contribution appearing in the *Economic Journal*. However, Clark's tenure on the Council came to an abrupt end when he felt it proper to resign when approached by Prime Minister Ramsay MacDonald who quixotically proposed that the two of them spend a long weekend at Chequers preparing a document which would rewrite economic theory and justify the case for protection.

Recognising his promise, Keynes stepped in and arranged for Clark to become a Lecturer in Economic Statistics at Cambridge. This appointment would fortify Clark's standing as an applied economist. While he was not part of the Cambridge "Circus", Clark had 'frequent conversations' with Keynes and saw how he was moving from *A Treatise on Money* to *The General Theory* (Clark 1983: 37). Clark summed up the process this way:

> In the *Treatise* the real issue was the difference between savings and investment and after 1930 it was just the opposite—to prove that savings were brought down to the level of investment. It took Keynes a long time and much effort to make that change. I was able to watch his mind at work while it was going on; this was between 1930 and 1932 (Clark in Higgins 1989: 298).

Despite the age difference, Keynes and Clark got on splendidly with the former encouraging Daniel Macmillan to publish Clark's first manuscript, *The National Income, 1924–31*. He told Macmillan in December 1931 that:

Clark's work, on this and other allied subjects, is quite outstanding, and that he is likely to become the recognised authority, in the course of time … Clark is, I think, a bit of a genius—almost the only economic statistician I have ever met who seems to me quite first class (Keynes to Macmillan, 2 December 1931, in Keynes 1979: 57, fn. 11).

When Keynes 'carefully' read the book, he told Clark:

I think it is *excellent*. An enormous step forward. I hope it is selling all right … You have quite convinced me that *gross* output, gross investment, gross savings, etc. is the natural way to work and not the net, and I have been re-writing my definitions and equations on these lines. I am sure it is an improvement (Keynes to Clark, 2 January 1933, in ibid.: 58; italics in original).

Clark replied: 'Dear Maynard, this is really rather fascinating. It certainly beats physics' (Clark to Keynes, 16 January 1933, in ibid.: 59).

Others shared in the enthusiasm. Henry Phelps Brown described *The National Income, 1924–31* as 'brave' and 'remarkable' (Phelps Brown 1933: 416). G.D.H. Cole praised the book, especially the last section, where Clark attempted 'to make the Keynes's formulae flesh and blood' (Cole to Clark, c.1932, CCP, BC, UO). In this respect, Philip Sargant Florence said Clark's empirics would be a proud achievement for the Cambridge School of Economics if it gave Keynes's theory added force (see Florence 1932: 114).

As noted, Clark used empirical data to support the Keynesian identities like saving and investment, aggregate costs of production compared with the general price level of output and even attempted an estimation of the multiplier. In his exposition, Clark showed that in 1931 the level of saving in the UK vastly exceeded the level of investment with the imbalance due to the depression and the preference of the saving classes to leave these balances idle. This under-investment begged for an increase in public spending to put these productive resources to work.

While most economists welcomed Clark's book on national income, it met with a hostile reception from those associated with the Royal Statistical Society and two economic statisticians, Arthur Bowley and Josiah Stamp, who had earlier attempted to estimate national income. Moreover, economic officialdom at the Treasury felt that Clark's estimates were unreliable. In the preface to his book, Clark complained about 'the disgraceful condition of British official statistics' (Clark 1932: vi) and the fact that he had been denied any funding assistance in his sole quest to determine the level of national income. Without such assistance, economics could not become a true science. He would repeat this complaint when he totally revised his book in 1937 with a new title, *National Income and Outlay* (Clark 1937a). Again, economists hailed its arrival but it failed to gain traction within policy-making circles. Clark bemoaned that he was still the only British scholar working in the field of national income measurement. However, if he was disappointed by the reception of his latest book, as suggested by Lepenies (2016: 34), Clark did not show it. On a related note, Patinkin (1976: 1113) has argued that despite his effusive praise for Clark, Keynes had 'reservations' about Clark's aggregate estimates and did not use any of his estimates of national income nor of the multiplier in *The General Theory*. Nevertheless, Markwell (2000: 41–42) pours doubt on Patinkin's view, arguing that Keynes had a great deal of respect for Clark, publicly complimenting him again in *How to Pay for the War* (Keynes 1940 [1972]: 381) for 'his brilliant private efforts'. Moreover, Keynes told Stamp that Clark 'deserved the V.C. for statistical courage' (Keynes quoted in Patinkin 1976: 1113).

For his part, Clark always regarded Keynes with almost filial devotion and wrote a moving tribute when Keynes died (see Clark 1947). To his dying days, Clark (1984: 80) would always profess that he 'knew Keynes well' and sought to uphold what he considered were the true interpretation of his doctrines. What particularly astounded Clark, who had become a neonatalist in the 1930s, was how Keynes in his 1937 Galton Lecture shrugged off his neo-Malthusian stance and now argued that population growth was necessary to underpin investment and consumption demand. The other version of Keynes which Clark liked to uphold was the fiscal conservative, as well as his lament about 'modernist stuff, gone wrong and turned sour and silly' and that the classical medicine still had a role to play once near full employment was reached (Keynes 1946: 186).

Meanwhile, Clark was part of an ensemble of Oxford economists who contributed a chapter to a volume edited by Cole entitled *What Everybody Wants to Know About Money*. In an avowedly Keynesian account, Clark (1933) argued the case for public works on slum clearance and a forward wage policy to underpin a monetary recovery. Interestingly, he argued that a deficit budget might have a harmful impact on business confidence. Robert Dimand (1988: 79) has argued that, of all those who had contributed to the volume, it was Clark who demonstrated an acute awareness of the income expenditure multiplier, though he gave no quantitative estimate of its power.

In five contributions that appeared in the *Economic Journal* over the period 1931–1937 Clark presented first, quarterly estimates of national income, and also estimations of the multiplier. In his 1937 article, he used an economic model to forecast the business future (see Clark 1937b). He predicted that

Britain was heading for an economic slump because investment spending had reached a peak by the end of 1936. Clark wrote about how the 'incentive to invest' (ibid.: 312) was governed by expectations of profit. In his model, he argued that a slump was likely in Britain unless the government took action with extra public spending.

Finally, within the Labour movement, Clark, together with Evan Durbin, Hugh Gaitskell and Douglas Jay, became members of a committee in June 1936 which laid down the intellectual foundations for Labour's socialist platform using Keynes's new theory. They emphasised especially the link between investment and employment in Labour's redesigned spending programmes to assist the unemployed (see Durbin 1985: 251). However, their policy recommendations were quite conservative and Clark compiled a statistical appendix to the report identifying a continuing high rate of structural and frictional unemployment. On this point, Clark agreed with Keynes's view that one could not press too much to achieve full employment and that a 'rightly distributed demand than of a greater aggregate demand' (Keynes 1982: 385) was appropriate as Britain recovered from the slump.

4   Australia

Offered the opportunity in 1937 to be a Visiting Lecturer for two terms at the University of Melbourne, Clark jumped at the chance. It would allow him to see where his father had first made his fortune. Clark had gone out to Australia on sabbatical and was expected to return to Cambridge in October 1938. Australia, however, got in the way; Clark became enchanted by the great southern land. The presence of a world-famous economist there attracted keen interest. Inevitably, he was soon offered a highly paid job within the Queensland Civil Service as State Statistician, Financial Adviser to the Treasury and Director of the Bureau of Industry. It was, he told Keynes, 'too remarkable an opportunity for putting economics into practice … I believe you yourself would have thought twice before rejecting an opportunity like that for putting some of your conclusions into practice' (Keynes 1983: 801). Taking the position meant turning his back on Britain, although Clark never expressed misgivings about the career switch. He had always fancied himself an economic scientist, not a theorist, 'content steadily to lay stone on stone in building the structure of ordered knowledge' (Clark 1940: viii). In any case, the purpose of economics is to improve the lot of mankind. Another reason why Clark plumped for Australia was because, as Hugh Dalton had rather pointedly reminded told him 'Cambridge…treated you like a helot' (Dalton to Clark, 19 March 1938, CCP, BC, UO) and that Keynes 'should have wangled you a Fellowship and not merely treated you as a statistical convenience' (Dalton to Clark, 28 January 1938, CCP, BC, UO). In Cambridge, news of Clark's defection was a 'bombshell' with 'realistic research' dealt 'a severe blow' (Robertson to Clark, 26 June 1938, CCP, FL, UQ). Clark continued to explain to Keynes the reasons for the switch; Queensland was a socialist state and apart from the weather, salary and lifestyle, Clark had a young family to care for. Nor were his official duties there as burdensome as they sounded. Indeed, his time in Brisbane would see a remarkable profusion of high-powered research flowing from his pen.

Meanwhile, the economic performance of the Soviet Union had been a source of fascination for socialists everywhere and Clark, who was vehemently anti-communist, was no exception. He had looked over Soviet economic statistics on the long voyage out to Australia after reading Michael Polanyi's (1935) article on the subject. Clark finished a long journal article and sent it to Keynes for comment. Keynes replied that was Clark's 'best effort so far in making bricks without straw' but cautioned that 'some of your orders of magnitude might not turn out right', given the secrecy of the Soviet state. Keynes added that, 'There must necessarily always remain a considerable doubt about the accuracy of the data' (Keynes to Clark, 23 July 1938, CCP, FL, UQ). It was published by Macmillan as a slim volume entitled *A Critique of Russian Statistics* (Clark 1939).

His second major undertaking during this period was *The Conditions of Economic Progress* (Clark 1940). The title was a derivative of Alfred Marshall's intended volume, *Progress: Its Economic Conditions*. In terms of personal effort and ingenuity, this was Clark's most definitive work. There were to be three editions, each completely revised. Phyllis Deane (1958: 371) said that the later versions were 'Essentially…the same book … [T]he framework of the first edition [had been] expanded by the addition of the miscellaneous ideas, notes and tables [needed to keep] the original results up to date'.

The book opened up a whole new vista of applied economics about the determinants of growth and material progress and why there were differing rates of growth for the thirty economies under Clark's microscope. He described it as 'a comparative study of the investigations which have been made in all the principal countries into national income, and economic factors bearing upon national income' (Clark 1940: vii). Paul Douglas (1941: 444) acknowledged its epic sweep, describing it as 'a tour-de-force of statistical economics'. Lionel Robbins considered it one of the 'great books of this century' (Clark to Marjorie Clark, 20 November 1947, Clark family letters) while John Hicks (1951: 3) described it as 'the most ambitious book on economics that had ever been written' in the sense that it took the world and all history as its province.

In the preface, Clark spelt out how he approached economics while also attacking the antics of his English counterparts. He felt that their preference for the theoretical rather than the scientific approach to economics was futile: 'It would be laughable, were it not tragic, to watch the stream of books and articles, attempting to solve the exceptionally complex problems of present-day economics by theoretical arguments, often without a single reference to the observed facts of the situation' (Clark 1940: viii). For Clark, economic research could only be done by 'the careful systemisation of all observable facts, the framing of hypotheses from these facts, prediction of fresh conclusions on the basis of these hypotheses, and the testing of these conclusions against further observable facts' (ibid.: vii–viii). These controversial passages were deleted from later editions because of the impetus in economics research towards empiricism. This had been triggered by the Second World War but also by the gathering realisation that the post-war challenge for economists was to address long-run problems of production, accumulation and growth (see Clark: 1951b: vii).

Clark wanted to demonstrate the long-term conditions necessary for a country to achieve material progress, which he equated with an improvement in economic welfare. Technically, the main achievement of *The Conditions of Economic Progress* was to compute the relative value of money in different countries or, more strictly, to establish the comparative real income per capita in thirty countries in terms of an artificial currency unit of constant purchasing power. As such, Clark was the first economist to present comparable estimates of real income across countries. He also used real income per head as a form of differentiation. This allowed Heinz Arndt (1979: 122) to compliment him for presenting convincing statistical evidence that revealed a 'gap' between rich and poor countries. Indeed, Clark discovered astonishing differences between levels of real income, revealing that the world was still 'a wretchedly poor place' (Clark 1940: 2), with the living standards of most of the planet's population inadequate; only a few industrialised countries—America, Britain, Germany, France and Germany—produced the bulk of global output. Most of the world's economies were underdeveloped, meaning that, even if all productive resources were employed, there would still be widespread poverty. He conceded, too, that overpopulation in a poor agricultural country could be quite 'disadvantageous' (ibid.: 6).

For Clark, the major cause of global poverty was a lack of capital expended on machinery, knowledge and skills and accessing natural resources (see Plimsoll 1941: 108). The wider ambit given to capital showed that Clark was reassessing its role in economic growth. Looking at what he called "The Morphology of Economic Growth" (Clark 1940: Chapter 10), Clark confirmed Sir William Petty's generalisation that, with economic progress, agriculture showed a relative decline in employment and national output as manufacturing grew more quickly. Eventually, manufacturing would be supplanted by the rise of the services sector. This evolving sectoral balance reflected the degree of development and maturity of an economy. The reallocation of the factors of production within the economy related to the interplay of both price and income elasticities for the products of all three sectors, together with the respective labour productivity for each sector. No doubt inspired by his earlier work with Allyn Young, Clark also found that large-scale production plants did not increase output per head; this was determined more by the relative rate of growth of the industry as a whole. In short, there was no tendency towards an optimum size of plant; in fact, increasing returns to scale could well be associated with a declining average size of the plant. Young spoke more of the cost savings to be made by the 'increasing specialisation and subdivision of processes' (Arndt 1992: 120). While big economies could prosper from this, so too could smaller economies which engaged in international trade by specialising in a number of manufactures or services.

Despite its grand ambition and leap into a new form of economic analysis, *The Conditions of Economic Progress* was something of a disappointment when it came to presentation, analytical punch and reasoning (see Maddison 2004). Reviewers fretted at its disorderly and fragmented nature, a paucity of headings, the maze of tables, and with the lack of an index and bibliography. While applauding it as a pioneering effort, Erwin Rothbarth (1941: 120) found Clark's book 'annoying' in its presentation, ambition and a 'certain vagueness as to its purpose' (ibid.)—whether it was a handbook of national income statistics or a treatise on the nature of economic progress.

Clark's third major undertaking during this period, *The Economics of 1960* (Clark 1942), again saw him taking the world as his oyster. More formally, his intention was to project how economic affairs may look by 1960. It would cover 'the most probable course of world populations, industrial development, prices, capital movements and interest rates' (ibid.: ix). For his part, Jan Tinbergen hailed it as a 'milestone in the development of econometrics' (Tinbergen to Clark, 15 January 1947, CCP, FL, UQ).

Clark predicted that, after the war, the terms of trade would turn in favour of primary producing countries. This argument went against some of the findings in *The Conditions of Economic Progress*. Clark's new prophecy was predicated on the belief that there would be an increased supply of manufactures on world markets as the old industrialised economies rebuilt their economies.

At the same time, Clark foreshadowed the industrialisation of countries such as China, Japan and India which would starve their rural sectors of capital and labour. This would amplify the oversupply of manufactures and, at the same time, exacerbate the shortage of primary products.

The other argument underlying Clark's findings was his view that the immediate post-war years would be a period of capital hunger. The capital accumulation by developed and developing economies alike meant that most nations would enjoy sustained full employment during the post-war period. Put another way, Clark was arguing that economic progress advances in long-run cycles rather than being interrupted by trade cycles and political and social upheavals. This was a heartening prognosis: there would be no secular stagnation, but rather a period of economic optimism with abundant capital and trade flows. This expansion was based on Clark adopting Kondratieff's theory of cycles. He adorned it with movements in investment, population, trade and the terms of trade. Clark posited that there were cycles of over-investment and under-investment, each spanning around 25 years, resulting in alternating periods of capital hunger and capital satiation. The post-war global economy was set for a period of reconstruction especially after the destruction caused by conflict. There would be a resumption of trade and investment accompanied by a big shift towards manufacturing as labour flowed to secondary and tertiary sectors. However, Clark was criticised for his grand long-run supply-side vision, along with his faith in economic determinism; there was no room in his analysis for the trade cycle or for macroeconomic policy (see Rosenstein-Rodan 1942: 544).

Notwithstanding criticism of his work, Clark was made a Fellow of the Econometric Society in 1944 in recognition of his pioneering statistical and empirical research. The year after, he contributed an article to *Econometrica* on the ideal size of cities (see Clark 1945a), a subject that had intrigued him since working with Carr-Saunders. Clark argued that the principal function of a city was the provision of the full range of services, including commercial, educational and cultural facilities as well as sheltered manufacturing such as food processing and construction materials, all of which are dependent upon an effective transport system. He then went on to claim that, on commercial criteria, a city need be no larger than 150,000 residents and certainly not any larger than 200,000, if car ownership was considered. Clark had found that municipal costs rose quickly once population approached big city levels. He informed Keynes of this 'drastic conclusion' about the ideal size of a city, arguing that this could justify spending 'a lot of money on redistributing the population to smaller towns'. However, he continued that 'the planners seem intent upon re-building the big cities in all their glory' (Clark to Keynes, 10

January 1945, Royal Economic Society Papers, LSE (RESP, LSE hereafter)). Clark had always held an antipathy towards urban conurbations given his attraction to distributism. As a distributionist, he favoured the decentralisation in all things, including industry, population and even political power. It was a philosophy that would continue to infuse his social and economic outlook.

Consistent with this philosophy against bureaucratism and concentrations of political power was an article that appeared in the *Economic Journal* in 1945. Entitled "Public Finance and Change in the Value of Money", Clark (1945b) argued that there was a natural tax threshold of 25% of national income and that attempts to tax beyond that would result in inflation. If the State tried to extract more than this, an inflationary process would be triggered which made the whole exercise self-defeating. Keynes had alluded to this tendency in the 1920s when talking about the depreciation of the French franc (see Harrod 1951: 374). It was a Queensland Premier who sparked the idea in Clark's mind about how mooted post-war expenditures on welfare meant unprecedented tax burdens in the future. Later, Clark furnished a proof in the form of a letter, with Keynes supporting his line of thinking, saying how he was strongly 'disposed to agree (that) 25 per cent taxation is about the limit of what is easily borne' (Keynes to Clark, 9 March 1945, RESP, LSE).

5   Epiphany

It was in Brisbane that Clark converted to Roman Catholicism which, he insisted, suited his social and moral outlook. Taking that leap meant that he dropped his Fabian beliefs, replacing them with Catholic social teaching. Critics noted that while Clark declared that his research was untainted, they suspected that he subordinated his thinking to the tenets of the Church. A keen observer of Clark's work, Heinz Arndt (1979: 123) noted that Clark's writings after his conversion, 'explicitly or implicitly', supported the teachings of the Catholic Church. One graphic example of this was when Clark served on the Papal Commission on Population, the Family and Birth Control. On that panel, he strongly upheld the Church's opposition to birth control outlined in the 1968 Papal Encyclical *Humanae Vitae* released by Pope Paul VI. The appointment to the Papal Commission was costly to Clark's academic reputation with critics drawing an association between his views on population and his allegiance to the Church. For his part, Clark held that his views on population growth were based on economic reasoning and not religious belief.

In post-war Australia, Clark had already caused controversy by advocating aggressive land settlement and denounced the protectionism afforded to manufacturing at the expense of the primary industries. Australia's food production was faltering because labour was being spirited away to facilitate an obsession of politicians to have industrialisation (Clark 1952: 68–69). In what was his last letter to Keynes, Clark reported how his relationship with Australian politicians and indeed economists had soured:

> As a prophet of greatly improved terms of trade for primary produce I ought to be very popular in Australia, but I am not. Everybody has his mindset on making Australia a manufacturing country. Not many people have realised that if we exclude imports of manufactures, we shall lose our ability to export primary produce (Clark to Keynes, 18 February 1946, RESP, LSE).

When his advice about decentralising economic activity and land settlement was squarely rejected by the Queensland government, Clark resigned from his executive post. For a few months, he dabbled in economic journalism and opened Australia's first business forecasting agency. Years earlier Harrod had asked Clark whether he ever considered returning to England (Harrod to Clark, 3 November 1944, RESP, LSE). He replied that he would willingly come back to England, 'a country for which I have great affection, but would I fit into it?', before adding that he had always felt 'a bit of a misfit' at Cambridge (Clark to Harrod, 5 May 1945, RESP, LSE). Clark's reference to 'fitting in' was reflective of the fact that he had undergone a huge change in ideological outlook. Certainly, to his old colleagues at Cambridge, Oxford and the Labour movement he was manifestly not the same man that had gone out to Australia in 1937. For his part, Clark always maintained that he had not changed his mind; it was the world that had moved on. Either way, it was as an Oxford economist that British audiences would soon see this new Colin Clark.

6   Oxford Reclaimed

Clark made an unexpected return to Oxford after he was appointed Director of the AERI. Before he started there in early 1953, he spent a term at the University of Chicago as a Visiting Professor where he gave a series of lectures on "The Development of Backward Economies: Taking Account of Population Problems". He was offered a permanent professorship at Chicago but declined because he did not want to bring up his family in a big American city.

While the ambit of the AERI encompassed the study of the economics of the production, distribution and consumption of agricultural products and rural industrial conditions, its brief had been broadened to include the processes of economic growth, more particularly the role of the agricultural sector in that process as well as the economics of irrigation and the dynamic interaction between food supplies and global population. It was on none of these matters, however, upon which Clark announced his presence back in England.

In a pamphlet, *Welfare and Taxation* (Clark 1954a), Clark told working men and women that, under Beveridge's welfare reforms, they would end up paying more taxes than they received in social benefits. The pamphlet created a furore in the British newspapers by suggesting that, if the welfare state was dismantled and families left to manage their own affairs, they would end up better off. Clark also argued that this would result in national production rising by 10% in two to three years. The National Health System, which had only been introduced in 1948, would be wound back except for those in serious ill health or who had been the victims of an accident. In Clark's schema, the State was to be given the minimum of powers and duties.

The intellectual origins for the pamphlet sprang not just from Hilaire Belloc's *The Servile State* (Belloc 1912) but John Stuart Mill and Catholic social teaching. Clark's solution involved a mixture of self-help and voluntarism: 'The citizen who owns property, educates his own children, insures against serious ill-health, unemployment and old age through independent trade unions and friendly societies which are under his control—such a man will be able to resist any future encroachments on his liberty' (Clark 1954a: 62). Apart from living with high taxation, Clark assumed, wrongly, that most people had had enough of 'the experiment' of universal health and the welfare state and much preferred to arrange their own social services. His main concern was the budgetary cost and bureaucracy that accompanied collective welfare.

As noted, the pamphlet created waves. However, the reception was mostly negative. One sympathetic response came from Milton Friedman, who found the general approach in *Welfare and Taxation* 'congenial', and stated that few people had examined the welfare state in such a fundamental way (Friedman to Clark, 30 March 1954, Milton Friedman Papers, Hoover Institution, Stanford University (MFP, HI, SU hereafter)). Clark's response to Friedman was an interesting one; he had discerned that, since the Second World War, there had been a slow and steady decline in the moral standards of British politics and society generally (Clark to Friedman, 9 April 1954, MFP, HI, SU). Put simply, Clark was referring to how politics was adulterating public policy. Another interested party was Arthur Seldon, who said that *Welfare and*

Taxation marked the first reaction against the welfare state and foretold how a new political movement would rise up against it. With the businessman Antony Fisher, Seldon would later establish the Institute of Economic Affairs (IEA). Clark involved himself with the Institute by being on its Advisory Board but also by authoring three Hobart Papers, entitled *Growthmanship* (Clark 1961), *Taxmanship* (Clark 1964) and *Poverty Before Politics* (Clark 1977a).

"Growthmanship" was described as 'an excessive preoccupation with growth, the advocacy of unduly simple proposals for obtaining it, and also the careful choice of statistics to prove that countries with a political and economic system, which you favour have made exceptionally good economic growth' (Clark 1961: 12). The term also applied to the use of statistics to measure growth performance. In post-war Britain, there had been continuing concern that the country's growth rate was inferior to that of its European counterparts. British investment rates were markedly lower than in Europe. This suggested that what was needed was simply more investment. Clark was critical of this logic, arguing that comparing rates of economic growth between different countries and over different times was too simplistic. Data purporting to show that countries with the highest investment rates had the highest growth rates was flimsy. In short, he argued, capital investment was a necessary but not sufficient condition for economic growth. There was no close correlation between investment and growth.

Economic growth, Clark stressed, 'should be a slow and gradual process' and attempts at 'forcing the pace' (ibid.: 13), with investment drives and attempts to expand purchasing power, would merely result in waste and, just as importantly, inflation. Empirically, Clark showed that investment in nationalised industries in economies such as Britain had been wasteful while a pattern of over-investment in developing countries was typical of tyrannical governments. He was dismissive, therefore, of claims that the Soviet Union had recorded strong growth rates because of high investment ratios. In any case, statistics about capital accumulation and growth were hard to interpret; some data showed that the amount of capital per unit of output could fall, thus discrediting the fashionable view that growth depends on prior investment. Clark duly compiled evidence from a number of countries showing that additions to investment had yielded only small additions to output. Moreover, a great deal of growth came from knowledge and innovations that were both capital-saving and labour-saving.

Two years later, Clark returned to the theme of excessive taxation in the IEA pamphlet, *Taxmanship* (Clark 1964). This contained his trademark views that high taxation impairs productivity and aggregate supply, as well as his espousal of the 25% tax limit, including Keynes's tacit support for it. Clark was still insistent that taxation levels, currently then around 40% of net national product, could be reduced if the British welfare system was dismantled and individuals allowed to make their own welfare provision. The 25% target could be reclaimed with a new mix of taxes, including an expenditure tax, taxes on capital and company profits, a land tax and a value-added tax. The company tax rate should be set at 10%, he argued, and, with a self-supporting welfare system, the maximum rate on incomes could set at 50%.

The pamphlet was re-issued in the 1970s and was given some traction by the worsening rate of inflation in the UK. Clark insisted that workers suffered neither money illusion nor tax illusion but were savvy to the value of their post-tax real wage. This meant that tax increases directly fed into wage increases. In an IEA forum on *The State of Taxation*, Clark (1977b: 25) expatiated on governments upholding social justice and how this meant respecting the rights of different groups but did not warrant attempting equality or the redistribution of funds from one group to another.

7   Development Economics

In 1984, the World Bank recognised Clark as a pioneer in development economics. He found himself alongside illustrious contemporaries such as Albert Hirschman, Gunnar Myrdal, Jan Tinbergen, Walt Rostow, Peter Bauer and Sir Arthur Lewis.

Even before he assumed the Directorship of the AERI in 1953, Clark had been one of the first development economists writing on comparative economic development, as seen in *The Conditions of Economic Progress* (see Rostow 1990; Arndt 1990). Moreover, Rostow (ibid.: 387–389) identified several additional unique contributions made by Clark. They can be summarised as: first, increasing returns and the public sector's role in economic development; second, the stages of agricultural productivity and rural-urban migration of labour; and, third, how population growth was a boon in promoting an increase in real income per capita. However, Rostow overlooked Clark's later work on transport and land use, on how the revolutions in land transport from the eighteenth century onward had overturned agricultural and industrial practices, and on how cities developed. For instance, the arrival of the railways meant that big cities could have a greater concentration of industry than before.

Two other volumes which earned Clark the status as an innovator in development economics were *The Economics of Subsistence Agriculture*, co-authored with Margaret Haswell in 1964, and *Population Growth and Land Use* (Clark 1967). Before these volumes, Clark had spent a fair part of the 1950s examining global food supplies and whether the Food and Agriculture Organisation's (FAO) dire findings of the extent of world hunger were true. Clark had been drawn to the issue by Lord Boyd-Orr (1950: 11), the first Director-General of the FAO, who had announced that 'a lifetime of malnutrition and actual hunger is the lot of at least two-thirds of mankind'. A querulous Clark (1951c, 1953, 1954b, 1962) embarked on gathering evidence on food supplies and human nutritional requirements to debunk Boyd-Orr's observation which he later described as 'the most incorrect statement of human history' (Clark quoted in Johns 1967: 2). It was Clark's thesis that population growth acted as a spur to agricultural improvement and that such growth preceded industrialisation. He presented many historical allusions showing a positive link between population expansion and economic progress. Despite this, Clark was irritated that the FAO continued to trade on fears that rising populations put pressure on the world's ability to feed itself. Over a 20-year period, Clark doggedly criticised the FAO's estimates of food requirements per head and of world hunger which, he argued, had been prepared to suit their own purposes (see Clark 1970: 30). He was astonished to hear FAO officials say that sometimes they made statements about the extent of world hunger first and then gathered evidence to support it.

Addressing the thirtieth British Liberal Summer School in 1956, Clark repudiated the prophets of doom who, he said, showed a complete lack of awareness of 'the simplest facts of geography and agriculture' and of 'the extraordinary rapidity' with which scarce materials and fibres could be replaced by substitutes (Clark quoted in Anonymous 1956). By 1957, the FAO had changed its tune, now claiming that half of the population in the developing world (as distinct from the entire world) was malnourished. They would continue to revise the figure downwards as Clark forensically examined their statistics.

It was at Oxford that Clark produced two outstanding works in development economics. *The Economics of Subsistence Agriculture*, co-authored with Margaret Haswell, looked at how the bulk of the world's population lived in less-developed countries and, embedded within a traditional agricultural setting, lacked basic amenities such as clothing, housing, medicine and education. However, it was transport which was identified as the overriding factor holding back agricultural productivity and perpetuating poverty.

The book considered how a subsistence cultivator at village level divided his time between production and leisure, land requirements, exchange and consumption preferences. Clark and Haswell underlined the evolution of agriculture, from pre-agricultural man, who required almost 90 square kilometres to obtain his food, to the primitive cultivator and, finally, to the settled cultivator, who required just one to five square kilometres.

This investigation into the economics of subsistence agriculture made Clark a physiocrat, believing that the agricultural sector had an important role to play in economic development. The authors advanced their "neo-Ricardian principle", positing that the proportion of the labour force able to be employed in non-agricultural activity was governed by the productivity of the agricultural sector. That is, the proportion of the labour force transferring to non-agricultural employment was a consequence, not a cause, of the increase in agricultural productivity.

Clark's second effort, *Population Growth and Land Use*, which appeared in 1967, was a treatise on population growth, emphasising that increases in population were the locomotive for technological innovation and industrial land use. Despite its faults and idiosyncrasies, the volume was described as a tour de force (Kirk 1968: 1,011), and its impact marked something of an Indian summer for Clark. *Population Growth and Land Use* certainly showed off his talents, not just as a statistician but also as an economist, historian and urban designer. A compendious, synthesised work drawing upon a wealth of sources, it encapsulated views on fecundity and fertility, mortality, long-run trends in world population, the sociology underpinning reproduction, and the economic consequences of population in terms of density and prosperity.

As the title denotes, the book adopts a long-run view focused on patterns of human reproductive capacity amongst nations and societies, population capacity, food supplies and urban densities. Given the temper of the times and concern about population outrunning food supplies, there was a contrarian twist in the preface where Clark stated: 'The principal problems created by population growth are not those of poverty, but of exceptionally rapid increases in wealth in certain favoured regions of growing population, their attraction of further population by migration and the unmanageable spread of the cities' (Clark 1967: xi). That is, the real problem facing humanity was no longer resources, but finding space for housing and industry in a bid to avoid rampant urbanisation.

Twenty years in the making, *Population Growth and Land Use* was, then, a 'personal statement' conveying Clark's earnestly held views about population, the use of the world's resources, urban development and economic growth. He qualified it as only a 'preliminary attempt' (Clark 1967: ix) at the interrelationship between population growth and economic growth. A second edition, released in 1977, included a new chapter highlighting the striking decline in fertility below the replacement level in many Western countries and in the socialist republics of Eastern Europe. This decline was attributed to deep-seated sociological factors, including the rise of the nuclear family, contraception, compulsory education and the prohibition of child labour.

Despite still having five years to run on his contract as Director of the AERI, Clark decided to leave Oxford in mid-1969 and return to Australia. Many might have been mystified as to why he wanted to leave Oxford, with all its trappings, and remove himself to the relative academic backwater of Australia. There were, however, some compelling reasons for his move. Monash University had offered him an honorary research position within its Department of Economics. More significantly, the Roman Catholic Archdiocese of Melbourne had set aside funds for him to head up his own research office which was to be called the Institute for Economic Progress. Lastly, Clark delighted in the prospect of spending his retirement in Australia.

Gavin McCrone (1989: 70), who knew Clark at Brasenose, observed that, given his many original contributions across a variety of areas, some figures at Oxford lamented that he had not been given a full chair in economics there. The same can also be said about neither Oxford nor Cambridge awarding Clark an honorary doctorate; it prompted Arthur Seldon (1977: 5) to observe that Clark can be said 'to have done Britain more honour than she did him'.

8   Conclusion

In the 1970s, Colin Clark would widen his critique against the Malthusians, including the Zero Population Growth movement as well as challenging the bleak, dystopian picture put out by the Club of Rome in its first report, *The Limits to Growth*, which appeared in 1972. His chemistry background proved useful in this regard. He was quick to point out that there was no chance of an exhaustion of resources since many were actually indestructible, meaning huge potential for recycling. Clark was also adamant that pollution was not directly related to population growth and was conquerable, though most societies were reluctant to devote the 1–2% of GDP needed, he felt, to abate it. He did warn, however, that economies could not continue to burn fossil fuels, especially coal, as a form of energy.

On the alleged global shortages of food, Clark (1970) turned Malthus on his head, warning that Western countries were facing the blight of early deaths from obesity. At the same time, he admitted that there were severe cases of malnutrition amongst children in India and elsewhere. He also continued to note how world fertility levels were turning down after an initial surge in the post-war years.

While Clark made further contributions to journals, wrote two books and indeed co-authored two others, none of this work would have the impact of his previous research. His last journal article, Clark (1985), on long-term cyclical economic change, was redolent of earlier works.

Clark died in Brisbane on 4 September 1989 surrounded by his large family of eight sons (seven of whom were Australian-born), one daughter and his loving wife, Marjorie. He was interred at Mount Gravatt Cemetery, Brisbane, with the headstone engraved with an inscription that summed up his life as an economist: 'Example is better than precept'.

References

Primary Sources

Clark family letters, courtesy of David Clark.
Colin Clark Papers, Fryer Library, University of Queensland.
Colin Clark Papers, Brasenose College, University of Oxford.
Milton Friedman Papers, Hoover Institution, Stanford University.
Royal Economic Society Papers, LSE.

Main Works by Colin Clark

Clark, C. (1929). 'A Graphical Analysis of the Unemployment Position, 1920–1928'. *Journal of the Royal Statistical Society*, 92(1): 74–99.
Clark, C. (1932). *The National Income, 1924–31*. London: Macmillan.
Clark, C. (1933). 'Investment, Savings and Public Finance'. Chapter IX in G.D.H. Cole (ed.) *What Everybody Wants to Know About Money*. London: Gollancz: 414–435.
Clark, C. (1937a). *National Income and Outlay*. London: Macmillan.
Clark, C. (1937b). 'National Income at Its Climax'. *Economic Journal*, 47(186): 308–320.
Clark, C. (1939). *A Critique of Russian Statistics*. London: Macmillan.
Clark C. (1940). *The Conditions of Economic Progress*. London: Macmillan.
Clark, C. (1942). *The Economics of 1960*. London: Macmillan.
Clark, C. (1945a). 'The Economic Functions of a City in Relation to its Size'. *Econometrica*, 13(2): 97–113.
Clark, C. (1945b). 'Public Finance and Change in the Value of Money'. *Economic Journal*, 55(220): 371–389.
Clark, C. (1947). 'Lord Keynes'. *Twentieth Century*, 1(4): 20–25.

Clark, C. (1949a). 'Soviet a "Backward Country": Australian's Analysis of Production'. *The Daily Telegraph (Sydney)*, 22 August.

Clark, C. (1949b). 'A System of Equations Explaining the United States Trade Cycle, 1921 to 1941'. *Econometrica*, 17(2): 93–124.

Clark, C. (1951a). 'Urban Population Densities'. *Journal of the Royal Statistical Society, Series A (General)*, 114(4): 490–496.

Clark C. (1951b). *The Conditions of Economic Progress*. Second edition. London: Macmillan.

Clark, C. (1951c). 'World Resources and World Population'. *Economia Internazionale*, 4(1): 15–40.

Clark, C. (1952). 'The Australian Crisis: Penalties of Over-Industrialisation'. *The Guardian*, 3 July: 68–69.

Clark, C. (1953). 'Population Growth and Living Standards'. *International Labour Review*, 68(2): 99–117.

Clark, C. (1954a). *Welfare and Taxation*. Oxford: Catholic Social Guild.

Clark, C. (1954b). 'World Supply and Requirements of Farm Production'. *Journal of the Royal Statistical Society*, 117(3): 263–291.

Clark, C. (1958). *Australian Hopes and Fears*. London: Hollis and Carter.

Clark, C. (1961). *Growthmanship: A Study of the Mythology of Investment*. London: Institute of Economic Affairs.

Clark, C. (1962). 'Future Sources of Food Supply: Economic Problems'. *Journal of the Royal Statistical Society*, 125(3): 418–448.

Clark, C. (1964). *Taxmanship*. London: Institute of Economic Affairs.

Clark, C. (1967). *Population Growth and Land Use*. London: Macmillan.

Clark, C. (1970). 'Too Much Food?'. *Lloyds Bank Review*, 95(January): 19–35.

Clark, C. (1977a). *Poverty Before Politics: A Proposal for a Reverse Income Tax*. London: Institute of Economic Affairs.

Clark, C. (1977b). 'The Scope For, and Limits of Taxation'. Chapter 2 in A.R. Prest (ed.) *The State of Taxation*. London: Institute of Economic Affairs: 19–28.

Clark, C. (1982). *Regional and Urban Location*. St Lucia, Queensland: University of Queensland Press.

Clark, C. (1983). 'Recollections of Keynes' *Economic Papers*, 2(3):33-41.

Clark, C. (1984). 'J.M. Keynes: Edwardian Elitist'. *Quadrant*, May: 80–83.

Clark, C. (1985). 'Is There a Long Cycle?'. *Banca Nazionale del Lavoro Quarterly Review*, 38: 307–320.

Clark, C. and M. Haswell (1964). *The Economics of Subsistence Agriculture*. London: Macmillan.

Pigou, A.C. and C. Clark (1936). *The Economic Position of Great Britain*. Special Memorandum No. 43. London: London and Cambridge Economic Service.

Other Works Referred To

Anonymous (1956). 'Enough Food To Go Round'. *The Guardian*, 4 August: 6.

Arndt, H.W. (1979). 'Colin Clark'. In D.L. Sills (ed.) *International Encyclopaedia of the Social Sciences: Biographical Supplement.* Volume 18. New York: Free Press: 121–124.

Arndt, H.W. (1990). 'Colin Clark as a Development Economist'. *World Development,* 18(7): 1,045–1,050.

Arndt, H.W. (1992). 'Stubbornly Defending the Free Trade Position'. *Economic Analysis and Policy,* 22(2): 117–126.

Belloc, H. (1912). *The Servile State.* London: T.N. Foulis.

Boyd-Orr, J. (1950). 'The Food Problem'. *Scientific American*, 183(2): 11–15.

Castles, I. (2014). 'Measuring Economic Progress: From Political Arithmetick to Social Accounts'. Chapter 12 in A. Podger and D. Trewin (eds) *Measuring and Promoting Well-Being.* Canberra: ANU Press: 271–280.

Deane, P. (1958). 'Review of *The Conditions of Economic Progress*, by C. Clark'. *Economic Journal*, 68(270): 370–371.

Dimand, R.W. (1988). *The Origins of the Keynesian Revolution.* Cheltenham: Edward Elgar.

Douglas, P.H. (1941). 'Review of *The Conditions of Economic Progress*, by C. Clark'. *Journal of the American Statistical Association*, 36(215): 443–444.

Durbin, E. (1985). *New Jerusalems: The Labour Party and Economics of Democratic Socialism.* London: Routledge and Kegan Paul.

Florence, P.S. (1932). 'Statistical Economics'. *The Cambridge Review*, 18 November: 114.

Harrod, R.F. (1951). *The Life of John Maynard Keynes.* London: Macmillan.

Healey, D.T. and B.J. McFarlane (1979). 'Colin Clark Reminisces: An Unscripted Discussion with Derek Healey and Bruce McFarlane'. Department of Economics Working Paper No. 12, University of Adelaide.

Hicks, J.R. (1951). 'Economist'. *The Guardian*, 8 May: 3.

Higgins, C. (1989). 'An Interview: Colin Clark'. *Economic Record*, 65(3): 296–310.

Johns, B. (1967). 'How Australia Can Aid World's Hungry'. *Sydney Morning Herald*, 16 September: 2.

Keynes, J.M. (1940) [1972]. *Essays in Persuasion.* Volume IX of *The Collected Writings of John Maynard Keynes.* London: Macmillan.

Keynes, J.M. (1946). 'The Balance of Payments in the United States'. *Economic Journal*, 56(222): 172–187.

Keynes, J.M. (1979). *The General Theory and After: A Supplement.* Volume XXIX of *The Collected Writings of John Maynard Keynes.* London: Macmillan.

Keynes, J.M. (1982). *Activities, 1931–1939.* Volume XXI of *The Collected Writings of John Maynard Keynes.* London: Macmillan.

Keynes, J.M. (1983). *Economic Articles and Correspondence: Investment and Editorial*. Volume XII of *The Collected Writings of John Maynard Keynes*. London: Macmillan.

Kirk, D. (1968). 'Review of *Population Growth and Land Use*, by C. Clark'. *American Sociological Review*, 33(6): 1,011–1,012.

Lepenies, P. (2016). *The Power of a Single Number: A Political History of GDP*. New York: Columbia University Press.

Maddison A. (2004). 'Macromeasurement Before and After Colin Clark'. *Australian Economic History Review*, 44(1): 1–34.

Markwell, D.J. (2000). 'Keynes and Australia'. RBA Discussion Paper 2000–04. Available at: https://www.rba.gov.au/publications/rdp/2000/pdf/rdp2000-04.pdf.

McCrone, R.G.L. (1989). 'Obituary of Colin Clark'. *The Brazen Nose: A College Magazine*, 24: 69–70.

Parker, J. (1982). *Father of the House: Fifty Years in Politics*. London: Routledge and Kegan Paul.

Patinkin, D. (1976). 'Keynes and Econometrics: On the Interaction Between the Macroeconomic Revolutions of the Interwar Period'. *Econometrica*, 44(6): 1,091–1,123.

Peters, G. (2001). 'Colin Clark (1905–1989): Economist and Agricultural Economist'. Queen Elizabeth House Working Paper No. 69, University of Oxford.

Phelps Brown, E.H. (1933). 'Review of *The National Income, 1924–31*, by C. Clark'. *The Oxford Magazine*, 9 February: 415–416.

Plimsoll, J. (1941). 'Review of *The Conditions of Economic Progress*, by C. Clark'. *Australian Quarterly*, 13(1): 104–109.

Polanyi, M. (1935). 'USSR Economics – Fundamental Data, Systems and Spirit'. *The Manchester School*, 6(2): 67–88.

Robbins, L. (1971). *Autobiography of an Economist*. London: Macmillan.

Rosenstein-Rodan, P.N. (1942). 'Review of *The Economics of 1960*, by C. Clark'. *International Affairs Review Supplement*, 19(10): 543–544.

Rostow, W.W. (1990). *Theorists of Economic Growth from David Hume to the Present*. New York: Oxford University Press.

Rothbarth, E. (1941). 'Review of *The Conditions of Economic Progress*, by C. Clark'. *Economic Journal*, 51(201): 120–124.

Seldon, A. (1977). 'Preface'. In *Poverty Before Politics*, by C. Clark. London: Institute of Economic Affairs: 3–6.

The Daily Telegraph (1989). 'Obituary: Colin Clark'. 5 September: 21.

Young, A.A. (1928). 'English Political Economy'. *Economica*, 22(March): 1–15.

Young, W. and F. Lee (1993). *Oxford Economics and Oxford Economists*. London: Macmillan.

17

P.W.S. Andrews (1914–1971)

John E. King

1   Introduction

Philip Walter Sawford Andrews was born on 12 March 1914 into an upwardly mobile working-class family. His father rose from being a railway shunter to retire as Chief Traffic Inspector at Southampton Docks, and his mother was an agricultural labourer's daughter who worked as a domestic servant before her marriage. After attending grammar school in the town, Andrews studied at University College, Southampton, graduating in 1934 with a Second Class degree in Economics. For the next three years, he remained at the College as a research student and temporary Lecturer, before moving to Oxford in 1937 at the invitation of D.H. Macgregor. Andrews would remain at Oxford for the next 30 years. At first, he worked on company accounts at the Oxford Institute of Statistics, and between 1938 and 1952 he was Secretary of the Oxford Economists' Research Group (OERG), which interviewed businessmen on a range of economic issues. A conscientious objector during the Second World War, Andrews took charge of undergraduate teaching at New College for the duration of the war, and he also became part of a Nuffield College research team that undertook economic and social surveys. Supported

I am grateful to Peter Earl and Lowell Jacobsen for helpful comments on an earlier draft.

J. E. King (✉)
La Trobe University, Melbourne, Victoria, Australia
e-mail: j.king@latrobe.edu.au

financially by Samuel Courtauld, Andrews carried out research into the rayon and footwear industries, with a particular interest in the relative efficiency of large and small firms. He became an Official Fellow of Nuffield in 1946. Six years later he founded the *Journal of Industrial Economics*, and worked as a consultant in court cases involving restrictive business practices.

As a teacher, Andrews 'was at his best in the cut and thrust of graduate seminars, from which former students conveyed his teachings to many parts of the world' (Corley 2004). Unusually among Oxbridge economists in the 1940s, he was a convinced Conservative, always concerned to defend the entrepreneur against 'the niggling denigration which tends to make him ashamed of his way of life merely because success brings profits and enriches his business as well as his country' (Andrews 1949a: xvi). In a similar vein, he described his co-authored biography of the car manufacturer Lord Nuffield as 'an act of piety' (Andrews and Brunner 1959: v). His lifestyle was no less conservative:

> Andrews dressed very conventionally, and kept his Hampshire burr to the end. A cultivated man, he adorned his handsome rooms in Nuffield with statues, paintings (some his own handiwork) and sculptures. He played the viola and read widely outside economics, especially in philosophy and literature; he would often bubble with enthusiasm over something new he had learned. Sensitive and in some ways immature, he could be genial and kind; friends and colleagues were warmed by his open, welcoming smile, but remained watchful for passing thunderclouds (Corley 2004).

Andrews was always something of an outsider at Oxford, and in retrospect it is surprising that he stayed there so long. His career might have benefitted had he followed Ronald Coase to the United States; he would have thrived in a supportive environment like the Harvard Business School. In 1967, Andrews left Oxford to head the Economics Department at Lancaster University, where in the following year he appointed me to my first academic job and for the first three years closely supervised my teaching of undergraduate microeconomics. He was a generous and supportive (if sometimes prickly) boss. Philip Andrews died of cancer on 5 March 1971 at his family home, near Carnforth. His extensive papers are now held at the London School of Economics.

2   Early Career

The OERG was the formative influence on Andrews' economic thinking (see Lee 1981, 1991). Its long and detailed interviews with prominent industrialists led to the publication of a series of studies, including several by Andrews himself (see Andrews 1937, 1940; Meade and Andrews 1938). Most influential was the famous paper by Hall and Hitch (1939) on price theory and business behaviour, which reported that business people set prices by adding a "pricing margin" to the average variable costs of production and then maintained these prices in the face of fluctuations in demand because of the penalties that the market would impose for changing them. The neoclassical equilibrium condition (marginal cost equal to marginal revenue) was unknown to practical business people, and irrelevant to the operation of the markets for manufactured products (see Andrews 1964: 33–34).

Andrews devoted the remainder of his career to developing a theory of the firm that would be consistent with the evidence that the OERG had uncovered, and by 1949 he began to publish the elements of his new theory of competitive oligopoly pricing. In an article in the local journal, *Oxford Economic Papers*, Andrews began by criticising 'such economists as Kalecki. They think in terms of monopoly where I think in terms of competition, and I do not see the gross profit margin as a simple index of monopoly power' (Andrews 1949b: 54). Much of the article is devoted to the theory of costs, with Andrews drawing on the work of the OERG to deny the orthodox belief that both short- and long-run cost curves are U-shaped. On the contrary, he maintained, average direct costs of production tend to be constant over a wide range of output so that (with average fixed costs falling continuously) the average total cost curve is downward-sloping at all relevant levels of output. Since firms tend to keep some reserve capacity to deal with unexpected emergencies, they rarely operate at a high enough level of output for average direct costs to rise significantly.

In dealing with costs in the long run, when the level of plant capacity is variable, Andrews distinguishes technical from managerial costs. Average technical costs will be constant since the firm can simply add more and more identical manufacturing capacity (more factories, with more machines). Any tendency for long-run average costs to rise must therefore come from the supposedly rising costs of management, which Andrews denies. The firm adapts to the problems posed by increased output through the adoption of different techniques of management (his term is 'levels of management'), giving a roughly horizontal long-run average total cost curve (ibid.: 75).

This explains what Andrews terms the 'normal-cost principle' of pricing. As the OERG had discovered, firms set prices by adding to their average direct costs a gross profit margin designed to cover overhead costs and provide the desired net profit at the expected level of output. Abnormal or temporary increases in costs (e.g. overtime payments) do not lead to increased prices; neither do prices fluctuate in response to changes in demand. For Andrews, the rationale for normal-cost pricing is as follows: Business people think in terms of long-run rather than short-run profits. Even in oligopolistic markets, they believe themselves to be operating in an intensely competitive environment, in which the entry of new producers from other industries is a constant menace. The threat of 'cross-entry', as Andrews would later term it, keeps prices down so that 'the tide of competition may leave little pools of abnormal profits behind it, but in the end, they tend to disappear' (ibid.: 88).

This was the clearest statement of Andrews' thinking on the theory of price in competitive oligopoly that he ever published. Nonetheless, it leaves a lot to be desired (see King 1988: 193–194). Important parts of his argument are confined to footnotes, with less significant issues occupying excessive space in the main body of the text. This is true in particular of Andrews' criticisms of earlier contributors to the academic debate on pricing under oligopoly, which are not at all systematic or comprehensive. The article itself seems not to have been widely read; it brought no published critical comments by other price theorists, from Oxford or elsewhere.

3   Manufacturing Business

Andrews' first and most influential book appeared in 1949. It seems to have been written less for an academic readership than for an audience of economically literate business people. 'It has been thought desirable', he wrote in the introduction, 'not to obscure the text with any detailed discussion of finer points of economic theory' (Andrews 1949a: xvi). The discussion of the existing literature on competition and pricing is again sketchy and unsystematic, and it seems the word "oligopoly" never makes an appearance (shamefully the book has no index, so it is impossible to be sure). Instead, Andrews begins with an account of the various legal forms of business ownership and continues first with a defence of capitalism against economists who exaggerate its monopolistic nature and then with a description of basic accounting practices, from which the concept of "gross profits" is derived. Next, Andrews provides a simple version of the *Oxford Economic Papers* account of short-run costs, interspersed with much more complicated remarks on the concepts of reserve and excess capacity (ibid.: 88–93). This is followed by an analysis of long-run costs, again derived from the journal article but with the implications explained more carefully: as average costs do not normally increase with output, an expansion in demand will generally not lead the firm to raise prices (ibid.: 136–137).

The core of the argument is set out in Chapter 5, where Andrews presents his price theory at some length. It is indeed a theory of oligopoly, in which firms are aware of their interdependence with their competitors, believe that they face a horizontal (perfectly elastic) long-run demand curve and are always concerned at the possibility of cross-entry by firms using similar materials or techniques. Under these conditions, the "costing-margin" that the firm adds to its "normal cost" of production to set the price is

> arrived at by competition or, in the case of a business man producing what he believes to be a unique product, by his idea of the margin at which he would, in the long run, have to face competition. It may formally be reached by quite elaborate calculations on the basis of existing costs, or it may be given by rule of thumb. But the consequences will be the same, in so far as, in either case, the level of the business man's average direct costs will determine his quoted price (ibid.: 158–159).

Andrews insists that although oligopoly is pervasive,

> the business world should be seen as competitive in the sense that in any market there will be a definite limit to the price which can be charged, and that any business man who exceeds this will lose his market, unless he is protected in some special way, as by legal restrictions (ibid.: 168).

The remainder of *Manufacturing Business* deals with selling costs, factor markets and a descriptive account of the business cycle, and is of much less theoretical interest.

The book was reviewed in four leading journals. In the *American Economic Review*, W. Rupert Maclaurin (1950) appeared not to realise that the chief contribution of *Manufacturing Business* was its analysis of price determination, missing its whole point. Meanwhile, V.W. Bladen wrote in the *Canadian Journal of Economics and Political Science* that, 'This is at the same time an exciting and a disappointing book. It is exciting in its origin and promise' (Bladen 1950: 263). But it was disappointing that confidentiality requirements had prevented the publication of much of the detailed empirical research that it relied upon:

This absence of concrete material makes the book disappointing. One wonders, at times, whether it would have been very different if the author had not had this extraordinarily rich material available to him. It seems at times as theoretical as the theoretical treatises which it criticises. It is disappointing too because of its unduly polemical tone: it is too defensive, too worried about the attacks on "monopoly". The result is just the opposite from what the author intends. He protests too much and thus raises doubts as to the validity of his interpretations. Yet it is still a challenging book which should not be neglected by economists (ibid.).

In *Economica*, LSE's Arnold Plant (1951) made the sardonic suggestion that it should be provided to students only along with a copy of George Stigler's impeccably neoclassical *Theory of Price*. Even less favourable was the ten-page review by Austin Robinson in the *Economic Journal*, which was harsh in tone and extremely critical of Andrews' thinking. Robinson regarded the normal-cost pricing principle as 'a wholly irrational ritualistic system of pricing' (A. Robinson 1950: 774), and *Manufacturing Business* itself as 'powerfully destructive not only of the newer accretions of imperfect competition but also of the whole body of economic reasoning' (ibid.: 771). Andrews' firms, he maintained, were actually engaged in long-term profit maximisation, which was a necessary condition for their survival; he had simply misinterpreted their price-fixing behaviour (see ibid.: 780). Robinson did not explain how Andrews could be 'fundamentally destructive of all the concepts of economics' (ibid.: 774) and, at the same time, guilty of nothing more than a clumsy restatement of orthodox ideas. The *Economic Journal* offered Andrews nothing more than a very brief right of reply, which he declined (see King 1988: 196–197).

In addition to these formal reviews, reference was sometimes made to Andrews by other writers on the theory of pricing in the early 1950s. None was as hostile as Austin Robinson had been, though Joan Robinson came close with her claim (in a footnote) that *Manufacturing Business* was 'full of dark sayings' (J. Robinson 1953: 590, fn. 2). Both Peter Wiles (1950) and E.H. Chamberlin (1952) took basically the same position as Austin Robinson had done, while Andrews was defended by one of his students, M.J. Farrell (1951, 1952) and by H.R. Edwards (1952); Farrell's first paper drew a brief reply from Austin Robinson (1951). But the strongest defence of normal-cost pricing came from Elizabeth Brunner, who had been Andrews' assistant and collaborator since 1942. She had a degree in English literature, and Brunner's very clear style of writing benefited their joint publications, which included books on the US Steel Company and the previously mentioned biography of

Lord Nuffield (see Andrews and Brunner 1951, 1959). Two years after the appearance of *Manufacturing Business*, Brunner published a lengthy article in which she carefully and systematically explained what the normal-cost theory of pricing had in common with orthodox models and where it broke with them (see Brunner 1952). The article appeared at a point in time when there were moves afoot to take away Andrews' Nuffield College Fellowship, and seems to have been largely responsible for preserving it even though it was published in the Italian journal *Economia Internazionale*, which was not widely read by academic economists in Britain. The book itself continued to sell reasonably well, with reprints in 1955, 1959 and 1963, but Andrews declined to rewrite it, or even to add a substantial new introduction.

4   Andrews' Later Work

It has often been noted that *Manufacturing Business* fell neatly between two stools, being too difficult for the lay (i.e. business) reader and not rigorous enough for an academic audience. The three "Netherlands Lectures" that Andrews delivered at the University of Groningen in May 1952 do not suffer from this problem, and instead constitute what is probably the best introduction to Andrews' way of thinking. They provide a 45-page summary of his ideas that is very clearly aimed at an academic audience (see Andrews 1952 [1993]: 175–219), supplemented by an extra 14 pages of 'letters on the marginalist controversy', some between Andrews and Roy Harrod, R.B. Hefleblower and Richard Kahn, and the remainder from Andrews to E.H. Chamberlin and to his publisher, Harold Macmillan (see ibid.: 219–232). The first lecture provides his own interpretation of Alfred Marshall, which he contrasts with that of A.C. Pigou, of whom Andrews is a strong critic. The second deals with the post-Marshallian analyses of monopoly, oligopoly, imperfect and monopolistic competition in the 1920s and 1930s, with particular reference to Chamberlin and to Joan Robinson, concluding with a discussion of the work of the OERG. The third and final lecture sets out Andrews' own ideas on price theory. The lectures are superior on all counts to both the 1949 *Oxford Economic Papers* article and the theoretical component of *Manufacturing Business*.

'My work has led me to rather different interpretations of Marshall', he notes early in the first lecture, 'from that which was normal in the inter-war years, although on several points it is consistent with the position sustained by two of Marshall's pupils – Professors [Dennis] Robertson and [D.H.]

MacGregor' (ibid.: 179). Andrews believed that Marshall himself was not very sympathetic to the neoclassical theory of atomistic equilibrium of the firm:

> Marshall retained the idea of a supply curve, and of a stable equilibrium between demand and supply conditions because such an idea conformed to reality, in so far as actual prices were stable in given conditions; also because, given changes in demand conditions, changes in the levels of market prices could be explained on the lines of systematic changes in supply conditions according to changes in the underlying cost conditions. But he could not retain the idea of full atomistic equilibrium of the firm. He did retain the notion of a competitive parity of price as between individual producers. But he had to recognise in manufacturing industries not only that costs would fall with the expansion of the industry owing to the increased exploitation of external economies, but that costs also fell because of the existence of internal economies. Many passages show that he was well aware that in actual fact manufacturing businesses would not tend to have higher costs if they could expand their sales but would frequently have lower costs (ibid.: 182).

Thus, Andrews concluded, Marshall's 'definition of competition was not that of perfect competition as we have come to know it in later textbooks or as it was already being presented in continental textbooks' (ibid.: 183). On the contrary, Marshall's definition 'was not in terms of homogeneous commodities sold in markets where preferences did not exist, but simply in term of the fundamental assumptions of freedom of entry and of parity of prices' (ibid.: 183–184). From this, Andrews concluded that pure competition 'should be seen as only a special case of Marshallian competition. The latter is the general case which he differentiates from pure monopoly, where freedom of entry was impossible and so the [price] parity condition could not apply' (ibid.: 184).

This led Andrews to make strong criticisms of many subsequent Marshall scholars. 'Later generations', he maintained, 'have interpreted the whole of Marshall in terms of pure competition analysis and have convicted him of error in the one field where he now seems to me to have been so original' (ibid.: 184–185); Pigou was especially culpable in this regard. Andrews pursued this theme in the second lecture, noting that '[t]he revolutionaries of the 1930s...went a good deal further in the assumptions which they postulated rather than justified. In approaching the problem, they were prisoners of the idea of full equilibrium in the individual business which had dominated the older traditional theories' (ibid.: 192). The problem was that the atomistic full equilibrium approach required that its marginal revenue should equal its marginal costs. If, therefore, a business was supposed to have falling marginal costs, it was necessary for it to be confronted by a falling marginal revenue curve, if it were to reach equilibrium in the output which it planned to place upon the market. This required a falling demand curve. The traditional theory which produced such a demand curve for the individual firm was, of course, the theory of monopoly (ibid.: 192–193).

Piero Sraffa (1926) had seen this very clearly, outlining what in the later published work especially of Joan Robinson would become the Cambridge theory of imperfect competition.

Andrews also commented critically on contemporary approaches to the theory of oligopoly, which had 'all been far too much concerned with short-period price-cutting to have general relevance to the problem of normal prices, since price-cutting is not a normal phenomenon' (Andrews 1952 [1993]: 199). 'At their most abstract level'—here he refers to von Neumann and Morgenstern (1944)—'they seem to me to have little relevance to price formation as ordinarily developed in established industries' (Andrews 1952 [1993]: 200). Similar criticisms applied to the work of Michał Kalecki and Peter Wiles. 'Other examples could be cited, and it would seem that, like the sorcerer's apprentice, we have become the victims of our own devices' (ibid.: 202).

In the third lecture, Andrews reported on his own efforts to escape from these devices: 'When I study a business I go to it, stay in it, and work, [so] to speak from the inside, so a wide range of experience may be available to me' (ibid.: 205). He spent some considerable time in each business, and insisted on being able to move around freely: 'It is from studies of this kind', he concluded, 'that my theories of price formation emerged gradually' (ibid.: 206). He began by assuming that 'all consumers of the product in question are other business men', so that the issue of consumer irrationality did not arise. However, 'I postulate that, other things being equal, the demand will *not* be distributed at random between suppliers, but that various customers will prefer to deal with particular producers and that each producer will have his circle of customers whose "goodwill" he enjoys' (ibid.: 208; italics in original). This, he always believed, was a rational response—"better the devil you know"—in an imperfect world where loyalty to a known reliable supplier makes more sense than choosing randomly when unknown rivals are quoting the same price.

In the long term, Andrews insisted, 'if there is to be equilibrium in the market, the prices of identical products must be identical'. But this 'does not imply any infinite elasticity of demand for the product of the individual business'. On the contrary, the attachment of buyers to one particular supplier 'implies that, at the given price, each business will at any one time have only a definite demand, which can be increased in given conditions only by the rather slow process of building up goodwill'. What Andrews terms the 'price line' for the product of any particular firm 'represents the maximum price which the business can charge if it is to retain its goodwill in the long run. This price will represent the lowest price any potential competitor would charge for a product of identical specification' (ibid.: 209).

So much for demand. On the question of costs, Andrews argues that, with given input prices, 'average direct costs will be constant over the range of output which the business is organized to produce' (ibid.: 210). He 'finds it difficult to accept' the 'simple U-shaped cost curve' of traditional theory, instead proposing 'a falling long-run average cost curve because of the influence of technical factors'. However, it is likely that 'such a curve will fall more steeply for increases from a relatively small scale, than it will for increases from a relatively much larger scale. The curve of long-run costs in our model may, therefore, be drawn as falling even more gently' (ibid.: 211).

The implications for pricing decisions are clear. The businessman 'will have no cost deterrent to increasing his scale to meet any permanent increase in demand but, equally, for any likely increase in demand he will not expect a substantial fall in his costs' (ibid.: 211–212). 'It will be seen that our model postulates no fine marginal balance, except in so far as the business will be doing the best it can, if it meets whatever demand comes its way to the limit of its capacity' (ibid.: 212). In setting price, the businessman needs to calculate

the estimated average direct costs of a product, and the margin which he proposes to add in order to get his quoted price – the gross profit margin, already mentioned. Since his direct costs will be given quantities, given the specifications, his pricing problem is to estimate the gross margin which it is safe for him to charge, revising his estimates downwards if he is forced to do so in order to meet competition ... The costing margins are therefore determined by estimates of potential competition (ibid.: 212).

Andrews insists that this does not entail that all businesses always cover all their costs. This distinguishes his version of mark-up pricing theory from that of Hall and Hitch (1939): '*There is no full-cost theory*. It will be quite normal for any business to have a proportion of products which, for long-run reasons or because of the nature of its market, it wishes to keep offering', even at a loss (ibid.: 213; italics added). Andrews concludes that, unless factor prices change, the prices set in this way will tend to be stable so that the overall price level will become unstable only in quite exceptional circumstances involving 'a general fall in demand' or 'great restriction of supply in the face of...a very strong demand' (ibid.: 214). On this important issue, he does agree with Hall and Hitch.

Andrews ends his lectures with

> one last methodological observation. I have been very much impressed by the way in which traditional theory has tended to stultify empirical research, in the field in which I am most interested. Even if the theory were right, this might have happened, in so far as it provided the student with rigid models, not set out in terms which would be recognizable when he worked inside a business. I have deliberately avoided too much model building, except of the simplest kind. I have tried hard to leave my theoretical work with the fuzzy edge which belongs to reality – in the sense that, within the simple models which I have constructed, I try always to analyse in [a] realistic manner, and with qualifications and examples given as soon as they become relevant (ibid.: 218–219).

However, it was precisely this 'fuzzy edge' that Andrews' critics would most strongly object to.

After 1952, he turned away from academia to work with businesspeople, whose company he found more congenial. Andrews' second, and last, important book did not appear until 1964. In *On Competition in Economic Theory*, he provided the detailed critical history of the theory of the firm since Marshall that should have come in the early chapters of *Manufacturing Business*, followed by a critique. Oligopoly is the most common market type, Andrews maintains, and the static marginalist equilibrium method used by the orthodox theory of the firm cannot deal adequately with it. There is no theoretical justification for the downward-sloping demand curve for the individual firm. 'Joan Robinson's demand functions have no analytical roots', he concluded. 'Her demand curves fall simply because she tells them to do so' (Andrews 1964: 22). In oligopoly, the firm cannot know its demand curve, which depends on the pricing policy of its competitors. Unless there is collusion between firms, marginalist pricing procedures are impossible. But collusion is also impossible unless entry is blocked (ibid.: 25–30). Potential cross-entry brings long-run considerations into the short run, destroying the short-run demand curves used by orthodox theorists and rendering cost and demand functions mutually dependent on each other. Thus, potential competition 'removes the ring fence which is necessary for the playing of classical and neoclassical games' (ibid.: 84).

On Competition was widely reviewed, in rather more favourable terms than *Manufacturing Business*, but with criticism of both the depth of the theoretical analysis and the neglect of similar ideas that had been developed in the United States and Europe. Writing in the journal *Kyklos*, J.B. Heath described the book as 'stimulating but endlessly frustrating ... Time and again [Andrews] takes us to the brink of new ideas and analyses which offer the prospect of further advances in this difficult subject, and then with masterly self-control restrains himself from taking the plunge' (Heath 1965: 710). 'Can it be hoped', T.A.B. Corley asked at the end of his review in *Economica*, 'that Mr. Andrews, with his long experience and intensive study of the subject, will now lay aside his work on restrictive practices, and give us the "foundations" that are so badly needed?' (Corley 1965: 472). Similarly, Derek Robinson—the third of this ilk to engage with Andrews between 1950 and 1965—regretted in the *Journal of Management Studies* that he 'does not, in the critique, directly state his own theoretical position'. 'The next step', Robinson concluded, 'is for Mr. Andrews to restate his own theoretical position in detail' (D. Robinson 1965: 237).

In the *American Economic* Review, E.T. Grether also complained about the absence in *On Competition* of a general theory that could then be applied to particular cases, making Andrews vulnerable to 'the pitfalls of rationalizing the status quo'. Grether also criticised the 'notable lack of reference' to the US literature on industrial organisation and the totally inadequate account of the work of Joe Bain (see Grether 1966: 1264). The final review, by the Cambridge economist Aubrey Silberston in the *Economic Journal* two years later, also objected to 'Mr. Andrews' dismissal of Bain's important work on new entry, in the course of two or three pages, on the grounds that Bain has not sufficiently taken into account potential competition from established businesses' (Silberston 1967: 866). Indeed, Andrews had not taken adequate account of the concept of "limit pricing" that could be found in Bain's book on *Barriers to New Competition* (Bain 1956), and later in a well-received book on *Oligopoly and Technical Progress* by the Italian theorist Paolo Sylos-Labini (1962). There was really no excuse for the omission, since both had been summarised—Sylos-Labini from the as then untranslated Italian version—by Franco Modigliani (1958) in the *Journal of Political Economy*.

5   Later Appraisals

Andrews published little after the appearance of *On Competition*, with failing health and his professorial duties at Lancaster putting paid to any possibility that he would write the treatise on the theory of the firm that he had earlier contemplated. On his death in 1971, the *Journal of Industrial Economics* published brief tributes from Michael Farrell (1971), Roy Harrod (1971), Philip Sargent Florence (1971) and Tom Wilson (1971). The most interesting (and also the most enigmatic) was that by Harrod, who had been the Chairman of the OERG when Andrews was its Secretary:

> Throughout the period of our collaboration, I saw a great deal of Philip. Our relations were always cordial and I found him an easy person to work with. Philip had certain problems in Oxford, which he used to discuss with me at some length. The time is not ripe for a reference to all that was involved. Perhaps, it never will be and the matter may be allowed to pass into oblivion. For my own part, I should like to say that I had much sympathy with Philip's point of view, and was deeply grieved that in his later years at Oxford he was not spared these difficulties, which ought not to have proved insoluble (Harrod 1971: 7).

Harrod pointedly avoided naming Andrews' enemies in Oxford, who were in fact John Hicks and Norman Chester (see Lee 1993: 22). Ironically, the earliest attempt to formalise the Andrews model, made by the Australian H.R. Edwards in 1955, had been in defence of his ideas against the very different analysis offered by Harrod (see Edwards 1955; Harrod 1952). This was purely diagrammatical, but in the year before Andrews' death a mathematical formalisation was provided by the Indian theorist Jagdish Bhagwati (1970), who commented favourably on both Andrews and Edwards; a rather simpler Andrewsian model was later provided by Gavin Reid (1979, 1981). Empirical evidence was also beginning to emerge in support of Andrews, with one sophisticated econometric study coming out strongly in favour of a constant rather than a U-shaped average cost curve (see Koot and Walker 1970).

Four years after Andrews' death, Brunner published *Studies in Pricing*, a book of five essays, two of which were the text of hitherto unpublished lectures from the mid-1960s in Paris and at Harvard and one that applied the theory of normal-cost pricing to the building industry (see Andrews and Brunner 1975). It was enthusiastically reviewed by Alfred Eichner, who maintained that Andrews' theoretical writings 'anticipate what has come to be recognised as the micro foundations of post-Keynesian theory' (Eichner 1978: 1,437). These important points of agreement included an emphasis on disequilibrium—perhaps "non-equilibrium" would be a better term—the absence of demand curves for the individual firm outside perfect competition, reserve capacity as standard business practice, price rigidity in the face of demand fluctuations, wage increases routinely passed on in higher prices through the costing process, and (most important) a mark-up model of pricing (see Lee 1998). Yet Andrews always kept his intellectual distance from first-generation Post Keynesians like Michał Kalecki and Joan Robinson, and with the solitary exception of one rather unimpressive chapter in *Manufacturing Business*, never paid any attention to the macroeconomic implications of his theory of the firm. It has to be said that his neglect of potential allies was not confined to Post Keynesians. He made no attempt to explore the possible affinities with Austrian economics, not even in the more moderate British version associated with George Shackle, and completely ignored the work of early behavioural economists like Herbert Simon, whose fundamental concept of "bounded rationality" had obvious similarities with Andrews' own thinking on the behaviour of the oligopolist (see King 1988: 202–204).

Several Post-Keynesian microeconomists did follow Eichner's lead and explore their intellectual links with Andrews, sometimes in considerable detail. As Fred Lee noted:

> [I]n the two decades since his death, increasing tendencies towards methodological debate in economics were followed by a steady growth of interest in Andrews' work, particularly among younger scholars, many of whom teach at newer universities. After discovering his contribution (often by chance), this younger generation of heterodox economists has tended to take the view that Andrews' research output was potentially revolutionary in its content and deserved to have made a bigger impact, especially with regard to developing a non-neoclassical theory of markets (Lee 1993: 29).

In Australia, a PhD was awarded to Juli Irving (1978) for her dissertation on Andrews and 'the unsuccessful revolution in economics'. Lee himself published widely on Andrews' work for almost two decades, beginning in 1981 with an assessment of the OERG and concluding in 1998 with a chapter on Andrews in his authoritative text on Post-Keynesian price theory (see Lee 1981, 1984, 1989, 1991, 1993, 1998: Chapter 5). He also co-authored two books, one on Oxford economics (see Lee and Young 1993) and the other on Andrews, which included twelve previously unpublished papers, among them the Groningen Lectures referred to above (see Lee and Earl 1993), together with a paper on 'the fate of an errant hypothesis', the normal-cost pricing doctrine, with an exhaustive eight-page bibliography (see Lee and Irving-Lessmann 1992).

Lee's lengthy introduction to the 1993 volume begins with a detailed intellectual biography of Andrews and continues with a perceptive extended summary of his contributions. The 1998 chapter ends with a penetrating one-paragraph critique, which notes that Andrews failed to provide a satisfactory explanation of the costing-margin, underestimated the role of social institutions such as trade associations and trade unions, and largely ignored consumer behaviour (see Lee 1998: 116). Peter Earl's long concluding chapter in the 1993 volume is more favourably inclined, drawing a clear parallel with John Maurice Clark's (1940) theory of "workable competition" and noting how many of Andrews' ideas had been 'reinvented' by later industrial economists, with the role of potential entry in constraining prices being rediscovered as "contestability" in the subsequent literature (see Earl 1993: 403–405). Earl praises Andrews' work on labour economics, in particular his early discussion of oligopsony, his treatment of labour as a "quasi-fixed factor" of production ten years before Walter Oi invented the term, and his analysis of internal labour markets with limited ports of entry a full two decades ahead of the supposedly pioneering work of Doeringer and Piore (see ibid.: 410–412). In the theory of the firm, Andrews had also anticipated the analysis of X-inefficiency and organisational slack later provided by Leibenstein (see ibid.: 414). But he had contributed to his own neglect with his poor writing style and his 'failure to build marketing coalitions' with scholars of similar theoretical inclinations (see ibid.: 420–421). As a result, Earl notes, 'many Post Keynesians give his work short shrift; citation is usually very brief, often comprising no more than a footnote mention' (ibid.: 407).

However, some attention does continue to be paid to Andrews in the second decade of the new century. In her account of developments in the Marshallian tradition in Oxford economics between 1947 and 1979, Lise Arena writes perceptively both on *Manufacturing Business* and on Andrews' role in the emergence of the new sub-discipline of industrial economics, focusing on the Nuffield seminars that he organised in the 1950s and early to mid-1960s (see Arena 2011: 253–256, 260–261). Lowell Jacobsen (2017) also revisits *Manufacturing Business* in an article that concentrates on the hostility of the reviews that it received from Arnold Plant and Austin Robinson. In a later paper, Jacobsen draws on two unpublished Robinson documents from 1982 which both offer retrospective criticisms of Andrews' ideas on pricing and price stability in response to the question: "What remains of full cost pricing?" (see Jacobsen 2018). Meanwhile, the classical-Marxian theorist Anwar Shaikh, in his massive treatise on *Capitalism: Competition, Conflict, Crises*, makes no fewer than 25 references to Andrews, including—amazingly—two direct comparisons with the work of Karl Marx, in the context of price-cutting competition and "full-cost pricing" (see Shaikh 2016: 318, 334). Of course, Andrews would not have been happy with either of these references to "full-cost pricing".

6   Conclusion

There were both political and personal reasons for the failure of Philip Andrews' challenge to economic orthodoxy (see King 1988: 205–206). In the late 1940s, socialist ideas were very influential among British economists, many of whom stressed the ubiquity of market failure and the need for comprehensive intervention by the State. In his defence of business and business people, Andrews was swimming against a powerful tide. At the personal level, he failed to work with or even acknowledge the achievements of potential allies, insisting instead that 'room is left for the anarchist who obstinately wants to work within the limitations of his own presuppositions and experience' (Andrews 1957: 71).

In his review of the 1993 book of essays, Robert Rothschild came to rather similar conclusions:

> The question is why Andrews' influence upon the direction subsequently taken by industrial economics turned out to be as modest as it did. Undoubtedly, his opaque exposition and the way in which he chose to present his ideas will have played a role, as will the fact that his model must have struck some of his contemporaries as underdetermined in a mathematical sense and others as susceptible to a mathematical interpretation which could be straightforwardly reconciled with the marginalist paradigm. Moreover, while Andrews' model seems to provide an intuitively appealing description of some aspects of business practice, it does not appear to offer a way into the analysis of many of the problems which are the legitimate concern of modern industrial economics. Strategic interdependence amongst oligopolists is one example of an area of research which the marginalist approach has rendered tractable in a way which would not have been possible within Andrews' framework. On a more personal level, Earl notes that Andrews was very much a "loner" who neglected to market his insights by establishing coalitions with like-minded economists, especially those working in the United States. In failing somehow to make an immediate impact he was denied the basis for influence in the longer term. Yet many of his insights have since been incorporated without acknowledgement in the work of others, or independently rediscovered by authors unfamiliar with them. Recent work on "contestability", for example, emphasises the role of potential competition as a source of market discipline and an inducement for existing firms to seek no more than competitive profits (Rothschild 1995: 196).

Similarly, Jacobsen notes that the emerging discipline of strategic management would benefit from an acknowledgement of Andrews' work on the 'two leading approaches to strategy (industrial organisation and resource-based)' (Jacobsen 2017: 205). Peter Earl, in his appraisal of the "new behavioural" economics of the 2017 Nobel Laureate Richard Thaler, regrets the lack of any reference in his writings on "fairness" in pricing decisions to the previous work of Marshall, the OERG and (especially) Philip Andrews (see Earl 2018: 119). Perhaps, half a century after his death, the obstinate anarchist will at last receive the recognition that he deserves.

References

Main Works by P.W.S. Andrews

Andrews, P.W.S. (1937). 'Post-War Public Companies: A Study in Investment and Enterprise'. *Economic Journal*, 47(187): 500–510.

Andrews, P.W.S. (1940). 'A Further Inquiry Into the Effects of Rates of Interest'. *Oxford Economic Papers*, 3(February): 33–73.

Andrews, P.W.S. (1949a). *Manufacturing Business*. London: Macmillan.

Andrews, P.W.S. (1949b). 'A Reconsideration of the Theory of the Individual Business'. *Oxford Economic Papers*, New Series, 1(1): 54–89.

Andrews, P.W.S. (1950). 'Some Aspects of Competition in Retail Trade'. *Oxford Economic Papers*, New Series, 2(2): 137–175.

Andrews, P.W.S. (1951). 'Industrial Analysis in Economics – With Especial Reference to Marshallian Doctrine'. Chapter IV in T. Wilson and P.W.S. Andrews (eds) *Oxford Studies in the Price Mechanism*. Oxford: Clarendon Press: 139–172.

Andrews, P.W.S. (1952a). 'Industrial Economics as a Specialist Subject'. *Journal of Industrial Economics*, 1(1): 72–79.

Andrews, P.W.S. (1952) [1993]. 'The Netherlands Lectures'. Chapter 5 in F.S. Lee and P.E. Earl (eds) *The Economics of Competitive Enterprise: Selected Essays of P.W.S. Andrews*. Aldershot: Edward Elgar: 175–232.

Andrews, P.W.S. (1957). 'The Business Enterprise as a Subject for Research: A Comment'. *Kyklos*, 10(1): 70–74.

Andrews, P.W.S. (1958). 'Competition in the Modern Economy'. Chapter 1 in G. Sell (ed.) *Competitive Aspects of Oil Operations*. London: Institute of Petroleum: 1–42.

Andrews, P.W.S. (1963). *Industrial Uses of Economic Theory*. Los Angeles: University of California Press.

Andrews, P.W.S. (1964). *On Competition in Economic Theory*. London: Macmillan.

Andrews, P.W.S. (1966). 'Proof of Evidence'. In R.E. Barker and G.R. Davies (eds) *Books are Different*. London: Macmillan: 513–607.

Andrews, P.W.S. and E. Brunner (1950). 'Productivity and the Business Man'. *Oxford Economic Papers*, New Series, 2(2): 197–225.

Andrews, P.W.S. and E. Brunner (1951). *Capital Development in Steel: A Study of the United Steel Company Ltd*. Oxford: Basil Blackwell.

Andrews, P.W.S. and E. Brunner (1959). *The Life of Lord Nuffield: A Study in Enterprise and Benevolence*. Oxford: Basil Blackwell.

Andrews, P.W.S. and E. Brunner (1962). 'Business Profits and the Quiet Life'. *Journal of Industrial Economics*, 11(1): 72–78.

Andrews, P.W.S. and E. Brunner (1965). *The Eagle Ironworks, Oxford: The Story of W. Lucy and Company Limited*. London: Mills & Boon.

Andrews, P.W.S. and E. Brunner (1966). 'Economic Aspects of the Net Book Case'. In R.E. Barker and G.R. Davies (eds) *Books are Different*. London: Macmillan: 75–85.

Andrews, P.W.S. and E. Brunner (1975). *Studies in Pricing*. London: Macmillan.

Andrews, P.W.S. and F.A. Friday (1960). *Fair Trade: Resale Price Maintenance Re-examined*. London: Macmillan.

Andrews, P.W.S. and F.A. Friday (1962). 'The Recent Controversy Over Resale Price Maintenance: A Rejoinder'. *Journal of the Royal Statistical Society, Series A (General)*, 125(4): 592–595.

Meade, J.E. and P.W.S. Andrews (1938). 'Summary of Replies to Questions on Effects of Interest Rates'. *Oxford Economic Papers*, 1(October): 14–31.

Other Works Referred To

Arena, L. (2011). 'The Marshallian Tradition of Industrial Economics in Oxford (1947–79): From Andrews' Contribution to the Emergence of Industrial Organization and Business Studies'. Chapter 13 in T. Raffaelli, T. Nishizawa and S. Cook (eds) *Marshall, Marshallians and Industrial Economics*. London: Routledge: 250–271.

Bain, J.S. (1956). *Barriers to New Competition*. Cambridge, MA: Harvard University Press.

Bhagwati, J.N. (1970). 'Oligopoly Theory, Entry-Prevention, and Growth'. *Oxford Economic Papers*, New Series, 22(3): 297–310.

Bladen, V.W. (1950). 'Review of *Manufacturing Business*, by P.W.S. Andrews'. *Canadian Journal of Economics and Political Science*, 16(2): 263–267.

Brunner, E. (1952). 'Competition and the Theory of the Firm'. *Economia Internazionale*, 5(August): 509–523 and 5(November): 727–745.

Chamberlin, E.H. (1952). '"Full Cost" and Monopolistic Competition'. *Economic Journal*, 62(246): 318–325.

Clark, J.M. (1940). 'Towards a Concept of Workable Competition'. *American Economic Review*, 30(2, Part 1): 241–256.

Corley, T.A.B. (1965). 'Review of *On Competition in Economic Theory*, by P.W.S. Andrews'. *Economica*, New Series, 32(128): 470–472.

Corley, T.A.B. (2004). 'Andrews, Philip Walter Sawford (1914–1971), economist'. *Oxford Dictionary of National Biography*. Available at: https://www.oxforddnb.com/view/10.1093/ref:odnb/9780198614128.001.0001/odnb-9780198614128-e-64196.

Earl, P.E. (1993). 'Epilogue: Whatever Happened to P.W.S. Andrews' Industrial Economics?'. In F.S. Lee and P.E. Earl (eds) *The Economics of Competitive Enterprise: Selected Essays of P.W.S. Andrews*. Aldershot: Edward Elgar: 402–427.

Earl, P.E. (2018). 'Richard H. Thaler: A Nobel Prize for Behavioural Economics'. *Review of Political Economy*, 30(2): 107–125.

Edwards, H.R. (1952). 'Goodwill and the Normal Cost Theory of Price'. *Economic Record*, 28(1–2): 52–74.

Edwards, H.R. (1955). 'Price Formation in Manufacturing Industry and Excess Capacity'. *Oxford Economic Papers*, New Series, 7(1): 94–118.

Eichner, A.S. (1978). 'Review of *Studies in Pricing*, by P.W.S. Andrews and E. Brunner'. *Journal of Economic Literature*, 16(4): 1,436–1,438.

Farrell, M.J. (1951). 'The Case Against the Imperfect Competition Theories'. *Economic Journal*, 61(242): 423–426.

Farrell, M.J. (1952). 'Deductive Systems and Empirical Generalisations in the Theory of the Firm'. *Oxford Economic Papers*, New Series, 4(1): 45–49.

Farrell, M.J. (1971). 'Philip Andrews and Manufacturing Business'. *Journal of Industrial Economics*, 20(1): 10–13.

Grether, E.T. (1966). 'Review of *On Competition in Economic Theory*, by P.W.S. Andrews'. *American Economic Review*, 56(5): 1,263–1,264.

Hall, R.L. and C.J. Hitch (1939). 'Price Theory and Business Behaviour'. *Oxford Economic Papers*, 2(May): 12–45.

Harrod, R.F. (1952). *Economic Essays*. London: Macmillan.

Harrod, R.F. (1971). 'Philip Andrews and the Oxford Economists' Research Group'. *Journal of Industrial Economics*, 20(1): 6–7.

Heath, J.B. (1965). 'Review of *On Competition in Economic Theory*, by P.W.S. Andrews'. *Kyklos*, 18(4): 709–710.

Irving, J. (1978). *P.W.S. Andrews and the Unsuccessful Revolution*. Unpublished PhD dissertation, University of Wollongong.

Jacobsen, L. (2017). 'P.W.S. Andrews' *Manufacturing Business* Revisited'. *Review of Political Economy*, 29(2): 190–208.

Jacobsen, L. (2018). 'Robinson, Andrews and the Oxford Economists' Research Group in Retrospect: "What Remains of Full Cost Pricing?"'. Mimeo, Baker University.

King, J.E. (1988). *Economic Exiles*. Basingstoke: Macmillan.

Koot, R.S. and D.A. Walker (1970). 'Short-Run Cost Functions of a Multi-Product Firm'. *Journal of Industrial Economics*, 18(2): 118–128.

Lee, F.S. (1981). 'The Oxford Challenge to Marshallian Supply and Demand: The History of the Oxford Economists' Research Group'. *Oxford Economic Papers*, New Series, 33(3): 339–351.

Lee, F.S. (1984). 'The Marginalist Controversy and the Demise of Full Cost Pricing'. *Journal of Economic Issues*, 18(4): 1,107–1,132.

Lee, F.S. (1989). 'D.H. MacGregor and the Firm: A Neglected Chapter in the History of the Post Keynesian Theory of the Firm'. *British Review of Economic Issues*, 11(24): 21–47.

Lee, F.S. (1991). 'The History of the Oxford Challenge to Marginalism, 1934–1952'. *Banca Nazionale del Lavoro Quarterly Review*, 44(179): 489–511.

Lee, F.S. (1993). 'Introduction: Philip Walter Sawford Andrews, 1914–1971'. In F.S. Lee and P.E. Earl (eds) *The Economics of Competitive Enterprise: Selected Essays of P.W.S. Andrews*. Aldershot: Edward Elgar: 1–34.

Lee, F.S. (1998). *Post Keynesian Price Theory*. Cambridge: Cambridge University Press.

Lee, F.S. and P.E. Earl (eds) (1993). *The Economics of Competitive Enterprise: Selected Essays of P.W.S. Andrews*. Aldershot: Edward Elgar.

Lee, F.S. and J. Irving-Lessman (1992). 'The Fate of an Errant Hypothesis: The Doctrine of Normal-Cost Prices'. *History of Political Economy*, 24(2): 273–309.

Lee, F.S. and W. Young (1993). *Oxford Economics and Oxford Economists*. London: Macmillan.

Maclaurin, W.R. (1950). 'Review of *Manufacturing Business*, by P.W.S. Andrews'. *American Economic Review*, 40(5): 968–970.

Modigliani, F. (1958). 'New Developments on the Oligopoly Front'. *Journal of Political Economy*, 66(3): 215–232.

Plant, A. (1951). 'Review of *Manufacturing Business*, by P.W.S. Andrews'. *Economica*, New Series, 18(69): 96–100.

Reid, G.C. (1979). 'An Analysis of the Firm, Market Structure and Technical Progress'. *Scottish Journal of Political Economy*, 26(1): 15–32.

Reid, G.C. (1981). *The Kinked Demand Curve Analysis of Oligopoly: Theory and Evidence*. Edinburgh: Edinburgh University Press.

Robinson, D. (1965). 'Review of *On Competition in Economic Theory*, by P.W.S. Andrews'. *Journal of Management Studies*, 2(2): 236–240.

Robinson, E.A.G. (1950). 'The Pricing of Manufactured Products'. *Economic Journal*, 60(240): 771–780.

Robinson, E.A.G. (1951). 'The Pricing of Manufactured Products and the Case Against Imperfect Competition: A Rejoinder'. *Economic Journal*, 61(242): 429–433.

Robinson, J.V. (1953). 'Imperfect Competition Revisited'. *Economic Journal*, 63(251): 579–593.

Rothschild, R. (1995). 'Review of *The Economics of Competitive Enterprise: Selected Essays of P.W.S. Andrews*, by F.S. Lee and P.E. Earl'. *Economic Journal*, 105(428): 195–196.

Sargant Florence, P. (1971). 'Philip Andrews and the Empirical Approach'. *Journal of Industrial Economics*, 20(1): 8–9.

Shaikh, A. (2016). *Capitalism: Competition, Conflict, Crises*. Oxford: Oxford University Press.

Silberston, A. (1967). 'Review of *On Competition in Economic Theory*, by P.W.S. Andrews'. *Economic Journal*, 77(308): 863–867.

Sraffa, P. (1926). 'The Laws of Returns Under Competitive Conditions'. *Economic Journal*, 36(144): 535–550.

Sylos-Labini, P.S. (1962). *Oligopoly and Technical Progress*. Cambridge, MA: Harvard University Press.

Von Neumann, J. and O. Morgenstern (1944). *Theory of Games and Economic Behavior*. Princeton, NJ: Princeton University Press.

Wiles, P. (1950). 'Empirical Research and the Marginal Analysis'. *Economic Journal*, 60(239): 515–530.

Wilson, T. (1971). 'Philip Andrews: Editor and Colleague'. *Journal of Industrial Economics*, 20(1): 3–5.

18

Hrothgar John Habakkuk (1915–2002)

F. M. L. Thompson

1   Introduction

An outstanding economic historian, greatly admired Principal of Jesus College, Oxford, for seventeen years, and a distinguished Vice-Chancellor of Oxford, Hrothgar John Habakkuk was born on 13 May 1915 in Barry, Glamorgan. His very rare name, which was to cause spelling problems for generations of undergraduates, he owed to a seventeenth-century ancestor's choice of surname, in which he had given free rein to the Welsh sense of affinity with Old Testament Prophets. Hrothgar, as he was always known by his friends before the 1970s, derived from the chance that his father, Evan Guest Habakkuk, happened to be reading *Beowulf* at the time of his son's birth, and this forename was also to cause trouble, not only with its spelling. Later on, as will transpire, he experienced the sea change of becoming "Sir John" and "John" as a response to the euphonics of a knighthood and to spare the anxieties over how to handle "Hrothgar" of a public which was increasingly unfamiliar with the *Beowulf* story. His mother, Anne, was by all accounts a strong and determined, not to say formidable, woman—in this most rationalist of

This chapter is reprinted from Thompson (2004) with the permission of the British Academy. I [Thompson] am grateful to Hrothgar's children, especially David and Alison, for providing me with information about his life, and letting me have copies of the MSS of his major speeches. My debt to Keith Thomas's Address at the Memorial Service is inadequately acknowledged in the footnote references.

F. M. L. Thompson (1925–2017)

families she told her son when he not unreasonably objected to going to Sunday school, that it was far better than mooning around the house reading the newspaper, and packed him off to good effect; well over three-quarters of a century later he remembered clearly that it was his Band of Hope teacher who first introduced him to St David.[1] Anne's mother, Hrothgar's maternal grandmother, died in 1884 when her daughter was eighteen months old, and this catastrophe—along with cheap American grain—drove his maternal grandfather, a Welsh-speaking Montgomeryshire farmer, to work in the Aberfan colliery. Hrothgar's paternal grandfather, a mining engineer, was killed in a mining accident in 1887. These family misfortunes gave Hrothgar an abiding sense that life is precarious and that chance may bring some unforeseen disaster. This—and of course the experience of coming to maturity in the 1930s—goes a long way towards explaining the streak of caution and circumspection in both his scholarship and university administration.

The move off the land and down the Aberfan mines was not an unmitigated downward slide for the family, as it provided the setting and means for Anne to become a pupil teacher at the age of thirteen, to go on to teacher training, and to become a school teacher in Barry. She always bitterly regretted that the general public-service rule of the times compelled her to abandon her teaching career on marriage. This undoubtedly was a powerful influence on Hrothgar's determination, when he had the opportunity, to further the education of women. The importance of education was the central lesson of his childhood. His father had been obliged to leave school at fourteen, but later through the support of an uncle was able to go to University College of Wales at Aberystwyth, although not able to afford to stay long enough to get an honours degree. After a spell of school-teaching, Evan Guest then became a local government official, as Secretary to the Education Committee of Barry Council and clerk to the governors of Barry County School and of its sister girls' school. This parental combination of learning and teaching furnished an upbringing in which books, serious discussion and argument, and a nonconformist ethic tempered with the agnosticism fostered by rationalist thinking were the main formation influences. His great schoolfriend, Bryan Hopkin—later Chief Economic Adviser to the Treasury—on his first visit to the Habakkuk home was disconcerted when Hrothgar asked him what he thought was the most important common element in the world's religions, not a subject which figured in the Hopkin household's normal discourse (nor a subject which much occupied Hrothgar's mind in later life).

---

[1] Sermon delivered by Habakkuk in Jesus College, Oxford, on St David's Day, 2000.

Alongside his family, Barry and Barry County School were the important formative factors in his early years. Barry, he later pointed out, as an entirely new town was very special in having a precise birthday: 14 November 1884 when the excavation of the dock and the construction of the Barry Railway began. Hrothgar's father, although born on a farm, was brought to live in Barry in 1886, and he was brought there because after his father was killed in a mining accident his mother remarried to a miner, who then came to work as a coal-tipper in the Barry dock. This was John Hughes, Hrothgar's step grandfather, still working as a tipper in the 1920s when step grandson talked with him at the docks.[2] Barry in the 1920s still felt like a pioneer town, its oldest inhabitants all incomers from the Welsh hinterland or from across the Severn (there was a regular paddle-steamer service between Weston-super-Mare and Cardiff), and something of the feeling of excitement, novelty, and intensity of living on a frontier in a boom town had survived the First World War, even though Barry had lost forever its pre-1914 atmosphere of headlong expansion as one of the largest coal-exporting ports in the world. Barry was being reinvented as a seaside resort with the beaches of Barry Island, but the docks and coal remained the core of the town's economy. Hrothgar recalled that an east wind on a Monday was still a major menace—the coal dust from the coal-tips played havoc with the washing on the clothes lines. The atmosphere was not all grime and hard work: a community was being forged by very active music, literary, and dramatic societies, sports clubs, and lively local politics. There is no record of any sporting interest—beyond a recollection of the town's devastation when the local doctor's horse, Little Titch, came last in the Derby—but Hrothgar did recall taking part when he was only ten years old in fierce arguments over the merits of candidates in a local council election; his performance as Orsino in *Twelfth Night* was long remembered; and he sang with gusto the school song, 'To our town where mighty Severn opens to the Ocean Blue…'

The institutions which shaped the community were the churches and chapels, more than forty of them, and the schools. The influence of the former is problematic, while that of Barry County School is unambiguous. It is true that in his St David's Day sermon Habakkuk spoke in personal terms of religion 'as we experienced it' in the inter-war years. He sang the great Welsh hymns, took to heart the message that 'we are pilgrims through a barren land', and witnessed the fervour and austerity of Welsh nonconformity at first hand. He experienced religion, however, as a moral code and system of ethics, not as something entailing faith, doctrine, theology, and worship; it provided a set of

---

[2] MS notes of a speech given by Habakkuk at the launch of *Barry: The Centenary Book*, by D. Moore (1984).

rules for the conduct of life. These rules were replete with prohibitions: 'There were a great many "thou-shall-nots" … There was no talk of self-fulfilment and a great deal about duty, obligation, and conformity'.[3] Undoubtedly these rules did much to shape Hrothgar's own work ethic and sense of duty; but at the same time their narrowness and joylessness contributed to his youthful rebellion against what he felt to be the parochialism of life in Barry.

Barry County School, on the other hand, was the gateway to the wider world. His father, as secretary to the governors, may have sat at a table in the playground collecting the admission fees from new boys, but Hrothgar got into the school entirely through his own success in the competitive scholarship examination. Barry had a notably progressive local education authority, and the County School had an outstanding headmaster, Major Edgar Jones, "the Thomas Arnold of Wales". Both the history masters, David Williams and Ifor Powell, later became university lecturers and professors, and they started a Barry tradition of schooling distinguished academic historians, which over the twentieth century included David Joslin (Cambridge Professor of Economic History, 1965–1970), Sir Keith Thomas FBA, and Martin Daunton FBA, as well as Hrothgar himself. His contemporary schoolfellows included Glyn Daniels, future Cambridge Professor of Archaeology, as well as Bryan Hopkin. He and Hrothgar in 1931 won two of the four "Geneva Scholarships" offered each year by the Welsh League of Nations Union to sixth-formers, scholarships which financed their attendance at a Summer School in Geneva devoted to the League of Nations and international relations. This cemented the Habakkuk-Hopkin axis and sharpened their interest in, and knowledge of, international affairs (see Hopkin 2003: 7). Together they won scholarships to St John's, Cambridge, in 1933, Hopkin to read Economics, Habakkuk History.

Hrothgar, already a teenage socialist who had been active in the school debating society, spent much time as a Cambridge undergraduate discussing politics, and went to many meetings with Bryan Hopkin—whose friendship doubtless kept him abreast, also, of the new economics of Keynes and Joan Robinson. Hrothgar was strongly anti-communist, having been greatly impressed by a talk in the local chapel early in 1933, given by Gareth Jones (son of headmaster Edgar Jones) who had just spent the winter in the Ukraine: he spoke of the catastrophic famine caused by forcible collectivisation that he had seen at first hand. Hrothgar was also influenced by his dock-side conversations with his step grandfather, who greatly disliked the local communists and thought they were dishonest rogues. At Cambridge he used to argue with

---

[3] Habakkuk sermon, St David's Day, 2000.

his brilliant contemporary John Cornford, the communist poet and womaniser later killed in the Spanish Civil War, whose irresponsibility shocked Hrothgar almost as much as his politics. 'What I most hated about the communists', he wrote in the last month of his life, 'was their millenarian element—the belief that a million or so deaths were well worth the coming of the age of prosperity and peace which they would inevitably bring about. I used to argue with Cornford whom I now think was much less sensible and well informed than my father's stepfather' (Habakkuk to Hopkin, 21 October 2002).[4]

Hrothgar's experience of "red Cambridge" was exhilarating, but limited: he had no contact with the famous Cambridge spies, though he did know George Barnard, also at St John's, 'the chief local commissar of the student Communist Party'—who ended up as Professor of Mathematics at Essex University and President of the Royal Statistical Society (see Hobsbawm 2002: 116).[5] The academic experience was decisive in shaping his life. Hrothgar distinguished himself in the Tripos, and what he remembered years later were the lectures of the Professor of Economic History, J.H. Clapham, packed with information, a descriptive treatment of Britain's economic history from before the Conquest to the end of the nineteenth century, replete with anecdotes and curious facts; but above all he recalled the sheer ebullience and intellectual excitement of Munia Postan's lectures, darting from nineteenth-century movements of capital and labour to fourteenth-century agrarian crises, and grounded in the latest Continental teachings of figures—Sombart and Bloch, for example— who were virtually unknown in Cambridge. It was, Hrothgar recalled in his address at the Memorial Service for Sir Michael Postan, 'an entirely fresh vision of economic history'.[6] All the same when he decided in 1936 to stay on at Cambridge to do historical research, he at first proposed as his field, for reasons he failed to recall, not any economic history, but Dutch Arminianism in the seventeenth century. He rapidly dropped that idea, and Clapham, who was to be his supervisor (but not for a PhD, for which he never registered, it not being the done thing at that time for high-fliers) suggested that he should research the Industrial Revolution in South Wales. He rejected that topic also, partly because he regarded the history of South Wales as parochial, and perhaps partly because in his socialist phase he was out of sympathy with the great industrial capitalists like the coal owner David Davies, the creator of Barry. Looking back in retirement it was a decision he rather regretted, maybe

---

[4] For a sympathetic, not to say adulatory, view of Cornford, see Hobsbawm (2002: especially Chapter 8).

[5] Habakkuk had picked up this reference, a sign of the enduring alertness of his mind, and his voracious reading (Habakkuk to Hopkin, 21 October 2002).

[6] Address delivered by Habakkuk at the Memorial Service for Sir Michael Postan, 13 February 1982 (*Peterhouse Record*, 1981/82).

a lost opportunity. For the rest of us it was a decision which cleared the way for Hrothgar to become the pioneering historian of English landownership, although he claimed that this happened completely by accident. Postan returned to Cambridge one day from the newly formed Northampton Record Office (virtually the single-handed creation of Joan Wake), where he had been immersed in manorial records, bubbling over with enthusiasm for the richness of the sources there, and announced that Hrothgar positively had to seize the opening for creating a completely new field of historical enquiry, the history of the eighteenth-century Northamptonshire gentry from their private family records.

When reminiscing in his eighties about this momentous step, he claimed it was taken entirely under the almost hypnotic influence of Postan's supremely confident and exuberant pronouncements. An interest in landowners, however, was not without some roots in Hrothgar's own youth, for he remembered as a boy speculating about the vivid contrast between the new Barry of the coal-tips and the old Barry of neighbouring Porthkerry Park, 'the almost feudal estate of Lord Romilly', where he often went walking. And he claimed that an interest in the effects of the marriages of Welsh heiresses to English and Scottish husbands was a question 'which occurred naturally to a schoolboy in Glamorgan in the 1920s when the Marquess of Bute, the Mackintosh of Mackintosh, the Earl of Dunraven, and the Earl of Plymouth were still great names'.[7] In later life, he wondered whether it had not been a mistake to plunge into the landownership subject at the deep end, into the vast piles of extremely wordy and abstruse title deeds—which were also physically difficult to handle—that formed the bulk of the available family records, when it might have been better to start with the more easily accessible printed private estate acts (a series starting in the later eighteenth century) with their random national coverage and their evidence about the legal deficiencies in the circumstances and powers of individual landowners which they were concerned to remedy.[8] It is certainly true that his path-breaking contributions to the history of landownership all came to derive fundamentally from close scrutiny of legal instruments—marriage settlements, wills, conveyances, and the like—where later historians would tend to use other sources, such as family or business correspondence, and estate accounts, as their starting points. Thus, it came about that Hrothgar was launched into research where the key to understanding the documents was some familiarity with the technicalities not

---

[7] MS notes of a speech given by Habakkuk at the launch of *Barry: The Centenary Book*, by D. Moore (1984) and Habakkuk (1984: 182).

[8] Video interview with Sir John Habakkuk by Negley Harte, 17 March 2001, for the Economic History Society series. Available at: https://www.ehs.org.uk/multimedia/interviews-with-historians.

simply of the laws of real property, but of obsolete laws of real property. For the rest of his life, he was enthralled—though not continuously—by this austere discipline: in his retirement in the 1980s, it is recorded, 'a colleague remembers seeing him in the Law Library [of the Bodleian], poring over abstruse works on land law, with, on his face, a look of beatific contentment'.[9]

The last four years of the 1930s were spent in preparing for his dramatic arrival on the academic scene (if overshadowed by other events), with the publication in 1940 of two substantial pieces, one an acutely perceptive treatment of an established subject, the chapter on "Free Trade and Commercial Expansion, 1853–1870" (Habakkuk 1940a) in the *Cambridge History of the British Empire*, and the other the highly original article on "English Landownership, 1680–1740" (Habakkuk 1940b) which opened up an entirely new field of study. In 1938 he became a Fellow of Pembroke College, and it is possible that his venture into imperial economic history arose out of lectures and tutorials [sc. supervisions in Cambridge] he was giving on nineteenth-century subjects. Although it was an excursion into territory to which he never returned, this chapter has all those qualities of clarity, lucidity, logical exposition, and judicious employment of economic theory, which were to become the hallmarks of his scholarship. Moreover, it contains distinct anticipations of concepts such as informal empire, and multilateral settlements of international payments, which were only to be fully articulated, many years later, by other historians. This capacity for initiating or anticipating future lines of enquiry and interpretation, cultivated by his mentor Postan, was also to be characteristic of Hrothgar's most influential work.

The bulk of his research time, however, was spent on the Northamptonshire records. Some of the time was in Lamport Hall, where Joan Wake was busy establishing a private enterprise county record office. Here Hrothgar was startled by the abrupt and hectoring manner with which Joan Wake treated a scruffily dressed old man who kept asking for her help in deciphering the medieval Latin script of documents he was studying, telling him he ought to try to master some elementary palaeographical skills before wasting her time. Curious to find out who the victim of this bullying was, Hrothgar stole a glance at the visitors' register, only to see the cryptic signature 'Spencer'. The hapless researcher was none other than the donor of most of the records Joan Wake had collected, engrossed in looking at his own family papers and enjoying her badinage. This episode doubtless led eventually to Hrothgar's gaining access to the Althorp muniments that had not yet been transferred to Lamport

---

[9] Address delivered by Keith Thomas at the Memorial Service for Sir Hrothgar John Habakkuk, 8 February 2003 (printed by All Souls College, Oxford): 13.

Hall, and to his legendary encounter with the law. It seems that in the early days of the blackout in the autumn of 1939, while hurriedly completing the research for his landownership article, he was working far into the evening when a policeman saw a light in the muniment room and a figure crouched by the safe. Asked what he thought he was doing, he replied that he was studying eighteenth-century landownership. Naturally such an implausible activity aroused the suspicions of a rural constable, who then demanded to know his name. On being told it as Habakkuk, he remarked, 'And I suppose your first name is Jehovah', to which the innocent reply was 'No, it's Hrothgar', which confirmed the constable's sense that he was being mocked. So, Hrothgar was marched off to the police station, where his attempt to establish his identity by citing the equally improbably named Munia Postan as his referee simply prolonged his detention, until straightforward Sir John Clapham could be contacted to vouch for him.

The seminal landownership article marked out both a lifelong interest and the starting point for a group of followers who have developed the modern history of the subject in the same way that followers of Postan developed the history of medieval landownership and tenure. In this article, he announced the social and economic significance of Orlando Bridgeman's invention of the legal device of trustees to preserve contingent remainders—the essential feature of what became known as "strict settlements" of landed families' estates, as distinct from the more easily overturned and unreliable instruments that family lawyers had been using before the Interregnum to provide for the line of possession and succession to estates. The purpose of these new-style trustees, normally created in the dispositions for succession to the family estates contained in the deed of settlement made on the marriage of the heir to an estate (hence known as "marriage settlements") or in his will, was to protect the rights of succeed of specified children, most probably as yet unborn, or of more remote relatives, and thus to prevent the owner for the time being (or tenant-for-life) from selling off the family estate, or frustrating these "remainders" through any other action. The relatively rapid adoption of this new form of settlement, which by the end of the seventeenth century had become normal practice in all landed families, Habakkuk argued, was a major factor in halting a previous tendency for landed estates to be broken up or subdivided through sales and inheritance patterns, and in establishing a new tendency for estates to be preserved intact from generation to generation, with younger sons and daughters provided for in portions secured as charges on the family estate, rather than in mini-estates or parcels of land carved out of father's property. Coupled with the willingness of the courts to uphold the "equity of redemption", which made lenders on mortgage more wary in calling in debts from landowners, these developments in land law, consolidated during the Restoration, played a major part in favouring the growth and security of large estates. At the same time, the argument ran, the greater landowners were better able to cope with the rising taxation of the Marlborough wars, especially with the new land tax, than either the country gentry or more especially the smaller freehold landowners—what remained of the former English peasantry. Hence, the sixty years after 1680 witnessed the rise of the landed aristocracy at the expense of both gentry and peasantry. Thus was sketched a neat counterpoint to the coming doctrine of the rise of the gentry as the key feature of the century 1540–1640, although Tawney's classic article was not published until a year after Habakkuk's.[10]

Over the following half century, the Habakkuk thesis of the rise of the great estates generated great interest, stimulating ever more rigorous research as more and more landowners' archives became accessible, and sustaining a large volume of publications, many of them increasingly controversial. In contrast to the sometimes vitriolic controversy over the "rise of the gentry" the debate over the "rise of the great landowners" developed rather slowly, and came to focus on the nature and effects of marriage settlements. Hrothgar enlarged on his views of marriage settlements in his 1949 paper to the Royal Historical Society, in which speculation on the effects on the wealth and landholdings of the recipients of the portions that brides brought to their marriages, through using them to acquire more land (somewhat to the neglect of the contrary effects on the fortunes of the brides' fathers), led to the further thesis that the class of greater landowners was in effect 'raising itself by its own bootstraps' (Habakkuk 1950: 28). Critical comments on his thesis came from C. Clay, J.V. Beckett, and Lloyd Bonfield, and with the arrival of feminism and gender history debate homed in on marriage settlements and was dominated by notable exchanges between Lawrence Stone and Eileen Spring.[11] Hrothgar took on board those findings of fresh research in the archives which he considered helpful, and as was his invariable habit paid little attention, at least in print, to the more combative and aggressive arguments, with the result that he was sometimes thought to be arrogant in not deigning to engage in controversy— quite the opposite of the truth, for he was by disposition courteous as well as diffident. Over the years, Hrothgar modified and altered his views about marriage settlements, and about the rise of the great estates, absorbing some of the findings of other scholars, and refining and sharpening his own analysis of

---

[10] By later standards it was an essay, or sketch, since it contained no footnotes or references. See Tawney (1941).

[11] The best guides to this literature are in Bonfield (1979, 1986: especially p. 342, fn. 7). See also Spring (1993).

their impact, until in his final statement much of the 1940 thesis was stood on its head.[12] Constant development of his thinking, rather than reiteration of a static position, was another of his strengths.

That is to jump ahead. The Second World War abruptly interrupted many careers. Hrothgar had a short spell with the code-breakers in Bletchley, but spent most of the war in the Board of Trade. It would indeed have been too good to be true if temporary civil servant Habakkuk had been involved with the crazy project known as, and misspelt as, Habakkuk. This was to have been an alternative to the Mulberry harbours: a floating airstrip 2000 feet long, weighing 2.2 million tons, and made of frozen seawater mixed with sawdust. It appealed strongly to Lord Mountbatten, but alas, Hrothgar was not the controller of sawdust, and the codename was adopted because the Old Testament book refers to 'a work which you will not believe though it be told to you' (see Lampe 1959: 128–162). It is only a little less astonishing to find that Hrothgar finished the war drafting briefs on the trade treaty negotiations which accompanied the Bretton Woods Conference on post-war international currency mechanisms.[13] This may well have sharpened his interest in the historical background of the pre-1914 operation of the gold standard and convertible currencies, but apart from that—and the cementing of his friendship with Postan (also a wartime civil servant, in the Ministry of Economic Warfare)—it is not easy to discern direct influences on his later academic career of his wartime experiences.

That is, if one excepts his meeting with Mary Richards, whose own wartime experiences, while waiting to go up to Girton, were in working with deprived children at the East End settlement, Cambridge House, where in 1944 she met Hrothgar who was also living there. It is reported that they first held hands on VE Day. Mary then took up her place at Girton, and they did not marry until after she graduated, in 1948. This was indeed the decisive event in Hrothgar's personal life, the foundation of a partnership of more than fifty years. Mary complemented Hrothgar: she came from the other side of the Bristol Channel; her upbringing was in an Anglo-Catholic family (her father was a priest, and she went to a convent school) and she remained an active Anglican; and although he wrote about technology, Hrothgar never moved beyond writing with pen and ink, with numerous additions and amendments pinned and paper-clipped to his manuscripts, while Mary was fluent on a typewriter, and later taught herself word-processing on a computer. So, she became Hrothgar's essential support, not only in their family life bringing up

---

[12] See below pp. 434–436.
[13] Video interview of Habakkuk by Harte.

four children, but also in his professional life. Her assistance when he was editor of the *Economic History Review* was especially valuable, since his spelling was pretty unreliable. She was an excellent hostess when he was Principal of Jesus, and Vice-Chancellor, 'a great believer in breaking up little groups at parties; though not everyone responded with equal enthusiasm to her cheerful invitation to "come across the room and meet the mathematicians"'.[14] In his retirement, it was Mary who urged him on to finish his great book on landowners, and who typed, revised, and indexed it. He was bereft when she died—mercifully, that was only a few months before his own death.

While Mary went to Girton, Hrothgar returned to Pembroke College, as Director of Studies in History and University Lecturer in Economics, his lectures on British economic history being directed at both economists and historians. He shared with Postan a special subject on the British economy, 1886–1938, a virtually contemporary subject well-suited to the home of Marshallian and Keynesian economics and a reminder that Hrothgar, as well as Postan, had no narrow chronological limits to his interests. His collaboration with Postan was close: in 1946 he became assistant editor of the *Economic History Review*, Postan having been sole editor since 1934, and in 1950 began a ten-year period as joint editor with Postan, inaugurating the continuing *Review* practice of joint editorship. This intensely active post-war period in Cambridge, which left precious little time for his own writing, saw his reputation advance to the point where his election to the Chichele Chair of Economic History at Oxford, in 1950, was an obvious choice, even though his publication record then stood at no more than three articles. Thereafter, although retaining certain Cambridge features in his work, he became devoted to Oxford, with the passionate loyalty of an adopted son.

He spent seventeen highly productive years in the Chichele Chair, regularly publishing an article a year while vigorously developing economic history at Oxford, especially through his graduate seminar; previously the subject had been left to London, Cambridge, Birmingham, Manchester, and Glasgow. He introduced the practice of having a full minute of each seminar paper and discussion, and as his first graduate student and seminar secretary I found this exercise an invaluable way of getting to grips with the take-off into self-sustained growth, trade cycle theory, Kondratiev cycles, and other mysteries. He continued to build his reputation in the Postan manner, through a string of articles, rather than through writing the large books favoured by his initial supervisor, Clapham; but it was the publication of his first book, in 1962, *American and British Technology in the Nineteenth Century*, which not only

---

[14] Thomas Memorial Address: 6.

consolidated his position as one of the leading figures on the international stage (alongside Postan he had been involved in the creation of the International Economic History Association in 1959), but also created a whole school of (mainly) American economic historians, who have paralleled in their vigour and significance the school of (mainly) British historians of landownership which grew out of his 1940 article. A posthumous article by Rothbarth in 1946 had initiated the academic discussion of the effects of labour scarcity on the American economy, but it was Habakkuk's book which launched this American cottage industry, and which drew upon economic theories dealing with the choice of techniques (see Rothbarth 1946; Habakkuk 1962a). This book was the fruit of lectures given in visits to Harvard, Columbia, and Berkeley, in which he speculated on the links between factor endowments and the frequently contrasting prevailing technologies in the two economies. It remains the most brilliant example of Hrothgar's historiographical methodology, the "marriage of history and theory" expressed in the elegant prose of a master of the logical deduction of theoretical explanations from concrete empirical observations. The starting point was the observations of British visitors to the United States in the 1850s that in specific industries, woodworking and small arms manufacture, the Americans were commonly using more advanced and more automatic machinery than their British counterparts. The general explanation Hrothgar offered was in terms of labour scarcity, specifically the comparative scarcity and high cost of unskilled labour in America attributable largely to the abundance of "free" land which attracted labour into farming; alongside this he argued for a secondary scarcity of capital to account for the "flimsy" and short-life nature of much American machinery and infrastructure (particularly noticeable in railway equipment) in comparison with British emphasis on solid and immensely durable machines. He toyed with cultural explanations, that something about American society produced more innovative and adventurous entrepreneurs than did Britain, only to reject them in favour of structural economic differences. This book confirmed his distinction as an economic historian of international importance, and was swiftly followed by his election as a Fellow of the British Academy in 1965 and as a Foreign Member of both the American Academy of Arts and Sciences and the American Philosophical Society.

Hrothgar did not make any further contributions to this technology debate and its close connections with the mechanics of the operation of the nineteenth-century Atlantic economy, beyond a 1962 article on the somewhat fortuitous complementarity of building cycles in Britain and America (Habakkuk 1962b). The large body of literature generated by the technology book was analysed by Peter Temin in the Festschrift for Hrothgar's seventieth birthday, paying generous tribute to him for having 'transformed the concept of labour scarcity...into a serious research topic' (Temin 1994: 257). It was Peter Temin, however, who—no doubt quite unintentionally—had scared Hrothgar away from having anything more to do with the subject. Already faintly alarmed by the rise of cliometrics, Temin's 1966 article "Labor Scarcity and the Problem of American Industrial Efficiency in the 1850s", which contained a formal theoretical presentation of Habakkuk's argument and a highly algebraic appendix that mounted a mathematical proof of inconsistencies and paradoxes in the Habakkuk treatment of labour scarcity, convinced Hrothgar that the practice of economic history, at least in the United States, had moved beyond his intellectual reach. Reflecting in old age, he claimed that the invitation in 1968 to become Principal of Jesus College came in the nick of time to prevent a serious collapse in his self-confidence as an economic historian; at the time it would have seemed more like a welcome change from the sometimes rather uncongenial life of All Souls.

He had, after all, other irons in the fire besides his interest in theories to explain the choice of technologies. Landownership, in England and in comparison with European countries with different property systems, had remained a strong interest in many of the articles he wrote while Chichele Professor. These ranged from the market in monastic lands in the sixteenth century through to the land market in the late eighteenth century, passing on the way the impact of the Civil War, Interregnum, and Restoration on landed estates, and developing theories about changing relationships between the rate of interest and the price of land which came to occupy a prime place in his thinking alongside the marriage settlements.[15] He was also developing a third main interest in historical demography and the relationships between population movements and economic growth (and decline). It would be an exaggeration to claim that he founded a third group of disciples for historical demography had many other influential contemporary leaders. But his 1953 article "English Population in the Eighteenth Century" (Habakkuk 1953) was as stimulating and path-breaking as his dramatic entries into the other two fields. When it was reprinted in 1965, the editors of the volume commented:

> It may be said to have marked the revival...of interest in the unsolved questions concerning population growth in the eighteenth century, and it influenced subsequent work by raising the possibility that this growth might after all have been due to changes in fertility to a much greater extent than had previously been thought possible (Glass and Eversley 1965: 269).

---

[15] There is a complete bibliography of his works in Thompson (1994: xi–xiii).

In 1953, the received view was that population growth in the second half of the eighteenth century was caused by a falling death rate brought about by medical and public health improvements. The notion that eighteenth-century medical improvements were considerable enough to have reduced mortality had been recently demolished, but a declining death rate resulting from improving living conditions and nutrition remained the favoured explanation. Habakkuk did not produce any new demographic evidence, but simply by reasoning power and logic, advanced arguments for supposing that a rising birth rate, consequent on a fall in the age at marriage or more likely a decline in the proportion of women who never married, could have been the mainspring of population growth. What mattered to him as an economic historian was whether economic developments produced population changes, or vice versa, and he satisfied himself that something like the run of abundant harvests, and cheap bread, of the 1730s and 1740s could well have produced earlier marriages and increased fertility.

He sharpened this argument in his 1958 article on "The Economic History of Modern Britain" (Habakkuk 1958) in which changes in fertility and nuptiality figured as the key mechanisms of population growth and in some circumstances the triggers of economic change while in others possibly its main consequences, and this thesis was developed to cover alternating and contrasting demographic trends over several centuries in Arthur Pool Memorial Lectures he gave in Leicester University in 1968.[16] Demographers, however, were sceptical of inference and hypotheses unsupported by new hard evidence, and generally remained attached to death rate explanations. Even those disposed to look at changes in fertility as the chief agent of change were doubtful about some of his unsupported speculations on their origins in rational calculations by parents about the eventual size of surviving families in the light of their supposed knowledge of infant mortality. As the most expert of the book's reviewers commented: 'In a field of study where new knowledge and new means of testing old hypotheses are both growing apace, it may prove to wear less well than some of Mr Habakkuk's earlier and excellent discussions of demographic, economic, and social structural history' (Wrigley 1973: 728). Nevertheless, when the new evidence eventually arrived, from a vast exercise in cooperative research in parish registers, family reconstitution, and back projection, it was Hrothgar's birth rate thesis which was broadly confirmed, albeit with modifications and refinements of both the chronology and the causal chain which he had originally proposed (see Wrigley and Schofield 1981).

---

[16] The Arthur Pool Memorial Lectures were published as Habakkuk (1971).

By 1981 he had long moved on from both technology and demography, increasingly occupied with university administration and politics from his position as Principal of Jesus. At All Souls he had been rather out of sympathy with the lack of academic seriousness of some of his colleagues, and frankly dismayed by the decision that the pioneer historian of the making of the English landscape, W.G. Hoskins, had been deemed not good enough to become a fellow. Since his early days in Oxford, Hrothgar had been in demand for public service, serving on the Grigg Committee on Departmental (Whitehall) Records, 1952–1954, the Advisory Council on Public Records, 1958–1970, and then on the Social Science Research Council, 1967–1971, and the National Libraries Committee, 1968–1969. This committee work with colleagues from other disciplines and different professions proved to be an excellent preparation for becoming an energetic and successful head of house, a position he regarded as 'the height of human felicity'.[17] If he had previously rather moved away from his Welsh origins, he rediscovered and acknowledged them from the Jesus perspective, at once recognising in the portrait of the Founder, Hugh Price, a reminder of the elderly Vale of Glamorgan farmers he had known as a boy. To coincide with his translation, he published an article in the *Welsh History Review* (see Habakkuk 1967).[18] In 1975, he became Principal of University College, Swansea. He would have ranked his greatest achievement as Principal the acceptance of the "Jesus scheme" in the early 1970s, under which five men's colleges were allowed to admit women undergraduates on a trial basis; this turned out to be a decisive move in Oxford's painfully slow recognition of women's education so that within a generation only one single-sex college was left in Oxford, that being a women's college. From a purely college standpoint, Hrothgar's cultivation of good relations with old members, crowned with the Edwin Stevens benefaction which enabled Jesus to house all its students for all of their three years in residence, would be his most memorable legacy.

Sometimes rather intimidating to undergraduates whom he would engage in intellectually taxing conversation at parties (where Mary would provide welcoming and less demanding small talk), Hrothgar was so clearly tolerant, liberal, and fair-minded that the student eruptions of 1968 caused him very little trouble. He took in his stride the attendance of a goldfish at Governing Body meetings, it being the solemnly elected President of the Junior Common Room, but was understandably exasperated when an ex-public schoolboy

---

[17] Thomas Memorial Address: 12.

[18] Habakkuk explained that he chose to examine the acquisitions of a group of Welsh soldiers because one of the history masters at Barry County School, David Williams, had endowed the Civil War period with a special interest which he [Habakkuk] never lost.

made the absurd claim that the College's charges were forcing him to live at "subsistence level", a state which Hrothgar had seen at first hand both in the breadlines of South Wales in the 1930s and in India in the 1960s. In 1973, he became the first Vice-Chancellor of Oxford from Jesus College for 275 years, and one of the early holders of the four-year term of office that had recently been introduced as one of the reforms recommended by the Franks Commission (1966). 'As Vice-Chancellor', it was remarked, 'he had the great advantage of usually being the most intelligent person in the room, as well as the one who had most closely studied the papers'.[19] Little wonder then that as a committed and skilful exponent of academic democracy he persuaded the endless committees of university governance to reach sensible, liberal, decisions on the issues of his time: a student sit-in at the Examinations Schools; a tied vote over a proposed honorary degree for Bhutto of Pakistan; above all, the beginnings of the slide in university funding which came as a shock after the post-Robbins (1968) euphoria. He was equally enchanted with the ceremonial dimension of vice-cancellarial life, developing into a much sought-after speaker with a fund of good stories from Barry and Cambridge days, and apparently relishing the experience of official limelight: 'We have quantities of photos', Mary wrote, 'of topping out a building in construction (Hrothgar's face contorted with passionate eloquence), or robed for some ultra-dignified occasion'.[20]

Unlike many of his successors he actively enjoyed being Vice-Chancellor. As he neared the end of his term, the Senior Proctor commented that 'when we took over, we expected to find a tired man, haggard, in the autumn of his office. We were left wondering if this was autumn, what on earth spring could have been like'.[21] 'Spring', as an interview in *The Times Higher Education Supplement* recorded in 1974, had seen him confessing to finding the administrative duties as Vice-Chancellor 'rather fun', even regarding the need for cheeseparing after the recent cuts in government funding 'almost with relish'.[22] There were moments, though, when the 'fun' was of the adrenalin-coursing, confrontational variety. There was once a demonstration in the Broad chanting 'Habakkuk out, Habakkuk out!' and with 500 booing students outside the Clarendon Building he and the University Registrar stood grasping their umbrellas ready to do battle. When the students invaded the Indian Institute, the Vice-Chancellor and Registrar with a posse went to Hertford College, got

---

[19] Thomas Memorial Address: 11.

[20] Mary Habakkuk to Thompson, 2 May 1993. He told some of these stories in the video interview with Harte.

[21] Quoted in Thomas Memorial Address: 12.

[22] *The Times Higher Education Supplement (THES)*, 7 June 1974: 7.

ladders, and climbed into the upper floor of the Institute, charging downstairs and evicting the invaders. Prudently, the Vice-Chancellor had been restrained from climbing the ladder; he insisted in the face of noisy demonstrations that nineteen students who had been identified among the invading force should be brought before the Proctors and be sent down for a year. Thus, was order restored.[23]

Energetic, resourceful, companionable, with a spring in his step that belied his sixty years, widely respected for the cogency and vigour of his defence of the idea of a "liberal university", in 1976, he was elected as the first Oxford Chairman of the Committee of Vice-Chancellors and Principals (later to rename itself Universities UK). He articulated for a wide audience his passionate, radical, and closely reasoned attachment to the independence of the institutions which embodied and protected the freedom of the world of learning, scholarship, research, and teaching, most notably in his great speech to the meeting of the International Association of Universities in Moscow in August 1975. He warned the 900 delegates from eighty-six countries that the role of universities as centres for the "unfettered exchange of ideas" was under increasing threat from the interference of governments using their control of the purse strings, with the increasing demands that universities should concentrate on activities relevant to national needs meaning that society could easily lose sight of the unique function of universities as centres of learning and free inquiry. He foresaw that the university population would continue to expand in the next twenty-five years, perhaps at a slower pace than before, until something approaching half of the age group were receiving a university education, many no doubt on courses less specialised than traditional honours degrees. He concluded that if, through this expansion,

> the university is compelled to conform to the views which happen to be fashionable or dominant at the moment, if it is induced to direct too many of its resources to meeting the immediate needs of society as these are interpreted by the State at a particular point of time—then we shall find that the ability of the university to perform its central function has been impaired, and its capacity to produce creative and original work weakened.[24]

Hrothgar received a knighthood in the 1976 New Year's Honours, and chose to be known as "Sir John". Americans, in particular, who had difficulty in coming to terms with either the spelling or the pronunciation of Hrothgar,

---

[23] Video interview with Lady Habakkuk by Pat Thane, 7 March 1997, archive at Girton College, Cambridge.
[24] *THES*, 22 August 1975: 1.

had for some time been in favour of the manageable "John". When he retired as Vice-Chancellor in 1977 (in the event he returned temporarily for a few months in 1978), it was reported that 'Sir John's final view from the top is gloomy' because of the squeeze on university finances and the implication that the government did not expect or want student numbers to grow.[25] Personally and as a historian he was far from gloomy. When he became Vice-Chancellor, he thought 'the trouble is that my subject is going econometric. By the time I finish being Vice-Chancellor it will be completely beyond me'.[26] He had been working on the recent history of the steel industry but he was never satisfied with this and it remained an unpublished manuscript when he died. In 1977, keen to resume activity as a scholar, it is true that he kept well clear of econometrics. Instead he returned directly to his academic starting point, English landownership; he became President of the Royal Historical Society, and in November 1977 delivered his first Presidential Address, "The Land Settlement and the Restoration of Charles II" (Habakkuk 1978). Remarkably, while the paper must have been written while he was still a full-time Vice-Chancellor, it dealt with an entirely fresh aspect of a subject on which he had published in the 1960s. The detailed exposition of the steps by which Charles and Hyde avoided any commitment to confirm the purchasers of confiscated crown, bishops', capitular, and delinquent lands, and manoeuvred the resumption of most lands without compensation, except for purchasers of incomes in possession on church lands, however, did not greatly modify the accepted view of the Restoration land settlement. The three succeeding Presidential Addresses (1978–1980) were devoted to "The Rise and Fall of English Landed Families, 1600–1800". In the main these were reworkings of some of his earlier contributions, in no clear sequence: (1) dealt with heiresses and the rise of large estates; (2) with private estate acts and sales by indebted landowners; and (3) returned to the sale of monastic lands, and the development of a market in land in the early seventeenth century. However, they did contain the delightful quotation:

Helmsley, once proud Buckingham's delight
Fell to a scrivener and a City knight.

The scrivener was the banker Charles Duncombe, typical new man of the 1690s, ancestor of the earls of Feversham, and the estate became Duncombe Park (see Habakkuk 1980: 216).

---

[25] *THES*, 30 September 1977: 31.
[26] *THES*, 7 June 1974: 7.

In his final three years at Jesus, he was also kept busy as Chairman of the Oxfordshire Health Authority, and then having retired as Principal of Jesus in 1984 Hrothgar, back at All Souls, gave the Ford Lectures the following year. Spurred on and assisted by Mary, these, much expanded and revised, were published in 1994 as *Marriage, Debt, and the Estates System: English Landownership, 1650–1950*. This great work of nearly 700 pages of text and more than 50 pages of endnotes is not so much a distillation of a lifetime's reflections on large questions concerning the social and economic dimensions of the history of England's long dominant landed class, as a cornucopia of a lifetime's accumulation of facts, quarried from an enormous range of archival and printed sources, about the marriages, debts, purchases, and sales of the landed aristocracy. It has to be said that this magnum opus attracted a mixed reception.[27] Reviewers were impressed by the extraordinary wealth of the material Hrothgar had collected over the years, by the clarity of his exposition of the inner workings of the English landed family and his mastery of the technicalities of the legal arrangements these involved, and by his readiness to revise some of his own earlier arguments. Thus it no longer seemed that the landed aristocracy was "raising itself by its own bootstraps", but rather that the operation of marriages and inheritances was constantly recirculating lands that were already within the "estates system", with families taking it in turns as it were from generation to generation to be gainers or losers, and from time to time estates passing out of the hands of great landowners and swelling the ranks of landed gentry through purchases by new men. While some welcomed the book as the definitive account of strict settlements, their functioning in preserving the "estates system", and the significance of that system (of gentry and magnate estates) for agriculture and much of industry and urban development, others were disappointed and even sharply critical. The criticisms were directed chiefly at the methodology of piling instance upon instance and largely leaving them to speak for themselves, and at the supposed superior air of being above the fray conveyed by Hrothgar's aversion from direct engagement with the debates and controversies—sometimes vociferous—which had been largely generated by his own work.

The book is densely packed, by no means a straightforward or easy read even for those well-acquainted with the field, and it requires close attention. That reveals that Hrothgar had taken on board all the modifications and alterations to his initial positions that he regarded as reasonable, and as for those arguments with which he disagreed—for example, on the scale and consequences of aristocratic indebtedness, on the openness of the elite, on the rise

---

[27] Major reviews were by Beckett (1996), Spring (1995), Bonfield (1996) and English (1996).

of affective marriage or on the treatment of the womenfolk of landed families—he simply allowed them to be flattened by implication through the massive weight of the evidence he presented. He demonstrated, for instance, with the chapter and verse of specific cases in which actual numbers were recorded in the deeds, that in eighteenth-century settlements it was normal for a widow's jointure (income for life) to equal about one-quarter of her husband's total income (as well as being 10% of the portion she brought on her marriage). This, he argued with some plausibility, was a reasonable substitute for a widow's common law right to dower of one-third of a husband's income, since enforcing dower and collecting it in rents had always involved legal and administrative costs, and a degree of uncertainty. He did not present this in the context of an academic debate not because he regarded himself as above the fray, but because he did not subscribe to the fashion for combative and aggressive scholarship. In his own modest words, 'I have not striven to identify the points on which my conclusions differ from those of other scholars' (Habakkuk 1994: vii).

The reservations about the methodology of the book were more serious. He had certainly moved a long way from the days when the "marriage of history and theory" had been the touchstone of his research. There is precious little theory in this book, except for lawyers' theory on the interpretation and impact of legal instruments. Indeed, with its evidence drawn from deeds, settlements, private acts and genealogies, rather than from letters, journals, diaries or estate accounts, it is in a sense more of a lawyer's book than a social or economic historian's book, and the material is often described in the lawyer's language of a particular case illustrating a general point. It is also true that Hrothgar's pronounced distrust of econometrics and quantification meant that he declined to do any counting and produced no tables or graphs so that the evidence is presented in a literary rather than a statistical framework. What had happened was that in the historian's continual tension between being a "lumper" or a "splitter" the accumulation of evidence had pushed Hrothgar more and more into the splitters' camp. What the evidence indicated was the great diversity of the experiences, and the behaviour, of landed families in their marriages, their children, heirs, and heiresses, their debts, their extravagances and economies, their purchases and sales of lands, and their good or bad luck. The 'diversity of experience', he had come to feel, 'makes the identification of representative behaviour and of dominant trends particularly difficult'. Despite the literally thousands of examples he had assembled, Hrothgar modestly concluded:

I do not, however, know enough about a sufficiently large number of families to specify the basis on which a…representative sample should be selected. I have therefore proceeded by example, As I am well aware, examples, even if tiresomely numerous, are not proof. And the method is particularly dangerous when, as in the case of the landed elite, behaviour was so diverse that it is possible to find an instance to illustrate the most implausible generalisation. All I can hope is that this work will make it easier to test hypotheses in a more systematic fashion (ibid.: x).

The result was a triumphant demonstration of the strengths of a perhaps somewhat old-fashioned historical empiricism, worthy of his original supervisor, Clapham, and provided future researchers with a vast body of data and, though buried in the fifty pages of endnotes, a quite extraordinary guide to the sources, and the literature, of the history of landownership. Moreover, some trends were established. There was change over time, essentially the result of demographic changes which saw a reduction in the infant mortality of the landed classes from the mid-eighteenth century, and a significant increase in life expectancy from the early nineteenth century, which together produced trends towards fewer failures of male heirs, more surviving daughters and younger sons, and longer delayed succession by eldest sons, all of which in turn had serious implications for the amount of family support, and hence debt, which an estate had to carry. Change as a result of major alterations in strict settlements did not come until the 1882 Settled Land Act— which Hrothgar somewhat cavalierly described as a conservative, technical, measure of land law reform unconnected with the contemporary liberal and radical attacks on the "land monopoly"—an Act which brought 'to an end the effectiveness of the strict settlement as a device to fuse a particular family into a particular estate, which had been its primary function since the seventeenth century' (ibid.: 646). The unchallengeable powers of sale conferred on tenants-for-life by this Act were used over the following decades to bend before the pressures of agricultural depression, death duties, and war, and the final chapter of the book is devoted to the decline of the landed interest from the 1880s to 1950. Circumspect to the end Hrothgar declined to accept the more extreme versions of the disappearance of landed estates, and concluded that 'the greater part of English agricultural land is still held in the form of units which are still recognizably estates'. He had explained "La Disparition du Paysan Anglaise" in 1965 (Habakkuk 1965); fittingly the final sentence of the great book is simply 'There is no English peasantry' (Habakkuk 1994: 704).

This was his last published work, though he continued to relish conversations about the long-term rate of interest and claimed merely to be waiting, with some impatience, for medievalists to supply him with rather more evidence for ruling rates of interest in the early middle ages than a single observation of the rate at which Simon de Montfort's forfeited lands were valued in 1265, before he could complete a monograph on the subject. He greatly enjoyed his years as a Distinguished Fellow of All Souls in the 1980s and 1990s, carrying on working in libraries well after the big book had been finished, keeping up with seminars where his interventions were as crisp and sharp as ever, and above all relishing conversations and gossip (never malicious) with friends, colleagues, and visitors. His relaxations remained what they had been in his prime a long walk every Sunday, often on Port Meadow, and reading Victorian novels and poetry.[28] In the final years his brisk, jaunty, step was stilled, but the quizzical look from under the bushy eyebrows and the wonderful voice of reason never left him. He moved to Somerset to be with his daughter Alison and to be near Mary, who had to go into a nursing home. He was bereft when she died in August, and barely three months later he himself died, on 3 November 2002. He was perhaps the last of the generation of historians who began to make their mark before the Second World War, one who rose to the summit of his profession through the exciting and innovative quality of his scholarship in three separate areas of historical enquiry, and who was a notable guardian of the institutions of the "liberal university" through his unruffled reasonableness. A Memorial Service was held in the University Church of St Mary the Virgin, Oxford, on 8 February 2003.

References

Main Works by Hrothgar John Habakkuk

Habakkuk, H.J. (1940a). 'Free Trade and Commercial Expansion, 1853–1870'. Chapter XXI in J. Holland Rose, A.P. Newton and E.A. Benians (eds) *The Cambridge History of the British Empire. Volume II: The Growth of the New Empire, 1783–1870*. Cambridge: Cambridge University Press: 751–805.

Habakkuk, H.J. (1940b). 'English Landownership, 1680–1740'. *Economic History Review*, 10(1): 2–17.

Habakkuk, H.J. (1950). 'Marriage Settlements in the Eighteenth Century'. *Transactions of the Royal Historical Society*, 32(December): 15–30.

---

[28] *THES*, 7 June 1974: 7. He never recorded any hobbies in *Who's Who*.

Habakkuk, H.J. (1953). 'English Population in the Eighteenth Century'. *Economic History Review*, 6(2): 117–133. Reprinted as Chapter 11 in D.V. Glass and D.E.C. Eversley (eds) (1965) *Population in History*. London: Edward Arnold: 269–284.

Habakkuk, H.J. (1958). 'The Economic History of Modern Britain,' *Journal of Economic History*, 18(4): 486–501.

Habakkuk, H.J. (1962a). *American and British Technology in the Nineteenth Century: The Search for Labour-Saving Inventions*. Cambridge: Cambridge University Press.

Habakkuk, H.J. (1962b). 'Fluctuations in House-Building in Britain and the United States in the Nineteenth Century'. *Journal of Economic History*, 22(2): 198–230.

Habakkuk, H.J. (1965). 'La Disparition du Paysan Anglaise'. *Annales*, 20(4): 649–663.

Habakkuk, H.J. (1967). 'The Parliamentary Army and the Crown Lands'. *Welsh History Review*, 3(4): 403–426.

Habakkuk, H.J. (1968). *Industrial Organisation since the Industrial Revolution*. Southampton: University of Southampton.

Habakkuk, H.J. (1971). *Population Growth and Economic Development since 1750*. Leicester: Leicester University Press.

Habakkuk, H.J. (1978). 'The Land Settlement and the Restoration of Charles II'. *Transactions of the Royal Historical Society*, 28(December): 201–222.

Habakkuk, H.J. (1980). 'The Rise and Fall of English Landed Families, 1600–1800: II'. *Transactions of the Royal Historical Society*, 30(December): 199–221.

Habakkuk, H.J. (1984). 'Marriage and the Ownership of Land,' in R.R. Davies, R.A. Griffiths, I.G. Jones and K.O. Morgan (eds) *Welsh Society and Nationhood: Historical Essays Presented to Glanmor Williams*. Cardiff: University of Wales Press: 178–198.

Habakkuk, H.J. (1994). *Marriage, Debt, and the Estates System: English Landownership, 1650–1950*. Oxford: Clarendon Press.

Other Works Referred To

Beckett, J.V. (1996). 'Family Matters'. *Historical Journal*, 39(1): 249–256.

Bonfield, L. (1979). 'Marriage Settlements and the "Rise of Great Estates": The Demographic Aspect'. *Economic History Review*, New Series, 32(4): 483–493.

Bonfield, L. (1986). 'Affective Families, Open Elites and Strict Family Settlements in Early Modern England'. *Economic History Review*, New Series, 39(3): 341–354.

Bonfield, L. (1996). 'Review of *Marriage, Debt, and the Estates System: English Landownership, 1650–1950*, by H.J. Habakkuk'. *American Historical Review*, 101(2): 483–484.

English, B. (1996). 'Review of *Marriage, Debt, and the Estates System: English Landownership, 1650–1950*, by H.J. Habakkuk'. *Agricultural History Review*, 44(1): 114–116.

Glass, D.V. and D.E.C. Eversley (eds) (1965). *Population in History*. London: Edward Arnold.

Hobsbawm, E. (2002). *Interesting Times*. London: Allen Lane.

Hopkin, B. (2003). *A Short Account of My Life*. Privately printed.

Lampe, D. (1959). *Pyke: The Unknown Genius*. London: Evans Brothers.

Spring, E. (1993). *Law, Land, and Family: Aristocratic Inheritance in England, 1300 to 1800*. Chapel Hill and London: University of North Carolina Press.

Rothbarth, E. (1946). 'Causes of the Superior Efficiency of USA Industry as Compared with British Industry'. *Economic Journal*, 56(223): 383–390.

Spring, D. (1995). 'Review of *Marriage, Debt, and the Estates System: English Landownership, 1650–1950*, by H.J. Habakkuk'. *Albion*, 27(3): 517–520.

Tawney, R.H. (1941). 'The Rise of the Gentry, 1558–1640'. *Economic History Review*, 11(1): 1–38.

Temin, P. (1966). 'Labour Scarcity and the Problem of American Industrial Efficiency in the 1850s'. *Journal of Economic History*, 26(3): 277–298.

Temin, P. (1994). 'Labour Scarcity and Capital Markets in America,' Chapter 10 in F.M.L. Thompson (ed.) *Landowners, Capitalists, and Entrepreneurs: Essays for Sir John Habakkuk*. Oxford: Clarendon Press: 257–273.

Thompson, F.M.L. (ed.) (1994). *Landowners, Capitalists, and Entrepreneurs: Essays for Sir John Habakkuk*. Oxford: Clarendon Press.

Thompson, F.M.L. (2004). 'Hrothgar John Habakkuk, 1915–2002'. *Proceedings of the British Academy*, 124: 90–114.

Wrigley, E.A. (1973). 'Review of *Population Growth and Economic Development since 1750*, by H.J. Habakkuk'. *Economic History Review*, 26(4): 726–728.

Wrigley, E.A. and R.S. Schofield (1981). *The Population History of England, 1541–1871*. London: Edward Arnold. Second edition published by Cambridge University Press, 1989.

19

David Worswick (1916–2001)

Rosalind Seneca

1   Introduction

My father, David Worswick,[1] was born on 18 August 1916 in Chiswick, London. His father, Thomas Worswick, was the son of a mining family in Ashton-in-Makerfield, Lancashire, who worked his way to Liverpool University, earning a BSc and an MSc. After distinguished war service, he became Director of Education at the London Regent Street Polytechnic where he devoted himself to the education and advancement of working-class students, a mission which David carried on. David's mother, Evelyn, née Green, studied History and English at Manchester University. Thomas and Evelyn had three sons and a daughter; David was the second son.

I would like to thank my sister, Eleanor Stanier, for materials and memories about David and also my brother, Richard Worswick, for a treasure trove of materials. I am also very grateful to Geoffrey Harcourt, my former supervisor at Cambridge in 1965–1966, who proposed my name for this project and gave me some enlightening comments and thoughts on the first draft. Finally, my husband, Joseph Seneca, organised and edited the entire manuscript for which I give him hearty thanks.

---

[1] His given names were George David Norman and his professional signature was G.D.N. Worswick.

R. Seneca (✉)
Cornelius, NC, USA

© The Author(s), under exclusive license to Springer Nature Switzerland AG 2021
R. A. Cord (ed.), *The Palgrave Companion to Oxford Economics*,
https://doi.org/10.1007/978-3-030-58471-9_19

As a boy, David attended the preparatory school, Colet Court (now St Paul's Juniors), and received a typical classical education of the time, including a large dose of Latin and Greek. He excelled in all his subjects, but was particularly gifted in mathematics. By the time he was twelve, he was promoted to the same class as his clever brother, Tom, who was two-and-a-half years older.

From Colet Court, David went on to attend St Paul's School, where also he excelled, until tragedy struck the family in the form of the sudden death of his father from meningitis in 1932. David was just fifteen. The awful blow was compounded by the embezzlement of his father's inheritance by a trusted friend, leaving the family in straightened circumstances. David's time at St Paul's was cut short. Nonetheless, with his mother's encouragement, he made his way via an Open Scholarship in Mathematics to New College, Oxford.[2] Subsequent scholarship funds made it possible for David to complete his degree in Mathematics with First Class Honours in 1937.

The early and sudden death of his father was one in a series of tragedies that David suffered in the following years. His younger brother, Dick, an RAF pilot in the Second World War, was lost over the North Sea in 1942. In 1948, David and his wife, Sylvia, lost their fourth child, Thomas Nigel, at birth. David had married Sylvia Walsh in 1940 and she became his lifelong support. They had three children, Eleanor Mary, Rosalind Sylvia and Richard David before Thomas.

Then in his early thirties, David began to go deaf and was diagnosed with otosclerosis, a disease of the middle ear. He had inherited the disease from his mother who was also deaf. This blow affected him throughout his life as he became deafer as he grew older. He was completely uncomplaining and open about it. In professional meetings, he would unclip the microphone of his hearing aid from his shirt pocket and place it on the table in the middle so he could hear comments from all sides. But it was a sore affliction, especially since he was a great lover of music and lost his capacity to hear it well in later life.

2   Starting Out

After completing his undergraduate degree, he faced the question of what to do next. As a gifted mathematician, David could have pursued his study in mathematics further. But he was deeply affected by the general

---

[2] See Artis (2003: 515).

unemployment and resulting dire poverty that afflicted the country during the Great Depression. Government policy of the time was ineffective. So, since further funding was available at Oxford, he enrolled for a Diploma in Economics and Political Science.

An influential tutor was Henry Phelps Brown with whom he later formed a lifelong friendship. Phelps Brown recognised the importance of assembling and analysing economic statistics before such information was routinely available and attempted to formulate such mathematical economic constructs as general equilibrium theory for non-mathematical students, albeit with varying success. He had, however, much in common with David's interests in both the economics of unemployment and mathematics. David earned his diploma with distinction.

With the outbreak of war, David applied for active military service but was rejected. He was then approached by Roy Harrod to take a position in the Oxford University Institute of Statistics (much later renamed the Oxford University Institute of Economics and Statistics) which had been founded to promote the use of statistics in social studies. This became an exciting place to work as a group of distinguished European economists, fleeing the Nazis, found their way to Oxford and were employed at the Institute. They were Fritz Burchardt, Ernst Schumacher, Thomas Balogh, Ludwig Lachmann, Kurt Mandelbaum and Michał Kalecki, whose theories about the causes of unemployment paralleled those of Keynes and were a great influence on David's thought.

To gain a sense of perspective about the importance of the "unemployment problem" to so many economists from the 1930s, it is worth looking back to 1929 when the stock market crashed on Wall Street. There followed an economic collapse in the US which immediately spread to the UK and around the world. The Great Depression lasted until the outbreak of the Second World War. In the UK, the unemployment rate reached 22% at its peak, although it rose as high as 75% in some parts of Northern England. There was dire poverty, malnutrition and illness among many groups.

It was in this world that David lived, first as a schoolboy and then as a student of economics. In this decade, Keynes and Kalecki independently developed similar theories that provided answers to the problem of unemployment for government policy. Their solution—to increase government spending—was almost immediately proved correct. Unemployment in England virtually disappeared by falling to 0.5% when the government ramped up to the fullest its expenditure on armaments. After the war, as government spending began to fall, the question arose of whether full employment could be sustained.

The concept of unemployment was itself complicated. Keynes, Kalecki and others focused on "involuntary unemployment" as the correct measure for the health of the economy and as the impetus for government policy. The involuntarily unemployed are those who are willing to work 'under existing conditions—wage rates, conditions of work and so on' (Harcourt 2012: 1) but cannot find a job. On its face, this would seem clear enough, but the definition immediately raises moral, statistical and policy questions. First, what groups does "willing to work" include?[3] If many unemployed have no work by choice then it can be argued that the social responsibility of society need not include them or be a trigger for government policy. This measure of unemployment would be relatively low.

Economic power is at issue here. In an extreme economic downturn, such as during the 1930s, all sections of society will gain from a government policy of full employment; workers will have jobs, business people (capitalists) will have higher profits, and there will be less social unrest. Also, if government policy increases public expenditure, as during the war, output will be increased. However, under less extreme national circumstances, as in the decades following the war, the issue will arise whether government expenditure will be maintained at previous levels when higher wages for workers may mean lower profits for capitalists. Also, in a country not at war, but with full employment, inflation is likely to become a problem. So there would be a public policy choice about how to balance inflation and unemployment. Tinbergen's insight was that you need one policy tool for each objective. Thus to maintain two economic goals, you need two policy tools. David's answer was that aggregate demand management could keep the economy at full employment and incomes policy could keep inflation under control (see Section 8 below).

David became a socialist during his time in Oxford. He joined the Labour Party during the war and helped set up the Oxford branch of the Fabian Society,[4] and for the rest of his life worked to understand and prevent involuntary unemployment. In the 1930s, Keynesian theories had mapped out the course for the government to maintain full employment during peacetime. Towards the end of the war, there was great optimism that economic depression was a thing of the past. In 1944, the BBC boldly broadcast—in a peak listening period on eight evenings over the space of a fortnight—a discussion on full employment. The programme was called "Jobs for All". David was in

---

[3] See Worswick (1976: 14).

[4] The Fabian Society is a British socialist organisation. It advocates democratic socialism through gradualist and reformist effort in democracies rather than by revolution. It was founded in 1884 and had an important influence on the Labour Party which grew from it.

the chair.[5] Each participant, from a wide variety of occupations, began by describing his or her background and personal experience, ranging from Donald Carson, 'a joiner by trade', Mary Lewis, 'a quarry man's wife', to the academic economist Maurice Dobb, a German, an American, manufacturers, industrialists, up to Sir William Beveridge himself. The discussion was wide-ranging. For example, Carson said, 'Well, there's just one thing I would like to ask—has the speaker been out of a job himself?' David replied, 'No, I have to admit I haven't'. 'I thought not!' was Carson's rejoinder. On occasion, the discussion became so heated that David had to call for order by striking a hammer on the table. The interest aroused among listeners was great and the broadcasts were published in a small book entitled "Jobs for All", with the royalties being given to the BBC's The Week's Good Cause.

At the Institute of Statistics, David published a series of papers about the war economy and he and his colleagues also considered the meaning of Keynesian theories for the post-war economy. The resulting book, *The Economics of Full Employment* (Burchardt et al. 1944), provided 'a statement of remarkable clarity and verve, which had no immediate real rivals for its combination of analytical insight and practical application' (Artis 2003: 516).

David's paper in this book entitled "Stability and Flexibility of Full Employment" introduced the idea of a wages policy, which later became more generally "incomes policy", to control the price level of a full employment economy, and showed him to be a true Keynesian macroeconomist. However, he was not beyond a foray into microeconomics when he published the solution to the consumer's optimisation problem with points rationing as well as income as constraints (see Worswick 1944).

3   Teaching and Academic Life: Introduction

In 1945, after the war had ended, David took a position, first as Lecturer and then immediately afterwards as Fellow in Economics at Magdalen College, Oxford. He became part of a distinguished group of fellows, which included Kenneth Tite in politics and Thomas Dewar ("Harry") Weldon in philosophy, who were to be joined by Frank Burchardt, who was, as noted, at the Institute of Statistics. They taught in the interdisciplinary field of Politics, Philosophy and Economics (PPE), introduced in 1920 because of the belief that, at the undergraduate level, none of these fields should be studied without reference to the others. Thus, for example, theories of reducing unemployment could

---

[5] See Sylvia Worswick's obituary of David (2001).

not be truly understood without reference to concepts of social justice. The ideas of the Utilitarians in philosophy influenced the development of consumer choice theory in economics. Also, as David was later to encounter, the politics behind the making of economic policy was influential in how eagerly the full employment goal was pursued by different members of the government. Students would study all three topics in their first year and could then reduce their topics to two for the last two years. The PPE degree at Oxford has become increasingly popular and the number of politicians, statesmen and journalists with PPE degrees from Oxford is remarkable.

In 1949, in the Oxford University Congregation, David put forward a proposal to postpone all University salary increases (with a few exceptions) for two years until 1951. The reason for this action of admitted self-denial was that it would be a 'noble and generous gesture' (Worswick quoted in *Oxford Mail* 1949: 2) to mirror the county's wage freeze in other sectors, that is, to support income's policy (see below, Section 8). The measure failed amid furious opposition, Sir Hugh Henderson stating that it 'was most unreasonable— almost a bizarre proposal, which might do serious damage to the interests of the University … We are being asked to do something which is plainly intolerable from the stand-point of the primary interest in our lives—that of the University' (Henderson quoted in ibid.). This was an example of David's tendency to assume that other people would, of course, be as self-denying as him. It was perhaps a naïve view, though he later more formally recognised that the clash between the public and the private interest was ubiquitous in making economic policy, especially the incomes policy. However, he was always disappointed when private interest dominated as much as it did under the government of Margaret Thatcher.

3.1   Teaching

The teaching method at Oxford consisted of a tutorial of usually between one to three students and his/her tutor and lectures at the University level which undergraduates from all colleges could attend. David's teaching schedule included both tutorials for Magdalen undergraduates as well as BPhil and DPhil students, and also lectures in economics at the University level. His room in Magdalen College was in the beautiful eighteenth century addition to the old college called the New Building. It looked out over a huge well-kept lawn and herbaceous border in the front and the deer park at the back. David's room was equally grand, on the upper floor in the front and middle of the building with the lawn view from two double windows with great shutters and window seats. This was where he held his tutorials.

David was, by the accounts of students and colleagues alike, a brilliant teacher. He gave one-hour tutorials from ten to one in the morning and four to seven in the late afternoon. He would eat lunch at home (across the High Street in number 62A) or in college depending on his schedule. (His salary included a number of free meals.) University lectures would also be part of his weekly schedule, as well as college meetings, PPE meetings and faculty meetings at times during term.

The reading list for economics was comprehensive, including mathematics and original treatises in economics such as *The Wealth of Nations* works by Joan Robinson, John Hicks and many others. A textbook on economics was recommended (Paul Samuelson's was the first). The level of teaching and final examination questions were very high. The student was required to have fully grasped the basic theory and to be able to discuss higher level questions in economics. David taught both microeconomics and macroeconomics and the mathematical formulations of each when they were required. Here's his student and later colleague at Magdalen, Kit McMahon, describing David's evolving thought about the uses of mathematics in economics:

When (David) started to study economics his first reaction was how easy it was. I remember vividly his typically self-deflating description of a hectic, stimulating week in which he devoured all eight hundred pages of Alfred Marshall's "Principles" turning all the arguments into equations—and pretty simple equations at that. And then it dawned on him that that was not the point. He came quickly to share the skepticism of Marshall himself (also a mathematician who took up economics because of his social concerns) … He used to enjoy quoting the great man: "Every economic fact…stands in relation to cause and effect to many other facts…and since it *never* happens that all of them can be expressed in numbers, the application of exact mathematical methods to those which can is nearly always a waste of time, while in the large majority of cases it is positively misleading" (italics in original).

McMahon continued:

The fact that David could clearly do the mathematics if he wanted to was a great strength in his arguments against those who increasingly tried to avoid the hard parts of economic problems by solving the easy parts with equations … He was from first to last a believer in political economy rather than economics and therefore that PPE was a genuine discipline rather than, as it was often taught in other colleges, three different subjects slung together (remarks made at David's memorial service, Magdalen College Chapel, Oxford, 20 October 2001).

In 1959, David published an article entitled "Mrs. Robinson on Simple Accumulation: A Comment with Algebra" (Worswick 1959). He says at the beginning of the article that 'The best reason I can give for making this translation is that I was driven to do it because I found myself coming adrift more than once in following her argument' (ibid.: 125). He congratulates Robinson 'for striving to examine each successive step [of] her argument afresh' in her book *The Accumulation of Capital*, but then says that there are 'still traces of the habitual modes of thought which turn out to be unnecessary...and which might well, if left unexposed, be seriously misleading' (ibid.).

Robert Solow used David's mathematical model in his volume, *Capital Theory and the Rate of Return*, although there was no comment from others nor from Joan Robinson herself. But then no one likes to be taken to task in public, and David should perhaps have known this.

The following are some more testimonials about David's style of teaching. Michael Artis writes:

> His style was to let the student find out for himself how a particular hypothesis "worked"—the joy of seeing the discovery in the student's face was one of the things that David savored. And the method worked to bring confidence to the student to analyse and solve a problem. It also ensured a better grasp of what was learnt than rote learning could ever do (Artis 2003: 517).

Here's Paul Dodyk, a Rhodes Scholar at Oxford:

> [David] was articulate, considerate, interesting and interested. He was never dictatorial, dismissive, sarcastic or coercive ... With David as your tutor, you wanted to learn. His suggested readings for our sessions were the beginning, not the limit of what I wanted to know. He taught, and caused me to learn, a great deal of economics. He also taught me that blowing the place up and starting over was probably not a great idea (remarks made at David's memorial service).

This comment reflects the fact that David was never a communist.

Here is another student, David Stout, writing in a letter to Sylvia after David's death:

> I had the luck to have David as a dear friend and example throughout my scrambled career. No one has remotely influenced me so much. I always wanted him to be there and he was. When I walked in funk and despair out of one of the Webb Medley papers, David walked me round the deer park and talked me back into the Examination Schools. He talked me into trying for a Prize Fellowship and helped me to learn to teach by his own example and his trust ... I not only loved being in David's company, I admired him and wanted to be like him. His gaiety and his honesty, his acuity and his sympathy I found unfailing.

Here again is Kit McMahon: 'He was the most un-pompous, unstuffy of men, and the best of colleagues' (remark made at David's memorial service).

3.2   Other Academic Life

Besides his teaching at Magdalen, David also gave classes for the Workers' Educational Association (WEA) in Oxford. This organisation had had a long history in the socialist life of the country as universities took it upon themselves to provide education for working-class adults who did not have the means or the opportunity to attend a university themselves.

Early on in his time at Magdalen, David was involved in a number of committees and outside activities (see Artis 2003: 522). In 1946, he sat on a working party on the lace industry which required many visits to Nottingham. In 1951, he was a member of a committee on the purchase tax and another on tax paid stocks. He was also an expert witness for the Registrar of Restrictive Trade Practices. In all these activities, he deepened his knowledge of the inner workings of the British economy about which he wrote later wrote with such insight in his books and papers.

Artis writes:

David had great clarity of mind and a lot of plain common sense as well as economic intuition … He could listen to others and whilst of strong opinions on some subjects himself he did not allow this to impair his dealings with others. These qualities recommended himself to numerous others who needed a job done, especially one with economic content (ibid.).

4   Research and Writing

In 1952, David joint-edited an important book of studies of economic development and policies in various fields in the UK for the years 1945–1950. His co-editor was Peter H. Ady, a Fellow of St Anne's College, Oxford. David wrote the introductory chapter summarising the British economy as it developed between 1945, the end of the war, and 1950. Experts, including Ady, were tapped to write on twenty-four different aspects of the economy during those years from "Direct Controls" to "Britain and the Sterling Area". It was a comprehensive volume. Ten years later, a companion volume compiled by the same editors was published, entitled *The British Economy in the Nineteen-Fifties* (Worswick and Ady 1962) which comprised thirteen broader categories from the "Terms of Trade" and "Fiscal Policy" to "Government and

Industry". Once again, David wrote an extensive introduction for the years 1950–1960. These two volumes were the first of their kind in Britain to describe the domestic economy, its development as a whole and in its parts and the prevailing government economic policy at the time. They were used as the first textbooks in applied economics by many students and they offered a comprehensive and detailed description of the different economic sectors as well as a discussion of policy in which David was particularly interested.

The UK post-war recovery following 1945 was a solid one. A Labour government under Clement Atlee had been elected and significantly maintained full employment through the maintenance of aggregate demand and physical controls over the markets where demand was greatest. Some increase in prices resulted. The balance of payments, so important in a small, open economy like the UK, was in surplus in 1950, the same year that Marshall Aid ended. There was still substantial pent-up demand dating from the war years, and a price and wage freeze in 1948 had succeeded in slowing the rate of rise of prices and money incomes.

Unfortunately, the Korean War in the early 1950s upset the applecart. It had a profound effect on the economy of the US. The short-lived 1948–1949 recession precipitated the devaluation of the British pound. There was a large increase in expenditure on armaments in the US which, in starts and stops, ultimately saved the economy from a further slump. Total expenditure on imports rose rapidly and a balance of payments deficit crisis resulted. Moreover, a rearmament programme in the UK led to some increase in taxes and proposed cuts in social services. A general election was called in 1951 and the Conservatives took over the reins of government.

In his introduction to the second volume on the British economy David chronicles the success of the post-war economic recovery through the 1950s, a period referred to as the Golden Age, mainly in reference to the continuation of full employment. However, his insight into government economic policy at the time is not so sanguine. At the end of his chapter, he notes three grounds of criticism. First, the goals of policy were viewed as achievable as separate entities rather than being interlinked. He quotes the government statement: 'First we must get rid of inflation and put the balance of payment right *before* we can increase production' (Worswick 1962: 72; italics in original). He notes that this notion implied that a fall in production could actually help in expanding the economy. This counts as a "nonsequence", to use his invented word much appreciated by his students who called such words "Worsicisms". As soon as attention was brought back to the full employment goal, prices were already rising.

The second criticism was that direct controls were made less clear which meant that private decision-makers such as banks were confused about what rules to follow. The third criticism of policy is that it relied far too much on an implied harmony of private and public economic interests. For example, David noted:

> Where does the loyalty of the trade union leader lie: to his members, who press him to get higher wages or to the Chancellor [of the Exchequer] who begs him to hold off? As for business, whose rationale is profit, the public good is a luxury which may be expensive and even ruinous.

He continued: 'Persuasion and reliance upon the acceptance of the "full duties of citizenship" may have some small part to play, but carried to any length they contradict the principles of private enterprise: in such a system it is illogical to expect them to succeed' (ibid.: 74).

The papers in the rest of the book address this conflict between the social conscience of economic actors and their private interest in great detail. But it was always David's concern for social justice and fairness that pitted him against the various Conservative governments when it came to formulating clear policies for the maintenance of full employment. This concern he maintained in his writing and teaching long before he left Oxford.

During his years at Magdalen, David was deeply involved in all aspects of university life. He was Chairman of the Board of the Faculty of Social Studies from 1948. He became an examiner for the PPE degree from 1949 to 1951 and was Senior Tutor for the Magdalen from 1955 and served as Vice President during 1963–1965. He dined regularly in college both at lunch and in the evenings and would return home in a convivial mood after the wine, delicious food and interesting conversation. It was no wonder that he loved his time at Magdalen.

In the 1950s, his son, Richard, became a chorister in the Magdalen College choir. He was not a boarder at Magdalen College School as the other choristers were. So every evening before practice and Evensong, he would walk out of the front door of 62A High Street where we lived and join the procession of choristers as they came down from Magdalen College School and over the bridge towards the College. David was a frequent member of the congregation in the chapel for Evensong even though he claimed he did not believe in any religion and was agnostic about the existence of God. But he was proud of Richard and he loved the wonderful hymns, anthems and prayers sung by the choir. His favourite anthem was "Splendente Te, Deus" by Mozart which was also sung at his memorial service.

There were two breaks in his teaching career. First, he was appointed in 1954 as a member of a team of three economists by the United Nations (UNCTAD) to advise the Turkish government on economic development. This entailed moving to Ankara, Turkey, in January with the whole family. Unfortunately, the Turkish government was not receptive to the suggestions of the team and after six months they ended their assignment. David spent the last three months of his appointment in Geneva.

The second break from Oxford occurred in the academic year 1962–1963, when David was invited to MIT as a Visiting Professor. Among his colleagues were Paul Samuelson and Robert Solow. One frequent topic of conversation was incomes policy. This was certainly on David's mind as the question of how to maintain full employment and at the same time prevent wage and price inflation in the long run became politically more difficult. Incomes policy involved pitting the private interest of wage earners and higher prices and profits for businesses against the public interest of controlling both types of increase.

After his time at MIT, he was offered a position as Professor of Economics at Manchester University, which he declined. Shortly thereafter, he was appointed as Director of the National Institute of Economic and Social Research (NIESR), a post for which he was eminently suited. Thus, in 1965, he began a new chapter of his life.

5   The National Institute

David's new position presented him with challenges in many different areas. The first was the need to maintain, support and keep the NIESR's economic forecasting model. This meant providing accurate quarterly and annual forecasts for the UK for a myriad of different variables, not simply GDP, employment, incomes, prices, wages and interest rates, but also the budget and the balance of payments, including the levels of exports and imports, as well as the exchange rates with many other currencies. This was ongoing, time-sensitive work.

The second was the supervision of a large number of studies about particular regions and industries in different parts of the country, the nature of structural unemployment and differing regional growth rates. The third challenge was to clarify the need for government policy, in particular to ask how to maintain full employment and wage and price stability in a changing world in which prices tended to keep rising. David's answer was some form of incomes policy. The relationship between those economists who stressed demand management as the main full employment policy tool and those who stressed monetary goals to contain inflation was continually strained. At issue were the economic facts themselves as they described how the economy worked, not only the different political interests at work in forming official policy.

The fourth challenge was to clarify the balance of payments issues associated with making an economic policy which would sustain full employment. The last issue, which he encountered immediately, was the issue of funding to support the work of the Institute itself. This involved constant communication with and presentations to different sources of funding: the government, in particular the Treasury, large American foundations like Ford and Rockefeller, and many smaller private business sources.

6   Economic Forecasting

Let us begin a more detailed discussion of these challenges with economic forecasting and the econometric model. Its importance as part of David's activities at NIESR can be measured by the fact that modelling and forecasting for the economy absorbed half the Institute's budget.

Before describing the history of NIESR's modelling and forecasting, it is appropriate to comment on David's fundamental approach to measurement, modelling and forecasting in economics as a field which he lays out in his paper, "Is Progress in Economic Science Possible?" (Worswick 1972). He first observes that economic variables are not like scientific entities which have clear and particular meanings like specific gravity. Economic variables such as tons of steel are ultimately proxies for value or utility in the minds of consumers. Workers are proxies for hours of human labour which may vary in different situations. Also, relationships between economic variables, such as the consumption function in which income determines consumption, result from human decision-making which varies over time and circumstances. Therefore, the attempt to describe the economy in terms of its inter-related variables through the use of statistical techniques such as econometrics, and to make projections about the future of path of the economy based on econometric modelling, is fraught with difficulty and ambiguity from the start.

As an example of the false accuracy of econometric relationships, David cites the case of the Phillips curve. Using data from 1861 to 1913, Phillips estimated a single equation relating the change in wage rates in the UK to the level of unemployment. This relationship was then used to incorporate later data and form a prediction that 2.5% unemployment could stop inflation. This was then linked to another idea that a higher level of unemployment would be favourable to economic growth. These two simplifications together were seized on by government policy makers to form the notion that increasing the unemployment rate could stop inflation and advance economic growth. This turned its head on the idea that the goal of policy should be to reduce unemployment because of the poverty and social distress it caused. David pointed out that the Phillips curve relationship continued to have traction with some economists and policy makers even during years when unemployment and inflation were rising simultaneously and, as David cogently put it, 'virtually every Phillips curve ever invented had jumped off the page' (ibid.: 82).

When David came to the National Institute, he encouraged its Executive Committee to come to a decision that not more than one half of its resources be devoted to the regular quarterly forecast of the British economy and the accompanying analysis. This was important in that it prevented the Institute from being drawn into the development of ever more complicated and costly econometric modelling at a time when such activity and its seemingly endless demands were coming into their own. It also allowed time and resources to be devoted to other lines of research previously outlined in Section 3.2.

When David took over the Directorship of NIESR, the forward estimates of the main components of GDP were not yet the result of an econometric model per se. Individual equations describing specific relationships were relied on, but these equations were not joined together in a simultaneous model (see Jones 1998: Chapter 4). During the 1960s, the building of a complete econometric model gradually took place. But the need to linearise the individual equations was difficult since many of the successful forecasting relationships were non-linear and did not perform as well when transformed into the linear context of the simultaneous model. However, in August 1969, a suitable simulation program was developed for a non-linear model with eleven equations which generated forecasts.

The job of improving forecasts was the focus of a large amount of work by the NIESR research team over a wide range of subjects as the scope and capacity of computers increased. David was involved as a member of the editorial board in overseeing the development of forecasting during his years as Director. Jones noted in 1998 that:

> Today, the [NIESR's forecasting] model can be described as having Keynesian features in the short term, but with classical long-run properties such that output is determined by the size of the labor force and the state of technology. Recent research has continued to refine the model along a number of different lines, each combining empirical validity with theoretical rigour (ibid.: 34).

In 1971, David wrote an extraordinarily clear and honest introduction to a book by M.J.C. Surrey called *The Analysis and Forecasting of the British Economy* which laid out the methods used at that time by the National Institute to produce quarterly forecasts. The book encompassed a discussion of all the variables and equations used in the Institute's econometric model. In his introduction, David discussed the various different contexts for viewing and understanding forecasting methods and outcomes. The idea, he says, is to be completely open about the methodology of forecasting so that the student or researcher can reproduce for herself the Institute's forecasts based on the information in the book. The quarterly estimates should be consistent in two ways: first, the rules of accounting should be maintained within each time period, and second, the relationships between different variables within and between periods should be consistent with the postulated structural equations. He notes that, in its essentials, the forecasting process has changed relatively little:

> The first step is to make estimates of the probable changes in certain "exogenous" variables, notably investment, exports, import prices and public expenditure, and to derive the remaining "endogenous" variables, such as consumption and the volume of imports, by using a model which is, in its essentials, a lagged multiplier combined with an "accelerator" for stock-building (Worswick 1971: 4).

He then points to the increasing importance of computers in obtaining forecasts rapidly from changing one or more exogenous variables (ibid.).

The next question is to ask whether the forecasts are any good. But now you have to ask what exactly is being tested? The reason for this second question is that the judgment of the (human) forecaster may be used to adjust forecasts in the light of special knowledge not reflected in the equations. This judgment is important in improving the accuracy of the forecast. But to test its accuracy the actual forecast must be used and the number of available forecasts may be too few for very exacting tests. At quarterly intervals, one would still hardly be satisfied with twelve such observations, still a small number, and certainly not just one. In particular, trends may be hard to detect.

Another difficulty arises when account is taken of the fact that forecasts are made on the basis of "unchanged policies". It may be that policies are changed within the forecast period in which case it would be perverse to compare the actual outcome directly with the original forecast. Of course, the econometric model could be re-estimated with the policy change included, or with other measurement changes in some of the variables over the forecast period. But now it is not clear at all what the meaning of the accuracy of the original forecast is. It is comparing apples with oranges.

Finally, David addresses the National Institute model itself as described in Surrey's book and notes that it is small. Many of the equations which comprise it are non-linear and all have to be constantly maintained in the light of data and policy changes. (He notes that a larger and more comprehensive linear econometric model was tried, but it performed badly.) He draws attention to the Phillips curve relationship which was used to predict unemployment but notes that the relationship had broken down, necessitating a change in the model.

The idea that the National Institute should undertake economic forecasting originated with economists within the Treasury, and there had been some movement of economists between the two institutions. But David stresses that the National Institute forecasts were 'wholly independent. This cannot be emphasized strongly enough' (ibid.: 13). This is typical of the way that David led the Institute. The formation of the forecasts was a team effort by the Institute forecasters, including David, but uninfluenced by outside voices.

Two newspaper articles by economic correspondents attest to the appropriateness of David's and the National Institute forecasting team's approach to forecasting. The first was by Peter Jay in *The Times* on 25 November 1971. He noted that the Institute's quarterly forecasts were central to the reputation of conventional national income (or "Keynesian") projections. These forecasts were widely published and reported, but often faced a lack of public understanding of what the forecasters were trying to do. Jay refers to David's 'fascinating, totally intelligible and elegant introduction to M.J.C. Surrey's book on forecasting' (Jay 1971: 25), discussed above. He describes David as 'a rare economist who throughout a long and distinguished academic career has combined a superior mathematical proficiency with an unquenchable skepticism about the ability of econometrics to displace political economy and seasoned judgement in the management of national economic affairs' (ibid.).

The second article, from *The Sunday Telegraph* on 8 September 1972, is by Patrick Hutber who also concurs with the National Institute's approach to forecasting and policy-making. He refers to a recent Institute forecast as a 'prediction of what may happen if things go on as they are' (ibid.: 21). The case discussed shows 'just how damaging the effects of the current inflation are liable to be. Left unchecked, accelerating inflation next year would mean that much of the higher consumer spending would be swallowed up in rising prices, so that demand would be lower, production rise less and unemployment stay painfully high' (ibid.). Hutber then traces out further outcomes of the forecast which he claims he has been saying himself 'until my voice gets hoarse and my typing fingers ache' (ibid.). Such approval from the press about National Institute forecasts was not infrequent.

7   Other National Institute Projects

The half of the Institute's time not devoted to forecasting was given to many other lines of activity.[6] For example, early on, David enlisted Arthur Brown from Leeds University to head a team of young researchers to work on regional issues. This resulted in *The Framework of Regional Economics in the United Kingdom* (Brown 1972).

The next project concerned the process of technological diffusion, a comparatively new research area. George Ray headed the project which also involved international comparisons involving cooperation with research institutes in five other countries. This project attracted David's involvement in particular. Besides a number of papers, the work resulted in a 1974 book entitled *The Diffusion of New Industrial Processes: An International Study* edited by Nasbeth and Ray. After that came *Industrialization and the Basis of Trade*, Batchelor et al. (1980) and *The Management of the British Economy 1945–60*, by Dow, subsequently extended and updated as *British Economic Policy, 1960–74: Demand Management*, edited by Blackaby. Meanwhile, Sig Prais and Peter Hart produced substantial work on industrial concentration, large firms and mergers. Eventually, this and Prais's continuing work won for the National Institute the accolade of designated research center from the Economic and Social Research Council. A number of conferences were also launched which were designed to explore leading issues in economic policy, including incomes policy (see below), demand management, deindustrialisation, and Britain's trade and exchange rate policy.

In its later stages, this research was shared with Chatham House and the Policy Studies Institute. Some fifteen books were published under this joint sponsorship before 1987 under the heading "Studies in Public Policy". David also visited the Brookings Institution (about which more below in Section 10 on funding at NIESR) and based the form of the NIESR's conferences and publications on the *Brookings Papers on Economic Activity*.

8   Incomes Policy

It is interesting that there is no discussion of incomes policy in the book (or the index) by David and Peter Ady, *The British Economy in the Nineteen-Fifties*, published in 1962. During the years following the Second World War and in the 1950s and 1960s, unemployment in the UK was low but rising

---

[6] This section draws on Artis (2003: 519–520).

slowly. It was 1.0% in June 1951 and rose to 2.2% in May 1969 (see Brittan 1976: 250). Each percentage point increase in unemployment represented 100,000 more people out of work. The individual social cost to an involuntarily unemployed person was high in terms of poverty and social distress, so the multiplication by 100,000 of such costs was considerable. Nevertheless, in terms of percentages, during the Great Depression in the 1930s when unemployment rates were between 10% and 20%, and in the decades subsequent to the 1960s (the number of unemployed persons in the UK rose to 3.5 million in 1986), a figure of 2.2% was considered to be relatively low.

During the post-war decades, Keynesian demand management were still in effect. That is, fiscal but also monetary policies designed to increase investment to plug the gap between aggregate demand and income were employed. However, policy makers were conscious of the fact that excessive aggregate demand might lead to rising wage costs as unions took advantage of their strong position in the labour market to push for higher money wages, in turn causing businesses to respond by increasing their prices. So the question became, how to maintain full employment without inflation? For a time, the Phillips curve seemed to provide an answer: if the level of unemployment were kept at 2.5%, or what was regarded as the natural rate of unemployment, then the rate of price rises would be stabilised. However, this empirical relationship soon collapsed as described in Section 4, and the conflict between maintaining full employment and keeping prices under control re-emerged.

In his 1991 book, *Unemployment: A Problem of Policy*, written after he had retired from the National Institute, David defined incomes policy as referring to

> measures intended to influence directly the level, or the rate of change, of money incomes, especially wages and salaries … Historically, wages policy and incomes policy were first discussed as a means to contain the cost inflation which accompanied the full employment which came to be taken for granted in the years following the war. Analytically it fitted comfortably into the Keynesian paradigm (ibid.: 118).

He then goes on to enumerate the various forms which incomes policy could take. For example,

> a highly centralized system in which all money wages were fixed by a single authority. At the other end of the spectrum the policy might consist of no more than jawboning, resorted to, at one time or another, by virtually every post-war Chancellor of the Exchequer, urging all concerned to exercise restraint in claims for higher wages or salaries. Incomes policies can be embodied in voluntary

agreements between workers and employers, or between workers and employers' organisations and the government, or they can be imposed by law. They can be permanent features of the economic landscape or they can be introduced temporarily in response to some economic crisis (ibid.: 119).

The problem with the systematic use of incomes policy in the decades following the Second World War was that, while it fitted the Keynesian model of analysing the economy, it did not fit the monetarist model which assumed full employment. But it was the monetarist model that was gradually adopted by policy makers in Conservative governments especially that of Margaret Thatcher. As a result of monetarism, the government was no longer committed to keeping the unemployment rate low, but rather to preventing prices from rising too fast. However, during the 1980s, both the unemployment rate and inflation were increasing at the same time.

Since it is important for understanding incomes policy to know how economists thought the economy worked, it is necessary to look both at the Keynesian and monetarist models. In *Unemployment: A Problem of Policy*, David devoted some time to considering the monetarist model and the evidence which should support it. He started with a discussion of the quantity theory of money (QTM) using the well-known equation $MV = PT$, where M is the quantity of money in circulation, V is the velocity of circulation, P is the price level and T is the number of transactions. If Q stands for real national income, then $MV = PQ$, where Q is an index number for output and P is an index number of prices, and thus, $PQ = Y$ is the nominal national income. If $m = \log M$ and we adopt the same notation for the other variables, we have the logarithmic form of the money equation as $m + v = p + q = y$. This equation can then be used to test empirically the strength of the relationships between the variables. There are two versions of the QTM, the first saying that the money stock and nominal income move together, and the second, older version asserting that the money stock and prices move together.

Brown (1983) tests the relationship between the money stock and money income for different countries and finds that there were fifteen and a half cases where money changes led income changes, there were fourteen and a half cases of simultaneity and five cases where income led money (the halves refer to a dead heat). When the relationship between the money stock and prices was measured there were eleven and a half cases where money led prices, five of simultaneity, and nine and a half where prices led money. David concluded that, 'Brown's data show that changes in the velocity of circulation from year to year are not so much less variable than the changes in money growth that velocity can reasonably be treated as a constant' (Worswick 1991: 145).

In 1982, Friedman and Schwartz published a massive study of *Monetary Trends in the United States and the United Kingdom*, covering the period 1867–1975 in the US and the UK. Time series were assembled for money stock, nominal national income, price deflators, interest rates, the sterling-dollar exchange rate and other variables. The data were "decycled" by an unusual device of triplets of neighboring cycle periods. *Monetary Trends* formed the agenda of a meeting of the Bank of England's Panel of Academic Consultants in October 1983. Besides Friedman and Schwartz, a number of journal reviews were discussed as well as two specially prepared papers by Hendry and Ericsson (1983) and by Brown (1983). The former concluded that a number of the assertions made by Friedman and Schwartz about their money demand equation 'were found to be without empirical support' (Hendry and Ericsson 1983: 82) and their failure to produce evidence pertinent to their main assertions 'leaves these devoid of credibility' (ibid.).

David commented that this was 'strong language' (Worswick 1991: 146). But he goes on to show that in his paper, Brown demonstrates that in the short run the growth of money income is not related to money. It is velocity, not money, which varies with money income growth within cycles and in the period between the world wars this relationship was particularly strong in the UK. Then Brown examined the question of how an expansion of money income is partitioned between changes in output and in price. He found that extra demand had gone mostly into output when there was spare capacity and into inflation when full employment was approached. David concludes by stating that: 'Finally, when Brown asks the question whether [Friedman and Schwartz] make their case that United Kingdom experience supports a simple quantity theory, with money controlling prices, and output controlled by other factors entirely', he says, "In a word, no"'(ibid.).

During the 1950s and 1960s,[7] a "Stop-Go" was in place in which the "Goes" were mainly encouraged by a relaxation of fiscal policy to raise output and employment and the "Stops" were most engineered by a tightening of monetary policy in the form of higher interest rates, restrictions on bank advances and a stiffening of controls on consumer credit. In 1964, the Labour government set up a National Board for Prices and Incomes (NBPI) whose primary aim was to control inflation. The Trades Union Congress (TUC) at first reluctantly agreed to participate, and the policy was initially voluntary—and ineffective. A six-month statutory freeze of wages and prices was imposed in the mid-1960s. However, when the Conservatives came to power in 1970, they abolished the NBPI. Prices began to rise especially after the floating of

---

[7] The following discussion is based on Worswick (1991: Chapter 13).

the pound in June 1972 which caused import prices to rise. The Conservatives undertook long negotiations with the TUC to set up a new incomes policy. These failed and the government imposed a wage freeze which remained in effect for the rest of the Conservative administration.

In 1973, there was a double energy crisis: war began in the Middle East and the Arab oil producers cut supplies which led to a quadrupling in the world price of oil. A Labour government was returned to power after a general election in the UK in February 1974 and proceeded to drop all wage controls, retaining only threshold agreements and a Price Commission.

This tit-for-tat tussle between Conservative and Labour governments over the type and severity of incomes policies in the face of continuing price rises lasted until the Thatcher government took office in 1979. By that time, unemployment was rising along with prices, and in 1986 the number of unemployed had reached 3.1 million. David's reaction to this figure was to point out that the accumulation of person-years of unemployment was substantially higher in 1986 than in the 1930s!

The failure of incomes policy to contain prices while preserving the level of employment was seen by David, and no doubt many others, as the failure of reasonable people in government, in the TUC and other policy makers to put the collective good ahead of personal advantage. David always expected people to do the right thing and not to act for themselves alone. So he was constantly disappointed when self-interest and disingenuousness (as in the monetarist mantra) at the top of government frustrated the collective good as he saw it. But then he was a socialist and put the interests of the ordinary people before those of the ruling classes. This, of course, was also a key difference between the Labour and Conservative parties.

9   The Balance of Payments

David addressed another constraint on the making of economic policy in Britain, namely the balance of payments. In a small open economy, trade is, of course, an important part of national economic activity. In his 1991 book, David employed his skills as a teacher to explain how trade affects the economy (Worswick 1991: 206–231). The classical model, first laid out explicitly by Ricardo, shows that barter between two countries benefits both. When that model is extended to take into account exports and imports trading at some exchange rate, the balance of trade (the value of exports minus imports) affects the internal economy, particularly output, employment, wages and the domestic price level. David laid out the case for a tariff as a means to increase employment in the protected industry. But he shows that it does not increase overall employment; it diverts employment into the protected industry and at the expense of a loss of real income to consumers.

In a small open economy, the difference between the value of exports and imports has been the focus of economic policy as another constraint on the attempt to maintain full employment and domestic price stability. David's 1981 article "The Money Supply and the Exchange Rate" rehearses the arguments of the policy debate between the Keynesians and the monetarists with respect to their different conclusions about the effects on the exchange rate and the balance of payments of changes in the money supply. For example, suppose there is a deficit in the balance of trade which policy makers believe will not correct itself soon enough. Then monetary policy could be undertaken to reduce the money supply and raise interest rates. This would cause an inflow of funds and a rise in the exchange rate causing a reduction in exports, a rise in imports and lower output and employment. On the other hand, if fiscal policy is tightened (higher taxes and/or lower government spending) in order to reduce demand for imports then domestic employment will fall as output is reduced. This is because the negative effects on output of a tighter fiscal policy (due to reduced consumption and investment) are likely to outweigh the upward effect on output due to lower imports.

In 1944, the Bretton Woods agreement fixed exchange rates to the US dollar. The IMF was set up at the same time to provide temporary funding for countries in deficit. The Marshall Plan also came into operation, providing significant amounts of aid from the US to the countries devastated by war. The explicit policy of maintaining full employment was affirmed by the UK government and led to a devaluation of sterling in November 1967. As noted, in 1972, sterling was allowed to float as the Bretton Woods system broke down. Devaluation had become another policy tool to help in achieving the goal of demand management when the balance of payments was also a significant policy objective along with full employment and only modest increases in prices.

10   The Problem of Funding

The problem of how to find financial support for an independent institute such as NIESR was present at its beginning and was still present when David became Director in 1965. The original grants from the Ford and Rockefeller foundations were ending and the UK Treasury, which had previously provided substantial funds, had decided that these should be directed away from forecasting in order to avoid the perception that the Institute's forecasts might be unduly influenced by the government. But, in 1965, David was invited to become a member of the Social Science Research Council (SSRC) under the Chairmanship of Michael Young. David accepted this position with the open recognition that the Institute would shortly be applying for SSRC funds. These funds were forthcoming in the form of programme and development grants and put the Institute's financing on a firmer footing for the next ten years. However, other applicants for SSRC funds objected to the priority of giving such generous funding to NIESR. A coup was attempted in the form of a proposal to establish a "British Brookings". This was an implied criticism of NIESR's policies which were viewed in Conservative circles as too Keynesian. At the same time, if adopted, the establishment of such a competitor would have probably completely bled the Institute's finances. Then it happened that one week David was asked to accept a cut of £200,000 for the Institute, and the next week he read an announcement that exactly the same amount of money was to be set aside for a "British Brookings". But as Artis states: 'David was always reasonable but never soft. He could defend his corner fiercely and did so on the occasion. In an atmosphere of considerable tension he had the decision reversed' (Artis 2003: 518–519).

As a by-product, NIESR joined forces with two other threatened institutes to arrange a series of conferences with eventual book publications to deal with various topics of the day, much like the practice of the Brookings Institution. However, shortly afterwards, Margaret Thatcher came to power and Treasury funding was run down. Other funding was eventually found and the Institute continued to produce quarterly forecasts and a substantial amount of research in a wide variety of topics, as has been detailed in Section 4.

11   Retirement

David retired from the Directorship of the National Institute in 1982 and moved back to Oxford with Sylvia. They bought a house at 25 Beechcroft Road in Summertown, North Oxford, where Sylvia created a third beautiful garden behind the house (the other two were at 62A High Street, Oxford, and at 7 Highmore Road, Blackheath, in London). From Summertown, David could cycle to Magdalen where he was appointed Fellow Emeritus and Sylvia could cycle to a school where she volunteered as a teacher of English as a second language. They were both very happy in their retirement and David's activities continued apace.

David turned down offers of teaching, noting that, 'I marveled at the confidence with which I had been prepared to teach a wide range of subjects a mere twenty years earlier' (Worswick quoted in Artis 2003: 521). One exciting opportunity came when he was made President of the Royal Economic Society. Among many other tasks, this involved organising a major international conference to recognise the centenary of the birth of John Maynard Keynes on 5 June 1883. The conference was held at King's College, Cambridge, in July 1983 and was attended by distinguished economists from all over the world. It came at a time when Keynes's macroeconomic ideas were under attack by Conservative policy makers with monetarist convictions in the UK and the US. So the large gathering of Keynesian economists created a particularly exhilarating atmosphere.

Many of the papers addressed the microfoundations of Keynes's theories, in particular by trying to explain the Walrasian and monetarist theories that predict that less than full employment is a disequilibrium circumstance which will disappear in the medium to long run. In his writing, David did not explicitly present or discuss the mathematical models supporting such arguments. The empirical evidence against them was perhaps enough for him. However, he recognised that the two main reasons for the economy getting stuck in unemployment are that money wages are sticky downwards and that the liquidity trap prevents interest rates from falling below a certain level. Lowering interest rates is supposed to encourage investment. Investment is in any case inelastic at low interest rates and certainly unaffected when the interest rate cannot fall any further. Therefore, increasing the money supply will be useless in this circumstance. Moreover, the Keynesian model does not provide an equilibrating mechanism for halting inflation once full employment has been achieved by demand management. This is why David always emphasised incomes policy as the only solution.

In that centenary year of 1983, I organised a "Keynes Day" at Drew University in Madison, New Jersey, where I was Associate Professor of Economics. The event took place in the Great Hall at Drew on 11 November. I had noticed that no celebration or even mention of Keynes was occurring in the US to mark the centenary of Keynes's birth. I invited my father to give the keynote lecture and a prominent post-Keynesian (American) economist, Paul Davidson from Rutgers University, to give the second lecture in the morning. After lunch, there was a panel discussion among the following economists: Lorie Tarshis, a former pupil of Keynes, who still possessed the class notes he had taken during Keynes's lectures in Cambridge, Robert Solow from MIT, Orley Ashenfelter from Princeton University and Leonard Silk, the economics editor of *The New York Times*.

David's talk addressed the 'practical results' of Keynes's theories. He first drew attention to Keynes's pre-Second World War approaches to economic issues. Keynes's book, *Economic Consequences of the Peace* (Keynes 1919 [1971]), warned that the harsh reparations imposed on the defeated Germany and its allies after the First World War would result in depression and political backlash in those countries. This, in fact, occurred and also led to the rise of fascism. Keynes's essay, "The Economics Consequences of Mr. Churchill" (Keynes 1925 [1972]), who was then Chancellor of the Exchequer in Britain, warned of the harm that a high exchange rate and adherence to the gold standard was doing to the UK economy.

David then turned to Keynes's post-war influence and, for the American audience he was addressing, emphasised the impact of the Bretton Woods Agreement of 1944 which set the terms of international exchange for a quarter of a century. Bretton Woods led to unprecedented growth and full employment in the advanced countries for twenty years after the war, the so-called Golden Age. At Bretton Woods, Keynes was the negotiator for Britain and Harry Dexter White represented the US. In the end, Keynes's ideas for an international central back and currency to be used by the bank were not adopted. Instead, White's more modest plan was put in place. The gold standard was abolished and currencies were to be tied to the dollar at fixed exchange rates; the dollar was then exchangeable for gold at \$35 an ounce. The fixed rates could be readjusted if a country's trade became too unbalanced. The IMF and the World Bank were formed to monitor trade and promote borrowing and lending between countries. However, Bretton Woods collapsed at the beginning of the 1970s and exchange rates were allowed to float freely. As noted, prices began to rise and the goal of full employment was not met. Rather, inflation control became the number one policy objective.

In his talk during the afternoon panel discussion, Robert Solow pointed out that Keynes's macroeconomic model delineating the relationship between aggregate economic variables such as national income, consumption, investment, savings, employment and so on led to an outpouring of attempts to measure them. The new field of econometrics was then used to test the relationships between these variables in the context of Keynes's structure of the economy. Empirical measures of the consumption function, the causes of investment and other relationships then burgeoned. Even though Keynes's influence on full employment policies may have waned, his legacy in the field of macroeconomic measurement and forecasting lives on.

David's scholarly writing continued apace after his retirement. In 1991, partly working from an office in the National Institute, he completed his book, *Unemployment: A Problem of Policy*. As the title indicates, David always believed that the persistence of medium to high levels of unemployment as occurred after the Golden Age was not the result of a macroeconomic and monetary theory that required maintaining a higher rate of unemployment as the only way to dampen inflation. Adjusting demand to maintain employment, accompanied by incomes policy that was needed to prevent rising wages and prices, was rejected by some economists and policy makers alike in favour of tight monetary policy and adjusting the balance of payments. In a later article entitled "Has Mass Unemployment Come to Stay?" (Worswick 1994), David concludes that

> the obstacles in the way of achieving (a full employment economy) are, I think, as much moral and political as they are economic. On the domestic front, sectional interests of all kinds must learn to refrain from pushing to the limits of their strength for what may appear to be their sectional advantage. In the international arena cooperation is necessary…but very hard to achieve … I am not so pessimistic as to give an unconditional Yes in answer to my original question. But in all honesty I have to say that I shall be agreeably surprised if we see the end of mass unemployment in the United Kingdom before the end of this century (ibid.: 21).

In 2000, the unemployment rate was 5.4% and fell in 2001, the year of David's death, to 5.1%. These figures are too high in David's moral terms compared with the Golden Age levels of below 2%. In the first decade of the twenty-first century, the unemployment rate climbed to 8.1% in 2011 due to the Great Recession. It then began to fall, standing at 4.1% in 2018, with 1.36 million people unemployed.

12   Activities and Honours

Before going to the National Institute, David pre-invented the Norrington Tables, which listed by college the results obtained by Oxford students in their final examinations (see Artis 2003: 522). These were published in the Oxford Magazine and were always much referred to. He discontinued these in 1963 and subsequently a similar list was produced by Sir Arthur Norrington, after whom the list was named. Later, David was invited to join a committee to review admissions to the University in the light of the creation in 1961 of the Universities Central Council on Admissions system.

He was a founding member of the Social Science Council and was President of Section F of the British Association in 1972. He served on the government's Committee on Policy Optimization in 1978 and from 1982 to 1990 he was on City University's Council. In 1975, David received a DSc from City University and was very pleased to be elected a Fellow of the British Academy in 1979. From 1986/1987 and 1988/1989, he served as Chairman of its Section 9. In 1981, he was awarded a CBE.

13   David's Broader Life

David had a broad range of interests besides economics. He was an enthusiastic walker and adored climbing the mountains and hills of Scotland and the Lake District. Many family holidays were spent in these beautiful places. Another passion was music. David loved all kinds of classical music which was all we ever heard on the radio or on records.

Perhaps a good way to end this "Life" is to quote from a piece written by David's grandson Robert, son of Eleanor and Tom Stanier. Tom read it at David's memorial service since Robert was in India. Robert Stanier had been an undergraduate at Magdalen College reading Greats:

> It was a late summer morning four years ago, and my tutor at the time, being a young and trendy type, suggested that we have the tutorial outside. So we sat down to discuss my essay on the grass in Longwall Quad. After a few minutes, though, I caught sight of David, wheeling his bicycle in through the gate. He put it on the bike stands and methodically locked it up, took off his helmet and his cycle clips and began to walk steadily around the path towards the SCR Dining Room to claim his free lunch. When he looked up, he caught sight of me waving and came towards us. My tutor was not quite sure what to make of this man. I explained that he was my grandfather and as David came across, he had a smile on his face. It was the day after the General Election and Labour had finally returned to power. I asked if he was pleased, and David said that he was, but he assured my tutor that New Labour was not really him; in fact he was not just Old Labour, he was Dinosaur Labour! My tutor laughed. Then, after a short conversation, David took himself off, and as he walked away, I caught my tutor looking away at him. He seemed partly in awe at this distinguished college figure who had been walking the quads of Magdalen for over fifty years yet was still completely on the ball, and partly amused: after all, David did strike a somewhat comic figure with his bright yellow sash to ward off traffic, and his trousers tucked into his socks and it was improbably bizarre that someone of his years would still be cycling into college.

As for me, I looked at David largely with pride. In part, I took pride in the simple fact that he was the oldest Fellow in the College and that he was my grandfather. Yet, I was also proud because he was someone who had not given up his principles, be they political—he was still supporting Labour and had got some reward at last—or just with regard to cycling; he was still using the bicycle stands long after all the other fellows were behind the steering wheels of their cars.

David died on 18 May 2001. I was as proud of him at his death as I was when he came to visit me in nursery school when I was three and brought me my lunch. He was deeply honest and taught us always to tell the truth, a lesson which has stood me in good stead throughout my life. The reason he eschewed joining any government as a policy maker was precisely that he did not want to compromise with the truth in any way. He was a dedicated teacher who cared passionately about his students and the lessons he taught them. He was consistently a public servant in many areas throughout his life. His writing was clear and accessible and always relied on the evidence as it was presented. He made his passionately held case for full employment policy whenever he could. He was disappointed that the Golden Age was never repeated because of his deep compassion for the unemployed. He was a good man who was much loved.

References

Main Works by David Worswick

Burchardt, F.A. et al. (1944). *The Economics of Full Employment*. Six Studies in Applied Economics Prepared at the Oxford University Institute of Statistics. Oxford: Basil Blackwell.

Worswick, G.D.N. (1944). 'Points, Prices and Consumers' Choice'. *Bulletin of the Oxford University Institute of Economics and Statistics*, 6(3): 33–49.

Worswick, G.D.N. (1959). 'Mrs. Robinson on Simple Accumulation: A Comment with Algebra'. *Oxford Economic Papers*, New Series, 11(2): 125–142.

Worswick, G.D.N (1962). 'The British Economy, 1950–1959'. Chapter 1 in G.D.N. Worswick and P.H. Ady (eds) *The British Economy in the Nineteen–Fifties*. Oxford: Clarendon Press: 1–75.

Worswick, G.D.N. (1971). 'Introduction'. In M.J.C. Surrey *The Analysis and Forecasting of the British Economy*. London: Cambridge University Press: 1–14.

Worswick, G.D.N. (1972). 'Is Progress in Economic Science Possible?'. *Economic Journal*, 82(325): 73–86. Reprinted as Chapter 2 in G.D.N. Worswick (ed.) (1972) *Uses of Economics*. Oxford: Basil Blackwell: 21–38.

Worswick, G.D.N. (ed.) (1976). *The Concept and Measurement of Involuntary Unemployment*. London: Allen & Unwin.

Worswick, G.D.N. (1981). 'The Money Supply and the Exchange Rate'. *Oxford Economic Papers*, New Series, 33(Supplement): 9–22.

Worswick, G.D.N. (1991). *Unemployment: A Problem of Policy*. Cambridge: Cambridge University Press/National Institute of Economic and Social Research.

Worswick, G.D.N. (1994). 'Has Unemployment Come to Stay?' *Contemporary British History*, 8(1): 1–22.

Worswick, G.D.N. and P.H. Ady (eds) (1952). *The British Economy, 1945–1950*. Oxford: Clarendon Press.

Worswick, G.D.N. and P.H. Ady (eds) (1962). *The British Economy in the Nineteen-Fifties*. Oxford: Clarendon Press.

Worswick, G.D.N. and J. Trevithick (eds) (1983). *Keynes and the Modern World*. Proceedings of the Keynes Centenary Conference, King's College, Cambridge. Cambridge: Cambridge University Press.

Other Works Referred To

Artis, M. (2003). 'George David Norman Worswick, 1916–2001'. *Proceedings of the British Academy*, 120: 515–524.

Batchelor, R.A., R.L. Major and A.D. Morgan (1980). *Industrialization and the Basis of Trade*. Cambridge: Cambridge University Press.

Blackaby, F.T. (ed.) (1978). *British Economic Policy, 1960–74: Demand Management*. Cambridge: Cambridge University Press/National Institute of Economic and Social Research.

Brittan, S. (1976). 'Full Employment Policy: A Reappraisal'. Chapter 13 in G.D.N. Worswick (ed.) *The Concept and Measurement of Involuntary Unemployment*. London: Allen & Unwin: 249–278.

Brown, A. (1972). *The Framework of Regional Economics in the United Kingdon*. London: Cambridge University Press/National Institute of Economic and Social Research.

Brown, A.J. (1983). 'Friedman and Schwartz on the United Kindgom'. In *Monetary Trends in the United Kingdom*. Bank of England Panel of Academic Consultants, Panel Paper No. 22. London: Bank of England: 9–43.

Dow, J.C.R. (1964). *The Management of the British Economy 1945–60*. London: Cambridge University Press/National Institute of Economic and Social Research.

Friedman, M. and A.J. Schwartz (1982). *Monetary Trends in the United States and the United Kingdom: Their Relation to Income, Prices, and Interest Rates, 1867–1975*. Chicago: National Bureau of Economic Research.

Harcourt, G.C. (2012). *Full Employment*. Discussion Papers 2012–39, School of Economics, University of New South Wales.

Hendry, D.F. and N.R. Ericsson (1983). 'Assertion Without Empirical Basis: An Econometric Appraisal of "*Monetary Trends in…the United Kingdom*" by Milton Friedman and Anna Schwartz'. In *Monetary Trends in the United Kingdom*. Bank of England Panel of Academic Consultants, Panel Paper No. 22. London: Bank of England: 45–101.

Hutber, P. (1972). 'How to Read the Various Forecasts … Mr. Rogaly Rolls About the Floor'. *The Sunday Telegraph*, 8 September: 21 and 23.

Jay, P. (1971). 'Clearing the Name of Economic Forecasters'. *The Times*, 25 November: 25.

Jones, K. (1998). *Sixty Years of Economic Research: A Brief History of the National Institute of Economic and Social Research*. London: National Institute of Economic and Social Research, Occasional Paper No. 52.

Keynes, J.M. (1919) [1971]. *The Economic Consequences of the Peace*. Volume II of *The Collected Writings of John Maynard Keynes*. London: Macmillan.

Keynes, J.M. (1925) [1972]. 'The Economic Consequences of Mr Churchill'. In *Essays in Persuasion*. Volume IX of *The Collected Writings of John Maynard Keynes*. London: Macmillan: 207–230.

Nasbeth, L. and G.F. Ray (eds) (1974). *The Diffusion of New Industrial Processes: An International Study*. London: Cambridge University Press/National Institute of Economic and Social Research.

Oxford Mail (1949). 'Academic Salaries To Go Up At Once'. 30 November: 2.

Solow, R.M. (1963). *Capital Theory and the Rate of Return*. Amsterdam: North-Holland.

Worswick, S. (2001). *Obituary of David Worswick*. Unpublished.

20

Ian Little (1918–2012)

Christopher Bliss and Vijay Joshi

1 Introduction

Ian Malcolm David Little, who died on 13 July 2012, at the age of 93, was one of Britain's foremost economists and, for a time, the world's most influential development economist. Ian had a mind of unusual penetration, subtlety and creative power. The quantity and quality of his scholarly output was impressive, and he wrote or edited around twenty books and about a hundred papers, some of which were path-breaking. He also made an impact beyond the groves of academe. His seminal writings undermined the orthodox postwar view that protectionism and dirigiste central planning were the road to prosperity for developing countries. He became, thereby, one of the intellectual leaders of the shift in most of these countries towards liberal trade policies, which made a major contribution to lifting millions of people out of

We thank the British Academy for its kind permission to reprint here our memoir "Ian Malcolm David Little, 1918–2012", *Biographical Memoirs of Fellows of the British Academy*, 2014, XIII, London: Oxford University Press: 315–349.

C. Bliss (✉)
Nuffield College, Oxford University, Oxford, UK
e-mail: christopher.bliss@nuffield.ox.ac.uk

V. Joshi
Merton College, Oxford University, Oxford, UK
e-mail: vijay.joshi@merton.ox.ac.uk

© The Author(s), under exclusive license to Springer Nature Switzerland AG 2021
R. A. Cord (ed.), *The Palgrave Companion to Oxford Economics*,
https://doi.org/10.1007/978-3-030-58471-9_20

poverty in the last quarter of the twentieth century. Astonishingly, he was not knighted.

This chapter is divided into several sections. The next section is an account of Ian's life, career and personality. Later sections discuss his writings in the main areas which bear his imprint: theoretical welfare economics; applied welfare economics (project evaluation); trade and development; and the Indian economy. The last section appraises his work as investment bursar of Nuffield College, Oxford.

2   Life, Career, Personality

The sketch of Ian's life below is an inferior substitute for his own 2004 account in *Little by Little* (hereafter *LbL*), a remarkable autobiography that combines detached frankness with dry humour. Another useful source for details of his life and views is *Collection and Recollections* (hereafter *CaR*), published in 1999, which reprints some of his articles (selected by him), interspersed with his later reflections.

Ian was born on 18 December 1918 into a large, upper middle class, family. He writes in *LbL* that his lineage both on his father's and his mother's side was devoid of intellectual distinction. A harsh judgement but, even if true, distinction as such was not lacking. His grandfather was a general in the British army, his father a brigadier general, and they both commanded the 9th Lancers. On his mother's side, he was descended from Thomas Brassey, the great Victorian entrepreneur, who built railways all over the world. The family was well-off. According to *LbL*, Ian's childhood home had

> 23 bedrooms…and an appropriate number of reception rooms, servants' rooms and offices and so forth. It stood in about four acres of garden. There were six cottages, housing four gardeners, the butler, the head groom … There were ten or more horses…two motor cars … Within the house, there were eight or nine servants making about 20 in all. This was all apart from the mixed farm of about 180 acres with another three cottages for the bailiff and other farm workers (*LbL* 2004: 10).

But family relationships were distant: 'It was Nanny who was the real parent' (ibid.: 15). After early instruction at the hands of a governess and a prep school, Ian went to Eton. He did quite well in examinations but was not regarded as a high-flier, partly because of his inability to learn by heart. He describes himself in *LbL* as painfully shy and fearful of sexual advances by older boys: he took up carpentry to avoid being in his house during the evening hours. He left school as soon as he was admitted to Oxford, because he was terrified of making the customary end-of-year speech to a gathering of parents. Travel during his gap year gave him 'some self-confidence which was woefully lacking' (*CaR* 1999: 5). All in all, while it would be an exaggeration to say that he suffered his Etonian education, he certainly did not much enjoy it.

Ian went up to New College, Oxford, to read Philosophy, Politics and Economics (PPE) in 1938. For some time, he was by his own account a hunting, drinking, gambling man, lacking any focus or direction. Things improved after the first two terms, when his intellectual interests were stimulated by philosophy tutorials with Isaiah (later Sir Isaiah) Berlin, and his friendship with Monty Woodhouse (later Lord Terrington). Even so, he writes in *LbL*, 'if it had not been for the war, I would not have got a first, perhaps not even a second' (*LbL* 2004: 43). Called up soon after war was declared, he served for nearly the full six years in the Airborne Forces Experimental Establishment of the Royal Air Force. At first, he flew autogyros, which were used to calibrate the ring of radar stations that warned of approaching enemy planes. Later, he was a test pilot and flew some hair-raisingly dangerous contraptions such as the "rotachute", an innovative rotary-wing device designed by Raoul Hafner to be a super-parachute for dropping airborne soldiers, and the "rotabuggy", also designed by Hafner, that was intended to convert a jeep into a flying machine by attaching a two-bladed rotor.[1] Much skill and courage was required in these obligatory adventures; he had several crashes and nearly met his death in one of them. Though he made light of the dangers (he compares himself in *LbL* to 'a sort of James Bond, before he was even conceived' (ibid.: 50)), the Air Force Cross that he was awarded towards the end of the war was clearly well deserved.

In 1945, he was demobilised with the rank of squadron leader and returned to undergraduate studies at New College. The war had changed him profoundly. Before, he had been an amiable playboy, uninterested in scholarship. Now, he threw himself into academic study and resolved to become an academic. He took papers in philosophy (tutors: Isaiah Berlin and Herbert Hart) and economics (tutor: Philip Andrews) and got an outstanding First in PPE in the summer of 1947, and then a scholarship to Nuffield College to do graduate work in economics. He chose economics over philosophy because it offered wider possibilities and, as he says in *LbL*, 'it seemed at the time that

---

[1] During the intervals between these test flights, Ian trained as a pilot of the Sikorsky helicopter that had just arrived in England.

philosophers were cleverer than economists and so the competition would be less severe' (ibid.: 77).

His graduate supervisor was the eminent J.R. (later Sir John) Hicks, but they got on very badly. Ian was critical of his supervisor's work and Hicks was so affronted that he tried, thankfully without success, to get Ian's scholarship discontinued.[2] Shortly thereafter, Ian was elected to a Prize Fellowship (a fellowship by examination) at All Souls College, Oxford. Isaiah Berlin is said to have remarked that Ian 'was the most ignorant person to get a fellowship at All Souls' (ibid.: 79). Presumably, he meant that his breadth of knowledge fell far short of a typical young fellow's, but he made up for that in superior analytical power. At All Souls, Ian finished in two years his doctoral thesis, *A Critique of Welfare Economics* (hereafter *A Critique*). Though it was largely self-directed, he acknowledged helpful conversations with William Baumol, Jan Graaff and Lionel McKenzie. The thesis was examined by Arthur (later Sir Arthur) Lewis and David Worswick. It was however rejected for publication by Macmillan.[3] This was a bad business decision: it was published instead by Oxford University Press (OUP) in 1950, became a classic, sold 70,000 copies, and established Ian's world reputation as an economic theorist. *A Critique* was motivated by a deep conviction that welfare economics had become a pretentious subject, insulated from good sense. What does it mean to say that one economic outcome is better for society than another? This is among the most basic, foundational questions in welfare economics. Ian demonstrated in *A Critique* that an ethical judgement about the distribution of income is intrinsic to any legitimate answer to this question, and that the search for some objective, value-free criterion of economic improvement is doomed to failure. While that is the justly famous central point of the book, we can see, retrospectively, that it made another advance. It clearly foreshadowed the theory of the second best, the idea that if one of the Pareto conditions is violated, satisfaction of one or all of the others would not, in general, constitute an improvement in efficiency. This proposition is stressed time and again in the middle chapters of *A Critique*, though a formal proof had to wait for the famous article by Richard Lipsey and Kelvin Lancaster in the *Review of Economic Studies*. Ian himself followed up *A Critique* in 1951 with a short

---

[2] On Hicks, see Creedy (2013).

[3] In *LbL*, Ian speculates that the referee was A.C. Pigou. The passage is worth quoting: 'The anonymous referee's report said that I seemed incapable of grasping the elementary distinction between the size of a cake and the way it is sliced. As it was a central and closely argued message of the thesis that no such distinction can be drawn, because one does not know the size of the cake until one knows how it is sliced, this was a frustrating comment. I do not know for certain who the referee was, but I think it was A.C. Pigou' (*LbL* 2004: 81).

paper in the *Economic Journal*, refuting the alleged superiority of direct over indirect taxes. This was a rigorous exercise in the economics of the second best, of which there is not, so far as we know, another such early example, except Jacob Viner's work on customs unions, which appeared at about the same time (see Viner 1950).

In 1950, Ian succeeded Anthony Crosland as Fellow and Tutor in Economics at Trinity College, Oxford. He was there for two years, during which he wrote two well-known papers: a review article (for which he retained a special fondness) in the *Journal of Political Economy* (Little 1952a) of Kenneth Arrow's *Social Choice and Individual Values*, and the paper on "Direct Versus Indirect Taxes" mentioned above. He was elected an Official Fellow of Nuffield College, Oxford, in 1952, and it remained his base thereafter, despite several spells away. After a year at Nuffield in which he wrote a policy-orientated book, *The Price of Fuel*, he was seconded in 1953 to Whitehall for two years as Deputy Director of the Economic Section of the UK Treasury, under Sir Robert Hall. This spell of government duty stimulated an abiding interest in problems of economic management and policy. He continued writing books and articles after his return to Nuffield. During 1955–1958, Ian directed and published (jointly with Richard Evely) a study of concentration in British industry, and wrote articles on capital theory, as well as (jointly with Robert Neild and C.R. Ross) a long memorandum of evidence for the Radcliffe Committee on monetary policy. In addition, he collaborated with Paul Rosenstein-Rodan on a study of nuclear energy in Italy. Looking back, he later described himself in this phase as lacking in focus. He was clearly still searching for an area of specialisation.

To this end, the Rosenstein-Rodan connection proved to be critical: he invited Ian to join the MIT India Project. The Project Team that went to India in 1958 consisted of Ian, George Rosen and Trevor Swan. Ian and Swan established a close relationship with Pitambar Pant, the head of the Perspective Planning Division of the Planning Commission, and became intimately involved with producing India's Third Five-Year Plan. The nine months in India were a turning point in Ian's career: thereafter, he became primarily a development economist.[4] For Ian, the road to Delhi was to be the road to Damascus. At that preliminary stage, however, his work did not depart much from contemporary orthodoxy, and was supportive of central planning. The India trip also got him interested in the economics of foreign aid. After a

---

[4] 'The nine months that I spent in India was a turning point in my career. I became a development economist. I felt that there were problems that an open-minded economist could help to solve; and the terrible poverty would greatly increase the value of any material improvement one could help to bring about. But this was not the main influence. I think this was simply that I liked India and Indians' (*LbL* 2004: 107).

three-month tour of Africa in 1963, funded by the Overseas Development Institute (ODI), he wrote two books on the subject (*Aid to Africa* and *International Aid*, the latter co-authored with Juliet Clifford). These were sympathetic to the objective of aid but expressed severe doubts about the absorptive capacity of African developing countries at that time.

The breakthrough in Ian's work on development came after his second trip to India in 1965, again on behalf of the MIT India Project. This time, relations with the Planning Commission turned out to be less cordial. So, Ian made his services available to the Bell Mission of the World Bank, which was visiting the country. As part of this consultancy, Ian was asked to do an economic appraisal of a heavy electrical plant in Bhopal. This project was a clear instance of plan-driven import substitution. If the Indian five-year plan model was soundly based, this project should have scored high marks. Ian came to the opposite conclusion. While doing the project evaluation, he realised that the investment made sense only if inputs and outputs were valued at domestic market prices. Valued at world prices, which are the true measures of opportunity cost in an open economy, the project was a waste of money. This was the seed from which sprouted his cardinal insight that economic progress in many developing countries had gone off the rails as a result of neglecting the use of foreign trade.[5] This idea was to provide the focus of Ian's work for the next ten years, during which he wrote two path-breaking books.

Both books were initiated during a two-year stint as Vice President of the OECD Development Centre in Paris from 1966 to 1968. They were written with others but Ian was the driving force. The first, *Industry and Trade in Some Developing Countries*, appeared in 1970 and was co-authored with Maurice Scott and Tibor Scitovsky. Using theory, as well as empirical evidence from six background country studies, it argued that trade controls, and inward-looking policies more generally, impose large economic costs and reduce employment

---

[5] 'My work on Bhopal was a major factor in changing my ideas about planning development. I concluded that this very large project was seriously flawed in conception, implementation, and current operations, and that it promised a very low rate of financial and social return. The project evaluation work of other members of the Bell Mission suggested that Bhopal was no exception. If planning threw up many projects that seemed to have a very low rate of return, belief in planning—anyway, planning as it was actually done was undermined. A related lesson was that one of the reasons for the low calculated rate of return was that the advantages of international trade were being neglected. This insight, blindingly obvious as it now appears, was then quite a revelation, for the ethos of development economics at the time prohibited any attention to the advantages of trade' (*LbL* 2004: 129). Note that Ian's change of view about economic planning constituted an abandonment of the earlier influence of Rosenstein-Rodan whose big push theory of economic development argued for rapid industrialisation on all fronts in economies with surplus labour in agriculture to take advantage of network effects. While undoubtedly well intended, the big push theory is toxic to rigorous and effective economic planning. It makes it acutely difficult to consider economic performance piecemeal, as any apparent local failings may be offset by network effects, which are easy to invoke but impossible to measure.

and growth. It advocated radical trade liberalisation, but not laissez-faire: it was explicitly in favour of using taxes and subsidies to offset domestic market failures. It also showed that some developing countries, notably South Korea and Taiwan, were already breaking out of economic stagnation on the basis of export-oriented policies. The book had a huge impact on development thinking and policy and its message has stood the test of time. There is now a wide consensus that an open trade policy is a necessary, though not a sufficient, condition of economic transformation.

Ian's other outstanding book on development, also initiated at the OECD, was *Manual of Industrial Project Analysis II, Social Cost-Benefit Analysis* (Little and Mirrlees 1969), published later in revised form as *Project Appraisal and Planning for Developing Countries* (Little and Mirrlees 1974). It was written in collaboration with James (later Sir James) Mirrlees and proposed an original and constructive scheme of social cost-benefit analysis for project evaluation, sensitive to foreign trade opportunities as well as distributional considerations. It had a major influence on the practice of project selection in the World Bank and elsewhere (see also Joshi 1972). Notably, Ian himself succeeded in persuading the Indian Planning Commission to set up a Project Appraisal Division.

For many years, Ian's work as a development economist did not give him entry to the UK development economics community. The circle of UK development economists was then a closed shop dominated by a "structuralist" view that held underdeveloped countries to be a separate family, to which orthodox (and especially neoclassical) methods had no application. The role of prices in economic development was underplayed because they were seen as chiefly to do with distribution, in which regard they could easily be offset by taxation and price regulation. That prices have crucial effects through the incentives that they create for action, however obvious that may now seem, was not then regarded as important.[6] If Ian's decision to become a development economist gave him no entry to the national community, it proved to be worth even less when it came to recognition in Oxford where, in the 1950s and 1960s, there were two regnant camps: Professor Hicks and his followers, and the development economics establishment led by Thomas (later Lord) Balogh. The former kept Ian at a distance, the latter met his ideas with active hostility.

Nuffield College was the sanctuary in which Ian flourished. Along with Max Corden, James Mirrlees and Maurice Scott, he made it a centre of

---

[6] This last description applies better to British thinking on development than to development theory worldwide. Albert Hirschman in particular based his theory of unbalanced growth on the idea that what the State does creates incentives and outcomes in the private unplanned sector of the economy.

excellence to which many of Oxford's brightest graduate students in economics gravitated.[7] Looking back on Ian Little's life, it is difficult not to feel some sadness and embarrassment for British economics. He rarely received the credit due to him, and even when granted it was often reluctantly delivered. *A Critique* was not generally recognised as the masterpiece it undoubtedly represents, and Hicks's churlish rejection of Ian's work was a disgrace. But it is in the field of development economics that the embarrassment is greatest, and it is in Oxford that it reached its peak. Ian was a giant of development economics, and the Oxford colleagues who rejected him and tried to lock him out were shown to be completely misguided. To assume that good ideas always win in the end is too optimistic. However, in the case of trade and development, Ian, notwithstanding his early rejection, has proved to be on the winning side.

In 1970, Ian was elected to the Professorship of the Economics of Underdeveloped Countries at Oxford, and in 1973 to a Fellowship of the British Academy. He resigned the Oxford Chair after four and a half years, in part because he was uncomfortable in the lecture theatre and hated public speaking. He then moved to Washington for two years as Special Adviser in the Development Economics Division of the World Bank. While there, he initiated a research project on small-scale manufacturing enterprises. (After he left, it made slow progress. He returned to the Bank for a few months in 1984 to write the overview.) He retired to Provence in 1978 but came back to live in Oxford after the death of his first wife.

Two of Ian's non-academic positions are noteworthy: board membership of the British Airports Authority (BAA) from 1968 to 1973, and investment bursarship of Nuffield College off and on (including a short stint after retirement).[8] As a member of the BAA board, he had a major influence in scuppering the mooted Third London Airport at Maplin. He argued that the Roskill Commission had greatly overestimated the benefits of a new airport by failing to consider the use of peak-load pricing at existing airports. The case for Maplin was at first accepted by the Heath government. But Ian advised Tony Crosland, in opposition in 1971, that at most one new runway was

---

[7] 'As already indicated, I was now in my own mind a development economist but this was not recognised in Oxford. With only two exceptions no postgraduate student of the subject, or from a developing country, was assigned to me by the university before I became "professor of the economics of underdeveloped countries" a decade later and acquired some say in the matter … However, Nuffield College always appointed a college supervisor for its students in addition to the university supervisor, and in this way, I did acquire a few students, the most famous of whom was Manmohan Singh, Finance Minister of India from 1991 to 1996' (*LbL* 2004: 114).

[8] He was also a member of the UN Committee for Development Planning from 1972 to 1975.

needed in the London area in the twentieth century. He describes the ensuing course of events as follows:

> Sometime early in 1974 I had a telephone call from Tony Crosland, then again a Minister, asking what he should do about Maplin. I said "ditch it". He did …
> If I had any decisive influence on this issue, I reckon I earned my somewhat niggardly salary many times over (*LbL* 2004: 145–146).

Ian was co-investment bursar at Nuffield College with Donald MacDougall from 1958 to 1962 and Uwe Kitzinger from 1962 to 1965, and investment bursar from 1968 to 1970 and 1990 to 1992.

In retirement, Ian remained active and intellectually vigorous and wrote several major books and articles. The first was *Economic Development: Theory, Policy, and International Relations* (Little 1982), a brilliant, insightful survey of the field of development economics. In 1984, he was invited by Anne Krueger, then Vice President of the World Bank, to design a large multi-country research project on the macroeconomic policies of developing countries. Seventeen countries were studied. Ian's involvement was considerable. He co-wrote the synthesis volume *Boom, Crisis and Adjustment* (Little et al. 1993) with Richard Cooper, Max Corden and Sarath Rajapatirana.[9] In addition, he co-wrote one of the country studies, *India: Macroeconomics and Political Economy, 1964–1991* (Joshi and Little 1994), with Vijay Joshi. This was shortly followed by another book co-authored with Joshi, *India's Economic Reforms, 1991–2001* (Joshi and Little 1996a). In his eighties, Ian edited two books, and wrote two others: *Ethics, Economics and Politics*, a concise introduction to the interrelationship of the three component subjects of PPE, and *Little by Little*, the personal memoir mentioned above. He was appointed CBE in 1997.

At Nuffield College, Ian inspired many pupils and colleagues. One of his great satisfactions was that his doctoral student and friend, Manmohan Singh, became Finance Minister and then Prime Minister of India, and instigated many of the reforms that Ian had advocated. Ian's conversational style was quiet and reflective, not flashy; its hallmarks were the discerning throwaway remark, the *mot juste*, and the brief but incisive comment that goes to the heart of the matter. Despite the economy of words, his presence was magnetic; and its impact is captured by Francis Seton when he writes: '[His] views, however modestly expressed, would command immediate acceptance for

---

[9] Developing-country macroeconomics is an area in which Ian could fairly be claimed to have had a major influence. We have left out any discussion of his contribution to this field to keep the length of this chapter within reasonable bounds. For Ian's thoughts on the subject and on the World Bank project, see *LbL* (2004: 172–173) and *CaR* (1999: 90–92 and 250–269).

their lucidity and independence. He had no need to seek effects, to hedge about, manipulate the waverers, or lobby the influential…nothing seemed more alien to him than showmanship, conformity, plodding exertion, or nail-biting discomfiture' (Seton 1990: 1). It is no surprise that this style did not endear him to the great and the good, and it may account for the fact that, like his illustrious ancestor Thomas Brassey, he received few of the honours in this country that one might have expected to come his way.

Ian's personality was complex. He was outwardly diffident but had an inner core of iron self-confidence. He was deeply serious and high-minded, but he was not a puritan; he loved the food, wine and sun of Provence. He was rather reserved but gave wonderful parties. He had no ear for music but a very good eye for the visual arts. He was well-born but un-snobbish, hated ostentation and pomposity, and believed in taxing wealth more harshly than any of the political parties do today (see Flemming and Little 1974). He was in some ways a correct English gentleman but there was also a wild streak in him, manifested by his love of fast cars and by the houses he designed and lived in, with their lethal spiral staircases. It was difficult to know what was going on behind his steely blue eyes, so people sometimes found him reticent or unapproachable, or even slightly frightening. But he was a warm and affectionate friend; and in the company of friends he would melt, and talk about people and events with ironic amusement. These apparently contradictory elements did not in any way add up to a fractured or inconsistent personality. They were held together by his personal integrity, his humane and liberal outlook, and his zest for life.

Ian married twice. Both his marriages brought him fulfilment, though different in kind. He met Doreen Hennessey, known to friends as Dobs, while he was in the Royal Air Force. They married in 1946. They were a stylish couple and gave sensational parties that came to be known in Oxford as the "parties for dancing economists". The marriage was not peaceful during its middle years because Dobs was battling alcoholism and depression, but its last fifteen years were serene. Dobs died in 1984. Life as a widower did not suit Ian and, as he often remarked, he was very lucky to meet and marry Lydia Segrave in 1991. With her, Ian became young again. They had two decades of a rewarding and contented life, travelling the world, visiting art museums, doing *The Times* crossword, seeing friends and working. Lydia sculpted and Ian continued to write. He was very proud of Lydia's talent as a sculptor. She survives him, together with his two stepchildren, and a son and daughter by his first marriage.

3   Theoretical Welfare Economics

A Critique of Welfare Economics was the major contribution from Ian Little in his early career as an economist. It can also take its place beyond doubt as one as the most important publications on economics from the decades of the early post-war years. It is striking then to note that it reads less as pure economics than do many comparable works of the time. The author is certainly an economist, thoroughly grounded in the history and theory of the economics of welfare. Yet more than any other writer in the field, with the possible exception of Kenneth Arrow, he is also a philosopher. We recognise this from his insistence that welfare economics is about ethics, and that this aspect of the subject cannot be disguised or evaded.

To appreciate this work, it must be seen in the context of its time. These were the years of the "New Welfare Economics". This was founded in the rejection of the "Old Welfare Economics" of Mill, Bentham and Marshall, which depended upon measurable utility. To these writers, it made sense to discuss whether it is a good idea to take £10 from a rich man to give the proceeds to a poor man, even if leakage created by this transfer reduced the poor man's gain to £3. A comparison of the marginal utility of money of the two parties provides a precise numerical answer. This kind of reasoning was a victim of the revolution in philosophical thinking that was logical positivism, and the ideas of the Vienna School. Taken to extremes, as it sometimes was, this new philosophy reached such bizarre conclusions as the refusal by the Oxford philosopher A.J. Ayer to admit to being an atheist on the ground that the proposition "There is no God" is untestable, and hence without meaning.

If arguments are valid only if they discuss exclusively the observable and the measurable, there is no room for cardinal utility. The tendency of an economics that adopted a positivist outlook was to eschew discussion of the distribution of welfare gains and losses, and to focus on efficiency, and the possibility of changes that could make everyone better off. One escape from the constraint of positivism was to confine attention to Pareto improvements of this kind. If a change could give the rich man £10 and the poor man £3, then surely it could be recommended, regardless of the measurement of utility. Here the problem is that changes that are Pareto improvements are quite unusual. Normally, there are losers, even with the most attractive interventions.

It is in response to this difficulty that John Hicks and Nicholas Kaldor came up with the concept that came to be called the Kaldor-Hicks criterion (the K-H test). According to this test, a change can be recommended if the gainers are able to compensate (bribe) the losers and still be better off. That looks appealing, but what exactly does it mean? Are we asked to accept that a change that passes the K-H test, plus the required compensation, is to be recommended? That is no more than a particular case of the Pareto test, and is similarly limited in scope. Instead of such a narrow application, the K-H test did not require that the compensation be paid.

Then Tibor Scitovsky showed that the reversal of a K-H improvement could also pass the K-H test. With inefficient states, well inside the production possibility frontier, there is plenty of surplus to pay compensation, so Scitovsky's finding is not unexpected. It is to this confusing tangle of ideas that Ian brought his sharp and precise intellect. In place of the K-H test, he proposes a two-item checklist for a change to count as a welfare improvement. First, it would produce a not-unfavourable redistribution of income; and secondly, the losers from the change could not bribe the gainers to vote against it. These two tests together define the "Little criterion". The second test takes care of Scitovsky's point.

The first three chapters of *A Critique* develop carefully and thoroughly the theory of welfare comparisons based on the choices made by individuals in market situations. It is shown how consistent choices can generate indifference curves (or behaviour curves) that provide a behavioural definition of "better off" for an individual consumer. The many difficulties that this approach encounters are noted at every step. Ian eventually relies on the possibility that the theory might work better for an average individual than for a particular genuine individual. One of the striking features of *A Critique* is its focus on the central field of a basic welfare economics. Its author refuses to be diverted towards extensions, such as dynamics, or the cardinal utility measures of von Neumann and Frank Ramsey. He is aware of this material, but chooses not to go down those side roads. As the reader will learn from *A Critique*, there is plenty to be done with the most elementary welfare economics; and the author does just that.

The balance between rigorous scepticism, and a determination to achieve what can be achieved, is perfectly captured in the short paragraph that closes Chapter III of the volume:

> We must not pretend that our analysis is anything but rough and ready. As we have already implied…it is particularly inapplicable in respect of choices between jobs, and different hours and kinds of work. Nevertheless, enough has, I think, been said to show that it would be foolish to dismiss the whole of welfare economics solely on the ground that the analysis of "individual" behaviour, on which it rests, is hopelessly at variance with the facts (Little 1950: 50).

Chapters IV and V of *A Critique* move on from the behaviour of individuals and the evaluation of individual welfare to the difficult fields of the distribution of welfare, interpersonal comparisons, and value judgements. This is economics, yes; but truly it is high-standard philosophy. Central to Ian's case is a head-on assault on the clear fact-value distinction of David Hume and G.E. Moore. These writers insisted that "is" propositions cannot yield "ought" propositions. The same distinction was the basis of Lionel Robbins's claim that when economists argue that the abolition of the Corn Laws was a good thing, this is not science. If the effect of the abolition was to harm landlords and benefit workers, the evaluation of that change depends upon the value judgement that the landlord losses count for less than the worker gains. The K-H test is designed to jump over that difficulty without confronting it. Ian allows himself no such easy ride. He shows in detail how slippery is the distinction between fact and value.

Central to his argument is the observation that terms such as "happy" or "better off" do not refer to the entirely subjective and personal, as it might be maintained does "tastes good". Even this last term cannot be completely subjective. A man who says that raw sewage tastes good is not truthful. Also, some terminology that appears to be no more than a value judgement reflects commonly understood criteria for its application. So, while the description "a good man" may be less precise than "a tall man", it is not available for anyone to use as he likes. To say that a mass murderer is a good man is simply to reveal linguistic incompetence. Now the sentence 'John would be happier if he gave up drinking' can be considered a positivist statement. One who insists on a rigid fact-value distinction cannot claim that this last sentence does not entail a value-loaded recommendation that John gives up drinking. Clearly, the positivist statement does imply a recommendation in favour of abstinence in John's case. A crucial conclusion of Ian's detailed analysis heads a list at the end of chapter IV: 'Interpersonal comparisons of satisfaction are empirical judgements about the real world, and are not, in any normal context, value judgements' (ibid.: 68).

Chapter VII is a short chapter devoted to the social welfare function, such as is proposed by Bergson and Samuelson. Little (1952a: 425) states that he has not taken note of Arrow's book on social choice (see Arrow 1951) because 'it has no relevance to the traditional theory of welfare economics'. This view is strange because Arrow arrived at his impossibility theorem after he had attempted unsuccessfully to arrive at a formal justification of the social welfare function. His analysis shows that, given his other axioms, one individual must be decisive concerning a pairwise choice, which violates his no-dictatorship axiom. This is quite similar to the conclusion reached by Little, who characterises the social welfare function as the objective of 'a Superman', that is, a dictator.

Chapters VIII and IX of *A Critique* examine the optimal conditions of production and exchange: equal marginal rates of substitution for different individuals or producers. Yet the important point delivered by these chapters is that the satisfaction of one of these conditions is not sufficient for an optimum, however defined, if other marginal conditions are not satisfied. For example, direct taxation is not necessarily superior to indirect taxation when direct taxation destroys the equality between the rates of transformation and substitution of leisure and goods. This type of argument is now always called the theory of the second best. Little is perhaps its originator, although a few would realise that. As he himself put it: 'Unfortunately for me, I did not name the theory!' (*CaR* 1999: 8).

Marginal conditions do not work when there are indivisibilities. A bridge across a river is either built or not built; one cannot have a little less bridge. Ever since Marshall, this problem has been treated by applying the theory of consumer surplus to focus on the difference in total utility that the bridge delivers. This approach was obviously undermined when cardinal utility was abandoned. Hicks applied much energy to rehabilitating the concept without cardinal utility, while Little took a different route, preferring direct ordinal assessments of lumpy changes. So, Hicks and Little differed sharply on two separate questions: the K-H test, and consumer surplus.

The remaining chapters of *A Critique* (XI-XIV) examine output and price policy for public enterprises; the valuation of national income; welfare theory and international trade; and welfare theory and politics. Chapter XV concludes. There are numerous sharp insights in these discussions, and also some intriguing surprises. Take, as an example of cutting analysis, the question of marginal-cost pricing for public enterprises. It is evident that the theory of the second best will take issue with a simplistic argument in favour of marginal-cost pricing. This is because with average costs far higher than marginal costs, as is typically the case with public enterprises, such as the railways, strict marginal-cost pricing leaves a large revenue gap to be filled. There is no non-distorting way of raising that revenue, so the case in favour of marginal-cost pricing collapses. Little goes further by showing marginal cost to be a slippery concept. In the short run, marginal cost oscillates wildly, as when the marginal cost of a rail journey varies according to how crowded are the carriages. In the extremely long run, marginal cost is much the same as average cost.

Given his espousal of the second best, one might expect Ian to reject the case for free trade. His actual position is more subtle and interesting. In the preface to the 2002 edition of *A Critique* he writes:

The basic fallacy is that the free trade dogma neglects the distribution of income. Fifty years later I can find no fault with this. However, I fear that the cursory reader might think that I believe that free trade generally worsens the distribution of wealth both between and also within countries. On the contrary, I believe that for most developing countries, especially the poorest, trade benefits the poor: this is because exports are relatively labour intensive, and raising the demand for labour reduces poverty (Little 2002a: xii).

A good way of assessing the weight of the contribution that is provided in *A Critique* is to ask what a contemporary undergraduate studying welfare economics would lose if told to read nothing but that one volume. The answer must be that this imagined student would not be badly disadvantaged. Of course, there are numerous other references that would benefit that individual. Ideally, he or she should certainly study some social choice theory, which does have relevance for classical welfare economics. Also, the welfare economics of risk and uncertainty, and intergenerational welfare, should not be neglected. Analysis using welfare weights, rejected by Hicks and only adopted later by Little, is moreover hugely valuable. Yet a must-have tool kit of welfare economics, with the correct emphasis on the distribution of welfare, is all to be found in the pages of *A Critique*.

4   Project Evaluation

Many economists if asked to nominate Ian's major contribution to development economics would select his work on project evaluation. Given that, it is notable that his entry to that field was almost accidental. It was not that he sought out the question of how to evaluate projects. Rather, the issue landed on his desk while he was with the OECD in Paris:

The other main product of my two years at the Development Centre was the OECD *Manual of Industrial Project Analysis*. This was jointly authored by myself and Jim Mirrlees. This was not the outcome of research that I had started. The Development Centre had already commissioned a French consultancy firm to produce such a manual, soon after it heard that the UN was doing so. A draft arrived which I thought terrible. I criticized it fundamentally, and revisions were promised. I considered the revised draft which eventually arrived to be still unacceptable. A small conference was called, most participants of which sided with me. But I had to threaten resignation to get the ball rolling. Baron [the then President of the OECD Development Centre] was convinced that my opposition simply stemmed from an Anglo-Saxon attitude (*LbL* 2004: 132).

Here, the discussion of the contribution made to project evaluation theory by Little and Mirrlees (henceforth L&M) will concentrate on their 1974 publication (henceforth *Project Appraisal*) rather than the original 1969 manual.[10] Two reasons support this choice. First, the 1974 book develops and presents their ideas more thoroughly and richly than the original. Secondly, the later publication responds in detail to the UNIDO *Guidelines* volume published between the two in 1972 (see Dasgupta et al. 1972). A comparison of the L&M approach and that of UNIDO is made difficult because the two volumes have distinct orientations. To put it simply, UNIDO is far more theoretical whereas L&M originated as a manual and remains as such in the developed 1974 exposition. A manual is literally something to be held in the hand, like a guide book for workers in the field. For this reason, the L&M exposition is intensely practical and offers detailed guidance concerning short cuts and approximations.

Fundamentally, L&M and UNIDO follow similar paths in that they adjust market-based returns by using shadow prices that are designed to better reflect social valuations. A difference between the two methods that received great attention is in itself of limited significance: the two systems use different numeraires (accounting units). The choice of a numeraire cannot of itself make a great difference. However, once a numeraire has been selected, conversion factors are required, that is, formulae to convert other values, such as wage rates, into values expressed in the numeraire. Then the details of conversion can make a substantial difference. The L&M numeraire is uncommitted social income measured at border prices, which contrasts with UNIDO's aggregate consumption measured at domestic market prices. To cut short what could become a lengthy discussion, it suffices to say that the L&M method is simpler and more reliable in practice. This is because it avoids the complex issue of deciding how far domestic market prices correctly reflect their contribution to consumption. In a highly distorted economy this is a complex exercise. L&M, on the other hand, avoid this tangled maze, either because if the good is traded one goes directly to the border price or, if it is not traded, its value can be measured at its marginal cost of production, broken down into its direct and indirect traded-good content (valued at border prices) and labour costs.

The focus of any project evaluation exercise is on the particular project and the numerical values associated with it. For that reason, the impression is too easily arrived at that the theory is entirely microeconomic, concerned only

---

[10] The two publications are the *Manual of Industrial Project Analysis, II, Social Cost-Benefit Analysis* (1969) and the *Project Appraisal and Planning for Developing Countries* (1974).

with the project itself. This would be a mistake, and it is a great merit of the L&M method that it shows in a clear light how the evaluation of the individual project must be embedded in a global perspective that reflects the entire economy. The point can be illustrated via the consideration of a crucial value in any social return calculation, the shadow price of labour. The L&M formula for the shadow wage (SWR) is derived from the following:[11]

$$SWR = m + (c' - c) + (1 - 1/s)(c - m)$$

where c' = value of consumption at market prices, including items that do not directly contribute to welfare such as transport costs; c = welfare-producing consumption; m = marginal productivity of the wage earner; and s = the value of uncommitted government income in terms of consumption.

The first term in the above equation is the marginal product of labour, the second term adds the costs of delivering consumption, such as transport costs, and the third term shows the increase in consumption of the marginal worker minus that part of it which is reckoned to be a benefit. The final total SWR is in domestic local-currency value. That must be converted to the numeraire (foreign exchange) by the application of the shadow exchange rate. This last number is an economy-wide value with which all project evaluators will be provided.

The derivation of the SWR illustrates beautifully some of the basic principles that underlie the L&M analysis. Wages display two contrary aspects. On the one hand, they are a welfare benefit; they provide workers and their families with consumption, and the higher they are the more consumption they provide. On the other hand, they are a cost to the national budget because each rupee of wage paid out might otherwise be applied to beneficial government expenditure. In a simple case, let (c' - c) be zero, so no additional resources are devoted to the provision of consumption. Also, let m equal zero because, for example, labour employed on the project comes from agriculture where the marginal worker adds nothing to output. Furthermore, assume that workers consume all their wages, there being no saving. These are not realistic assumptions, but they help to show the principles of SWR calculation in a clear light. Then the formula for the SWR reduces to the following:

$$SWR = (1 - 1/s)w$$

---

[11] See Little and Mirrlees (1974: 271). The formula shown in the text is not quite correct given the definitions of the variables at the top of the same page. This problem has been taken care of here by the provision of different definitions of the variables to make the formula correct.

where w is the market wage rate that the project will have to pay. Note that the SWR is below the market wage rate. This implies that public sector projects evaluated positively by the L&M method will be more labour intensive than would be a similar project chosen to maximise profit in the private sector.

Another important value for the accurate assessment of projects is the accounting rate of interest (the ARI), the number that measures how future numeraire values are weighted relative to current numeraire values. This rate of interest may vary over time, but the discussion concentrates reasonably on the case where it is nearly constant. The role of the ARI is to act as a gatekeeper for the projects being assessed. It must not accept too many, when taxes would have to rise sharply, and present consumption would be depressed excessively. Equally, it must not accept too few, when welfare-increasing possibilities would be wasted. The questions at issue here are easier to answer in a classroom on a blackboard than in reality. The two fundamental effects that need to be taken into account are the rate at which per capita consumption will rise, and the root discounting of the future that reflects the impatience of the planner (or the population). Growth of per capita consumption argues for weighting future consumption more lightly. Impatience adds an additional effect in the same direction. These two effects together generate an ARI that should be equated to the rate of return on the marginal project—the one that only just gets accepted. L&M discuss an interesting, although special, case in which the return on private investments provides a useful estimate of the ARI.

The OECD *Manual* was hugely influential. It generated important empirical studies that applied its methods in the field.[12] It also played a crucial role in promoting formal rule-based project evaluation methodology in the World Bank. For many years in that institution, project evaluation and Little/Mirrlees became synonymous. These successes were in sharp contrast to the largely hostile reception of the OECD *Manual* in Britain, and notably in Oxford. As Little writes:

> The OECD *Manual* was strongly attacked by the development establishment, especially the Oxford branch. The essential principle it promoted was that, in considering the costs and benefits of domestic production of something, both export possibilities and the alternative of satisfying domestic demand by importing should be carefully considered. The implied insistence on trying to use international trade optimally was anathema to those who had been taught that free trade was a colonial tyranny designed to ensure that developing countries would forever produce only primary commodities … Since those days relatively open

---

[12] See, inter alia, Little et al. (1970), Scott et al. (1976) and Stern (1972).

trading policies have become more widely practised in developing countries, and few would now deny the benefit of such policies. But I myself continue to be reviled as The Great Satan in some development schools (*LbL* 2004: 138).

The critiques of L&M pursued many arguments, these of variable merit. The February 1972 edition of the *Bulletin of the Oxford University Institute for Economics and Statistics* was devoted entirely to a symposium concerned with the OECD *Manual.* Several of these papers, including one by Vijay Joshi, took a favourable view of L&M, and the paper by Nicholas Stern on an application to tea farming in Kenya provided a valuable example of the L&M method in practice. Partha Dasgupta's paper compared the OECD and UNIDO manuals. In contrast, the long paper by Frances Stewart and Paul Streeten is not unlike a prolonged artillery assault on L&M (see Stewart and Streeten 1972).[13] Elsewhere, a paper by Amartya Sen explored the issue of irrational (or at least immovable) government policies (see Sen 1972), a point also stressed by Stewart and Streeten.

Leading issues raised by the Oxford critics of L&M are the following: irrational governments; economic linkages; and non-traded goods. It was claimed that L&M assume that the government of the country to which project evaluation is applied is as rational and detached as the authors themselves. Another assertion is that L&M ignore the multiple linkages—forward, backward, and sideways—that are characteristics of underdeveloped countries. The final claim from the prosecution is that L&M give insufficient weight to non-traded goods and fail to price them correctly.

In the final paper in the *Bulletin of the Oxford University Institute* issue, Little and Mirrlees provide a vigorous and robust reply to their critics. They agree that recommendations may be conditional on a rational government response but note that the implication of an irrational response is often contained in the recommendation. Thus, if the project evaluator recommends the adoption of a scheme to manufacture motor vehicles domestically, provided that the engines are imported, this implies, and that could be made explicit, that the scheme should not be adopted if the government insists on all production being domestic. On linkages, L&M confirm their scepticism concerning their universality and measurability, yet point out that if a linkage is evident and important it becomes part of the project, to be assessed with other components of the same. They underline their flexibility concerning the shadow pricing of non-traded goods, such as electricity supply in many

---

[13] All the other papers (except Sen's) mentioned in this and the succeeding paragraph are to be found in the same issue of the journal.

countries. Non-traded goods can often be priced by their opportunity costs in terms of traded goods. If that is not possible, the values in domestic prices can be translated to border values using the conversion factor that already figures in their analysis. Notable in the L&M response is how, rather than mounting new arguments, the authors usually point their critics to what is already there in the *Manual*.

The 1970s were the years when project evaluation based on cost-benefit analysis was at its high point, both in developed and developing countries. Since then, its status has declined, although it is still used (or abused).[14] A leading problem that emerged when institutions such as the World Bank tried to impose the method is that project evaluation proved to be strongly liable to manipulation. As L&M show clearly in their writing, estimates and guesses have important parts to play. That opens the door to biased estimates designed to achieve a particular result—usually the acceptance of a dubious project. A senior Indian civil servant once told one of the authors of this memoir that, given the book of rules, he and his colleagues could arrange for almost any favoured project to get over the finishing line. In fact, the bias affecting project evaluation is two-sided. Governments receiving aid favour certain projects and will twist the assessment process to favour those schemes. Lenders also have their own biases. They are not paid for turning down projects; their job is to lend money. So, a rigorous tough approach to project proposals does not suit donors any more than recipients. Little was sharply aware of the problems created when political forces encroach on project evaluation. He writes: 'The main difficulty facing cost-benefit analysis is that large public, or publicly subsidized, investments are a source of prestige, patronage, and kick-backs for those in power, and their relatives and cronies. They do not want their projects submitted to hard-nosed appraisal by economists' (*LbL* 2004: 142).

Aside from the problems of manipulation discussed above, there is another major reason why cost-benefit analysis on L&M lines has declined in importance. A leading motivation for the L&M approach, and the same could be said of the UNIDO method, is to surmount the misleading price signals prevalent in highly distorted economies, especially those subject to strong and unbalanced trade protection. All this has become far less important as developing countries have become more open, their markets less interfered with, and their tariffs and controls diminished, often to levels below those of rich industrial countries. A great deal of credit for this belongs to Ian and to

---

[14] A current case in point is the claimed benefits of the proposed hugely expensive high-speed rail link in the United Kingdom between London and Birmingham, and points north. The benefits concerned are hard to measure and highly impressionistic. The costs are massive, and sometimes neglected. This is an exercise more in political persuasion than in genuine evaluation.

economists who thought on similar lines. So, perhaps Little, the trade and protection specialist, was the executioner of Little, the project evaluation innovator. If that is the case, he would probably not have minded.

5   Trade and Development

So influential have been the ideas of Ian Little, and parallel thinkers, on the role of trade in economic development that it is difficult now to recover the intellectual climate of early post-war economic thinking on this topic. To put it simply, an orthodoxy of that time held that trade was ineffective, unnecessary, and a dangerous break on development. This view was underpinned by the belief that the way to economic advancement took the form of industrialisation, and that this required the protection of infant industries from foreign competition. One finds this kind of thinking in many newly independent countries, but it is well illustrated with India because that country produced one of the most articulate expressions of anti-trade thought.[15] Two ideas powered this philosophy. First, it was felt that colonialism had hampered Indian industrialisation for selfish reasons, a claim that was not without foundation, and that policy should now reverse that tendency. Secondly, self-sufficiency was seen to be an ideal, supposedly because it offered more security than the perils of dependence on trade.

For India, the Soviet Union provided a model of successful economic development for a large country based on forced industrialisation and little international trade with the capitalist West. There was an appreciation of undoubted Soviet successes, including the defeat of Nazi Germany, rapid growth, and impressive development of some sectors. For example, the Soviet Union had by a long way the world's largest shoe industry. However, there was less understanding of the severe deficiencies of the Soviet economy. Agriculture was a disaster sector, the victim of forced confiscation of output, collectivisation, and discriminatory pricing. The delivery of consumer goods was extremely poor. Even those millions of shoes were in wrong sizes and styles. Crucially, the basic mechanism of the planning system was misguided. Output was crudely measured with quantity counting for much more than quality. Producers operated with soft budgets, encouraging them to waste such inputs as they could obtain. For such a lavishly forested nation to suffer a timber shortage was an astounding achievement. The closed nature of the economy

---

[15] The Prebisch-Singer hypothesis that held that the terms of trade would inevitably move against primary product exports was another argument for industrial self-sufficiency.

implied that economic planning was directed to achieving targets without the question of whether national comparative advantage favoured those outputs ever being considered.

Indians, like everyone else, were in a poor position to view the true nature of the Soviet economy, hidden as it was behind propaganda and misleading statistics. Had they been able to enjoy a clearer view they could have drawn useful lessons concerning economic management and economic planning. Among these lessons would have been the danger of grandiose projects undertaken without proper assessment of costs and benefits. Another lesson would have been the cost of neglecting export opportunities. Had forestry not been starved of inputs, the Soviet Union could have exported timber to its benefit rather than failing to meet even domestic needs. Finally, the five-year plan model, under which growth targets for various sectors were laid down in advance, led to the misallocation of scarce inputs and the underweighting of consumer needs.

Whatever the problems of economic planning, it was required in some form by newly independent countries. Hardly anyone thought that simply introducing laissez-faire would produce the results required. The question was what form should planning take, and, in particular, in what direction it should point economic development? Should it favour heavy industry over light? What place should it give to international trade, to imports and to exports? Little was a product of his time, and he started out firmly in favour of economic planning. However, over time, experience and sharp observation modified his views. Autobiographies too often take the form of a prolonged monologue on the lines of 'I was always right, and everyone else was wrong'. This was foreign to Ian's character. He freely admitted to alterations in his position:

> I am widely regarded as having shifted from uncritical belief in *dirigiste* planning to excessive trust in the price mechanism. Apart from the adjectives, this is broadly true. All economists are conversant with the faults of the price mechanism, some would suppress it altogether. Many liberals, including myself, wanted to tinker with it, and to rely on government to implement the tinkering. We were slow to realize that the most prevalent reason for market failure was government itself. Governments were driven by false economic ideology—heavy industry, protection, and import substitution—and also became increasingly self-serving and corrupt. My own change in emphasis is obvious … It was driven by experience and research. However, although the change is insidious from 1960 to 1990, my India visit of 1965 was a watershed. It led directly to my

research programme at the OECD, and hence to increasing emphasis on free trade and the reduction of domestic controls (*CaR* 1999: 81).

Ian's evolving views on trade and development were laid out extensively and provided with solid empirical support in the fine volume that he co-authored with Tibor Scitovsky and Maurice Scott, henceforth *Industry and Trade*. This volume draws together the conclusions of several OECD studies of individual countries—Brazil, India, Mexico, Pakistan, the Philippines, and Pakistan. The essence of the approach adopted in this volume is the following. Beginning students of economics learn that the advantages of international trade lie in the exploitation of comparative advantage: a country should do what it does relatively best, and rely on imports for what it does badly. It then seems clear that numerous qualifications destroy this simple conclusion. Among these are terms of trade that vary with the volume of exchange, externalities and infant industry considerations, issues of income distribution, and more. In *Industry and Trade*, we find a forensic analysis of the multiple effects of protection and economic planning biased towards heavy manufacturing, and hence inevitably biased against agriculture and light manufacturing. Most importantly, this policy obliterates the possibility of taking advantage of opportunities for exports, that is, exactly those exports that have proved to be the foundation of economic growth in the successful East Asian countries, such as South Korea and Taiwan.

Industry and Trade is a volume that cannot be fairly summarised in a short chapter. It examines the issues involved in great depth and breadth. However, picking out some of its leading points gives a good sense of its contributions. Chapters 2 and 5 discuss the magnitude of protection, and distinguish between the "nominal" rate of protection (how much protection raises domestic prices), and effective protection (how far protection permits the value added in production to exceed what it would be in its absence). Effective protection is often far higher than its nominal cousin, and sometimes, when outputs are more heavily protected than inputs, even allows activities with negative value added at world prices to survive.

Chapter 6 looks at the pernicious consequences of reliance on controls, a characteristic of a planned, and overplanned, economy. Widespread controls on investment and other activities are costly and they blunt private initiatives. Entrepreneurs gain more from playing the planning system than from innovation and productivity improvements. Industrialisation has aggravated income inequalities. The extra profits made in industry are not a net gain to the community. Protection of large-scale industry implies the anti-protection of light industry and agriculture, sectors in which incomes are low. Chapter 2 notes that a major source of saving and investment is the profits of heavy industry inflated by protection. These profits are invested to a great extent in the same industries that generated them, thus adding force to the bias against light manufacturing and agriculture. Protection biased in favour of heavy industry is bad for employment and the full utilisation of capital. Finally, and crucially, the protection of heavy industry leads to the neglect of comparative advantage. This echoes points made above concerning biases in the Soviet system.

6   The Indian Economy

Ian Little's connection with India extended for more than fifty years and was the inspiration for a good deal of his work after he wrote *A Critique*. We have already covered his first visit in 1958, while he was favourably disposed to Indian planning, and his second visit in 1965, when he became disillusioned with it. A major reason for the disillusionment was that he became convinced of the falsity of "elasticity pessimism", which was one of its central tenets. This change of view, in conjunction with his field experience in project analysis, strongly influenced his thinking on methods of project selection for developing countries. The first fruits of this can be seen in "Public Sector Project Selection in Relation to Indian Development", an article that was published in an obscure book in 1969.[16] Many of his distinctive ideas, in particular the use of world prices as shadow prices for tradable goods, later refined in collaboration with James Mirrlees, can be found in this seminal piece. More generally, Ian's second thoughts on India's development strategy, along with early evidence of the success of export-oriented growth in the "Gang of Four", prompted him to mount the large OECD project on trade and industrialisation policies in developing countries. Six countries were selected for close examination; one of these was India. The volume on India, written by Jagdish Bhagwati and Padma Desai and published in 1970, became a classic in its own right. Following the OECD project, and until his retirement, Ian did not work directly on India but maintained his strong links with the country.

After he retired, Ian wrote extensively about the Indian economy. This came about as a result of the project on macroeconomic policy in developing countries that he initiated at the World Bank in the mid-1980s. He wrote the India volume with Vijay Joshi as his co-author, and it was published by OUP

---

[16] The article was written in 1965. One of the authors of this memoir attended the seminar in Nuffield College at which it was presented and remembers the mixture of admiration and outrage with which it was greeted. The article was published as Little (1969); it has since been reprinted in *CaR*.

in 1994 under the title *India: Macroeconomics and Political Economy, 1964–1991*. This was the first systematic assessment of Indian macroeconomic policies from the death of Pandit Nehru until the inauguration of the liberalising reforms of 1991. The book was divided into three parts. Part One was an introduction to India's history, institutions and markets. Part Two examined four major macroeconomic crises that the country experienced during this period—in 1965–1967, 1973–1975, 1979–1981, and 1990–1991. To put it very crudely, the first three crises were mainly the result of exogenous events, in particular droughts and oil price increases. The fourth was different. It resulted from the pursuit of unsustainable fiscal policies during the 1980s. The authors analysed in depth the causes and resolution of the crises, with particular attention to the shortcomings of stabilisation policy. Part Three was concerned with longer-term trends in policy. Separate chapters were devoted to fiscal, monetary, and trade and payments policies, and to the connection between macroeconomic policy and long-run growth. A distinctive contribution of the book was that it demonstrated a link between microeconomics and macroeconomics in the Indian context. Before this book, the fashionable view about Indian economic policy was that it was unsound microeconomically but sound macroeconomically, and that these phenomena were positively related—in other words, the controls that led to microeconomic inefficiency helped to attain macroeconomic stability. In contrast, one of the central conclusions of the book was that India's control system was not only microeconomically inefficient but macroeconomically perverse. In *CaR*, Ian writes about this book, 'It was the first and only full macroeconomic history of India since the death of Nehru and will, I hope, prove to be the definitive study of the period' (*CaR* 1999: 92).

By the time that book was published, India had embarked on an ambitious reform programme designed to move the economy towards greater openness and market orientation. Joshi and Little got a grant from the Overseas Development Administration to carry out an appraisal of this programme. The book that resulted—*India's Economic Reforms, 1991–2001* (Joshi and Little 1996a)—was the first systematic assessment of India's reforms. It went into seven impressions and made a significant impact. There were five chapters, apart from an introductory and a concluding chapter. Chapter 2 on stabilisation policy showed that government deficits and debt were on an unsustainable track, and that fiscal consolidation was imperative. On balance-of-payments policy, it was supportive of India's decision to opt for a managed exchange rate, buttressed by targeted capital controls, and by occasional sterilisation of reserve accumulation, in order to prevent excessive exchange rate appreciation caused by exuberant capital inflows. This policy proved its worth during the build up to the East Asian crisis of 1997. Chapters 3–5 undertook a critique of structural reform. The authors took the view that while India had made a good beginning, the reforms were partial and incomplete. On trade and indirect taxation, they argued that India should move to a uniform value-added tax, harmonised between the central government and the states, with few exemptions, supplemented by a uniform tariff no higher than 10% for industry as well as, more controversially, for agriculture.[17] They drew attention to the superabundance of government subsidies, explicit and implicit. Fertilisers, fuel, electricity, irrigation water, and many other goods and services that are not public goods were sold well below their costs of production. The beneficiaries were preponderantly the better off sections of society. Winding up these subsidies would improve resource allocation and yield more than enough fiscal savings to compensate the poor. On industrial policy, the book argued for privatising state-owned enterprises producing tradable goods. In these sectors, international competition would annul the main argument for nationalisation—namely the possibility of monopolistic exploitation. Public sector enterprises producing non-tradables should be broken up into competitive and naturally monopolistic elements. The former should be privatised; the latter could be privatised or left in State ownership, but in either case independent regulation was essential. The economy's poor infrastructure, which was mainly in State ownership, was identified as a critical constraint on growth. The book also argued strongly that liberalising output markets was not enough. Factor markets needed reform. Company laws, labour laws and urban land law had combined to make the economy highly inflexible and to impede labour-demanding, inclusive growth. Chapter 6 considered the social sectors. It argued that well-designed public employment schemes were superior to food subsidies (distributed via the highly inefficient public distribution system) as instruments of poverty alleviation.

Since the book was written, India's reform programme has made significant progress. But many shortcomings remain, including a bias against employment and the continuing presence of counterproductive subsidies. These failings were clearly identified and analysed in the 1996 book.

---

[17] The authors recognised that there is a theoretical case for non-uniformity but preferred a uniform rate for various pragmatic reasons. On agricultural trade liberalisation, they argued that it would raise prices and profits for farmers producing the principal crops. This would enable the elimination of various ill-judged subsidies to agriculture. The rise in output prices would hurt the poor but they could and should be compensated by direct transfers, which would require reform of the public distribution system. These changes would not be easy but the net benefits would be large.

7   Ian as Investment Bursar

Ian Little's experience of portfolio investment began with his appointment as one of the two investment bursars at Nuffield College in 1958. At that date, Nuffield ceased to be a department of the University and became responsible for the management of its own funds. Ian served with Donald (later Sir Donald) MacDougall, and subsequently with Uwe Kitzinger. The College's broker was Vickers da Costa, and its Chairman, Ralph Vickers, advised the bursars directly, this advice being delivered via a daily telephone call that reported on the state of the market. The performance of the College's investments in the first four years, with Ian partly in charge, was outstanding. This owed much to Ralph Vickers' unusual investment skills. He studied company reports with forensic care, an approach that had served Keynes well when he was a successful investor, as it did later for Warren Buffett.

Vickers was an extraordinary individual. His warmth and huge generosity gave him friendships with left-leaning academics despite his own right-wing politics and his support for apartheid South Africa. He was an active and daring investor. He was not afraid to select the unorthodox and to bet on relatively short-run movements. Riding price bubbles is notoriously dangerous, and it is a measure of Vickers' judgement and intuition that it protected him and his clients from the worst perils of high-risk investment. A striking example of this comes from a time long after Little had ceased to be an investment bursar. Vickers put the College into Asil Nadir's *Polly Peck* conglomerate, to show a considerable profit, and got out of that stock in good time before the company was exposed as a sham and went bust. The daily telephone conversations with Vickers were hugely enjoyable, but resulted inevitably in too much trading ("churning" as it is now called), a bad investment strategy, though profitable to a broker on commission for trades.

One of the investment trusts that served the College well was the Vickers da Costa Insecs (Investing in Success) fund. This fund was based largely on the principle of investing in firms that had shown a high rate of growth of earnings per share in the past. This strategy was surprisingly successful for some time. The success is surprising because the policy is based on two assumptions. First, it is assumed that earnings are positively serially correlated. Secondly, the strategy only succeeds if stock prices do not reflect that correlation, as what would now be called the efficient markets hypothesis would require. The serial correlation of earnings is such a natural and intuitive idea that it takes an unusual intellect to question it. That intellect was Ian Little's. As he writes: 'However, I was unhappy that there was no statistical proof that past growth was a good predictor of future growth. I feared that our success might be based on an illusion, which could not last' (*LbL* 2004: 113).

The result of these ruminations was a short paper with the eye-catching title of "Higgledy-Piggledy Growth", published in November 1962, and subsequently a small book co-authored with A.C. Rayner, published in 1966, *Higgledy-Piggledy Growth Again*. These studies destroyed the notion that there are growth stocks whose future earnings performance can be predicted from the past. This discovery was embarrassing because Ian was an Insecs Director (a position from which he resigned shortly thereafter) and because his findings could be seen as ungrateful in view of the great benefits that had accrued to Nuffield from its investment in Insecs. As Ian writes: 'Donald MacDougall also thought I was "rather letting the side down". I did not see it that way, as I did not believe success could continue for long if based on error. Perhaps I also thought that an academic scholar should put the dissemination of truth before profits' (*LbL* 2004: 113). As it happens, opinion in the City was catching up with Ian's thinking. The fashion for growth stocks was soon in decline, and the analysis of company prospects became far more sophisticated. Ian's friendship with Ralph Vickers survived this history, and he became a Director of the General Funds Trust, the other big beast in the Vickers da Costa stable.

8   Conclusion

Looking back at any major economist the leading question is: what did he do that will last? Here, Ian Little's major impact is his argument that prices matter, and that standard economic theory must be adapted to the particular features of developing countries, not abandoned altogether. Today, this is the orthodox view, so that many would not think of it as coming from Little, and a few other writers, such as Scitovsky and Scott. That is what happens with many leading contributions: They are first rejected as false, then dismissed as obvious.

References

Main Works by Ian Little

Evely, R. and I.M.D. Little (1960). *Concentration in British Industry: An Empirical Study of the Structure of Industrial Production, 1935–1951*. Cambridge: Cambridge University Press.

Flemming, J.S. and I.M.D. Little (1974). *Why We Need a Wealth Tax*. London: Methuen.

Joshi, V. and I.M.D. Little (1989). 'Indian Macroeconomic Policies'. Chapter 13 in G. Calvo, R. Findlay, P. Kouri and J. Braga de Macedo (eds) *Debt, Stabilization and Development: Essays in Memory of Carlos Diaz-Alejandro*. Oxford: Basil Blackwell: 286–308.

Joshi, V. and I.M.D. Little (1994). *India: Macroeconomics and Political Economy, 1964–1991*. Washington, D.C. and Delhi: Oxford University Press.

Joshi, V. and I.M.D. Little (1995). 'Future Trade and Exchange Rate Policy for India'. Chapter 4 in R. Cassen and V. Joshi (eds) *India: The Future of Economic Reform*. Delhi: Oxford University Press: 53–70.

Joshi, V. and I.M.D. Little (1996a). *India's Economic Reforms, 1991–2001*. Oxford and Delhi: Clarendon Press.

Joshi, V. and I.M.D. Little (1996). 'Macroeconomic Management in India, 1964–1994'. Chapter 10 in V.N. Balasubramanyam and D. Greenaway (eds) *Trade and Development: Essays in Honour of Jagdish Bhagwati*. London and New York: Palgrave: 171–194.

Little, I.M.D. (1949). 'A Reformulation of the Theory of Consumer's Behaviour'. *Oxford Economic Papers*, New Series, 1(1): 90–99.

Little, I.M.D. (1949). 'The Valuation of the Social Income'. *Economica*, New Series, 16(61): 11–26.

Little, I.M.D. (1949). 'The Foundations of Welfare Economics'. *Oxford Economic Papers*, New Series, 1(2): 227–246.

Little, I.M.D. (1950). *A Critique of Welfare Economics*. Second edition, 1957. Oxford: Clarendon Press.

Little, I.M.D. (1951). 'Direct Versus Indirect Taxes'. *Economic Journal*, 61(243): 577–584. Reprinted as Chapter 8 in R.A. Musgrave and C.S. Shoup (eds) (1959) *Readings in the Economics of Taxation*. Homewood, IL: Richard D. Irwin: 123–131.

Little, I.M.D. (1952a). 'Social Choice and Individual Values'. *Journal of Political Economy*, 60(5): 422–432.

Little, I.M.D. (1952). 'Fiscal Policy'. Chapter 8 in G.D.N. Worswick and P.H. Ady (eds) *The British Economy, 1945–1950*. Oxford: Clarendon Press: 159–187.

Little, I.M.D. (1953). *The Price of Fuel*. Oxford: Clarendon Press.

Little, I.M.D. (1957). 'Classical Growth'. *Oxford Economic Papers*, New Series, 9(2): 152–177.

Little, I.M.D. (1960). 'The Strategy of Indian Development'. *National Institute Economic Review*, 9(1): 20–29.

Little, I.M.D. (1961). 'The Real Cost of Labour, and the Choice Between Consumption and Investment'. *Quarterly Journal of Economics*, 75(1): 1–15.

Little, I.M.D. (1962). 'Higgledy Piggledy Growth'. *Bulletin of the Oxford University Institute of Economics and Statistics*, 24(4): 387–412.

Little, I.M.D. (1962). 'A Critical Examination of India's Third Five-Year Plan'. *Oxford Economic Papers*, New Series, 14(1): 1–24.

Little, I.M.D. (1962). 'Fiscal Policy'. Chapter 8 in G.D.N. Worswick and P.H. Ady (eds) *The British Economy in the Nineteen-Fifties*. Oxford: Clarendon Press: 231–300.

Little, I.M.D. (1964). *Aid to Africa: An Appraisal of UK Policy for Aid to Africa South of the Sahara*. Oxford: Pergamon Press.

Little, I.M.D. (1965). 'Welfare Economics, Ethics and Essentialism: A Comment'. *Economica*, New Series, 32(126): 223–225.

Little, I.M.D. (1969). 'Public Sector Project Selection in Relation to Indian Development'. In A.V. Bhuleshkar (ed.) *Indian Economic Thought and Development*. London: C. Hurst: 228–258.

Little, I.M.D. (1971). 'Trade and Public Finance'. *Indian Economic Review*, New Series, 6: 119–132.

Little, I.M.D. (1979). 'Welfare Criteria, Distribution and Cost-Benefit Analysis'. In M.J. Boskin (ed.) *Economics and Human Welfare: Essays in Honor of Tibor Scitovsky*. New York: Academic Press: 125–131.

Little, I.M.D. (1979). 'An Economic Reconnaissance'. Chapter 7 in W. Galenson (ed.) *Economic Growth and Structural Change in Taiwan: The Postwar Experience of the Republic of China*. Ithaca, NY: Cornell University Press: 448–507.

Little, I.M.D. (1980). 'Distributive Justice and the New International Order'. Chapter 3 in P. Oppenheimer (ed.) *Issues in International Economics*. London: Oriel Press: 37–53.

Little, I.M.D. (1981). 'The Experience and Causes of Rapid Labour-Intensive Development in Korea, Taiwan Province, Hong Kong and Singapore and the Possibilities of Emulation'. Chapter 2 in E. Lee (ed.) *Export-Led Industrialisation & Development*. Geneva: ILO: 23–45.

Little, I.M.D. (1982a). *Economic Development: Theory, Policy, and International Relations*. New York: Basic Books.

Little, I.M.D. (1982). 'Indian Industrialization Before 1945'. Chapter 21 in M. Gersovitz et al. (eds) *The Theory and Experience of Economic Development: Essays in Honor of Sir W. Arthur Lewis*. London: George Allen & Unwin: 356–371.

Little, I.M.D. (1987). 'Small Manufacturing Enterprises in Developing Countries'. *World Bank Economic Review*, 1(2): 203–235.

Little, I.M.D. (1992). 'Ethics and International Economic Relations'. Chapter 4 in B. Barry and R.E. Goodin (eds) *Free Movement: Ethical Issues in the Transnational Migration of People and Money*. Hemel Hempstead: Harvester Wheatsheaf: 48–58.

Little, I.M.D. (1996). 'India's Economic Reforms, 1991–1996'. *Journal of Asian Economics*, 7(2): 161–176.

Little, I.M.D. (1996). *Picking Winners: The East Asian Experience*. London: Social Market Foundation.

Little, I.M.D. (1999). *Collection and Recollections: Economic Papers and their Provenance*. Oxford: Clarendon Press.

Little, I.M.D. (2002a). *A Critique of Welfare Economics: A Retrospective Reissue.* Oxford: Oxford University Press.

Little, I.M.D. (2002). *Ethics, Economics and Politics: Principles of Public Policy.* Oxford: Oxford University Press.

Little, I.M.D. (2004). *Little by Little.* Privately printed.

Little, I.M.D. and J.M. Clifford (1965). *International Aid: A Discussion of the Flow of Public Resources from Rich to Poor Countries with Particular Reference to British Policy.* London: George Allen & Unwin.

Little, I.M.D. and K.M. McLeod (1972). 'The New Pricing Policy of the British Airports Authority'. *Journal of Transport Economics and Policy*, 6(2): 101–115.

Little, I.M.D. and J.A. Mirrlees (1969). *Manual of Industrial Project Analysis in Developing Countries, II, Social Cost-Benefit Analysis.* Paris: OECD.

Little, I.M.D. and J.A. Mirrlees (1972). 'A Reply to Some Criticisms of the OECD Manual'. *Bulletin of the Oxford University Institute of Economics and Statistics*, 34(1): 153–168.

Little, I.M.D. and J.A. Mirrlees (1974). *Project Appraisal and Planning for Developing Countries.* London: Heinemann.

Little, I.M.D. and J.A. Mirrlees (1991). 'Project Appraisal and Planning Twenty Years On'. *Proceedings of the World Bank Annual Conference on Development Economics*. Washington, D.C.: World Bank: 351–382.

Little, I.M.D. and D.G. Tipping (1972). *A Social Cost-Benefit Analysis of the Kulai Oil Palm Estate, West Malaysia.* Paris: OECD.

Little, I.M.D., T. Scitovsky and M. FG. Scott (1970). *Industry and Trade in Some Developing Countries: A Comparative Study.* London: Oxford University Press. Also French and Spanish translations.

Little, I.M.D., D. Mazumdar and J.M. Page Jr. (1987). *Small Manufacturing Enterprises: A Comparative Study of India and Other Economies.* Oxford: Oxford University Press.

Little, I.M.D., R.N. Cooper, W.M. Corden and S. Rajapatirana (1993). *Boom, Crisis, and Adjustment: The Macroeconomic Experience of Developing Countries.* New York: Oxford University Press.

Rayner, A.C. and I.M.D. Little (1966). *Higgledy Piggledy Growth Again: An Investigation of the Predictability of Company Earnings and Dividends in the UK, 1951–1961.* Oxford. Blackwell.

Other Works Referred To

Arrow, K.J. (1951). *Social Choice and Individual Values.* New York: John Wiley & Sons. Second edition, 1963.

Bhagwati, J.N. and P. Desai (1970). *India: Planning for Industrialization.* London: OECD.

Creedy, J. (2013). 'John Richard Hicks, 1904–1989'. *Biographical Memoirs of Fellows of the British Academy*, XII: 215–231.

Dasgupta, P.S., S.A. Marglin and A.K. Sen (1972). *Guidelines for Project Evaluation.* New York: UNIDO.

Joshi, V. (1972). 'The Rationale and Relevance of the Little-Mirrlees Criterion'. *Bulletin of the Oxford University Institute of Economics and Statistics*, 34(1): 3–32.

Lipsey, R.G. and K. Lancaster (1956–1957). 'The General Theory of Second Best'. *Review of Economic Studies*, 24(1): 11–32.

Scott, M. FG., J. MacArthur and D.M.G. Newbery (1976). *Project Appraisal in Practice: The Little/Mirrlees Method Applied in Kenya.* London: Heinemann.

Sen, A.K. (1972). 'Control Areas and Accounting Prices: An Approach to Economic Evaluation'. *Economic Journal*, 82(325): 486–501.

Seton, F. (1990). 'Ian Little – A Salute *Inter Vivos*'. Chapter 1 in M. FG. Scott and D. Lal (eds) *Public Policy and Economic Development: Essays in Honour of Ian Little.* Oxford: Clarendon Press: 1–9.

Stern, N.H. (1972). *An Appraisal of Tea Production on Small-Holdings in Kenya: An Experiment with the Little/Mirrlees Method.* Paris: OECD.

Stewart, F. and P. Streeten (1972). 'Little-Mirrlees Methods and Project Appraisal'. *Bulletin of the Oxford University Institute of Economics and Statistics*, 34(1): 75–91.

Viner, J. (1950). *The Customs Union Issue.* New York: Carnegie Endowment for International Peace.

21

W.M. Gorman (1923–2003)

Patrick Honohan and Peter Neary

1   Introduction[1]

William Moore Gorman, known to all as "Terence", died in Oxford on 12
January 2003. The greatest Irish economist since Edgeworth, he was, like
Edgeworth, totally unknown to the general public, both in his native country
and in Britain where he made his career. He was the purest of pure theorists,
whose life was devoted to scholarship and teaching, and whose work of for-
bidding technical difficulty was incomprehensible to most of his contemporaries. Yet, paradoxically, he was always concerned with applied issues, and the
tools and theorems he developed have had a lasting influence on empirical work.

---

[1] This chapter is reprinted from Honohan and Neary (2003) with the kind permission of *The Economic
and Social Review*.

P. Honohan (✉)
Trinity College Dublin, Ireland
e-mail: phonohan@tcd.ie

P. Neary
Department of Economics, Oxford, UK
e-mail: peter.neary@economics.ox.ac.uk

© The Author(s), under exclusive license to Springer Nature Switzerland AG 2021
R. A. Cord (ed.), *The Palgrave Companion to Oxford Economics*,
https://doi.org/10.1007/978-3-030-58471-9_21

503

2   The Life

Gorman was born in Kesh, County Fermanagh, on 17 June 1923. His father, a veterinary surgeon, died when Gorman was young, and so he was raised by his mother, spending part of his childhood in what was then Rhodesia. He liked to recount that it was his African nanny who rejected William as a not very Irish name and rechristened him Terence, by which he was thereafter universally known. Back in Ireland, he attended Mount Temple College in Dublin and Foyle College in Derry before going up to Trinity College Dublin in 1941. He served as a Rating and then Petty Officer in the Royal Navy from 1943 to 1946, and then returned to Trinity where he graduated in Economics in 1948 and in Mathematics in 1949.[2] After Trinity, Gorman moved to Britain where he held a succession of posts at leading economics departments. From 1949 to 1962, he taught at the University of Birmingham, which was a leading centre for theoretical research in the 1950s, with Frank Hahn and Maurice McManus among his colleagues. In 1962, he was appointed to a chair in economics at Oxford and in 1967 he moved to a chair at the London School of Economics, where he played a central role in the development of a taught Master's programme in Econometrics and Mathematical Economics, then a rarity outside the United States. He returned to Oxford in 1979 as an Official Fellow of Nuffield College, becoming Senior Research Fellow in 1984 and Emeritus Fellow in 1990. He also spent periods as Visiting Professor at several US universities, including Iowa, Johns Hopkins, North Carolina and Stanford. Meanwhile, honours and awards were piling up, most notably the Presidency of the Econometric Society in 1972, as well as Fellowship of the British Academy, membership of Academia Europaea, honorary foreign membership of the American Academy of Arts and Sciences and of the American Economic Association, and honorary doctorates from University College London and the Universities of Birmingham and Southampton. In Ireland too his achievements were recognised, with an honorary doctorate from the National University of Ireland in 1986 and an Honorary Fellowship from

---

[2] Gorman always spoke fondly of the then Whately Professor in Trinity, George Duncan. In a late paper on the Le Chatelier Principle, which appeared in a Festschrift for Ivor Pearce, Gorman wrote: 'I would like to praise George Duncan…who introduced me to economics as an engine of thought, and who, in particular, taught me to expect the result that I will attempt to prove, and that in one of the first lectures of the first term of my first year in Trinity College Dublin'. Gorman continued, with his characteristic bluntness, that Duncan was 'a man in many ways like Ivor [Pearce] who might have become just as distinguished had he known more mathematics. He could not make head nor tail of the accelerator: but taught us about what have come to be known as Arrow-Debreu goods in one of his first lectures' (Gorman 1984: 1 and 16).

Trinity College Dublin some years later. After retirement, he continued to live in Oxford, also spending summers in County Cork with his wife Dorinda, whom he had met at Trinity, until in his last years when illness impaired his mobility.

3   The Work

It was sometimes said that Gorman published relatively little, and it is true that many of his papers circulated for years in mimeo form, some of them to be rescued by the editors of his *Collected Works* (see Blackorby and Shorrocks 1995). However, as the bibliography at the end of this paper shows, even his published output was formidable, and would have satisfied the most demanding research assessment exercise. Gorman's own summary of his principal contributions is worth quoting in full:

> James Davidson at Foyle College, Derry, and George Duncan at Trinity College Dublin, taught me to think of mathematics and economics as styles of thought, not collections of theorems, and Birmingham taught me to think of the social sciences as a unity with history as one way of holding them together. My research has accordingly been devoted to the end of flexible modelling, that is, to allow economists to immerse themselves in their data and in the opinions of other social scientists, and then to choose forms which seem capable of handling this information. This has been even more true of my teaching, largely through workshops for students beginning research (Gorman quoted in Blaug 1986: 328).

A reader unfamiliar with Gorman's works might interpret this as the manifesto of a woolly inter-disciplinarian. But the key phrase is 'flexible modelling'. Gorman was younger than Hicks, who in *Value and Capital* relegated his mathematics to appendices, and Samuelson, who in his *Foundations* proselytised about the value of a mathematical approach to economics. To Gorman, technical difficulty was taken for granted, though not an end in itself. Most of his research pursued the goal of using whatever tools were appropriate (and frequently developing new ones) in order to throw light on a central issue in economic theory: the links between individual preferences and market behaviour. Here we comment on some of the main topics which he illuminated.

3.1   Aggregation

In his first published paper, Gorman (1953), he provided the definitive answer to a key question in economics: when does a society of utility-maximising individuals behave as if it was a single individual? In other words, when does a community indifference map exist? He showed that a necessary and sufficient condition is that, assuming all individuals face the same prices, their income-consumption or Engel curves should be parallel straight lines. Thus, for individual (or household) h, the Hicksian demand function for good i should take the following form:[3]

$$x_i^h(p,u) = f_i^h(p) + u^h g_i(p) \qquad (21.1)$$

The location of the h superscripts on the right-hand side is crucial. Individuals can differ greatly in their responses to price changes as far as the f_i^h functions are concerned. However, their differences must be independent of income (or utility): all individuals must have the same g_i function, so that at the margin they have identical responses to changes in u. Hence, aggregate demands have the same form as (21.1):

$$X_i(p,u) = F_i(p) + U g_i(p) \qquad (21.2)$$

where X_i, F_i and U are the sums over all individuals of the corresponding micro terms.

Gorman returned to this question in Gorman (1961a), now using the much more powerful tools of duality which he and others had developed in the interim. This short paper is bedtime reading by contrast with the 1953 paper, yet it contains what is probably his best-known contribution. Here Gorman derived an explicit expression for the form of preferences which give rise to linear Engel curves. He showed that individual h's expenditure function must take the simple form:

$$e^h(p,u^h) = f^h(p) + u^h g(p) \qquad (21.3)$$

---

[3] This result was independently obtained by Antonelli (1886) and Nataf (1953). However, taken together, Gorman (1953) and (1961a) provide an explicit characterisation of the preferences which are consistent with exact aggregation.

where the functions $f^h(p)$ and $g(p)$ are homogeneous of degree one in prices (so ensuring that this property is exhibited by the expenditure function itself), and their derivatives equal the coefficients in (21.1). They have nice interpretations: $f^h(p)$ is the expenditure needed to reach a reference utility level of zero, while $g(p)$ is the price index which deflates the excess money income $e^h(p,u^h) - f^h(p)$ needed to attain a level of utility or real income u^h. Inverting (21.3) gives utility as a function of prices and expenditure:

$$v^h\left(p,I^h\right) = \frac{I^h - f^h\left(p\right)}{g\left(p\right)} \qquad (21.4)$$

which Gorman called 'the polar form of the underlying utility function' (ibid.: 54). With this unconventional term, Gorman was drawing attention to the fact that using what we would now call the indirect utility function amounts to switching from Cartesian to a form of polar coordinates in describing the indifference surface. Specifically, expenditure I may be taken as analogous to the radius and the vector of prices p to the angle in solid geometry. In any case, the term "Gorman polar form" has come to be universally applied to the functional form in (21.4).[4]

By construction, the Gorman polar form plays a central role in consumer theory, and it has also been hugely important in empirical work. On the one hand, special cases with particular functional forms for $f^h(p)$ and $g(p)$ proved amenable to estimation, even before the advent of high-speed computers. Gorman himself showed that, if the marginal propensities to consume (which equal $p_i g_i/g$) are constant, then the function $g(p)$ can be written as a geometric mean of prices:

$$g\left(p\right) = \prod p_i^{\rho_i}, \quad p_i = \rho_i g_i / g, \quad \sum \rho_i = 1 \qquad (21.5)$$

The linear expenditure system, developed by R.C. Geary amongst others, is a further special case, corresponding to the combination of (21.5) with a linear form for $f(p)$.[5] On the other hand, Gorman's results did not prove a barrier to extending the theory to more general demand systems which avoid the implausible restrictions on income effects of (21.3). Muellbauer (1975) showed that a richer family of demand systems could be generated if the traditional requirement, used by Gorman, that aggregate demands behave like

---

[4] Blackorby et al. (1978) appear to have been the first to refer to it as such.
[5] See Neary (1997) for further discussion and references.

the sum of individual demands, was replaced by the weaker requirement that they generate only the same budget *shares*. This in turn has spawned a huge empirical literature applying members of Muellbauer's family and its extensions, such as the "Almost Ideal Demand System" of Deaton and Muellbauer (1980).

Gorman (1968a) also explored the conditions that must be satisfied for the existence of an aggregate stock of a fixed factor such as capital. The necessary and sufficient condition turns out to be formally very similar to that for aggregation of demands over individual consumers. Each firm must have a restricted profit function similar in form to (21.3), where utility is replaced by a function of the amount of capital used by the firm. In his own words, this result 'certainly does not help justify the practice of fitting aggregate production functions' (ibid.: 167). This contribution of Gorman to the capital theory controversies of the 1960s lacked the fireworks of those that emanated from the two Cambridges (England and Massachusetts), but it is probably of more lasting importance.

3.2   Separability

'Suppose you were interested in the demand for tomatoes in Ireland' (Gorman 1987: 305). Thus, begins Gorman's article on separability in the *Palgrave Dictionary of Economics*, recalling his own early applied work, characterised by his widow Dorinda as involving 'careering around Dublin on a bike, looking in greengrocers' windows' (private communication). For him, separability assumptions were what allowed the researcher to abstract from the mass of institutional detail accumulated on such trips: detail that could conceivably be relevant, but was certainly going to make analysis impossibly complex. 'Separability', he wrote, 'is about the structure we are to impose on our model: what to investigate in detail, what can be sketched in with broad strokes without violence to the facts' (ibid.).

As for the researcher, so also for the household or the enterprise. Practical decision-making often calls for shortcuts relative to full intertemporal optimisation of a preference function. Gorman was confident that in reality most households engage in two-stage budgeting, in which the family budget is first allocated between broad classes of spending (clothing, food, etc.) and then choices are made within each class.

How good is this as a way of making decisions? Each of the two stages is problematic. Can the first-stage allocation safely be made just on the basis of some price aggregates for each class of goods, and without looking at the relative prices of all goods? Even if the first-stage allocations are correct, can the choice of goods within each class safely be made without reference to the prices on offer or quantities chosen of goods in other classes? It turns out that the validity of such a procedure for achieving the optimum requires that the household's utility function satisfy some fairly drastic separability restrictions—more stringent than had been recognised in the literature.

In particular, Strotz (1957) had argued that a sufficient condition for two-stage budgeting is that the household's utility function be separable, that is, expressible in the form:

$$u = F\left[v_1(x_1), v_2(x_2), \ldots, v_n(x_n)\right] \tag{21.6}$$

where x_r denotes the vector of consumption in class r. Gorman showed that, while necessary, separability is not sufficient.[6] In addition, it is required that the sub-utility functions, which Gorman called "specific satisfaction functions", v_r, enter utility either additively or through an intermediate function which is homogeneous of degree one in its components.[7]

That these constraints were severe was for Gorman 'in a sense a good thing' (Gorman 1959a: 475); since (he knew) households did adopt two-stage budgeting, it must be that their preferences were so restricted. Knowledge of this fact would ease the task of applied researchers wishing to estimate the relevant parameters.

What motivated Gorman here was the tension between two goals of economic modelling. On the one hand, the conceptual need for a coherent and psychologically or organisationally credible theoretical representation of decision-making; on the other hand, the operational need to have a workable algebraic representation of this behaviour. The basic assumptions of utility theory are too weak to yield specific functional forms or to make many predictions about individual or aggregate behaviour. Further assumptions are

---

[6] See Gorman (1959a). Gorman had refereed Strotz's paper but (according to the account he gave to Blackorby and Shorrocks (1995: 31)) his report, handwritten and covered with strawberry jam, was disregarded by the editor, Robert Solow!

[7] More precisely, the condition is that the utility function must be expressible in one of the following three forms, where f is homogeneous of degree one:

(1) $u = F(v_1, v_2)$ (the case where there are only two classes)
(2) $u = F[v_1, f(v_2, \ldots, v_n)]$ (all but one class can be grouped into a homogeneous function)
(3) $u = F[v_1 + \ldots + v_d + f(v_{d+1}, \ldots, v_n)]$ (classes 1 to d and a homogeneous function grouping the remaining classes all enter additively).

needed if real progress is to be made in applied economics, but these assumptions must be more-or-less reasonable. Looking from the other side, it is evident that simple algebraic representations of behaviour are needed for applied econometrics. Simplicity is also needed if the theory is to be mathematically manipulated to yield further predictions. But all such uses are empty if the algebraic specification implies incoherent decision-making. In practice, most of the algebraic representations with which demand and production theory deal are linear functions of prices or quantities, or are simple transformations of linear functions. Here questions of separability become central.

An interesting example of how specific separability assumptions could help in underpinning a linear representation of behaviour is provided by Gorman's 1982 paper "Facing an Uncertain Future". In this paper, Gorman's goal is to show that the assumptions required to justify a linear representation of the intertemporal objective function are much weaker and more credible than had hitherto been recognised in the literature.

For a static environment, Allais, Samuelson, Von Neumann and Morgenstern and others had presented the conditions under which decision-making under conditions of uncertainty could be represented as the maximisation of a linear function—a weighted average—of the various alternative possibilities.[8] The key assumption in this expected utility hypothesis, Samuelson's weak independence axiom (or "sure thing principle"), is one of separability.

If we widen the focus to intertemporal decisions (still under uncertainty), can we get as simple an objective function with equally weak assumptions? The objective function that is commonly—indeed almost universally used—is a double sum:

$$\sum_{s}\sum_{t} f^{st}\left(y_{st}\right) \qquad (21.7)$$

where y_{st} is the vector of flows which occur in period t if state s occurs.[9] Can we derive such a simple form from assumptions that are as mild and acceptable as those underlying expected utility? If we are prepared to assume an extended version of the sure thing principle, so that it applies over time as well as between uncertain states of the world, we will get this double summation

---

[8] The weights are usually interpreted as subjective probabilities, an interpretation which Gorman found unhelpful: 'Frequently they seem to me to obscure, rather than enlighten' (Gorman 1982: 215).

[9] We often make the further simplification $f_{st}(y_{st}) = \delta_s\, r_t\, y_{st}$, where δ is a probability and r a discount factor, but Gorman does not force such an interpretation.

form of the objective function. But Gorman points out that extending weak independence in this way is logically problematic.

Before doing so, he notes that such an extension to a second dimension is permissible in the case of a social welfare function under uncertainty, where households rather than time are the extra dimension. Thus, if social welfare is increasing in every household's utility, if each household is "self-regarding",[10] and if Samuelson's weak independence axiom holds, then, drawing on a powerful theorem from an earlier paper of his on the structure of utility functions (see Gorman 1968b),[11] Gorman shows that the social welfare function can be expressed in the same double summation form as (21.7), except with y_{sh} as the consumption of household h in state of the world s instead of y_{st}. These simple and acceptable[12] assumptions are thus all that is needed to produce 'Bentham and Bernoulli at a stroke' (Gorman in Blackorby and Shorrocks 1995: 212).

However, to assume that households or firms are not only able to calculate their utility over all possible future states of the world but assert independence over each set of states of the world and time periods is a step too far for Gorman. Such an argument 'assumes from the outset that we are all very bright, and especially so at computation' (ibid.: 214). Instead, he proposes the contrary idea, that 'we are all pretty limited beings, only able to hold a few things in our minds at a time…and that organisations are collectively quite as limited as their members' (ibid.). Specifically, he assumes that 'we look ahead two periods in detail, summarising the impact of our choices on more distant prospects in a single figure' (ibid.). He then proceeds to show that this, partially myopic but more realistic, vision of decision-making, embodying a very weak (undemanding) form of intertemporal separability, is enough to generate the double summation form of the objective function.

Here, Gorman has armed applied econometricians with a justification for doing what they had always intended—use a linear functional form. The behavioural assumptions are somewhat restrictive, but also characteristically down-home: the firm is planning for now and next year, and for a general sense of what it will bequeath in later years. If that is not how firms and households behave exactly, it seems, at the same time, to be not too unrealistic.

---

[10] That is, considers only its own consumption; this is what gives separability or independence in the additional dimension.

[11] The theorem states that if two separable sets overlap in their membership, then their intersection and differences are also separable. In the social welfare case, the overlapping arises because the separable (self-regarding) individuals are all involved in states of the world to which Samuelson's weak independence axiom applies; in the intertemporal choice case the separability is induced by the partial myopia mentioned below.

[12] He was of course fully aware of the continuing controversy over the weak independence axiom for choice under uncertainty and the fact that it has been rejected by many empirical experiments.

3.3   Characteristics

Separability may be justified between goods that satisfy widely different needs. However, for other goods, it is their close similarities that attract attention. It is not on the basis of their essence that a consumer will choose between goods, but on the basis of the satisfaction they will produce. Even for closely related goods, this in turn may depend on more than one characteristic.

Switching from tomatoes to eggs in deference to his original audience for the topic—an agricultural economics seminar at the Iowa State College of Agriculture and the Mechanic Arts in 1956—Gorman entitled his first paper on the topic of characteristics "A Possible Procedure for Analysing Quality Differentials in the Egg Market" (this paper finally appeared in 1980). Ever concerned with the interests of the applied economist, he saw the paper as a response to the need of Iowan farmers to understand what drove price differentials for eggs of different qualities.

The basic idea is simple: consumers buy different varieties of eggs solely for certain measurable characteristics (for example, he suggests, their vitamin content). If only two characteristics are relevant, then, given arbitrary prices, we may expect that at most two varieties of eggs will be bought by any given consumer; if three characteristics are relevant, at most three varieties.[13] Only in the "degenerate case", where the relative prices happened to be just right, would the consumer be indifferent between three or more varieties. But—and here is where things get interesting—as soon as we consider market equilibrium, the prices will not be arbitrary: the degenerate case will prove to be the normal one, as it is '*the only case in which every type of egg could find a sale*' (ibid.: 844; italics in original). This degenerate case can be characterised by a shadow price q_j of characteristic j such that, if purchased variety i delivered quantity a_{ij} of characteristic j, the price p_{it} of each variety i at each time t should always equal the value of the sum of its characteristics measured at the shadow prices:

$$p_{it} = \sum_j a_{ij} q_{jt} \qquad (21.8)$$

---

[13] Determined by the tangent of the consumer's indifference curve with the convex hull of the affordable combinations of the two characteristics.

Building on this insight, essentially an argument from the assumption that market prices should not embody arbitrage opportunities, Gorman proposed an empirical research agenda. The specific quantity of each characteristic delivered by each variety, though measurable for the consumer, is unknown to the researcher, as are the shadow prices. But a sufficiently long time series on the prices of different varieties could allow both to be identified, even if the prices were also somewhat influenced by other, less important, elements. If the number of varieties is I and the number of characteristics J, then price data for T time periods yields IT data points to estimate $I + J$ parameters. Statistical techniques such as factor analysis are available for such analysis. Gorman sensed that many of these ideas were already known,[14] but the arbitrage argument seems to be original to him.

For all his warmth towards the challenges faced by applied econometricians, Gorman had little real interest in pursuing applied empirical work. His attempts to operationalise the characteristics model on an ambitiously large scale using quarterly regional data on the consumption of over a hundred categories of food for 1956–1971 proved somewhat inconclusive (see Boyle et al. 1977).

Yet the characteristics model has assumed an empirical life of its own: far from egg or tomato markets, this insight now underpins the most widely used asset-pricing models in modern finance theory.[15] After all, most financial assets are closely substitutable, and investors' choices between them are largely driven by their potential to deliver a relatively small number of yield characteristics. Whereas Markowitz (1959) asserted that investors were seeking to balance portfolio risk and return, measured by mean and variance, modern theories allow the goals of investors to be unmeasured characteristics of the stream of future returns. Market-clearing prices of the various assets must, in these theories, be adapted to the shadow prices of these characteristics in the market, just as Gorman saw. Thus, such price processes are estimated by factor analysis-type methods (Campbell et al. 1997). Even the famous option pricing model of Black and Scholes (1972) and Merton (1973) appeals to precisely the same arbitrage logic so lucidly presented by Gorman more than fifteen years earlier.

---

[14] The idea of hedonic indexes can indeed be traced back to Waugh (1928). Griliches (1961) advocated their use for the US CPI, and this suggestion was acted on from 1984. A recognition of more rapid and systematic quality change has led to the increasingly widespread use of such price indices.

[15] It has also been applied in a great variety of other fields, notably through the later work of Lancaster (1966).

3.4   Duality

Over and above his substantive contributions, a recurring theme in Gorman's writings was the need to select the appropriate technical tools for the problem at hand. Typically, this meant using "dual" tools, functions defined over prices rather than quantities. As households and firms typically take prices as given, it is much easier to understand their behaviour in terms of expenditure, cost and profit functions than in terms of primal utility and production functions. The latter only take account of tastes and technology, the former add optimising behaviour. Gorman was not alone in advocating this approach, but he was one of its most ardent proponents. The great virtue of duality is that it avoids matrix inversion, which he called 'the only technically difficult operation in general equilibrium theory' (Gorman 1986a). Even a cursory comparison between modern textbooks and Hicks's *Value and Capital* or Samuelson's *Foundations* shows how much more powerful are dual methods.

A nice example of the value of the dual approach was Gorman's contribution to the issue of household equivalence scales. Such scales, which attempt to correct consumption patterns for differences in household composition, had been used for years in applied budget studies, though without any theoretical foundation. Barten (1964) pioneered the exploration of such scales in the context of utility theory. But Barten used the primal approach, expressing utility as a function of consumption per "equivalent adult", where the scale which determines equivalence varies between commodities. Gorman (1976) argued that the insight of an 'otherwise obtuse' schoolmaster he once had put it better: 'When you have a wife and baby, a penny bun costs threepence' (ibid.: 215). Leaving aside the banality (and, to a modern ear, the sexism) of the aphorism, Gorman noted that it gets to the heart of the issue: differences in household composition are better thought of as altering the effective prices which must be paid, rather than the effective number of consumers. This approach, implemented using the expenditure function, led to a substantial simplification and extension of Barten's results.[16]

Expenditure and profit functions are usually the appropriate tools. However, in some problems, quantities may be the exogenous variables. In

---

[16] Muellbauer (1974) independently rederived Barten's results using the dual approach.

such cases, the appropriate technical tool is the distance function, defined implicitly as the scalar by which an arbitrary consumption bundle must be deflated to yield a target level of utility: $u[q/d(q,u^0)] = u^0$. This can be viewed as the natural inverse of the direct utility function. But it also turns out to bear a dual relationship to the expenditure function. Just as (by Shephard's Lemma) the price derivatives of the expenditure function equal the optimal quantities, so the quantity derivatives of the distance function equal the optimal shadow prices. Gorman developed this concept in full, independently of others. In Gorman (1965a), he gave what appears to be the first statement of the duality between cost and distance functions, while in Gorman (1970a) he examined the properties of the distance function in detail. These papers however remained unpublished, so modern treatments typically give precedence to Debreu (1951) and Malmquist (1953) and pass over Gorman's pioneering explorations.

Gorman's emphasis in all this was on the need for careful thought about which theoretical tools were appropriate for a particular problem. As he wrote in unpublished notes for a 1986 seminar at University College Dublin, doing economic theory 'is like eating an apple pie. If you know there is one in the fridge, and where the light switches are, there is nothing to it. Look around when you next visit a strange house, in case you should feel hungry in the night' (Gorman 1986b).

4   Conclusion

Gorman wrote in his first paper: 'In writing this article I have been torn between a desire for rigour and a desire for simplicity, and each has had to be sacrificed in part to the other' (Gorman 1953: 63, fn. 1). Even to today's technically trained economists, his writings seem characterised more by rigour than by simplicity. Yet Gorman's legacy, carried on in part by generations of students to whom he devoted so much of his time and attention, is a set of results and tools which make it immeasurably easier for future economists 'to tailor models for particular problems and particular data' (Gorman 1987: 305).

References

Main Works by W.M. Gorman[17]

Collected Works

Blackorby, C. and A.F. Shorrocks (eds) (1995). *Separability and Aggregation: Collected Works of W.M. Gorman*. Volume 1. Oxford: Clarendon Press.

Other

Boyle, J.R., W.M. Gorman, and S.E. Pudney (1977). 'The Demand for Related Goods: A Progress Report'. Chapter 2c in M.D. Intriligator (ed.) *Frontiers of Quantitative Economics*. Volume IIIA. Amsterdam: North–Holland: 87–101. Invited paper at the Third World Congress of the Econometric Society.

*Gorman, W.M. (1953). 'Community Preference Fields'. *Econometrica*, 21(1): 63–80.

Gorman, W.M. (1955). 'The Intransitivity of Certain Criteria Used in Welfare Economics'. *Oxford Economic Papers*, New Series, 7(1): 23–35.

Gorman, W.M. (1957). 'Convex Indifference Curves and Diminishing Marginal Utility'. *Journal of Political Economy*, 65(1): 40–50.

Gorman, W.M. (1957). 'How Surprising is a Chain of Coincidences?'. *Metroeconomica*, 9(2): 112–115.

Gorman, W.M. (1957). 'A Note on "A Revised Theory of Expectations"'. *Economic Journal*, 67(267): 549–551.

Gorman, W.M. (1957). 'Some Comments on Professor Hicks' *Revision of Demand Theory*'. *Metroeconomica*, 9(3): 167–180.

Gorman, W.M. (1958). 'Tariffs, Retaliation, and the Elasticity of Demand for Imports'. *Review of Economic Studies*, 25(3): 133–162. Reprinted as Chapter 12 in M.J. Farrell (ed.) (1973) *Readings in Welfare Economics*. London: Macmillan: 167–196.

*Gorman, W.M. (1959a). 'Separable Utility and Aggregation'. *Econometrica*, 27(3): 469–481. Reprinted as Chapter 16 in K.J. Arrow (ed.) (1971) *Selected Readings in Economic Theory from Econometrica*. Cambridge, MA: MIT Press: 326–338.

Gorman, W.M. (1959). 'The Effect of Tariffs on the Level and Terms of Trade'. *Journal of Political Economy*, 67(3): 246–265.

Gorman, W.M. (1959). 'Are Social Indifference Curves Convex?'. *Quarterly Journal of Economics*, 73(3): 485–496.

Gorman, W.M. (1960). 'Tariffs and Trade in a Two-Good World'. *International Economic Review*, 1(3): 223–229.

---

[17] Articles denoted with an asterisk are included in Blackorby and Shorrocks (1995).

*Gorman, W.M. (1961). 'On a Class of Preference Fields'. *Metroeconomica*, 13(2): 53–56.

Gorman, W.M. (1961). 'Elasticity of Demand for Imports with Close, but Imperfect Substitutes'. *International Economic Review*, 2(3): 371–376.

Gorman, W.M. (1963). 'Additive Logarithmic Preferences, A Further Note'. *Review of Economic Studies*, 30(1): 56–62.

*Gorman, W.M. (1964). 'More Scope for Qualitative Economics'. *Review of Economic Studies*, 31(1): 65–68.

Gorman, W.M. (1965a). 'Production Functions in Which the Elasticities of Substitution Stand in Fixed Proportions to Each Other'. *Review of Economic Studies*, 32(3): 217–224.

Gorman, W.M. (1965). 'Professor Friedman's Consumption Function and the Theory of Choice'. *Econometrica*, 32(1/2): 189–197.

Gorman, W.M. (1967). 'Tastes, Habits and Choices'. *International Economic Review*, 8(2): 218–222.

*Gorman, W.M. (1968a). 'Measuring the Quantities of Fixed Factors'. Chapter 5 in J.N. Wolfe (ed.) *Value, Capital and Growth: Papers in Honour of Sir John Hicks*. Edinburgh: Edinburgh University Press: 141–172.

*Gorman, W.M. (1968b). 'The Structure of Utility Functions'. *Review of Economic Studies*, 35(4): 367–390.

*Gorman, W.M. (1968). 'Conditions for Additive Separability'. *Econometrica*, 36(3/4): 605–609.

Gorman, W.M. (1971). 'Preference, Revealed Preference, and Indifference'. Chapter 5 in J.S. Chipman, L. Hurwicz, M.K. Richter and H.F. Sonnenschein (eds) *Preferences, Utility and Demand: A Minnesota Symposium*. New York: Harcourt Brace Jovanovich: 81–113.

Gorman, W.M. (1976). 'Tricks with Utility Functions'. Chapter 11 in M.J. Artis and A.R. Nobay (eds) *Essays in Economic Analysis*. Cambridge: Cambridge University Press: 211–243. Invited address to the 1975 Association of University Teachers in Economics Conference.

Gorman, W.M. (1980). 'A Possible Procedure for Analysing Quality Differentials in the Egg Market'. *Review of Economic Studies*, 47(5): 843–856. First circulated as Journal Paper No. 2319, Iowa Agricultural Experiment Station, November 1956.

*Gorman, W.M. (1981). 'Some Engel Curves'. Chapter 1 in A. Deaton (ed.) *Essays on the Theory and Measurement of Demand in Honour of Sir Richard Stone*. Cambridge: Cambridge University Press: 7–30.

Gorman, W.M. (1984). 'Le Chatelier and General Equilibrium'. Chapter 1 in A. Ingham and A. Ulph (eds) *Demand, Equilibrium and Trade: Essays in Honour of Ivor F. Pearce*. London: Macmillan: 1–18.

*Gorman, W.M. (1986). 'Assembling Efficient Organizations?'. Chapter 8 in W.P. Heller, R.M. Starr and D.A. Starrett (eds) *Uncertainty, Information and Communication: Essays in Honor of Kenneth J. Arrow*. Volume III. Cambridge: Cambridge University Press: 213–228.

*Gorman, W.M. (1987). 'Separability'. In J. Eatwell, M. Milgate and P. Newman (eds) *The New Palgrave: A Dictionary of Economics*. Volume 4. London: Macmillan: 305–311.

*Gorman, W.M. (1990). 'More Measures for Fixed Factors'. In G.D. Myles (ed.) *Measurement and Modelling in Economics*. Amsterdam: North–Holland: 381–409.

Gorman, W.M. and G.D. Myles (1987). 'Characteristics'. In J. Eatwell, M. Milgate and P. Newman (eds) *The New Palgrave: A Dictionary of Economics*. Volume 1. London: Macmillan: 403–406.

Unpublished Works[18]

Gorman, W.M. (1959c). 'The Demand for Fish: An Application of Factor Analysis'. Paper read to the Amsterdam meeting of the Econometric Society; Discussion Paper A.6, Faculty of Commerce and Social Science, Birmingham University, September.

Gorman, W.M. (1960b). 'A Note on Hotelling's Method of Extracting the Latent Roots and Vectors of a Matrix'. Discussion Paper A.12, Faculty of Commerce and Social Science, Birmingham University, September.

*Gorman, W.M. (1965). 'Consumer Budgets and Price Indices'. Unpublished typescript.

*Gorman, W.M. (1970a). 'Conditions for Generalised Additive Separability'. Discussion Paper No. 9, Department of Economics, London School of Economics, September.

*Gorman, W.M. (1970). 'Quasi Separable Preferences, Costs and Technologies'. Paper read at Harvard University, November.

Gorman, W.M. (1972). 'Sketch for the Demand for Related Goods'. Presidential Address to the Econometric Society.

*Gorman, W.M. (1982). 'Facing an Uncertain Future'. Technical Report No. 359, Institute for Mathematical Studies in the Social Sciences, Stanford University, January.

Gorman, W.M. (1986a). 'Unpublished Notes for a Seminar at University College Dublin'. 12 March.

Other Works Referred To

Antonelli, G.B. (1886). *Sulla Teoria Matematica dell'Economia Politica*. Pisa: Tipografia del Folchetto. English translation, 'On the Mathematical Theory of Political Economy', Chapter 16 in J.S. Chipman, L. Hurwicz, M.K. Richter and H.F. Sonnenschein (eds) (1971) *Preferences, Utility and Demand: A Minnesota Symposium*. New York: Harcourt Brace Jovanovich: 333–360.

---

[18] As explained in the text, much of Gorman's work was never published, although many previously unpublished papers were collected in Blackorby and Shorrocks (1995). This brief selection includes only those papers which he included in his curriculum vitae of 1985 or which are discussed in the text.

Barten, A.P. (1964). 'Family Composition, Prices and Expenditure Patterns'. In P.E. Hart, G. Mills and J.K. Whitaker (eds) *Econometric Analysis for National Economic Planning*. London: Butterworth: 277–292.

Black, F. and M. Scholes (1972). 'The Valuation of Option Contracts and a Test of Market Efficiency'. *Journal of Finance*, Papers and Proceedings, 27(2): 399–417.

Blackorby, C., R. Boyce and R.R. Russell (1978). 'Estimation of Demand Systems Generated by the Gorman Polar Form: A Generalization of the S-Branch Utility Tree'. *Econometrica*, 46(2): 345–363.

Blaug, M. (1986). *Who's Who in Economics: A Biographical Dictionary of Major Economists 1799–1986*. Second edition. Sussex: Wheatsheaf Books.

Campbell, J.Y., A.W. Lo and A.C. Mackinlay (1997). *The Econometrics of Financial Markets*. Princeton, NJ: Princeton University Press.

Deaton, A.S. and J. Muellbauer (1980). 'An Almost Ideal Demand System'. *American Economic Review*, 70(3): 312–326.

Debreu, G. (1951). 'The Coefficient of Resource Allocation'. *Econometrica*, 19(3): 273–292.

Griliches, Z. (1961). 'Hedonic Price Indexes for Automobiles: An Econometric Analysis of Quality Change'. In *The Price Statistics of the Federal Government*. Report No. 3, General Series, No. 73. New York: National Bureau of Economic Research: 173–196.

Honohan, P. and J.P. Neary (2003). 'W.M. Gorman (1923–2003)'. *The Economic and Social Review*, 34(2): 195–209.

Lancaster, K.J. (1966). 'A New Approach to Consumer Theory'. *Journal of Political Economy*, 74(2): 132–157.

Malmquist, S. (1953). 'Index Numbers and Indifference Surfaces'. *Trabajos de Estadistica*, 4(2): 209–242.

Markowitz, H. (1959). *Portfolio Selection: Efficient Diversification of Investments*. New York: John Wiley.

Merton, R.C. (1973). 'Theory of Rational Option Pricing'. *Bell Journal of Economics and Management Science*, 4(1): 141–183.

Muellbauer, J. (1974). 'Household Composition, Engel Curves and Welfare Comparisons Between Households: A Duality Approach'. *European Economic Review*, 5(2): 103–122.

Muellbauer, J. (1975). 'Aggregation, Income Distribution and Consumer Demand'. *Review of Economic Studies*, 42(4): 525–543.

Nataf, A. (1953). 'Sur des Questions d'Agrégation en Économétrie'. *Publications de l'Institut de Statistique de l'Université de Paris*, 2, Fasc., 4: 5–61.

Neary, J.P. (1997). 'R.C. Geary's Contributions to Economic Theory'. Chapter 3 in D. Conniffe (ed.) *Roy Geary, 1896–1983: Irish Statistician*. Dublin: Oak Tree Press and The Economic and Social Research Institute: 93–118.

Strotz, R.H. (1957). 'The Empirical Implications of a Utility Tree'. *Econometrica*, 25(2): 269–280.

Waugh, F.W. (1928). 'Quality Factors Influencing Vegetable Prices'. *Journal of Farm Economics*, 10(2): 185–196.

22

W. Max Corden (1927–)

John Martin

1   Introduction

Max Corden was born in August 1927 in what was then the German city of Breslau, capital of Silesia. It is now a Polish city called Wroclaw after it was ceded to Poland after the Second World War. His birth name was Werner Max Cohn. His parents, Rudolf and Katia Cohn, were Jewish but were not practising, unlike Rudolf's older brother Willy. The Jewish community in Breslau at the time of Corden's birth was the third largest in Germany after Berlin and Frankfurt.

Rudolf's father Louis and his brother Moritz had built a successful business in Breslau. They owned a significant building close to the central square of Breslau, part of which was occupied by a clothing store called Trautner. The building was not damaged during the war and still exists today. Rudolf took over the management of Trautner in 1932, but after the Nazis came to power, he was obliged to relinquish this position in 1937 and sell the business.

The advent of the Nazis to power in Breslau had a huge effect on Corden's family, as it did on all Jewish families in that terrible epoch. Corden's older brother, Gerhart, was a teenager and at risk of anti-semitic violence. His

I am very grateful to John Creedy, Vijay Joshi, Dermot McAleese and Peter Oppenheimer for their comments on an earlier version of this paper. I alone am responsible for any remaining errors.

J. Martin (✉)
Ville D'Avary, France

parents decided to send Gerhart abroad to England in 1937 where their mother had a sister, Aunt Elli, who played a major role in getting the rest of the family out of Germany and to safety.

1.1   A Lucky Escape

In his memoirs, Corden (2018: 17) states that he was aware of the anti-semitic attitudes at the time stirred up by Nazi propaganda but that he himself did not experience it directly. However, when his father was sacked from his post as manager and made unemployed, the family began to make active preparations to emigrate. As part of this process, Max was also sent to England in early 1938 where he was met by his Aunt Elli and, like his older brother, enrolled in an English preparatory school. It is noteworthy that at the tender age of ten, Max travelled alone to England by boat and train. In Corden (ibid.: 12–13), he describes the adventure in matter-of-fact terms, but it vividly illustrates his resilience and determination.

Things came to a head for the family after the terrible events of *Kristallnacht* on the 9 November 1938. All over Germany, Jewish synagogues and businesses were sacked and destroyed. Thousands of Jewish men were arrested and sent to concentration camps. Max's father, Rudolf, was one of them: he was imprisoned in Buchenwald. However, luck was at hand for the family in the person of Aunt Elli. She had managed to secure visas for the family to emigrate from Germany to Australia. With these precious visas in hand, Max's mother was able to get Rudolf released from Buchenwald. The parents then went to England and met up with their two sons. On 16 December 1938, they all boarded a liner at Southampton bound for Australia, finally settling in Melbourne towards the end of January 1939.

Unfortunately, a much more tragic fate awaited Max's Uncle Willy Cohn and his family. Willy was a high school teacher who lost his job when the Nazis came to power because he was an active social democrat. Willy was a historian and author of numerous articles about the history of German Jews. He was also an avid diarist who documented in great detail life for the Jewish community in Breslau under the Nazis. Unlike Rudolf, Willy was very reluctant to leave Germany though his three older children did so.[1] When he had made up his mind to leave, war broke out. Willy, his second wife, Trudi, and their two youngest daughters, Susanne (aged nine) and Tamara (aged three), were rounded up with a thousand other Jews from Breslau on 21 November

---

[1] See Corden (2018: 31–37) for a discussion of the reasons why Willy did not follow his younger brother in seeking to leave Germany until it was too late.

1941. They were shipped by train to Kaunas (in Lithuania) where they were all murdered on arrival by an extermination squad. Miraculously, Willy's diaries survived the war and were later published first in Israel and then in Germany.[2] They are regarded as one of the most compelling descriptions of what life was like for Jews in Germany under the Nazis.

After the family had settled in Melbourne, they quickly anglicised their names: Cohn became Corden, Werner became Warner, Gerhart became Gerald. However, Corden (ibid.: 46) makes it clear that Warner never stuck as his first name and he was always henceforth known as "Max". In 1942, Corden entered Melbourne High School, a selective State school, and he graduated from it in 1945, winning a prize as well as a scholarship to the University of Melbourne. His favourite subject at school was history. But, as he recounts in his memoirs, his father advised him against studying history at university. Instead, he urged Max to study commerce with the aim of getting a well-paid job after graduation. Luckily the commerce course at Melbourne University involved a lot of economics so that is how Corden became an economist. History's loss was to prove economics' gain, thanks to the wise advice of Rudolf Corden.[3]

His development as an economist during his undergraduate years was much influenced by his careful reading of two seminal books: *The Economics of Imperfect Competition* by Joan Robinson and *The Economics of Welfare* by A.C. Pigou. In a conversation about his life and work, Corden testified about the impact these books had on his life's work: 'The first launched me into partial equilibrium diagrams and the second, with its emphasis on market failure and the use of taxes and subsidies to correct for externalities, became a kind of ancestor of my later book *Trade Policy and Economic Welfare*' (Corden in Coleman 2006: 381).

After graduating with a First in 1949, Corden did not initially consider an academic career. Instead, he joined the management and research unit of a major Melbourne newspaper, *The Argus*, and explored the possibility of becoming a journalist. But he kept his academic options open too by enrolling part-time for a Master's degree at Melbourne. His thesis topic was "The Economics of the Australian Press". It resulted in Corden's first published

---

[2] The German version of Willy Cohn's diaries covering the years from 1933 to his death in November 1941 was edited by Professor Norbert Conrads and published in 2006 (see Cohn 2006). An abridged version of the diaries was published in English by Stanford University Press (see Cohn 2012).

[3] Even though he chose to follow his father's advice and not become a historian, Corden's love of history has influenced much of his economics writings. Many of his works cite historical parallels for their topics—witness the many such references in Corden (1974, 1997a) and the Appendix on the history of the effective protection concept in Corden (1971a).

economics article—Corden (1952–1953)—in the prestigious British journal, the *Review of Economic Studies*. This article also had a bonus effect of catching the eye of two leading international economists who were later to become key mentors for Corden: Harry Johnson and James Meade.

2   LSE and NIESR (1953–1957)

In 1952, the then Head of the Economics Department at Melbourne, Wilfred Prest, suggested to Corden that he should go to the UK to do postgraduate studies at the London School of Economics (LSE) and apply for a British Council scholarship. Corden notes in (2018: 92) that he wrote in haste on his application form that his research area was to be transport economics.

Corden first encountered James Meade through reading his books, especially *The Balance of Payments* (Meade 1951) and *A Geometry of International Trade* (Meade 1952). When he arrived at LSE, Corden immediately requested Meade for his PhD supervisor. Thanks in part to his published paper, Meade accepted this request. Transport economics was dropped swiftly in favour of international economics, a most serendipitous choice. Corden (2018: 97–102) makes it clear that Meade made a lasting impression on him, both as a person and as an economist. During this period, Meade was writing his second volume on *The Theory of International Economic Policy: Trade and Welfare* (Meade 1955), and Corden read the proofs of it.

Given his immigrant background, it is perhaps unsurprising that Corden's choice for his thesis topic was related to the economics of immigration: the title was "Population Increase and Foreign Trade". It was much influenced by the writings of Harry Johnson on the effects of growth on the terms of trade, and by Meade's work.[4]

While he was at LSE, Corden became interested in issues surrounding protection, especially sparked by his reading of the 1929 Brigden Report on the cost of protection in Australia. He published two papers on the topic, both of which made an impact. The first, Corden (1957), presents what is now the standard treatment of the welfare cost of a tariff in a small country using a diagram which combines domestic demand and supply curves for the importable and highlights the deadweight loss in the form of the well-known Harberger triangles. The second paper, Corden (1957), uses a neat diagram to first make a simple, but important, point about trade policy: a production subsidy is a superior instrument to a tariff if the objective is to achieve a given

---

[4] Corden (1956) is drawn directly from his thesis.

level of industry output or employment. The underlying assumption here is that there is a positive externality associated with production, that is, there is a divergence between the marginal private and social cost of production. This is a nice example of the theory of domestic distortions. The central insight is that any policy intervention should be targeted as close as possible to the source of the distortion. Corden then proceeds to drop the small-country assumption and considers the impact of varying the terms of trade. In the latter case, he shows that the goal of protecting a given sector requires a combination of policy instruments, namely an optimum tariff with a production subsidy. The optimum tariff is needed to deal with varying terms of trade and the subsidy to ensure that output or employment is at the desired level.[5] Harry Johnson did much to publicise these two papers among the international economics fraternity.

One feature of these two papers which would become typical of Corden's approach to economics is the clever use of diagrams. As he put it: 'I'm naturally inclined to diagrams … The fact is everybody loves them when you do them, provided they are simple' (Corden in Coleman 2006: 386).

2.1 Mentors and Friends

In his memoirs, Corden (2018: 102) singles out Harry Johnson as his second great mentor after James Meade and calls him his 'Patron Saint'. Indeed, as we shall see below, Johnson was the key figure behind Corden going to Oxford.

There was a vintage crop of graduate students at LSE when Corden was there. He made several close friends whose subsequent work had an impact on his own research. In Corden (ibid.: 104–106), he singles out Kelvin Lancaster, Richard Lipsey and Tad Rybczynski. The famous Lipsey and Lancaster (1956–1957) paper on second-best theory had a major impact on Corden (see Corden 1974, 1997a). Rybczynski, as every student of international economics knows, gave his name to one of the canonical theorems of the Heckscher-Ohlin-Samuelson model, and it has featured prominently in several of Corden's papers.

John Black became another invaluable friend. Corden met him through the Oxford-Cambridge-LSE seminar at a time when Black was a student at Nuffield College, Oxford. Black read many of Corden's writings while they were being drafted. In his memoirs, Corden credits Black with saving him from numerous errors (see Corden 2018: 103–104).

---

[5] This article and its results predate the well-known Bhagwati and Ramaswami (1963) paper, a point stressed in Johnson (1965).

During this period, LSE attracted several outstanding students from abroad who later achieved renown in international economics. These students were drawn to the School by the possibility of working with Meade. They included Peter Kenen, Richard Cooper and Robert Mundell (a future Nobel Prize winner in Economics). All became close friends of Corden.

When his British Council scholarship expired, Corden joined the National Institute of Economic and Social Research (NIESR) as a Research Fellow for two years. Together with Margaret Hemming, he published a theoretical paper on import controls as an instrument to influence the balance of payments (see Hemming and Corden 1958). This paper, in turn, served as the genesis of a much more widely cited paper of Corden's via a diagram showing how countries could achieve internal and external balance through a combination of expenditure-switching and expenditure-reducing policies (see Corden 1960). The diagram in question was the Swan diagram with its so-called four zones of economic unhappiness, where the twin objectives of internal and external balance are not achieved (see Swan 1955). Corden also highlighted the fact that a similar diagram was developed by Salter (1959) which showed how an economy's production and consumption of traded and non-traded goods could vary in response to relative price changes.[6] Combining these two diagrams yields the Salter-Swan model of internal and external balance which has subsequently been much used to analyse numerous issues in international economics. Corden (1960) can rightly claim credit for popularising this model.

During this period in London, Corden married his fiancée Dorothy (née Martin) whom he had met in Melbourne and who had followed him to England. Dorothy was a wonderful person, charming and kind, a committed Anglophile and the perfect life companion for Max.

3   Return to Australia (University of Melbourne, 1958–1962; ANU, Canberra, 1962–1967)

Returning to Australia, Corden devoted most of his research to tariff policy in that country, inspired by his reading of the Brigden Report and his papers on the cost of protection. Australian industry was then very heavily protected by tariffs and quotas. Shortly after his return to Australia, Corden gave a major

---

[6] Salter (1959) uses the small-country assumption of fixed terms of trade to aggregate importables and exportables as traded goods.

lecture on his suggestions for reforms to Australian protectionism with the aim of reducing its costs. He advocated two major reforms: (1) quotas should be replaced by tariffs; and (2) tariffs should be shifted gradually towards a uniform ad valorem rate.[7]

In order to support his arguments for reform, Corden dug deeply into the logic behind the highly complex Australian system of protection. This led him to stress the issue of *tariff escalation* and, from this, he made the case for measuring protection in terms of the *effective protection rate*, that is, protection in relation to value added rather than imports or output.[8]

3.1   Effective Protection

The basic formula for the effective rate of protection (ERP) on a simple one importable good using one traded input is:

$$ \text{ERP}_i = \left(t_i - a_{ij} t_j \right) / \left(1 - a_{ij} \right) \tag{22.1} $$

where t_i = nominal tariff rate on good i, t_j = nominal tariff rate on input j and a_{ij} = share of input j in cost of good i at free trade prices.[9]

If $t_i > t_j$, $\text{ERP}_i > t_i$;
If $t_i = t_j$, $\text{ERP}_i = t_i = t_j$;
If $t_j < t_i$, $\text{ERP}_i < t_i < t_j$;
If $t_i < a_{ij} t_j$, $\text{ERP}_i < 0$.[10]

The ERP measure can be extended to cover all taxes and subsidies affecting both importables and exportables. It permits a single measure to sum up the net effect of all trade and non-trade taxes and subsidies on the value added in a particular activity. There are, of course, many theoretical and empirical complications associated with the ERP concept. A number of these are addressed

---

[7] Corden (2018: 113–123) argues that he was perhaps a bit too timid in these recommendations and that he should have added a third reform, devaluation of the Australian dollar, to help stabilise industrial output and employment. His writings on Australian trade policy during this period are collected in Corden (1997b).

[8] Corden notes that he first came across the effective protection concept in Barber (1955).

[9] Since the data on input shares for ERP calculations are derived from input-output tables which include the nominal tariff rates on both outputs and inputs, these are used for actual calculations of ERPs rather than the free trade values.

[10] The case of negative value added attracted much attention in the empirical literature and many instances of this were discovered, especially in developing countries (see Greenaway and Milner 2003).

specifically in Corden (1966), one of his best known and most cited papers.[11] In this paper, he spells out the general equilibrium implications of the ERP concept and introduced non-traded goods explicitly into the model. The crucial insight concerning general equilibrium effects is that *relative* rather than *absolute* levels of ERPs matter in determining resource shifts induced by protection. Also, in the presence of non-tradeables, one needs to take account of exchange rate changes in order to assess whether a particular sector is protected relative to non-tradeables. The paper further discusses the "substitution problem" which arises when one drops the assumption of *fixed* input coefficients (the a_{ij}'s in Equation 22.1). In this case, changes in relative prices will lead to substitution between material inputs and labour and capital which, in turn, will change the input coefficients. These general equilibrium issues surrounding the ERP concept generated a very large literature which Corden (1971a) sought to address (see below).

Subsequent to Corden (1966, 1971a), an extensive empirical literature sprang up calculating ERPs for a large number of countries, both developed and developing. This reflected a growing concern about the costs of protection and a widespread desire to boost export-led growth as a development strategy instead of relying upon import substitution. A great impetus to the measurement of ERPs in developing countries was given by the World Bank, under the leadership of Bela Balassa who popularised its measurement and use in developing strategies to boost industry and growth.[12]

However, the heyday of ERP measurement came to an end in the late 1970s and early 1980s with the rapid development and spread of *computable general equilibrium* (CGE) models. These promised to provide better estimates of resource allocation shifts than ERPs precisely because they took into account all of the general equilibrium interactions which ERPs could not. Nevertheless, CGE models also have their own problems since they rely upon assumptions about agents' behaviours which may often be unrealistic and empirical estimates of a large number of key parameters which are often subject to wide margins of uncertainty. Despite the theoretical and empirical critiques levied against ERPs, Greenaway and Milner (2003), after an extensive literature survey, argue that ERPs are still a useful measurement tool to guide policy reforms of the systems of protection in developing countries.

---

[11] A first draft of this paper was submitted to the *Economic Journal* and rejected for publication. Corden then sent it to Harry Johnson who made many suggestions for improvements and advised Corden to submit it to the *Journal of Political Economy*. The rest is history.

[12] An OECD Development Centre study by Little et al. (1970) was also very influential in highlighting the role of ERPs in industrial development strategies in developing countries.

In sum, Corden's nine years at Melbourne and Australian National University (ANU) were very productive. Not only did he make significant contributions to the ongoing debate on the costs of protection in Australia, but he also made a major theoretical contribution to the debate on how protection should best be measured. His 1966 article provided the key theoretical foundations upon which the whole subsequent edifice of ERP measurement and use in policy analysis is based. This paper brought him to the attention of trade theorists everywhere.

However, we cannot conclude our review of Corden's work in Australia during this period without citing his 1965 Princeton survey of recent developments in trade theory (Corden 1965). It proved to be a great hit with teachers and students and was much appreciated by two Nobel Prize winners in Economics, Bertil Ohlin and John Hicks (see Corden 2018: 136). Indeed, the latter's appreciation of the survey played a role in Corden's arrival at Oxford in 1967.

4   Oxford, 1967–1976

In his memoirs, Corden refers to his stay at Oxford as "The Very Best Years" (Corden 2018: Chapter 13). Once again, his 'Patron Saint' Harry Johnson was instrumental in this move. It was he who first suggested to Corden that he should apply for the Nuffield Readership in International Economics which was due to become vacant shortly on the retirement of Roy Harrod. Corden was reluctant at first, but spurred on by Dorothy and by Johnson, he submitted an application. Both Johnson and John Hicks were members of the panel for the post and it was duly offered to Corden.

Thus began an extremely productive period for Corden who published three major books during his time at Oxford as well as numerous articles. He also had, as we shall see below, a major impact on the graduate teaching of international economics at Oxford.[13] The three books, all published by Oxford University Press, were as follows:

(1) *The Theory of Protection*, published in 1971;
(2) *Trade Policy and Economic Welfare*, published in 1974; and
(3) *Inflation, Exchange Rates and the World Economy*, published in 1977 after Corden had returned to Canberra (considered in Section 4 briefly below).

---

[13] In the interests of transparency, the author should note that he was privileged to be supervised by Corden when he was a graduate student at Nuffield from 1972 to 1975.

The Theory of Protection is essentially Corden's seminal 1966 paper on effective protection writ large. In it, he takes all of the basic elements of that article and expands them, showing how the ERP fits into a general equilibrium framework. He also treats the many critiques and issues which arose out of the ERP concept. Many of the theoretical critiques of the ERP centred around the so-called substitution problem which arises when one relaxes the assumption of fixed coefficients between the traded inputs and final output. If the underlying production functions are *separable*, substitution between the traded inputs and labour and capital is unbiased and the concept of value added is meaningful. In this case, Corden shows that measurement of the ERPs using input coefficients post-protection will have a bias arising from the substitution effects. The bias will tend to overstate the "real" ERPs. A more fundamental problem arises for the ERP concept if production functions are not separable since in that case it is unclear if value added can be readily defined. While Corden (1987) acknowledges these critiques, he still mounts a defence of the utility of the concept in terms of giving policy makers some guidance as to the direction of possible resource shifts and the costs of protection.

The Theory of Protection is the most dense of Corden's books. While it contains the Corden trademark of many diagrams, it also uses a lot of algebra to support its arguments. It remains an essential reference for any economist interested in the theoretical foundations of the ERP and how best to interpret actual measurements.

On the other hand, *Trade Policy and Economic Welfare* is undoubtedly Corden's magnum opus in the field of trade policy. It is very much influenced by Meade's *Trade and Welfare*, as the title indicates; it is also imbued by the spirit of Pigou's classic, *The Economics of Welfare*.[14] The expository style is vintage Corden. The writing is clear, the assumptions are well-defined and the implications of relaxing them explored thoroughly. There are over 60 diagrams in the book, giving full rein to Corden's skill with geometry.

Trade Policy and Economic Welfare aims to give a full overview of the *normative* theory of trade policy. It has a strong political economy flavour as it puts much focus on the income distribution effects of trade policies. In addition to reviewing the standard trade arguments for intervention (terms of trade, infant industry, senescent industry, etc.), it also treats various dynamic aspects of trade policy (some of which foreshadow themes in the endogenous growth

---

[14] Johnson (1965) is another important influence on the book.

literature) and has a novel treatment of the productivity impacts of protection building upon the concept of X-efficiency.[15]

The book is innovative in its treatment of policy interventions in the presence of so-called domestic distortions which arise whenever there is a divergence between marginal private and social costs/benefits. It carefully traces out what Corden calls a 'hierarchy of policies' (Corden 1974: 28–31), i.e. interventions to remedy the given distortion in question: policy interventions are ranked in order as first-best, second-best, third-best and so on in terms of the level of welfare attainable. As Corden recognises, this ranking method is not just applicable to trade policies but it can be fully generalised to public policy interventions in all economic fields.

A significant innovation in the book is the concept of the 'conservative social welfare function'. This embodies an explicit distributional goal. As Corden (ibid.: 107) puts it, 'any significant absolute reductions in real incomes of any significant section of the community should be avoided'. This implies that workers and/or localities which suffer significant real income losses as a result of a public policy intervention should be compensated for these losses. The concept is a precursor to current concerns about "loss aversion" and "fairness". It should also be pointed out that, while lip service is paid to the compensation principle by many academic economists and policy makers, it is usually the case that compensation does not materialise for the losers or, if it does, it covers only a small portion of their losses. Given the current preoccupations about the negative side effects of globalisation and the apparent willingness of the Trump administration to launch trade wars, it would be timely to give more weight to the conservative social welfare concept and put it into practice.

Trade Policy and Economic Welfare has proved to be the most influential of Corden's books. The first edition remained in print for over 20 years and a revised second edition was issued in 1997. According to Google Scholar, it is the second most cited of Corden's publications, racking up nearly 2,100 citations, nearly twice as many as those recorded for *The Theory of Protection*.[16]

4.1 The Switch of Research Focus

Having completed his two major books on protection and trade policy and a manuscript on customs union theory which he decided was not original

---

[15] Both Corden (1970) and Martin (1978) treat X-efficiency as referring to the *intensity of managerial effort* and examine how it is likely to be impacted by trade policy.

[16] Taken from Google Scholar, 24 April 2021.

enough to be published, Corden made what he calls his 'Big Switch' in the mid-1970s away from trade theory to focus most of his future research in the field of open-economy macroeconomics. He did not abandon the field of trade theory entirely, continuing for more than two decades to publish occasional articles and one major survey (see below). But he sought a new challenge and the switch was undoubtedly influenced by the major shocks which hit the world economy in the early 1970s: the collapse of the Bretton Woods fixed exchange rate regime in 1971 which ushered in a new era of floating rates, the surge in world oil prices in 1973 and the partly resultant higher inflation rates in Organisation for Economic Co-operation and Development (OECD) countries.

In his first real venture into this new field, Corden (1972a) tackled the issue of European monetary integration. The Werner Report in 1970 pushed for the completion of economic and monetary union in the then European Economic Community within a decade. Corden's essay analyses the theoretical issues which would need to be addressed as part of a European monetary union. It highlights the costs of such a union for the participating countries, focusing on the means of achieving macroeconomic equilibrium that could be needed under such a regime. It considers the conditions under which a *real exchange rate adjustment* would deal with the internal balance problem. This would require sufficient flexibility in domestic prices and wages in order to ensure the necessary adjustments in the absence of either large offsetting fiscal transfers from other members of the union and/or sufficient labour and capital mobility to fulfil Mundell's (1961) condition for an optimum currency area.

The essay was both innovative and influential at the time. But given the hindsight of what actually happened after the formation of the eurozone in 1999 and the major sovereign debt crisis of 2009–2012 which almost brought it to its knees, it misses some crucial issues. Corden (2018) notes that it does not discuss the key issue of whether the formation of a monetary union would actually increase the probability of asymmetric shocks hitting the members. It also does not consider the so-called death loop problem when growing private debts are linked directly to sovereign debts via the banking system in the absence of a full banking union and a common sovereign debt mutualisation scheme. Nonetheless, the essay still contains useful policy insights as the euro celebrates its 20th anniversary with some of the basic design flaws that Corden identified still unresolved.[17]

Corden's third Oxford book was his first in his new field. Besides European monetary integration, *Inflation, Exchange Rates and the World Economy*

---

[17] See Eichengreen (2019) for a recent exposition of these design flaws.

discusses balance-of-payments theories; inflation and exchange rates; and the international adjustments to the 1973 oil price shock. A particular focus throughout the book is on the role of the exchange rate as a policy instrument. The book proved to be very popular and went through three editions. The third edition was expanded to include a discussion of selected issues arising in a world with flexible exchange rates and capital mobility, namely the international transmission of shocks, the nature of the international macro-system that evolved after the collapse of the Bretton Woods system and the possibilities of macroeconomic policy coordination among OECD countries.

4.2   Notable Articles Published During the Oxford Years

As noted above, Corden chose not to publish his customs union manuscript; instead, he published two articles based on it. In Corden (1972b), he departed from previous literature by assuming that the formation of the union would generate *internal* economies of scale for firms in the participating countries. The paper assumes that the countries forming the union are "small", that is, they face given terms of trade. He then shows that, while the standard concepts from customs union theory of trade creation and trade diversion still hold, two new concepts can be added: (1) a *cost reduction effect* which arises as a result of lower costs of production in the union countries; and (2) a *trade suppression effect* which occurs when imports from non-union countries are replaced by more expensive imports produced by newly formed firms based in the union.

The second paper, Corden (1976), deals with the topic of non-uniform tariffs. It shows how a shift in the pattern of imports post-union may lead to a welfare gain if the pre-union tariff on the importable in one of the union partners is higher than the union's common external tariff. In this case, reducing the former tariff to the level of the latter will raise welfare, while reducing it beyond that level will reduce welfare.

One other article published during Corden's Oxford period deserves special mention even if it deals neither with a trade and protection topic nor with an issue in international macroeconomics. Rather it deals with a development topic, namely the phenomenon of urban unemployment in developing countries, as exemplified by the well-known Harris-Todaro model (see Harris and Todaro 1970). Corden and Findlay (1975) use standard trade-theoretic diagrams to analyse the important phenomenon of urban (so-called wait) unemployment in developing countries where many young people prefer to remain unemployed or work in informal jobs while waiting to secure a permanent job, often in the public sector. The paper also discusses various policy options to tackle the problem. This article has proved to be very popular in the development literature: it is ranked sixth in terms of Corden's citations by Google Scholar.

Corden has often used the Salter model as an expository device in his writings. Jones and Corden (1976) show how the Salter diagram, which uses the small-country assumption to aggregate goods into composites of traded and non-traded goods, can be used to investigate how policies such as a devaluation can impact the relative price of traded to non-traded goods, that is, the real exchange rate. The Salter model has subsequently been used by many international economists to discuss policies aimed at achieving internal and external balance.

4.3 Impact on Oxford Economics via Teaching and Graduate Supervision

Max Corden's impact on Oxford economics was not confined to his writings. His lectures, his graduate seminar and his conscientious supervision of graduate students all contributed to create a fertile environment in which work on international economics flourished at Oxford during his time there and subsequently. Besides giving an annual lecture series to graduates, he organised a regular graduate seminar at Nuffield in international economics with support from two colleagues, Vijay Joshi and Peter Oppenheimer.[18] Joshi describes the impact of the Corden seminar as follows:

> What I would highlight about Max is the huge difference he made to graduate teaching of economics at Oxford (Jim Mirrlees also played a major role). I remember very well the style of graduate teaching in international economics in the pre-Max era. There were no lectures to speak of. There were seminars but they were quite casual affairs with Sir Roy Harrod and Maurice Scott seated in armchairs. A student would read a paper, which no one had read, and of which no one other than the speaker had a copy. After the student had finished, there was a desultory discussion. This was not a useful way to teach the subject (though both Harrod and Scott were of course distinguished economists). Max changed all that with German efficiency and Australian informality. I still

---

[18] Corden also briefly organised a graduate seminar on welfare economics with John Hicks. Professor John Creedy, who attended this seminar during the academic year 1971–1972, has this to say about Corden's role in it: 'Max ran the seminars pretty much as he ran the trade seminars. He was fully in charge, and his emphasis was always on clarity. I have never seen anything before or since to match Max's way of leading seminars. I looked forward to every one—and it was necessary to get there early to get a seat' (personal communication to the author, 14 January 2019).

remember his international economics seminar fondly, with Max leaping up and down to draw diagrams and make things crystal clear. For students, he was a godsend (author, personal communication, 2 November 2018).

The seminars were meticulously organised. The topics for each term were published in advance. Papers were delivered by students or visiting academics. When a student presented a paper, it was reviewed in draft by Corden and the final version was then distributed in advance to the seminar participants. After the seminar was over, the discussions would often continue in Corden's room at Nuffield over drinks. As the author can testify from personal experience, presenting a paper at the Corden seminar could be a daunting experience for a student but Corden was always gracious and kind to the presenters even when they made mistakes. He never showed off his own mastery of the subject but always tried to make the exposition of the underlying arguments as clear as possible.[19]

Corden's renown attracted many leading international economists to Oxford, either to give presentations to the seminar or to stay for longer periods as visitors at Nuffield. During his own sojourn in Oxford from 1972 to 1977, the author remembers visits from such luminaries as Robert Baldwin, Jagdish Bhagwati, Rick Brecher, Alan Deardorff, Carlos Diaz-Alejandro, Ronald Findlay, Jacob Frenkel, Herbert Grubel, Ron Jones, Charles Kindleberger, Peter Lloyd, Fritz Machlup, Steve Magee, Michael Mussa, Robert Stern and Wolfgang Stolper.

Corden also took his supervisory duties very seriously. Many of the graduate students he supervised went on to have distinguished careers in academia, international organisations and elsewhere. For example, Paul Collier has described his experience of being supervised by Corden:

Max supervised my thesis and I remain in debt to him for what I learnt. In those days, I was a ferment of ideas, mostly inchoate and muddled. Martin Wolf, then as now a model of clarity, would walk around Nuffield with me, listening to my confusion before interjecting an illuminating "what you really mean is". Max raised these lessons in clarity of thought to the highest professional level. He taught me how to think my ideas through to their conclusion, and most importantly, how to express them clearly. I recall such an occasion when, surely driven to exasperation, but as always determined to relate to his students in the most kindly and helpful manner, he responded to one of my wilder passages of analy-

---

[19] The international economics seminar lapsed several years after Corden's departure from Oxford. However, it was revived in 2006 by Peter Neary and is still going strong. Neary is currently a Professor at Oxford and a Fellow of Merton College. He is one of the world's leading trade theorists.

sis: "Paul, you write economics as if it were poetry". At the time, entirely mistakenly, I found the notion that I was bestowing the glamour of poetry on the dismal science quite appealing. But I gradually faced up to the intellectually demanding process of clarity (author, personal communication, 31 January 2019).[20]

During his time at Oxford, Corden was also instrumental in founding the International Economics Study Group (IESG) with David Wall (Sussex University). The founding committee also included John Dunning, Brian Hindley, Tim Josling and Harry Johnson. The Group no longer exists, but for many years it organised regular seminars at LSE and an annual conference which brought together international economists from all over the UK and abroad.

5   Return to Australia: The ANU, 1977–1986

In late 1976, Corden left Oxford to return to Australia to take up the post of Head of the Economics Department in the Research School of Pacific Studies at the ANU in Canberra. Family reasons motivated this move: his mother and Dorothy's mother were both elderly and living in Melbourne and they also felt that their daughter Jane would benefit from the move. Shortly after they returned to Canberra, Harry Johnson died and Corden wrote his obituary for *The Times*.[21]

After his return to Australia, Corden was much engaged in public policy debates. In his position as President of the Economic Society of Australia, he became very active in the debate on wage inflation and unemployment which followed a wage explosion under the Whitlam Government in 1974–1975 and later under the Hawke Government. In his Presidential Address, he argued that, under the centralised wage determination system in Australia, the main driving force behind inflation was unions pushing for a target real wage which, in turn, led to higher unemployment.[22] Subsequently, Corden and Dixon (1980) argued that a way out of the dilemma was to aim for an agreement under which unions would moderate their nominal wage demands in return for the government cutting taxes so as to maintain real after-tax wages.

---

[20] Martin Wolf wrote the Foreword to Corden's memoirs. In it, he states that 'Max was far and away the best teacher and expositor I met during my time at Oxford' (Wolf in Corden 2018: ix).

[21] Corden (1984a) reviewed Johnson's major contributions to trade theory.

[22] In Corden (1979), he coined the term "union-voluntary unemployment" to describe this phenomenon.

This argument had some impact on the so-called Accord which the unions struck with the Hawke Government in 1983.

During this period in Australia, Corden wrote what was to become one of his most influential papers dealing with the phenomenon of Dutch Disease. His interest in the topic went back to his days in Oxford when he became involved in the heated debate about the impact of the discovery of North Sea oil and gas reserves on the UK economy, notably on the tradeables sector.[23] Corden (1981a) was his first published paper on the topic and it dealt explicitly with the British case. However, in 1979, on a visit to Oxford, Corden began to explore theoretically with his former Oxford student, Peter Neary, the impacts of a booming sector on resource allocation shifts, factor prices and the exchange rate. The phenomenon of the co-existence within the tradeables sector of a booming sector with one that lags behind is a very common one in both developed and developing countries. Corden and Neary (1982) set out to analyse the phenomenon using the standard tools and models of trade theory, ignoring monetary complications and focusing entirely on the impact of a booming sector on real variables.

Their basic model is a variant of the Salter model with an economy producing two traded goods (energy and manufacturing) and one non-traded good (services). They assume a small, open-economy framework for the traded goods; the price of the non-traded good is assumed to be flexible and determined by domestic demand and supply. Two further simplifying assumptions are made: (1) trade is always in balance overall; and (2) there are no distortions in goods or factor markets. The paper then considers a sequence of models characterised by different degrees of intersectoral factor mobility. It begins with the case of a Ricardo-Viner model in which each of the three sectors uses a single *specific* factor in production as well as a factor which is perfectly mobile between sectors. This particular assumption is relaxed later in the paper.

The paper highlights two key effects of a boom: (1) a *resource movement effect*; and (2) a *spending effect*. The former occurs when a booming sector (say energy) draws in mobile factors from other sectors in response to higher marginal productivity of factors. The spending effect results from the higher real income due to the boom. This raises the demand for services, increasing their price and leading to a *real exchange rate appreciation*, the latter being the relative price of traded to the non-traded good. In the Ricardo-Viner model, the boom leads to a decline in manufacturing (deindustrialisation). However, in

---

[23] In Corden (2018), he acknowledges that two of his Australian colleagues, Bob Gregory and Richard Snape, had treated a similar issue following an Australian mining boom in the 1970s.

the other models which allow for intersectoral mobility of more than one factor, the deindustrialisation outcome is sometimes reversed.

Corden and Neary's study has proved to be an extremely influential paper. For both authors, it is by far their most cited paper according to Google Scholar: it records not far off 4,200 citations for it.[24] Part of its success comes from the clever mix of methods it uses: neat diagrams in the Corden manner together with a detailed mathematical presentation of the various models and derivation of the main results by Neary. The paper is a prime example of the principle of comparative advantage being put into practice by two of the profession's leading trade theorists.

Over and above the neatness of the methods used in the paper, its popularity owes much to the enduring nature of the topic. Booming sectors arise continually in different settings and they are not just tied to the discovery and extraction of natural resources (e.g. the financial sector in the UK). They give rise to significant resource shifts between sectors, shifts in sectoral income distribution and changes in real exchange rates. Corden and Neary's analysis remains a key reference for all those interested in the many possible impacts of a booming sector on the real economy.[25]

Corden (1985b) was another notable output during the ANU years. It surveys the *normative* side of trade theory and updates and extends the discussion in Corden (1974) to take account of key developments since that was written.

6   Move to the US: The IMF and SAIS, 1986–2002

In late 1986, Corden left ANU to take up a two-year appointment as a Senior Adviser in the Research Department of the IMF.[26] Towards the end of his stint at the Fund, Corden, strongly encouraged by Dorothy, accepted a Professorship at the Johns Hopkins School of Advanced International Studies (SAIS) in Washington, D.C. His main responsibility at SAIS was teaching. Corden (2018) makes it abundantly clear that he enjoyed this and, just as in his Oxford days, he was much appreciated by his students at SAIS—winning teaching awards in several years. However, he also pursued his research in international macroeconomics, not least co-authoring (with his former

---

[24] As of 24 April 2021.

[25] Corden (1984c) is a less technical survey of this literature. It also discusses policy implications, notably what would be the optimal intervention to protect a lagging sector.

[26] See Corden (2018: 181–186) for a description of his time at the Fund and the topics he worked on during that period.

Nuffield colleague Ian Little plus Richard Cooper and Sarath Rajapatirana) a book summarising the results of a major World Bank project on macroeconomic developments in 18 developing countries.

In Little et al. (1993), Corden wrote three chapters dealing mainly with inflation and exchange rate policies. In order to make his analysis more coherent, he focused on six countries with episodes of very high inflation, namely Argentina, Brazil, Chile, Indonesia, Mexico and Turkey. His stint at the IMF provided him with much useful background information to enable him to discuss the policies and varied experiences of these countries. The book did have an impact: it is the tenth most cited of Corden's publications on Google Scholar.

Corden (1994) was originally intended to be the fourth edition of *Inflation, Exchange Rates and the World Economy*. However, he decided to write a new and bigger book instead. It has four main sections: (1) open-economy macroeconomics, (2) the European Monetary System (a precursor to the euro) and monetary integration, (3) the managed-floating, high-capital-mobility nonsystem and (4) protection and competitiveness.

One topic treated in the book has contemporary resonance: Does the current account matter? The Trump administration continually cites current account imbalances with the US's major trading partners such as China, Canada, Mexico and the EU as justification for large tariff hikes. Corden (ibid.) would classify this argument under what he calls 'the Old View' of the current account with the rider that President Trump's concern is with the loss of manufacturing jobs in the US which he attributes to unfair competition. The 'New View' takes a different tack. It treats the current account as the net outcome of saving and investment choices, both private and public. A current account deficit can be caused by an increase in investment or a drop in savings or a combination of both. Indeed, it could be caused by a combination of a larger public sector deficit and weak private investment. Thus, the large Trump tax cut in 2018 might well result in a larger current account deficit and lower employment in US manufacturing, even though there might be some gains in employment in specific sectors such as autos and steel which have experienced steep tariff increases.[27]

In September 2000, Corden gave the Ohlin Memorial Lecture in Stockholm on the topic of exchange rate regimes. These lectures formed the basis of his final academic book. Corden (2002) sets out a framework against which the choice of a specific exchange rate regime can be assessed. It first outlines the

---

[27] See Corden and Garnaut (2018) for a discussion of the likely economic impacts of the Trump tax cut and tariff hikes.

theory and then reviews the experiences of various countries in Latin America, Asia and Europe in terms of their choices of exchange rate regimes.

The book opens with three alternative approaches to the choice of exchange rate regime and monetary policy: the nominal target, the real target and exchange rate stability. The nominal anchor comes into play when a country seeks to curb high inflation. With a real target approach, a country seeks to achieve a real goal, either output or employment. The third approach seeks to stabilise expectations.

Corden then discusses the pros and cons of three exchange rate regimes: a free float, a fixed rate and a fixed but adjustable rate. The country case studies enable him to analyse how selected countries in the different regions reacted to asymmetric shocks under alternative exchange rate regimes. This leads Corden to conclude that countries should avoid opting for a fixed but adjustable regime since they have often collapsed with very serious negative impacts on the real economy. At the same time, he draws the agnostic conclusion that countries need not opt for either a truly fixed rate regime or a free float.

7   The Final Return to Melbourne

In late 2002, Corden retired from SAIS and returned with Dorothy to live in Melbourne. Their return was motivated by concern for Dorothy's health as she had begun to exhibit symptoms of Alzheimer's disease. Dorothy's condition deteriorated over the years and she died in 2010 in a nursing home. She and Max were married for over 50 years and they were a devoted couple. Dorothy's kindness to Max's students, as the author can testify, was something none of them will forget. Sadly, their daughter Jane died in Melbourne in 2019 after a short illness.

After their return to Australia, Corden was made a Companion of the Order of Australia, the highest grade of the Order. It was awarded 'for service as a leading international economist, particularly in the areas of international trade and finance policy development' (Corden 2018: 207). He has received many other awards including Fellow of the British Academy, President of the Economic Society of Australia and membership of the Group of Thirty from 1982–1990. His alma mater, the University of Melbourne, has renamed the Department as the Arndt-Corden Department of Economics, joining Max's name with that of another distinguished economist and Jewish emigrant from Breslau, Heinz Arndt. The University has also established an Annual Corden Lecture in his honour and the list of speakers to date includes many leading international economists, some of them former students of Corden. Recently, in a fitting tribute, Nuffield College has established a Max Corden Scholarship in International Economics.

Martin Wolf, in his Foreword to Corden's memoirs, calls him 'Australia's greatest living economist' (Wolf in ibid.: ix). A recent profile of Corden in an Australian national newspaper referred to him as 'a national treasure' (*The Australian Financial Review*, 14–15 April 2018: 45). In addition, as all his students and multitude of friends and admirers all over the world will attest, Corden is not merely a great economist but also a wonderful person. He is without malice and is free from the oversized ego which many great economists acquire. In his nineties, he continues to be active and engaged in economics—witness a recent published paper, co-authored with Ross Garnaut, on the economic consequences of President Trump's policies (see Corden and Garnaut 2018). Australia is known as the "Lucky Country" and there is no doubt that this expression is apt where Max Corden is concerned. But Oxford can also count itself lucky to have been the scene of some of his most notable contributions to international economics.

References

Main Works by Max Corden

Corden, W.M. (1952–1953). 'The Maximisation of Profit by a Newspaper'. *Review of Economic Studies*, 20(3): 181–190.

Corden, W.M. (1956). 'Economic Expansion and International Trade: A Geometric Approach'. *Oxford Economic Papers*, New Series, 8(2): 223–228.

Corden, W.M. (1957). 'The Calculation of the Cost of Protection'. *Economic Record*, 33(64): 29–51.

Corden, W.M. (1957). 'Tariffs, Subsidies and the Terms of Trade'. *Economica*, New Series, 24(95): 235–242.

Corden, W.M. (1960). 'The Geometric Representation of Policies to Attain Internal and External Balance'. *Review of Economic Studies*, 28(1): 1–22.

Corden, W.M. (1965). *Recent Developments in the Theory of International Trade*. Princeton University Essays in International Economics No. 7, International Finance Section. Princeton: Princeton University.

Corden, W.M. (1966). 'The Structure of a Tariff System and the Effective Protective Rate'. *Journal of Political Economy*, 74(3): 221–237.

Corden, W.M. (1967). 'Monopoly, Tariffs and Subsidies'. *Economica*, New Series, 34(133): 50–58.

Corden, W.M. (1970). 'The Efficiency Effects of Trade and Protection'. Chapter 1 in I.A. McDougall and R.H. Snape (eds) *Studies in International Economics: Monash Conference Papers*. Amsterdam: North-Holland: 1–17.

Corden, W.M. (1971a). *The Theory of Protection*. Oxford: Oxford University Press.

Corden, W.M. (1971). 'The Effects of Trade on the Rate of Growth'. Chapter 6 in J.N. Bhagwati, R.W. Jones, R.A. Mundell and J. Vanek (eds) *Trade, Balance of Payments, and Growth: Papers in International Economics in Honor of Charles P. Kindleberger*. Amsterdam: North-Holland: 117–143.

Corden, W.M. (1972a). *Monetary Integration*. Princeton University Essays in International Finance No. 93, International Finance Section. Princeton: Princeton University.

Corden, W.M. (1972b). 'Economies of Scale and Customs Union Theory'. *Journal of Political Economy*, 80(3, Part 1): 465–475.

Corden, W.M. (1974). *Trade Policy and Economic Welfare*. First edition. Oxford: Oxford University Press.

Corden, W.M. (1975). 'The Costs and Consequences of Protection: A Survey of Empirical Work'. In P.B. Kenen (ed.) *International Trade and Finance: Frontiers for Research*. Cambridge: Cambridge University Press: 51–92.

Corden, W.M. (1976). 'Customs Union Theory and the Non-Uniformity of Tariffs'. *Journal of International Economics*, 6(1): 99–106.

Corden, W.M. (1977). *Inflation, Exchange Rates and the World Economy*. Oxford: Oxford University Press.

Corden, W.M. (1979). 'Wages and Unemployment in Australia'. *Economic Record*, 55(1): 1–19.

Corden, W.M. (1981a). 'The Exchange Rate, Monetary Policy and North Sea Oil: The Economic Theory of the Squeeze on Tradeables'. *Oxford Economic Papers*, New Series, 33(Supplement): 23–46.

Corden, W.M. (1981). 'Exchange Rate Protection'. Chapter 2 in R.N. Cooper, P. Kenen, J. de Macedo and J. van Ypersele (eds) *The International Monetary System under Flexible Exchange Rates: Global, Regional and National: Essays in Honor of Robert Triffin*. Cambridge, MA: Ballinger: 17–34.

Corden, W.M. (1983). 'The Logic of the International Monetary Non-System'. Chapter 3 in F. Machlup, G. Fels and H. Müller-Groeling (eds) *Reflections on a Troubled World Economy: Essays in Honour of Herbert Giersch*. London: Macmillan: 59–74.

Corden, W.M. (1984a). 'Harry Johnson's Contributions to International Trade Theory'. *Journal of Political Economy*, 92(4): 567–591.

Corden, W.M. (1984b). 'The Normative Theory of International Trade'. Chapter 2 in R.W. Jones and P.B. Kenen (eds) *Handbook of International Economics*. Volume 1. Amsterdam: North-Holland: 63–130.

Corden, W.M. (1984c). 'Booming Sector and Dutch Disease Economics: Survey and Consolidation'. *Oxford Economic Papers*, New Series, 36(3): 359–380.

Corden, W.M. (1985). *Protection, Growth and Trade: Essays in International Economics*. Oxford: Basil Blackwell.

Corden, W.M. (1987). 'Effective Protection'. In J. Eatwell, M. Milgate and P. Newman (eds) *The New Palgrave: A Dictionary of Economics*. Volume 3. London: Macmillan: 102–106.

Corden, W.M. (1991). 'Strategic Trade Policy'. Chapter 14 in D. Greenaway, M. Bleaney and I.M.T. Stewart (eds) *Companion to Contemporary Economic Thought*. London: Routledge: 274–290.

Corden, W.M. (1992). *International Trade Theory and Policy: Selected Essays of W. Max Corden*. Aldershot: Edward Elgar.

Corden, W.M. (1993). 'Exchange Rate Policies for Developing Countries'. *Economic Journal*, 103(416): 198–207.

Corden, W.M. (1994). *Economic Policy, Exchange Rates and the International System*. Oxford: Oxford University Press.

Corden, W.M. (1997a). *Trade Policy and Economic Welfare*. Second edition. Oxford: Oxford University Press.

Corden, W.M. (1997b). *The Road to Reform: Essays on Australian Economic Policy*. Lane Cove: Addison Wesley.

Corden, W.M. (2002). *Too Sensational: On the Choice of Exchange Rate Regimes*. Cambridge, MA: MIT Press.

Corden, W.M. (2018). *Lucky Boy in the Lucky Country: The Autobiography of Max Corden, Economist*. London: Palgrave Macmillan.

Corden, W.M. and P. Dixon (1980). 'A Tax-Wage Bargain in Australia: Is a Free Lunch Possible?'. *Economic Record*, 56(154): 209–221.

Corden, W.M. and R.F. Findlay (1975). 'Urban Unemployment, Intersectoral Capital Mobility and Development Policy'. *Economica*, New Series, 42(165): 59–78.

Corden, W.M. and R. Garnaut (2018). 'The Economic Consequences of Mr Trump'. *Australian Economic Review*, 51(3): 411–417.

Corden, W.M. and J.P. Neary (1982). 'Booming Sector and De-industrialisation in a Small Open Economy'. *Economic Journal*, 92(368): 825–848.

Corden, W.M. and S.J. Turnovsky (1983). 'Negative International Transmission of Economic Expansion'. *European Economic Review*, 20(1–3): 289–310.

Hemming, M.F.W. and W.M. Corden (1958). 'Import Restriction as an Instrument of Balance-of-Payments Policy'. *Economic Journal*, 68(271): 483–510.

Jones, R.W. and W.M. Corden (1976). 'Devaluation, Non-Flexible Prices and the Trade Balance for a Small Country'. *Canadian Journal of Economics*, 9(1): 150–161.

Little, I.M.D., R.N. Cooper, W.M. Corden and S. Rajapatirana (1993). *Boom, Crisis and Adjustment: The Macroeconomic Experience of Developing Countries*. Oxford: Oxford University Press.

Other Works Referred To

Barber, C.L. (1955). 'Canadian Tariff Policy'. *Canadian Journal of Economics*, 21(4): 513–530.

Bhagwati, J.N. and V.K. Ramaswami (1963). 'Domestic Distortions, Tariffs and the Theory of Optimum Subsidy'. *Journal of Political Economy*, 71(1): 44–50.

Cohn, W. (2006). *Kein Recht, Nirgends, Tagebuch vom Untergang des Breslauer Judentrums, 1933–1941*. Edited by Norbert Conrads. Cologne: Bohlau.

Cohn, W. (2012). *No Justice in Germany: The Breslau Diaries, 1933–1941*. Edited by Norbert Conrads and translated by Kenneth Kronenberg. Stanford: Stanford University Press.

Coleman, W. (2006). 'A Conversation with Max Corden'. *Economic Record*, 82(259): 379–395.

Eichengreen, B. (2019). 'The Euro at 20: An Enduring Success but a Fundamental Failure'. *The Conversation*. Available at: https://theconversation.com/the-euro-at-20-an-enduring-success-but-a-fundamental-failure-108419.

Harris, J.R. and M.P. Todaro (1970). 'Migration, Unemployment and Development: A Two-Sector Analysis'. *American Economic Review*, 60(1): 126–142.

Greenaway, D. and C. Milner (2003). 'Effective Protection, Policy Appraisal and Trade Policy Reform'. *The World Economy*, 26(4): 441–456.

Johnson, H.G. (1965). 'Optimal Trade Intervention in the Presence of Domestic Distortions'. In R.E. Baldwin et al. *Trade, Growth, and the Balance of Payments: Essays in Honor of Gottfried Harberler*. Amsterdam: North-Holland: 3–34.

Lipsey, R.G. and K. Lancaster (1956–1957). 'The General Theory of Second Best'. *Review of Economic Studies*, 24(1): 11–32.

Little, I.M.D., T. Scitovsky and M. FG. Scott (1970). *Industry and Trade in Some Developing Countries: A Comparative Study*. London: Oxford University Press.

Martin, J.P. (1978). 'X-Inefficiency, Managerial Effort and Protection'. *Economica*, New Series, 45(179): 273–286.

Meade, J.E. (1951). *The Theory of International Economic Policy, Volume I: The Balance of Payments*. London: Oxford University Press.

Meade, J.E. (1952). *A Geometry of International Trade*. London: Allen & Unwin.

Meade, J.E. (1955). *The Theory of International Economic Policy, Volume II: Trade and Welfare*. London: Oxford University Press.

Mundell, R.A. (1961). 'A Theory of Optimum Currency Areas'. *American Economic Review*, 51(4): 657–665.

Salter, W.E.G. (1959). 'Internal and External Balance: The Role of Price and Expenditure Effects'. *Economic Record*, 35(71): 226–238.

Swan, T.W. (1955). 'Longer-Run Problems of the Balance of Payments'. Paper delivered at the Congress of the Australian and New Zealand Association for the Advancement of Science. Reprinted as Chapter 24 in H.W. Arndt and W.M. Corden (eds) *The Australian Economy: A Volume of Readings*. Melbourne: Cheshire: 384–395.

23

Derek Robinson (1932–2014)

Ken Mayhew

1   Introduction[1]

The son of a coal miner, Derek Robinson was brought up in Barnsley and entered the Civil Service in a clerical post straight from school. His background is fundamental to understanding his work as an economist. He was fond of telling how his line manager in London asked him not to answer the office phone because of the poor impression his Yorkshire accent might give. He became a union activist there and as a consequence won a union scholarship to Ruskin College, Oxford, after which he went on to Lincoln College, Oxford, where he obtained a First in Philosophy, Politics and Economics (PPE). After a brief spell teaching at Sheffield University, Robinson took an appointment at the Oxford University Institute of Economics and Statistics where he remained for the rest of his career, simultaneously holding a Fellowship at Magdalen College. Although he revelled in Oxford college life, he continued to embrace his trade union routes. A regular at the annual conference of the Trades Union Congress (TUC), he was on first name terms

---

[1] Much of the biographical material on Derek Robison is taken from two obituaries I wrote not long after his death. They can be found in the January 2015 *Newsletter* of the Royal Economic Society (Mayhew 2015a) and in the September 2015 issue of the *Economic and Labour Relations Review* (Mayhew 2015b).

K. Mayhew (✉)
Oxfordshire, UK
e-mail: ken.mayhew@pmb.ox.ac.uk

with most of the prominent union leaders of the time who recognised someone who believed in the union movement but who was prepared to criticise its shortcomings and mistakes. By the same token, employers saw in him an academic who would treat each case on its merits, who would objectively examine the facts before coming to any conclusions or recommendations without fear or favour. Robinson was a researcher whose main concern was the practicalities and realities of the labour market, practicalities and realities that he believed too many theoreticians ignored or assumed away. This approach meant that his contribution was as strong, if not stronger, in the corridors of Whitehall as in the groves of academe.

When he arrived at the Institute of Economics and Statistics in 1961, the golden era of industrial relations at Oxford represented, amongst others, by Hugh Clegg, George Bain, Allan Flanders and Alan Fox was in full swing. Though Clegg, Bain and Flanders subsequently decamped to the University of Warwick, Robinson maintained and enhanced the study of industrial relations at Oxford alongside Bill McCarthy and Arthur Marsh. The three of them never worked together and the other two were not economists, but Robinson regarded the study of labour economics and industrial relations as inextricably intertwined. He was very firmly an institutionalist.

2   Imperfect Labour Markets

In 1971, Doeringer and Piore produced their influential book on internal labour markets in the US. Robinson, often in collaboration with his colleague at the Institute, Kenneth Knowles, had been independently developing his own ideas in this area and on the workings of local labour markets more generally. A year before Doeringer and Piore, Rees and Shultz had published *Workers and Wages in an Urban Labor Market* (Rees and Shultz 1970). Studying workers in Chicago, they ran regressions for a variety of occupational groups of individual earnings against a series of variables describing individual characteristics and a series of variables describing the characteristics of the firm in which the individuals worked. The latter were of substantial statistical significance. Whilst Adam Smith's concept of equalising wage differentials provided, at least in theory, a textbook explanation as to why similar employers in the same geographical location could pay apparently similar workers very different wages, Rees and Shultz argued that their results suggested that more complex forces were at work. Employers were not simply the prisoners of external market forces—they were not wage takers. This was entirely consistent with the argument of Doeringer and Piore. To an extent, the firm's labour market was an administered one operating with some freedom from external labour market constraints.

Robinson's detailed studies of mainly manufacturing firms in Coventry and Liverpool had led his thinking in the same direction. For the time, Rees and Shultz had an unusually rich data set of individuals describing their characteristics and those of the firms that employed them. Such data were not available to UK researchers, who often had to rely on broad averages of earnings by occupation and firm. Even when individual pay data could be extracted from employers, there was little or no further information on the individuals concerned. Data extraction was itself a major research endeavour, as illustrated by the work of Robinson and Knowles, but also by similar research by MacKay et al. (1971) on local labour markets in Glasgow and Birmingham. Their observations chimed with those of Doeringer and Piore and of Rees and Shultz but, given the data limitations, were inevitably less scientifically based.

However, Robinson went beyond the reporting of data and started to explore why firms were not simply wage takers but had some discretion in the wages they offered. Important here is the inability or unwillingness of workers to respond to signals from alternative employers. Embedded in Robinson's writings is discussion of why such a supply response might be limited—lack of information, mobility costs and efficiency wages. His investigation of local labour markets made it clear that workers often lacked basic information about starting salaries for apparently equivalent jobs in the same town. However, perhaps more important than this were two other sources of informational imperfections. The first relates to Smith's concept of compensating differentials. Workers found it difficult to assess the non-wage and non-monetary benefits of working for a different employer. Even more significant was a time dimension. Even if an individual believed that she could assess the immediate impact of a potential job move, it was difficult to assess what the future in the new firm would hold for her. This depended so critically on things which could only be ascertained once a job had been taken up—how well she got on with her managers and fellow workers, how ruthless or otherwise her managers were when she made mistakes, how readily good performance was recognised in the form of extra pay or other rewards or promotion. Faced with such uncertainties, it might be quite rational for an individual not to respond to the lure of higher starting pay elsewhere—the rationality of irrationality or, as it became known, "bounded rationality".

At first sight, the issue of mobility costs might not seem relevant for studies of local labour markets. Yet, moving from one firm to another even in a moderately sized town, let alone a large city, can involve increases in travel to work expenses and complicate childcare and other family responsibilities. Over and above these costs, Robinson and others emphasised the "psychic" costs of changing firms. People contemplating such a move might be concerned about losing contact with friends and colleagues at their current workplace, about leaving their social circle for a new and largely unknown community. In other words, he saw the firm as a social community as well as an economic entity. The third constraint on supply responses was the consequence of efficiency wages. Employers differentiated between workers in the same occupational category, recognising that some were more capable and productive than others and being willing to pay them "over the odds" in order to attract and retain them. Taken to the extreme, this implies that the only truly homogenous unit of labour is a single person, throwing the then typical textbook model into some confusion.

This imperfect supply response frees employers from the constraints of a perfectly competitive local labour market but, if that was all there was to it, the employer would, at least to an extent, be a monopsonist. However, Robinson was also aware of the literature on labour as a quasi-fixed factor of production, as pioneered by Walter Oi (1962). Employers may train workers in skills that are to an extent specific to his firm. They can pay (at least in part) the costs of that training because they calculate that the worker will be reluctant to leave the firm. Imagine someone is hired whose market value of marginal product (VMP) is 100. After training, that person's VMP rises to 150 but only in that firm. Therefore, the employer can start to recoup the costs by paying the person less than 150 but more than 100 and the worker is likely to stay. A sort of bilateral monopoly has been created: The employer is the only employer who demands this particular bundle of skills and the relevant group of workers are the only people who possess them. As a consequence, there is no unique equilibrium wage; there is scope for bargaining.

Robinson understood the fundamental imperfections in the labour market long before they became so central in academic thinking. Like Doeringer and Piore, he envisaged internal labour markets as administered markets often characterised by limited ports of entry, rewards for length of tenure and well-defined promotion ladders. Importantly, he understood that unions would have had relatively little room for bargaining or bargaining power over wage-related matters at the workplace but for the existence of internal labour markets. Often, unions used this bargaining power to shape the institutions of the internal labour market—for example, by encouraging limited ports of entry or rewards for seniority. Although Robinson worked mainly on the internal labour markets of firms (horizontal internalisation), he also stressed the importance of similar forces at work to create and intensify occupational internal labour markets (vertical internalisation).

3   Trade Unions

Robinson started his career at a time when trade union power in Britain was significant and increasing. Immediately after the Second World War, trade union density (the percentage of the workforce unionised) stood at about 44%. From the late 1960s, it started to increase and reached its peak in 1979 when 55% of employees were union members. In the same year, about three-quarters of workers were covered by collective agreements. There were two reasons why the coverage figure was so much higher than membership. The first was that in many workplaces, individuals who chose not to join a union were nevertheless beneficiaries of the wages negotiated by the recognised union. The second was that workers in the public sector, large swathes of manufacturing and in parts of private services were covered by national agreements, which in the case of the private sector were multi-employer. As a consequence, an employee in a non-union firm, which at least complied with the rates set by the relevant national agreement, was covered by that agreement.

It was against this backdrop that Robinson believed that wages and wage structures were capable, to an extent, of being "administered". Notions of fairness and the exercise of bargaining power could play a fundamental role. Many years later, Atkinson (1999) wrote about pay norm models based on social codes, examples of which are solidaristic wage bargaining in Sweden and sectoral collective bargaining in the Netherlands, which effectively limited the dispersion of pay. This belief that there was room for social choice in constructing wage structures motivated much of Robinson's work. It underlay the many commissions he undertook for the International Labour Organisation (ILO), the findings of some of which were published, including his report on civil service pay in Africa and his comparison of occupational pay structures in Singapore and elsewhere.

His belief in unionism was firmly based in the liberal-pluralist tradition. This was at the heart of the report of the Donovan Commission published in 1968. To give Donovan its full title, it was the Royal Commission on Trade Unions and Employers' Associations (1968), set up by the government to investigate the problems of industrial relations and what could be done to mitigate them. This was in response to concerns about the UK's relatively slow growth rates and attempts to diagnose the reasons why. Prominent among these reasons was the view that the industrial relations system was functioning inefficiently. The Donovan Report's stated operating assumptions were that workers had a right to a say in decisions affecting their everyday working lives and that an efficient collective bargaining system was the most appropriate way of ensuring this. Remarkably to modern eyes, these were relatively uncontentious assumptions to most of the political establishment of the day. This version of pluralism emphasised that there was an irreducible minimum of issues where there was bound to be a fundamental conflict of interest between worker and employer. It would be pointless and indeed illiberal to pretend otherwise. The aim should be to mediate such conflicts of interest as efficiently and costlessly as possible. The Commission recognised that reform was needed and believed that this could be achieved voluntarily. It saw the underlying problem as a structural one. UK industrial relations had developed into a dual system. As we have seen, in most of private manufacturing and in some private services as well as in the public sector there was an infrastructure of national bargaining. In the private sector, this bargaining was multi-employer. For example, in engineering, the Engineering Employers' Federation negotiated with an amalgam of the relevant unions to agree basic rates of pay for a variety of grades as well as some other minimum terms and conditions. It was then open to individual employers to offer more, whether as a result of local bargaining or by fiat. The 1950s and 1960s saw a massive growth of this company or even establishment wage bargaining. Accompanying this was an increase in the number of shop stewards—ordinary workers at the establishment who took on trade union duties. Increasingly, it was at the establishment that wages were determined. The problem was that all of the rules and procedures that helped bargaining work remained at the national level and so there was the potential for chaos. In the relatively tight labour markets of the 1960s, shop stewards used their bargaining power to pursue their wage demands. There was a rising trend of strike activity and most of these strikes were unofficial, that is, not sanctioned by the national union leaders.

Donovan's voluntaristic solution was essentially to bureaucratise the shop steward movement in an approach that became dubbed "giving up control to regain control". Giving up control meant relinquishing managerial prerogative over a whole range of issues. By giving shop stewards full information about finance, production and marketing and about future plans and by, to an extent, making all of these things part of the bargaining process, they could make bargaining more of a non-zero-sum game. The vast majority of shop stewards, Donovan believed, were reasonable individuals who could be made to see that the interests of their members more often coincided with those of management than not.

Robinson firmly believed in the essence of this approach and that wage determination should be achieved, as far as possible, through collective bargaining. In part, it was this desire to make collective bargaining work that led him to become one of Barbara Castle's advisers when she became Secretary of

State for Employment in the Harold Wilson Labour government of the late 1960s. Robinson was influential in the production of the famous, some would and did say infamous, White Paper entitled *In Place of Strife* (1969). However, as a result of Cabinet infighting and sustained union opposition, it never found its way on to the statute books. It was in many respects a more radical and coherent intervention than Edward Heath's Industrial Relations Act of 1971 that rapidly entered the demonology of the union movement. Strong though his belief in liberal pluralism and in voluntarism was, Robinson belonged to a group within Labour circles who believed that on their own these elements might not be enough. Something was needed to control the militant extremists amongst the shop stewards and in some union head offices. This was what *In Place of Strife* was intended to do. It proposed that the Secretary of State could order an employer to recognise a union or unions for bargaining purposes and that there should be a cooling-off period and/or a ballot of members before a strike could be called. An Industrial Board was proposed, which would have judicial power to impose penalties on any organisation or anyone failing to comply with such orders.

Union opposition to both *In Place of Strife* and Heath's subsequent legislation was in large part motivated by concern that the customary legal foundations of unionism were being threatened. Since the early years of the twentieth century, the UK had been unusual among developed countries in having what Otto Kahn-Freund (1972) called an abstentionist tradition. Rather than having their rights and obligations defined by statute, British unions gained their abilities to function through the operation of tort law. A tort is a civil wrong. Trade unions essentially had immunity from actions in tort taken by another party when they were engaged in or in contemplation of a trade dispute. Many union activists, as well as senior figures in the Labour government, resented the intrusion of the law, since they saw it as threatening this abstentionist tradition.

This episode seems to place Robinson very much on the right wing of the Labour Party. His involvement in government department discussions about the introduction of a national minimum wage and about tackling gender pay gaps would, in the late 1960s, have appeared to put him closer to the union movement. This was not in fact the case, at least as far as the national minimum wage was concerned. When, in early 1968, its possibility was discussed with the TUC, Castle's Department was met with indifference and, in some cases, outright opposition. There were two strands to this opposition. The first was very much linked to the reaction to *In Place of Strife*. This was an anxiety to keep the law out of industrial relations and to preserve "free collective bargaining". The second related to wage differentials between different groups of workers. Differentials between the skilled and less skilled had remained remarkably stable for the first forty years of the twentieth century, but they narrowed noticeably during the Second World War. Subsequently, through the 1950s and 1960s, these differentials widened and those unions representing more skilled workers were worried that a national minimum wage might compress differentials again. Meanwhile, policy makers speculated that in order to avoid this compression, skilled workers would simply obtain compensating increases. If this indeed happened, then a national minimum wage award designed to improve the relative pay position of the low paid would have no such effect. This possibility alarmed many in official circles because, it was calculated, knock-on effects such as these would triple or even quadruple the impact on the national wage bill. Against such opposition, legislation to promote a national minimum wage did not see the light of day and it was only thirty years later that the UK saw its introduction.

Interestingly, it would appear that officialdom exhibited very little concern about possible impacts on employment. This was in stark contrast to the prevailing orthodoxy among academic economists. For them, monopsony was a rare occurrence. They had been brought up on textbooks that defined it in ways such as "a single employer in a remote geographical area". Unsurprisingly, therefore, they tended to underplay its significance. It was a number of years later that more sophisticated ideas about monopsony emerged from authors such as Card and Krueger (1997). Evidently, however, Robinson was fairly relaxed about negative employment effects. Undoubtedly, this was because of his research on local labour markets. As we have seen, this made it clear to him that worker supply response was often limited. It was inelastic labour supply curves which subsequently formed the basis of more nuanced developments of monopsony theory from the likes of Card and Krueger, which in turn made the mainstream of the profession more relaxed about potential adverse employment effects of minimum wage legislation.

Whilst Castle's minimum wage plans came to naught, another important pay intervention came into law shortly before the Labour government left office in 1970. This was the Equal Pay Act. Coming fully into force in 1975, the Act declared that an employer was obliged to ensure that:

(a) for men and women employed on like work, the terms and conditions of one sex are not in any respect less favourable than those of the other; and
(b) for men and women employed on work rated as equivalent, the terms and conditions of one sex are not less favourable than those of the other in any respect in which the terms and conditions of both are determined by the rating of their work.

Of necessity, these requirements applied to individual employers. Robinson (1998a) realised that women were often concentrated by firm or occupation and that the Equal Pay Act could do little for them.

4   Incomes Policy and the Pay Board

When the Conservatives, led by Edward Heath, entered office in 1970, Robinson's central role in Whitehall seemed over, at least until and if Labour regained power. With the exception of accepting the need to enforce the equal pay legislation, Heath explicitly set his face against interference in the private sector wage determination process and specifically against the incomes policies that had been such a prominent feature of Labour's period of office between 1964 and 1970. Instead, he introduced the so-called N-1 policy whereby each successive public sector wage settlement was meant to be 1% lower than the previous one, in the hope that this would encourage moderation in private wage settlements. However, faced with simultaneously rising unemployment and inflation, Heath did a major U-turn. Initially, he tried to persuade the TUC and the Confederation of British Industry to enter into some form of voluntary wage and price restraint. When these attempts failed, he declared a wages and prices freeze in November 1972. In April 1973, the second phase of his policy was announced and with it the establishment of two bodies charged with monitoring and implementation—the Pay Board and the Prices Commission. Robinson was appointed one of two Deputy Chairmen of the Pay Board. Despite Robinson's very clear Labour Party background and involvement, it is said that Heath and his advisers recognised that few, if any others, combined intimate knowledge and experience of running incomes policy with his understanding and engagement with the trade union movement.

Robinson's expertise was derived in large part from his time working as a senior economic adviser for the National Board for Prices and Incomes under the previous Labour government. It was established in 1965. This was not the first venture into something that might be called an incomes policy. The Atlee government had attempted to impose a wage freeze from 1948 to 1951. In 1956, the Conservative administration had tried to obtain voluntary restraint in price and wage increases, while in July 1961 the Conservatives started a series of voluntary measures of pay restraint for the private sector, with the guidelines being compulsory for the public sector and the Wages Councils (independent bodies set up to establish minimum pay rates and other terms and conditions in areas of employment where trade union representation was weak or non-existent). So, administered wage restraint was not the preserve of the Labour Party. However, it was in the second half of the 1960s that a Labour government almost institutionalised incomes policy. On entering office in 1964, it obtained TUC support to adopt a guideline of 3–3.5% for wage increases. This proved inadequate to constrain pay inflation and so a complete standstill was imposed in 1966. Importantly, for the first time, pay restraint became fully statutory. Thereafter, slightly more relaxed limits were set until the Labour government left office, but with the statutory element remaining.

In the short life of the Pay Board, Robinson became a nationally known figure. Ironically, given his background, the coal miners are central to the story. Coal mining was a nationalised industry. A miners' strike in 1972 caused wholesale disruption to the UK economy to the extent that, in order to cope with limited energy supplies, a three-day working week had to be instituted. So powerful were the miners that the government essentially caved in and yielded to almost all of their demands. Effectively, it was the miners who smashed the N-1 policy, ultimately leading the government to move to a statutory, second phase policy, in April of the following year. This second phase, which attempted to impose a limit on pay increases of £1 plus 4% per week, was superseded by a slightly more generous third phase, with a limit of 7% or £2.25, whichever was the larger. In the autumn of 1973, the miners received an offer that was within the limits set by the third phase. They rejected it and called an overtime ban, which was followed by a strike in early 1974. The Chairman of the Pay Board, Sir Frank Figgures, launched an inquiry into miners' pay and appointed Robinson to lead it. Simultaneously, Prime Minister Heath called a general election under the slogan "Who Governs Britain?" Robinson's report found that the miners' claim was largely justified. Unfortunately for Heath, the report, which was scheduled for publication shortly after the election, leaked a few days before polling day. Heath narrowly lost the election, and Labour secured a more substantial victory in a second election later in the year. As a consequence, Heath was ousted as leader of the Conservatives by Margaret Thatcher. It is said that Heath believed that the leak fatally undermined his electoral strategy and that he blamed Robinson for it and for his election defeat. Certainly, the national press fuelled such speculation, alighting on the fact that Robinson's father still worked for the Coal Board and emphasising his own trade union background. The truth of the matter was never discovered.

The new Labour government accepted the findings of Robinson's report, abolished the Pay Board and, with it, Robinson's Whitehall job. In the summer of 1974, Labour launched its own brand of incomes policy. This was initially voluntary, but this was found to be insufficient and so resort was had to statutory measures. Many commentators have argued that, just as with Heath, it was its failed incomes policies that were, in large part, responsible for Labour's election defeat in 1979. With the arrival of Margaret Thatcher in Downing Street, incomes policies were assigned to the dustbin of history. Shortly after the demise of the Pay Board, Robinson was appointed Chair of the Social Science Research Council (the precursor of the Economic and Social Research Council), holding the post from 1975 to 1979. After that, he played a little further part in national public life. However, for most of the rest of the 1970s, Robinson did contribute to local policy-making as Chair of the Oxfordshire and Buckinghamshire District Manpower Committee and as head of a committee on local unemployment.

Today's graduate students in economics have hardly heard the term incomes policy and yet in the 1960s and 1970s it was a central tool in the management of the economy. Why were economists like Robinson so wedded to this now discredited policy tool? In the 1960s, the Phillips curve had become regarded as a menu for policy choice, as Albert Rees put it. In making policy interventions, governments could choose to trade off unemployment and inflation. Though unemployment in the first half of the 1960s was relatively low in Britain, ministers and civil servants were children of the Great Depression and put huge weight on keeping it low. This was true even for those of them who accepted the synthesis provided by Samuelson (1955). Samuelson essentially argued that in the longer run, the classical model worked to produce full employment via flexible wages and prices but in the short run the economy was Keynesian. Naturally, policy emphasised the short run and was still biased towards keeping unemployment low.

Friedman's famous 1968 article on the expectations-augmented Phillips curve did not really change this bias amongst most policy makers and certainly not for Robinson. By the late 1960s and into the 1970s, they were witnessing a period of rising inflation and unemployment. Increasingly, elements of the economics profession were influenced by the implications that Friedman drew from the expectations-augmented Phillips curve. The long-run Phillips curve was vertical at the natural rate of unemployment. Any single short-run Phillips curve is drawn for a given level of price expectations. A government that attempts to run the economy below the natural rate will cause money wages and prices to rise, thus shifting the Phillips curve outwards, reflecting a new higher level of price expectations. Thus, all that has been achieved is a short-run reduction in unemployment. The economy will be driven back to the natural rate but now with higher nominal inflation. Of course, many in the profession were unconverted, including Robinson.

Following Keynes's own line, they argued that there were multiple equilibria and, if effective demand were insufficient, there would be involuntary unemployment. On their own, wage and price flexibility were not enough to rectify this (see Farmer 2020). Later in his career, Robinson departed from his usual publishing arena and collected his thoughts on neoclassical economics in general and on monetarism in particular in his book *Monetarism and the Labour Market* (Robinson 1986a).

However, whilst rejecting Friedman's approach, Robinson worried that injections of demand could be dissipated in inflation. Cost-push inflation dominated his thinking, as it did of many others at the time. The two main drivers were import prices and wages. The oil price hike together with earlier increases in other commodity prices provided a dramatic example of the impact of import prices in the early 1970s. Unions, intent on trying to maintain real wages, demanded and obtained a compensating rise in nominal wages, which in turn employers passed on in prices, thus creating a vicious spiral of inflation. Wage bargaining could, and did, also provide a primary impetus in this cost-push world. Unions aiming for an increase in real wages achieved above inflation pay rises, only for employers to pass on the cost in their prices, again potentially causing an inflationary spiral. These fears reached their peak in the early to mid-1970s. As the Appendix at the end of this chapter shows, from 1973 until 1981 retail price inflation was in double-digits in every year except one, peaking in 1975 at nearly 25%. In many more years than not, earnings inflation exceeded price inflation.

It was one thing to take an anti-classical view of the world and to be concerned about cost-push inflation and quite another to believe that incomes policies were a sensible tool of economic management. Indeed, many left-leaning academics were sceptical. Reviewing Robinson's collection of essays, *Incomes Policy and Capital Sharing in Europe* (Robinson 1973), McCarthy (1974: 668) commented somewhat tartly that Robinson's most interesting conclusion was that, 'Incomes policy has little hope of success until governments realize that by resorting to such instruments they are setting out to "change basic and deeply rooted attitudes"'. Is this a fair appraisal of Robinson's views? In attempting to answer this question, a good starting point is Robinson's own definition of an incomes policy:

> Comprehensive incomes policies can be more or less formal and more or less stringently applied. Nevertheless, they can fairly easily be grouped together generically to produce a family of policies which, although they range from statutory enforceable policies to a voluntary Social Contract, have certain features in common. Firstly, there is a norm which specifies the permissible rate of

increase in pay. Secondly, there is usually, although not always, some provisions for additional increases in specified cases, either by applying certain pre-determined rules or as a result of special examination or recommendation by some approved body (Robinson and Mayhew 1983: 7).

The essential point to understand when assessing Robinson's approach is that, at the time, he could not foresee a situation when collective bargaining was *not* the dominant mechanism by which pay was determined. At the same time, unemployment was rising to frighteningly high levels and inflation sometimes seemed in danger of getting out of control. In this climate, Robinson saw a limited defence of conventional incomes policy, which was one of timing. It could delay inflationary pressures with, he established, very limited allocative costs. One potential problem raised by some commentators at the time was that once a given policy was lifted, the reaction, known at the time as "bounce back", of the relevant actors would be such as to produce even greater inflation than there would have been in the absence of the policy. Again, Robinson demonstrated that this was far from an inevitability. Therefore, both as an academic and policy adviser, he devoted himself to mas-sively detailed work on the design of policy—on how and why to allow for exceptions, on how to set pay limits, and on how restraint should be gradually relaxed and finally lifted. Arguably, he had no peer in these respects.

Nevertheless, in some ways, McCarthy's interpretation of Robinson's think-ing was correct. He believed that structural and attitudinal changes were needed to improve the performance of the labour market. Robinson empha-sised that, strangely, this was not so far removed from the thinking of the followers of Friedman. Friedman indeed thought that the economy had to be run at the natural rate of unemployment in order to achieve stability of infla-tion. However, he also stressed that if a government judged that this level of unemployment was unacceptably high, it needed to resort to structural mea-sures to reduce it. In many respects, this was what Thatcherite policy was subsequently all about. Furthermore, just as much as Thatcher, Robinson understood that changing the balance of power between unions and employ-ers might well be a vital ingredient in such reforms. He also recognised that social security reform, either by reducing the level of out-of-work benefits or by tightening eligibility criteria, could change the reservation wage and make the trade-off between unemployment and inflation less severe. What set Robinson apart from most economists of the time was a belief that a perma-nent incomes policy might itself achieve structural reform. In 1983, he wrote that he had 'no doubt that the apparent gains and losses of a comprehensive incomes policy look far more favourable when compared with the results of the present package of government policy measures which include unemployment of well over three million' (Robinson and Mayhew 1983: 138). He continued: 'The depressing feature of the present policy discussion is the refusal of trade unions to recognise that there are serious problems in reconciling counter inflationary policies with high employment. Some structural or attitudinal changes are imperative' (ibid.) and that:

> Attitudes and value judgments cannot be changed overnight. They are more likely to be changed if those whose perceived self-interests are to be adversely affected can be persuaded that the new criteria and standards are generally acceptable and acceptable to those whose opinions the adversely affected groups regard as legitimate or reasonable. To this end we would hope that trade unions might be persuaded to participate in an incomes policy. If they do not, there seems little prospect of them achieving their other objectives (ibid.: 139).

In other words, Robinson fully recognised a need for structural reform. However, as late as the early 1980s, he still saw unions as a vitally powerful force in the UK economy. This was unsurprising given that, as we have seen, union density had reached its highest ever level at the end of the previous decade. Furthermore, the miners went on strike twice in the early 1980s, causing major industrial and political disruption. Thatcher felt too weak to take them on during the strike of 1982. It was only during the second strike in 1984 that she went on the offensive, bolstered by massive stockpiles of coal. Moreover, Robinson retained his political stance that collective bargaining was the best way of determining wages in an economy that desired a balance of power between workers and employers in order to produce distributional fairness. He saw a long-run incomes policy as a central tool for achieving this by persuading the union movement to moderate short term, sectional thinking in favour of taking a longer-term, more coordinated stance. His research on pay determination elsewhere, particularly in the Netherlands and Northern Europe, encouraged him in this view. Freeman and Medoff's paper (1979) on the two faces of unionism chimed with Robinson's take on the role of unions. Freeman and Medoff contrasted the monopoly face of unions where bargaining was a zero-sum game with the collective voice face. In the right environment, where bargaining could be across an extensive range of issues, the expression of the collective voice could provide employers with a range of information about the concerns, observations and suggestions of their employees which could enable a non-zero-sum game. It was this which Robinson believed could be achieved in a carefully designed and implemented national incomes policy. He was realistic about the extremism, often politically motivated, of some union leaders. That is why he had always believed that some legislative interference was necessary.

5   Conclusion

Whether any of this was ever achievable, we will never know. Such potential experiments became irrelevant after Thatcher won the second miners' dispute of 1984 and the country embarked on a very different type of structural reform and the union movement lost members and power year by year. This perhaps was one of the reasons why, in his later years, Robinson concentrated so much of his effort on missions, largely to developing countries, for the ILO. There his views that bargaining structures were capable of being changed and that wage outcomes to some extent should be administered had a more sympathetic audience than in the UK. However, some of Robinson's thinking also has a strange resonance with economic debate in Britain today. His ambition to reform wage bargaining was based on a belief that the market set only broad limits and was motivated by the contemporary anxieties about both the level of inflation and the inflation/unemployment trade off. Today and in more recent times, concern about inequality has caused some economists to suggest that intervention in a now very different wage determination process is both desirable and feasible.

Robinson was primarily an institutionalist, researching industrial relations as much as conventional labour economics. Some contemporaries accused him of neglecting theory—indeed of being positively hostile to it. This was unfair. What he despised was theory from those who had little or no knowledge of the institutions and history of the labour market. Sometimes, he was possibly too frank in expressing his contempt but he was intent on nurturing and protecting political economy. This reflected not just a view about what researchers should be doing but a view about what undergraduate education should be about. For many years, the Oxford PPE syllabus had a "bridge" optional paper between Politics and Economics entitled "Labour Economics and Industrial Relations". In the 1970s through until the early 1990s, when industrial relations issues were such a prominent part of the national political debate, it was one of the most popular options. Robinson taught it for many years. He recognised that the vast majority of his students were not going to become professional economists and that indeed the specifics of what they had learnt in Oxford economics courses would soon be forgotten once they had moved into the world of work. Certainly, they needed to learn technical aspects of the subject but this should not lead to the undergraduate syllabus simply being a piece of watered-down professional training. Professional preparation, in that sense, was the preserve of the Master's degree. He saw his role as developing students' general intellectual and cognitive capabilities through studying subjects they found interesting. That is what would remain with them in later life. He wanted his students to learn to think critically and carefully, to assemble and use evidence effectively and to write persuasively.

Perhaps this influence on generations of undergraduate and graduate students, some of whom *did* go on to work on labour matters (whether as academics, public servants or union activists), together with his early insights into the workings of an imperfectly competitive labour market, are his two lasting legacies.

Appendix 1: The Retail Price Index (RPI) and Unemployment in the UK, 1960–1985

	RPI (%)	Unemployment (million)
1960	1.8	0.37
1961	4.4	0.34
1962	2.6	0.45
1963	1.9	0.54
1964	4.8	0.39
1965	4.5	0.34
1966	3.7	0.35
1967	2.5	0.55
1968	5.9	0.57
1969	4.7	0.57
1970	7.9	0.60
1971	9.0	0.74
1972	7.7	0.83
1973	10.6	0.59
1974	19.1	0.59
1975	24.9	0.90
1976	15.1	1.22
1977	12.1	1.31
1978	8.4	1.30
1979	17.2	1.23
1980	15.1	1.56
1981	12.0	2.42
1982	5.4	2.79
1983	5.3	3.04
1984	4.6	3.16
1985	5.7	3.27

References

Main Works by Derek Robinson

Knowles, K.G.J.C. and D. Robinson (1962). 'Wage Rounds and Wage Policy'. *Bulletin of the Oxford University Institute of Economics and Statistics*, 24(2): 269–329.

Knowles, K.G.J.C. and D. Robinson (1964). 'Some Concepts Relevant to the Consideration of the Engineering Wage Settlement of November 1963'. *Bulletin of the Oxford University Institute of Economics and Statistics*, 26(2): 93–111.

Knowles, K.G.J.C. and D. Robinson (1969). 'Wage Movements in Coventry'. *Bulletin of the Oxford University Institute of Economics and Statistics*, 31(1): 1–21.

Knowles, K.G.J.C. and D. Robinson (1969). 'Wage Movements in Coventry, Appendix II'. *Bulletin of the Oxford University Institute of Economics and Statistics*, 31(2): 145–152.

Paukert, F. and D. Robinson (eds) (1992). *Incomes Policies in the Wider Context: Wage, Price and Fiscal Initiatives in Developing Countries*. Geneva: ILO.

Robinson, D. (1961). 'Wage-Rate Differentials Over Time'. *Bulletin of the Oxford University Institute of Economics and Statistics*, 23(4): 367–378.

Robinson, D. (1963). 'Wage Rates, Wage Income and Wages Policy'. *Bulletin of the Oxford University Institute of Economics and Statistics*, 25(1): 47–76.

Robinson, D. (1967). 'Low Paid Workers and Incomes Policy'. *Bulletin of the Oxford University Institute of Economics and Statistics*, 29(1): 1–29.

Robinson, D. (ed.) (1970). *Local Labour Markets and Wage Structures*. London: Gower Press.

Robinson, D. (1973). *Incomes Policy and Capital Sharing in Europe*. London: Croom Helm.

Robinson, D. (1983). 'Indirect and Partial Measures'. *Oxford Bulletin of Economics and Statistics*, 45(1): 105–125.

Robinson, D. (1986a). *Monetarism and the Labour Market*. Oxford: Oxford University Press.

Robinson, D. (1986). *Introduction to Economics*. London: ICSA Publishing.

Robinson, D. (1987). 'How Inflexible Are Negotiated Wages in Britain?'. *Oxford Bulletin of Economics and Statistics*, 49(1): 37–57.

Robinson, D. (1990). *Civil Service Pay in Africa*. Geneva: ILO.

Robinson, D. (1998a). 'Differences in Occupational Earnings by Sex'. *International Labour Review*, 137(1): 3–31.

Robinson, D. (1998). 'A Comparison of Occupational Wage Structures in Singapore and Other Countries'. Chapter 18 in C.Y. Lim and R. Chew (eds) *Wages and Wages Policies: Tripartism in Singapore*. River Edge, NJ: World Scientific Publishing: 279–324.

Robinson, D. and K. Mayhew (1983). 'Introduction' and 'Conclusions'. *Oxford Bulletin of Economics and Statistics*, 45(1): 3–13 and 127–139.

Robinson, D. and A.G. Wilson (1966). 'A Note on Calculating Average Compound Rates of Growth'. *Bulletin of the Oxford University Institute of Economics and Statistics*, 28(4): 241–246.

Rosewell, B. and D. Robinson (1980). 'The Reliability of Vacancy Statistics'. *Oxford Bulletin of Economics and Statistics*, 42(1): 1–16.

Other Works Referred To

Atkinson, A.B. (1999). *Is Rising Inequality Inevitable? A Critique of the Transatlantic Consensus*. Helsinki: UNU/WIDER.

Card, D. and A.B. Krueger (1997). *Myth and Measurement: The New Economics of the Minimum Wage*. Princeton: Princeton University Press.

Doeringer, P.B. and M.J. Piore (1971). *Internal Labor Markets and Manpower Analysis*. Lexington, MA: D.C. Heath.

Farmer, R. (2020). 'The Importance of Beliefs in Shaping Macroeconomic Outcomes'. *Oxford Review of Economic Policy*, 36(3): 711–722.

Freeman, R.B. and J.L. Medoff (1979). 'The Two Faces of Unionism'. *Public Interest*, 57(Fall): 69–93.

Friedman, M. (1968). 'The Role of Monetary Policy'. *American Economic Review*, 58(1): 1–17.

In Place of Strife: A Policy for Industrial Relations (1969). Cmnd. 3888. London: HMSO.

Kahn-Freund, O. (1972). *Labour and the Law*. London: Stevens.

MacKay, D.I. et al. (1971). *Local Labour Markets Under Different Conditions*. London: Allen & Unwin.

Mayhew, K. (2015a). 'Derek Robinson'. Royal Economic Society *Newsletter*, Issue No. 168, January: 24. Available at: https://www.res.org.uk/uploads/assets/uploaded/2cb6ccaa-6ad5-42a4-9039f2b717289957.pdf.

Mayhew, K. (2015b). 'Derek Robinson, 9 February 1932–1 September 2014'. *Economic and Labour Relations Review*, 26(3): 490–492.

McCarthy, W.E.J. (1974). 'Review of *Incomes Policy and Capital Sharing in Europe*, by D. Robinson'. *Economic Journal*, 84(335): 668–669.

Oi, W.Y. (1962). 'Labour as a Quasi-Fixed Factor'. *Journal of Political Economy*, 70(6): 538–555.

Rees, A. and G.P. Shultz (1970). *Workers and Wages in an Urban Labor Market*. Chicago: University of Chicago Press.

Report of the Royal Commission on Trade Unions and Employers' Associations, 1965–1968 (1968). Cmnd. 3623. London: HMSO.

Samuelson, P.A. (1955). *Economics: An Introductory Analysis*. Third edition. New York: McGraw-Hill.

24

David F. Hendry (1944–)

Neil R. Ericsson

1   Introduction

David Hendry has made—and continues to make—pivotal contributions to the econometrics of empirical economic modelling, economic forecasting, econometrics software, substantive empirical economic model design, and economic policy. This chapter reviews his contributions by topic, emphasising the overlaps between different strands in his research and the importance of real-world problems in motivating that research.

David Forbes Hendry was born of Scottish parents on 6 March 1944 in Nottingham, England, where his parents were temporarily relocated for the war effort. After an unpromising start in Glasgow schools, David obtained an

The author is a staff economist in the Division of International Finance, Board of Governors of the Federal Reserve System, Washington, D.C. 20551, USA, a Research Professor of Economics, Department of Economics, The George Washington University, Washington, D.C. 20052, USA, and an Adjunct Professor at the Paul H. Nitze School of Advanced International Studies (SAIS), Johns Hopkins University, Washington, D.C. 20036, USA. The views in this chapter are solely the responsibility of the author and should not be interpreted as reflecting the views of the Board of Governors of the Federal Reserve System or of any other person associated with the Federal Reserve System. The author is grateful to Cambridge University Press and Elsevier for permission to draw on material in Ericsson (2004, 2017), and to Jennifer Castle, Mike Clements, Robert Cord, David Hendry, Fred Joutz, Jaime Marquez, Andrew Martinez, and Tara Sinclair for helpful comments and suggestions.

N. R. Ericsson (✉)
Federal Reserve Board, Washington, D.C., USA
e-mail: ericsson@frb.gov

© The Author(s), under exclusive license to Springer Nature Switzerland AG 2021   **563**
R. A. Cord (ed.), *The Palgrave Companion to Oxford Economics*,
https://doi.org/10.1007/978-3-030-58471-9_24

MA in Economics with First Class Honours from the University of Aberdeen in 1966. He then went to the London School of Economics (LSE) and completed an MSc (with distinction) in Econometrics and Mathematical Economics in 1967 and a PhD in Economics in 1970 under Denis Sargan. His doctoral thesis, "The Estimation of Economic Models with Autoregressive Errors", provided intellectual seeds for his future research on the development of an integrated approach to modelling economic time series. David was appointed to a Lectureship at LSE while finishing his thesis and to a Professorship at LSE in 1977.

In 1982, David moved to the University of Oxford as a Professor of Economics and a Fellow of Nuffield College. At Oxford, he has also been Acting Director for the Institute of Economics and Statistics (1982–1984), Leverhulme Personal Research Professor of Economics (1995–2000), ESRC Professorial Research Fellow (2003–2006), and Chair of the Department of Economics (2001–2007). He is currently the Director of the programme Economic Modelling (EMoD; Institute for New Economic Thinking at the Oxford Martin School, 2010–) and the Co-Director of the programme Climate Econometrics (2015–). He also helped design the University's Resource Allocation Model.

Much of David's research has focused on constructing a unified methodological approach to empirical modelling of economic time series. His 1995 book, *Dynamic Econometrics*, is a milestone on that path. General-to-specific modelling is an important aspect of this empirical methodology, which has become commonly known as the "LSE" or "Hendry" approach. David is widely recognised as the most vocal advocate and ardent contributor to this methodology. His research also has aimed to make this methodology widely available and easy to implement, both through publicly available econometrics software packages that embed the methodology (notably, PcGive and OxMetrics) and by substantive empirical applications of the methodology. As highlighted in many of his papers, David's interest in methodology is driven by a passion for understanding how the economy works and, specifically, how best to carry out economic policy in practice.

David's research has many strands. They include deriving and analysing methods of estimation and inference for non-stationary time series; developing Monte Carlo methods for investigating small-sample properties of econometric techniques; exploring alternative modelling strategies and empirical methodologies; analysing concepts and criteria for viable empirical modelling of time series; developing software for econometric analysis, culminating in model selection procedures utilising machine learning; evaluating these developments in simulation studies and in empirical investigations of consumer expenditure, money demand, inflation, and the housing and mortgage markets; and reassessing the history of econometric thought.

Over the last three decades, and in tandem with many of his developments in model design, David has reassessed the empirical and theoretical literature on forecasting, leading to new paradigms for generating and interpreting economic forecasts. He developed a taxonomy of forecast errors and a theory of unpredictability that have yielded valuable insights into the nature of forecasting. He has also provided new perspectives on many existing forecasting techniques, including mean square forecast errors, add factors, leading indicators, pooling of forecasts, and multi-step estimation. In addition, David has developed new forecast tools, such as forecast encompassing, and he has improved existing ones, such as nowcasting and robustification to breaks.

David's enthusiasm for econometrics and economics permeates his teaching and makes his seminars notable. Throughout his career, he has promoted innovative uses of computers in teaching and, following the birth of the PC, he helped pioneer live empirical and Monte Carlo econometrics in the classroom and in seminars. To date, he has supervised over 40 PhD theses, with numerous professional collaborations with his former doctoral students and other colleagues.

David has held many prominent appointments in professional bodies. He has served as President of the Royal Economic Society; editor of the *Review of Economic Studies, Economic Journal*, and *Oxford Bulletin of Economics and Statistics*; associate editor of *Econometrica* and the *International Journal of Forecasting*; President (Section F) of the British Association for the Advancement of Science; Chairman of the UK's Research Assessment Exercise in economics; and special adviser to the House of Commons, both on monetary policy and on forecasting. He is a chartered statistician, co-founder of *Econometrics Journal*, and a Fellow of the British Academy, the Royal Society of Edinburgh, and the Econometric Society. Among his many awards and honours, David has received the Guy Medal in Bronze from the Royal Statistical Society, eight honorary doctorates, a Lifetime Achievement Award from the ESRC, the Isaac Kerstenetzky Scholarly Achievement Award, and a knighthood from Her Majesty The Queen. The ISI lists him as one of the world's 200 most cited economists, and he is a Thomson Reuters Citation Laureate. In addition to his academic talents, David is an excellent chef and makes a great cup of cappuccino!

The remainder of this chapter focuses on key contributions by David: the econometrics of empirical economic modelling (Section 2), econometrics software (Section 3), forecasting (Section 4), empirical analysis (Section 5), and Oxford connections (Section 6).

2   Economics, Econometrics, and Empirical Modelling

'The three golden rules of econometrics are test, test, and test; that all three rules are broken regularly in empirical applications is fortunately easily remedied' (Hendry 1980: 403). This quote from David's 1979 Inaugural Lecture at LSE is a common thread throughout his writings. He has authored or co-authored three books that are milestones in his contributions to the development of the econometrics for empirical economic modelling: *Dynamic Econometrics* (Hendry 1995), *Co-integration, Error Correction, and the Econometric Analysis of Non-stationary Data* (Banerjee, Dolado, Galbraith and Hendry 1993), and *Empirical Model Discovery and Theory Evaluation* (Hendry and Doornik 2014). The titles to these books aptly serve as the titles to the subsections herein.

2.1   *Dynamic Econometrics*

Dynamic Econometrics provides a systematic framework for empirical modelling of economic data, focusing on economic time series. Drawing on a likelihood approach, this book lays out the economic and statistical underpinnings for empirical modelling, develops a typology of dynamic models, and ties the statistical theory of reduction to exogeneity, model evaluation, diagnostic testing, encompassing, and model design. The concept of a data generation process (DGP) is central to the theory of reduction, which implies that empirical models are derived from that DGP, rather than being autonomous constructs. This framework also allows a direct and unified analysis of many traditionally ad hoc "problems" in econometrics, such as residual autocorrelation and heteroscedasticity, simultaneity, measurement errors, data mining, misspecification, nonsense regressions, causality, expectations, structural breaks, and the Lucas critique. Constructively, Hendry (1995) provides a progressive research strategy for empirical econometric modelling that embodies both economic theory and data features, explicitly allowing for evolution in the data's structure and in economic theory itself. The empirical studies in Section 5 exemplify that progressive research strategy, and Hendry and Nielsen (2007) further develop the likelihood basis for this approach.

David's education set the stage for *Dynamic Econometrics*. He was motivated to study economics in Aberdeen and then in London because he saw unemployment, living standards, and equity as important issues. A scientific approach to their understanding required quantification, however, which led him to econometrics—and thence to econometric methodology—to determine what could be learnt from non-experimental empirical evidence. In David's view, if econometrics could develop good models of economic reality, economic policy decisions could be significantly improved. Since policy requires causal links, economic theory plays a central role in model formulation. However, being highly abstract and simplified, economic theory could not be the sole basis for model formulation. Data and their analysis are crucial, with much variation in the data being due not to economic factors but to "special events" such as wars and major changes in policy, institutions, and legislation. Failure to account for these special events can obfuscate the role of economic forces in an empirical model.

Then, as now, the "conventional" approach to modelling was to write down the economic theory, collect variables with the same names (such as consumers' expenditure for consumption), develop mappings between the theory constructs and the observations, and then estimate the resulting equations. That approach often ignored institutional aspects and inter-agent heterogeneity, as well as inherent conflicts of interest between agents on different sides of the market. Nevertheless, economists often believed their theories to such an extent that they retained them, even when the theories were strongly rejected by the data.

David had learned that the conventional approach did not work well empirically and that the straitjacket of that approach meant that one understood neither the data nor economic behaviour. Instead, David tried a more data-based approach, in which economic theory provided guidance rather than a complete structure—but that approach required developing concepts of model design and modelling strategy.

David's approach has four basic stages, beginning with an economic analysis to delineate key economic factors. The next stage embeds those factors in a general empirical model that also allows for other potential determinants and relevant special features. Then, the congruence of that general model is tested. Finally, the general model is simplified to a parsimonious undominated congruent final selection that encompasses the original model, thereby ensuring that all reductions (aka simplifications) are valid.

Chris Gilbert (1986) contrasted the conventional approach and David's approach, nicknaming the two as the "Average Economic Regression" (AER) and "Professor Hendry's Econometric Methodology". While the latter is often known as the "LSE" or "Hendry" approach, David is the first to acknowledge that many other individuals have also contributed to it and that not all of those individuals have been at LSE. Moreover, David himself has now spent most of his professional career at the University of Oxford, not LSE.

When David began developing his approach, the first tractable cases for general-to-specific modelling were linear dynamic single equations, where a key issue was choice of appropriate lag length. That said, the general-to-specific principle applies to all econometric modelling, albeit with some complications for nonlinear settings; see Trivedi (1970), Mizon (1977) and Hendry (1984a) for early empirical and theoretical contributions. Many other aspects followed, such as developing a taxonomy for model evaluation, orthogonalising variables, and recommencing an analysis at the general model if a rejection occurs. Additional developments expanded this approach to system modelling, in which several (or even all) variables are treated as endogenous; see Hendry, Pagan and Sargan (1984). Cointegration is easily analysed as a reduction in this framework. So is encompassing of the VAR and determining whether a conditional model entails a valid reduction; cf. Mizon (1995) and Hendry (1997). David's empirical research embodies these features of model construction, as Section 5 details. Sections 2.3 and 3 discuss how his approach could be and was automated with machine learning, resulting in the Autometrics feature of his and Jurgen Doornik's econometrics software package OxMetrics.

Dynamic Econometrics is the largest single project in David's professional career, and it had several false starts. In 1972, the large Italian public holding company IRI invited David and his former LSE classmate Pravin Trivedi to publish (in Italian) a set of lectures on dynamic modelling. In preparing those lectures, David and Pravin became concerned that conventional econometric approaches camouflaged misspecification. Rather than resulting directly in a book, that process laid out a research agenda that included a general analysis of misspecification, as in Hendry (1973, 1975); the unified treatment of econometric estimators, in Hendry (1976); and empirical model design, systematised in Hendry and Richard (1982, 1983) and Hendry (1983, 1987a).

In the 1980s, David visited Duke University on a regular basis and again attempted to write the book—this time with Bob Marshall and Jean-François Richard. Common factors, the theory of reduction, equilibrium correction, cointegration, encompassing, and exogeneity had already clarified the empirical analysis of individual equations; and powerful software with recursive estimators implemented the ideas.

Modelling complete systems raised new econometric and operational issues, so David and colleagues wrote the software package PcFiml, now part of OxMetrics; see Section 3. PcFiml ensures that system modelling begins with the unrestricted system, which is first checked for congruence. Modelling then reduces that system to a specific model thereof, tests over-identification, and encompasses the VAR; see Hendry, Neale and Srba (1988), Hendry and Mizon (1993), and Doornik and Hendry (1994). This work paralleled and drew on concurrent developments in system cointegration by Søren Johansen, Katarina Juselius, and others in Copenhagen; see Johansen (1988, 1995), Johansen and Juselius (1990), and Juselius (2006). A daunting list of topics still remained, including general-to-specific modelling and diagnostic testing in systems, model reliability, and the role of inter-temporal optimisation theory. Bob and Jean-François became more interested in auctions and experimental economics, so their co-authorship lapsed.

In the late 1980s, David circulated a first full draft of *Dynamic Econometrics* for comments, drawing extensively on help from Duo Qin and Carlo Favero. In Oxford, Duo had transcribed David's course lectures, themselves based on earlier draft chapters, and Carlo had drafted answers for the solved exercises. The final manuscript still took years more to complete.

As published, *Dynamic Econometrics* systematically covers a vast array of topics in econometric modelling and is almost 1000 pages long, 6 cm thick, and heavy—which David has jokingly remarked makes it useful as a doorstop. David dedicated the book to his wife Evelyn and their daughter Vivien. The dedication was much more than perfunctory. Evelyn and Vivien not only facilitated time to work on ideas and visit collaborators, tolerated numerous discussions on econometrics, and corrected grammar; Vivien—a professional economist in her own right—worked through analyses and helped debug the software.

Dynamic Econometrics notably and deliberately omitted several major strands of David's research, as they were being published elsewhere. Those strands include Monte Carlo methodology, in Hendry (1984b) and Hendry, Neale and Ericsson (1990); numerical issues and econometric software, in Hendry (1976), Hendry and Srba (1977, 1980), and Doornik and Hendry (1992, 1994); the history of econometrics, in Hendry and Morgan (1995); forecasting, in Clements and Hendry (1994, 1998a, b, 1999a, 2002a); and cointegration in Hendry (1986a), Banerjee and Hendry (1992a), and Banerjee, Dolado, Galbraith and Hendry (1993). On the last, *Dynamic Econometrics* lacks an extensive discussion of cointegration—a surprising omission, given David's interest in and major contributions to cointegration and equilibrium correction. However, because (co)integrated series can be reduced to stationarity, much of *Dynamic Econometrics* assumes stationarity, allowing *Dynamic Econometrics* to focus on modelling per se. Fittingly, the next subsection turns to cointegration.

2.2   Co-integration, Error Correction, and the Econometric Analysis of Non-stationary Data

David's early exposure to and understanding of error correction models—what are now called equilibrium correction models—lay the foundation for his contributions to cointegration, including the book by Banerjee, Dolado, Galbraith and Hendry (1993) titled *Co-integration, Error Correction, and the Econometric Analysis of Non-stationary Data*. In the late 1960s and early 1970s, David had learned from the equilibrium correction models in Sargan (1964) how to model in differences and in levels of economic variables. A decade prior to Sargan's paper, Bill Phillips (1954)—of Phillips curve fame and also at LSE—had analysed integral, proportional, and derivative control in formulating economic policy. Phillips's framework was also equilibrium correction; see in addition Smith (1926) and Mills (2011).

In the early 1970s, David, with James Davidson, began modelling UK consumers' expenditure in an equilibrium correction framework, eventually published as Davidson, Hendry, Srba and Yeo (1978). At the same time, David and Gordon Anderson were modelling building societies, which are the British analogue of the US savings and loans associations. David discussed that work in his invited presentation at the August 1975 Toronto Econometric Society World Congress, showing that a system of equilibrium corrections could offset non-stationarity; see Hendry and Anderson (1977).

A major turning point came shortly thereafter during David's sabbatical in the USA. In November 1975, Chris Sims and the Minneapolis Fed sponsored a conference "New Methods in Business Cycle Research". In a presentation at the conference, Clive Granger critiqued the then common poor econometrics of static regressions involving trending data, showing in particular that a high R^2 and a low Durbin–Watson statistic were diagnostic of misspecification and indicative of a nonsense regression in the sense of Yule (1926). As an alternative, Clive proposed modelling differences of the variables, as advocated by Box and Jenkins (1970).

David was a discussant for Clive's presentation. While sympathetic to Clive's critique, David thought that the common factor interpretation of error autocorrelation—in combination with equilibrium correction models—resolved the problem of nonsense regressions better than did differencing. Moreover, equilibrium correction models retained the economics. Clive's and David's presentations were subsequently published in the conference volume as Granger and Newbold (1977) and Hendry (1977).

At the conference, Clive was sceptical about relating differences to lagged levels, as in an equilibrium correction framework, and he doubted that the correction in levels could be stationary. Differences of the data did not have a unit root, whereas their lagged levels did. Investigating that issue helped Clive discover cointegration, with results published initially in Granger (1981, 1986), Granger and Weiss (1983), and Engle and Granger (1987). In his Nobel Prize Lecture, Clive gives an amusing account of his interchange with David at the Minneapolis conference:

> A colleague, David Hendry, stated that the difference between a pair of integrated series could be stationary. My response was that it could be proved that he was wrong, but in attempting to do so, I showed that he was correct, and generalized it to cointegration, and proved the consequences such as the error-correction representation … (Granger 2004: 363).

Clive's development of cointegration also resolved the debate between modelling in levels and modelling in differences, as David discussed in Hendry (2004).

In mid-1983, David visited Rob Engle and Clive Granger in San Diego and returned to Oxford all enthused about testing for cointegration. That rapidly resulted in one of the very first empirical applications of the Engle–Granger test for cointegration—Hendry and Ericsson (1983), later published as Hendry and Ericsson (1991a); see Section 5.3.

David's interest in cointegration led to an explosion of research activity: two special issues on cointegration for the *Oxford Bulletin of Economics and Statistics*, published as Hendry (1986a) and Banerjee and Hendry (1992a); a number of papers, including Banerjee, Dolado, Hendry and Smith (1986), Hendry (1986b), Hendry and Neale (1988, 1991), Banerjee and Hendry (1992b), and Campos, Ericsson and Hendry (1996); and the book by Banerjee, Dolado, Galbraith and Hendry (1993). The last was prompted in part by innovative mathematical statistics that use Wiener processes to help describe the limiting distributions of unit-root processes, as developed by Phillips (1986, 1987), Stock (1987), Johansen (1988), Chan and Wei (1988), and others. David felt that the power and generality of that new approach would dominate the future of econometrics, especially since some proofs became easier, as with the forecast-error distributions in Clements and Hendry (1996a, b).

The key insight with cointegration, though, was conceptual. In the Granger representation theorem in Engle and Granger (1987), the data are integrated and cointegrated because the number of distinct equilibrium correction terms is less than the number of decision variables. Johansen (1988) formalised that property as reduced-rank feedbacks of combinations of levels onto growth rates. Cointegration also explained and helped reinterpret many earlier results.

For instance, in Sargan (1964), the equilibrium relationship involved real wages relative to productivity, with the measured disequilibrium determining future wage rates, given current inflation rates. Likewise, in Davidson, Hendry, Srba and Yeo (1978), disequilibrium between consumers' expenditure and income affected future growth in expenditure; and Hendry (1980) showed that "nonsense regressions" could be both created and detected.

2.3   *Empirical Model Discovery and Theory Evaluation*

Hendry (1995) laid the framework for empirical model evaluation and design, and Banerjee, Dolado, Galbraith and Hendry (1993) provided the statistical framework for dealing with cointegration. However, the actual construction of a model by manually simplifying from general to simple was tedious, time-consuming, and fraught with error, not least because there often were many simplification paths to follow. David's initial empirical studies—of consumers' expenditure, money demand, and the mortgage and housing markets—highlighted those challenges and difficulties; see Section 5. A twofold serendipity for David led to remarkable breakthroughs in empirical modelling. First, general-to-specific modelling could be automated in computer software with machine learning. Second, the number of potential variables being considered could be more than the number of observations. Hendry and Doornik's (2014) book *Empirical Model Discovery and Theory Evaluation* provides the theoretical, statistical, computational, and empirical basis that integrates those breakthroughs.

The first serendipity occurred at a Carnegie–Rochester conference in November 1996. David was the discussant of Faust and Whiteman (1997), who critiqued the Hendry approach to modelling, with David's formal reply published as Hendry (1997). One of the conference participants was Kevin Hoover, who knew David from Oxford when he (Kevin) was writing his DPhil at Nuffield College in the early 1980s. Over drinks, Kevin expressed scepticism about general-to-specific modelling, with David pointing to the success of his and others' various empirical modelling efforts. After the conference, Kevin and his student Stephen Perez set out to scientifically challenge David's claim by constructing a computer-based simulacrum of what general-to-specific modellers did in practice, focusing on path search and diagnostic testing. Much to Kevin's surprise, the simulacrum worked well—phenomenally well in fact—and well beyond even David's own hopes and expectations; see Hoover and Perez (1999).

David immediately saw the potential of this computer-automated approach that employed machine learning. David and his colleague Hans-Martin Krolzig built on Kevin and Stephen's achievement, developing the econometrics package PcGets ("Gets" for "general to specific"). Subsequently, David and Jurgen Doornik embedded and enhanced that modelling approach directly in their econometrics package PcGive as the routine Autometrics; see Section 3 for further details.

The second serendipity arose through Jan Magnus and Mary Morgan's (1999) econometric modelling competition, in which they invited researchers to analyse two datasets, following different modelling approaches. One dataset was of the US demand for food from 1929 to 1989, building on Tobin's (1950) empirical analysis through 1948. Most investigators discarded the data for the inter-war period and for the Second World War as being too difficult to model. For example, a standard demand model fitted over the whole sample delivered positive price elasticities.

David was a late entrant in the competition, serving as discussant to Siegert (1999), who had analysed the data acting "as if" he were David. In David's follow-up, published as Hendry (1999) and to be reprinted in Ericsson (2021), David aimed to replicate Siegert's and others' findings for the post-war subsample while actually using the whole sample. After all, more data should be better than less, if used in the right way. David thus estimated a given model over the whole sample, including indicator variables (one-off dummy variables for individual observations) for all observations up to the beginning of the post-war period. Several of those indicator variables were highly significant. Three were associated with a food programme in the USA during the Great Depression. Unsurprisingly, the food programme affected the demand for food. The other significant indicator variables were for years during the Second World War.

David then reversed the whole procedure, estimating the model over the whole sample but including indicators for the post-war period. That was equivalent to estimating the model over the first part of the sample. A few post-war indicators were marginally significant, as the corresponding Chow test revealed.

Finally, David estimated the model over the whole sample, including the indicators selected in the two subsample estimations. Of those indicators, only those for the food programme and the Second World War were significant, and they had clear economic explanations. By including just those indicators, the whole sample could be adequately captured by a single model. The large data variability during the inter-war period and the Second World War also greatly reduced the estimated economic parameters' standard errors relative to those in the same model estimated on the post-war period alone.

In the process, David had included an indicator for every observation, albeit in two large blocks. Model selection could handle more potential variables than there are observations—something previously believed to be impossible, both theoretically and empirically. All indicators *could* be considered. The key was realising: just not all of them at once.

There are precursors to this approach in the literature. For reference, the canonical case for this problem in model selection is impulse indicator saturation (IIS), in which the set of candidate explanatory variables includes a dummy variable for each observation. The solution to this canonical case is implicit in several existing techniques. For instance, as Salkever (1976) shows, the Chow (1960) statistic for testing predictive failure can be calculated by including zero-one indicator variables for all observations in the forecast period and then testing those indicators' joint significance. Recursive estimation is another example. Its "forward" version can be calculated by estimating the model, including an indicator variable for every observation in the latter part of the sample, and then sequentially removing the indicators, one indicator at a time. Both forward and backward versions of recursive estimation can be calculated in this fashion. Together, they require indicators for all observations in the sample and thus analyse as many potential variables as there are observations. Andrews' (1993) unknown breakpoint test and Bai and Perron's (1998) generalisation thereon are also interpretable as specific algorithmic implementations of saturation techniques.

To understand IIS's properties, Hendry, Johansen and Santos (2008) considered a stylised version of IIS with a split-half sample, similar to what David undertook empirically in Hendry (1999). Under the null hypothesis that there are no outliers or breaks in the DGP, IIS incurs only a small loss of efficiency. For example, for a sample size of 100, on average one impulse indicator out of the 100 total would be significant at the 1% significance level. Because an impulse indicator merely removes one observation from the sample, the method is 99% efficient under the null hypothesis. IIS is almost costless, despite searching across 100 indicators.

Under the alternative hypothesis, IIS can detect multiple outliers and location shifts (aka structural breaks). Castle, Doornik and Hendry (2012) demonstrate high power for multiple location shifts that are "large enough". Importantly, IIS can detect breaks that are near or at the ends of the sample. That circumvents an implicit shortcoming of the Andrews and Bai–Perron procedures. Johansen and Nielsen (2009) generalise the theory of IIS to include autoregressive distributed-lag models with or without unit roots and prove that IIS does not affect the rate of convergence of other parameter estimates to their population values.

IIS adds blocks of dummies to estimation and model selection. IIS can consider many blocks, thereby allowing many different alternatives to be considered. This feature of IIS has remarkable implications. Under the null hypothesis, an indicator for a given observation is significant only if it is discrepant. Its significance does not depend particularly on how or how often the indicators are split into blocks, provided that the blocks are large and that multiple search paths are explored.

The alternative hypothesis of multiple unmodelled breaks or outliers is equally important. For ease of discussion, assume two outliers. Detection of one outlier (the first, say) can be difficult unless the other outlier is accounted for. Failing to include that second outlier in the model induces a larger estimated error variance, making the first outlier appear less significant than it actually is. Hence, there is a need to include sufficient indicators to capture all actual outliers.

Hoover and Perez (1999) showed the advantages of multiple-path contracting searches that are guided by encompassing evaluations. Moreover, the block-search algorithm can be generalised to include candidate variables such as standard economic variables, and not just impulse indicators. Purely contracting searches are not always possible, but the principle of examining many large blocks remains. Blocks help avoid inadvertently eliminating variables that are correlated with already selected variables, and blocks help detect effects that are camouflaged by breaks.

Block searches allow selecting jointly across lag length, functional form, relevant variables, and breaks, even when doing so implies that the number of candidate variables is greater than the number of observations. Such block searches can still be implemented, so long as the number of variables in each block is smaller than the sample size. Block searches can be iterated—and with changing composition—to allow many alternatives to be considered. Under the null, estimates of the parameters of interest are still relatively efficient. Under the alternative, it is particularly important to consider all of these complications jointly because they are likely to be connected. As with cointegration, proofs of distributional results involve additional mathematics, such as an iterated one-step approximation to the Huber-skip estimator; see Johansen and Nielsen (2013, 2016).

Other procedures tend to address just one or a few issues, rather than all of them at once. Nonparametric statistics can determine functional form but, in so doing, assume constant parameters, accurate measurements, and inclusion of all relevant variables. Robust statistics can tackle contaminated data but assume an otherwise correct specification. Step-wise regression and Lasso may easily detect a single omitted variable but can fail badly under multiple misspecifications. Those techniques lack a mechanism that ensures capturing all relevant outliers and breaks. The block-search approach aims at considering all complications together. As Hendry and Johansen (2015) show, it can do so without distorting the distribution of the parameter estimates of a correct theory-specified model. In yet another moment of serendipity, David and Søren discovered this result while trying to prove something else.

Hendry and Doornik (2014) thus integrate the computer-automated model selection approach launched by Hoover and Perez (1999) and the IIS technique formulated in Hendry (1999), enhancing and generalising both. Hendry and Doornik (2014) document that automated approaches such as Autometrics avoid the pernicious properties of many earlier approaches, which employed poor algorithms and inappropriate criteria for model selection and evaluation. Whether starting from a large model that nests the DGP or from a model that is the DGP itself, model search à l'Autometrics retains roughly the same relevant variables, and it obtains a controlled average number of irrelevant variables. Hendry (2015) and Castle and Hendry (2019) show at an intuitive level how these tools are accessible for empirical macroeconometric modelling of economic time series, illustrating with equations for wages, prices, unemployment, and money demand in the UK.

3   Econometrics Software

Operational econometric methods require computer software. David recognised this early on when writing his PhD thesis, so he wrote code in Fortran for the techniques that he was developing. David parlayed that code into a suite of mainframe software programs called AUTOREG, the most prominent being the single-equation package GIVE (for "Generalized Instrumental Variables Estimation"). GIVE served as a precursor to David's PC-based program PcGive. The programs in AUTOREG lay the framework for David and Jurgen Doornik's current software package OxMetrics, which includes PcGive. This section discusses how David's development of econometric software parallels and embodies his and others' innovations in econometric methodology, facilitated by extensive collaboration and by improvements in computing technology. Hendry and Doornik (1999) provide a brief history.

David had three reasons for developing econometrics software: to facilitate his own research, seeing as many techniques were not available in other packages; to ensure that other researchers did not have the excuse of unavailability; and for teaching. Early versions of GIVE demonstrated the computability of FIML for systems with high-order vector autoregressive errors and latent-variable structures. At LSE, David and his research officer Frank Srba expanded David's initial version of AUTOREG to include new techniques, especially a rapidly expanding battery of model diagnostic (misspecification) tests.

David saw diagnostic testing as a key aspect of empirical model building, functioning in much the same way that a medical doctor would run examinations and tests on patients to diagnose what was troubling them. Tests for predictive failure—along with numerous other diagnostics being developed at the time—were promptly implemented in AUTOREG; see Hendry and Srba (1977, 1980). At the time, few empirical economic models were subjected to much diagnostic scrutiny: it was typical to report just an R^2 and the Durbin–Watson statistic. In seminars and workshops, and in meetings at HM Treasury, the Bank of England, and elsewhere, David would question these untested assumptions in other authors' empirical models and volunteer to check out their models in GIVE, which quickly became known as Hendry's "model destruction program" (in the words of Meghnad Desai).

Shortly after moving to Oxford, David ported the mainframe program GIVE to a PC-based "PcGive", a menu-driven version initially on an IBM PC 8088 using a rudimentary MS-DOS Fortran compiler; see Hendry (1986c, 1987b). That conversion took about four years, with his research officer Adrian Neale writing graphics in Assembler. One immediate benefit was a practical, graphical implementation of recursive estimation and testing procedures—a major leap forward for analysing parameter constancy.

Jurgen Doornik then translated PcGive to C++ and implemented it as a Windows-based package with a front end (GiveWin), modules for single-equation and system estimation and testing (PcGive and PcFiml), Monte Carlo simulation (PcNaive), and specialised modules for modelling volatility, discrete choice, panels, ARFIMA, and X12ARIMA; see Doornik and Hendry (2001). Jurgen subsequently converted PcGive to his Ox language, enabling further additions by anyone writing Ox packages; see Doornik (2001).

Motivated by Hoover and Perez's (1999) results on computer-automated model selection, David and Hans-Martin Krolzig designed the PcGive-based econometrics software package PcGets, expanding on Hoover and Perez's tools for model selection; see Hendry and Krolzig (2001). PcGets's simulation properties confirmed many of the earlier methodological claims about general-to-specific modelling; and, through machine learning, PcGets provided significant time-savings to the researcher, especially for large problems; see Hendry and Krolzig (1999, 2005). David and Jurgen then embedded and enhanced PcGets's modelling approach in PcGive as the routine Autometrics; see Doornik and Hendry (2007) and Doornik (2008, 2009). Improvements to PcGive and the suite of OxMetrics packages continue unabated, as the most recent release in Doornik and Hendry (2018) testifies. The software manuals are substantial works in themselves, providing extensive discussion of the econometric and methodological underpinnings to the software's implementation.

PcGive embodies several important features for David, and for modellers generally. First, the software is flexible and accurate, with the latter checked by standard examples and by Monte Carlo. Second, it has rapidly incorporated new tests and estimators—sometimes before they appeared in print. Examples include Sargan's common-factor test, the system-based tests of parameter constancy from Hendry (1974) and Kiviet (1986) and their recursive equivalents, the Johansen (1988) reduced-rank cointegration procedure, general-to-specific model selection, and IIS and its generalisations. Notably, other commercially available software packages are only starting to implement IIS, in spite of its power for detecting breaks and outliers. Third, while OxMetrics is interactive, it also generates editable batch code of user sessions, helping replication and collaboration—and combining the best of both batch and interactive worlds.

Empirical modelling still requires the economist's value added, especially through the choice of variables and the representation of the unrestricted model. The machine-learning algorithm Autometrics confirms the advantages of good economic analysis through excluding irrelevant effects and (especially) through including relevant ones. Excessive pre-simplification, as might be suggested by some economic theories, can lead to a badly misspecified general specification with no good model choice from simplification. Fortunately, little power is lost from some overspecification with orthogonal regressors, and the empirical size remains close to the nominal one.

For David, automatic model selection is a new and powerful instrument for the social sciences, akin to the introduction of the microscope in the biological sciences. Already, PcGets and Autometrics have demonstrated remarkable performance across different (unknown) states of nature, with Monte Carlo data generating processes being found almost as often by commencing from a general model as from the DGP itself. Retention of relevant variables is close to the theoretical maximum, and elimination of irrelevant variables occurs at the rate set by the chosen significance level. The selected estimates have the appropriate reported standard errors, and they can be bias-corrected if desired, which also down-weights adventitiously significant coefficients. These results essentially resuscitate traditional econometrics, despite data-based selection. Peter Phillips (1996) has made great strides in the automation of model selection using a related approach; see also Haldrup, Hendry and van Dijk (2003).

4   Forecasting

A forecast is any statement about the future. Such statements may be well founded, or lack any sound basis; they may be accurate or inaccurate on any given occasion, or on average; precise or imprecise; and model-based or informal ... Since [a forecast] is merely a statement about the future, anything can be forecast ... (Clements and Hendry 2002b: 2).

This quote from the introduction to David and Mike Clements' 2002 book *A Companion to Economic Forecasting* emphasises just how widespread forecasts are—whether as ex ante or ex post forecasts, or as "projections", alternative simulations, or policy scenarios. As such, forecasts play key roles in economic decision-making by consumers, by firms, and by governments. David's own involvement in economic forecasting evolved from making forecasts (Section 4.1) through an understanding of the nature of forecasts (Section 4.2) to designing ways in which forecasts can be improved (Section 4.3).

4.1   Making Forecasts

David has made economic forecasts throughout his professional career. His early experiences in forecast failure motivated him to examine the roles of forecasts in economics, and thence to understand forecasts qua forecasts and seek out how to improve them.

David first became interested in forecasting in 1964 as an undergraduate at the University of Aberdeen. He was very much influenced by the empirical economic models of Klein (1950) and Tinbergen (1951), who had suggested the feasibility of forecasting future outcomes. In his undergraduate thesis, David estimated a regression model for annual UK consumers' expenditure given current income and lagged expenditure—painstakingly worked out on a mechanical calculator. Using the whole-sample parameter estimates, he calculated a "forecast" of the last observation to see how close it was to the outcome—in effect, evaluating the last residual of his estimation period. The forecast and the outcome were reasonably close, but unsurprisingly so because the observation that was forecast was in the estimation sample, and hence the corresponding forecast error was included in the sum of squared residuals that least-square estimation minimised.

A few years later, when writing his PhD thesis under Denis Sargan at LSE, David developed a small macro-model of the UK economy that included an equation for consumers' expenditure. David's forecasts from that model did not fare well. In late 1967, he calculated ex ante forecasts of consumers' expenditure for the next two quarters: 1968Q1 and 1968Q2. When actual expenditure was later reported by the Central Statistical Office, David's model had massive forecast failure and, in his own words, it took him years to understand why such forecast failure is commonplace.

That particular forecast failure arose from a change in economic policy. During 1968Q1, the Chancellor of the Exchequer (i.e. the UK finance minister) threatened to increase Purchase Tax—essentially, a sales tax—if consumers did not "behave themselves" and spend less. Consumers responded by spending more, especially on durable goods. So, in the next quarter, the Chancellor duly increased Purchase Tax, and consumers' expenditure fell. David's model did not account for the Chancellor's policy threat, the policy's implementation, or consumers' responses to both. Consequently, the model's forecasts failed badly. Forecast failure notwithstanding, David's model was subsequently published in Hendry (1974), which included a new test for predictive failure that generalised Chow's (1960) single-equation predictive failure test to systems, albeit in a χ^2 version rather than the F version that Kiviet (1986) later developed.

Other economists were also evaluating forecasts from macro-models, and their contributions stimulated David's own thinking on the topic. Charles Nelson in particular wrote two influential papers on ex ante forecasts: Nelson (1972) and Cooper and Nelson (1975). Using methods proposed by Box and Jenkins (1970), Nelson and Cooper showed that forecasts from univariate time-series models could beat forecasts from large empirical economic models such as the FRB–MIT–PENN model. From an LSE perspective, such large models treated dynamics inadequately, often simply as autocorrelated errors in static equations. David suspected that, in a trade-off between misspecified dynamics and omitted economics, models that included only dynamics could forecast better. Empirically, David found that simple dynamic models did indeed forecast better than static economic models, even though the latter embedded economic theory whereas the former did not.

This debate on forecast performance motivated David to investigate the nature of predictive failure. Why did models built from even the best available economics using the latest econometrics and fairly good data not produce useful forecasts? In Hendry (1979), David attributed ex post predictive failure to model misspecification. Chong and Hendry (1986) then developed forecast-encompassing statistics, a technique for comparing different models' forecasts. This approach is feasible even if the models themselves are unavailable, as is common with proprietary models and for judgmentally based forecasts. Hendry (1986d) looked at forecasting from dynamic systems, mainly to improve the power to test models.

The forecast failures documented in Hendry (1974, 1979) and elsewhere actually signalled a different source of forecasting problems with econometric models: unanticipated changes in the DGP. Those forecast failures also suggested that it was possible to develop a general theory of economic forecasting in which the forecasting model was misspecified for a DGP that itself was nonconstant over time. These realisations came after a long hiatus, and they lead to the next section.

4.2   Understanding Forecasts

Until the early 1990s, David had viewed forecasting as an activity subsumed by model design. That perspective arose naturally from the taxonomy of information for empirical model evaluation and design in Hendry and Richard (1982), and from the framework for exogeneity in Engle, Hendry and Richard (1983). While these developments were central to improvements in empirical modelling, they did hamper David's understanding of forecasting as a separate discipline in its own right. Moreover, the ubiquity of predictive failure was discouraging.

Policy rekindled David's interest in forecasting and led to major breakthroughs in the understanding of forecasts—particularly through the development of a taxonomy for the sources of forecast error. The catalyst was the 1991 enquiry by the UK Parliament's Treasury and Civil Service Committee into "Official Economic Forecasting"; see the Treasury and Civil Service Committee (1991a, b). As a backdrop to the enquiry, forecasts by HM Treasury missed the 1987 boom in the UK economy and subsequently missed the sharp economic downturn in 1989, with the resulting policy mistakes combining to induce high inflation and high unemployment.

Evidence submitted to the parliamentary Committee included many forecasts from many forecasters and dozens of ex post forecast evaluations that tried to sort out why forecasts had gone wrong. Forecasts from different models frequently conflicted, and the underlying models often suffered forecast failure. As Makridakis and Hibon (2000) and Clements and Hendry (2001) later argued, those realities could not be explained within the standard paradigm that forecasts were the conditional expectations of the variables being forecast. Empirics dominated theory in the enquiry. In fact, there was almost no theory of economic forecasting presented. At the time, most theories of forecasting were from the physical and statistical sciences. Those theories typically assumed data ergodicity and so were not necessarily relevant to economic forecasting, where intermittent structural breaks are a key data feature.

David submitted evidence on economic forecasting to the parliamentary Committee. Preparation of his report—detailed in Hendry (1991) and to be published in Ericsson (2021)—led to a broader understanding of the subject. David subsequently produced a torrent of insightful evaluations of many existing forecast techniques, including error correction models and cointegration, mean square forecast errors, add factors, leading indicators, pooling of forecasts, multi-step estimation for forecasting, and forecast competitions; see Clements and Hendry (1998b, 1999a) in particular. David also developed a theory of forecasting, which included a taxonomy of forecast errors (initially sketched out in Hendry (1991)) and a theory of unpredictability with implications for parsimony, congruence, and aggregation; see Clements and Hendry (2005a, b), Hendry and Mizon (2014), and Hendry and Hubrich (2011). From that theory of forecasting, David was able to develop and refine tools such as intercept correction, robustification, and nowcasting to improve forecasts themselves; see Section 4.3.

David's renewed interest in forecasting resulted in a remarkable and continuing collaboration with his then DPhil student Mike Clements. Motivated by the encouraging developments in Hendry (1991), David and Mike sought to develop analytical foundations for understanding ex ante forecast failure when the economy is subject to structural breaks, and the forecasts are from misspecified and inconsistently estimated models that are based on incorrect economic theories and selected from inaccurate data. Everything was allowed to be wrong, but the investigator did not know that.

Despite the generality of this framework, David and Mike derived many interesting results about economic forecasting, as shown in Clements and Hendry (1993) and Hendry and Clements (1994a, b). The theory's empirical content matched the historical record, and it suggested how to improve forecasting methods. Estimation per se was not a key issue. The two important features in their framework were allowing for misspecified models and incorporating structural change in the DGP. With that combination, causal variables need not beat non-causal variables at forecasting. In particular, extrapolative methods could win at forecasting, as shown in Clements and Hendry (1999b).

The implications are fundamental. Ex ante forecast failure should not be used to reject models. A model well-specified in-sample could forecast poorly—and worse than an extrapolative procedure—so the debate between Box–Jenkins models and econometric models needed reinterpretation.

In this context, Clements and Hendry (1998a) brought to the fore the difference between equilibrium correction and error correction. The first induces cointegration, whereas in the latter the model adjusts to eliminate forecast errors. A cointegrated system—which has equilibrium correction—will fore-cast systematically badly when its equilibrium mean shifts, with the cointe-grated system continuing to converge back to the old equilibrium. By contrast, devices such as random walks and exponentially weighted moving averages embody error correction. While an error correction model will temporarily misforecast when an equilibrium mean shifts, it will then adjust relative to the new equilibrium mean. Mike and David's insight explained why the Treasury's cointegrated system had performed so badly in the mid-1980s, following the sharp reduction in UK credit rationing. It also helped Clements and Hendry (1996a) demonstrate the advantageous property of intercept corrections to offset such shifts. Hendry and Ericsson (2001) and Castle, Clements and Hendry (2019) offer highly intuitive nontechnical introductions to forecast-ing and their uses, challenges, and benefits. Clements and Hendry (2002a) give a compendium.

David's initial collaborations with Mike Clements, however, examined mean square forecast errors (MSFEs), a standard tool for comparing forecasts from different models. Clements and Hendry (1993, 1995) questioned their value and generated considerable controversy—the discussants' published comments on Clements and Hendry (1993) are longer than the paper itself. Cointegration was the origin of these two papers.

At its inception in the early 1980s, cointegration had demonstrated many real advantages—in modelling, in economic understanding, and in interpre-tation. Engle and Yoo (1987) then discovered that imposing cointegration significantly improved forecasts in terms of MSFEs. This result seemed to show yet additional value from cointegration—in forecasting. Clements and Hendry (1995) replicated Engle and Yoo's Monte Carlo experiments and found that, to the contrary, imposing cointegration did not appear to reduce MSFEs. This discrepancy in results arose because Engle and Yoo (1987) had calculated MSFEs for the variables' levels whereas Clements and Hendry (1995) had calculated MSFEs for the cointegrating combination. Inadvertently, Clements and Hendry (1995) had discovered that data transformations affected MSFEs. Additionally, rankings across models often depended more on the choice of data transformation, and less on whether or not cointegra-tion was imposed, or even whether the model included the equilibrium cor-rection term.

Clements and Hendry (1993) formalised algebraically these properties of MSFEs. The ranking of different models' forecasts could alter, depending upon whether and how the variables being forecast were transformed. Ericsson (2008) illustrated this problem by comparing forecasts in levels and forecasts in differences for two models of crude oil spot prices. For forecasts of the level of oil prices, the MSFE for the first model was more than four times that for the second model. However, for forecasts of the change of oil prices, the MSFE for the first model was less than half that for the second model. Thus, a simple transformation of the variable being forecast altered the MSFE ranking of the models, with no change to the models, to the forecasts, or to the underlying data. Furthermore, the oil price example illustrated that, for a given model, the MSFE was not invariant to the transformation from levels to differences. Clements and Hendry (1993) showed that MSFEs lack robustness when the data are transformed, when forecasts are multivariate, and when forecasts are multi-step ahead. All three situations are common in economics.

Clements and Hendry (1993) also showed that useful comparison of MSFEs required highly restrictive assumptions about the forecasts—namely, that the forecasts must be of a single specific variable just one step ahead. Data transformations, multivariate forecasts, and multi-step-ahead forecasts are all outside that limited structure because they imply a vector of forecasts. Clements and Hendry (1993) discussed how the predictive likelihood generalises the MSFE for a vector of forecasts. Moreover, predictive likelihood is the only direction-invariant measure, as it does not depend on nonsingular linear scale-preserving transformations of the system. Even so, predictive likelihood has not been used much for forecast evaluation. Wallis (1993) pioneered its use, but its practical implementation was hindered because its calculation seemed to require having sufficient observations on all the multi-step-ahead forecast errors in order to estimate their variance–covariance matrix. Results in Abadir, Distaso and Žikeš (2014) encouraged David to revisit predictive likelihood in Hendry and Martinez (2017), where they show that one can evaluate multi-step-ahead system forecasts with relatively few forecast errors. Explicit loss functions also have come back into favour, as in Granger (2001) and Barendse and Patton (2019).

Because MSFEs are widely used for comparing forecasts, David and Mike became interested in the forecasting competitions organised by Spyros Makridakis, which at that time was the M3 competition, hosted by the *International Journal of Forecasting*. Many different time series were divided into subperiods, each of which was then forecast by many methods, albeit usually only one step ahead. Various evaluation criteria were applied to each forecasting device on each dataset to find which methods had the best ex post forecast performance as measured by the chosen criteria. Those methods with the best forecast performance then "won" the competition. Because parsimonious methods such as damped trend often did well, whereas less parsimonious methods such as econometric models often did poorly, Makridakis and Hibon (2000) concluded that parsimony was key to good forecast performance.

David could not understand why parsimony per se should make models do so well at forecasting. After all, the sample mean of a variable's level is parsimonious, but it is often a dreadful forecast of the variable's future values. To understand the empirical results in the M3 competition and, more generally, to help interpret the problems that arise in economic forecasting, David and Mike developed a general analytical framework that describes a taxonomy for forecast errors. Initially, David and Mike solved the taxonomy for vector autoregressive models and simple time-series models. More recently, David has considered open dynamic simultaneous systems and nonlinear formulations.

The taxonomy delineates all possible sources of forecast error—nine sources in total. These sources derive from the three components of a model:

(1) Unobserved terms,
(2) Observed stochastic variables, and
(3) Deterministic terms.

The first component is what the model fails to explain, and it thus includes mismeasurement of the data at the forecast origin, omitted variables, and the innovation errors in the DGP. The second and third components characterise what is modelled, and they often correspond to the slope parameter and the equilibrium mean. Each of the model's three components is itself subject to three potential problems:

(a) Estimation uncertainty,
(b) Misspecification, and
(c) Change in the DGP's parameter values,

leading to a 3×3 array of possibilities and implying nine sources of forecast error.

The taxonomy has immediate implications: the consequences of forecast error depend on the sources of forecast error, and the taxonomy allows deriving the effects of each source for a given forecasting device. For instance, the combination (3)+(c) is an out-of-sample structural break involving deterministic terms, as with a change in the equilibrium mean. For equilibrium correction models, that particular combination results in systematic misforecasting. That problem is fundamental, pernicious, and common in economic forecasting. Such predictive failure due to a location shift is easily detected because it induces forecast bias and increases the MSFE, noting that the MSFE includes the squared shift in the mean. Other sources of forecast error can deteriorate forecast performance as well, but they are often harder to detect and with more benign effects. If forecast errors arise from multiple sources, interactions between sources may also matter.

More generally, the taxonomy reveals which sources of forecast error most affect each forecasting method, thus clarifying why some methods outperform or underperform others, and when. For intermittent location shifts, all methods misforecast at the break. However, after the breakpoint, methods that are not robust to such breaks tend to make systematic forecast errors, whereas robust methods get the forecasts back on track; see Hendry and Doornik (1997).

The taxonomy also shows that rankings of forecasts should not depend particularly on the number of parameters in either the model or the DGP, whereas the rankings do depend on the robustness of the forecasting devices to structural breaks. The design of forecast competitions such as M3 happened to favour robust devices by having many short forecasting subperiods with intermittent location shifts in the data, thus giving the impression that parsimony per se was advantageous in forecasting. Clements and Hendry (2001) showed that many of the key empirical results in the M3 competition were derivable from the taxonomy of forecast errors. Clements and Hendry (1994, 1998b, 1999a, 2006) give comprehensive derivations and analyses of the taxonomy.

One major insight about forecasting came during a seminar in which David was explaining a very early version of the taxonomy. David noticed that the change in the slope coefficient [(2)+(c) above] was multiplied by the deviation of the data at the forecast origin from the data's equilibrium mean. Consequently, if forecasting happened to start when the data were in equilibrium, changes in the slope parameter would not affect the forecast errors. Indeed, if the mean of the data stayed constant and the forecast origin were accurately measured, forecasts would not be systematically biased—even if all the other problems were present. Conversely, out-of-sample location shifts would systematically bias the forecasts, even if the forecast model were the in-sample DGP itself. That realisation in the middle of the seminar astonished David as much as the seminar participants!

Hendry and Mizon (2000a, b) found additional implications of the taxonomy: the best explanatory model need not be the best for forecasting, and the best policy model could conceivably be different from both. Some structural breaks—such as shifts in equilibrium means—are inimical to forecasts from econometric models but not from robust forecasting devices, which themselves may well not explain behaviour. However, such shifts need not affect the relevant policy derivatives. For example, the effect of interest rates on consumers' expenditure could be constant, despite a shift in the target level of savings due to (say) changed government provisions for health care in old age. After the shift, altering the interest rate still could have the expected policy effect, even though the econometric model misforecasted. Because econometric models can be robustified against such forecast failures, it may prove possible to use the same baseline causal econometric model for forecasting and for policy.

This analytical framework represents considerable progress in developing a general theory of forecasting. It does not assume how the model is estimated, how badly misspecified it is, or what changes occur in the economy. Many aspects still need more research, though, including how to forecast breaks, how to best select forecasting models for realistic economic processes, and how to improve forecasts—the next topic.

4.3   Improving Forecasts

The taxonomy clarified the sources of predictive failure. The taxonomy also led to and formalised new techniques that robustify forecasts after structural breaks and that augment robust devices with information from economic models. Robustification led to research on nowcasting and, from a completely different route, impulse indicator saturation. Hendry (2006) develops and systematises robustification methods, which include intercept correction, pooling, leading indicators, and differencing. These four tools and nowcasting serve as foci for discussing David's contributions to improving forecasts.

Intercept Correction: In addition to investigating the many aspects of forecasting discussed in Section 4.2, David and Mike Clements re-examined the ubiquitous forecast tool known as "add factors". Add factors are now interpretable as a form of intercept correction and hence are a potentially useful method for robustifying forecasts against the effects of structural breaks. This interpretation contrasts with David's earlier harsh views on add factors, as one example illustrates. Peter Hooper was presenting forecast results on the Fed's Multi-country Model at a Fed workshop in 1985, and David was highly critical of Peter's adjustment of the forecasts with add factors. At the time, David remarked: 'Why adjust forecasts if the model is good?'. David's views on add factors have evolved enormously since then.

Some history helps put that evolution in perspective. Klein (1971) discussed *that* add factors might improve economic forecasting, but he gave no theory explaining *why* they might do so. There was no such theory at the time.

Much later, David and Mike Clements realised that some types of add factors might mitigate forecast failure that was caused by location shifts at the start of the forecast period. Clements and Hendry (1996a) showed analytically and in practice how intercept correction could improve forecasts in the face of location shifts. Intercept correction differences the forecast error that would have occurred otherwise and thereby removes the original forecast error's systematic component. Consequently, intercept correction is a valuable tool in the face of location shifts.

Pooling: Combining or "pooling" forecasts provides another tool for robustifying forecasts. Bates and Granger (1969) proposed combining forecasts as a mechanism for improving forecast performance. Chong and Hendry (1986) later showed that pooling is unnecessary under the null of forecast encompassing but could improve forecasting when (e.g.) neither of two forecasts forecast-encompassed the other forecast. Bates and Granger provided the intuition: in that situation, each forecast model has information that the other model does not. Pooling combines the information in the models' forecasts. Bates and Granger did not address the question of whether pooling forecasts was better than utilising the information from both models in a nesting model and generating forecasts from that model. Hendry and Clements (2004) showed that there was not a unique answer. It can pay to pool forecasts in some situations and not in others.

Pooling is often viewed as being benign at worst, serving as insurance against bad forecasts by averaging across a range of forecasts. It does carry an important caveat, though: a single poor forecast can ruin the average. Imagine having a set of good models, along with one poisonous model. Averaging the forecast of the poisonous model with those of the good models can poison the pooled forecast. If the poisonous models are eliminated—through model selection, say—then averaging over the forecasts from just the remaining models may reduce the risk a little; see Hendry and Doornik (2014: 286).

In the literature, model averaging is often over all possible models that arise by either including or excluding the variables from a given set of explanatory variables. Most of those models are "poisonous" because they are distorted by omitted variables, unmodelled nonlinearities, intermittent location shifts, etc. One has to be careful which forecasts one averages across, and how that averaging is carried out. In their submission to the recent M4 forecast competition, Doornik, Castle and Hendry (2020a) designed pooled forecasts with computer-automated model selection, aiming to embody key features learned from the taxonomy.

Forecasts from different models may also be of value in themselves. Divergence of different models' forecasts can indicate breaks that are occurring and hence can serve as "canaries in a coal mine". The Bank of England has used a suite of models in this manner, as Hatch (2001) discusses in Hendry and Ericsson (2001). When models are sufficiently different, they need not all be affected in the same way by a major unanticipated shift. Including robust forecasting devices in the suite of models can help, too. Robust devices are not affected systematically once the breakpoint is past, although they will still misforecast as the break hits.

Leading Indicators: Leading indicators are yet another tool aimed at improving forecasts. Emerson and Hendry (1996) found that the variables selected as leading indicators changed all too often, suggesting that they did not lead for very long. Also, picking leading indicators by maximum in-sample correlation was unreliable. Emerson and Hendry concluded that using only leading indicators for economic forecasting was not a fruitful route to pursue.

That said, leading indicators could have some role in forecasting. For instance, a cointegrated system can be written as a set of differenced variables that are explained by lagged cointegrating combinations and lagged differenced variables. That system is interpretable as a system of leading indicators because its endogenous variables depend on past outcomes. Also, higher frequency information may improve forecasting performance, with that information acting as a leading indicator. Moreover, leading indicators may help predict turning points and breaks, as in Birchenhall, Jessen, Osborn and Simpson (1999).

Differencing: Hendry (2006) shows that predictive failure is an inherent issue for econometric models and that differencing is a natural solution for robustifying those models' forecasts. To put differencing in context, Hendry notes that virtually all standard economic models are equilibrium correction models, including dynamic stochastic general equilibrium (DSGE) models, New Keynesian Phillips Curve models, structural vector autoregressions, and so-called error correction models. When the equilibrium mean alters, the model's equilibrium correction term pushes the model's forecasts back towards the old equilibrium—not the new one—inducing the sort of systematic predictive failure that is often seen in practice. Intercept correction—and hence differencing—can robustify the forecast of an equilibrium correction model because it serves as a good proxy for such shifts in the equilibrium. Hendry (2006) formalises this. Castle, Clements and Hendry (2013, 2015) illustrate it empirically with an assessment of robustified US GDP forecasts.

The taxonomy of forecast errors also provides insights on why differencing a model robustifies the model's forecasts. From the taxonomy, few things can go wrong in forecasting a variable if the forecasting model for the second difference of that variable has no parameters and no deterministic terms, thereby eliminating the sources of forecast error in (3) and (a) above. If the data do not accelerate, the second difference of the variable being forecast has a mean of zero, implying that the first difference of the current-dated variable (or the current growth rate) is an unconditionally unbiased forecast for its future value. Because that current growth rate is the current value and not the future one, such a "forecast" device never really forecasts. However, the current growth rate will be close to the future growth rate in the absence of acceleration.

The first difference of the dependent variable has another interpretation as well: it is a single measure that aggregates almost all the information needed in forecasting its future value. The explanation requires a slight digression. In David's view, economists build congruent, encompassing, cointegrated models to test theories, understand the economy, and conduct policy analysis. These models also need to account for breaks and other non-stationarities. For forecasting, though, these models can be differenced to eliminate deterministic terms such as intercepts and location shifts. Doing so introduces the current growth rate in the model for forecasting the future growth rate, and the current growth rate depends on the cointegrating relationship as a feedback term. This new system thus retains the economics and the policy-relevant causal information that underlie the original model. Also, differencing the model introduces the first difference of the model's other economic variables.

Moreover, because the current growth rate itself is generated by the DGP, it necessarily includes relevant variables for forecasting the future growth rate. By contrast, a model of the current growth rate is a simplification of the DGP and need not include the relevant variables that determine the current growth rate. When forecasting, there is also no need to disentangle the DGP's individual components that enter the current growth rate—unlike when modelling or for policy analysis. The data themselves provide the basis for forecasting. As a practical implication, differencing creates a system that is robust after location shifts because the current growth rate includes all stochastic and deterministic shifts, and also any variables omitted from the forecast model. Moreover, use of the current growth rate to forecast the future growth rate obviates the need to estimate model parameters.

Hendry (2006) derives yet another, related interpretation of the current growth rate, as arises from the standard representation of the vector equilibrium correction model (VEqCM). In the simplest VEqCM, the future growth rate of the dependent variable is forecast by its mean growth rate (the VEqCM's intercept) and the current disequilibrium (the deviation of the cointegration vector from the equilibrium mean). Both the mean growth rate and the current disequilibrium employ full-sample estimates of the model's parameters. In the differenced VEqCM (or DVEqCM), however, the mean growth rate is estimated by the current growth rate, and the disequilibrium is estimated by the deviation in the cointegrating relation from its previous value. Both terms in the DVEqCM are estimates that use only current-dated observed growth rates, although the cointegrating coefficients themselves need to be estimated with a longer sample.

Forecasts from the VEqCM itself use fixed values of two key VEqCM components—the mean growth rate and the equilibrium mean—shifts in which can cause forecast failure. By contrast, forecasts from the DVEqCM use the current period's observations to estimate those key components and so may be more relevant for forecasting than using the full historical sample.

This approach generates a class of "data-based" forecasting devices that could utilise a single observation (as in the DVEqCM), a subset of observations (as in rolling regressions), or the full sample (as in the VEqCM); see Martinez, Castle and Hendry (2021). The choice of sample highlights a trade-off between precision in estimation and rapid adaptation. As harbingers to these developments in forecasting, Hendry and Ericsson (1991b) and Campos and Ericsson (1999) formulated such data-based predictors in empirical modelling. Other similar approaches, such as in Phillips (1995), adapt the forecasts to location shifts through automated variable reselection and parameter estimate updating. Eitrhein, Husebø and Nymoen (1999) empirically document implications of the taxonomy by comparing real-world forecasts from Norges Bank's macro-model RIMINI with forecasts from simple robust devices, finding that the latter often won at four quarters ahead but lost out at a longer forecast horizon; see also Bårdsen, Eitrheim, Jansen and Nymoen (2005).

Nowcasting: The taxonomy of forecast errors also has implications for nowcasting. David and Mike Clements started thinking about nowcasting in a more structured way when they were consulting for the UK Statistics Commission and evaluating how the UK's Office for National Statistics calculated its flash estimates of the national accounts; see Clements and Hendry (2003). Nowcasting can imply measurement errors of the forecast origin, that is, the combination (1)+(a) from Section 4.2. Sometimes, those errors are systematic and large, as with official economic statistics during the 2008 financial crisis and the more recent COVID-19 pandemic. Improved methods of nowcasting can help reduce real-time forecast problems that arise from mismeasuring the forecast origin.

Large data revisions during the financial crisis and COVID-19 pandemic are not surprising in light of the methods used to produce flash estimates. For example, in the USA and the UK, a flash (or "advance") estimate of quarterly GDP growth is released about a month after the quarter's end, and that flash estimate is derived in part from many disaggregate components. Observations on some disaggregate components become available too late for inclusion in the flash estimate, so those missing components are "infilled", based on interpolation models such as Holt–Winters (a form of exponential smoothing).

Such infilling can work reasonably well during times of steady and uniform growth across the economy. However, sudden changes in data behaviour—as occurred during the financial crisis—can make interpolation methods inappropriate. They led to flash estimates of aggregate economic growth that were systematically above the final data in the downturn and systematically below the data in the upturn—often by several percentage points per annum; see Ericsson (2017). In 2008, these mismeasurements made it difficult for policymakers to ascertain the timing and extent of the crisis, as Stekler and Symington (2016) and Ericsson (2016) discuss.

Systematic errors such as these have led to proposed improvements in nowcasting, as documented in Mazzi and Ladiray (2017). The taxonomy delineates what does and what does not cause forecast failure and so has direct implications for nowcasting; see Castle, Hendry and Kitov (2017). When a statistical agency estimates (say) GDP growth from a set of disaggregate components, the agency could check whether previous forecasts of those components are close to their now known outcomes. If they are not, a location shift may be responsible, so any missing disaggregates could be infilled, taking into account information about the recent break. Considerable contemporaneous information is available for nowcasting, including surveys, Google Trends, mobile phone data, prediction markets, and previous historically similar episodes. All could be used to improve the accuracy of forecast-origin estimates. Automatic model selection can help do so, as by building forecasting models of the disaggregated series. An alternative approach is to summarise the information from large numbers of variables by using principal components or factors: see Forni, Hallin, Lippi and Reichlin (2001), Artis, Banerjee and Marcellino (2005), Stock and Watson (2011), and Castle, Clements and Hendry (2013). Regardless, nowcasts that utilise such additional information could be created before the end of the reference period, thereby reducing the delay with which flash estimates appear.

The coronavirus pandemic poses a global challenge—medically, socially, politically, and economically. To better inform decision-making, Jennie Castle, Jurgen Doornik, and David Hendry have been generating short-term (one-week-ahead) forecasts for confirmed cases and deaths from COVID-19; see Castle, Doornik and Hendry (2020a) and Doornik, Castle and Hendry (2020b, 2021). Jennie, Jurgen, and David select their forecast models by Autometrics, incorporating generalisations of impulse indicator saturation. In addition, Castle, Doornik and Hendry (2020b) have been making medium-term (multi-week) forecasts from models utilising path indicator saturation (PathIS)—a new saturation technique that saturates across paths, similar to the designer breaks in Pretis, Schneider, Smerdon and Hendry (2016). Both the short-term and medium-term forecasts combine key elements of David's contributions outlined in Sections 2, 3 and 4, including model design through machine learning with diagnostic testing and saturation techniques, and forecast design through robustification in light of the forecast taxonomy. Notably, these forecasts perform well relative to some standard epidemiological models.

In retrospect, David's attitude towards economic forecasting—and the profession's attitude as well—has shifted significantly over the last three decades, and for the better. Many top econometricians are now involved in the theory of forecasting, including Frank Diebold, Hashem Pesaran, Peter Phillips, Lucrezia Reichlin, Jim Stock, Timo Teräsvirta, Ken Wallis, and Mark Watson. Their technical expertise as well as their practical forecasting experience is invaluable in furthering the field. As the taxonomy illustrated, mathematical treatment can help understand economic forecasts, with key developments summarised in the books by Hendry and Ericsson (2001), Clements and Hendry (2002a, 2011), and Elliott, Granger and Timmermann (2006).

5   Empirical Analysis

Empirical analysis often motivated David's new developments in econometric methodology, as when Ericsson, Hendry and Prestwich (1998) were modelling UK money demand on an extended dataset. That analysis led to a formal treatment of expansions of information sets, itself laying the groundwork for saturation techniques. Conversely, David would also almost immediately apply new methodological developments to ongoing empirical analyses, as when incorporating the Engle–Granger cointegration test into Hendry and Ericsson's (1983) empirical analysis of UK money demand. While David's empirical analyses cover many aspects of the economy for many countries and regions, five modelling endeavours stand out: housing and mortgage markets, consumers' expenditure, money demand, television advertising, and climate change. This section examines those endeavours.

5.1   Mortgage and Housing Markets

David's professional interest in UK housing and mortgage markets began in the early 1970s, when he and Gordon Anderson were modelling building societies—the British analogue of US savings and loans associations. Hendry and Anderson (1977) nested the long-run solutions of existing empirical equations, using a formulation related to Sargan (1964), although the link to Denis's work was only clarified much later in Anderson and Hendry (1984).

David's interest in the housing market arose from a forecasting puzzle. During 1972, UK house prices rose dramatically in response to a major increase in mortgage lending by building societies. David later checked how well his house-price model would have forecast through that period. When forecasting a few quarters after the then largest-ever increase in UK house prices, the model predicted a fall in prices, while prices actually continued to rise substantially. Nevertheless, coefficients estimated over the pre-forecast period were almost identical to those estimated over the whole sample, and the whole-sample residuals were homoscedastic, so there appeared to be little evidence of parameter nonconstancy.

David finally resolved this conundrum over a decade later, when he and Mike Clements were developing the general theory of forecasting. That theory distinguishes between "internal breaks" (shifts in the model's parameters) and "external breaks" (shifts in the unmodelled included variables). A change in multicollinearity among the model's variables leaves estimated coefficients almost unchanged but can greatly increase MSFEs, contrasting with the irrelevance of multicollinearity to forecast uncertainty when multicollinearity is constant. This problem with multicollinearity cannot be solved by orthogonalising the model's variables or by eliminating relevant multicollinear variables. The latter can lead to even worse forecasts. However, updating parameter estimates with new data can reduce MSFEs. For UK house prices, the correlations of mortgage lending with disposable income, interest rates, and inflation altered markedly when mortgage lending itself increased. Despite the accrual of more information from changes in multicollinearity, the MSFE also increased, in line with the general theory of forecasting.

Model nonlinearities proved central to explaining house-price bubbles. Through David's interest in the natural sciences, he had learned that Van der

Pol's cubic differential equation could describe heartbeats and that heartbeats could manifest sudden surges. Changes in UK house prices seemed rather like heartbeats so, in his model, he included the cube of the excess demand for housing, as represented by the cube of lagged house-price inflation. As Hendry (1984a) showed, the cube was significant. The formulation had difficulties, though. It predicted some large jumps in house prices that did not materialise. Also, it implied that large changes in house prices were explosive. In practice, though, once the market was far from equilibrium, excessively high or low house-price-to-income ratios drove the market back towards equilibrium, as followed after the UK housing bubble in the late 1980s. Richard and Zhang (1996) improved on David's nonlinear formulation by using a cubic in the observed deviation from the long-run equilibrium rather than the cube of house-price inflation.

In related research, Ericsson and Hendry (1985) showed that the price of new housing piggybacked on the price of existing houses in an equilibrium correction framework that also accounted for construction costs, housing units still under construction, and the cost of financing. Hendry (1986c) modelled the construction sector, focusing on the determination of starts and completions of houses.

5.2   Consumers' Expenditure

In modelling UK consumers' expenditure, David adopted a modelling approach similar to that in Hendry and Anderson (1977) by seeking a consumption function that served to interpret the equations from the major UK macro-models and explain why their proprietors had picked their particular specifications. The resulting paper—Davidson, Hendry, Srba and Yeo (1978), often referred to as DHSY—has become one of David's most cited papers. DHSY adopted a "detective story" approach, using a nesting model for the different models' variables, valid for both seasonally adjusted and unadjusted data, and with up to five lags on all the variables to capture dynamics. Reformulation of that nesting model delivered an equation that Hendry and von Ungern-Sternberg (1981) later reinterpreted in light of Phillips (1954, 1957) and called an error correction model. Under error correction, if consumers made an error relative to their plan by overspending in a given quarter, they would later correct that error.

Some historical background helps illuminate DHSY's approach. David first had access to computer graphics in the early 1970s, and he was astonished by the graphs of real UK consumers' expenditure and income. Expenditure manifested vast seasonality, with double-digit percentage changes between quarters, whereas income had virtually no seasonality. Those seasonal patterns meant that expenditure was much more volatile than income on a quarter-to-quarter basis. Two implications followed. First, it would not work to fit a model with first-order lags (as David had done in Hendry (1974)) and hope that seasonal dummies plus the slight seasonality in income would explain the seasonality in expenditure. Second, the general class of consumption-smoothing theories such as the permanent-income and life-cycle hypotheses seemed misfocused. Consumers were inducing volatility into the economy by large inter-quarter shifts in their expenditure, so the business sector must be a stabilising influence. Moreover, as discussed in Section 4.1, the equation for consumers' expenditure in Hendry (1974) had dramatically misforecast the first two quarters of 1968, suggesting the need for respecification.

In developing their own model, DHSY examined several ingredients that were necessary to explain other modellers' model selections: their modelling approaches, data measurements, seasonal adjustment procedures, choice of estimators, maximum lag lengths, and misspecification tests. DHSY first standardised on unadjusted data and replicated models on that. While seasonal filters leave a model invariant when the model is known, they can distort the lag patterns if the model is data-based. DHSY then investigated both least squares and instrumental variables estimation but found little difference. Few of the then reported evaluation statistics were valid for dynamic models, so such tests could mislead. Most extant models had a maximum lag of one, and they had short-run marginal propensities to consume that seemed too small to reflect agent behaviour. DHSY tried many blind alleys (including measurement errors) to explain these low marginal propensities to consume. DHSY then showed that equilibrium correction explained the low marginal propensities to consume by the induced biases in partial adjustment models. DHSY designed a nesting model, which explained all the previous findings, but with the puzzle that it simplified to a differenced specification, with no long-run term in the levels of the variables. Resolving that conundrum led to the equilibrium correction mechanism. DHSY's "Sherlock Holmes" approach was extremely time-consuming and was rarely repeated subsequently; but it did stimulate research into encompassing, that is, trying to explain other models' results from a given model's perspective.

Even with DHSY's wide-ranging and highly systematic modelling approach, a significant model reformulation occurred just before publication. An earlier version of DHSY's model explained real consumers' expenditure given real income, and that model significantly over-predicted expenditure through the 1973–1974 oil crisis. Angus Deaton (1977) had just established a role for inflation in a consumption function if agents were uncertain as to whether relative prices or absolute prices were changing. Deaton's formulation suggested adding inflation and its lags to that earlier DHSY specification. Doing so explained the over-prediction. This result was the opposite to what some other economic theories suggested—namely, that high inflation should induce pre-emptive spending because inflation is an opportunity cost of holding money. Inflation did not reflect money illusion. Rather, it implied the erosion of the real value of liquid assets. Consumers did not treat the nominal component of after-tax interest as income, whereas the UK government's statistical office did, and so disposable income was being mismeasured. Adding inflation to DHSY's equation corrected that.

DHSY made enormous advances empirically and methodologically. However, it did miss some key issues, including the equivalence of equilibrium correction models and cointegration (discussed in Section 2.2); the implications of seasonality in the data for annual differences in the model; the role of liquid assets in determining consumers' expenditure; and the insights of Phillips (1954, 1957) on proportional, integral, and derivative control rules. Collaboration with Thomas von Ungern-Sternberg identified and sorted through the last three issues and resulted in Hendry and von Ungern-Sternberg (1981), or HUS.

In DHSY, the equilibrium correction term was the four-quarter lag of the log of the ratio of expenditure to income, and it was highly seasonal. However, seasonal dummy variables were insignificant if one used Scheffé's method. About a week after DHSY's publication, Thomas von Ungern-Sternberg added seasonal dummies to that equation and, with conventional t-tests, found that they were highly significant. Care was clearly required with multiple-testing procedures. Those results on seasonality stimulated an industry on time-varying seasonal patterns, periodic seasonality, and periodic behaviour, with many contributions by Denise Osborn (1988, 1991).

Also, DHSY found that liquid assets were not significant in their model: that result arose from a subtle form of misspecification. HUS showed that, in an equilibrium correction formulation, imposing a long-run unit elasticity of expenditure with respect to income leaves no room for liquid assets. Methodologically speaking, DHSY were testing from simple to general, and not general enough. Once the long-run income elasticity was derestricted, liquid assets were significant in DHSY's equation. HUS interpreted the role of liquid assets as a Phillips-type integral correction mechanism. Moreover, the combined effect of liquid assets and real income on expenditure added up to unity in the long run.

After DHSY and HUS, David produced a whole series of papers on consumers' expenditure. Davidson and Hendry (1981) found that lagged variables, as derived from HUS, were significant in explaining current changes in UK consumers' expenditure. HUS's model thus encompassed the Euler-equation approach in Hall (1978). Subsequent papers by David checked the constancy of the models and extended them. Hendry (1983) modelled annual inter-war UK consumers' expenditure, obtaining results similar to the post-war quarterly relations in DHSY and HUS, despite large changes in the correlation structure of the data. Mizon and Hendry (1980) and Hendry (1992a) developed models of consumers' expenditure in Canada and France respectively; Hendry (1999) modelled inter-war and post-war US food expenditure; and Hendry (1994) revisited HUS with yet additional data. Hendry, Muellbauer and Murphy (1990) re-examined DHSY on an extended information set, finding that additional variables mattered—a result consistent with econometric theory in Sargan (1975) and White (1990). With an increasing sample size or information set, noncentral t-statistics become more significant, so models expand. These results also highlighted some of the challenges of empirical work. General-to-specific methodology provides guidelines for building encompassing models, but advances between studies are frequently simple-to-general, putting a premium on creative thinking.

5.3   Money Demand

David has analysed money demand in many contexts, including narrow and broad money demand for both the UK and the USA. These analyses stimulated and were stimulated by interactions with various governmental bodies, and they resulted in significant press coverage as well.

David's first money-demand study—Hendry and Mizon (1978)—responded to work on quarterly narrow money (M1) and broad money (M3) demand by Graham Hacche (1974), then at the Bank of England. In back-to-back publications in the *Economic Journal*, Courakis (1978) criticised Hacche (1974) for differencing data in order to achieve stationarity, and Hendry and Mizon (1978) proposed testing the restrictions imposed by differencing with Denis Sargan's new common-factor test, later published as Sargan (1980). Additionally, Hendry and Mizon (1978) developed an equilibrium correction representation for quarterly M3, using the Bank's data. The common-factor restriction in Hacche (1974) was rejected, and the equilibrium correction term in Hendry and Mizon's (1978) model was significant.

Hendry and Mizon (1978) implicitly assumed that both the equilibrium correction term and the differences in their model would be stationary—despite no concept of cointegration—and that the significance of the equilibrium correction term was equivalent to rejecting the imposed common factor from differencing. Also, Hacche (1974) was specific to general in its approach, whereas Hendry and Mizon (1978) argued for general-to-specific modelling, which was also the natural way to test common-factor restrictions using Sargan's determinantal conditions. Sargan's COMFAC algorithm was already included in David's software program GIVE, with a Monte Carlo study of COMFAC appearing in Mizon and Hendry (1980).

A subsequent Bank of England study—of the monetary aggregate M1 by Richard Coghlan (1978)—considered general dynamic specifications, but they still lacked an equilibrium correction term. In Hendry (1979), David responded by showing how narrow money acts as a buffer for agents' expenditures, but with target ratios for money relative to expenditure, deviations from which prompt adjustment. That target ratio depended on the opportunity costs of holding money relative to alternative financial assets and to goods, as measured by interest rates and inflation respectively.

Hendry (1979) also highlighted problems confronting a simple-to-general approach, including the misinterpretation of earlier results in the modelling sequence, the impossibility of constructively interpreting test rejections, the many expansion paths faced, the unknown stopping point, the collapse of the strategy if later misspecifications are detected, and the poor properties that result from stopping at the first non-rejection. These criticisms dated back to Anderson (1962) at least, but many modellers seemed unaware of them at the time. Parameter nonconstancy was another key difficulty with earlier UK money-demand equations. The model in Hendry (1979), however, was empirically constant over a sample with considerable turbulence after the introduction of Competition and Credit Control regulations in 1971.

Hendry (1979) served as the starting point for subsequent papers on UK M1, including Hendry (1985), Hendry and Ericsson (1991b), Ericsson, Hendry and Tran (1994), and Doornik, Hendry and Nielsen (1998). Despite a very general initial model, that research obtained a simple specification with only four key variables, which measured the opportunity costs of money against goods and other assets, adjustment costs, and the money market's disequilibrium.

Stimulated in part by several extended visits to the USA, David turned to modelling US M1, with results published in Baba, Hendry and Starr (1992). As background, Goldfeld (1976) had recorded a supposed breakdown in US money demand in the early 1970s, so it was natural to implement models for US M1 similar to those that David had developed for UK M1. Andrew Rose, who was David's MPhil student at Nuffield College in the early 1980s, showed how econometric methodology contributed to Goldfeld's results. Goldfeld had modelled money demand as a partial adjustment model and had imposed short-run price homogeneity. Both of those features are dynamic restrictions and were rejected on the data. Rose (1985) started with a more general dynamic specification without those restrictions, modelled from general to specific, and found a money-demand model that was empirically constant over Goldfeld's sample and for several years thereafter.

However, even Rose's model showed parameter instability in the early 1980s. Many new financial instruments had been introduced, including money market mutual funds, CDs, and NOW and SuperNOW accounts. David hypothesised that these unaccounted-for financial innovations were the cause. Ross Starr also thought that long-term interest-rate volatility had changed the maturity structure of the bond market, especially when the Fed implemented its New Operating Procedures. Because high interest rates then became associated with high variances, a high long-term rate was no longer a signal to buy bonds: interest rates might go higher still and induce capital losses. This phenomenon suggested calculating a certainty-equivalent long-term interest rate—that is, the interest rate adjusted for risk.

Otherwise, David's approach to modelling US M1 was similar to his approach to modelling UK M1, with M1 being determined by the private sector, conditional on interest rates set by the central bank and the banking sector. The estimated long-run income elasticity for the USA was one half—consistent with the theory of transactions demand developed in Baumol (1952) and Tobin (1956), but contrasting with the estimated long-run elasticity of unity for the UK in Hendry (1979). That difference in elasticities could be explained by convenient and inexpensive overdraft facilities then available in the UK but not in the USA.

David's model of US M1 generated controversy. Seminar presentations at the Fed produced a number of challenges from the audience, including the claim that the Fed had engineered a monetary expansion for Richard Nixon's re-election. Dummy variables for that period were insignificant when added to David's model: agents were willing to hold that money at the prevailing interest rates, and confirming valid conditioning. The model was also criticised for its lag structure, which captured average adjustment speeds in a large and complex economy. Some economists still regard the final formulation as too complicated, perhaps believing in a world that is inherently simple. Other economists were concerned about data mining, although data mining per se would be hard-pressed to produce the large t-values found, however many search paths were explored. The variables might proxy unmodelled effects, but their large t-statistics would be highly unlikely to arise by chance alone.

Modelling annual UK broad money demand generated even more controversy for David. In 1982, Milton Friedman and Anna Schwartz published their book *Monetary Trends in the United States and the United Kingdom*; and it had many potential policy implications. Early the following year, the Bank of England asked David to evaluate the econometrics in Friedman and Schwartz's volume for the Bank's Panel of Academic Consultants. Neil Ericsson was David's research officer at the time, and their initial examination revealed much. Methodologically, Friedman and Schwartz's approach was deliberately simple-to-general, commencing with bivariate regressions, generalising to trivariate regressions, etc. Testing their equations found considerable misspecification, including parameter non-constancy, an anathema to money-demand equations. Also, Friedman and Schwartz had phase-averaged their annual data in an attempt to remove business cycles, but phase averaging still left highly autocorrelated, non-stationary series. Because filtering (such as phase averaging) imposes dynamic restrictions, David and Neil analysed both the phase-average data and the original annual data. In late October, David presented the research in Hendry and Ericsson (1983) to the Bank's Panel. Luminaries and rising stars in UK academia and government participated, including Chris Allsopp, Michael Artis, Andrew Bain, David Begg, Arthur Brown, Willem Buiter, Terry Burns, Ian Byatt, Alec Cairncross, Forrest Capie, Nicholas Dimsdale, Charles Goodhart, Jeroen Kremers, Rachel Lomax, R.C.O. Matthews, Ken Wallis, Geoffrey Wood, and David Worswick.

It is helpful to put that meeting at the Bank in historical context. Monetarism was at its peak. Margaret Thatcher—then Prime Minister—had instituted a regime of monetary control, as she believed that money caused inflation, precisely the view put forward by Friedman and Schwartz (1982). From this perspective, a credible monetary tightening would rapidly reduce inflation because expectations were rational. In fact, inflation fell slowly in Britain, whereas unemployment leapt to levels not seen since the 1930s. The UK House of Commons' Treasury and Civil Service Committee on Monetary Policy—which David had advised in Hendry (1981a, b)—had found no evidence that monetary expansion was the cause of the high inflation in the 1970s. If anything, inflation caused money, whereas money was almost an epiphenomenon. The structure of the British banking system made the Bank of England a "lender of first resort", and so the Bank could only control the quantity of money by varying interest rates.

Shortly after the meeting of the Bank's Panel of Academic Consultants, Hendry and Ericsson (1983) received considerable press coverage, starting with the British newspaper *The Guardian* and spilling over into other newspapers around the world. Chris Huhne—*The Guardian*'s economics editor at the time—had seen Hendry and Ericsson (1983), and he deemed the evidence therein central to the policy debate. On 15 December 1983, *The Guardian* published two articles about Friedman and Schwartz (1982). On page 19 of the newspaper, Huhne had authored an article that summarised—in layman's terms—the critique by Hendry and Ericsson (1983) of Friedman and Schwartz (1982). David and Chris had discussed Hendry and Ericsson (1983) at length beforehand, and Chris's article—"Why Milton's monetarism is bunk"—provided an accurate statement of Hendry and Ericsson (1983) and its implications. In addition, *The Guardian* decided to run a front-page editorial on Friedman and Schwartz (1982) with the headline "Monetarism's guru 'distorts his evidence'". That headline summarised Huhne's view that it was unacceptable for Friedman and Schwartz to use their data-based dummy variable for 1921–1955 and still claim parameter constancy of their money-demand equation. Rather, the statistical, numerical, and economic significance of that dummy variable actually implied nonconstancy, as Goodhart (1982) also discussed. Moreover, Hendry and Ericsson (1983) had shown that Friedman and Schwartz's money-demand equation was empirically nonconstant, even with their dummy variable. Nonconstancy undermined Friedman and Schwartz's policy conclusions. Chris later did a TV programme about the debate, spending a day at David's house filming.

Hendry and Ericsson (1983) started a modelling sequence that included Longbottom and Holly (1985), Escribano (1985), and (after a prolonged editorial process) Hendry and Ericsson (1991a). Attfield, Demery and Duck (1995) subsequently claimed that the money-demand equation in Hendry and Ericsson (1991a) had broken down on data extended to the early 1990s, whereas Friedman and Schwartz's specification was constant. To compile a coherent statistical series over the extended sample period, Attfield, Demery and Duck (1995) had spliced several different money measures together, but they had not adjusted the corresponding measures of the opportunity cost. With that combination, the model in Hendry and Ericsson (1991a) did indeed fail. Ericsson, Hendry and Prestwich (1998) showed that that model remained constant over the whole sample with an appropriate measure of opportunity cost, whereas the model of Friedman and Schwartz failed. Escribano (2004) updated the equation from Hendry and Ericsson (1991a) through 2000 and confirmed its continued constancy.

Ericsson, Hendry and Hood (2016) subsequently examined the US money-demand equations in Friedman and Schwartz (1982), finding substantial empirical shortcomings, even by Friedman's own criteria, such as subsample properties. Ericsson, Hendry and Hood (2016) highlighted difficulties with Friedman and Schwartz's simple-to-general methodology and showed that Friedman and Schwartz's final US money-demand equation had nonconstant parameters and that its residuals were heteroscedastic, even though that equation's estimation included an adjustment for the heteroscedasticity induced by the phase averaging of the annual data. Furthermore, Friedman and Schwartz's data adjustment for the USA's increasing relative financial sophistication did not adequately capture the financial changes that occurred in the sample.

5.4   Television and Ofcom

David also worked with the UK government's Office of Communications (Ofcom) on forecasts of net advertising revenue for the TV broadcasting network ITV. These forecasts had significant policy consequences and are of interest in their own right.

Ofcom is the British government agency responsible for regulating the UK telecommunication and postal industries, including the licensing of UK TV broadcasting. In 2004, Ofcom needed to price the renewal of the advertising licence for ITV, the oldest and biggest commercial TV network in the UK. The licence fee had been specified to be calculated from forecasts of discounted net advertising revenue (NAR) over the subsequent decade.

Hendry (1992b) had developed a VEqCM for key variables in forecasting NAR—hours broadcast, audience reach, and the price of advertising time. David subsequently improved that VEqCM using PcGets. Ofcom then augmented that new VEqCM by forecasts from a macro-model for variables such as GDP, company profits, interest rates, and inflation.

In forecasting NAR, Ofcom initially preferred to forecast from that augmented VEqCM, rather than from the corresponding DVEqCM. Ofcom was concerned with how the differencing in the DVEqCM would eliminate long-run relationships from the VEqCM. However, representatives from the advertising industry described recent breaks in TV advertising that arose from innovations such as video recorders, Internet advertising, and alternative TV channels. Those breaks would be difficult to model with available data, yet they could cause systematic forecast failure by the VEqCM. David persuaded Ofcom that differencing the VEqCM would robustify their forecasts, removing effects of those location shifts but retaining long-run information; see Section 4.3.

Ofcom published forecasts for NAR over 2004–2014 in Raven, Hoehn, Lancefield and Robinson (2004: Figure 6.5). Forecasts were calculated from three models: a "long-run trend" model, the VEqCM, and the corresponding DVEqCM. Those models' forecasts were respectively increasing, relatively flat, and slightly declining over time. Robustification was consequential because of recent unmodelled shifts. Robustification by differencing the VEqCM removed location shifts in excluded variables such as the introduction of personal video recorders, which had reduced TV advertising revenue.

These forecasts were key to setting policy: Ofcom set a lower licence fee because the DVEqCM forecasts showed NAR declining, rather than increasing. However, while the DVEqCM did perform the best of the three models ex post, even its forecasts proved too optimistic. Many of the variables included in the DVEqCM themselves experienced unanticipated location shifts during the forecast period. For instance, in the wake of the financial crisis, actual GDP and profits were much lower than forecast, poignantly illustrating that unanticipated location shifts can induce systematic forecast errors.

5.5   Climate Change

David has had a long-standing interest in the natural sciences, including palaeontology and geology. From his readings on these topics and from discussions with experts, David became concerned about anthropogenic influences in climate change and the economic consequences thereof. At the time, much climate science was nonstochastic and scenario-driven, so David saw a role for econometrics in advancing understanding and driving policy.

Hendry (2011)—David's initial foray into climate econometrics—examines geologic evidence on climate change and its role in great extinctions. Relatedly, Castle and Hendry (2020) derive the causal role of atmospheric CO_2 levels in past Ice Ages. Hendry and Pretis (2013) turn to relatively recent evidence from the Mauna Loa Observatory, using IIS and automatic model selection across a wide range of climatic and economic variables to determine the extent to which anthropogenic sources increase atmospheric CO_2. Their model controls for a number of natural carbon sources and sinks—such as vegetation, temperature, weather, and dynamic transport—and determines the additional anthropogenic contributions from industrial production, business cycles, and shocks. The anthropogenic sources are significant contributors to changes in atmospheric CO_2. Pretis and Hendry (2013) illustrate how advances in econometric methodology can improve existing studies of global warming. Pretis, Schneider, Smerdon and Hendry (2016) develop saturation procedures using "designer breaks" to detect and identify volcanic eruptions, some of which created strong albeit temporary climatic changes.

In 2015, David and Felix Pretis received a £660,000 grant from the Robertson Foundation to support their research programme Climate Econometrics, ably managed by Angela Wenham. The programme serves as a key catalyst for wide-ranging econometric advances in climate change, with several recent developments. Pretis (2020) shows the equivalence of energy balance models and cointegrated vector autoregressions. David's former DPhil student Andrew Martinez (2020a) uses a multidisciplinary approach with automated model selection to show that larger errors in a hurricane's predicted landfall increase the hurricane's damages; see also Martinez (2020b). Hendry (2020) and Castle and Hendry (2020) model CO_2 emissions in the UK over the last century and a half using saturation techniques and automatic model selection. Over the last several decades, UK emissions have dropped dramatically to pre-1900 levels, even while real income increased manyfold, with legislation and technological improvements being key factors in the reduction. To paraphrase the title of David's 2020 paper ("First In, First Out"), Britain was the first country into the Industrial Revolution—then producing a large share of global anthropogenic CO_2 emissions—and Britain is now becoming one of the first countries out. On 22 April 2017, Britain had its first full day in over a century with no electricity being produced by coal-fired plants. In April 2020, electricity production in Britain went for 18 consecutive days coal-free. While climate change remains a major global challenge, progress can be made. Modern dynamic econometric analysis can shed light on climate change and help guide policy.

6   Oxford Connections

David spent the first decade and a half of his professional career in London at LSE—first as a student in the MSc and PhD programmes, then as a Lecturer and Professor. In January 1982, he moved to Nuffield College, Oxford. He has been at Nuffield ever since. Nuffield College itself is a college of only graduate students in the social sciences and, as such, attracted remarkable students and colleagues, many becoming co-authors on David's research projects.

The move to Oxford appealed to David for many reasons. Oxford provided a good research environment with many excellent economists, it had bright students, and it was a lovely place to live. David and Evelyn's daughter Vivien was about to start school, and Oxford schools were preferable to those in Central London. Amartya Sen, Terence Gorman, and John Muellbauer had all recently moved to Oxford; Jim Mirrlees was already there. Steve Nickell and David Cox were soon to arrive.

In Oxford, David was initially also the Acting Director of the Institute of Economics and Statistics. The Institute transmogrified into the University's Department of Economics in 1999, which David later chaired. In 2007, the

Department was the focus for David's Festschrift, published as Castle and Shephard (2009).

When David arrived in Oxford, the University had no economics department, and no undergraduate economics degree either. Economics was college-based rather than university-based, it lacked a building, and it had little secretarial support. PPE—short for Philosophy, Politics, and Economics—was the major vehicle through which Oxford undergraduates learnt economics. With the creation of a department of economics, the University moved to a more integrated teaching programme at both the graduate and the undergraduate levels. Even so, the University still has no undergraduate programme strictly in economics: only PPE and E&M (Economics and Management).

The Institute of Economics and Statistics also housed the *Oxford Bulletin of Economics and Statistics*, which David began editing. He saw that a shift in focus would benefit the journal, and this was helped by commissioning two timely special issues on cointegration that attracted the profession's attention—Hendry (1986a) and Banerjee and Hendry (1992a); see Section 2.2. Some people then nicknamed the journal the *Oxford Bulletin of Cointegration*, reflecting the pivotal and highly cited articles on cointegration that it published.

Research funding proved critical to David's activities in Oxford. Although many of his research grant applications for forecasting were rejected, he was awarded two personal Research Fellowships: one from the Leverhulme Trust for five years, and one from the Economic and Social Research Council for three years. These Fellowships bought out some of his teaching responsibilities, enabling him to develop the general theory of forecasting. Additionally, James Martin and George Soros generously funded his programme Economic Modelling (EMoD)—James Martin through the Oxford Martin School, and George Soros through the Open Society Foundations and the Institute for New Economic Thinking (INET). The initial five-year grant for EMoD supported Oxford economics faculty and post-doctoral research fellows in analysing difficulties that empirical modelling, economic analysis, policy, and forecasting confront with rapid unanticipated changes. INET extended David's EMoD grant for three more years jointly with John Muellbauer, and the Robertson Foundation awarded a grant for David and Felix Pretis's programme Climate Econometrics.

Research topics at EMoD and Climate Econometrics are manifold. They include analysing the mathematical and statistical bases for expectations formation and inter-temporal optimisation when economic agents face unanticipated breaks, and developing methods of empirical model discovery that can handle multiple intermittent shifts. EMoD also investigated inequality in wealth and income, established a web-based database of civilisation's progress (www.ourworldindata.org), modelled immigration into Norway, and formulated alternative macro-models with financial channels. At Climate Econometrics, saturation methods for detecting breaks are isolating the effects of volcanic eruptions on temperature, detecting policy-driven shifts in CO_2 emissions, and helping to model increases in sea level. The overriding theme is to develop approaches appropriate to a world undergoing rapid unanticipated changes, and to improve forecasting methods in such a setting.

7   Conclusion

David Hendry has made path-breaking contributions to econometrics: in modelling, in forecasting, in software, and in policy. Hendry (1995), Banerjee, Dolado, Galbraith and Hendry (1993), and Hendry and Doornik (2014)—three pioneering books on econometric methodology, cointegration, and model design—set the foundations for systematic empirical economic modelling with machine learning. David has applied that approach to a wide range of substantive empirical studies, including on consumers' expenditure, mortgage and housing markets, money demand, and climate change.

In economic forecasting, David and Mike Clements developed a taxonomy of forecast errors that has yielded valuable insights into the nature of forecasting. David—often with Mike and (more recently) Jennie Castle—has provided new perspectives on many existing forecast techniques, including mean square forecast errors, add factors, leading indicators, pooling of forecasts, and multi-step estimation. David has also developed new forecast tools, such as forecast encompassing, and he has improved existing ones, such as nowcasting and the robustification of forecasts to breaks.

David's studies in modelling and forecasting have had direct implications for economic policy. Practical implementation and assessment in modelling, forecasting, and policy require computer software, and David and Jurgen Doornik's suite of software packages continues to embody best-practice econometrics. Overlaps are common between different strands in David's research, with the analysis of real-world problems motivating and benefiting from that research.

References

Main and Cited Works by David F. Hendry

Anderson, G.J. and D.F. Hendry (1984). 'An Econometric Model of United Kingdom Building Societies'. *Oxford Bulletin of Economics and Statistics*, 46(3): 185–210.

Baba, Y., D.F. Hendry and R.M. Starr (1992). 'The Demand for M1 in the USA, 1960–1988'. *Review of Economic Studies*, 59(1): 25–61.

Banerjee, A., J.J. Dolado, J.W. Galbraith and D.F. Hendry (1993). *Co-integration, Error Correction, and the Econometric Analysis of Non-stationary Data*. Oxford: Oxford University Press.

Banerjee, A., J.J. Dolado, D.F. Hendry and G.W. Smith (1986). 'Exploring Equilibrium Relationships in Econometrics Through Static Models: Some Monte Carlo Evidence'. *Oxford Bulletin of Economics and Statistics*, 48(3): 253–277.

Banerjee, A. and D.F. Hendry (eds) (1992a). *Testing Integration and Cointegration*, Special Issue, *Oxford Bulletin of Economics and Statistics*, 54(3).

Banerjee, A. and D.F. Hendry (1992b). 'Testing Integration and Cointegration: An Overview'. *Oxford Bulletin of Economics and Statistics*, 54(3): 225–255.

Banerjee, A. and D.F. Hendry (eds) (1996). *The Econometrics of Economic Policy*, Special Issue, *Oxford Bulletin of Economics and Statistics*, 58(4).

Banerjee, A. and D.F. Hendry (eds) (1997). *The Econometrics of Economic Policy*. Oxford: Blackwell Publishers.

Barnett, W.A., D.F. Hendry, S. Hylleberg, T. Teräsvirta, D. Tjøstheim and A. Würtz (eds) (2000). *Nonlinear Econometric Modeling in Time Series: Proceedings of the Eleventh International Symposium in Economic Theory*. Cambridge: Cambridge University Press.

Campos, J., N.R. Ericsson and D.F. Hendry (1996). 'Cointegration Tests in the Presence of Structural Breaks'. *Journal of Econometrics*, 70(1): 187–220.

Campos, J., N.R. Ericsson and D.F. Hendry (eds) (2005). *General-to-Specific Modelling*. Volumes I and II. Cheltenham: Edward Elgar.

Castle, J.L., M.P. Clements and D.F. Hendry (2013). 'Forecasting by Factors, by Variables, by Both or Neither?'. *Journal of Econometrics*, 177(2): 305–319.

Castle, J.L., M.P. Clements and D.F. Hendry (2015). 'Robust Approaches to Forecasting'. *International Journal of Forecasting*, 31(1): 99–112.

Castle, J.L., M.P. Clements and D.F. Hendry (2019). *Forecasting: An Essential Introduction*. New Haven and London: Yale University Press.

Castle, J.L., J.A. Doornik and D.F. Hendry (2012). 'Model Selection When There Are Multiple Breaks'. *Journal of Econometrics*, 169(2): 239–246.

Castle, J.L., J.A. Doornik and D.F. Hendry (2020a). 'COVID-19 Short-Term Forecasts'. Oxford: University of Oxford. Available at: https://www.doornik.com/COVID-19/.

Castle, J.L., J.A. Doornik and D.F. Hendry (2020b). 'Medium-Term Forecasting of the Coronavirus Pandemic'. Draft, Oxford: Nuffield College, University of Oxford, May.

Castle, J.L. and D.F. Hendry (eds) (2017). *Sir Clive W. J. Granger Memorial Special Issue on Econometrics, European Journal of Pure and Applied Mathematics*, 10(1).

Castle, J.L. and D.F. Hendry (2019). *Modelling Our Changing World*. Cham, Switzerland: Palgrave Macmillan.

Castle, J.L. and D.F. Hendry (2020). 'Climate Econometrics: An Overview'. *Foundations and Trends in Econometrics*, 10(3–4): 145–322.

Castle, J.L., D.F. Hendry and O. Kitov (2017). 'Forecasting and Nowcasting Macroeconomic Variables: A Methodological Overview'. Chapter 3 in G.L. Mazzi and D. Ladiray (eds) *Handbook on Rapid Estimates: 2017 Edition*. Luxembourg: European Union: 53–120.

Chong, Y.Y. and D.F. Hendry (1986). 'Econometric Evaluation of Linear Macroeconomic Models'. *Review of Economic Studies*, 53(4): 671–690.

Clements, M.P. and D.F. Hendry (1993). 'On the Limitations of Comparing Mean Square Forecast Errors'. *Journal of Forecasting*, 12(8): 617–637 (with discussion).

Clements, M.P. and D.F. Hendry (1994). 'Towards a Theory of Economic Forecasting'. Chapter 2 in C.P. Hargreaves (ed.) *Nonstationary Time Series Analysis and Cointegration*. Oxford: Oxford University Press: 9–52.

Clements, M.P. and D.F. Hendry (1995). 'Forecasting in Cointegrated Systems'. *Journal of Applied Econometrics*, 10(2): 127–146.

Clements, M.P. and D.F. Hendry (1996a). 'Intercept Corrections and Structural Change'. *Journal of Applied Econometrics*, 11(5): 475–494.

Clements, M.P. and D.F. Hendry (1996b). 'Multi-Step Estimation for Forecasting'. *Oxford Bulletin of Economics and Statistics*, 58(4): 657–684.

Clements, M.P. and D.F. Hendry (1998a). 'Forecasting Economic Processes'. *International Journal of Forecasting*, 14(1): 111–131 (with discussion).

Clements, M.P. and D.F. Hendry (1998b). *Forecasting Economic Time Series*. Cambridge: Cambridge University Press.

Clements, M.P. and D.F. Hendry (1999a). *Forecasting Non-stationary Economic Time Series*. Cambridge, MA: MIT Press.

Clements, M.P. and D.F. Hendry (1999b). 'On Winning Forecasting Competitions in Economics'. *Spanish Economic Review*, 1(2): 123–160.

Clements, M.P. and D.F. Hendry (2001). 'Explaining the Results of the M3 Forecasting Competition'. *International Journal of Forecasting*, 17(4): 550–554.

Clements, M.P. and D.F. Hendry (eds) (2002a). *A Companion to Economic Forecasting*. Oxford: Blackwell Publishers.

Clements, M.P. and D.F. Hendry (2002b). 'An Overview of Economic Forecasting'. Chapter 1 in M.P. Clements and D.F. Hendry (eds) *A Companion to Economic Forecasting*. Oxford: Blackwell Publishers: 1–18.

Clements, M.P. and D.F. Hendry (2003). 'Report of a Scoping Study of Forecasting in the National Accounts at the Office for National Statistics'. Annex A in *Forecasting in the National Accounts at the Office for National Statistics*, Statistics Commission Report No. 12, December. London: Statistics Commission.

Clements, M.P. and D.F. Hendry (2005a). 'Guest Editors' Introduction: Information in Economic Forecasting'. *Oxford Bulletin of Economics and Statistics*, 67(Supplement): 713–753.

Clements, M.P. and D.F. Hendry (eds) (2005b). *Information in Economic Forecasting*, Specifal Issue, *Oxford Bulletin of Economics and Statistics*, 67(Supplement).

Clements, M.P. and D.F. Hendry (2006). 'Forecasting with Breaks'. Chapter 12 in G. Elliott, C.W.J. Granger and A. Timmermann (eds) *Handbook of Economic Forecasting*. Volume 1. Amsterdam: Elsevier: 605–657.

Clements, M.P. and D.F. Hendry (eds) (2011). *Oxford Handbook of Economic Forecasting*. Oxford: Oxford University Press.

Davidson, J.E.H. and D.F. Hendry (1981). 'Interpreting Econometric Evidence: The Behaviour of Consumers' Expenditure in the UK'. *European Economic Review*, 16(1): 177–192 (with discussion).

Davidson, J.E.H., D.F. Hendry, F. Srba and S. Yeo (1978). 'Econometric Modelling of the Aggregate Time-Series Relationship Between Consumers' Expenditure and Income in the United Kingdom'. *Economic Journal*, 88(352): 661–692.

Doornik, J.A., J.L. Castle and D.F. Hendry (2020a). 'Card Forecasts for M4'. *International Journal of Forecasting*, 36(1): 129–134.

Doornik, J.A., J.L. Castle, and D.F. Hendry (2020b). 'Statistical Short-Term Forecasting of the COVID-19 Pandemic'. *Journal of Clinical Immunology and Immunotherapy*, 6, 5, 046.

Doornik, J.A., J.L. Castle, and D.F. Hendry (2021). 'Short-Term Forecasting of the Coronavirus Pandemic'. *International Journal of Forecasting* (in press).

Doornik, J.A. and D.F. Hendry (1992). *PcGive Version 7: An Interactive Econometric Modelling System*. University of Oxford, Oxford: Institute of Economics and Statistics.

Doornik, J.A. and D.F. Hendry (1994). *PcFiml 8.0: Interactive Econometric Modelling of Dynamic Systems*. London: International Thomson Publishing.

Doornik, J.A. and D.F. Hendry (2001). *PcGive Version 10 for Windows*. Five volumes. London: Timberlake Consultants Press.

Doornik, J.A. and D.F. Hendry (2007). *PcGive 12: Empirical Econometric Modelling*. Volume I. London: Timberlake Consultants Press.

Doornik, J.A. and D.F. Hendry (2018). *PcGive 15*. Three volumes. Richmond, UK: Timberlake Consultants Ltd.

Doornik, J.A., D.F. Hendry and B. Nielsen (1998). 'Inference in Cointegrating Models: UK M1 Revisited'. *Journal of Economic Surveys*, 12(5): 533–572.

Emerson, R.A. and D.F. Hendry (1996). 'An Evaluation of Forecasting Using Leading Indicators'. *Journal of Forecasting*, 15(4): 271–291.

Engle, R.F., D.F. Hendry and J.-F. Richard (1983). 'Exogeneity'. *Econometrica*, 51(2): 277–304.

Ericsson, N.R. and D.F. Hendry (1985). 'Conditional Econometric Modeling: An Application to New House Prices in the United Kingdom'. Chapter 11 in A.C. Atkinson and S.E. Fienberg (eds) *A Celebration of Statistics: The ISI Centenary Volume.* New York: Springer-Verlag: 251–285.

Ericsson, N.R., D.F. Hendry and S.B. Hood (2016). 'Milton Friedman as an Empirical Modeler'. Chapter 6 in R.A. Cord and J.D. Hammond (eds) *Milton Friedman: Contributions to Economics and Public Policy.* Oxford: Oxford University Press: 91–142.

Ericsson, N.R., D.F. Hendry and K.M. Prestwich (1998). 'The Demand for Broad Money in the United Kingdom, 1878–1993'. *Scandinavian Journal of Economics,* 100(1): 289–324 (with discussion).

Ericsson, N.R., D.F. Hendry and H.-A. Tran (1994). 'Cointegration, Seasonality, Encompassing, and the Demand for Money in the United Kingdom'. Chapter 7 in C.P. Hargreaves (ed.) *Nonstationary Time Series Analysis and Cointegration.* Oxford: Oxford University Press: 179–224.

Haldrup, N., D.F. Hendry and H.K. van Dijk (eds) (2003). *Model Selection and Evaluation,* Special Issue, *Oxford Bulletin of Economics and Statistics,* 65(Supplement).

Hendry, D.F. (1973). 'On Asymptotic Theory and Finite Sample Experiments'. *Economica,* New Series, 40(158): 210–217.

Hendry, D.F. (1974). 'Stochastic Specification in an Aggregate Demand Model of the United Kingdom'. *Econometrica,* 42(3): 559–578.

Hendry, D.F. (1975). 'The Consequences of Mis-specification of Dynamic Structure, Autocorrelation, and Simultaneity in a Simple Model with an Application to the Demand for Imports'. Chapter 11 in G.A. Renton (ed.) *Modelling the Economy.* London: Heinemann Educational Books: 286–320 (with discussion).

Hendry, D.F. (1976). 'The Structure of Simultaneous Equations Estimators'. *Journal of Econometrics,* 4(1): 51–88.

Hendry, D.F. (1977). 'Comments on Granger-Newbold's "Time Series Approach to Econometric Model Building" and Sargent-Sims' "Business Cycle Modeling Without Pretending to Have Too Much *A Priori* Economic Theory"'. In C.A. Sims (ed.) *New Methods in Business Cycle Research: Proceedings from a Conference.* Minneapolis, MN: Federal Reserve Bank of Minneapolis: 183–202.

Hendry, D.F. (1979). 'Predictive Failure and Econometric Modelling in Macroeconomics: The Transactions Demand for Money'. Chapter 9 in P. Ormerod (ed.) *Economic Modelling: Current Issues and Problems in Macroeconomic Modelling in the UK and the US.* London: Heinemann Education Books: 217–242.

Hendry, D.F. (1980). 'Econometrics—Alchemy or Science?'. *Economica,* New Series, 47(188): 387–406.

Hendry, D.F. (1981a). 'Comment on HM Treasury's Memorandum, "Background to the Government's Economic Policy"'. In House of Commons (ed.) *Third Report from the Treasury and Civil Service Committee, Session 1980–81, Monetary Policy.* Volume 3. London: Her Majesty's Stationery Office: 94–96 (Appendix 4).

Hendry, D.F. (1981b). 'Econometric Evidence in the Appraisal of Monetary Policy'. In House of Commons (ed.) *Third Report from the Treasury and Civil Service Committee, Session 1980–81, Monetary Policy*. Volume 3. London: Her Majesty's Stationery Office: 1–21 (Appendix 1).

Hendry, D.F. (1983). 'Econometric Modelling: The "Consumption Function" in Retrospect'. *Scottish Journal of Political Economy*, 30(3): 193–220.

Hendry, D.F. (1984a). 'Econometric Modelling of House Prices in the United Kingdom'. Chapter 8 in D.F. Hendry and K.F. Wallis (eds) *Econometrics and Quantitative Economics*. Oxford: Basil Blackwell: 211–252.

Hendry, D.F. (1984b). 'Monte Carlo Experimentation in Econometrics'. Chapter 16 in Z. Griliches and M.D. Intriligator (eds) *Handbook of Econometrics*. Volume 2. Amsterdam: North-Holland: 937–976.

Hendry, D.F. (1985). 'Monetary Economic Myth and Econometric Reality'. *Oxford Review of Economic Policy*, 1(1): 72–84.

Hendry, D.F. (ed.) (1986a). *Econometric Modelling with Cointegrated Variables*, Special Issue, *Oxford Bulletin of Economics and Statistics*, 48(3), August.

Hendry, D.F. (1986b). 'Econometric Modelling with Cointegrated Variables: An Overview'. *Oxford Bulletin of Economics and Statistics*, 48(3): 201–212.

Hendry, D.F. (1986c). 'Empirical Modeling in Dynamic Econometrics'. *Applied Mathematics and Computation*, 20(3/4): 201–236.

Hendry, D.F. (1986d). 'The Role of Prediction in Evaluating Econometric Models'. *Proceedings of the Royal Society of London, Series A*, 407(1832): 25–34 (with discussion).

Hendry, D.F. (1987a). 'Econometric Methodology: A Personal Perspective'. Chapter 10 in T.F. Bewley (ed.) *Advances in Econometrics: Fifth World Congress*. Volume 2. Cambridge: Cambridge University Press: 29–48.

Hendry, D.F. (1987b). *PC-GIVE: An Interactive Menu-Driven Econometric Modelling Program for IBM-Compatible PC's*. Version 4.2. University of Oxford, Oxford: Institute of Economics and Statistics and Nuffield College, January.

Hendry, D.F. (1991). 'Economic Forecasting: A Report to the Treasury and Civil Service Committee', 12 July. Submitted to the House of Commons, *Memoranda on Official Economic Forecasting*, Treasury and Civil Service Committee. Session 1990–91. London: Her Majesty's Stationery Office.

Hendry, D.F. (1992a). 'Assessing Empirical Evidence in Macroeconometrics with an Application to Consumers' Expenditure in France'. Chapter 13 in A. Vercelli and N. Dimitri (eds) *Macroeconomics: A Survey of Research Strategies*. Oxford: Oxford University Press: 363–392.

Hendry, D.F. (1992b). 'An Econometric Analysis of TV Advertising Expenditure in the United Kingdom'. *Journal of Policy Modeling*, 14(3): 281–311.

Hendry, D.F. (1993). *Econometrics: Alchemy or Science? Essays in Econometric Methodology*. Oxford: Blackwell Publishers.

Hendry, D.F. (1994). 'HUS Revisited'. *Oxford Review of Economic Policy*, 10(2): 86–106.

Hendry, D.F. (1995). *Dynamic Econometrics*. Oxford: Oxford University Press.

Hendry, D.F. (1997). 'On Congruent Econometric Relations: A Comment'. *Carnegie-Rochester Conference Series on Public Policy*, 47(December): 163–190.

Hendry, D.F. (1999). 'An Econometric Analysis of US Food Expenditure, 1931–1989'. Chapter 17 in J.R. Magnus and M.S. Morgan (eds) *Methodology and Tacit Knowledge: Two Experiments in Econometrics*. Chichester: John Wiley and Sons: 341–361.

Hendry, D.F. (2000). *Econometrics: Alchemy or Science? Essays in Econometric Methodology*. New edition. Oxford: Oxford University Press.

Hendry, D.F. (2004). 'The Nobel Memorial Prize for Clive W. J. Granger'. *Scandinavian Journal of Economics*, 106(2): 187–213.

Hendry, D.F. (2006). 'Robustifying Forecasts from Equilibrium-Correction Systems'. *Journal of Econometrics*, 135(1–2): 399–426.

Hendry, D.F. (2011). 'Climate Change: Lessons for Our Future from the Distant Past'. Chapter 2 in S. Dietz, J. Michie and C. Oughton (eds) *The Political Economy of the Environment: An Interdisciplinary Approach*. Abingdon: Routledge: 19–43.

Hendry, D.F. (2015). *Introductory Macro-Econometrics: A New Approach*. London: Timberlake Consultants Ltd.

Hendry, D.F. (2020). 'First In, First Out: Econometric Modelling of UK Annual CO_2 Emissions, 1860–2017'. Economics Discussion Paper No. 2020–W02, Oxford: Nuffield College, University of Oxford, February. Available at: http://www.nuffield.ox.ac.uk/economics/Papers/2020/2020W02_CO2UKEmissionsModel20.pdf.

Hendry, D.F. and G.J. Anderson (1977). 'Testing Dynamic Specification in Small Simultaneous Systems: An Application to a Model of Building Society Behavior in the United Kingdom'. Chapter 8c in M.D. Intriligator (ed.) *Frontiers of Quantitative Economics*. Volume 3A. Amsterdam: North-Holland: 361–383.

Hendry, D.F. and M.P. Clements (1994a). 'Can Econometrics Improve Economic Forecasting?'. *Swiss Journal of Economics and Statistics*, 130(3): 267–298.

Hendry, D.F. and M.P. Clements (1994b). 'On a Theory of Intercept Corrections in Macroeconometric Forecasting'. Chapter 8 in S. Holly (ed.) *Money, Inflation and Employment: Essays in Honour of James Ball*. Aldershot: Edward Elgar: 160–182.

Hendry, D.F. and M.P. Clements (2004). 'Pooling of Forecasts'. *Econometrics Journal*, 7(1): 1–31.

Hendry, D.F. and J.A. Doornik (1997). 'The Implications for Econometric Modelling of Forecast Failure'. *Scottish Journal of Political Economy*, 44(4): 437–461.

Hendry, D.F. and J.A. Doornik (1999). 'The Impact of Computational Tools on Time-Series Econometrics'. In T. Coppock (ed.) *Information Technology and Scholarship: Applications in the Humanities and Social Sciences*. Oxford: Oxford University Press: 257–269.

Hendry, D.F. and J.A. Doornik (2014). *Empirical Model Discovery and Theory Evaluation: Automatic Selection Methods in Econometrics*. Cambridge, MA: MIT Press.

Hendry, D.F., J.A. Doornik and I. Hiroya (2006). *Empirical Econometric Modelling Using PcGive 10*. Tokyo: Nippon-Hyoron-Ska (in Japanese).

Hendry, D.F. and N.R. Ericsson (1983). 'Assertion Without Empirical Basis: An Econometric Appraisal of "Monetary Trends in…the United Kingdom" by Milton Friedman and Anna Schwartz'. In *Monetary Trends in the United Kingdom*. Bank of England Panel of Academic Consultants, Panel Paper No. 22. London: Bank of England: 45–101.

Hendry, D.F. and N.R. Ericsson (1991a). 'An Econometric Analysis of UK Money Demand in *Monetary Trends in the United States and the United Kingdom* by Milton Friedman and Anna J. Schwartz'. *American Economic Review*, 81(1): 8–38.

Hendry, D.F. and N.R. Ericsson (1991b). 'Modeling the Demand for Narrow Money in the United Kingdom and the United States'. *European Economic Review*, 35(4): 833–881 (with discussion).

Hendry, D.F. and N.R. Ericsson (eds) (2001). *Understanding Economic Forecasts*. Cambridge, MA: MIT Press.

Hendry, D.F. and K. Hubrich (2011). 'Combining Disaggregate Forecasts or Combining Disaggregate Information to Forecast an Aggregate'. *Journal of Business and Economic Statistics*, 29(2): 216–227.

Hendry, D.F. and S. Johansen (2015). 'Model Discovery and Trygve Haavelmo's Legacy'. *Econometric Theory*, 31(1): 93–114.

Hendry, D.F., S. Johansen and C. Santos (2008). 'Automatic Selection of Indicators in a Fully Saturated Regression'. *Computational Statistics*, 23(2): 317–335, 337–339.

Hendry, D.F. and H.-M. Krolzig (1999). 'Improving on "Data Mining Reconsidered" by K. D. Hoover and S. J. Perez'. *Econometrics Journal*, 2(2): 202–219.

Hendry, D.F. and H.-M. Krolzig (2001). *Automatic Econometric Model Selection Using PcGets 1.0*. London: Timberlake Consultants Press.

Hendry, D.F. and H.-M. Krolzig (2005). 'The Properties of Automatic *Gets* Modelling'. *Economic Journal*, 115(502): C32–C61.

Hendry, D.F., M. Marcellino and G.E. Mizon (2008). *Encompassing*, Special Issue, *Oxford Bulletin of Economics and Statistics*, 70(Supplement).

Hendry, D.F. and A.B. Martinez (2017). 'Evaluating Multi-Step System Forecasts with Relatively Few Forecast-Error Observations'. *International Journal of Forecasting*, 33(2): 359–372.

Hendry, D.F. and G.E. Mizon (1978). 'Serial Correlation as a Convenient Simplification, Not a Nuisance: A Comment on a Study of the Demand for Money by the Bank of England'. *Economic Journal*, 88(351): 549–563.

Hendry, D.F. and G.E. Mizon (1993). 'Evaluating Dynamic Econometric Models by Encompassing the VAR'. Chapter 18 in P.C.B. Phillips (ed.) *Models, Methods, and Applications of Econometrics: Essays in Honor of A. R. Bergstrom*. Cambridge, MA: Basil Blackwell: 272–300.

Hendry, D.F. and G.E. Mizon (2000a). 'On Selecting Policy Analysis Models by Forecast Accuracy'. Chapter 5 in A.B. Atkinson, H. Glennerster and N.H. Stern (eds) *Putting Economics to Work: Volume in Honour of Michio Morishima*. London: STICERD, London School of Economics: 71–119.

Hendry, D.F. and G.E. Mizon (2000b). 'Reformulating Empirical Macroeconometric Modelling'. *Oxford Review of Economic Policy*, 16(4): 138–159.

Hendry, D.F. and G.E. Mizon (2014). 'Unpredictability in Economic Analysis, Econometric Modeling and Forecasting'. *Journal of Econometrics*, 182(1): 186–195.

Hendry, D.F. and M.S. Morgan (eds) (1995). *The Foundations of Econometric Analysis*. Cambridge: Cambridge University Press.

Hendry, D.F., J.N.J. Muellbauer and A. Murphy (1990). 'The Econometrics of DHSY'. Chapter 13 in J.D. Hey and D. Winch (eds) *A Century of Economics: 100 Years of the Royal Economic Society and the Economic Journal*. Oxford: Basil Blackwell: 298–334.

Hendry, D.F. and A.J. Neale (1988). 'Interpreting Long-Run Equilibrium Solutions in Conventional Macro Models: A Comment'. *Economic Journal*, 98(392): 808–817.

Hendry, D.F. and A.J. Neale (1991). 'A Monte Carlo Study of the Effects of Structural Breaks on Tests for Unit Roots'. Chapter 8 in P. Hackl and A.H. Westlund (eds) *Economic Structural Change: Analysis and Forecasting*. Berlin: Springer-Verlag: 95–119.

Hendry, D.F., A.J. Neale and N.R. Ericsson (1990). *PC-NAIVE: An Interactive Program for Monte Carlo Experimentation in Econometrics*. Version 6.01. Oxford: Institute of Economics and Statistics and Nuffield College, University of Oxford.

Hendry, D.F., A.J. Neale and F. Srba (1988). 'Econometric Analysis of Small Linear Systems Using PC-FIML'. *Journal of Econometrics*, 38(1/2): 203–226.

Hendry, D.F. and B. Nielsen (2007). *Econometric Modeling: A Likelihood Approach*. Princeton: Princeton University Press.

Hendry, D.F., A. Pagan and J.D. Sargan (1984). 'Dynamic Specification'. Chapter 18 in Z. Griliches and M.D. Intriligator (eds) *Handbook of Econometrics*. Volume 2. Amsterdam: North-Holland: 1,023–1,100.

Hendry, D.F. and M.H. Pesaran (eds) (2001). *Special Issue in Memory of John Denis Sargan 1924–1996: Studies in Empirical Macroeconometrics*, Special Issue, *Journal of Applied Econometrics*, 16(3), May–June.

Hendry, D.F. and F. Pretis (2013). 'Anthropogenic Influences on Atmospheric CO_2'. Chapter 12 in R. Fouquet (ed.) *Handbook on Energy and Climate Change*. Cheltenham: Edward Elgar: 287–326.

Hendry, D.F. and J.-F. Richard (1982). 'On the Formulation of Empirical Models in Dynamic Econometrics'. *Journal of Econometrics*, 20(1): 3–33.

Hendry, D.F. and J.-F. Richard (1983). 'The Econometric Analysis of Economic Time Series'. *International Statistical Review*, 51(2): 111–148 (with discussion).

Hendry, D.F. and N. Shephard (eds) (1997). *Cointegration and Dynamics in Economics*, Special Issue, *Journal of Econometrics*, 80(2), October.

Hendry, D.F. and F. Srba (1977). 'The Properties of Autoregressive Instrumental Variables Estimators in Dynamic Systems'. *Econometrica*, 45(4): 969–990.

Hendry, D.F. and F. Srba (1980). 'AUTOREG: A Computer Program Library for Dynamic Econometric Models with Autoregressive Errors'. *Journal of Econometrics*, 12(1): 85–102.

Hendry, D.F. and T. von Ungern-Sternberg (1981). 'Liquidity and Inflation Effects on Consumers' Expenditure'. Chapter 9 in A.S. Deaton (ed.) *Essays in the Theory and Measurement of Consumer Behaviour: In Honour of Sir Richard Stone*. Cambridge: Cambridge University Press: 237–260.

Hendry, D.F. and K.F. Wallis (eds) (1984). *Econometrics and Quantitative Economics*. Oxford: Basil Blackwell.

Martinez, A.B., J.L. Castle and D.F. Hendry (2021, forthcoming). 'Smooth Robust Multi-Horizon Forecasts'. *Advances in Econometrics*.

Mizon, G.E. and D.F. Hendry (1980). 'An Empirical Application and Monte Carlo Analysis of Tests of Dynamic Specification'. *Review of Economic Studies*, 47(1): 21–45.

Pretis, F. and D.F. Hendry (2013). 'Comment on "Polynomial Cointegration Tests of Anthropogenic Impact on Global Warming" by Beenstock et al. (2012)—Some Hazards in Econometric Modelling of Climate Change'. *Earth System Dynamics*, 4(2): 375–384.

Pretis, F., L. Schneider, J.E. Smerdon and D.F. Hendry (2016). 'Detecting Volcanic Eruptions in Temperature Reconstructions by Designed Break-Indicator Saturation'. *Journal of Economic Surveys*, 30(3): 403–429.

Other Works Referred To

Abadir, K.M., W. Distaso and F. Žikeš (2014). 'Design-Free Estimation of Variance Matrices'. *Journal of Econometrics*, 181(2): 165–180.

Anderson, T.W. (1962). 'The Choice of the Degree of a Polynomial Regression as a Multiple Decision Problem'. *Annals of Mathematical Statistics*, 33(1): 255–265.

Andrews, D.W.K. (1993). 'Tests for Parameter Instability and Structural Change with Unknown Change Point'. *Econometrica*, 61(4): 821–856.

Artis, M.J., A. Banerjee and M. Marcellino (2005). 'Factor Forecasts for the UK'. *Journal of Forecasting*, 24(4): 279–298.

Attfield, C.L.F., D. Demery and N.W. Duck (1995). 'Estimating the UK Demand for Money Function: A Test of Two Approaches'. Mimeo. Bristol: Department of Economics, University of Bristol, November.

Bai, J. and P. Perron (1998). 'Estimating and Testing Linear Models with Multiple Structural Changes'. *Econometrica*, 66(1): 47–78.

Bårdsen, G., Ø. Eitrheim, E.S. Jansen and R. Nymoen (2005). *The Econometrics of Macroeconomic Modelling*. Oxford: Oxford University Press.

Barendse, S. and A.J. Patton (2019). 'Comparing Predictive Accuracy in the Presence of a Loss Function Shape Parameter'. Discussion Paper No. 909. Oxford: Department of Economics, University of Oxford, November.

Bates, J.M. and C.W.J. Granger (1969). 'The Combination of Forecasts'. *Operational Research Quarterly*, 20(4): 451–468.

Baumol, W.J. (1952). 'The Transactions Demand for Cash: An Inventory Theoretic Approach'. *Quarterly Journal of Economics*, 66(4): 545–556.

Birchenhall, C.R., H. Jessen, D.R. Osborn and P. Simpson (1999). 'Predicting US Business-Cycle Regimes'. *Journal of Business and Economic Statistics*, 17(3): 313–323.

Box, G.E.P. and G.M. Jenkins (1970). *Time Series Analysis: Forecasting and Control*. San Francisco: Holden-Day.

Campos, J. and N.R. Ericsson (1999). 'Constructive Data Mining: Modeling Consumers' Expenditure in Venezuela'. *Econometrics Journal*, 2(2): 226–240.

Castle, J.L. and N. Shephard (eds) (2009). *The Methodology and Practice of Econometrics: A Festschrift in Honour of David F. Hendry*. Oxford: Oxford University Press.

Chan, N.H. and C.Z. Wei (1988). 'Limiting Distributions of Least Squares Estimates of Unstable Autoregressive Processes'. *Annals of Statistics*, 16(1): 367–401.

Chow, G.C. (1960). 'Tests of Equality Between Sets of Coefficients in Two Linear Regressions'. *Econometrica*, 28(3): 591–605.

Coghlan, R.T. (1978). 'A Transactions Demand for Money'. *Bank of England Quarterly Bulletin*, 18(1): 48–60.

Cooper, J.P. and C.R. Nelson (1975). 'The Ex Ante Prediction Performance of the St. Louis and FRB–MIT–PENN Econometric Models and Some Results on Composite Predictors'. *Journal of Money, Credit, and Banking*, 7(1): 1–32.

Courakis, A.S. (1978). 'Serial Correlation and a Bank of England Study of the Demand for Money: An Exercise in Measurement Without Theory'. *Economic Journal*, 88(351): 537–548.

Deaton, A.S. (1977). 'Involuntary Saving Through Unanticipated Inflation'. *American Economic Review*, 67(5): 899–910.

Doornik, J.A. (2001). *Ox 3.0: An Object-Oriented Matrix Programing Language*. London: Timberlake Consultants Press.

Doornik, J.A. (2008). 'Encompassing and Automatic Model Selection'. *Oxford Bulletin of Economics and Statistics*, 70(Supplement): 915–925.

Doornik, J.A. (2009). 'Autometrics'. Chapter 4 in J.L. Castle and N. Shephard (eds) *The Methodology and Practice of Econometrics: A Festschrift in Honour of David F. Hendry*. Oxford: Oxford University Press: 88–121.

Eitrheim, Ø., T.A. Husebø and R. Nymoen (1999). 'Equilibrium-Correction Versus Differencing in Macroeconometric Forecasting'. *Economic Modeling*, 16(4): 515–554.

Elliott, G., C.W.J. Granger and A. Timmermann (eds) (2006). *Handbook of Economic Forecasting*. Volume 1. Amsterdam: Elsevier.

Engle, R.F. and C.W.J. Granger (1987). 'Co-integration and Error Correction: Representation, Estimation, and Testing'. *Econometrica*, 55(2): 251–276.

Engle, R.F. and B.S. Yoo (1987). 'Forecasting and Testing in Co-integrated Systems'. *Journal of Econometrics*, 35(1): 143–159.

Ericsson, N.R. (2004). 'The ET Interview: Professor David F. Hendry'. *Econometric Theory*, 20(4): 743–804.

Ericsson, N.R. (2008). 'Comment on "Economic Forecasting in a Changing World" (by Michael Clements and David Hendry)'. *Capitalism and Society*, 3(2): 1–16.

Ericsson, N.R. (2016). 'Eliciting GDP Forecasts from the FOMC's Minutes Around the Financial Crisis'. *International Journal of Forecasting*, 32(2): 571–583.

Ericsson, N.R. (2017). 'Economic Forecasting in Theory and Practice: An Interview with David F. Hendry'. *International Journal of Forecasting*, 33(2): 523–542.

Ericsson, N.R. (ed.) (2021, forthcoming). *Celebrated Econometricians: David F. Hendry*, Special Issue, *Econometrics*.

Escribano, A. (1985). 'Non-linear Error-correction: The Case of Money Demand in the UK (1878–1970)'. Mimeo. La Jolla, CA: University of California at San Diego, December.

Escribano, A. (2004). 'Nonlinear Error Correction: The Case of Money Demand in the United Kingdom (1878–2000)'. *Macroeconomic Dynamics*, 8(1): 76–116.

Faust, J. and C.H. Whiteman (1997). 'General-to-specific Procedures for Fitting a Data-admissible, Theory-inspired, Congruent, Parsimonious, Encompassing, Weakly-exogenous, Identified, Structural Model to the DGP: A Translation and Critique'. *Carnegie-Rochester Conference Series on Public Policy*, 47(December): 121–161.

Forni, M., M. Hallin, M. Lippi and L. Reichlin (2001). 'Coincident and Leading Indicators for the Euro Area'. *Economic Journal*, 111(471): C62–C85.

Friedman, M. and A.J. Schwartz (1982). *Monetary Trends in the United States and the United Kingdom: Their Relation to Income, Prices, and Interest Rates, 1867–1975*. Chicago: University of Chicago Press.

Gilbert, C.L. (1986). 'Professor Hendry's Econometric Methodology'. *Oxford Bulletin of Economics and Statistics*, 48(3): 283–307.

Goldfeld, S.M. (1976). 'The Case of the Missing Money'. *Brookings Papers on Economic Activity*, 3: 683–730 (with discussion).

Goodhart, C.A.E. (1982). '*Monetary Trends in the United States and the United Kingdom*: A British Review'. *Journal of Economic Literature*, 20(4): 1,540–1,551.

Granger, C.W.J. (1981). 'Some Properties of Time Series Data and Their Use in Econometric Model Specification'. *Journal of Econometrics*, 16(1): 121–130.

Granger, C.W.J. (1986). 'Developments in the Study of Cointegrated Economic Variables'. *Oxford Bulletin of Economics and Statistics*, 48(3): 213–228.

Granger, C.W.J. (2001). 'Evaluation of Forecasts'. Chapter 6 in D.F. Hendry and N.R. Ericsson (eds) *Understanding Economic Forecasts*. Cambridge, MA: MIT Press: 93–103.

Granger, C.W.J. (2004). 'Time Series Analysis, Cointegration, and Applications'. In T. Frängsmyr (ed.) *The Nobel Prizes 2003*. Stockholm: Almqvist and Wiksell International: 360–366.

Granger, C.W.J. and P. Newbold (1977). 'The Time Series Approach to Econometric Model Building'. In C.A. Sims (ed.) *New Methods in Business Cycle Research: Proceedings from a Conference*. Minneapolis, MN: Federal Reserve Bank of Minneapolis: 7–21 (with discussion).

Granger, C.W.J. and A.A. Weiss (1983). 'Time Series Analysis of Error-correction Models'. In S. Karlin, T. Amemiya and L.A. Goodman (eds) *Studies in Econometrics, Time Series, and Multivariate Statistics: In Honor of Theodore W. Anderson*. New York: Academic Press: 255–278.

Hacche, G. (1974). 'The Demand for Money in the United Kingdom: Experience Since 1971'. *Bank of England Quarterly Bulletin*, 14(3): 284–305.

Hall, R.E. (1978). 'Stochastic Implications of the Life Cycle–Permanent Income Hypothesis: Theory and Evidence'. *Journal of Political Economy*, 86(6): 971–987.

Hatch, N. (2001). 'Modeling and Forecasting at the Bank of England'. Chapter 8 in D.F. Hendry and N.R. Ericsson (eds) *Understanding Economic Forecasts*. Cambidge, MA: MIT Press: 124–148.

Hoover, K.D. and S.J. Perez (1999). 'Data Mining Reconsidered: Encompassing and the General-to-specific Approach to Specification Search'. *Econometrics Journal*, 2(2): 167–191 (with discussion).

Johansen, S. (1988). 'Statistical Analysis of Cointegration Vectors'. *Journal of Economic Dynamics and Control*, 12(2/3): 231–254.

Johansen, S. (1995). *Likelihood-based Inference in Cointegrated Vector Autoregressive Models*. Oxford: Oxford University Press.

Johansen, S. and K. Juselius (1990). 'Maximum Likelihood Estimation and Inference on Cointegration—With Applications to the Demand for Money'. *Oxford Bulletin of Economics and Statistics*, 52(2): 169–210.

Johansen, S. and B. Nielsen (2009). 'An Analysis of the Indicator Saturation Estimator as a Robust Regression Estimator'. Chapter 1 in J.L. Castle and N. Shephard (eds) *The Methodology and Practice of Econometrics: A Festschrift in Honour of David F. Hendry*. Oxford: Oxford University Press: 1–36.

Johansen, S. and B. Nielsen (2013). 'Outlier Detection in Regression Using an Iterated One-step Approximation to the Huber-skip Estimator'. *Econometrics*, 1(1): 53–70.

Johansen, S. and B. Nielsen (2016). 'Asymptotic Theory of Outlier Detection Algorithms for Linear Time Series Regression Models'. *Scandinavian Journal of Statistics*, 43(2): 321–381 (with discussion and rejoinder).

Juselius, K. (2006). *The Cointegrated VAR Model: Methodology and Applications*. Oxford: Oxford University Press.

Kiviet, J.F. (1986). 'On the Rigour of Some Misspecification Tests for Modelling Dynamic Relationships'. *Review of Economic Studies*, 53(2): 241–261.

Klein, L.R. (1950). *Economic Fluctuations in the United States, 1921–1941*. Cowles Commission Monograph No. 11. New York: John Wiley.

Klein, L.R. (1971). *An Essay on the Theory of Economic Prediction*. Chicago: Markham Publishing Company.

Longbottom, A. and S. Holly (1985). 'Econometric Methodology and Monetarism: Professor Friedman and Professor Hendry on the Demand for Money'. Discussion Paper No. 131. London: London Business School.

Magnus, J.R. and M.S. Morgan (eds) (1999). *Methodology and Tacit Knowledge: Two Experiments in Econometrics*. Chichester: John Wiley and Sons.

Makridakis, S. and M. Hibon (2000). 'The M3-Competition: Results, Conclusions and Implications'. *International Journal of Forecasting*, 16(4): 451–476.

Martinez, A.B. (2020a). 'Forecast Accuracy Matters for Hurricane Damage'. *Econometrics*, 8(2): 1–24.

Martinez, A.B. (2020b). 'Improving Normalized Hurricane Damages'. *Nature Sustainability*, 3(7): 517–518.

Mazzi, G.L. and D. Ladiray (eds) (2017). *Handbook on Rapid Estimates: 2017 Edition*. Luxembourg: European Union.

Mills, T.C. (2011). 'Bradford Smith: An Econometrician Decades Ahead of His Time'. *Oxford Bulletin of Economics and Statistics*, 73(2): 276–285.

Mizon, G.E. (1977). 'Inferential Procedures in Nonlinear Models: An Application in a UK Industrial Cross Section Study of Factor Substitution and Returns to Scale'. *Econometrica*, 45(5): 1,221–1,242.

Mizon, G.E. (1995). 'Progressive Modeling of Macroeconomic Time Series: The LSE Methodology'. Chapter 4 in K.D. Hoover (ed.) *Macroeconometrics: Developments, Tensions, and Prospects*. Boston, MA: Kluwer Academic Publishers: 107–170 (with discussion).

Nelson, C.R. (1972). 'The Prediction Performance of the FRB–MIT–PENN Model of the US Economy'. *American Economic Review*, 62(5): 902–917.

Osborn, D.R. (1988). 'Seasonality and Habit Persistence in a Life Cycle Model of Consumption'. *Journal of Applied Econometrics*, 3(4): 255–266.

Osborn, D.R. (1991). 'The Implications of Periodically Varying Coefficients for Seasonal Time-series Processes'. *Journal of Econometrics*, 48(3): 373–384.

Phillips, A.W. (1954). 'Stabilisation Policy in a Closed Economy'. *Economic Journal*, 64(254): 290–323.

Phillips, A.W. (1957). 'Stabilisation Policy and the Time-forms of Lagged Responses'. *Economic Journal*, 67(266): 265–277.

Phillips, P.C.B. (1986). 'Understanding Spurious Regressions in Econometrics'. *Journal of Econometrics*, 33(3): 311–340.

Phillips, P.C.B. (1987). 'Time Series Regression with a Unit Root'. *Econometrica*, 55(2): 277–301.

Phillips, P.C.B. (1995). 'Automated Forecasts of Asia-Pacific Economic Activity'. *Asia-Pacific Economic Review*, 1(1): 92–102.

Phillips, P.C.B. (1996). 'Econometric Model Determination'. *Econometrica*, 64(4): 763–812.

Pretis, F. (2020). 'Econometric Modelling of Climate Systems: The Equivalence of Energy Balance Models and Cointegrated Vector Autoregressions'. *Journal of Econometrics*, 214(1): 256–273.

Raven, J., T. Hoehn, D. Lancefield and B. Robinson (2004). *Economic Analysis of the TV Advertising Market*. London: PricewaterhouseCoopers LLP. Available at: https://www.ofcom.org.uk/__data/assets/pdf_file/0018/23913/tvadvmarket.pdf.

Richard, J.-F. and W. Zhang (1996). 'Econometric Modelling of UK House Prices Using Accelerated Importance Sampling'. *Oxford Bulletin of Economics and Statistics*, 58(4): 601–613.

Rose, A.K. (1985). 'An Alternative Approach to the American Demand for Money'. *Journal of Money, Credit, and Banking*, 17(4, Part 1): 439–455.

Salkever, D.S. (1976). 'The Use of Dummy Variables to Compute Predictions, Prediction Errors, and Confidence Intervals'. *Journal of Econometrics*, 4(4): 393–397.

Sargan, J.D. (1964). 'Wages and Prices in the United Kingdom: A Study in Econometric Methodology'. In P.E. Hart, G. Mills and J.K. Whitaker (eds) *Econometric Analysis for National Economic Planning*. Volume 16 of *Colston Papers*. London: Butterworths: 25–54 (with discussion).

Sargan, J.D. (1975). 'Asymptotic Theory and Large Models'. *International Economic Review*, 16(1): 75–91.

Sargan, J.D. (1980). 'Some Tests of Dynamic Specification for a Single Equation'. *Econometrica*, 48(4): 879–897.

Siegert, W.K. (1999). 'An Application of Three Econometric Methodologies to the Estimation of the Income Elasticity of Food Demand'. Chapter 16 in J.R. Magnus and M.S. Morgan (eds) *Methodology and Tacit Knowledge: Two Experiments in Econometrics*. Chichester: John Wiley and Sons: 315–340.

Smith, B.B. (1926). 'Combining the Advantages of First-Difference and Deviation-From-Trend Methods of Correlating Time Series'. *Journal of the American Statistical Association*, 21(153): 55–59.

Stekler, H.O. and H. Symington (2016). 'Evaluating Qualitative Forecasts: The FOMC Minutes, 2006–2010'. *International Journal of Forecasting*, 32(2): 559–570.

Stock, J.H. (1987). 'Asymptotic Properties of Least Squares Estimators of Cointegrating Vectors'. *Econometrica*, 55(5): 1,035–1,056.

Stock, J.H. and M.W. Watson (2011). 'Dynamic Factor Models'. Chapter 2 in M.P. Clements and D.F. Hendry (eds) *Oxford Handbook of Economic Forecasting*. Oxford: Oxford University Press: 35–59.

Tinbergen, J. (1951). *Business Cycles in the United Kingdom, 1870–1914*. Amsterdam: North-Holland.

Tobin, J. (1950). 'A Statistical Demand Function for Food in the USA'. *Journal of the Royal Statistical Society, Series A*, 113(2): 113–141.

Tobin, J. (1956). 'The Interest Elasticity of Transactions Demand for Cash'. *Review of Economics and Statistics*, 38(3): 241–247.

Treasury and Civil Service Committee (1991a). *Memoranda on Official Economic Forecasting, Session 1990–91*, House of Commons. Two volumes. London: Her Majesty's Stationery Office.

Treasury and Civil Service Committee (1991b). *Official Economic Forecasting, Minutes of Evidence, Session 1990–91*, House of Commons. London: Her Majesty's Stationery Office.

Trivedi, P.K. (1970). 'The Relation Between the Order-Delivery Lag and the Rate of Capacity Utilization in the Engineering Industry in the United Kingdom, 1958–1967'. *Economica*, New Series, 37(145): 54–67.

Wallis, K.F. (1993). 'On the Limitations of Comparing Mean Square Forecast Errors: Comment'. *Journal of Forecasting*, 12(8): 663–666.

White, H. (1990). 'A Consistent Model Selection Procedure Based on *m*-Testing'. Chapter 16 in C.W.J. Granger (ed.) *Modelling Economic Series: Readings in Econometric Methodology*. Oxford: Oxford University Press: 369–383.

Yule, G.U. (1926). 'Why Do We Sometimes Get Nonsense Correlations Between Time Series?—A Study in Sampling and the Nature of Time Series'. *Journal of the Royal Statistical Society*, 89(1): 1–64.

25

Avner Offer (1944–)

Joshua Getzler

1 Introduction

Avner Offer's abundant scholarship may be divided into a number of streams. In his first two monographs, he developed fresh analyses of the course of British and imperial history from the 1870s to the Great War (Offer 1981, 1989), using as a fulcrum the idea of control of land as simultaneously the most basic factor of production and a potent source of political and cultural power. In his next two books, he analysed the rise of consumer society in the United States and the United Kingdom after 1950 (Offer 2006), and the links between high economic theory and market ideologies that from the early 1970s helped to disrupt and displace social democracy (Offer and Söderberg 2016). Extending these projects, Avner then turned to the historical evolution of finance and its penetration into pension, health and housing provision (Offer 2012a, 2014a, 2017a, 2018). He has also maintained a long-standing interest in the economics and culture of land ownership in Britain and in the visual representations of landscape. Any one of his contributions would be a substantial scholarly achievement. This chapter outlines the formative experiences and main writings of a world-renowned economic historian and searches for some keys as to how to understand his body of work taken as a whole.

J. Getzler (✉)
St Hugh's College, Oxford University, Oxford, UK
e-mail: joshua.getzler@law.ox.ac.uk

Avner is a fine historical writer, and his skills of narrative, evocation and exposition have assured him a readership beyond academia (e.g. *The Economist* 2006; James 2006; Venook 2016). He is as much a political economist and social scientist as a historian. Implicit as well as explicit models of social behaviour and economic structure and careful appraisal of data are always in play in his work, propelling and shaping the enquiry. Alongside formal causal models and quantitative analysis, Avner has deployed behavioural models going beyond the constrained maximisation constructs of economic theory. Key organising ideas in his work have included the quest for status and esteem, the mutually supportive functions of reason and emotion through instincts of altruism, empathy and reciprocity, the dilemmas of choice over time, the challenges of myopia and infirmities of self-control, and the social organisation of risk-bearing, risk-sharing, cooperation and conflict (Offer 2012a, b). He has always sought out moral, psychological and cultural explanations to challenge and enrich classical and neoclassical economic models based on methodological individualism. This wide theoretical curiosity, allied to high skill in archival work and devotion to empirical verification, has helped him to make original contributions to some of the oldest questions of political economy and economic history, such as aggregate and sectoral growth, demographic and class change, technological diffusion, specialisation and trade, the operation of markets (and States) in factor, capital and consumer goods (Offer 1980, 1991, 1993), the institutional evolution of property rights (Offer 1977, 1994) and the definition and measurement of welfare (Offer 1997, 2003).

Avner's life story is very different to that of his peers in British economic history and political economy. That story can give clues about the ideas that have animated the work of this highly original scholar. He was born in Mandatory Palestine in 1944 (Offer 2014b: 13–33; Nunan 2012) and grew up in Kibbutz Yifat in the Jezreel Valley, the heartland of Israel's communal agricultural settlements which had been founded by Jewish immigrants from Eastern Europe some two decades before. His father had come from Odessa in 1928, escaping the turmoil of the first decade of the Soviet Union. Avner's mother was born in Palestine, her forbears also coming from the Black Sea region. The young Zionist immigrants regarded Palestine as more than a place of refuge; here was an opportunity to pursue a revolution in the condition of the Jewish people, for an existential transformation. The settlements of the Jezreel Valley cultivated a new way of life for an ancient and harried people. Members abandoned their native languages to speak a revived Hebrew. They discarded inherited culture, heritage and religious traditions, rebelled against the bourgeois and shtetl legacies, and submerged individual need in the imperatives of the modern Zionist collective: "To build and to be built by the land", as the Zionist slogan went.

Yet there was something old-fashioned in Avner's upbringing in the utopian kibbutz. From his parents and also his schooling, he could imbibe high European culture alongside the austere values of pioneering and egalitarian Labour Zionism, which had its own secular canon of song, dance and ritual, much of it distilled from the German *Wandervogel* and East European folk culture. There was plenty of classical music to hear and fine literature to read, especially Russian classics in translation. Avner's mother was a talented poet and sculptor, and his father was intermittently an ambassador for the kibbutz movement, taking the family for sojourns abroad. Two and a half years in Canada and New York as a child aged five to eight helped form and cement Avner's easy command of English and this was followed, a decade later, by five months in Moscow at age 17, where he failed to learn much Russian, saving him from the risk of being tempted into the study of Soviet history and politics in later life, as he wryly acknowledged looking back over his career (Nunan 2012). These youthful memories may have affected his political outlook as well: he had early seen the superpower rivals at the peak of their confidence and success, expanding his awareness of the wider world beyond the confines and conformities of the pioneering State of Israel. A lifelong immunity to the extremes of market fundamentalism and dogmatic socialism might be ascribed to these youthful experiences of America and the Soviet Union, a kind of ideological inoculation. Other economic historians, including his close colleague and predecessor in the Chichele Professorship of Economic History at Oxford, Charles Feinstein, have been attracted to one or both poles; Avner has remained a resolute social democrat.

On the brink of military service in 1962, Avner developed a liking for photography and soon showed not only devotion to the art but also rare skill and talent. He thought that this might be his vocation after army service. Avner served for 11 years as a conscript and reservist in a paratroop reconnaissance infantry unit, seeing action in Jerusalem in the Six-Day War of 1967, and then in the Jordan Valley and the Sinai in the aftermath of that conflict, leading up to and including the 1973 Yom Kippur War. He captured his soldiering experiences of 1967 in an extraordinary series of photographs of soldiers and civilians, both Jewish and Arab, caught in the vice of war, images that were widely exhibited and published at the time and winning him first prize at the 1968 Tel Aviv Museum exhibition of "Photographs from the Six-Day War". His photograph of the paratroopers of his own unit advancing up the road to the Lion's Gate of the Old City of Jerusalem on their way to the Temple Mount nearby was one of the great images of the war and was widely reproduced. Avner collected these images into a memoir of the war written immediately afterwards, but only published in 2014. The book, entitled *Burn Mark* (Offer 2014b), can be viewed not only as an intimate record of a crucial campaign, but also a paean to past youth and camaraderie, a remembrance of the fallen and an elegy for a country that was to shed its innocence and diminish its ideals in the long years of conflict.

The jolt of the 1967 victory and the expansion of its borders gave Israel a burst of confidence, even euphoria, with shadows and doubts suppressed. As a loyal scion of the labour movement that still dominated Israeli society, Avner worked after the war as a farmer and pioneer both in his home kibbutz and in the new settlement of Sde Boker in the Negev Desert in the south of the country, where the founding premier David Ben-Gurion, by then in his eighties, resided in political retirement. Avner worked on nature conservation for an NGO and subsequently spent three years leading a field survey of the nature and landscapes of the Southern Sinai for the country's Nature Reserves Authority. During this period of Israel's strength and growth, Avner also perceived that the occupation of Palestinian land and domination of its people, excoriated by Ben-Gurion but embraced by most of the political elite, was leading Israel into a dead end. His unease was deepened by the constant rumbling of attritive war on Israel's extended borders, which absorbed the energies and took the lives of many of his generation.

In 1969, Avner embarked on studies at the Hebrew University of Jerusalem, a seat of learning still under the influence of the Germanic academic culture of its founding professors. He read geography, including a strong quantitative element, as a preparation for further conservation work, and also history as a key to understanding the sources of Israel's growing geopolitical and social predicaments. Avner studied with some of the scholarly greats of that era such as Jacob Talmon, who wrote a notable book on totalitarianism and populist democracy (Talmon 1952), and who courageously opposed the occupation of Palestinian territories. Through Talmon's study of the Rousseauian general will, Avner seems to have picked up a sense of the uneasy relationship between liberalism, democracy and nationalism at the birth of modern politics. He also developed a strong interest in history and philosophy of science and the logic of scientific discovery and explanation, and wrote a dissertation on Darwin. Israel's strong schools of behavioural economics and strategic bargaining were also then emerging, with scholars such as Daniel Kahneman, Amos Tversky and Robert Aumann in Jerusalem producing seminal insights into rationality beyond simple maximisation models. Avner remembers the ferment and excitement associated with those new ideas on the Jerusalem campus. Methodological concerns from these first years of study would come back into play much later when Avner turned his attention to the scientism of modern economic theory.

Avner graduated with high honours in 1973 and decided to accept a scholarship for study abroad, choosing the University of Oxford. He chose Britain over America as he wanted to study British imperialism and politics as determinants of Israeli history. He experienced this move to Britain in his late twenties as much as a severance from the encompassing world of the kibbutz as a parting from Israel. Avner had come to the conclusion that egalitarian kibbutz society, whilst admirable and just, was perhaps past its heroic stage and did not hold out sufficient challenges for the young. Moreover, his worries about the direction of the country were deepening as the dominant Israeli Labour Party became mired in corruption and infighting. He arrived on a scholarship at St Antony's College, Oxford, in the autumn of 1973 to commence doctoral studies on land ownership in England from 1870 to the First World War and after. He was supervised first by the Industrial Revolution historian Peter Mathias at Oxford and then by Michael (F.M.L.) Thompson from London University, author of classic works on English landed society and one of the foremost economic and social historians in the United Kingdom. Perhaps the study of a very different, deeply rooted and traditional landed society, a stark contrast to the socialist kibbutz, would help him make sense of the world from which he sprang.

Avner's first Oxford term was soon interrupted by a call back to military service on the fierce Sinai front of the 1973 war. He found himself fighting under the command of Ariel Sharon on the banks of the Suez Canal right up to the moment of ceasefire. Grateful to be alive, he returned to Oxford to bury himself in his research, producing his first monograph on *Property and Politics 1870–1914* in 1981, completed as a Junior Research Fellow at Merton College. Avner sensed that, after the trauma of the 1973 war, the political mood in Israel was hardening and the compromises necessary to make peace were beyond reach. He and his generation of the 1960s had paid a toll in war service, and, despite the field victories, the future road was dark. More time away made good sense, and he took up a Lectureship in the Department of Economics at the University of York, where he taught economic and social history alongside Feinstein who led the department. Feinstein was a pioneer of the new quantitative economic history with a virtuoso ability to gather and fine-tune the historical national accounts, the bedrock for empirical appraisal of macroeconomic performance (Offer 2017b).

Avner worked at York for a decade and his family enjoyed living there. His York phase was divided by a productive three-year research sojourn at the Australian National University in Canberra, where he became fast friends with the distinguished social historians Kenneth and Amirah Inglis. The family flourished in the balmy environment of mid-1980s Australia, and there Avner researched and wrote his second monograph (Offer 1989), which described the agrarian origins of the First World War and traced the deeper structures of the far-flung pre-war British Empire. In 1991, he was appointed to a senior position back at Oxford, as a Reader and Professorial Fellow at Nuffield College, moving in 2000 to the Chichele Chair in Economic History at All Souls College in succession to Feinstein and held earlier by Mathias.

At Oxford, Avner helped build up a powerful economic history group which included Feinstein, Knick Harley, Jane Humphries and Robert Allen. The team also included Nicholas Dimsdale, Paul David and other stars. At the time, this may have been the premier economic history group in the world, with new graduate courses attracting an international student body, and a constant stream of distinguished visitors and research collaborators. Avner contributed to the programmes with energy and commitment, helping to launch many scholarly and professional careers. He revelled in collegiate life, where the generations mixed at a common table, bonded by a common purpose, and trusting in the good sense and sound motivations of one other. The life of the college was 'the closest I could find to a kibbutz', Avner said more than once.

In this latter phase, his attention turned to the social and cultural shape of late capitalism and the ideologies of political economy, resulting in a widely read and warmly reviewed monograph on affluence, well-being and post-war capitalism (Offer 2006). He later embarked on a study, joining with the younger Swedish scholar Gabriel Söderberg, which took the history of the Nobel Prize in Economics as a framework to explore the meaning and impact of modern economic theory (Offer and Söderberg 2016). Avner spent several periods in America to study and experience at close hand the epicentre of world capitalism, finding the manufacturing culture of Detroit, even in its decline, as interesting as New York as a financial and cultural capital. These latter works analysed and documented the undermining of individual self-control and satisfaction in consumer society, and the neglect of community, solidarity and social obligation by modern economics.

Avner retired from the Chichele Chair in 2011. Freed from full-time teaching and administration, he continued to work on more recent issues in political economy, tracing the displacement of social democracy by market liberalism in the West, particularly the Anglosphere, from 1970 to the present. He also explored the trajectories along which finance has affected the organisation of housing, welfare and government. His work on the historical problem of quality of life has evoked wide interest beyond the academy, with governments in the United Kingdom, Sweden and Israel keen to learn from his work.

In "retirement", the flow of vigorous work has not abated—rather the opposite. Avner remains as a stalwart presence and beneficial force at Oxford, always ready to give attention and good advice to students and colleagues, and continuing with a considerable effort of teaching and supervision. Beyond the university community, he has also contributed as a public intellectual with occasional forays into policy. His main vocation remains as a scholar, and his influence as a writer and communicator in his discipline is exceeded by none. We now turn to investigate more closely that body of work.

2   Land, Tenures and the Property State

Property and Politics 1870–1914 (Offer 1981) is a work of high ambition that was acknowledged by reviewers on publication as a stunning debut. Here, Avner aimed to anatomise English society before the Great War by working through the relationships of landed wealth and income, taxation, regulation, private and municipal enterprise, land and credit markets, professional human capital (with a special focus on lawyers and clerics), local and national politics and the cultural and ideological dimensions of landholding. The material covered was dense, but skilfully ordered with ideas drawn from classical and modern political and economic theory. In the Offerian vision, Adam Smith's rational actors seek approbation and acceptance from their status as property holders, as well as maximisation of incomes. Ricardo's capitalists avoid competition and capture rents from property ownership. Pareto's elites partake of a culture of "romantic residues" derived from past forms of economic life and property. Bentham's State regulates and stabilises the allocation of resources by conferring property rights, with owners paying a portion of their wealth to maintain the State which establishes and protects their property. Henry George's land monopolists extract unearned increments from industry and labour as towns expand and the economy grows. Rousseau, who is accorded the first and last lines of the book, describes property as a coercive source of inequality, the original worm of self-regard, destroying the pre-lapsarian world of natural community. Underpinning the entire study was a basic problem in political theory from Hobbes and Locke, through Rousseau, to Mill and Marx: How can fallen man civilise an unequal property-holding world through politics?

To make sense of it all, Avner developed his own theory of "tenures", or claims by groups to privileged status and income by virtue of their cohesion as owners or professionals. Tradition and expertise vest these groups with lucrative control of resources and skills. The first part of the book, entitled "Law as Property", is the main instantiation of the tenure thesis and threw light on some highly technical aspects of the development of property law and practice (elaborated earlier in Offer 1977). Lawyers were the tenured professional group par excellence, extracting a share of social wealth by their monopoly control of legal transactions, especially land conveyance. These ideas of rent seeking and regulatory capture were deployed at the same time that they were first being modelled more formally in the United States. Land law reform, pre-eminently land registration as a rationalisation of conveyancing, was the proving ground for lawyers' independent, self-governing professional status. Edwardian solicitors' incomes were threatened by a downturn of the property cycle and by overcrowding of the profession. Self-interested solicitors, organised under the umbrella of the Law Society, blocked attempts by Benthamites and Liberals to institute a system of land registration as a quick, cheap and secure form of recording and conveying titles, a system that reformers held to be clearly superior to common law conveyance by deed. The lawyers disagreed, claiming that their arcane techniques were beyond the reach or understanding of non-professionals. The legislation that finally emerged in 1922–1925 was designed to rationalise property law on the legal professionals' terms. It solved a string of particular problems and assisted in the liberal commodification and clarification of land entitlements, but also preserved the lucrative role of lawyers in executing title searches, land contracts and conveyances. Self-interested professionalism thus defeated the public interest, and Britain's economy remained saddled with high legal transaction costs for the remainder of the twentieth century.

These conceptions of monopolistic human capital and professional identity, cartelisation and rent seeking exerted a wide influence amongst economic, social and legal historians in the decades that followed (see, for example, Perkin 1989 and Anderson 1992). Avner's critique of the professions came from the left but chimed with the Thatcherite assault on establishment and professional formations in the 1980s. At the same time, his critical account of the lawyers' promotion of their own interests attracted rebuttals or demands for adaptation by scholars who found value in the pre-modern sensibilities of the old learned professions (Anderson 1992; Pottage 1994; riposte from Offer 1994).

Moving from legal to political authority, Avner was also interested in the reciprocal nature of State authority and property prerogatives. In the liberal (Lockean, Kantian) equation, the representative State exists to protect and manage property, which requires taxation and administration—but not redistribution, which is seen as an illegitimate violation of vested rights beyond the reach of politics. How is that line to be held in modern times when the State's power rests on a growing franchise, and the public realm, both local and national, is called upon to shoulder new and heavy tasks of military and welfare investment? This was the conundrum that led to the People's Budget of 1909 and the constitutional crisis that followed, and launched a deeper crisis of State legitimacy in Britain that fluctuated in intensity but that has never really ended.

Avner went on in *Property and Politics* to describe the mounting conflict between town and country, Liberals and Tories, capitalists and rentiers, over who should bear taxation burdens necessary to support the modern welfare and warfare state, and who should reap the benefits of expanding social wealth expressed in rising property values. He deployed quantitative data to describe wealth distributions, modes of land ownership and levels of income and taxation over the period covered by the volume, dissecting high politics and the motivations of leading actors, giving due weight to the social and cultural dimensions of ownership in the politics of property. In later quantitative work, Avner showed that economic payoffs could not explain the premium prices commanded by land, a gap which he explained in terms of the social and political status and self-esteem that command of acres or houses conferred on the owner (Offer 1980, 1991). He went on to examine the reduction or abolition of rates, the capping of local government taxation, the sell-off of public housing and promotion of private home ownership to reshape the electorate, the channelling of savings via profit-taking banks into the domestic land market (Offer 2014a, 2017a), and the opening of property ownership to investors as a store of value and leveraging opportunity, which effected a febrile boom in both commercial and domestic land markets in Britain. Current work in progress shows how mass home ownership in the twentieth century could only be achieved by means of government mandates, sanctions and subsidies.

3   Food, Empire and War

Avner's next historical project, *The First World War: An Agrarian Interpretation* (Offer 1989) was situated in the same fin de siècle as *Property and Politics*, but ranged across a much wider terrain. Here, Avner examined international food supply as a factor in the course of late Victorian imperialism and the run up to, outbreak, prosecution and settlement of the Great War. During the "first globalisation" of 1870–1914, Britain outsourced much of its food supply to overseas suppliers, as did Germany, albeit to a lesser extent. This new international division of labour exposed the maritime supply routes of food and essential raw materials to naval blockade. This gave rise to international tensions which were instrumental in setting off the First World War and affected the way it was fought and concluded.

Avner began by examining the German food economy during the war, assessing the fragility of domestic and imported supplies, and carefully reconstructing the quality of food and calorific intake over time. He then linked this to data on illness, mortality and morale, both on the front and at home, concluding that the sense of deprivation and uncertainty incurred by food stress, including the ill will caused by competition for food resources and coercive rationing by the State, were more significant factors in understanding Germany's defeat than the insult to health during this protracted period of hardship. These discoveries marked the beginning of Avner's quest to find secure economic-historical measures of welfare that go beyond the commodity standard of living.

The book then turned its focus to the Allies where the picture was very different. Across a century or more of specialisation in trade and industry, Britain had run down its domestic food economy and become dependent on cheap food imports—which explained the country's mediocre food culture in modern times. Britain's manufactured exports did not cover the cost of its food and raw material imports, a gap bridged by services and income from overseas assets, and vouchsafed by financial and naval power. Wheat was the essential staple, and Avner explored the migration of Britons to the prairies and pastures of the Dominions, showing how the bonds of trade, kinship and shared culture held together a vast imperial system of food production and transport. He then demonstrated that the deepening of the British food trading economy between the metropole and peripheries of empire affected the social structure of both. Large land ownership in Britain, with its tenant farmers and impoverished wage labourers, could not compete with the yeoman farmers of the Dominions, who enjoyed land abundance and strong incentives to work for economic independence on their homesteads. A similar analysis of settler capitalist societies had been developed by Avner's Canberra colleague Donald Denoon a few years earlier (Denoon 1983). In sum, British farming declined, starved of investment and labour, whilst colonial and North American farming flourished. Impoverished British workers moved to the wealthier colonies in search of better lives. Changes in land use and agrarian pricing affected wage levels and opportunities for capital investment. These developments help explain the migration cycles of the pre-war period, the development of social democracy in the Dominion societies, their exposure to the ebb and flow of capital movements and commodity prices, and the heightened class conflict and angry politics in the British metropole.

Avner then analysed the social and economic development since the mid-nineteenth century of the three main breadbaskets supplying Britain—Australia, Canada and the United States, offering glimpses also of South American export production, and contrasting these with subsistence systems in Russia and India. Wheat was like petroleum—a bulk-traded international good, not easily replaced, and cheap to transport in highly responsive markets. Avner highlighted an interesting dualism in the wealthy wheat-exporting societies: a high-wage settlement and well-developed public goods, combined with fear of competition from Asia and considerable racial animus. The inefficient constraints on free labour migration in the Pacific Rim was an economic puzzle whose answer lay not only in the relations of inside and outside labour markets but also in terms of the colonial insistence on a white racial identity and imperial defence. When war broke out, the Dominions leapt to the defence of the mother country and sent their youth to die across the oceans in Europe and the Middle East at rates comparable to the losses of the British and French.

The second half of the book focused on military strategy and the economics of blockade. Avner demonstrated, through painstaking research in the British and German archives, how the pre-war leadership of Britain and Germany were each conscious that they had surrendered their food self-sufficiency through economic specialisation, and came to fear the other's capacity to cut vital food supplies. On both sides, therefore, political and military elites strove to neutralise the mutual threat of starvation by means of military and naval superiority. After two years of stalemate in the trenches, Germany made the fateful decision to launch economic war against a staggering Britain by starting the U-boat campaign against mercantile shipping. By bringing America into the war, the submarine campaign guaranteed German defeat, and a tight food blockade helped to bring the Central Powers to their knees.

The global story of international food production and trade added a new dimension to this much-studied history of strategic miscalculation and descent into the Great War, and also gave a new twist to economic theories of empire, moving explanation away from the Hobsonian theory of capital export and under-consumption as the taproot of imperial expansion. Avner suggested that military planning on the German side with its fatalistic commitment to decisive action regardless of the consequences overcame civilian rationality both in the initial attack of 1914, and the "second decision for war" being the 1917 U-boat campaign (Offer 1995). The story on the British side was more complicated; the civilian and naval planners expected to win a long war by means of blockade and had good reasons to avoid being drawn into a land war. The pre-war Liberal government attempted to deter and constrain the Germans by means of a naval build-up and a bellicose posture. When Germany failed to read the signals and threw the dice in August 1914, Britain was drawn into a continental commitment.

Avner also highlighted the social contract on the home front as a factor in understanding the course of the war. The nation state in all combatant countries placed heavy demands on its populations and had to offer a modicum of equality in return. German officialdom was more coercive and less inclined to rely on moral appeals and market incentives to discipline production and ration consumption. Avner argued that resentment about the inequality of burdens leached the authority of the German State and undermined the war effort. In contrast, the British home front remained more or less intact. With the hardships of the Allied food blockade extending into the winter of 1918–1919, accompanied by the flu epidemic, German civil society was gravely weakened; this, together with the punitive Allied victory settlement, left a poisonous political legacy post-war. The idea of unequal burdens and coercion as destructive of polity was to recur in Avner's later social and economic analyses.

4   Wealth and Time, Self-control and Satisfaction

Avner's third major project, *The Challenge of Affluence*, shifted ground in both the time periods studied and techniques applied. It also reached for an economic as well as a historical audience and was very widely read, reviewed, praised and criticised. The subject was the affluent and hedonistic consumer society that emerged in the United States and Britain after 1950. The book kicks off with the core argument: 'Affluence breeds impatience, and impatience undermines well-being' (Offer 2006: 1). Avner here took aim at the core assumption of neoclassical economics that people were the best judges of their own good. The criticism went beyond the usual behavioural and game-theoretic qualifications of expressed preference utilitarianism, viz. that bounded rationality and coordination problems could impede the instrumental attainment of goals. Avner was more interested in the plentiful social-psychological and survey evidence where people reported stagnation or decline of their happiness levels even as they satisfied their wants. This observation has long been a staple of moralising literature and psychology; Wilde quipped in his 1892 play *Lady Windermere's Fan* that it was a much worse tragedy to get what you want than not; Freud in *Studies in Hysteria* three years later suggested that the task of psychoanalysis was to help modern man attain merely common unhappiness, and there is certainly a tradition in utilitarian ethics of identifying higher and lower forms of well-being (Gintis 2007). Could a rigorous social science of the relation of want-satisfaction to happiness be charted? Avner advanced a new testable hypothesis: that the flow of abundant and novel material and experiential pleasures of late capitalism can undermine the quality of life as evidenced by the indices of reported levels of subjective well-being. Consumption in the affluent society strains the consumer's capacity to assimilate, enjoy and attend to meaningful life experience, with deleterious effects on intimacy, health and life satisfaction. Material abundance and overexposure to marketing intensified the intrinsic preference for immediate satisfaction, and consequent surges of over-stimulation swamped the capacity for enjoyment. The key to well-being was to bring stimulation into alignment with the capacity for enjoying it.

Avner deployed models of hedonic experience and consumer and household decision-making in a series of original test cases examining sources of pleasure (and pain) as varied as advertising, car ownership, dissemination of consumer durables, body weight and self-control, occupational status, inequality, sex and family life. Key to his approach was the problem, being worked out in behavioural economics, of hyperbolic discounting, a form of hedonic myopia that makes temporally distant but significant rewards far more difficult to build into a calculus of decision-making than immediate pleasures or avoidances of pain or effort. Modern affluence had diffused compelling but potentially harmful consumer satisfactions through society, promoting poor-quality foods which caused an obesity crisis inimical to health and self-esteem, and particularly afflicting the poor whose futures were much more uncertain than those of the wealthy. Two chapters examined the frenzy for bigger and gaudier automobiles; Detroit had preferred to manipulate desire by means of unremitting but superficial novelty over investment in durable engineering and safety. The advent of mass auto-ownership contributed to congestion, pollution, suburbanisation and the breakdown of community; a private good generated public bads. Another chapter, co-researched with Sue Bowden, examined the temporal diffusion of domestic consumer durables—cleaning, cooking and entertainment devices—and found that "time-using" entertainment appliances, television and radio, diffused more rapidly than "time-saving" ones, which reduced the workload of housewives. The time saved from housework was transferred into watching television. Consumption was promoted by highly proficient and manipulative advertising that wore a "mask of intimacy", but ubiquitous commercial speech ultimately undermined trust in all information in the public space and debased the public good of truth and sincerity, of mutual expectations of honesty.

An important bridge between instrumental theories of rational choice and a secular concept of the good life was found in the work of the psychologist George Ainslie. In *Picoeconomics* (1992), Ainslie modelled the individual as involved in a constant process of bargaining between inter-temporal states of motivation, setting up "commitment devices" to enforce internal deals prioritising future states over near-field pleasures, and repressing self-cheating. Avner demonstrated how the historian and social scientist could expose the cultural inheritance of commitment devices that stinted and gave savour to experience, that afforced the Ainsliean internal deals; and conversely, one could measure the negative impact on utility when such commitments were weakened or abandoned. The temptations of myopia were traditionally countered by social commitment devices like table manners, education, mortgages, marriages, insurance and pensions. Heightened consumer choices and stimuli undermined communal and institutional commitment devices that had slowed down consumption, delayed satiation and maintained appetite and anticipation. The old curbs had constrained immediate pleasures and maintained a more sustainable sense of well-being.

Avner charted changes in family structure, as the patient staging of courtship, sexual initiation and marriage gave way to impatience and restlessness in relationships, with women and children the main victims. Another source of ill-being was the rise in inequality and extension of status ladders. Much well-being is generated by being able to compare oneself favourably to others, and to one's past self. Modern consumer capitalism set up a privatised acquisitive arms race that diminished a rough equality of basic goods and made people at the bottom feel like losers, even though they were consuming more than generations past.

The book's chapter on obesity (based on Offer 2001) explicitly treated the condition as a challenge to the rationality assumption in economics. People regret the overeating that makes them obese even as it happens, and then strive to undo the result by means of slimming and medical treatment. A follow-up analysis demonstrated that English-speaking countries have much higher rates of obesity than European welfare states and shows that overeating is a response to the competitive pressures of market liberalism, to economic insecurity rather than (as argued by others) to inequality (Offer et al. 2010).

Avner's achievement in *The Challenge of Affluence* was to apply a novel combination of behavioural, decisional and welfare models across a varied historical canvass composed of carefully gathered and measured data: 'I have woven the argument from the whole range of evidence: this is both social science and history' (Offer 1989: 11). The book could also be read as a sustained attack on much of modern economics and the public policies that economics supports or justifies. Data showed that economic growth and increased GDP per head did not promote subjective happiness. Indeed, efforts to increase prosperity measured in material terms might actively undermine the capacity for well-being.

What, then, was the appropriate measure of happiness? Myopic limitations on rationality and the unmanageable abundance of information prevented the self-referential individual from properly assessing all available options across any longer period of time; in modern economic theory, everything was driven by individual choice, but social science had also generated plentiful evidence that meaningful maximising of utility over time was impossible. Instead, Avner embraced an older political—or better, moral—economy. In an influential article (Offer 1997, developed in Offer 2006: Chapter 5), he introduced the concept of "the economy of regard", in which aspiration was guided not by self-interest but by a quest for approbation. Exchange was started by a unilateral gift which elicited a discretionary response, starting off a cycle of mutually beneficial reciprocity. The idea originates in Smith's *Theory of Moral Sentiments*. In another article, Avner showed that the concept of "sympathy" was an intrinsic capacity which was required to establish a social order driven by our concern for the good opinion of others (Offer 2012b).

Avner's arguments were criticised by many economists, reasserting their well-rehearsed intuitions that more was not less, that choices were empowering and the meeting of needs and wants was generally pleasant (Gintis 2007). Such critics may have missed that Avner was really cleaving to an adapted utilitarianism, expanding the measures of happiness to include inter-subjective experience, self-esteem and approbation derived from mutuality and obligation. He also, in effect, displaced instrumental rationality, the efficient adaptation of means to reach discretionary goals. Instead, he preferred a model of judgement and taste guided by culture as a good in itself, and also better suited to deal with the decisional challenges of time discounting and future uncertainty. Friendly critics (Oswald and Powdthavee 2007) suggested that there was a sting in the tail of such social measures of well-being and reason: in an affluent society of impatient, over-consuming, miserable and ill individuals, one's self image and canons of judgement, born of comparison to others, might settle into a low equilibrium, normalised by one's social surrounds and expectations. This insight has been supported by later research on the flaws of contemporary capitalism, especially with the decline of meaningful work, the fraying of community and the unavailability of decent health care causing increased "deaths of despair" in contemporary America (Case and Deaton 2020).

5   The Market Turn

Avner acknowledged that his 2006 study of affluence did not cover the complementary topics of public goods and collective welfare provision. In his next period of research, he entered this fray and carried the enquiry forward into recent decades of intellectual, political and financial history. Avner analysed the turn to market definition of social relations that had taken place since the 1970s, both in high economic theory and in political discourse and action. Avner observed how the "market turn" had eviscerated social democracy, which he conceived as a pooling of life risks and production of public goods brokered by a trusted State. The ring-fencing of risk and smoothing of life-cycle earnings by non-market institutions (social insurance) has been replaced by market organisation of housing, education, health, employment and retirement through deregulated financial institutions. Politically difficult cross-generational welfare pacts have been replaced by unreliable contractual intra-generational savings and insurance deals. Arguing for the depoliticisation of an inefficient mixed economy, these reforms brought financial gains and political power for a small elite, matched by insecurity and stagnant incomes for the rest, with the result that the whole system regularly tipped into crisis.

There was an intellectual story to be told. In *The Nobel Factor*, a co-authored study of the origins and history of the Nobel Prize in Economics, written with Gabriel Söderberg, Avner showed how the Riksbank, the Swedish central bank, had set up and paid for the Prize from the late 1960s with the purpose of celebrating economic theorising that questioned the social democratic consensus of high tax and transfer and strong public goods. The coterie of Swedish economists controlling the award of the Prize were discreet and nuanced as they set to work. Survey data showed that some two-thirds of the economics profession had a left-of-centre policy orientation but approximately half the prizes went to conservative economists, including Friedrich von Hayek, George Stigler, Milton Friedman, James Buchanan and Robert Lucas. These awards enhanced the credibility of their free market theories and their often aggressively conservative or libertarian politics. Most of the other prizes went to liberal economists such as Paul Samuelson, Robert Solow, Kenneth Arrow and Joseph Stiglitz, who nevertheless were committed to the assumptions of neoclassical economics. Only one prize went to a social democrat, Gunnar Myrdal, from Sweden, though behaviourists such as Daniel Kahneman and Elinor Ostrom who received awards also stood somewhat outside the liberal consensus.

Avner found much to deplore in the post-war development of economic science, with the Chicago School from Friedman to Lucas, and the wider (and somewhat different) circle of economists associated with Hayek and the Mont Pelerin Society. The moral and political values of conservative economics presented it as a "Just World" theory, in which the market gives everyone what they deserve, regardless of their prior endowments and how these might have been obtained. As Friedman put it: 'The ethical principle that would directly justify the distribution of income in a free market society is, "To each according to what he and the instruments he owns produces"' (Friedman 1956: 1). The consequence is indifference to inequality. Prestigious branches of economic theory (such as optimal taxation and public choice) give precedence to policies based on the purported efficiency of imagined free markets over the proven benefits of social equity and public goods. In other words, economic theory can too easily serve as a "warrant for pain" (Offer 2014c).

In his solo and collaborative writings on the technical content of modern economic theory, Avner engaged with two main approaches which are inconsistent with each other. One is "good faith economics", which scales up the discretionary choices of omniscient individuals into a socially optimal general equilibrium. This is a harmony theory in which there is no conflict of interest. Alternatively, in "bad faith economics", information is asymmetric and limited and everyone has an incentive to cheat. Good faith economics is unrealistic but specifies optimal policy solutions. Bad faith economics is more realistic but is empirically indeterminate and is unattractive ethically. Neither provides reliable guidance for policy.

Can society do better? Hayek argued that it was impossible for any form of social management to encompass the richness of information handled smoothly by the market. In recent writings, Avner has produced powerful counterarguments to this based on the heuristics of time discounting and collective decision-making in conditions of uncertainty to make a positive case for public goods and social insurance (Offer 2003, 2012a, 2018). He names these "prudential goods" and shows how wealthy societies have historically expanded the production of such goods to form some 40% of the economy. Prudential goods are hardened into institutionally protected entitlements for good reason: not as illegitimate use of public power for sectional rent seeking, but rather as commitment devices to overcome market failures and coordination costs, to extend time horizons, to pool risks and benefits and help individuals smooth life-cycle earnings, and to achieve economies of scale. Since the 1970s, hostility from the high economic theorists, consumer restlessness, political boredom and division, and short-termism by politicians currying electoral favour combined to undermine investment in prudential goods, resulting in breakdowns in societal order that ultimately harmed individual prosperity for the majority or for large minorities—a price that the electorate seemed willing to pay or at least unwilling to recognise.

In recent work, Avner develops a new theory of the private-public boundary. The efficiency attributes of the market are only available for short-term projects whose duration is determined by the break-even time horizon defined by the prevailing interest rate. The higher the interest rate, the shorter this time horizon. If a project has a longer break-even, it cannot be undertaken by profit-making business on its own. It needs to be undertaken directly by society (through public enterprise or not-for-profit), or by a "franchise" whose profit is underwritten by society. Between them, these social and hybrid forms of enterprise cover more than half of aggregate economic activity. Competitive markets are important enclaves, but cannot provide a template for society.

One corollary of pervasive public and hybrid economic activity is widespread corruption which has increased in line with marketisation and financialisation. A possible solution to such problems is indicated by the successful "integrity revolution" which took place in Northwestern Europe in the second third of the nineteenth century. This was achieved by aligning the interests of public servants with their occupational codes, and worked well for about a century until the privatisation of public services and the introduction of competitive incentives into those remaining in the public sector. Payment by results in the public service set up a conflict between the self-interest of officials and the public good. Meanwhile, the privatised utilities and services continued to depend on government support. This support extends to the very heart of capitalism, the financial system which relies on central bank clearing, regulation, credit and bailouts (Offer 2018, and current work in progress). Here was a tragic irony: myopic choice amplified by sectional interests and accelerated by economic ideology is strong enough to undo the commitment devices installed historically to counter it. The linked crises of 2020 in public health and the macroeconomy highlight what is at stake.

6   Conclusion

Some of the dominant themes of classical and New Economic History concerned economic performance across time, defined in terms of growth, expansions of productive capacity through technology or organisation, rising standards of living, demographic expansion and power relations and material distributions mediated by class, race and gender. Surveying Avner's work as an integrated whole, he has embraced these questions in his research programme, especially in his first phase of work, but he has also taken them in new directions. He has focused on the paradoxes and pathologies of modern economic growth, observing how social and military conflict, the search for security, status and identity, and the fragility of well-being, make the judgments of political economy more, not less, difficult even in a world of technological change and material plenty. But the picture is not all dark: Avner's narratives and analyses are leavened with the sense that social and individual choice can always take new courses, that goodwill, mutuality and cooperation are just as common as self-interest, rivalry and conflict, and that a prudent social democracy supporting a secure and genial citizenry is, despite all, quite possible.

We may ponder how life experience, education, culture, identity and memory will shape the intellectual life of a particular scholar or writer, and how valuable it is for the reader to know something of the life of an author or creator. Avner's life and formation outside the liberal Anglo-American consensus, in the first decades of socialist Israel, is surely a large element shaping his historical and economic vision, his sense of what most needs explaining. We can leave the last word on this puzzle to Avner himself, who offered these lines to readers of his 1989 work on the First World War, at the close of the preface (Offer 1989: ix):

> A decade or so spent as a farmer, soldier, public servant and student in Israel in the 1960s and 1970s prepared me to perceive the agrarian, military and mental patterns of the Edwardian Empire. Those years also exposed me to some of the faces of war.
>
> Clouds float across my window
> In many towns, on many desks,
> then seasons, years—a decade yet?
> A mound of paper binds me in the net
> of puzzles that research might yet unravel
> and memories that I am ever striving to forget.

References

Main Works by Avner Offer

Offer, A. (1977). 'The Origins of the Law of Property Acts, 1910–25'. *Modern Law Review*, 40(5): 505–522.

Offer, A. (1980). 'Ricardo's Paradox and the Movement of Rents in Britain, c.1870–1910'. *Economic History Review*, New Series, 33(2): 236–252.

Offer, A. (1981). *Property and Politics 1870–1914: Landownership, Law, Ideology and Urban Development in England*. Cambridge: Cambridge University Press.

Offer, A. (1989). *The First World War: An Agrarian Interpretation*. Oxford: Oxford University Press.

Offer, A. (1991). 'Farm Tenure and Land Values in England, c.1750–1950'. *Economic History Review*, New Series, 44(1): 1–20.

Offer, A. (1993). 'The British Empire, 1870–1914: A Waste of Money?'. *Economic History Review*, New Series, 46(2): 215–238.

Offer, A. (1994). 'Lawyers and Land Law Revisited'. *Oxford Journal of Legal Studies*, 14(2): 269–278.

Offer, A. (1995). 'Going to War in 1914: A Matter of Honor?'. *Politics & Society*, 23(2): 213–241.

Offer, A. (1997). 'Between the Gift and the Market: The Economy of Regard'. *Economic History Review*, New Series, 50(3): 450–476.

Offer, A. (2001). 'Body Weight and Self-Control in the United States and Britain Since the 1950s'. *Social History of Medicine*, 14(1): 79–106.

Offer, A. (2003). *Why Has the Public Sector Grown So Large in Market Societies? The Political Economy of Prudence in the UK, c.1870–2000*. Oxford: Oxford University Press.

Offer, A. (2006). *The Challenge of Affluence: Self-Control and Well-Being in the United States and Britain Since 1950*. Oxford: Oxford University Press.

Offer, A. (2012a). 'The Economy of Obligation: Incomplete Contracts and the Cost of the Welfare State'. Discussion Papers in Economic and Social History, University of Oxford, 103(August). Available at: https://pdfs.semanticscholar.org/a673/f0e499acb03a343b6a303ccc3de82e7e3192.pdf?_ga=2.191585325.601989749.1591885991-635948987.1548679853.

Offer, A. (2012b). 'Self-Interest, Sympathy and the Invisible Hand: From Adam Smith to Market Liberalism'. *Economic Thought*, 1(2): 1–14.

Offer, A. (2014a). 'Narrow Banking, Real Estate, and Financial Stability in the UK, c.1870–2010'. Chapter 9 in N. Dimsdale and A. Hotson (eds) *British Financial Crises Since 1825*. Oxford: Oxford University Press: 158–173.

Offer, A. (2014b). *Burn Mark: A Photographic Memoir of the Six Day War*. Oxford: Lintel Press.

Offer, A. (2014c). 'A Warrant for Pain: *Caveat Emptor* vs the Duty of Care in American Medicine, *c.*1970–2010'. Chapter 15 in N. Morris and D. Vines (eds) *Capital Failure: Rebuilding Trust in Financial Services.* Oxford: Oxford University Press: 332–349.

Offer, A. (2017a). 'The Market Turn: From Social Democracy to Market Liberalism'. *Economic History Review*, 70(4): 1,051–1,071.

Offer, A. (2017b). 'Charles Hilliard Feinstein (1932–2004)'. Chapter 46 in R.A. Cord (ed.) *The Palgrave Companion to Cambridge Economics.* London: Palgrave Macmillan: 1,027–1,044.

Offer, A. (2018). 'Patient and Impatient Capital: Time Horizons as Market Boundaries'. Discussion Papers in Economic and Social History, University of Oxford, 165(August). Available at: https://www.economics.ox.ac.uk/materials/working_papers/4670/165-avner-offer.pdf.

Offer, A., R. Pechey and S. Ulijaszek (2010). 'Obesity Under Affluence Varies by Welfare Regimes: The Effect of Fast Food, Insecurity, and Inequality'. *Economics & Human Biology*, 8(3): 297–308.

Offer, A. and G. Söderberg (2016). *The Nobel Factor: The Prize in Economics, Social Democracy, and the Market Turn.* Princeton: Princeton University Press.

Other Works Referred To

Ainslie, G. (1992). *Picoeconomics: The Strategic Interaction of Successive Motivational States Within the Person.* Cambridge: Cambridge University Press.

Anderson, J.S. (1992). *Lawyers and the Making of English Land Law 1832–1940.* Oxford: Clarendon Press.

Case, A. and A. Deaton (2020). *Deaths of Despair and the Future of Capitalism.* Princeton, NJ: Princeton University Press.

Denoon, D. (1983). *Settler Capitalism: The Dynamics of Dependent Development in the Southern Hemisphere.* New York: Oxford University Press.

The Economist (2006). 'The Perils of Prosperity: Can You Be Too Rich?'. 27 April. Available at: https://www.economist.com/books-and-arts/2006/04/27/the-perils-of-prosperity.

Friedman, M. (1956). 'The Distribution of Income and the Welfare Activities of Government'. Lecture delivered at Wabash College, 20 June. Available at: https://miltonfriedman.hoover.org/friedman_images/Collections/2016c21/MFlecture_06_1956_5.pdf.

Gintis, H. (2007). 'Economic Growth and Well-Being: A Behavioural Analysis'. *Economic Journal*, 117(521): F445–F459.

James, O. (2006). 'Workaholic Consumerism is Now a Treadmill and a Curse'. *The Guardian*, 2 May. https://www.theguardian.com/commentisfree/2006/may/02/comment.politics1.

Nunan, T. (2012). 'Interview with Avner Offer'. 28 July. Available at: https://docs. google.com/viewer?a=v&pid=sites&srcid=ZGVmYXVsdGRvbWFpbnxhdm9m ZmVyfGd4OmVjNjRhMmRhNzliMzA1Zg.

Oswald, A.J. and N. Powdthavee (2007). 'Obesity, Unhappiness, and *The Challenge of Affluence*: Theory and Evidence'. *Economic Journal*, 117(521): F441–F459.

Perkin, H. (1989). *The Rise of Professional Society: England Since 1880*. Abingdon: Routledge.

Pottage, A. (1994). 'The Measure of Land'. *Modern Law Review*, 57(3): 361–384.

Talmon, J.L. (1952). *The Origins of Totalitarian Democracy: Political Theory and Practice During the French Revolution and Beyond*. London: Secker & Warburg.

Venook, J. (2016). 'The Political Slant of the Nobel Prize in Economics'. *The Atlantic*, 9 October. Available at: https://www.theatlantic.com/business/archive/2016/10/ nobel-factor-offer-soderberg/503186/.

26

John Muellbauer (1944–)

John Duca

1   Introduction[1]

John Muellbauer is a distinguished Oxford economist who has made notable, especially applied, contributions in the economics of demand analysis, consumption, housing and financial stability, and in macroeconomics more generally. His influential co-authored paper, "An Almost Ideal Demand System", published in 1980, was selected as one of the best 20 papers published in the first 100 years of the *American Economic Review*. It was prominently mentioned by The Royal Swedish Academy of Sciences, amongst his publications, when the paper's co-author, Angus Deaton, was awarded the Nobel Prize in Economics in 2015. Their highly regarded book, *Economics and Consumer Behaviour*, also published in 1980, has been widely used in graduate courses and cited over 7,000 times.[2] The book is considered a modern classic: it was described as a landmark by Blundell (1988) more than three decades ago, and this was reiterated by Besley (2016; see also Besley et al. 2011). John's research

---

[1] Please note that the views expressed in this chapter are those of the author and are not necessarily those of the Federal Reserve System.

[2] As reported by Research Papers in Economics (RePEC).

J. Duca (✉)
Oberlin College, Ohio and Federal Reserve Bank of Dallas, Dallas, TX, USA
e-mail: jduca@oberlin.edu

© The Author(s), under exclusive license to Springer Nature Switzerland AG 2021
R. A. Cord (ed.), *The Palgrave Companion to Oxford Economics*,
https://doi.org/10.1007/978-3-030-58471-9_26

spans theory and empirics, and it emphasises the importance of using empirical evidence to assess the former while requiring the latter to be well-grounded in theory.

Two prominent themes have pervaded John's research: addressing theoretical consistency and reducing misspecification in empirical models, partly by incorporating institutional heterogeneity across countries and over time; and using evidence to engage in policy debates. These considerations have motivated his development of theory-based, empirical frameworks, flexible enough to encompass an eclectic set of influences and insights, and yet sufficiently tractable to avoid the curse of dimensionality and be able to yield robust and reliable estimates. This emphasis on consistency, completeness and practicality has played a role in his interests evolving from mainly microeconomics to macroeconomics. Since the early 1980s, a major focus of his research has been modelling aggregate consumption and housing markets and analysing the role of housing in the wider economy. More recently, his research has broadened to cover the interconnections between macroeconomics and financial stability.

John has long engaged in prominent policy debates in the UK. These include the UK's supposed productivity growth revolution of the early 1980s, Thatcher's misconceived poll tax of the late 1980s and the collapse of the UK savings rate in the 1980s. He argued that the UK's departure from the Exchange Rate Mechanism (ERM) was inevitable in 1992[3] and explained why Britain should not adopt the euro as its currency. He has made influential and significant contributions over many years to debates about reforming UK housing policy. Through newspaper articles and VoxEU, he has engaged a wider audience in macroeconomic policy debates, for instance, on inflation and exchange rate pass-through (Muellbauer and Aron 2008; Aron and Muellbauer 2014a, b), a prescient article on the imminence of a housing-led recession (Muellbauer 2008a), early articles encouraging credit easing by central banks during the global financial crisis (Muellbauer 2008b, c), Eurobonds and the Eurozone's sovereign debt crisis (Muellbauer 2011), monetary policy lessons from Japan (Muellbauer and Murata 2011), fiscal policy lessons and the UK's 'lost generation' (Muellbauer 2014a), "QE for the People" (Muellbauer 2014b, 2016a), and the failure of central bank models (Muellbauer 2016b).

John has combined an Oxford tradition of robust econometric testing with a Cambridge tradition of developing the implications of the insights of John

---

[3] Two days before the UK was forced to leave the ERM, the *Financial Times* published John's oped explaining why the exchange rate was unsustainable. In the immediate aftermath, in another oped, he argued that the outcome would be benign, forecasting correctly that inflation would be subdued.

Maynard Keynes and Richard Stone. His work also extends later insights on wealth and asset prices from Franco Modigliani, James Tobin and Robert Shiller, on expectations from Robert Hall, and on credit constraints from George Akerlof and Joseph Stiglitz. His many honorary distinctions include election as a Fellow of the Econometric Society in 1975, a Centre for Economic Policy Research (CEPR) Research Fellow in 1983, a Fellow of the British Academy in 1997, and a Fellow of the European Economic Association in 2006. John has also served on the editorial boards of the *Review of Economic Studies* and *Econometrica*, inter alia.

2   Origins, Education and Career

John Muellbauer was born in a hamlet in the foothills of the Alps in south-west Bavaria. His father, Norbert, was a scientist in the field of electronics, who had lost his wartime scientist's exemption from military service owing to strongly anti-Nazi views. His mother, Edith Gruber, hailed from Vienna, where she studied piano at the Vienna Conservatory of Music, but later had to work as a laboratory assistant. To survive the Nazi era, she and her spouse obscured the Jewish heritage of her father, who had been a City Councillor in Vienna. In the early 1950s, John's parents took advantage of an opportunity for his father in the electronics industry, and the family emigrated to the UK, first to South Wales and later to London. Aided by a diligent teacher and the efforts of his mother, John quickly learned English and was able to excel in his entrance exams to grammar school, later gaining admission to King's College, Cambridge.

As an undergraduate at Cambridge, his tutors in economics included Christopher Bliss, Frank Hahn, Robin Marris and Luigi Pasinetti, and he enjoyed studying sociology with John Goldthorpe.[4] The young lecturer, Charles Goodhart, influenced his thinking on balance sheets and monetary transmission. Following Cambridge, John pursued his PhD at Berkeley. Lectures from the Nobel Laureate Dan McFadden introduced him to duality theory, which John drew on in his early solo-authored contributions to economics and in his joint work with Angus Deaton. He studied econometrics with Dale Jorgenson and Edmond Malinvaud, and statistics with Henry Scheffé. Two other Berkeley giants were particularly influential. One was Aaron Gordon, whose coverage of business cycles emphasised econometric analysis of the major components of GDP and the role of financial crises,

---

[4] Both Bliss and Goldthorpe were later colleagues of John at Nuffield College.

drawing on Kindleberger's and Minsky's early work. The second was Robert ("Bob") Hall, who supervised John's dissertation on applying hedonics and index number theory to measuring prices for consumer and producer durable goods; his later work on the consumption Euler equation, Hall (1978), posed challenges addressed by John's subsequent time series contributions.

Following his graduate studies at Berkeley, John returned to the UK to begin a long and distinguished career as an academic. He has a son (and three grandchildren) from his first marriage, and a daughter from his subsequent marriage to Janine Aron, an Oxford economist and co-author.

John began in academia as a Lecturer at Warwick in 1969, moving in 1972 to Birkbeck College, where colleagues included Richard Portes, A.G. ("Bertie") Hines, John Broome, and later, Dennis Snower. He was a Lecturer, then Reader, and finally Professor of Economics at Birkbeck.[5] In 1981, he moved to Nuffield College, Oxford, as Official Fellow (1981–2011), Senior Research Fellow (2012–present) and Professor of Economics (1997–present). Over the years, his Nuffield colleagues included a sextet of Sirs, Tony Atkinson, David Cox, Andrew Dilnot, David Hendry, James Mirrlees and Stephen Nickell, and other distinguished academics, including Steve Bond, Terence Gorman, Paul Klemperer, Meg Meyer, Bent Nielsen, Avner Offer, Neil Shephard, Hyun Shin and John Vickers. This range of talents, the interdisciplinary atmosphere of an outstanding graduate social science college and interaction with its students provided a highly stimulating environment. The College freed John to pursue research he judged important, independently of the fashions of the time. It also enabled him to interact with visiting fellows from the world outside academia. John served on the Investment Committee throughout his time at Nuffield until 2016 and was the Investment Bursar for 13 years, including during the bursting of the dotcom bubble in 2000–2002 and the global financial crisis and its aftermath during 2008–2016. He taught for over 30 years on the Oxford MPhil programme and supervised MPhil and DPhil students, many of whom have become eminent economists. He has also been a Senior Research Fellow at the Institute for New Economic Thinking at the Oxford Martin School (2012–present), which under the respective leaderships of Eric Beinhocker and Ian Goldin have taken an interdisciplinary, collaborative approach to new levels, addressing the most important problems of the age.

Apart from his academic career, John's engagement in policy debate has included an active role in advising policy makers. In the UK, he served on the

---

[5] While in London, John began interacting with Terence Gorman and Dennis Sargan, and also started a long friendship and professional association with David Hendry, later also a Fellow at Nuffield.

Chancellor's group of economic advisers in 1990 and played an important role on the Retail Price Index Advisory Committee in 1993–1996. He provided a central part of the case in 1997–1998 for why the UK failed to meet the Treasury's "five economic tests" for entering the Eurozone.[6] For many years, he served on the expert housing panel advising the relevant ministry and has been an expert witness for the House of Lords and the Treasury Select Committee. He and Janine Aron produced six reports from 2009 to 2014 for the UK government's housing ministry on mortgage arrears and repossessions (see, for example, Aron and Muellbauer 2016). He has engaged widely with many central banks on policy, modelling and research issues since 2000. In the early 2000s, he assisted the Bank of England in measuring credit conditions (see Fernandez-Corugedo and Muellbauer 2006). For the South African Reserve Bank (SARB), he and Aron assembled the first time series of household balance sheets for any emerging market economy (see Aron and Muellbauer 2006), now regularly published by the SARB and used in their core model. Together, they have contributed over 20 policy-relevant research papers on South Africa, including on monetary policy, forecasting output and inflation, modelling consumption and debt, and measuring exchange rate pass-through, for example, see Aron and Muellbauer (2000, 2002, 2012, 2013a) and Aron et al. (2014a). John has also worked with charitable foundations and think tanks such as Shelter, the Joseph Rowntree Foundation, the Nuffield Foundation, the Resolution Foundation, the Institute for Public Policy Research and the National Institute of Economic and Social Research, and international organisations, including the World Bank, the Organisation for Economic Co-operation and Development (OECD) and the Bank for International Settlements (BIS).

Since the global financial crisis, John's hitherto less fashionable macroapproach has received significant and increasing attention. This began with an invited presentation to the 2007 Jackson Hole conference on "Housing, Housing Finance, and Monetary Policy" (see Muellbauer 2007) and a request from the BIS in 2009 to evaluate the policy-modelling framework conventional among central banks (see Muellbauer 2010). Since 2006, a research collaboration on macro-financial linkages, housing and financial stability proved fruitful with John Duca at the Dallas Fed, later including Anthony Murphy (see Duca et al. 2010, 2011, 2016, 2019; Duca and Muellbauer 2014). John was awarded a Wim Duisenberg Fellowship at the European Central Bank (ECB) for collaboration with ECB, Bundesbank and Banque de France researchers to develop better models for macro-financial linkages (see

---

[6] See https://en.wikipedia.org/wiki/Five_economic_tests.

Geiger et al. 2016; Chauvin and Muellbauer 2018). SARB Research Fellowships during 2018–2020 have supported work with Aron on the SARB's new financial stability mandate (see Aron et al. 2019a, b).

3   Muellbauer's Contributions to Economics

The early contributions of John Muellbauer centred on accurately modelling household behaviour and measuring welfare at the microeconomic level. His interests later evolved towards a greater focus on macroeconomics, extending beyond household economics. The bulk of his work has entailed crafting well-grounded empirical implications of consumer and macroeconomic theory, then reconciling and interpreting reliable empirical patterns with sensible modifications of neoclassical and efficient market theory to account for credit constraints, uncertainty and open economy considerations.

3.1   Early Precursors to the AIDS Model and *Economics and Consumer Behaviour*

Many of John's early publications contained the individual building blocks that he and Angus Deaton combined to develop their famous Almost Ideal Demand System (AIDS) model. These include the use of duality theory to formulate indirect utility functions (or cost functions) that are more amenable to generating estimable demand functions than are direct utility functions. Using the cost function representation of preferences made it possible to discuss the impact of taste and quality change on consumer cost of living indices in a more elegant and compelling way than hitherto (see Muellbauer 1975). It also permitted a translation of the framework for defining household equivalence scales, proposed by Prais and Houthakker (1955) and Barten (1964), into cost functions (see Muellbauer 1974a, 1977, 1980). This allowed welfare comparisons across households of different compositions, the measurement of the "cost of children" (also see Deaton and Muellbauer 1986) and incorporation of the differential impact of relative price movements and of household composition in the measurement of welfare and inequality (see Muellbauer 1974b).

A second important application of duality theory was to devise forms of preferences that could be aggregated across households, while being less restrictive than then-prevailing frameworks used by economists. The earlier, seminal contributions of Gorman and Stone had imposed identical linear

Engel curves such that the marginal propensities to consume of particular classes of goods and services were invariant to levels of income. This assumption is convenient in permitting aggregation across households into aggregate demand functions but is contrary to empirical evidence.

The research that led to the AIDS model began with a 1974 Birkbeck working paper, triggered by John's concern about the distributional impact of inflation, entitled "The Political Economy of Price Indices". John made a remarkable discovery in asking the question: whom does an index such as the retail price index (RPI) represent, or where in the income distribution could one find a household with expenditure patterns similar to the weights used in the RPI? With identical linear Engel curves, such a representative household would have had average income, which is restrictive. John generalised the concept of the representative household, leading to a new class of preferences and a more general representative income level (see Muellbauer 1975, 1976). This research spawned a new literature in demand analysis discussed below. Though not published at the time, the 1974 paper also generated a research on "social cost of living indices", for example, Jorgenson and Slesnick (1983) (see Muellbauer 2019a, b, for the paper and its historical context).

In his 1976 *Econometrica* paper, John asks what form of preferences, shared by all consumers, would allow budget share equations defined for the aggregate of consumers to be represented simply by budget share equations driven by prices and the income of a single representative consumer. He characterised this income concept—in general—as a function of prices and of the entire income distribution of individual consumers. This characterisation of "community preferences" imposed less restrictive assumptions than used earlier by Gorman. John gave the name "generalised linearity" (GL) to this form of preferences. Under GL preferences, budget share equations are linear, but now in a *general* (non-linear) function of prices and income common to each budget share equation. In his 1975 article in the *Review of Economic Studies*, the same problem was studied with the further requirement that the income of the representative consumer be independent of relative prices, depending only on the underlying income distribution across consumers. This "price independent generalized linearity" (which he christened PIGL) meant that the budget share equations are linear in a general power function of income, whose form is the same for all consumers. A special case arose where the function was logarithmic, which he named "the PIGLOG case". Subsequent empirical micro-evidence suggested that the PIGLOG case was in fact the best fitting in the PIGL class.

PIGLOG imposes the condition that expenditure shares be linear in log income, which allows Engel curves in the level of income to be non-linear.

This is more realistic than the assumptions made in the linear expenditure system (LES) of Stone. The PIGLOG specification allows aggregate behaviour across consumers to be modelled as though it emanated from a single maximising agent. Nevertheless, PIGLOG implies that that aggregate behaviour depends not only on average income, but also on its distribution. With reliable time-series data on income distribution, PIGLOG also provides a way of linking aggregate behaviour and the income distribution.

The work described in Muellbauer (1975, 1976) inspired a new literature that extended forms of Engel curves and of preferences, with useful aggregation and other properties. Gorman (1981) introduced the notion of the rank of a system of Engel curves. Rank 1 corresponds to homothetic preferences where budget shares do not depend on the level of total expenditure. Rank 2 includes linear Engel curves and GL, the latter being the necessary and sufficient condition for the representative household concept discussed above. Engel curves of Rank 3 further extend functional forms, and with useful aggregation properties (see Lewbel 1988, 1989, 1991). The "Quadratic Expenditure System" of Howe et al. (1979) is an example of such an extension of GL, while the translog form of demands of Jorgenson et al. (1982) is an application within the GL class.

3.2   The AIDS Framework

Addressing the need for a general but accessible empirical specification for econometric studies, Muellbauer and Deaton made a tremendous contribution to economics in developing their Almost Ideal Demand System. The AIDS framework is rare in being both well-grounded in economic theory and empirically tractable and flexible for estimating a broad range of consumer behaviour. By drawing on Muellbauer's earlier work on duality theory, aggregation and PIGLOG preferences, building on the 1970s literature on flexible functional forms (see Diewert 1971), and combined with Deaton's econometric insights, the AIDS framework derives demand specifications that can be aggregated across households and estimated using linear techniques. When it was created, it had several features which made it attractive relative to its two main competitors for estimating demand systems—the linear expenditure system of Stone, and the "Rotterdam model" associated with Henri Theil and Anton Barten.

From a theoretical perspective, the AIDS framework has four major, desirable properties for a system of demand functions for different types of goods, while assuming that households are rational and specifying a form of heterogeneity enabling aggregation across households. The least technical of these properties ("additivity") implies that individual demands will add up to satisfy an overall budget constraint. Three technical attributes stemming from maximising behaviour could easily be imposed: homogeneity in prices and income, symmetry in the cross-price responses, and a condition on the matrix of cross-price derivatives.[7] Symmetry implies that the marginal effect of a change in the price of good A on the demand for another good B is the same as the marginal effect of a change in the price of good B on the demand for good A, for a given level of utility. One implication of the matrix condition is that a higher price of a good should not increase the demand for that good (holding utility constant). These features are shared by Stone's LES, but they follow in the AIDS framework with preferences less restrictive than the Stone-Geary utility form assumed by the LES approach. An advantage over the Rotterdam model is that the AIDS framework can be derived from well-behaved preferences while still having much of the empirical flexibility of the Rotterdam model.

The AIDS framework proved especially suited for a wide range of empirical applications. The flexibility and limited restrictions imposed by the AIDS model made it popular for analysing the demand for various goods. As it is nearly linear, the component demands in AIDS can be estimated independently. If used with a well-specified aggregate price index, ordinary least squares suffices to estimate each component or the whole system.

Deaton and Muellbauer (1980a: 312) eloquently summarise their paper's contribution:

> Our model, which we call the Almost Ideal Demand System (AIDS), gives an arbitrary first-order approximation to any demand system; it satisfies the axioms of choice exactly; it aggregates perfectly over consumers without invoking parallel linear Engel curves; it has a functional form which is consistent with known household-budget data; it is simple to estimate, largely avoiding the need for non-linear estimation; and it can be used to test the restrictions of homogeneity and symmetry through linear restrictions on fixed parameters.

For all these reasons, the paper has, according to RePEC, been cited in over 1,400 publications.

The extensive application of the AIDS approach rests partly on the ease with which expenditure shares of broad categories of goods and services can be modelled. Moreover, if consumer preferences are weakly separable, then

---

[7] This third property is that the Slutsky matrix of all derivatives of the Hicksian demand functions be negative semi-definite.

the AIDS, like other demand systems, can model expenditure on goods within a broad expenditure category independently of how spending is allocated across the goods in other expenditure categories. The separability assumption also makes the AIDS framework useful for empirically modelling portfolio behaviour (see Barr and Cuthbertson 1991; Blake 2004). Separability[8] allows for a hierarchy of decision-making where a household chooses an overall portfolio size, then an allocation across different categories of assets and liabilities, and then particular instruments within each of these categories.

As with any framework, there are limitations to the AIDS. In applications that condition on average income without considering distributional shifts, it implicitly assumes that the distribution does not change over time. Another shortcoming in some implementations is the use of a simple approximation of the underlying price index to deflate nominal income (rather than taking further steps in a simple iterative procedure,[9] or implementing a full systems estimation). Thirdly, expenditure shares are not always linear in log income, as noted by Banks et al. (1997), who developed a variant of the AIDS framework allowing for quadratic Engel curves, which they dubbed QUAIDS. The appeal and applicability of the AIDS model, along with the development of variants to address its weaknesses, have made it a widely used framework in empirical analysis. Indeed, three and a half decades after its publication, Besley (2016: 381) described it as a 'cornerstone of demand estimation'.

3.3   *Economics and Consumer Behaviour*

John has made noteworthy contributions in modelling consumption. Especially important was his 1980 book co-authored with Angus Deaton entitled *Economics and Consumer Behaviour* (Deaton and Muellbauer 1980b). This classic of the literature was designed both as a comprehensive textbook for graduate economics and as a reference work for economists. The first part provides readers with a well-organised and accessible introduction to consumer choice and duality theory. Duality theory is then used to derive cost functions, including those underlying the demand functions that Stone–Deaton's graduate adviser—estimated in his classic LES. The authors then introduce the AIDS framework and a simple but effective application. The

---

[8] Separability is a testable hypothesis. Chauvin and Muellbauer (2018) model components of household balance sheets, including liquid assets and two types of debt, and reject the hypothesis on aggregate data.

[9] A simple iterative procedure gives first-stage estimates of the parameters using an approximation to the price index, and the price index can be updated with these parameter estimates. Several steps usually result in estimates close to the full information maximum likelihood estimates of the system.

book, from the start, effectively integrates theoretical and empirical analysis, a relatively rare achievement in economics.[10] Thereafter, there are extensions to analysing labour supply and durable goods purchases.

The second part of the book reviews the conditions needed for demand components to be separable and for demand to be aggregated across consumers—both featured prominently in John's early publications in refereed journals. This sets the stage for the third section of the book, on consumer index numbers, Engel curves, and the analysis of social welfare.

The fourth part of the book provides a mix of theoretical and empirical extensions, covering topics involving labour supply, intertemporal choice, consumption and income dynamics, the demand for durables, discrete choice, credit rationing and uncertainty. Deaton and Muellbauer were prescient in introducing readers to the relevance of these topics—which preoccupied economic research in the following decades—and to tools to allow them to be addressed with better integration of theory and empirical practice.

A particular achievement of the book was highlighting the contributions and shortcomings of the then prevailing representative agent and perfect markets version of the life-cycle/permanent income hypothesis (LCH/PIH). At the micro-level, the book documented how empirical tests of the basic tenets of the theory were rejected using this framework. Deaton and Muellbauer pointed to the need to incorporate credit constraints, heterogeneity in preferences, and uncertainty into an LCH/PIH framework in order to better reconcile micro-theory with empirical evidence. In so doing, their book helped many in the economics profession (especially those of us in graduate school) to make sense of the implications of research on imperfect information and financial frictions unfolding in the following decades.[11]

3.4   Evolution Towards Macroeconomics

In the 1970s, partly in response to the high unemployment rates of the period, much work was done on the macroeconomics of "disequilibrium" or "fixed-price" macro, for example, in the excess supply/excess demand regime-switching models of Barro and Grossman (1971), Drèze (1975, 1987) and Malinvaud (1977). Muellbauer and Portes (1978a, b) introduced an element of forward-looking behaviour, previously missing, into these models

---

[10] This balance of theory and practice reflects the tremendous influence of Stone and the "British empirical tradition".

[11] This integration of the micro and macro aspects of consumption also marked the early stages of how Muellbauer's research focus shifted from microeconomics to macroeconomics.

illustrated with an attractive diagrammatic apparatus. Muellbauer and Winter (1980), in an empirical application of the ideas to UK manufacturing employment, relaxed the closed economy assumption found in many models, and the assumption that the entire economy was in one given regime. The fixed-price approach later fell out of favour with the profession as it lacked convincing explanations of pricing, the economics of labour market search and how agents' expectations were formed.

3.5   Productivity Growth, Labour and Capacity Utilisation

Following Thatcher's rise to power in 1979, enormous changes took place in the UK economy. Dramatic financial liberalisation sowed the seeds of the later consumption and house price boom, tough economic measures were enacted to lower inflation, and, together with reforms of labour market regulation, these changes eventually destroyed the power of the trade unions. From 1979 to 1986, around a third of employment in UK manufacturing disappeared. Some—in particular the government—claimed a revolution had begun in productivity growth. To assess such claims, Mendis and Muellbauer (1984) and Muellbauer (1986, 1990) examined evidence on productivity growth in UK manufacturing accounting for hard-to-measure changes in labour and capacity utilisation, and measurement problems in value-added.[12] Assuming a stable distribution of actual hours around normal hours, the authors derived the mean of actual hours relevant for measuring productivity from the observed upper tail, which produced convincing results. Part of the productivity gain in UK manufacturing was genuine, but output per head substantially overestimated the gains. Thus, measured productivity growth proved sensitive to controlling for utilisation rates. In his critical assessment of real business cycle models, Muellbauer (1997) suggested that the pro-cyclical movement of supposed "productivity shocks" driving such models was largely due to mismeasurement—from omitting variation in utilisation rates.

3.6   Explaining Aggregate Consumption…

In the 1980s, John's research interests shifted to the macroeconomics of consumption and the role of the open economy, building on his microeconomic

---

[12] Labour hoarding is hard to measure as paid-for hours and actual hours of work can diverge. Paid-for overtime is a good indicator of the upper tail of the distribution of actual hours.

work on consumption and aggregation. This occurred against a backdrop of large macroeconomic and exchange rate cycles in the UK. Hall (1978), in his landmark paper on the implications of the LCH/PIH model of consumption under rational expectations and the absence of credit constraints, showed that the intertemporal optimality condition, the Euler equation, implied that the growth rate of consumption should be unpredictable.[13] Muellbauer (1983) tested this consumption model on UK data and rejected Hall's hypothesis. After accounting for a structural break associated with the shift from fixed to flexible exchange rates in 1971, he found instead that important marginal information about consumption was contained in lagged consumption and lags in income. The rejection could not be attributed to either time variation in the real interest rate or to violations of the perfect credit markets assumption in the form of shifts in the proportion of credit-constrained households. This led John to suspect that other factors, such as household balance sheets, were involved; a more complete specification of a consumption function was necessary to be consistent with aggregate time-series data.

In a related paper, Muellbauer (1988) investigated whether habit formation in consumption could explain why consumption was sensitive to past lags of income in the presence of lagged consumption. Habit describes the notion that the utility from consumption in a period depends to a significant extent on consumption levels in surrounding periods. He tested two forms of habit formation, one he dubbed rational and the other, myopic, and found evidence supporting the latter. This inspired John to work further on modelling consumption allowing for lagged adjustment towards target or equilibrium consumption and to apply equilibrium- or error-correction models of time-series consumption, in extensions of the Davidson et al. (1978) equilibrium correction model for consumption.

3.7 …Then to Both Housing and Consumption

John was amongst the very first economists to analyse how housing booms and busts could influence consumption and to consider wider interactions between housing and the economy, for example, labour markets and migration. His work was influenced by the large swings in UK house prices during the 1970s and 1980s. In a paper on why the UK personal sector saving rate had collapsed, Muellbauer and Murphy (1989) proposed a consumption function incorporating many of the elements of the "credit-augmented

---

[13] Hence, consumption follows a so-called Martingale process.

consumption function" of John's later work with various co-authors. In an equilibrium correction framework, the long-run solution for the log of non-durable consumption was specified as a function of the log of non-property income, the log of the relative price of non-durables and durables, and ratios to income of liquid assets, debt and illiquid assets, sometimes split into housing and financial assets. The model controlled for interest rates, demography and a proxy for income uncertainty. Crucially, tests overwhelmingly rejected the restriction that household wealth portfolios could be summarised in a single net worth statistic. Interaction effects also proved highly significant, either with illiquid assets or with housing wealth, each with an increasing ogive dummy representing financial liberalisation (zero up to 1981 then rising to 0.95 in 1988). The results indicated that financial liberalisation made illiquid assets, and especially housing, far more spendable. Drawing on these findings, Muellbauer and Murphy (1990) explained how an increased ability of households to borrow against rising home equity could make consumption highly vulnerable to booms and busts in house prices, especially in an open economy where capital inflows could indirectly bolster mortgage-equity withdrawal (MEW). Subsequently, David Miles, a doctoral student of John's and former member of the Bank of England's Monetary Policy Committee, developed this insight (see Miles 1992).

A comprehensive survey paper on consumption by Muellbauer and Lattimore (1995) proposed consumption functions that allowed for sluggish adjustment and controlled for real interest rates, uncertainty, expected future income growth, wealth and housing wealth interacted with credit conditions. By including liquidity, credit constraints, uncertainty and expectations effects, they incorporated insights not only from Hall (1978), but also from Deaton (1991) and Carroll (1992) on buffer-stock saving, and the literature on credit constraints associated with Akerlof, Jaffee, Stiglitz and Weiss. This survey paper influenced the consumption function adopted in the large Federal Reserve FRB-US model introduced in 1996,[14] although the model unfortunately did not build in the recommended credit channel influences or wealth disaggregation.

The common practice in the empirical literature on consumption is still to aggregate all forms of household financial and housing assets minus all debt into one wealth variable, namely net worth. Muellbauer and Lattimore (1995), as did Muellbauer and Murphy (1989), noted that using total net

---

[14] For example, FRB-US used the recommended wealth to income form of wealth effects, which gives a far better approximation than the commonly used log wealth formulations and a high discount rate to formulate permanent income given the perceived riskiness of income.

worth ignores substantial costs to households if they fail to meet debt obligations, a risk leading many households in practice to put greater (negative) weight on a unit of debt than on a unit of gross assets. Disaggregating net worth at least into liquid assets minus debt, illiquid assets (such as pension wealth) and housing wealth reflects differences in the marginal propensities to consume of these different components. Another argument for separating out housing wealth is that housing is both a consumption good and an asset, and intertemporal choice theory then implies that it should be treated differently from financial wealth. This research was a precursor to the studies of Mian et al. (2013) and Mian and Sufi (2018) on the US consumption boom and bust of the mid-2000s to early 2010s.

The related question of what determines house prices was studied by Muellbauer and Murphy (1997). They inverted the demand for housing services, as in Poterba's (1984) classic house price model, and found that easier mortgage credit conditions—in the presence of controls for real interest rates and expected income—bolstered house prices. The first time the inverse demand approach was applied to spatial house price determination was in Cameron et al. (2006a), which explained variations in regional house prices with a system of inverted demand equations. Prices in each region depend not just on same-region incomes and housing stocks, but also on those of other regions. Consequently, there are cross-regional spillover or "ripple" effects of house price changes. An implication of this spatial analysis is that *where* additional housing is constructed, it may have a substantial effect on national house prices. Muellbauer (2019c) applied these ideas to a model of Parisian house prices: as in London, prices in Paris proved to be more sensitive to interest rates and credit conditions than elsewhere in the country.

An innovative feature of John's research has been his emphasis on the important double role for credit conditions in influencing both house prices and consumption, partly via the collateral role of housing wealth (e.g. borrowing against housing equity can contribute to swings in consumption across housing price booms and busts). In much of his research on housing and consumption, John has tried account for changing credit conditions by improving measures of difficult-to-observe credit availability. Beginning with a 2000 working paper, published in revised and updated form as Aron and Muellbauer (2013a), a technique of extracting a measure of credit conditions as a latent variable common to several equations was developed. This first application was to two equations for consumption and household debt in South Africa.[15]

Fernandez-Corugedo and Muellbauer (2006) used the latent variable method in a 10-equation system for aggregate debt and proportions of mortgage loans in high loan-to-value and high loan-to-income tranches to extract a mortgage credit conditions index for the UK. Duca and Muellbauer (2014) christened the technique, "latent interactive variable equation system" (LIVES), since the interaction of credit conditions with housing wealth or the house price-to-income ratio is a crucial feature of the credit channel. Applying the method to the US, they showed that the interaction of the fall in house prices and the contraction of credit after 2007 explained the sharp fall in consumption relative to income. More generally, their paper emphasised the importance of household balance sheets. Consistent with Brainard and Tobin's (1968) vision of integrating finance and monetary policy into macro-models, and to incorporate a more modern Bernanke-Gertler-Gilchrist type of household financial accelerator, they explained methods for endogenising household balance sheets in plausible and tractable ways.

Cognizant of the heterogeneity in financial regulations and development across economies, Muellbauer and his collaborators have applied the LIVES method to several other countries, including Australia (Muellbauer and Williams 2012), Canada (Muellbauer et al. 2015), Germany (Geiger et al. 2016) and France (Chauvin and Muellbauer 2018). For most countries, Muellbauer and his co-authors used a spline approach[16] to estimate the time variation in the effect of non-price terms of both mortgage and consumer (non-real estate-secured) credit on consumption. The inclusion of credit conditions through the LIVES methodology in aggregate, time-series models of consumption addresses an omitted variable bias found in conventional models of consumption. For most countries, this notably improves model fit and raises the speed of adjustment of actual to equilibrium consumption levels from implausibly slow to more plausible. Japan and Germany are exceptions since credit conditions for households underwent little change in Japan and only moderate changes in Germany.

In his 2007 Jackson Hole Symposium article, John warned of the downside risk that the housing-fuelled US consumption boom of the mid-2000s would unwind in a bust. In a study of the US, the UK and Japan, Aron et al. (2012),

---

[15] The time lapse before publication was due to the construction of a set of time-series estimates of household balance sheets for South Africa, the first for an emerging market economy (see Aron and Muellbauer 2006; Aron et al. 2008).

[16] In Duca et al. (2012), they instead used the Kalman filter to measure the latent variable in a two-equation model for consumption and mortgage refinancing.

Muellbauer and co-authors show how credit-augmented, generalised consumption models outperform the "barebones" LCH/PIH models in those countries experiencing substantial financial liberalisation or substantial innovations in lending, by controlling for critical time-variation in credit constraints, uncertainty and the composition of disaggregated household wealth and debt. The mortgage-equity channel is not uniform, ranging from large impacts in the financially liberalised UK and US, to small, negative impacts in Japan, with onerous down-payment requirements for a mortgage and without the possibility of borrowing against housing equity. The impact of a housing bust for the macroeconomy and for financial stability thus critically depends on the architecture of credit markets and the type of shocks experienced. Moreover, the effect of housing wealth on consumption is largely a collateral effect, consistent with much micro-evidence.

Differences in the structure of household balance sheets and in the intertemporal elasticity of substitution can affect the magnitude and even the sign of the direct impact of real interest rates on consumption. In Japan, household bank and saving deposits were huge, while debt levels were relatively low and relatively few households owned equities. A fall in real interest rates then reduced the consumption of pensioners and those saving for retirement by more than it increased the consumption of debtors. Thus, monetary policy in Japan is likely to be much less effective than in the UK or the US. This paper was awarded the Kendrick Prize for the best macroeconomic paper in the *Review of Income and Wealth* in 2012 and 2013.

In countries with more complete data, Muellbauer and his co-authors were able to develop measures specific to mortgage availability. For the UK and the US, loan-to-value ratios were constructed for first-time homebuyers—the marginal homebuyers in most countries—whose housing wealth, unlike that of previous owners, is not directly affected by earlier capital gains or losses on housing. Incorporating such measures greatly improves house price models for countries where mortgage constraints have notably varied, as in the UK and the US (see Duca et al. 2011, 2016).

3.8   Housing and the Regional Economy

In the 1990s, John became interested in links between housing and the wider economy. Cameron and Muellbauer (1998) studied regional migration and commuting in the UK, revealing multiple influences of the housing market. Earlier research ignoring the role of housing had shown remarkably small effects of earnings and unemployment differentials on migration in the

UK. However, when the effect of housing cost differentials and expectations of relative house price appreciation were included, relative unemployment rates and real earnings became far more relevant for migration.[17]

Cameron and Muellbauer (2001) examined the determination of UK regional unemployment and earnings differentials, revealing the heterogeneous influence of house prices on different types of employment. This threw doubt on the view that higher owner-occupation is a major cause of higher unemployment, as suggested by Blanchflower and Oswald (2013). Papers by Cameron et al. (2006a, b) became key inputs into the then British government's "Housing Affordability Study". The main elements of a general equilibrium model were assembled so that, for example, the impact of earnings growth on regional housing affordability could be simulated, taking account of feedbacks via migration and commuting. This work could form the basis of a model of "regional evolutions" for the UK (i.e. how regions evolve economically and interact with each other and the national economy), which Blanchard and Katz, in a famous 1992 paper, had suggested needed to be analysed in a general equilibrium system. Sadly, Gavin Cameron, a sufferer from cystic fibrosis, died in 2007. In 2008, Muellbauer and Murphy guest-edited an issue of the *Oxford Review of Economic Policy* on "Housing and the Economy", contributing a detailed assessment that surveyed the many interactions between housing and the economy.

3.9   Financial Stability and Macroprudential Policy

John's work on the impact of financial liberalisation on consumption and housing inspired his contributions to the literature on financial stability and macroprudential policy. He has emphasised the need for better models of macro-financial linkages (see Duca et al. 2010, forthcoming; Muellbauer 2010; Duca and Muellbauer 2014; Hendry and Muellbauer 2018; Muellbauer 2018a; Aron et al. 2019a). In a paper for the BIS,[18] critical of the conventional wisdom, Muellbauer (2010) noted that in dynamic stochastic general equilibrium (DSGE) models without financial frictions, asset prices act merely as a proxy for income growth expectations, with no causal role. His UK aggregate consumption evidence strongly contradicts this finding, for all possible discount rates, and both for a perfect foresight and an empirical rational expectations approach to measuring income expectations. By contrast, his

---

[17] These findings were confirmed in Cameron et al. (2006b) which examined gross as well as net migration flows.

[18] Given at its Eighth Annual Conference in 2009 on "Financial System and Macroeconomic Resilience: Revisited".

"credit-augmented consumption function" explains the data well. The BIS paper reported new evidence on the striking rejection on aggregate data of the consumption Euler equation central to all DSGE models; it showed that UK micro-evidence on households in different age groups is consistent with the generalised consumption model. The limitations of newer DSGE models with financial frictions and housing, and the business cycle implications of amplification mechanisms and non-linearities operating via households and residential construction, were explained. The paper then suggested economet-ric methodology appropriate for designing better evidence-based central bank policy models. Hendry and Muellbauer (2018) reiterated these themes, also addressing the failure of rational expectations in the presence of structural breaks. In a detailed analysis of models at the Bank of England, they explained how the Bank's DSGE-based empirical models had failed before, during and after the global financial crisis.

Since the financial crisis, there has been an explosion of research into hous-ing markets. In a comprehensive review of the literature and policy implica-tions of international house price cycles, Duca et al. (forthcoming) discuss within financial sector contagion and amplification, the transmission mecha-nism to the real economy, and feedback loops from the real economy back to the financial sector. These features link with recent developments in macro-prudential policy and risk monitoring. They find the real estate and financial crisis affected the US economy not only by hurting residential construction and consumption (via MEW), but also by impairing the functionality of finance from both financial intermediaries (indirect finance) and securities markets (direct—and ultimately indirect finance). A holistic approach should understand the supply side of housing markets and how institutional differ-ences in supply as well as in credit market structures influence outcomes. It is imperative for policy makers and the economics profession to address critical gaps in data, on general and mortgage credit standards, as well as measures of the housing stock and the land component of house prices. Omission of such factors often leads researchers to draw misleading conclusions from simplistic housing models, for example, on whether house prices are overvalued (see Muellbauer 2012), important for assessing risks to financial stability.

Emphasis on the importance of institutional differences and the need to avoid "one-size-fits-all" thinking is an ever-present theme in John's research. The macro implications of Anglo-German housing and credit market differ-ences (see Muellbauer 1992) was an important reason why Maclennan et al. (1998) argued strongly that the UK did not meet the criteria for a common currency area with major Continental European economies and, hence, did not belong in the Eurozone. In Muellbauer (2018b), he draws on the same cross-country comparisons for ideas to solve the UK housing affordability problem, which has had unfortunate implications for cross-sectional and intergenerational inequality.

3.10   Inflation

In Aron and Muellbauer (2013b), the authors demonstrate that conceiving of inflation as a process of adjustment of relative prices could improve policy makers' forecasts. Given differences in underlying market conditions, market prices do not move in lockstep, with some prices adjusting with lags to different domestic conditions, including labour costs, house prices and international influences. By setting out an equilibrium correction model for the price *level*, an approach pioneered by Sargan (1964), Aron and Muellbauer are better able to model and forecast the time series of US inflation.[19] An application to an emerging market country of similar ideas showed how disaggregated components can additionally improve forecasting accuracy (see Aron and Muellbauer 2012).

As with the bulk of John's research, this inflation analysis nicely blends the need to address aggregation and measurement issues with those of developing estimable and robust empirical specifications that are flexible enough to account for several important drivers and for variation in the speed at which the prices of different categories of items adjust towards their equilibrium paths. International influences on the price level and hence on inflation were the theme of Aron et al. (2014b), an analytical survey of the exchange rate pass-through literature with special reference to emerging market countries.

4   Conclusion

John Muellbauer's accomplishments in economics are noteworthy in terms of both their depth and their breadth. Few economists have contributed significantly both to micro- and macroeconomics, as well as to theory and empirical analysis. The range of the topics and debates he has engaged in are exceptionally varied. Another rare quality has been his ability to address both academic questions and related policy debates—with a knack for spotting large macroeconomic imbalances before they were widely acknowledged, even in policy circles. John has also had the courage and persistence to address unfashionable

---

[19] In Muellbauer (2018a), he returned to this theme from a post-crisis perspective, suggesting that changing firm concentration in the US was another driver of the long-run price level.

subjects over decades both in academia and in policy, eschewing a rational expectations and efficient markets outlook that ignored the role of institutions such as credit and housing market architecture. Since the global financial crisis, his contribution has been increasingly recognised. Also exceptional is that John's empirical analyses span many diverse countries, including both advanced and emerging market economies. The applicability of his microframeworks, housing and consumption models, and his macroprudential policy insights, ensure that his body of work will long continue to benefit both the economics profession and policy makers.

References

Main Works by John Muellbauer

Aron, J., J.V. Duca, J. Muellbauer, K. Murata, and A. Murphy (2012). 'Credit, Housing Collateral, and Consumption: Evidence from Japan, the UK, and the US'. *Review of Income and Wealth*, 58(3): 397–423.

Aron, J., G. Farrell and J. Muellbauer (2019a). 'Financial Stability and the Housing Market in South Africa'. Working Paper, South African Reserve Bank.

Aron, J., G. Farrell and J. Muellbauer (2019b). 'Macroprudential Governance and Communication for Financial Stability in South Africa'. Working Paper, South African Reserve Bank.

Aron, J., G. Farrell, J. Muellbauer and P. Sinclair (2014a). 'Exchange Rate Pass-through to Import Prices and Monetary Policy in South Africa'. *Journal of Development Studies*, 50(1): 144–164.

Aron, J., R. Macdonald and J. Muellbauer (2014b). 'Exchange Rate Pass-Through in Developing and Emerging Markets: A Survey of Conceptual, Methodological and Policy Issues, and Selected Empirical Findings'. *Journal of Development Studies*, 50(1): 101–143.

Aron, J. and J. Muellbauer (2000). 'Personal and Corporate Saving in South Africa'. *World Bank Economic Review*, 14(3): 509–544.

Aron, J. and J. Muellbauer (2002). 'Interest Rate Effects on Output: Evidence from a GDP Forecasting Model for South Africa'. *IMF Staff Papers*, 49(S1): 185–213.

Aron, J. and J. Muellbauer (2006). 'Estimates of Household Sector Wealth for South Africa, 1970–2003'. *Review of Income and Wealth*, 52(2): 285–307.

Aron, J. and J. Muellbauer (2012). 'Improving Forecasting in an Emerging Economy, South Africa: Changing Trends, Long-Run Restrictions and Disaggregation'. *International Journal of Forecasting*, 28(2): 456–476.

Aron, J. and J. Muellbauer (2013a). 'Wealth, Credit Conditions and Consumption: Evidence from South Africa'. *Review of Income and Wealth*, 59(S1): S161–S196.

Aron, J. and J. Muellbauer (2013b). 'New Methods for Forecasting Inflation, Applied to the USA'. *Oxford Bulletin of Economics and Statistics*, 75(5): 637–661.

Aron J. and J. Muellbauer (2014a). 'Exchange Rate Pass-Through in Developing and Emerging Markets'. VoxEU, 14 September. Available at: https://voxeu.org/article/exchange-rate-pass-through-developing-and-emerging-markets.

Aron J. and J. Muellbauer (2014b). 'Exchange Rate Pass-Through Using Highly Disaggregated Micro-Data'. VoxEU, 16 September. Available at: https://voxeu.org/article/exchange-rate-pass-through-using-highly-disaggregated-micro-data.

Aron, J. and J. Muellbauer (2016). 'Modelling and Forecasting Mortgage Delinquency and Foreclosure in the UK'. *Journal of Urban Economics*, 94(July): 32–53.

Aron, J., J. Muellbauer and J. Prinsloo (2008). 'Estimating the Balance Sheet of the Personal Sector in an Emerging Market Country, South Africa 1970–2003'. Chapter 10 in J.B. Davies (ed.) *Personal Wealth from a Global Perspective*. UNU-WIDER Studies in Development Economics. Oxford: Oxford University Press: 196–223.

Cameron, G. and J. Muellbauer (1998). 'The Housing Market and Regional Commuting and Migration Choices'. *Scottish Journal of Political Economy*, 45(4): 420–446.

Cameron, G. and J. Muellbauer (2001). 'Earnings, Unemployment, and Housing in Britain'. *Journal of Applied Econometrics*, 16(3): 203–220.

Cameron, G., A. Murphy and J. Muellbauer (2006a). 'Was There a British House Price Bubble? Evidence from a Regional Panel'. Discussion Paper 5619, CEPR.

Cameron, G., A. Murphy and J. Muellbauer (2006b). 'Housing Market Dynamics and Regional Migration in Britain'. Discussion Paper 5832, CEPR.

Chauvin, V. and J. Muellbauer (2018). 'Consumption, Household Portfolios and the Housing Market in France'. *Economie et Statistique/Economics and Statistics*, 500–502: 157–178.

Deaton, A. and J. Muellbauer (1980a). 'An Almost Ideal Demand System'. *American Economic Review*, 70(3): 312–326.

Deaton, A. and J. Muellbauer (1980b). *Economics and Consumer Behaviour*. Cambridge: Cambridge University Press.

Deaton, A. and J. Muellbauer (1986). 'On Measuring Child Costs: With Applications to Poor Countries'. *Journal of Political Economy*, 94(4): 720–744.

Duca, J.V. and J. Muellbauer (2014). 'Tobin LIVES: Integrating Evolving Credit Market Architecture into Flow-of-Funds Based Macro-Models'. Chapter 2 in B. Winkler, A Van Riet and P. Bull (eds) *A Flow-of-Funds Perspective on the Financial Crisis*. Volume II. London: Palgrave Macmillan: 11–39.

Duca, J.V., J. Muellbauer and A. Murphy (2010). 'Housing Markets and the Financial Crisis of 2007–2009: Lessons for the Future'. *Journal of Financial Stability*, 6(4): 203–217.

Duca, J.V., J. Muellbauer and A. Murphy (2011). 'House Prices and Credit Constraints: Making Sense of the US Experience'. *Economic Journal*, 121(552): 533–551.

Duca, J., J. Muellbauer and A. Murphy (2012). 'How Financial Innovations and Accelerators Drive Booms and Busts in US Consumption'. Mimeo, University of Oxford. Available at: http://www.iariw.org/copenhagen/duca.pdf.

Duca, J.V., J. Muellbauer and A. Murphy (2016). 'How Mortgage Finance Reform Could Affect Housing'. *American Economic Review*, 106(5): 620–624.

Duca, J.V., J. Muellbauer and A. Murphy (forthcoming). 'What Drives House Prices? International Experience and Policy Issues'. *Journal of Economic Literature*.

Fernandez-Corugedo, E. and J. Muellbauer (2006). 'Consumer Credit Conditions in the UK'. Working Paper 314, Bank of England.

Geiger, F., J. Muellbauer and M. Rupprecht (2016). 'The Housing Market, Household Portfolios and the German Consumer'. Working Paper 1904, European Central Bank.

Hendry, D.F. and J. Muellbauer (2018). 'The Future of Macroeconomics: Macro Theory and Models at the Bank of England'. *Oxford Review of Economic Policy*, 34(1–2): 287–328.

Maclennan, D., J. Muellbauer and J. Stevens (1998). 'Asymmetries in Housing and Financial Market Institutions and EMU'. *Oxford Review of Economic Policy*: 14(3): 54–80.

Mendis, L. and J. Muellbauer (1984). 'British Manufacturing Productivity 1955–1983: Measurement Problems, Oil Shocks and Thatcher Effects'. Discussion Paper 32, CEPR.

Muellbauer, J. (1974a). 'Household Composition, Engel Curves and Welfare Comparisons Between Households: A Duality Approach'. *European Economic Review*, 5(2): 103–122.

Muellbauer, J. (1974b). 'Inequality Measures, Prices and Household Composition'. *Review of Economic Studies*, 41(4): 493–504.

Muellbauer, J. (1975). 'Aggregation, Income Distribution and Consumer Demand'. *Review of Economic Studies*, 42(4): 525–543.

Muellbauer, J. (1976). 'Community Preferences and the Representative Consumer'. *Econometrica*, 44(5): 979–999.

Muellbauer, J. (1977). 'Testing the Barten Model of Household Composition Effects and the Cost of Children'. *Economic Journal*, 87(347): 460–487.

Muellbauer, J. (1980). 'The Estimation of the Prais-Houthakker Model of Equivalence Scales'. *Econometrica*, 48(1): 153–176.

Muellbauer, J. (1983). 'Surprises in the Consumption Function'. *Economic Journal*, 93(Supplement): 34–50.

Muellbauer, J. (1986). 'Productivity and Competitiveness in British Manufacturing'. *Oxford Review of Economic Policy*, 2(3): i–xxv.

Muellbauer, J. (1988). 'Habits, Rationality and Myopia in the Life Cycle Consumption Function'. *Annales d'Économie et de Statistique*, 9(January–March): 47–70.

Muellbauer, J. (1990). 'Aggregate Production Functions and Productivity Measurement: A New Look'. Chapter 6 in G.D. Myles (ed.) *Measurement and Modelling in Economics*. Amsterdam: North-Holland: 157–203. Discussion: 204–218.

Muellbauer, J. (1992). 'Anglo-German Differences in Housing Market Dynamics: The Role of Institutions and Macro Economic Policy'. *European Economic Review*, 36(2–3): 539–548.

Muellbauer, J. (1997). 'Business Cycles'. *Oxford Review of Economic Policy*, 13(3): 1–18.

Muellbauer, J. (2007). 'Housing, Credit and Consumer Expenditure'. In *Housing, Housing Finance, and Monetary Policy: A Symposium Sponsored by the Federal Reserve Bank of Kansas City*. Kansas City: Federal Reserve Bank of Kansas City: 267–334.

Muellbauer, J. (2008a). 'Housing Wealth and Consumer Spending'. VoxEU, 20 July. Available at: https://voxeu.org/article/housing-led-recession-making.

Muellbauer, J. (2008b). 'The Folly of the Central Banks of Europe'. VoxEU, 27 October. Available at: https://voxeu.org/article/folly-central-banks-europe.

Muellbauer, J. (2008c). 'Time for Unorthodox Monetary Policy'. VoxEU, 27 November. Available at: https://voxeu.org/article/unorthodox-monetary-policy-central-banks-stabilising-speculators.

Muellbauer, J. (2010). 'Household Decisions, Credit Markets and the Macroeconomy: Implications for the Design of Central Bank Models'. Working Paper 306, Bank for International Settlements.

Muellbauer, J. (2011). 'Time for Euro Bonds—But with Conditions'. VoxEU, 12 October. Available at: https://voxeu.org/article/time-euro-bonds-conditions.

Muellbauer, J. (2012). 'When Is a Housing Market Overheated Enough to Threaten Stability?'. In A. Heath, F. Packer and C. Windsor (eds) *Property Markets and Financial Stability*. Sydney: Reserve Bank of Australia: 73–105.

Muellbauer, J. (2014a). 'Six Fiscal Reforms for the UK's "Lost Generation"'. VoxEU, 25 March. Available at: https://voxeu.org/article/six-fiscal-reforms-uk-s-lost-generation.

Muellbauer, J. (2014b). 'Combatting Eurozone Deflation: QE for the People'. VoxEU, 23 December. Available at: https://voxeu.org/article/combatting-eurozone-deflation-qe-people.

Muellbauer, J. (2016a). 'Helicopter Money and Fiscal Rules'. VoxEU, 10 June. Available at: https://voxeu.org/article/helicopter-money-and-fiscal-rules.

Muellbauer, J. (2016b). 'Macroeconomics and Consumption: Why Central Bank Models Failed and How to Repair Them'. VoxEU, 21 December. Available at: https://voxeu.org/article/why-central-bank-models-failed-and-how-repair-them.

Muellbauer, J. (2018a). 'The Future of Macroeconomics'. In *The Future of Central Banking: Festschrift in Honour of Vítor Constâncio*. European Central Bank. Available at: https://www.ecb.europa.eu/pub/pdf/other/ecb.futurecentralbankingcolloquiumconstancio201812.en.pdf.

Muellbauer, J. (2018b). 'Housing, Debt and the Economy: A Tale of Two Countries'. *National Institute Economic Review*, 245(1): 20–33.

Muellbauer, J. (2019a). 'Historical Introduction to the Political Economy of Price Indices,' *Cyprus Economic Policy Review*, 13(1): 31–34.

Muellbauer, J. (2019b). 'The Political Economy of Price Indices'. *Cyprus Economic Policy Review*, 13(1): 35–56.

Muellbauer, J. (2019c). 'A Tale of Two Cities: Is Overvaluation a Capital Issue?'. Chapter 5 in R. Nijskens, M. Lohuis, P. Hilbers and W. Heeringa (eds) *Hot Property: The Housing Market in Major Cities*. Cham: Springer: 51–62.

Muellbauer, J. and J. Aron (2008). 'US Price Deflation on the Way'. VoxEU, 10 October. Available at: https://voxeu.org/article/don-t-worry-about-inflation-worry-about-deflation.

Muellbauer, J. and R. Lattimore (1995). 'The Consumption Function: A Theoretical and Empirical Overview'. Chapter 5 in M.H. Pesaran and M.R. Wickens (eds) *Handbook of Applied Econometrics*. Volume 1. Oxford: Blackwell: 187–267.

Muellbauer, J. and K. Murata (2011). 'Mistaken Monetary Policy Lessons from Japan'. VoxEU, 21 August. Available at: https://voxeu.org/article/mistaken-monetary-policy-lessons-japan.

Muellbauer, J. and A. Murphy (1989). 'Why Has UK Personal Saving Collapsed?'. Credit Suisse First Boston, July.

Muellbauer, J. and A. Murphy (1990). 'Is the UK Balance of Payments Sustainable?'. *Economic Policy*, 5(11): 348–395.

Muellbauer, J. and A. Murphy (1997). 'Booms and Busts in the UK Housing Market'. *Economic Journal*, 107(445): 1,701–1,727.

Muellbauer, J. and A. Murphy (2008). 'Housing Markets and the Economy'. *Oxford Review of Economic Policy*, 24(1): 1–33.

Muellbauer, J. and R. Portes (1978a). 'Macroeconomics with Nonclearing Markets'. Chapter 16 in W.H. Branson (ed.) *Macroeconomic Theory and Policy*. New York: Harper & Row: 337–372.

Muellbauer, J. and R. Portes (1978b). 'Macroeconomic Models with Quantity Rationing'. *Economic Journal*, 88(352): 788–821.

Muellbauer, J., P. St-Amant and D. Williams (2015). 'Credit Conditions and Consumption, House Prices and Debt: What Makes Canada Different?'. Bank of Canada, Staff Working Paper 2015–40.

Muellbauer, J. and D. Williams (2012). 'Credit Conditions and the Real Economy: The Elephant in the Room'. In *Property Markets and Financial Stability*. BIS Papers No. 64. Basel: Bank for International Settlements: 95–101.

Muellbauer, J. and D. Winter (1980). 'Unemployment, Employment and Exports in British Manufacturing: A Non-Clearing Markets Approach'. *European Economic Review*, 13(3): 383–409.

Other Works Referred To

Banks, J., R. Blundell and A. Lewbel (1997). 'Quadratic Engel Curves and Consumer Demand'. *Review of Economics and Statistics*, 79(4): 527–539.

Barr, D.G. and K. Cuthbertson (1991). 'An Interdependent Error Feedback Model of UK Company Sector Asset Demands'. *Oxford Economic Papers*, New Series, 43(4): 596–611.

Barro, R.J. and H.I. Grossman (1971). 'A General Disequilibrium Model of Income and Employment'. *American Economic Review*, 61(1): 82–93.

Barten, A. (1964). 'Family Composition, Prices and Expenditure Patterns'. In P.E. Hart, G. Mills and J.K. Whitaker (eds) *Econometric Analysis for National Economic Planning*. Volume 16. Colston Papers. London: Butterworths: 277–291.

Besley, T. (2016). 'The Contributions of Angus Deaton'. *Scandinavian Journal of Economics*, 118(3): 375–396.

Besley, T., A. Case and C. Paxson (2011). 'Angus Deaton Symposium—Introduction'. *Economic Journal*, 121(554): F119–F122.

Blake, D. (2004). 'Modelling the Composition of Personal Sector Wealth in the UK'. *Applied Financial Economics*, 14(9): 611–630.

Blanchflower, D.G. and A.J. Oswald (2013). 'Does High Home-Ownership Impair the Labor Market?'. NBER Working Paper 19079. Cambridge, MA: National Bureau of Economic Research.

Blundell, R. (1988). 'Consumer Behaviour: Theory and Empirical Evidence—A Survey'. *Economic Journal*, 98(389): 16–65.

Brainard, W.C. and J. Tobin (1968). 'Pitfalls in Financial Model Building'. *American Economic Review*, Papers and Proceedings, 58(2): 99–122.

Carroll, C.D. (1992). 'The Buffer-Stock Theory of Saving: Some Macroeconomic Evidence'. *Brookings Papers on Economic Activity*, 23(2): 61–156.

Committee for the Prize in Economic Sciences in Memory of Alfred Nobel (2015). 'Scientific Background on the Sveriges Riksbank Prize in Economic Sciences in Memory of Alfred Nobel 2015: Angus Deaton: Consumption, Poverty and Welfare'. Stockholm: The Royal Swedish Academy of Sciences. Available at: https://www.nobelprize.org/uploads/2018/06/advanced-economic-sciences2015.pdf.

Davidson, J.E.H., D.F. Hendry, F. Srba and S. Yeo (1978). 'Econometric Modelling of the Aggregate Time-Series Relationship between Consumers' Expenditure and Income in the United Kingdom'. *Economic Journal*, 88(352): 661–692.

Deaton, A. (1991). 'Saving and Liquidity Constraints'. *Econometrica*, 59(5): 1,221–1,248.

Diewert, W.E. (1971). 'An Application of the Shephard Duality Theorem: A Generalized Leontief Production Function'. *Journal of Political Economy*, 79(3): 481–507.

Drèze, J.H. (1975). 'Existence of an Exchange Equilibrium Under Price Rigidities'. *International Economic Review*, 16(2): 301–320.

Drèze, J.H. (1987). 'Underemployment Equilibria: From Theory to Econometrics and Policy'. Presidential Address, First Congress of the European Economic Association, *European Economic Review*, 31(1–2): 9–34.

Gorman, W.M. (1981). 'Some Engel Curves'. Chapter 1 in A. Deaton (ed.) *Essays on the Theory and Measurement of Demand in Honour of Sir Richard Stone*. Cambridge: Cambridge University Press: 7–30.

Hall, R.E. (1978). 'Stochastic Implications of the Life Cycle-Permanent Income Hypothesis: Theory and Evidence'. *Journal of Political Economy*, 86(6): 971–987.

Howe, H., R.A. Pollak and T.J. Wales (1979). 'Theory and Time Series Estimation of the Quadratic Expenditure System'. *Econometrica*, 47(5): 1,231–1,247.

Jorgenson, D.W., L.J. Lau and T.M. Stoker (1982). 'The Transcendental Logarithmic Model of Aggregate Consumer Behavior'. Chapter 3 in R.L. Basman and G. Rhodes (eds) *Advances in Econometrics*. Volume 1. Greenwich, CT: JAI Press: 97–238.

Jorgenson, D.W. and D.T. Slesnick (1983). 'Individual and Social Cost-of-Living Indexes'. Chapter 4 in W.E. Diewert and C. Montmarquette (eds) *Price Level Measurement*. Ottawa: Statistics Canada: 241–323.

Lewbel, A. (1988). 'Exact Aggregation, Distribution Parameterizations, and a Nonlinear Representative Consumer'. Chapter 7 in G. Rhodes and T. Fomby (eds) *Advances in Econometrics*. Volume 7. Greenwich, CT: JAI Press: 253–290.

Lewbel, A. (1989). 'Exact Aggregation and a Representative Consumer'. *Quarterly Journal of Economics*, 104(3): 621–633.

Lewbel, A. (1991). 'The Rank of Demand Systems: Theory and Nonparametric Estimation'. *Econometrica*, 59(3): 711–730.

Malinvaud, E. (1977). *The Theory of Unemployment Reconsidered*. Oxford: Blackwell.

Mian, A., K. Rao and A. Sufi (2013). 'Household Balance Sheets, Consumption, and the Economic Slump'. *Quarterly Journal of Economics*, 128(4): 1,687–1,726.

Mian, A. and A. Sufi (2018). 'Finance and Business Cycles: The Credit-Driven Household Demand Channel'. *Journal of Economic Perspectives*, 32(3): 31–58.

Miles, D. (1992). 'Housing Markets, Consumption and Financial Liberalisation in the Major Economies'. *European Economic Review*, 36(5): 1,093–1,127.

Poterba, J.M. (1984). 'Tax Subsidies to Owner-Occupied Housing: An Asset-Market Approach'. *Quarterly Journal of Economics*, 99(4): 729–752.

Prais, S.J. and H.S. Houthakker (1955). *The Analysis of Family Budgets*. Cambridge: Cambridge University Press.

Sargan, J.D. (1964). 'Wages and Prices in the United Kingdom: A Study in Econometric Methodology'. In P.E. Hart, G. Mills and J.K. Whitaker (eds) *Econometric Analysis for National Economic Planning*. Volume 16. Colston Papers. London: Butterworths: 25–54, with discussion.

27

Paul Collier (1949–)

David Fielding

1   Early Life

The values that shape Sir Paul Collier's work were formed at an early age. The son of a pork butcher, he grew up in working-class Sheffield as its traditional industries began to decline, studying at the local State grammar school but also working in his parents' shop. (Economic policy making is often compared to the making of sausages, but he is perhaps the only person in the world who is professionally qualified to comment on this comparison.) He grew up in the impoverished deindustrialising north of England, but the grammar school system provided him with an education that would lead to a professional life engaged with the causes of poverty.

After completing school, Paul won a place at Trinity College, Oxford, but the beginning of his university education in 1967 was not entirely auspicious. He was enrolled to read Law, a subject that he soon found to be entirely unsuitable for him, and his college was comprised almost entirely of boys from elite private schools, who were not always entirely welcoming to butcher's boys. Fortunately, there was little in the way of formal administrative structure at Oxford, so the tutors at Trinity accepted without question his

I am grateful to Paul for a conversation that informs this chapter.

D. Fielding (✉)
Global Development Institute, University of Manchester, Manchester, UK
e-mail: david.fielding@manchester.ac.uk

R. A. Cord (ed.), *The Palgrave Companion to Oxford Economics*,
https://doi.org/10.1007/978-3-030-58471-9_27

decision to switch from Law to Philosophy, Politics and Economics (PPE) in his first term.

Equally fortunately, Paul met Keith Griffin, the Oxford don who introduced him to development economics. Oxford already had an established group of researchers working on the economics of South Asia, but there was very little research on Africa. Under Keith's supervision, Paul worked on his first piece of development economics research: a study on Malawi, written for an undergraduate essay prize. This led to an interview with Patrick Minford for a position in Malawi funded by the Overseas Development Administration, the precursor to the Department for International Development. The interview was successful, but Paul was prevented from taking up the position by a decline in his father's health: his first graduate position was back in the butcher's shop.

2   Doctoral Research

Eventually, Paul returned to Oxford for postgraduate study at Nuffield College. The subject of his doctoral thesis (the economics of customs unions, supervised by Max Corden) was motivated not by a passion for the theory of international trade, but by a perception that at that time, only a "mainstream" economics postgraduate education would give him the intellectual tools needed for a career in development economics. The thesis led to two publications highlighting the importance of the way in which commodities are aggregated in theoretical models of customs union formation (see Collier 1979a, 1985). These papers are purely theoretical and strictly neoclassical: they introduce extra layers of complexity into the standard analysis of customs unions originally developed by Viner (1950) and Lipsey (1957), but do not stray beyond the boundaries of standard trade theory with perfectly competitive markets. In the original Vinerian theory, which was based on a model with two commodities ("imports" and "exports"), calculation of the welfare effects of customs union formation was based on the concepts of "trade creation" and "trade diversion". Begin with a world in which each country is imposing tariffs on imports from the others. If two of the countries form a customs union, then there are aggregate welfare gains from the increased trade between them that follows from the abolition of intra-union tariffs. However, the customs union also creates a wedge between the consumer price of imports from inside the union relative to those from outside and the relative producer price. As a consequence, importers may switch from a low-cost producer outside the union to a high-cost producer inside the union, and this entails a welfare loss.

Paul's main contribution was to extend the analysis to a case of more than two commodities, making it possible to analyse the reallocation of resources (and of consumption) not just between imports and exports, but also between different types of import, and between different types of export. In this case, the traditional categories of trade creation and trade diversion become redundant, and the aggregate welfare effects of customs union formation depend on the elasticities of production and consumption between different types of import (and export), not just imports as a whole and exports as a whole. The analysis of customs union formation demonstrates Paul's ability as an economic theorist, but it does not reflect the interests apparent in his later work. For example, there is no analysis of the effect of customs union formation on income distribution or poverty through Stolper-Samuelson effects.

3   Labour Markets, Natural Resources and Poverty in East Africa

On completion of his thesis in 1976, Paul was appointed to a University Lectureship and a Fellowship at Keble College, where he tutored a number of future academic economists, most notably Tim Besley. His research at Keble might have seemed at first to be completely unrelated to his doctoral work. He was commissioned to write a World Bank report on labour markets and poverty in Tanzania. This provided his first experience of fieldwork in Africa, and his first opportunity to conduct applied economics research, using household survey data at a time when such data were still unfashionable. The Tanzanian study was followed by a similar commission in Kenya, this time with Deepak Lal, and a study of Dutch Disease in Nigeria funded by the International Labour Organisation. In fact, the academic publications that resulted from this work (*Labour and Poverty in Rural Tanzania* (Collier et al. 1986), which won the Edgar Graham Prize, and *Labour and Poverty in Kenya, 1900–1980* (Collier and Lal 1986)) were very much connected to international trade theory, stressing the importance of location and capability-based comparative advantage in explaining economic outcomes. The insight that theory explaining variation in the wealth of nations can be applied at a different scale, in order to explain variation in the wealth of peasant farmers, is important to the broader discipline, not just to development economics.[1]

---

[1] During this period of Paul's career, he also collaborated with Colin Mayer, although their research was not directly connected to Paul's other work. One of their papers anticipates Oxford's current trials with regard to undergraduate admission procedures by modelling the determinates of admission into the PPE programme in 1978. One remarkable feature of their results is the high degree of discrimination against

Despite the many differences between the studies of Kenya and Tanzania and the earlier work on customs unions, there are some similarities in the style of the economic analysis. In both cases, existing theory was extended by the addition of more moving parts, and this sometimes led to radically different policy conclusions. One example is the study of migration and unemployment in Tanzania (see Collier 1979b). The starting point for the analysis is the Harris-Todaro model, in which a persistent gap between urban formal-sector wages and rural wages creates an incentive for rural workers to migrate to cities in order to look for work (see Harris and Todaro 1970). In equilibrium, there is a pool of urban workers who are either unemployed or underemployed in the informal sector, but the prospect of high-wage formal-sector employment keeps them from returning home to work. In such a world, a government policy that expands the urban formal sector will also increase the number of people who chose to migrate and are unemployed or work in the informal sector. Paul extended the model by making explicit the distinction between unemployment and informal sector employment, and by allowing for a heterogeneous labour force, distinguished by characteristics, such as education, that affect their ability to migrate. In the extended model, an expansion of the formal sector can induce a more-than-proportional increase in the reservation wage of migrants, and therefore a net fall in the total number of people who are unemployed or in the informal sector. Analysis of evidence from Tanzania between 1969 and 1975 indicates that the expansion of the formal sector did indeed tend to depress the total number of unemployed and informally employed migrants.

The work on Kenya and Tanzania also included one of the first serious studies of the dynamics of African income distribution (see Collier and Lal 1984). This study showed that remittances from urban migrants to their rural families tended to mitigate rural income inequality. Remittances and other sources of non-farm income were particularly important as a source of funds for investment, given the absence of credit markets for small farmers. Here, in Kenya and Tanzania, the work showed an acute awareness of the ways in which individual markets and government policies had failed (see also Collier 1983), but the analysis of radical State failure that was to be so important in later work was still far over the horizon.

The research in Kenya and Tanzania was conducted during the middle of the coffee boom in the late 1970s. Coffee is the countries' main cash crop, and

---

older applicants, which seems to have escaped media attention. The other paper critiques the 1989 World Bank *World Development Report* and its policy recommendations with regard to financial liberalisation (see Collier and Mayer 1986, 1989).

a steep rise in world prices led to a large increase in coffee revenue, at least some of which made its way into the hands of peasant farmers. The visible consequences of the boom, such as more bicycles on the street and better quality rooves, stimulated Paul's interest in the way in which economic policy might enhance or detract from the potential benefits of such a windfall. The offer of World Bank funding for further fieldwork in Kenya and Tanzania prompted him to make a career-changing decision. He resigned his Fellowship at Keble, which came with substantial undergraduate teaching responsibilities, in order to take up a less well-paid Fellowship at St Antony's College, with no such responsibilities and therefore the freedom to travel to East Africa for long periods. Since then, his academic life has been devoted to research, engagement with policymakers, and postgraduate education; those undergraduates who knew him as a tutor and lecturer are all now in their 50s.

A large part of the fieldwork in East Africa involved tracking down official government publications that were not available abroad. Detective work and a certain amount of arm-twisting were required to locate data that had been stored in a single hard copy or tape. The efforts were not always successful—for example, the 1968 Tanzanian household budget survey had disappeared without trace—but the work provided the empirical foundation for two monographs co-authored with David Bevan and Jan Gunning, one with a microeconomic focus (*Peasants and Governments* (Bevan et al. 1989)) and one with a macroeconomic focus (*Controlled Open Economies* (Bevan et al. 1994)). Using East Africa as a case study, this work explores the consequences of government controls in small open economies that are subject to large external shocks.

Peasants and Governments is notable for its use of household panel data: to my knowledge, the only other panel dataset in development economics that dates back to the 1970s is from India (see Baulch 2011).[2] The construction of the panel involved locating and interviewing households who had taken part in previous government surveys. The method was not perfect—for example, there was no way to control for the sample selection bias due to households who had migrated and were therefore untraceable—but it is among the earliest examples of a research method that has since become ubiquitous in development economics. By using panel data, Paul and his colleagues could track the response of small farmers to changing economic conditions during the coffee boom. Government policy in Kenya differed markedly from that in Tanzania, so the study also sheds light on the consequences of different policy

---

[2] Otherwise, the earliest panel dataset for Africa is the Côte d'Ivoire Living Standards Survey, which began in 1985.

regimes. In Kenya, the prices of most locally consumed goods were determined by the market, and although there was a wedge between the farmgate coffee price and the international price, the Coffee Board of Kenya, which acted as a middleman, passed on most of the international price increase to farmers. The panel data evidence indicated that farmers saved most of their temporary windfall, demonstrating some degree of forward-looking behaviour. Most of the saving was in the form of fixed capital investment (bicycles and rooves being two of the most visible examples), but large variations in the rates of return to different types of investment suggested the existence of information asymmetries or some other type of capital market failure. In Tanzania, most prices were controlled and the supply of goods was rationed, inhibiting the production of cash crops and delivering outcomes much further from the first best than in Kenya.

Controlled Open Economies is among the first substantial empirical studies in development macroeconomics that take dynamics seriously, working through some of the macroeconomic implications of the results in *Peasants and Governments*. The analysis of Kenya focuses on the macroeconomic consequences of the coffee farmers' windfall income. As elaborated in *Peasants and Governments*, farmers saved in the form of physical assets, lacking access to reliable financial institutions. Much of this physical capital was not internationally tradeable, so there was a steep rise in the relative price of non-tradeable capital goods, in other words, a form of Dutch Disease. The analysis of Tanzania focuses on the macroeconomic consequences of the extensive price controls there.

The publication of *Peasants and Governments* and *Controlled Open Economies* coincided with the genesis of the Centre for the Study of African Economies at Oxford, which is now arguably the most influential research institute of its kind in the world. The Centre began with a small amount of industry funding in 1989, obtained through the success of the two monographs, and became sustainable with the award of a £2 million Economic and Social Research Council Grant over 1991–2001. The Centre owes its existence to Paul's vision and leadership, although the success of its early years was also due to the work of David Bevan. Subsequent directors of the Centre have included Jan Gunning, Marcel Fafchamps and, most recently, Stefan Dercon, who was one of Paul's first graduate students.

4   Time at the World Bank

By the end of the millennium, Oxford had finally accepted the idea of academic promotion, so Paul was now a full professor, with Oxford as his permanent home. His one sustained period away from Oxford was as Research Director at the World Bank between 1998 and 2003. He was instrumental in the expansion of the Bank's range of survey datasets, which had previously focused almost entirely on households, but which now include surveys of firms and public services. His work with Bank colleague David Dollar is one of the most influential contributions to the aid effectiveness literature (see Collier and Dollar 2002, 2004). This literature arouses the emotions of development economists in the same way that climate change arouses the emotions of the rest of the world, and consensus has proved hard to achieve. Nevertheless, Paul's work in this field, emphasising the role of recipient government institutional capacity in determining the impact of aid expenditures, was a key factor in the World Bank's movement away from traditional aid conditionality. Previous work by Dollar and Craig Burnside, examining the cross-country association between per capita GDP growth and aid inflows, had suggested that the positive influence of aid on growth was diminished when governance in the recipient country (as measured by, for instance, the International Country Risk Guide) was poor (see Burnside and Dollar 2000). The Collier-Dollar papers examined this relationship in more detail and worked out the implications for an international allocation of aid allocation designed to minimise poverty across the globe. Of necessity, this allocation involves channelling aid to countries with a relatively high incidence of poverty and relatively good governance, which is good news for Ethiopia but a bleak outlook for the Central African Republic. However, this bleakness was to stimulate later work, described below.

5   The Economics of Civil Wars

Before moving to Washington, Paul began his research collaboration with Anke Hoeffler on the causes and consequences of civil wars. The series of papers that they published, beginning in 1998, marks a turning point in Paul's research, with a much greater emphasis on political economy. The focus on political economy was the fruit of a long-running conversation with Robert Bates, the Harvard political economist whom Paul first met in the late 1980s, and whose work concentrates on violence and State failure in Africa (see, for example, Bates 2014). Paul and Anke's work highlights economic insights into civil war combatants' incentives and constraints, which are used to explain the pattern of intra-State conflict observed since the end of the colonial era. It is part of a trend of increasing engagement between development economists and political scientists.[3] Serendipitously, political scientists such as James Fearon, Stathis Kalyvas and Nicholas Sambanis were beginning to take an interest in correlates of intra-State conflict at the same time as Paul and Anke, and this has led to the creation of a genuinely interdisciplinary field. Just as Paul's earlier work, which applied the methods of mainstream economics to the problems of resource-poor countries, was part of the re-engagement of development economics with the mainstream, so his later work is part of the re-engagement of economics with other social sciences, with development economics and economic history in the vanguard.

The conceptual framework underpinning Paul and Anke's initial research on civil wars, published in 1998, drew on the work of Herschel Grossman (1995) and Jean-Paul Azam (1995). Potential rebels are rational: everything else being equal, the probability that they will take up arms is increasing in the probability of victory, which is decreasing in the incumbent government's per capita tax-raising powers. These powers are increasing in per capita GDP and in the proportion of GDP made up of natural resource revenue. (The production of natural resources is geographically concentrated, so the administrative costs of taxing it are lower.) However, potential tax revenue is also a prize that can incentivise rebels to take more risks, so the effect of per capita GDP and the natural resource share on the incidence of civil war is indeterminate a priori, and the empirical relationships could be non-monotonic. The main innovation in the 1998 paper was the idea that the ability of rebels to co-ordinate opposition to the government depends on the ethnic composition of the country. With complete ethnic homogeneity, there is no opportunity for the rebels to exploit disadvantaged minority groups. On the other hand, if there are very many ethnicities, co-operation between different rebellious groups is likely to be more difficult to achieve. The relationship between civil war incidence and ethnic fractionalisation can therefore be expected to have an "inverted-U" shape. Empirical analysis of cross-country panel data suggested not only a non-monotonic relationship between economic conditions and civil war incidence, but also the inverted-U relationship with ethnic fractionalisation.

---

[3] The other highly influential work of this kind is by Açemoğlu, Johnson and Robinson, although Paul and Anke were first off the mark: see Collier and Hoeffler (1998) and Açemoğlu et al. (2001). The better-known civil war paper (with over 8,000 citations) is Collier and Hoeffler (2004).

The better-known 2004 paper is a refinement of the original empirical analysis. Ethnic fractionalisation, now interpreted as a correlate of the propensity for social grievance, is measured in several different ways. This reinterpretation of the ethnic fractionalisation measure is conceptually significant. In the 1998 paper, all of the theory remained within the bounds of rational choice economics, and all of the correlates of civil war were interpreted in terms of the economic costs and benefits of belligerence. In the 2004 paper, there is an implicit acknowledgement that war is at least partly a function of attitudes, and attitudes are shaped by social and political processes. In addition, the paper allows for alternative sources of grievance, including religious fractionalisation, income inequality and inequality in the distribution of land. It also includes a more extensive set of correlates of the cost of waging war, some of which (e.g. male education rates, a proxy for the reservation wage of soldiers) suggest scope for policy interventions to reduce the long-run incidence of conflict.

Hundreds of papers later, this literature is arriving at more nuanced results. For instance, ethnic fractionalisation appears to be an important predictor for certain types of intra-State conflict but not others (see Hegre and Sambanis 2006), and while religious fractionalisation was not found to be a significant correlate of civil war incidence in early studies, certain types of religious difference do now appear to be associated with violence (see Basedau et al. 2016). Economic theories jostle with political theories in interpretation of the data, and reading lists on the subject are correspondingly eclectic. Moreover, as highlighted in another early paper by Paul, civil war is itself a cause of poverty, and so a vicious circle of conflict and poverty can prevent a country from ever developing: in the jargon of development economics, it is a "low-level development trap" (see Collier 1999).

6   Fragile States

Paul and Anke's work on civil wars was the starting point for a broader investigation into the political economy of different causes of persistent underdevelopment. This work, informed by Paul's former undergraduate student, Tim Besley (see, for example, Besley and Persson 2011), aims to account for the different underlying causes of State fragility. First, there is a connection between the literature on civil wars and the literature on the "natural resource curse".[4] Compared with other types of economic activity, mineral production

---

[4] The resource curse literature is surveyed in Frenkel (2010), Collier and Venables (2010) and Ross (2015).

tends to be highly geographically concentrated, and intensive in physical rather than human capital. Therefore, minerals are highly lootable, creating an incentive not only for corruption and criminality, but also for violent conflict: war is a continuation of rent-seeking by other means. Evidence for the association between the incidence of civil war and mineral dependence appears in studies by Paul and Anke and by James Fearon (see Collier and Hoeffler 2005; Fearon 2005). Such rent-seeking behaviour (along with Dutch Disease, as outlined in *Controlled Open Economies*) leads to disinvestment in other sectors of the economy, and an even greater reliance on minerals: another vicious circle. Secondly, Paul's work with Steve O'Connell has highlighted the particular challenges facing landlocked resource-poor countries. These countries' international trade connections depend not just on the ability of their maritime neighbours to maintain adequate port facilities with good regional road and rail connections, but also on the quality of governance in these neighbours, and the absence of roadblocks created by protectionist central governments or by corrupt local officials. The misery caused by a country's poor governance can easily spread beyond its borders (see Collier and O'Connell 2007; Collier 2007a).

At this point, Paul's research might seem to paint a rather depressing picture: countries that are landlocked, or that have a history of war, or that rely heavily on natural resources, can become persistently impoverished and have persistently poor government. Under these conditions, on average, foreign aid has had very little effect. Paul's work with Lisa Chauvet does something to alleviate this depression by investigating the variation in foreign aid effectiveness around this mean. Their most striking result is that the effectiveness of World Bank aid is highly dependent on the amount of time devoted by Bank staff to preparation and supervision. When more time is given, the project is much more likely to be successful, and this effect is significantly larger in the aftermath of civil conflict. There is also some evidence that aid to build infrastructure is more likely to succeed than is aid for education. Investment in physical capital is a better bet than investment in human capital, although the long-run returns to successful human capital investment are likely to be especially high, if it creates the capacity for countries to provide efficient supervision of their own. A balanced donor investment portfolio might reasonably include some of both (see, for example, Chauvet et al. 2010).

In many of Paul's contributions over the years, the angel is in the detail. Vinerian customs union theory is a fine thing, but it will lead to mistaken policy conclusions if its simplistic aggregation of commodities is taken at face value. The Harris-Todaro model is equally fine. However, it too will lead policymakers astray if the aggregation implicit in its characterisation of labour markets is not relaxed. Even more importantly, the finding that aid is relatively ineffective in poor policy environments, on average, is not to be taken as a counsel of despair, but rather as a reason to disaggregate aid in poor policy environments, in order to discover the correlates of variation around the mean.

7   A Wider Audience

In the last decade or so, Paul has written a number of books aimed at a wider audience, including *The Bottom Billion* (Collier 2007b), which provides an overview of his work in political economy, emphasising the importance of effective policy to deal with poverty in fragile States. This book won the Lionel Gelber, Arthur Ross, Corine, and Estoril Global Issues book prizes. *Wars, Guns and Votes: Democracy in Dangerous Places* (Collier 2009) draws on Paul's work on the causes of civil war, while *The Plundered Planet: How to Reconcile Prosperity with Nature* (Collier 2010) focuses on the challenges of creating institutions for the international management of natural resources. Two later books represent a decisive rejection of neoclassical economics as an overarching theory of human society (while retaining a role for neoclassical economics in the analysis of specific markets or institutions). *Exodus* (Collier 2013) makes a case for immigration controls, while *The Future of Capitalism* (Collier 2018), inspired partly by Colin Mayer's book *Prosperity* (Mayer 2018), argues for the cultivation of social norms and social institutions that limit the tendency of free markets to generate inequality. To the extent that these norms are based on loyalty to geographically defined communities, *The Future of Capitalism* espouses a form of patriotism similar to that advocated by George Orwell in *The Lion and the Unicorn: Socialism and the English Genius* (Orwell 1982).[5] To the extent that inequality has a geographical dimension (with fragile cities in otherwise non-fragile States), the book highlights the importance of economic geography and urban planning.

Much of Paul's most recent academic work connects to the themes in *The Future of Capitalism*. His work in political economy explores the consequences for economic development of the evolution of the culture in which social norms are embedded. He argues that there is no reason to expect cultural evolution to be socially optimal: there is no invisible cultural hand, and equilibria embodying the predatory cultures of Gordon Gekko or Mobutu Sese Seko are to be expected (see Collier 2017a). Here, there is a suggestion that

---

[5] Although the S-word is missing from the original title of Paul's book, the German version is entitled *Sozialer Kapitalismus*.

cultural development traps can be observed in industrialised countries as well as in the global South. A theory of cultural development traps has not yet been elaborated in detail, but the model of class formation and identity choice in Collier (2020), which builds on Akerlof (2017), may provide a starting point. Paul's work with Tony Venables on economic geography employs the tools of neoclassical economic theory to motivate the case for urban planning and redistribution (see Collier and Venables 2018). Larger, relatively productive cities generate bigger economic rents, but the share of rents accruing to land in these cities is relatively low (and the share accruing to skilled labour is relatively high). Land values *understate* the rents that have accrued to the most prosperous cities: much of the rent appears in the form of high white-collar wages. Taxing this rent in order to fund urban development in fragile cities is not only egalitarian but also economically efficient. Later papers explore the policy consequences of this conceptual framework and its implications for development economics (see Collier and Venables 2016, 2017; Collier 2017b).

Although Paul's five-year stint at the World Bank was his only sustained period away from Oxford, he has continued to engage with policy making. For example, he led the preparation of the natural resource management and corporate tax avoidance sections of the 2013 G8 meeting in the UK, and the design of the Compact for Africa (an initiative to attract international businesses to the continent) at the 2017 G20 meeting in Germany. He currently co-directs the Commission on State Fragility, with Tim Besley. In 2008, he was awarded a CBE for services to scholarship and development, and in 2014, he received a knighthood for services to promoting research and policy change in Africa.

8   Conclusion

The development of Paul's research over the last 50 years reflects some trends in economics as a whole (albeit there are enclaves that resist these trends). Neoclassical economic theory is no longer ubiquitous, but remains as a tool to be used in specific circumstances, and there is an increasing awareness of the importance of engaging with (and sometimes provoking) academics from other social sciences. The website of Oxford's Blavatnik School of Government, which is Paul's current academic home, quotes him as saying: 'Recently, interchanges between social psychology and economics have broadened what is accepted as rational behaviour. Culture can provide a fresh framework with different motivations and other-regarding values—such as esteem, fairness, hatred—and narratives that can influence expected behaviours' (Collier quoted in Blavatnik 2017).

This is not a point of view that could easily have been predicted from Paul's first work on customs unions. It reflects the fact that much of the broadening of academic economics over the last 30 years can be traced through the work of individual economists: it is an age effect at least as much as a cohort effect. The new eclecticism is seen most clearly in Paul's work with Pedro Vincente on intimidation and corruption during African election campaigns. Their theoretical work to explain the conditions under which intimidation and corruption appear has a strongly neoclassical flavour, with rational electoral candidates making strategic decisions about the employment of their resources on the basis of the expected costs and benefits of different types of electoral manipulation (see Collier and Vincente 2012). The applied work which follows, and which is motivated by a search for practical policies to reduce the incidence of electoral manipulation, has a rather different flavour, drawing on the experimental methods of behavioural economics to test the effectiveness of different policy interventions in Nigeria and Mozambique (see Collier and Vincente 2014; Aker et al. 2017).[6]

Notwithstanding this eclecticism, Paul's current work is driven by the same enthusiasm that motivated his undergraduate essay on Malawi, even if the undergraduate's unbridled optimism about the ability of economics to solve the problems of the post-colonial world has disappeared. Last, but not least, several generations of graduate students are indebted to him for his thoughtful support and encouragement. The family tree of his PhD children, grandchildren, great-grandchildren and great-great-grandchildren has not been documented, but it is surely extensive.

References

Main Works by Paul Collier

Aker, C.J., P. Collier and P.C. Vincente (2017). 'Is Information Power? Using Mobile Phones and Free Newspapers During an Election in Mozambique'. *Review of Economics and Statistics*, 99(2): 185–200.

---

[6] Collier and Sterck's study (2018) exhibits a different type of eclecticism, combining arguments from applied ethics with neoclassical economic theory in order to address questions about international financial support for HIV treatment in Africa.

Bevan, D., P. Collier and J.W. Gunning (1989). *Peasants and Governments: An Economic Analysis*. Oxford: Clarendon Press.

Bevan, D., P. Collier and J.W. Gunning (1994). *Controlled Open Economies: A Neoclassical Approach to Structuralism*. Oxford: Oxford University Press.

Chauvet, L., P. Collier and M. Duponchel (2010). 'What Explains Aid Project Success in Post-Conflict Situations?'. Policy Research Working Paper 5,418. Washington, D.C.: World Bank.

Collier, P. (1979a). 'The Welfare Effects of Customs Union: An Anatomy'. *Economic Journal*, 89(353): 84–95.

Collier, P. (1979b). 'Migration and Unemployment: A Dynamic General Equilibrium Analysis Applied to Tanzania'. *Oxford Economic Papers*, New Series, 31(2): 205–236.

Collier, P. (1983). 'Malfunctioning of African Rural Factor Markets: Theory and a Kenyan Example'. *Oxford Bulletin of Economics and Statistics*, 45(2): 141–172.

Collier, P. (1985). 'Commodity Aggregation in Customs Unions'. *Oxford Economic Papers*, New Series, 37(4): 677–682.

Collier, P. (1999). 'On the Economic Consequences of Civil War'. *Oxford Economic Papers*, 51(1): 168–183.

Collier, P. (2007a). 'Poverty Reduction in Africa'. *Proceedings of the National Academy of Sciences*, 104(43): 16,763–16,768.

Collier, P. (2007b). *The Bottom Billion: Why the Poorest Countries are Failing and What Can Be Done About It*. Oxford: Oxford University Press.

Collier, P. (2009). *Wars, Guns and Votes: Democracy in Dangerous Places*. New York: Harper Collins.

Collier, P. (2010). *The Plundered Planet: How to Reconcile Prosperity with Nature*. London: Allen Lane.

Collier, P. (2013). *Exodus: How Migration Is Changing Our World*. Oxford: Oxford University Press.

Collier, P. (2017a). 'Culture, Politics, and Economic Development'. *Annual Review of Political Science*, 20: 111–125.

Collier, P. (2017b). 'Africa's Prospective Urban Transition'. *Journal of Demographic Economics*, 83(1): 3–11.

Collier, P. (2018). *The Future of Capitalism: Facing the New Anxieties*. London: Penguin.

Collier, P. (2020). 'Diverging Identities: A Model of Class Formation'. *Oxford Economic Papers*, 72(3): 567–584.

Collier, P. and D. Dollar (2002). 'Aid Allocation and Poverty Reduction'. *European Economic Review*, 46(8): 1,475–1,500.

Collier, P. and D. Dollar (2004). 'Development Effectiveness: What Have We Learnt?'. *Economic Journal*, 114(496): F244–F271.

Collier, P. and A. Hoeffler (1998). 'On Economic Causes of Civil War'. *Oxford Economic Papers*, 50(4): 563–573.

Collier, P. and A. Hoeffler (2004). 'Greed and Grievance in Civil War'. *Oxford Economic Papers*, 56(4): 563–595.

Collier, P. and A. Hoeffler (2005). 'Resource Rents, Governance, and Conflict'. *Journal of Conflict Resolution*, 49(4): 625–633.

Collier, P. and D. Lal (1984). 'Why Poor People Get Rich: Kenya 1960–1979'. *World Development*, 12(10): 1,007–1,018.

Collier, P. and D. Lal (1986). *Labour and Poverty in Kenya, 1900–1980*. Oxford: Clarendon Press.

Collier, P. and C. Mayer (1986). 'An Investigation of University Selection Procedures'. *Economic Journal*, 96(Supplement): 163–170.

Collier, P. and C. Mayer (1989). 'Financial Liberalization, Financial Systems, and Economic Growth'. *Oxford Review of Economic Policy*, 5(4): 1–12.

Collier P. and S.A. O'Connell (2007). 'Opportunities and Choices'. Chapter 2 in B.J. Ndulu, S.A. O'Connell, R.H. Bates, P. Collier and C.C. Soludo (eds) *The Political Economy of Economic Growth in Africa, 1960–2000*. Cambridge: Cambridge University Press: 76–136.

Collier, P., S. Radwan and S. Wangwe (1986). *Labour and Poverty in Rural Tanzania*. Oxford: Clarendon Press.

Collier, P. and O. Sterck (2018). 'The Moral and Fiscal Implications of Antiretroviral Therapies for HIV in Africa'. *Oxford Economic Papers*, 70(2): 353–374.

Collier, P. and A.J. Venables (2010). 'Natural Resources and State Fragility'. Working Paper 2010/36. Robert Schuman Centre for Advanced Studies. Florence: European University Institute.

Collier, P. and A.J. Venables (2016). 'Urban Infrastructure for Development'. *Oxford Review of Economic Policy*, 32(3): 391–409.

Collier, P. and A.J. Venables (2017). 'Urbanization in Developing Economies: The Assessment'. *Oxford Review of Economic Policy*, 33(3): 355–372.

Collier, P. and A.J. Venables (2018). 'Who Gets the Urban Surplus?'. *Journal of Economic Geography*, 18(3): 523–538.

Collier, P. and P. Vincente (2012). 'Violence, Bribery, and Fraud: The Political Economy of Elections in Sub-Saharan Africa'. *Public Choice*, 153(1–2): 117–147.

Collier, P. and P. Vincente (2014). 'Votes and Violence: Evidence from a Field Experiment in Nigeria'. *Economic Journal*, 124(574): F327–F355.

Other Works Referred To

Açemoğlu, D., S. Johnson and J.A. Robinson (2001). 'The Colonial Origins of Comparative Development: An Empirical Investigation'. *American Economic Review*, 91(5): 1,369–1,401.

Akerlof, R. (2017). 'Value Formation: The Role of Esteem'. *Games and Economic Behavior*, 102(March): 1–19.

Azam, J.-P. (1995). 'How to Pay for the Peace? A Theoretical Framework with References to African Countries'. *Public Choice*, 83(1–2): 173–184.

Basedau, M., B. Pfeiffer and J. Vüllers (2016). 'Bad Religion? Religion, Collective Action, and the Onset of Armed Conflict in Developing Countries'. *Journal of Conflict Resolution*, 60(2): 226–255.

Bates, R.H. (2014). *Markets and States in Tropical Africa: The Political Basis of Agricultural Policies*. Los Angeles: University of California Press.

Baulch, B. (2011). 'Household Panel Data Sets in Developing and Transition Countries'. Mimeo, Chronic Poverty Research Centre. Available at: http://www.chronicpoverty.org.

Besley, T. and T. Persson (2011). 'Fragile States and Development Policy'. *Journal of the European Economic Association*, 9(3): 371–398.

Blavatnik (2017). 'Faculty Spotlight: Paul Collier'. Blavatnik School of Government, University of Oxford. Available at: https://www.bsg.ox.ac.uk/research/faculty-spotlights/faculty-spotlight-paul-collier.

Burnside, C. and D. Dollar (2000). 'Aid, Policies, and Growth'. *American Economic Review*, 90(4): 847–868.

Fearon, J. (2005). 'Primary Commodity Exports and Civil War'. *Journal of Conflict Resolution*, 49(4): 483–507.

Frenkel, J.A. (2010). 'The Natural Resource Curse: A Survey'. NBER Working Paper 15,836. Cambridge, MA: National Bureau of Economic Research.

Grossman, H.I. (1995). 'Insurrections'. Chapter 8 in K. Hartley and T. Sandler (eds) *Handbook of Defense Economics*. Volume 1. Amsterdam: North-Holland: 191–212.

Harris, J.R. and M.P. Todaro (1970). 'Migration, Unemployment and Development: A Two-Sector Analysis'. *American Economic Review*, 60(1): 126–142.

Hegre, H. and N. Sambanis (2006). 'Sensitivity Analysis of Empirical Results on Civil War Onset'. *Journal of Conflict Resolution*, 50(4): 508–535.

Lipsey, R.G. (1957). 'The Theory of Customs Unions: Trade Diversion and Welfare'. *Economica*, New Series, 24(93): 40–46.

Mayer, C. (2018). *Prosperity: Better Business Makes the Greater Good*. Oxford: Oxford University Press.

Orwell, G. (1982). *The Lion and the Unicorn: Socialism and the English Genius*. London: Penguin.

Ross, M.L. (2015). 'What Have We Learned About the Resource Curse?'. *Annual Review of Political Science*, 18: 239–259.

Viner, J. (1950). *The Customs Union Issue*. New York: Carnegie Endowment for International Peace.

28

Anthony J. Venables (1953–)

Gianmarco I. P. Ottaviano

1 Introduction

At the time of writing, Anthony J. Venables ("Tony" hereafter) is still active as BP Professor of Economics at Oxford, Fellow of New College and Director of the Oxford Centre for the Analysis of Resource-Rich Economies (OxCarre). However, while Oxford has featured strongly in his academic life, Tony's career has also been influenced by time spent at other institutions.

Tony hails from Newport, South Wales, now in industrial decline but a prosperous steel town in the 1950s and 1960s with maritime traditions dating back to the Romans. He was the scion of an upper-middle-class dynasty that had run a successful family business for a century from the 1870s to the 1970s. The founder, John Cashmore, had realised that the tidal reach of the River Usk was ideal for ship scrapping as large vessels could easily navigate upstream. By 1937, his firm had become a major employer in the area, handling iron and steel, dealing with new and rebuilt machinery, works dismantling and ship-breaking. "Everything Iron and Steel" became its logo. Apart from its strong tidal waters, Newport had other advantages, from business

I am grateful to Tony Venables for useful materials and discussions, and to Isabella Fausti for outstanding research assistance.

G. I. P. Ottaviano (✉)
Bocconi University, Bologna, Italy
e-mail: gianmarco.ottaviano@unibocconi.it

expertise in coal exporting to the spin-offs of maritime trade. The adoption of modern working practices and new technology in metal cutting also helped. The firm had several competitors in the UK, but only a few were of a comparable size. What Cashmore seems to have feared more was foreign competition, describing 'busy, keen and happy workers doing their best to retain in this country a business that is threatened and attacked by continental competition' (Cashmore quoted in Dyer 2011). It was indeed foreign competition that ended the ship-breaking business in the 1970s, albeit not as a result of competition from Continental Europe: today the largest ship-breaking yards are in the Far East.

While Newport was declining, Tony's mind was elsewhere. He went to boarding school in Bath, taking mathematics, history and economics as specialisms. It was the late 1960s, so everybody Tony's age thought they would change the world. Tony was no exception and remembers being really excited by the book written by Jagdish Bhagwati on the economics of underdeveloped countries (see Bhagwati 1966). In 1969, he was offered admission to Cambridge University when he was still only 16 but took it up when 18 after a "gap year" teaching in Botswana. Looking back, Tony is not sure that Newport influenced him much. However, as we will see, there are surprising coincidences between Tony's home town, local family business and his research interests.

By 1974, Tony had been awarded his BA in Economics at Clare College, Cambridge, and was ready to start graduate studies at Oxford, where he first obtained his BPhil (now called MPhil) in Economics at St Antony's College in 1976 and then his DPhil in Economics at Worcester College in 1984. There were two main influences during this period. The first was college life. Tony was at St Antony's: nomen est omen, or rather simply the result of having 'been advised while at Cambridge that Nuffield was too dull!' (private correspondence). At that time, St Antony's was an extremely lively place for political argument (and it seems good parties, too). The second influence was Hywel Jones, his main MPhil supervisor for core teaching. Jones was an excellent communicator, with whom Tony used to go drinking and talking economics one evening a week along with other young fellows, such as Nicholas Crafts and Robert Eastwood. Jones had just finished writing an introduction to modern theories of economic growth (see Jones 1976) and introduced Tony to the Oxford grandees James Mirrlees (Nobel Prize winner in 1996) and Joseph Stiglitz (Nobel Prize in 2001).

Mirrlees became the sole supervisor of Tony's BPhil thesis on "The Impact of Technical Progress on Less Developed Economies: A Theoretical Reappraisal", which remained unpublished and contained an application of optimal control methods. Of those days, Tony remembers how Mirrlees 'set demanding standards and taught rigour' (private correspondence), while interactions with Stiglitz were more informal. Tony had an office opposite Stiglitz's in the Institute of Economics and Statistics, and it was Stiglitz who triggered Tony's early work on imperfect competition. In Tony's words: 'Joe was of course inspirational in his unique way' (ibid.). Mirrlees and Stiglitz got Tony into economics: up to then, he had planned to become 'Secretary General of the UN, not an academic' (ibid.). Nonetheless, according to Tony, he did not really learn to write academic papers until the year he spent at the University of British Columbia in 1982–1983. There he had rich interactions with Charles Blackorby, William Schworm, David Donaldson as well as with Margaret Slade and Ashok Kotwal. In particular, Tony spent quite some time trying to persuade Blackorby and Schworm that much of the complicated aggregation analysis they were working on at the time was just an application of factor price equalisation. He eventually managed to win them over, as shown by Blackorby et al. (1993).

In 1984, Tony was appointed Research Fellow of the Centre for Economic Policy Research (CEPR), a pan-European research network set up that year in the image of the US National Bureau of Economic Research (NBER). Ten years later, Tony would become Co-Director with Richard Baldwin of the CEPR's International Trade Programme, and eventually one of its Trustees in 2013. As for many a young scholar in Europe since 1984, Tony's involvement in the CEPR's activities at an early stage of his career was fundamental to him getting international exposure. Especially at that time, young faculty did not have research grants or developed networks of contacts. Being part of the CEPR allowed him to meet renowned scholars, some of whom eventually became regular co-authors, such as Richard Baldwin, Paul Krugman, James Markusen, Victor Norman and Alasdair Smith. It was from Norman in particular that Tony learnt international trade theory, sharing with him the Yrjö Jahnsson Lectures on the same subject in 1989. They also started writing a textbook together that, while still unpublished, greatly benefited Tony's graduate students at LSE, where Tony was Professor of International Economics and Director of the Globalization Programme at the Centre for Economic Performance (CEP) from 1992 to 2007, and also at the University of Southampton, where he had been Eric Roll Professor of Economic Policy from 1988 to 1992, following previous appointments as Lecturer in Economics at the University of Essex (1978–1979) and the University of Sussex (1979–1988).

Interactions within the CEPR had a strong positive influence on Tony's penchant for topical policy analysis. At the turn of the century, Tony's deep interest in policy-relevant issues and commitment to economic development motivated his appointments first as research manager in the World Bank's Development Research Group (DECRG) from 1998 to 1999 and then as Chief Economist in the UK's Department for International Development (DFID) from 2005 to 2008. His activity at the World Bank overlapped with his old mentor Stiglitz's momentous term as Senior Vice President for development policy and Chief Economist.

After DFID, it was time for Tony to return to Oxford, where he remains. It is at Oxford that the different threads of his research have been woven together in studies on natural resources and development patterns through an eclectic mix of trade, development, urban and resources economics, as well as new collaborations with Frederick van der Ploeg, the Research Director of OxCarre, and Paul Collier of the Centre for the Study of African Economies (CSAE).

In what follows, I will discuss Tony's contributions to economics, organising them along three broad themes: international trade (Section 2), economic geography (Section 3) and economic development (Section 4). Section 5 will conclude.

2   International Trade[1]

The Nobel Prize in Economics has been awarded to scholars in international trade twice, in 1977 to James Meade and Bertil Ohlin jointly, and in 2008 to Paul Krugman. Tony's work on the subject starts from where Ohlin and Meade ended and has been instrumental to Krugman's success.

What determines the pattern of international trade? What are the associated welfare gains and losses? What are the sources of these gains and losses? Can individual incentives to trade diverge from societal objectives? Should governments intervene to promote or restrict international trade? Questions like these have always been at the core of the debate on trade down the years (indeed, over many centuries; see Irwin 1996). In the last few decades, they have gained new salience, in Europe and elsewhere. The world first embraced globalisation after the Second World War but then with the new century it caved into renewed protectionist pressures and resurgent nationalistic tendencies due to disenchantment with the globalised economy, especially after the financial crisis of 2008.

---

[1] Parts of this section draw on Behrens and Ottaviano (2011).

The ideas underpinning Krugman's Nobel Prize were the products of this roller coaster period, just like those motivating Meade and Ohlin were the product of an earlier period. To understand why, it is useful to divide the recent history of international trade relations into two waves of globalisation (see Baldwin and Martin 1999). The first started in the mid-nineteenth century and ran up the eve of the First World War. It roughly coincided with the Second Industrial Revolution, during which new manufacturing, transportation and communication technologies diffused from Great Britain to Continental Europe and a small set of other countries worldwide. The result was the emergence of an industrialised "North", exporting manufactures to a less developed and often colonised "South" in exchange for raw materials and primary products. This is the period in which John Cashmore and many others built their business fortunes through a mix of animal spirits, modern working practices and new technology.

During this first wave of globalisation, due to North-South international specialisation in production, international trade was characterised by the exchange of different goods between structurally different countries. In economics, such an intersectoral pattern of trade soon found two robust theoretical explanations at the core of what later came to be known as traditional trade theory (TTT). Both explanations highlighted the role of relative cost differences (comparative advantages) between countries, predicting that a country would export the goods that it is able to produce at relatively lower costs. The two explanations differed, however, in terms of the sources of cost differences, which were to be found in the uneven international distribution of either technologies (Ricardian model) or relative factor endowments (Heckscher-Ohlin model). It was for their contributions to the theory of comparative advantage that Ohlin and Meade were (belatedly) awarded the Nobel Prize in 1977.

The second wave of globalisation began to gain momentum just after the Second World War, and it is still going on despite changing moods about its merit, especially in places with fading manufacturing traditions, like Newport. In this period, further technological improvements in production, transportation and communication technologies, and their steady diffusion to a growing number of countries, brought a substantial change in international trade patterns. These started to be dominated by the exchange of similar goods between structurally similar "northern" countries, sharing roughly the same technologies and relative factor endowments. The rise of this type of intra-industry trade between rich countries created a conundrum for the traditional theories based on comparative advantage as these explained bilateral trade flows in terms of differences between trading partners (see Linder 1961; Grubel and

Lloyd 1975; Greenaway and Milner 1986). How to explain that similar countries actually traded more than dissimilar countries? This was the key question
in international trade when Tony was attracted to models of imperfect competition and trade constructed by Stiglitz and Norman, although his initial
interest was motivated much more by the "rich welfare effects" of trade that
imperfectly competitive models could allow for in the wake of work by
Michael Spence (1976a, b).[2]

The counterfactual predictions of the Ricardian and Heckscher-Ohlin
models were derived from two specific simplifying assumptions: constant
returns to scale at the firm level and perfect competition in all markets. These
assumptions anchored those models to the standard Arrow-Debreu paradigm
of general equilibrium theory in which incentives to trade arise only when
traders have different individual assessments of the relative values of the trans-
acted goods. The larger the difference in those assessments, the higher their
incentives to transact and thus the volumes of trade. Vice versa, individuals
sharing the same assessments have no incentive to trade. This is indeed the
case for countries sharing the same technologies and relative factor endowments, as their autarky relative prices are identical.

While it was clear that the Arrow-Debreu assumptions were putting a
straitjacket on the ability to explain the structure of world trade, for a long
time the lack of tractable general equilibrium models with increasing returns
to scale and imperfect competition hampered progress in international trade
theory. This state of affairs started to change in the late 1970s when new partial equilibrium models of oligopoly and monopolistic competition were borrowed from industrial organisation and transplanted to the general equilibrium
framework of international trade theory (see Helpman 1984a). By the end of
the 1970s and the beginning of the 1980s the so-called new trade theory
(NTT), which would transform the field, had been born (see, for example,
Krugman 1979, 1980; Dixit and Norman 1980; Markusen 1981; Brander
and Krugman 1983; Helpman 1984b).

With the benefit of hindsight, it is now clear that what had held international trade theory back had been its "obsession" with general equilibrium.
This obsession is easily explained and justified by the fact that the assessment
of the effects of trade liberalisation on a national economy necessarily requires
an understanding of what happens to factor incomes and prices. In other
words, 'you want a general-equilibrium story, in which it is clear where the
money comes from and where it goes' (Fujita and Krugman 2004: 141).

---

[2] Spence was awarded the Nobel Prize in 2001.

At the same time, even armchair evidence makes it clear that a theoretical account of the structure of world trade cannot fly without a model of firm behaviour. By assumption, however, in the perfectly competitive Arrow-Debreu paradigm, the boundaries of the firm are undetermined. A firm, whatever that may be in an Arrow-Debreu world, is just a production function and, as such, has no "behaviour" whatsoever. Yet, as John Cashmore would testify, firm behaviour is important in many respects: firms decide whether to launch new products and dispense with old ones, where to produce and where to sell their goods, whether to compete in prices or quantities, how to organise their operations and so on.

The key that eventually unlocked the door of general equilibrium with imperfect competition was the monopolistically competitive model by Krugman (1980), heralded in earlier unpublished work by Norman (1976). The idea of monopolistic competition is a rather old one, dating back at least to the early 1930s. Chamberlin (1933) introduced the idea of "large group competition", where firms retain some monopoly power thanks to product differentiation, yet are small in the aggregate economy. The idea that firms are small in the economy can be made precise by assuming that there is a "continuum" of firms. In such a setting, firms are aware that they are price makers as they face finitely elastic demand for their products while their behaviour has no impact on market aggregates like gross domestic product (GDP), the number of firms, consumer income and price indices.

Such "non-strategic" behaviour allows one to sidestep a myriad of thorny technical problems that arise once we seriously think about oligopoly in general equilibrium, such as the existence of equilibria or diverging conclusions depending on whether firms maximise profits or the welfare of their shareholders by choosing prices or quantities. Though one may argue that the properties of monopolistic competition are rather special and may limit the generality of the analysis, they offer the advantage of laying out a clear framework within which macroeconomic issues can be parsimoniously examined. Thanks to the theoretical and empirical success of monopolistically competitive models in accounting for the exchange of similar goods between structurally similar "northern" countries, comparative advantage is today usually viewed as driving specialisation at the industry level, whereas product differentiation and economies of scale are utilised to explain what drives specialisation at the product level.

Trade and gains from trade then arise not only because international exchange allows countries to specialise according to comparative advantage, but also because it increases the variety of products available and reduces the market power of domestic firms, thus leading to smaller markups, lower prices as well as larger quantities consumed. With increasing returns to scale, larger quantities serve to reduce prices not only because markups fall but because average production costs fall as well.

TTT and NTT are clearly complementary and in the 1980s their synthesis provided a unified view of international trade, changing the way economists understand the patterns, the gains and the sources of international trade (see Dixit and Norman 1980; Helpman and Krugman 1985). It also enriched the way that economists understand the effects of trade policies (see Helpman and Krugman 1989) and how trade barriers affect economic growth (see Grossman and Helpman 1993), economic geography (see Fujita et al. 1999 and Baldwin et al. 2003) and foreign direct investment (see Markusen 2004; Barba et al. 2006).

For his contributions to NTT (and to the so-called new economic geography (NEG)), Krugman was awarded the Nobel Prize in 2008. Tony's contribution to the body of work that led to Krugman's Nobel is substantial, starting with key studies on the TTT-NTT synthesis, such as Venables (1987) and later Markusen and Venables (2000). Of particular relevance is the trilogy of articles published in the *Journal of International Economics* in the 1980s (see Venables 1982, 1984, 1985), which became reference points for subsequent generations of trade scholars. For instance, one can read Melitz and Ottaviano (2008) who point out that almost all the rich welfare effects of trade featured in the "new" NTT literature with heterogeneous firms, developed in the wake of Melitz (2003), had been already identified in the "old" NTT literature with representative firms. In particular, the welfare gains from additional product variety as well as the asymmetric welfare gains of trade induced by differences in country size and trade costs had been highlighted by Krugman (1980). Krugman (1979) had also shown how trade can induce pro-competitive effects in a model with monopolistic competition and endogenous markups, while Markusen (1981) had formalised and highlighted the pro-competitive effects from trade due to the reduction in market power of a domestic monopolist. Horstmann and Markusen (1986) and Venables (1985) had extended this modelling framework to the case of oligopoly with free entry (while maintaining the assumption of a homogeneous traded good). These papers had also emphasised, among other things, how free entry could generate welfare losses for a country unilaterally liberalising imports by "reallocating" firms towards the country's trading partners. Venables (1987), a paper not in the trilogy but on which Tony had already been working in parallel when visiting the University of British Columbia in 1982–1983, had shown how this effect can be generated in a model with monopolistic competition and product differentiation with exogenous markups. The new NTT models additionally captured the welfare effects stemming from changes in average productivity based on the selection of heterogeneous firms into domestic and export markets. More recently, Haaland and Venables (2016) have discussed some of those models' policy implications in another paper in the *Journal of International Economics* that echoes Venables (1982) after more than 30 years.

The third paper of the 1980s trilogy hints at what would arguably become Tony's most important contribution to economics and his ongoing passion: the study of the interactions between geography, development and trade. Specifically, Venables (1984) developed a model of trade with monopolistic competition in which small perturbations in the parameters radically change the number and type of equilibria. For certain parameter values, the model exhibits multiple stable equilibria. In some of them, sectoral specialisation across countries is not complete and intra-industry trade takes place. In others, specialisation is complete and there is no intra-industry trade. This suggested that, differently from TTT, NTT models could lead to path dependency, lock-in effects and suboptimal outcomes in patterns of international trade and development, an insight at the core of the NEG.

3   Economic Geography[3]

The sectoral specialisation of countries, and of regions and cities within countries, is the result of firms' location decisions. A firm's location decision gives rise to an economic problem when two things are true. First, the shipment of goods and factors across space is costly. Second, production fragmentation is also costly, that is, there are increasing returns to scale at the plant level. The former gives physical substance to the concept of space. Together with the latter, it generates an economic trade-off between market proximity and production concentration that makes location choices non-trivial. Scotchmer and Thisse (1992) call this the "folk theorem of spatial economics".

However, while fundamental, these two ingredients are incompatible with the perfectly competitive paradigm that still dominated much of mainstream economics (and TTT) in the late 1970s and early 1980s. Starrett (1978) highlighted this theoretical impasse in his "spatial impossibility theorem": if space is homogenous, there does not exist any competitive equilibrium with shipments between distant locations. A policy-relevant implication is that any analysis trying to explain how economic interactions per se shape the

---

[3] Parts of this section draw on Ottaviano (2003) and Ottaviano (2019a).

economic landscape has to abandon the assumption of perfect markets and the associated efficiency property of market equilibrium.

There are many ways out of this impasse: while there is only one way to be perfect, there are many ways to be imperfect. Most obviously, a first solution is to acknowledge that space is not homogenous. Places differ in terms of their relative abundance of natural resources, proximity to natural means of communications and climatic conditions. This is the way out investigated by TTT. However, it looks like an inadequate explanation of the dramatic differences in economic development that one observes even between areas that are not very different in terms of those exogenous properties. In other words, there must be something more going on which is inherent to the functioning of economic interactions. This point was raised quite forcefully by Marshall (1890), who stressed the role of both localised technological and pecuniary externalities. Both concepts stem from the standard textbook situation in which market prices incompletely reflect the cost and utility values of the interactions between economic agents. However, while the problem with technological externalities is that some effects of the interactions are not priced at all, with pecuniary externalities the problem lies in price distortions due to the presence of market power. Accordingly, while the former can be transmitted by sheer proximity, the transmission of the latter requires market transactions.

Localised pecuniary externalities are at the core of NEG. Eventually, their comparative advantage lies in the possibility of relating their emergence to a set of well-defined microeconomic parameters. This has proven to be quite difficult in models based on the concept of technological externalities as these still remain mostly "black boxes" (see Duranton and Puga 2004), although some progress has been made by, among others, Storper and Venables (2004). Differently, building on NTT, starting in the late 1980s NEG managed to show how pecuniary externalities arise in sectors characterised by relevant trade costs (due to transportation as well as to administrative and cultural barriers), increasing returns to scale, and monopolistic competition. In those sectors, when a new firm begins producing in a certain location, it increases local demand for upstream activities ("market expansion effect") and local supply for downstream ones ("market crowding effect"). It generates a pecuniary externality insofar as the firm bases its entry decision on its own profit and this, due to imperfect competition, does not perfectly reflect all the changes in the payoffs of upstream and downstream activities.

Agglomeration takes place when the final impact of the market expansion effect dominates the impact of the market crowding effect (see Krugman 1991; Krugman and Venables 1995; Venables 1996). Consider, for instance, the situation depicted by Venables (ibid.), which predates Krugman and Venables (1995) in terms of working paper versions. There are three vertically linked activities: intermediate production, final production and consumption. For simplicity, assume that final production uses only intermediate inputs, intermediate production employs only labour and workers are the only source of final demand. If, for any reason, a new firm starts producing intermediates, it will increase labour demand and intermediate supply. Due to excess demand and supply, respectively, wages will go up while intermediate prices will fall. This is bad news for the other intermediate producers (market crowding effect). However, it is good news for final suppliers, who experience falling production costs and higher demand by richer workers. As new final producers are induced to enter the market, the expansion of final production will feed back into stronger intermediate demand so that intermediate suppliers will also benefit (market expansion effect). When the latter effect dominates the former, both final and intermediate firms will end up agglomerating in the same place.

This mechanism was not new when Tony constructed his model. For example, it had been described by both Marshall (1890) and Ohlin (1933). The crucial contribution of Tony's model and thus of NEG was that the mechanism in question was translated into a general equilibrium model with solid microeconomic foundations. As a result, the evolution of the spatial landscape was related to microeconomic parameters: agglomeration is more likely to take place in sectors where increasing returns are intense, market power is strong, customers and suppliers are easily mobile and trade costs are low. The reason is that more intense returns to scale and stronger market power weaken the market crowding effect, while more mobile customers and suppliers amplify the market expansion effect. On the other hand, lower trade costs reduce both market expansion and market crowding effects, but the latter more than the former.

The impact of trade liberalisation is arguably the central insight of NEG models. At first sight, it did not sound that new as it was reminiscent of Kaldor (1970), who predicted the loss of the industrial base of a less developed region facing trade liberalisation with respect to a more developed one. However, NEG models provided a more detailed understanding of how the economic landscape evolves as trade impediments are gradually eliminated. NEG models showed that lower trade impediments affect the balance between market expansion and market crowding effects in a very nonlinear way. In particular, they may cause self-reinforcing uneven development between growth centres and stagnant peripheries as economic activities agglomerate in the former and shun the latter. Only the congestion of immobile resources and non-tradable inputs can stop the emergence of self-sustaining "core-periphery" patterns. Moreover, processes of circular causation like the one described by Venables (1996) can sustain multiple spatial equilibria and thus make the spatial economy settle in a suboptimal equilibrium due to path dependency, self-fulfilling expectations and lock-in effects, factors which remind one of Venables (1984).

These insights were "iconoclastic" when they made it into the public policy discourse, especially in Europe. The late 1980s and early 1990s were crucial years for the project of European integration of "One Market, One Money" (Commission of the European Communities 1990). The project was based on a promise of inclusive development that would benefit all regions of the Old Continent, in particular the least prosperous ones. The promise rested on the expectation that lower barriers to the international movement of goods, labour and capital in an integrating Europe would eventually lead to regional convergence in prices, factor returns and thus living standards between and within countries.

This expectation mainly derived from neoclassical growth arguments founded on the assumptions of constant returns to scale and perfectly competitive markets. In some of their more sophisticated versions, these arguments acknowledged the long-term horizon in which convergence would take place but considered, if not convergence, at least regionally balanced growth as the inevitable final outcome of economic integration. This can be seen as the economic essence of the "European dream" (see Ottaviano 2019b). On the one hand, as economic growth is typically driven by what happens in a limited number of dynamic geographical areas that lead the way, any leap forward along the development path requires the geographical concentration of economic activities and thus an ineluctable division of areas in more and less developed countries. The emergence of an economic "core" and an economic "periphery" are two sides of the same coin. On the other hand, the implied polarisation of the economic landscape is not an issue as long as the success of more dynamic areas automatically ends up also benefiting less dynamic ones. If the core grows, the periphery will eventually grow too. As time goes by, the wealth gap between the two remains constant and may even shrink as long as it is easier to follow than to lead the way. In this respect, European integration promotes inclusive development. It not only allows for the concentration of economic activities in the most dynamic regions that are the engines of growth, but also facilitates the diffusion of such growth to the least dynamic areas thanks to their belonging to a common economic space.

NEG forcefully made the point that the foregoing did not need to be the only ineluctable outcome (see Baldwin and Venables 1995; Krugman and

Venables 1996). A quarter of a century later, the promise of inclusive development does not seem to have been kept, and the strengthening of regional imbalances is increasingly becoming a threat not only to social cohesion but also to the political stability of the European Union, as possibly heralded by Brexit. Almost 30 years since the introduction of the Single Market, the iconoclastic insights of NEG can still help understand the causes of this lack of geographical convergence. Tapping the coherent body of results systematised by Fujita et al. (1999), Fujita and Thisse (2002) and Baldwin et al. (2003) would be an obvious starting point.

4   Economic Development

After contributing to the theory and policy of international trade and economic geography, by the end of the 1990s Tony was back to his original passion for economic development, and since then his research on trade, economic geography and economic development have increasingly come together as one with the usual strong emphasis on policy issues. A common theme is the crucial implication of Starrett's impossibility theorem that any explanation of the geographical patterns of economic development we observe in reality is necessarily based on some kind of market imperfection and thus necessarily implies that the market mechanism alone is not able to deliver an optimal economic landscape (see Henderson and Venables 2009). Ottaviano and Thisse (2001) call this the "spatial question": any positive model of economic geography necessarily raises normative issues.

A prominent example of how the study of the interactions among trade, geography and development can lead to new useful insights on what holds some countries back economically can be found in Redding and Venables (2004). This paper starts from the observation that, despite increasing international economic integration, the vast cross-country disparities in per capita have not been bid away by the mobility of manufacturing firms and plants. While there are many potential reasons for the reluctance of firms to move production to low wage countries, including endowments, technology, institutional quality and geographical location, Redding and Venables focus on the last and emphasise two main mechanisms. One is the distance of countries from the markets in which they sell output ("demand access"), and the other is distance from countries that supply manufactures and provide the capital equipment and intermediate goods required for production ("supply access"). Transport costs or other barriers to trade mean that more distant countries suffer a market access penalty on their sales and also face additional costs on imported inputs. Therefore, firms in these countries can only afford to pay relatively low wages, even if, for example, their technologies are the same as those elsewhere. By estimating a structural NEG model à la Fujita et al. (1999) using cross-country data on per capita income, bilateral trade and the relative price of manufacturing goods, Redding and Venables (2004) provide evidence that the geography of access to markets and sources of supply is statistically significant and quantitatively important in explaining cross-country variation in per capita income. This finding is robust to controlling for a wide range of factors, including economic, geographical, social and institutional. Geography matters through the mechanisms emphasised by NEG, and the estimated coefficients are consistent with plausible values for the model's structural parameters.

In the same vein, Limão and Venables (2001) note that the real costs of trade, due to transport and various frictions in doing business, are important determinants of a country's ability to fully participate in the world economy. Remoteness and poor transport and communications infrastructure act to isolate countries, inhibiting their participation in global production networks such as those Tony investigated subsequently in Baldwin and Venables (2013). Using different datasets to investigate the dependence of transport costs on geography and infrastructure, Limão and Venables (2001) find that infrastructure is an important determinant of transport costs, especially in landlocked countries. In particular, analysis of African trade flows reveals that their relatively low level is largely due to poor infrastructure.

At a finer level of disaggregation, Collier and Venables (2016) evaluate the importance of infrastructure (in particular infrastructure for connectivity) in the development of fast-growing cities. They argue that the value of infrastructure goes well beyond the "user benefits" of standard cost-benefit appraisal, as infrastructure supports an economic environment in which the potential of cities, that is, scale, specialisation and agglomeration, can best be achieved. They then turn to the policies that are required to support infrastructure investment, looking at public finance, governance, urban density and turning finally to the wider national context. Within the same conceptual framework, Henderson et al. (2016) explore the factors that may underlie the non-functionality of many cities in the developing world. Lall et al. (2017) try to understand why cities in Sub-Saharan Africa are experiencing rapid population growth but their economic growth has not kept pace as other regions have reached similar stages of urbanisation at higher per capita GDP.

An important concern about some developing countries is their mishandling of natural resources. This concern had already attracted Tony's attention at an early stage of his career. In particular, when he started publishing his

NTT trilogy in 1982, he also published a paper on the macroeconomic implications of a resource discovery in an open economy (see Eastwood and Venables 1982). Fast forward and the analysis of resource-rich economies again became prominent in his research agenda when he went back to Oxford in 2007 as Director of OxCarre.[4]

Countries with substantial non-renewable natural resource wealth face special opportunities and challenges. Research undertaken by Tony with other Oxford economists, notably Frederick van der Ploeg and Paul Collier, has contributed to understanding these challenges and to improving policies for resource management, particularly in developing economies. Of particular impact has been their study of the relationship between resource wealth and conflict, the short- and medium-run management of instability in revenue streams (see van den Bremer and van der Ploeg 2013), trade issues (see Ruta and Venables 2012), the experience of particular countries (see Collier et al. 2010; Venables 2011), and long-run decisions about saving, investing and consuming revenues. Through this research, Tony's team has been influential in shaping the policy positions of international financial institutions, particularly the IMF, and in contributing to policy debates within countries, particularly in the newly resource-rich nations of Africa.

Another focus has been the management of the foreign exchange windfall that is often generated by resource revenues. At the aggregate level, these revenues can help to finance three things: current expenditure, domestic investment and the acquisition of foreign assets (e.g. through a sovereign wealth fund). OxCarre research has shown that the balance between these different types of spending depends on a number of factors including the following: the ethical weighting of income accruing to different generations to the constraints on public funds and the supply of capital; the need to avoid an inflationary resource boom to exchange rate overvaluation and Dutch disease; a country's capacity (institutional and economic) to absorb extra expenditure; and the need to insulate an economy from volatility in world commodity prices to the need for spending decisions to be robust to different politico-economic environments. Analysis of how best to manage the trade-offs between these factors has been the subject of van der Ploeg and Venables (2011, 2013), Collier et al. (2010), van den Bremer and van der Ploeg (2013) and van der Ploeg and Poelhekke (2009).

OxCarre research on the use of natural resource revenues has challenged the conventional wisdom of using the permanent income hypothesis (PIH) to guide decisions about how revenues are spent. In particular, Tony's team has

---

[4] The following discussion of Tony's work on natural resources is drawn from OxCarre (2013).

constructed a dynamic model of a developing economy that is capital constrained (because households and government are unable to borrow at the world interest rate) and on a growth path towards development. They have shown that in this setting the optimal policy is not to follow the PIH prescription of using revenues to accumulate long-run foreign assets, but rather to balance higher investment in the domestic economy (particularly infrastructure) with a relatively large increment to current consumption to address the poverty of the current generation (see van der Ploeg and Venables 2011). This research has also addressed issues relating to short- and medium-run economic management, analysing the impact of resource revenue on the structure of the economy, its implications for the exchange rate and how to manage these implications (see van der Ploeg and Venables 2013).

This body of research has outlined a strategy for resource revenue management that prioritises investment in physical (and human) assets in the domestic economy, supplementing these with foreign savings vehicles designed to mitigate the effects of volatility and in which revenues can be "parked" until absorptive capacity problems are solved. It also outlines the importance of concurrent domestic economic reform—for example, preparing the economy to overcome absorption constraints and how to handle a resource boom—and the microeconomic detail of the interaction between the public and private sectors. The importance of this line of research lies in the fact that the core analysis suggests a use of revenues quite different from the PIH prescriptions that have underpinned the policy advice of the Fiscal Affairs Department of the IMF and influential country-based organisations, such as the Norwegian Oil for Development programme. Indeed, it has influenced the policy debate within a range of countries through advice offered to ministers and engagement in debates within civil society and NGOs. The WTO in its *World Trade Report 2010* (WTO 2010) has also used Tony's research insights, as has the IMF despite its attachment to the PIH. The impact on policy design within countries has been achieved in particular by advice provided through the Natural Resource Charter (NRC), established in 2009 by an independent team of experts to provide guidance on the management of natural resources. The NRC has been adopted or otherwise endorsed by a broad range of organisations, governments and NGOs: the World Bank, the IMF, Norway, Australia, Zimbabwe, the African Development Bank and the Africa Progress Panel. The UK government has given its support to the NRC through DFID (see DFID 2009).

5   Conclusion

The best way to summarise Tony's research contributions to economics is to build on his own assessment of how research at the juncture of trade, geography and development has evolved in the last few decades. In an unpublished paper written to celebrate the 30th birthday of the CEPR (see Venables 2013), he looked back to take stock of what had been achieved by the International Trade Programme he had also co-directed for a decade:

> In the 30 years since the CEPR was launched the word "globalisation" has come in and out of fashion; the ratio of world trade to GDP has doubled, foreign direct investment has grown even faster, communications technology has been transformed and trade liberalization—unilateral, regional and multilateral— have all made progress (Venables 2013: 9).

Continuing:

> Trade matters for two reasons. One—that of classical international economics—is that it enables a country to get its consumption more cheaply; exports in line with comparative advantage fund the import of goods with comparative disadvantage. The other is that trade can be a catalyst for other changes, going far beyond switching suppliers of some goods. Trade brings larger markets, interaction with a wider group of people and access to new technologies. These can change performance across the wider economy and may have implications many times greater than comparative advantage alone. These "wider" effects of trade have been at the forefront of much trade research in the last 30 years; they have brought an intellectual excitement to the field, have deepened understanding of important phenomena, and have made issues of trade (and spatial economics more generally) of relevance to a broader range of policy makers ... Further, there are three areas in which research on these wider effects of trade has made progress. They are as follows: market integration—firms, competition and scale; geography and the location of economic activity; trade and development. In each of these areas there has been interaction between researchers and policy makers. This is two-way; research insights have shaped policy, and policy makers have shaped the worldview and the priorities of researchers (ibid.: 1).

Nevertheless:

> Research questions—on the evolution of firms, the quantification of gains and the ways in which to lever the most from export activities—remain. However, the last 30 years of research has seen unprecedented innovation, theoretical and

empirical and has established the centrality of trade—within and between countries—to overall economic performance. Economies work better if spatial barriers to interaction are reduced (ibid.: 9–10).

Tony has been a crucial contributor to this wave of 'unprecedented innovation'. His legacy is in his research, but also in his students and in particular the younger scholars he has interacted with especially at the Centre for Economic Performance (CEP) during his time at LSE. Among others, these scholars include Mary Amiti, Gilles Duranton, Simona Iammarino, Niko Matouschek, Henry Overman, Diego Puga, Steve Redding, Francisco Requena-Silvente, Daniel Sturm, Karen Helene Ultveit-Moe and Marina Wes. I had Tony as my MSc supervisor at LSE in 1992–1993. That was when Paul Krugman could also often be found at the School, NEG was taking off and, in terms of world research on "geography and trade", several researchers across Europe were leading the pack. My own research trajectory owes a lot to those glory days.

References

Main Works by Anthony J. Venables

Baldwin, R. and A.J. Venables (1995). 'Regional Economic Integration'. Chapter 31 in G.M. Grossman and K. Rogoff (eds) *Handbook of International Economics*. Volume 3 Amsterdam: North-Holland: 1,597–1,644.

Baldwin, R. and A.J. Venables (2013). 'Spiders and Snakes: Offshoring and Agglomeration in the Global Economy'. *Journal of International Economics*, 90(2): 245–254.

Barba Navaretti, G. and A.J. Venables (2006). *Multinational Firms in the World Economy*. Princeton: Princeton University Press.

Blackorby, C., W. Schworm and A.J. Venables (1993). 'Necessary and Sufficient Conditions for Factor Price Equalization'. *Review of Economic Studies*, 60(2): 413–434.

Collier, P., F. van der Ploeg, M. Spence and A.J. Venables (2010). 'Managing Resource Revenues in Developing Economies'. *IMF Staff Papers*, 57(1): 84–118.

Collier, P. and A.J. Venables (2016). 'Urban Infrastructure for Development'. *Oxford Review of Economic Policy*, 32(3): 391–409.

Eastwood, R.K. and A.J. Venables (1982). 'The Macroeconomic Implications of a Resource Discovery in an Open Economy'. *Economic Journal*, 92(366): 285–299.

Fujita, M., P. Krugman and A.J. Venables (1999). *The Spatial Economy: Cities, Regions, and International Trade*. Cambridge, MA: MIT Press.

Haaland, J.I. and A.J. Venables (2016). 'Optimal Trade Policy with Monopolistic Competition and Heterogeneous Firms'. *Journal of International Economics*, 102(September): 85–95.

Henderson, J.V. and A.J. Venables (2009). 'The Dynamics of City Formation'. *Review of Economic Dynamics*, 12(2): 233–254.

Henderson, J., A.J. Venables, T. Regan and I. Samsonov (2016). 'Building Functional Cities'. *Science*, 352(6,288): 946–947.

Krugman, P. and A.J. Venables (1995). 'Globalization and the Inequality of Nations'. *Quarterly Journal of Economics*, 110(4): 857–880.

Krugman, P. and A.J. Venables (1996). 'Integration, Specialization, and Adjustment'. *European Economic Review*, 40(3–5): 959–967.

Lall, S.V., J.V. Henderson and A.J. Venables (2017). *Africa's Cities: Opening Doors to the World*. Washington, D.C.: World Bank.

Limão, N. and A.J. Venables (2001). 'Infrastructure, Geographical Disadvantage, Transport Costs and Trade'. *World Bank Economic Review*, 15(3): 451–479.

Markusen, J.R. and A.J. Venables (2000). 'The Theory of Endowment, Intra-Industry and Multi-National Trade'. *Journal of International Economics*, 52(2): 209–234.

Redding, S. and A.J. Venables (2004). 'Economic Geography and International Inequality'. *Journal of International Economics*, 62(1): 53–82.

Ruta, M. and A.J. Venables (2012). 'International Trade in Natural Resources: Practice and Policy'. *Annual Review of Resource Economics*, 4: 331–352.

Storper, M. and A.J. Venables (2004). 'Buzz: Face-to-Face Contact and the Urban Economy'. *Journal of Economic Geography*, 4(4): 351–370.

Van der Ploeg, F. and A.J. Venables (2011). 'Harnessing Windfall Revenues: Optimal Policies for Resource-Rich Developing Economies'. *Economic Journal*, 121(551): 1–30.

Van der Ploeg, F. and A.J. Venables (2013). 'Absorbing a Windfall of Foreign Exchange: Dutch Disease Dynamics'. *Journal of Development Economics*, 103(July): 229–243.

Venables, A.J. (1982). 'Optimal Tariffs for Trade in Monopolistically Competitive Commodities'. *Journal of International Economics*, 12(3–4): 225–241.

Venables, A.J. (1984). 'Multiple Equilibria in the Theory of International Trade with Monopolistically Competitive Commodities'. *Journal of International Economics*, 16(1–2): 103–121.

Venables, A.J. (1985). 'Trade and Trade Policy with Imperfect Competition: The Case of Identical Products and Free Entry'. *Journal of International Economics*, 19(1–2): 1–19.

Venables, A.J. (1987). 'Trade and Trade Policy with Differentiated Products: A Chamberlinian-Ricardian Model'. *Economic Journal*, 97(387): 700–717.

Venables, A.J. (1996). 'Equilibrium Locations of Vertically Linked Industries'. *International Economic Review*, 37(2): 341–359.

Venables, A.J. (2011). 'Economic Integration in Remote Resource Rich Regions'. Chapter 7 in R.J. Barro and J.-W. Lee (eds) *Costs and Benefits of Economic Integration in Asia*. New York: Oxford University Press.

Venables, A.J. (2013). 'The Wider Gains from Trade'. Unpublished paper.

Other Works Referred To

Baldwin, R., R. Forslid, P. Martin, G. Ottaviano and F. Robert-Nicoud (2003). *Economic Geography and Public Policy*. Princeton: Princeton University Press.

Baldwin, R.E. and P. Martin (1999). 'Two Waves of Globalisation: Superficial Similarities, Fundamental Differences'. NBER Working Paper No. 6,904. Cambridge, MA: National Bureau of Economic Research.

Behrens, K. and G. Ottaviano (2011). 'General Equilibrium Trade Theory and Firm Behaviour'. Chapter 5 in D. Bernhofen, R. Falvey, D. Greenaway and U. Kreickemeier (eds) *Palgrave Handbook of International Trade*. London: Palgrave Macmillan: 119–159.

Bhagwati, J. (1966). *The Economics of Underdeveloped Countries*. London: Weidenfeld & Nicolson.

Brander, J. and P. Krugman (1983). 'A "Reciprocal Dumping" Model of International Trade'. *Journal of International Economics*, 15(3–4): 313–321.

Chamberlin, E. (1933). *The Theory of Monopolistic Competition*. Cambridge, MA: Harvard Univesity Press.

Commission of the European Communities (1990). 'One Market, One Money: An Evaluation of the Potential Benefits and Costs of Forming an Economic and Monetary Union'. Directorate-General for Economic and Financial Affairs, *European Economy*, 44(October).

DFID (2009). *Eliminating World Poverty: Building Our Common Future*. Cmnd. 7656. London: HMSO.

Dixit, A.K. and V.D. Norman (1980). *Theory of International Trade: A Dual, General Equilibrium Approach*. Cambridge, MA: Cambridge University Press.

Duranton, G. and D. Puga (2004). 'Micro-Foundations of Urban Agglomeration Economies'. Chapter 48 in J.V. Henderson and J.-F. Thisse (eds) *Handbook of Regional and Urban Economics. Volume 4: Cities and Geography*. Amsterdam: North-Holland: 2,063–2,117.

Dyer, J. (2011). 'John Cashmore: Everything Iron and Steel'. Available at: http://www.newportpast.com/jd/cashmore.htm.

Fujita, M. and P. Krugman (2004). 'The New Economic Geography: Past, Present and Future'. *Papers in Regional Science*, 83(1): 139–164.

Fujita, M. and J.-F. Thisse (2002). *Economics of Agglomeration*. Cambridge: Cambridge University Press.

Greenaway, D. and C. Milner (1986). *The Economics of Intra-Industry Trade*. London: Basil Blackwell.

Grossman, G.M. and E. Helpman (1993). *Innovation and Growth in the Global Economy*. Cambridge, MA: MIT Press.

Grubel, H. and P. Lloyd (1975). *Intra-Industry Trade: The Theory of Measurement of International Trade in Differentiated Products*. New York: John Wiley.

Helpman, E. (1984a). 'Increasing Returns, Imperfect Markets, and Trade Theory'. Chapter 7 in R.W. Jones and P.B. Kenen (eds) *Handbook of International Economics. Volume 1: International Trade*. Amsterdam: North-Holland: 325–365.

Helpman, E. (1984b). 'The Factor Content of Foreign Trade'. *Economic Journal*, 94(373): 84–94.

Helpman, E. and P. Krugman (1985). *Market Structure and Foreign Trade: Increasing Returns, Imperfect Competition and the International Economy*. Cambridge, MA: MIT Press.

Helpman, E. and P. Krugman (1989). *Trade Policy and Market Structure*. Cambridge, MA: MIT Press.

Horstmann, I.J. and J.R. Markusen (1986). 'Up the Average Cost Curve: Inefficient Entry and the New Protectionism'. *Journal of International Economics*, 20(3–4): 225–247.

Irwin, D.A. (1996). *Against the Tide: An Intellectual History of Free Trade*. Princeton, NJ: Princeton University Press.

Jones, H.G. (1976). *Introduction to Modern Theories of Economic Growth*. New York: McGraw-Hill.

Kaldor, N. (1970). 'The Case for Regional Policies'. *Scottish Journal of Political Economy*, 17(3): 337–348.

Krugman, P. (1979). 'Increasing Returns, Monopolistic Competition, and International Trade'. *Journal of International Economics*, 9(4): 469–479.

Krugman, P. (1980). 'Scale Economies, Product Differentiation, and the Pattern of Trade'. *American Economic Review*, 70(5): 950–959.

Krugman, P. (1991). 'Increasing Returns and Economic Geography'. *Journal of Political Economy*, 99(3): 483–499.

Linder, S.B. (1961). *An Essay on Trade and Transformation*. New York: John Wiley.

Markusen, J.R. (1981). 'Trade and the Gains from Trade with Imperfect Competition'. *Journal of International Economics*, 11(4): 531–551.

Markusen, J.R. (2004). *Multinational Firms and the Theory of International Trade*. Cambridge, MA: MIT Press.

Marshall, A. (1890). *Principles of Economics*. London: Macmillan.

Melitz, M.J. (2003). 'The Impact of Trade on Intra-Industry Reallocations and Aggregate Industry Productivity'. *Econometrica*, 71(6): 1,695–1,725.

Melitz, M.J. and G. Ottaviano (2008). 'Market Size, Trade, and Productivity'. *Review of Economic Studies*, 75(1): 295–316.

Norman, V. (1976). 'Product Differentiation and Trade'. Unpublished manuscript. UK Economic Study Group, University of Warwick, UK.

Ohlin, B. (1933). *Interregional and International Trade*. Cambridge, MA: Harvard University Press.

Ottaviano, G. (2003). 'Regional Policy in the Global Economy: Insights from New Economic Geography'. *Regional Studies*, 37(6–7): 665–673.

Ottaviano, G. (2019a). 'Comments on: Spatial Agglomeration and Superstar Firms: Firm-Level Patterns from Europe and the US, by L. Alfaro, M.X. Chen and H. Fadinger'. ECB Forum 2019 Proceedings. Available at: https://www.ecb.europa.eu/pub/conferences/shared/pdf/20190617_ECB_forum_Sintra/presentation_Ottaviano.en.pdf.

Ottaviano, G. (2019b). *Geografia Economica dell'Europa Sovranista*. Bari: Laterza.

Ottaviano, G. and J.-F. Thisse (2001). 'On Economic Geography in Economic Theory: Increasing Returns and Pecuniary Externalities'. *Journal of Economic Geography*, 1(2): 153–179.

OxCarre (2013). 'Managing Natural Resource Revenue in Developing Economies'. Submission to UK Research Excellence Framework 2014.

Scotchmer, S. and J.-F. Thisse (1992). 'Space and Competition: A Puzzle'. *Annals of Regional Science*, 26(3): 269–286.

Spence, M. (1976a). 'Product Differentiation and Welfare'. *American Economic Review*, Papers and Proceedings, 66(2): 407–414.

Spence, M. (1976b). 'Product Selection, Fixed Costs, and Monopolistic Competition'. *Review of Economic Studies*, 43(2): 217–235.

Starrett, D. (1978). 'Market Allocations of Location Choice in a Model with Free Mobility'. *Journal of Economic Theory*, 17(1): 21–37.

Van den Bremer, T. and F. van der Ploeg (2013). 'Managing and Harnessing Volatile Oil Windfalls'. *IMF Economic Review*, 61(1): 130–167.

Van der Ploeg, F. and S. Poelhekke (2009). 'Volatility and the Natural Resource Curse'. *Oxford Economic Papers*, 61(4): 727–760.

WTO (2010). *World Trade Report 2010: Trade in Natural Resources*. Geneva: WTO Publications.

29

Paul David Klemperer (1956–)

Huw Dixon

1   Introduction

Paul Klemperer was born in Southampton, England, in 1956. At the age of
six, he moved to Birmingham with his parents who were both academic scientists: his mother Ruth at Aston University and father Hugh at the University
of Birmingham.[1] He went to the local Bournville Primary School and later
won a scholarship to King Edward's School. From an early age, Klemperer
was fascinated by geometry. On his teenage bedroom wall hung a poster of
Albrecht Dürer's engraving *Saint Jerome in His Study*. The engraving did not
catch his attention because of his interest in Jerome's translation of the Hebrew
Old Testament and Greek New Testament into the Latin around 400 CE. It
was the geometry of perspective (of which Dürer was a pioneer): the way the
parallel lines met at a point in the background. This interest in geometry was
to be a lasting influence on how Klemperer thought about the issues and
problems he studied later in life. He was admitted to study Mathematics at
Cambridge University in 1975, and for his final year he switched to the
Engineering Tripos, in order to be able to focus on more applicable

---

[1] His family did not follow the musical career of his distant relative, the conductor Otto Klemperer.

H. Dixon (✉)
Cardiff Business School, Cardiff, UK
e-mail: DixonH@cardiff.ac.uk

mathematics, especially operations research (OR). Before going to Cambridge, he had vacations: For IBM in Birmingham, where he developed an early computer-aided design program. He also worked during his university vacations: For IBM again, for Monsanto in its world headquarters in St Louis, the United States, and for BP in London (all doing programming and OR).

At the end of the course in 1978, he was eager to get back into the real world, joining Arthur Andersen and Co.'s management consulting division in London (this was subsequently spun off as Accenture). His most significant project was a secondment of about a year to the Department of Health and Social Security. It had developed a complex linear-programming model to allocate resources both within the National Health Service (NHS) and among the NHS and local authorities (who delivered social care) and housing authorities (then a different level of local government). Unfortunately, the model was so complex that no one really understood it, so no one really trusted its answers. His most important contribution was to develop a much simpler model, which not only generated very similar answers but also brought out the intuition clearly, so users trusted the answers and could understand the effects of modifying the assumptions or changing the resources available. The work done in this period later led to Klemperer and McClenahan (1981). Klemperer's ability to make the complex simple to be comprehensible to policy makers was to stand him in good stead later in life when he advised the Bank of England during the financial crisis.

In 1980, Klemperer was awarded a Harkness Fellowship to pursue a two-year MBA at Stanford University. However, at an early stage, he decided he wanted to do a PhD, which he started in 1982 and completed in 1986. The faculty members advising his doctorate were Tim Bresnahan, John Roberts and Jeremy Bulow. Bulow not only advised on the thesis research but also started joint work with Klemperer that resulted in his first two economics papers (see Bulow et al. 1985a, b).

At the end of 1984, Klemperer moved back to England to take up a post as Lecturer in Operations Research and Mathematics at Oxford, based at St Catherine's as college Tutor in Economics. He was to remain in Oxford for the rest of his career to date. He became a Reader in 1990 and moved to Nuffield College in 1995 becoming the Edgeworth Professor of Economics following the retirement of the first Edgeworth Professor Sir James Mirrlees. He inherited not only the post but also the room and some of the furniture from Mirrlees. Klemperer remains in this post at the time of writing.

Klemperer's research can broadly be divided into two main parts. The first is oligopoly theory, interpreted in a wide sense, with 20 or so publications covering the decade at St Catherine's. His best-known research in oligopoly theory is on switching costs. The second part is auction theory, which started with the renewal of his partnership with Jeremy Bulow (see Bulow and Klemperer 1996) and continues to the present.

Klemperer's work in auction theory led to his involvement in public policy. This included designing the auction for the sale of the British 3G Telecom Licences in 2000 and later the design of artificial markets for the Bank of England (and other central banks) to make loans to commercial banks for assets of differing quality (including toxic assets) in the aftermath of the financial crisis.

In this chapter, I will first deal with the two stages of Klemperer's research and then go on to look at his involvement advising public bodies about designing auctions.

2   Oligopoly

The research career of Paul Klemperer started with two articles with his Stanford supervisor Jeremy Bulow and Yale economist John Geanakoplos (see Bulow et al. 1985a, b). The most revolutionary paper was the first: "Multimarket Oligopoly: Strategic Substitutes and Complements". The idea of a strategic complement (substitute) is defined by the cross-partial derivative of the payoff function. In a symmetric payoff game, the payoff U of each player depends on their own action (x) and that of the other player (y): $U(x, y)$. The strategies of the two players are strategic complements (substitutes) depending on whether the cross-partial derivative is strictly positive (negative):

$$\frac{d^2U}{dxdy} > 0 \quad \text{Strategic complements}$$

$$\frac{d^2U}{dxdy} < 0 \quad \text{Strategic substitutes}$$

Why is the cross-partial derivative so important? Because the reaction function is defined by the (necessary) standard first-order condition that the derivative of the chosen action is zero. In the case of strategic complements, the reaction function will be upward sloping (as in the usual case of price competition with differentiated products): in the case of strategic substitutes the reaction function will be downward sloping (as is typically the case in homogeneous Cournot oligopoly). However, price competition can sometimes lead to strategic substitutes and quantity competition to strategic complements.

This very simple classification turned out to have a fundamental importance in terms of how oligopoly models behave—the paper applied the idea to a variety of settings. Its key insight led to the development of a whole literature on supermodular games, which generalised the notion of strategic complementarity for payoff functions that were not twice continuously differentiable.

The other paper "Holding Idle Capacity to Deter Entry" applied the classification of strategic complements and substitutes to Avinash Dixit's model of entry deterrence (see Dixit 1980). Dixit's model had assumed an incumbent firm would always reduce output if a new firm was to enter, but Bulow et al. (1985b) showed that this depended on the post-entry oligopoly game being one of strategic substitutes: if the goods were strategic complements, then the incumbent might install capacity, in order to expand output if entry occurs, but leave it idle if no entry occurs. The idea of strategic complementarity went on to have a life of its own and became a term used widely across economics, including macroeconomics.

Klemperer teamed up with his future wife Margaret Meyer[2] (see Klemperer and Meyer 1986) to write a paper on the foundations of price versus quantity competition. Suppose that firms can choose whether to set price (and supply the quantity demanded) or choose quantity (and let the price be determined by the market). Furthermore, suppose there is a demand system linking the prices and outputs demanded of the firms. In the absence of uncertainty, firms are indifferent between setting a price or quantity. They face a demand curve and simply choose the profit maximising point on that curve (where marginal revenue equals marginal cost). The action of firm A does influence the demand curve for firm B, and hence firm B's best response. However, the best response can be attained by choosing either price or quantity. There are thus four types of (pure strategy Nash) equilibria with no uncertainty: the two firms both choose price, both choose quantity or one choses price and the other quantity. Bertrand and Cournot are both equilibria, as is the mixed price and quantity setting case. With demand uncertainty, matters are rather different. Firms will in general have a strict preference for setting price or quantity. The preference will depend on a variety of factors: the shape of the demand curve, the marginal cost curve and the size of shocks. For example, a steep marginal cost curve makes quantity choice more attractive, and a flatter marginal cost curve favours price. If the model is symmetric, then the factors will influence both firms in the same way and tend to make the mixed equilibria less likely. The

---

[2] They were to marry in 1989 and have three children.

nature of technology, demand and uncertainty will lead to either price- or quantity-setting equilibrium being chosen.

In two further papers, Klemperer and Meyer looked at equilibria in reaction functions (Klemperer and Meyer 1988) and supply functions (Klemperer and Meyer 1989). The 1988 paper, "Consistent Conjectures Equilibria: A Reformulation Showing Non-Uniqueness", contributed to the literature on consistent conjectures which had been a topic rekindled by Timothy Bresnahan's 1981 paper. Bresnahan was an Assistant Professor at Stanford in the period of Klemperer's PhD. The conjectural variation (CV) acts to alter the first-order conditions for the optimal response and hence acts as a shift variable for the firm's reaction function. By varying its CV, in effect a firm can move its reaction function. Firm A treats the reaction function of its competitor B as given: there will be a (unique) point on the other firm's reaction function that yields the highest profit for firm A. This point will be where there is a tangency between the iso-profit curve of firm A and firm B's reaction function. It can then choose its reaction function (via its CV) so that its own reaction function passes through this optimal point. Firm B can reason in the same way. What Klemperer and Meyer showed was that: (a) the equilibrium in reaction functions involves (Bresnahan) consistent conjectures (the conjectural variation equals the slope of the other firm's reaction function); and (b) the equilibrium is highly non-unique in that almost any output pair corresponds to an equilibrium. The result rested on a geometrical intuition. If you pick any output pair, iso-profit curves of both firms pass through that point. The reaction functions that support this are the tangents to the iso-profit curves at that point. Neither firm can increase its profits by changing its reaction function given the other's choice.

In the 1989 paper, "Supply Function Equilibria in Oligopoly Under Uncertainty", Klemperer and Meyer revisited the issue of the strategic choice of whether to set a price or quantity. This time, however, they argued that since neither a fixed price nor a fixed quantity allows a firm to adapt optimally to demand shocks, it is natural for firms to use more general supply functions as strategic variables; they therefore looked at equilibrium in supply functions. Uncertainty then acted to restrict the choice of supply functions to choices that ensured ex-post optimality in the face of the supply functions of competitors and uncertain demands. Klemperer and Meyer's supply function analysis has frequently been used since, in both theoretical and applied work. In particular, it has been used to study electricity markets in which producers offer supply functions specifying the quantities of energy they are willing to supply at different prices. More generally, the equilibrium supply functions of firms which supply a market are precisely (a constant minus) the equilibrium bidding schedules of bidders in a uniform-price multi-unit auction, so the 1989 paper also contributed to the development of multi-unit auction theory.

2.1   Switching Costs

The title of Klemperer's 1986 PhD at Stanford was "Markets with Consumer Switching Costs", which gave rise to a series of publications on switching costs in different contexts (these and other papers he reviewed in Klemperer 1995a). The idea that the presence of lump sum costs (pecuniary or psychic) paid by consumers when changing seller might make markets less competitive was not new. However, a rigorous dynamic modelling of the switching costs was new.

Ex ante homogeneous products may, after the purchase of one of them, be ex post differentiated by switching costs including learning costs, transaction costs or artificial costs imposed by firms, such as repeat-purchase discounts. The non-cooperative equilibrium in an oligopoly with switching costs may be the same as the collusive outcome in an otherwise identical market without switching costs. However, the prospect of future collusive profits leads to vigorous competition for market share in the early stages of a market's development. The model thus explains the emphasis placed on market share as a goal of corporate strategy (Klemperer 1987a: 375).

In his paper "The Competitiveness of Markets with Switching Costs" (Klemperer 1987b), Klemperer modelled a two-period model with two firms. Switching costs can arise in the second period if consumers decide to switch from one seller to the other. Customers are modelled in a locational setting with the sellers at either end of the street. Customer demand in the first period is given by prices and linear transport costs. In the second period, there is an additional switching cost. The prices in the first period are influenced not only by maximising profit in that period but also by building up a customer base for the second period. It is in the second period that the firms can exploit the monopoly power created by the switching costs. The model allows for rational expectations on the part of consumers who can predict the second period pricing decisions by firms. Even though there are no switching costs in the first period, demand is less elastic in that period than if there were no switching costs in the second period. Consumers realise that the seller with the larger consumer base in period 1 will extort higher prices in period 2 and so are less attracted to the low-priced seller than they would be without switching costs. So, although prices will be lower in period 1 than in period 2, they may be higher in both periods because of the switching costs.

"Entry Deterrence in Markets with Customer Switching Costs" (Klemperer 1987c) also looked at a two-stage game, but where the only mover in the first period was an incumbent, who could influence the second stage entry game. The key here was the ability of the incumbent to build up a captive customer base (captive due to switching costs); modelling was of Cournot oligopoly with firms choosing quantities. Switching costs were captured by making second period purchases depend on the first period (positively). In the first period, the incumbent may over-invest in output to lock in customers and so deter any entry (or reduce the entrant's output) in the second period. However, for some parameter values, the incumbent prefers to deter entry by under-investing in output, thus committing to competing aggressively for new customers with any entrant in the second period (Klemperer named this phenomenon limit over-pricing).

"Welfare Effects of Entry into Markets with Switching Costs" (Klemperer 1988) showed that the presence of switching costs can lead to excessive entry that reduces social welfare. This is even possible if new entrants have lower costs than incumbents. The mechanism is that 'a large amount of social surplus is dissipated by the consumers' cost of switching to the new competitor' (ibid.: 164). This phenomenon can even occur if industry output increases, resulting in lower prices. However, Klemperer cautioned that in spite of his results: 'Probably most entry into markets with switching costs is socially desirable' (ibid.).

In "Price Wars Caused by Switching Costs", Klemperer (1989) extended the switching cost model to four periods. In the first two pre-entry periods, the monopolist sets up shop. In period three, a fringe of competitors enters (treating the incumbent's output as given) and there is the threat of additional fringe entry in period four. The path of prices over time is then traced. In the final period, with the switching costs, prices tend to rise to a higher level. Firms have just one period left to exploit all of their monopoly power. In period three, entry drives a price war. New entrants and the incumbent lower prices to build up or maintain their customer base to exploit in the final period. The effect of entry is to lower prices in period three relative to the pre-entry periods (and the incumbent may also lower prices in period two, immediately prior to the new entry). 'In our model of a market in which consumers have switching costs, the entry of new firms leads to a price war, and we have argued that this conclusion is robust' (ibid.: 415).

In a paper with his then-student, Alan Beggs (Beggs and Klemperer 1992), "Multi-Period Competition with Switching Costs", the switching costs approach was generalised to an infinite-period version of the duopoly model found in Klemperer (1987b). Firms have a discount rate and customers turn over, with some dying to be replaced with new-born customers. The paper established the conditions for existence of a symmetric steady-state equilibrium and showed that equilibrium prices will be higher when there are switching costs than when they are absent. Indeed, the net present values of firms' profits are usually larger—even for a new entrant which has no customer base—when there are switching costs.

In a paper with Kenneth Froot titled "Exchange Rate Pass-Through When Market Share Matters" (Froot and Klemperer 1989) took the basic idea of switching costs that market share in one period can lock in demand to subsequent periods, and applied it to the classic issue of exchange rate pass-through. They found that:

> Foreign firms may either raise or lower their dollar export prices when the dollar appreciates temporarily (i.e., the pass-through may be perverse) and import prices may be more sensitive to expected future than to current exchange rates. We explore whether expected future exchange rates provide a clue to the puzzling recent behavior of US import prices (ibid.: 637).

Indeed, the paper had an empirical dimension that was not usual in the other papers on switching costs, in that it looked at data on import and export prices between the major economies in the 1980s.

In his 1992 paper "Equilibrium Product Lines: Competing Head-to-Head May Be Less Competitive", Klemperer took a model where consumers face shopping costs, which mean that consumers prefer to shop at fewer outlets. In this case, Klemperer showed that in equilibrium, firms may prefer to offer identical product ranges so that customers will only choose one shop to visit. This head-to-head competition can lead to higher prices. If they are only shopping at one outlet, it requires a bigger price incentive for a consumer to switch outlets or shop at both outlets. If firms offer distinct product ranges, consumers shop at both outlets and can respond to quite small price differentials. This line of thought went against some then-established economic models where firms maximise product differentiation in order to increase monopolistic markups. However, Klemperer argued that his model fitted with the marketing literature which identified umbrella branding (selling goods in related markets under the same brand name) and brand extension (selling new brands under an established brand name).

The issue of product lines, variety and welfare was explored in a paper with another of his students at the time, Jorge Padilla (see Klemperer and Padilla 1997), titled "Do Firms' Product Lines Include Too Many Varieties?" A firm that offers an additional product can capture business from rival firms for other products when consumers prefer to concentrate their purchases at a single supplier. This may lead firms to offer excessive product variety from the social standpoint. A firm may even completely foreclose competing firms from the market by introducing a new product. Restricting the ability of firms to offer new products could increase welfare. Klemperer and Padilla even applied the model to the then live policy debate about Sunday trading, arguing that 'if—as many shopkeepers argue—customer loyalty to shops is important, then [under certain conditions] shops will open for a socially excessive number of hours' (ibid.: 483).

Gilbert and Klemperer (2000) developed an equilibrium theory of rationing. In a simple model of pricing, a monopolist would never want to set a price in which all consumer demand was not met (a price with rationing). The argument is simple: the monopolist can make more money by raising the price and selling the same output. However, Gilbert and Klemperer considered a two-stage set-up where consumers have to make an upfront investment to enter the market. In this case, the monopolist might want to *precommit* to keep the price low in order to encourage more consumers to enter. Although ex post the rationing is inefficient, it can yield higher profits if the firm is able to commit to it. This paper was later developed in the context of auction theory in Bulow and Klemperer (2002).

Klemperer's interest in oligopoly theory was not just theoretical. He wanted to apply his theoretical ideas to policy and his opinion was sought after. He was an adviser to the US Federal Trade Commission 1999–2001 (adviser on merger and competition cases and policy) and also a member of the UK Competition Commission 2001–2005 (and later adviser 2006–2014). He also undertook an applied analysis of the major economic issues raised by the 1997 Tobacco Resolution and the ensuing proposed legislation that were intended to settle tobacco litigation in the United States (see Bulow and Klemperer 1998). In addition, Klemperer wrote about the appropriate breadth of patent or copyright protection (see Klemperer 1990), stimulated by a debate about whether Japan's very narrowly defined patents took unfair advantage of American technology, and he has contributed to subsequent public policy debate in this area (see Klemperer 2004a).[3]

---

[3] Klemperer also contributed to the UK government's 2006 *Gowers Review of Intellectual Property*.

3   Auctions in Theory

'Auction Theory is one of economics' success stories. It is of both practical and theoretical importance: practical because many of the world's most important markets are auction markets…; theoretical because lessons from auction theory have led to important insights elsewhere in economics' (Klemperer 2004b: 1).

A new line of study started with Klemperer in the mid-1990s, coinciding with a renewal of an old partnership with Jeremy Bulow. However, it is important to note that Klemperer had already used an auction framework both in his 1987 paper with Peter Cramton and Robert Gibbons (see Cramton et al. 1987) and in Klemperer and Meyer (1989), discussed above. Significantly, for future research, the Cramton et al. paper was inspired by the Federal Communications Commission's allocation of licences for cellular telephone franchises and also the Federal Aviation Administration's allocation of landing slots. Cramton et al. showed that achieving the optimal allocation involved payments depending on all bids and not just the winning bidder paying—this is very different to standard auction mechanisms such as first- or second-price auctions. However, they also showed that standard mechanisms can achieve the efficient outcome if the initial partner shares are close enough to equal.

The title of Bulow and Klemperer (1994), "Rational Frenzies and Crashes", does not mention auctions, but is about a Dutch auction where a seller has multiple units to sell and starts from a high price. Buyers have a valuation for buying one unit coming from a common distribution, which is known. The key point is that buyers can choose to bid or delay. If at least one buyer offers to buy at the current price, the other buyers are also asked if they wish to buy at the current price. This simple auction is solved using revenue equivalence. What Bulow and Klemperer showed is that once one person has bid and been allocated a unit, others may wish to also buy since removing the unit purchased will raise the price buyers can expect to pay. This case of multiple purchases at a single price is a frenzy. However, if unexpectedly few bidders then participate in the frenzy, the information that that reveals about demand means the price has to fall a long way to tempt another bidder to make an offer—a crash. Although derived for a specific model, Bulow and Klemperer believe the lessons will apply to a wide range of models.

In their 1996 paper "Auctions Versus Negotiations", Bulow and Klemperer pose the question: when selling a firm, should you employ 'an auction with no reserve price or an optimally-structured negotiation with one less bidder? We show under reasonable assumptions that the auction is always preferable' (ibid.: 180). However, the paper is as important for the way it models the auction process in terms of a monopoly, and looks at *marginal revenues* instead of prices. The price is the value of the bidder; the quantity is defined by the cumulative density of the bidder's value. Marginal revenue (MR) is then the derivative of price times quantity, with the optimal price for the monopolist occurring when MR is zero (assuming the seller has no cost). The analogy works because,

> just as the expected revenue from a take-it-or-leave-it price can be calculated by multiplying that price by the probability of sale at that price, expected revenue can also be found by taking the area under the MR curve for all the values in excess of the take-it-or-leave-it price. The seller may be thought of as receiving, in expectation, the MR of the buyer when it is positive, and zero when the buyer's MR is negative (ibid.: 183–184).

This approach was originally developed by Bulow and Roberts (1989) for bidders with independent private values, but the Bulow and Klemperer paper shows how to extend the approach to all auctions in which bidders' signals are independent, whether values are private or common or something in between, and then—a key insight—to all ascending auctions, whether or not bidders have independent signals. So, the expected revenue from any ascending auction is given by the marginal revenue of the bidder with the highest signal.

The Bulow and Klemperer paper also shows the usefulness of this approach. Using marginal revenue analysis, it is simple to show what was not otherwise obvious: that so long as all bidders are serious (in the sense that their valuations exceed the seller's actual value), then adding an extra (serious) bidder to an ascending auction with no reserve price will, under mild conditions, always increase expected revenue more than adding the use of a reserve price.[4]

Klemperer went on to promote his view that 'connections between auction theory and standard economic theory run deeper than many people realise' (Klemperer 2000: 2) and applied the auction-theoretic perspective to a wide variety of applications, in his aptly titled Econometric Society World Congress lecture, "Why Every Economist Should Learn Some Auction Theory". Put simply, Klemperer believes that many markets can be understood as equivalent to particular type of auction markets. Alternatively, auctions are a way of

---

[4] Bulow and Klemperer also use a similar marginal revenue approach to examine the effect of price controls on rent-seeking and consumer welfare (see Bulow and Klemperer 2012). They further highlighted the importance of attracting new entrants in their paper "Why Do Sellers (Usually) Prefer Auctions?" (Bulow and Klemperer 2009).

setting up a market. A well-designed auction can yield a desirable outcome where for some reason no market exists.

In Klemperer (1998), "Auctions with Almost Common Values: The 'Wallet Game' and Its Applications", he considered the following classroom experiment: two students are picked, each checks how much is in his or her wallet; the combined contents of the wallets are then auctioned to the two students using an English auction. The problem for each student is that they only know the value of their own wallet, not the value of the other student's wallet. There are many equilibria to this, but only one symmetric equilibrium (both bidders offer up to twice what was in their own wallet). Klemperer went on to consider situations where bidders have almost common values: that is one bidder has a slightly higher value. He found that small differences in valuations would lead to far from symmetric outcomes. In terms of the Wallet Game, suppose player 1 has a small advantage (he gets a bonus of £1 if he wins). Even this tiny advantage can mean that player 1 always wins the Wallet Game, which is very unlike the symmetric equilibrium. In practice, many economic situations might involve situations where there is a small advantage. In a takeover, one firm might have a toe hold, leading it to bid more aggressively and lead to other bidders being discouraged due to an increased winner's curse (see Bulow et al. 1999). Alternatively, in a takeover contest, one of the firms might have more synergies to exploit than others. Klemperer argued that this applied to the 1995 takeover of Wellcome by Glaxo: Glaxo had more to gain than other potential bidders such as Zeneca and Roche. Glaxo made a first bid and the others dropped out. Possible ways around these problems included sealed-bid auctions or multi-stage auctions such as his Anglo-Dutch auction proposal (see Klemperer 1995b).

In "The Generalized War of Attrition", Bulow and Klemperer (1999) used the Revenue Equivalence Theorem from auction theory to solve the case where N+K firms were competing for N prizes. Such wars of attrition occur when a number of firms are competing for a fixed number of slots (for example, firms competing to supply wireless telephony in major US cities) or where there is a battle to control a new technology and set the standards. Previous analysis had focused on the two-firm case. Bulow and Klemperer instead looked at the more general natural oligopoly case: 'The natural oligopoly case yields a striking result: there is "instant sorting", so K-1 firms will exit immediately, leaving only N+1, or one too many firms to battle for the N prizes' (ibid.: 177). This instant sorting result is a general feature of these games.

Bulow and Klemperer (2002), "Prices and the Winner's Curse", developed themes from Klemperer (1998). In particular, they showed how in ascending-price auctions increasing supply might in fact lead to higher prices because it encourages weaker bidders to participate, since the greater supply alleviates the winner's curse they face. More active bidders can result in a higher price. Furthermore, when there are even small deviations from common value, the auction can behave very differently from the common value auction. This insight was to have important implications when it came to designing auctions in practice because in real life, pure common values are almost never found. It is a case of economic theorists spending time looking at the case that is easy to solve. If auction theorists want to produce relevant models, they need to stop looking at the simple models and look at something more realistic. Even small deviations from the simple case can lead to very different outcomes.

4   Auctions in Practice

In an interview, Klemperer explains his fascination with auctions: 'I thought that if we couldn't understand auctions, then we probably couldn't understand how the whole economy works. But by learning about auctions, we could learn about more complex environments, and auction models could be the building blocks for modelling more complex economic systems' (Klemperer in Petropoulos 2015). Klemperer (2002a, 2003) discussed the pitfalls of moving from theory to practice. In his opinion, 'most of the extensive auction literature…is of second order importance for *practical* auction design. The literature largely focuses on a fixed number of bidders who bid non-cooperatively' (Klemperer 2002a: 170; italics in original). In contrast, 'what matters in auction design are the same issues that any industry regulator would recognise as key concerns: discouraging collusive, entry-deterring and predatory behaviour. In short, good auction design is mostly good elementary economics' (ibid.: 169–170). There was thus a link between the development of real-life auctions and the extensive research Klemperer had made in industrial organisation (IO) issues reviewed in Section 2 and his work with real-world regulation and competition policy in the United States and the United Kingdom.

Klemperer has been involved in advising governments on many issues, but by far the highest profile policy engagements were applying auction theory to real auctions. Specifically, he has been closely involved in two very high-profile auctions.

4.1   The Biggest Auction Ever

The first auction was "The Biggest Auction Ever: The Sale of the British 3G Telecom Licences" (Binmore and Klemperer 2002). The biggest ever auction was held in the United Kingdom over the months of March and April 2000 and involved the sale of the third generation (3G) mobile spectrum licences. Klemperer was part of a team with other members, including Ken Binmore, Tilman Börgers, Jeremy Bulow, Philippe Jehiel and Joe Swierzbinski (this was the result of a successful bid for the assignment by the ESRC Centre for Learning and Social Evolution based at UCL; Klemperer's role was as the auction specialist). The team had started to advise the British government on the design of the auction three years earlier in 1997. The starting point was the view that 'a well-designed auction is the method most likely to allocate resources to those who can use them most valuably' (ibid.: C75). The only practical alternative was a beauty contest: government officials or experts choosing the most attractive bid, a process notoriously open to issues of political and legal influences. Auctions could also raise a lot of money for the public purse.

The aims of the UK auction were to assign the spectrum efficiently, to promote competition and to realise the full economic value. The auction was designed to meet these objectives taking into account the specific features of the British telecoms market. Early on in the process, the team recognised that it was very important to encourage entry and not to restrict competition to the existing 2G suppliers. Whilst the possibility of a royalties-based payment scheme was considered, this was ruled out as inferior to the one-off sunk cost payment which would involve less distortion in the operations of 3G after the auction.

The government initially proposed that the auction should be for a fixed number of four licences with no bidder getting more than one licence. Since the then current number of 2G incumbents was also four, there was a real concern that no potential entrant would be willing to bid against the (likely much-stronger) incumbents in an ascending auction—precisely the concern that Klemperer had raised in his 1998 Wallet Game paper discussed above—and that a pure sealed-bid auction would risk substantial inefficiency. So, the team went for a version of Klemperer's (1995b, 1998) Anglo-Dutch auction: the four licences would be auctioned with an English ascending price auction until there were five bidders left. Then the five bidders would make a sealed bid for the licences and the four highest would get the licences and pay the fourth highest bid. In the end, however, the government decided to issue five licences. As such, since one licence was the most any one firm could be allocated, at least one new entrant would be guaranteed to win, and a simultaneous ascending auction was used.

The auction was a great success from the perspective of the government raising revenue. There were 13 bidders at the start of the process. In the end, the new entrant (Hutchison Whampoa, under the brand 3 Mobile) won the largest licence A, the four incumbents the other licences with total revenue of $34bn, which was used by Chancellor Gordon Brown to pay down the public debt. Binmore and Klemperer found that 'Auction design is a matter of "horses for courses", not one size fits all; each economic environment requires an auction design that is tailored to its special circumstances' (Binmore and Klemperer 2002: C94).

There were, however, many critics in the popular press who argued that the weakness of the auction was the (standard economists') belief that, since the auction payments were sunk costs, the prices consumers would pay in the United Kingdom would be unaffected. Soon after the auction, *The Guardian* newspaper ran an article titled "Consumers Pay the Price in 3G Auction", claiming, 'Those countries which opted for the beauty contest route—namely France, Portugal, Spain, Norway and Finland—face no such embarrassing post mortems and are likely to enjoy far more sophisticated 3G services as a result' (Osborn 2000: 33).[5] These fears do not seem to have been borne out in practice.[6] There was also a telecoms crash in 2001 in which the market value of shares in telecommunications companies across the developed world fell significantly and many jobs were lost in the UK and elsewhere. But Klemperer argued that the auction itself was not at fault: he pointed out that some of the firms that fared worst in the telecoms crash were ones who had bid unsuccessfully in the United Kingdom (citing NTL); that the fees paid in all the European 3G auctions amounted to only one-fortieth of the losses in the crash they allegedly caused; that the US telecoms sector lost more than four times as much money in the crash as its European counterpart (although there were no 3G auctions in the United States); and that the mobile industry lost a greater percentage of value in the crash than fixed-line operators (which suffered no auctions) (see Klemperer 2002b: 21).

Klemperer (2002a, c, 2003) explained why he thought the British auction was much more successful in meeting its objectives than most of the other 3G auctions held in Europe (there were almost simultaneous auctions held in

---

[5] For Klemperer's view on the state of auction theory at the turn of the century, see Klemperer (1999).

[6] For example, Park et al. (2011: 118) argue that the 'results show no evidence to support claims of negative effects of spectrum auctions [on consumers] in the mobile communications market'.

Austria, Germany, Holland, Italy and Switzerland): '[M]any auctions—including some designed with help of leading academic economists—have worked badly' (Klemperer 2002a: 169). His judgement about the other European spectrum licence auctions was that, 'These other auctions were fiascos primarily because they were poorly designed' (ibid.). Auctions are often wide open to collusion. For example, in a German ascending auction in 1999 two bids were made by two large German telecoms companies which meant they had half each. The companies then stopped bidding, which in Klemperer's analysis was collusive 'live and let live' (ibid.: 171) behaviour. The other key issue in practice is to allow entry to occur in the auction process rather than restricting auctions to incumbents. 'In an ascending auction, there is a strong presumption that the firm that values winning the most will be the eventual winner, because even if it is outbid at an early stage, it can eventually top any opposition' (ibid.: 172). So, Klemperer believes that in many contexts an ascending auction favours stronger firms and incumbents against weaker firms and potential entrants. A good auction design needs to address these issues.

4.2   The Financial Crisis and the Product-Mix Auction

In the financial crisis, a new problem faced central banks. Central banks have a role as lender of last resort and from time to time need to provide liquidity to commercial banks and so on. As Bagehot had described it, the central bank made loans to solvent banks in return for collateral assets. In the past, since solvency implied that the value of assets was at least as great as liabilities, this was a straightforward procedure. However, the 2007 banking crisis[7] was different to what had happened in the previous half century: it was a systemic crisis that affected many banks and was in part triggered by the general uncertainty of some asset values and in particular some assets were held to be toxic (possibly worth very little). Banks had stopped lending to each other because of the uncertainty about the value of each other's balance sheets and required the Bank of England to step in and provide liquidity. The new problem faced by the Bank was how to allocate and price the liquidity provided given that some of the collateral on offer would be less than perfect. As Klemperer described it, after the 2007 Northern Rock bank run: 'The Bank of England wanted urgently to supply liquidity to banks and was therefore willing to accept a wider-than-usual range of collateral, but it wanted a correspondingly

---

[7] The crisis is often thought of as beginning with the collapse of Lehman Brothers in September 2008, but the September 2007 Northern Rock bank run—Britain's first bank run since the 1800s—was one of the early signs of trouble.

higher interest rate against any weaker collateral it took' (Klemperer 2010a: 526).

Paul Klemperer had a solution to the problem. It originated from his belief that auctions could act like markets, and that if you knew what the efficient or desired market outcome looked like, then an auction could be devised to yield the desired market outcome. In this case, the market Klemperer had in mind was one of competitive markets simultaneously clearing for different qualities of asset. He dubbed the auction the *Product-Mix auction*, the theory of which was written up in a 2008 Nuffield College Working Paper (see Klemperer 2008) and was eventually published in a slightly revised form as "The Product-Mix Auction: A New Auction Design for Differentiated Goods" (Klemperer 2010a). Banks needed an auction design that was quick to execute and not like the long drawn out 3G licence auction of 2000.

Let us assume that the collateral has two standards according to credit rating criteria: strong and weak. Bidders make sets of bids, with each bid specifying a quantity of money to be borrowed from the central bank and two prices, one price (the interest rate the bidder will pay) for each type of collateral the bidder might use. (If the bidder has only one type of collateral available it bids zero on the other type.) These bids make a demand curve for the liquidity supplied by the central bank. There are several banks bidding for liquidity from the central bank, which provides an element of competition. If there were only one bank, it could offer the lowest possible interest rate on just the weakest (worst) collateral. With more than one bank, this unattractive bid will be outbid, even if the other banks are bidding for the other collateral, because the auction decides the prices and quantities, given the bids, in both the strong and weak collateral markets at the same time.

The exact way the central bank decides to do this will depend on its objectives. It may have a fixed supply, or be willing to vary the quantity supplied with the interest rate. Either way, the auction can determine prices for each collateral, and how the supply is allocated across the two markets. The central bank can express its preferences in terms of its supply function: if it is unwilling to accept much weak collateral it can require a premium over the strong collateral that is increasing in the amount of weak collateral accepted.

In the auction, there is only one price for each type of collateral (uniform pricing), as in a competitive market. The central bank chooses a minimum cut off price for each collateral and accepts at most one offer from each bid, with all offers at or above the cut-off paying the cut-off price. Again, this mimics the competitive market where all demand for any good is met at the same price and all those with positive demands above this price get what they ask for (as in a standard competitive market, this is the source of consumer, i.e.

bidder, surplus). If the prices offered for the two collaterals in a bid are both above the cut-off price, the collateral that maximises the bidder's surplus is chosen. Each bidder can make multiple bids.

The product-mix auction proved to be a hit with the Bank or England: Governor Mervyn King said that the auction was 'a marvellous application of theoretical economics to a practical problem of vital importance to financial markets' (King quoted in R.D. 2012). In order to understand the importance of Klemperer's product mix auction one has to consider what the central bank would have done without it. The US Treasury had previously simply fixed either the price (interest rate) or quantity of different types of asset. In this case, it is easy to make a poor choice of price or quantity, since the auctioneer cannot condition on the information that is generated by the bids in Klemperer's design. Klemperer argues that it is best to have a single auction for all products (types of collateral) as it enables the central bank to use all the information to decide how much of each product to allocate. It also means bidders automatically use the collateral that is best for them given the auction prices, whereas they would have to guess which auction was best for them to bid in if the products were sold in separate auctions. The product-mix auction also reduces the market power of bidders as there is competition between buyers across the different products.

The Bank of England went on to develop the product-mix approach: in 2014, it no longer predetermined the total quantity and introduced more than two types of asset. Iceland also planned, and programmed, a version of the auction in 2015, although the plan to use it was dropped in the 2016 political crisis (see Klemperer 2018). Part of the reason for the success of the product-mix auction was that it can be explained in terms of a simple supply and demand figure (for the two asset-type case at least), which was easily understood by policy makers in the central banks. This was made possible by Klemperer having developed the idea that auctions are a form of market which itself is often easier to understand than what can often be complicated auction theory. This talent for making complex ideas and models simple harks back to his experience in designing allocation mechanisms for the NHS in the late 1970s. Complex models are unlikely to be accepted by policy makers unless they can be explained simply. This is a talent few academic economists possess.

In addition, Klemperer developed simple software which could be used to implement his ideas: *Product-Mix Auction Software*, which is free to use.[8] It includes options for maximising efficiency (the aggregate of the auctioneer's and bidders' profits) or maximising the auctioneer's profits. Also, the software

---

[8] The software can be downloaded at: http://pma.nuff.ox.ac.uk/.

includes the possibility of discriminatory (pay-as-bid) pricing replacing uniform pricing. In the *Version for Budget-Constrained Bidders*, Klemperer shares the design he developed for the Icelandic government. This version can be applied to situations where a country's creditors exchange their claims (nominal amounts of debt) for a choice among new debt instruments, or an acquired firm's shareholders exchange their holdings (numbers of shares) for a choice of cash or new shares. The software is developed with another of his students, Elizabeth Baldwin.[9]

Klemperer has also worked on auctions in other aspects of public policy. In 2002, he advised the UK government on the world's first auction for greenhouse gas emissions reductions, working with Nobel prize-winner Eric Maskin. He also participated in the meeting that drafted the Potsdam Memorandum to the 2007 UN Climate Change Conference in Bali (see Klemperer 2007, 2010b). Klemperer has also been on the Environmental Economics Academic Panel to the UK's Department of the Environment (Defra).

5   Conclusion

Paul Klemperer continues to innovate with ideas relating to new hybrid capital for banks in order to increase financial stability (see Bulow and Klemperer 2015); a new approach to modelling preferences and equilibrium based on geometry (see Baldwin and Klemperer 2019); the effect of price controls on rent-seeking and consumer welfare (see Bulow and Klemperer 2012); and continues to seek improvements in auctions (see Erdil and Klemperer 2010). However, it is possible to look back over his career from the perspective of 2019. One often finds when one looks at successful people and their lives that things just seem to effortlessly come together, with different parts reinforcing each other. This may be something of an ex-post rationalisation of what are unconnected random events. However, the temptation is very strong when one considers how the elements of Klemperer's research and auction design fit together almost perfectly.

His early experience in the world of consultancy and working for firms like IBM, Monsanto and Arthur Andersen gave him experience of real-world problems and the need to explain and apply complex ideas in a simple way. Whilst he started as a mathematician at Cambridge, he switched to

---

[9] In addition to being the main (usually, only) supervisor of around 15 doctoral students who have gone on to Professorships, Klemperer supervised the Master's theses that were the first research of many other students who went on to distinguished careers, such as Jon Levin, Eric Budish, and Shengwu Li (Professors at Stanford, Chicago, and Harvard, respectively, at the time of writing).

engineering because he wanted to apply mathematical ideas. However, driven by intellectual curiosity, he ended up at Stanford from 1980 to 1984, moving from MBA to PhD. Stanford was buzzing with ideas at that time and inspired much of Klemperer's research for the following decade and beyond; from strategic complements and substitutes to work on consistent conjectures and switching costs, Klemperer developed new ideas and approaches to problems both with co-authors and as sole author. If one met Paul during this period, as I did, one would have described him as an IO economist with a theoretical bent. He developed the understanding of market power over time, oligopolistic interaction and entry. His papers almost always have simple mathematical examples, diagrams which explain in a clear way what are often very abstract models and reasoning.

The next stage of his career was dominated by auction theory. There were of course many very smart theorists researching in this field. Klemperer soon developed his own way of understanding auctions as markets. In his view, most auction theorists looked at the details of special cases that assumed away the issues found in real-life auctions. Whilst there are techniques and insights that are central to auction theory, such as revenue equivalence, you need to go further to understand real auctions, considering the factors found in real markets such as collusion, entry and asymmetric equilibria. This is what Klemperer proceeded to do. He was involved in two large and important auctions: as a team member in the 2000 3G spectrum auction in the United Kingdom and later as the sole designer of the product-mix auction for the Bank of England in the wake of the financial crisis. This built upon his previous work in industrial economics and oligopoly theory. The importance of being able to explain solutions in a simple way was an essential part of his success in persuading central bankers and policy makers to adopt his advice. Part of his ability to do this was his geometric intuition which enabled him to depict simple cases in diagrams.

Indeed, Klemperer has become something of an apostle of auction theory. In his opinion, all economists should know some auction theory. Since one can think of an auction as a market, understanding auctions can help us understand markets and vice versa. Auctions can be set up to obtain efficient or desirable outcomes where markets fail or are absent. However, the design of auctions needs a sound grasp of how markets work. Klemperer has proven himself not only an apostle of the theory but also a wizard of auction design.

References

Main Works by Paul Klemperer

Baldwin, E. and P. Klemperer (2019). 'Understanding Preferences: "Demand Types", and the Existence of Equilibrium with Indivisibilities'. *Econometrica*, 87(3): 867–932.

Beggs, A. and P. Klemperer (1992). 'Multi-Period Competition with Switching Costs'. *Econometrica*, 60(3): 651–666.

Binmore, K. and P. Klemperer (2002). 'The Biggest Auction Ever: The Sale of the British 3G Telecom Licences'. *Economic Journal*, 112(478): C74–C96.

Bulow, J., J. Geanakoplos and P. Klemperer (1985a). 'Multimarket Oligopoly: Strategic Substitutes and Complements'. *Journal of Political Economy*, 93(3): 488–511.

Bulow, J., J. Geanakoplos and P. Klemperer (1985b). 'Holding Idle Capacity to Deter Entry'. *Economic Journal*, 95(377): 178–182.

Bulow, J., M. Huang and P. Klemperer (1999). 'Toeholds and Takeovers'. *Journal of Political Economy*, 107(3): 427–454.

Bulow, J. and P. Klemperer (1994). 'Rational Frenzies and Crashes'. *Journal of Political Economy*, 102(1): 1–23.

Bulow, J. and P. Klemperer (1996). 'Auctions Versus Negotiations'. *American Economic Review*, 86(1): 180–194.

Bulow, J. and P. Klemperer (1998). 'The Tobacco Deal'. *Brookings Papers on Economic Activity*, 29(Microeconomics): 323–394.

Bulow, J. and P. Klemperer (1999). 'The Generalized War of Attrition'. *American Economic Review*, 89(1): 175–189.

Bulow, J. and P. Klemperer (2002). 'Prices and the Winner's Curse'. *RAND Journal of Economics*, 33(1): 1–21.

Bulow, J. and P. Klemperer (2009). 'Why Do Sellers (Usually) Prefer Auctions?'. *American Economic Review*, 99(4): 1,544–1,575.

Bulow, J. and P. Klemperer (2012). 'Regulated Prices, Rent Seeking, and Consumer Surplus'. *Journal of Political Economy*, 120(1): 160–186.

Bulow, J. and P. Klemperer (2015). 'Equity Recourse Notes: Creating Counter-Cyclical Bank Capital'. *Economic Journal*, 125(586): F131–F157.

Cramton, P., R. Gibbons and P. Klemperer (1987). 'Dissolving a Partnership Efficiently'. *Econometrica*, 55(3): 615–632.

Erdil, A. and P. Klemperer (2010). 'A New Payment Rule for Core-Selecting Package Auctions'. *Journal of the European Economic Association*, 8(2/3): 537–547.

Froot, K. and P. Klemperer (1989). 'Exchange Rate Pass-Through When Market Share Matters'. *American Economic Review*, 79(4): 637–654.

Gilbert, R. and P. Klemperer (2000). 'An Equilibrium Theory of Rationing'. *RAND Journal of Economics*, 31(1): 1–21.

Klemperer, P. (1987a). 'Markets with Consumer Switching Costs'. *Quarterly Journal of Economics*, 102(2): 375–394.

Klemperer, P. (1987b). 'The Competitiveness of Markets with Switching Costs'. *RAND Journal of Economics*, 18(1): 138–150.

Klemperer, P. (1987c). 'Entry Deterrence in Markets with Consumer Switching Costs'. *Economic Journal*, 97(Supplement): 99–117.

Klemperer, P. (1988). 'Welfare Effects of Entry into Markets with Switching Costs'. *Journal of Industrial Economics*, 37(2): 159–165.

Klemperer, P. (1989). 'Price Wars Caused by Switching Costs'. *Review of Economic Studies*, 56(3): 405–420.

Klemperer, P. (1990). 'How Broad Should the Scope of Patent Protection Be?'. *RAND Journal of Economics*, 21(1): 113–130.

Klemperer, P. (1992). 'Equilibrium Product Lines: Competing Head-to-Head May Be Less Competitive'. *American Economic Review*, 82(4): 740–755.

Klemperer, P. (1995a). 'Competition When Consumers Have Switching Costs: An Overview with Applications to Industrial Organization, Macroeconomics, and International Trade'. *Review of Economic Studies*, 62(4): 515–539.

Klemperer, P. (1995b). 'Comments on "Putting Auction Theory to Work"'. Discussant's comments on Paul Milgrom's 1995 Churchill Lectures, Working Paper, Oxford University.

Klemperer, P. (1998). 'Auctions With Almost Common Values: The "Wallet Game" and Its Applications'. *European Economic Review*, 42(3–5): 757–769.

Klemperer, P. (1999). 'Auction Theory: A Guide to the Literature'. *Journal of Economic Surveys*, 13(3): 227–286.

Klemperer, P. (2000). 'Why Every Economist Should Learn Some Auction Theory'. Econometric Society World Congress lecture, 11 August. Available at: https://pdfs.semanticscholar.org/9fec/3d2db6feb81f8bc246fca7598a0aeadab125.pdf.

Klemperer, P. (2002a). 'What Really Matters in Auction Design'. *Journal of Economic Perspectives*, 16(1): 169–189.

Klemperer, P. (2002b). 'The Wrong Culprit for Telecom Trouble'. *Financial Times*, 26 November: 21.

Klemperer, P. (2002c). 'How (Not) to Run Auctions: The European 3G Telecom Auctions'. *European Economic Review*, 46(4–5): 829–845.

Klemperer, P. (2003). 'Alfred Marshall Lecture: Using and Abusing Economic Theory'. *Journal of the European Economic Association*, 1(2/3): 272–300.

Klemperer, P. (2004a). 'America's Patent Protection Has Gone Too Far'. *Financial Times*, 2 March: 19.

Klemperer, P. (2004b). *Auctions: Theory and Practice*. Princeton: Princeton University Press.

Klemperer, P. (2007). 'What Is the Top Priority on Climate Change?'. 13 December. Available at: https://voxeu.org/article/climate-change-innovation-key.

Klemperer, P. (2008). 'A New Auction for Substitutes: Central-Bank Liquidity Auctions, "Toxic Asset" Auctions, and Variable Product-Mix Auctions'. Working Paper, Nuffield College, University of Oxford.

Klemperer, P. (2010a). 'The Product-Mix Auction: A New Auction Design for Differentiated Goods'. *Journal of the European Economic Association*, 8(2–3): 526–536.

Klemperer, P. (2010b). 'What Is the Top Priority on Climate Change?'. Chapter 19 in H. Schellnhuber et al. (eds) *Global Sustainability: A Nobel Cause*. Cambridge: Cambridge University Press: 233–242.

Klemperer, P. (2018). 'Product-Mix Auctions'. Working Paper, Nuffield College, Univesity of Oxford.

Klemperer, P. and J. McClenahan (1981). 'Joint Strategic Planning Between Health and Local Authorities'. *Omega*, 9(5): 481–491.

Klemperer, P. and M. Meyer (1986). 'Price Competition vs. Quantity Competition: The Role of Uncertainty'. *RAND Journal of Economics*, 17(4): 618–638.

Klemperer, P. and M. Meyer (1988). 'Consistent Conjectures Equilibria: A Reformulation Showing Non-Uniqueness'. *Economics Letters*, 27(2): 111–115.

Klemperer, P. and M. Meyer (1989). 'Supply Function Equilibria in Oligopoly Under Uncertainty'. *Econometrica*, 57(6): 1,243–1,277.

Klemperer, P. and A. Padilla (1997). 'Do Firms' Product Lines Include Too Many Varieties?'. *RAND Journal of Economics*, 28(3): 472–488.

Other Works Referred To

Bresnahan, T. (1981). 'Duopoly Models with Consistent Conjectures'. *American Economic Review*, 71(5): 934–945.

Bulow, J. and J. Roberts (1989). 'The Simple Economics of Optimal Auctions'. *Journal of Political Economy*, 97(5): 1,060–1,090.

Dixit, A. (1980). 'The Role of Investment in Entry-Deterrence'. *Economic Journal*, 90(357): 95–106.

Osborn, A. (2000). 'Consumers Pay the Price in 3G Auction'. *The Guardian*, 17 November: 33.

Park, M., S.-W. Lee and Y.-J. Choi (2011). 'Does Spectrum Auctioning Harm Consumers? Lessons from 3G Licensing'. *Information Economics and Policy*, 23(1): 118–126.

Petropoulos, G. (2015). 'Product-Mix Auction—How Auction Theory Came to the Rescue During the Banking Crisis: Interview with Paul Klemperer'. *The TSEconomist*. September. Available at: https://tseconomist.com/archive/september-2015/production-mix-auction-how-auction-theory-came-to-the-rescue-during-the-banking-crisis-interview-with-paul-klemperer/.

R.D. (2012). 'A Golden Age of Micro'. *The Economist* (online). Available at: https://www.economist.com/free-exchange/2012/10/19/a-golden-age-of-micro.

30

John Vickers (1958–)

Peter Sinclair

1   Introduction

Research, teaching, editing, consulting, industry, finance, public service and university administration are the eight principal activities that economists may undertake in their professional careers. Many do two or three of these. Just a few, at some point or other, might end up having done as many as four or five. But very rarely more. At various stages of his life, John Vickers has done all eight, and with real distinction.

The structure of this chapter is as follows. Sections 2, 3, 5, 6, 7, 8, 9, and 10 explore each of those activities. The sequence starts with industrial experience (Section 2) and turns to consulting (Section 3). Then Section 4 goes back to Vickers' early life and studies up to the end of his undergraduate course at Oxford. Section 5 is substantial; it covers research and research partnerships, as well as academic papers specifically within the general area of industrial organisation. Editing, a briefer section, follows at Section 6, and then finance at Section 7. Public service is discussed in Section 8, teaching in Section 9, and the last of the eight activities, university administration, forms the subject matter of Section 10.

P. Sinclair (1946–2020)

© The Author(s), under exclusive license to Springer Nature Switzerland AG 2021
R. A. Cord (ed.), *The Palgrave Companion to Oxford Economics*,
https://doi.org/10.1007/978-3-030-58471-9_30

2   Industry

Vickers' industrial experience took the form of some 16 months with Shell, undertaken directly after the completion of his undergraduate degree in 1979. This was at a turbulent time. The period 1979–1981 witnessed a great surge in oil prices. The macroeconomy's two-way interactions with energy prices appeared quite manic. Then, as now, they were not particularly well understood. Shell is an Anglo-Dutch giant. As fossil fuel exporters come lately to the game, both its parent countries experienced sharp real exchange rate appreciation. Most Organisation for Economic Co-operation and Development (OECD) countries saw rising unemployment, as well as elevated inflation.

The aftermath of the Organization of the Petroleum Exporting Countries' (OPEC) oil price hikes offered a deeper insight about the nature and teaching of economics. Keynes's *General Theory* in 1936 led to the division of our subject into two separate sub-disciplines, micro and macro. From the Second World War onwards, in universities across the world, professional economists would all too often get encouraged to specialise on one side or the other of this mental canyon. Much of microeconomics became a land of topology, lemmas and theorems directed formally at narrow issues in sharp focus. Much of macroeconomics degenerated into a crude form of impressionism, with vivid splashes of colour around little more than a sad little income-expenditure diagram view of the world.

Vickers is one of many economists who considered that development as retrograde. Microeconomics provides the best instruments for analysing problems logically and systematically. Macroeconomics offers the grandest canvas for portraying those problems. The way that these two areas have for so long been taught is unhelpful, because it makes them seem distinct and unrelated. But in fact, they are complementary. Vickers once suggested half-jestingly in conversation that good macroeconomics might be defined as that branch of microeconomics that deals with the mechanics of aggregation. He agreed with Robert Solow's oft-quoted opinion, that the absence of micro-foundations in macro was probably much less alarming than the absence of macro-foundations in micro. Reflections on the oil crises of the 1970s revealed the essential unity of economics.

The oil markets were exceptionally interesting for a young economist then. Most of the raw material was extracted in a few countries with low costs, but there was a fringe of smaller producers where costs, both fixed and variable, were quite large. The products were not greatly differentiated. Competition was evident, but qualified. In some respects, its market structure resembled a classic oligopoly. Countries were quantity setters, with many attempting to control prices, sometimes with great success for a while, within the umbrella of an international cartel (OPEC). Vertical separation was a prominent feature: transportation, refining and selling were the preserve at that time of just seven huge companies, of which Shell was one.

Since oil in the ground is an asset, and reserves are subject to an unknown upper limit, intertemporal choices and uncertainty are central. Vickers' experience with Shell and the enigmas of the oil markets built a firm foundation for his later research on the dynamics of oligopoly. Section 5 of this chapter will consider his path-breaking papers with Harris and others on patent races and innovation in duopolistic environments. Pondering oil markets in 1979–1980 may well have helped to influence that research agenda.

3   Consulting

No less influential for Vickers' later career than his time at Shell was the serendipity of being invited in the summer of 1979 to assist on a consulting project by his undergraduate economics tutor at Oriel College, Derek Morris. Morris, along with others, formed a very powerful team. They included Jeremy Lever QC and Carl Christian von Weizsäcker, and other lawyers and economists, right at the frontiers of the modern theories of industrial organisation and regulation, who would also become lifelong friends. What brought the group together was the task of advising IBM on how best to prepare for a case that the company realised would later be brought against it, by the European Commission (EC). This was Vickers' first experience of economic consulting. The EC had alleged that IBM was employing anti-competitive practices, in contravention of the prohibition of abuse of market dominance in the Treaty of Rome. The team advising IBM had to furnish arguments to demonstrate that it really wasn't.

In the end, the issue was eventually settled out of court. The multifaceted case provided the young Vickers with a window into a set of intriguing questions at the intersection of law, welfare economics and firms' behaviour. Probing the dynamics of competition would in due course come to frame a major part of his career, as researcher and no less, later on, as regulator. In 2008, Vickers wrote about the later Microsoft case in *Competition Policy International* (Vickers 2008).

One immediate consequence was meeting a member of the team, Jeremy Lever. Lever had been a Fellow of All Souls College, Oxford, for over 20 years.

Having heard about Vickers' Finals results, Lever encouraged him to sit the examination for a Prize Fellowship there. Vickers did so and was duly elected. That was in November 1979. Vickers has retained his links with All Souls. Forty years later, he has already served as its Warden for over a decade.

4   Early Life

This is to run too far ahead, however. Let us move now to the start. Where did John Vickers grow up? Where did he go to school? He was born on 7 July 1958. He and his brother spent their boyhoods close to the centre of Eastbourne, by train an hour or so south of London, on the Sussex coast. While nearby Brighton, its western brother, is raffish, Eastbourne is a town of elegance, now gently fading. It nestles in a dell, sheltered by a range of magnificent hills, "the Seven Sisters". His family ran a shop selling numerous objects of considerable utility for both residents and holidaymakers, such as handbags and umbrellas. His father served for over 50 years on its town council, chaired its finance committee and took his turn as mayor.

Vickers was educated first at Meads Church of England Primary School and then from age 11, at Eastbourne Grammar School for boys. The Grammar School is now a sixth form college. Both it and its sister institution for girls, the High School, were State schools. They charged no fees but were selective. To enter, you needed to do well in an examination based on language, logic, puzzles and maths. In Eastbourne, the pass rate was about 25%. The quality of the education was high. In the sixth form, Vickers took four A level courses: Mathematics, Advanced Mathematics, History and a combined course in Economics and Politics. For nearly all pupils, Maths A Level was partnered with Physics and Chemistry, and not with subjects from the humanities or social science stable. The school had to go to some trouble to alter its timetable to permit the unusual combination which their star student had requested. It is much to their credit that they did accommodate him.

Economics was well taught by an Oxford graduate, Ronnie Ladbroke. Ladbroke would sport a Marylebone Cricket Club (MCC) tie. He was a keen cricketer. Vickers shared that enthusiasm, as both player and spectator. Cricket, with its numerous complexities and fascinating uncertainties which make game theory look almost pedestrian by comparison, has profound appeal to many economists. Though he did not know it at the time, it was also an abiding interest for two of Vickers' future Oxford economist colleagues, Michael Bacharach and Walter Eltis. Ladbroke had imbibed his economics at University College Oxford, partly from the future Prime Minister, Harold

Wilson. Wilson was at that time a recently graduated researcher, working for Lord Beveridge, the main architect of Britain's modern welfare state.

Among the other staff at Eastbourne, one of Vickers' maths teachers was said to have worked in his youth with Barnes Wallis, the father of the Dambusters' bouncing bomb. History was taught impressively by Ken Reed, a Cambridge graduate, and an unusual and charismatic individual with sophisticated views. Reed enlivened his course by introducing his pupils to Marx and Popper. History for Reed was so much more than "just one damned thing after another".

Eastbourne Grammar School sent alumni to Oxford and Cambridge occasionally and knew little about how to navigate their admissions process. The school advised Vickers, who was keen to study Philosophy, Politics and Economics (PPE), to apply to Magdalen College, Oxford. Two of Magdalen's PPE tutors were very forceful talkers, inclined to admire that quality in others; they could well have misinterpreted Vickers' reserve and brevity at interview. Assured later that they would certainly have offered him a place, Vickers was trumped with a scholarship by Oriel College. So, that is where he went up, in 1976, three months after his 18th birthday.

Oriel's tutors at that time were Jonathan Barnes (philosophy), Derek Morris (economics) and Christopher Seton-Watson (politics). The first-year course involved all three subjects. After that you could stay with all three or you could drop one, to extend your study of the other two. In her final two years, a PPEist could choose to do no economics or to allocate anything from one-quarter to effectively three-quarters of her time to that subject. Vickers was committed to economics from the start. He had at first expected to drop philosophy. But he was so taken by it that, when the time came, he opted to forego politics instead.

Oriel was a friendly, united college. Vickers was sufficiently popular and respected to be elected secretary of Oriel's Junior Common Room. Sport consisted mainly of cricket, supplemented by croquet and by bridge, where he partnered his philosophy tutor. Two of his four optional Finals papers were Philosophy of Language with Jonathan Barnes, and Philosophy of Mind, with David Charles, who succeeded Barnes after he moved to Balliol College. The other two were in economics. One was the Economics of Industry (Oxford's quaint term for industrial organisation (IO)), which he studied with Derek Morris. The other was Money, with Peter Sinclair at Brasenose. Nearly all of Vickers' subsequent professional work and research were to fall within the ambit of those two optional papers. Sinclair was, by chance, one of the PPE examiners in 1979, and can testify to the fact that Vickers' examination results were simply stellar. He was widely agreed to have gained the highest set of first-class marks in PPE since the war.

5   Research

This section begins by describing several of the main events that occurred in John Vickers' career in the years shortly after 1981. In Section 5.1, the focus is on his postgraduate studies, and the main research that he conducted in industrial organisation in the years that followed is explored in Sections 5.2, 5.3, 5.4, and 5.5.

5.1   Academic Apprenticeship

As a Prize Fellow of All Souls, Vickers was quite free to undertake postgraduate study if he wished, or to pursue a non-academic career. We saw how he started working with Shell. But from October 1981, he enrolled into Oxford's two-year MPhil course in Economics. The programme consisted of compulsory work in microeconomics and macroeconomics, followed by three optional papers in special subjects, drawn from quite a long list. One of the three optional papers could be dropped if you decided to conduct original research, and write an MPhil thesis; and that is what Vickers chose to do. The MPhil thesis could then form the foundation of a doctoral thesis at Oxford. Candidates who did really well in the MPhil were permitted to progress to that, if they wished.

Despite the difference in terminology, therefore, the MPhil cum DPhil programme was broadly similar to the comprehensives-plus-thesis package in a top economics department in the US. With Mirrlees, Sen and Stiglitz all teaching on the Oxford programme at about that time, its quality was outstanding. The modern MPhil syllabus had been shaped by Mirrlees soon after arriving in Oxford in 1968. Oxford's comparative advantage in those days lay in theoretical topics, and especially so in the areas of uncertainty, information, incentives, agency theory and welfare economics. Mirrlees, Sen and Stiglitz would all later be awarded Nobel Prizes. Vickers interacted with all these, and others; Stiglitz was a colleague of his, who returned periodically, in All Souls. Mirrlees and Sen worked at Nuffield College, barely six minutes' walk away from All Souls. But his principal tutor, his thesis adviser, was not in Oxford. That was Partha Dasgupta, who was then at LSE, and would later move to Cambridge. Dasgupta would point Vickers to powerful new research from scholars he knew well, like Maskin, Hart and Hammond. Dasgupta was interested in a vast range of topics, including welfare, agency, games, innovation and the dynamics of competition.

Vickers' MPhil thesis was completed by 1983. It formed the foundation of his DPhil, titled "Patent Races and Market Structure", which was submitted successfully in 1985. This doctorate became the springboard of many later articles and a long programme of research. Three early papers (Harris and Vickers 1985a, b, 1987) were co-authored with Christopher Harris. Harris was a brilliant Oxford mathematics graduate from Corpus, who had gone on to study economics. He and Vickers were on the MPhil at the same time, and both came top of their class, with Harris ahead by a nose for the thesis prize.

5.2   Research in Industrial Organization: The Harris-Vickers Collaboration

In the years that followed, Harris and Vickers went on to develop their ideas further. The Harris and Vickers partnership was to bear much fruit. Vickers admits modestly that while he has a good nose for an interesting problem, cracking it rigorously can call for yet greater mathematical skills than he himself might muster. They continued to work together, collaborating in their 1993 paper with Christopher Budd, and with Philippe Aghion for a 1997 paper. Later on, Vickers and Harris built on that work with Aghion and Peter Howitt in tackling a central question in the theory of endogenous growth (Aghion et al. 2001): What is the relationship between competition between firms, and technological progress? A further Harris and Vickers paper appeared in 1995. All but three of these six papers were published in the *Review of Economic Studies*. The fourth, their first in print, Harris and Vickers (1985a), had appeared in the field journal, the *Journal of Industrial Economics*, the 1997 paper with Aghion appeared in the *European Economic Review*, and the last, with its focus on natural resources, would come out in the *RAND Journal of Economics*.

Various models of endogenous growth can involve externalities, or population growth, or fossil fuel extraction, once one of these phenomena is allowed not just to influence, but genuinely to interact with, the standard dynamics of aggregate output and capital. Still more appealing in the view of many, and absolutely consistent with the phenomenon of Harrod-neutral technical progress, is the evolution of human capital and the role of training in economic growth, which was first demonstrated rigorously by Lucas (1988). But what interested Vickers was technological progress. For many years, economic growth models had treated it as a mysterious exogenous parameter, if they allowed for it at all. Meanwhile, most of the IO literature about innovation tended to focus, alas, on the narrow canvas of partial equilibrium. So, technological progress would become the most celebrated member of the endogenous growth family of models. But in 1985, hints from Arrow's concept of learning by doing aside, that lay some years in the future.

Technological progress took three stages for Vickers—first, research, then discoveries and finally, implementation and diffusion. He was convinced that inventors are typically not loners. Observation and history teach that most of them, whether successful or no, are far from solitary; rivalry is involved; there is a race. That is precisely what Vickers set out to model initially alone and soon with Harris.

The framework was deliberately kept as simple as possible. There are two inventors. They are running in the same race towards the same objective—discovering a particular new product or process. The one who will get there first will scoop all the cream, by securing the patent or the prize. What is needed in the race is not just stamina, which they both have, but effort, which is privately costly. At some early stage in the race, they might conceivably be running together, or, more likely, one may be ahead of the other, possibly by a whisker, possibly by more. One question is this: If one of them is in front, does he supply more effort than the rival behind him, or less? Another question: Does the gap between the two runners tend to widen, or to narrow, as the race proceeds?

What are the answers? If there is symmetry between the two runners, if they are patient, and if the race has two stages, the one in front always supplies more effort at stage one; and the effort gap goes up as the distance between them widens. These answers are general. In a many-stage race, the same findings hold in particular examples. If the runners are impatient (or equivalently, if the prize is discounted over time), the desire to get there sooner makes the front runner try even harder. These are the findings proved in the 1993 paper with Budd, which introduces, and focuses upon, the challenging extension to uncertainty.

The setting of the 2001 paper with Aghion and Howitt, as well as Harris, combines elements of the important Aghion and Howitt *Econometrica* 1992 paper—which, along with Lucas (1988) on training and Romer (1990) on invention, constitutes the core of modern endogenous growth theory—with the Harris and Vickers (1987) paper summarised above. In Aghion et al. (2001), the runners already produce products, but the extent to which those products compete with each other can vary. The runners do not just observe each other; it is possible that they can imitate each other as well. Innovation proceeds incrementally, step by step.

The key question here is this: Will the growth rate tend to increase with (a) closer competition in the product market, and (b) the probability of imitation? At the risk of oversimplification, one can state that the answer to (a) is yes, usually. To (b), the answer is yes, but for sure only if it is low enough, and definitely not if it is too high. If a policy maker seeks to maximise growth, therefore, we welcome stronger competition in the product market—ironically, because that whets the competitors' desire to escape it—but she should turn her face strongly against anything but a low chance of imitation. Too much copyright infringement definitely needs to be stopped. But all that presumes, of course, that faster growth is good for welfare, which the Aghion and Howitt (1992) paper shows could quite possibly be false. You can have too much growth in that model, where the winner takes all, at least until she is usurped at the frontier by someone else.

Research racing was not the only field that Vickers explored while completing his doctoral thesis. There were others. Six further articles appeared in 1985 and 1986 (Vickers 1985a, b, c, d, 1986a, b), varying in length, but all single authored, and devoted mainly to aspects of theory and policy in oligopolistic markets. One was first given at a Royal Economic Society (RES) conference and chosen for publication in the *Economic Journal*. Here, Vickers (1985a) looked at why the owner of a firm, call it A, in a Cournot oligopoly, whose main concern is the firm's profits, might want to employ an aggressive manager with a quite different objective. If the manager disregarded costs, she would raise her firm's output. If each of the rival firms, owner-managed by assumption, continued to set its output to maximise its profit, taking all other firms' outputs as given, it would cut back, earn less profit. But A's profits would go up, even though the industry's total profits would drop. The moral was this: If you want to make as much profit as possible, try to do something else, so long as your rivals don't! Vickers' aggressive manager makes her firm behave rather like a Stackelberg leader.

The other members of this quartet of early, single-authored papers included a crisply written survey of modern oligopoly theory much read by students (Vickers 1985b), as well as others on predation (Vickers 1985c) and preemptive patenting (Vickers 1985d).

5.3   The Vickers-Yarrow Collaboration

But theory was not everything. In the real IO world in Britain, the mid-1980s witnessed a radical new institutional development. This was denationalisation, or, as it became known, privatisation. This complemented Vickers' interest in the rarefied world of abstract models of invention and innovation. What should an economist make of the case for privatisation in principle? Was it a good or a flawed application of agency theory in practice? Was the sale of State assets being handled well? What was the best form of regulation for privately run natural monopolies, and were the new instruments of regulation going to work satisfactorily? Vickers was intrigued by these questions forming in his mind and found that George Yarrow, an economics tutor at Hertford College, Oxford, shared his curiosity. The partnership with Yarrow was to be the second great collaboration in IO in which John Vickers participated.

At the same time fellowship as these thoughts were starting to form, the Fellow Warden of Nuffield College had approached Vickers informally to tell him that there was a vacant fellowship there. The post was named after a former Fellow and eminent economist, Sir Roy Harrod. Vickers applied, and was elected to the Fellowship, in the Economics of Business and Public Policy, on 1 October 1984. He relinquished his Prize Fellowship at All Souls, half a mile to the east, but would retain his connections there. Alongside his work with Harris on patent races, therefore, Vickers started to collaborate with Yarrow on the intriguing new field, the economics of privatisation.

They started with a well-received booklet, *Privatisation and the Natural Monopolies* (Vickers and Yarrow 1985), which dissected the issues dispassionately. Then came a long book, *Privatization: An Economic Analysis* (Vickers and Yarrow 1988a), published by MIT Press, which received very wide attention. Thorough and probing, yet accessible to all, it at once became the canonical work for economists on this subject. It described and appraised the mechanics of the various ways of selling shares in previously nationalised companies; it considered when some form of regulation was required when a business faced limited competitive pressures; and it contrasted various ways of achieving that, including the UK's favoured RPI-x approach to price setting and alternatives employed in the US, and focused on knotty other problems like the optimum length of a franchise period.

Translations into Spanish and Chinese later brought that book to the attention of some two billion more potential readers. These two Vickers and Yarrow publications were meanwhile succeeded swiftly by another, a journal special issue, then book, co-edited with his politics colleague at Nuffield, Vincent

Wright, on the politics of privatisation in Europe (Vickers and Wright 1989). Vickers and Yarrow continued to publish together on aspects of privatisation, and in non-UK based journals: two papers in the *European Economic Review* on regulation (Vickers and Yarrow 1988b) and on electricity pricing (Vickers and Yarrow 1991a), in *Economic Policy* again on electricity (Vickers and Yarrow 1991b), and a more wide-ranging discussion in the *Journal of Economic Perspectives* (Vickers and Yarrow 1991c). Vickers' publications also include some papers on privatisation written by himself alone.

Many other productive collaborations that various scholars undertook with Vickers were also occurring in this period. One was with Paul Stoneman, and another, Michael Waterson. Both were at Warwick. Stoneman and Vickers (1988) focused upon technology policy while Vickers and Waterson (1991), and a paper with Giacomo Bonanno (a postdoctoral Nuffield student who had moved to UC Davis) (Bonnano and Vickers 1988), were both on vertical relationships. Yet others were with current or former Oxford colleagues, most prominently Donald Hay (Hay and Vickers 1988) and John Kay (Kay and Vickers 1988). These were devoted to aspects of regulation.

5.4   But Why Industrial Organization—and Why the Need for Umpires to Ensure Fair Play?

Why did Vickers concentrate so much of his research upon aspects of IO? Also, what was his general attitude to issues of competition? Economics lies at the interface of many different subjects. Two such are psychology and engineering. Engineering is key to the production of a good. Psychology helps to inform us about what causes people to buy things, and what that may do to their sense of pleasure and well-being. Economics throws its light, instead, on that moment when such goods change hands. What determines the volume of output and sales? Why are the prices what they are? How can we best understand and explain why these quantities and prices ebb and flow, and evolve over time? The answers to these questions are the basis of any economic analysis. It immediately emerges that sellers constitute a big part of the answers. Are they numerous? Knowledgeable? Observant? In cahoots with each other? Restrained by conventions, or by laws? Do they compete, and if so, when, and how?

Those on the outside right of politics claim that markets are nearly always as close to perfect as it is possible to get. From their bases in Chicago, Illinois, and elsewhere, they maintain that any dispute is typically best settled by applying the principle of caveat emptor. Regulation, they declare, is rarely if ever needed. It is just one more "conspiracy in restraint of trade". If a seller misbehaves, everyone will soon know about it, and he will not survive, and he knows that, so he will not. They conclude that no sensible seller will therefore ever act against his own interest. By contrast, those on the far left see producers as exploitative. They pay their staff much too little. They craftily con buyers into buying things they may well not need, and at exorbitant prices. Mainly because of indivisibilities of various types, they cite plenty of reasons for increasing returns. They therefore see state-run monoliths as the main solution to such problems. For them, powerful regulators can be very useful in the wings, ever ready to police and punish those few private firms that it happens to be inconvenient to abolish.

Between these two extremes, of reactionary Chicago on the one side, and Bolshevism on the other, lies a great middle ground where Vickers is to be found. The vast majority of economists are at home with him in that middle area, too. Their views might differ in some details. But what they agree upon is that markets are games where, like cricket, you definitely do need the services of an umpire. An umpire might have to intervene only quite rarely. De minimis non curat lex, they admit, though you can quibble about what constitutes minimal. But she, the umpire, has to be there to apply clear rules, to monitor, to be vigilant and to help prevent foul play. There should be a simple set of sanctions when infractions are observed. A game is a battle tamed. The umpire is in position to spot and stop chicanery and belligerence, and, above all, to ensure that all the play is fair.

Vickers' activities were to centre more and more on umpiring. The issue of umpiring figured, as we have seen, in the publications with Yarrow and others. It would feature, as we shall see below, in many of the books Vickers co-edited and would be crowned with his position as Chief Umpire (Chairman) at the Office of Fair Trading (OFT) and later as Chair of the Vickers Commission. Moreover, the concepts underlying so much "foul play" would constitute the research that Vickers would continue to conduct, over many years, with Mark Armstrong. The Armstrong and Vickers partnership is the subject with which this section now concludes.

5.5   The Armstrong-Vickers Research Partnership

The terrain between the Elysian field of perfect competition and the quagmire of unassailable monopoly is forbiddingly large and rather messy. There are two main clumps of terra firma. One is monopolistic competition, where lots of firms all produce something just a little bit different, in location or non-spatial characteristics. A basic, stripped-down version of the Dixit and Stiglitz (1977) paper has been borrowed extensively to illuminate trade theory, growth, unemployment and public finance. Afforced by the algebraically brilliant but absurdly implausible device of Calvo pricing, it underpins all standard work on monetary policy transmission and the dynamics of inflation. It is easily adapted and relies greatly on symmetry. This is mostly a story of niches. The spatial aspect of monopolistic competition, which mostly begins with Hotelling (1929) and Salop (1979), deals with bigger entities. It is now a cornerstone in the grand edifice of the economic theory of politics.

Monopolistic competition has a more complex and very powerful rival. This is oligopoly, competition among the few. Like monopolistic competition (where the substitution elasticity between varieties can range widely), oligopoly embraces perfect competition and monopoly as limiting cases. Unlike monopolistic competition, it takes interdependency very seriously. Competition may vary in intensity and character. It extends to the hypothetical warfare between an incumbent monopolist and a would-be entrant.

Vickers' first journal publications had, as we saw above, already been devoted to aspects of oligopoly. This was followed by others, extending Cournot's oligopoly model in various directions, for example, when players' costs differ. That leads to heterogeneity in their market shares, a phenomenon which is commonly observed but rarely explained systematically. Oligopoly featured centre stage in two major sole-authored papers by Vickers in 1995 (one of which appeared in *Oxford Economic Papers* (Vickers 1995a), and the other in the *Review of Economic Studies* (Vickers 1995b), and also in an earlier one in 1989 (Vickers 1989).

Oligopoly and monopoly, regulation and IO applications of principal-agent problems have been among the main settings for Vickers' research with Mark Armstrong. Their collaboration has stretched over three decades. The first paper they published together was on price discrimination (Armstrong and Vickers 1991). So far, the duo have published no less than fifteen academic journal papers together. Most (Armstrong and Vickers 1991, 1993, 1998, 2000, 2001, 2010a, b, 2012, 2015, 2018a, b) have no other co-authors. But Simon Cowan (Oxford) and Ray Rees (Warwick) joined them for one each in 1995 (Armstrong et al. 1995a and Armstrong et al. 1995b respectively), and Jidong Zhou (now at Yale) for two (Armstrong et al. 2009a, b). There is also one new Armstrong and Vickers Oxford Discussion Paper (Armstrong and Vickers 2018b). Embryos of others nestle, no doubt, in the pipeline that will appear in due course.

One of the most celebrated Armstrong and Vickers papers (2010b) appeared in *Econometrica*. It is a valuable contribution to agency theory, which

James Mirrlees (Armstrong's DPhil supervisor and John Vickers' colleague) had helped to invent some 35 years before. But it starts with a key issue in regulation, the criterion for deciding whether a merger is good or bad for social welfare. One reason for the link is the fact that regulators often operate in the dark, for the firms they monitor may be able to conceal aspects of what they are doing. No ordinary mortal can spot everything that happens on the cricket field. A second umpire (like the square-leg umpire in a cricket match) can help. But even that will not ensure perfect vision.

In the very simplest Cournot oligopoly, for example, a horizontal merger is always bad for consumers. Fewer firms entail a higher price and hence lower welfare for the people who buy the product. The two firms that merge will shrink, reducing their aggregate profits provided that there are still one or more other players left in the industry, but lifting the profits a little for those other players. If there were just two duopolists in the same industry, with entry restricted, they gain from a merger, and consumers typically suffer (but might just conceivably not, if that meant that there were now big cost-reducing synergies to exploit, for example). In more complex cases, where the merging firms operate in different industries or have vertical links, you could, for instance, see a merger reducing consumer surplus straight away but raising producer surplus by a larger amount. What is more, profits may get invested; that should raise consumers' welfare in the future; and even if there were no extra investment, should profit recipients really be excluded from the notion of society's welfare? What should be done in such cases? The question of how social welfare is defined becomes critical, therefore, for deciding whether the merger should proceed.

This paper is rigorous and understandably quite abstract. It generalises the question. The utility of principal P depends upon one of a selection of actions, N, by an agent A. N is chosen by A from a longer list, L, but P cannot see what is in N. P needs to choose a list M of all the possible acts that he, P, permits A to do. The two lists, M and N, are subsets of L. Before acting, A tells P what he proposes to do. So, how does P choose M? It is not good enough for P to say, 'Choose what you like from list M': A might go for something that is not best from P's standpoint. The authors prove various results about P's optimal list M. The regulation analogy is this. Suppose P says, 'Do what you like so long as the merger increases welfare defined as consumer surplus plus producers' profit (which P would like maximised)'. That is not good enough from P's standpoint: a merger could increase welfare by that definition by greatly raising the merged firms' profits, partly at the expense of consumers. So, the competition authority umpire should restrict list M to actions that raise consumer surplus on its own—P knows the firms will not do anything to damage their combined profits. There is an echo here of Vickers' demonstration in 1985 that the profit-seeking owner of a firm in a Cournot oligopoly can gain by getting a manager who seeks to maximise not profit, but total revenue. There is still more in Armstrong and Vickers (2010b), for example, on dynamics and the effects of the discounting of future payoffs at different rates.

This *Econometrica* paper extends knowledge by providing solid analytical foundations for an important point. Like all the Armstrong and Vickers papers, it is rigorous and meticulous. While the inevitable technicalities make it challenging to digest, for example, for regulators and lawyers, there are other highly accessible publications that Armstrong and Vickers have recently written. Key points are made directly, and, whenever possible, in plain English. Three examples are their 2018 multiproduct pricing paper in the *Journal of Political Economy* (Armstrong and Vickers 2018a), their discussion of how contingent charges affect consumers' welfare in the *Journal of Economic Literature* (Armstrong and Vickers 2012), and a paper in the *American Economic Review: Insights*, on price discrimination in the presence of captive customers (Armstrong and Vickers 2019).

The first of these three compares Cournot oligopoly with both regulated and unregulated monopoly, when the firms produce more than a single product. This paper fills quite a big gap: there can be very few firms which are large enough to influence the prices of what they produce and yet make and sell only one single good. Among other results, Cournot equilibrium, they find, meets a famous test of efficiency (see Ramsey 1927). Multiproduct pricing is the norm. Even more relevant, perhaps, to real-world concerns is the problem of contingent charges, like big penalties that most banks charge for unauthorised overdrafts. Here, Armstrong and Vickers show that such charges tend to redistribute from uninformed customers to informed ones, and go on to ask what welfare economics has to say about that.

So many of Vickers' academic publications have been co-authored with Armstrong that it is easy to miss some of the fruit from other partnerships. There were many. Space precludes including most of them. But one such that clearly merits a mention is a paper which appeared in the *American Economic Review* on third-degree price discrimination by monopolists (see Aguirre et al. 2010). This appeared in the same year as the contingent charges paper. Many large firms sell different units to different people at different prices, and the IT revolution has often made this more common than it was. Is the practice harmful or beneficial for social welfare? Also, what does it mean for a firm's overall level of output? These are big policy questions. The Aguirre et al. paper is devoted to answering them. Like the work carried out by Armstrong, Yarrow and Harris, and all the papers that Vickers wrote alone or with others, it is addressed to a serious issue that matters, and on which economic analysis can throw a powerful light.

6   Editorial Work

Academic journal papers are almost never anonymous. Transatlantic conventions and increasingly ruthless inter-university competition have come to displace the traditional British view that publicity is embarrassing, and that bragging is an unpardonable sin. Morris Zapp has triumphed over Philip Swallow, even in Rummidge and Oxbridge. But there is still one activity that stays anonymous: refereeing for journals. Diligent and helpful referees are the unsung heroes of the academic profession.

When an editor sends out a paper to referees, she hopes for a clear cut and reasonably timely verdict on the quality of a submission. Best of all, she welcomes a report that will assist the author(s) even when, perhaps especially when, that verdict is a recommendation to reject. Without breaking confidences, your author is delighted to report that John Vickers is an outstandingly thorough referee. He dislikes the thought of work pending; he invariably replies speedily and decisively. Granted, he is not alone in these virtues, but it grieves one to state that there are many others who lack them. The worst kind of referee report, which editors receive too often, might run like this:

> I am sorry it has taken me so long to work through this paper, and to give you my recommendation. I wish I could put my finger more precisely on why I am not very impressed by it. Some of the paper is familiar or obvious, but other parts are hard going. The derivation of equations could be explained a bit better, in my view. The authors could benefit from studying several recent Discussion Papers written on related subjects. A suitably revised version might just pass muster, but I confess to being somewhat unenthusiastic.

No editor ever gets a report like that from Vickers.

In cricketing terms, referees are the fielders, submitters do the batting and editors bowl. Vickers bowled for the *Review of Economic Studies* for three years as assistant editor and served on its editorial board for a dozen. He bowled for *Oxford Economic Papers* as a member of the editorial board for about fourteen, chairing it for five. He bowled for the *European Economic Review*, editing its Papers and Proceedings for 1993. Other journal boards that have enjoyed his service include the *Journal of Industrial Economics* and the *Journal of Regulatory*

Economics. He has also co-edited books. The first was *Strategic Behaviour and Industrial Competition*, which he co-edited in 1986 with Martin Slater, and Morris and Sinclair, his undergraduate tutors (Morris et al. 1986). A year later, *The Economics of Market Dominance* appeared, which Donald Hay and he co-edited (Hay and Vickers 1987). Two years after that, Vickers and Vincent Wright edited *The Politics of Privatization in Western Europe* (Vickers and Wright 1989). The bowling and the batting were both of high standard in all three. A special issue of the *Journal of Industrial Economics* came next, in 1991; this was on vertical relationships, which he edited with Michael Waterson (Vickers and Waterson 1991).

7   Finance, Money and Banking

Firms need capital as an input; they borrow and pay interest and dividends. Banks, which borrow, lend and create money, are, like other financial intermediaries, firms in their own right as well. Firms and banks are both micro and macro faces. Each have been partly reshaped by agency theory, asymmetric information, contract theory and games, as well as by certain advances in econometric methods. It is no accident that the interrelated disciplines of IO and monetary economics should have attracted scholars interested in both their union and their intersection. In earlier generations, Edgeworth, Marshall, Hicks, Friedman, Baumol and Shubik are prominent examples.

Vickers' first publication in the area of monetary economics appeared in *Oxford Economic Papers* in 1986. It was agency theory applied to a central banker, who might be "dry", a determined inflation fighter, or he could be "wet", that is, concerned to keep employment high. But would a closet wet masquerade as a dry, Vickers asked, and try to conceal his preferences to stop inflation expectations running away, and if he did, would he get away with it?

Like John Flemming, who went on to be the Bank of England's Chief Economist in 1980, Vickers saw another side of finance for two years as investment bursar of his then college, Nuffield. He also looked at the economics of profit sharing with Colin Mayer (Mayer and Vickers 1996). Then came six influential papers in the *Bank of England Quarterly Bulletin*, when Vickers was the Bank of England's Chief Economist. All of these articles (Vickers 1998, 1999a, b, c, 2000a, b) were highly topical. They covered inflation targeting in 1998, shortly after its introduction in the UK; the euro; monetary union and economic growth; and the relationships between monetary policy and asset prices, economic models, and the supply side. Shortly after the global financial crisis erupted in September 2008, we see a 2010 BIS paper on central banks and competition authorities (Vickers 2010a), the Report of the Independent Commission on Banking (Vickers Commission 2013) which he chaired, and then three papers, among them Vickers (2012, 2014), which were devoted to the subjects of banking reform, and taxing and regulating banks.

The Vickers Commission was a landmark, in the UK and well beyond. It surveyed the various possible causal factors that underlay the global financial crisis. There were many. New accounting rules about marking to market, and permission to book now anticipated profits for future years; record low interest rates, held too long after 2001; the invention and profusion of fiendishly clever financial derivatives that hid various horrors; the 1999 repeal of the Glass-Steagall Act 1933 that had kept US investment and retail banking well apart. These and others are entertainingly discussed in a "The Financial Crisis: Whodunnit?" lecture delivered by Howard Davies in New Zealand in 2009 (Davies 2009).

However, two conclusions stood out. The banks that had failed had inadequate capital to withstand a large fall in the value of their loan assets, and those which had been "too big to fail", and been bailed out, or taken into state ownership, had survived because their indispensable retail banking activities had been jeopardised by huge losses in their investment banking wing. The Commission's main recommendations were therefore that banks should be required to hold a great deal more capital, and that retail banking should be insulated by Chinese walls from any speculative investment banking activities.

The banking crisis of late 2008 and 2009 was a massive earthquake. It was comparable in scale and gravity only to the Great Depression of the early 1930s, which would have numerous aftershocks, spread over many years. So, the Vickers Commission worked fast. Its final report was issued in September 2011. The urgency of safeguarding the British economy from any future banking crisis led the five members of the Commission, supported by a small team of civil servants, to cover a great deal of ground. The government at first reacted speedily. It initiated legislation on the day of publication. But it is sad to note that subsequent progress has been much less rapid. Vickers' disappointment is expressed in a 2016 paper in the *Journal of Financial Regulation* (Vickers 2016). This was followed by a VOX essay (Vickers 2017) on the disturbing recent decline, to ratios often far lower than in 2008, in many banks' equity valuations relative to the book values of their capital. Banks' capital requirements have been moving upwards, but, as Vickers notes, they are based on the perilously unhelpful accounting fiction of book value. This is a theme pursued in Vickers (2019).

8   Public Service

There can be few, if any, academic economists in Britain with such a long and distinguished record of public service as John Vickers, for which he received a knighthood in 2005. This began in the early 1990s, with memberships of panels for the European Commission, HM Treasury, Oftel, the Hansard Society, and the Department of Trade and Industry. It reached its climax with his fifteen months as Chair of the Independent Commission on Banking, which was mentioned in Section 7.

Before that, we have seen how he had nearly three years as Chief Economist of the Bank of England. He worked closely with Mervyn King, then Deputy Governor, and then Governor Eddie George. In this period, he served, among other bodies, on its Monetary Policy Committee which sets Bank Rate, its key policy instrument that influences all interest rates in sterling. From 2000 to 2005, after leaving the Bank, Vickers was head (first Director General, then Chair) of the OFT. Both his main academic area of interest, IO, and a subsidiary one, monetary economics, were covered by these positions. The Chair of the Vickers Commission would crown his career of public service. It combined both of them.

The OFT headship occurred in a busy period. In the realm of publications, it switched Vickers' activity away from monetary economics to competition law. Two of his papers in this area appeared in 2003 and 2004, in the *European Competition Law Review* (Vickers 2003, 2004). Another was devoted to the economics of consumer law (Vickers 2005a). Two others followed a little later in the *European Competition Journal* (Vickers 2006, 2007), and sandwiched between, among other things, a 2005 *Economic Journal* paper on a core law-and-economics topic, market power abuse (Vickers 2005b). In 2010, the *Economic Journal* also published his Presidential Address to the RES, on property rights (Vickers 2010b). In the US, where Vickers has had links (with Princeton, Harvard, Stanford and Chicago), law and economics are natural bedfellows. Law doctorates there are replete with economics, right to the gunnels. But in Britain, alas, it is deplorably hard to study both subjects to a high level, let alone contribute to scholarship in both. Vickers shows how, with hard work, it can be done.

9   Teaching

The outside world, like posterity, knows scholars from what they write. But inside a university, it is teaching that is most noticed, most remembered and most keenly judged. Vickers' teaching began with a Lectureship at Merton College, Oxford, covering for its tutor's leave. University lectures followed swiftly, when he had been appointed to the Harrod Fellowship at Nuffield. That particular position did not actually oblige him to lecture. But he chose to. It was lucky for that generation of Oxford's postgraduate students that he did. They greatly enjoyed his lectures and rated him among Oxford's very best. At this point, word processing was in its infancy, and some lecturers, like their predecessors had done for seven centuries, simply talked. But Vickers then produced handouts, written in his crystal-clear Italic script and photocopied for everyone. Good final year undergraduates specialising in IO also attended and learnt much.

As Drummond Professor, Vickers' lecture portfolio broadened. The MPhil course on Public Economics had eschewed environmental economics, for example; Vickers filled this lacuna himself. He had seven years in that position before his periods of leave, at the Bank of England and the OFT, and three after his return in 2005. One teaching activity he took outside Oxford in the latter period was to deliver a course of lectures for the RES Easter School. The audience was a highly selected thirty-four-strong group of PhD students and young lecturers, from all over the UK and beyond, who were specialising in IO; the numbers included a few specialists from the Treasury and the Bank of England. At the time, Vickers was suffering from a severe throat infection, and could barely speak. Most lecturers would have tried to get someone to deliver the material in their stead. But not Vickers. His dozen lectures were all carefully prepared, with handouts, copies of research papers and other documents, which were made available to everyone; he could supplement these by drawing diagrams and deriving equations on whiteboards, and somehow he was able to deliver short sentences in answer to questions and converse in whispers at coffee and meal breaks over the two days of his part of the school.

While President of the RES from 2007 to 2010, Vickers arranged that its annual Easter School could be supplemented by a new Autumn School, in order to strengthen the position of advanced research in macroeconomics in UK universities. The Autumn Schools thrived for three years, until a later President of the RES, the first for decades never to have observed or participated as an RES Easter School lecturer, decided that other priorities took precedence, so the Autumn Schools were sacrificed and the Easter Schools cut back.

After his return to Oxford, one lecture that Vickers undertook was the initial one for the first-year undergraduate course in Macroeconomics. The audience was large—well over 300. Most Drummond Professors restricted themselves to postgraduate teaching. At Cambridge, and in many distinguished US universities, it is traditional for many of the senior professoriate to welcome the daunting challenge of lecturing to beginners. The University of Oxford was not a place where something should be done for the first time, but Vickers thought that he should take it on. His students were fortunate.

10   University Leadership

In 2008, Vickers was elected Warden of All Souls, which he had joined as a Prize Fellow twenty-nine years before, and to which his Drummond Chair was attached. He was only the second economist to head the College, which had been founded almost six centuries earlier. In the past, he has served Oxford as a Trustee of Rhodes House, and as a Delegate of the University Press and Chair of its Finance Committee. Beyond Oxford, he has been President of the Institute of Fiscal Studies and of the British Association for the Advancement of Science (Section F), as well as of the RES. At the time of writing, he is President of the European Association for Research in Industrial Economics. Moreover, his academic research and publications continue unabated. His is a career of rare distinction.

References

Main Works by John Vickers

Aghion, P., C. Harris, P. Howitt and J. Vickers (2001). 'Competition, Imitation and Growth with Step-by-Step Innovation'. *Review of Economic Studies*, 68(3): 467–492.

Aghion, P., C. Harris and J. Vickers (1997). 'Competition and Growth with Step-by-Step Innovation: An Example'. *European Economic Review*, 41(3–5): 771–782.

Aguirre, I., S. Cowan and J. Vickers (2010). 'Monopoly Price Discrimination and Demand Curvature'. *American Economic Review*, 100(4): 1,601–1,615.

Armstrong, M., S. Cowan and J. Vickers (1995a). 'Nonlinear Pricing and Price Cap Regulation'. *Journal of Public Economics*, 58(1): 33–55.

Armstrong, M., R. Rees and J. Vickers (1995b). 'Optimal Regulatory Lag under Price Cap Regulation'. *Revista Espanola d'Economia*, 12(1): 93–116.

Armstrong, M. and J. Vickers (1991). 'Welfare Effects of Price Discrimination by a Regulated Monopolist'. *RAND Journal of Economics*, 22(4): 571–580.

Armstrong, M. and J. Vickers (1993). 'Price Discrimination, Competition and Regulation'. *Journal of Industrial Economics*, 41(4): 335–359.

Armstrong, M. and J. Vickers (1998). 'The Access Pricing Problem with Deregulation: A Note'. *Journal of Industrial Economics*, 46(1): 115–121.

Armstrong, M. and J. Vickers (2000). 'Multiproduct Price Regulation under Asymmetric Information'. *Journal of Industrial Economics*, 48(2): 137–160.

Armstrong, M. and J. Vickers (2001). 'Competitive Price Discrimination'. *RAND Journal of Economics*, 32(4): 579–605.

Armstrong, M. and J. Vickers (2010a). 'Competitive Non-Linear Pricing and Bundling'. *Review of Economic Studies*, 77(1): 30–60.

Armstrong, M. and J. Vickers (2010b). 'A Model of Delegated Project Choice'. *Econometrica*, 78(1): 213–244.

Armstrong, M. and J. Vickers (2012). 'Consumer Protection and Contingent Charges'. *Journal of Economic Literature*, 50(2): 477–493.

Armstrong, M. and J. Vickers (2015). 'Which Demand Systems Can be Generated by Discrete Choice?'. *Journal of Economic Theory*, 158(Part A): 293–307.

Armstrong, M. and J. Vickers (2018a). 'Multiproduct Pricing Made Simple'. *Journal of Political Economy*, 126(4): 1,444–1,471.

Armstrong, M. and J. Vickers (2018b). 'Patterns of Competition with Captive Customers'. Department of Economics, University of Oxford, Discussion Paper Series, Number 864.

Armstrong, M. and J. Vickers (2019). 'Discriminating Against Captive Customers'. *American Economic Review: Insights*, 1(3): 257–272.

Armstrong, M., J. Vickers and J. Zhou (2009a). 'Consumer Protection and the Incentive to Become Informed'. *Journal of the European Economic Association*, 7(2–3): 399–410.

Armstrong, M., J. Vickers and J. Zhou (2009b). 'Prominence and Consumer Search'. *RAND Journal of Economics*, 40(2): 209–233.

Bonnano, G. and J. Vickers (1988). 'Vertical Separation'. *Journal of Industrial Economics*, 36(3): 257–265.

Budd, C., C. Harris and J. Vickers (1993). 'A Model of the Evolution of Duopoly: Does the Asymmetry Between Firms Tend to Increase or Decrease?'. *Review of Economic Studies*, 60(3): 543–573.

Harris, C. and J. Vickers (1985a). 'Patent Races and the Persistence of Monopoly'. *Journal of Industrial Economics*, 33(4): 461–481.

Harris, C. and J. Vickers (1985b). 'Perfect Equilibrium in a Model of a Race'. *Review of Economic Studies*, 52(2): 193–209.

Harris, C. and J. Vickers (1987). 'Racing with Uncertainty'. *Review of Economics Studies*, 54(1): 1–21.

Harris, C. and J. Vickers (1995). 'Innovation and Natural Resources: A Dynamic Game with Uncertainty'. *RAND Journal of Economics*, 26(3): 418–430.

Hay, D. and J. Vickers (eds) (1987). *The Economics of Market Dominance*. Oxford: Basil Blackwell.

Hay, D. and J. Vickers (1988). 'The Reform of UK Competition Policy'. *National Institute Economic Review*, 125: 56–68.

Kay, J. and J. Vickers (1988). 'Regulatory Reform in Britain'. *Economic Policy*, 3(7): 286–343.

Mayer, C. and J. Vickers (1996). 'Profit-Sharing Regulation: An Economic Appraisal'. *Fiscal Studies*, 17(1): 1–18.

Morris, D., P. Sinclair, M. Slater and J. Vickers (eds) (1986). *Strategic Behaviour and Industrial Competition*. Oxford: Oxford University Press.

Stoneman, P. and J. Vickers (1988). 'The Assessment: The Economics of Technology Policy'. *Oxford Review of Economic Policy*, 4(4): i–xvi.

Vickers, J. (1985a). 'Delegation and the Theory of the Firm'. *Economic Journal*, 95(Supplement): 138–147.

Vickers, J. (1985b). 'Strategic Competition Among the Few—Some Recent Developments in the Economics of Industry'. *Oxford Review of Economic Policy*, 1(3): 39–62.

Vickers, J. (1985c). 'The Economics of Predatory Practices'. *Fiscal Studies*, 6(3): 24–36.

Vickers, J. (1985d). 'Pre-Emptive Patenting, Joint Ventures, and the Persistence of Oligopoly'. *International Journal of Industrial Organization*, 3(3): 261–273.

Vickers, J. (1986a). 'The Evolution of Market Structure When There is a Sequence of Innovations'. *Journal of Industrial Economics*, 35(1): 1–12.

Vickers, J. (1986b). 'Signalling in a Model of Monetary Policy with Incomplete Information'. *Oxford Economic Papers*, New Series, 38(3): 443–455.

Vickers, J. (1989). 'The Nature of Costs and the Number of Firms at Cournot Equilibrium'. *International Journal of Industrial Organization*, 7(4): 503–509.

Vickers, J. (1995a). 'Concepts of Competition'. *Oxford Economic Papers*, New Series, 47(1): 1–23.

Vickers, J. (1995b). 'Competition and Regulation in Vertically Related Markets'. *Review of Economic Studies*, 62(1): 1–17.

Vickers, J. (1998). 'Inflation Targeting in Practice: The UK Experience'. *Bank of England Quarterly Bulletin*, 38(4): 368–375.

Vickers, J. (1999a). 'EMU: A View from Next Door'. *Bank of England Quarterly Bulletin*, 39(1): 98–101.

Vickers, J. (1999b). 'Economic Models and Monetary Policy'. *Bank of England Quarterly Bulletin*, 39(2): 210–216.

Vickers, J. (1999c). 'Monetary Policy and Asset Prices'. *Bank of England Quarterly Bulletin*, 39(4): 428–435.

Vickers, J. (2000a). 'Monetary Policy and the Supply Side'. *Bank of England Quarterly Bulletin*, 40(2): 199–206.

Vickers, J. (2000b). 'Monetary Union and Economic Growth'. *Bank of England Quarterly Bulletin*, 40(3): 288–296.

Vickers, J. (2003). 'Competition Economics and Policy'. *European Competition Law Review*, 24(3): 95–102.

Vickers, J. (2004). 'Merger Policy in Europe: Retrospect and Prospect'. *European Competition Law Review*, 25(7): 455–463.

Vickers, J. (2005a). 'Economics for Consumer Policy'. *Proceedings of the British Academy*, 125: 287–310.

Vickers, J. (2005b). 'Abuse of Market Power'. *Economic Journal*, 115(504): F244–F261.

Vickers, J. (2006). 'Market Power in Competition Cases'. *European Competition Journal*, 2(Supplement No. 1): 3–14.

Vickers, J. (2007). 'Competition Law and Economics: A Mid-Atlantic Viewpoint'. *European Competition Journal*, 3(1): 1–15.

Vickers, J. (2008). 'A Tale of Two EC Cases: *IBM* and *Microsoft*'. *Competition Policy International*, 4(1): 2–32.

Vickers, J. (2010a). 'Central Banks and Competition Authorities: Institutional Comparisons and New Concerns'. Bank for International Settlements, Working Paper No. 331.

Vickers, J. (2010b). 'Competition and Property Rights'. *Economic Journal*, 120(544): 375–392.

Vickers, J. (2012). 'Some Economics of Banking Reform'. *Rivista di Politica Economica*, 4, 11–35.

Vickers, J. (2014). 'Banking Reform in Britain and Europe'. Chapter 12 in G. Akerlof et al. (eds) *What Have We Learned? Macroeconomic Policy After the Crisis*. Cambridge, MA: MIT Press: 155–164.

Vickers, J. (2016). 'The Systemic Risk Buffer for UK Banks: A Response to the Bank of England's Consultation Paper'. *Journal of Financial Regulation*, 2(2): 264–282.

Vickers, J. (2017). 'Consequences of Brexit for Competition Law and Policy'. *Oxford Review of Economic Policy*, 33(Supplement No. 1): S70–S78.

Vickers, J. (2019). 'The Case for Market-Based Stress Tests'. *Journal of Financial Regulation*. Available at: https://academic.oup.com/jfr/advance-article-abstract/doi/10.1093/jfr/fjz008/5583757.

Vickers Commission (2013). *The Independent Commission on Banking: The Vickers Report*. Available at: https://researchbriefings.parliament.uk/ResearchBriefing/Summary/SN06171#fullreport.

Vickers, J. and M. Waterson (1991). 'Vertical Relationships: An Introduction'. *Journal of Industrial Economics*, 39(5): 445–450.

Vickers, J. and V. Wright (eds) (1989). *The Politics of Privatisation in Western Europe*. London: Frank Cass.

Vickers, J. and G. Yarrow (1985). *Privatisation and the Natural Monopolies*. London: Public Policy Centre.

Vickers, J. and G. Yarrow (1988a). *Privatization: An Economic Analysis*. Cambridge, MA: MIT Press.

Vickers, J. and G. Yarrow (1988b). 'Regulation of Privatised Firms in Britain'. *European Economic Review*, 32(2–3): 465–472.

Vickers, J. and G. Yarrow (1991a). 'Reform of the Electricity Supply Industry in Britain: An Assessment of the Development of Public Policy'. *European Economic Review*, 35(2–3): 485–495.

Vickers, J. and G. Yarrow (1991b). 'The British Electricity Experiment'. *Economic Policy*, 6(12): 187–232.

Vickers, J. and G. Yarrow (1991c). 'Economic Perspectives on Privatization'. *Journal of Economic Perspectives*, 5(2): 111–132.

Other Works Referred To

Aghion, P. and P. Howitt (1992). 'A Model of Growth Through Creative Destruction'. *Econometrica*, 60(2): 323–351.

Davies, H. (2009). 'The Financial Crisis: Whodunnit?'. *Reserve Bank of New Zealand Bulletin*, 72(3): 69–75.

Dixit, A.K. and J.E. Stiglitz (1977). 'Monopolistic Competition and Optimum Produce Diversity'. *American Economic Review*, 67(3): 297–308.

Hotelling, H. (1929). 'Stability in Competition'. *Economic Journal*, 39(153): 41–57.

Lucas, R.E., Jr. (1988). 'On the Mechanics of Economic Development'. *Journal of Monetary Economics*, 22(1): 3–42.

Ramsey, F.P. (1927). 'A Contribution to the Theory of Taxation'. *Economic Journal*, 37(145): 47–61.

Romer, P.M. (1990). 'Endogenous Technological Change'. *Journal of Political Economy*, 98(5, Part 2): S71–S102.

Salop, S.C. (1979). 'Monopolistic Competition with Outside Goods'. *Bell Journal of Economics*, 10(1): 141–156.

Notes on Contributors

Lise Arena is a tenured Associate Professor at the CNRS-Université Côte d'Azur Research Institute GREDEG (France) where she obtained her PhD in Management. She also holds a DPhil in Modern History from the University of Oxford. Her major research interests are the history of management and the role of digital artefacts and practices in social organisation. Her recent work in the history of management has been published in *Entreprises et Histoire* and *History of Economic Ideas*.

Vincent Barnett is an independent scholar based in the UK who has written extensively on the history of economic thought, on Russian history and on media history. He has published various articles in journals such as *Evolutionary and Institutional Economics Review*, *Journal of Economic Issues* and *History of Political Economy*, and he is the editor of the Routledge *Handbook of the History of Global Economic Thought* (2015). He has also published articles on the economic history of organised crime, including in the *Journal of Popular Television*, and recently contributed various entries to the *Encyclopedia of Evolutionary Psychological Science* on the links between economics and evolutionary psychology.

Robert J. Bigg was educated in Southampton and at Clare College, Cambridge, and spent many subsequent years in information systems. His main research focus was the development of Cambridge monetary thought before *The General Theory*, including *Cambridge and the Monetary Theory of*

R. A. Cord (ed.), *The Palgrave Companion to Oxford Economics*, https://doi.org/10.1007/978-3-030-58471-9

Production (1990). He is a contributor to *The New Palgrave: A Dictionary of Economics* and is working on a study of Sir Theodore Gregory's work and some other pre-Keynesian economists.

Christopher Bliss has been at the University of Oxford since 1977. He is Emeritus Fellow at Nuffield College, Oxford. Bliss holds a PhD from Cambridge University. He has been a managing editor of various leading economics journals, including the *Review of Economic Studies*, *Oxford Economic Papers* and the *Economic Journal*. His books include *Capital Theory and the Distribution of Income* (1975) and *Trade, Growth, and Inequality* (2007).

Robert A. Cord is an independent researcher in economics. His specialist area of interest is the history of economic thought and, within this, the history of macroeconomics. His published books include *Reinterpreting the Keynesian Revolution* (2012), *Milton Friedman: Contributions to Economics and Public Policy* (co-edited with J. Daniel Hammond; 2016), *The Palgrave Companion to Cambridge Economics* (editor; 2017) and *The Palgrave Companion to LSE Economics* (editor; 2018), and his articles have appeared in the *Cambridge Journal of Economics* and the *History of Political Economy*. Cord is also managing editor of the Palgrave series *Remaking Economics: Eminent Post-War Economists*, which includes volumes on James Buchanan and Paul Samuelson. He holds a PhD from Cambridge University.

John Creedy is Professor of Public Economics and Taxation at Victoria Business School, Victoria University of Wellington, New Zealand. He was previously the Truby Williams Professor of Economics at Melbourne University, Australia. He has held chairs in economics at Pennsylvania State University in the US and Durham University in the UK. He has published extensively in public economics, labour economics, income distribution and the history of economic analysis.

Huw Dixon has been Professor of Economics at Cardiff Business School since 2006. His research interests initially centred on oligopoly theory, particularly developing Bertrand-Edgeworth models to allow for convex costs. Later, he was one of the first economists to introduce imperfect competition into macroeconomics, initially in static settings and later developing dynamic models of entry and variable markups. He has also developed methods for using micro-price data for measuring nominal rigidity. Dixon has been an editor of the *Economic Journal* and the *Review of Economic Studies*.

John Duca is the Danforth-Lewis Professor of Economics at Oberlin College and a part-time Vice President at the Federal Reserve Bank of Dallas. He is an applied macroeconomist, whose work has focused on the consumption, housing, labour and portfolio behaviour of households, incorporating roles for credit constraints, transaction costs, innovations and regulation. For over 30 years, Duca has served as an economist in the Federal Reserve System. Duca graduated with a PhD in Economics from Princeton and a BA in Economics from Yale.

Walter Eltis (1933–2019), a graduate of Emmanuel College, Cambridge, and an Oxford D.Litt., was a Research Fellow of Exeter College, Oxford (1958–1960), a Lecturer at Exeter and Keble (1960–1963), and then a Tutorial Fellow in Economics, with a linked University post, at Exeter from 1963 to 1988. Subsequently, he was Economic Director and Director General of the National Economic Development Office and Chief Economic Adviser to the President, at the Board of Trade. Eltis's articles appeared in the *American Economic Review* and the *Economic Journal*, amongst others. His books included *Growth and Distribution* (1973), *Britain's Economic Problem: Too Few Producers* (with R. Bacon; 1976), *The Classical Theory of Economic Growth* (1984), *Keynes and Economic Policy* (with P. Sinclair; 1988), *Classical Economics, Public Expenditure and Growth* (1993), *Britain's Economic Problem Revisited* (1996), *Condillac, Commerce and Government* (ed. with S.M. Eltis; 1998), and *Britain, Europe and EMU* (2000).

Neil R. Ericsson is Principal Economist, Division of International Finance, Board of Governors of the Federal Reserve System; Research Professor in the Department of Economics, The George Washington University; and Adjunct Professor at the Paul H. Nitze School of Advanced International Studies (SAIS), Johns Hopkins University. He holds a BA in Economics from Yale University, and an MSc in Econometrics and Mathematical Economics and a PhD in Economics from the London School of Economics (LSE). He has published more than 80 papers on econometric methods, theory, and modelling; empirical economics; and economic forecasting. He has also edited three books: *Testing Exogeneity* (1994, with John S. Irons), *Understanding Economic Forecasts* (2001, with David F. Hendry) and *General-to-Specific Modelling* (2005, with Julia Campos and David F. Hendry).

David Fielding is Professor of Development Economics at Manchester University's Global Development Institute and until recently was Professor of Economics at the University of Otago in New Zealand, where he still holds a visiting position. He was an undergraduate at Keble College when Paul Collier was Keble's Fellow and Tutor in Economics, and was later one of Collier's DPhil students. Fielding's early work focused on the macroeconomics of the francophone monetary unions in West Africa. His later work includes research on the economics of violent civil conflict, the role of altruism and trust in economic development, and the economics of inter-group contact.

Valpy FitzGerald is Emeritus Professor of International Development Finance, and Fellow of St Antony's College, at the University of Oxford. He read Philosophy, Politics and Economics (PPE) at Oxford, followed by a PhD in economics at Cambridge on optimal investment planning. FitzGerald was Assistant Director of Development Studies at Cambridge (1972–1979) and Professor of Development Economics at The Hague (1979–1992), before returning to Oxford, where he worked with Frances Stewart on the relationship between war and underdevelopment, and became Head of the Oxford Department of International Development (2007–2012). He continues to research the macroeconomic determinants of income distribution in the Kaleckian tradition and is a member of the Independent Commission on the Reform of International Corporate Taxation.

Joshua Getzler took first degrees in Law and History at the Australian National University and read for his doctorate at Oxford. His work concerns the evolution of property rights, including water claims and native title, trusts and fiduciary accountability, corporate and Crown liabilities, and the history of the judiciary. He has taught at St Hugh's College and the Oxford Faculty of Law since 1993, where he is Professor of Law and Legal History. Getzler has served as a visiting researcher and teacher at universities in Australia, Israel and the US. He is co-editor of the OUP monograph series *Oxford Legal History*.

Andrew Graham is Executive Chair and Chair of the Academic Council of The Europaeum, an association of 17 of the leading universities in Europe, and a Trustee of Reprieve. He was formerly Fellow and Tutor in Economics at Balliol College, Oxford, 1969–1997, Acting Master of Balliol, 1997–2001, and Master of Balliol, 2001–2011. He was Economic Assistant to Thomas Balogh from 1966 to 1968, Economic Adviser to the Prime Minister, 1968–1969, and Senior Economist in the Prime Minister's Policy Unit (on leave from Oxford), 1974–1976. In 2001, he founded the Oxford Internet Institute and, in 2010, the Balliol Interdisciplinary Institute.

David F. Hendry is Co-Director of Climate Econometrics and Senior Research Fellow of Nuffield College, University of Oxford. He was previously Professor of Economics at Oxford and of Econometrics at LSE. He was knighted in 2009 and received a Lifetime Achievement Award from the Economic and Social Research Council (ESRC) in 2014. He is an Honorary Vice President and past President of the Royal Economic Society; Fellow of the British Academy, Royal Society of Edinburgh, Econometric Society, Academy of Social Sciences, *Econometric Reviews* and *Journal of Econometrics*; Founding Fellow, International Association for Applied Econometrics;

Foreign Honorary Member of the American Economic Association (AEA) and American Academy of Arts and Sciences; and Honorary Fellow of the International Institute of Forecasters. He has received eight honorary doctorates, is a Thomson Reuters Citation Laureate and has published more than 200 papers and 25 books.

Patrick Honohan is an Honorary Professor of Economics at Trinity College Dublin, a non-resident Senior Fellow at the Peterson Institute for International Economics and a Research Fellow of the Centre for Economic Policy Research (CEPR). He was Governor of the Central Bank of Ireland from 2009 to 2015. Previously, Honohan spent 12 years on the staff of the World Bank where he was a senior adviser on financial sector issues. During the 1990s, Honohan was a Research Professor at Ireland's Economic and Social Research Institute. In the 1980s, he was Economic Adviser to the Taoiseach (Irish Prime Minister) Garret FitzGerald. A graduate of University College Dublin, Honohan holds a PhD in Economics from the London School of Economics.

Lowell Jacobsen is the Elizabeth Harvey Rhodes Professor of International Business at Baker University, the oldest university in Kansas. He holds a PhD in Economics from Edinburgh University, where he specialised in industrial organisation under the supervision of Gavin Reid. Over the past few years, Jacobsen's research has focused on deepening the intellectual roots of strategic management by examining the works of Marshall and such disciples as Andrews, Coase, Loasby, Macgregor, Penrose, Robertson and Austin Robinson. His publications include two critically acclaimed research monographs, *The Small Entrepreneurial Firm* (1988) and *Profiles in Small Business: A Competitive Strategy Approach* (1993) (both with Gavin Reid) in addition to many journal articles.

Vijay Joshi is Emeritus Fellow of Merton College, Oxford. His main areas of research interest and publication are macroeconomics, international economics and development economics. He has written several books on India's economic development, of which the most recent is *India's Long Road: The Search for Prosperity* (2017). His non-academic appointments have included Economic Adviser in the Ministry of Finance in India and Special Adviser to the Governor of the Reserve Bank of India. He was a Director of the J.P. Morgan Indian Investment Trust from 1996 to 2012.

John E. King is Emeritus Professor at La Trobe University and Honorary Professor at Federation University Australia. His principal research interests are in the history of heterodox economic thought, especially Marxian political economy and post-Keynesian economics. Recent publications include *The Distribution of Wealth* (2016; with Michael Schneider and Mike Pottenger) and *A History of American Economic Thought* (2018; with Samuel Barbour and James Cicarelli). His latest book, *The Alternative Austrian Economics*, dealing with the history of socialist economic thought in Austria between 1904 and the present day, was published in 2019 by Edward Elgar.

Frederic S. Lee (1949–2014) was a prolific and influential economist. He authored and edited numerous books, articles, book chapters, reviews and entries on microeconomics and price theory and, with Warren Young, wrote *Oxford Economics and Oxford Economists* (1993). He taught at the University of California Riverside, Roosevelt University, De Montfort University and the University of Missouri-Kansas City. He was editor of the *American Journal of Economics and Sociology* and President of the Associations for Institutional Economics and for Evolutionary Economics. His PhD was from Rutgers University.

John Martin completed his undergraduate economics degree at University College Dublin. He then did postgraduate studies at Nuffield College, Oxford, where he became a Research Fellow, and a Lecturer in Economics at Merton College and The University of Buckingham. In 1977, he joined the Organisation for Economic Co-operation and Development (OECD) in Paris. At the OECD, he worked in both the Economics Department and the Employment, Labour and Social Affairs Directorate where he was Director until his retirement. He was the founding editor of the *OECD Employment Outlook* and also edited the *OECD Economic Outlook*. He has published extensively in international trade and labour economics.

Ken Mayhew is Emeritus Professor of Education and Economic Performance at the University of Oxford, Emeritus Fellow in Economics at Pembroke College, Oxford, and Extraordinary Professor of Education and Economic Performance at Maastricht University. For over 15 years, he was Director of SKOPE, an ESRC-funded multidisciplinary research centre on skills, knowledge and organisational performance based at Oxford and Cardiff. He has spent most of his career as an academic in Oxford. His first job was in Her Majesty's Treasury and he served a stint as Economic Director of the UK's former National Economic Development Office. He is a member of the Armed Forces Pay Review Body.

Alex Millmow is Associate Professor in Economics at the School of Business, Federation University Australia. His research interests include the making of the Australian economics profession and the role of economic ideas in steering public policy. In 2004, he completed his doctorate at the Australian National University on "The Power of Economic Ideas: The Rise of

Macroeconomic Management in Australia", which was subsequently published. Millmow has published over 50 journal articles, including for the *Economic Record, Economic Papers, Economic Analysis and Policy* and the *History of Economics Review.* He is the President of the History of Economic Thought Society of Australia (HETSA). In 2017, Millmow published *A History of Australasian Economic Thought.* He is writing a biography of Colin Clark.

Peter Neary is Professor of Economics at the University of Oxford and a Professorial Fellow of Merton College. Educated at University College Dublin and Oxford, he was Professor of Political Economy at University College Dublin from 1980 to 2006. He is the author of *Measuring the Restrictiveness of International Trade Policy* (with Jim Anderson; 2005) and of various scholarly articles, mainly on international trade. He is a Research Fellow of CEPR and Centre for Economic Studies(ifo) (CESifo), a Fellow of the British Academy and the Econometric Society, and a Member of Academia Europaea and the Royal Irish Academy. He was President of the European Economic Association in 2002 and of the Royal Economic Society in 2017–2018.

Bent Nielsen is Professor of Economics at the University of Oxford and Fellow of Nuffield College. He has published more than 50 papers on age-period-cohort analyses, co-explosiveness and cointegration, outlier detection, time series specification tests and unit testing, as well as a textbook on econometric modelling.

Avner Offer is Chichele Professor Emeritus of Economic History at Oxford, Emeritus Fellow of All Souls College and Fellow of the British Academy. He initially studied land tenure and the economics of war, with *Property and Politics 1870–1914* (1981) and *The First World War: An Agrarian Interpretation* (1989). Subsequently, he focused on consumption and the quality of life with *The Challenge of Affluence: Self-Control and Well-Being in the United States and Britain Since 1950* (2006) and on the social determinants of obesity. His latest book is *The Nobel Factor: The Prize in Economics, Social Democracy and the Market Turn* (2016).

Gianmarco I. P. Ottaviano is Professor of Economics and Boroli Chair in European Studies at Bocconi University, having previously taught at LSE and the University of Bologna. He holds a BA in economics from Bocconi University, an MSc in economics from LSE and a PhD in economics from the Université Catholique de Louvain. He has co-authored many works in international trade, urban economics and economic geography with a special emphasis on the competitiveness of firms in the global economy and the effects of immigration and offshoring on employment and wages.

Rosalind Seneca (née Worswick) was born in 1944 in Oxford, England. She attended Oxford High School for Girls. In 1966, she graduated in Economics from Newnham College, Cambridge, and in the same year emigrated to the US. In 1971, she earned a PhD in Economics from the University of Pennsylvania. Seneca held academic positions at Hunter College of the City University of New York (CUNY), Columbia University and Drew University, where she was Chair of the Economics Department for eight years. She is the author of several articles and co-authored an economics textbook on government regulation of industry. Since her retirement, Seneca has written a novel and a memoir.

Peter Sinclair (1946–2020) was a Fellow of the Office for National Statistics and a consultant at the Bank of England. He was Emeritus Professor of Economics at the University of Birmingham and Emeritus Fellow of Brasenose College, Oxford. Sinclair held Visiting Professorships at Queen's University and the University of British Columbia in Canada and the University of the Witwatersrand in South Africa, was managing editor of *Oxford Economic Papers* for a decade and chaired the Royal Economic Society's Easter School for 22 years. Many of his research papers and books were devoted to climate change, unemployment, taxation, trade, and monetary economics and policy.

Frances Stewart is Emeritus Professor of Development Economics, University of Oxford. She was Director of the Oxford Department of International Development (1993–2003) and the Centre for Research on Inequality, Human Security and Ethnicity (2003–2010). She has an honorary doctorate from the University of Sussex and received the Leontief Prize for Advancing the Frontiers of Economic Thought from Tufts in 2013. Her primary recent research interests are horizontal inequalities, conflict and human development. Among many publications, she is the lead author of *Horizontal Inequalities and Conflict: Understanding Group Violence in Multiethnic Societies* (2008) and *Advancing Human Development: Theory and Practice* (2018).

F. M. L. Thompson (1925–2017) was a distinguished economic historian, much of whose work was devoted to elucidating the experience of the English landed classes in the nineteenth and twentieth centuries. Born in 1925, Thompson undertook military service during the war and only then went to Oxford to read History. From 1951, he was appointed to the staff of University College London: until his retirement he worked entirely in the colleges of the University of London, latterly as Director of the Institute of Historical Research from 1977 to 1990. His best-known book was *English Landed Society in the Nineteenth Century* (1963). Thompson was elected a Fellow of the British Academy in 1979 and gave the Ford Lectures at Oxford in 1994.

Jan Toporowski is Professor of Economics and Finance at SOAS University of London and holds visiting appointments at International University College, Turin, Italy, and the University of Bergamo, Italy. He studied Economics at Birkbeck College, University of London and the University of Birmingham. Toporowski has worked in fund management, international banking, central banking and economic consultancy. He has written nearly 300 articles, books and papers on finance, monetary theory and macroeconomics, including two volumes of intellectual biography on Michał Kalecki.

John Vint is Emeritus Professor at Manchester Metropolitan University (MMU) and Honorary Professor at Perm State University, Russia. He was formerly Head of Department at MMU and has taught at universities in the UK and North America. His research interests lie in the history of political economy specialising in the work of John Stuart Mill and Harriet Martineau. In 1993, Vint won the Joseph Dorfman Award for the best dissertation in the history of economic thought and published a book in 1994 based on his doctorate entitled *Capital and Wages*. For 18 years, he was the editor of the *History of Economic Thought Newsletter* and has been the Chair of the Martineau Society since 2014.

Warren Young is Emeritus Professor of Economics at Bar-Ilan University, Israel. He has published and edited books and articles on the history of modern macroeconomics and growth theory, the history of the Federal Reserve, international macroeconomics, energy economics and the economy of Israel. He is the author, with the late Fred Lee, of *Oxford Economics and Oxford Economists* (1993). Young was an adviser to the Archives Project, Federal Reserve Bank of Minneapolis. He was a Visiting Professor at the Tepper School of Business, Carnegie Mellon University and the Center for Economic Efficiency, Arizona State University. Young holds a PhD from the University of Cambridge.

Index[1]

---

[1] Note: Page numbers followed by 'n' refer to notes.